Tensile Structures

Design, Structure, and Calculation

of Buildings of Cables, Nets, and Membranes

Tensile Structures

Design, Structure, and Calculation

of Buildings of Cables, Nets, and Membranes

Edited by Frei Otto

The MIT Press
Cambridge, Massachusetts, and London, England

First published in German under the title *Zugbeanspruchte Konstruktionen,*
Volume 1 Copyright © 1962, Volume 2 Copyright © 1966 by
Ullstein Verlag GmbH, Frankfurt/M-Berlin.
Translated from the German by D. Ben-Yaakov and T. Pelz of the
Israel Program for Scientific Translations.

First MIT Press paperback edition, combining Volumes 1 and 2, March 1973

ISBN 0 262 15013 1 (hard)
ISBN 0 262 65005 3 (paperback)

Library of Congress catalog card number: 73–3123

CONTENTS

Tensile Structures

Volume 1

Frei Otto: Pneumatic Structures

Rudolf Trostel: Calculation of Membranes

Frei Otto: Tension Anchoring in the Foundations

The engineering and mathematical research required to complete Vol. 1—which extended from 1957 to 1960—was rendered possible by Peter Stromeyer of L. Stromey & Co., Constance, Germany.

The following participated in research at the Development Center for Lightweight Structures, Berlin-Zehlendorf: Ingrid Otto (Berlin), John Koch (St. Louis), Frederick Miles (Urbana) and Hans Wehrhahn (Berlin). Dieter Hilliges (Berlin) assisted with the drawings of the mathematical section and checked the formulas. Walter Bird, Victor Lundy, Carl Koch, and many others supplied valuable material.

I should like to express my particular gratitude for the understanding and trust of the publishers, for the support of my research, for the cooperation and assistance of all participants, and for all suggested improvements.

The Author.

Designs by the author are marked by an asterisk in the text.

The figures are separately numbered on all double pages. If the figure is mentioned on the same double page, only the figure number is given; otherwise the page number is also given.

FOREWORD

It is the intention of this work, the first volume of which is herewith presented, to report on tensile structures, indicate the present state of their technical development and to provide new stimuli for further exploration. The use of tensile structures is rapidly expanding. Many details important for a fundamental understanding are not yet established. It would be too early to attempt to provide fundamental rules for the entire field, but in certain specialized subsections some summarizing statements can be ventured. For this reason the contributions of several specialists from various related disciplines will be presented; whatever is common knowledge will be touched upon somewhat briefly while the more urgent problems will be discussed in greater detail. The treatment of structure (construction as well as design), form, and methods of calculation will be addressed to both architects and engineers.

In general, tensile structures are more readily put up than pressure- or elasticity-dependent structures because they are not subject to buckling, denting, or tipping effects. However, construction materials of extremely great tensile strength in the form of wires or fibers, which are unknown in the field of pressure construction, are available.

We shall deal here mostly with constructions which to a large extent consist of tensile components, such as cables, nets, or membranes.

The oldest examples of tensile structures are tents and suspension bridges. Today they are supplemented by the tensile supporting surfaces for roof constructions made of nets and membranes or of tractive three-dimensional rope configurations, and also tower and suspended-housing structures.

The primary impulse for engineering projects employing tensile structures was provided in the past century by Roebling and his suspension bridges, followed by those of Ammann, Leonhardt, Steinman, and Strauss. In the field of tensile-supporting structures Bird, Jawerth, Laffaille, Lanchester, Maculan, Norwicki, Sarger, Severud, Le Ricolais, Zetlin, and many others worked out new fundamental theories.

Extensive literature is available only within the realm of heavy-duty suspension bridges. The tensile supporting structures were first dealt with in the book *Das hängende Dach,* the manuscript of which originated in 1950–1953 as a doctoral dissertation at the Technical Institute of Berlin and was published by Ullstein in 1954. This field has in the meantime broadened out to such an extent, largely through suggestions stimulated by this publication, that a mere revised edition can no longer be considered. For this reason a wider framework had to be found, which would encompass the entire concept of tensile structures.

The search for structures demanding a minimum of material and time arises from the desire to be extremely economical with the energy available. This search has often led to surprising results. It is the task of every builder to provide, to utilize, and to extend living space. In this the construction materials are means to an end, although they often have the disadvantage of taking up space themselves or, because of their rigidity, oppose the natural trend toward change. To minimize or to eliminate these disadvantages is a task of prime importance.

Berlin, August 1962

Frei Otto

CONTENTS

About the contents of Volume 1

The first volume contains three chapters on themes of special and topical interest.

The first deals with pneumatic structures, largely tensile surfaces. Membranes resisting tensile forces are stiffened by differences of air or liquid pressure and form envelopes in the shape of halls, roofings, silos, dams, etc. The problems are presented by means of illustrations, clearly arranged and supplemented by the text.

The chapter "Calculation of Membranes" deals with the basic principles of statics of membranes; these experiments are not limited to pneumatic membranes but apply to membranes under any type of load. It thus presents a summary of the membrane theory of shells.

The end of the first volume deals with "Tension Anchoring in the Foundations". The low weight of tension-loaded structures and the considerable tensile forces acting raise new problems, especially if these forces are directly applied to the foundations. New possibilities for efficient solutions to these problems are pointed out.

Frei Otto · Tensile Structures · Volume 1

Definition and Characteristics

"Pneumatic structures" are structural forms stabilized wholly or mainly by pressure differences of gases, liquids, foam, or material in bulk. We shall deal here with tensile-stress structural forms such as membranes or nets. A familiar example is the balloon, which is a slack envelope stabilized by gas pressure, enabling it to withstand not only the gas pressure itself, but also to take up other loads.

Tensile-stress pneumatic structures can be readily made from light, collapsible, very strong membranes. Such structures have very little weight and are therefore of much greater practical importance than structures undergoing compressive or bending stresses under pneumatic loads.

Tensile-stress pneumatic structures are part of the large group of suspended and stretched structures. They differ, however, substantially from both heavy hanging structures such as suspension bridges and light prestressed membranes and nets, although these groups are closely related and their boundaries cannot always be precisely defined.

In pneumatic structures the pressure difference causes prestressing if unbalanced forces are present when no loads act and weight is neglected. This is the case if a completely closed container, such as a balloon, is filled with gas under pressure. In open containers a liquid by its own weight can stretch the skin and stabilize the shape. Such a system is considered *not prestressed,* since no stresses occur when no loads act and weight is neglected.

The distinctive feature of a tensile-stress structure is the container-shaped membrane. This can be obtained in many ways. It is possible, for example, to form bubbles in a *liquid* exhibiting marked surface tension or skin-forming properties (soap emulsion, certain plastics).

It is also possible to inflate highly *elastic* skins, such as rubber, which after deflating return to their original shape (toy balloons).

With highly *plastic* building materials, such as certain plastic foils, pneumatic loading may cause permanent deformations.

Of particular importance are inflated, *only slightly deformable* skins (rubberized heavy fabrics, wire nets, metal sheets, etc.), which must be given the required shape before inflating.

The deformations under load depend to a large extent on the *elasticity* of the material. For example, the shape of a rubber balloon will change much more than that of a glass-fabric balloon subjected to the same load under identical conditions. The rigidity of the structure increases with the modulus of elasticity. Whereas other tensile-stress structures are employed mainly in solving structural problems arising in above-surface and underground constructions, pneumatic structures have a wide application in many technical fields. The same structural shape can often be utilized in different ways. Our discussion of the structural form and the kind of loading will therefore take precedence over the consideration of possible uses.

Development

Pneumatic structures are one of the fundamental structural forms in nature. They have a wide application in plant, and particularly in animal, life. We find them not only in fruits, air bubbles, and blood vessels, but also in the skin kept taut by muscle tissue and blood pressure, and largely supported, in addition, by a skeleton resistant to bending or compression. Animal and man exhibit the essential features of a lightweight structure: tension in pneumatically slightly prestressed skins and fibres enables them to support broadly distributed surface loads, while all compressive and bending stresses are locally concentrated. It is not by coincidence that many man-made pneumatic structures resemble biological forms. Pneumatic structures, developed along lines dictated by purely technical considerations, are meeting the justified and growing demand that technology abandon its abstract, anorganic-mathematical conception, though not its scientific basis, in favor of a conception nearer to organic life.

The sail is probably man's earliest pneumatic structure, although its theory presents many difficulties. Pressure differences, determined by aerodynamic laws, act on a slack membrane and give it a shape which, from a structural and an aerodynamic point of view, must be favorable for the different wind directions. The shape of the sail was perfected by the experience of centuries. The latest advances in the field of stretched membranes have opened new possibilities, but the time of the sailing vessel is past. It remains to be seen whether the sail will still be of importance in the future. Perhaps it will capture other fields, such as large wind-driven power plants, etc. Other familiar pneumatic structures, known for a long time, are water hoses and various containers for liquids. The closed balloon also has a long history. In 1783 the Montgolfier brothers realized that the difference in density between warm and cold air is sufficient to stabilize a balloon envelope. This shows the extent of empirical knowledge available at that time. Toy balloons, automobile tires, dirigibles, parachutes, collapsible boats, air cushions, inflatable and upholstered furniture, high-pressure containers, and water reservoirs, today form the basis of a large industry.

It is almost impossible to trace the history of pneumatic structures since in no other type of tensile-stress structures were there so many interacting directions of development. For instance, we encounter the same problems in the design of automobile tires or collapsible boats as in pneumatic structures, but such problems are tackled by engineers specializing in completely different subjects, with almost no contact between them. The British engineer Frederick William Lanchester appears to have been the first to advocate the use of inflated spherical domes to roof large areas.

A patent, granted to him in 1917, contains the principal details of pneumatic structures. Lanchester, who died only a few years ago, never succeeded in realizing any of his projects. In the United States attempts to advance the development of this type of structure were made by Herbert H. Stevens, but a real breakthrough was achieved only after the war, when Walter Bird built many pneumatic structures, mainly of spherical or cylindrical shape, and contributed greatly to their perfection. Pneumatic structures of all kinds are now being developed by many firms, such as Birdair, Schjeldahl, Irving, U.S. Rubber, Goodyear, Texair, Stromeyer, Krupp, Seattle Tent and Awning, and CID Air Structures. There is no doubt that pneumatic structures will be the only economically feasible buildings in extraterrestrial regions.

Pneumatic structures as auxiliary structural elements have been known since the mid thirties. Rubber balloons were used as formwork for concrete shells by Wallace Neff in the U.S.A., while Buckminster Fuller made use of pneumatic principles in the erection of rib-shell domes.

In the course of research undertaken in connection with writing this book, several new structures were developed, such as pneumatically stretched skins with internal drainage and interior walls, new containers for liquids, and, in particular, new methods of dam construction, as well as "sail-shells" and pneumatic skins stiffened with plastics.†

Pneumatic structures not only permit solving old problems, but they also open the way to entirely new applications, which could not have been possible without them. It should not be forgotten that we are only at the beginning of a new development and that much practical experience has still to be gained. Where empirical knowledge is still lacking, one should thoroughly acquaint oneself with the theoretical foundation and then approach practical applications by way of experimental work. During the last few years there were some serious setbacks due to work on pneumatic structures being attempted without the necessary theoretical knowledge. Although these structures appear simple, their design cannot be properly understood without intensive study.

Soap Bubbles

The study of soap bubbles greatly helps the understanding of pneumatic structures. In each soap bubble or agglomeration of soap bubbles the membrane stresses are equal at each point and in every direction, if we neglect infinitesimal stress differences caused by the weight of the bubble skin. A vertical bubble skin of uniform thickness will be slightly more stressed at its top than at its bottom. This can also be deduced from Eq. (12.2) on page 290. Stresses are equalized by flow so that peaks cannot occur. When two unequally stressed bubbles unite to form a twin bubble, the stresses are instantaneously equalized. Soap bubbles always assume shapes having the smallest possible surface; they are "minimum areas" (cf. p. 292).

It is reported that bubbles made from soapsuds to which glycerin has been added can be kept for a very long time in dust-free air in hermetically sealed containers. There are many new synthetic foam formers which, in aqueous solution, are suitable for bubble formation.††

† Where the originator of a construction or design is not specifically mentioned, his name could either not be ascertained, or else the example is considered to be generally known. The author's original developments and ideas are marked with an asterisk. Where not otherwise indicated, the photographs, drawings, and reports of experiments are from the author's Development Center for Lightweight Structures.

†† C. V. Boys, *Soap Bubbles, Their Colours and the Forces which Mould Them.* New York, Dover Publications, Inc., 1911/1959.

Unfortunately soap bubbles have limited dimensions, and it is almost impossible to measure them with ordinary instruments, since they burst at the slightest touch. Photographic form-analysis methods may be used, but these require elaborate equipment if accuracy is to be sufficient.

Soap-bubble shapes in gravity-free space are of particular interest, since their shape is determined solely by skin stresses and is not affected by the weight of the membrane. Despite the extremely small thickness of the membrane (less than 1/1,000 mm), its weight influences the shape of the bubble. In a soap membrane stretched on a horizontal ring the sag is clearly visible. The influence of the membrane weight varies inversely with the ratio between admissible surface tension and bulk density.

As already stated by Boys, permanent bubbles can be formed from plastic materials that harden after some time; however, it is difficult to prevent distortions during hardening. Two-component plastic of the hardening type, or drying plastic solutions, may also be used.

The possibility of forming large domed structures by inflating liquid plastic was investigated by General Electric† and Günter Günschel.†† Whether suitable materials for this purpose will become available depends on future developments in the field of plastics.

Bubbles blown from softened glass are very stable, but it is extremely difficult to obtain a uniformly stressed membrane, since usually its thickness and temperature vary and weight effects are considerable. Therefore, glass bubbles form minimum areas only in exceptional cases.

Any shape which a soap bubble can assume can also be obtained as a pneumatic structure. Any envelope, forming an enlargement to scale of a soap-bubble shape can be made of slightly deformable skins, such as glass fabric or paper. If the membrane weight is neglected, such an envelope will be uniformly stressed at every point and in every direction when inflated, provided, of course, that its original shape is preserved by means of correct preparation.

It has been established that membranes made of materials that have a tendency to flow when under permanent stresses or to stress equalization (like most building materials in use), retain their shape and geometrical similarity for a long time only when the membrane stresses (for the permanent or primary state of stress) are uniform at each point and in each direction.

Soap-bubble-shaped structures are well-suited to the primary state of stress though not necessarily so if additional loads are applied. When searching for shapes that are satisfactory both with and without external loads we shall, in practice, often deviate from the soap-bubble shape. In the following section we shall first discuss, in general, closed soap membranes under internal pressure. When dealing with the various structural shapes, we shall treat the corresponding soap-bubble shapes in greater detail.

† *Architectural Forum* 3/1959

†† *Europäisches Bauforum* 12/1960

Flying soap bubbles

In a weightless state the free bubble assumes an exactly spherical shape (Fig. 1). If the internal pressure is p and the radius r, the membrane stress at any point and in any surface direction will will be $n_0 = pr/2$.

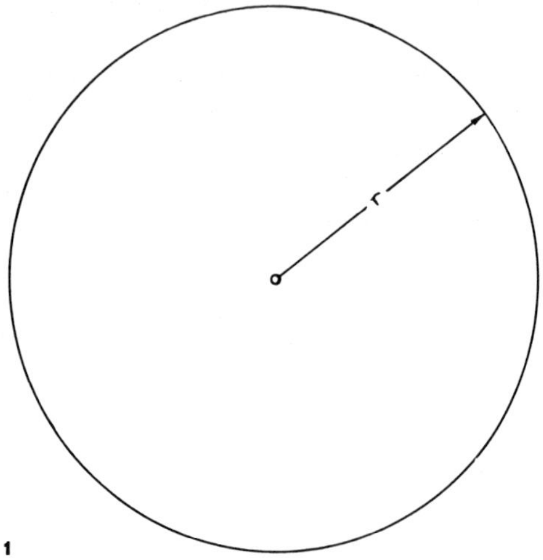

1

Since drag and weight of a bubble depend on its surface area, soap bubbles of different size (Fig. 2) having equally thick walls,

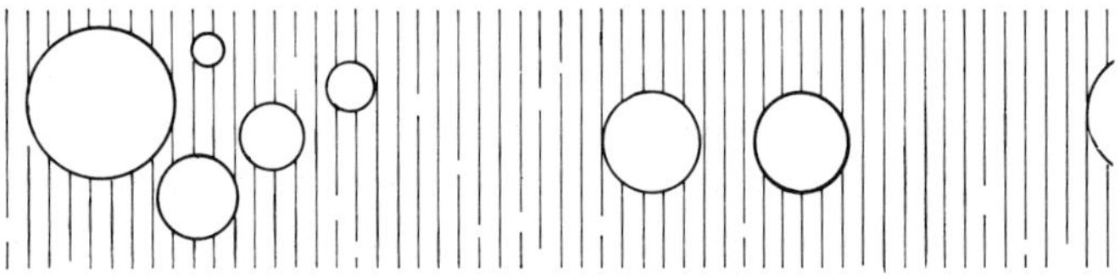

2 and 3

will descend at the same speed in still air. The internal pressure of small bubbles will then be higher than that of large bubbles. The speed of descent is higher for thick-walled than for thin-walled bubbles (Fig. 3).

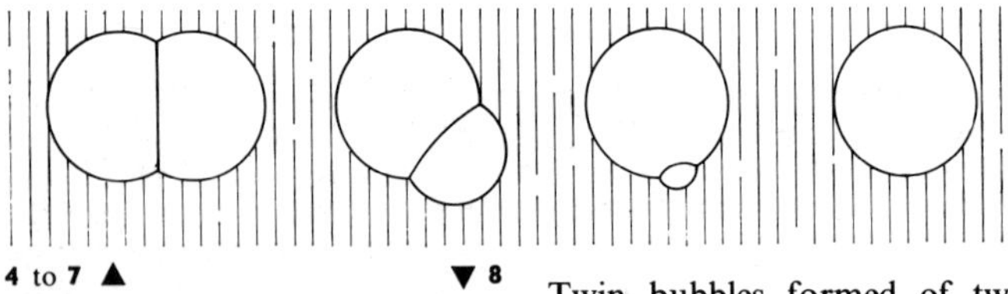

4 to 7 ▲

▼ 8

Twin bubbles formed of two equal bubbles descend with their common axis horizontal (Fig. 4). If, however, the two bubbles are unequal, the inclination of their common axis increases with the difference in size (Figs. 5 to 7). This is due to the displacement of the center of aerodynamic forces and can be seen clearly in Fig. 8.

A twin bubble (Fig. 9) consists of two spherical segments with a plane dividing diaphragm. The following is found to hold true for all soap bubbles: not more than three skins can be in contact along one line, and they will form angles of 120° with each other. The geometric shape is thus given exactly.

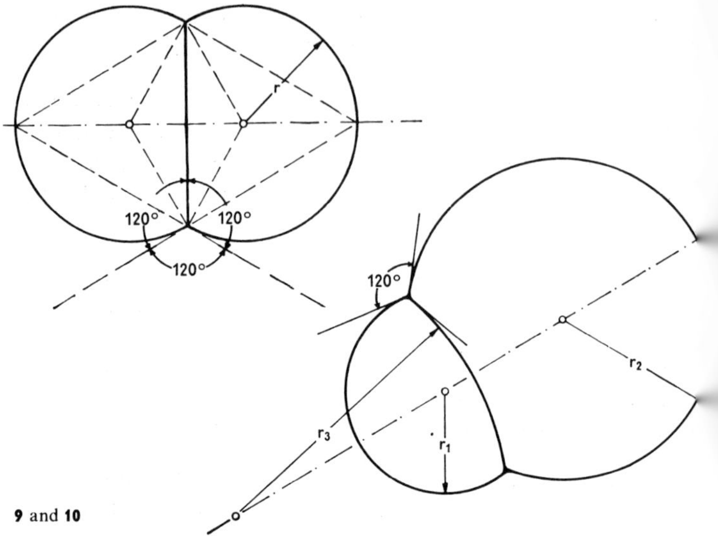

9 and 10

If two soap bubbles of different diameters form a twin bubble (Fig. 10), the diaphragm is curved. If the membrane stresses are equal, the gas pressure p in the smaller bubble is higher than that in the larger bubble. The relationship between the radii r_1, r_2, r_3 is given by:

$$n = \frac{p_1 r_1}{2} = \frac{p_2 r_2}{2} = \frac{(p_1 - p_2)\, r_3}{2}$$

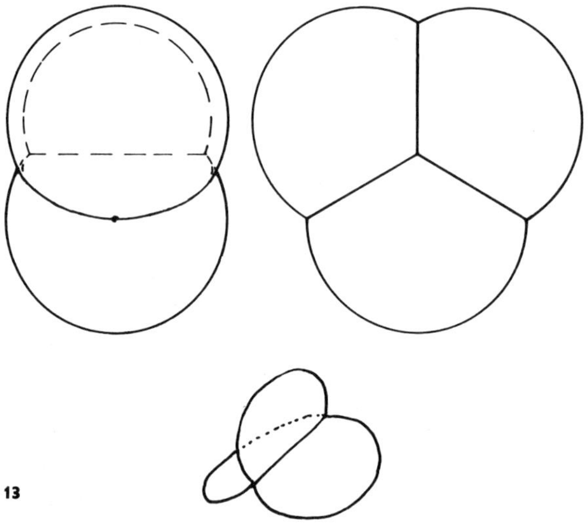

11 to 13

Figures 12 and 11 show, respectively, the plan and the elevation of three connected bubbles of equal size. It can be seen that there are, altogether, six membrane surfaces, namely three spherical segments and three planes. The three planes meet in a straight line passing through the center (Fig. 13).

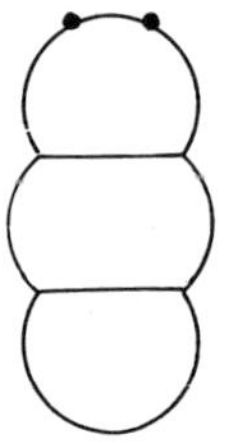

14

Free-flying bubbles always have a minimum surface area. Bubbles can only be strung (Fig. 14) if they are suspended from a ring.

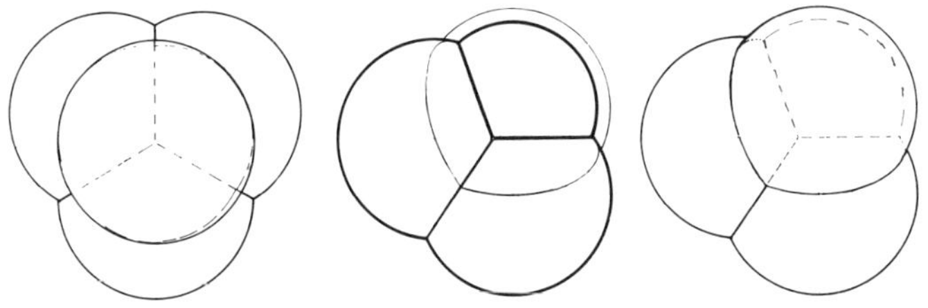

15 to **17**

Four equal soap bubbles (Figs. 15, 16, and 17) have a common point of contact in the center. The six contact planes intersect in four straight lines which meet in the center (Fig. 18) forming equal angles.

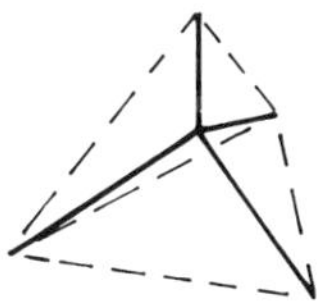

18

Irrespective of size and arrangement, not more than four bubbles can be in direct contact with one another.
If the bubbles are unequal, the lines and planes of contact are curved.
Five bubbles cannot all be in direct contact with one another.

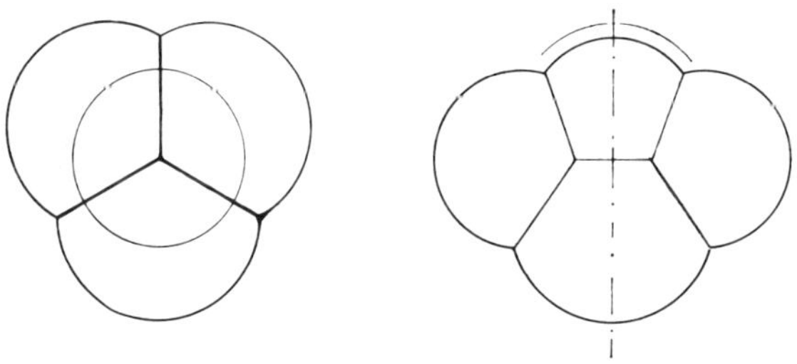

19 and **20**

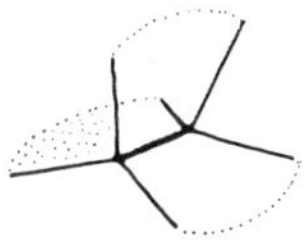

21

Five equal bubbles form three internal contact planes which intersect in a line lying completely in the interior. (Transverse section — Fig. 19, longitudinal section — Fig. 20, sketch of the interior membranes — Fig. 21.)

22

Four approximately equal bubbles may surround a fifth small internal bubble (Fig. 22) which will have the shape of a regular pyramid with slightly curved edges and surfaces.

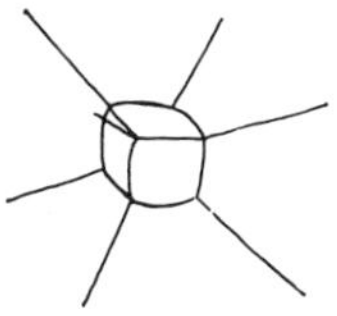

23

Six bubbles can surround a cube-shaped bubble in an axially symmetric arrangement (Fig. 23).

24

Floating soap bubbles

The laws governing bubble formation are more easily studied on floating than on free-flying soap bubbles. It should also be remembered that phenomena observed in bubbles do not necessarily apply to larger structures. The behavior of bubbles and foams is determined by molecular forces which act only over small distances. In spite of this, soap bubbles may be used as models for larger pneumatic structures, since, if the shape of the bubble is reproduced exactly to scale, the membrane stresses in the unloaded state will be the same at every point and in every surface direction.

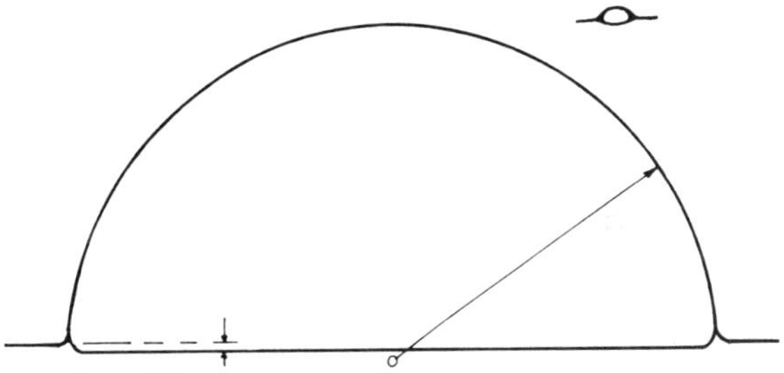

25 (above right) and **26**

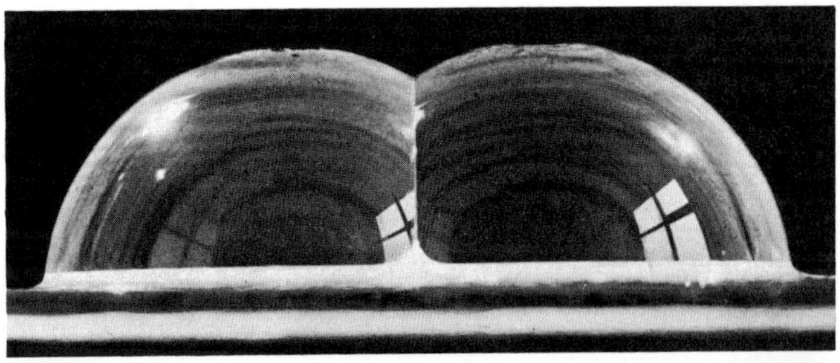

27 ▲

▼ **28**

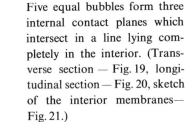

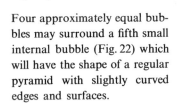

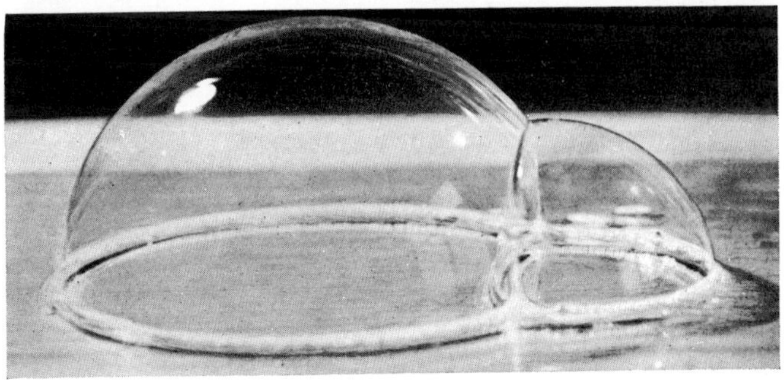

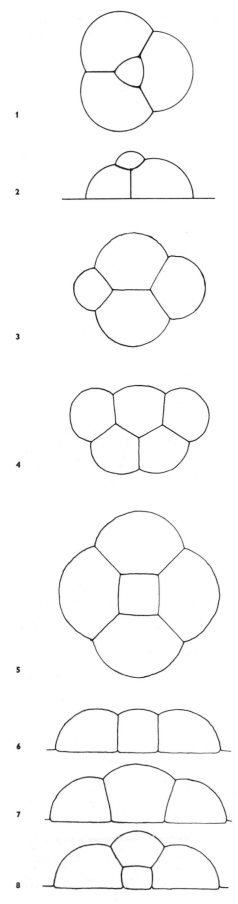

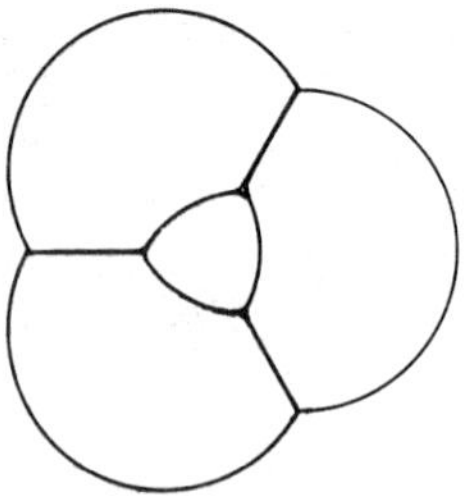
1

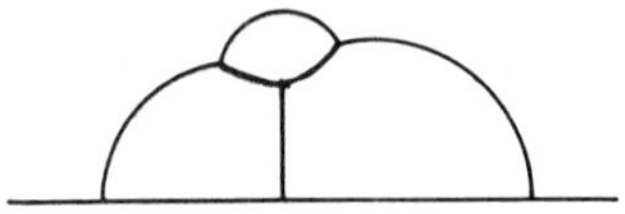
2

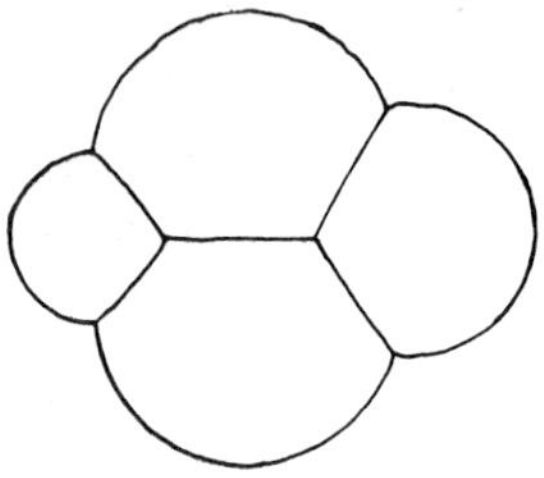
3

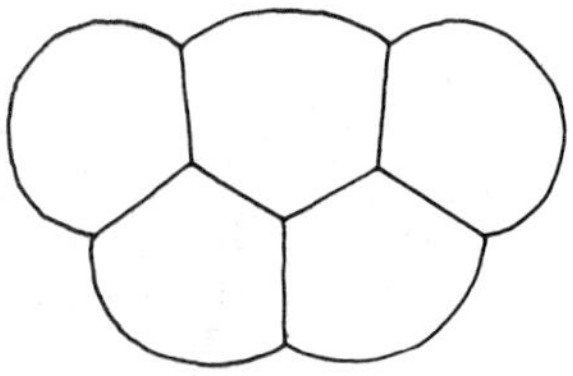
4

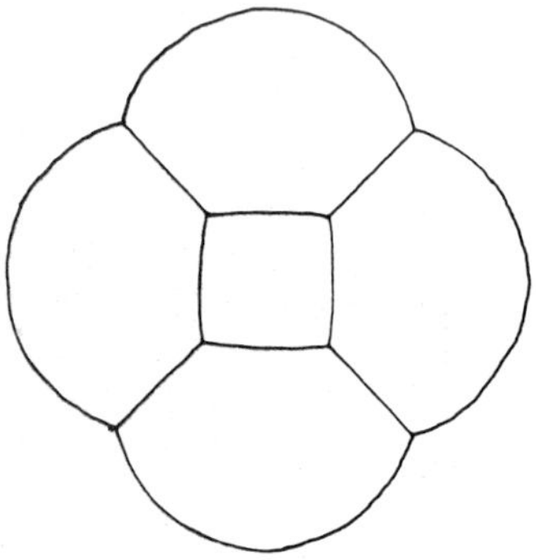
5

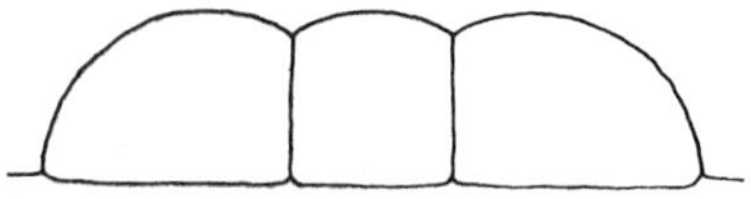
6

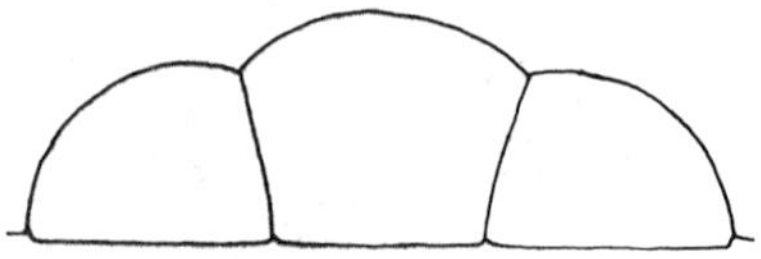
7

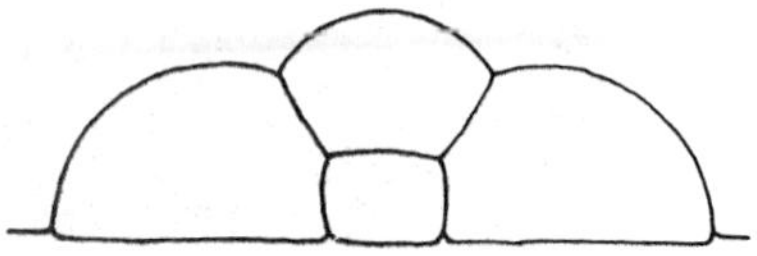
8

The floating bubble (Fig. 26, p. 13) is a hemisphere. The water level is lower inside the bubble than outside it. For equal membrane thicknesses small bubbles (Fig. 25, p. 13) have higher internal pressures, and the bubble base is curved. Very small bubbles are floating spheres of air.

The water rises at the base of the bubble, as can be seen in the detailed side view (Fig. 24, p. 13). Floating twin bubbles (Fig. 27, p. 13) have a plane vertical partition. If the bubbles are unequal (Fig. 28, p. 13) the partition is curved (photos by Butter and Sauter).

Three connected floating bubbles assume a typical shape (Fig. 22) on top of which a fourth "riding" bubble can be placed (Figs. 1 and 2).

Four floating bubbles (Fig. 3) cannot all be in contact with one another.

Five floating bubbles frequently form double rows, one of two and the other of three bubbles (Fig. 4); or they may group themselves around a small central bubble (Fig. 5).

If this central bubble grows, the shape of the cross section changes (Figs. 6 and 7). If the central bubble grows excessively, then it will either become a riding bubble, or a new, sixth bubble will be formed beneath the original central bubble (Fig. 8).

Many combinations with inside bubbles are possible. For instance, three large bubbles may enclose two unequal internal bubbles in an asymmetrical arrangement (Fig. 9).

Two small internal bubbles can easily be inserted at the points of contact of four bubbles (Fig. 10).

Three large and three internal bubbles become joined in a strictly geometric pattern (Fig. 11); an additional internal bubble may form in the center (Fig. 12).

Six bubbles of approximately the

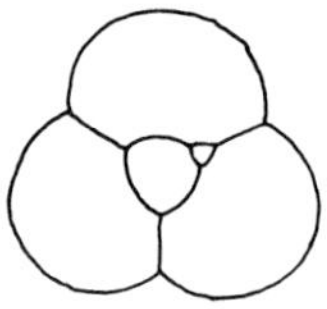
9

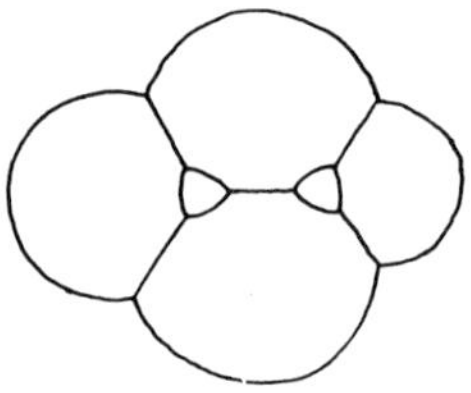
10

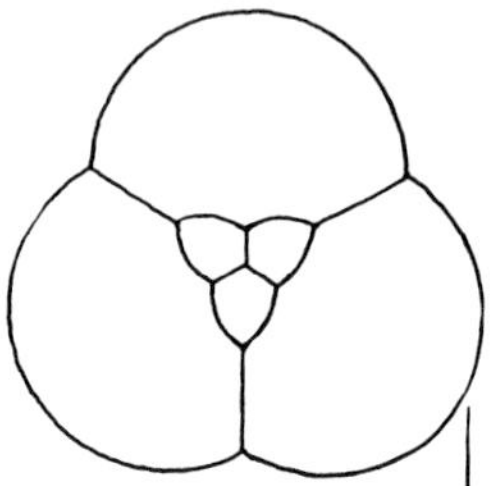
11

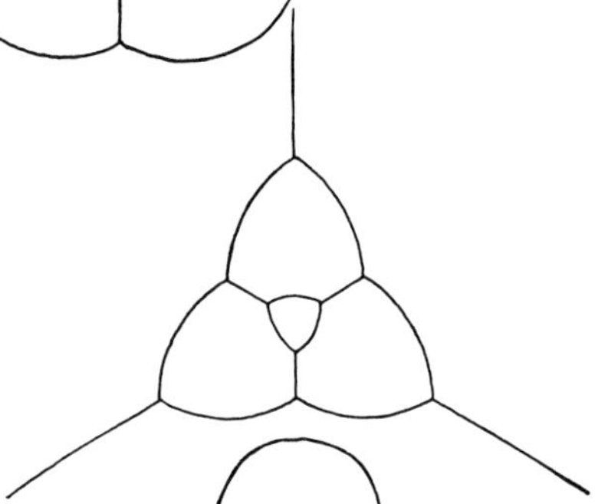
12

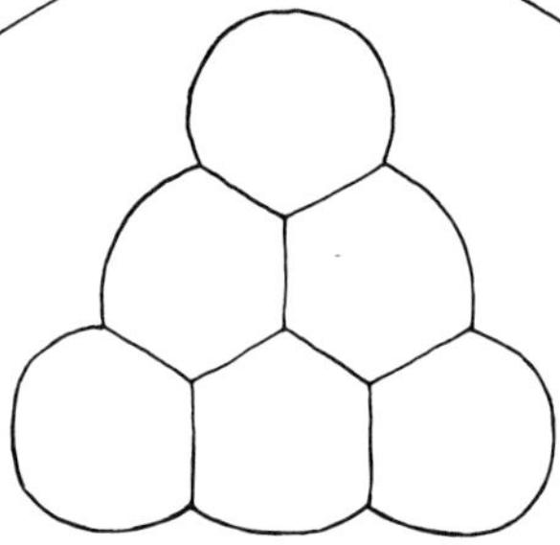
13

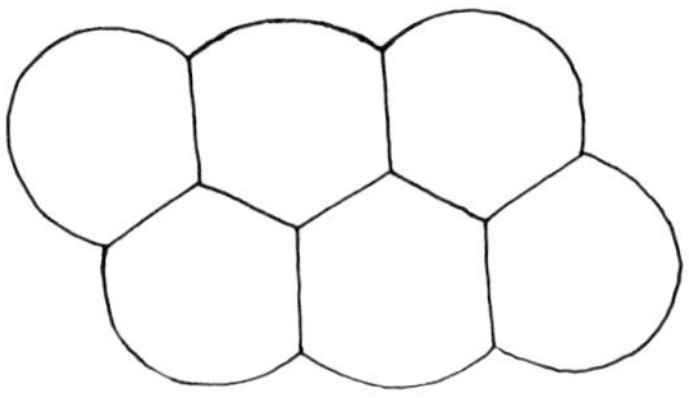
14

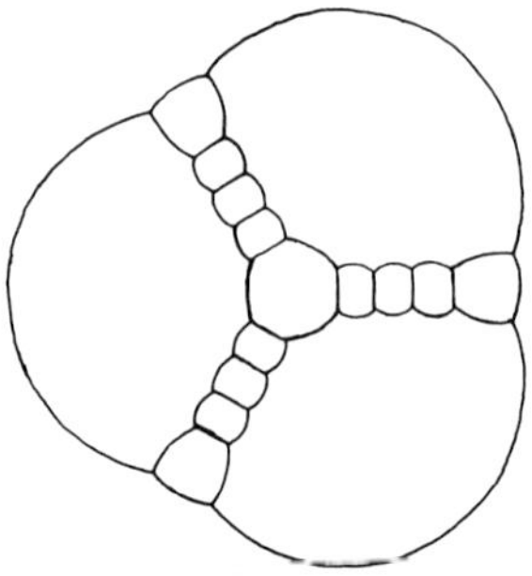
15

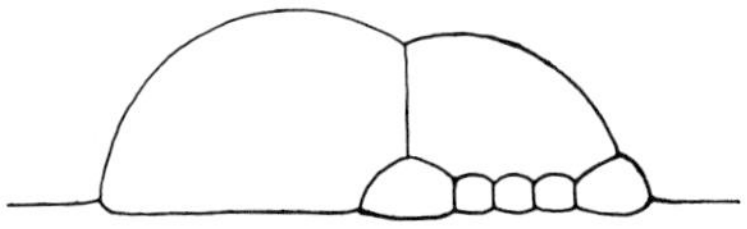
16

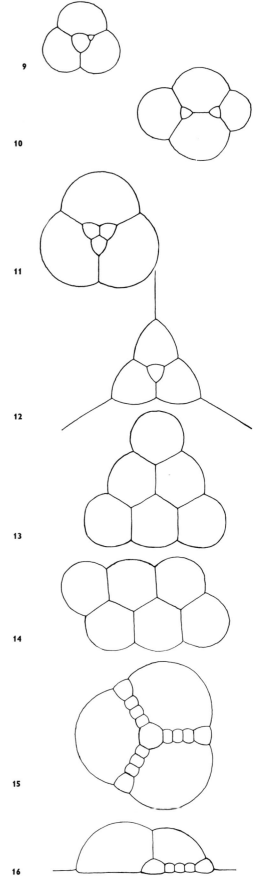

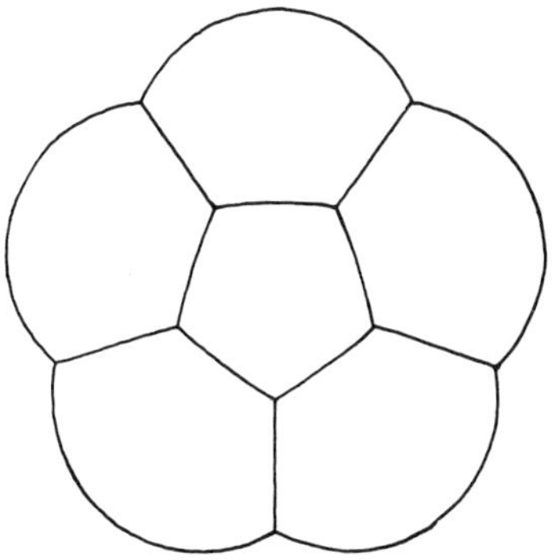

17

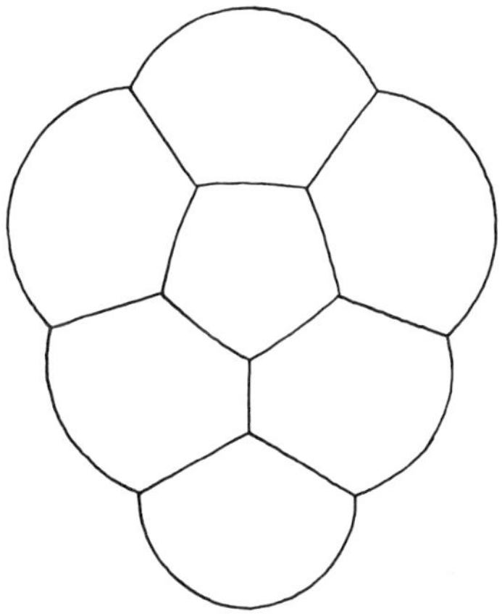

18

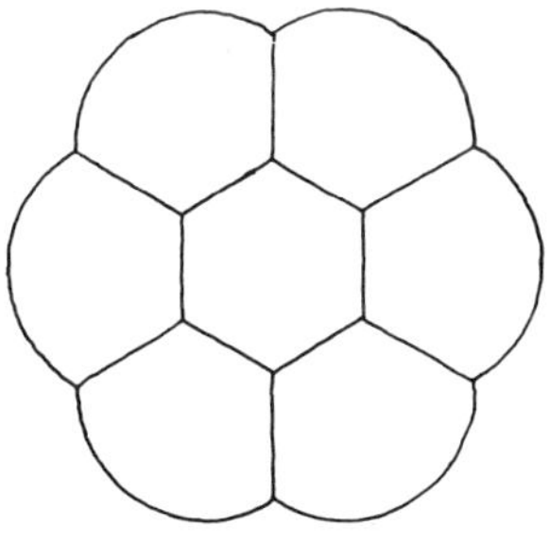

19

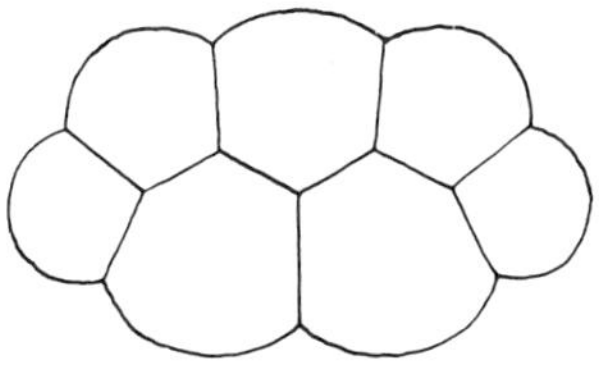

20

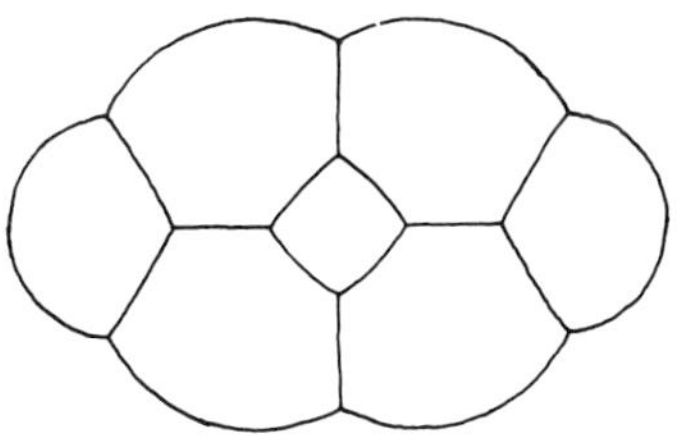

21

same size may arrange themselves either centrally (Fig. 13), or in rows (Fig. 14).

In a group of three bubbles, strings of small bubbles may be formed at the points of contact between the inside walls and the water. This can be seen in plan (Fig. 15) and section (Fig. 16). At contact lines such small bubbles always form continuous chains.

Five bubbles may arrange themselves around a central bubble (Fig. 17).

Seven approximately equal bubbles (Fig. 18) often form a similar arrangement with one of the bubbles placed eccentrically; alternatively, six bubbles may surround a hexagonal central bubble (Fig. 19).

Eight bubbles may group themselves in many ways: they may, for instance, form rows (Fig. 20), or surround internal bubbles symmetrically (Fig. 21).

Groups of floating bubbles generally assume an overall outline as rounded-off as possible. Long rows quickly agglomerate into compact masses (Figs. 3 to 5, p. 16).

The series of photographs of floating soap bubbles show the grouping of three large bubbles (Fig. 22), a large bubble riding on three others (Fig. 23), a fourth internal bubble beneath the riding bubble (Fig. 24), four bubbles with a fifth central bubble (Fig. 25, as in Fig. 6), with an additional internal bubble (Fig. 26, as in Fig. 8), and, finally, the most frequent arrangement of five bubbles (Fig. 27). (Soap bubbles in a black container, which were formed from a transparent solution, were photographed against the light.)

When a large number of floating bubbles of equal volumes (Figs. 1 and 2, p. 16) are grouped together, they assume a hexagonal shape; the system thus encloses a maximum space with a minimum membrane surface.

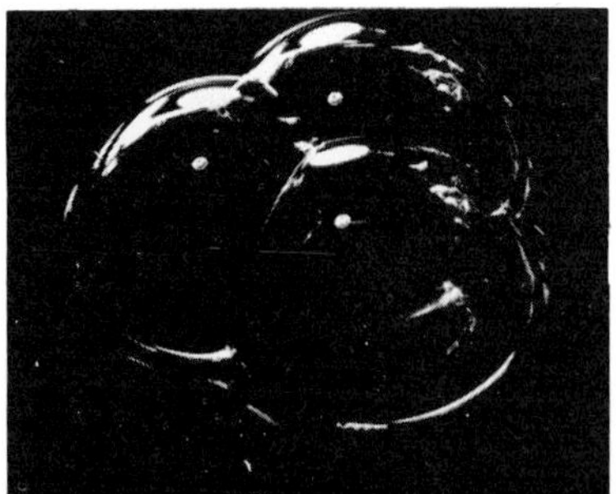

22

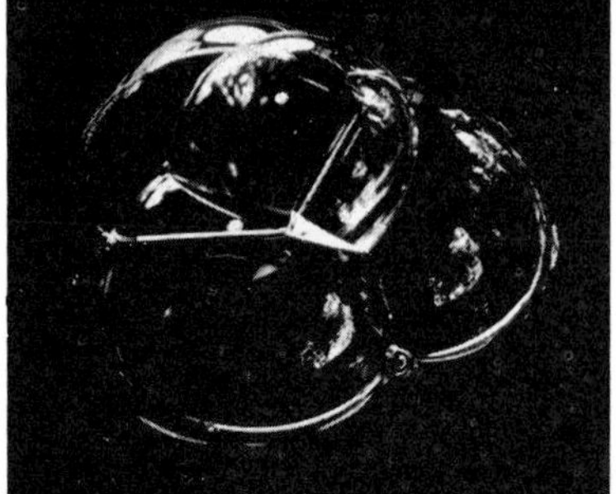

23

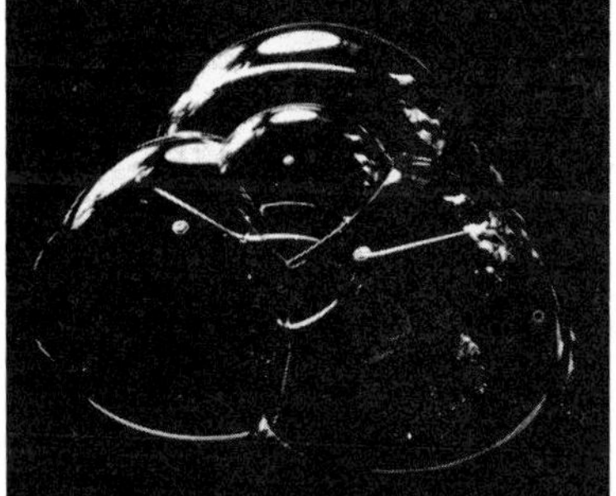

24

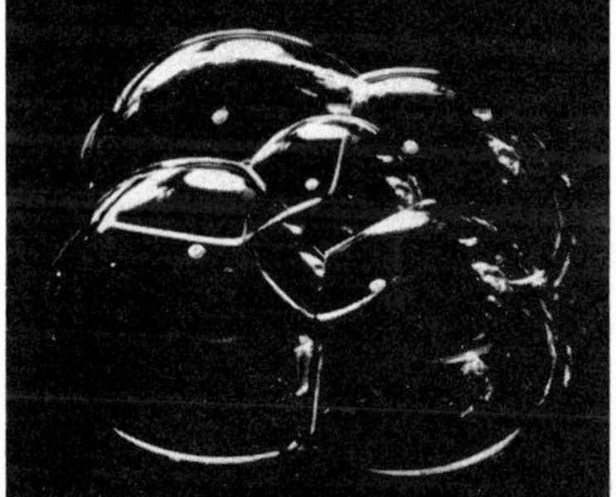

25

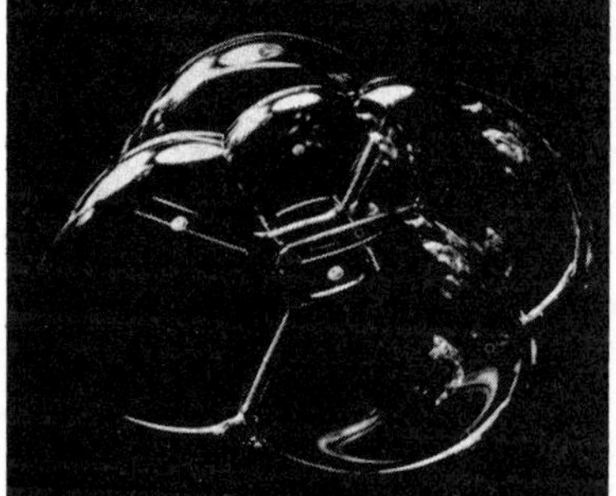

26

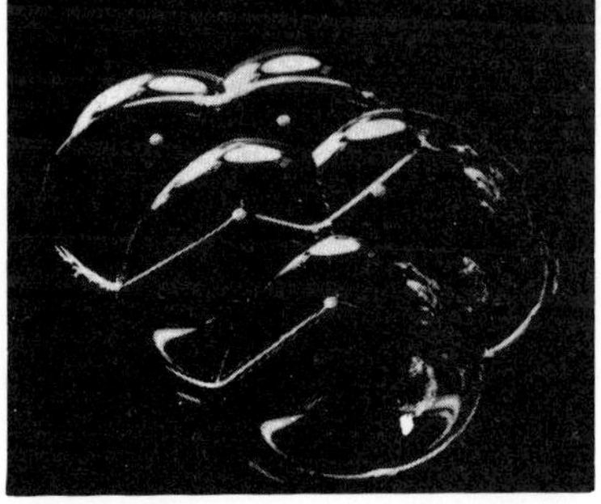

27

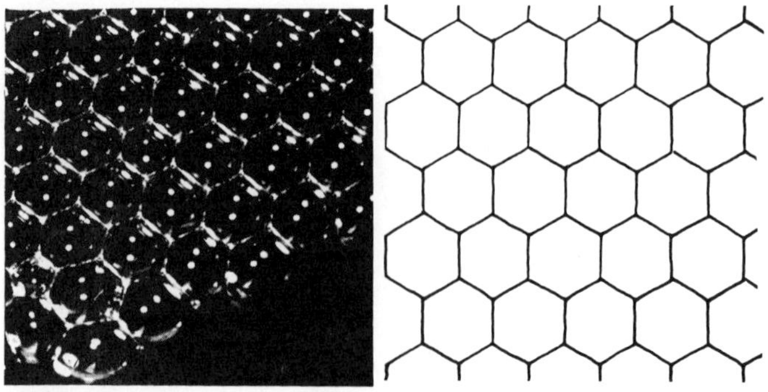

1 and 2

Long soap-bubble clusters quickly agglomerate into compact masses (Figs. 3 to 5).

It can be seen from the sections through soap-bubble agglomerations (Figs. 6 and 7), that if the lower layer is sufficiently extensive, it can support a second layer.

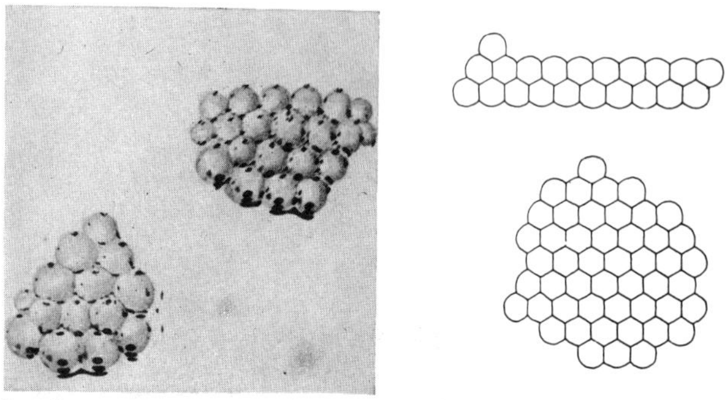

3 to 5

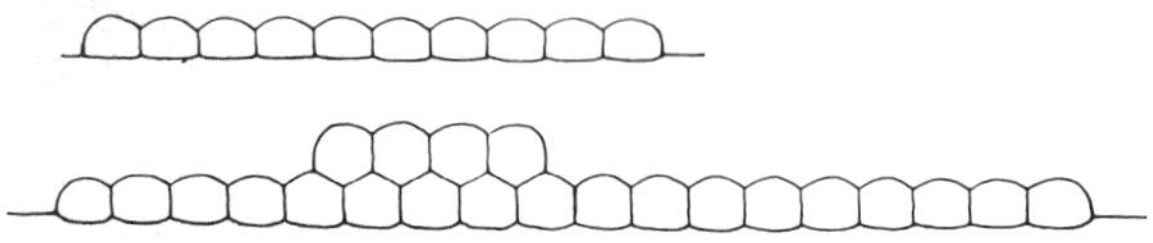

6 and 7

8

9

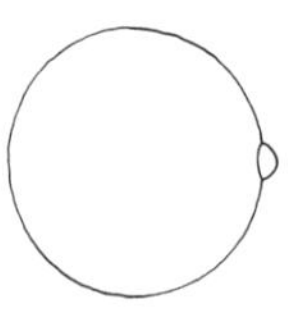

10

Small soap bubbles enclose a large bubble like a ring (Figs. 8 to 11). (This is a convenient model for a large pneumatic factory shed surrounded by smaller workshops.)

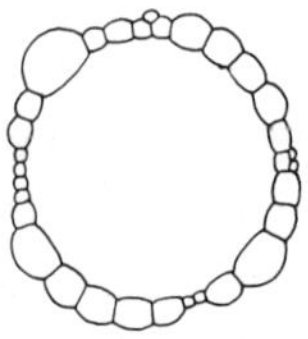

11

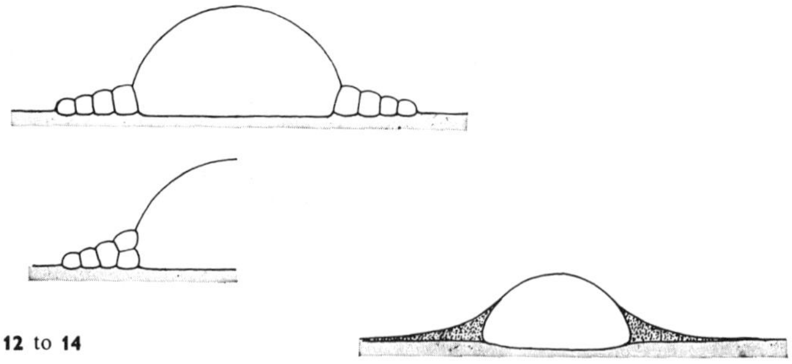

12 to 14

If there are small bubbles they will group themselves in several rings around a large central bubble (Fig. 12), the inner bubble rings often forming two layers (Fig. 13). Extremely small bubbles, as in foam, frequently agglomerate as shown in (Fig. 14).

A free floating bubble (Fig. 15) will rapidly approach an inclined plane and ascend it (Fig. 16) until the center of the sphere lies on the line of contact between the plane and the water. This is true for any angle of inclination of the plane (Figs. 17 and 18).

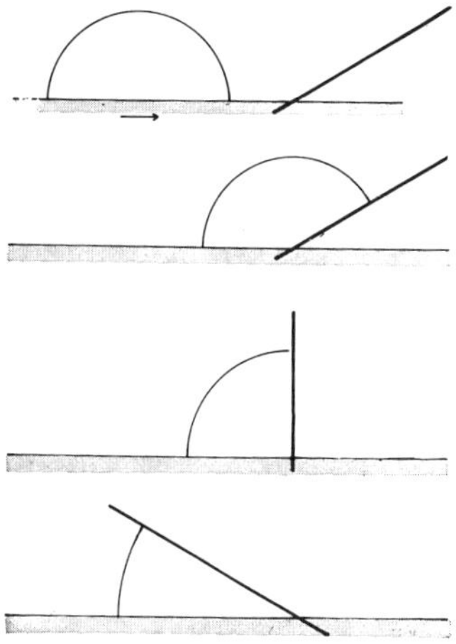

15 to 18

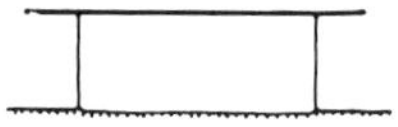

19

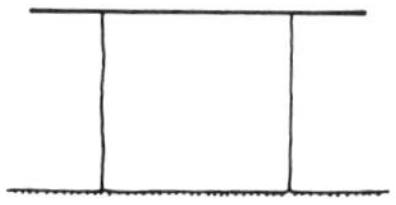

20

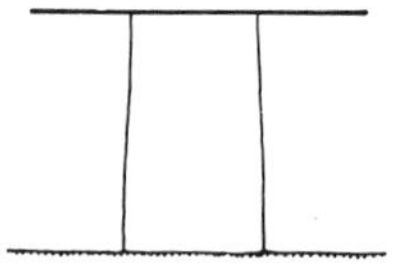

21

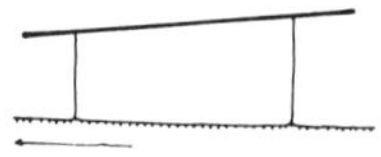

22

23 ▼

If the top of a floating bubble is touched with a horizontal surface, a cylinder is formed (Fig. 19). Thus, in the presence of internal pressure, a cylinder may also be a minimum area.

If the top surface is raised (Fig. 20), the cylinder will retain its shape, though only up to a certain height (Fig. 21).

If the surface is inclined, the cylindrical bubble moves in the direction of the lowest point (Fig. 22).

Photograph 23 shows a floating cylindrical soap bubble in contact with the horizontal underside of a piston just inside its rim (photo by Butter and Sauter).

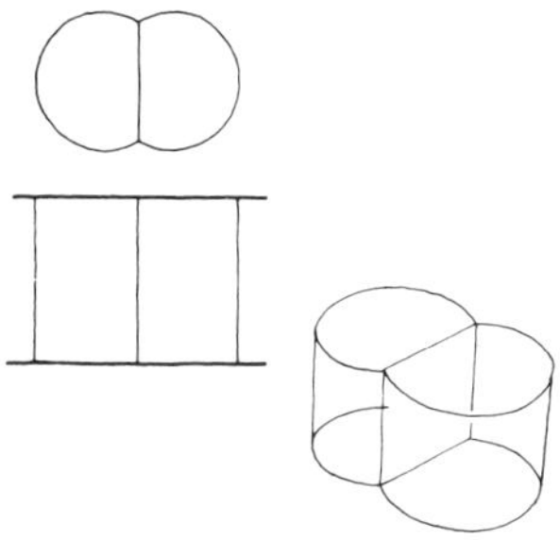

24 to 26

27 ▶

Twin bubbles between plane parallel surfaces (Figs. 24 to 26) form prismatic bodies consisting of two cylindrical segments with a plane internal partition. If the distance between the surfaces is increased beyond a certain point, the bubbles abruptly assume the shape of an hourglass (Fig. 27) (photo by Butter and Sauter).

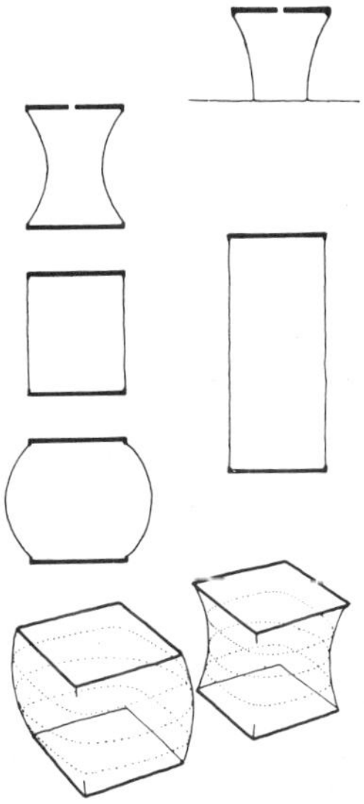

28 to 34

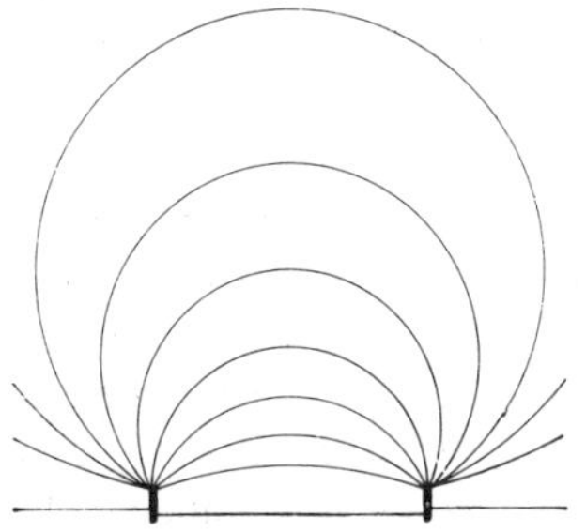

35 ▲ ▼ 36 and 37

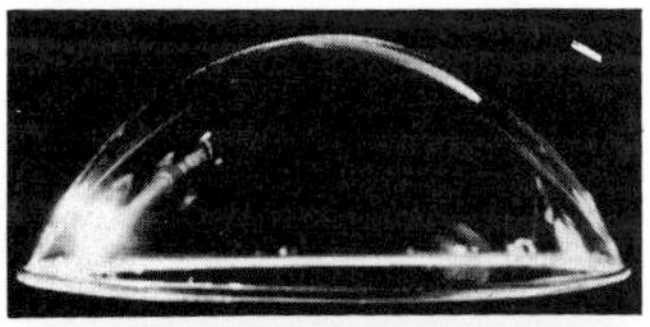

Various soap-bubble shapes

When not pneumatically stressed, the surface of revolution formed by soap skins stretched between an open ring and a water surface (Fig. 28), or between two rings (Fig. 29) is a catenoid (see p. 295).

If the internal pressure is increased, the bubble assumes first the shape of a cylinder (Figs. 30 and 31) and then that of a barrel (Fig. 32).

Similar processes can be observed also with noncircular frames (Figs. 33 and 34), but the bubbles do not have prismatic shapes. However, irrespective of the internal pressure, the bubbles tend to assume circular cross sections in the center.

When a soap bubble is blown up on a ring, it passes through many stages, in all of which it forms spherical segments (Fig. 35). This is also shown in photographs 36 and 37 (by Butter and Sauter).

Bubbles can have an infinite number of shapes. They can be stretched between frames that are mutually inclined at any angle, or between curves of arbitrary shape: in each case a bubble of definite shape is formed. However, multiple bubbles may assume different forms, even with the same boundary conditions.

Four bubbles inside a ring assume the form of a cushion within a rigid frame (Fig. 38) (photo by Butter and Sauter). Soap bubbles may be stretched over any frame of arbitrary shape (Fig. 39), though not always to any height. A soap bubble can form on an annulus. We obtain a pneumatic shape in which almost half the surface has a saddle-shaped curvature (Fig. 40). A soap bubble may even form on a frame with interior points (Fig. 41). The membrane is drawn down in the neighborhood of each point and has a saddle-shaped curvature. The slope of the skin, α, at the lowest point (Fig. 42) cannot exceed a certain value since otherwise stress uniformity could not be maintained.

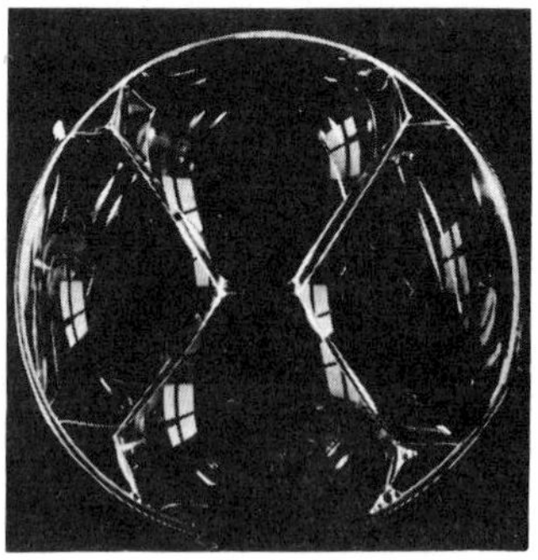

38

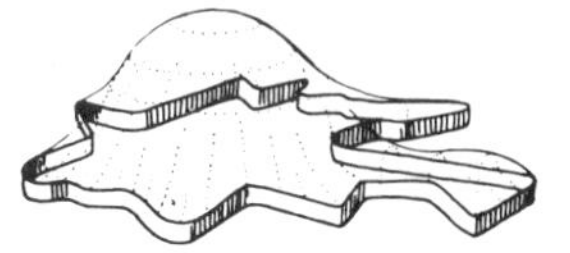

39

40

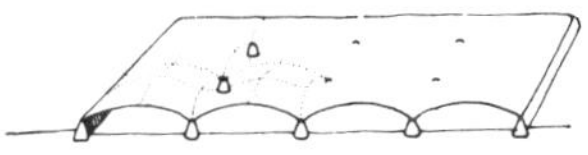

41

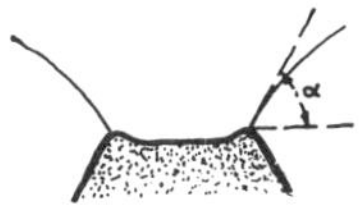

42

Foam

Foam is an agglomeration of bubbles (Fig. 43). Foam made of rubber, plastics, cement, minerals, metals, or glass has lately been increasingly adopted as a building material in addition to its use as insulation. When its pores are closed, foam has a pneumatic load-carrying capacity. In general, foams exhibit a large number of different bubble shapes. All these bubbles form multi-angular bodies. The use of hard foams as building and insulating material was widely advocated after the war by the author. Their enormously increased use is, however, a chance development, due more to the search for markets for certain synthetic materials. Foam offers great possibilities in the structures of the future, mainly as a center layer in sandwich panels, or in combination with skins stretched over it.

▼ 43

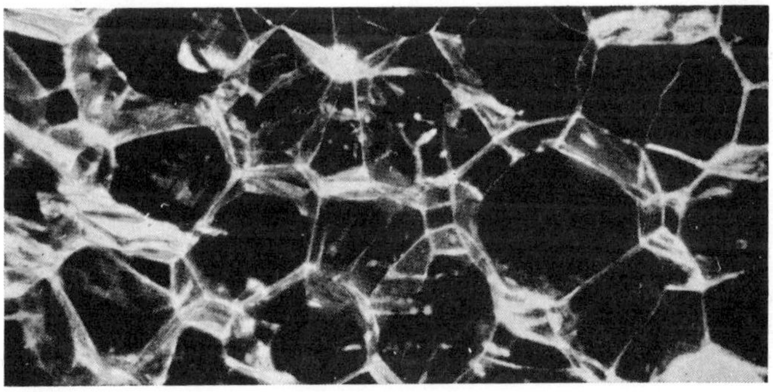

Laws Governing the Formation of Pneumatically Stretched Skins

There are countless soap-bubble shapes, all of which conform to the general condition of stress uniformity.

1

This number can still be increased if stress differences are admitted (Fig. 1). Nevertheless, only a fraction of all the imaginable shapes can be formed pneumatically.

Pneumatic shapes are characterized by double-curvature surfaces. Saddle-shaped and single-curvature surfaces are less frequently formed than spherical surfaces. Plane surfaces are impossible in actual practice.

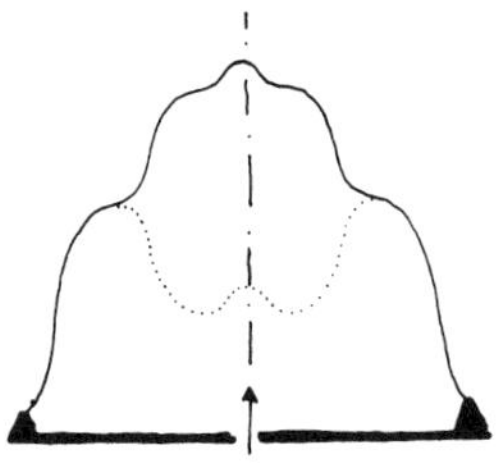

2

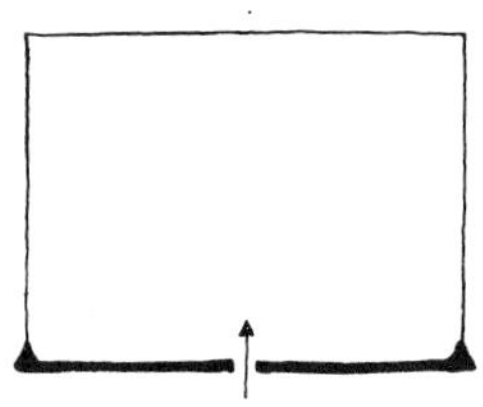

3

It is obvious that a membrane, shaped as shown by the dotted lines in Figure 2, will be forced outward as soon as internal pressure is applied. The shape shown by the dotted lines cannot, therefore, be formed pneumatically.

If we have a semicylinder made of pliable but inelastic skin and having a flat top (Fig. 3) and we apply internal pressure to it, the top will bulge outward (Fig. 4), and pleats will appear. The top of the cylinder becomes a surface of revolution, with zero circumferential stresses in the region of the pleats.

A pneumatic skin can be shaped like a flattened ball (Fig. 6) deviating only slightly from a sphere. In a body of revolution (Fig. 5), the membrane is not stressed in a tangential direction (parallel of latitude) if the radius of curvature is equal to half the distance P–N. If the radius of curvature becomes smaller—pleats will appear (see pp. 186-187). If such a body of revolution is formed, it will be noted that even with low elasticity or deformability of the skin, the shape has a tendency to become spherical. The reason for this is that the radial stresses at the apex of such a body are theoretically infinite.

4

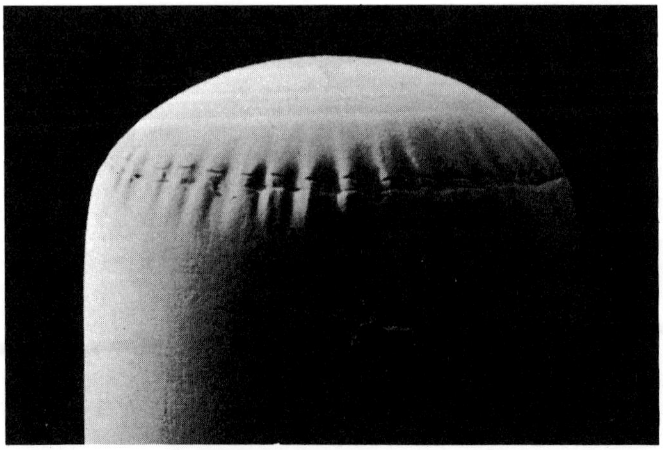

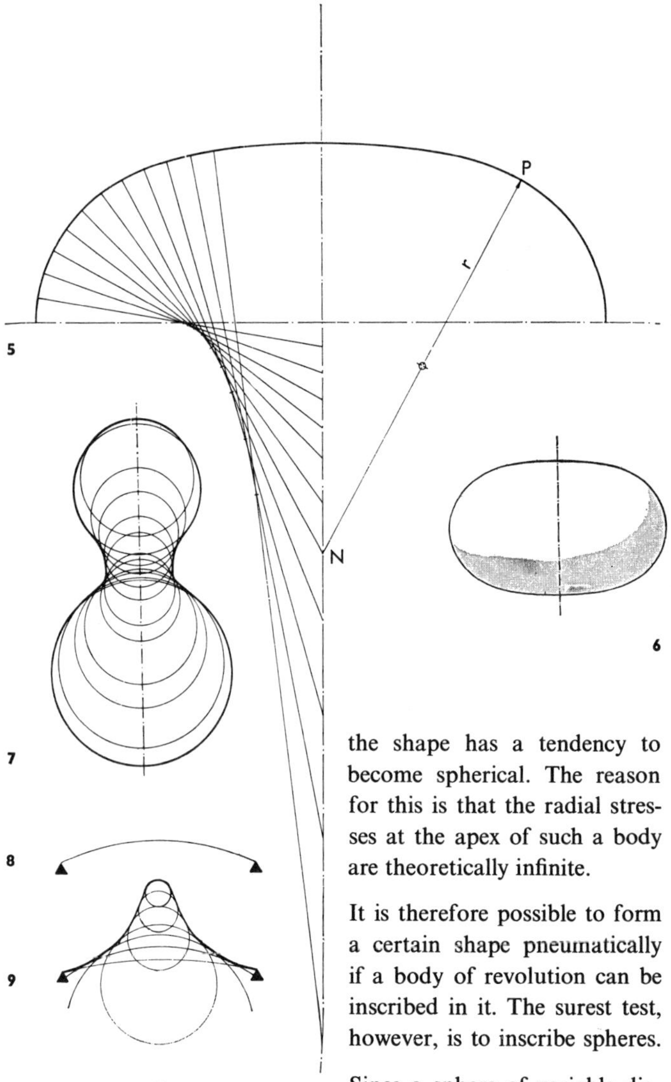

5

6

7

8

9

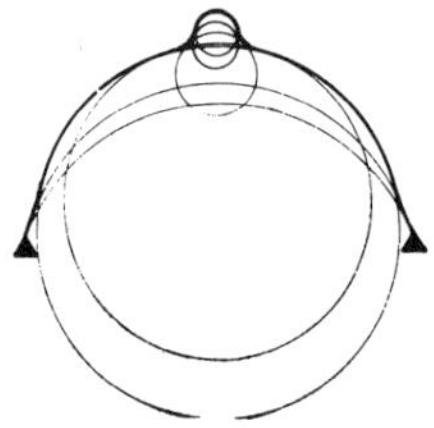

10

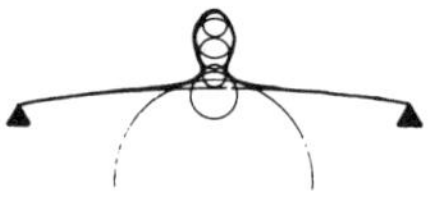

11

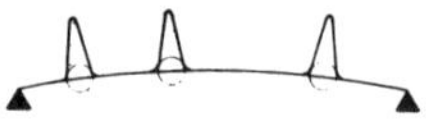

12

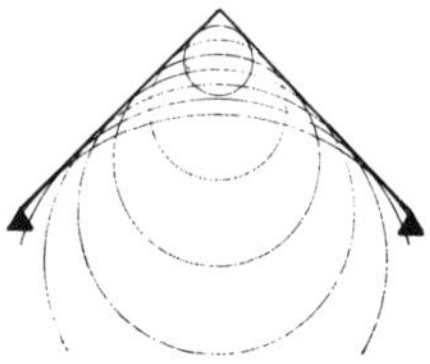

13

It is therefore possible to form a certain shape pneumatically if a body of revolution can be inscribed in it. The surest test, however, is to inscribe spheres.

Since a sphere of variable diameter can be moved along an axis (Fig. 7), the enveloping surface can be formed pneumatically. With the aid of inscribed spheres it can be ascertained whether different shapes (Figs. 8 to 13) can be formed pneumatically. The spheres can move along any curve (Fig. 14), provided the radius of curvature of the latter is not too small in relation to the diameter of the sphere. Branches can be constructed in the same manner.

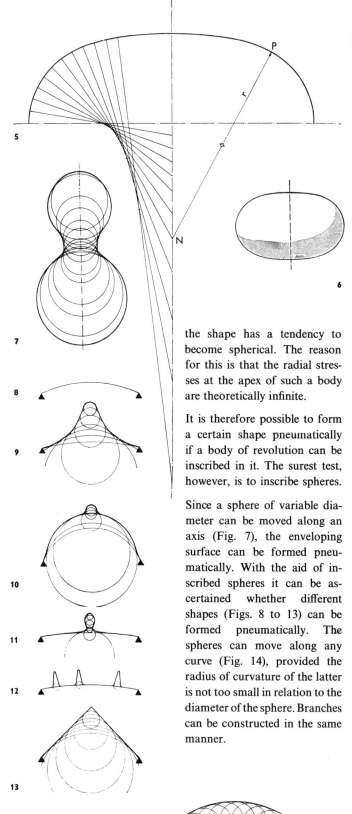

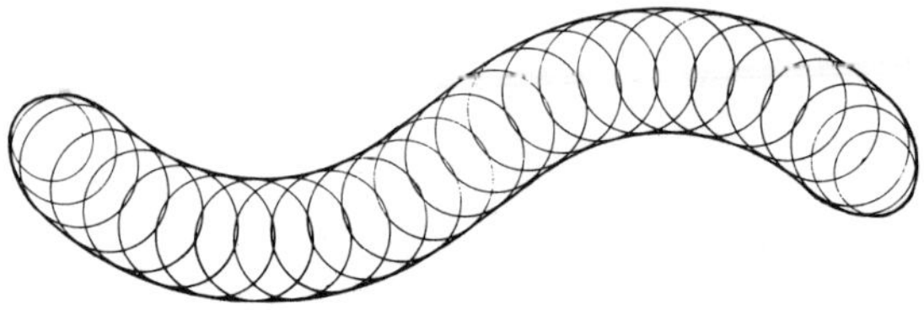

14

Buildings with Internal Pressure

Lanchester's concept of inflatable domes originated more than forty years ago, and may have been preceded by even earlier, forgotten ideas. It was unacceptable to builders of the old school, since it belonged to a completely different domain of thought. The load-carrying cable was not accepted because of its lack of rigidity. Only after development lasting almost a hundred years it gradually took its place in structural engineering. The idea of using air to carry loads appears even today like a utopia to many people. Pneumatic structures are tensile-stressed, and are therefore closely related to other suspended structures, although there exist basic differences. All other building structures can be traced to three main groups, namely, column-and-beam structures, arch structures, and suspended structures, but this is more difficult to do in the case of pneumatic structures. The expression "airborne structures" is appropriate for most pneumatic structures. Let us imagine a slightly vaulted dome membrane under internal pressure. In the

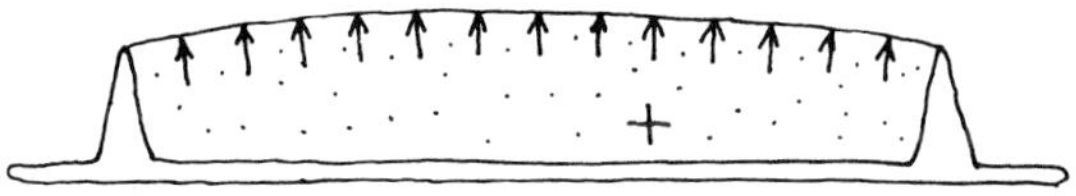

15

absence of wind or snow the internal pressure (Fig. 15) causes a stress in the membrane. With a uniform snow load, the membrane stress decreases, vanishing theoretically when the external load becomes equal to the internal pressure. (We have neglected here the fact that the weight of the snow acts vertically, while the internal pressure acts normal to the surface.) We have, therefore, the unusual case of a carrying structure being free of stress under a positive load: the load is borne by the air.

Although we do encounter more or less uniformly distributed snow loads on flat surfaces, other loads, in particular wind loads, are unevenly distributed.

With nonuniform moving loads (Fig. 19), membrane stresses cannot be avoided. Such loads greatly influence the design of pneumatic buildings.

In a test model, a horizontal rubber membrane was made to sag under a water load (Fig. 20). The water was then removed by applying pressure under the membrane. At a certain stage (Fig. 21), the left side of the membrane already bulged upward, while the water still pressed it down on the right. After all the water had been removed, the membrane assumed a uniformly convex shape (Fig. 22).

We can apply the concept of pneumatic structures with tensile-stressed skins not only to envelopes subjected to positive, but also

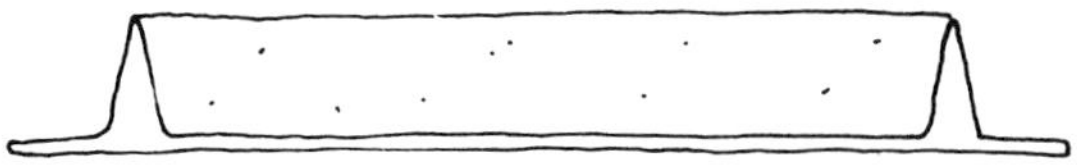

16

to negative pressures,* and adapt the air pressure to the applied loads. We can then give an even better explanation of the manner in which pneumatic structures operate using a plane unstressed membrane. Assume that the membrane (Fig. 16) weighs 1.0 kg/m^2: in the absence of an external load, an internal pressure of 1 kP/m^2 = 1 mm water column = 0.0001 atm will be enough to keep the skin stress-free.

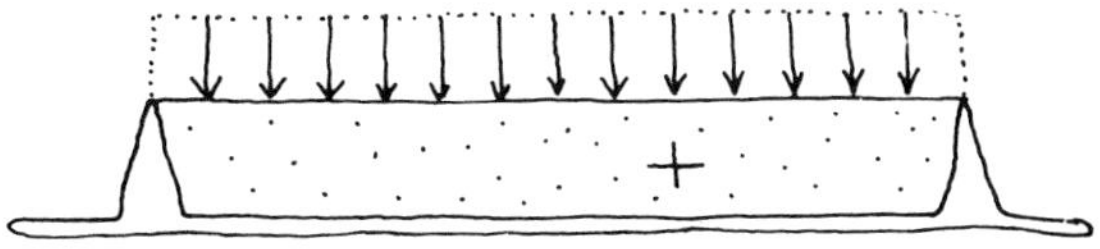

17

A uniformly distributed snow load of 75 kg/m^2 (Fig. 17) can be balanced by an internal pressure of 76 mm water column so that the skin remains stress-free.

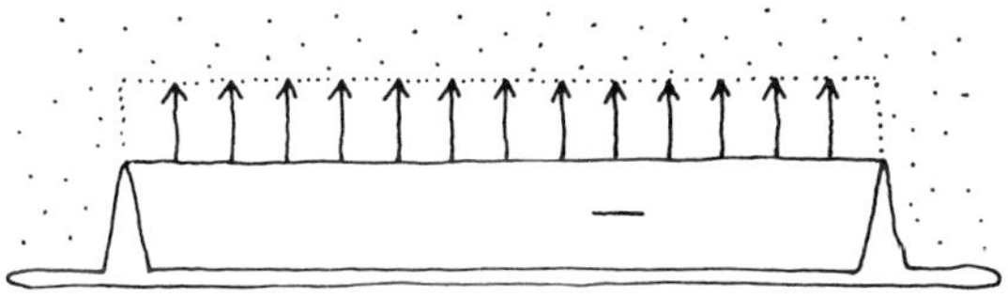

18

The action of the wind on such a building will give rise to an upward force (Fig. 18). If we assume this lift to be uniformly distributed and acting on the skin with a negative pressure of 60 kg/m^2, then, in order to keep the skin unstressed, an internal negative pressure

19

of 59 mm of water column must be applied. The membrane acts in this case only as a separating layer, and can be as thin as desired.

20

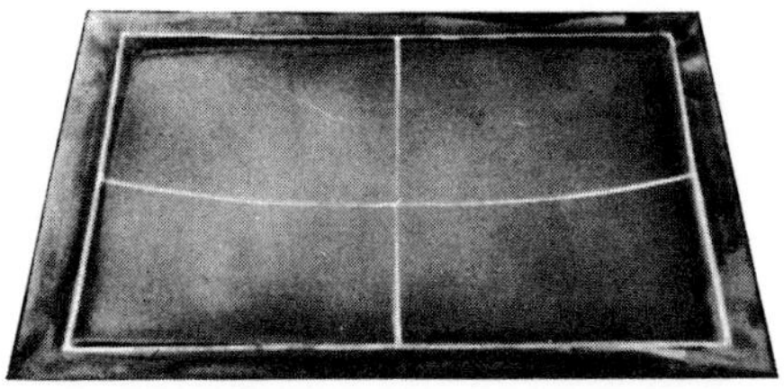

21

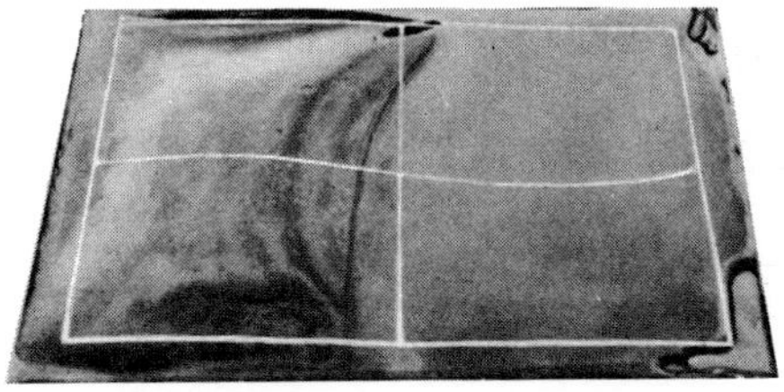

22

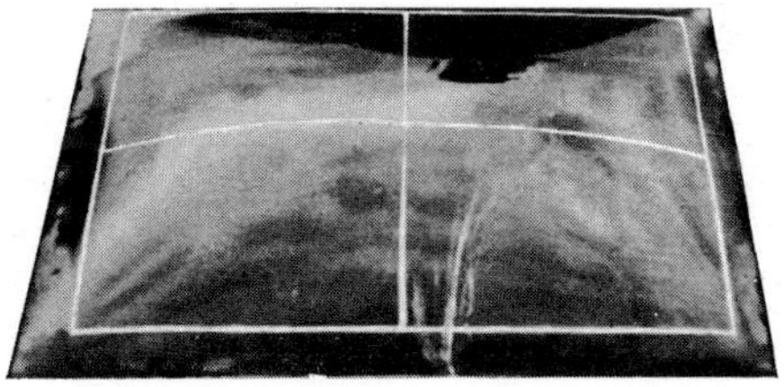

Another fundamental difference between pneumatic and other structures is that, for pneumatic membranes, there is no theoretical maximum span as determined by strength, elasticity, specific weight, or any other property.

Stresses in ordinary structures should not be larger than those corresponding to 1.3 times the breaking length (breaking stress/specific weight), since, otherwise, the structure would collapse under its own weight.† In pneumatic structures, however, this value may be exceeded.

Thus, it is theoretically hardly possible to span a distance of over 36 km with a steel cable; a shell of 10 km diameter, even if built with the best materials according to optimum design, would not be able to sustain its own weight. On the other hand, one can imagine a membrane supported by pressure differences, which would realize Buckminster Fuller's dream of "universal space" and could be of any size: for example, a closed envelope surrounding the earth. Although this would hardly be of any practical use, we shall, perhaps, some day build such an envelope around small artificial or natural satellites to maintain a synthetic climate within.

The Safety of pneumatic buildings under internal pressure

Lanchester already pointed out that pneumatic buildings are safer than any other form of structure. The main advantage of the pneumatically stretched membrane is its small weight; even with spans

1
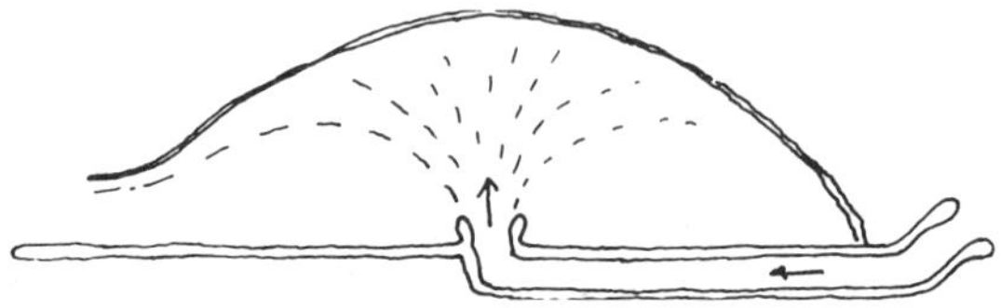

2
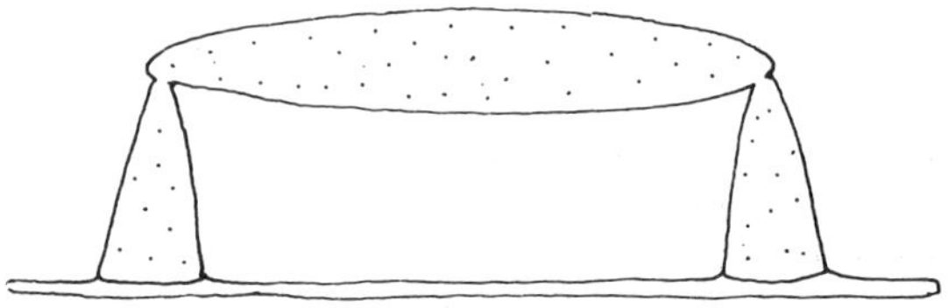

of more than 100 m, the weight of the structure does not exceed 3 kg/m^2.

Even if the compressed air supply should fail, it would take a long time for large envelopes to collapse, since the enclosed air can leak out only slowly. Even large holes and tears are not dangerous. Although the pressure drops quite rapidly, the force due to the weight of the membrane is so small that, in large envelopes, it may take days before the enclosed air escapes even if the openings are large. Wind or temperature differences may delay or completely stop the process of deflation. Snow loads, on the other hand, accelerate it. If the compressed air supply is adequate, permanent openings can even be left in pneumatic structures (Fig. 1).

Even if the envelope should collapse, this would not seriously interfere with the movement of people inside the building, particularly if poles or exhibition objects retain the envelope. Large pneumatic structures will of course have emergency compressors to maintain the internal pressure should the main supply fail.

† F. Otto, Berlin, Bauwelt Verlag 1954 [now Ullstein Fachverlag]

Spherical envelopes can be computed and designed with great precision. If we, nevertheless, compare the consequences of a tear in the envelope with those of the failure of a rigid concrete structure designed for the same safety factor, the differences due to structural weight become obvious.

The effects of high pressure on man

Irrespective of the span, a constant pressure of 20 mm of water column, which corresponds to an interior load of 20 kP/m^2 is normally employed today to maintain the shape of a structure. In most cases pressure of not more than 80 or 100 and not less than −60 mm water column is required. Man can withstand constant pressures in the range between 0.2 atm (12,000 m altitude) to 3 atm (30 m below water level).

In pneumatic structures a maximum pressure differential of 80 mm water column corresponds to a difference in altitude of only about 55 m; the ordinary load of 20 mm water column corresponds to a height of only 15 m. Even sensitive persons do not notice such small pressure variations, which are of the same order of magnitude as those caused in many houses by the wind. Higher pressures may be fleetingly noticed when hurrying through an air lock (revolving door). No health hazard is presented by a continuous stay in a pneumatic structure, even if very strict standards are applied.

Pneumatically stretched structures whose interior space is under normal pressure

All pneumatic structures have cavities in which the pressure is above that of the surrounding air. In principle it is not important whether these cavities are accessible, or whether they are closed balloons. Nevertheless, there exist differences between the two types. In the former case, air locks must generally be provided.

Buildings not under internal pressure generally consist of closed envelopes (Fig. 2) which, when inflated, become rigid and enclose rooms shaped like slabs, arches, or shells. Usually, these structures require a considerably larger membrane area and a much higher pressure than balloons with air locks and are far more expensive. In many structures both types are used, often combined with other structural methods. In this book only the most important examples will be mentioned.

3

The Spherical Surface

The pneumatically stretched spherical membrane (Fig. 3) is a minimum area well known for its applications (balls, balloons, gas containers, satellites). In the future its importance will probably be still greater. In Paris, in 1844, the French engineer, Marey-Monge, built a hydrogen container in form of a balloon having a 0.1 mm thick copper skin (Fig. 4; photo from *Illustrated London News*, 1844), which was perhaps a forerunner of the first balloon satellite of the U.S. Space Program.

The balloon satellite Echo I (Fig. 6; photo by DPA) was ejected in a folded state from the space rocket, and then inflated to a spherical shape through the expansion of the residual air in the balloon envelope. The balloon also contained a mixture consisting of 4.5 kg benzoic acid and 9 kg anthraquinone, which gradually evaporated and served as a continuous source of gas, keeping the balloon inflated. The balloon envelope

4

6

5

consisted of transparent glossy foil 0.127 mm thick, made of esters of polyterephthalic acids, which was treated with aluminum vapors in order to increase its reflective properties. Radio signals at frequencies up to 20,000 MHz were reflected with a loss of only 2%. The diameter of the balloon was 30 m, and its surface area 2,800 m^2. It was assembled from 82 parts. The foil had a specific weight of 1.4 kP/dm^3 and was designed to withstand temperatures between $-60°$ and $+130°$ C. The breaking stress was 18-25 kP/mm^2 in the longitudinal, and 14-20 kP/mm^2 in the transverse direction. The corresponding strains were between 50 and 130% in either direction.

The satellite was folded into a ball 107 cm in diameter and inserted into a magnesium container (Fig. 5; photo from *Kunststoffberater* 10/1960), which was placed in the tip of a three-stage Delta-I rocket and ejected two minutes after release of the third stage. Echo I had the brightness of a star of magnitude O.

Perfectly spherical balloons can exist only in gravity-free space. The influence of the weight of the envelope on the shape of the balloon depends on the internal pressure. This is particularly noticeable in partly inflated balloons, especially if they carry

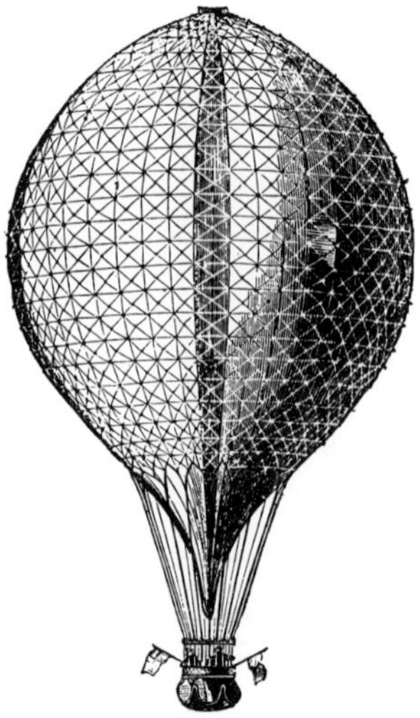

1

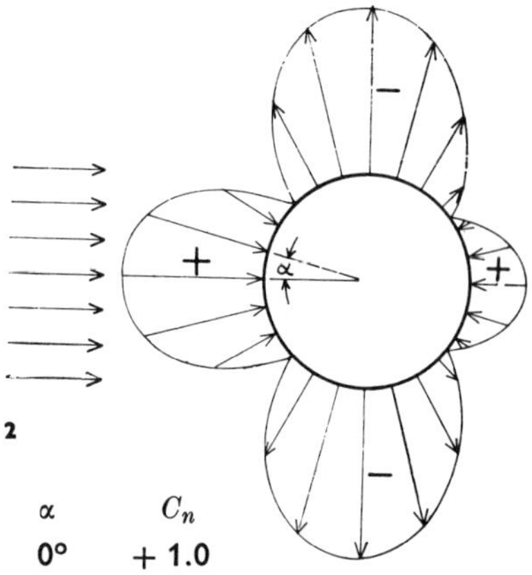

2

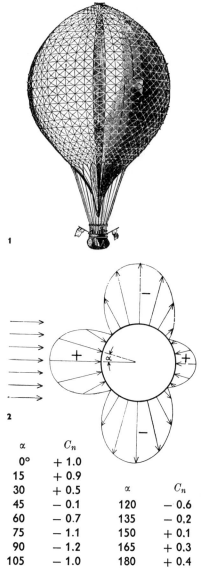

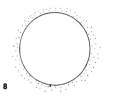

α	C_n	α	C_n
0°	+ 1.0		
15	+ 0.9		
30	+ 0.5		
45	– 0.1	120	– 0.6
60	– 0.7	135	– 0.2
75	– 1.1	150	+ 0.1
90	– 1.2	165	+ 0.3
105	– 1.0	180	+ 0.4

3

4

a payload. The shape of such balloons deviates markedly from the spherical, assuming the traditional drop-like balloon shape (Fig. 1; from *Illustrated London News,* 1844). The balloon envelope is covered with a net (Fig. 3; photo by Ullstein-Eckert) so as to distribute, over the largest possible surface, the weight of the gondola and thus avoid load peaks. The drop-like shape is most noticeable in hot-air balloons, in which the internal pressure is zero at the bottom of the envelope and increases toward the vertex.

Hot-air balloons have the typical shape of water containers (see page 122). Excessive prestressing of the balloon skin, caused by internal pressure, should be avoided, since this results in loss of lift. However, the rigidity of the structure is thereby reduced. The drag on a sphere, with the wind on all sides, is $W = C_n q F$, where q is the static pressure, F is the cross-sectional area, and $C_n = 0.2$ is the drag coefficient.

The coefficient C_n, referring to the surface of the sphere, is given in Fig. 2 and in the table (from SIA-Norm 160). A sphere is a body with little air resistance. The amount of water inside a sphere floating in water affects its shape only slightly (Figs. 5 to 7). This fact can be utilized in drinking-water containers. Not only heavily stressed pneumatic spheres, submerged in earth or water (Fig. 8), but also skins, only partly filled with sand (Fig. 9), (e.g.: gas containers), have organically linked anchorages. Spheres resting on small areas are frequently guyed with ropes (Fig. 4; photo from *Populäre Mechanik*). A free-floating balloon is almost held in position with three guy ropes (Fig. 10), in particular when anchored in a saddle-shaped membrane or cable net (Fig. 11). Balloons on high-guyed poles (Fig. 12)

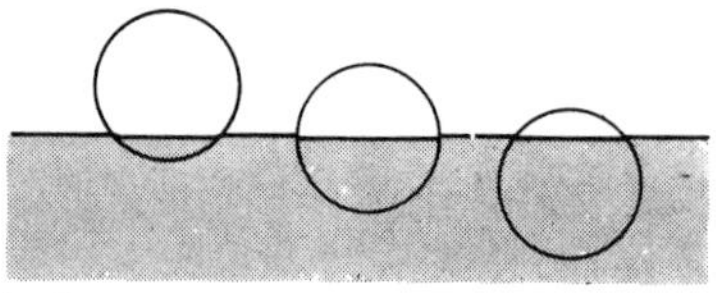

5 to 7

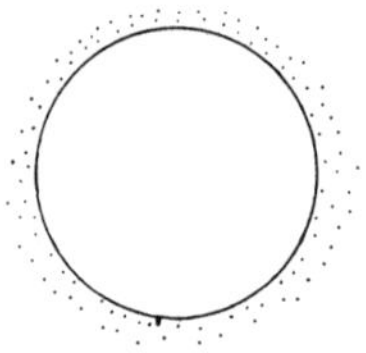

8

9

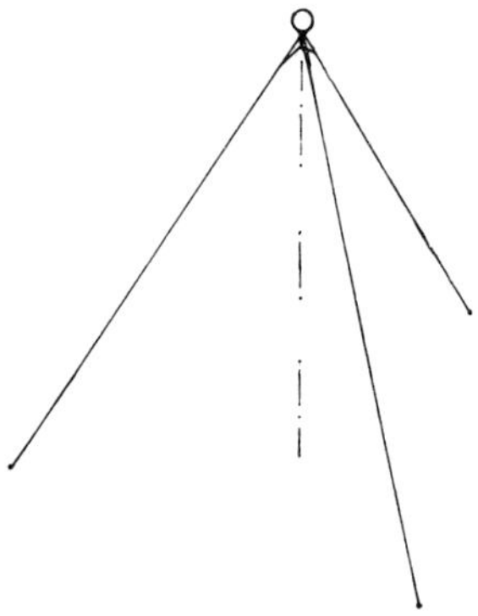

10

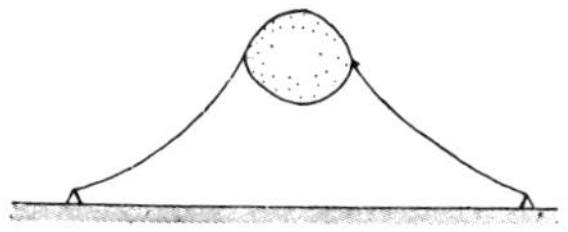

11

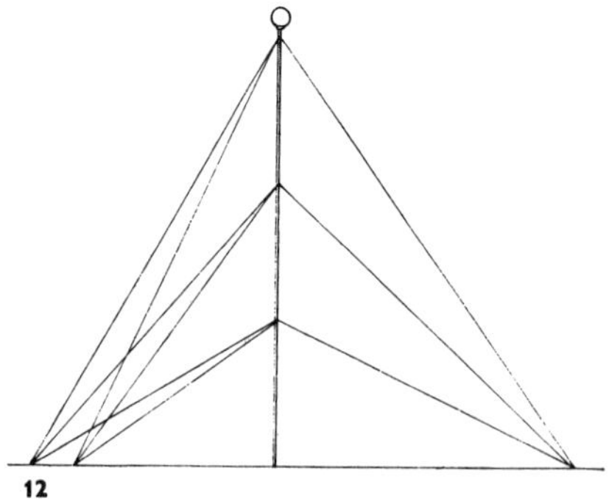

12

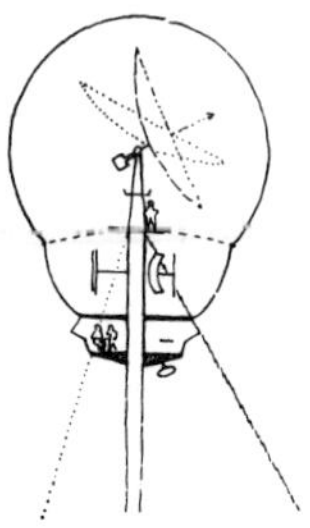

13

14

15

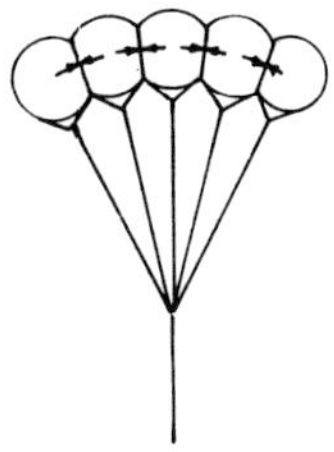
16

17

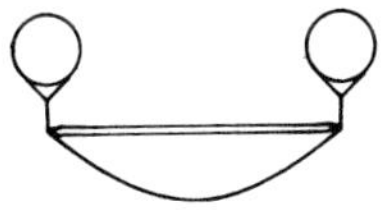
18

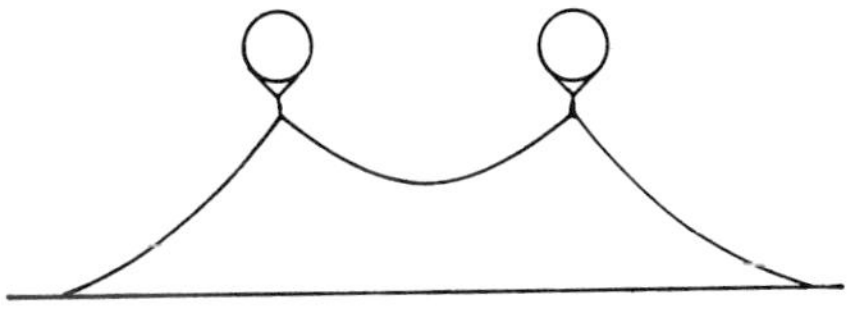
19

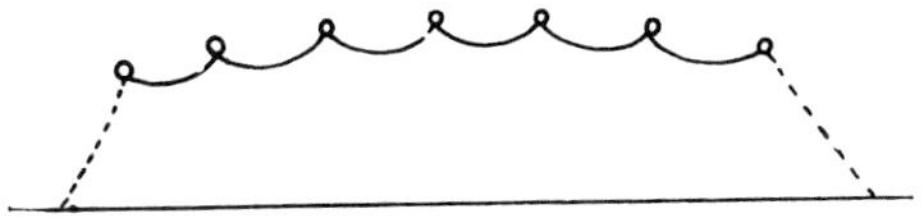
20

are best anchored to the latter by means of internal membranes, an example of which can be seen in Fig. 13 which shows a section through a radar dome. For high-pressure storage (Fig. 21) of gases or fluids, balloons are anchored* on the ocean floor and filled or emptied from the surface. Two balloons (Fig. 14), connected by a cable, move toward each other until they are in contact (Fig. 15). Balloons in clusters press against each other (Fig. 16).

It is difficult to suspend cable nets or even single cables freely, since the horizontal forces due to the cables have to be overcome. These can be balanced by propulsive force (Fig. 17). Struts (Fig. 18), particularly if designed as pneumatic cylinders, may also be used. However, all structures that are intended to take up compressive stresses are very costly if the span is large. It is simpler to suspend rope nets between two barrage balloons (Fig. 19). When cables or cable nets are suspended from great heights, the use of many small balloons may reduce the horizontal forces (Fig. 20). Small floating balloons (Fig. 22) may carry fertile soil in nets or perforated foils.* (Legend of Fig. 22: A-balloon of plastic foil filled with air, B-valve, C-foil with a few distributed holes, D-sand, E-water level, F-humus, G-plants).

The water level in the soil, and thus the moisture content, is regulated by varying the degree of inflation of the balloons.

Planting such floating fields† permits the cultivation of regions having excessive water surfaces. Even tidal basins can be cultivated. Large waves break at the edges of floating nets. In particular, new reservoirs (Fig. 23) can provide areas for cultivation at comparatively low cost (about \$1.50 per m^2). Before water storage begins, the soil is deposited in situ on floating fields.

† *Bauwelt* 21/1958.

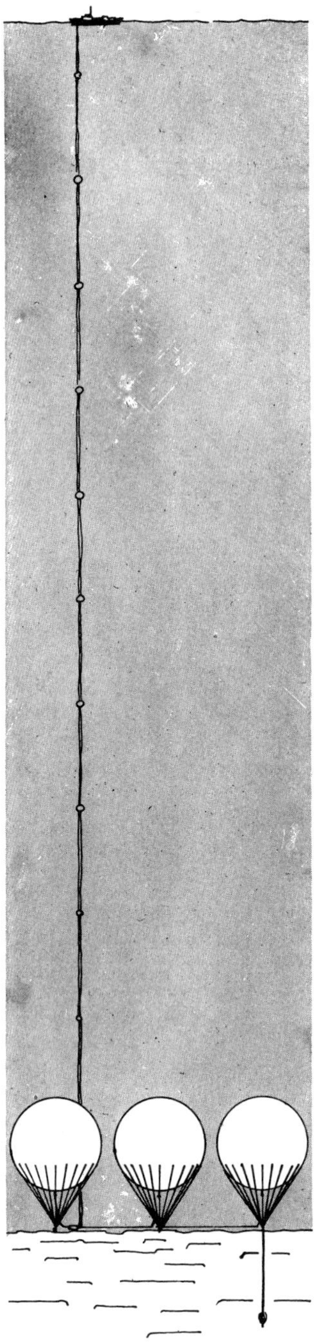
21 ▲

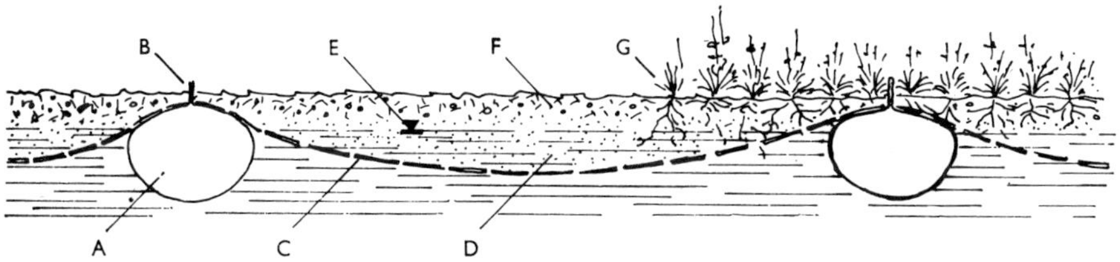

22 ▲

▼ 23

1

3

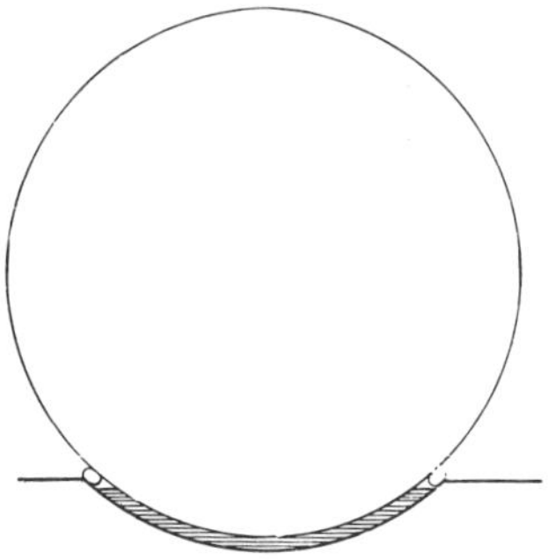

2 ▲

High-pressure steel tanks for gases are rigid shell structures when the internal pressure is zero. However, under pressure, they act as pneumatically stressed spherical surfaces which can sustain pressures up to 200 atm. These tanks (Fig. 1; photo from *Der Bauingenieur* 7/1955) are constructed by welding steel plates together. Concentrated loads should be avoided. Here too, the best way of retaining the spherical shape is by means of water. Fig. 2 shows a floating steel balloon, retained and centered by a hose.*

▼ 4

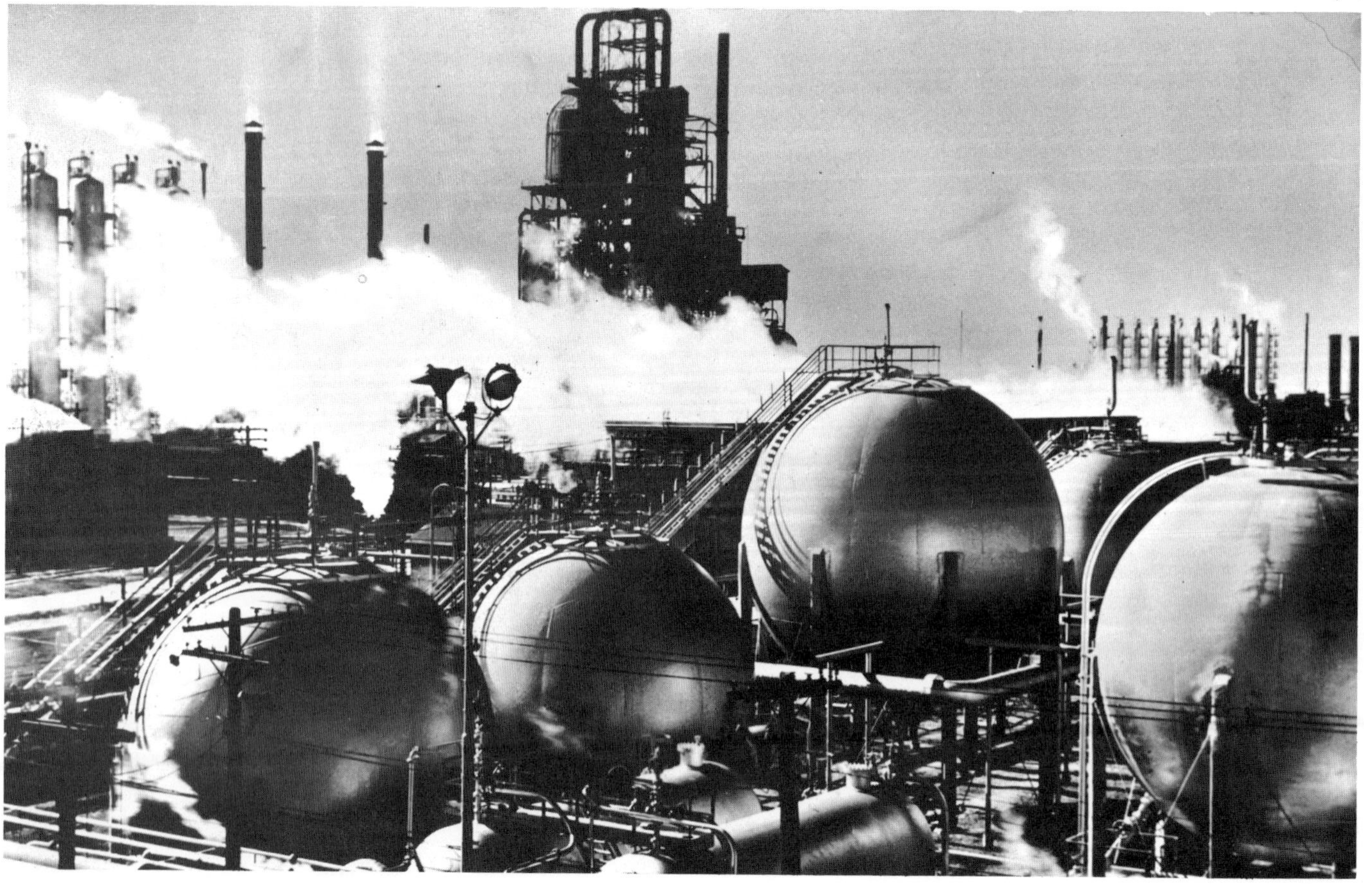

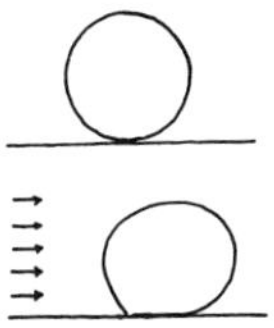

5 and 6

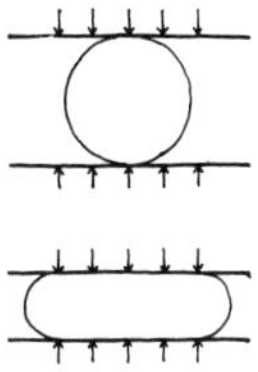

7 and 8

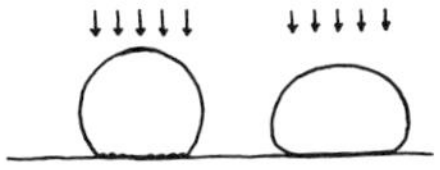

9 and 10

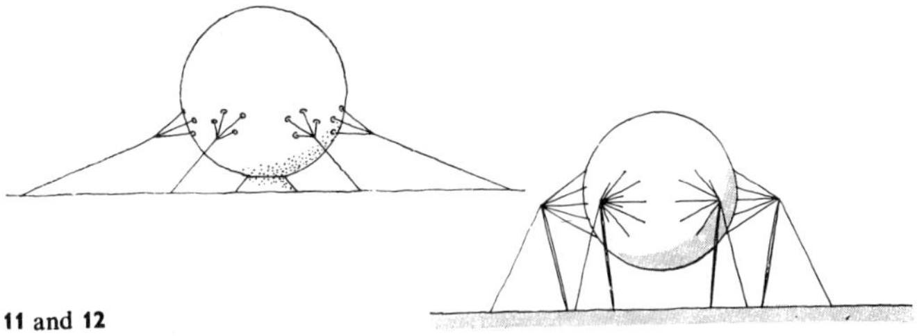

11 and 12

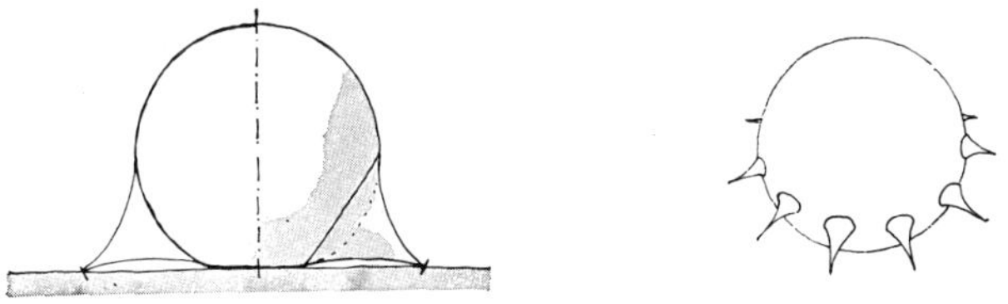

13 and 14

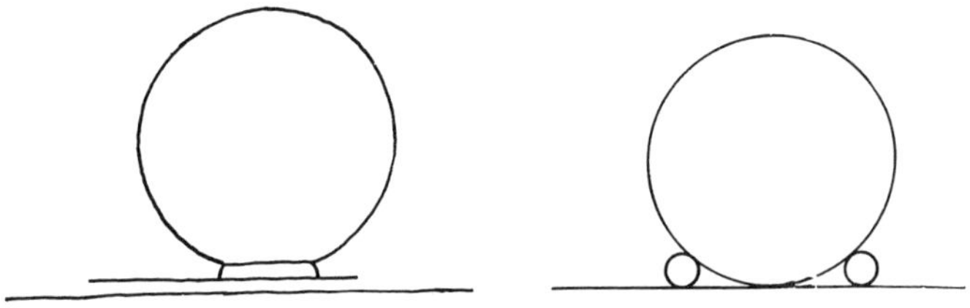

17 and 18

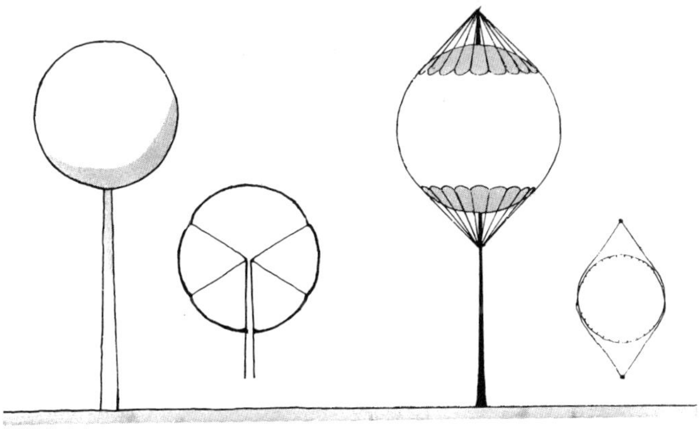

19 to 22

High-pressure containers are extensively used in industry today (Fig. 3; photo from *Acier* 9/1960 and photo by Deutscher Stahlbauverband).
A sphere anchored to the ground at a single point becomes greatly deformed by the wind (Figs. 5 and 6). The elasticity of the membrane of the sphere greatly affects the membrane stresses due to loads and the deformation of the sphere. A rubber ball acts like a spring: although the internal pressure and the stresses do not vary greatly, the ball becomes elastically deformed under load (Figs. 7 and 8). A skin possessing little elasticity retains its shape under load, but tends to form wrinkles (Fig. 9), in contrast to an elastic skin (Fig. 10).
The overturning and rolling-away of a sphere can be prevented by means of guy ropes (Fig. 4, p. 22), which should be attached to the membrane at as many points as possible (Fig. 11). Not directly supported spheres are anchored in a similar manner (Fig. 12).
Membranes attached to the sphere in circles can act like spread wires (Figs. 13 and 14). With the help of at least four cables the sphere can be maintained freely in space (Fig. 15).
The dimensions of the base of the sphere greatly affect its stability. A pneumatically stressed torus provides a good support (Figs. 17 and 18). A balloon on top of a mast can either be retained by internal ties (Figs. 19 and 20) or suspended from external wires (Fig. 21) connected either to the membrane or to two intersecting cable nets (Fig. 22).
Steel balloons are frequently suspended from poles (Fig. 16) but this causes large membrane stresses at the points of suspension, which can be avoided if a cable net is used as support (Fig. 23). Light balloons can be secured against flying away by the use of two cable nets (Fig. 24).

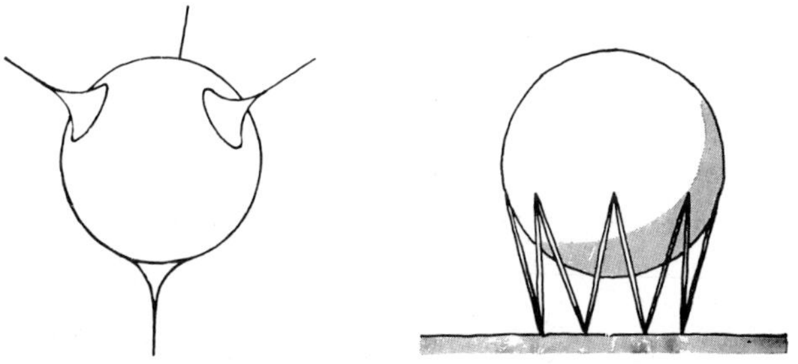

15 and 16

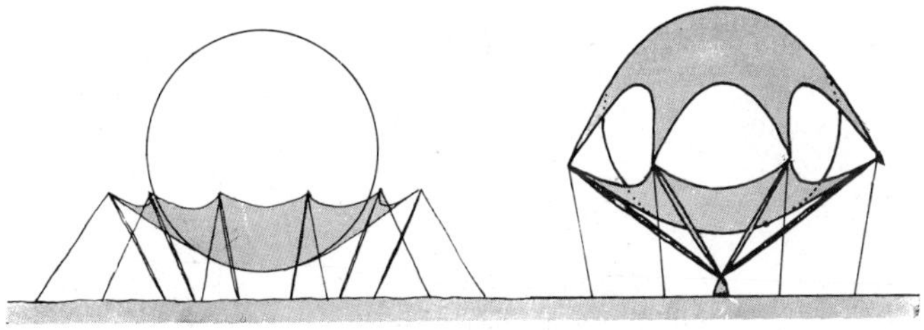

23 and 24

1

Use of spherical surfaces in space exploration

The successes of rocket technology in recent years indicate the coming of space travel in the near future. Many new challenges are presenting themselves to engineers and architects. Artificial satellites are unanchored weightless space structures, liable to generate artificial gravity phenomena by means of their own rotation.

Perfect mastery of all problems of extraterrestrial construction is a prerequisite for the survival of the space traveler. Man will not only travel in space to collect technical and scientific data, but will also consider the colonization of newly reached heavenly bodies as soon as this is technically and physically possible.

The conditions for the support of life on other planets are unknown. In the absence of any standard for comparison, we must expect great difficulties. On many small natural and artificial satellites, and above all on the moon, the protection of an atmosphere is lacking. Survival of space travelers is only possible if human beings can be successfully protected from cosmic rays. Due to their weight, the use of metals, proof against cosmic rays and heat, is not always possible, and the high sensitivity of plastics to ultraviolet and other rays still prevents their application despite the latest developments. In the 30 m diameter "Echo I" balloon satellite, (Fig. 6, p. 21) an attempt to protect the polyterephthalic acid ester foil was made by treating it with vaporized aluminum.

It can be expected that the textile industry will produce foils, cloths and materials for protection and insulation, which in correct combination, will meet these new requirements.

The removal of payloads from the gravitational field of the earth requires an exceptionally high expenditure of energy. Only very light structures can be considered, and therefore, tensile-stress structures should be given pride of place. Pneumatic hulls are required to overcome the large pressure differences. When breathing pure oxygen for an extended period of time human beings need a minimum pressure equal to about 0.25 atm. Every spaceship, extraterrestrial structure, or space suit must be able to withstand a pressure of 2,500 kP/m^2.

The structures must be collapsible into a very small volume, and provide maximum safety in their inflated condition. Pneumatic structures with multiple outer skins and, possibly, multiple internal compartments, provide a high degree of safety against damage.

Due to the especially favorable distribution of membrane stresses and the large ratio of enclosed space to surface, spherical skins are of particular interest; however, many other forms are also important (Fig. 1).

It is clear that we shall soon utilize the indigenous products of other planets to protect ourselves inside pressure hulls with a simulated earth climate. At the beginning, however, we shall only be able to rely on materials brought from earth.

On planets lacking oxygen human habitation will depend on finding means to produce oxygen. Cultivation of algae under pneumatically stressed skins is being considered.

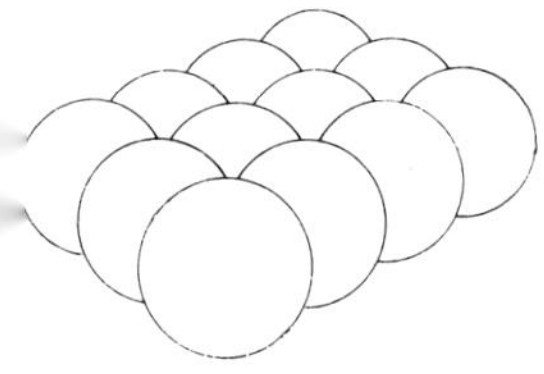

2

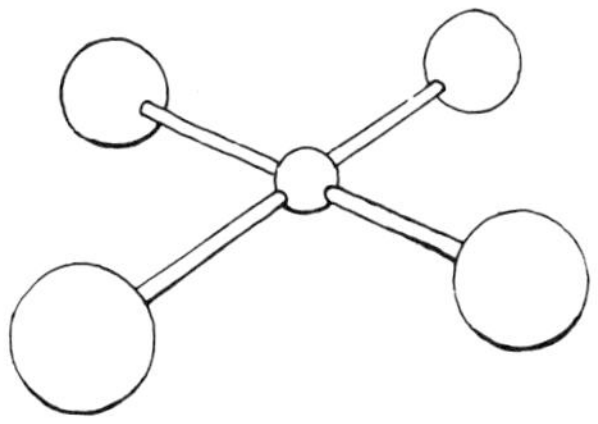

7

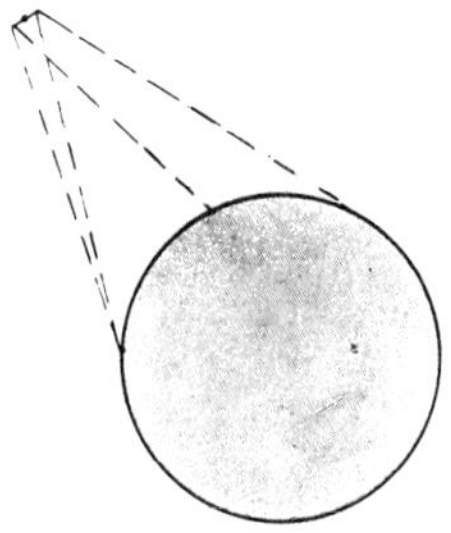

8

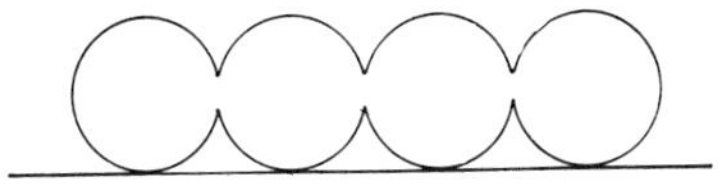

3

9

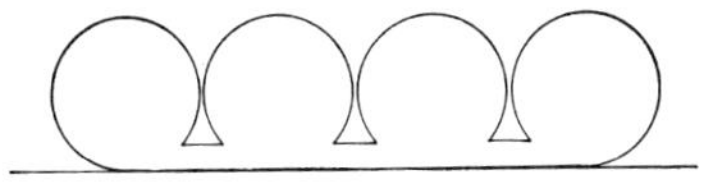

4

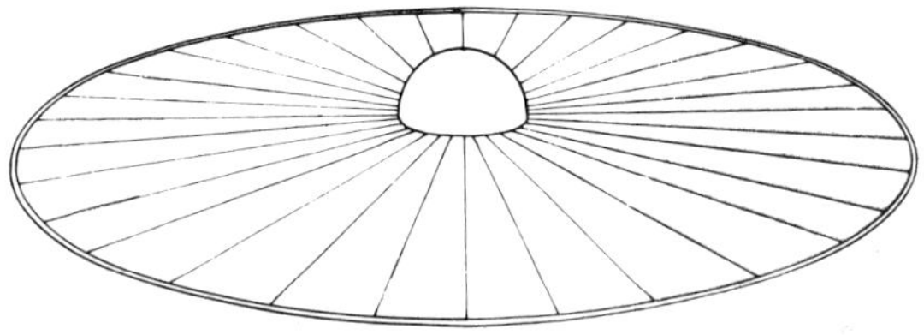

10

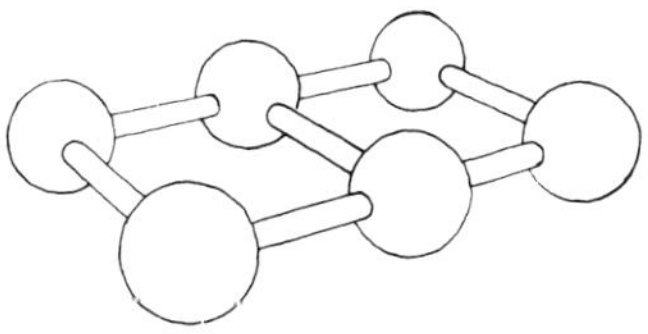

5

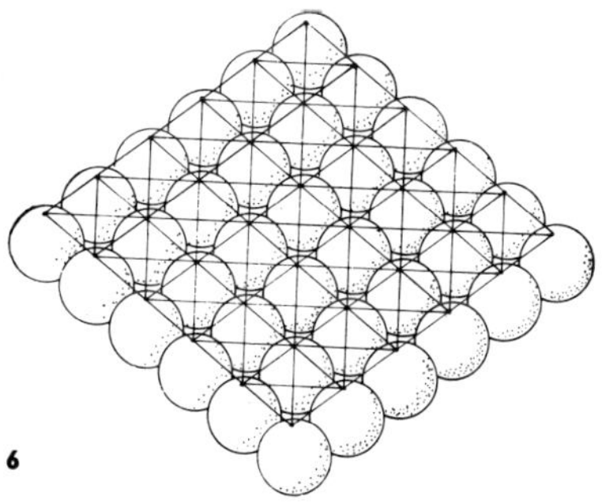

6

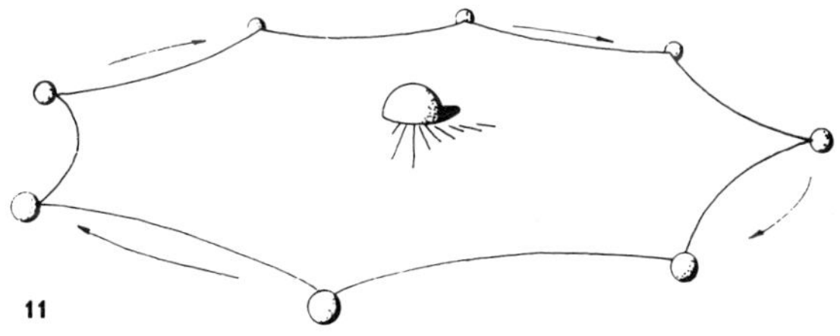

11

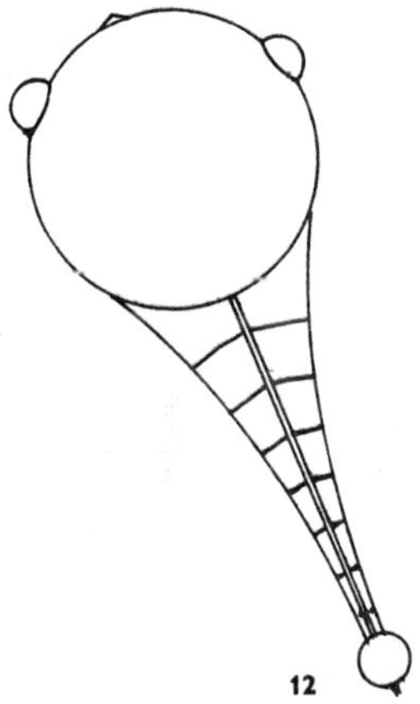

12

Small spherical units (Fig. 2) can easily be assembled to form buildings of any dimensions. Spheres directly in contact (Fig. 3) require no connecting gangways; the latter can, however, be useful, if through insertion of pneumatic cylinders (Fig. 4) larger safety distances are obtained (Fig. 5). Structures of various shapes (Fig. 8) can be created with cables and large numbers of spheres in contact.

The slowly rotating satellite design of Fig. 7 consists of pneumatically stressed spherical envelopes and connecting cylinders. Satellites serving as reflecting surfaces (Fig. 8) for terrestrial radio communications should possess maximum surface areas at great heights. Section 9 and view 10 show a reflecting satellite with a central spherical capsule and an outer pneumatic torus keeping the aluminum foil taut. Peripheral weights or spherical capsules (Fig. 11) may be used to stretch the foil. The position of the membrane can be altered by moving masses on the periphery and thus causing precessional motion. A thin strut, secured against buckling by means of ropes, connects two pneumatic spheres in the satellite design (Fig. 12). Only a few of the many designs possible have been described here.

It is the architect's task to make the new environment permanently livable. This cannot be done solely by creating the technical conditions, but requires an understanding of human beings and, especially, of the emotional problems of the astronaut.

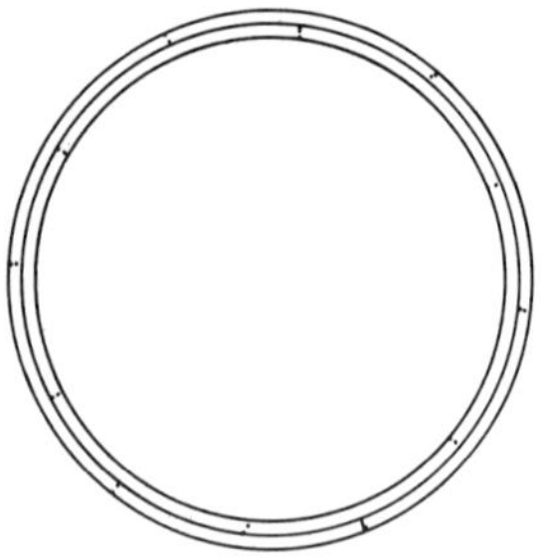
1

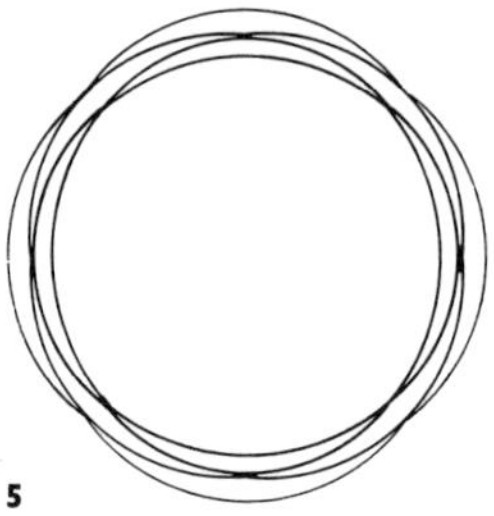
5

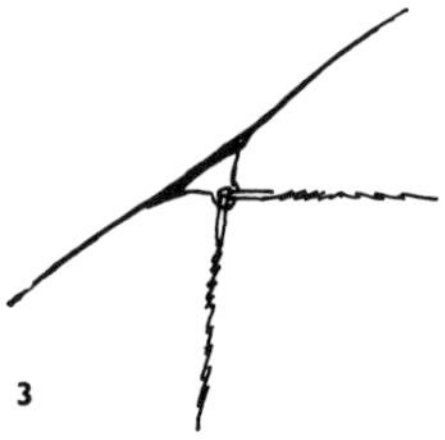
3

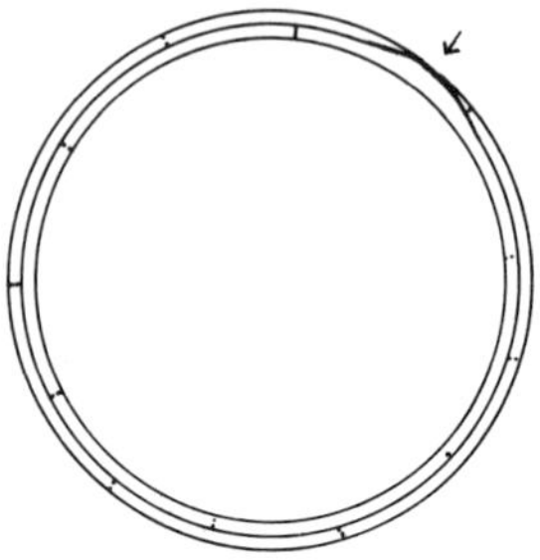
2

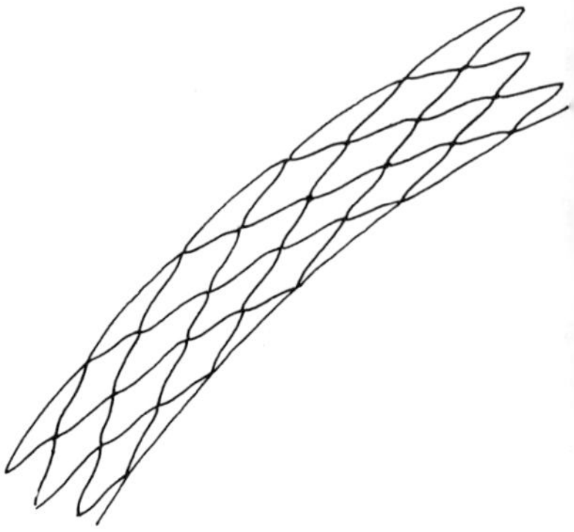
6

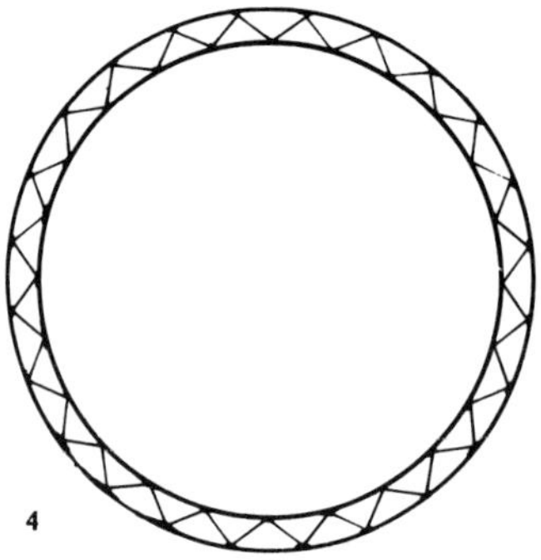
4

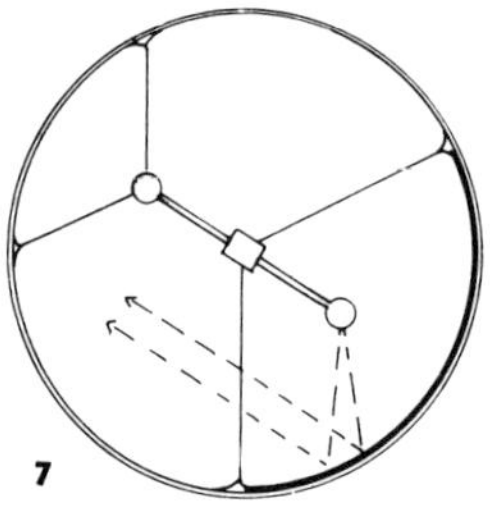
7

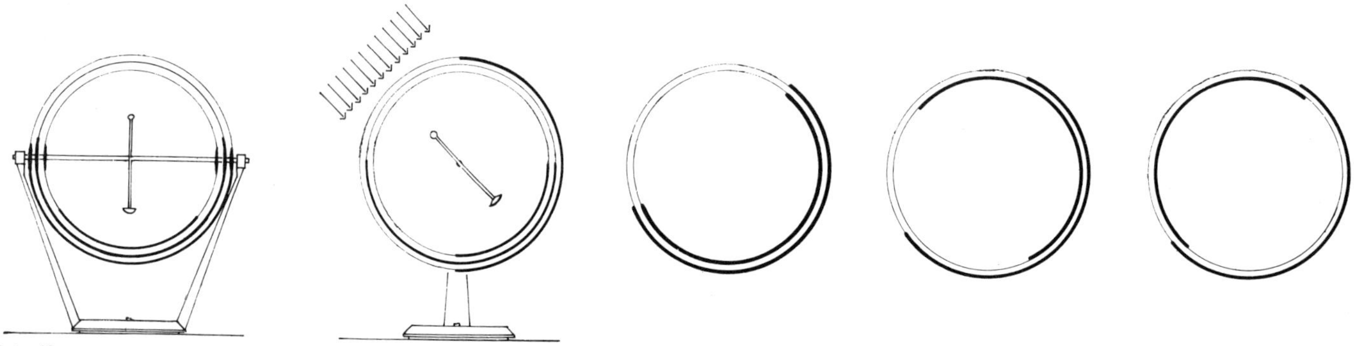
8 to 12

In a sphere (Fig. 1) with a triple outer skin the individual skins are elastically joined at several points. If the resistance to diffusion is equal everywhere the pressure in the hollow spaces decreases from the center outward.

Each of the three membranes is then approximately equally loaded by internal pressure. If the outer membrane is punctured (see arrow Fig.2) the pressure drops in the outer hollow. Due to internal pressure, the central membrane is pressed against the leak and closes* it. Even punctures caused by small meteorites in which all three membranes are pierced can, with ingenuity, be automatically closed.

Double envelopes (Figs. 3 and 4) linked by cables possess high stability. The same applies to spherical envelopes having four skins (Fig. 5) which are joined at several points or along lines: safety increases with a greater number of envelopes. (Fig. 6).

The structural safety of shells that are to house men must be particularly great, since a sudden lowering of pressure will cause instant death. Multiple envelopes in combination with cell-like partitions offer the best protection against injury to the outer skin, and it is even possible to anticipate making repairs while the structure is in a stressed state.

Further examples of the application of multiple spherical skins are devices to collect and utilize cosmic radiation.* Three pneumatically stressed spherical envelopes (Figs. 8 and 9) can be rotated on an axis and moved with respect to one another. Part of the inner envelope forms a mirror, while one half of each outer envelope is

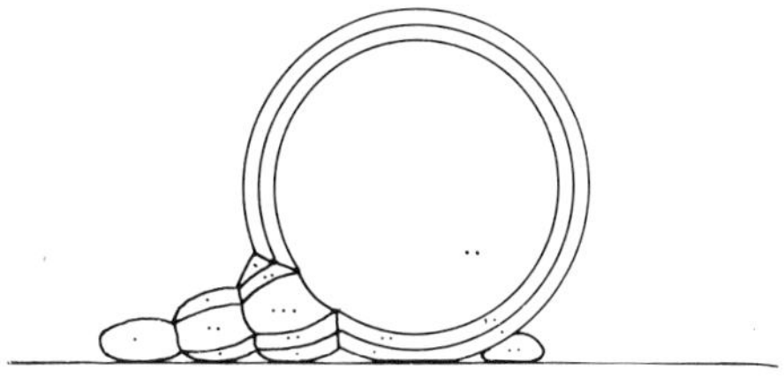

13

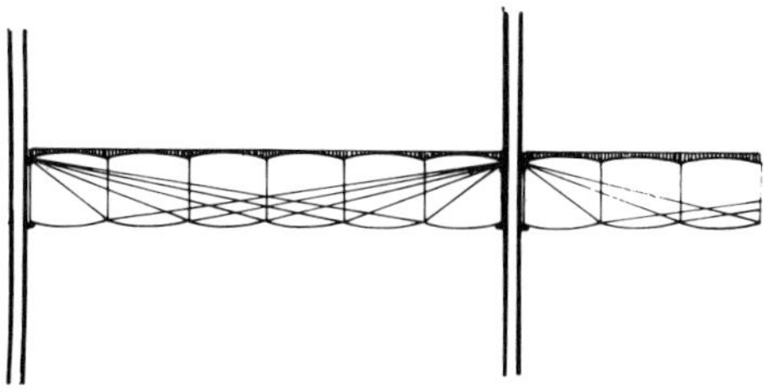

16

14

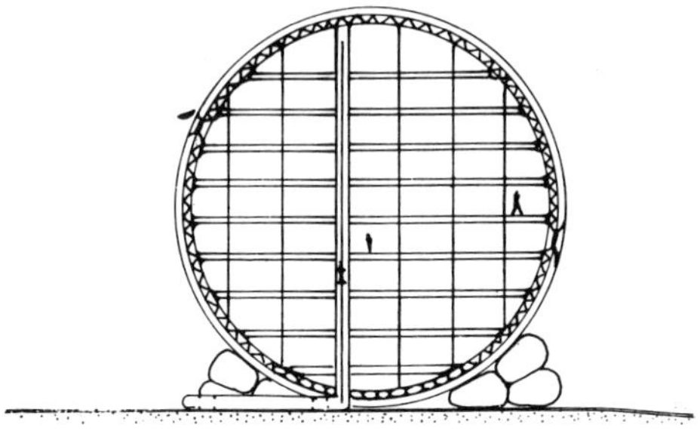

15

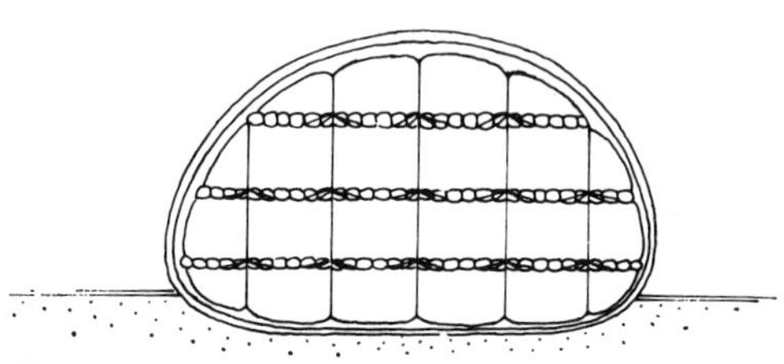

17

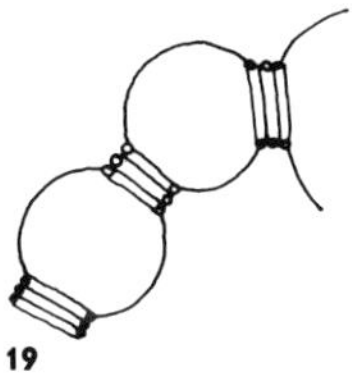

19

21

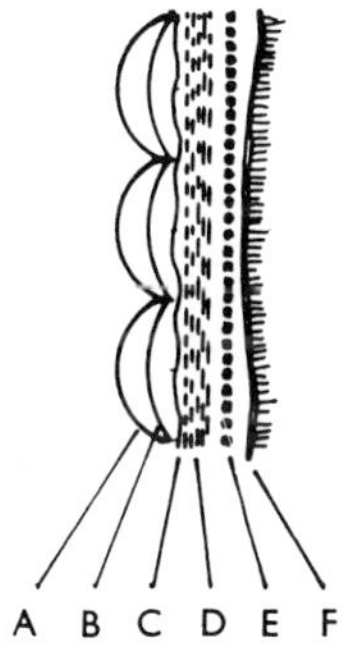

23

18

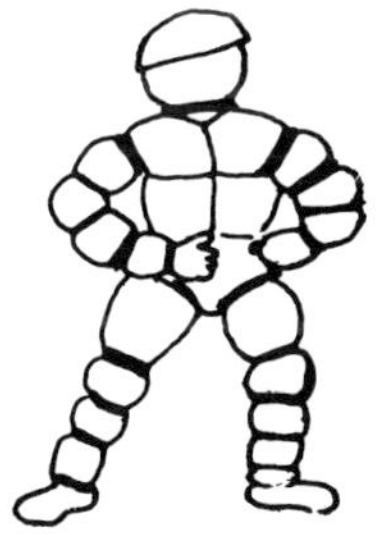

20

22

capable of reflecting the radiation. The entering radiation can thus be accurately regulated (Figs. 10, 11, 12).

The directional radiator (Fig. 7) has a pneumatically stressed spherical envelope whose inner surface forms a reflector. The device is not carried on an axis but is held by internal ties. In Fig. 13 an envelope with triple skins is also provided with three pressure locks as a safety precaution. The dots indicate pressure distribution. Such safety measures are necessary for prolonged human occupancy, but since so little is known about living conditions, nothing can yet be said about the best form of a dwelling. One can imagine spherical envelopes which could be joined to form orbiting structures, or could land on the surface of the moon (Fig. 14). Buildings of several stories could be erected (Fig. 15 and 18) using decks constructed of pneumatic pads with internal guy ropes (Fig. 16). If the decks are suspended from cables the structure will assume the shape of a water drop lying on a horizontal surface (Fig. 17).

Great care is required in the design of space suits; the rigidity of large space envelopes is best ensured by internal pressure. Space suits should, however, possess as little rigidity as possible in order not to interfere with movement. Spheres (Figs. 19 and 20) are therefore linked by means of flexible connecting hoses; alternatively, suits may be assembled from a large number of grooved pneumatic surfaces (Figs. 21 and 22). Section 23 shows: A—outer, B—intermediate, C—inner membrane, D—thermal insulation, E—humidity and pressure equalizer, F—human skin.

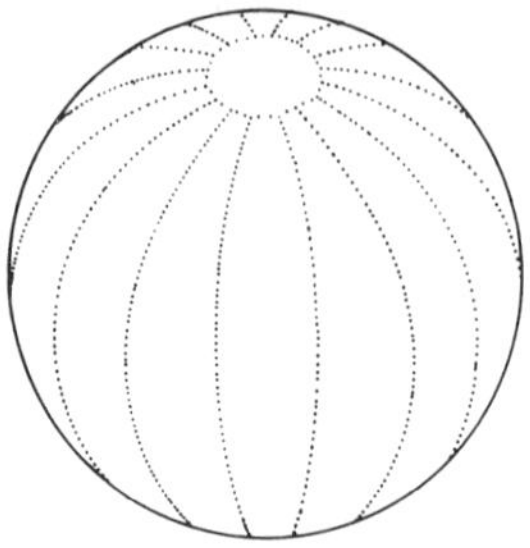

1

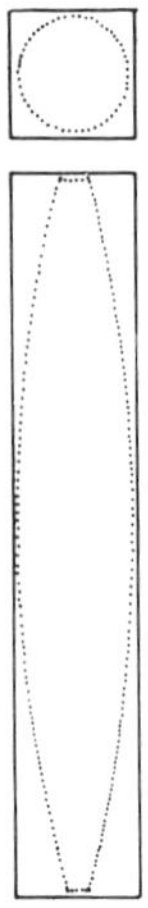

2 and 3

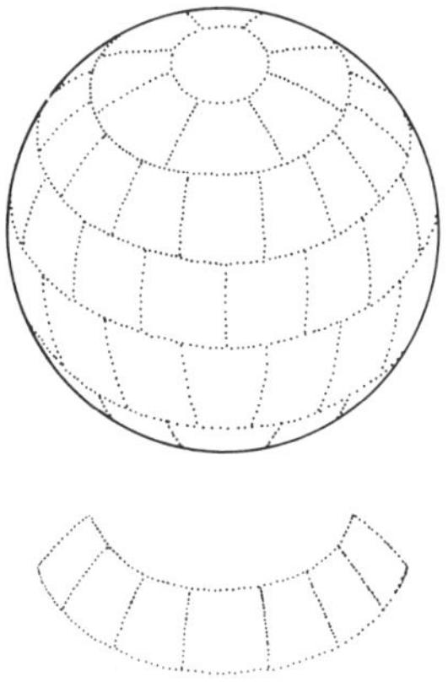

4 and 5

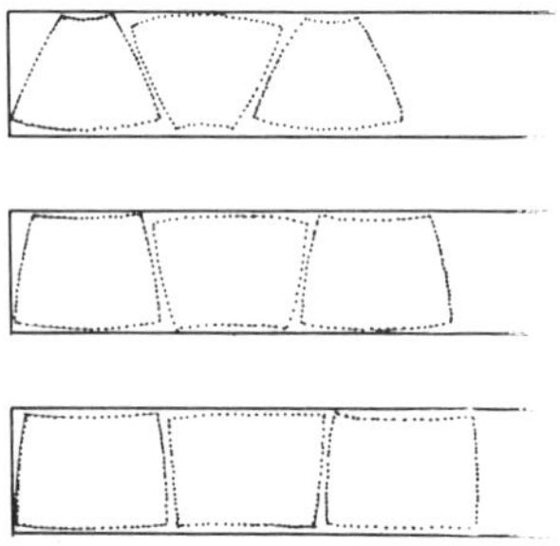

6 to 8

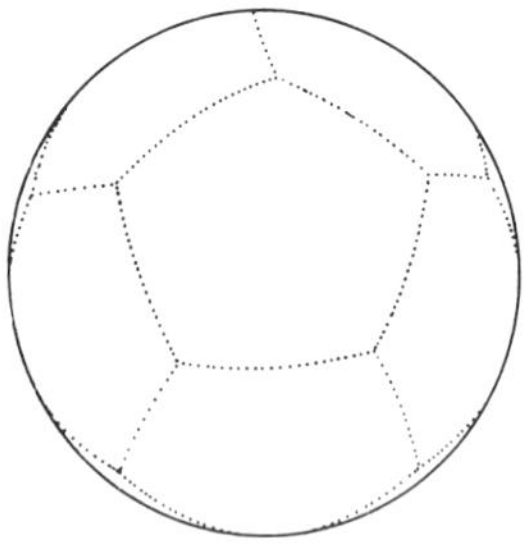

9 and 10

The subdivision of spherical surfaces

Skins forming spherical surfaces or parts thereof possess double curvature. In general, they are assembled from flexible, only slightly deformable foils or fabric, which may have simple curvature.

In order to form a spherical surface it is necessary to divide the material into smaller areas which themselves are plane or possess simple curvature. The less deformable a material is, the smaller these areas have to be. A sphere formed of sheet rubber requires far fewer individual parts than one of spun glass fabric. The individual areas may have different shapes. They are often oval, triangular, or trapezoidal. To obtain three-dimensional curvature, the edges must form arcs of circles in most cases. The normal state of tension in which uniform stresses act in all directions is important for the cutting pattern of the spherical surface. There are no "preferred" directions on the surface. The directions of the cloth fibers cannot, however, be arbitrarily changed at the seams. If very expensive material is used, low wastage should be aimed at; if labor costs are high, the lengths of the seams should be reduced.

Dividing the sphere by great circles (Fig. 1) results in few seams and a clear design. However, much wastage occurs, as can be seen by superimposing the two shapes on a length of material (Figs. 2 and 3).

When dividing the surfaces into zones of latitude (Figs. 4 and 5) each zone is assembled in trapezoidal pieces. This method yields small wastage (Figs. 6 to 8) and the additional advantage of smaller uninterrupted lengths in which the fabric can tear (straight lines from seam to seam); however, the drawback is that the seam lengths are great.

Subdividing the surface of a sphere (Figs. 9 and 10) into identical parts is possible up to a maximum of 120 equal triangles (Figs. 11 and 12).† Buckminster Fuller's work on spherical structures leads to a better understanding of the possibilities of subdividing spherical surfaces. The economics of the different methods of subdivision vary from case to case. The weight of large skin sections is often considerable. Since gas-tight connections are known, large skins (Fig. 13) are divided into simple parts (Fig. 14) which can be assembled by ordinary methods. Parts with an area of more than 600 m² require special contrivances since otherwise they are difficult to handle.

† Stuart, *On the Orderly Subdivision of Spheres,* Student Publications, North Carolina State College, Raleigh, Vol. 5/1.

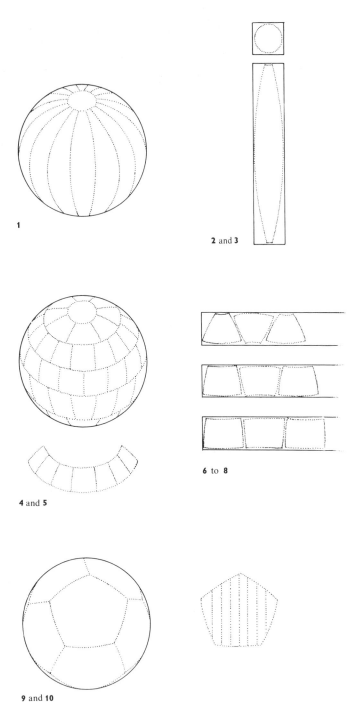

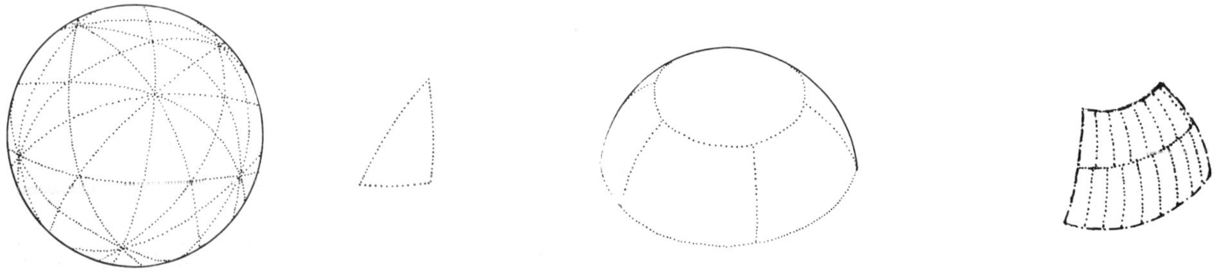

11 to 14

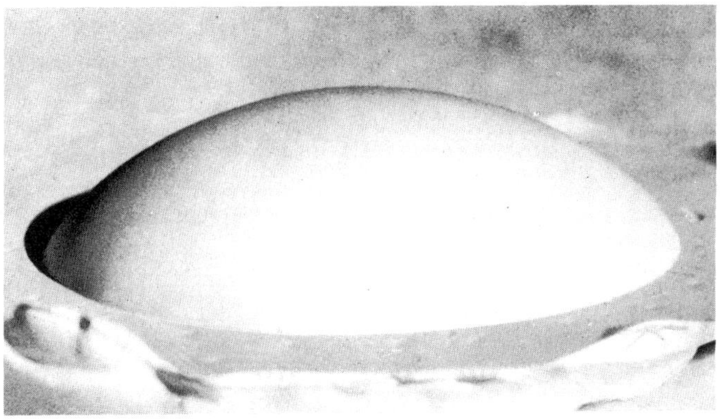

15

The Pneumatically Stretched Dome

Sections of spherical membranes are important in structural engineering. Low domes (Fig. 15) are used to span large areas. Hemispheres are suitable for buildings of greater height and can withstand large pressure differences as, for instance, in the project* for extraterrestrial buildings (Fig. 25). Three-quarter spheres have become known principally as hulls for radar stations. In the project* shown in Fig. 26 the membrane serves to close a tower. For equal internal pressures the membrane stress depends solely upon the diameter (Figs. 16 to 22). All the spheres are equally stressed. The hemisphere covers the largest ground surface. The three-quarter sphere has the greatest height. The higher, however, the spherical dome, the greater is the influence of live loads on the stresses (see p. 195ff).

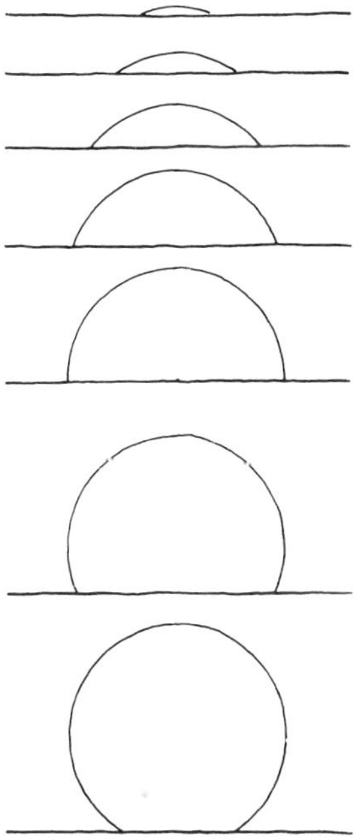

16 to 22

The two domes in Figs. 23 and 24 cover equal surfaces. In the upper figure, the radius, and therefore the membrane stresses, are twice as large as in the lower figure. With equal interior pressures the former membrane and its foundation must be twice as strong as the latter. The surface area of the former dome, however, is far smaller than that of the latter. The effect of wind loads on the former dom

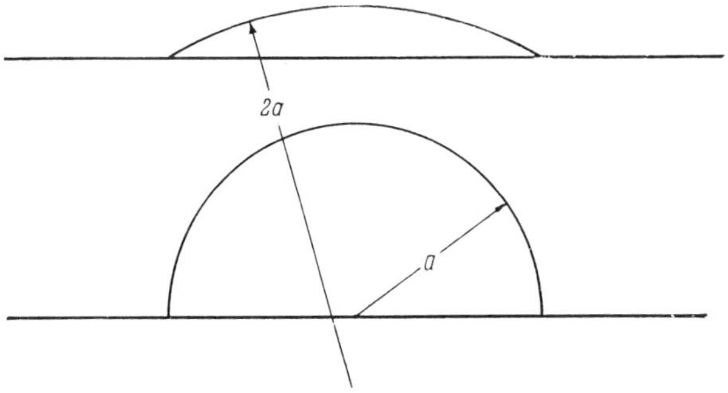

23 and 24

25

is also less. The economics of construction are very similar for both forms. The correct application of the design herein illustrated depends mainly upon other considerations, such as height of interior, heating, acoustics, etc.

26

During inflation of a highly elastic membrane (Fig. 27) the various stages from a flat to a full dome are passed through. The hemisphere has the smallest radius.

27

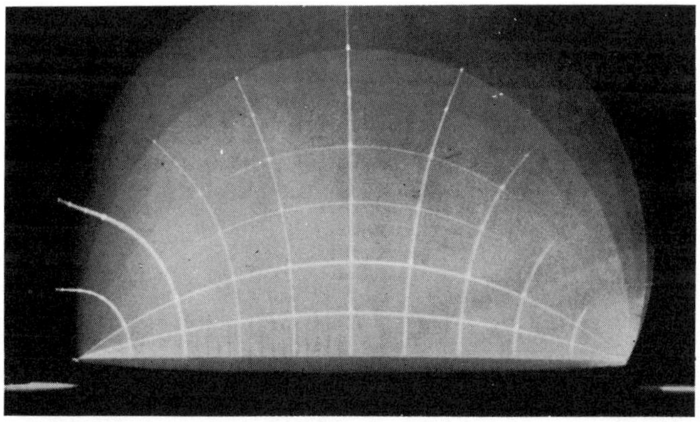

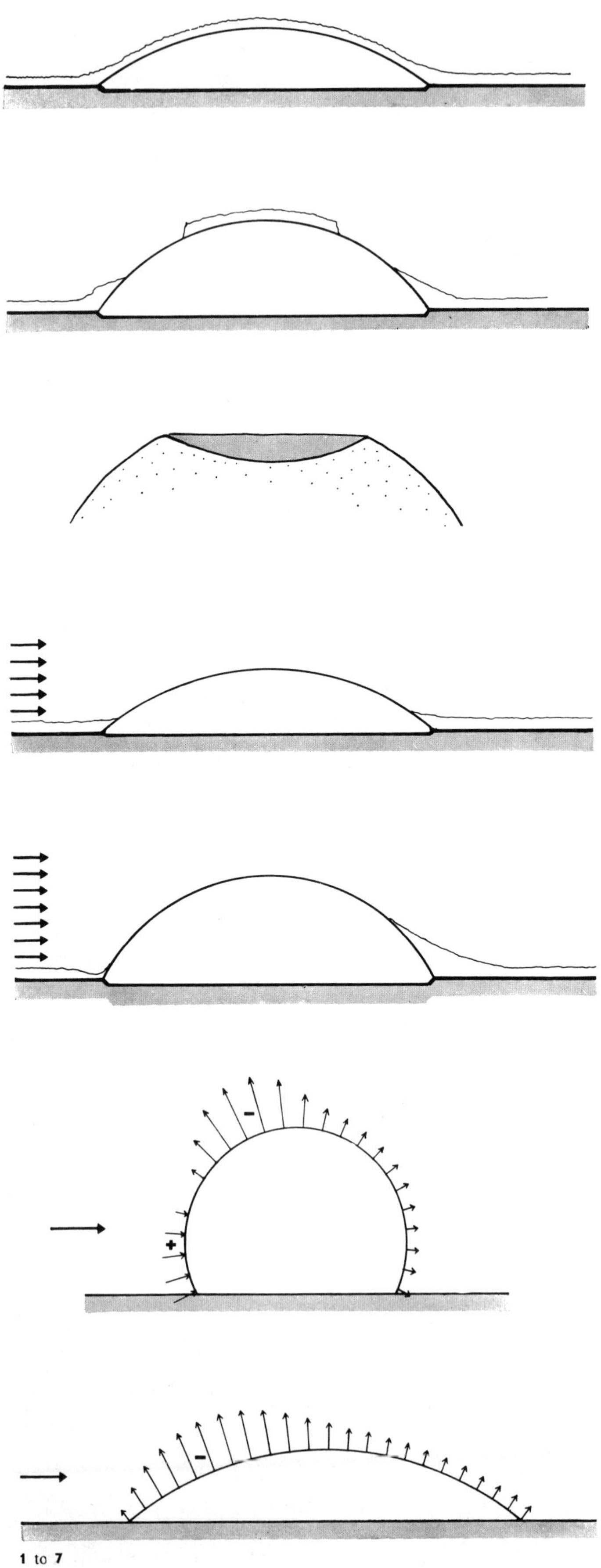

1 to 7

Live loads on domes

Only on very flat domes and in the absence of wind can a snow load of uniform thickness form over the entire surface (Fig. 1). Incidentally, good results have been obtained on membrane structures with melting off snow by internal heating, to prevent snow loads.

Snow slides off the sides of higher domes (Fig. 2). When the skin is elastic and smooth, internal pressure pulsations can accelerate this process. Surface roughness hinders sliding off. Large nonuniform loads may arise if only part of the snow has slid off.

While rain normally does not collect in water sacks even at very low internal pressures, water may, under unfavorable conditions, accumulate in an existing snow cover (Fig. 3).

When wind and snow act simultaneously (Fig. 4) snow will not normally be deposited on flat domes. On higher domes snow will usually be deposited only on the lee side.

Only during hail storms can an ice crust be observed on the weather side. Unfortunately, the clearly existing laws governing the deposition of snow on roofs have not yet been investigated.

A three-quarter sphere (Fig. 6) has a small positive-pressure zone in the direction of the wind. The dome will be forced in at this point if the internal pressure is insufficient. However, this can be avoided by letting the dynamic head of the wind act on the inside of the hull, possibly through a wind funnel. The remaining surface of the three-quarter sphere is under negative pressure.

A flat dome (Fig. 7) is in general completely under negative pressure. Even a slight wind can stabilize a flat dome. No internal pressure is then necessary. High wind velocities cause large membrane stresses. Although the sphere appears to be thoroughly analyzed aerodynamically, many problems still remain concerning sections of spheres (domes), especially if these structures are large. Wind-tunnel tests cannot provide design criteria directly. The behavior of natural wind is scarcely known in detail. It is known that velocity and direction can change within seconds, without any law being apparent. It may happen that gusts strike only part of a building. Largely asymmetrical dynamic loadings have therefore to be reckoned with.

The effect of tornados and water spouts on buildings is also incompletely known. Loads of 300 kP/m^2 and more may arise. Even in regions subject to tropical storms structures are generally not made tornado-proof since the probability that a building will be in the path of a tornado or water spout in its lifetime is very small. However, pneumatic buildings can be designed to be thoroughly tornado-proof.

Projects:

Walter W. Bird initiated the American development of pneumatic domes (radomes) for radar stations.

Highly sensitive instruments are located in the center of the sphere and transmit radio waves almost without resistance through the light nonmetallic envelope. The first unit, built in 1955, for a radar system in Canada, provided many important lessons (Fig. 8; photo by Cornell Aeronautical Laboratory). Development started in 1946. Many experiments were undertaken. Figure 11 on page 33 shows W. Bird on top of an experimental dome 16 m in diameter, erected on a concrete base at the Cornell Aeronautical Laboratory.

8

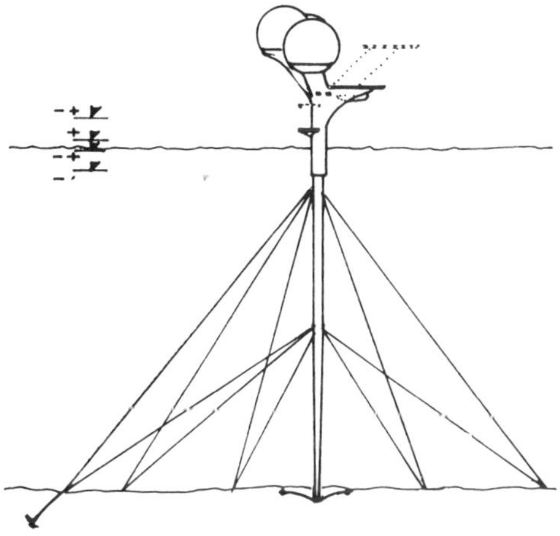

9

11 ▲

▼ 12

10

1 ▲ ▼ 2

3 ▲

▼ 4

This dome was ordered by the U.S. Air Force and built for General Electric (photo by Cornell Aeronautical Laboratory).
Inflated domes on artificial steel islands have withstood the strongest Atlantic storms (Figs. 10 and 12, p. 33; photos by Ullstein, D.P.A). The design of the steel structure for such "islands" is very difficult. In stormy seas, in earthquake zones, or on unstable ground, light, thin structures are necessary. They are shown in the design sketches* (Fig. 9, p. 33) for an artificial island with a revolving top and adjustable platform serving as a landing stage and heliport which is planned for installation in more than 90-m-deep water as part of the Civilian Air Safety Program.
Bird built five large exhibition domes for the U.S. Army which will later be used as rocket workshops. The central dome has a diameter of 49.5 m and is 28 m high; the diameters of the smaller domes are only 33 m. Each building is well provided with entrances and exits. Large objects such as rockets, pipes, etc., are "locked in" through a long, rigid, cylinder-shaped structure. The central dome is shown during inflation. On the extreme left of Figure 1 a semirigid entrance can be recognized (photos by Birdair).
Air photo 2 shows the installation in plan. The compressed air plant is recognizable at the right of the large dome. This building was well patronized during the inaugural exhibition. A map of the earth decorates the central dome (Fig. 3) inside which (Fig. 4) a Juno II rocket was erected. The passages to the neighboring domes and the division of the dome surface can be clearly seen
For the town office of a big corporation, Schjeldahl built a dome of transparent polyester foil, erected on a light timber platform at

roof height. Entry to the structure is from beneath (Fig. 1).

The pavillion of Pan American Airways at the 1958 World's Fair in Brussels was built by Irving (Figs. 2 and 3). The light envelope has two revolving doors and is painted to represent a globe. It is circled by a viewing gallery of reinforced concrete. This was the first pneumatic structure to be shown to the general public in Europe.

Air houses 6.5 m in diameter, made of PVC coated nylon cloth, were erected on the campus of the University of Kentucky (Fig. 4; photo from *Life*). In a project* for a city on an island group in the Antarctic (Fig. 5) a large spherical dome with transparent skin shelters a residential community with interior harbors, administrative offices and small industries. The envelope itself will not need to be heated since, due to the reduced heat loss from the earth, the climate inside will correspond to that of temperate zones. The houses are heated by a central heating plant and are located in the middle of a park whose trees create a more congenial environment. The trees also contribute to air purification, air conditioning, and sound absorption, as do the sails hung from the underside of the dome. The enclosed air is continuously renewed by ventilation. Air pressure will be maintained by wind pressure, blowers, and temperature differences. The air-conditioning plant with its intake openings will be located at the perimeter of the dome. All exhaust gases will be led directly to the outside. The airport, main harbor, and radio transmitting station will be located outside the envelope but will be accessible from the interior.

1 ▲

2 ▲

▼ 3

4 ▲

▼ 5

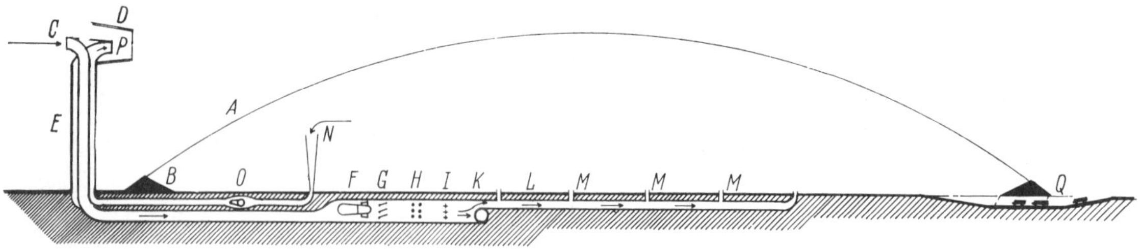

1

The economics of power and heat are important in the maintenance of pressure and climate inside large envelopes. New problems in air conditioning arise in large envelopes (Fig. 1) since air currents and the possibility of condensation give rise to zones having different inner climates. This effect can be considerable in spaces exceeding 500 m in span.

In the book *Das hängende Dach* (Ullstein Fachverlag 1954) the problem of large envelopes was treated for the first time. It was proposed to span valleys in the Alps and cover large settlements in the Arctic with cable nets.† Since these books became known, large envelopes have been widely discussed. With their aid, high agricultural yields can be obtained in cold zones. The large spans permit use of heavy farm machinery. Atomic energy can be used for heating the air and, in particular, the ground, by means of underground pipes. Pneumatically supported domes are especially suited for this purpose. Even with large spans a normal pressure of about 25 mm (water column) can be maintained. Only under special conditions (snow loads) will a higher pressure be required.

Normally, large blowers are used (Fig. 2). These maintain a uniform internal pressure at any height (Fig. 3). As will be shown later, temperature differences between the inside and the outside cause the air pressure to vary with height. Dynamic wind pressure can easily be utilized to inflate the dome (Fig. 4). Ordinarily, any wind speed exceeding 4 m/sec suffices to maintain the shape of a low pneumatic dome. High wind speeds (15 m/sec) cause heavy loads on the surface of the dome, which can be reduced through subjecting the inside to negative pressures (Fig. 5).

† U. Conrads and E. Sperlich, *Phantastische Architektur*, Stuttgart, Hatje, 1960.

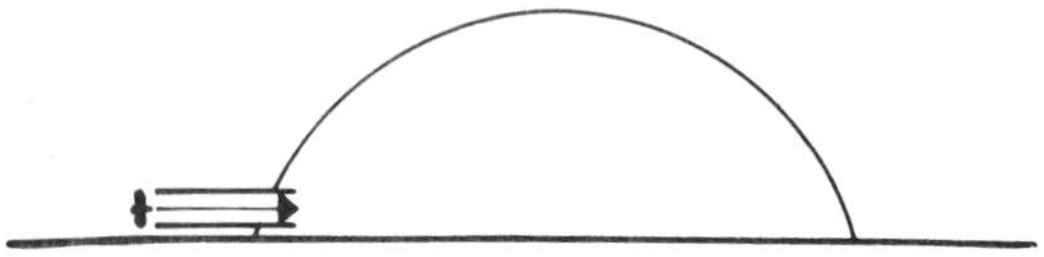

2

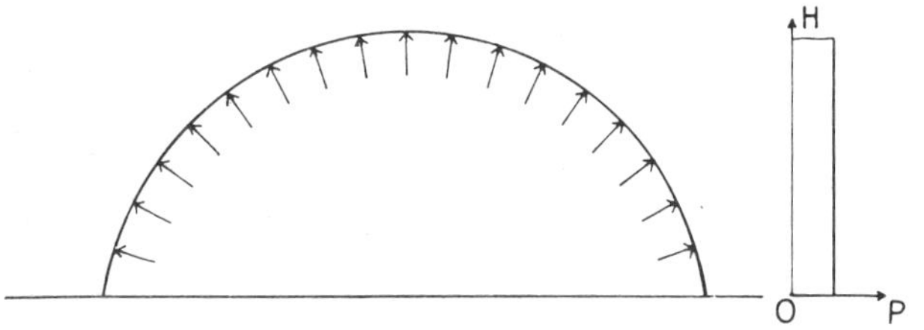

3

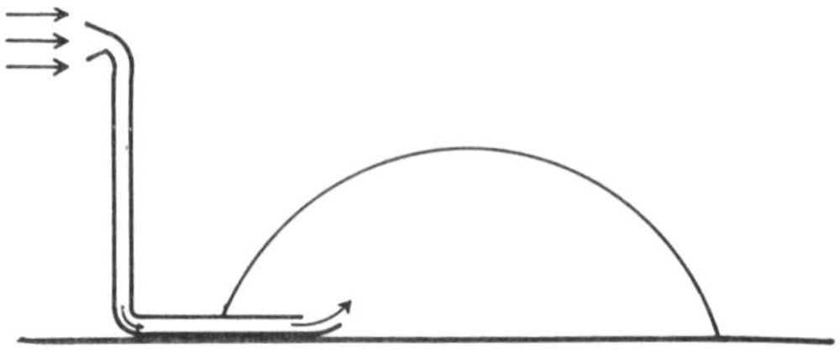

4

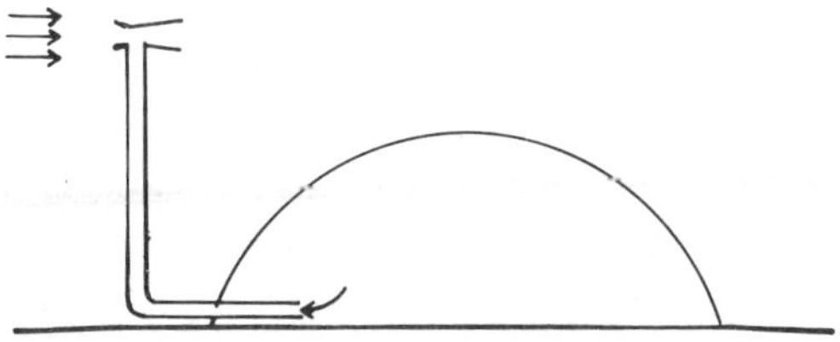

5

Figure 1, p. 38 shows:

A Membrane of heavy fabric or wire with transparent plastic coating.

B Annular foundation.

C Air inlet in air-conditioning tower having rotatable cap.

D Guide-vane annulus to adjust position of cap.

E Heat exchange in air-conditioning tower. In winter the used air heats the fresh air in a counter-flow arrangement.

F Blower.

G Air baffles.

H Heating and cooling plant.

I Humidifier.

K Ring main.

L Underground distribution line, serves also to heat ground.

M Warm air discharge.

N Used air extraction

O Pressure regulation valve.

P Exhaust discharge.

Q Air lock accessible to trucks.

6

In a project for a large industrial complex (1957-58)* near the intersection of a superhighway and a canal, the city center with administrative, cultural, and office buildings, the harbor, and industry located between canal and superhighway, are planned so that the city can undergo orderly growth. The plastic skin of the domes which are 750 m in diameter is reinforced with embedded steel wires. It is coated with aluminum so as to be translucent and to prevent both the emission or absorption of too much radiant energy (Figs. 6 and 7).†

† *Deutsche Bauzeitung* 7/1960.

7

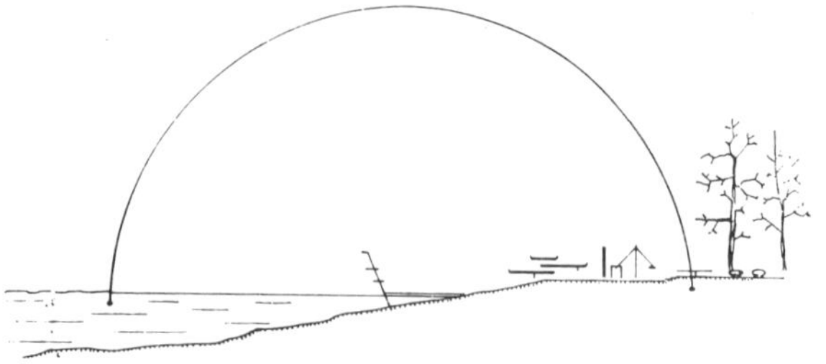

1

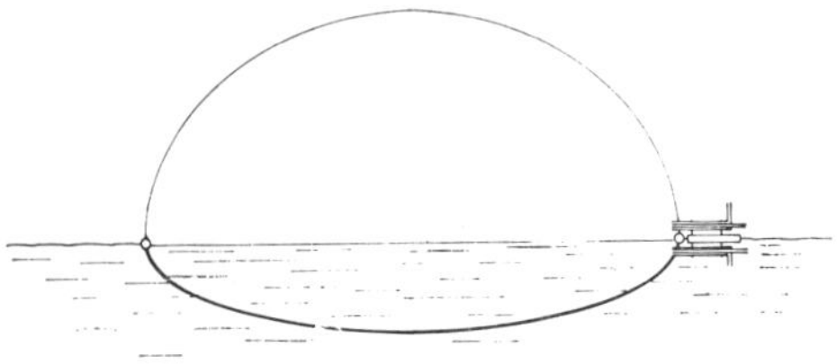

2

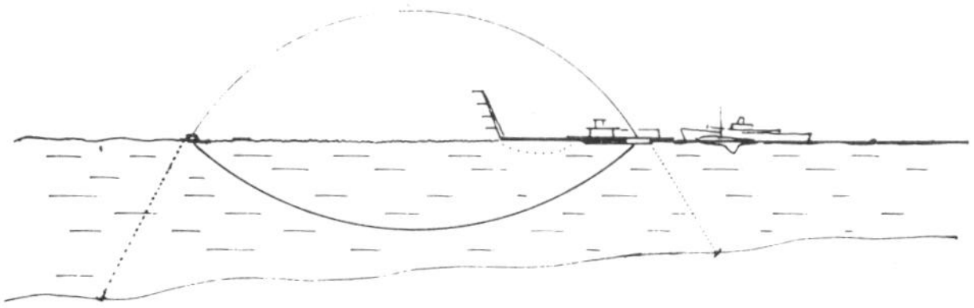

3

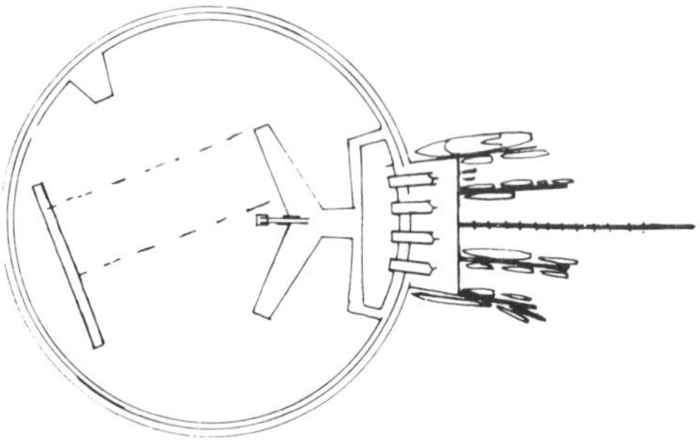

4

5

It can be expected that pneumatic structures will in the future be increasingly used for sports buildings, especially swimming pools. The intention is to extend the season (e.g., on beaches (Fig. 1), but permanent structures for use in winter can also be considered. In a design by Gilbert Hirt and Willi Ramstein, a large plastic dome covers a round, open-air swimming pool with a central diving tower (Fig. 5). Attention should also be called to the sketch submitted by U. v. Altenstadt in a contest for a swimming-pool structure in Hamburg in 1961.†

Freely floating domes (Fig. 2), enclosing a large area of water* would be particularly economical. If the inner and outer waters are separated by a pneumatic insulating double membrane, the higher summer temperature of the pumped-in surface water can be maintained for a longer period. The colder water at the bottom of the envelope is pumped out of the pneumatic envelope and replaced by surface water. Continuous circulation of water through heat exchangers is possible. Solar radiation passing through the transparent membrane heats the inside air and water, though auxiliary heating may be necessary in winter. The membrane is anchored to a buoyant hose ring or to a floating steel thrust collar, as in the design* for a large outdoor bath (Figs. 3 and 4). Large clear lakes near bigger cities located in a temperate climate are best suited for such projects since they cost only a fraction of the usual covered pools. Although they may be less luxurious than the latter, there is a more direct contact with nature (Fig. 6).

† *Bauwelt* 51/52, 1961.

6

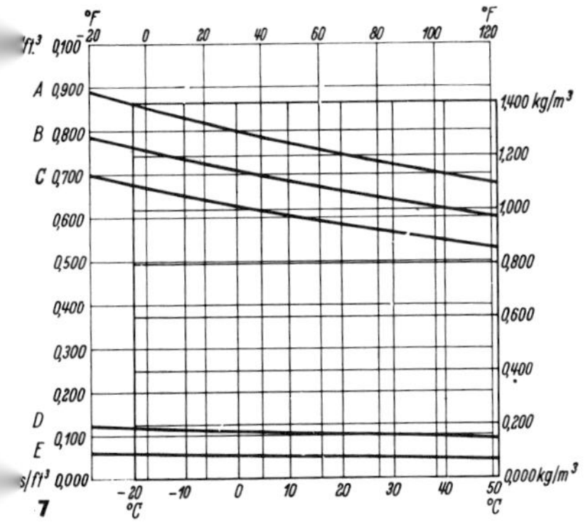

7

Specific weight of air as a function of temperature

A = air at 0 m
B = air at 1,000 m
C = air at 2,000 m
D = helium at 0 m
E = hydrogen at 0 m

9 and 10

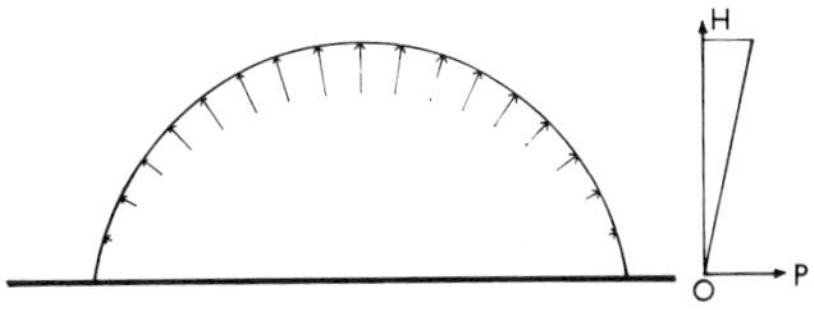

11

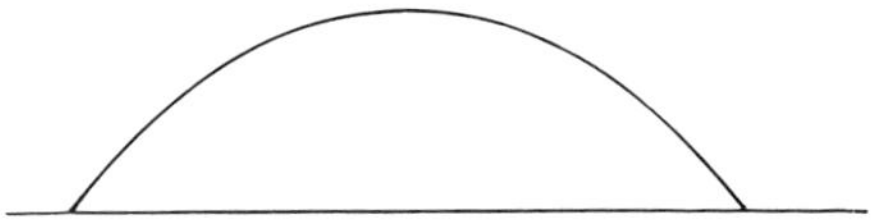

12 and 13

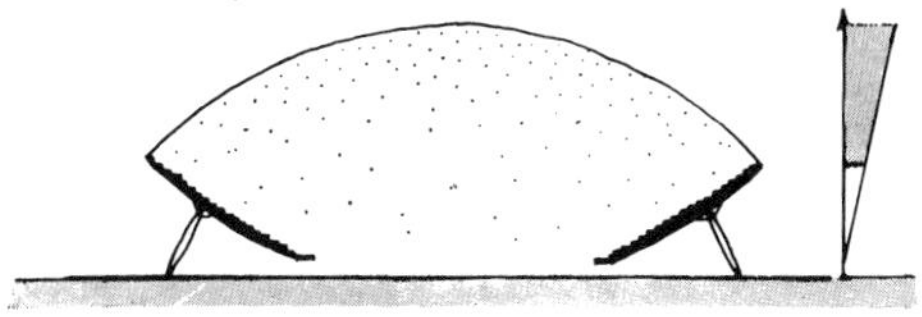

14 and 15

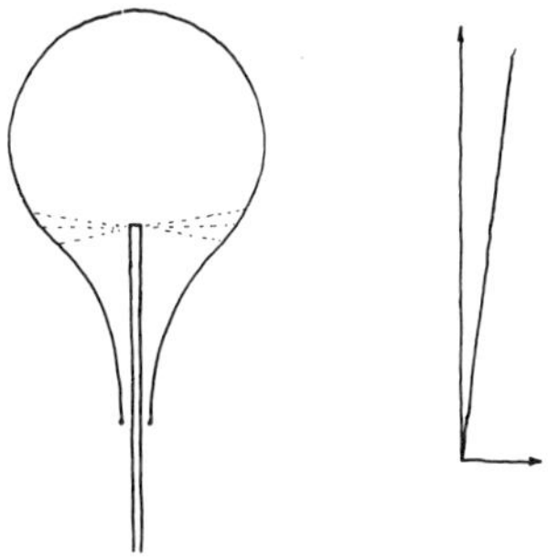

16

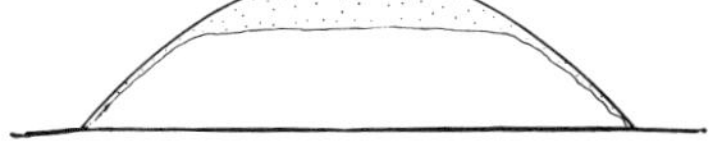

17

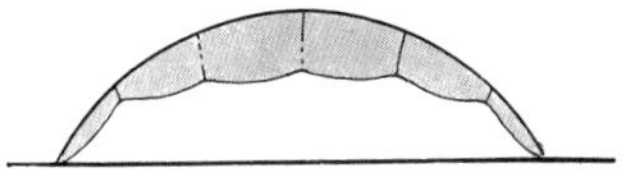

18

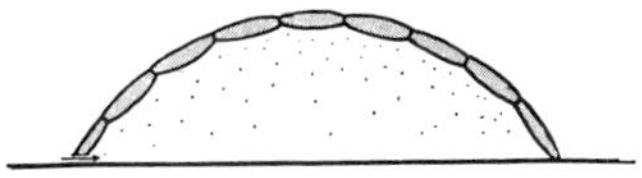

19

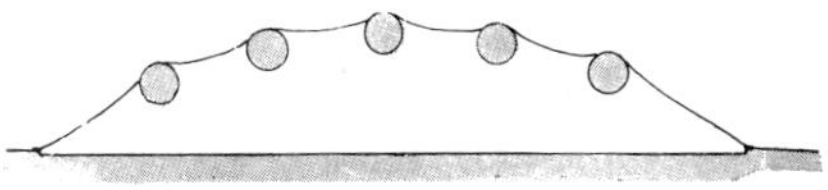

Domes borne by hot air or gases

Hot air in a dome creates an ascending lift (Fig. 9), due to the temperature differential with respect to the outer air. At the points of entry the air pressure is zero; it reaches its maximum at the apex of the dome (Fig. 10). The greater forces at the apex are taken up bettei when the curvature is increased at that point (Fig. 11). In some cases, such as when roofing a stadium (Fig. 12), the points of contact with the outer air are located so low that at the periphery the membrane (Fig. 13) is already subject to noticeable internal pressure. Although this type of dome does not require artificial internal pressure, under special load conditions this can be provided by compressors. A similiar case is a hot air balloon at the tip of a rod (Figs. 14 and 15).

If a dome has a double membrane (Fig. 16), and the interspace is filled with hot air or a light gas (e.g., helium), an air or gas cushion is formed at the apex of the dome, unless this is prevented by a special shape of the inner membrane, or if the latter is suspended from the outer membrane (Fig. 17). Figure 18 shows a double membrane formed by chambers filled with light gas. Figure 19 shows balloons carrying a domed membrane.

It can be seen from Table 7 that small differences in temperature suffice to maintain the shape of an envelope. It is known that the dead weight of an ordinary fabric membrane (approximately 500 g/m²) is held at a height of 10 m when the temperature difference is a mere 10°C.

In a shopping center designed by Richard Wolf of the University of Illinois, under the supervision of Frederick D. Miles (Fig. 8, helium was to be introduced between two membranes.

8

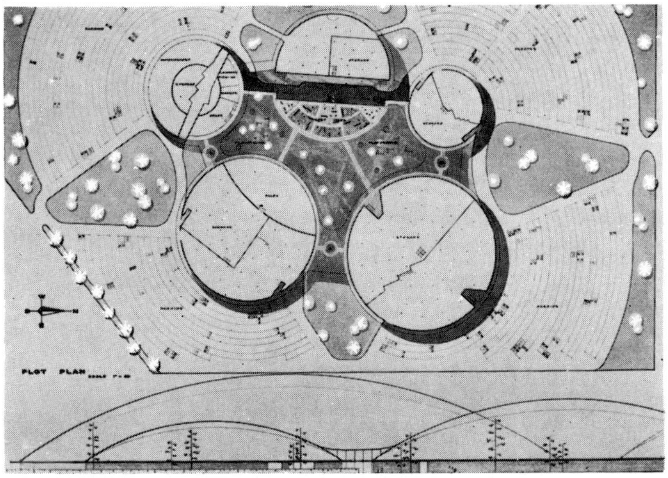

1

2

3

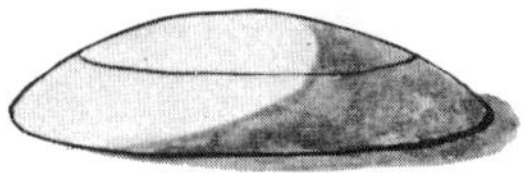

4

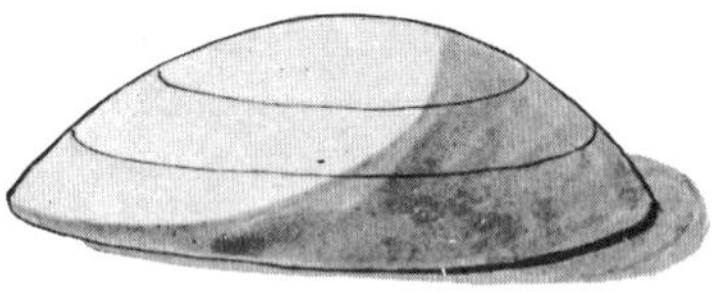

5

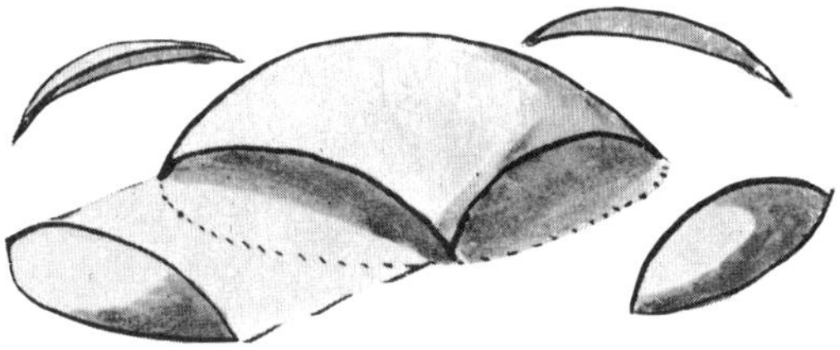

6

7

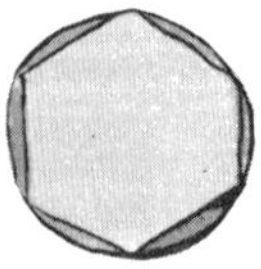

8

9

Spherical segments and combined shapes

Spherical domes need not rest on plane bases. Pneumatically tensed membrane domes can have widely varying boundaries. In a town-planning project* for a science center (Fig. 1), a spherical dome envelops a mountain top. The membrane extends into the valleys and follows the configuration of the terrain.

A small, shallow dome, (Fig. 2) is enlarged by attaching annular strips (Figs. 3 and 4). Since the radii are equal, and provided the interior pressure is the same, all three domes have equal membrane tensions and hoop forces at the base line, despite differing spans.

Four domes (Fig. 15) form a row and are connected by openings. The result is a long continuous inner space.

The five-part dome is highly adaptable (Fig. 5). The large central section has a square floor plan (Fig. 6) and is bordered by four identical sections.

Such subdivided spheres can be joined ad infinitum when mounted on a fixed grid. If four domes converge centrally, internal drainage becomes necessary. Anchored structures with internal drainage will be discussed further on pp. 90 to 105.

A hexagonal dome (Figs. 7 and 8), with six fixed points and six lateral sections can be adapted to a hexagonal grid (Fig. 18). In this case, three domes meet at the inner points.

By suitable subdivision (Fig. 9) spherical segments can be adapted to square or hexagonal grids, and to different elevations.

At the juncture of two domes a bracing cable (Fig. 11) must take up the forces. At fabric joins (Fig. 12) internal pressure causes sealing of the seam when a strip of fabric is applied.

Wall membranes (Fig. 13) can be suspended from roof channels to partition the inner space. Pneumatic structures with partitions are discussed in detail on pp. 101 to 105.

When connecting spherical and cylindrical segments (Fig. 16), structures in an "open" grid are obtained, enclosing inner courts.
In an adaptable design* for an exhibition, spherical segments of various shapes form an isolated single dome, a double dome, or a large assembly consisting of 13 units.

The different structures assembled of identical elements are connected by a pedestrian area. A square 30-m grid was used together with 16 identical roof elements, 28 identical lateral partitions, and 18 bracing cables: Figure 10 gives a lateral view, Fig. 14 an oblique bird's-eye view, and Fig. 17, the ground-plan model.

A floating residential and industrial town in the Arctic is designed* on the same principle (Figs. 18 to 20), but a hexagonal 60 m grid is used. The base and foundation of the light 1 to 3 story buildings is a hard foam (polystyrol) layer covered with wooden planks. The town can be expanded at will. Figure 18 is the ground plan, Fig. 19 the cross section, and Fig. 20 a panoramic sketch.

10

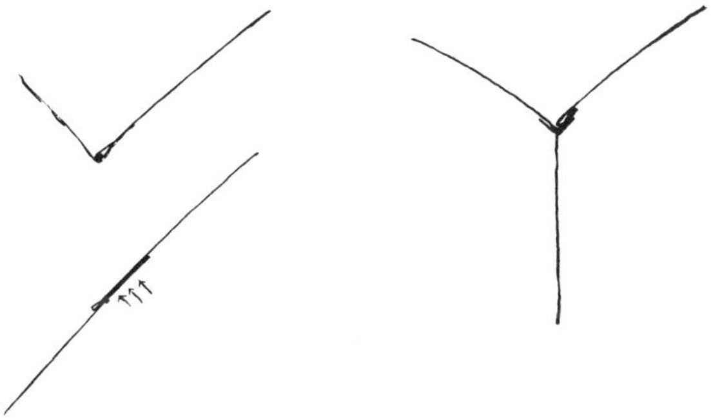
11 to 13

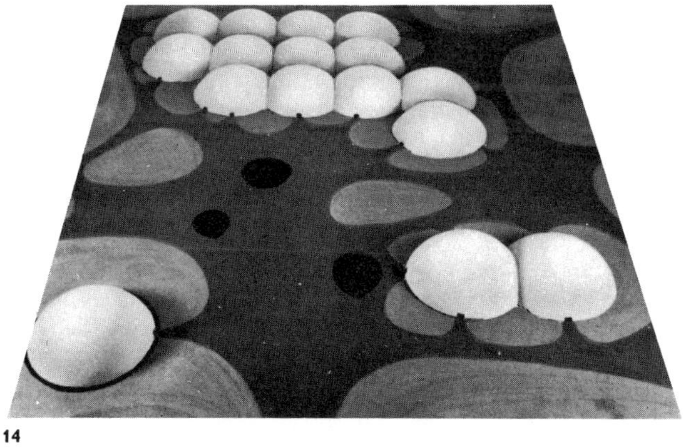
14

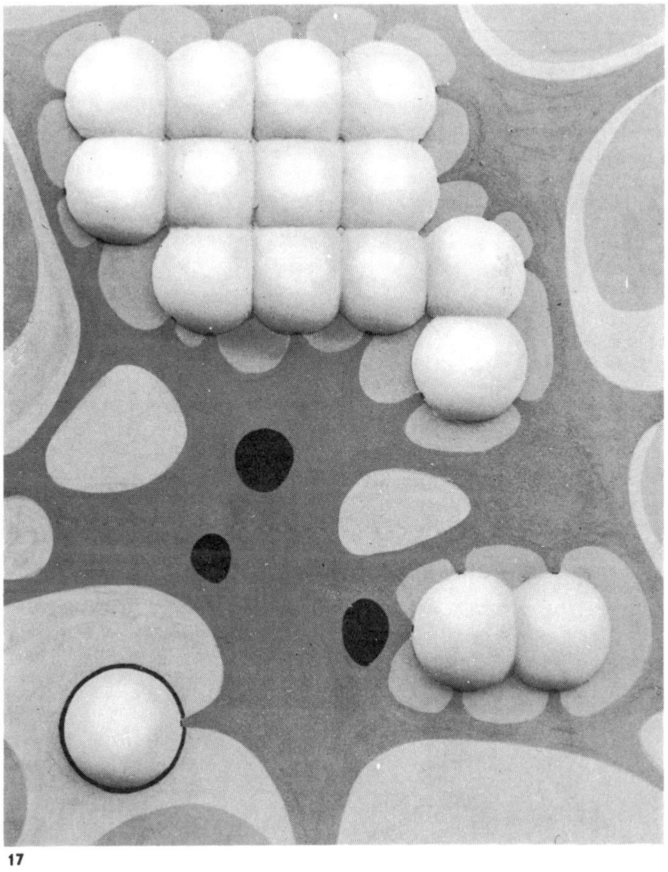
17

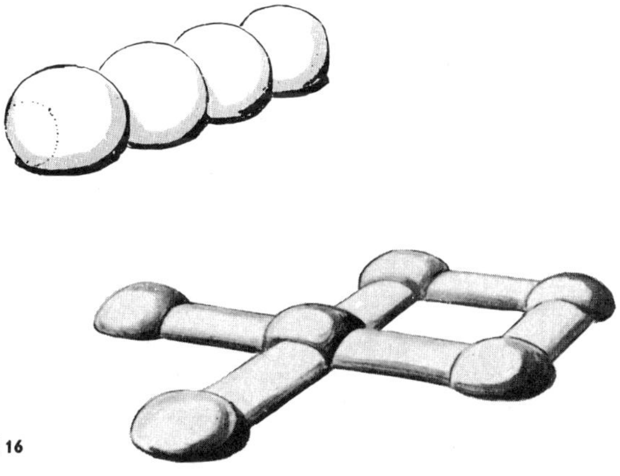
15 and 16

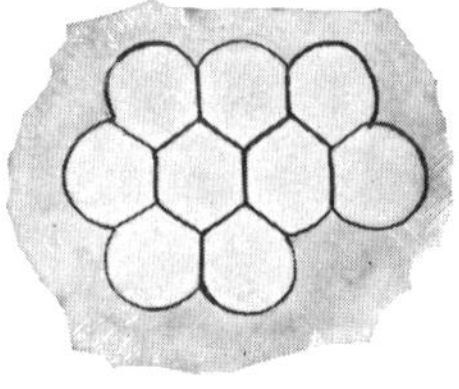
18

19

20

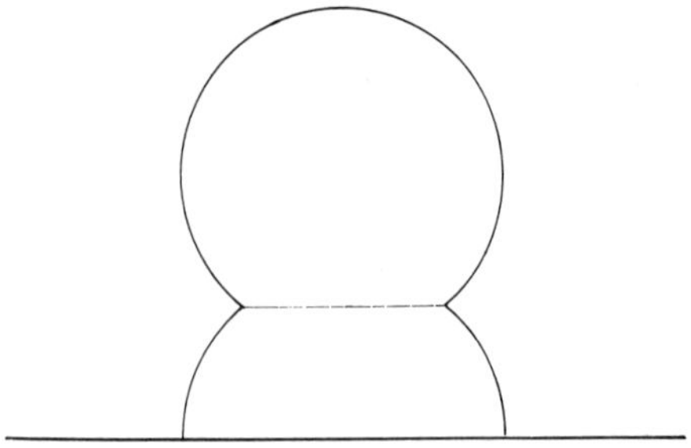

1

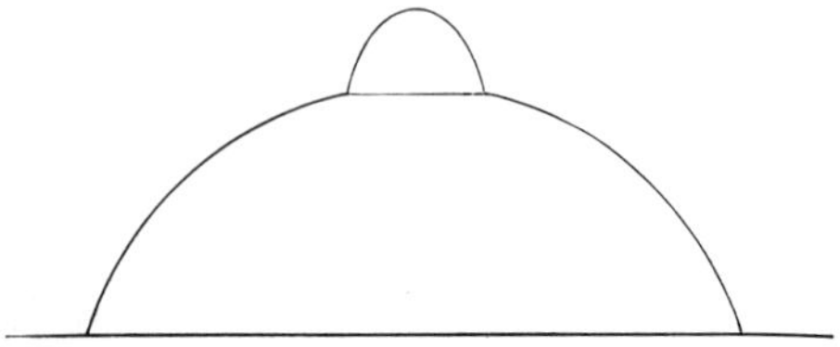

2

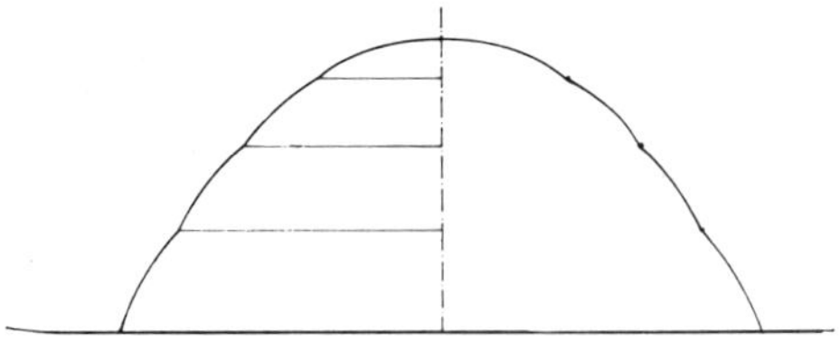

3

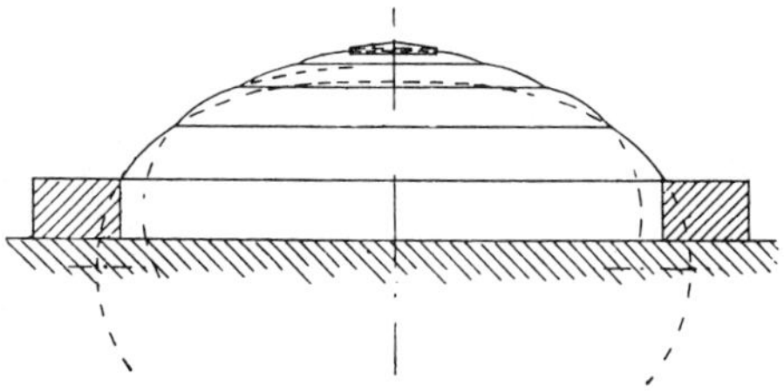

4

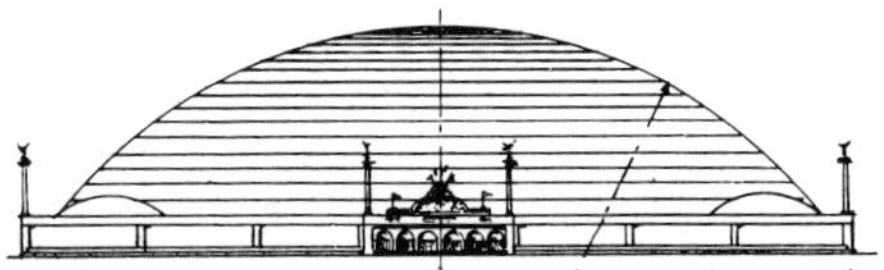

5

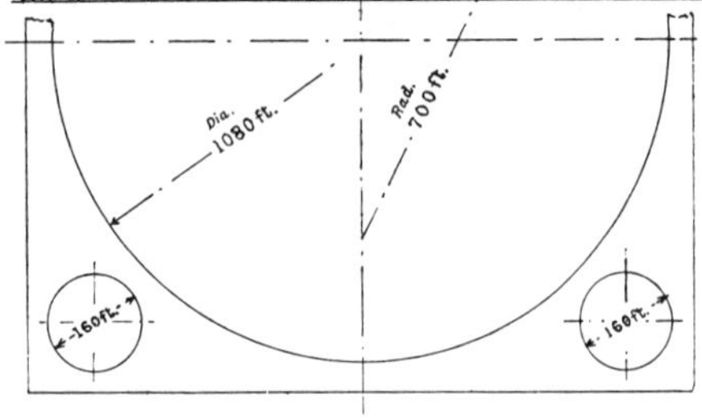

6

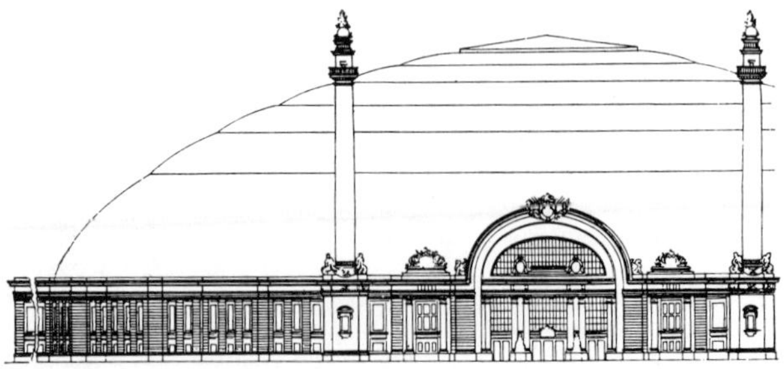

7

Domes with Cables and Cable Nets

If the membranes of pneumatically tensed spherical domes are made of plastic-coated fabric of natural, synthetic, or mineral fiber, it is generally difficult to obtain collapsible (i.e.; flexible) single-layer membranes with a tensile strength exceeding 6 t/m. Taking into account the necessary safety factors, such fabrics can only be used for spherical domes with radii of curvature up to 50 m.

Greater radii of curvature necessitate multiple membranes, reinforcing cables, or wire and web inserts in order to attain the required strength.

A row of spheres as in Fig. 15, p. 43, can also be arranged vertically (Fig. 1), resulting in tower-like structures.

A small transparent skylight dome is separated from a large flat dome by means of an annular cable (Fig. 2). The membrane tensions in the flat part are considerably greater than in the skylight. When designing such structures the laws cited on p. 18 must be observed.

This applies particularly when fairly small radii of curvature are to be attained in rather flat domes (Fig. 3) by means of horizontal cables.

In his first works (patented in 1917 and 1919) and in his lecture in 1938 before the Manchester Association of Civil Engineers on the subject of spans, Lanchester described horizontal cables, partly also in combination with radial cables (Figs. 4 to 7). The figures are from a reprint of the lecture by Butterly and Wood, Manchester. Lanchester suggested domes with diameters of up to 650 m and rigid skylights. His tarpaulin domes were to rise above stone buildings.

Together with his patent claims, this lecture by Lanchester is the first basic work on pneumatic structures.

The use of horizontal reinforcing cables is generally economical only for high domes in which the larger hoop forces appear as meridional forces.

For shallower domes, radial cables are generally far more effective than horizontal ones. Very small radii of curvature can appear in the membrane between the cables. Consequently, the cables take up most of the forces.

The five-cable dome* (Fig. 8) possesses strongly curved, drop-like membranes with marked contour lines (Fig. 10). View 11 and the curves seen in Fig. 12 show that the structure is comparatively low with an interior of strongly plastic differentiation.

The largest (at present) pneumatic membrane with radial cables was erected by the Schjeldahl Company, Northfield, Minnesota (Figs. 9 and 13; photos by Schjeldahl). It is a grain silo 60 m in diameter. The grain is retained by a wooden wall.

8 ▲

10 ▲

▼ 11

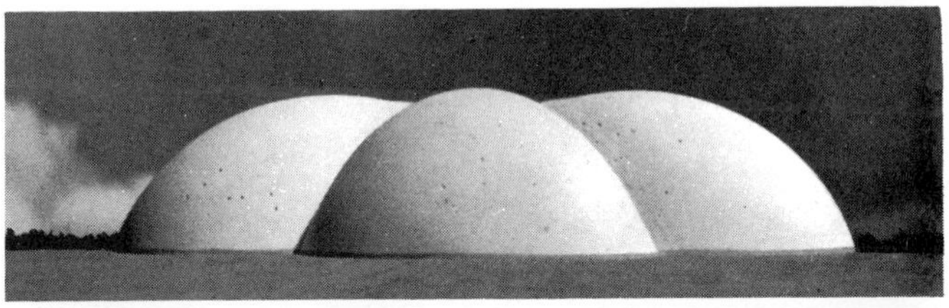

9

12

▼ 13

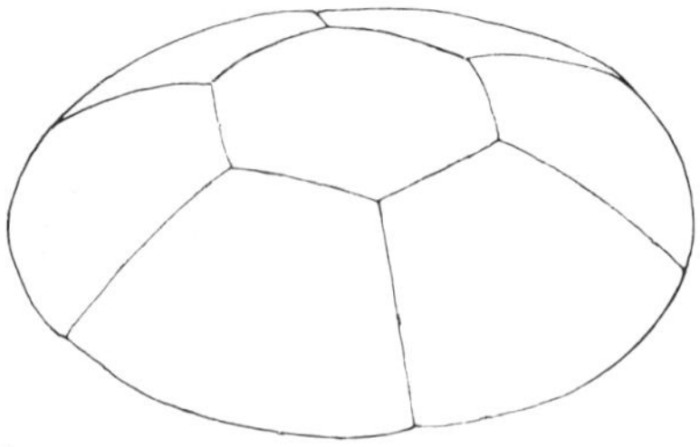
1

2

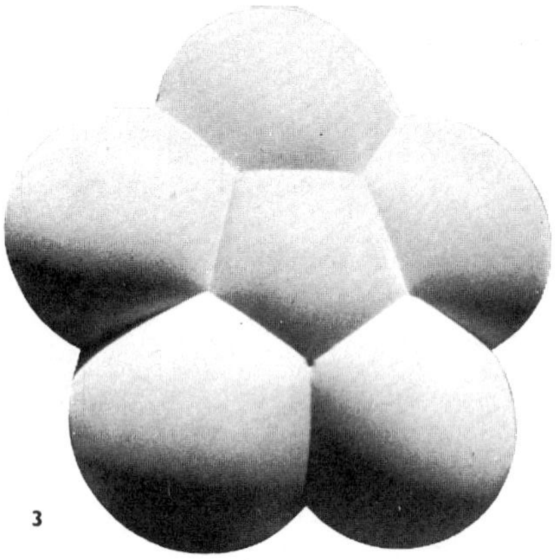
3

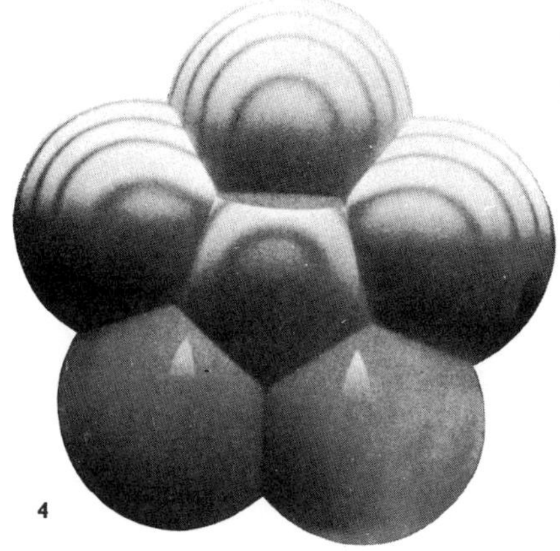
4

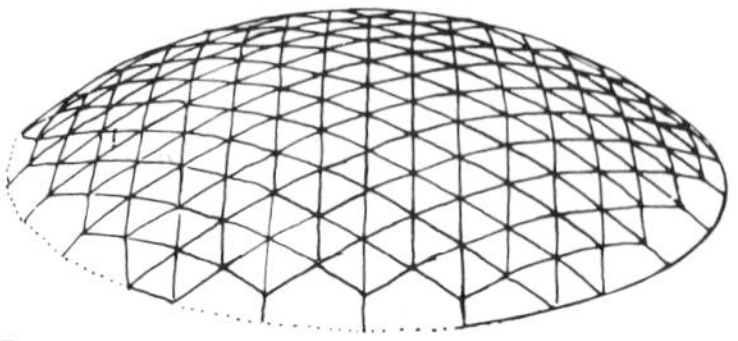
5

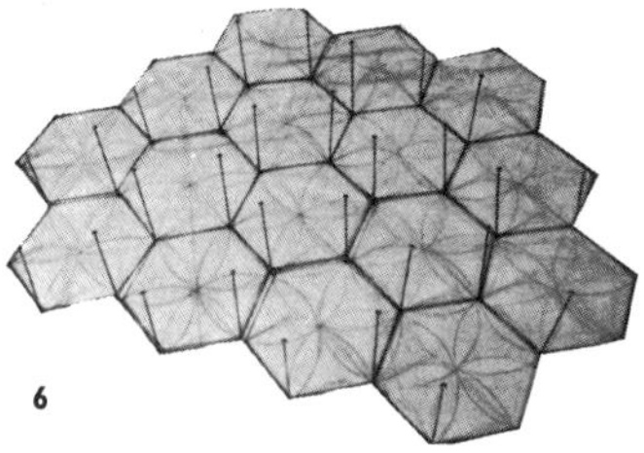
6

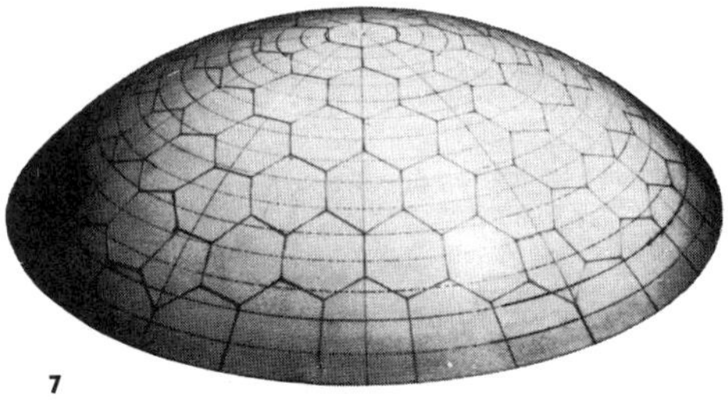
7

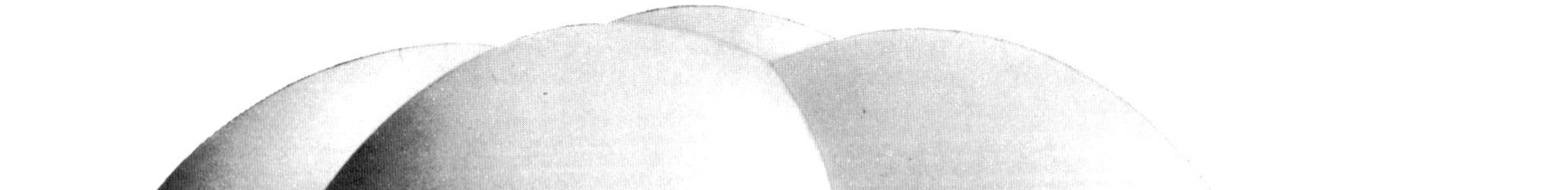
8

A combination of cable net and membrane is especially effective when the net is of approximately uniform mesh and the intermediate membrane sections have nearly the same radii of curvature.

A dome (Fig. 1), is easily spanned by a seven-mesh net.

A model membrane of very pronounced shape was stretched experimentally over the same ground plan as the project in Fig. 8, p. 45. Figure 3 is a top view, Fig. 2 shows the vertical sections, and Fig. 4 the contour lines. Figure 8 presents a lateral view.

It is best to use nets which can be manufactured in series. This applies particularly to nets of hexagonal, square, or rectangular shape in the extended plane position. In the spatially curved laminar form, the angles of intersection at the cable crossings of such nets change. The nets can often be given a considerable double curvature.

Experimental models frequently necessitate a high model accuracy of the net (Fig. 6), which is spanned over a rigid model dome (Fig. 7) in order to determine the anchoring points. The inflated dome was then formed of a transparent membrane (Fig. 16).

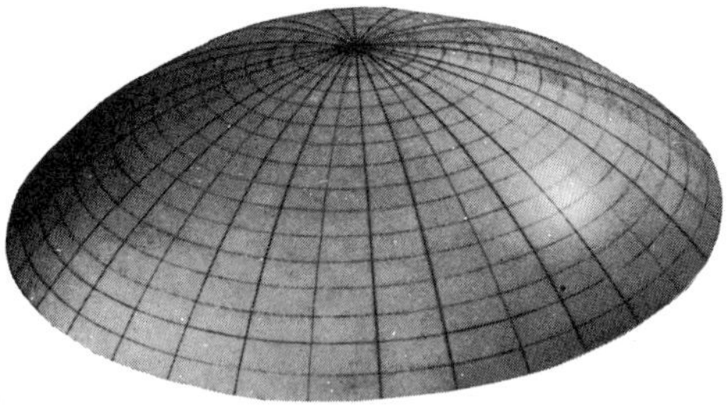

9

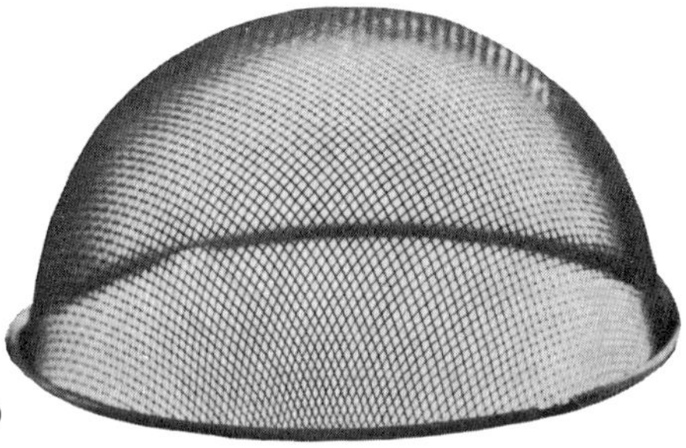

10

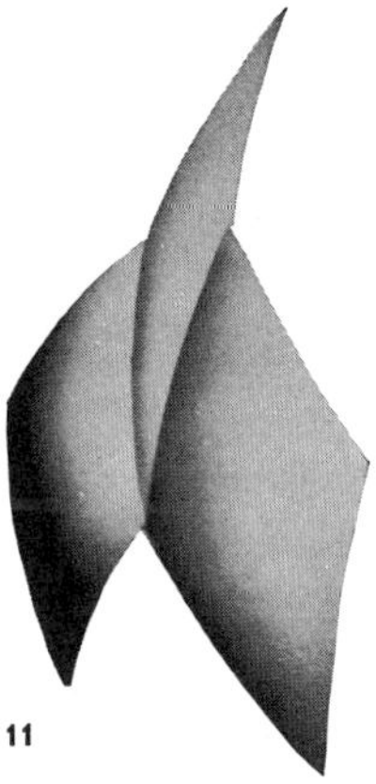

11

12

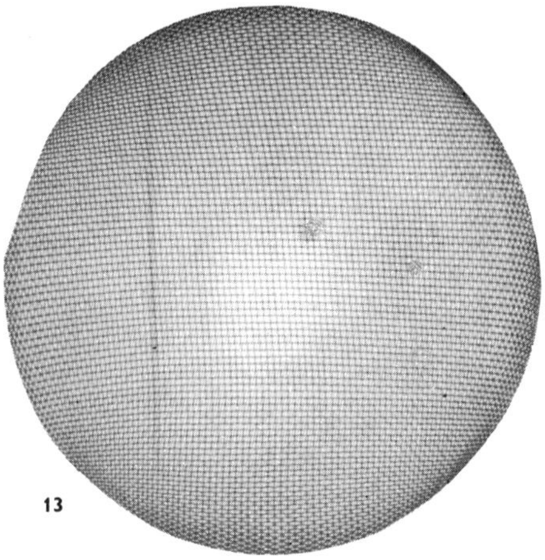

13

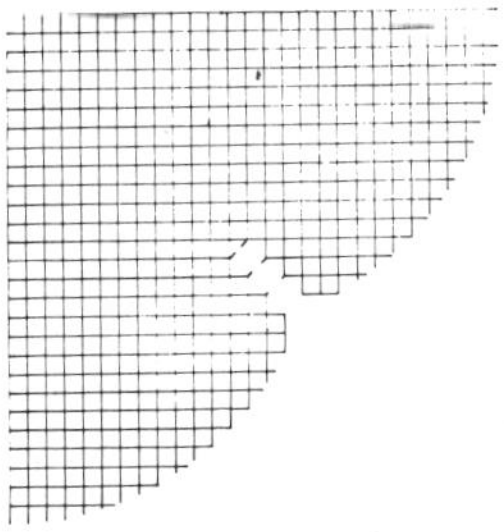

14

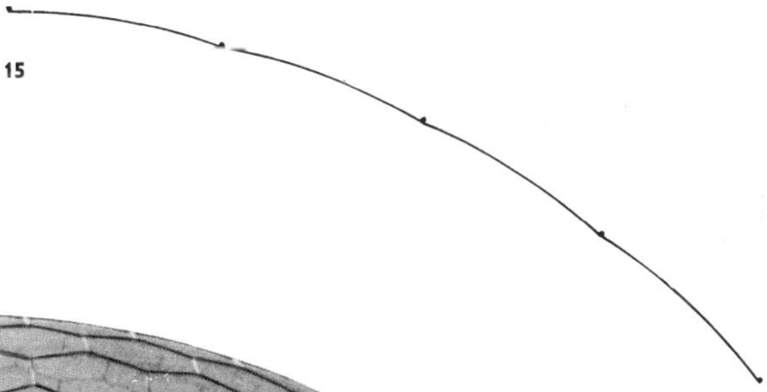

15

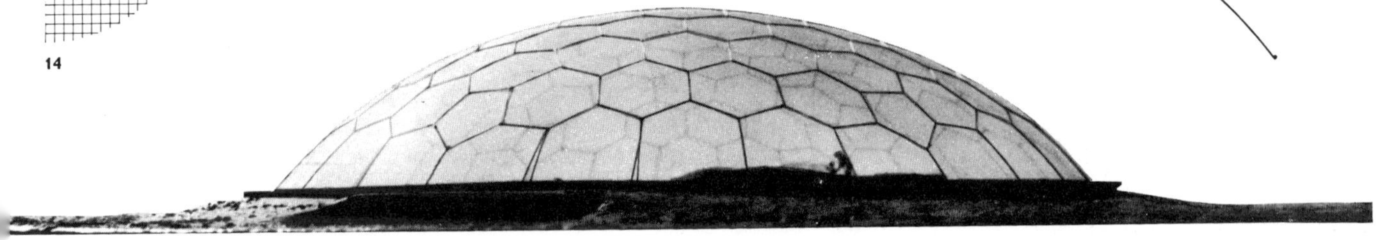

16

Nets of triangular mesh (Fig. 5) are fixed in form and cannot constitute plane surfaces. Their rigidity is slightly higher than that of quadrilateral and hexagonal nets.
Nets consisting of latitudinal and longitudinal circles (Fig. 9) have widely differing mesh shapes. Square nets used for forming round domes (Fig. 10) show lesser or greater angular deviations at four points (Fig. 13) depending on whether the domes are flat or high. This can also be seen in the photographs 11 and 12 of parts of another design.

A specially designed cable net (Fig. 14) can prevent excessive angular deviations, especially in fairly high domes.

A cross section through a membrane with cable-net bracing (Fig. 15) shows how the membrane is pushed against the net by internal pressure. The shape of the cable net is hardly affected. The cables form practically straight lines between their junctions. This prevents the accumulation of the rain water. Except at the summit the dome is inclined everywhere. This guarantees drainage.

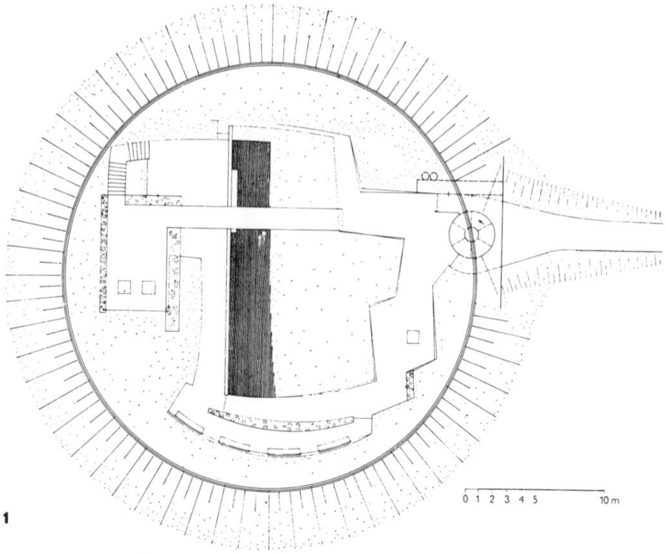

1

4

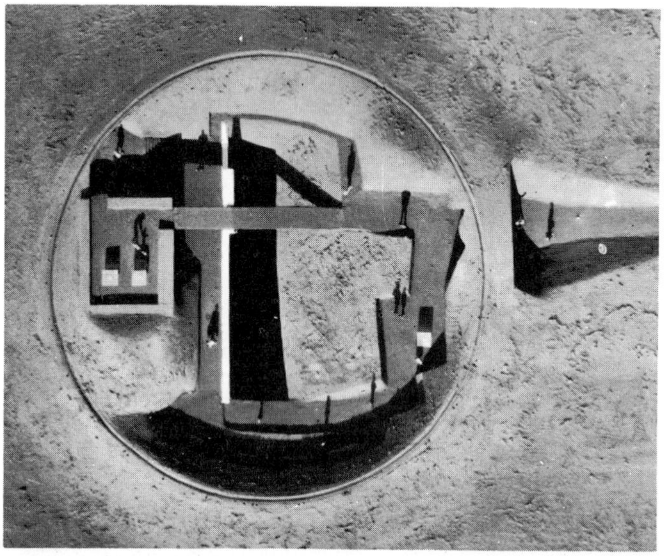

2 ▲

▼ 3

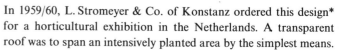

In 1959/60, L. Stromeyer & Co. of Konstanz ordered this design* for a horticultural exhibition in the Netherlands. A transparent roof was to span an intensively planted area by the simplest means.

Leisurely observation of the flowers was to be possible even at peak visiting hours. Visitors enter the structure from below, ascend a ramp, and cross a bridge over a pond. The strongly contoured terrain can be surveyed from an elevated position. Photographs and films related to the exhibition are shown in a separate closed room.

The revolving door at the entry and exit has an additional air lock at one side for larger items. There is an emergency exit on the other side with outward-opening rubber doors, on which the pressure is equalized. The blower is also near the entrance and ensures the maintenance of pressure, cooling, and heating. Since the plastic skin of the roof is tightly sealed, several vents serve to increase air circulation. The cable net has a comparatively narrow mesh. The membrane which is 0.5 mm thick must be renewed annually. The figures show a cross section through the pavilion (Fig. 5), the ground plan (Fig. 1), a ground-plan photo of the terrain (Fig. 2), and a ground-plan photo with the pneumatic envelope installed (Fig. 3).

This cable-reinforced pneumatic structure was thoroughly investigated on a model, taking the following factors into account: the proposed terracing of the terrain (Figs. 12 and 13), the external appearance (Fig. 4), and the inflating process (Figs. 8 to 11), which, in the presence of external wind, causes the dome to rise asymmetrically (Fig. 10). In the longitudinal section (Fig. 6), No. 1 represents the foundation ring; 2, the air duct; 3, the plastic skin; 4, the cable net, and 5, the air lock. The edge is simply formed and detachable.

The cables of the net are directly attached to deeply buried anchor plates. They pass over a wooden ring to which the membrane is nailed. This ring forms a gutter to drain the water of condensation.

A special sealing skin leads obliquely into the ground (Fig. 7).

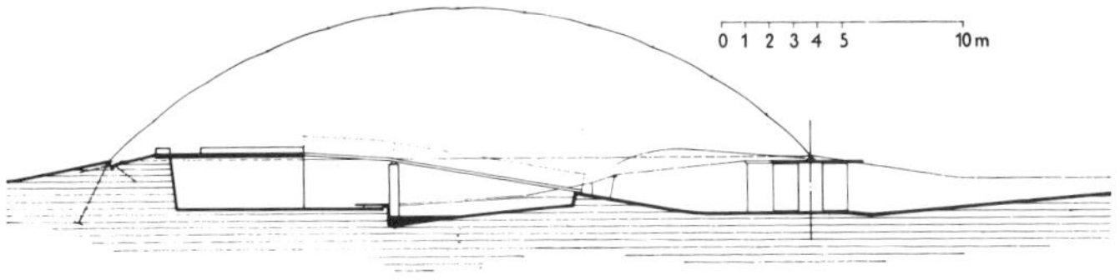

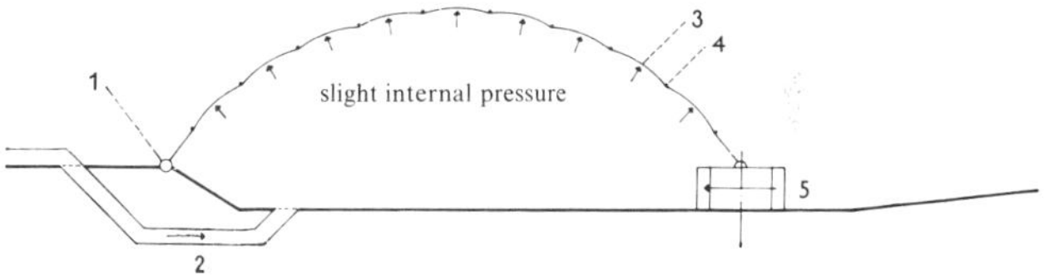

5 and 6

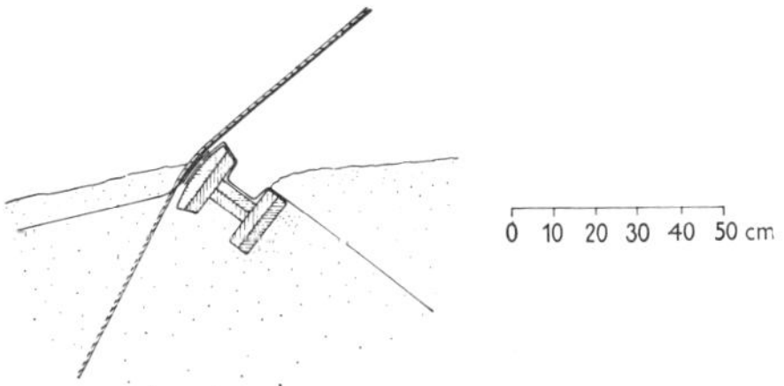

7

8 to 11 ▼

▼ 12

▼ 13

4

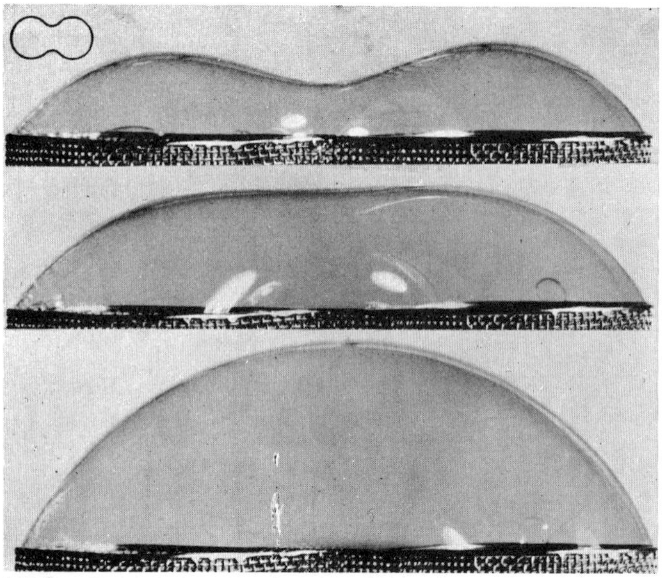

1 to 3

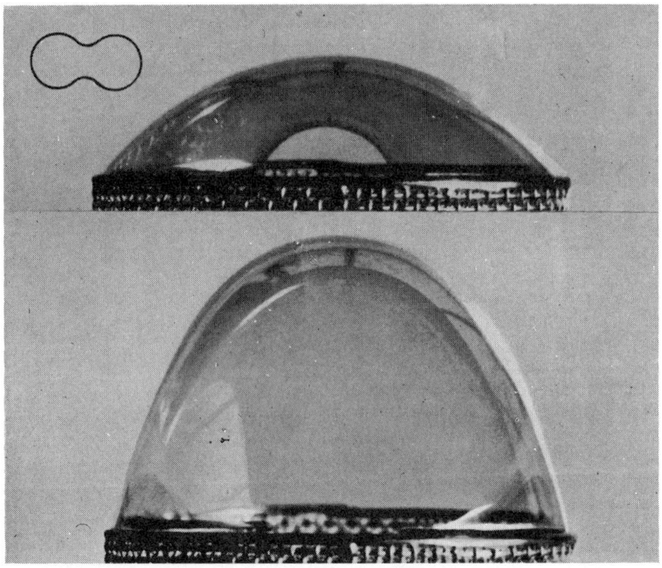

4 and 5 ▲ ▼ 6 to 8

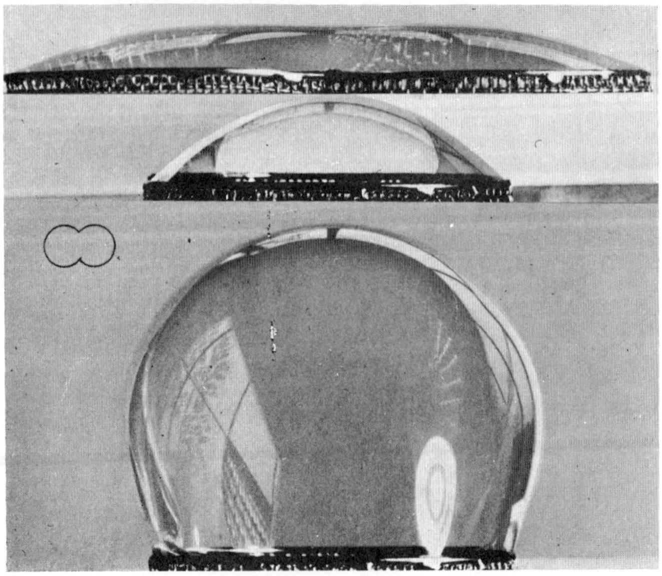

Double Domes

When a soap bubble is blown above a dumbbell-shaped base plan, two domes of gentle transition are formed initially. This can be clearly seen in the side views (Fig. 1), and from the front (Fig. 4).

It should be noted that in this case the minimum surface of the soap bubble forms a pronounced saddle. This constriction, which appears in spite of uniform membrane tension, disappears with increasing volume (Figs. 2, 3 and 5). A saddle shape remains only in the immediate vicinity of the constriction at the base.

If the same test is repeated with a base consisting of two connected three-quarter circles without partition, as shown in Fig. 8 at the upper left, the saddle surface can hardly be noticed. This is seen in side view (Fig. 6) and front views (Figs. 7 and 8), at different heights of the bubble. The membrane at first extends outward in a nearly horizontal direction near the turned-in points of the base and then slopes upward steeply. A very small saddle surface is formed. The sharp points of the base affect the shape of the minimum surface much less than the gentle curves in the first experiment.

A double dome with gradual transition can be of interest in many design problems.

In a project for a hangar* (Fig. 9) on a mountain top, the double dome is directly connected with fixed structures adjusted to the contours of the terrain and the design requirements. These structures also contain the entrances with their air locks. In the experimental model (Figs. 10 to 12), a flat rubber membrane was marked with a square grid. When inflated, the grid permitted an exact photographic record of the resulting shape.

Unless a sharply intersecting cable causes a clear separation of the two halves, a gently sloping saddle is formed even on an angular base, as shown in Fig. 13. This can be seen in the double dome on the right of Fig. 10 on p. 43. Domes with gradual transitions can be assembled to form long rows (Fig. 14).

If the constrictions of a dumbbell-shaped base meet at the center (Fig. 15), two separate shapes are formed. For one half of the base (Fig. 15), the minimum surface is shown as a soap bubble in Fig. 19 (plan), and in Fig. 20 (side view). The saddle surface is clearly visible, although not very large.

A particularly interesting design, by architect Victor Lundy, for an exhibition of the U.S. Atomic Energy Commission is shown in pp. 52 and 53. The pavilion was designed by Walter Bird, assisted by Severud, Elstad, and Krueger as consultant engineers. Acoustics were handled by Bold, Beranek, and Newman. The fully transportable structure is 91 m long, 38 m wide, and 19 m high, and has a total weight of 28 tons. It was designed for a touring exhibition which opened in South America on November 1st, 1960. A report appeared in *Architectural Forum* of November 1960, and also by Bandel, in *Bauingenieur* 4/1961. We will here refer expressly to these publications. The design combines several principles, providing both increased safety and the shape aimed at by the architect.

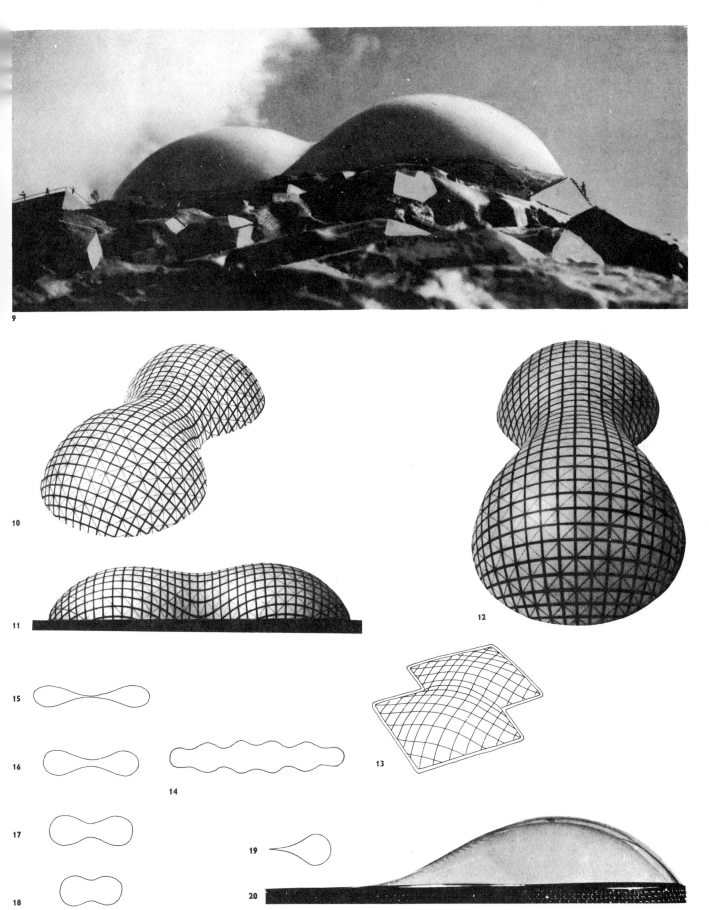

9

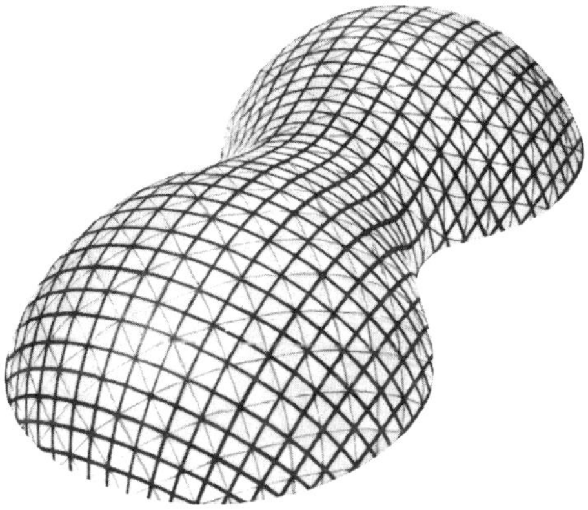
10

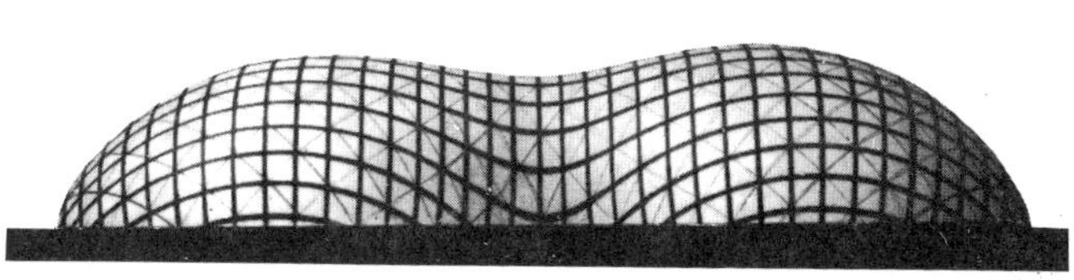
11

12

15

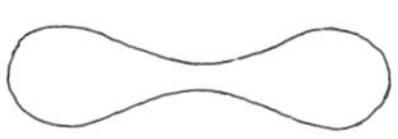
16

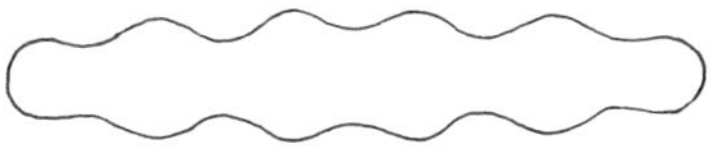
14

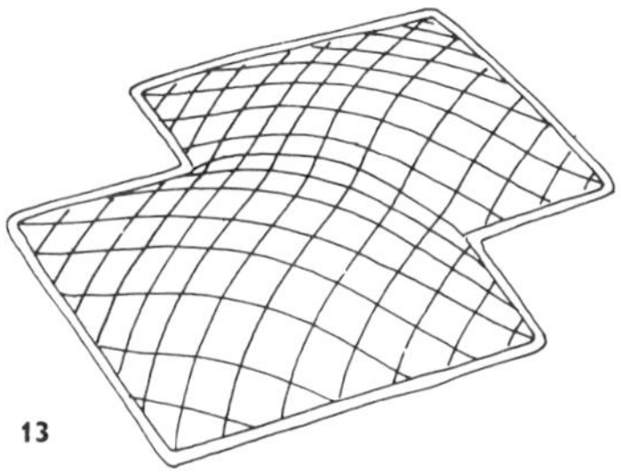
13

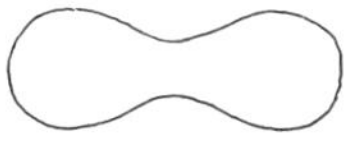
17

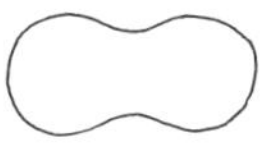
18

19

20

1

3

2

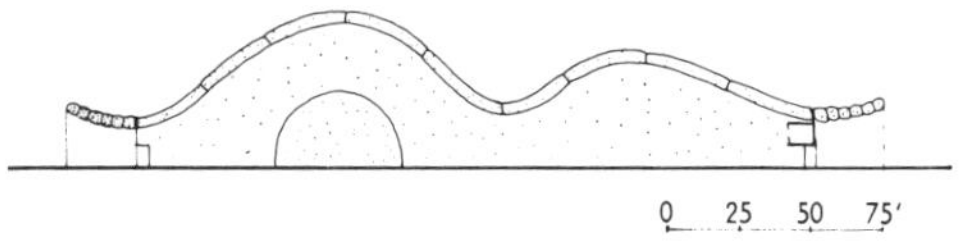

4

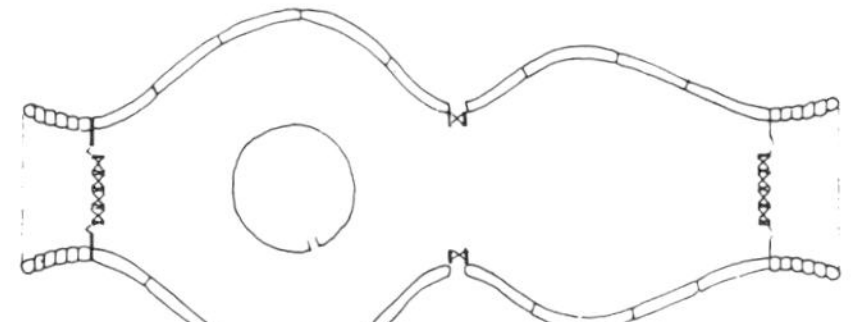
5

Section 4 and plan 5 show that the central part consists of two large domes connected by a saddle-shaped piece. This is a true double dome with gradual transition. The two domes differ in height and width. The interior (Figs. 2 and 3) is pressurized and enclosed by a double membrane. Entry is through revolving doors mounted in rigid end frames. The interior pressure is maintained at 49 mm water column. The pressure in the interspace is 38 mm water column. The clearance between the two membranes is 1.2 m, providing better heat insulation and constituting an additional safety measure. The interspace is partitioned into individual chambers. Should the membrane be damaged at any point, the ensuing loss

▼6

7

of tension is restricted to a limited area. However, the clearance between the membranes is too large to achieve self-sealing as explained on pp. 28 and 29. Air pressure in the interior and in the interspace is maintained by separate blowers.
The structure contains a cinema with three hundred seats, and a further pneumatic dome which forms the transparent cover of an experimental nuclear reactor. One pneumatic structure thus surrounds another. This inner dome is shown in Figs. 2 and 4. The internal pressure is highest inside the small spherical dome for the reactor. The public moves in a region of intermediate pressure. The pressure is lowest in the interspace. The pressure gradient acts outward from the center and ensures the correct tension of each membrane. The structure requires a concrete foundation and can be assembled in 3 to 4 days; inflation takes 30 minutes. The membranes are anchored to a pipe retained in the concrete foundations. The photographs show the structure at its first erection in Rio de Janeiro after November 1st, 1960.

The curved domes of the central section have roofed, open entrance halls on either side of the longitudinal axis outside the rigid end frames. These halls consist of curved, inflated hoses and constitute a pneumatic "cushion structure," which will be discussed later (see p. 106). These entrances are also under pneumatic tension but are based on a quite different principle. Although these halls

8

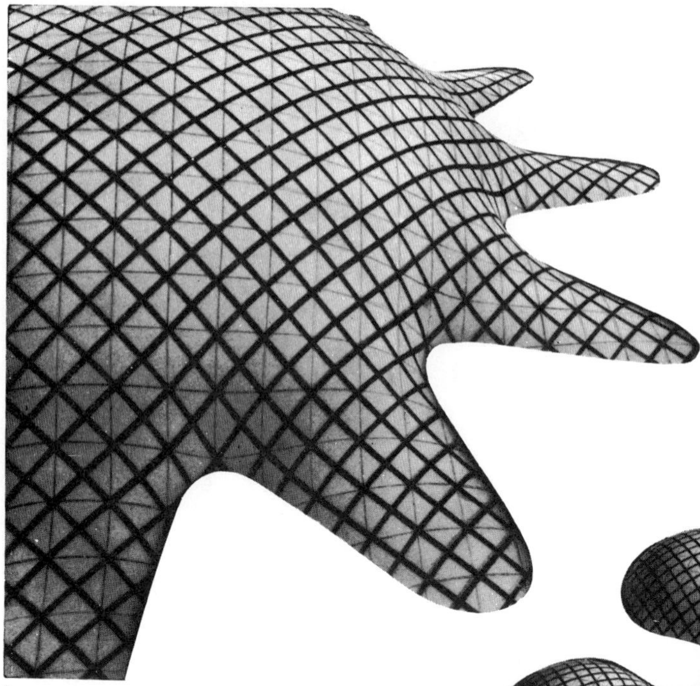

1

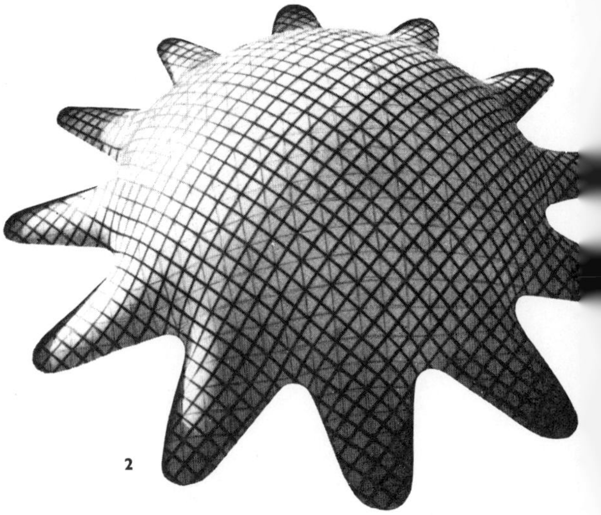

2

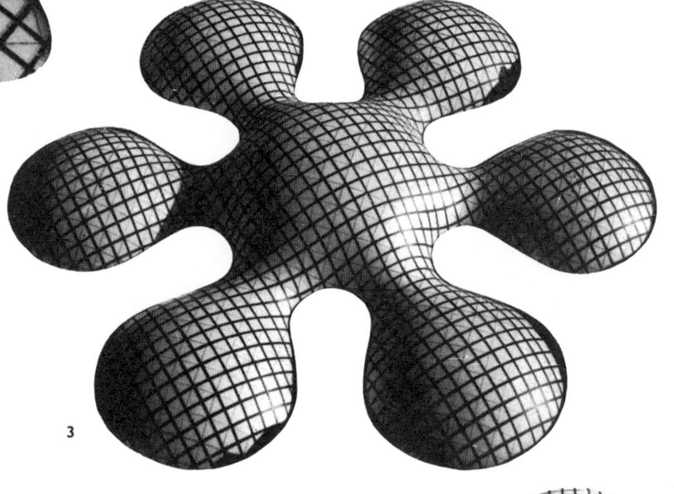

3

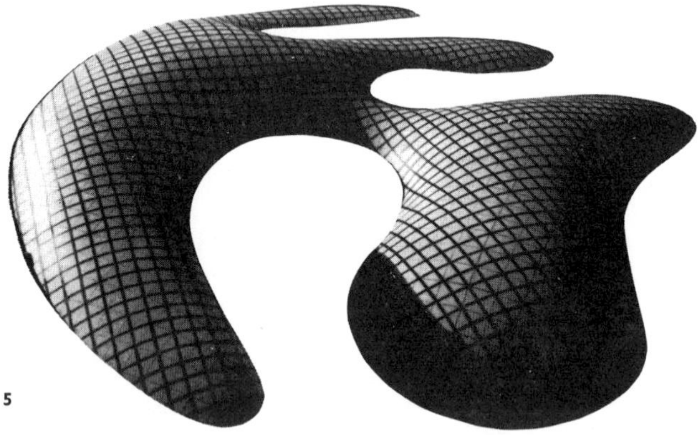

5

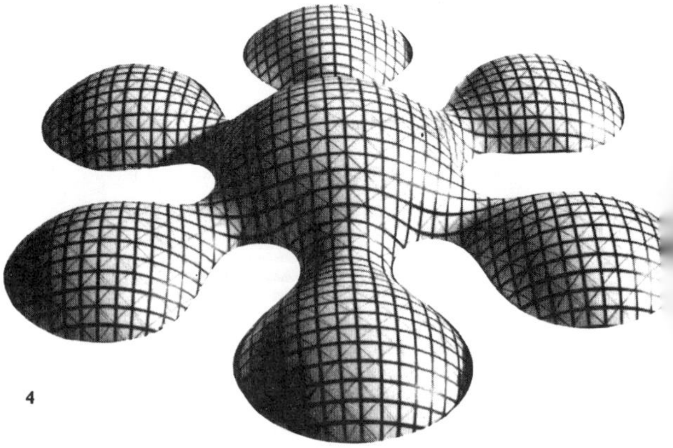

4

are not pressurized since they are open to the outside, they can be transformed into air-locks by attaching fabric walls to the outer borders in order to introduce large objects during the assembly of the exhibition. The cushion unit is structurally connected with the pressurized double sphere by means of the rigid frame.
This notable pneumatic structure provided a great deal of experience. The different pneumatic principles make comparison possible. Problems of space (extraterrestrial) construction can also be investigated.

The pavilion was the first practical attempt to go beyond the usual shapes of pneumatic structures, limited to spherical domes and cylinders. (All photographs were provided by Victor Lundy.)

Domes, spanning free-form ground plans

The shape of structures on free-form ground plans was studied in a series of experiments. Thin rubber membranes marked with double grids were inflated and assumed a shape very similar to a

6

7

8

minimum surface. The experiments were not limited to determining the laws governing membranes spanning large, continuous foundations of arbitrary shape, but were intended to reveal the appearance of saddle surfaces. These are comparatively rare in pneumatic structures and extend only over part of the total surface.

In the membrane spanning a star-shaped plan (Figs. 1 and 2), the influence of the plan curves is only marked in their immediate vicinity. The inner part of the dome itself hardly differs from a spherical dome which would form above a circular ring.

A star-shaped plan with widened ends makes the constrictions and saddle surfaces appear clearly (Figs. 3 and 4). The membrane is higher at the center than at the lateral domes. Even if the surface areas were equal, the curvature of the membrane, due to the constrictions, would cause the central dome to rise above the lateral domes. This experiment also revealed that pneumatic structures are unrivaled in adaptability. Any plan shape can be spanned by a pneumatically tensed membrane. However, the resulting shapes frequently differ in usefulness and structural efficiency.

As an example, Fig. 5 shows a membrane spanning an amoeba-shaped plan. Under the effect of internal pressure, the membrane has different heights, depending on the corresponding free mean span. The membrane has mainly a domed curvature, with some saddle surfaces and unilaterally curved transitions.

These experiments with highly deformable membranes are also important for structures made of less deformable material (e.g., coated glass fiber quilt) in which, for the same design and conditions, the stresses are similar to those appearing in highly deformable materials.

Domes with partly thickened membranes

Gradual constrictions are also attained by thickening the membrane at certain points. Despite approximately equal membrane tensions, larger forces can be taken up in regions of greater thickness (e.g., at double walls, etc.). If a rubber membrane is reinforced with a three-pronged star (Fig. 6), a tripartite dome with gradual transitions is formed (Fig. 7); this is particularly visible along the transverse lines (Fig. 8).

If a star-shaped cable reinforcement were used instead, sharp-edged constrictions (valleys) would form. By arranging several cables, or using strips of netting, gradual transitions can also be obtained with cable nets (comp. p. 68, Fig. 1).

Well-rounded bulges also ensure a gradual change in direction of the membrane stresses near the constrictions. In practice it is difficult to obtain a gradual thickening of the membrane. It is best to double or triple the original membrane by glued-on strips. It is thus possible to reinforce the membrane not only at constrictions, but also over large highly loaded surface areas, such as parts of a membrane having smaller radii of curvature than the remaining structure at the same internal pressures. It should be noted that each overlapping, sewn or glued seam constitutes a doubling, marked by a gradual constriction at an appropriate internal pressure. Seams act like a reinforcing net.

Domes, whose lateral boundaries do not lie in a plane

Domes can also extend over non-level plans. The number of possible designs is infinite; many are of practical importance.

Indeed, the pneumatic dome is a most adaptable structure. It can assume many shapes and is nearly unrivaled in its suitability for different requirements. When economy of material is desired, i.e., when the sum of all forces acting in the membrane and at the edges and, therefore, on the foundations are to be kept at a minimum, any desired edge curve has a corresponding membrane shape which, within certain limits, is the most suitable. For larger projects these shapes have to be investigated by model studies carried out with soap bubbles blown over the plan, or by inflating membranes of rubber or airtight fabrics.

Sketches of some designs* have been reproduced to clarify this point. The upper edge of a sports stadium with earthen walls (Fig. 1) must be adjusted to the lines of sight. In most cases this edge will be a closed spatial curve which can be spanned by a pneumatic dome without difficulty, even in existing structures.

In design (Fig. 2) a pneumatically tensed dome spans an inner court formed by a circular building roofed by an undulating shell which also acts as a counterweight to the pneumatically tensed membrane in the center.

A large climatic envelope (Fig. 3) spans the juncture of two mountain valleys. At some points the membrane extends far into the valleys, but leaves the adjoining wooden slopes uncovered.

Acoustic considerations may require membrane domes with vertical or inclined undulating edges (Figs. 4 and 5). Entrances, windows, and connections to other buildings can be provided in the illustrated example, by different design of the undulating edge formed by rigid rods, each peak being separately guyed.

Cable-reinforced domes on free-form ground plans

The design for a theater* is an example of a rounded dome supported by cable nets.

First, a rubber membrane (Figs. 12 to 14) was inflated over the plan of a classical amphitheater. It was found that, despite comparatively high membrane tensions, the height was insufficient, particularly above the stage.

A better shape (Figs. 6 to 9) was obtained by supporting the rubber membrane with cables. The ground plan (Figs. 11 and 16) was adapted to the new conditions. Four cables are anchored behind the upper row of seats and connected with a spatially curved cable which runs above the separation line of stage and hall. The model was permanently set by injecting plaster under pressure into a rubber membrane. All details could thus be accurately studied.

The entrances, lobbies, and administrative offices, as well as the restaurant, are arranged like terraces in one- and two-storied buildings adapted to the terrain and provided with flat roofs for strollers. The revolving stage is equipped with screens and adjustable partitions. There is also a curved safety wall which forms an upright and movable cylindrical shell (see Section Fig. 10).

Acoustic conditions were judged to be much better than in the first experiment. The possibility of supporting the six membrane surfaces between the main cables by cable nets was investigated in order to obtain a fine surface structure for further improvement of the acoustics.

This pneumatic form can also be used as an inverted shell carrying compressive loads. The cables then act as rigid bracing arches. Their curvatures can be experimentally determined exactly only by weight tests with membranes, or quickly, though only approximately, by means of pneumatic tests.

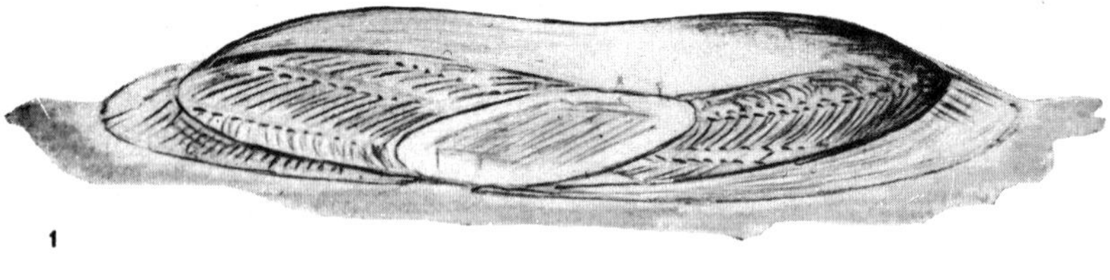

1

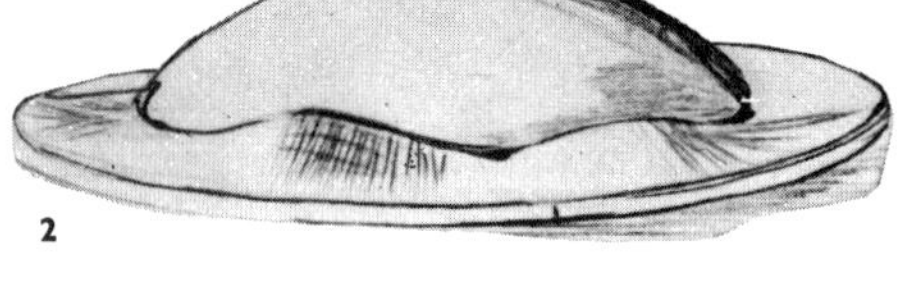

2

3

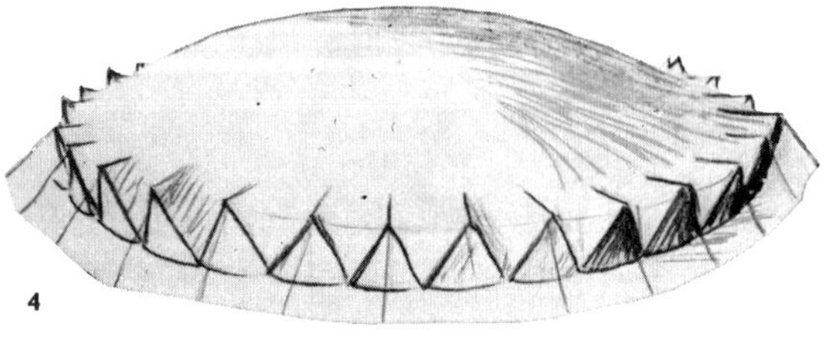

4

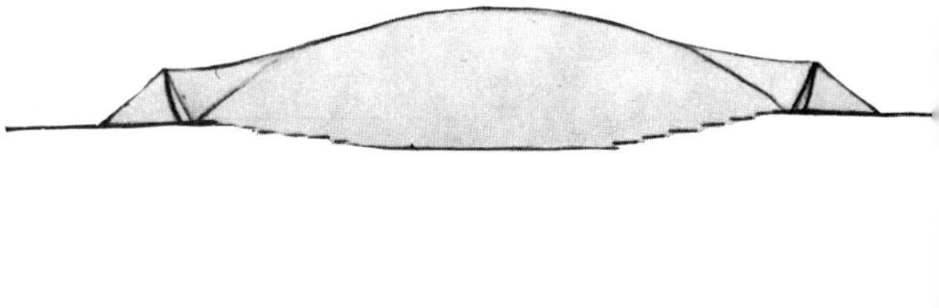

5

6 to 9

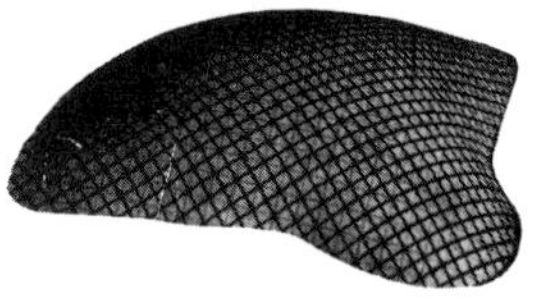

12

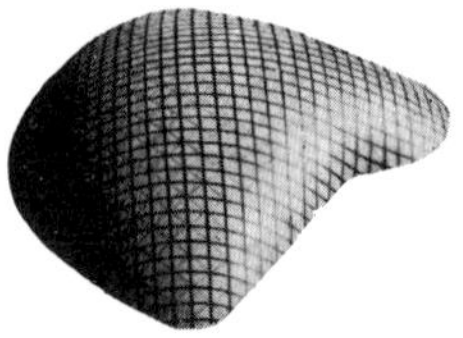

13

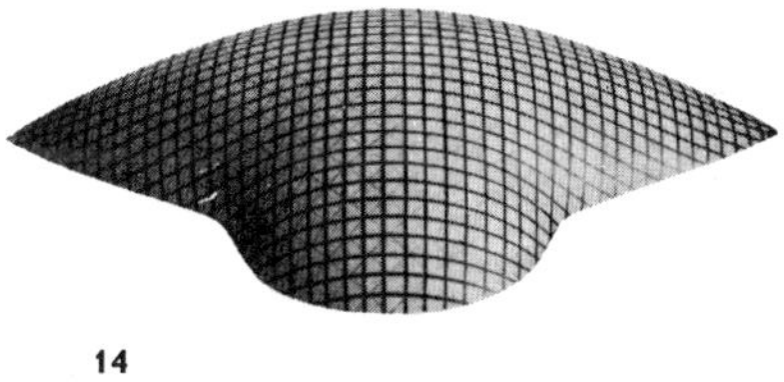

14

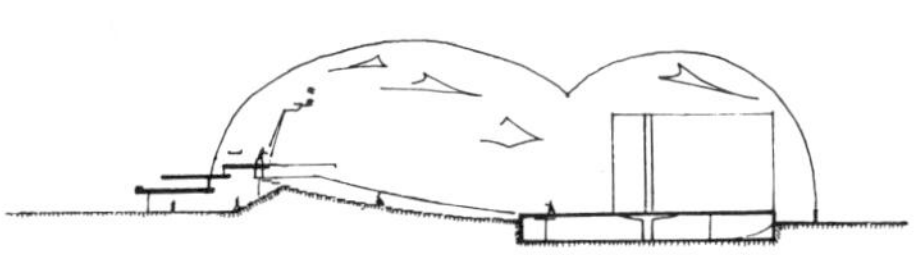

10

15 ▲

▼ 16

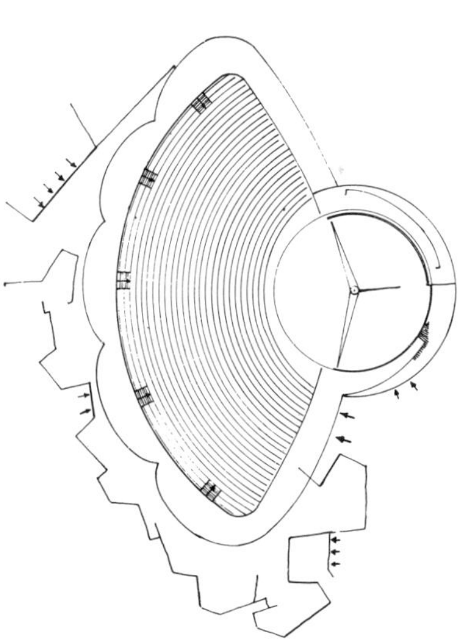

11

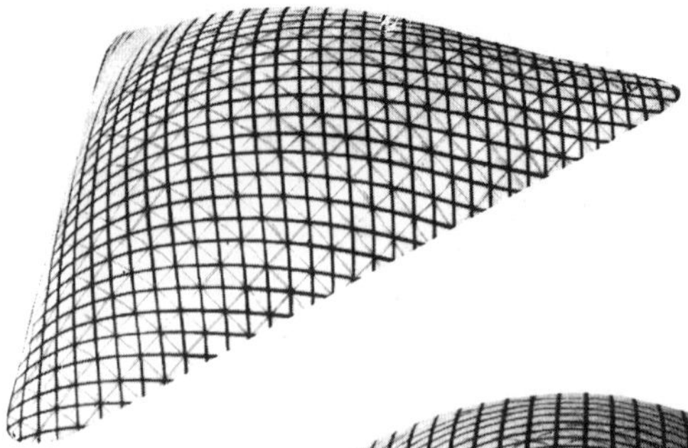

1

2

Domes Spanning Polygonal Ground Plans

Pneumatically stretched membranes spanning triangular outlines

Inflation of rubber membranes or blowing of soap bubbles over a triangular base yields shapes with marked saddle surfaces near the corners. Consequently, their vertical sections have points of inflection which can be connected by a curve on the membrane extending from side to side; this curve cuts off the corners. At each point of the saddle-shaped region the membrane curvature vanishes in two directions.

Figure 1 shows a rubber membrane, marked with a double grid and inflated over an equilateral triangle. Figure 2 is the side view of this

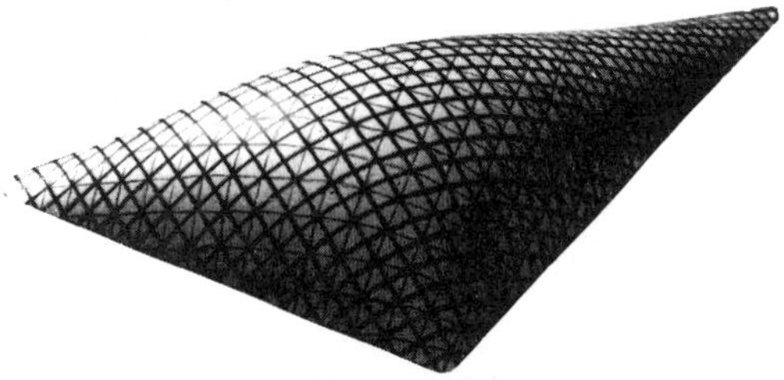

3

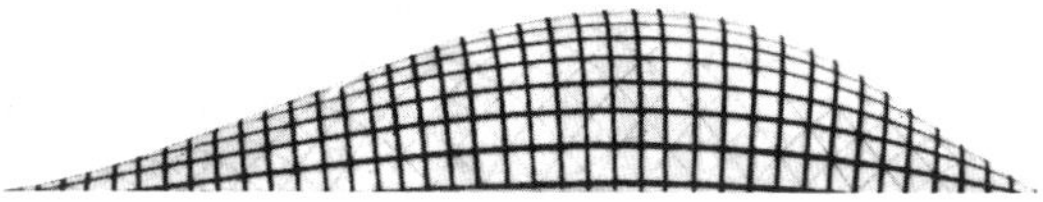

4

model from the apex. Figure 3 shows an asymmetrical membrane over a 30° right triangle. The summit of the dome lies approximately above the centroid of the triangle. In isosceles triangles with very acute angles, the summit moves away from the apex toward the short side. In tests with a rubber membrane whose plan (Fig. 6) shows the contoured lines (Fig. 7 is the side view), the summit is located approximately above the point which divides the perpendicular bisector of the short side at the ratio 1:5. This is clearly seen from the shadow cast by a vertical grid (Fig. 5). During a soap-bubble test on an acute-angled isosceles triangle (Figs. 8 and 9), a similar off-center summit was observed; when the soap bubble expanded, the summit moved away from the short side toward the centroid.

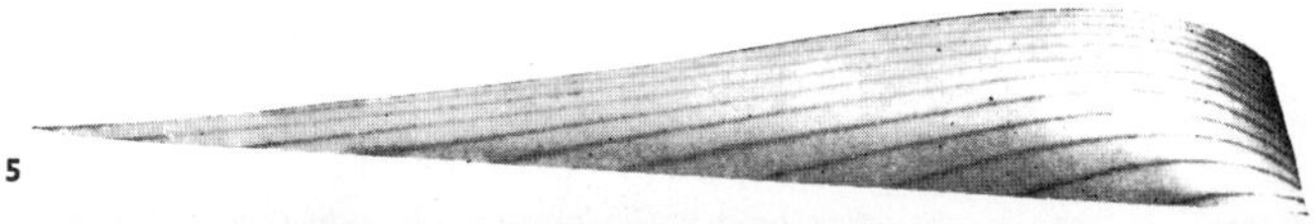

5

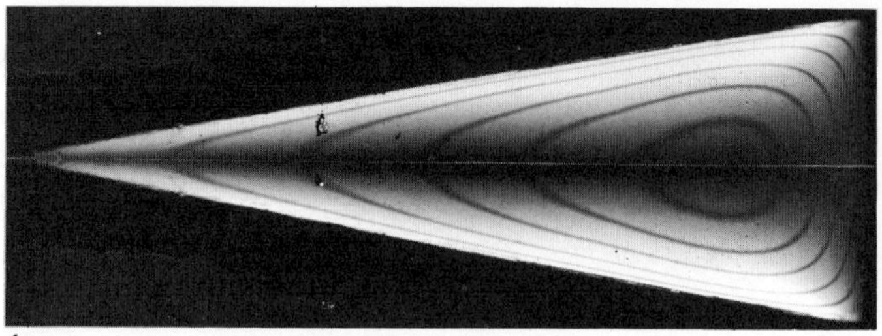

6

Triangular tensed pneumatic membranes can, for example, be used to line trussed roofs or wall panels. In practice, slightly deformable membranes, e.g., coated fabrics, are used. If such membranes are cut to a shape corresponding with that of the rubber membrane or soap bubble, a uniform distribution of tensions will be obtained if conditions are identical. However, this uniformity disappears when further inflation of these only slightly deformable membranes is attempted through increased pressure. Folds perpendicular to the bisectors of the angles, may then appear near the corners of the triangle. This indicates a reduced tension in the saddle-shaped region in the direction of the downward sag. All membrane forces are transmitted along the shortest path to the bisector of the angle.

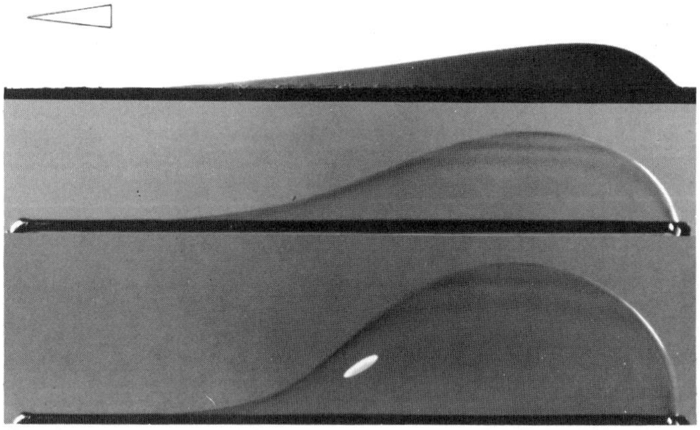

7 to 9

Membranes spanning quadrilateral ground plans

Such a plan gives rise to an interesting dome shape. This is already known from curved glass panes. At present, this shape is obtained during mass production of skylight domes of acryl resins (plastics) by clamping flat panels into square or quadrilateral frames and then deforming them by applying pressure while they are in the thermoplastic state.

This shape can frequently be observed in a sail when fabric is mounted in a frame and wind-loaded.

In the test, shown in Fig. 10, a rubber membrane spans a plan with rounded-off corners. The double grid clearly reveals the curvature in the directions parallel and diagonal to the edges. By rounding-off the corners, saddle surfaces can be entirely or partly avoided, should

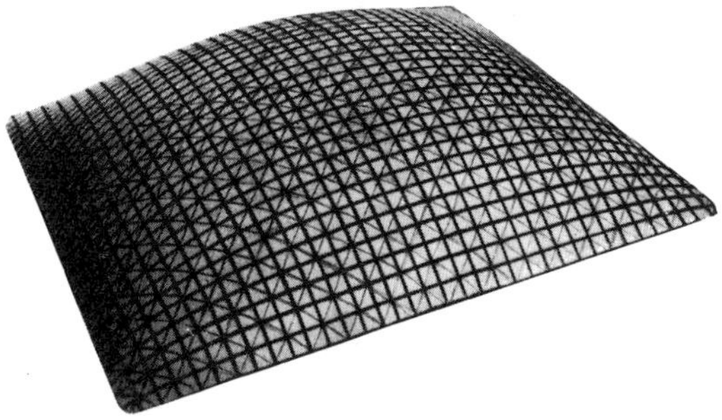

10

this be necessary for certain materials. The curvatures of the membrane surface differ at each point in the two directions, except at the center of the dome, where they are equal and of the same sign in all directions. Toward the edge of the frame a surface is formed, whose principal curvature in the immediate proximity of the frame lies in only one direction. The curvature parallel to the edge is prevented through the influence of this surface. The saddle surfaces at the corners are clearly visible.

A soap bubble blown on a square base constitutes a minimum surface. The photographs show the inflation of the soap bubble (Figs. 14 to 17) viewed from the side and (Figs. 18 to 21) the diagonal. All pictures were taken with a telephoto lens. The views can,

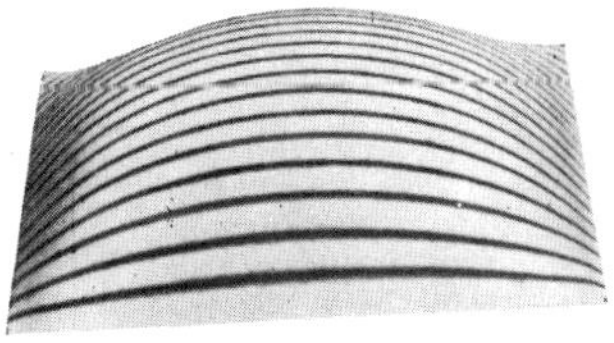

11

12

13

therefore, also be regarded as undistorted cross sections and evaluated accordingly.

It is not possible to inscribe a circle in any of the photographed soap-bubble sections; however, at very low internal pressures, the surface of the dome approximates the segment of a large sphere; at very large volumes it is theoretically equal to a full sphere of large diameter.

The soap-bubble section along the diagonal of the square (Figs. 18 to 21) has a typical bell shape. The bubbles were blown on a perfectly square base with sharp corners, as were those in Figs. 11 to 13 in which a rubber membrane was stretched under the pressure of freshly

14

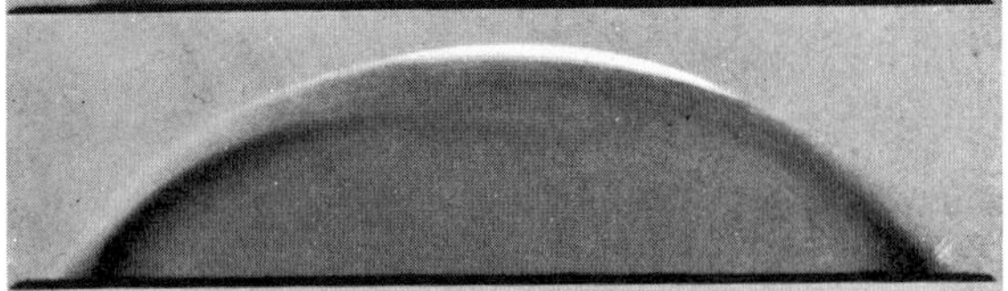

15

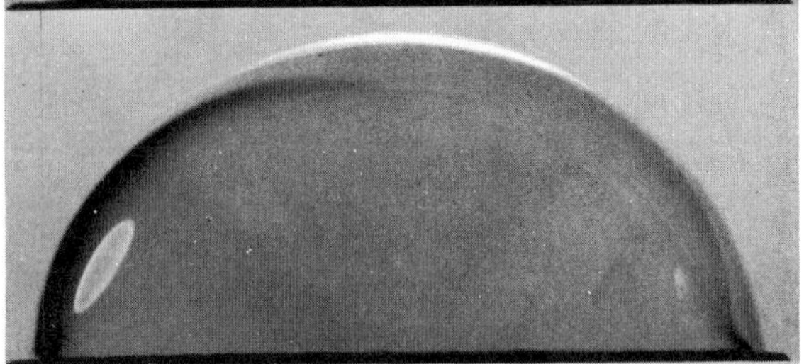

16

17

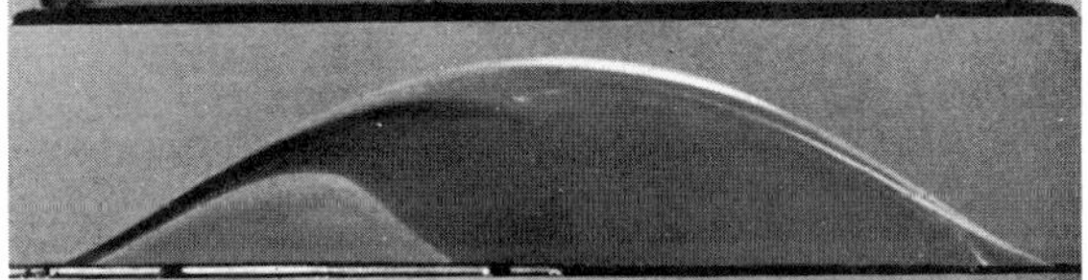

18

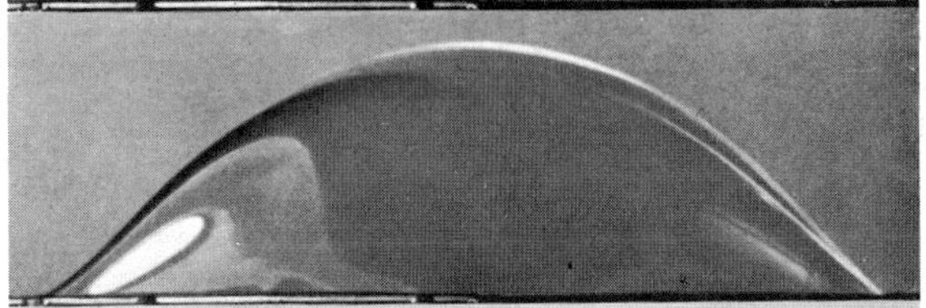

19

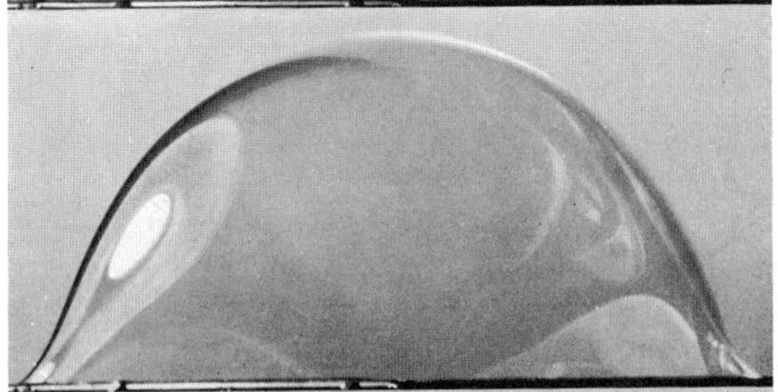

20

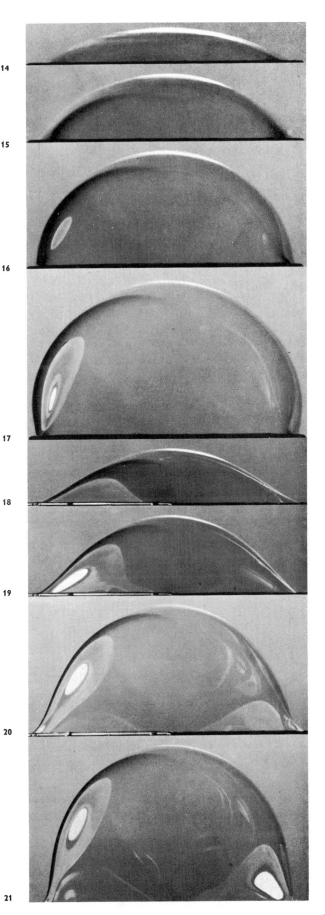

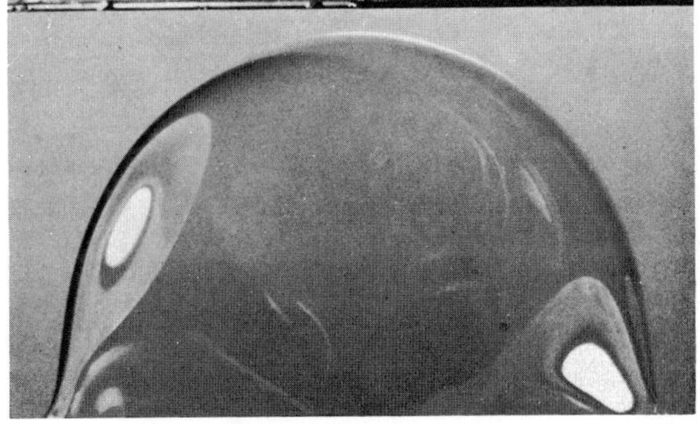

21

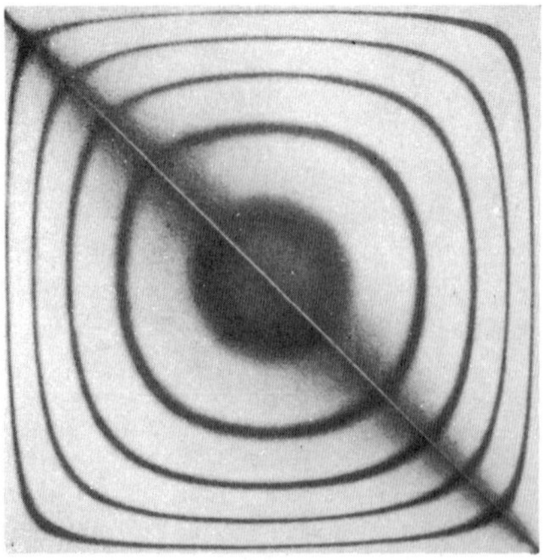

1

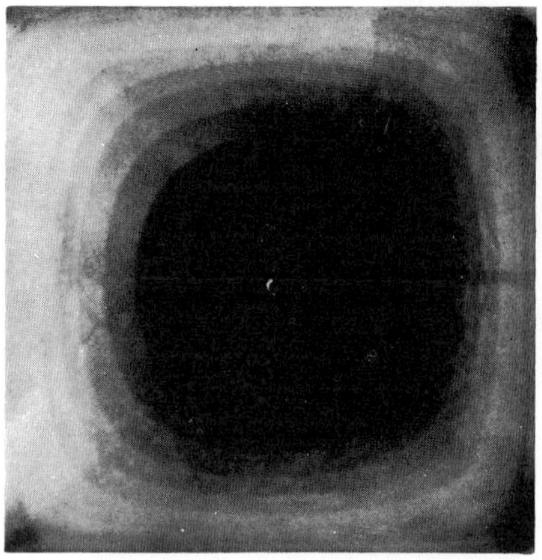

2

prepared liquid plaster. A shadow was then cast by vertical lines on the hardened form to bring out the sectional planes. During photography, the plane of the camera was vertical, i.e., parallel to these sectional planes. The sections are therefore shown undistorted; each, however, appears to a different scale, as determined by the laws of perspective.

The contour lines (Fig. 1) were also brought out by using a sunlight grid. Since only one half of the model could be depicted in this way, the other was added symmetrically as a photo montage. The contour lines can also be determined with great accuracy by means of a contour sensor, though this is very time-consuming. A further method is to cover the form or negative impression with a dark liquid (Fig. 2) to various heights. The different phases were recorded in a multiple-exposure photograph. The impression was made with fabric-reinforced, polyester casting resin. The contour lines are clearly visible.

The pneumatically tensed dome on a square plan is of particular interest, since the contour lines show a harmonic transition from square to circle.

A generally applicable process was used to determine the cross sections exactly. A vertical light plane (Fig. 6) is projected upon the model to be examined; a thin profile line is thus obtained. The model can be moved at will in relation to this light plane, or turned about the center, and the individual phases are then recorded by multiple exposures. In the case considered, the model was rotated around the center by 15° after each exposure (Fig. 3). The inner line represents the cross section parallel to the sides, and the outer line the diagonal section. Since the photographic plane of the camera was vertical, the sections are undistorted and shown to the same scale as in the diagonal view of the model (Fig. 4) during the experiment.

A rubber membrane measuring 20 × 20 cm, stretched in a square frame, was examined for indentation sensitivity by applying a load of 100 g acting on an area of 100 mm^2 (Fig. 5). It was found that the measurable depth of indentation was similar at all points of the membrane, and that markedly "hard" or "soft" points could not be detected. A parallel experiment with rubberized fabric proved that the influence of the fabric is very great, but difficult to determine, since the mounting of the fabric leads to inaccuracies which can not easily be eliminated.

The example of a pneumatic membrane used to enclose a greenhouse in a northern climate (Fig. 7) demonstrates how the envelope follows the straight-bordered fields in the valley, but adjusts to the terrain on the slopes. The slope faces south and is terraced.

In a project to convert an old skyscraper (Fig. 8), a membrane on a square ground plan forms the new rooftop over a large, high space split into numerous levels.

3 and 4

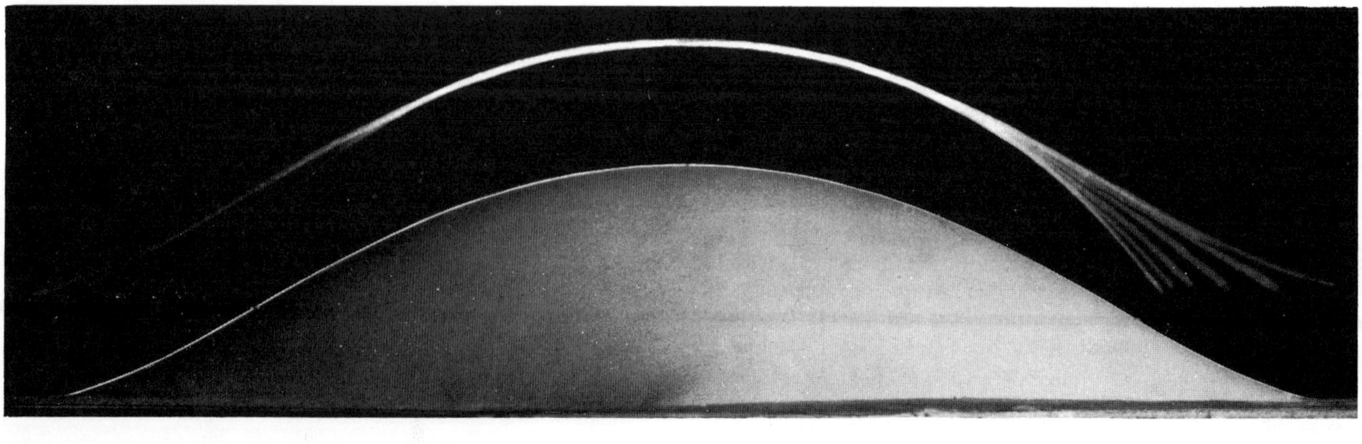

5

7

The plan over which a membrane is inflated need not be horizontal or lie in one plane. It may be inclined, vertical, or uneven. In the example illustrated (Fig. 9), a dome spans a spatial rectangle. In a square frame which has sides raised in the center (Fig. 10), the slopes toward the corners impart a capped shape to the membrane. The saddle surfaces occurring in this case can be eliminated.

Obviously, membranes can be arranged in series over triangular, square (Fig. 11), quadrilateral, and hexagonal (Fig. 12) frames. Many other forms can be created from these basic systems by varying the edge line.

Different types of domes, easily adapted to the requirements of a structure (Fig. 13), can be obtained by membranes on square plans supported by cable nets.

If a membrane spanning a square plan is supported by a cable net, the resulting shape approximates a minimum surface. However, cutouts in the cable net (Fig. 14) can produce separate bulges in the membrane, forming small, superimposed domes (see also p. 69).

An example of a membrane spanning a square plan is a design* for a warehouse serviced by trucks and ships. The transit depot is a plot of 750 × 750 m bordered by two heavily traveled roads. The open harbor serves for the rapid transfer of goods from ship to truck. The warehouse is formed by a large pneumatic membrane

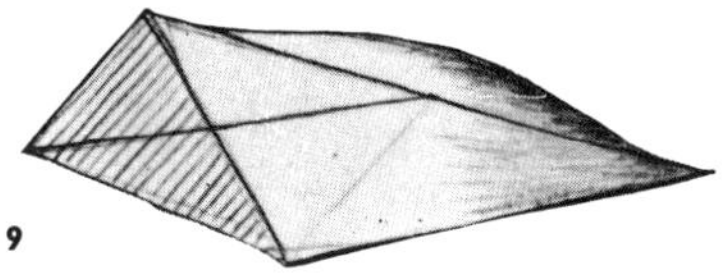

9

8

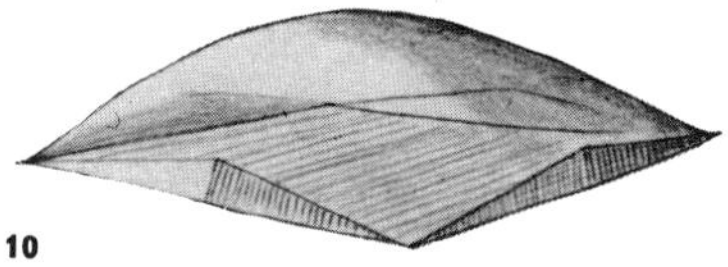

10

11

12

6

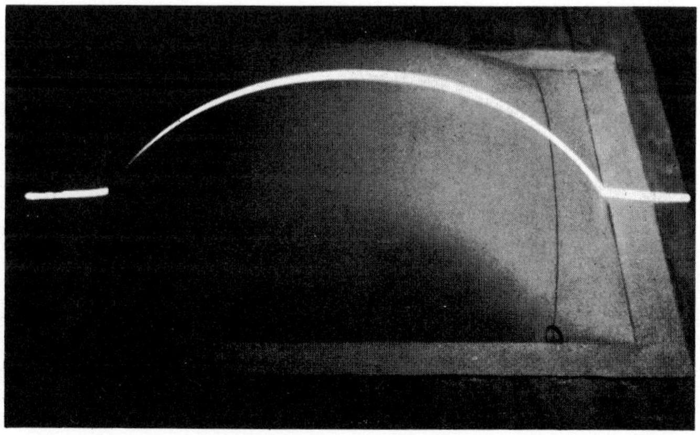

13

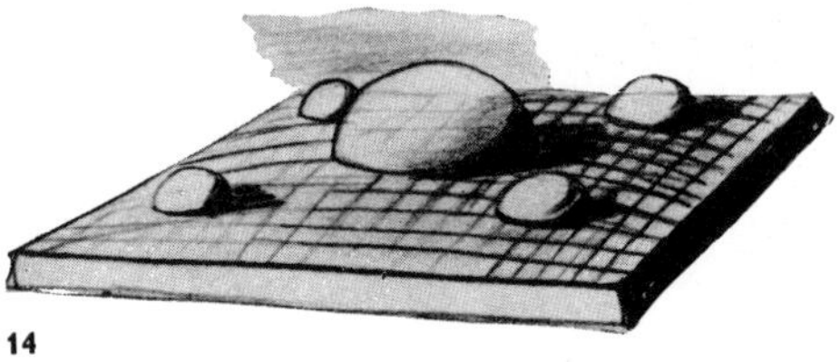

14

1

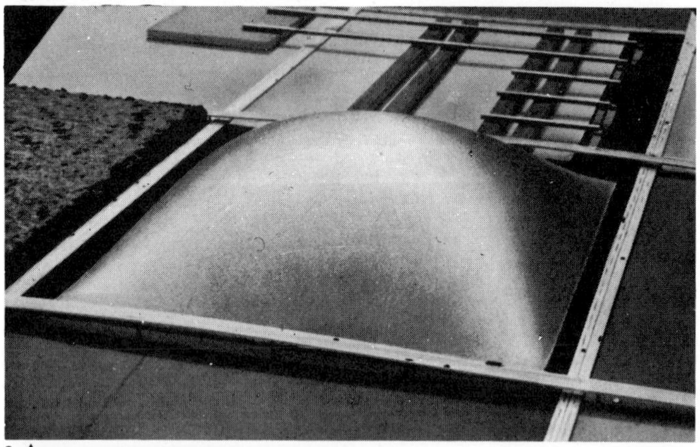

2 ▲

spanning a square plan, and provided with a surrounding drainage channel. Ships enter the small covered harbor through an airlock. Access to the open outer harbor and transit depot is through four long sheds which are equipped to handle perishable goods. The goods are stacked inside the warehouse or stored on shelves accessible from all sides. The plan view of the model (Fig. 1), shows the location of the project. Figure 2 is an oblique view from above, and Fig. 3 a view from the harbor at eye level.

A further example is the project* for a plant manufacturing agricultural machinery. This is planned as a large, square structure, in which a two story building containing workshops and offices encloses a large assembly area spanned by a pneumatically tensed, transparent membrane. The vaporized aluminum coating admits sufficient light. Two highly loaded intersecting cables lower the roof in order to economize on heating; they pass through the surrounding buildings and are anchored deep in the ground. The forces acting on the membrane which covers the four areas between the cables are much lower. The membrane is anchored at its edge to the inner rim of the massive roof of the building. The resulting shape was in this instance also thoroughly investigated, using a model with a rubber membrane.

Figure 4 is a view of the model from the front; Fig. 5 an oblique view; Fig. 6 a section through the plant; Fig. 11 a plan view of the model; Fig. 12 a view of the installation at night with the membrane illuminated from the inside; Fig. 13 an inclined view from above; Fig. 7 the model with front lines projected parallel to the outer edges, and Fig. 8 the model with diagonal lines which clearly reveal the curvature. The contour lines in Fig. 10 have been rendered visible by projection and photomontage. They bring out clearly the effect of the two main cables.

Sketch 9 shows how the membrane is supported by a cable net.
Both projects prove that pneumatic membranes are quite practical, meeting the demands of city planning, or the need to use right angles when employing support-girder constructions or panel assembly in adjacent buildings.

3

4 and 5

6

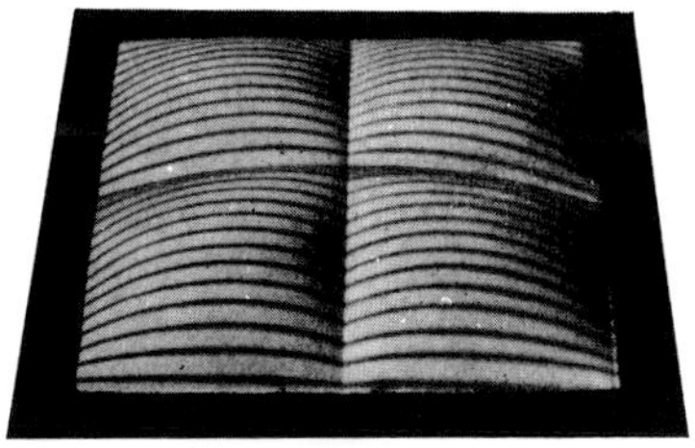

7

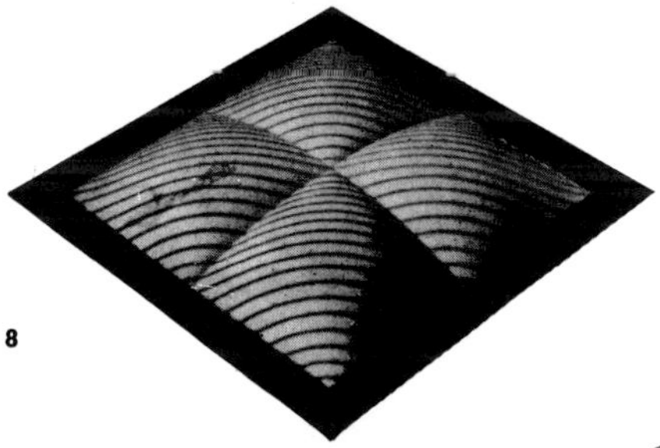

8

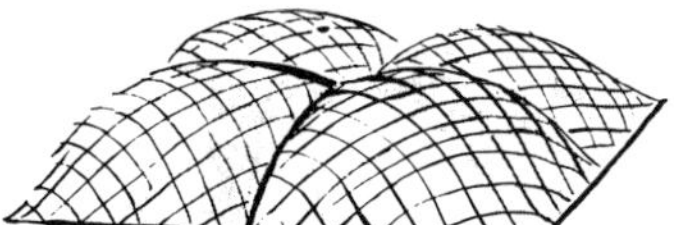

9

10

11

12 ▲

▼ 13

2

3

1

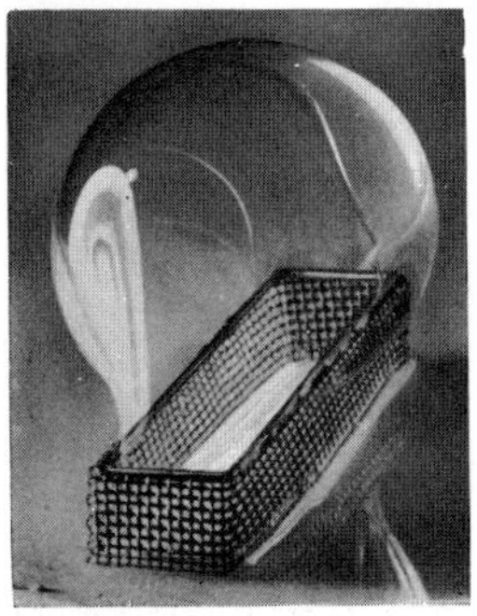

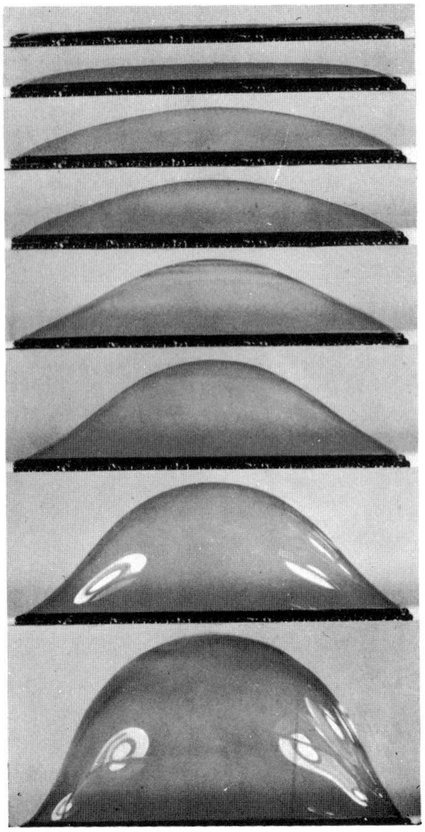

4 to 11

12

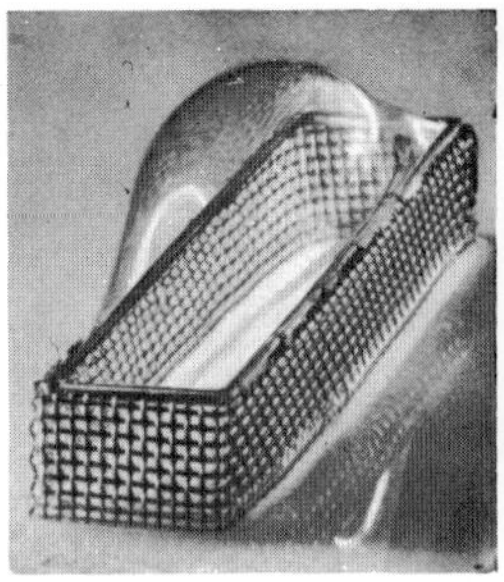

14

13

Membranes spanning quadrilateral outlines

A pneumatic membrane spanning an oblong rectangle differs from that spanning a square. When inflating a soap bubble it can be seen how the membrane, which initially has an almost cylindrical curvature (Figs. 4 and 5), increasingly assumes a spherical shape in the middle, the center of curvature rising above the base plane. This becomes clear when viewing the long side (Figs. 10 and 11), as well as from the associated lateral view (Fig. 13), and the general view (Fig. 1). (Broadside views, Figs. 4 to 11, narrow-side views, Figs. 2, 3, 12 and 13; general views, Figs. 1 to 14.) The sphere appears to be trying to break through at the top. The rectangular shape is maintained only near the base line.

When observing Figure 13 carefully it can be seen that the cross section of the soap bubble is by no means circular, but has a smaller radius of curvature in its lower part. The longitudinal extension of the bubble at its base appears to pull down the central spherical shape and press it onto the base line.

A parallel test with a rubber membrane gave a nearly cylindrical shape (Fig. 16) at the beginning of the experiment, drawn down only at its ends, but everywhere of uniform height. This can be seen from the broad-side view (Fig. 15) and from the narrow-side views (Figs. 17 and 18). The membrane was lightly tensed in the flat state before inflation, and marked with two grids to indicate curvature.

When attempting to inflate such a membrane beyond the shape forming a semicylinder at the center, the following phenomena may occur: during further testing, spontaneous spherical bulging was observed. This can be seen from the narrow side view (Fig. 24), from a view somewhat to one side (Fig. 25), from obliquely above (Fig. 26), and in the top view of the membrane center (Fig. 27). A comparatively thick rubber membrane stretched above an oblong rectangle was cast in plaster of Paris under considerable pressure so that the dead weight of the liquid plaster exerted little influence on the membrane. All plaster-reinforced membranes depicted in this book were inverted in the experiment to remove ascending air bubbles from the region of the outer skin.

In this experiment the described cylindrical shape was observed at first, but then it suddenly became spherical. The height of the remaining parts of the membrane even decreased due to the bulging of the central sphere. During expansion of the latter, the sudden increase in volume caused a reduction in pressure. At this stage the experiment was ended and the plaster allowed to harden. Raising the pressure again to the maximum recorded shortly before the formation of the sphere would have been impossible, since the latter would have burst. The observed phenomenon is not accidental but easily explained: a membrane has greatest strength in the hemispherical or semi-cylindrical form. If it expands further, the center or axis of curvature rises above the plane of the plan, and the radii of curvature become larger than the corresponding plan radii.

At equal internal pressure the membrane tensions are therefore greater than before and, thus, also the dilations.

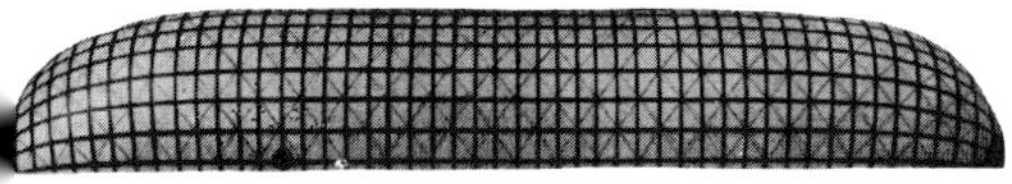
5

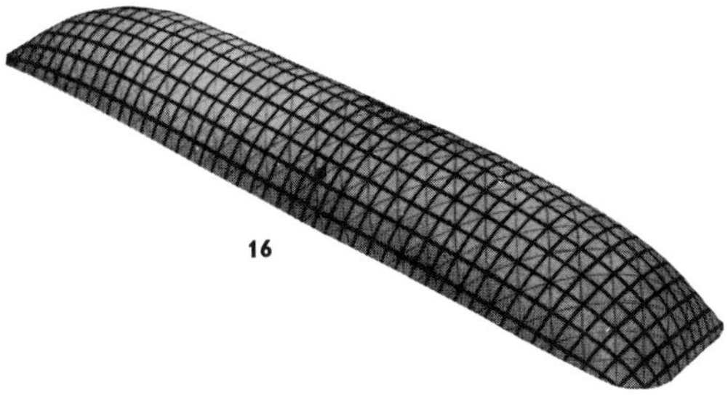
16

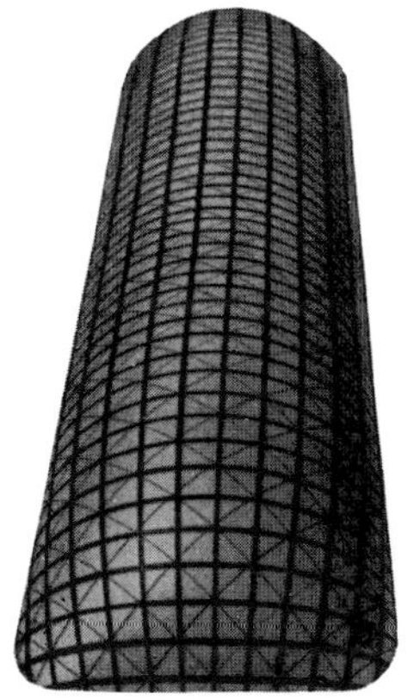
17

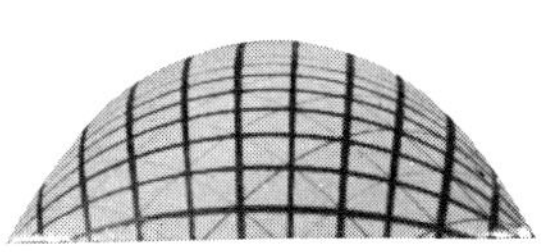
18

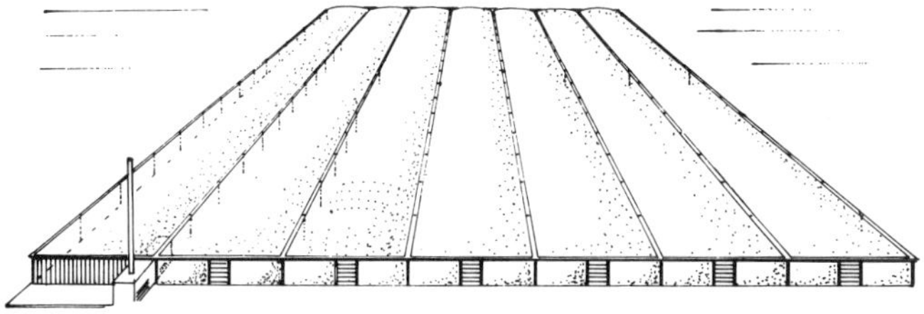
19

20

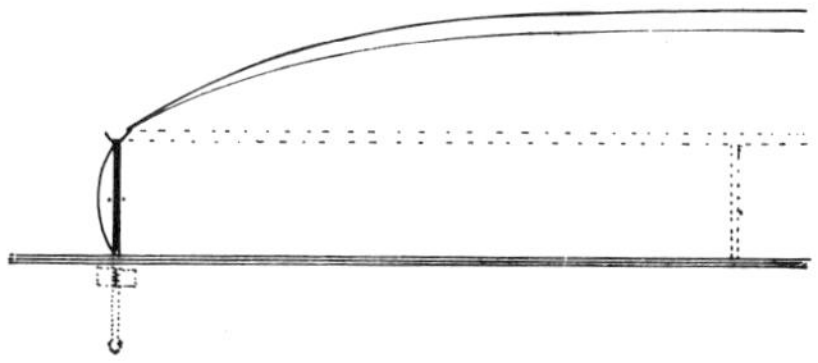
21

22

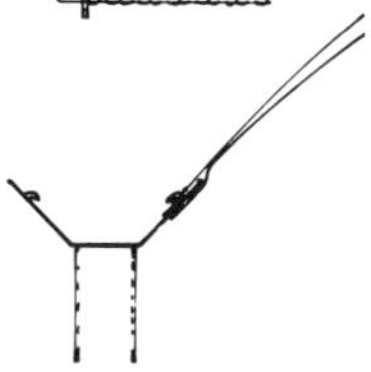
23

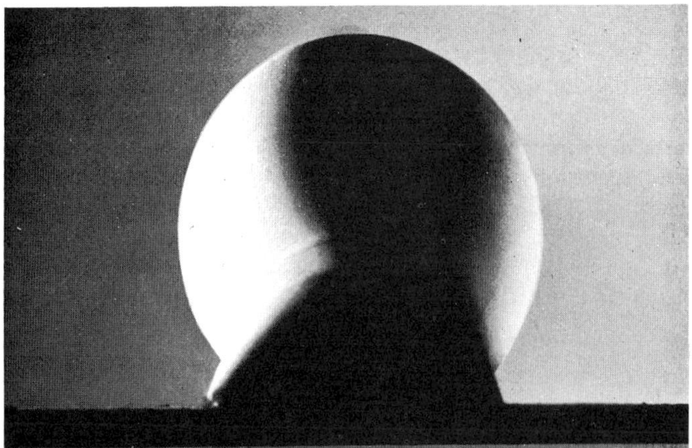
24

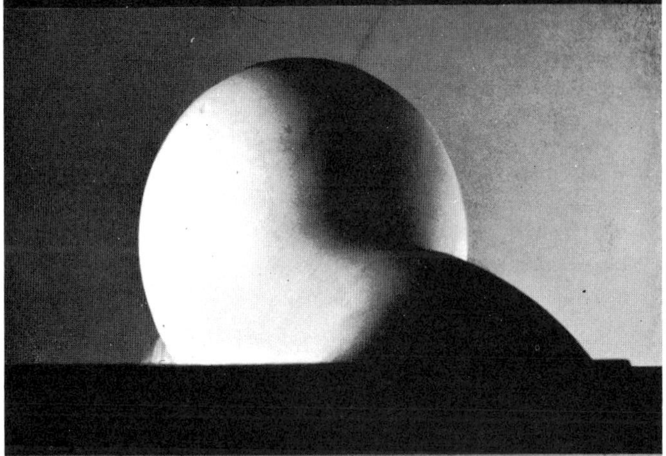
25

26

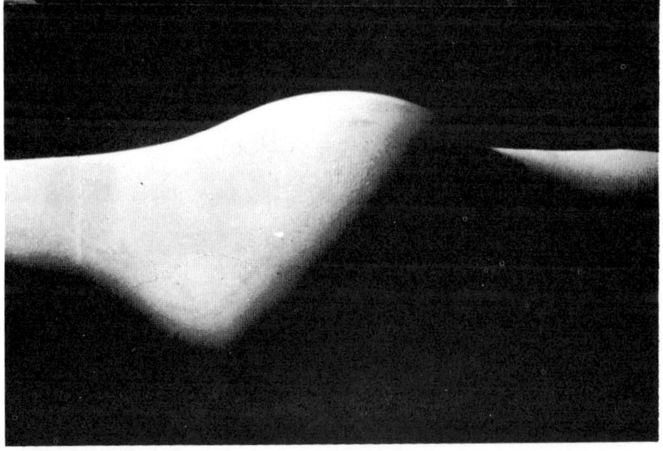
27

A greenhouse project* (Fig. 19) for an agricultural experimental station in Southern Germany has a pneumatically tensed thin double membrane only 0.5 mm thick, spanning a long series of adjoining rectangular plans (Fig. 22, p. 65). Even when assuming that the outer membrane is renewed annually before winter to save cleaning, the method is economical for this type of greenhouse. With particularly thin membranes or larger spans the outer skin can be reinforced by a net. The second membrane is primarily a heat insulator. It has been proved that such double membranes also have greater rigidity under wind pressure.

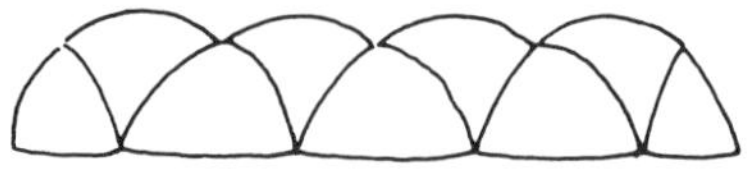

4

The membranes are stretched in light, transportable frames. It can be seen from the

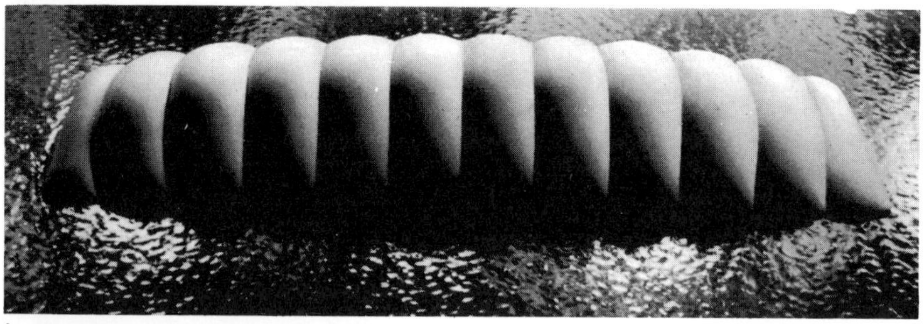

1

2

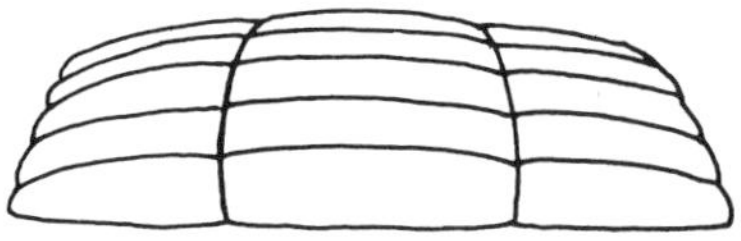

5

3 ▼

sections (Figs. 20 and 21, p. 65), and from the detail (Fig. 23, p. 65) that these frames consist of a sheet-metal trough with hooks and tubular supports.

Cable-reinforced membranes spanning quadrilateral plans

Study of cable-reinforced membranes spanning quadrilateral plans reveals many structural possibilities and forms, only some of which can be shown here.
Transverse cables form the simplest arrangement, as seen in the experimental model (Figs. 1 to 3). A considerable double curvature can appear between the cables without saddle surfaces forming when the membranes are sufficiently inflated.
If the cables divide the plan area into triangles (Fig. 4), a series of more or less pronounced triangular domes results depending on internal pressure and design. Cables

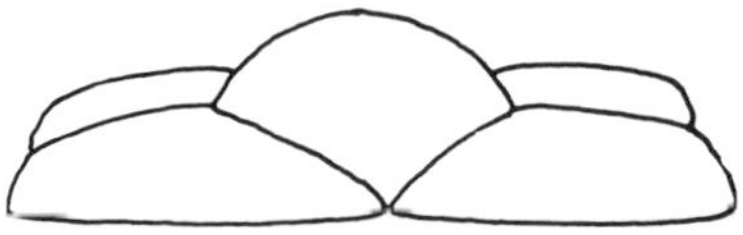

6

7

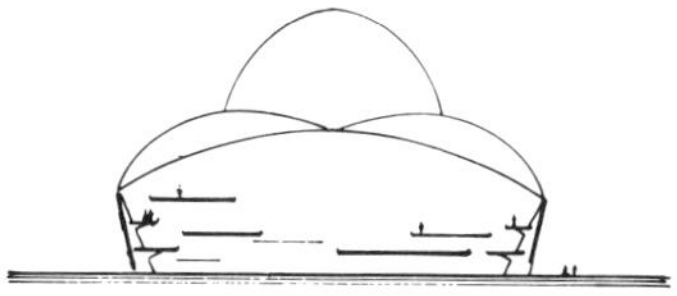
8

forming a quadrilateral grid (Fig. 5) permit considerable variation in the shape of the pneumatically tensed skin by length adjustments. The cables in Fig. 6 form a central rhomboid from which another dome rises still higher.

Cross section 8 shows a project* for an exhibition in which a pneumatically tensed roof is spanned between two parallel walls which are slightly inclined outward. The roof is supported by eight intersecting cables between which three domes rise to a greater height. The interior of the structure has many stands and galleries at various

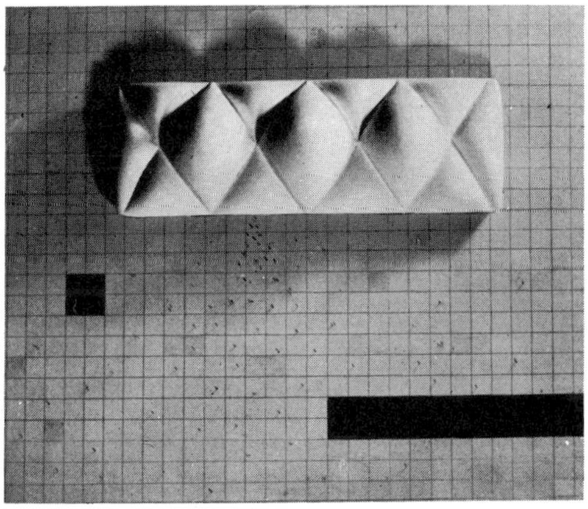
9

11

elevations (Fig. 10). The varied spaces created are combined into an internal and external entity by the dominant roof form.

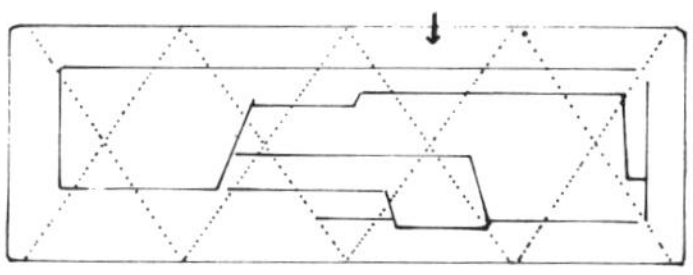
10

The completely enclosed structure stands freely in an open space (Fig. 9) and is accessible at only one point through a man-size entrance. The roof is white and the walls brick-red. This model was also prepared with a pneumatically tensed rubber membrane between cables, and finally set in plaster.

▼ 12

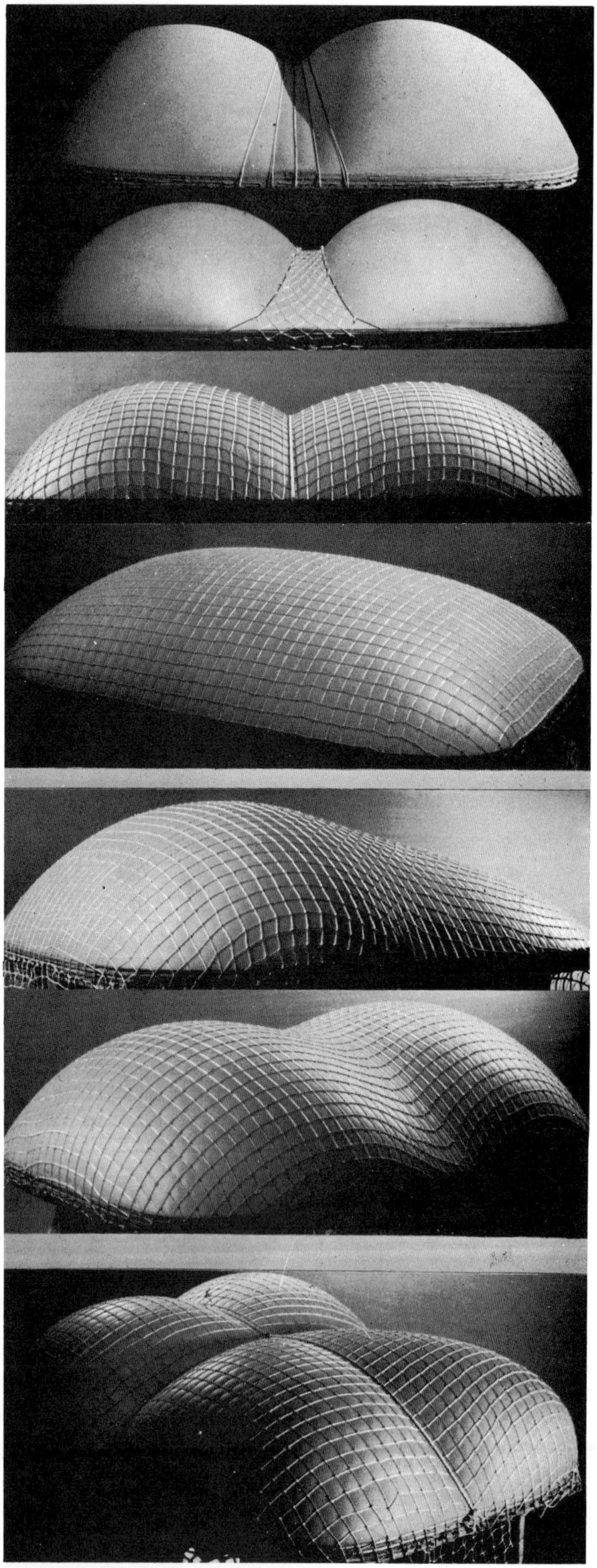

1 to **7**

Various cable and cable-net shapes spanning quadrilateral plans with rounded corners

It was previously mentioned that the most varied forms can be created on any plan by combining membranes and cables or cable nets. The photographs of the test series on these pages merely hint at the infinite possibilities.

A group of five parallel cables (Fig. 1) of different lengths prevents complete bulging. A rounded constriction can be formed by adjusting the cable lengths. The parallel cables can also be connected by transverse cables so that the constriction is retained by a net anchored over a sufficient spread along the base.

Whereas a diagonal net between strong lateral cables (Fig. 2) prevents bulging of the membrane between the cables, it cannot cause a gradual rounding.

A combination of membrane, cable net, and individual shaping cables is of great practical importance. The action of a single transverse cable within a net can be seen in Fig. 3. The cable net alone is shown in Fig. 4. The latter is not only capable of assuming a shape approximating a minimum surface, but can form many different shapes (Figs. 5 and 6) if the tension of the lateral cables is altered. However, even if combined with cables, these shapes must conform to the basic laws of formation (Fig. 7).

In the tests a net of uniform mesh was used. Changing the mesh angles while maintaining comparatively uniform distribution of tension allowed the development of widely different shapes.

We also investigated the behavior of a membrane after we cut a square hole in the covering cable net. The view from above in Fig. 8 shows that the cut assumes a roughly circular shape. At this point, the membrane bulges out into a separate small dome (Fig. 12).

When an octagonal hole is bordered by a cable (Figs. 9 and 13), the latter forms a nearly circular ring, and the raised dome a cap.

Using a cable net of uniform mesh with an octagonal ring-reinforced cutout, we investigated the insertion of a second radial net into a net with a uniform square grid. In principle, such a combination of cable nets poses no problems, and provides many new possibilities which can only be hinted at. By using eight radial cables and one central annular cable (Figs. 10 and 14), a shallow superimposed dome results when the cables are tightened. The height of this dome can be easily altered by shortening or lengthening the cables. Off-center and other forms are also possible.

In the next experiment (Figs. 11 and 15) another annular cable was used to form a more conical dome.

The tensions in the superimposed domes remain comparatively low when the forces in the cable net are taken up by an annular cable.

The formation of small separate domes is of particular advantage when fitting skylight domes in large-span structures which are made of opaque membranes that can be walked on.

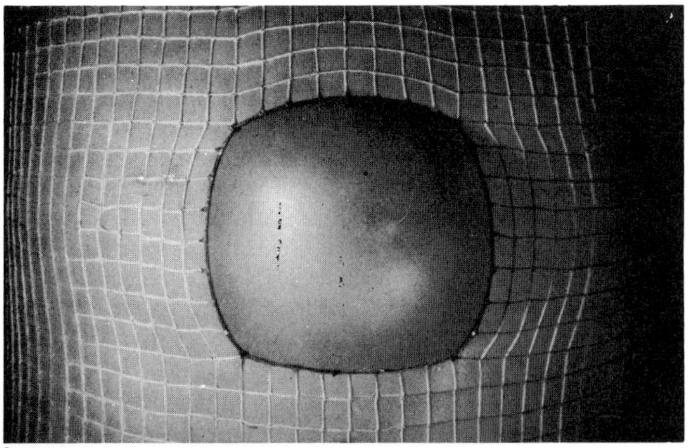

8

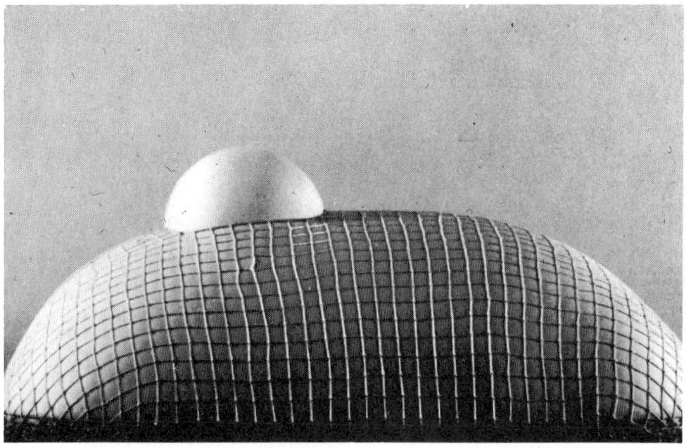

12

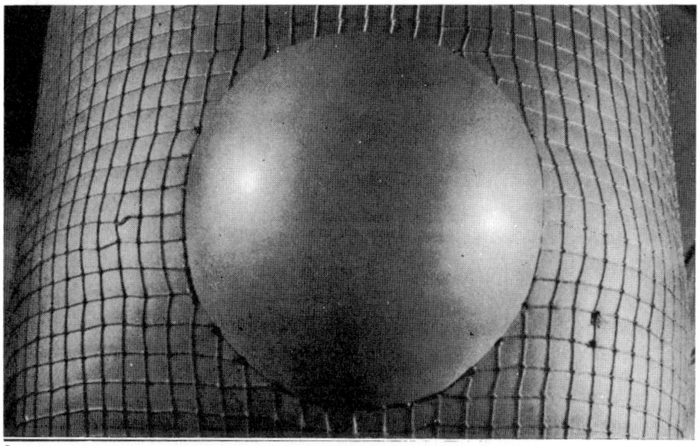

9

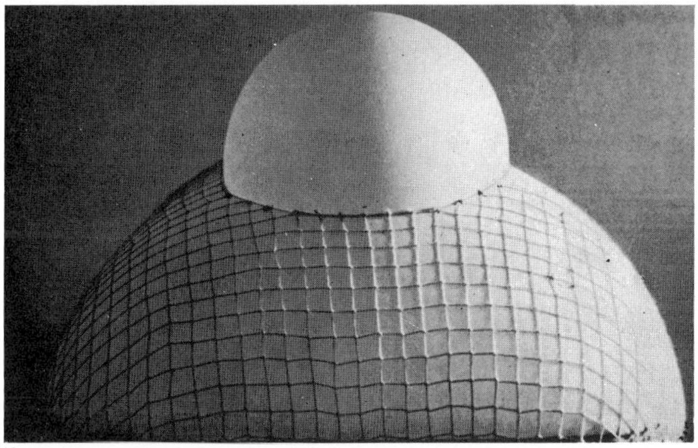

13

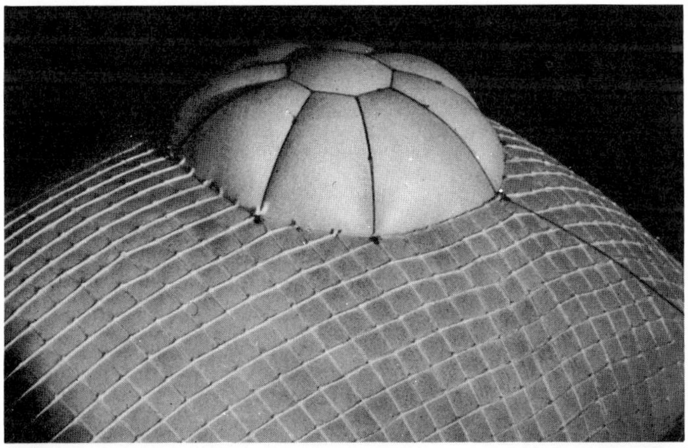

10 ▲ ▼ 11

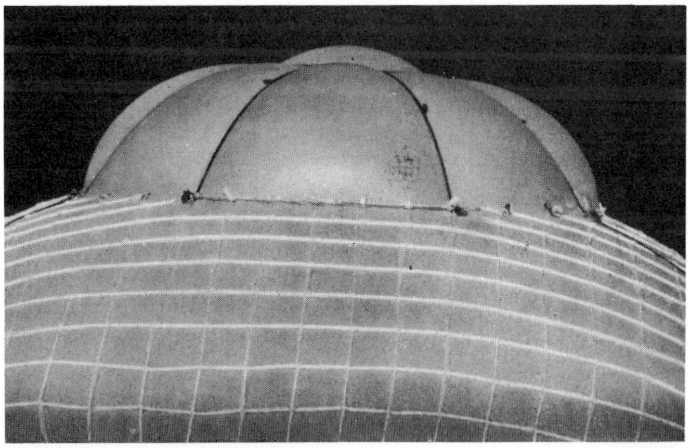

14 ▲ ▼ 15

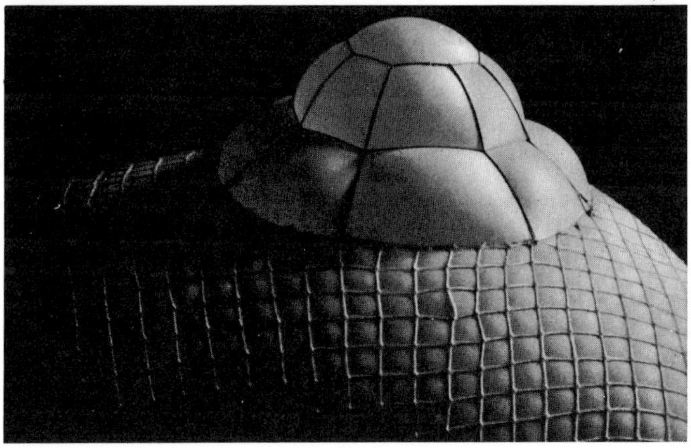

1 ▲

▼ 2

The Cylindrical Membrane

Any long, flexible, tubular membrane is cylindrical in the center, regardless of whether the ends are closed by circular disks (Fig. 3) or by any other surface (Fig. 4).

Of all prismatic bodies of considerable length, only the cylindrical membrane is suitable as a pneumatic structure. Rims deviating from circles only influence the shape of the pneumatic body at the cylinder's ends.

The flexible cylindrical membrane is widely used for various types of hoses; the best known are fabric fire hoses, or hot-air hoses. Internal pressure increases the stiffness of the cylinder. Since this mostly undesirable stiffness depends mainly on the elasticity of the membrane, elastic materials must be used for flexible hoses. Rubber predominates, usually reinforced by two diagonally wound crossing, layers of corded silk.

3

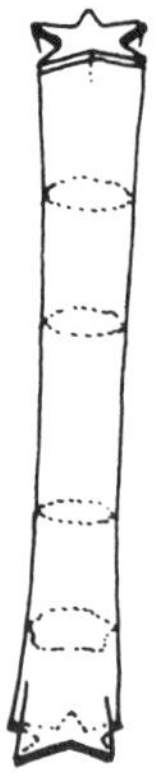

4

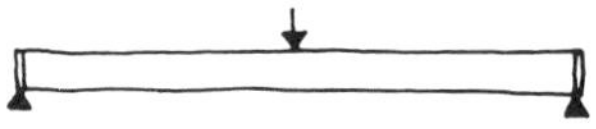

5

6

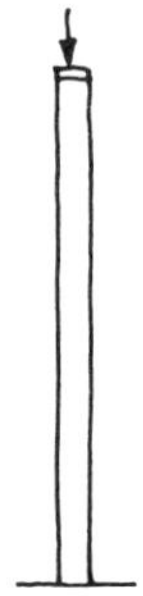

7

Rubber hoses of small diameters usually retain their shape without internal pressure.

Rigid cylinders retaining their shape without internal pressure are well known. Examples are oil tanks (Fig. 1, photo by Esso) and distillation columns (Fig. 2; photo by BASF).

In the absence of internal pressure, rigid cylinders have only to support their own weight and useful loads. The highest stresses usually occur at maximum internal pressure; the cylinders then behave essentially like pneumatically stressed cylindrical membranes.

A flexible cylindrical membrane maintains its shape under internal pressure and also exhibits resistance to bending (Fig. 5), buckling (Fig. 7), and torsion (Fig. 6) which depends on internal pressure, wall thickness, and the elasticity of the material. The higher the modulus of elasticity of the material, the smaller are the load-induced deformations.

If pneumatically tensed flexible cylindrical membranes are bent, the outer fibers are tensed and the inner relieved. Folds only occur

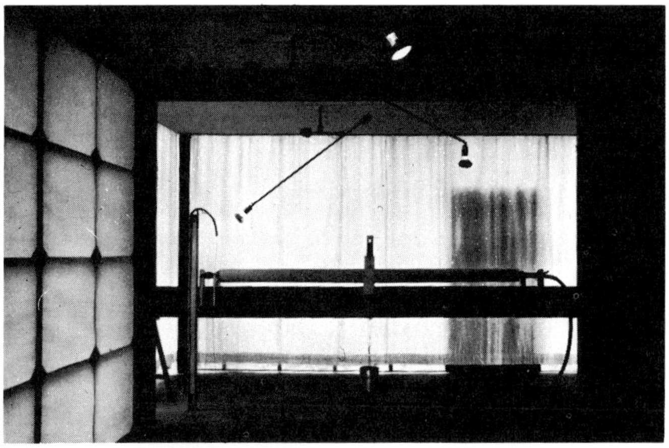

8

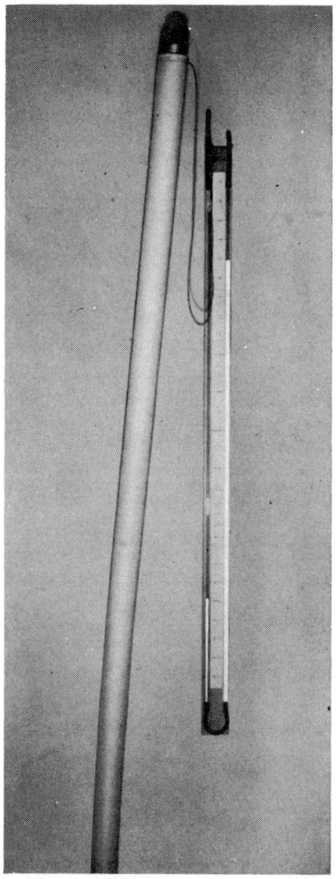

9 ▲

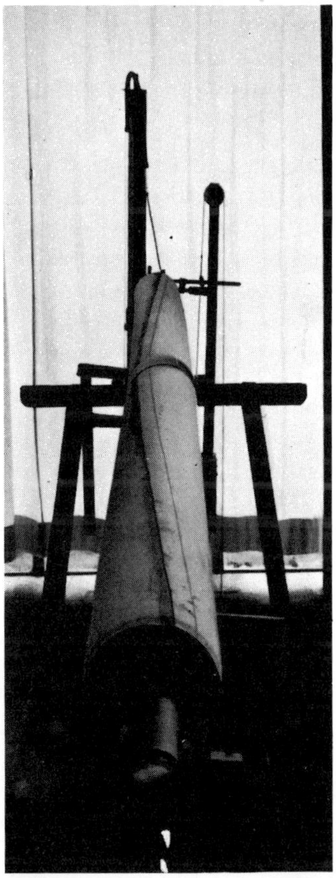

10 ▲

▼ 11

(Fig. 12) when the compressive forces in the inner fibers can no longer be counterbalanced in the longitudinal direction by the tension due to the internal pressure. When folds occur the rigidity of the hose is greatly reduced. It can even be entirely squeezed together (Fig. 13) so that a flexible hinge results. Consequently, the structural elements are not overstressed when such pneumatic cylindrical membranes are over-loaded. However, pinching can easily lead to dangerous pressures in hoses which contain liquids or gases.

Pronounced constrictions of the surface reduce the rigidity of thick hoses so that even quite small radii of curvature are possible without the hose being pinched (Figs. 14 and 15). In bending, buckling, and torsion, the elastic properties of the hose material are of great importance. This is not so for transverse compression of a long cylinder (Fig. 16) if the internal pressure is maintained at a constant level, e.g., by connecting to a compressed-air tank. However, if the cylindrical membrane is closed on all

12

13

14

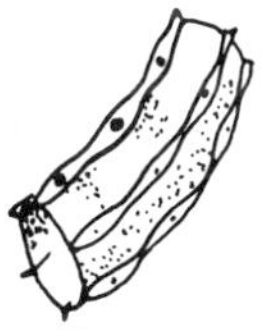

15

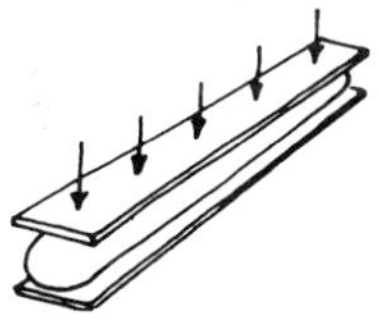

16

sides, highly elastic membranes (e.g., rubber) are deformed to a greater extent than less elastic membranes, since the latter expand less when the internal pressure rises during compression. Pneumatically tensed cylindrical membranes form excellent suspensions for vehicles and machines which are essentially influenced by the internal pressure. The spring rate is variable and not linear. Even with small loads pronounced deformation occurs due to the small contact surface. The greater the load, the smaller becomes the deformation in relation to the load. Cylindrical membranes are thus superior to steel springs in vehicle suspensions.

To study the behavior of pneumatically tensed cylinders under various types of loading, a series of tests were carried out in the Development Center for Lightweight Structures, Berlin. A slender rod, built-in at one end and loaded by a weight is shown in Fig. 9 at the instant of buckling. Figures 8 and 10 show a torsion experiment (see also p. 234).

1 to 5

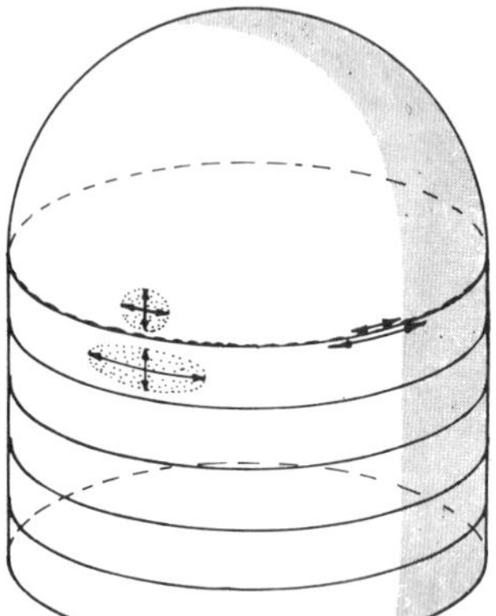

6

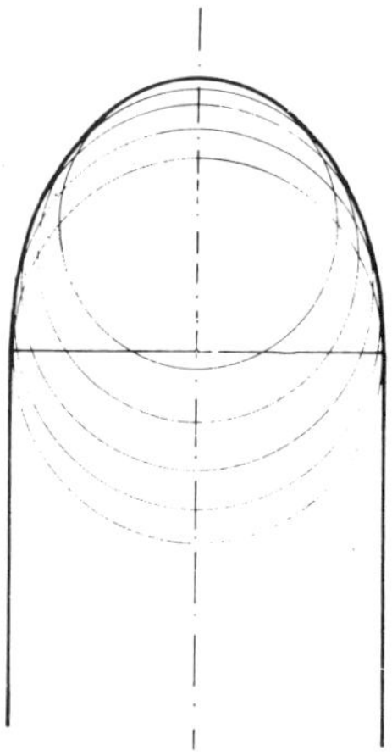

7

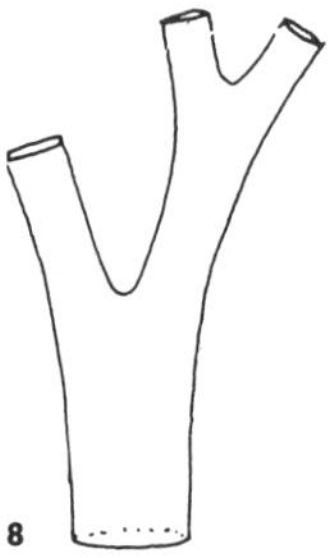

8

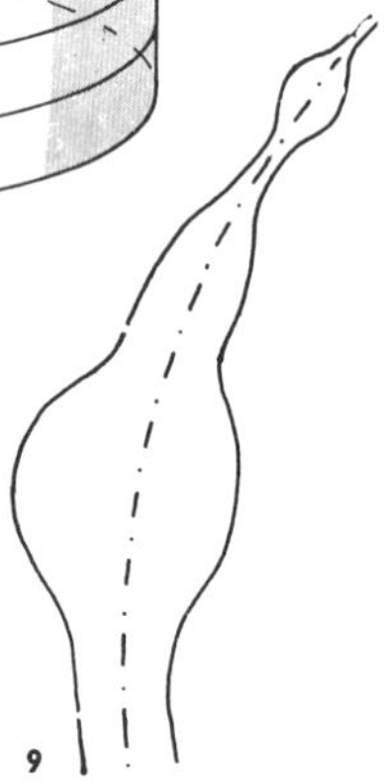

9

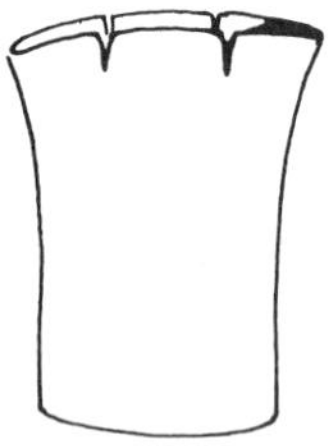

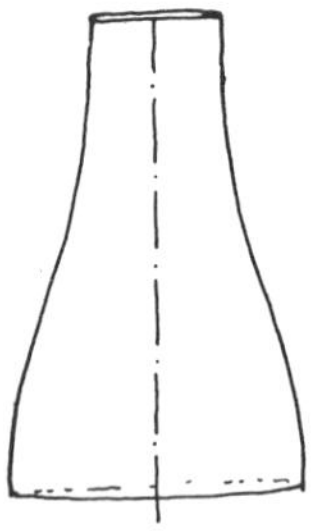

11

12

10 ▲ ▼ 14 13 ▲ ▼ 15

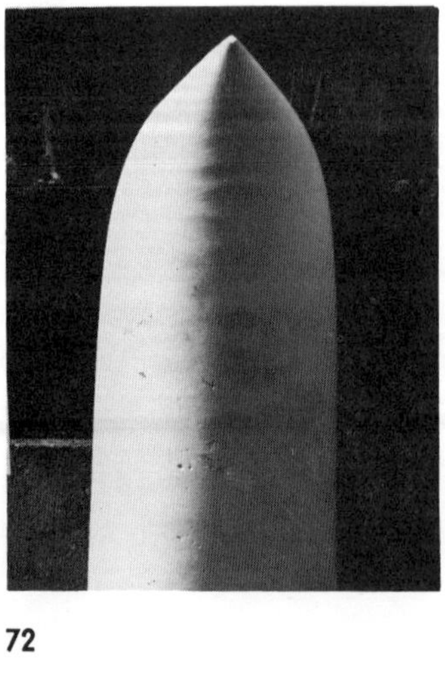

If p is the internal pressure and r the radius of curvature, the membrane tension of a cylindrical skin in the direction parallel to the cylinder axis is

$$n_\theta = \frac{pr}{2}$$ and, at right angles to it, i.e., along the circumference, $$n_\phi = pr,$$

if the cylinder ends are not clamped.

The tensions in the circumferential direction, therefore, are double those in the longitudinal direction. A cylinder made of material having equal rigidity in either direction, as for example, most sheet metals, will fail longitudinally when subjected to excessive loads, i.e., it will tear in the direction normal to the principal stress. The reinforcing of cylindrical boilers by hoops or by overlapping joints is justified if a material cannot be used whose strength in the circumferential direction is double that in the longitudinal direction. Even when using cylindrical shells as rigid structural elements to prevent bending or buckling, the highest loads in the shell occur in the transverse direction.

In a cylindrical shell or membrane the ends may have various shapes. Figure 1 shows a superimposed three-quarter sphere, Fig. 2 an onion-shaped dome. Both are connected to the cylinder by annular cables. Ogives (Fig. 3) and many other shapes are possible when they follow the laws of formation (p. 18) and are not subjected to compression or bending. However, bending stresses may act on a flat end (Fig. 4), and compressive stresses on an end which is formed by a membrane with a thrust collar (Fig. 5).
If, for example, a cylinder is closed by a hemisphere, the force diagram (Fig. 6) shows that the hoop stresses near the joint between sphere and cylinder differ. At equal thicknesses, the cylindrical membrane undergoes greater deformations than the spherical membrane. The resulting distortions can be avoided by adapting the material or by changing the hemisphere to a gradually tapering axisymmetrical shape (Fig. 7).

Closing a cylindrical membrane by transverse seams is very simple. Internal pressure causes the known shape (Figs. 14 and 15). Except in highly elastic materials, folds are unavoidable if the cut is not adapted to the special circumstances (Fig. 10). Taperings (Figs. 9 and 11) and branches (Fig. 8) can generally be designed to be free from compressive stresses. This is necessary to obtain an economical shape for large pressure conduits, (e.g., Y-pipes for power plants). A further advantage is that aerodynamic and hydrodynamic conditions generally favor this design.

When the internal pressure rises, a cylindrical skin with a longitudinal thickening on one side (Fig. 12) bends due to differing elastic deformations of the skin (Fig. 13), forming an arc of a circle (see pp. 88 and 89).

Lateral thrust on a cylinder due to the wind depends on the ratio of length to diameter. The resistance coefficients are shown in Fig. 16 (SIA Norm 160). Wind pressure tends to flatten a pneumatically tensed cylindrical skin at right angles to the direction of the wind.

Despite the long and varied history of the use of pneumatically tensed cylindrical skins, the possibilities are still practically unlimited. For example, Fig. 18 is the cross section of a floating bridge* which carries a road over a long and deep stretch of water.

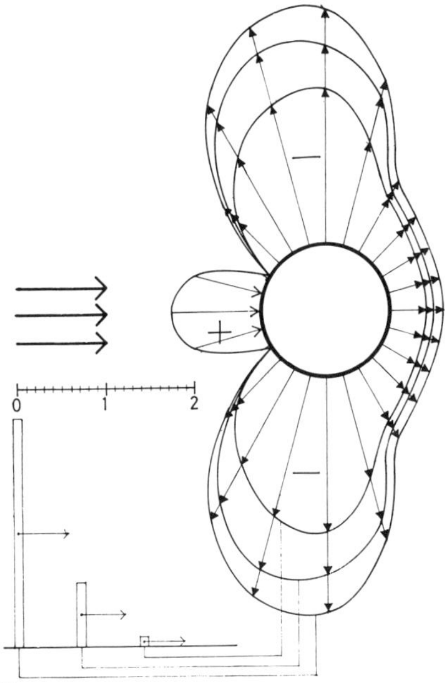

16

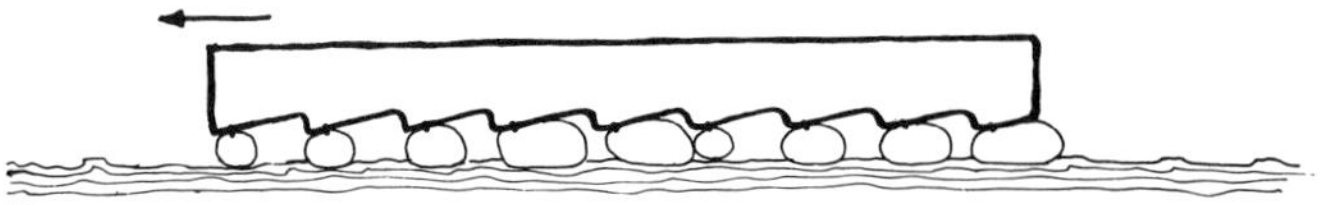

20

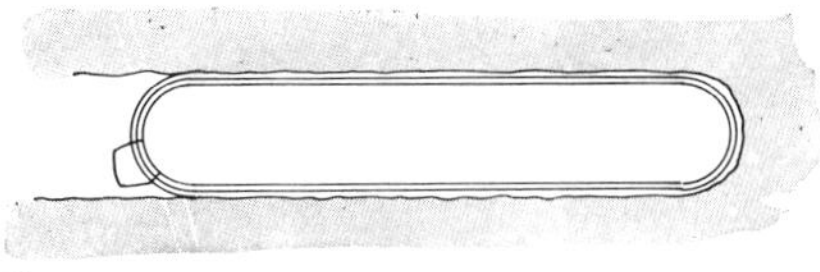

21

22

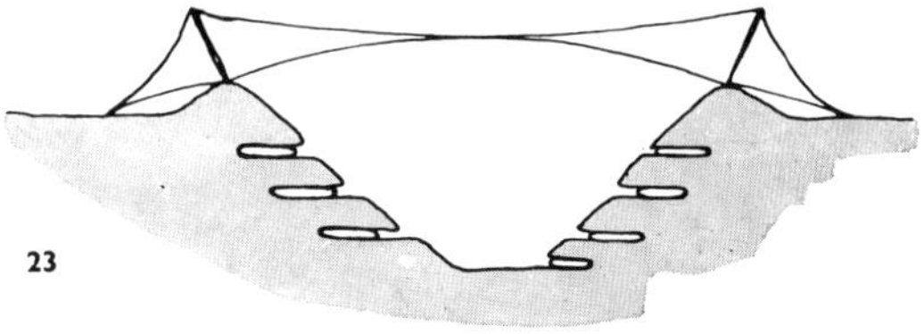

23

24

The bridge is formed by a pneumatically tensed, cylindrical skin, longitudinally divided by two horizontal partitions. The upper space serves for ventilation, the central carries the traffic, and the lower contains water ballast. The road surface has an adequate structural rigidity forming a continuous beam. Underwater anchors retain the hose which is entered through pressure locks. A tunnel stabilized by internal pressure is feasible under water only down to a certain depth. At a greater depth (Fig. 19) pure underwater construction becomes possible but not necessary. A hyperboloidal membrane (e.g., a cable net with ultra-heavy fabric lining) is stretched between heavy rigid rings (Fig. 17) and pneumatically loaded by external water pressure. Recently developed materials permit the design of floating bridges and underwater tunnels which can hardly be improved upon and are very easy to assemble.

The use of alternately inflatable hoses for moving very heavy loads over soft ground is shown in Fig. 20.

Figures 21 to 23 show the use of cylindrical shapes with multiple membranes for increased radiation protection of extraterrestrial projects* located in galleries driven into strongly fissured rocks.

To make a hose press,* to be used, for example, to glue together a stack of wooden boards, high internal pressure is generated inside a double hose (Fig. 24). Since a double hose is continuously invertible it permits continuous driving of galleries* in heterogeneous and collapsible rock formations (Fig. 25). The gallery is lined with a

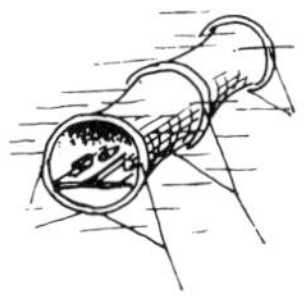

17

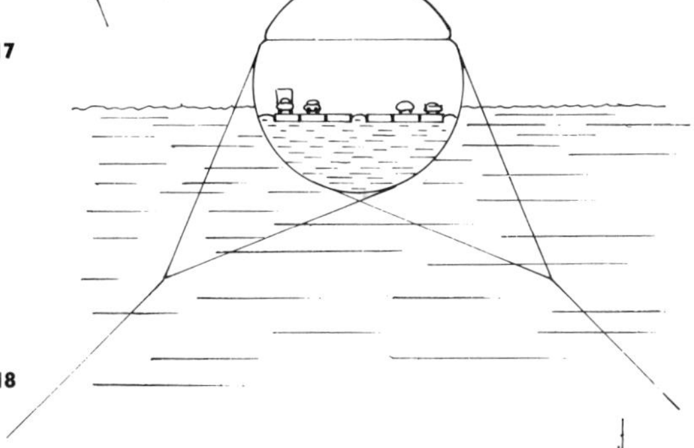

18

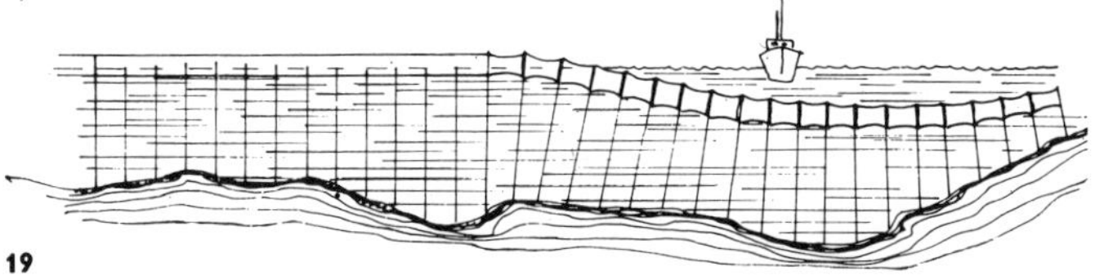

19

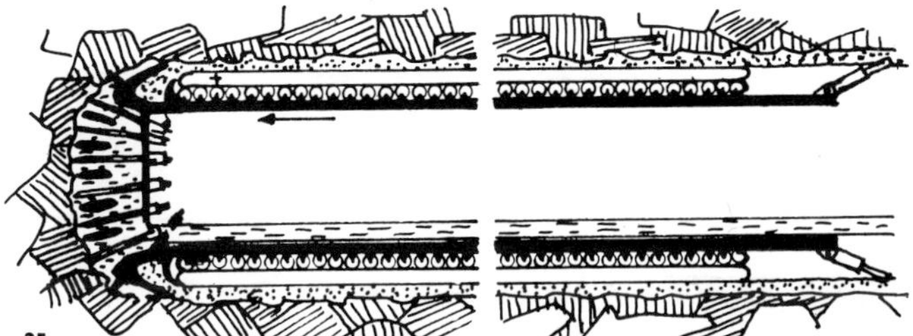

25

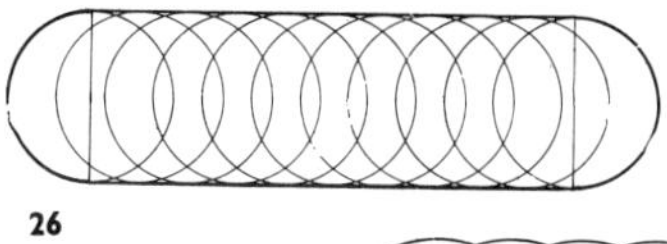

26

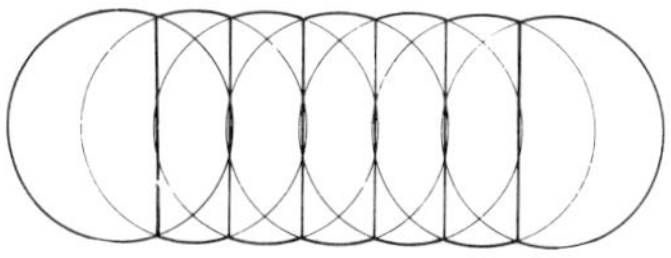

27

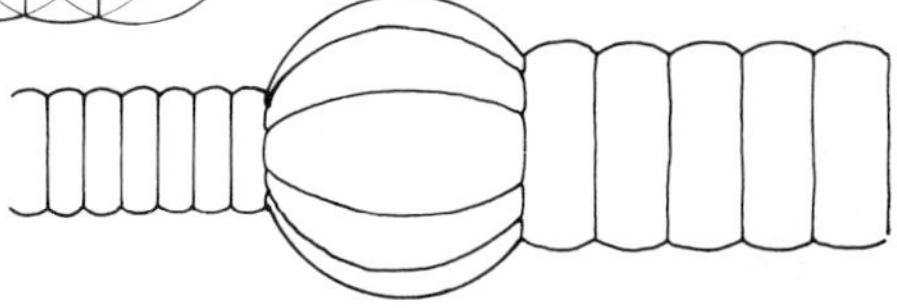

28

1

2 ▲

▼ 3

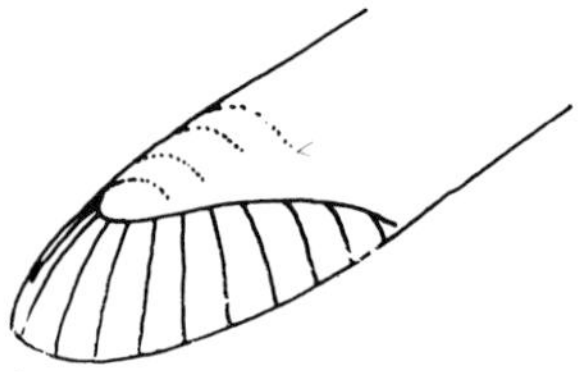

4

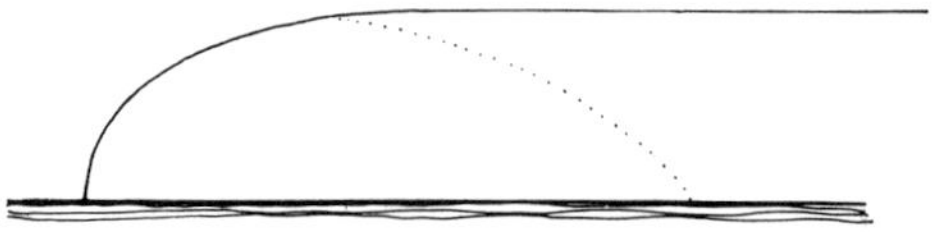

5

6

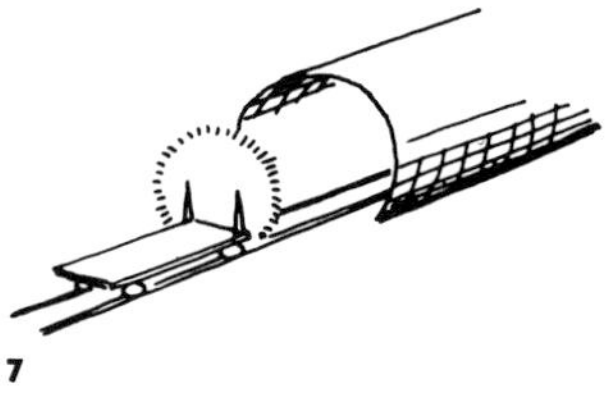

7

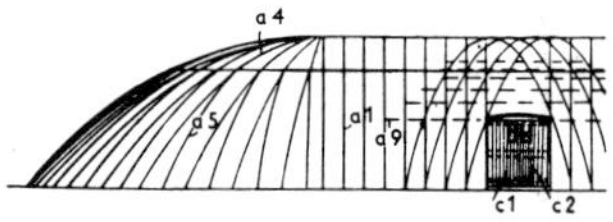

8

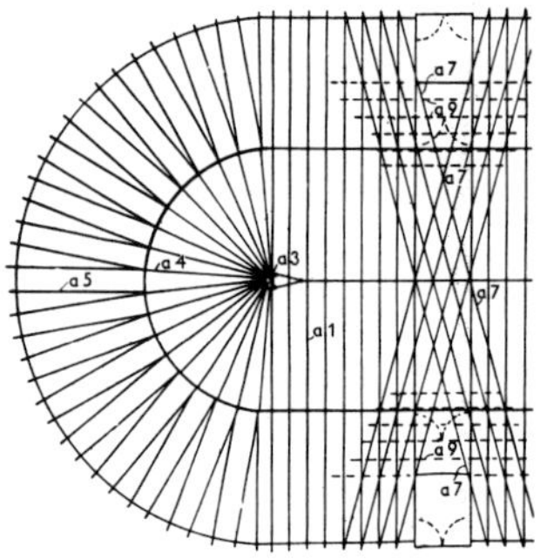

9

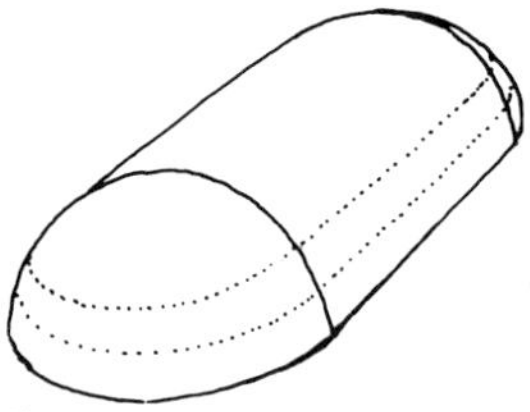

10

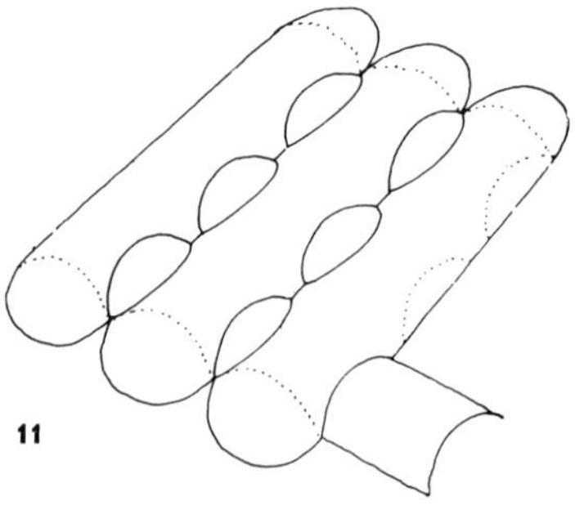

11

12

high-compression-resistant steel tube with a head, which permits drilling, blasting, and crushing of rock under mountain water- or flushing-water pressure. The resulting debris is pumped out of the gallery. Fast setting concrete is injected directly at the head at high pressure and immediately tamped by the hose press. During inversion the hose press is displaced in relation to the steel tube. It is maintained in the same position by a large number of small band rollers, or by an annular hose arrangement illustrated in Fig. 20, p. 73. The steel cylinder is advanced by hydraulic presses located at one end. The entire gallery head up to the end of the steel tube is tightly sealed against water pressure. It is possible to work under high rock- or water pressure.

A cylindrical membrane can be imagined as a series of spheres with infinitely small spacing (Fig. 26, p. 73). If the spacing is increased, the higher tension at the constrictions must be taken up by cables (Fig. 27, p. 73). By means of cables it is possible to combine cylindrical or spherical shapes to form tubular structures (Fig. 28, p. 73). Large cylindrical skins of coated heavy fabric are already being used as floating transports for liquids, e.g., oil (Figs. 1 and 2; photo by Glanzstoff). Inflated rafts and pontoons composed of cylindrical skins are well known (Fig. 3; photo by Ballonfabrik Augsburg). Composite cylinders can form large rigid surfaces.

Semicylinders

A cylinder cut lengthwise is highly suitable for many structural problems because of its simple cut, especially for very long buildings. However, even in this case a spherical shape should not be connected directly to the cylinder. There exist many possible ways of closing it off so that the tensions become uniform, for example, as shown in Figs. 4 and 5.

Cross section 6 shows the design of a pneumatically tensed cylindrical membrane for snow tunnels which are increasingly needed for main traffic links in polar areas. Unless a special ventilation duct is connected to the cylinder, the exhaust gases of the vehicles must be removed by increased air circulation. In horizontal conveyors, high-velocity wind can be used to drive rail vehicles (Fig. 7). Lanchester, in his patent of 1917 (Figs. 8 and 9; drawing by Lanchester), explained how the ends of a cylindrical membrane can be closed with dome and cable reinforcements, using diagonal cables and a connecting cable between the centers of the separated domes.

Cylinders and composite shapes, just like domes, can also be altered by attaching lateral strips, provided the radii of curvature remain unchanged (Fig. 10). Cylinders can be assembled in series at will and interconnected by corresponding cutouts in the membrane (Fig. 11), or provided with vertical partitions (Fig. 12).

Many designs and projects with cylindrical skins have recently been carried out. Several examples follow:

It is generally attempted to locate the entrance at the front (Fig. 13; photo by Texair, and Fig. 14; photo by Krupp).

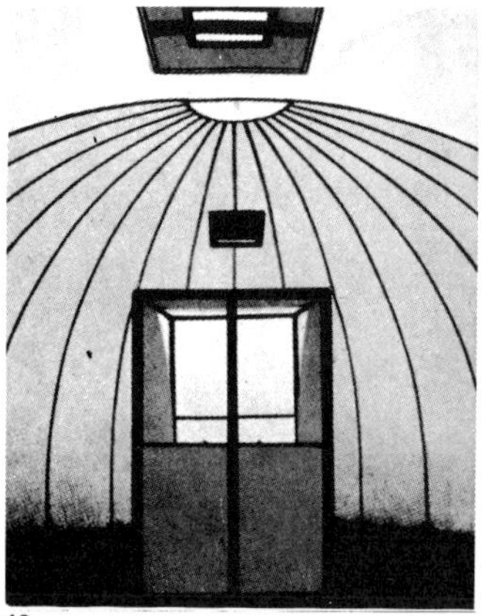
13

14

15

16

17

18

19

20

21 ▲

22 ▲

▼ 23

▼ 24

In cooperation with engineers at the Colorado School of Mines,† John S. Renehart designed a pneumatic cylinder, protected by an overhead radiation shield, for a moon project (Figs. 15 and 16, p. 75).

Until now the longest cylinder was constructed by Schjeldahl as an assembly hall for balloons and other pneumatic structures (Figs. 17 and 18, p. 75; works photos). A roof was also built of large steel sheets clad with aluminium (Figs. 19 and 20, p. 75; from *Populäre Mechanik*).

Rigid end disks are generally economical only for smaller projects, e.g., greenhouses (Figs. 21 and 22, p. 75; photos by Schjeldahl), or for small swimming pools closed at the ends by glass walls (Figs. 23 and 24, p. 75; (photos by Schjeldahl).

Figure 1 shows how the pneumatic skin is checked shortly before the experimental erection of a semicylindrical balloon with round domed ends (works photo by U.S. Rubber Company). The actual membrane is attached to a water-filled circular hose. When attached to such a hose the balloon can be inflated without anchoring it directly to the ground. In order to counter all possible loads, primarily wind pressure, the weight of the water ballast must be considerable. The design of the water hose is very simple, but great care must be taken with the hose. When filling the circular hose, the water pressure increases with deformation and imparts the desired rigidity. However, since the hose is rigid it leaves hollows where it bridges uneven terrain. This causes leakages which must be closed by fabric strips. Since the anchor forces in the cylindrical part are twice as high as those in the dome, the cross section of the hose must be adjusted accordingly.

Texair built a well-designed exhibition pavilion in France (Fig. 2; works photo by Texair).

A light revolving door is fitted in front (see internal view Fig. 13, p. 75. The foundation hose can be weighted both with water and with stones.

1

2 ▲

▼ 3

† *Architectural Forum* 3/1959.

In one of Walter Bird's designs (Fig. 3; photo by Birdair) the terminal domes are opaque membranes, whereas the cylindrical part is highly transparent in order to obtain a light-flooded interior. The structure is firmly anchored to the building site.

The interiors of pneumatically tensed cylindrical membranes rarely have good acoustics, but are still superior in this respect to spherical domes.

Cylindrical membranes are suitable for many structural purposes and constitute a highly economical form of transportable roofing.

The Seattle Tent and Awning Company made simple envelopes to permit the building of houses in winter (Fig. 4; works photo). Even a large one-family house can be completed inside such a heated envelope at very low outside temperatures. Envelopes for such hibernal constructions must meet very high standards due to rough handling at the building site. Very tough fabric is therefore used, or thin short-life foil which is discarded after a few times. There is no doubt that the pneumatic principle is admirably suited to winter-construction envelopes of most types. The possibilities have not yet been fully exploited.

It should be mentioned that a design method* has been developed for winter-construction envelopes which permits the shape to be changed even under internal pressure and the envelope to grow with the structure. The outer membrane is made of standardized large awnings with variably wide overlaps. The membrane is forced against a cable net by the internal pressure.

The interior effect of a large exhibition hall (Fig. 5; photo by Texair) conveys the spatial impression of a transparent cylindrical membrane. Vents can be seen in the ceiling.

Walter Bird made transportable roofs for small summer pools (Fig. 6) in the form of transparent semi cylinders with simple flap doors. These structures are also directly anchored in the ground. The high humidity inside causes condensation on the cold outer skins. The condensate runs down the skin and is collected at the bottom.

4

5 ▲

▼ 6

7▲ ▼4

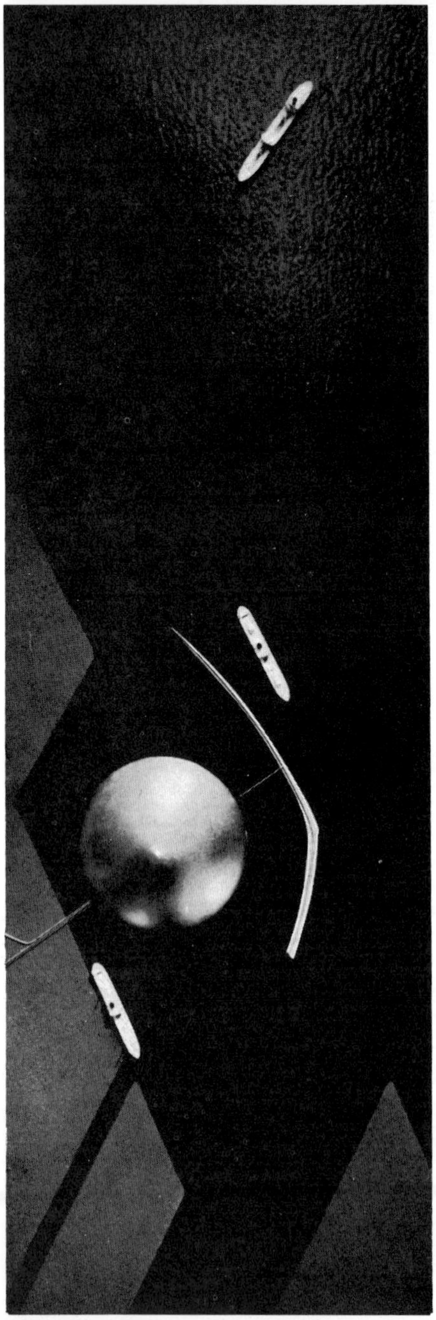

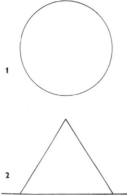

1

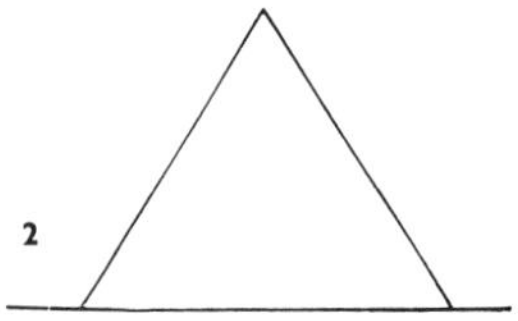

2

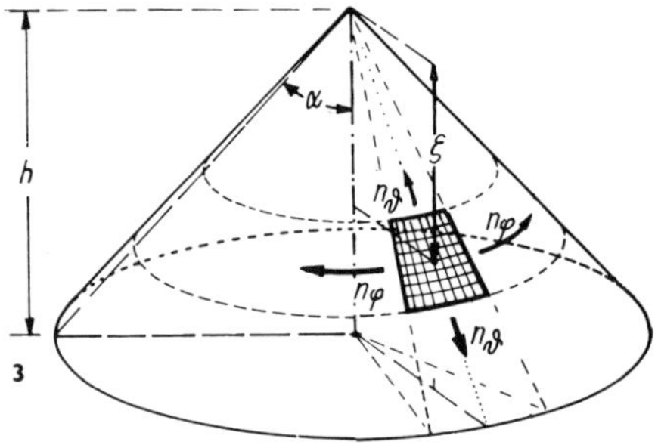

3

Pneumatically Tensed Conical Surfaces

The pneumatic formability of conical surfaces has already been shown in Fig. 13, p. 18. Cones have circular bases (Fig. 1) and triangular elevations (Fig. 2). The equations for the membrane tensions show that the hoop forces n_ϕ(Fig. 3) are always twice as large as the tensions n_θ in the direction of the generator. The tensions vanish at the apex of the cone and are greatest at its base.

The apex of a cone is soft and subject to considerable deformation by external loads. A cone is best truncated as in the support springs of a platform carried by pneumatic, conical membranes (Fig. 5), or rounded off as shown in the section through the apex of a cone (Fig. 6) into which spheres, gradually decreasing in size, are inscribed.

By rounding off with gradually changing curvature, stress discontinuities in the conical membrane are avoided. This has already been explained when discussing the closing of cylindrical skins (see p. 72).

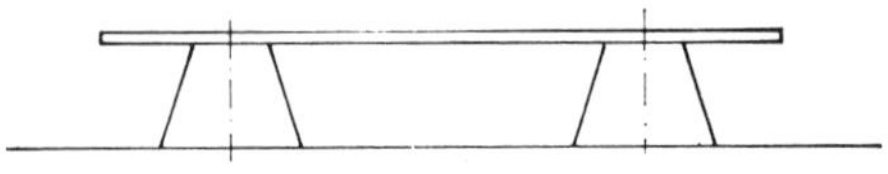

5

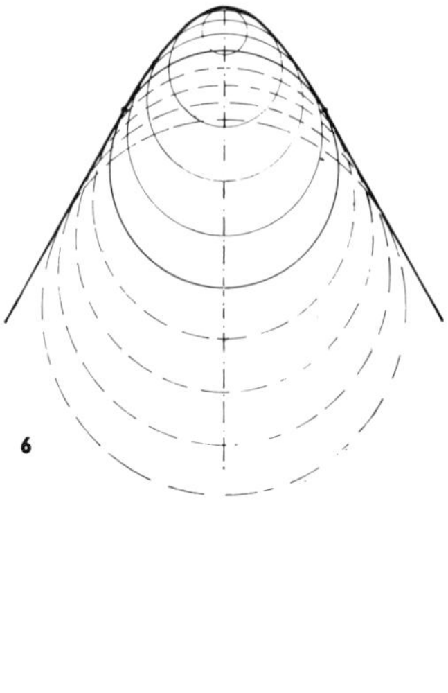

6

$$n_\theta = p\xi \frac{\sin\alpha}{2\cos^2\alpha}$$

$$n_\phi = 2n_\theta$$

$p =$ internal pressure

See Fig. 3 and pp. 207-214.

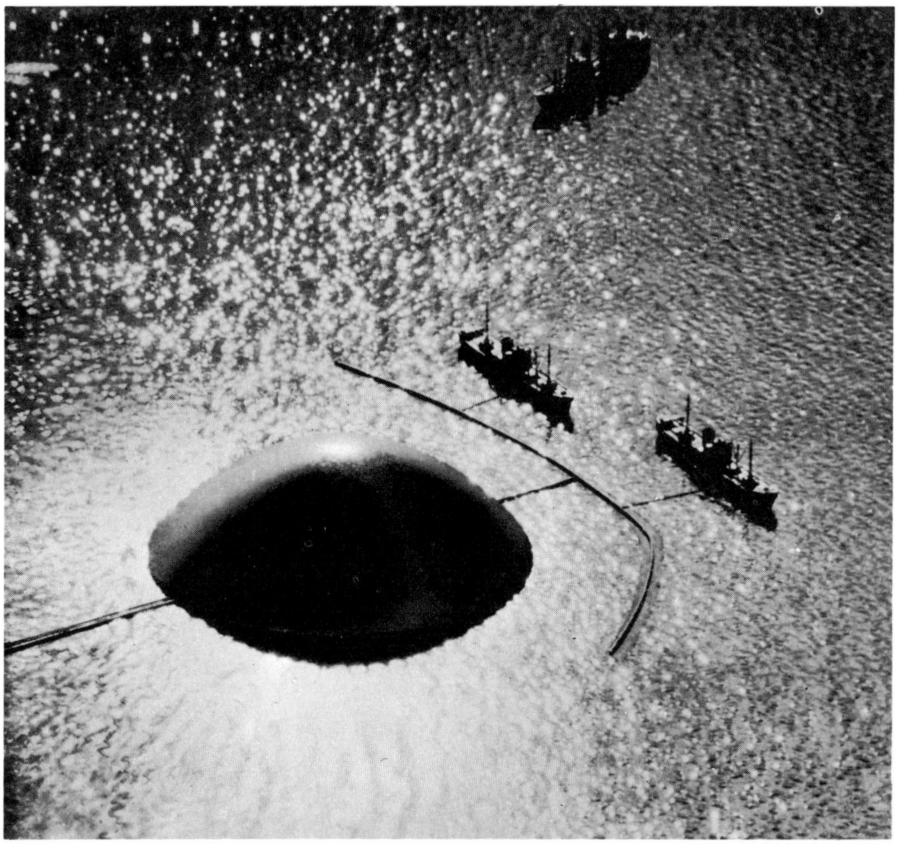

8

A conical surface is simply curved. This has the advantage of being simple to cut with little waste of material even when the apex of the cone is slightly rounded off.

The rounded off, pneumatically tensed conical membrane has numerous uses. For example, it is suitable for the stabilization of warm air in winter.

Furthermore, snow slides off the sloping surface. The interior acoustics of conical membranes are notably superior to those of hemispherical domes.

Two projects* for storing goods in bulk are shown. In Fig. 14, p. 81, the piled material is protected against the weather by a pneumatically tensed membrane with a similar slope. Such installations are suited for bulk goods sensitive to moisture, e.g., cement, gypsum, sulfur, and grain. In view of the great significance of reserves in overcoming shortages and storing surpluses, large storage installations have assumed increasing importance in the last decades.

To save valuable land, the first project for a structure covering a simple conical pile (Fig. 7) was planned in a shallow sea bay. This has the further advantage that the bottom membrane rests on smooth, soft sand. The foundation is a circular ring anchored somewhat deeper than the base of the structure. The bottom membrane prevents the entry of sea water; it floats on the surface when the silo is empty and is pressed to the

9

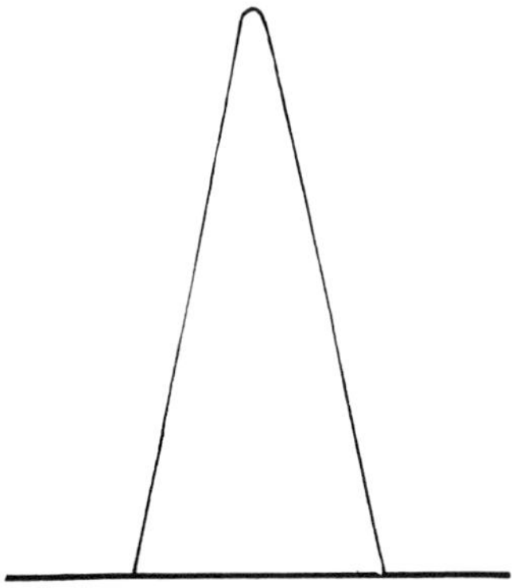

10

11

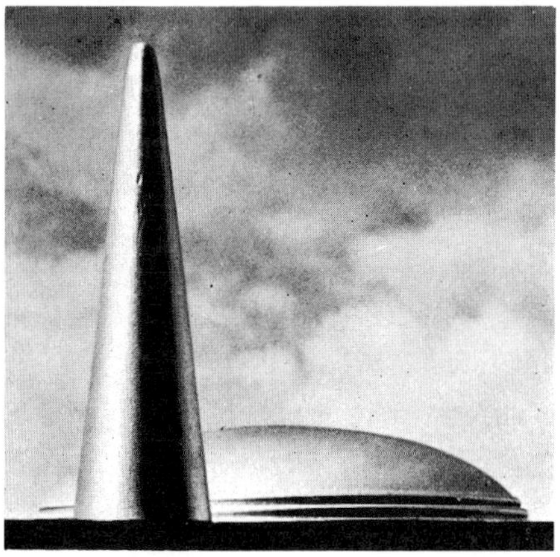

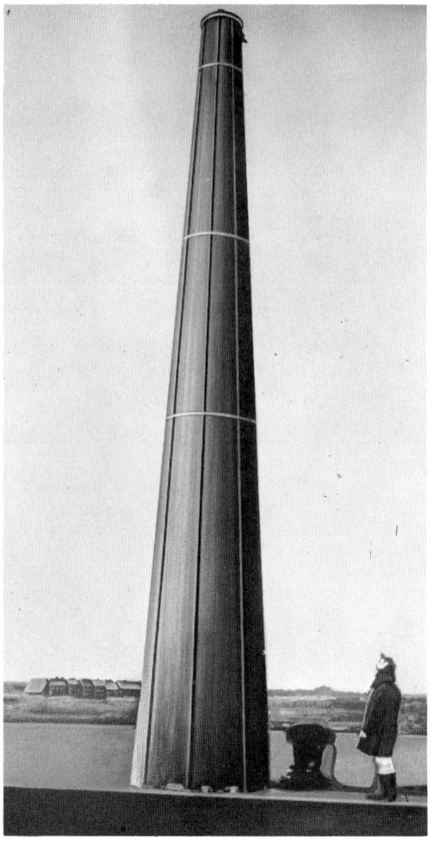

1

2

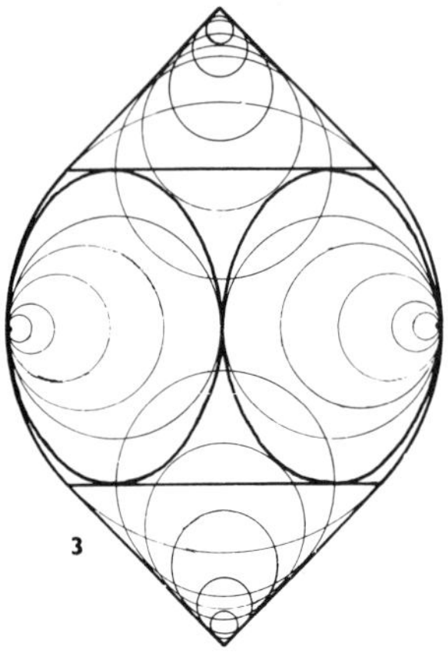

3

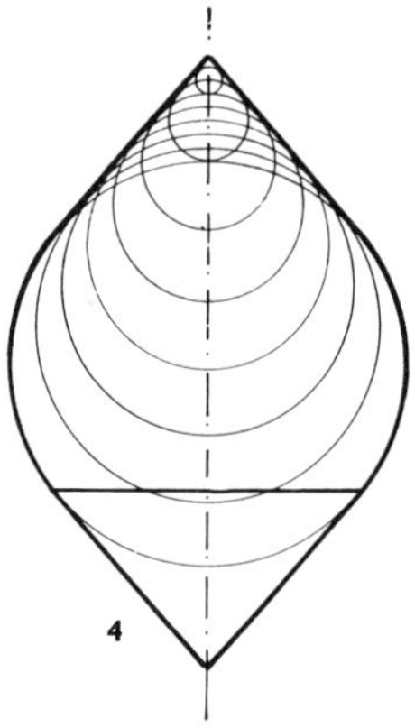

4

5

bottom only by the weight of the bulk goods. The silo is initially emptied by a pneumatic elevator moving along its periphery, and then by suction at the center, the collecting action of the buoyant bottom membrane facilitating discharge. For reasons of safety, the bottom membrane is made of two layers, with an intermediate layer of plastic foam. A breakwater protects the structure against waves and allows ships to lie alongside and fill or discharge the silo which is directly connected to land by conveyors. Figure 7 on p. 78 is a side view, Fig. 4 on p. 78 is a view from above, and Fig. 8, on p. 79 an oblique bird's eye view. The double silos in Figs. 5 and 11 are of similar design. The latter is intended for grain; it is intended to be erected on very cheap and poor land and not in the sea.

In order to avoid having to inflate the entire vast membrane for a small quantity of bulk goods, strips can be fitted to the inflated membrane and tension anchors adjusted to ensure expansion of the membrane with increasing charge.

Pointed cones (Fig. 9, p. 79) permit the erection of tower-like structures of comparatively high rigidity against wind action. The project* in Figs. 10 and 11 on p. 79 uses a pointed cone to mark a fully mobile dome-shaped place of worship for an ecclesiastical convention.

In the United States a large experimental tower has already been erected (Fig. 1; from

10

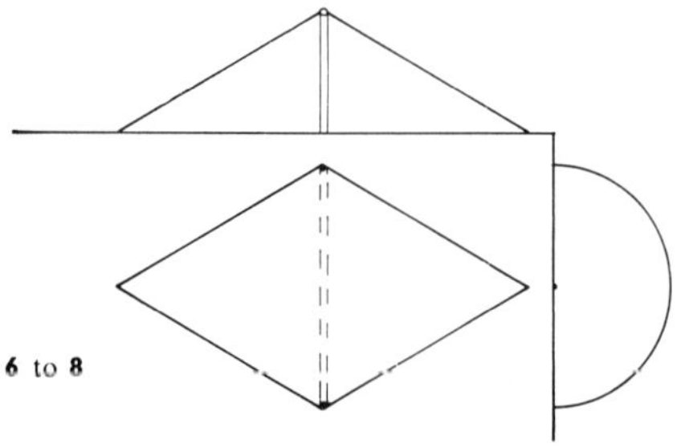

6 to 8

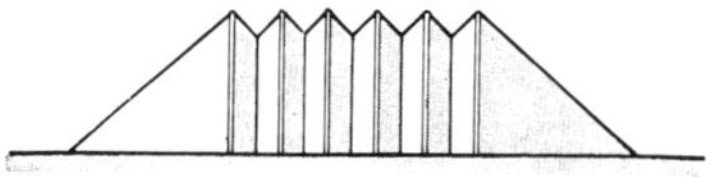

9

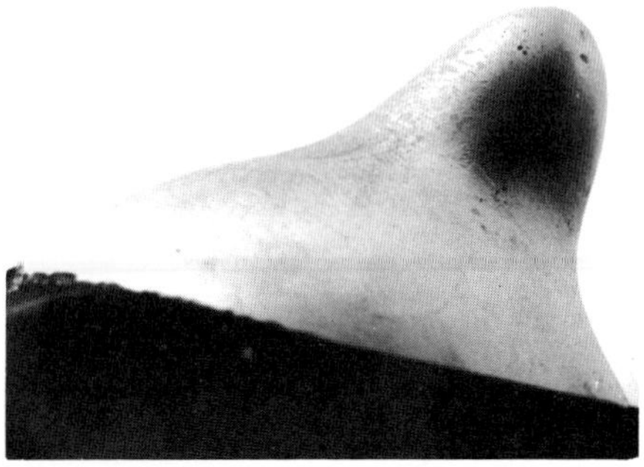

11

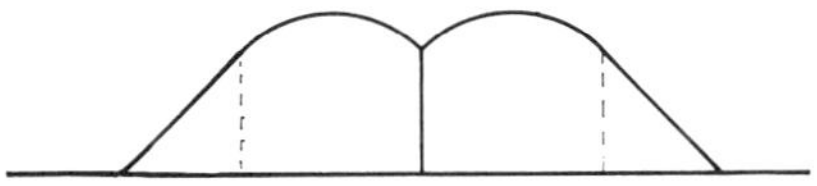

12

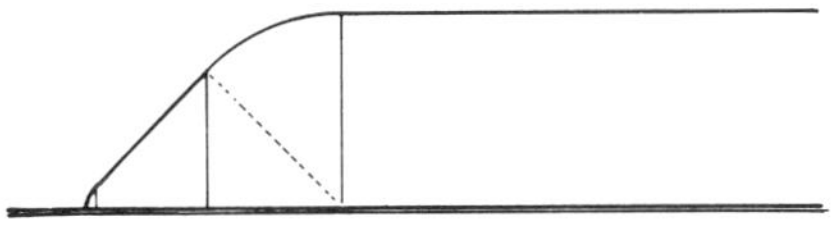

13

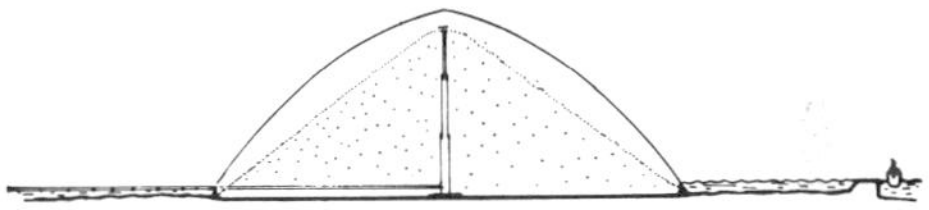

14

Architectural Forum 7/1959), and subjected to the most varied types of loading.

Pneumatically tensed conical membranes can also be combined into various forms, but the laws of formation (see p. 18) must not be disregarded. In Fig. 4 a circular ring connects two cones. In Fig. 2 a hexagonal body is shown from above and in Fig. 3 from the side. The six cones have right-angled points and are mounted on a spherical shape. The primary use of such structures is for containers, since they are usually simple to cut and possess considerable stability when correctly shaped.

If the cones join as shown from the side in Fig. 6, in the plan in Fig. 7, and from the front in Fig. 8, the junction is subjected to compression and must be rigid. This is also necessary if a number of cones or truncated cones are connected (Fig. 9), though not in the modified form seen from the side in Fig. 12, where the conical ends are attached to central spherical segments. When connecting cones and cylinders (Fig. 13) a spherical strip is a suitable transition.

With straight generators, various conical structures (Fig. 10) can be derived from cones.

Since the hoop forces of a cone exceed the forces acting in the direction of the generator, annular cables are provided (Fig. 15); however, the use of cable nets permits the most varied forms, regardless of whether the shapes are axisymmetrical (Fig. 16), or branched (Fig. 17).

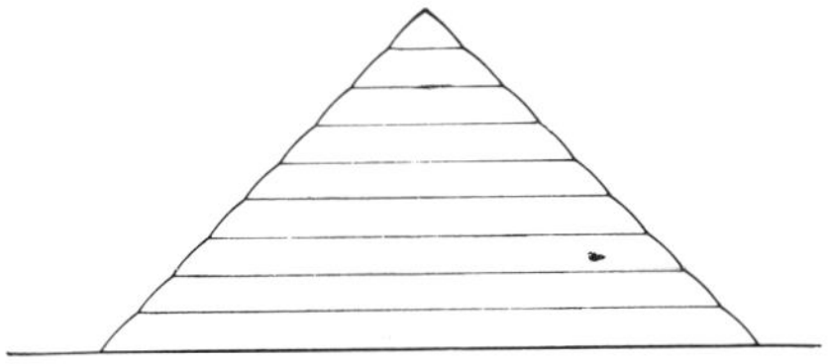

15

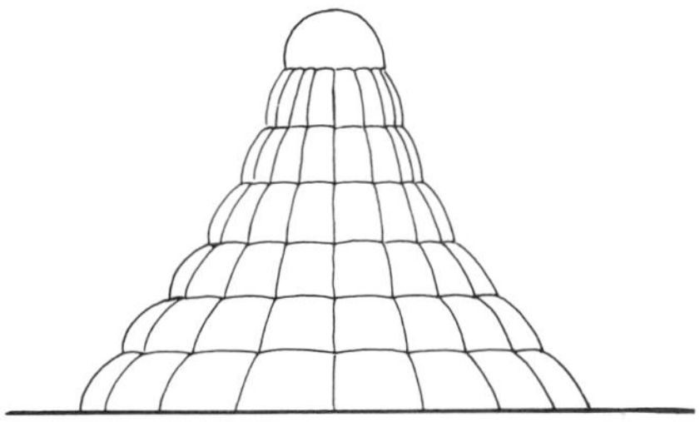

16

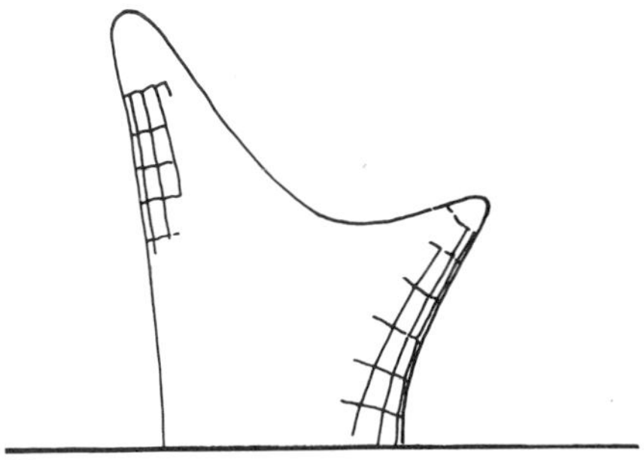

17

1 to 6 ▲ ▼ 7 to 12

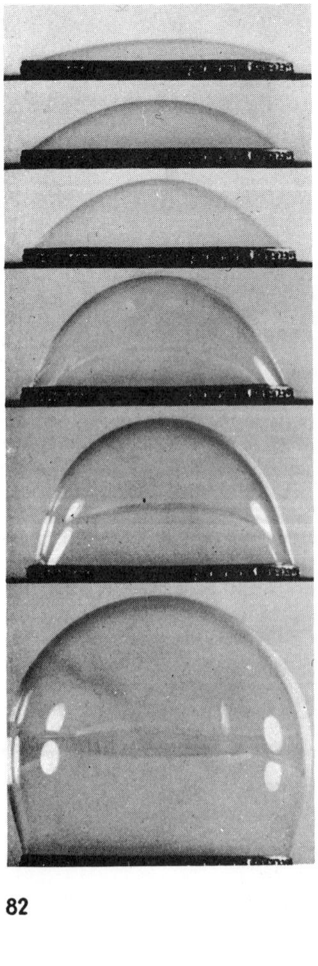

13

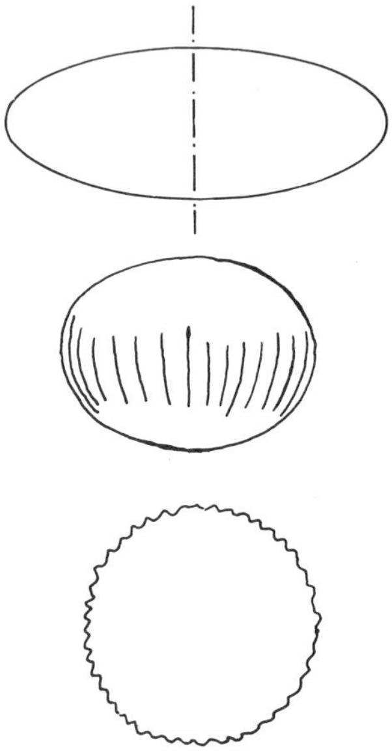

14 to 16

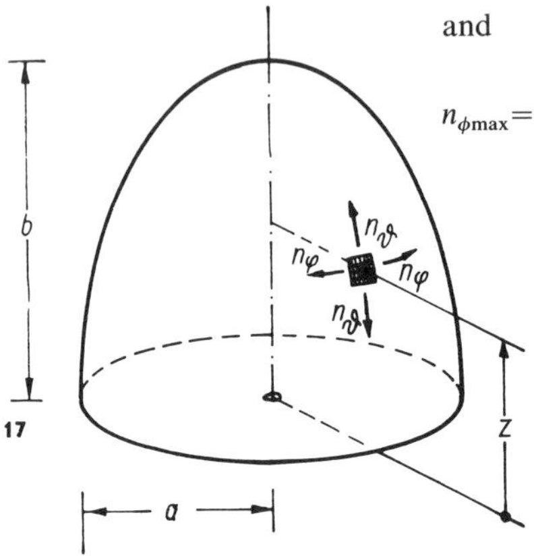

17

$$n_\theta = \frac{pa}{2b^2}\sqrt{b^4 + (a^2 - b^2)z^2}$$

$$n_\phi = \frac{pa}{b^2}\sqrt{b^4 + (a^2 - b^2)z^2}$$

$$\left[1 - \frac{a^2b^2}{2\left[b^4 + (a^2 - b^2)z^2\right]}\right]$$

For $z = 0$ we have:

$$n_{\theta\max} = \frac{pa}{2}$$

and

$$n_{\phi\max} = pa\left[1 - \frac{1}{2}\left(\frac{a}{b}\right)^2\right]$$

18

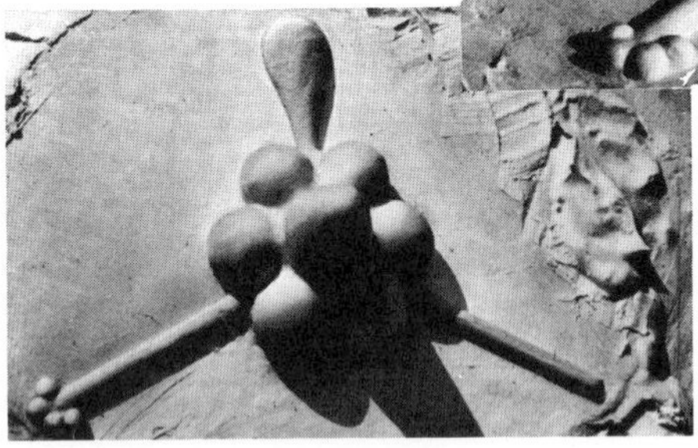

19

20

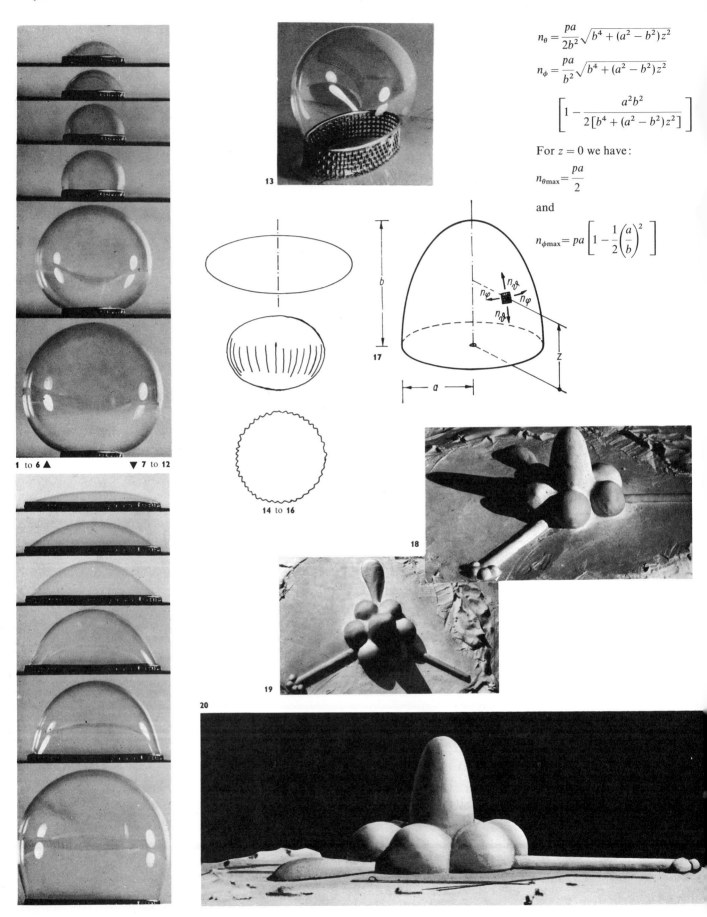

Spindle-shaped Forms

As shown on pp. 186/187, an ellipsoid can be formed pneumatically when the axis of rotation ($2b$) is longer than the maximum diameter ($2a$). If the axis of rotation is less than the maximum diameter, the hoop tensions decrease becoming zero for $b = a/\sqrt{2} = 0.7071\,a$. If the axis of rotation becomes shorter still, as in the ellipsoid in Fig. 14, then folds will be unavoidable. The side view will then resemble Fig. 15, and the plan, Fig. 16. If a soap bubble is blown above an elliptical base (Fig. 13; viewed from the narrow side in Figs. 1 to 6 and from the broad side in Figs. 7 to 12), the bubble will resemble the segment of an ellipsoid, if its height remains small. However, an ellipsoid cannot form a minimum surface. Further expansion of the bubble rapidly leads to a spherical shape.

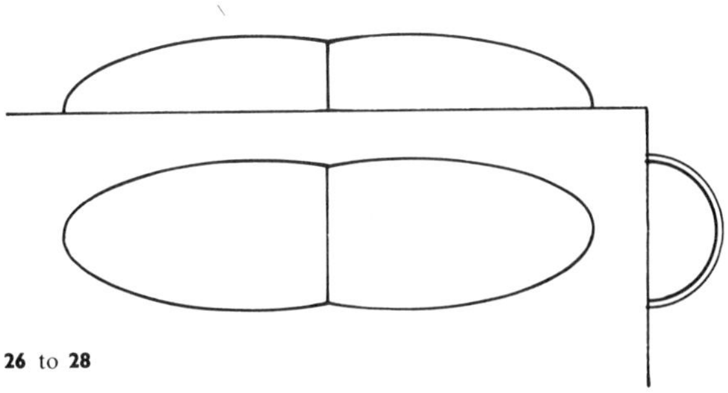

26 to **28**

The tension distribution in the ellipsoidal membrane renders it of interest for various structural problems, e.g., for roofing oblong floor plans (Figs. 21 to 23).

Apart from this longitudinally bisected ellipsoid, different segments (Figs. 24 and 25) can be used for special purposes (comp. the shapes of models Figs. 29 to 33), showing envelopes enclosing oblong and inclined objects). Ellipsoids can also be joined to form different shapes (Figs. 26 to 28). In the project depicted in Figs. 18 to 20,* a slender bisected ellipsoid constitutes the nucleus of an installation surrounded by six domed workshops. All parts of the installation, including the cylindrical annexes and the drop-shaped assembly hall, are made safe by multiple membranes.

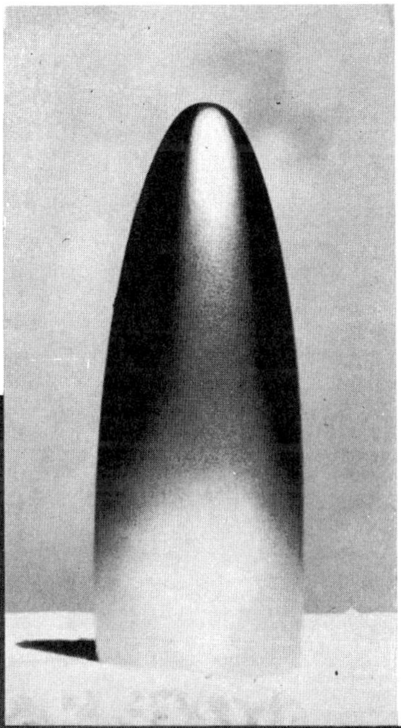

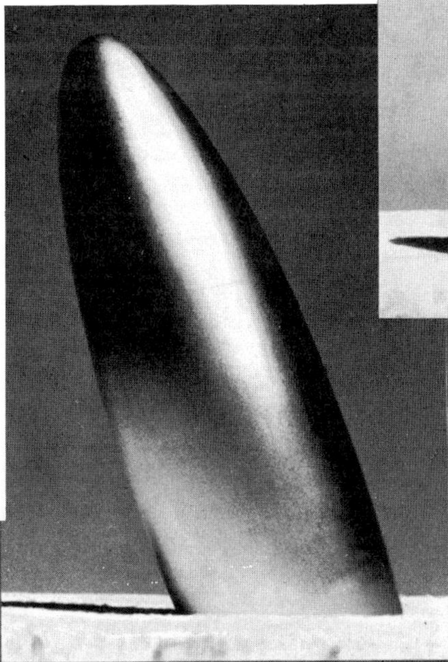

29 to **33**

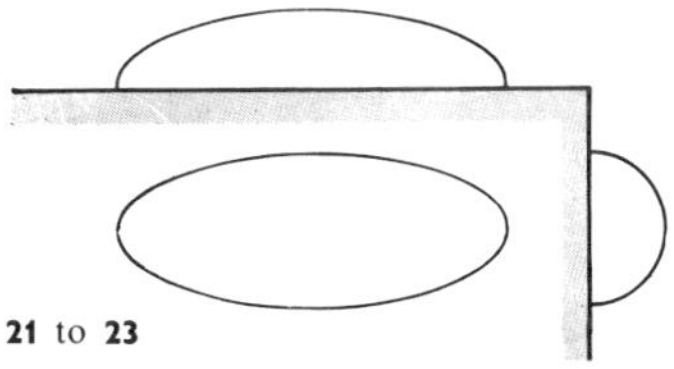

21 to **23**

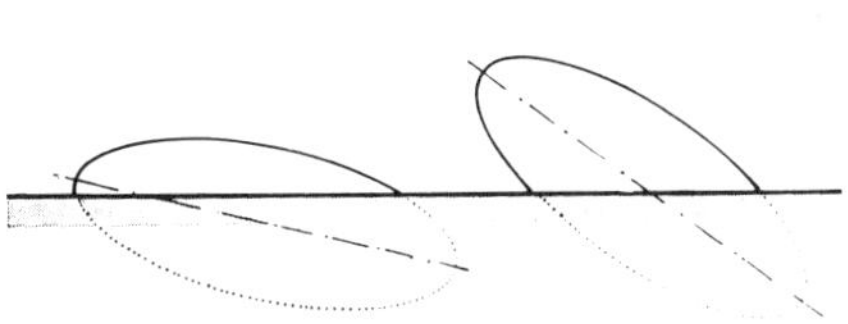

24 and **25**

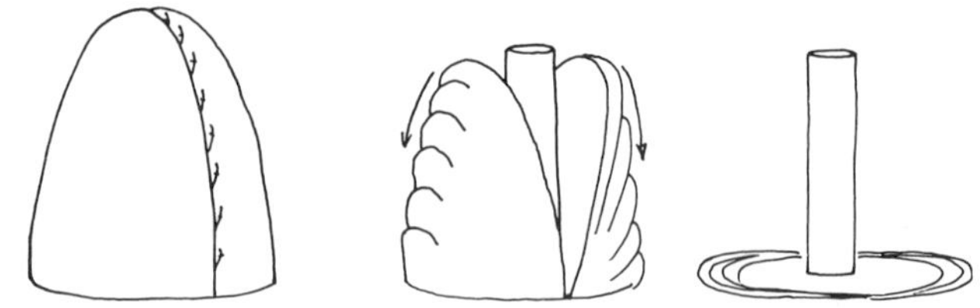

1 to 3

4

5

6 ▲

▼ 7

Various spindle-shaped bodies

Pneumatically tensed membranes can form protective envelopes around large objects and be quickly removed when necessary. The envelope collapses when a quick-closing seam is ripped (Figs. 1 to 3) and lies folded on the ground in circles when there is no wind.

Pneumatically formed spindle-shaped bodies are unlimited in number. Primarily they are transitions from cones, cylinders, ellipsoids, and spheres, illustrated by the reinforced model of a preformed rubber membrane (Figs. 4 and 5), or the various drop shapes which have found applications particularly in aeronautical construction and ship building. Captive balloons, now used for advertising (Fig. 6; photo by Ballonfabrik Augsburg), supported intricate barrage nets during the war. The nonrigid airship, (Fig. 7; photo by Ballonfabrik Augsburg) is one of the oldest airship designs. Internal pressure renders the skin sufficiently rigid to support gondolas, engines, and rudders.

The fuselage of modern stratospheric passenger planes (Fig. 8; photo by PAA) is subject to considerable pneumatic loading. The interior of the oblong shell must be maintained constantly at ground-level air pressure, although the external pressure at great heights may only be 20% thereof. Consequently, the pneumatic load on the cabin is $0.8\,\text{atm} = 8\,\text{m}$ water column $= 800\,\text{kP/m}^2$. Cabins, like spaceships, are designed with safety factors large enough so that pressure differences of one atmosphere can be withstood.

An easily transportable aircraft hangar* (Fig. 9) consists of bisected oblong and domed elements shaped like a large plane, thus preventing large spans and excessive membrane tensions. The hangar is very light ($0.8\,\text{kg/m}^2$) and transportable by air. The rapid activation of small auxiliary airfields therefore becomes possible. Before inflation, the membrane is drawn over the plane like a wrapping.

The assembly hall in Fig. 10 is of similar design.

A proposed safety bumper* (Fig. 11) for automobiles has a curved, pneumatically tensed, oblong membrane.

A further proposal (Fig. 12) is for a pressurized motor lifeboat of oblong shape, with tanks for ballast and drinking water. When the sea is calm, the design of the double membrane causes the shape to be maintained without internal pressure. The membrane takes up impacts resiliently and renders the boat unbreakable. A supertanker* is shown in Figs. 13 and 14 in cross section and from the side. It consists of a multilayered ultra-heavy membrane reinforced by cable netting, and maintains its streamlined shape by the pressure of the cargo (oil or water ballast with an air bubble).

A mast is the only rigid component: it carries the cabin for the crew of four, the remote controls, and, on outriggers, the underwater turbines and rudders of this fully automated ship. The floating resort hotel* (Fig. 15) is roofed by a completely transparent pneumatically tensed membrane above the terraced cabins and sundecks. The aerodynamic resistance of the ship is also considerably reduced. Only the afterdeck is not spanned.

8

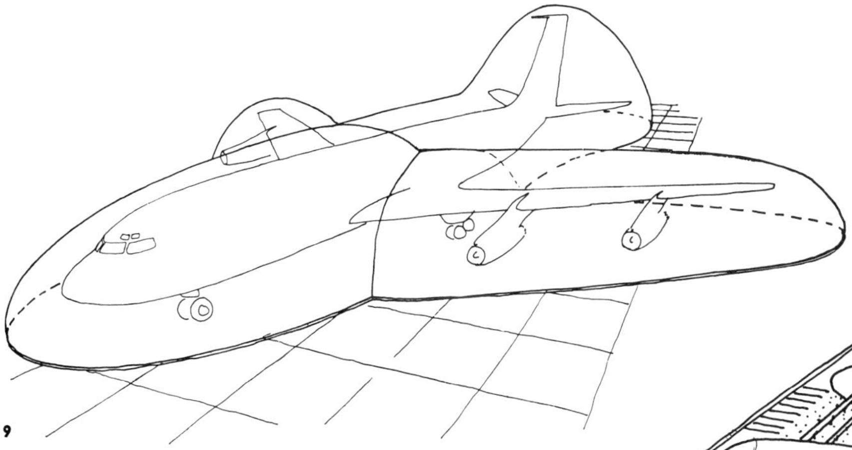
9

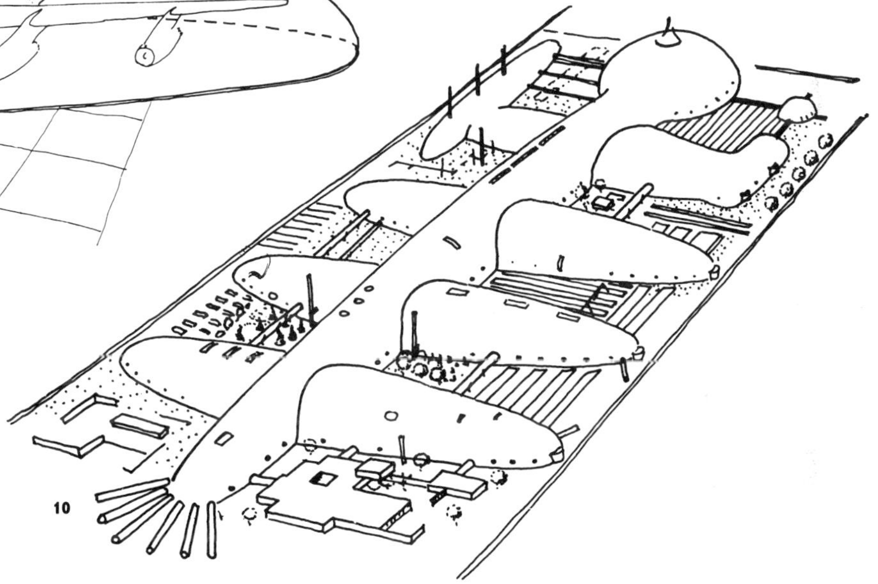
10

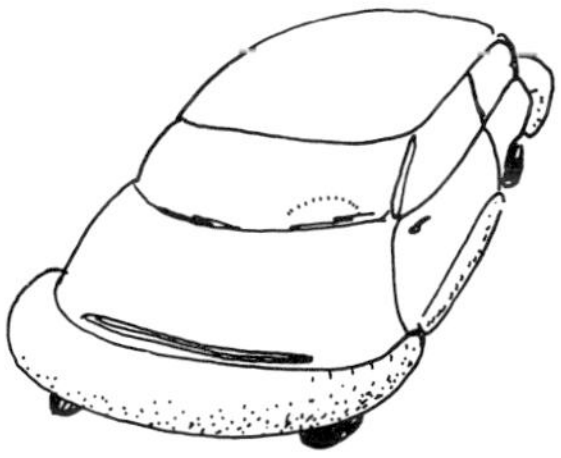
11

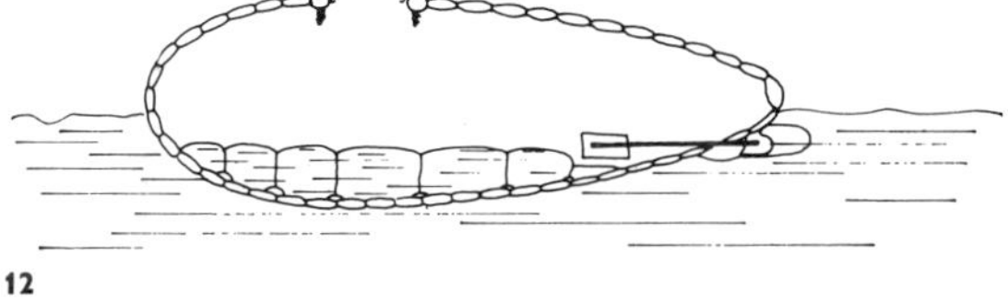
12

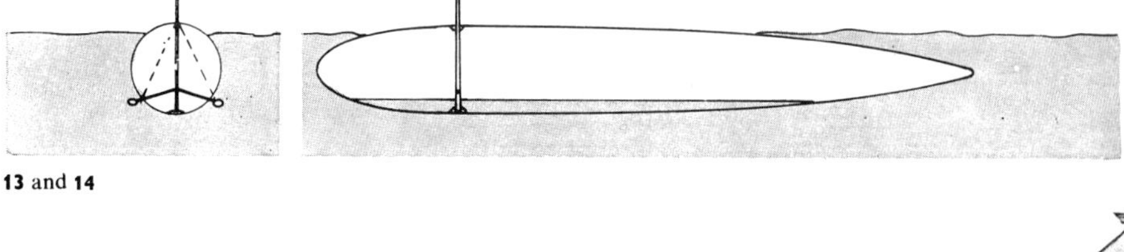
13 and **14**

15

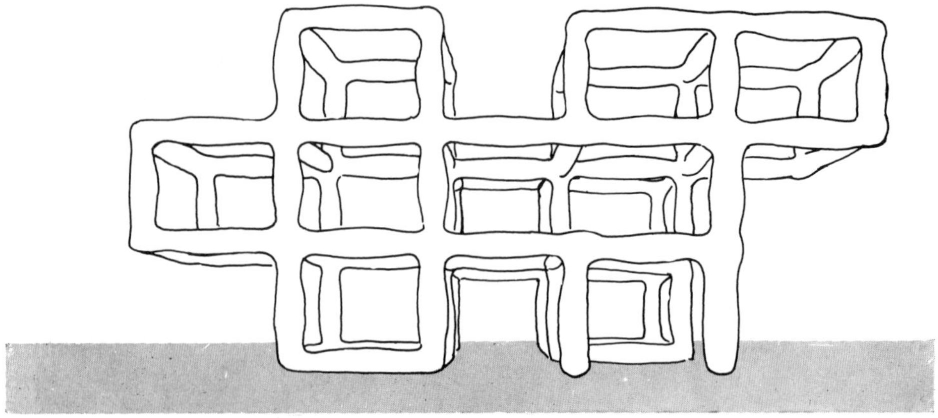

1

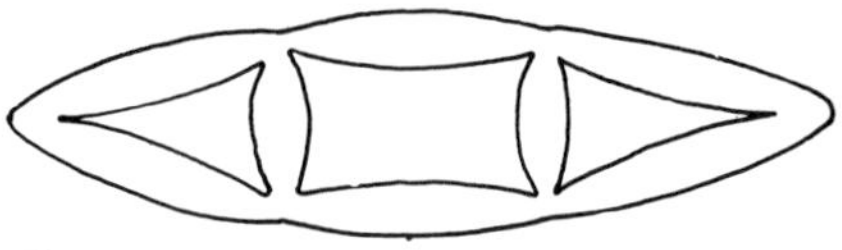

7

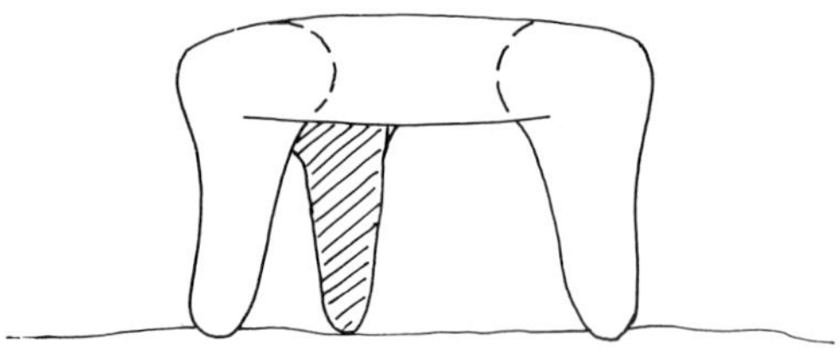

2

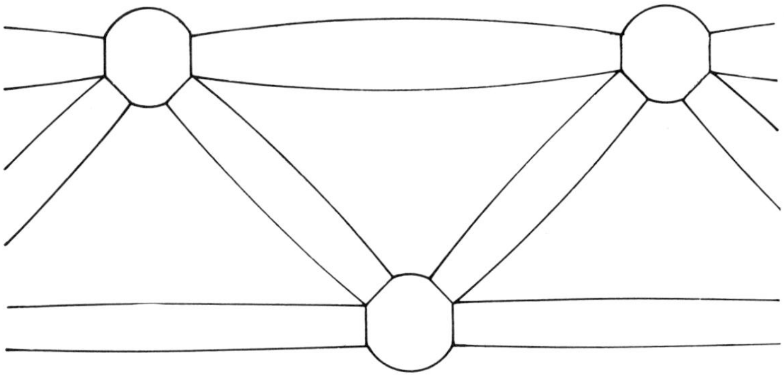

8

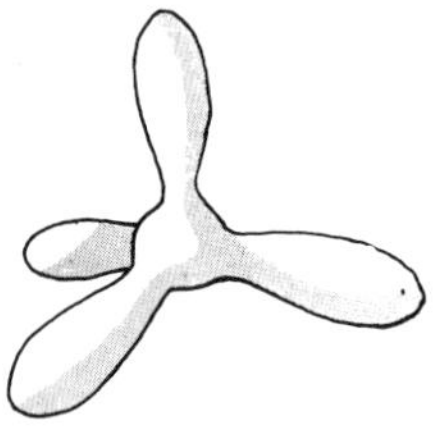

3

9

4 to 6

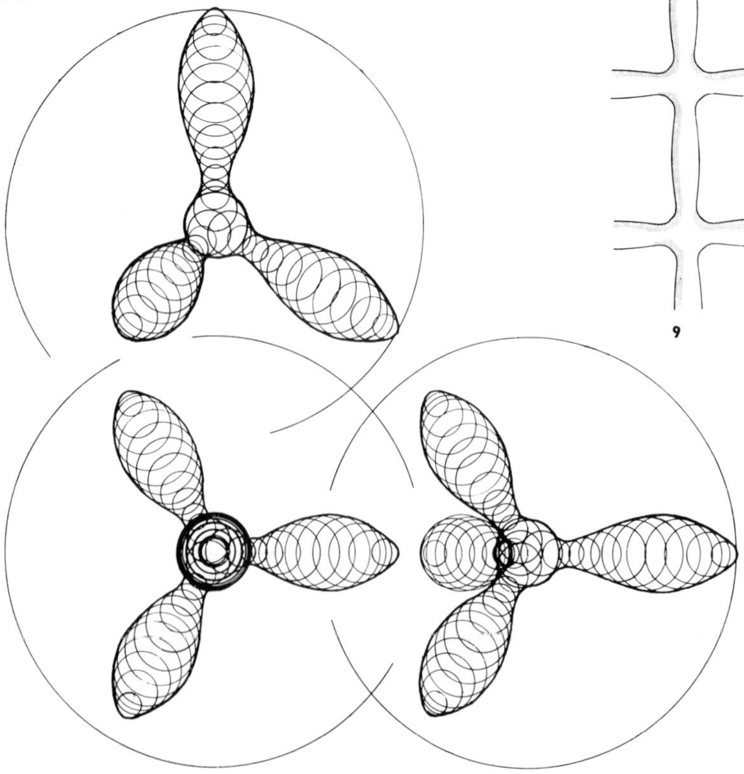

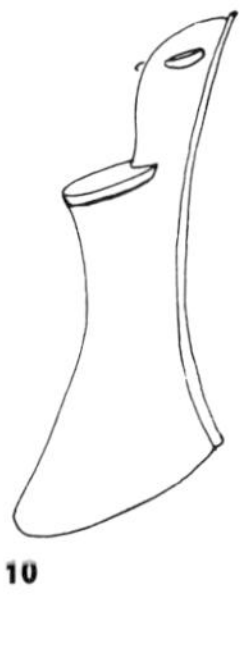

10

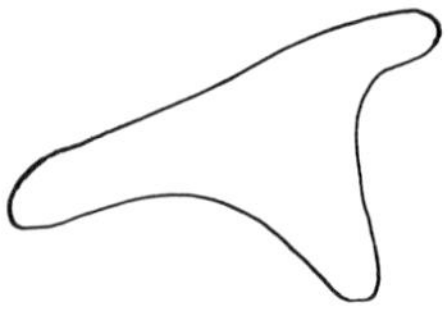

11

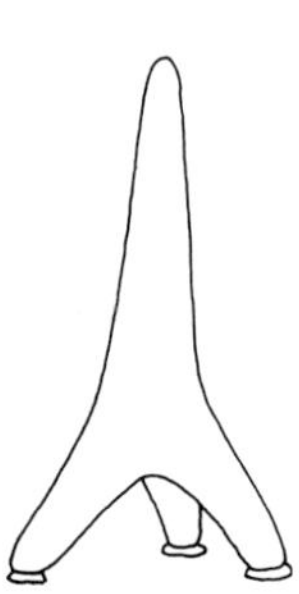

12

Pneumatically Tensed Lattice Structures

Large lattice structures can be built of cylindrical and spindle-shaped pneumatically tensed membrane struts.

When the internal pressure is high enough, cylindrical membranes become quite rigid. By enlarging the strut diameter at possible buckling points a pneumatic system can be adapted to the prevailing forces. Pneumatically tensed structures cannot resist highly concentrated loads. The loads should be distributed over large areas when they act at the well rounded-off strut ends or girder nodes.

Struts hinged at both ends should, if possible, be thickened at the center. Such shapes can be created with soap bubbles. For example, an oblong bubble can be formed between two rings arranged in one plane (Figs. 14 and 15), or one above the other (Figs. 16 to 18). If pneumatically tensed rod-shaped membranes are clamped at both ends, as in a system of thick struts (Figs. 1 and 9), the diameter is largest at the node; a constriction follows, and a bulge forms in the center of the strut.

It is too early to determine the economic feasibility of such structures if high internal pressure must be maintained continuously. They are undoubtedly of great value if liquids or plastic substances which harden under pressure (plastics, foams, foam concrete) can be injected and the permanent membrane tension maintained, even if small tears should appear. Collapsible lattice structures which can be rapidly inflated are a very attractive proposition. These proposals* are merely a superficial survey of the unlimited possibilities.

In a design for an exhibition pavilion a ring upholding the roof is supported by three columns (Fig. 2), or a rigid lattice girder is formed (Fig. 7). Entire lattice structures (Fig. 8) forming triangles, can be assembled, the nodes forming spheres. Figures 3 to 6 show the four-armed isogonal basic element of a spatial lattice; Figures 10 to 12 show several pylon- and bridge-like structures. An experimental dome with pneumatically tensed hollow cylindrical struts, built by Buckminster Fuller, is shown in Fig. 13.

13

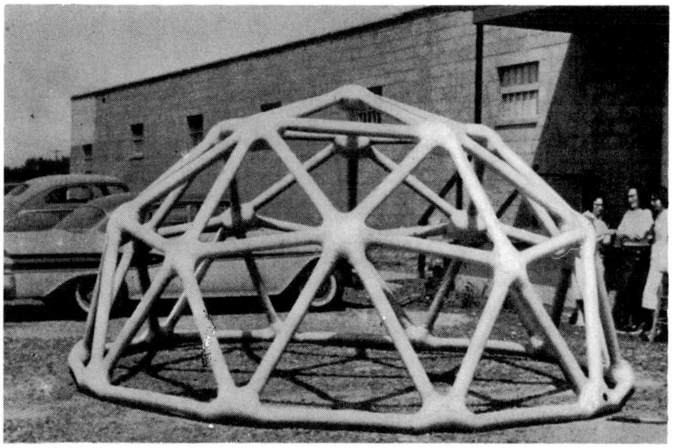

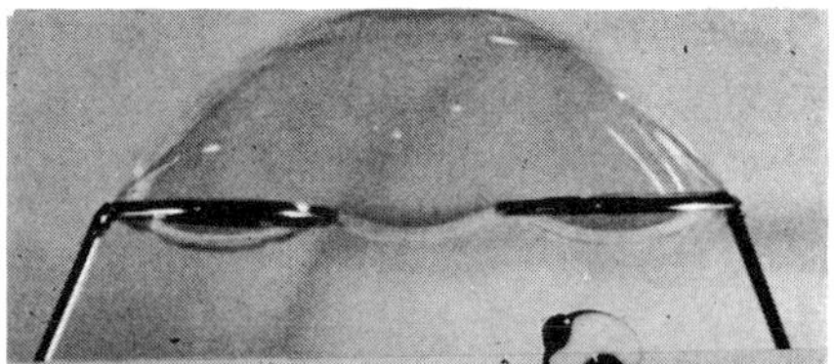

14

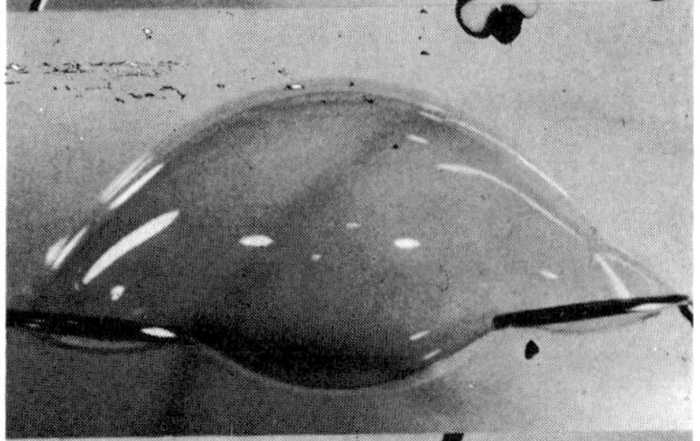

15

16

17

18

The Circular Hose (Torus)

The torus (Figs. 1 and 2) can also be designed as a pneumatic membrane, a well-known example being the vehicle tire. A circular hose or torus can be imagined as the tangential surface formed by an infinite number of spheres strung in a circle. The tensions in the direction of the circle are equal at all points (Fig. 3). The membrane forces n_θ, normal to this direction, are greater at the inner wall than on the outside (Fig. 4). The surface of a torus is doubly curved in the same sense (dome-like) on the outside and in opposed senses (saddle-like) on the inside.

The saddle surface of the inside part has a smaller area than the outside, which is not a saddle surface. The torus differs from all other pneumatically tensed membranes by this characteristic saddle-shaped region. The circle on which the spheres forming the torus are strung need not be in the same plane (Fig. 5), nor need the spheres have equal diameter (Fig. 6). Here, too, unlimited variations are possible, subject to the general laws of formation (p. 18), and to those particular to closed hoses.

When a rubber hose is overloaded, the phenomenon observed is similar to that explained on p. 65 for a rubber membrane spanning an oblong rectangle. The hose bulges spherically at some point, and as the tensions at the bulge increase more rapidly than elsewhere, further expansion and bulging will ensue. If the pressure is maintained the hose will inevitably burst. Because of the tendency to bulge, torii must either be membranes of low deformability (e.g., coated fabrics), or be reinforced by cording if made of rubber. This is generally true for automobile tires and has already been discussed for cylindrical hoses.

Upright toroidal sections can be used as structural arches (see p. 150).

The longitudinally bisected torus can also be used to span plans of circles or circular segments. It is even possible to obtain circular minimum surfaces, as can be seen from the side views in Figs. 7 and 8 and the corresponding plan (Fig. 9). The cross section of these minimum surfaces is not circular. Compared to a hose of circular cross section, the area of the saddle-shaped interior is smaller. Furthermore, there is no horizontal section at which the membrane is vertical both on the outside and on the inside: consequently, a closed torus free of this limitation cannot be

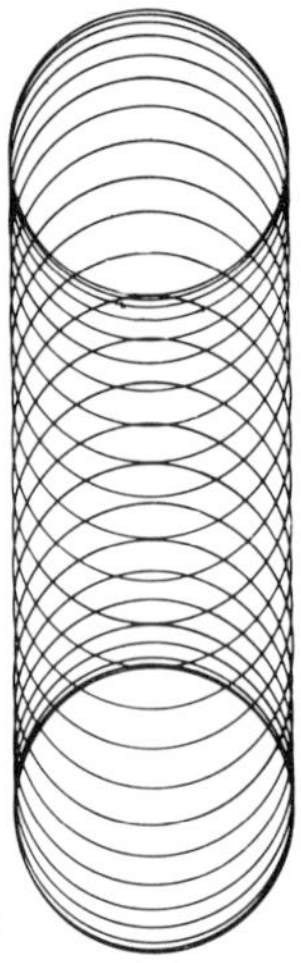

1

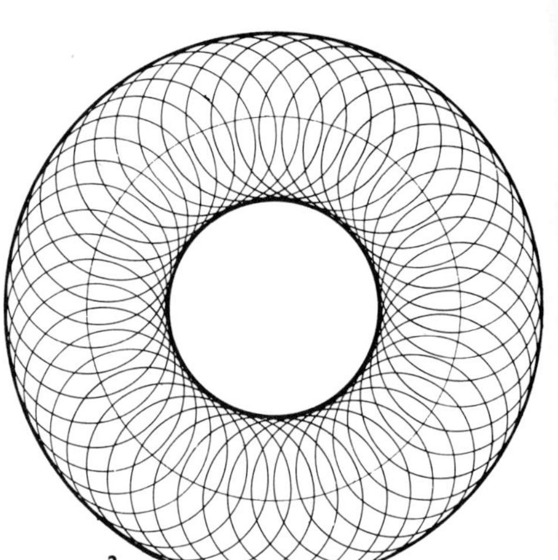

2

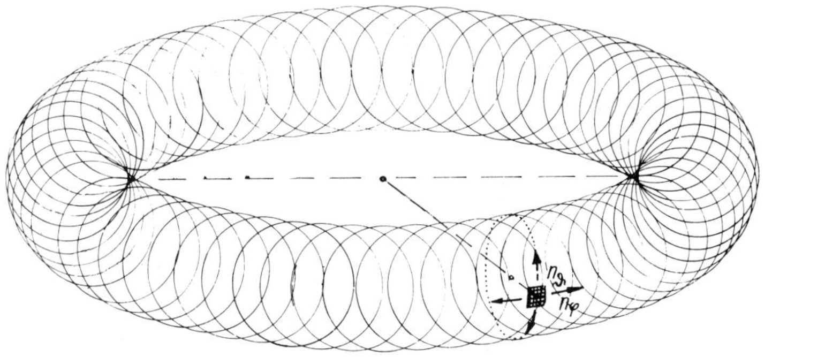

3

In general $\quad n_\theta = \dfrac{pr}{2}\,\dfrac{2+\kappa\sin\theta}{1+\kappa\sin\theta} \qquad n_\phi = p\dfrac{r}{2} \qquad \kappa = r/R$

On the outside: $\quad n_\theta\left(\dfrac{\pi}{2}\right) = \dfrac{pr}{2}\,\dfrac{2+\kappa}{1+\kappa}$

At the center: $\quad n_\theta(0) = n_\theta(\pi) \approx pr$

On the inside: $\quad n_\theta\left(-\dfrac{\pi}{2}\right) = \dfrac{pr}{2}\,\dfrac{2-\kappa}{1-\kappa}$

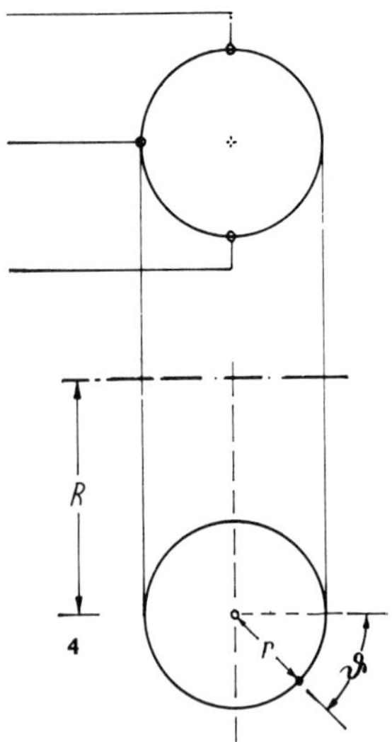

4

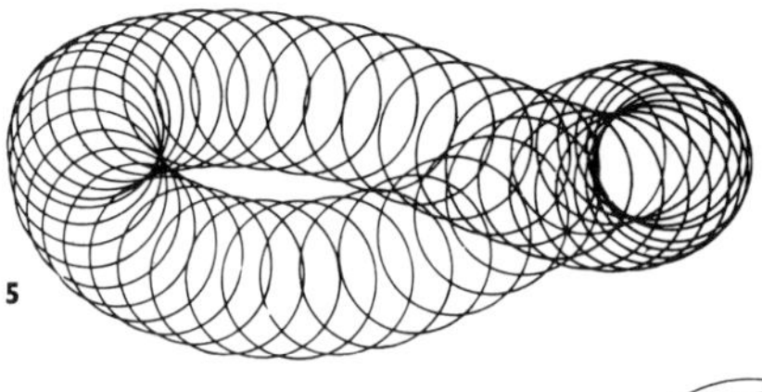

5

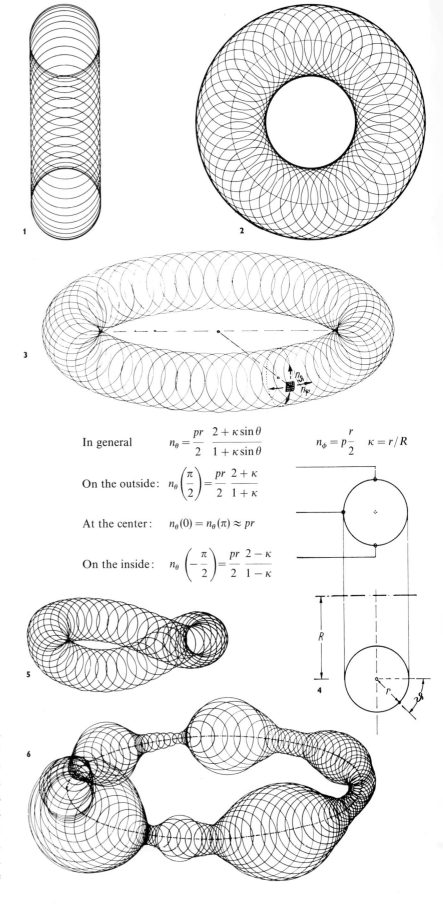

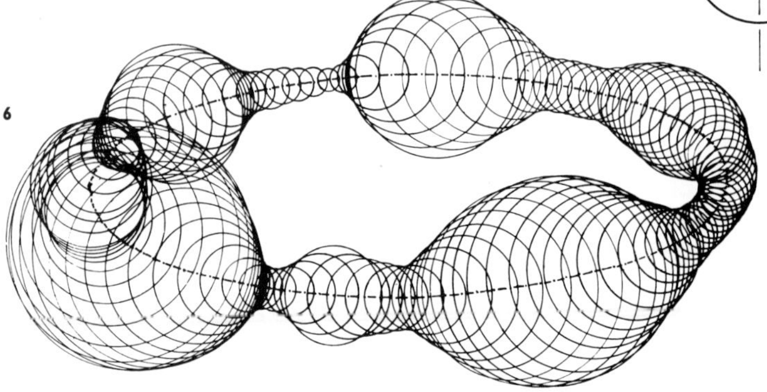

6

7

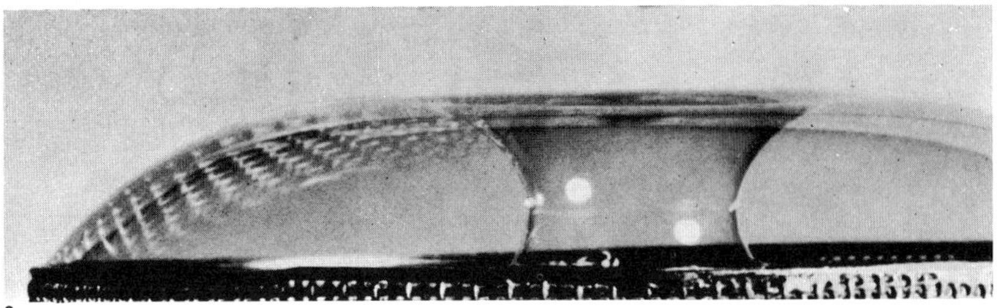

8

formed as a minimum surface. A minimum surface spanning a circular plan can rise only to a certain height, which is shown approximately in Fig. 8. When inflated further, the minimum surface suddenly assumes the shape of a dome which curves above the outer ring without touching the inner ring; in most cases a small inner dome spans the inner ring. If this inner ring is asymmetrically arranged, as shown in Fig. 10 by the sketch for this experiment (the arrows indicate the direction from which views 11 and 12 were taken), a membrane with a pronounced asymmetric deformation results. A minimum surface with two internal circles (Fig. 13) could also be formed. Figure 14 shows the view from the side. Such a form always remains flat. When inflated further, the membrane immediately contracts to a spherical bubble.

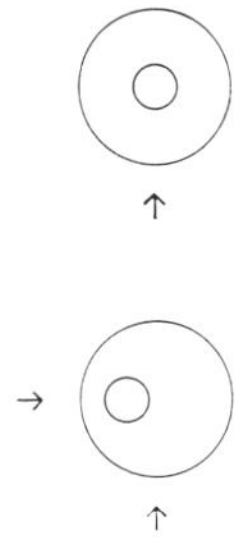

9 and 10

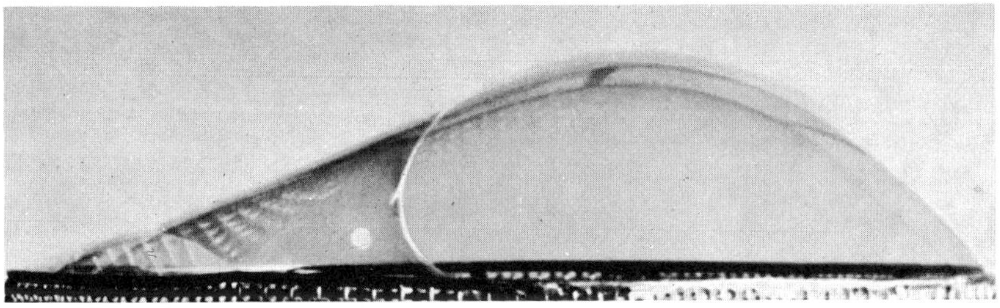

11

12

13

14

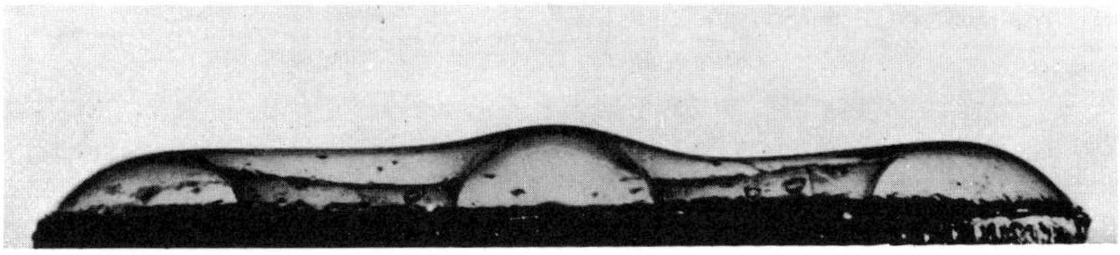

Figures 15 to 18 show toroidal shapes made of elastic membranes and radial cables. The use of cables or cable nets can greatly increase the number of shapes possible with circular torii.

15

16

17 ▲

▼ 18

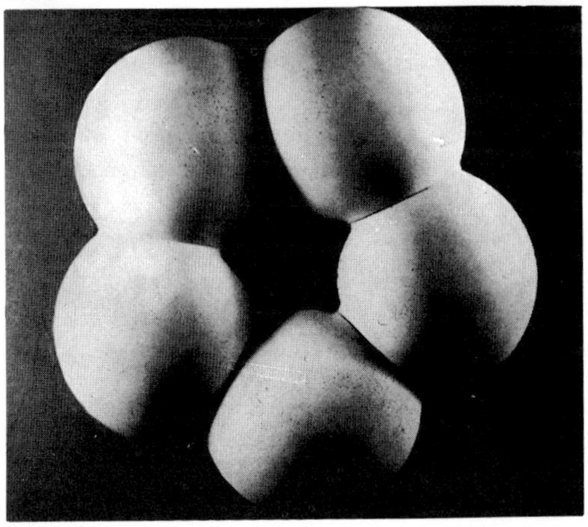

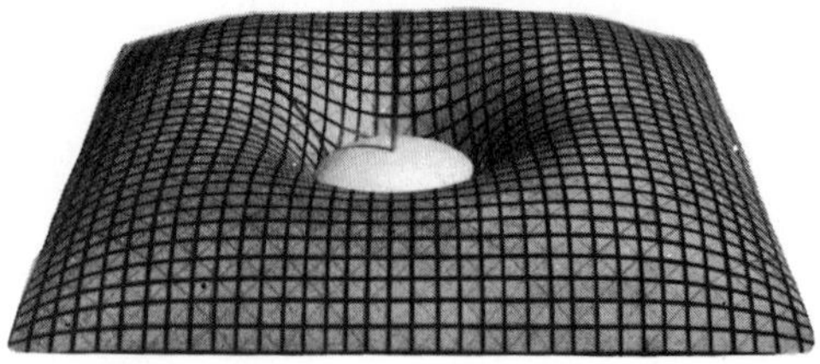
1

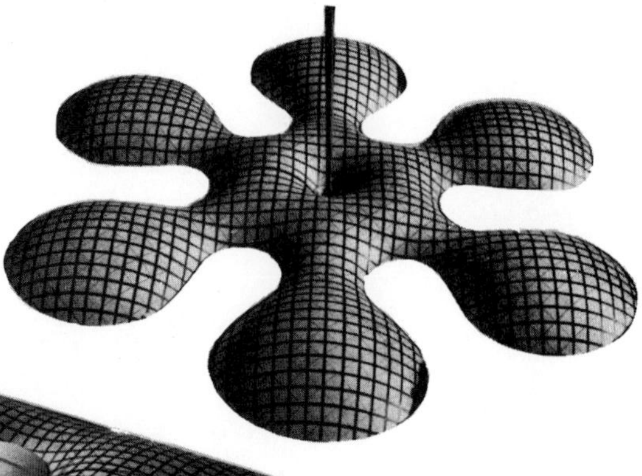
4

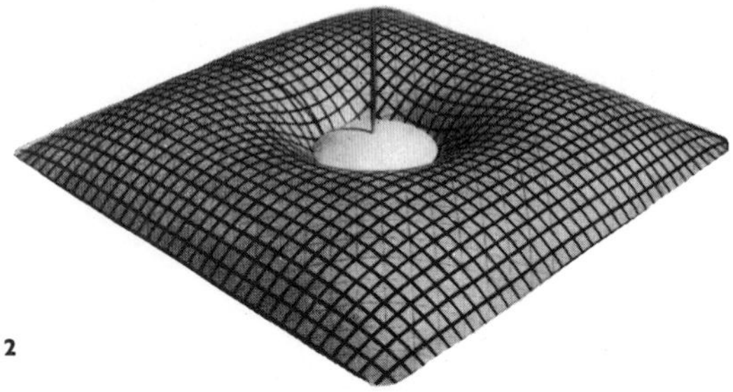
2

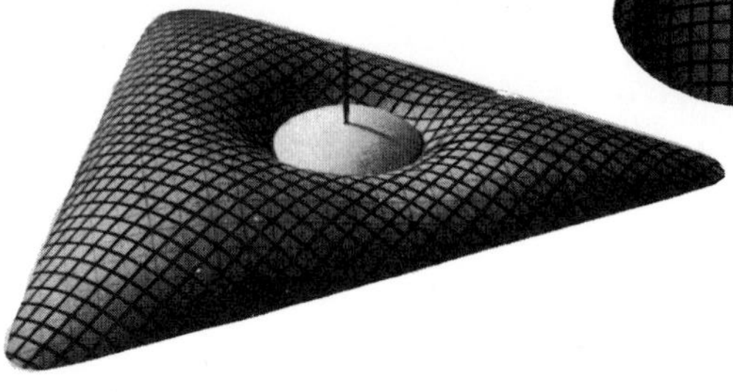
3

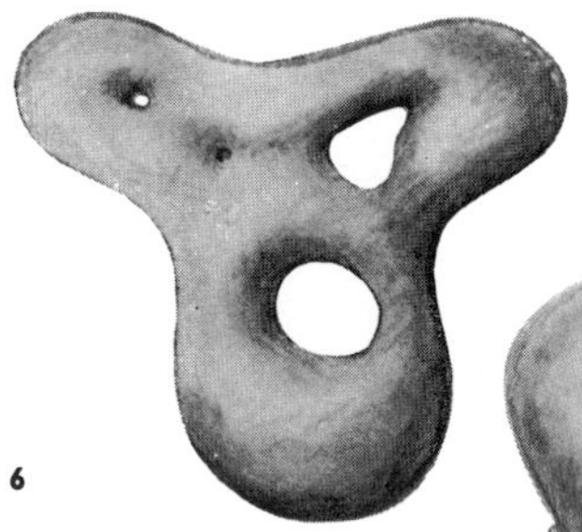
6

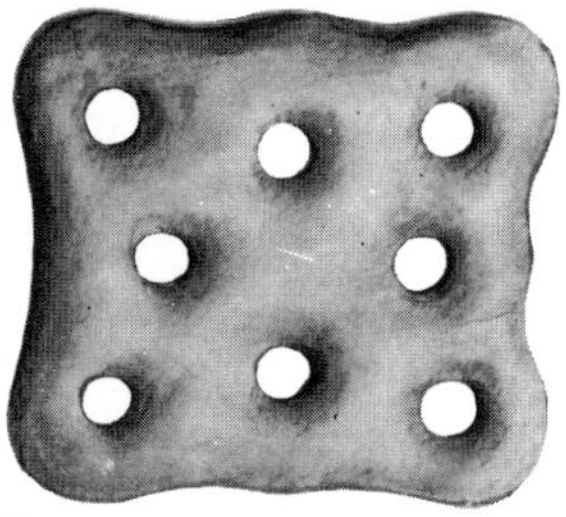
5

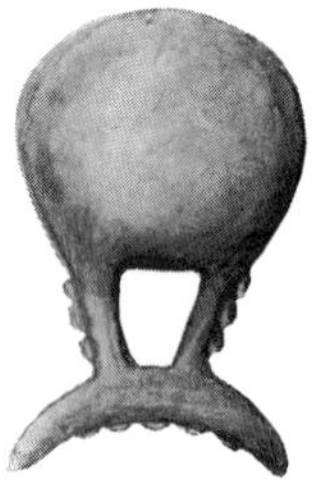
7

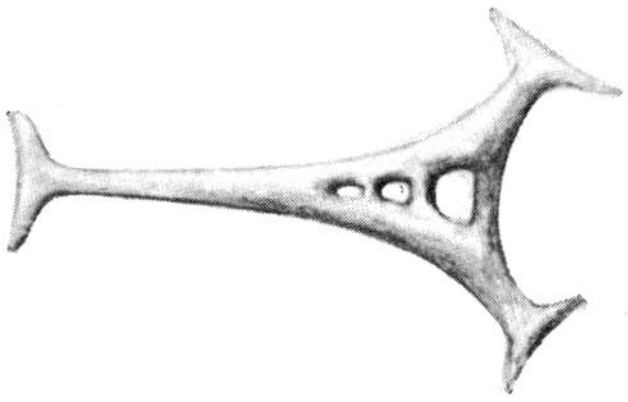
9

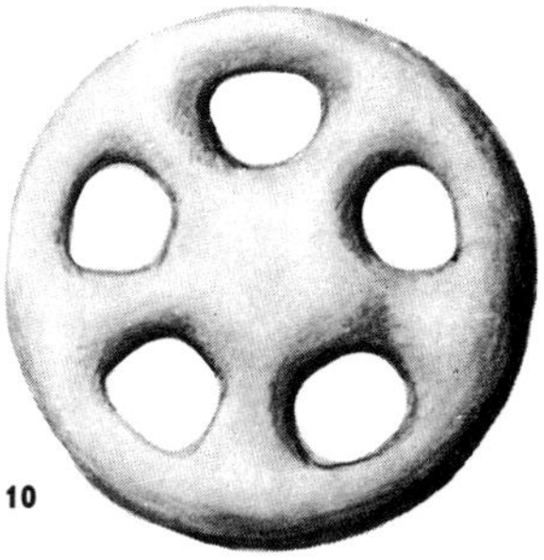
10

11

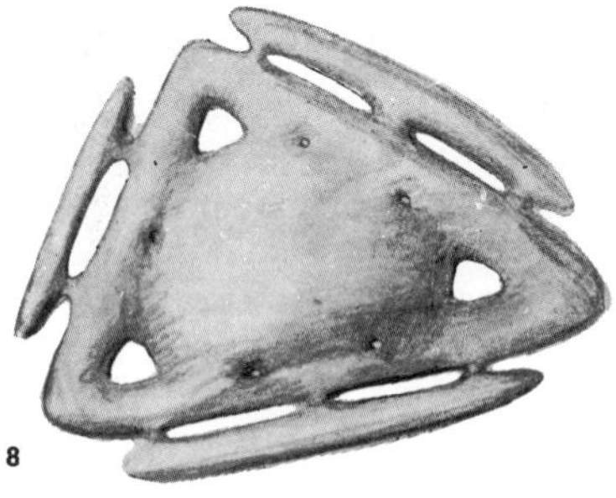
8

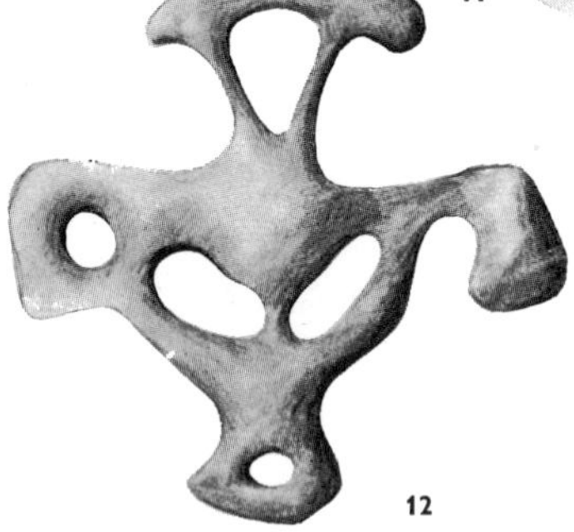
12

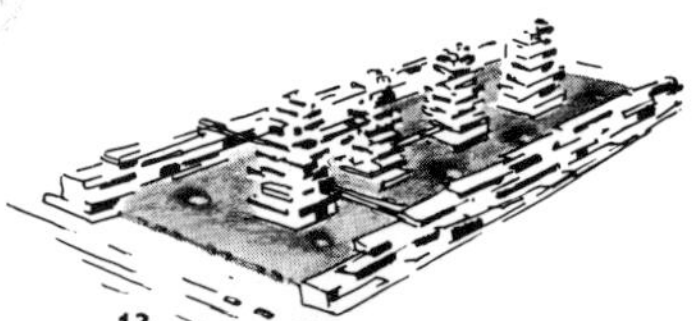
13

14

Pneumatically Tensed Membranes with Internal Drainage

Comparatively low structures are often required to roof very large areas. Shallow-arching pneumatically tensed membranes are generally subject to high tensions caused by the large radius of curvature. If it is possible to anchor the membrane, not merely at the edge, but also at one or several points in the center, the spans and radii of curvature are reduced with a consequent decrease of the membrane tensions. The resulting structures are highly economical. All pneumatic roof structures anchored at internal points or along internal closed lines require roof drainage, unless the overall slope of the membrane is greater than that of the funnel-shaped inclines created by the attachments. This design is therefore suitable without special drainage for vertical or steeply inclined walls. The experimental models (Figs. 1 and 2) show a rubber membrane spanning a square plan and held down at the center. In the immediate vicinity of the lowest point a saddle-shaped axisymmetrical surface is formed (as previously observed with the torus, see p. 88), which appears similarly also on a triangular plan (Fig. 3). Membranes on star-shaped plans (Fig. 4) have very small effective areas. This causes greater bulging of the membrane near the points of attachment.

15

16

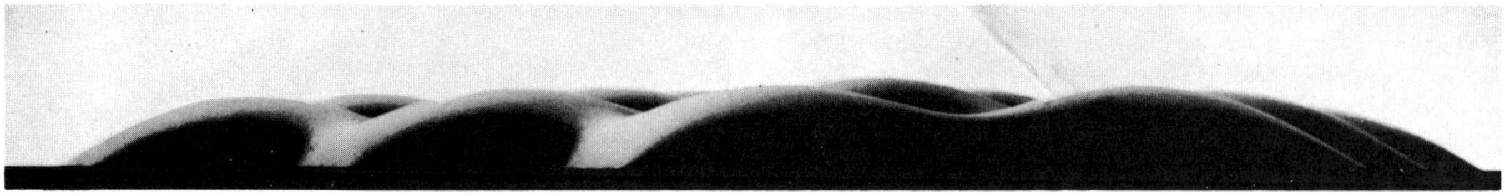

17 ▲

▼ 18

As a rule, the smaller the central supports, the greater are the membrane tensions. If the membranes are anchored over comparatively large central areas, enclosed internal courts result. This can be seen in the regularly shaped plan (Fig. 5) or in the roofing of a shopping street between fixed buildings (Figs. 13 and 14); in this case the membrane is anchored to the ground and drained at ten points. The pneumatically tensed membrane is attached to the buildings laterally. The transparent membrane covers greenery planted beneath it. Pneumatically tensed membranes are admirably suited for roofing traffic routes, especially pedestrian paths. Innumerable different forms with internal drainage are possible, be they wheel-shaped plans for factories (Fig. 10). or amoeba-shaped structures (Figs. 6 and 12) which might be required for exhibition areas that have old trees or buildings to contend with. Figure 7 shows the plan of a circus tent with wide entrances, internal cloakrooms and a shopping street. Figure 8 shows a large multi-purpose hall with low entrance halls and a large internal auditorium. Figure 9 shows the roofing of a shopping lane for pedestrians, and Fig. 11 the planting of greenery in courts enclosed by the membrane.

Tension-loaded pneumatic structures that are anchored at various points, are almost an inversion of shells that stand on columns, and are placed under compressive stress. The essential difference is that tensile loads appear at the points of support, but these loads can be taken up by ordinary cables or hoses. Since no buckling will occur, such structures can therefore be very long. Figures 15 to 18, p. 91, illustrate model studies for a design consisting of a pneumatically tensed membrane with internal drainage at the internal points of a hexagonal grid. The experimental model is a plaster impression made from a rubber membrane.

The resulting shape was rendered visible by means of parallel vertical shadow planes (Fig. 16, p. 91) which were subsequently photographed from various angles but with the camera always held vertically. This ensured an undistorted record of the cross sections.

The pronounced constrictions at the sixteen internal points and the gradual curvature of the membrane in the other regions can be recognized easily. In the hexagonal membrane structure all contour lines are curved, forming circles around the low points and around the apexes of the domes.

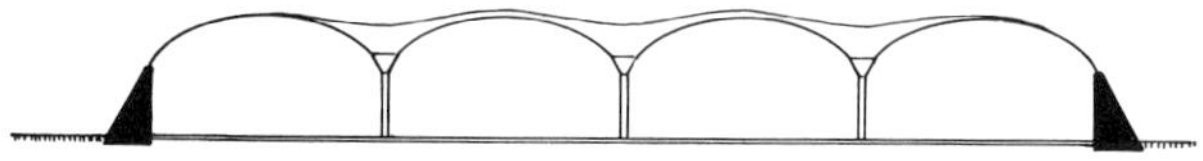

1

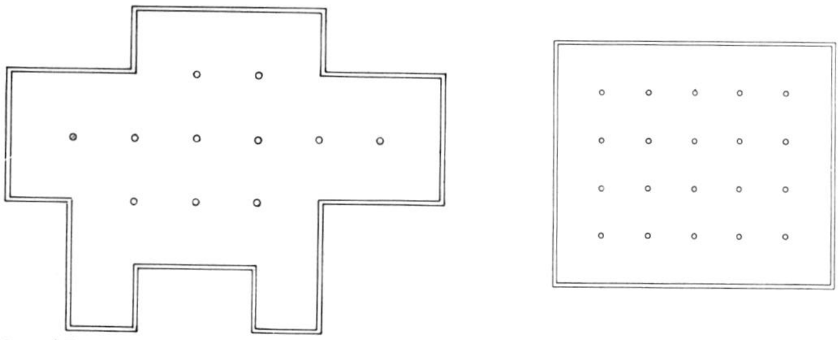

2 and 3

This unique type of roof construction, reminiscent of a snow or glacier landscape, can be seen on p. 91: in plan (Fig. 15), from the side, (Fig. 17) and obliquely from above, (Fig. 18).

A membrane roof spanning a square grid is very simple in design, as seen in cross section (Fig. 1) which shows a membrane with rigid lateral attachment and internal drainage. The boundaries of the membrane can be perfectly geometrical (Fig. 3), or they can follow the grid lines arbitrarily (Fig. 2).

The project in Figs. 4 to 8 shows a rectangular membrane anchored at twelve points in the foundation plane. The largest fixed bulges are of approximately equal height.

Such a shape assumes importance when the membrane must be reinforced to form a rigid shell resistant to compression and bending. Figure 4 shows part of the roof skin. The top view of the model (Fig. 5) brings out the plan. Sections through the plaster model are seen in Figs. 6 to 8: the left side of Fig. 6 shows the section through a high point; in Fig. 7 the section passes half-way between the high points, while in Fig. 8 it passes through two low points. The constrictions of the membrane are clearly visible.

4

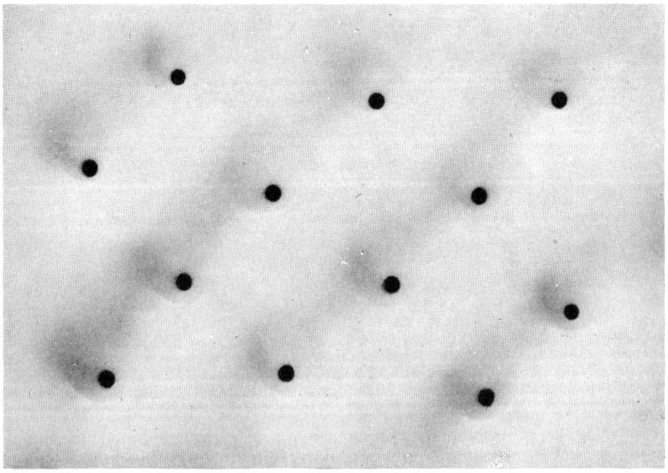

5 ▲

▼ 6 to 8

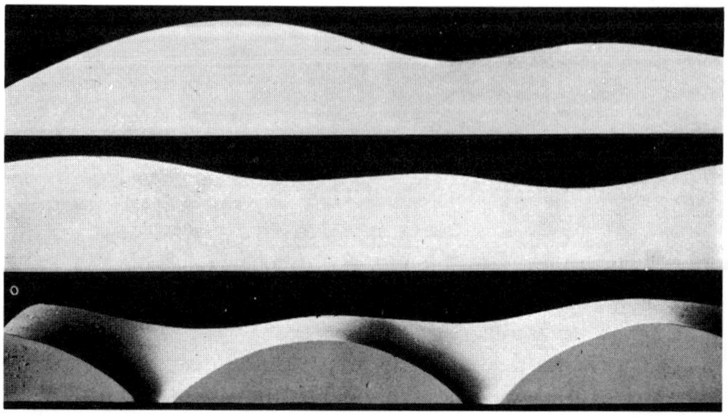

The design of the edges of the internal drain and of the foundation has a considerable bearing on the whole structure and on building costs.

Figure 9 is a section through a greenhouse set on sandy soil and covered by a transparent membrane with internal drainage. A membrane is also laid beneath the humus layer, and is positively connected with the roof membrane at the inner drainage points and along the outside edge. The humus layer thus forms a simple anchoring weight.

The floor membrane simultaneously permits moisture control of the soil. It has already been shown in Fig. 23 on p. 23 how floating fields can be created with inflated spheres.

The roofing of such cultivations by pneumatically tensed membranes with internal drainage is seen from the side in Fig. 10. A net of small open mesh floats on the water and carries the humus layer; it is supported both by inflated balloons and by the roof membrane

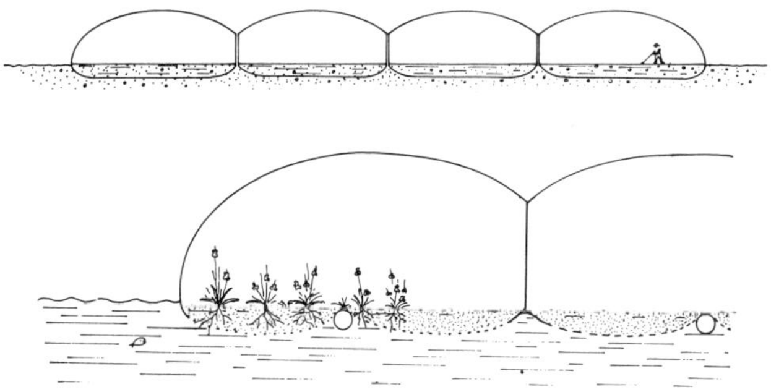

9 and **10**

itself which spans the floating fields and is immersed to a depth of approximately 15 cm at the edges.

Since soil and air temperatures of many greenhouses in moderate and northern climates must be maintained above the freezing point, roofed floating cultivations are economical from the point of heating. In particular, above deep waters which do not freeze, the interior temperature can be maintained at that of the deep water (which generally approximates the annual mean) by merely circulating the water without auxiliary heating, even when the outside temperature is very low.

In greenhouse and exhibition structures on firm ground, the roof and wall surfaces must often be separated because materials of different transparency and color are to be used, or because entrances, windows, or ventilation equipment are to be inserted. Figure 11 shows the system of a roof with an external frame that is anchored in the ground by cables. Both the wall membrane and the roof assume the shapes of curving domes. The roof is designed as a transparent membrane. At the central point of support it is attached to a rigid ring that is connected to a funnel and a drainage hose and

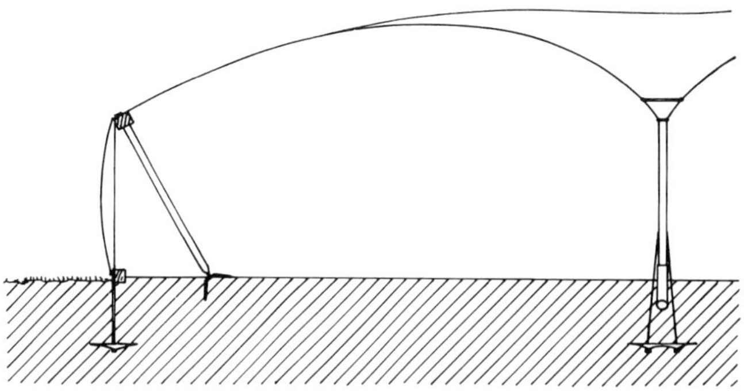

11

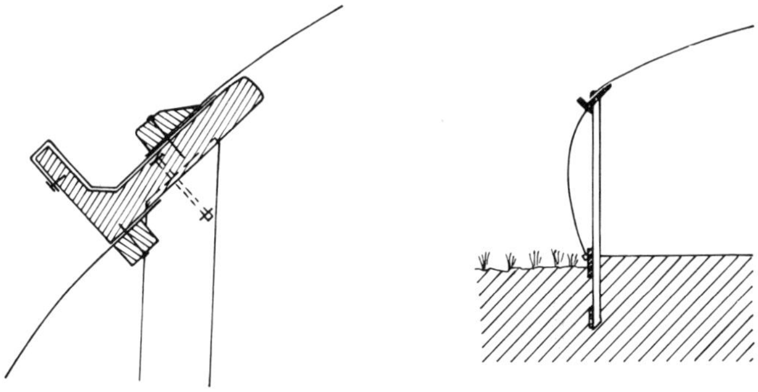

12 and **13**

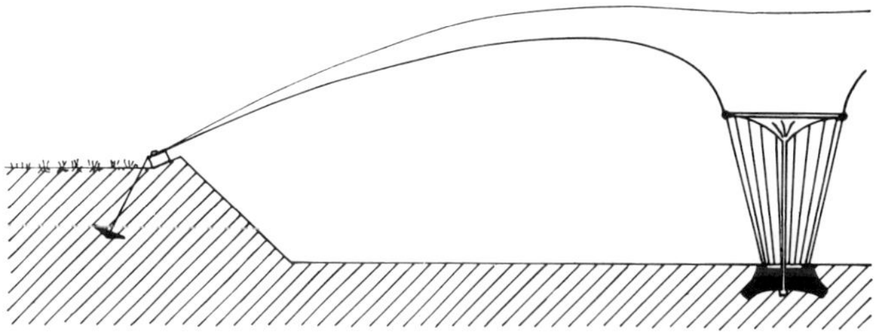

14

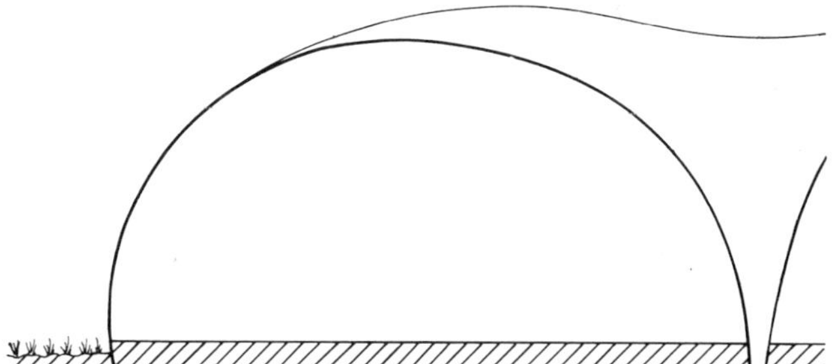

15

16 ▼

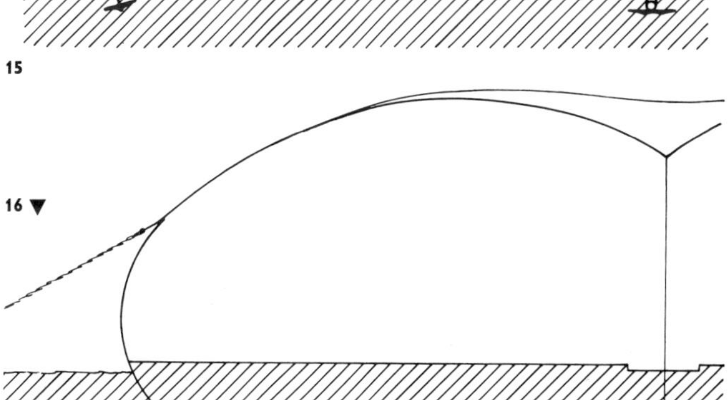

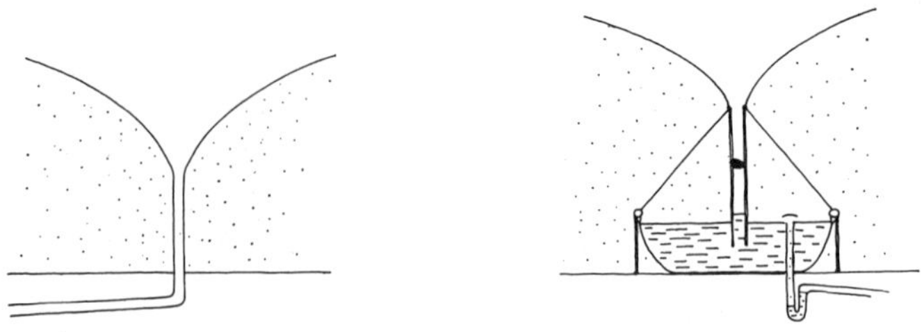

1 and 2

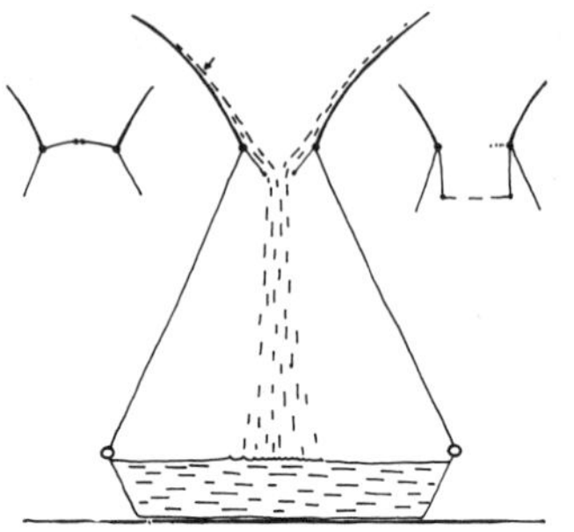

3 to 5

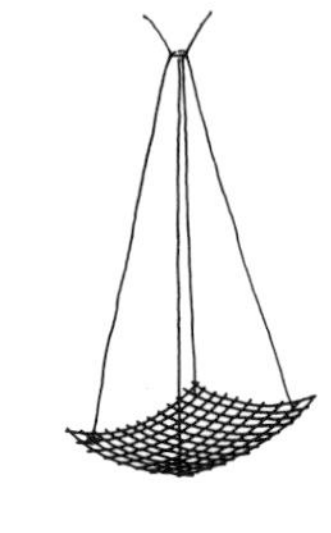

10

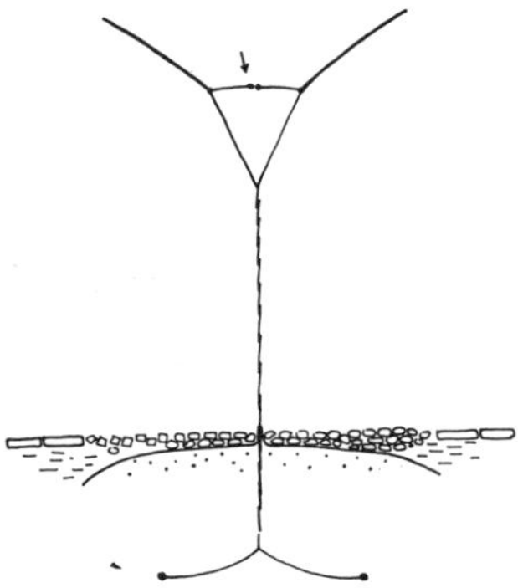

6

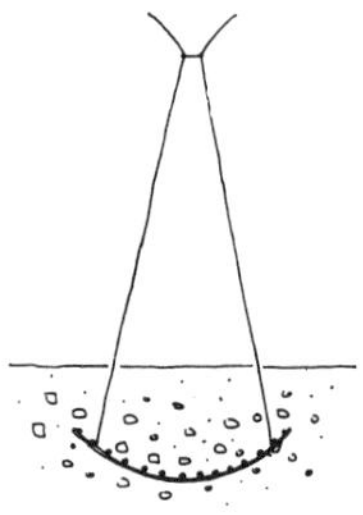

11

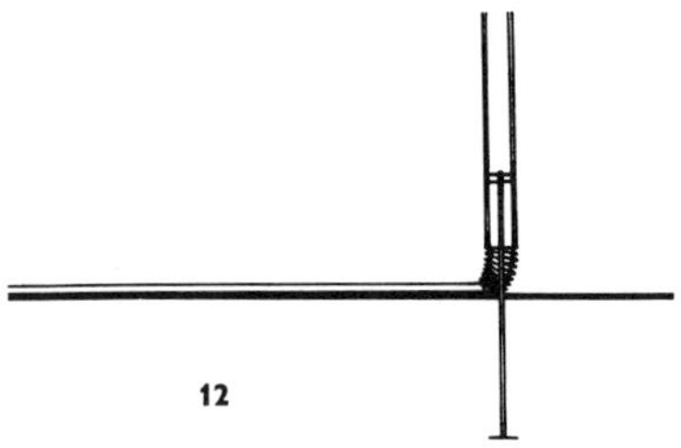

12

7 to 9 ▼

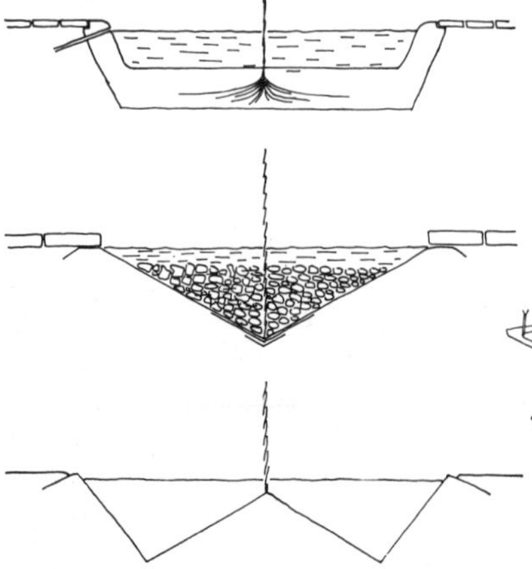

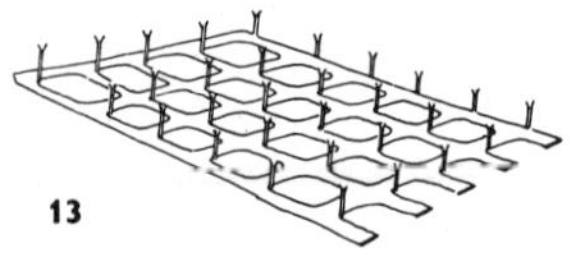

13

also transmits the forces to a tie rod anchored in the foundation. The drainage system is not affected by the internal pressure of the structure. Easy access to the drainage point is ensured through special openings at the funnel.

In small buildings with low spans the outer frame, especially when very low, can be made of a built-in steel or, more economically, wood construction (Figs. 12 and 13, p. 93) to which the roof and wall membranes are nailed. In nurseries "earth houses" rising slightly above ground level with a below-ground planting area are quite popular (Fig. 14, p. 93). In this example the roof membrane is nailed to a wooden rim and attached in the center to a tubular steel ring that is closed by a separate membrane. This ring is anchored with many thin cables to a tie rod in the ground, thus resembling a parachute. The ring transmits the anchor forces to the membrane over a considerable portion of its length. Consequently, membrane tensions are low. Rigid rims are not always necessary. The membrane can be attached to the foundations right at the edge and can form the drainage point at the center (Fig. 15, p. 93). Considerable spatial curvatures occur. Using guy ropes with special anchors (Fig. 16, p. 93), the tensions in the membrane roof can be maintained at a higher level than those in the lateral walls. This gives a flatter roof.

Figures 1 to 13 show various possibilities of internal drainage and their foundations. Usually rainwater flows directly into a conduit (Fig. 1) without contact with the interior. Figure 2 schematically depicts a design which can be used for transportable halls and greenhouses. The membrane is attached to a steel ring secured to a water tank by cables. The drainage pipe ends below water level and is thus unaffected by internal pressure. The container has an overflow and the usual U-shaped odor trap which also acts as a seal against internal pressure. The design in Figs. 3 to 5 is very similar, if the tubular steel ring is provided with a membrane closed by a rubber band which normally forms a hermetic seal at the internal drainage point (Fig. 3), but opens during rainfall due to the pressure of the liquid and discharges the water into a tank (Fig. 4), or into an internal drain. The inner membrane is a cylindrical skin (Fig. 5). It can be opened fully and collapses into folds when closed. Fairly large amounts of snow can be carried without overloading. A particularly simple design of this type with a separate valve membrane (arrow) is seen in Fig. 6. Rainwater runs down the cable into

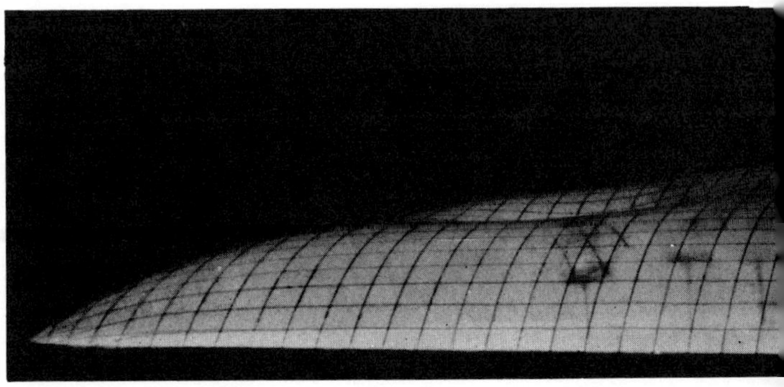

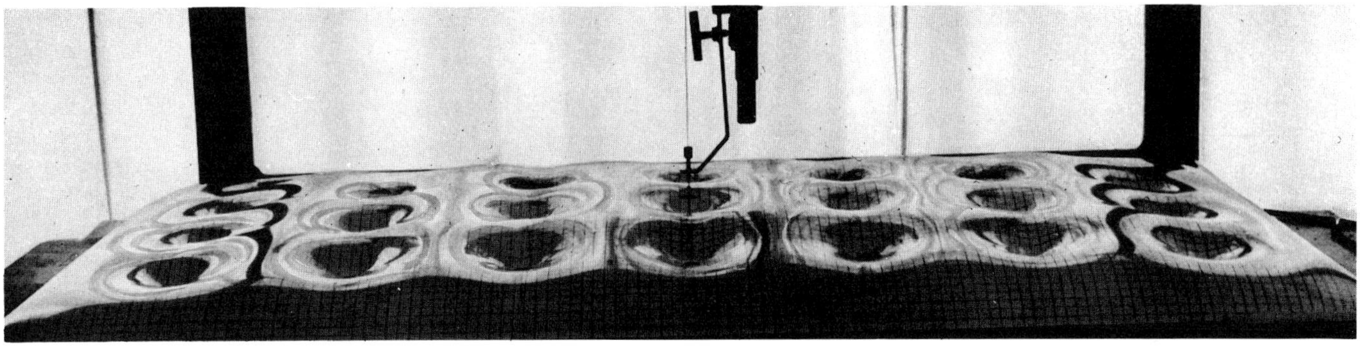

14

a gravel-covered seepage layer. The cable is anchored to a base membrane that is stretched on a compression ring and buried. The foundation in Fig. 7 shows a cable whose separate strands are directly anchored in a water-filled concrete tank; in Figs. 8 and 9 the cable is anchored to gravel-filled sheet-metal funnels which receive the rainwater and have run-offs. A simple method is to attach the anchor cables to ordinary corrosion-proof reinforcement mats of structural steel that are buried in the soil and loaded with gravel (Figs. 10 and 11). A special technique* was developed in 1958 for mobile exhibition halls which must be erected on different area roofings and is independent of the configuration of the enclosed terrain; the tie rods can be sunk into any type of soil, or even under water without the slightest difficulty. The span between drainage points determines the forces in the membrane. In membrane roofs for greenhouses 7 to 15 m spans are practical, while for heavy fabrics, 15 to 40 m and for membranes with reinforcing cable nets 60 m spans are preferable. Spans of 100 to 500 m are economically possible, and spans of several kilometers are technically possible.

For the economical erection of such roofs it is preferable to join

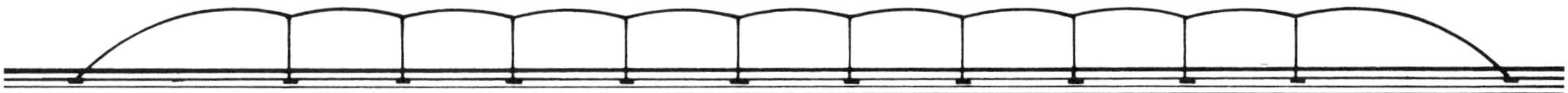

15 ▲

▼ 16

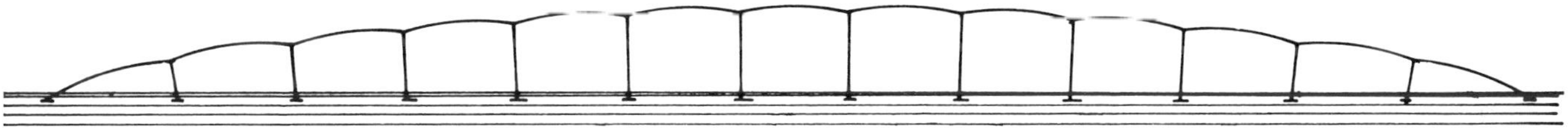

sites. The drainage pipes are directly connected to the tie rods (Fig. 12), but the pipes drain into a two-layered floor (Fig. 13) which is made of fairly thick plastic foil welded at the edges, the upper foil being covered with tough carpeting. The capacity of such a drainage system is considerable. A swelling of the carpet can scarcely be noted even in heavy rain.

The section through a roof with internal drainage at uniform spacings is shown in Fig. 15. Such a structure can be extended at will at a uniform average height. It is one of the most economical large-uniform sections. The edges will generally require special elements which can also be standardized. The system shown in Fig. 16 avoids special edge elements. The membrane is directly anchored to the foundations. The following experiments on a model of a large greenhouse correspond approximately to this sectional form. A large, rectangular roof is divided into squares and provided with 28 internal drainage points (Fig. 14).

The side views (Fig. 17, p. 95 and Figs. 1 and 10, p. 96) show that the resulting structure is so shallow that it is very hard to photo-

▼ 17

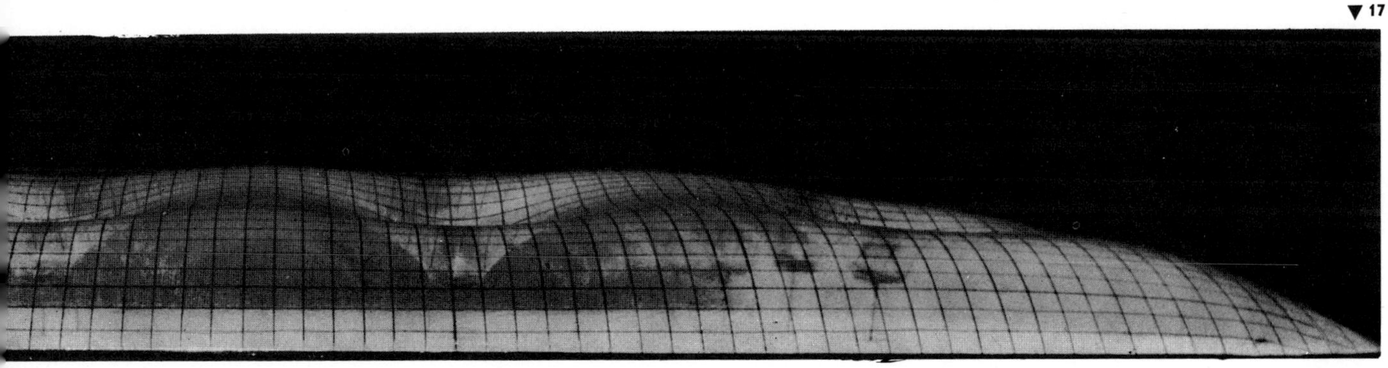

1

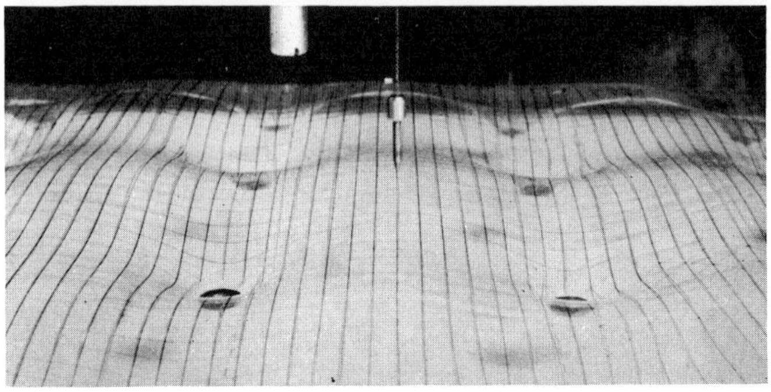

2

graph. Hardly any other structural form provides halls of similar transparent delicacy (Fig. 3). The anchor cables in this design are sheathed with a tight elastic rubber hose which can expand under the pressure of rainwater.

Several experimental models gave a comparatively accurate idea of the shape of the pneumatically tensed membrane and of its features.

In Figures 2 and 7 of the experiment the sectional shapes have been rendered visible by means of drawn lines. Since the lines marked on

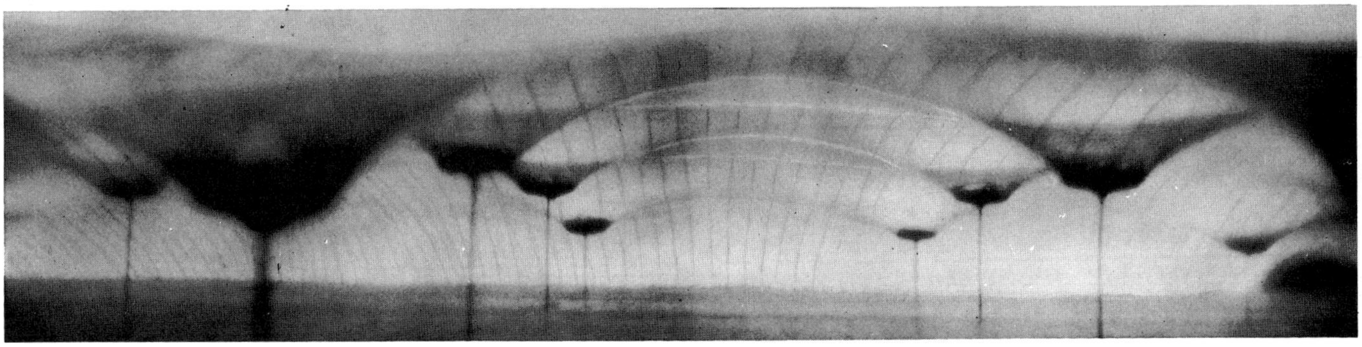

3

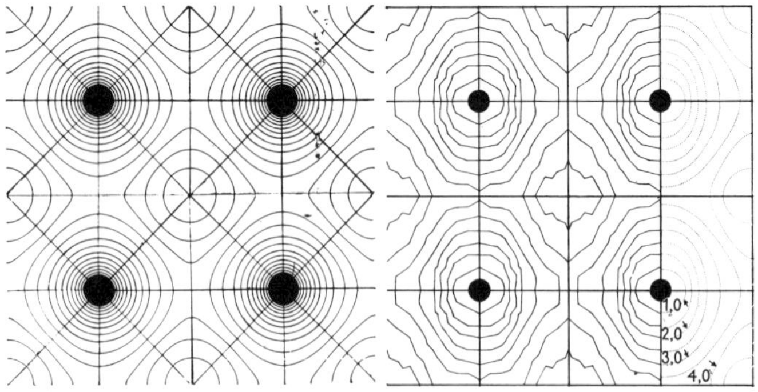

4 and 5

▼ 6

the initially flat membrane stretched over the base plate have moved upward almost exclusively along vertical planes, the slopes of the membrane indicate the tensions. The contour lines (Fig. 6) at the center of the model were established by a plumb line (Fig. 2) suspended from a flat ground marble plate used as a reference plane.

Figure 4 shows the contour lines in a membrane of uniform average height. The contour lines in the immediate neighborhood of the lowest and highest points are circles. Measurement of the indenta-

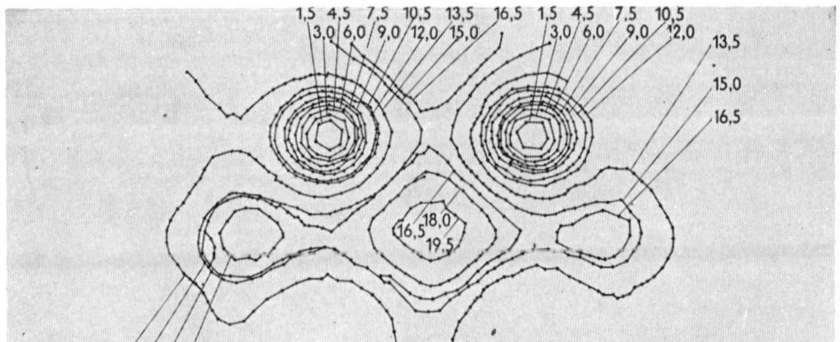

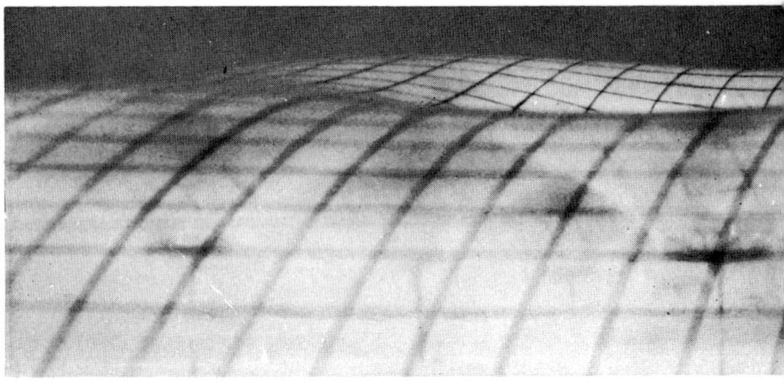

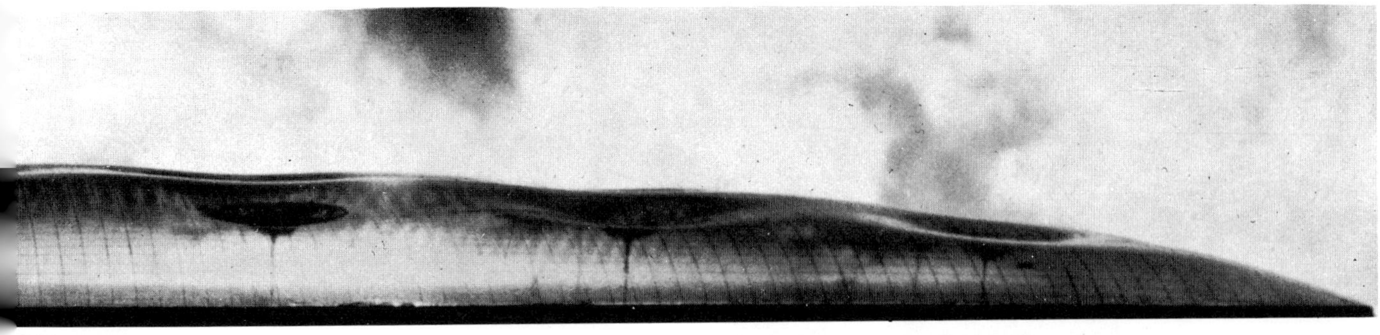

7 ▼

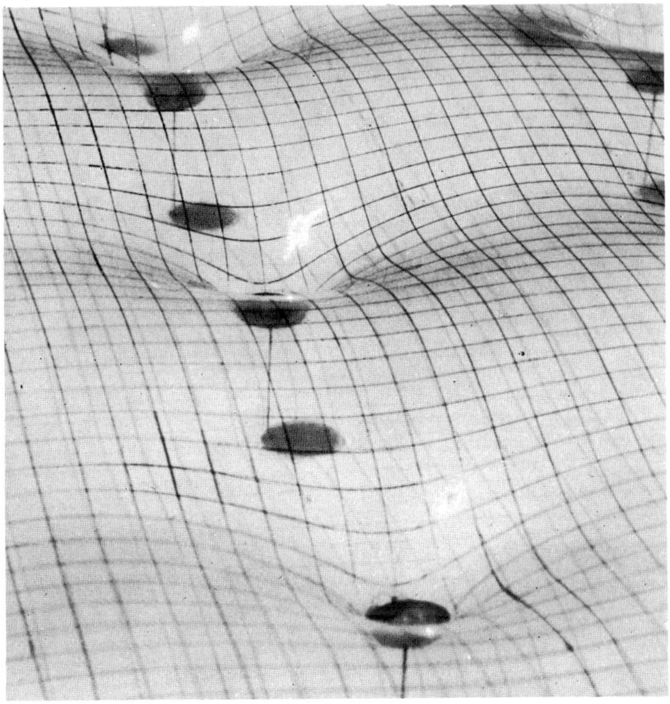

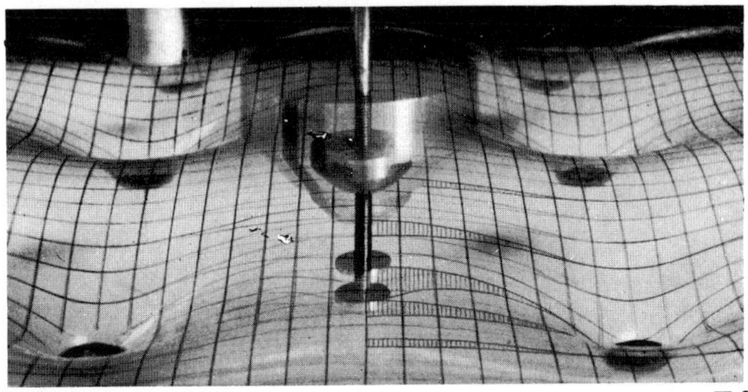

8 ▲

▼ 9

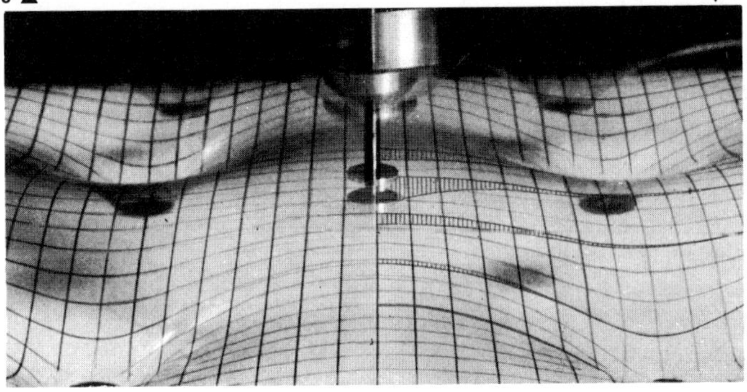

tion under a concentrated load was especially interesting. At a constant internal pressure the model was subjected to a load of 150 g acting on a disk $100\,mm^2$ in area. Internal pressure was maintained at 100 mm of water column. The distances between the lowest points were 80 mm. The indentation depths at the center of measured points are given in millimeters in Fig. 5. The lines of equal indentation depth were drawn starting from this region. The lines of equal deformation tendency corresponded approximately to the contour lines.

Figures 8 and 9 show the measuring of the indentation depth (a load of 150 g on a $100\,mm^2$ disk) as photographed in each phase and recorded in the loaded and unloaded states, using double exposures. The upper of the two double lines corresponds to the unloaded and the lower to the loaded state. Under constant internal pressure lowering of the membrane was observed everywhere with no bulging. To mark the displacements several grid lines to the right of the load points were drawn out thickly and their areas of displacement cross-hatched vertically.

▼ 10

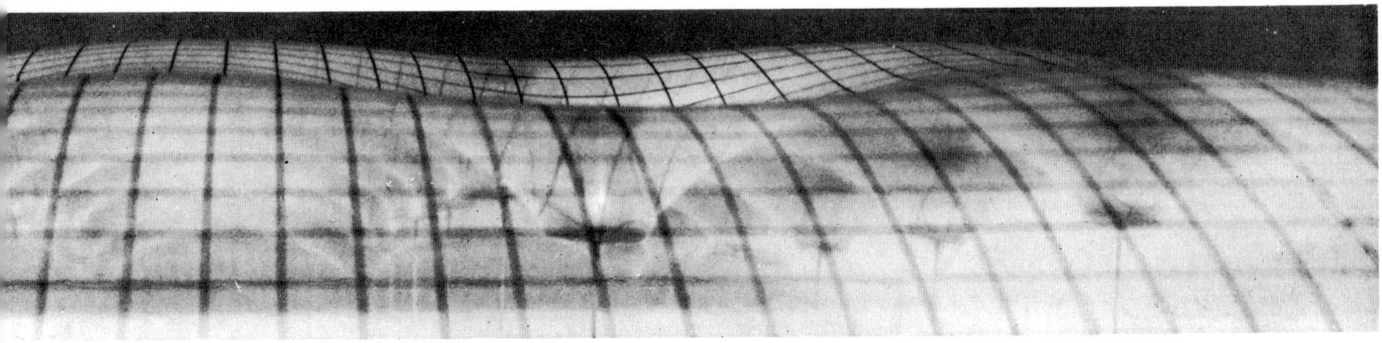

7

1

The possible variations in the shape of pneumatically tensed membranes that have internal drainage, are considerable. This is illustrated by the adjacent sectional views. In Figure 2 the membrane encloses an inner court on the left, rising toward the right where it is held at its deepest point by a cable. The section through a central structure (Fig. 3) shows a domed membrane which is being pressed down at the edge by the internal drainage so that a passage is created around the central dome. In the section through the asymmetrical space envelope (Fig. 4), varying interiors are created by the different distances between drainage points. The section in Fig. 7 shows a fairly high membrane with pronounced spatial curvature. Drainage is no longer vertical. In the sections through the edge and one internal point of a large auditorium (Fig. 9), the membrane hose opens at a low point near the floor and encloses a directly ventilated inner court which is accessible through air locks.

In the section through an exhibition hall (Fig. 5), drainage is not accomplished vertically but follows the cable line, ending at the edge of the hall. The advantage of low membrane spans is exploited without interrupting the free span of the hall. A similar design of a very high and extensive roof is shown in cross section (Fig. 8) in which the drainage points are combined in pairs.

Addiss, Kniffin, and Childs, of the Yale School of Architecture designed, under the supervision of the author, a project for a multi-purpose structure which was intended to serve as an exhibition and convention hall in Chicago. It was to be erected over the shal-

2

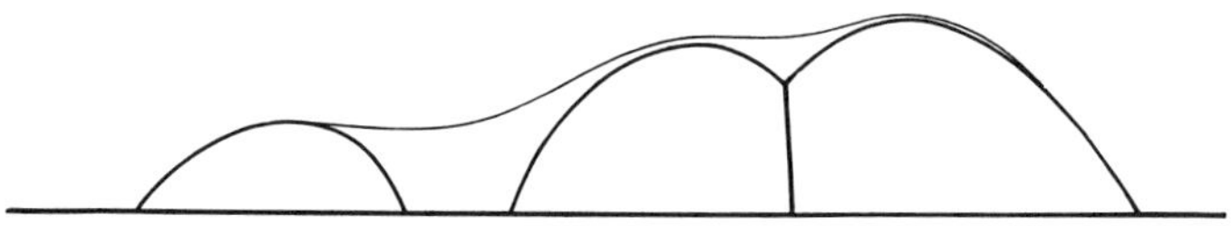

3

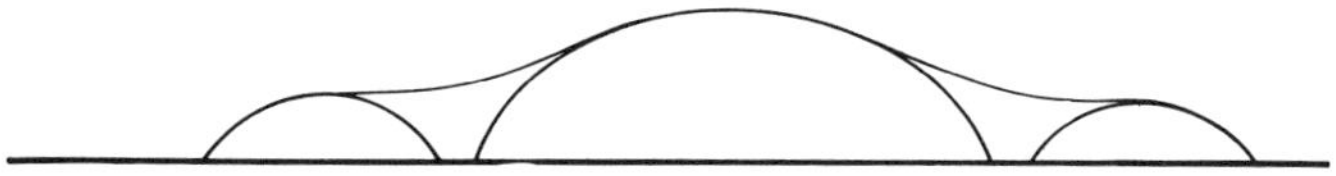

4

5

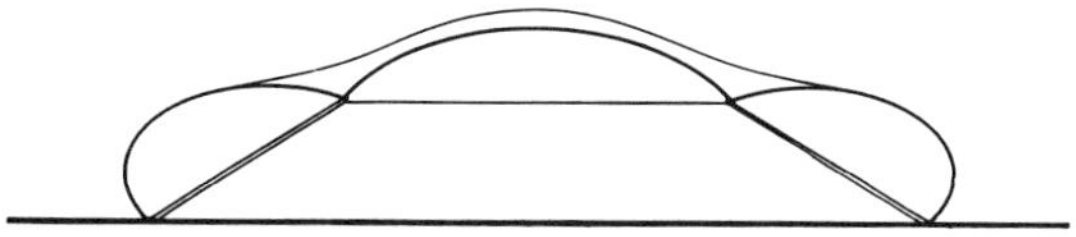

6 ▼

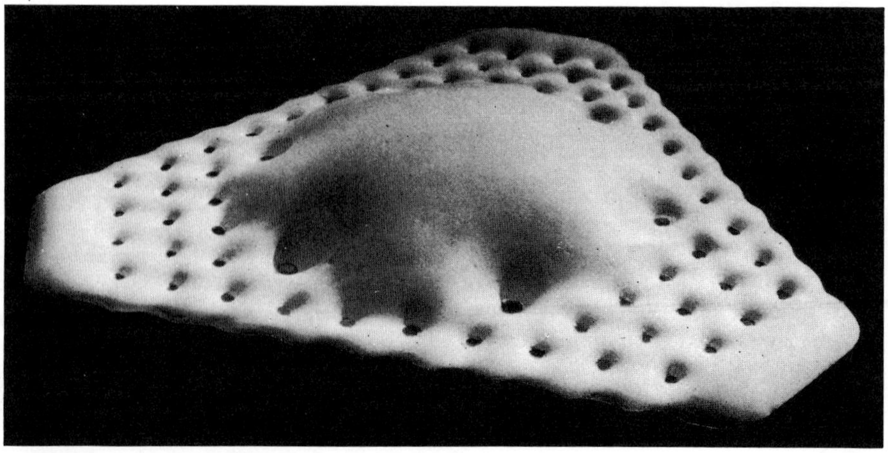

low waters of Lake Michigan near the Navy Pier, i.e., directly in the center of the town. A hexagonal, pneumatically tensed membrane with maximum side length of 300 m rises above a flat, packed foundation. The membrane roofs small chambers along the edge, where it is held low by many internal drainage points; the center is a large hall with a span of over 200 m (Fig. 6). The resulting shape was thoroughly investigated on a model. Since the large central span induces considerable tensions, the membrane was doubled and tripled toward the center, as shown in Fig. 10. The side views in Figs. 1 and 11 show the gently curving shape of this structure which was intended to form a foreground to the city, in the lake. The central dome is not a "cap," since it is undulating at the edge due to the large internal drainage points. This is an advantage acoustically. The roof of the large dome is of fabric reinforced with coated steel wire netting. A second membrane is suspended 2 to 4 m underneath in order to allow heating and cooling in the manner shown in Fig. 7 on p. 108. The interspace is accessible, and provides storage for lighting and sound equipment.

Membrane tensions increase considerably toward the internal drainage points. It is necessary to reinforce the membrane at these points and this is done best with cables. If, for example, the roof is formed by a cable net of square mesh as shown in Fig. 2 on p. 100, radial cable nets, which permit concentration of their strength at the lowest points, can be introduced without difficulty.

Since square and hexagonal nets can become

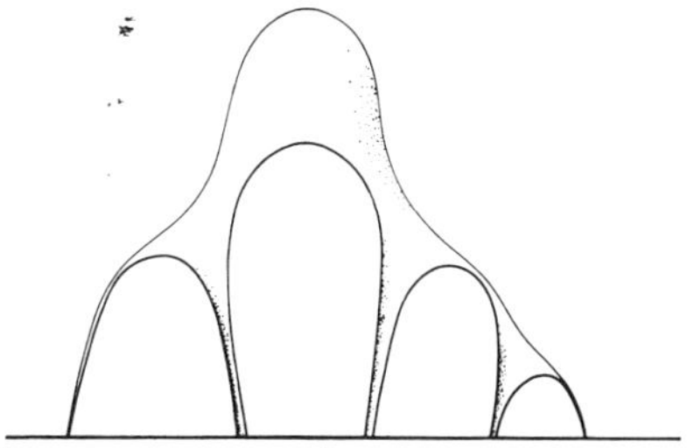

7

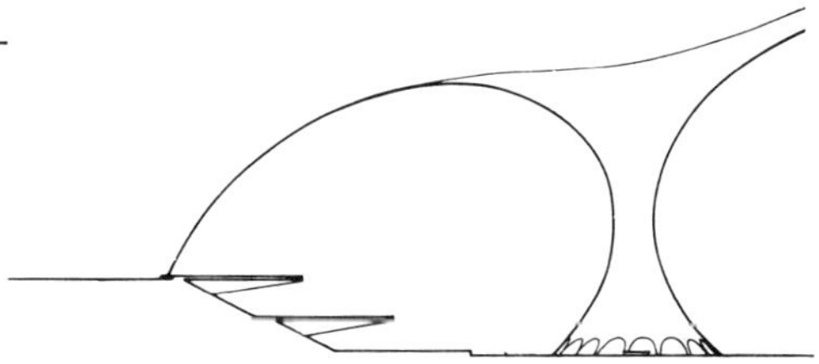

9

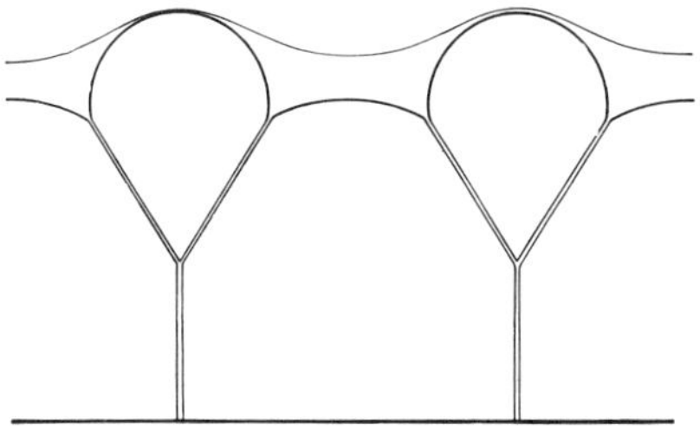

8

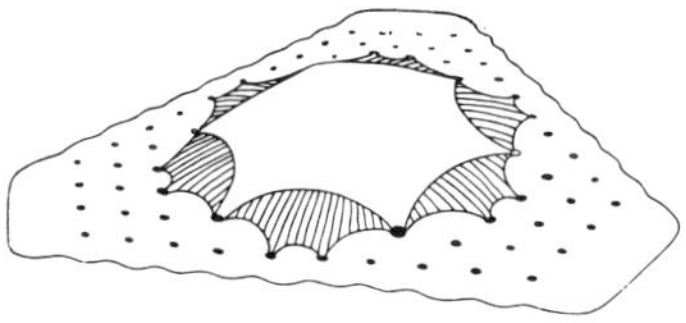

10

▼ 11

spatially curved also at constant mesh sizes, nets prefabricated in quantity can be used in the actual roof area. These nets could be closed by membranes.

In the project for a convention hall, Fig. 1 shows the internal view, Fig. 3 the roof plan, and Fig. 4 a side view of a deep point. The roof membrane is made of coated heavy fabric with good heat insulation properties.

The internal drainage points are formed by a radial cable net with a transparent lining.

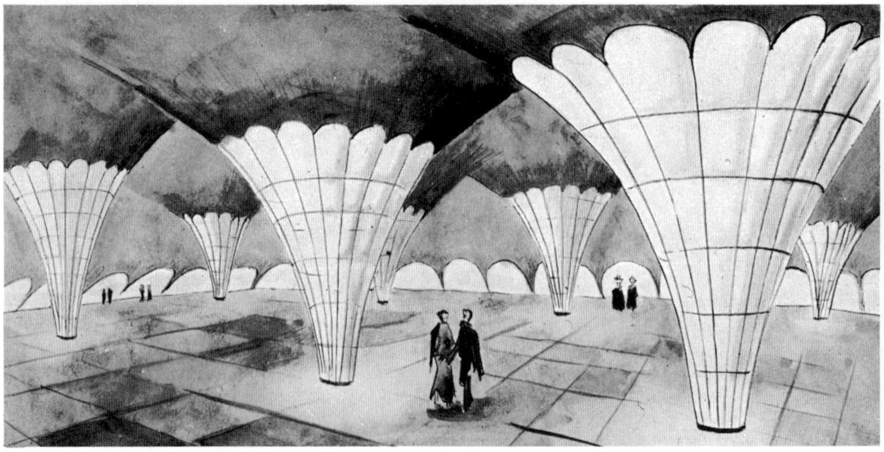

1

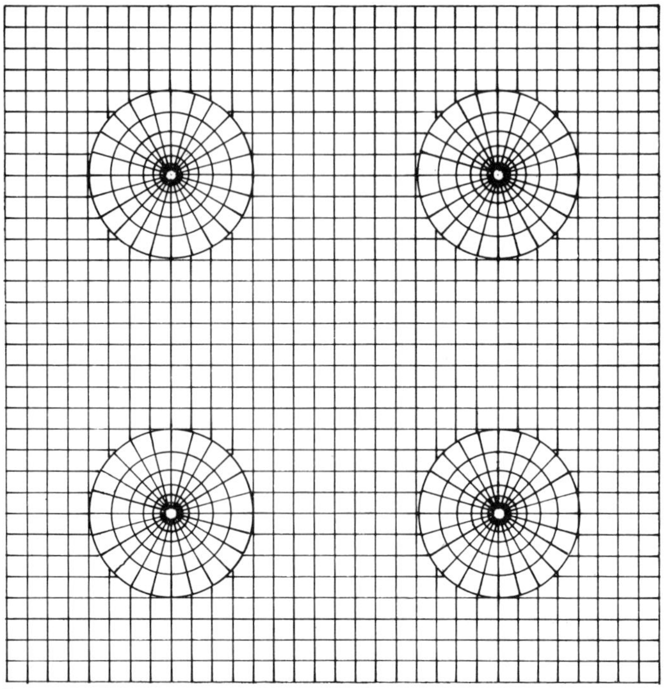

2

3

The cables of the radial net transmit the forces to the roof membrane via an annular cable.

The interior is illuminated through the transparent lining at the drainage points. It has already been stated that reinforcing the roof with cable nets gives a faceted appearance to the surface, as shown in section (Fig. 5) of one part of the large roof expanse (Fig. 6).

Large spans for pneumatic structures are best realized with the use of supporting cable nets.

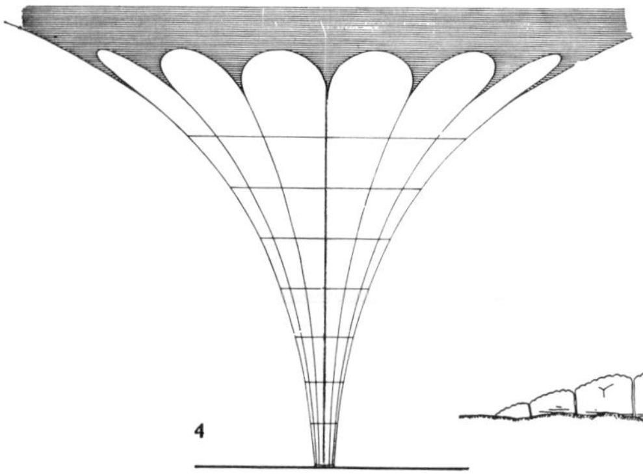

4

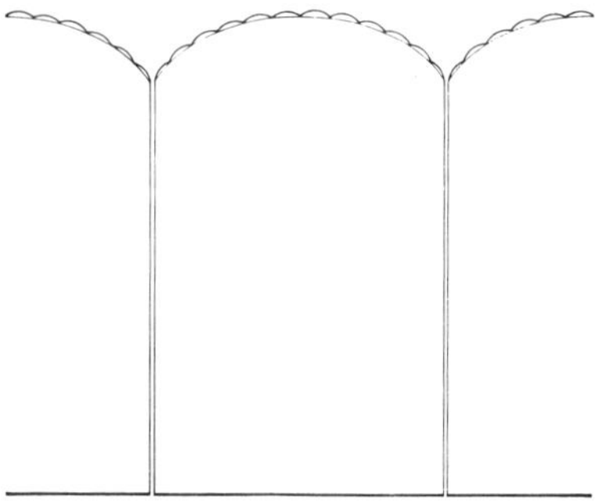

5

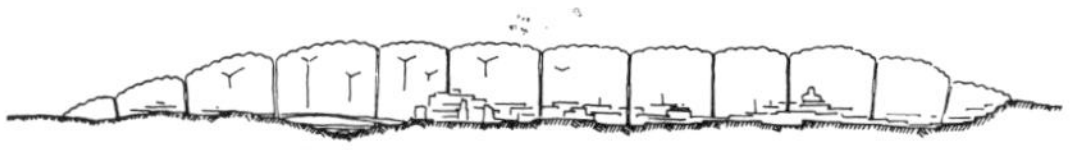

6

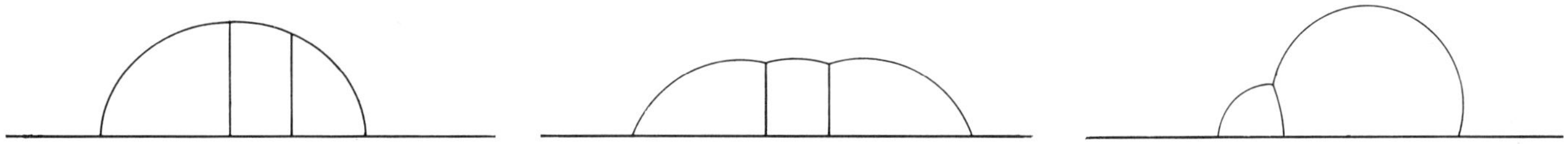

7 to **9**

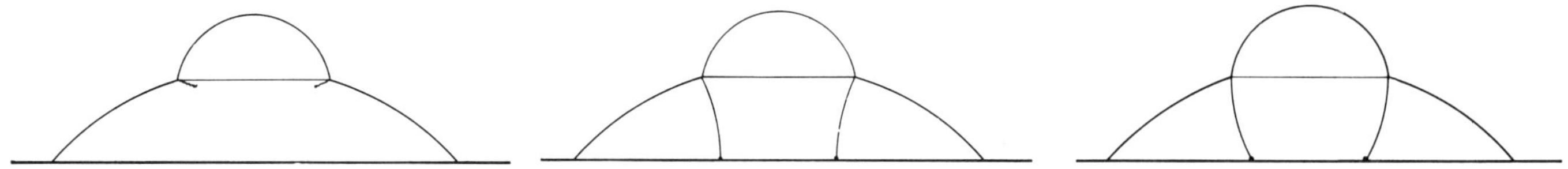

10 to **12**

Pneumatic Structures with Interior Partitions

If partitions are suspended from a pneumatically tensed membrane (Fig. 7), they hang down because of their own weight and deform the membrane only slightly. When anchored to the ground and tensed (Fig. 8), they become part of the pneumatic structure. If the air pressure on both sides of the structure is equal, plane, simply curved, or doubly curved, saddle-shaped surfaces form. If the air pressures differ, e.g., as in Fig. 9, the partition assumes a hemispherical shape. Partitions may be required for many reasons, e.g., to obtain variable subdivisions, to influence the distribution of forces acting on the roof membrane, and to regulate the drainage. Figures 10 to 12 show a movable partition closing off the interior of a pneumatically tensed dome. The partition is kept folded on an annular cable near the roof and can be lowered. When the pressures inside and outside the partition are equal, a smoothly stretched skin is obtained when the membrane is attached to the foundations and ballasted with a weight or a water-filled hose. If the interior has to be at a higher pressure, a spherically bulging partition is suitable (Fig. 12).

When two pneumatically tensed spherical membranes connected by a bracing cable must be provided with a partition at their juncture (Fig. 13), an initially flat membrane can be used. When the pressures differ in the two parts of the structure the membrane will tend to curve toward the part at lower pressure.

Resilient connections between the individual membrane parts permit bulging through controlled surface expansion. The membrane must be divided at one or at several places so that it can be raised to the roof (Fig. 14). The partition (Fig. 15) is designed as a spherical membrane whose curvature is continuous with that of one of the two roof membranes. It is thus possible (Fig. 16) to release entirely the pressure beneath one of the two roof domes.

When the pressure is equal in both parts of the structure the partition assumes a saddle shape. A hemispherical partition can be drawn up to the roof valley in one piece, as shown in Fig. 18. Such a partition can be inverted and can be attached at two base lines.

If, for example, a flat membrane is inserted as a partition between two spherical segments under the same internal pressure,

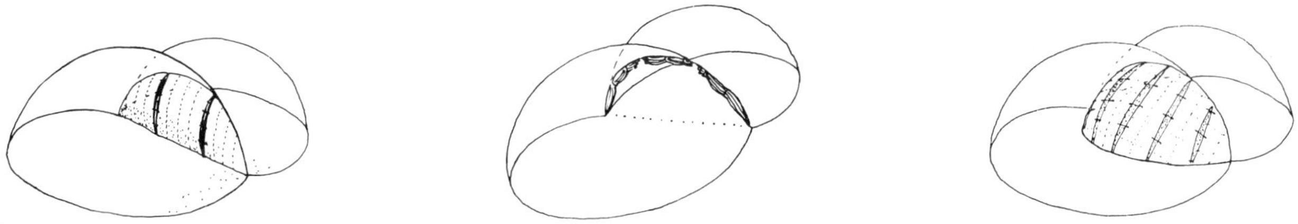

13 to **15**

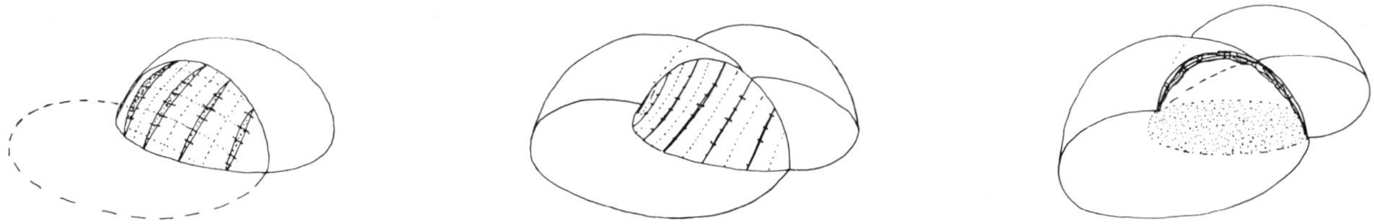

16 to **18**

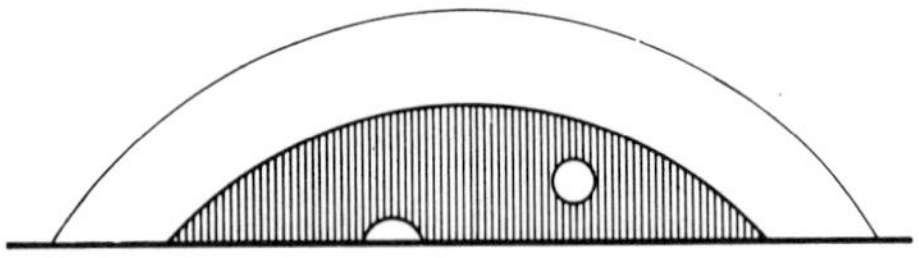

1

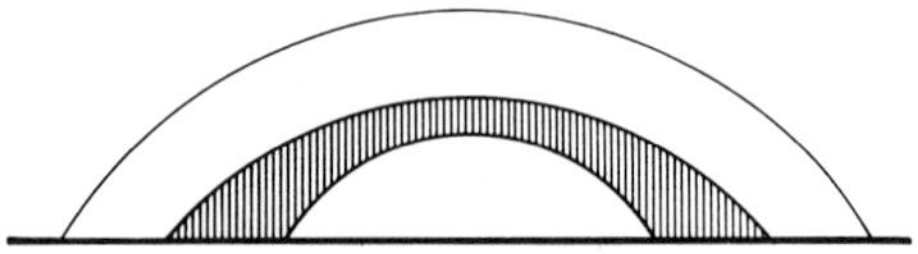

2

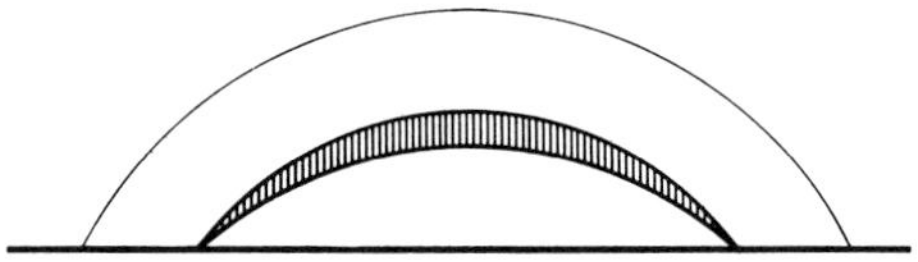

3

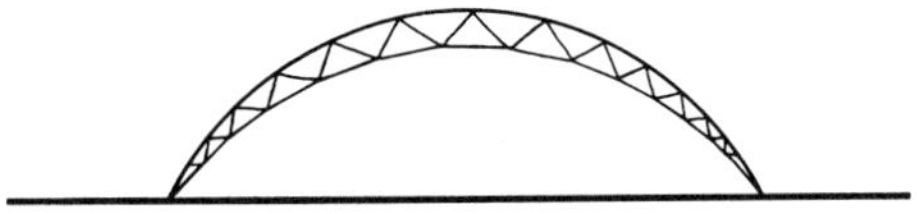

4

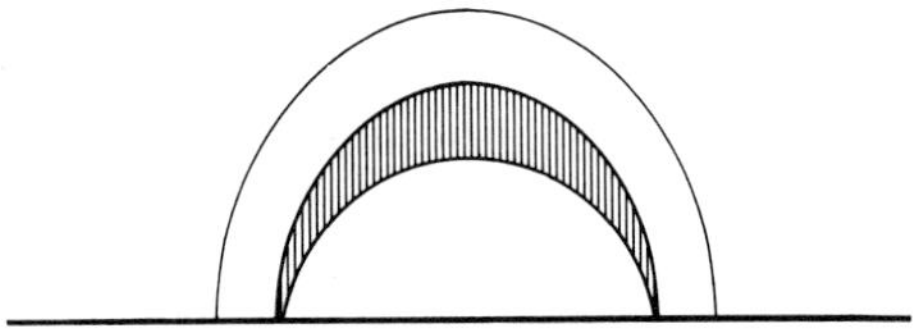

5

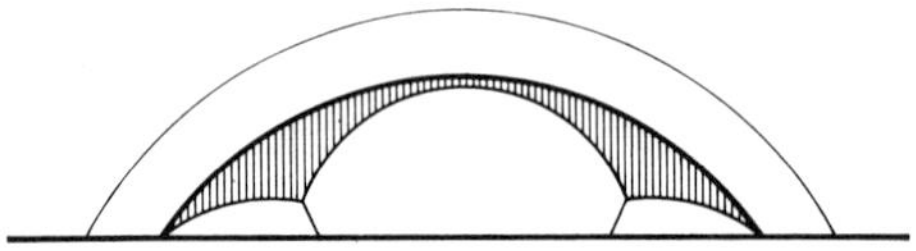

6

7 ▼

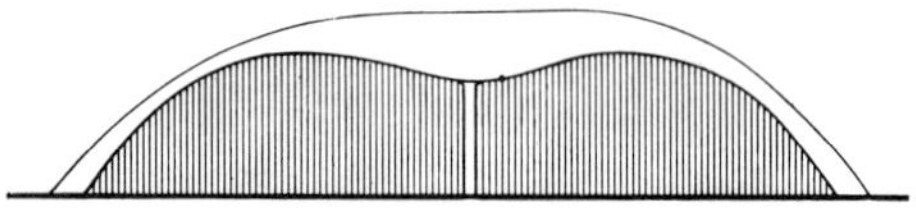

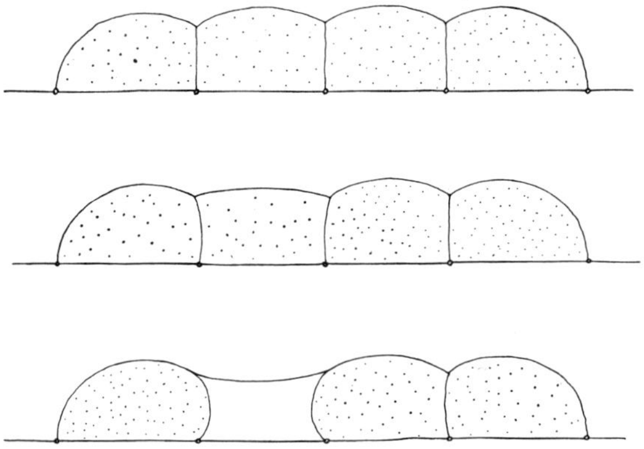

9 to 11

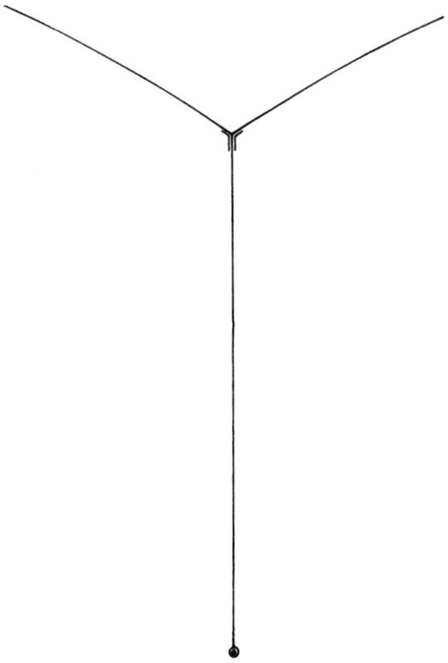

8

openings can be cut (Fig. 1) which must be bordered by cables. If the tensions in a membrane are equal in all directions, such windows or doors are circular. If the tensions differ, the boundary lines are elliptical.

In Figure 2 the entrance has been considerably widened and in Fig. 3 it has the same width as the ground plan, and the partition has been reduced to a minimum. A partition may be replaced by cables (Fig. 4) forming a lattice framework. A partition increases the rigidity of the pneumatic structure. This is of advantage with side winds and is often necessary in tall buildings (Fig. 5). Considerable forces can occur at the valley line of the juncture between two domes. A partition below the valley can take up these forces. If the partition is bordered

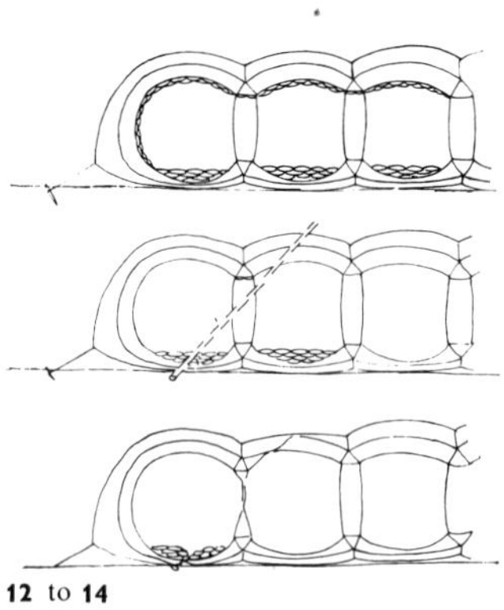

12 to 14

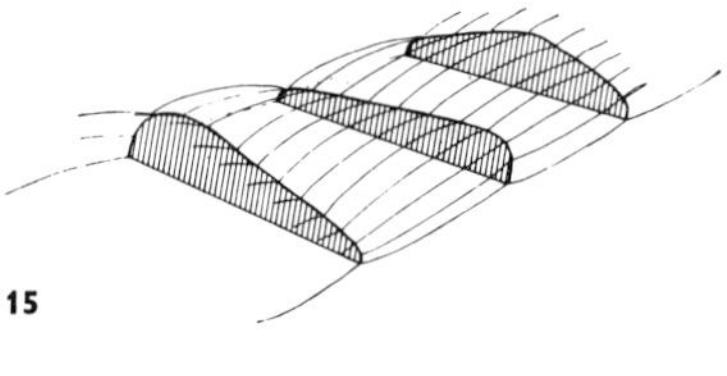

15

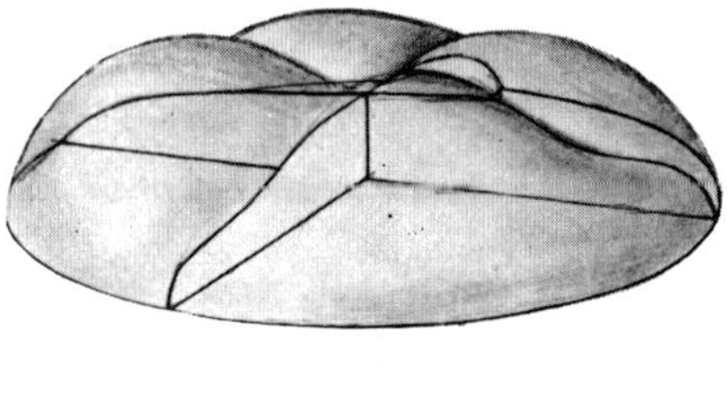

16

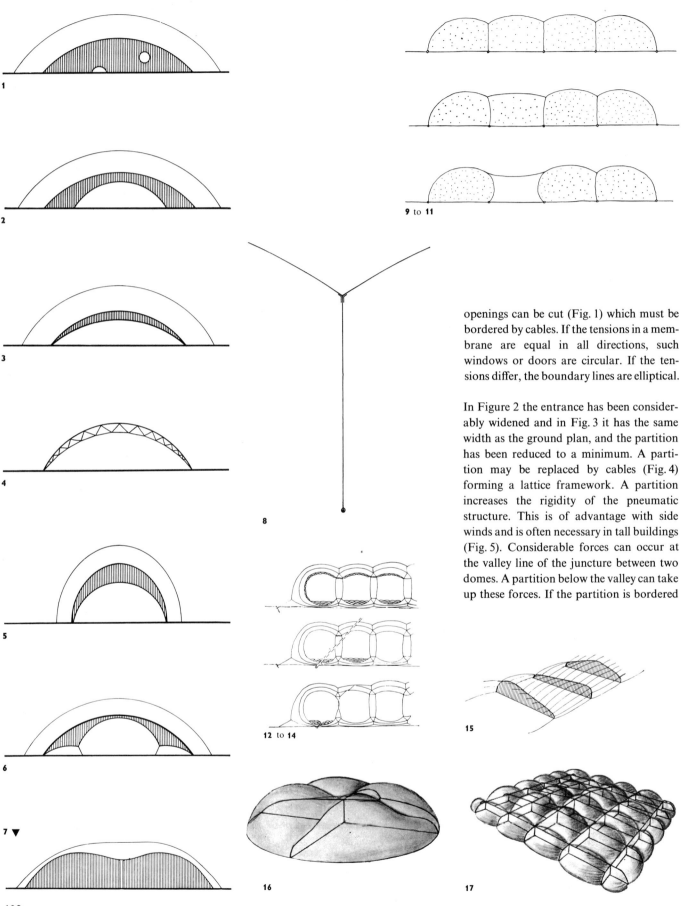

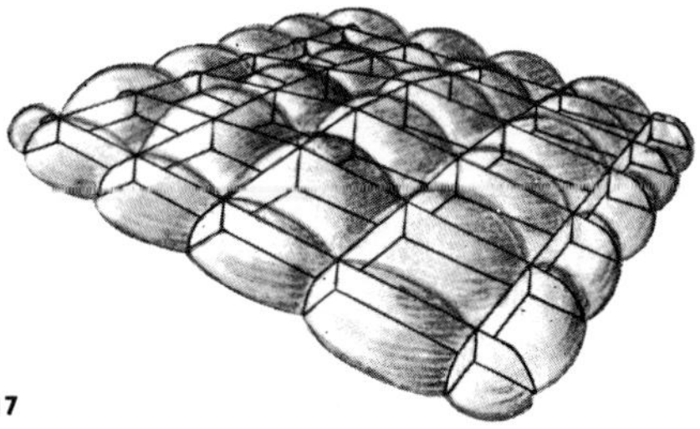

17

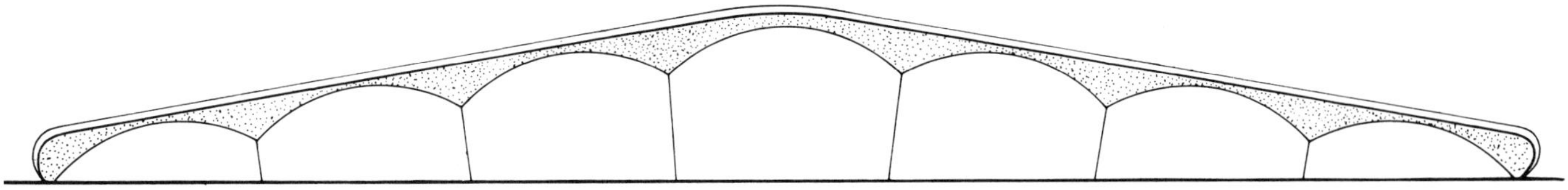

18

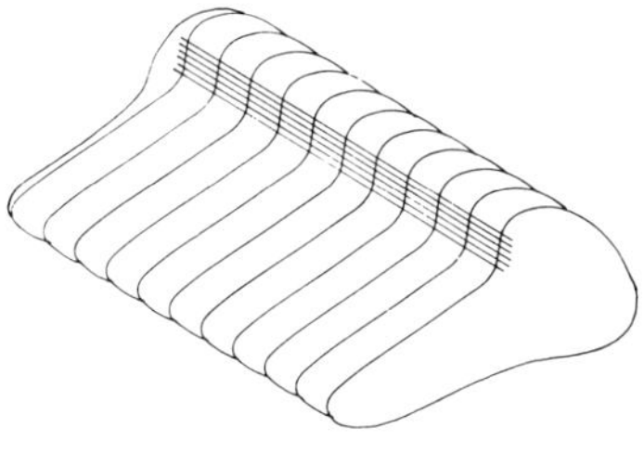

19

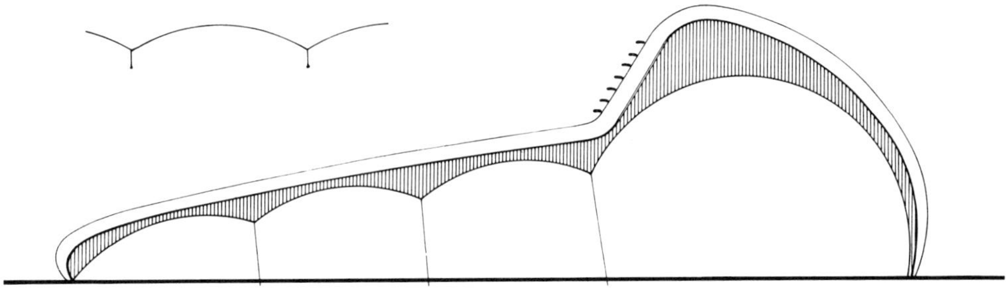

20 and 21

by cables, the latter transmit the forces to the anchoring points in the foundations. In design 6 the edge cables of the partition have a smaller radius of curvature than the roof valley. The free span is reduced by the two internal anchorings.

Partitions can have simple or double curvature; they will, therefore, largely determine the surface shape of a pneumatically tensed membrane. Membranes can also be convex downward, with internal drainage inside the partitions (Fig. 7). Figure 8 shows the connection of a partition to the roof. The partition is supported by a cable. Partitions can divide a large pneumatic system into many individual cells which, in the presence of pressure differences, undergo varying deformations in accordance with the rigidity of the material (Fig. 10). Even when the pressure is released from one or more cells it is possible to prevent the roof membrane from sagging to the floor (Fig. 11). A multicellular structure of this type provides great safety, which is increased by double or triple membranes (Fig. 12). Figure 13 shows the line of destruction which could be caused, for example, by a meteorite in an extraterrestrial structure. Figure 14 shows the automatic closing of the holes because of the internal pressure (comp. Fig. 2, p. 28). Partitions in a pneumatic system (Fig. 15) can also intersect (Fig. 16). In the sketches for a multicellular flat structure (Fig. 17) eleven partitions intersect. They are highest at the center of the structure and slope downward to the sides. A pneumatically tensed membrane rises on a square base above each frame formed by the partitions. The walls form straight roof valleys along which the rainwater drains to the outside. One of the most important features of partition membranes is that straight or inclined valleys can be obtained with their aid. This was done as shown in the section through a large envelope design (Fig. 18), in which the structure is highest at the center and gradually slopes downward to the sides. The great influence of such partitions on the shape of pneumatic structures is illustrated by Fig. 19 on p. 103, which shows a production hall. Figure 20, p. 103, is a cross section, and Fig. 21, p. 103, is a longitudinal section through the roof.

With circular or annular plans it is not always necessary to anchor the cables bordering the partitions to the foundations. They

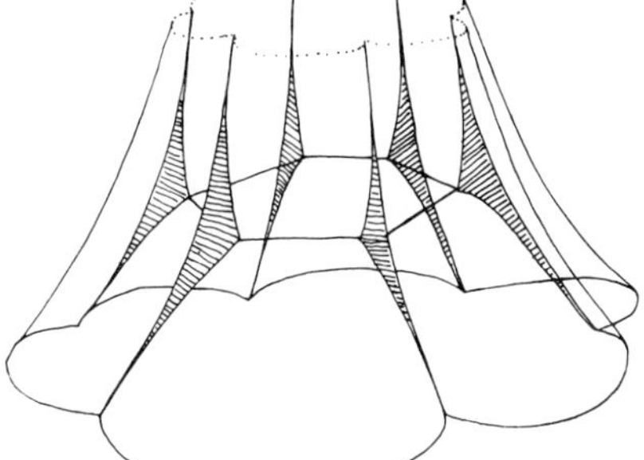

22

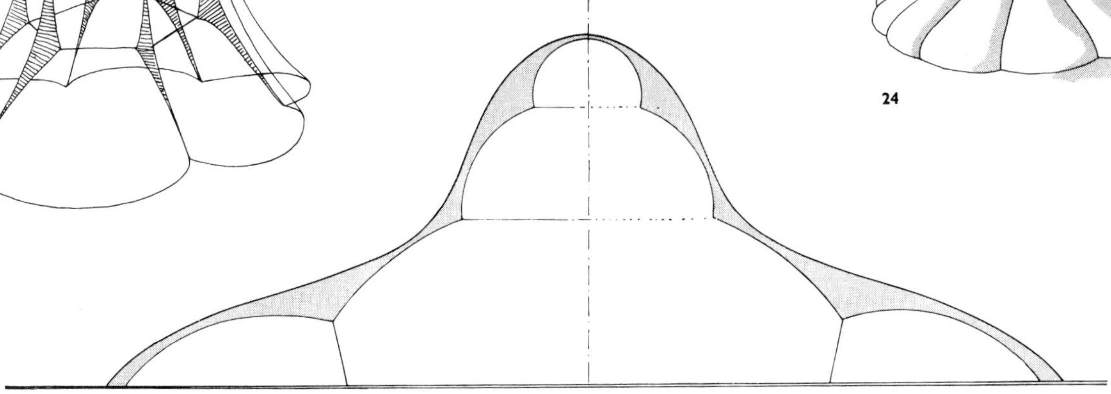

23

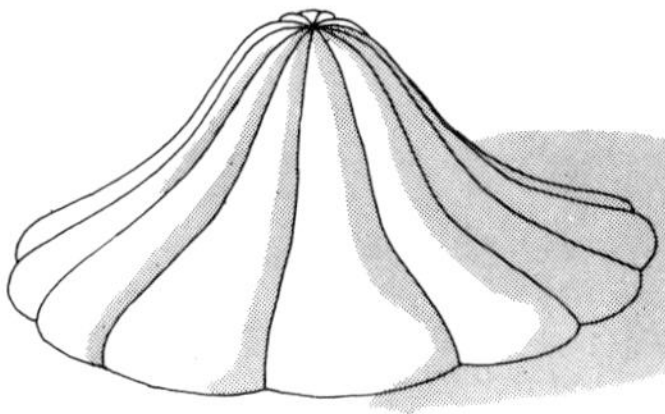

24

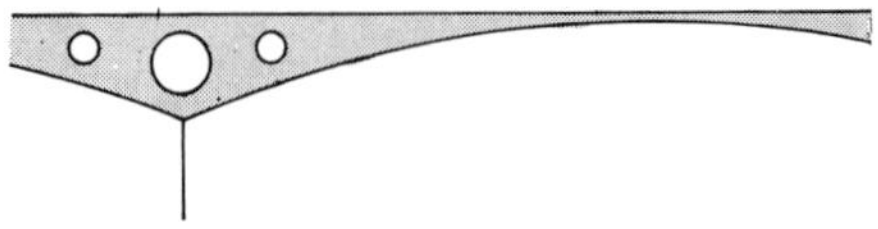

1

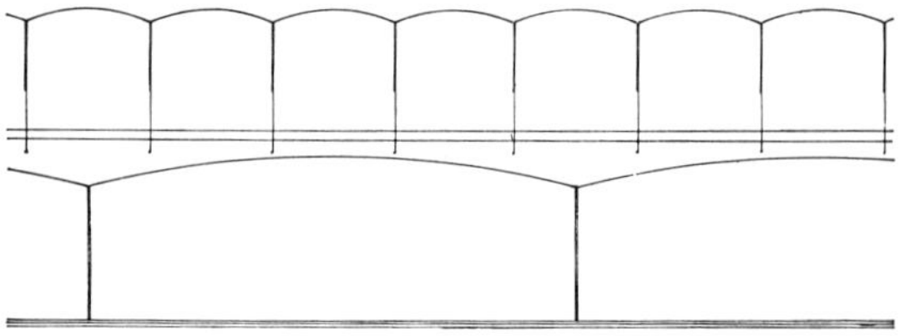

9

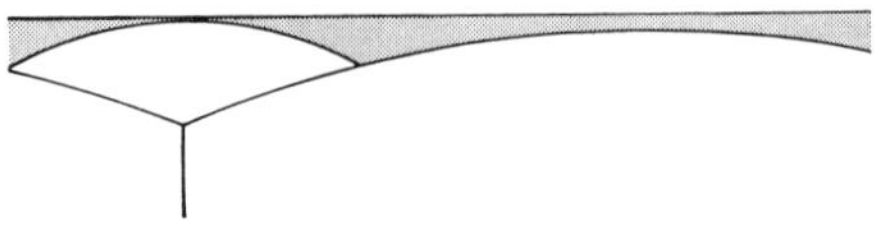

2

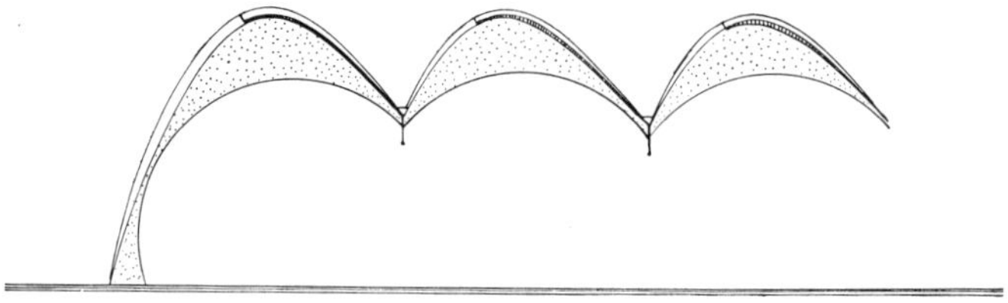

10

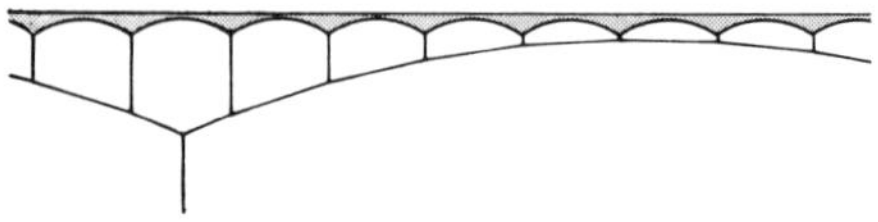

3

can also be attached to annular cables (Fig. 22, p. 103) in order to obtain equilibrium. This is also illustrated in the section through a dome in Fig. 23, p. 103, and in the sketch (from above) in Fig. 24 of the same page. Partitions are not under direct pneumatic stress when the pressure is equal on both sides. They are flat, prestressed membranes and can be treated as such. Their surface area can be reduced to a minimum by cutting out holes (Fig. 1), or arches (Fig. 2). Numerous small ropes, which are attached like a suspension bridge to a single cable via vertical connecting cables (Fig. 3), considerably reduce the area of the partition. Greater stability is provided by diagonal cables (Fig. 4), or fanned cables (Figs. 5 and 6), or close-meshed cable nets (Fig. 7). When taking up compressive forces acting, for example, on a rigid structural panel, it is often advisable to distribute the supporting points as in the branches of a tree. This permits the shortest possible effective lengths and thus minimizes buckling, and also imparts greater rigidity to the system. See Fig. 8 on the left. With tension-loaded supports this leads to greater cable lengths than are necessary for direct connecting lines (Fig. 8, right). Partitions bordered in their entirety by cables can also intersect and form a triangular, square, or hexagonal mesh. This can be seen in the project (Fig. 11), for a shed hall with longitudinal (Fig. 9) and transverse (Fig. 10) partitions.

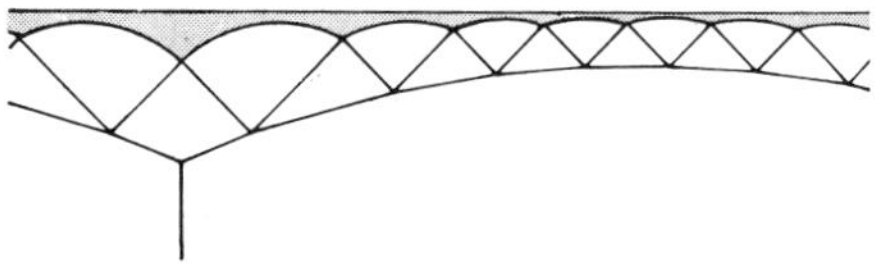

4

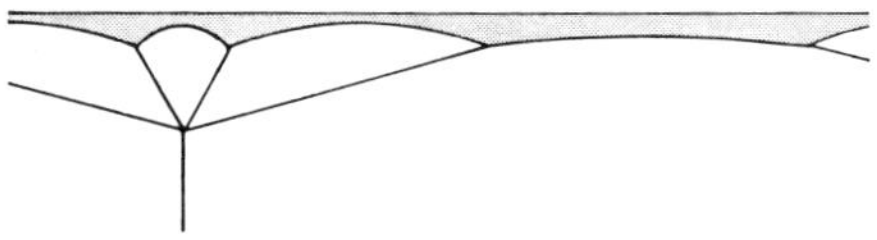

5

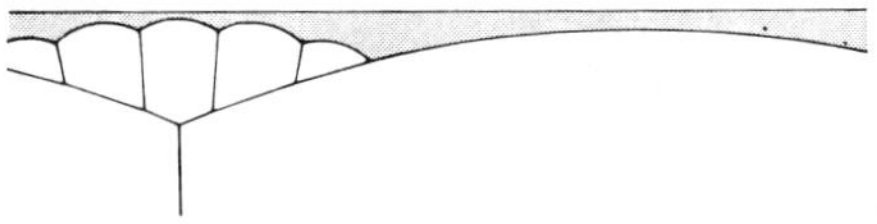

6

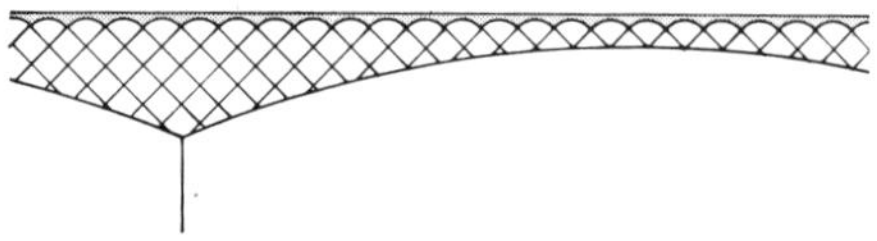

7

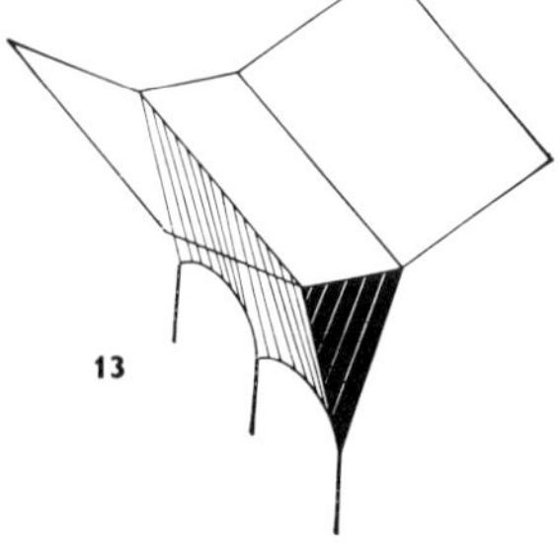

13

8 ▼

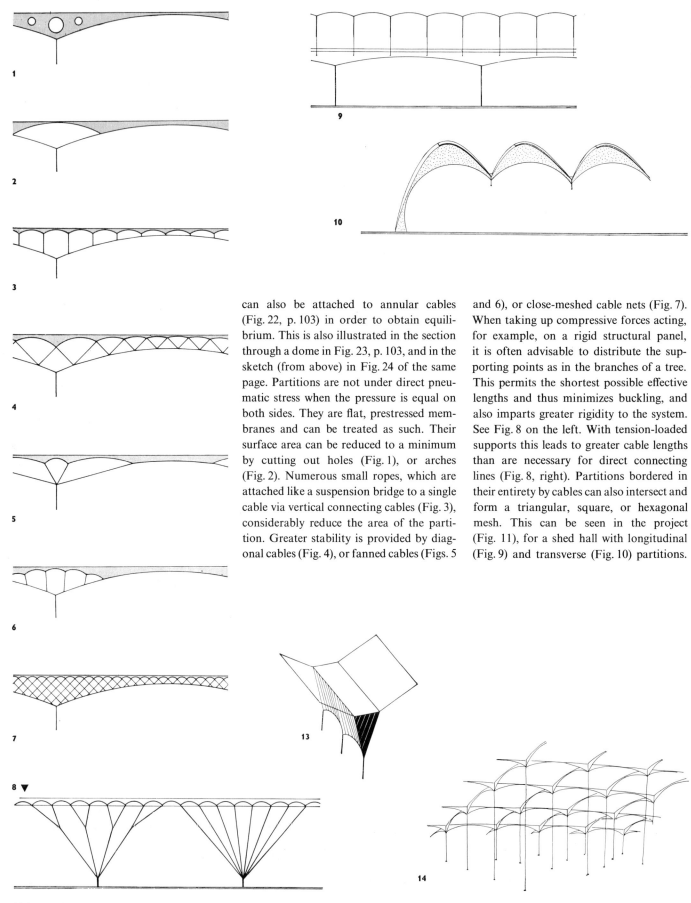

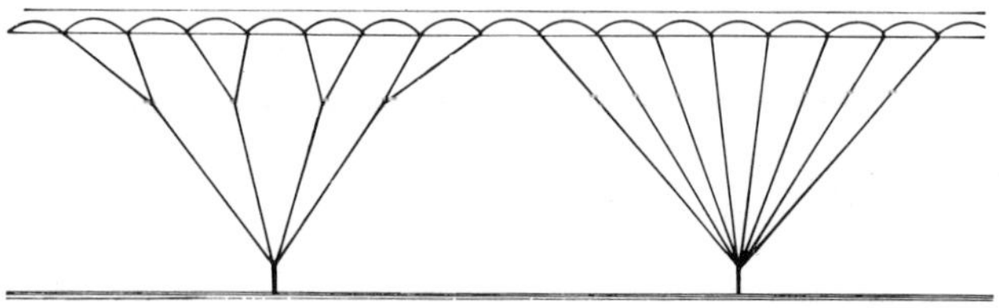

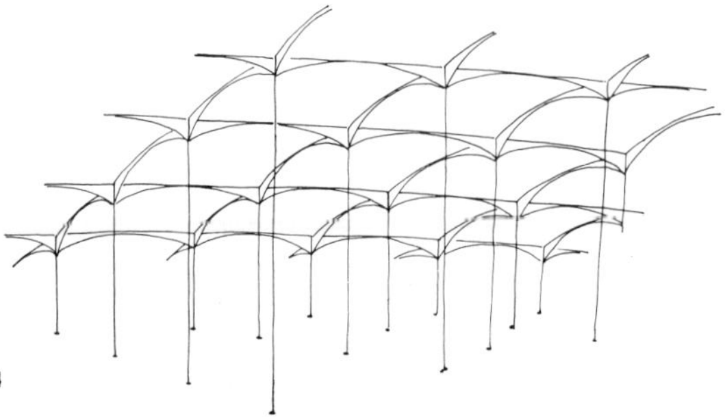

14

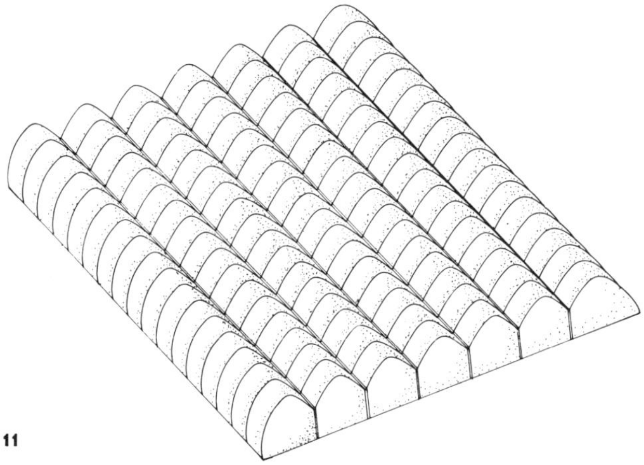

11

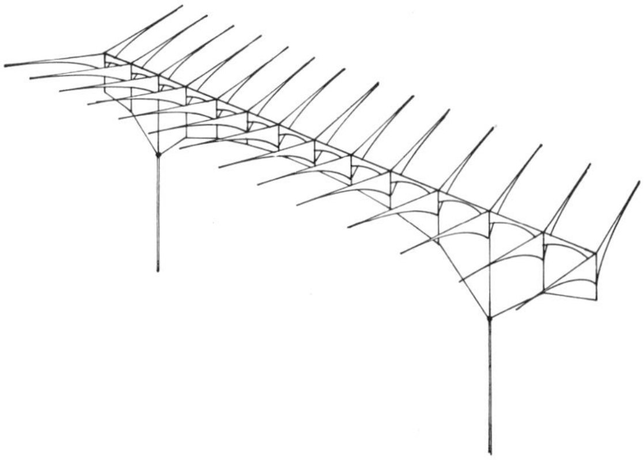

12

The transverse partitions are anchored to the longitudinal partitions. This can be done in various ways: an example is shown in Fig. 12. In order to obtain space for pipes and achieve a gentler rounding of the valleys the partition can be doubled so that it encloses a triangular channel (Fig. 13). Figure 16 shows a longitudinal section of a large-area envelope* for a greenhouse with intersecting partitions bordered by cables throughout. Figure 17 is the corresponding cross section; all internal spans—A—are equal. The section curves gently for drainage. The internal view (Fig. 14) shows the method of construction. Figure 15 gives a bird's eye view of the project, and Fig. 18, an oblique side view.

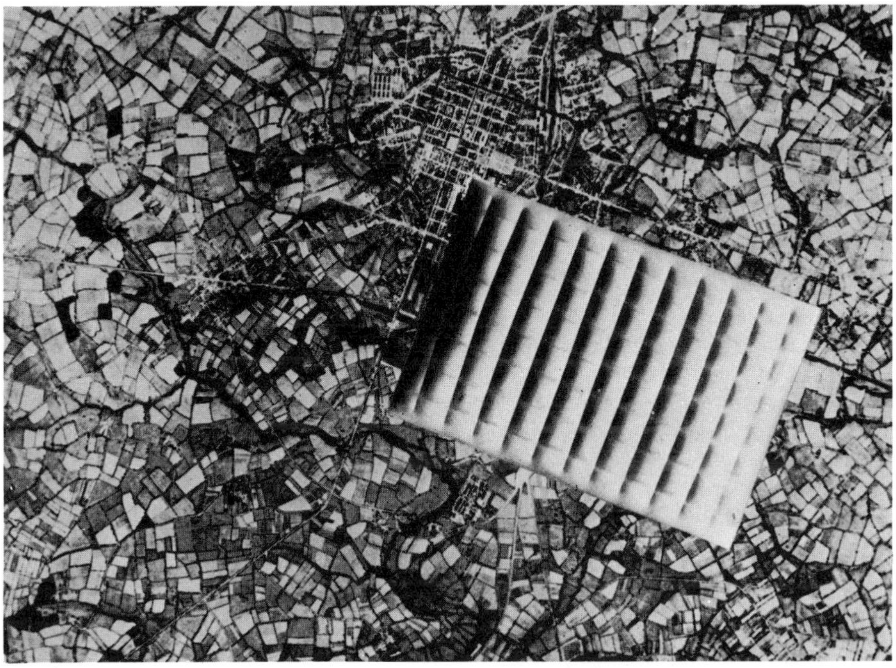

15 ▲

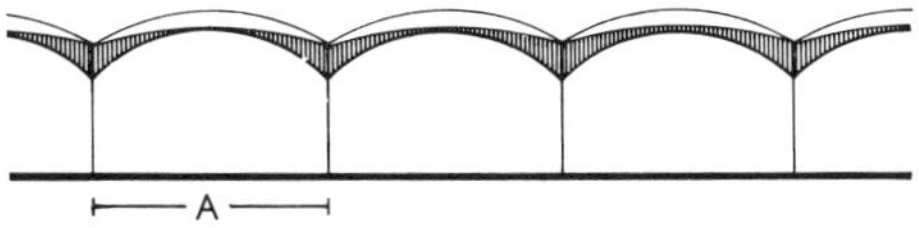

◀ 16

17 ▲

▼ 18

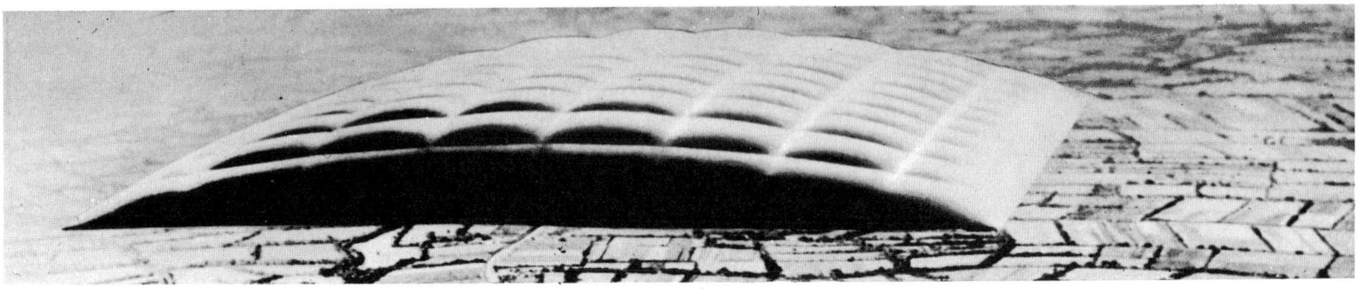

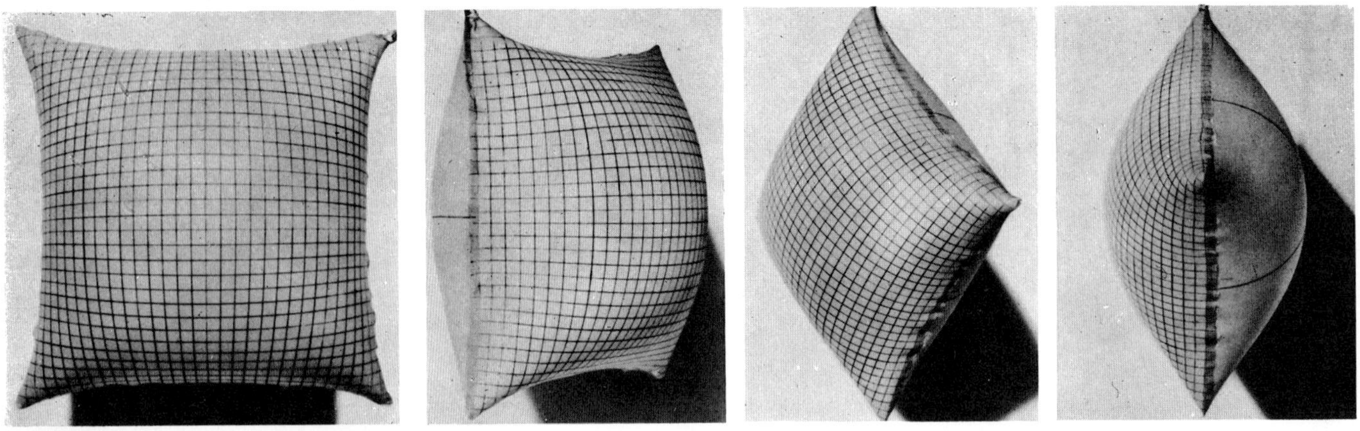

1 to 4

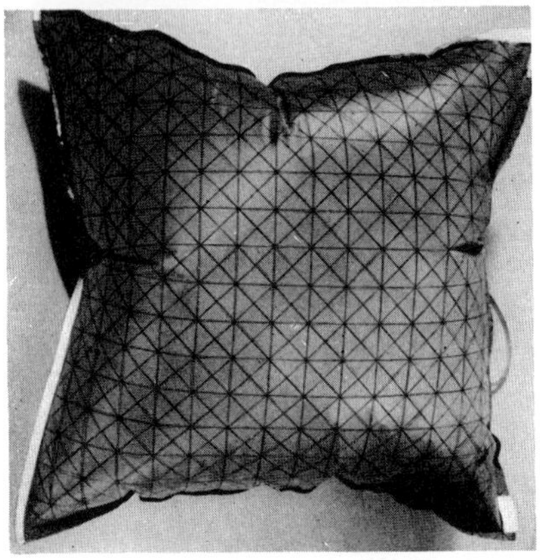

5

Cushion Structures

Pneumatically tensed envelopes that are closed on all sides and have a comparatively flat shape, will be referred to as cushion structures. If, for example, an envelope, consisting of two square rubber membranes joined at their edges, is placed under pressure, the resulting shape will approximate a body of rotation to which four cones are attached. This can be seen in Figs. 1 to 4. At the beginning of inflation folds form along the edge, but these disappear when the rubber expands. Deformations are rendered visible by the grid inscribed in the untensed state. The membranes are under greatest tension in the center. If, however, a material of low deformability such as balloon silk is used, edge folds, typical for cushions, appear (Fig. 5). These can be avoided by a suitable cut. One of the innumerable applications of such cushions is as floats inside concrete pipes during the underwater laying of a sewage conduit (Fig. 6; photo by Stromeyer). When two initially flat, triangular rubber membranes with concave edges are joined to form an inflatable envelope (Figs. 7 and 8), a cushion of comparatively large span but small height is obtained. There are various ways to prevent the spherical bulging of a closed envelope under internal pressure. For example, a flat shape can be obtained by external pressure application (Fig. 9). In this way large forces can be produced with ordinary cushions of welded membranes, as, for example, in load tests (Fig. 10), the cushion being placed between the ground and the test panel supported from above. To obtain greater travel, flat cushions of high load capacity alternate with rigid panels (Fig. 11). Stretching the cushions (Figs. 12 and 13), or attaching them to frames (Fig. 14) is particularly effective. The inflated cushion exerts bending loads on the frame. The latter can have various shapes (Fig. 15). The membranes increase the rigidity of the frame in its plane. When external forces (Fig. 16; thick arrows), act at the corners of the frame, major deformations are taken up by increased membrane tensions in the regions

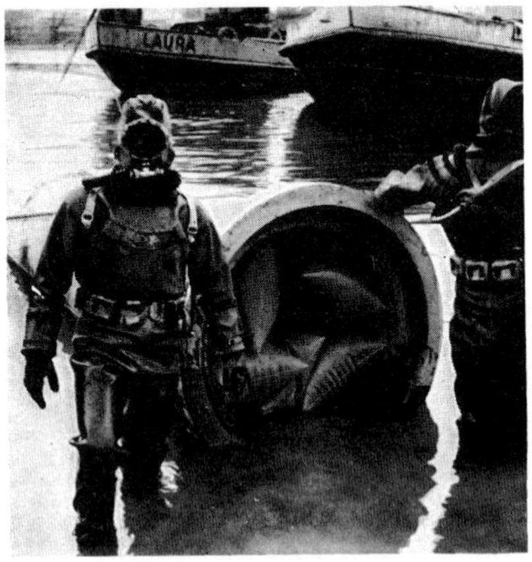

6 ▲ ▼ 7

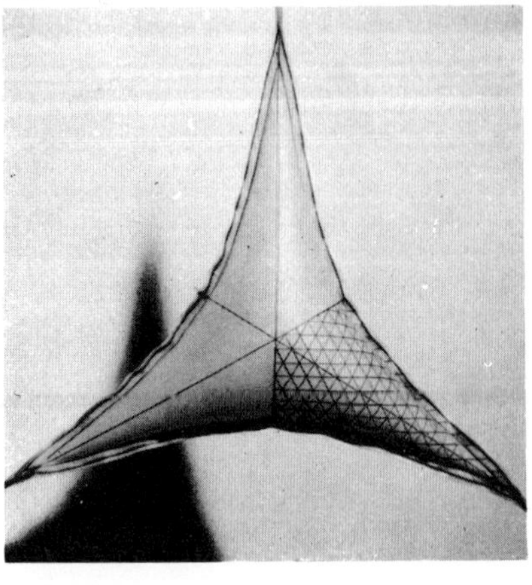

8

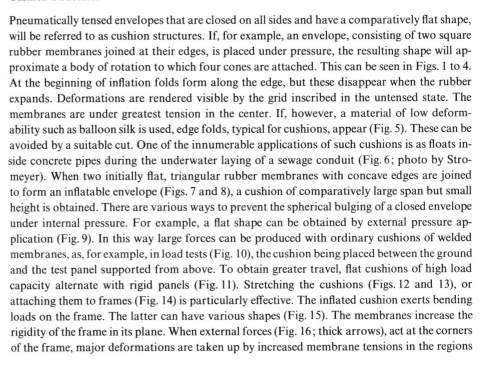

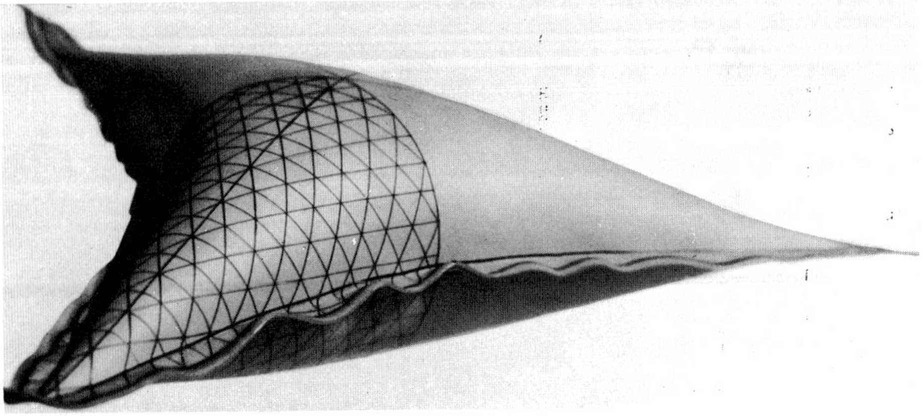

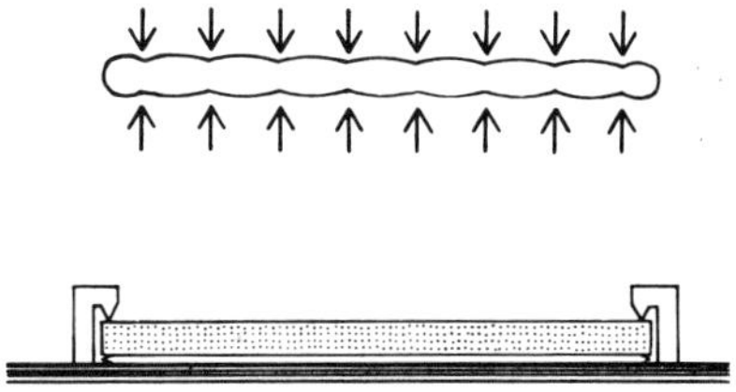

9 and 10

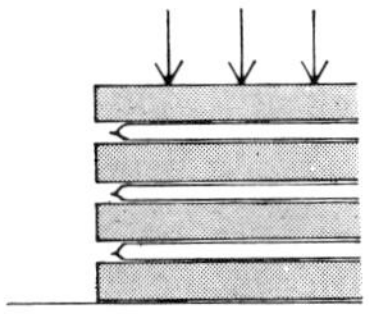

11

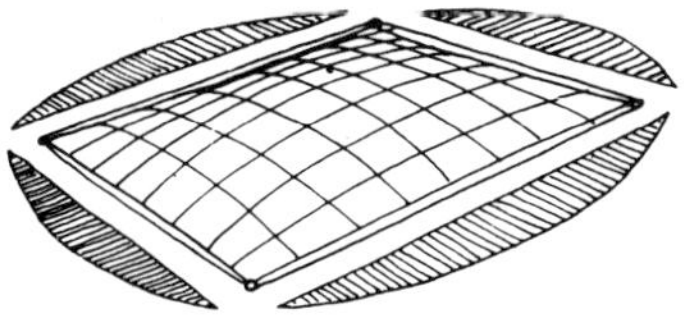

14

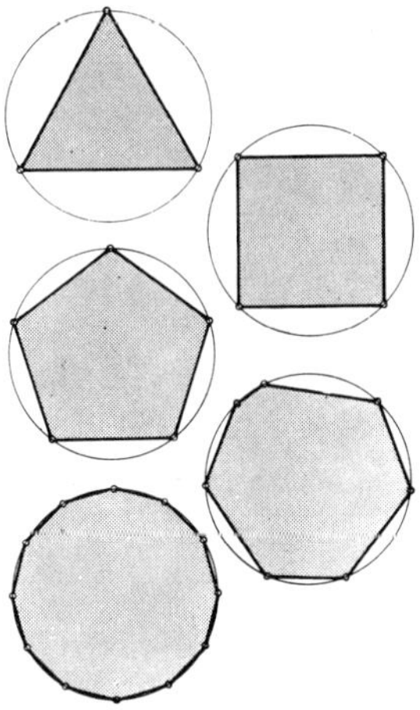

17 to 21

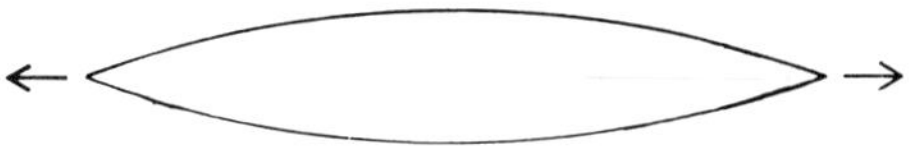

12

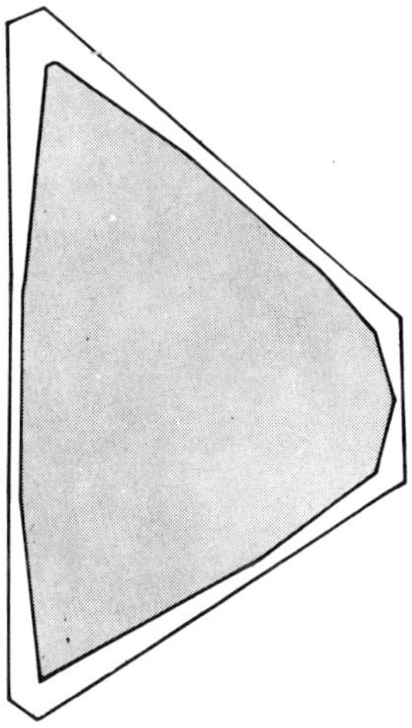

15

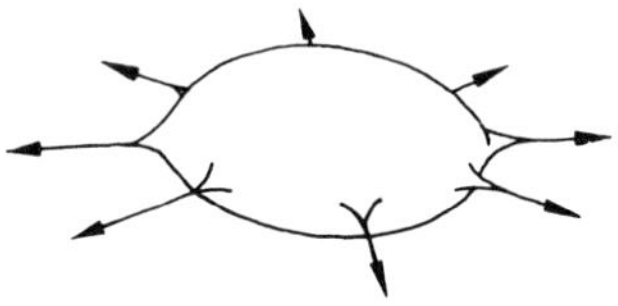

13

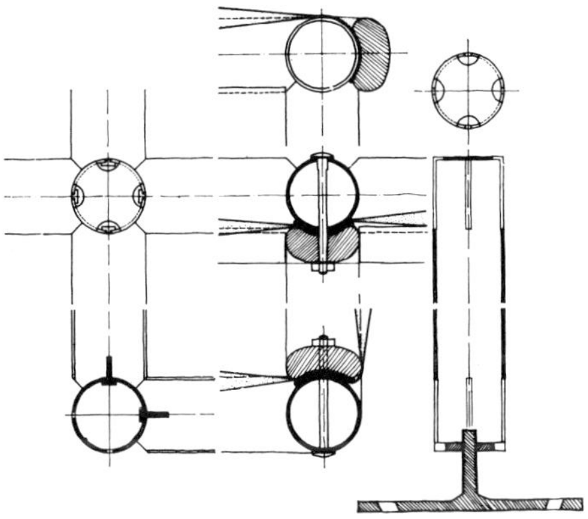

22

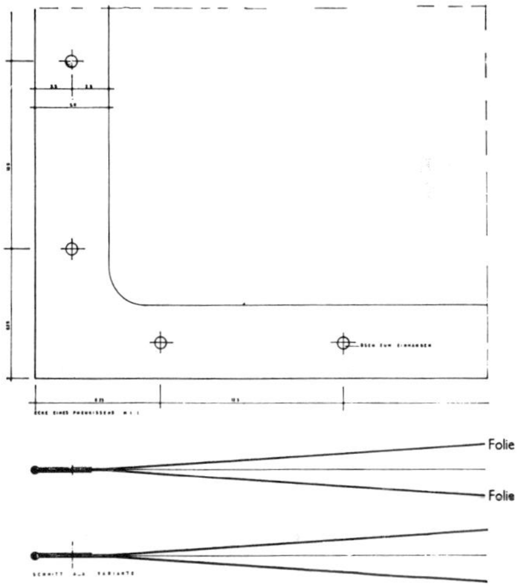

23 to 25

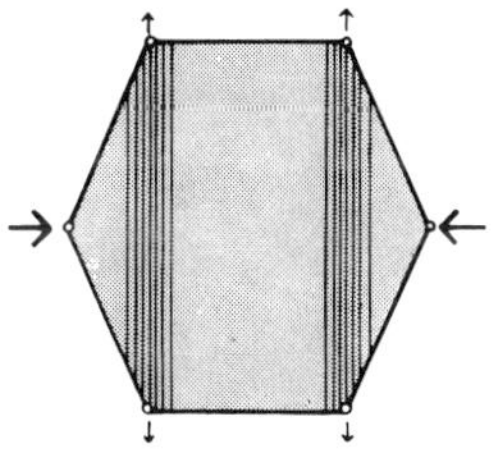

16

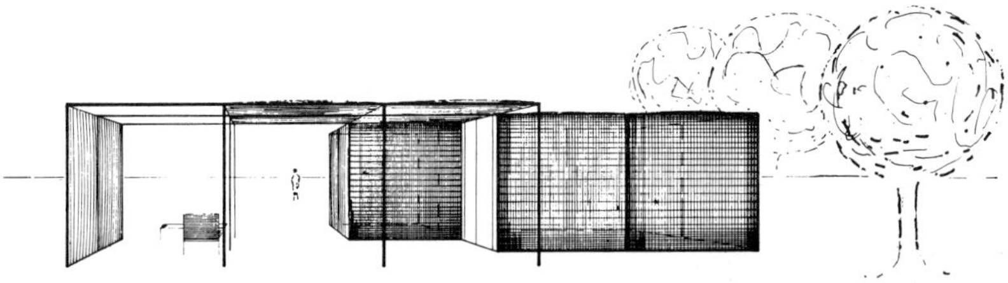

26

27 and 28

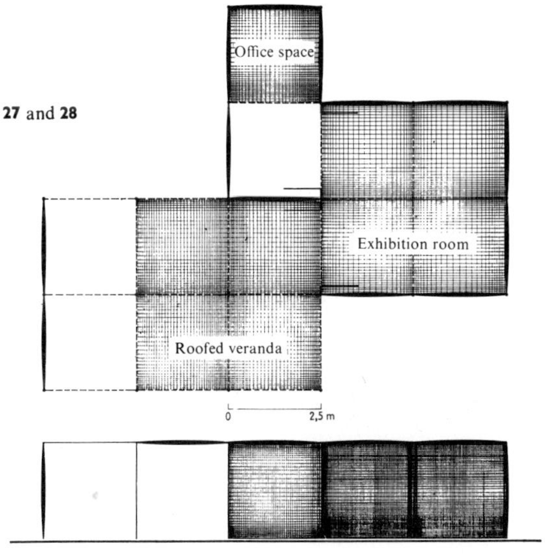

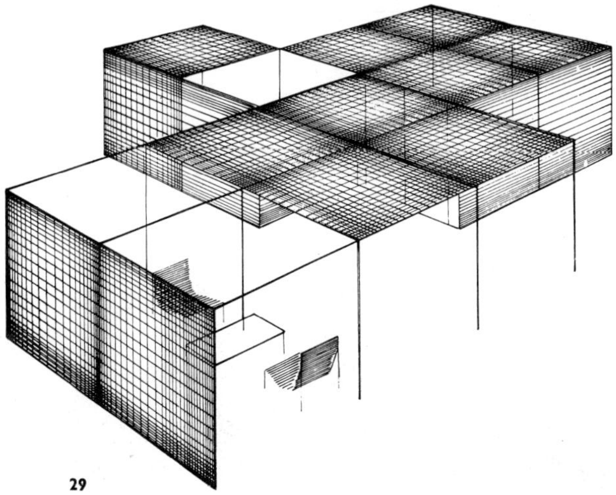

29

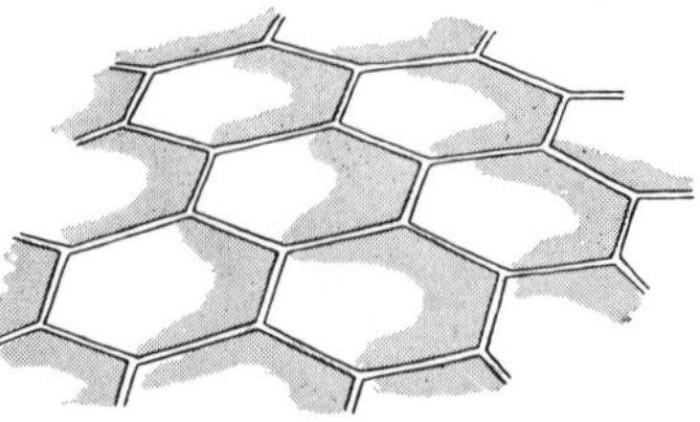
1

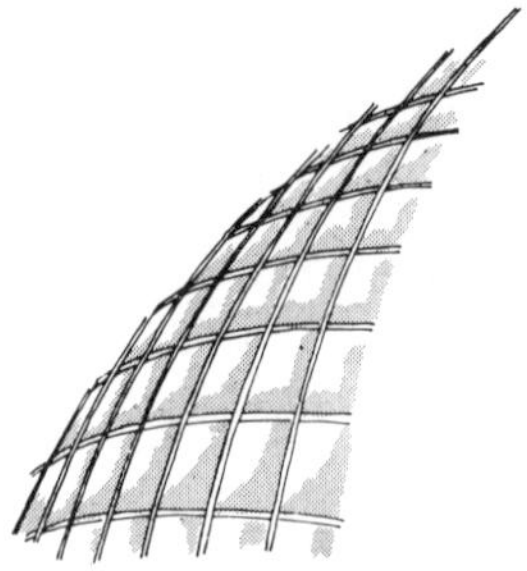
2

3

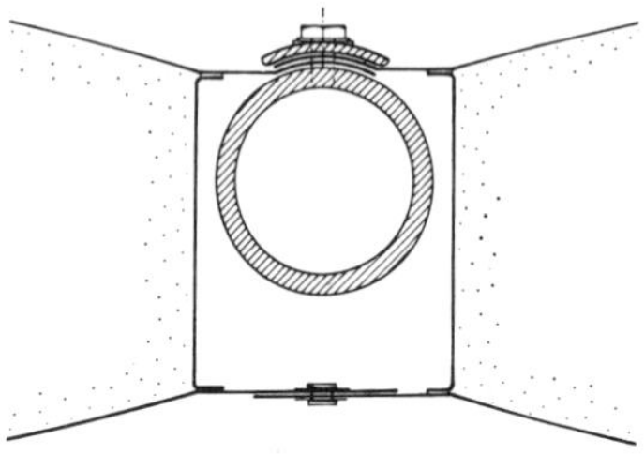
4

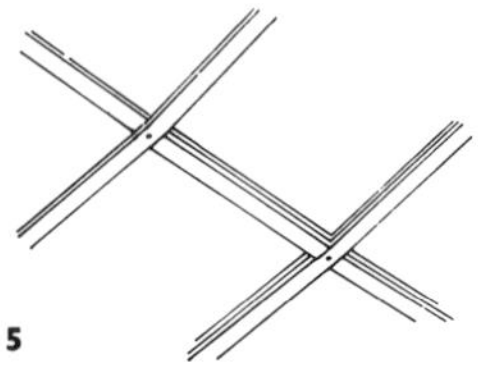
5

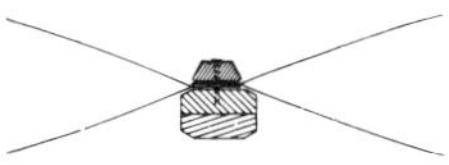
6

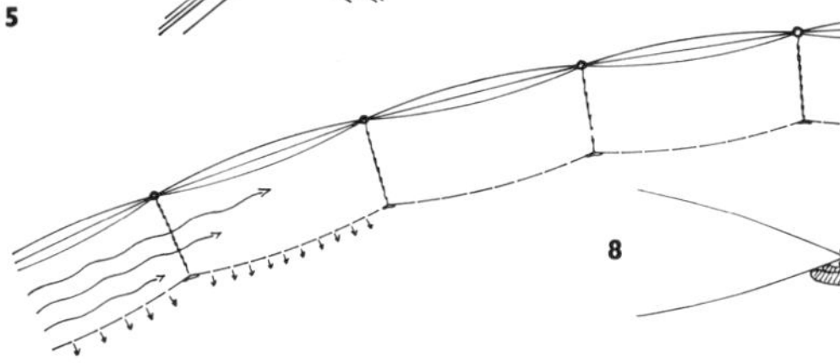
7

8

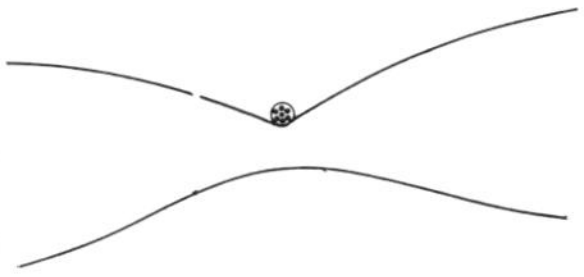
9

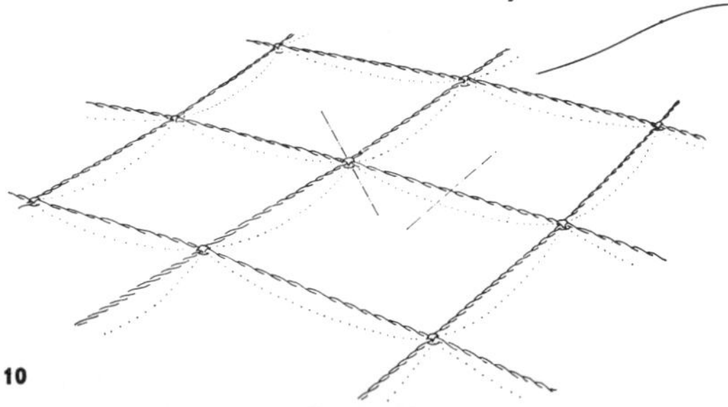
10

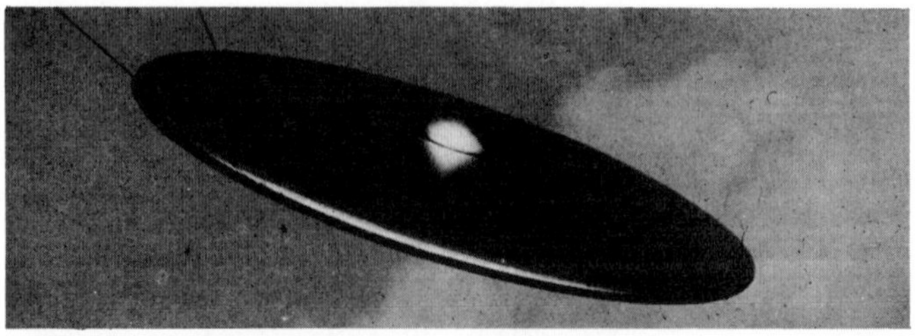
11 ▲

▼ 12

shown lined. The bending moments at the corners of hinged frames (Figs. 17 to 21, p. 107) are lowered by reducing the dimensions. An example of a cushion structure between rigid frames is the design* of a Stromeyer exhibition pavilion, shown here in a quick montage procedure. Plan (Figure 27, p. 107) and elevation (Fig. 28, p. 107) are based on a 2.5 m grid. The perspectives, (Figs. 26 and 29) and the structural details in Fig. 22, on p. 107 show the awning-type double membranes with glued edges (Figs. 23 to 25, p. 107), clamped in a tubular steel frame with wooden laths.

Pneumatically tensed cushions are particularly suitable for panels that close lattice structures. The spaces of a grid dome are covered with transparent cushions. For thermal insulation, the cushions (Fig. 1) can be clamped to the structure in such a way that they prevent the steel from providing a thermal short circuit (Fig. 4).

Figure 3 shows a dome of rectangular section shapes and triangular assembly, and Fig. 2 a dome of wooden laths with four-cornered equilateral mesh. The intersecting laths are bolted together (Fig. 5); the cushions are secured with wooden laths and bolts (Fig. 6).

Extra linings (Fig. 7) can be suspended from tubular or cable structures that are filled in with cushions. The lining prevents cooling at the boundaries of the interior, by enabling hot air to be injected into the interspace (wavy arrows). The outer cushions are triple membranes, for better heat insulation. The inner membrane is connected to the structure by cables, which cause it to form bulges; it may also be tensed pneumatically by the injected hot air. The cladding of a cable net (Fig. 10) is shown in the sections through the center of a cable and through a node (Figs. 8 and 9); two membranes are joined at the cable intersection by means of a welded-on grommet. Internal pressure causes the lower membrane to appear as if it were supported at many points, while the upper membrane is pressed against the cables. The individual air cushions are interconnected.

A pneumatically tensed double membrane may also be stretched in a ring, as shown in section (Fig. 14). Thermal insulation and frame rigidity are increased by the membrane if an additional flat membrane is inserted in the center (Fig. 15). The number of membranes can be raised at will (Fig. 16). Figure 17 shows an elevation and Fig. 18 a section of a project* for an orbiting reflector with an inner spherical envelope protected by a multiple membrane, and a double membrane stretched across a ring; Figs. 11 and 13 are photographs of the model. A modification of this design is also protected against radiation (Fig. 19). In such a structure the outer ring can be a pneumatically tensed hose (Fig. 20) in which the internal pressure must, however, be higher than that in the cushion. It was found in the experimental model (Fig. 12) that elastic membranes cause deformation of the compression ring during inflation, which leads to out-of-plane buckling (Fig. 21); the dotted lines mark the original shape of the ring and its axes. This phenomenon depends largely on the elasticity of the membrane. If, for example, an only slightly deformable material is used such as sheet metal, glass-fiber reinforced fabric, etc., and it is preformed to hemispheres, then pneumatic tension increases the rigidity of the ring. Sketches 28 to 31

13

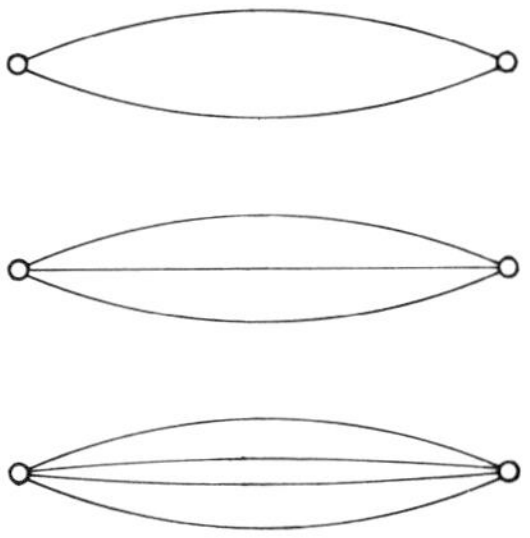
14 to 16

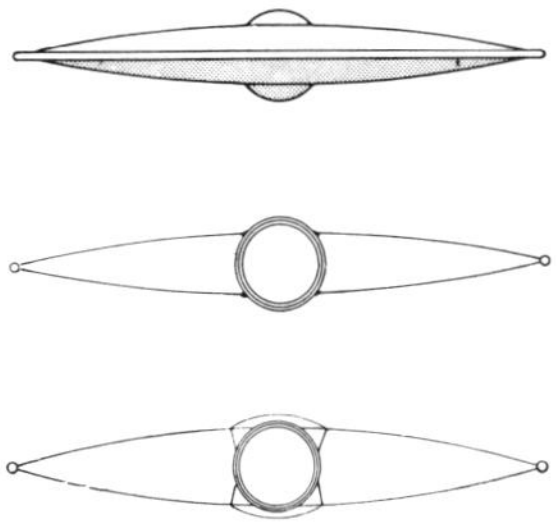
17 to 19

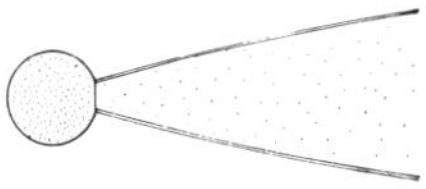
20

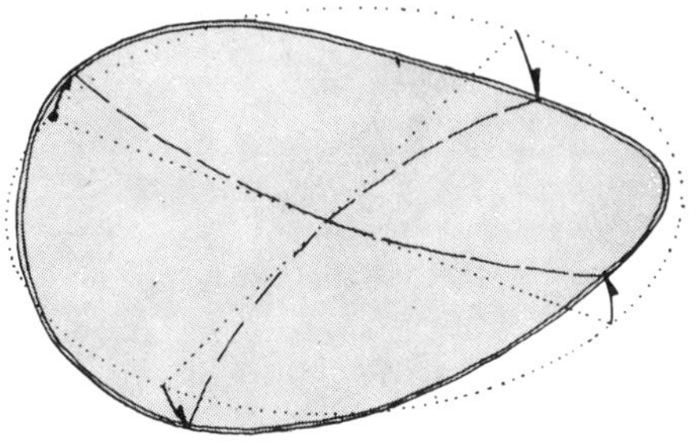
21

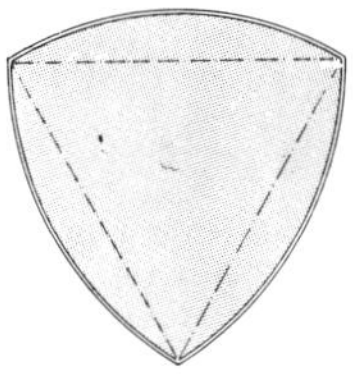
22

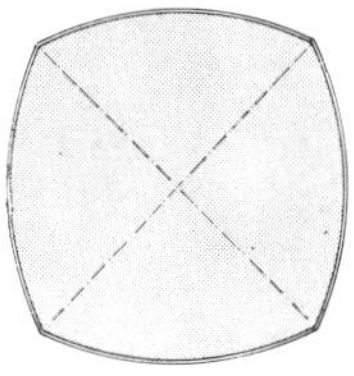
23

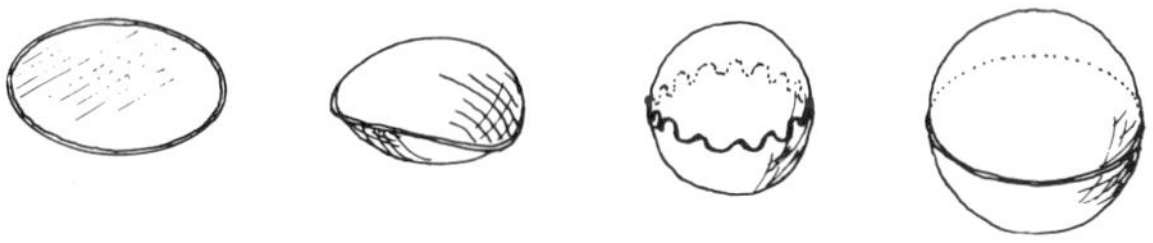
28 to 31

32

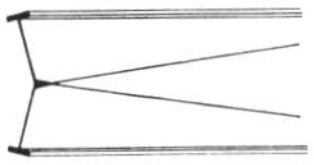
33

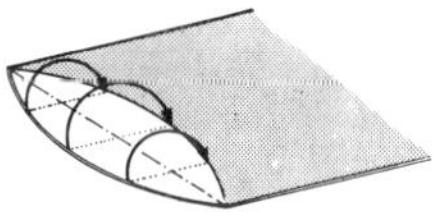
34

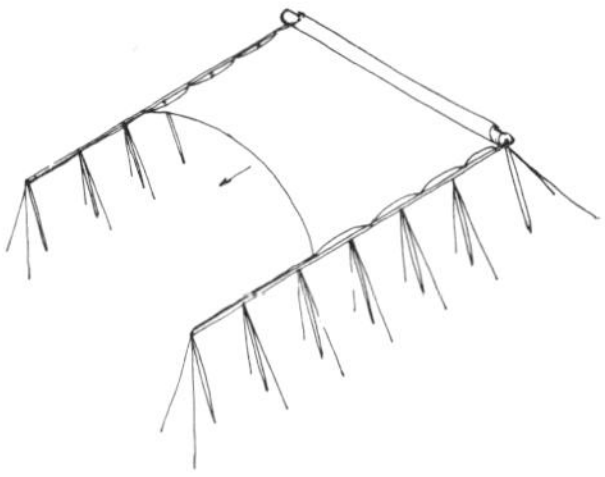
36

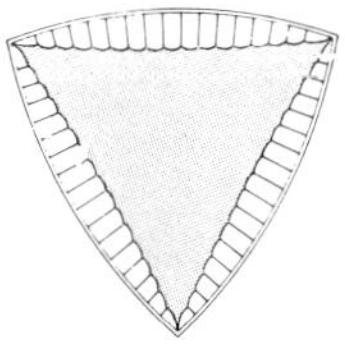
24

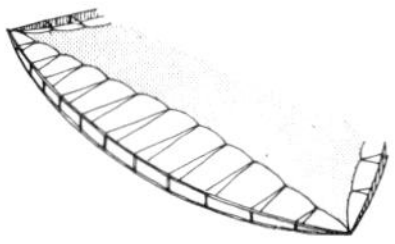
25

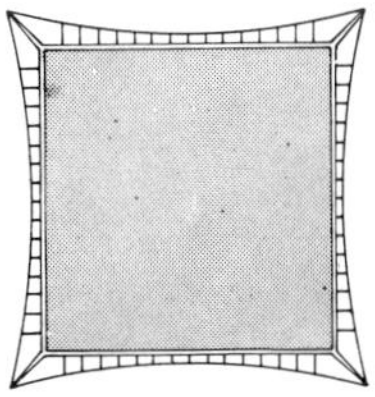
26

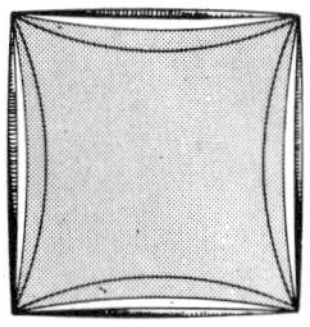
27

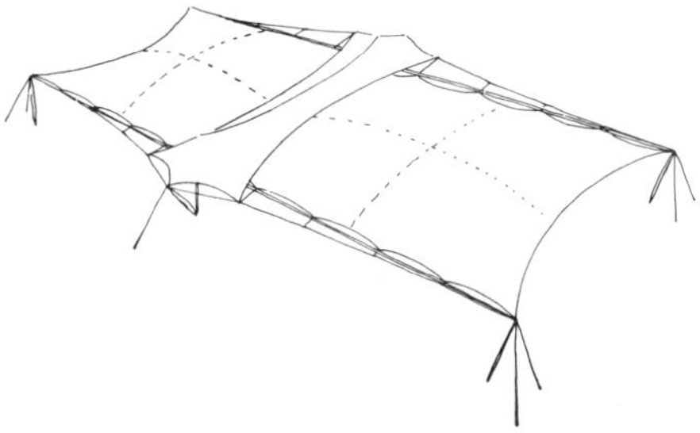
35

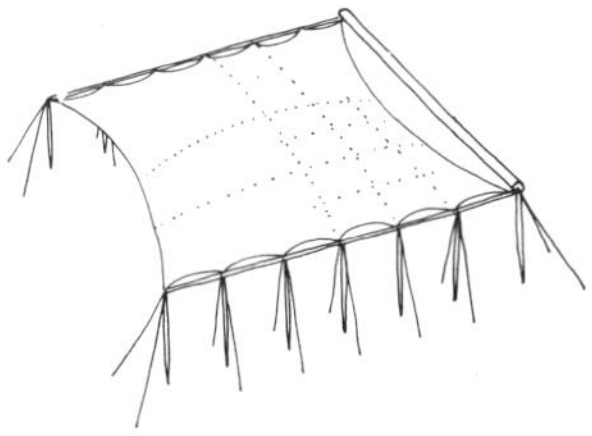
37

show the inflation of a rubber cushion stretched in a very soft ring: at first the ring is deformed until it buckles completely; upon further inflation it straightens again, being finally subjected to tensile forces like the membrane.

Since the stiffening effect is greater for thick than for flat cushions, the ring (Fig. 32) may be thinner for the former than for the latter, for which it must be particularly resistant to bending (Fig. 33). If a double membrane is attached along an arch, there is a danger of inversion along the line of suspension (Fig. 34). In this case (Figs. 22 and 23), the forces exerted can be taken up by cables arranged diagonally or as chords between the membranes. The arches in Figs. 24 and 25 act like rigid girders. The double membrane is attached to the lower chord which is constructed as a cable. The system shown in Fig. 26 is a square frame with compression members whose flexure is prevented by a suspended structure, whereas in the system shown in Fig. 27 the frame is subjected to compressive forces, since the membranes are attached to cables connecting the corners of the frame.

Double membranes with edge cables suspended between rigid frames provide a simple design for sliding roofs. In Figure 36 the double membrane is wound on a roller to the right; it can be pulled out between two rails on guyed masts, by means of a cable tackle. To prevent flutter, it is inflated during the unrolling. It is shown inflated in Fig. 37.

1

In the project sketch* for roofing a roller-skating rink (Fig. 35, p. 109), the double membranes are folded under the center of a special protective roof formed from a prestressed membrane. From this position they are unfolded toward both sides.

Before Walter Bird tackled larger projects he built radar domes in the form of pneumatic cushion structures on rings (Fig. 1).

The biggest cushion yet built roofs the 2,000-seat open-air auditorium of the Boston Arts Center Theater (1959) (Figs. 2 and 3). It was designed by the architects Carl Koch and Margaret Ross.

Structural analysis was performed by Paul Weidlinger; it was built by Walter Bird. The cushion is 7 m thick in the center and has a diameter of 44 m; it is bordered by cables and suspended in a compression ring 70 cm high mounted on steel beams supported by rods (Figs. 4 and 5). Two compressors behind the stage provide constant air pressure of approximately 25 mm of water column. It was initially the intention to use the cushion roof as a form for a permanent concrete dome.

Figure 8 shows the actual cushion structure. Figures 6, 7 and 9 show the finished building, whose outer walls were built by a local firm. During the great Boston hurricane of 1960 the outer walls were heavily damaged, but the cushion structure remained intact.

If cable-edged cushions are stretched between fixed points, the latter can be connected by a frame (Fig. 3, p. 112), whose members lie outside the cushion.

However, internal connections are also possible (Figs. 4 and 5, p. 112). This provides shorter total and effective lengths (unsupported lengths over which

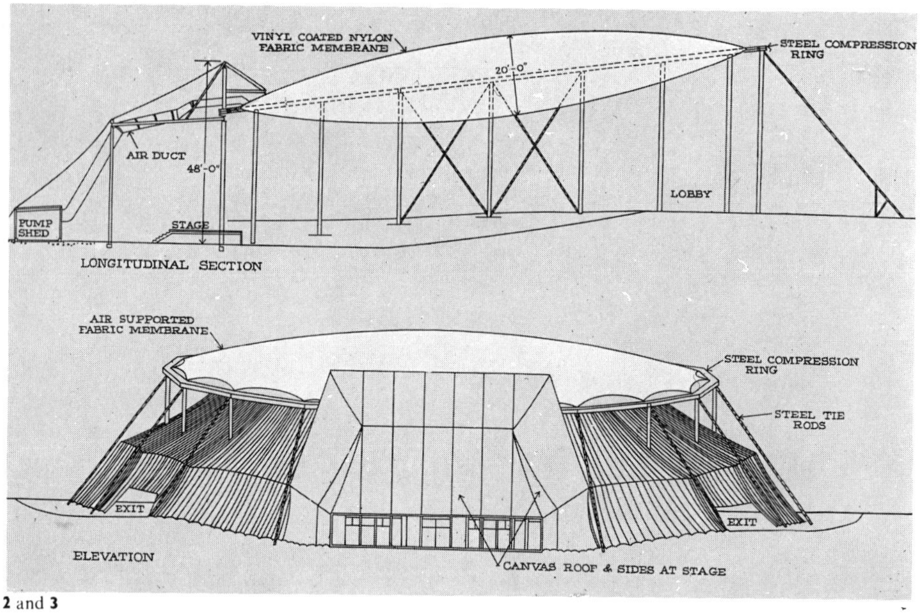

2 and 3

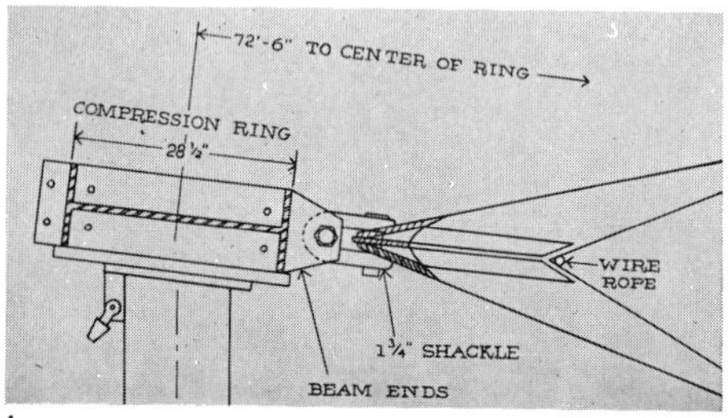

4

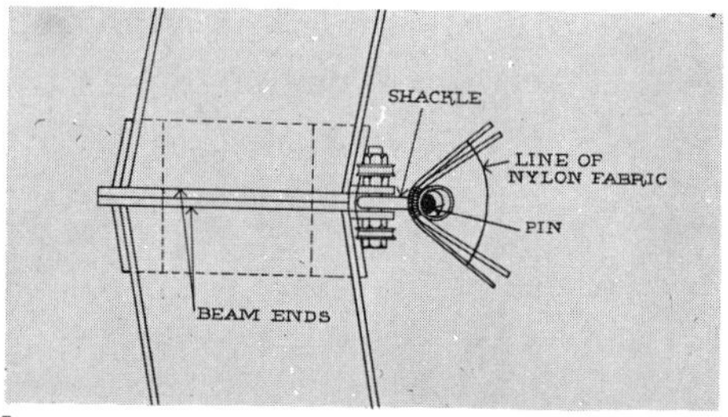

5

6 ▲

▼ 7

8 ▲

▼ 9

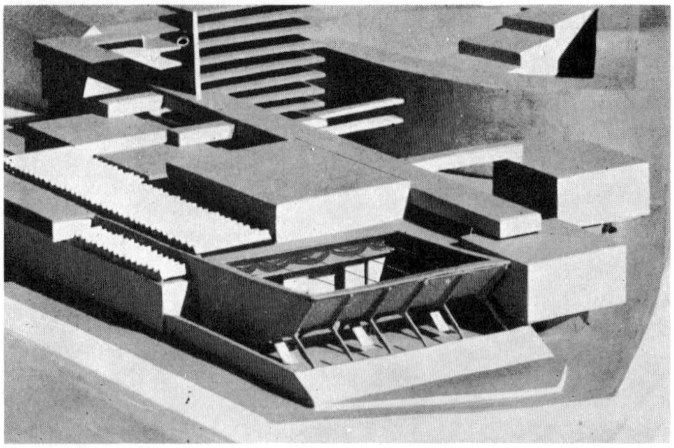

2

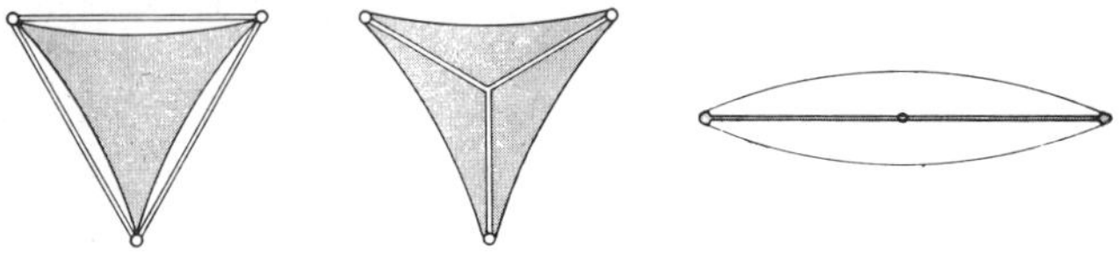

3 to 5

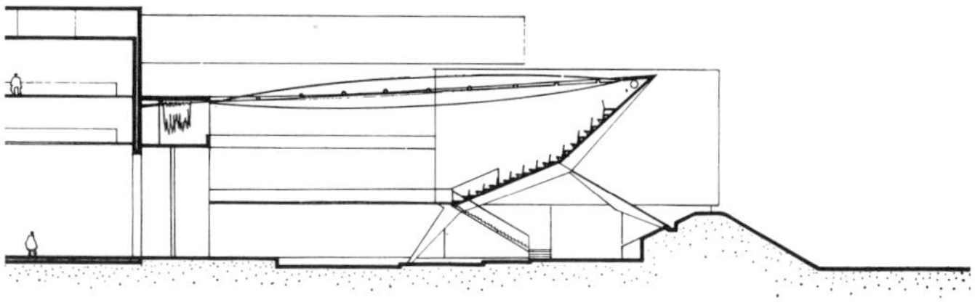

16

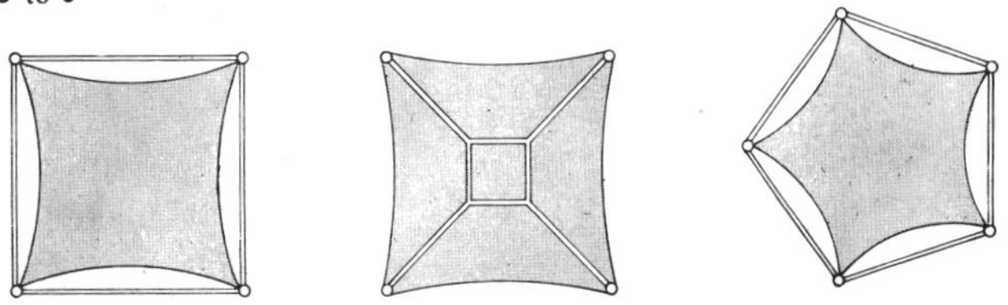

6 to 8

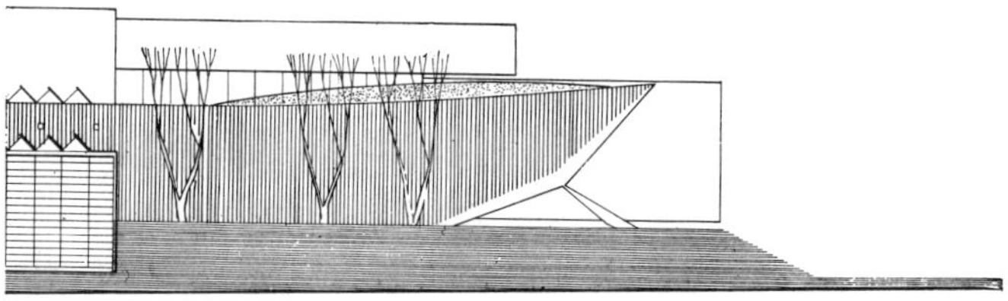

17

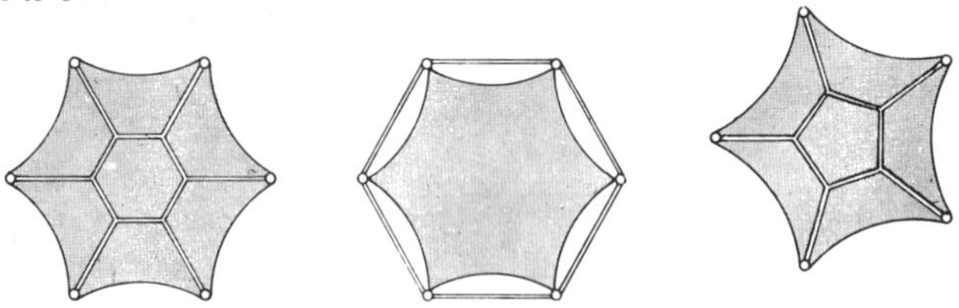

9 to 11

14 ▶

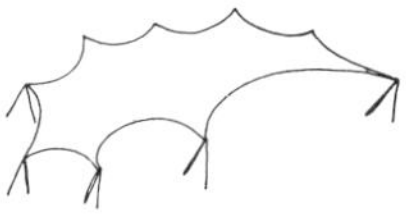

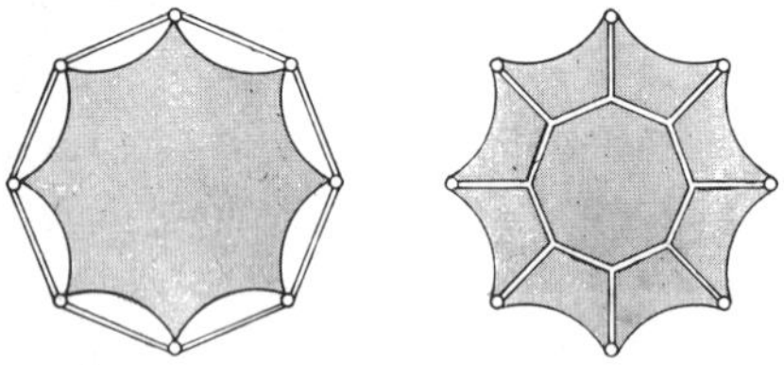

12 and 13

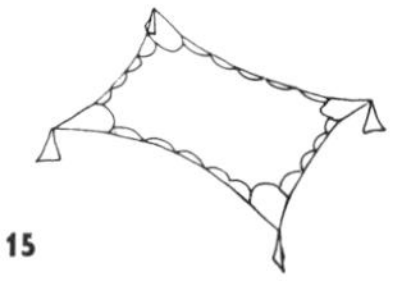

15

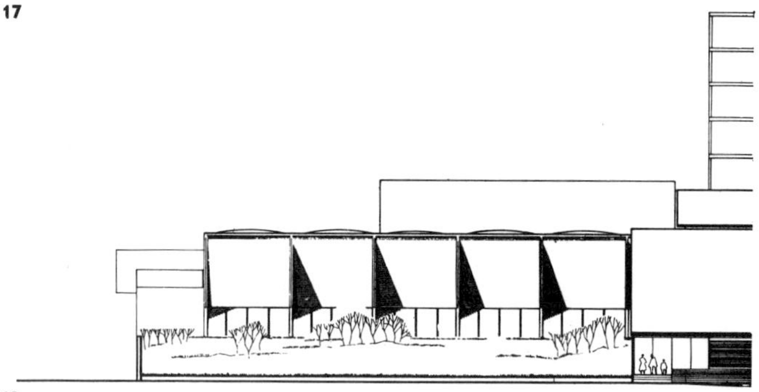

18

buckling can occur) of the rods within the plane of the system. The same is true for a square arrangement (Fig. 6), in which the compressive forces are taken up inside the cushion (Fig. 7). This causes a somewhat greater total length of the rods, but significantly shortens the effective lengths. This also applies to a five-point shape (Figs. 8 and 11), though not to six points, where the total length is the same both for an outer frame (Fig. 10) and for internal diagonal connections. The shortest effective lengths are obtained in the arrangement shown in Fig. 9. With eight points the circumference of the outer frame (Fig. 12) is always shorter than any arrangement of internal connections, which may, however, be useful when leading to shorter effective lengths (Fig. 13). The larger the number of fixed points, the more advisable is an annular frame.

Cushions stretched between frames may also consist of several units, e.g., the five cushions which were to cover an open-air studio for Radio Free Berlin (competition project* 1960). They can be seen in cross section, Fig. 16, in the folded (left) and opened position. (Comp. views 17 and 18 of the structure, and photographs of models [Fig. 1] in the folded and [Fig. 2] in the opened position.)

Cushions between built-in abutments are shown in Figs. 19 to 22 with photographs of a triangular, cable-edged cushion* between concrete supports, Figs. 23 to 25 of a project* with pentagonal cushions between built-in steel tubes. Inflated cushions bordered by cables may span the most varied ground plans (Fig. 14), or may be inserted into a free cable system (Fig. 15).

19

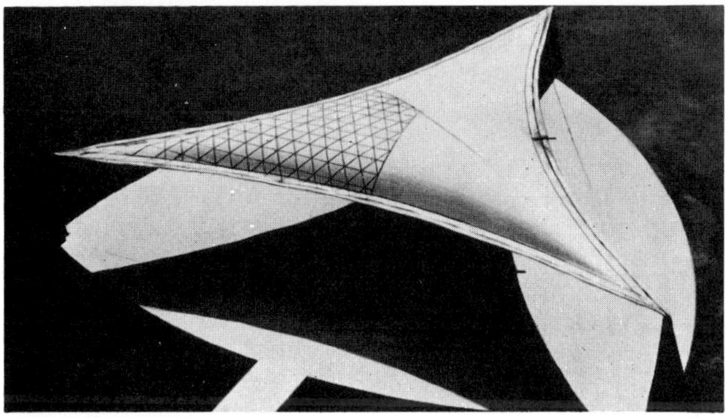

20

21

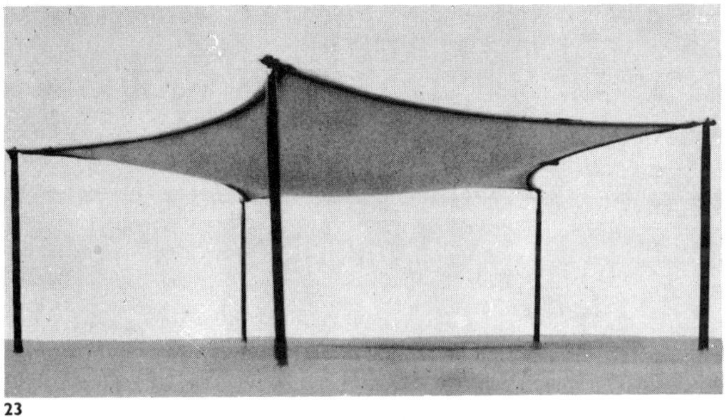

23

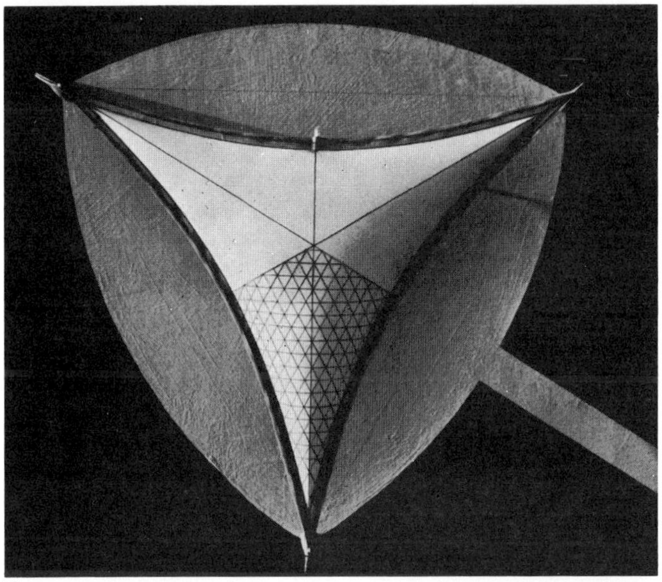

22

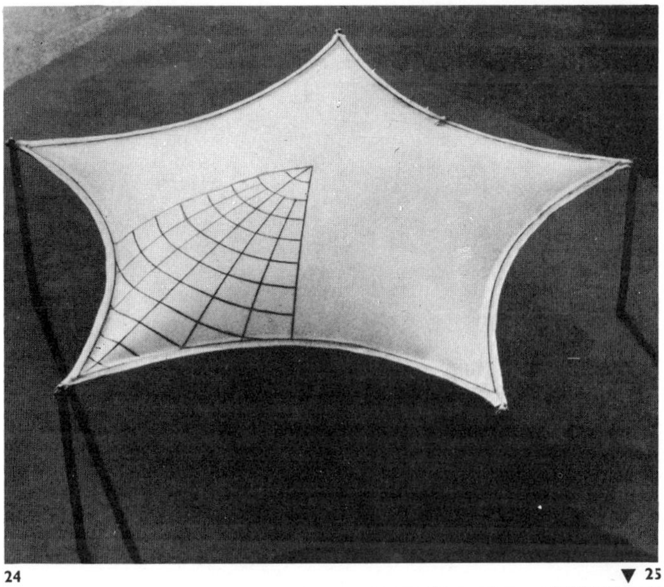

24

▼ 25

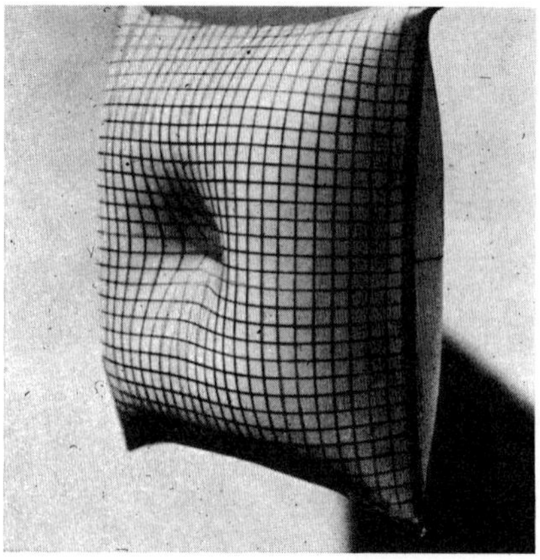
1

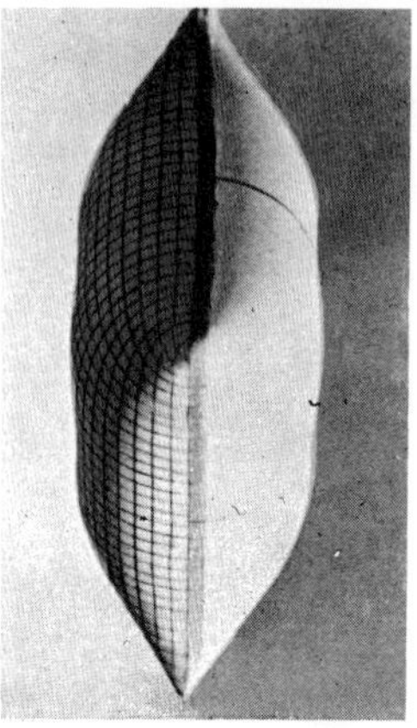
2

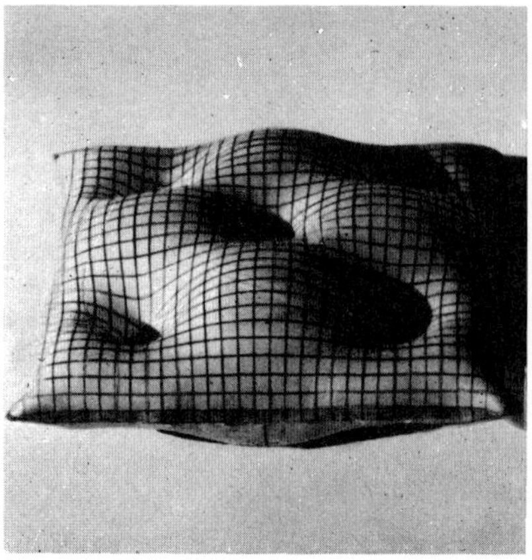
3

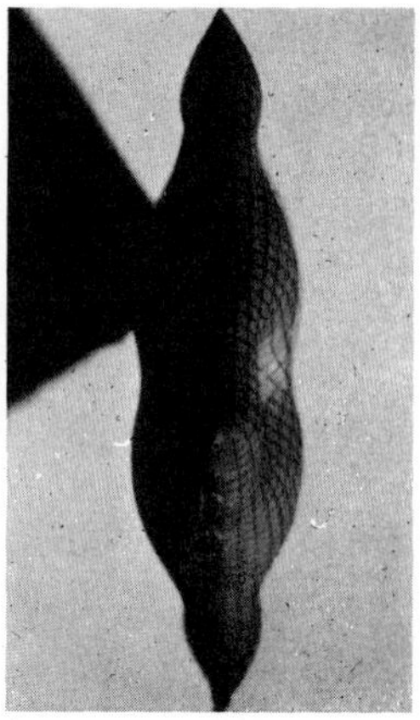
4

A further possibility for obtaining flat, pneumatic cushions is to insert interior connections between the membranes. The square rubber cushion in Figs. 1 and 2 is held together at the center. The greater the number of internal connections, the flatter the cushion becomes. The cushion in Figs. 3 and 4 (diagonal view) has five connecting points. The membranes can be joined either directly (Fig. 5) or by internal cables (Fig. 6). Mattresses are the best known type (Fig. 7). This led to the development of a mass-produced cushion* consisting of two transparent plastic sheets* welded together at the edge and at some points in the center and stretched in frames (Fig. 8). They are used as insulating windows and can also be made of three (Fig. 9) or four layers (Fig. 10). They are produced as a continuous web and wound on rollers. The cut edges are glued before they are fastened to the frames. The basic unit of the Stromeyer emergency house* (Fig. 11; drawings by John Koch) is a small dome, 5 m in diameter. These domes can be joined together to form dwelling units on a hexagonal grid (Fig. 12 and 13). The outer skin is an inflated triple membrane (Fig. 9) which has a certain rigidity for insulation and weather protection purposes. It is supported by six internal intersecting sheet-metal arches which can be rolled up like measuring tapes.

The structure retains its shape without internal pressure. The unit weighs approximately 60 kg. A doorsill renders the envelope buoyant when inflated.The units are of such rugged construction that they

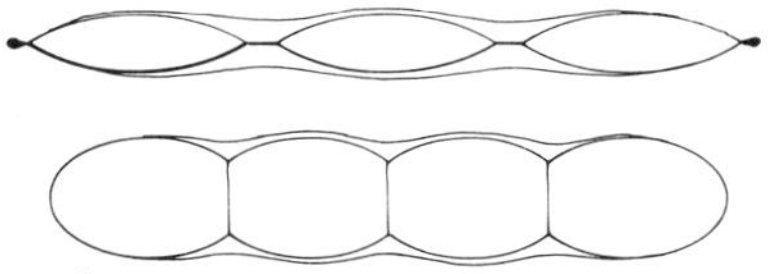
5 and 6

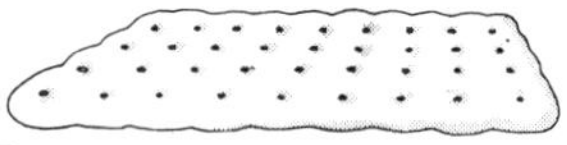
7

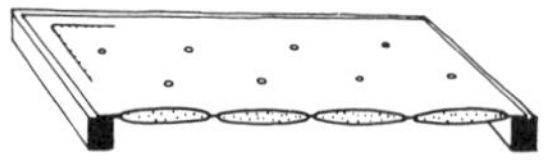
8

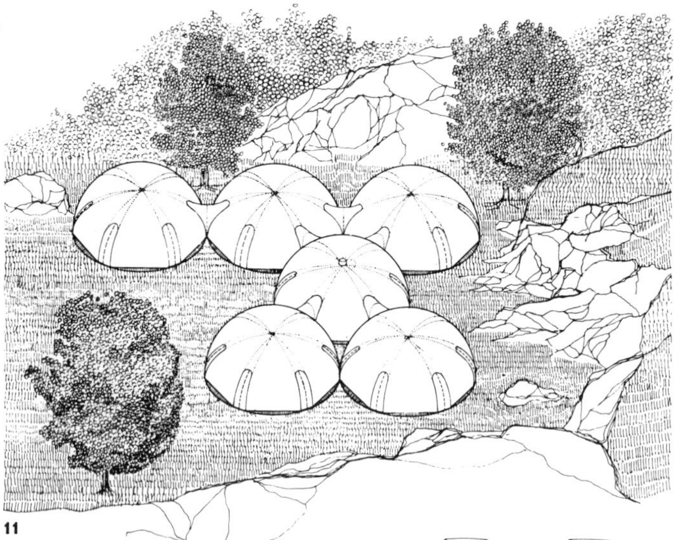
11

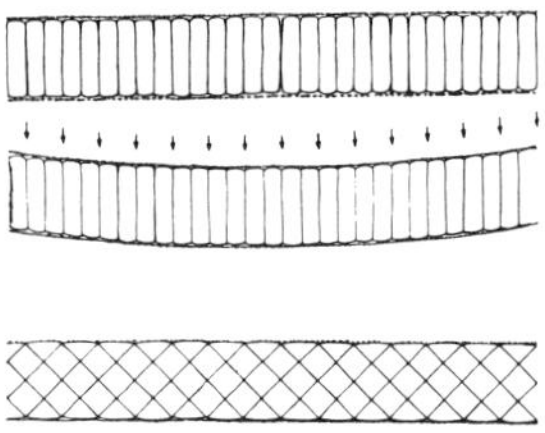
14 to 16

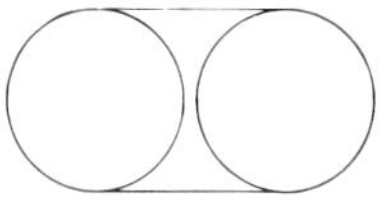
17

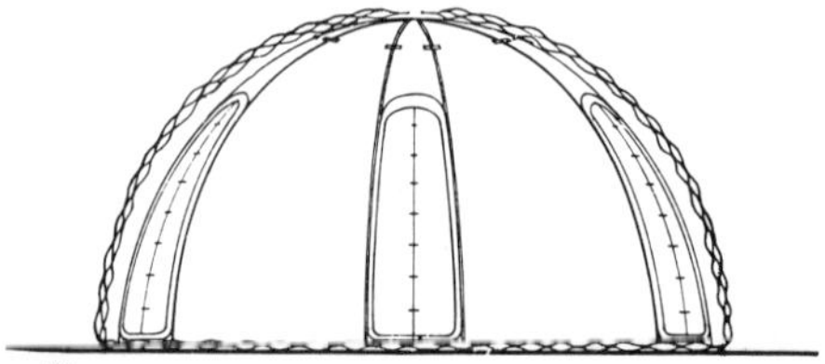
12

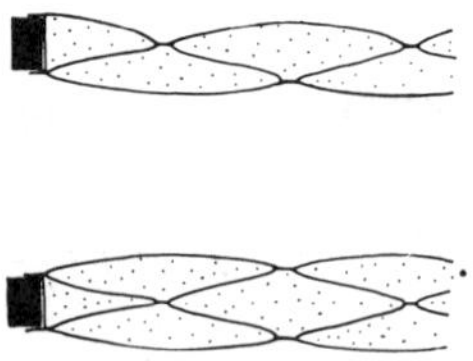
◀ 9 and 10

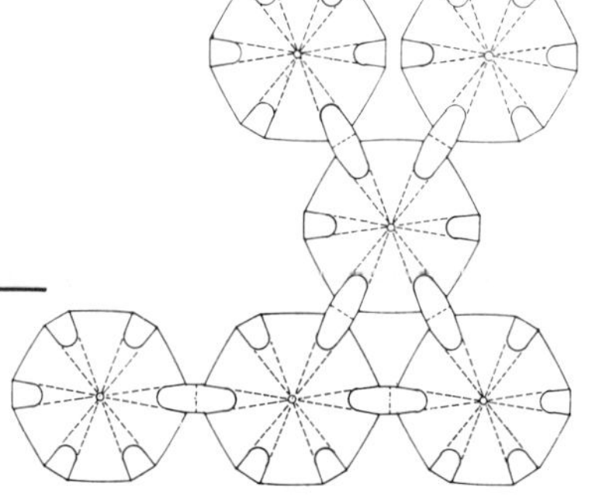
13 ▶

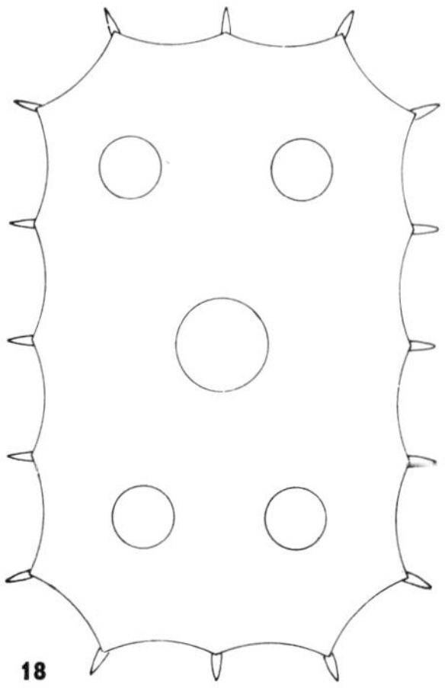
18

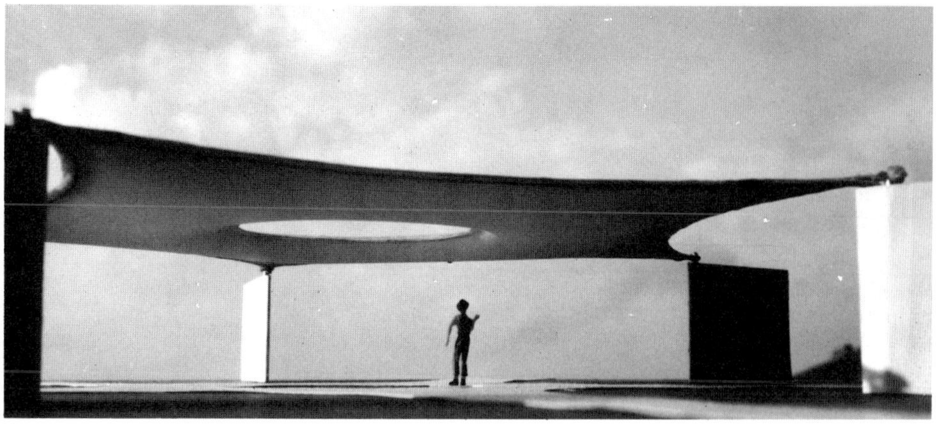

19

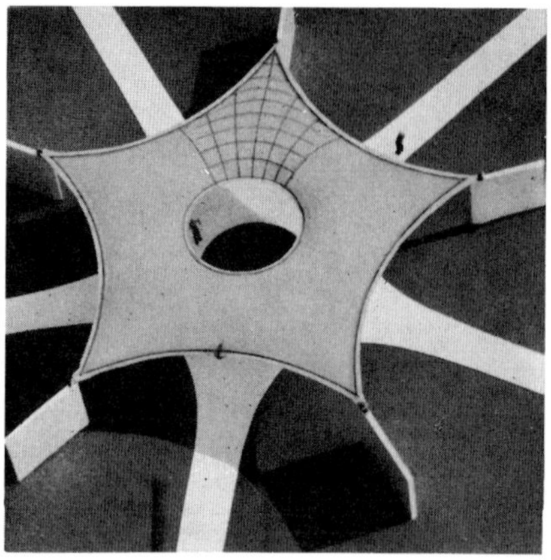

20

can be airdropped in their packings without a parachute. They can be erected by untrained personnel.

Every ring-shaped area (Fig. 17) is a cushion with zero thickness in the center. Consequently, double membranes can be drawn together not merely at points but also along circular lines which border apertures. This can be seen in the plan (Fig. 18) of a structure with 5 cutouts, and in photographs of the model of a design* for a hexagonal, cable-edged cushion roof with a central aperture (Figs. 19 and 20).

Both Goodyear and Wingfoot have designed cushions with plane-parallel surfaces held in shape by a large number of internal threads (see the section, Fig. 14). Such mats can be manufactured in a single weaving process and subsequently provided with an airtight coating. They are called "pneumatic sandwich panels." However, their rigidity under load is small (Fig. 15). Rigidity is increased* when the cords are inserted diagonally (Fig. 16). The aerodynamic shape of the air mattress (Fig. 21) is effected by nylon threads (photo by Goodyear). Buckminster Fuller, in cooperation with Berger Brothers of New Haven, constructed very light domes of pneumatic sandwich panels (Fig. 23 to 26; works photos). If cushions with internal struts are stretched in a frame, as shown in section, Fig. 3 on p. 116, light transportable structural elements result which can be tightly packed and assembled to form the most varied structures (Figs. 1 and 2, p. 116). Cushions become especially

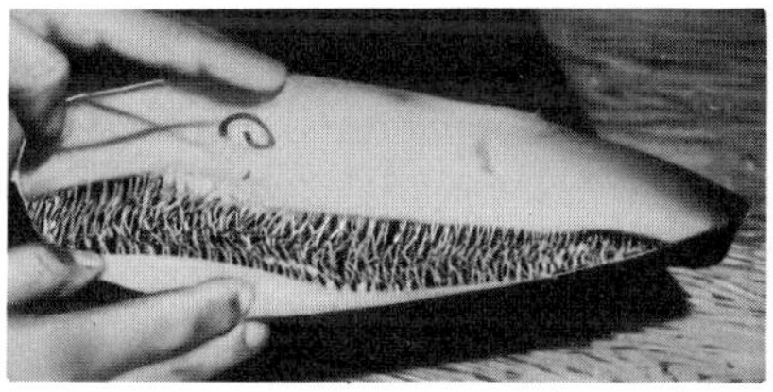

21 ▲ ▼ 22

24 ▲

23 ▼

25 ▼

26 ▶

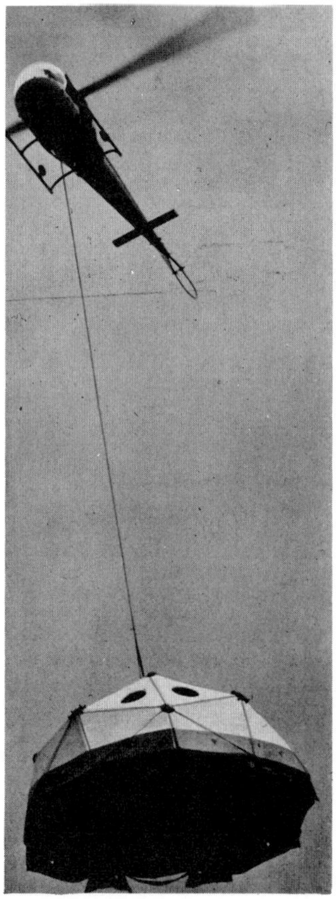

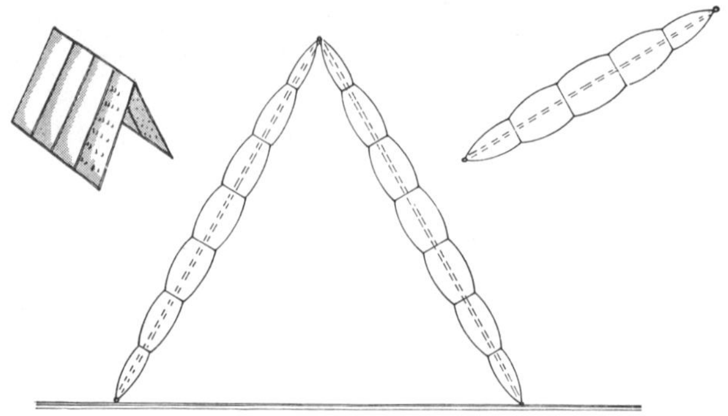

1 to 3

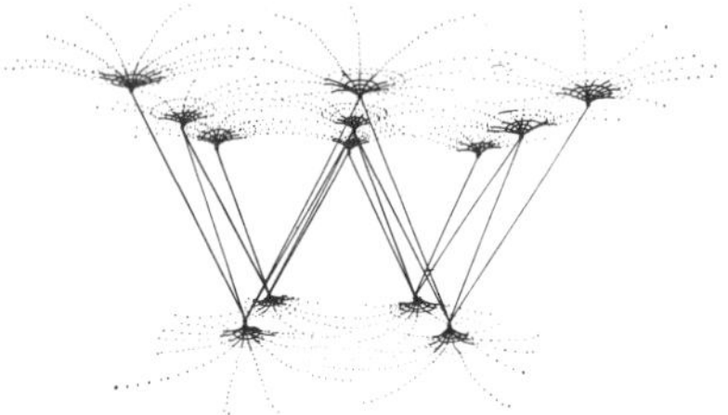

4

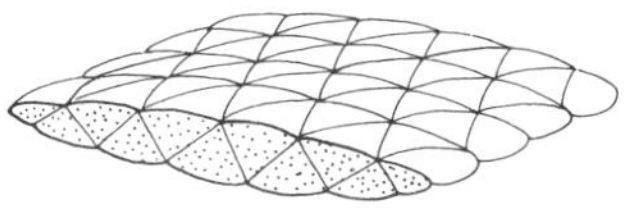

5

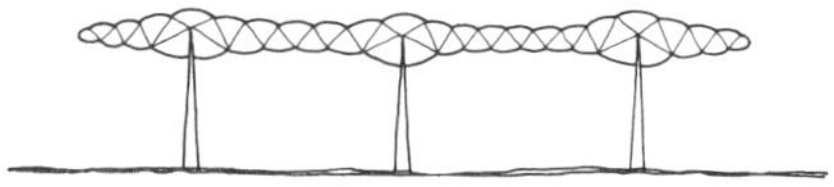

6

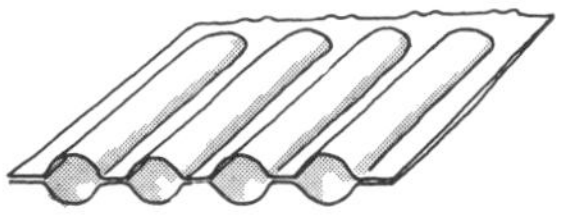

7

8

9

10

11

◄ 12

13 ▲

▼ 14

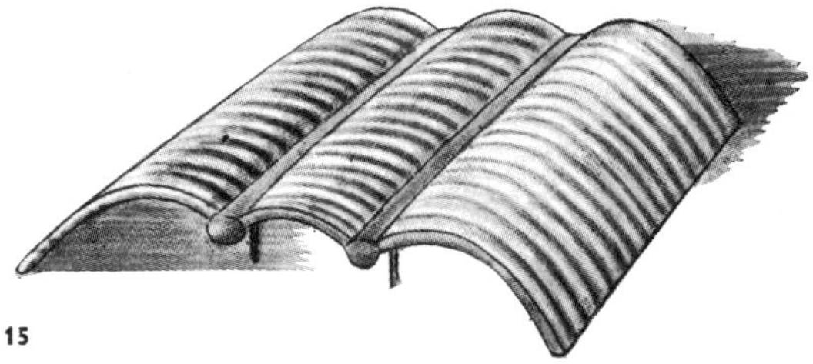

15

16

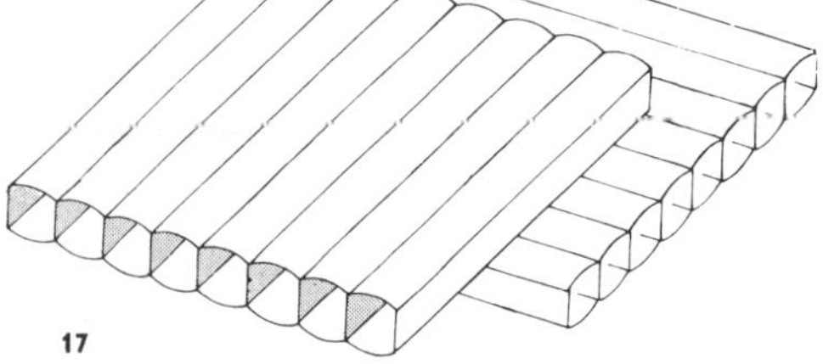

17

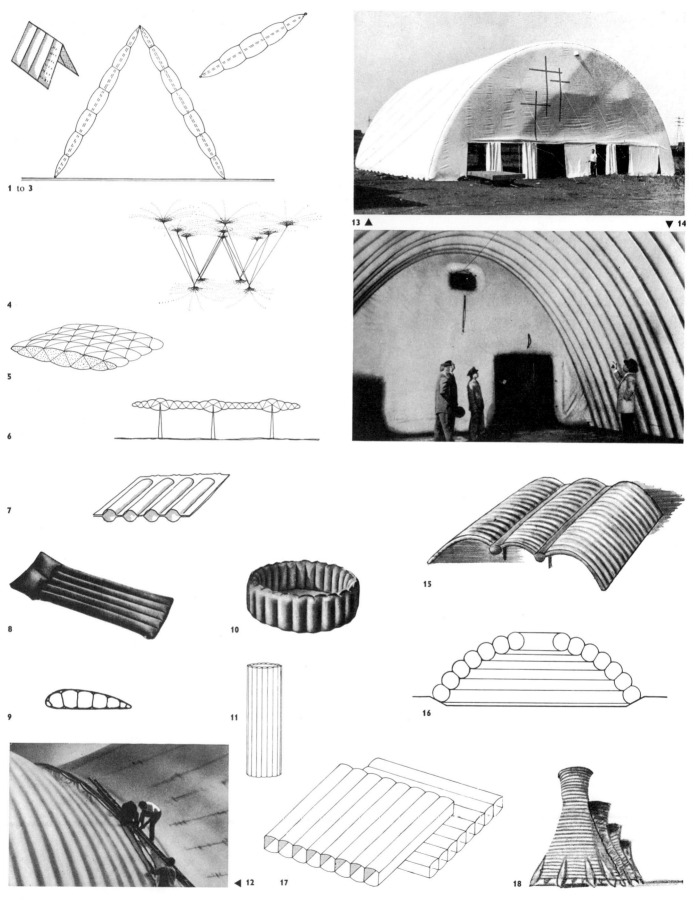

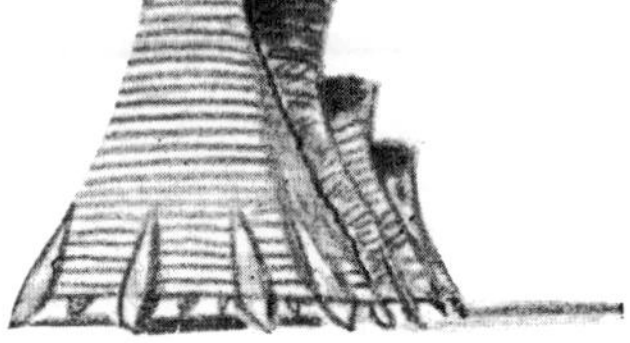

18

19 ▲

▼ 20

rigid (Fig. 4, p. 116) when the internal struts (Fig. 5, p. 116) form a lattice. Such structures can be used for many purposes. Even point-like supports arranged along the inner cable bracing (Fig. 6) are possible.

Cushion structures can be assembled easily from cylinders by welding membranes together along straight lines (Fig. 7). This procedure is well known for air mattresses (Fig. 8). (Figure by Stromeyer). As long ago as 1941 the author designed inflatable aeroplanes with wings of cylindrical hoses (Fig. 9). Several years ago such a plane actually flew in the United States (Fig. 22, p. 115; photo from *Architectural Forum*). If slender cylinders are connected so as to form a tube whose interior is also under pressure (Fig. 11), the resulting system is rigid in bending as compared to an ordinary cylindrical envelope. Lately, shallow pools for children (Fig. 10; photo by Metzeler) with walls of joined, vertical cylinders or cylindrical hoses have been produced. Rigid panels can be made by rotating successive layers of cylinders through 90° with respect to each other (Fig. 17). By joining circular hoses many different designs are possible, for example domes (Fig. 16), or hyperboloidal shells (Fig. 18) consisting of torii of different diameters. The formation of cylindrical shells (Fig. 15) from toroidal segments is very simple.

The barrel vault of the Mission church in Fig. 13; (photo by Birdair) was assembled from toroidal segments, as was the pneumatic pavilion built by Goodrich (Fig. 14; photo from *Architectural*

1 ▲ ▼ 2

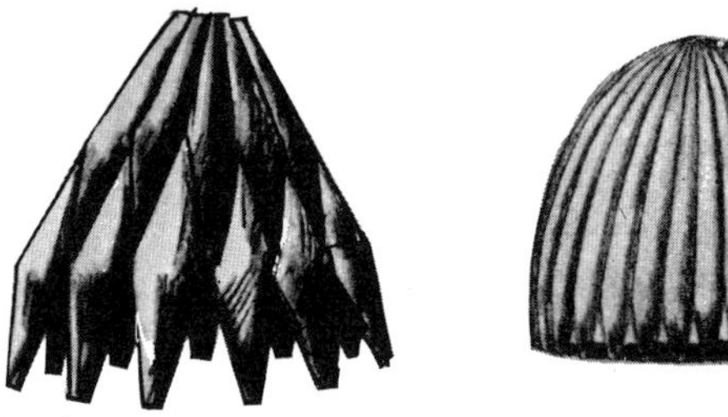

3 and 4

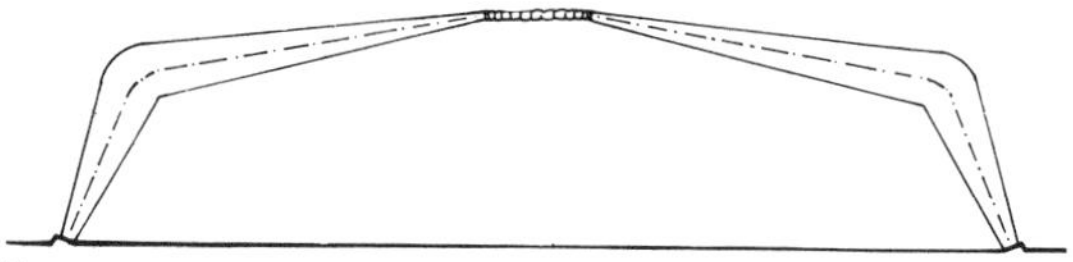

5

6

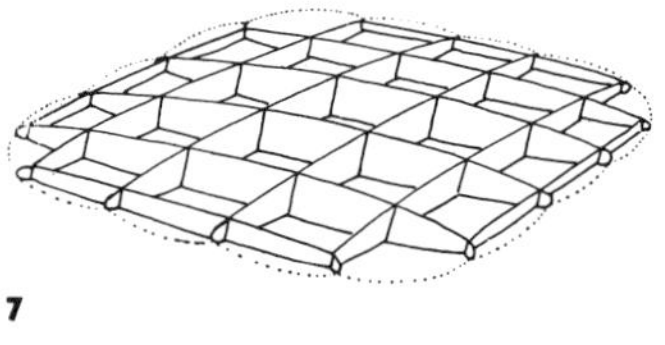

7

8

9

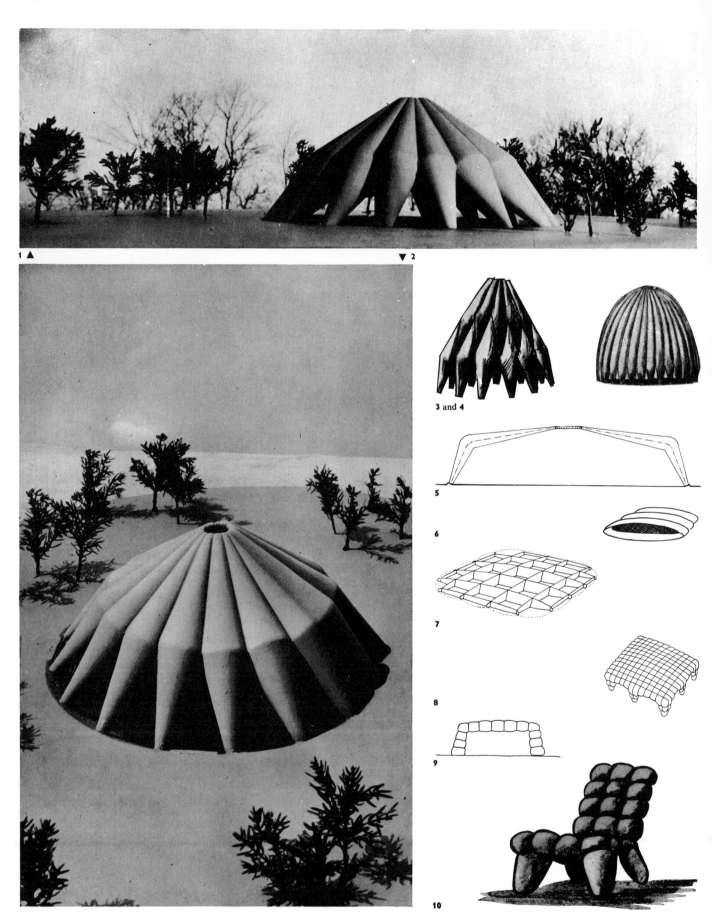

10

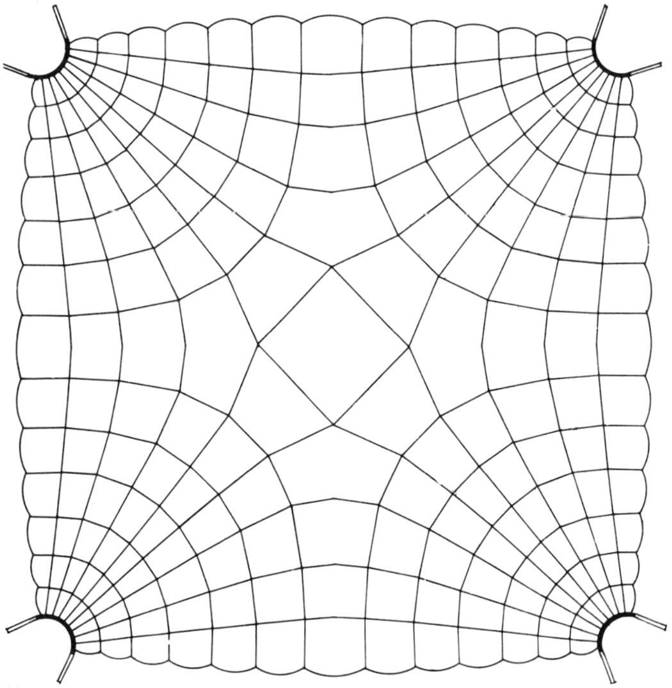

11

12

13

14 to 16 ▶

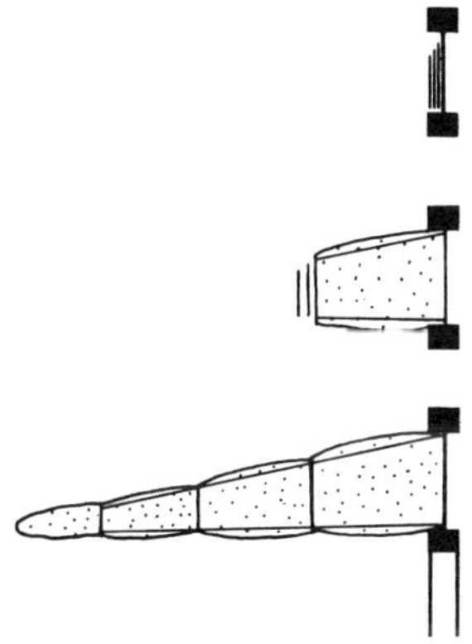

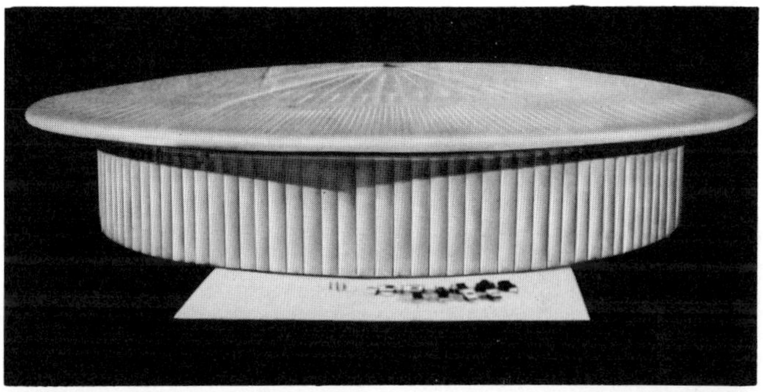

17 ▲

▼ 18

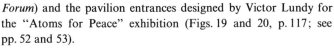

Forum) and the pavilion entrances designed by Victor Lundy for the "Atoms for Peace" exhibition (Figs. 19 and 20, p. 117; see pp. 52 and 53).

Joined cylinders behave like arches and were covered by an external awning (Fig. 12, p. 116). Pneumatically tensed hollow conical bodies are also well suited for the construction of envelopes. Double cones can be staggered like brickwork (Fig. 3), or simply placed side by side as in the project for a beach pavilion* (Figs. 1 and 2). This design is very simple, since the double cones are easily manufactured. They are all interconnected at their common contact point and can therefore be inflated together. The blower is below the foot of one of the cones. Since the membrane is highly airtight and the double cones are closed on all sides, a small blower is sufficient. The structure is open on all sides.

Figure 5 shows a section through a circular hall formed of double cones bent at an angle and placed side by side. The roof surface is closed down to the bend. The footings are similar to those in the beach pavilion in Figs. 1 and 2. The dome in Fig. 4, whose joined double cones have a curved axis, is also very similar.

1 ▲

▼ 2

▼ 3

If, for example, pneumatic cushions are assembled from cylinders which touch not merely along a line, but along a surface, we obtain "partitions" (Fig. 17, p. 116) which are located within the structure and are mainly plane surfaces, since the air pressure on both sides is substantially equal. The partitions may consist of flexible membranes which are admirably suited to the manufacture of flat cushions (Fig. 6, p. 118). They can also consist of porous open fabric whose weft should make an angle of less than 45° with the neutral axis. Intersecting partitions forming individual air chambers are especially worth mentioning (Fig. 7, p. 118). Highly rigid cushions whose thickness can vary with the magnitude of the bending moment, can be made. The use of such cushions for a roof structure is illustrated in Fig. 8 on p. 118 and in the cross section, Fig. 9 on p. 118 of a similar building. Additional cushions have been fitted to the panel as footings or side walls. Nearly any shape can be obtained as seen by the example of a chair in Fig. 10, p. 118. Nevertheless, the laws of formation governing pneumatically tensed membranes must be adhered to for the entire system if folds are to be avoided. The rigidity of cushions which form plane panels can, within certain limits, be varied with the magnitude of the bending moments by changing the number of partitions. Figure 11, p. 119 shows the plan of a panel which is thicker at its center than at the edges and corners. It is held at the corners by four built-in supports designed as curved shells. The structure of a roof of arbitrary size that has central supports is very similar; a part of it is shown in Fig. 12, p. 119.

Cushion structures with closed compartments can form overhanging or free roofs (Fig. 13, p. 119) which can be extended or retracted by internal pressure alone (Figs. 14 to 16, p. 119). The individual compartments are pressurized successively to prevent sag, since

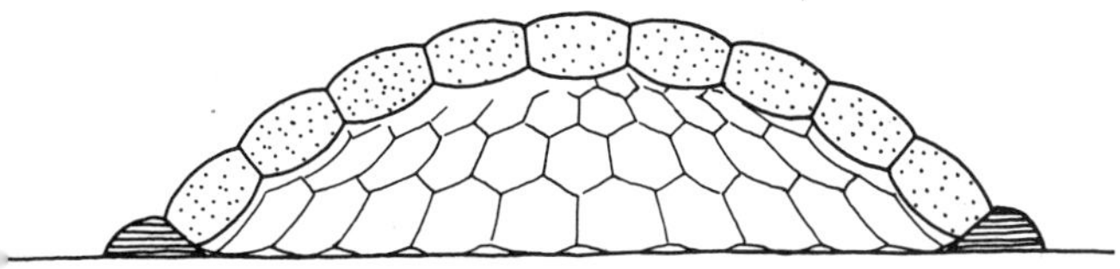

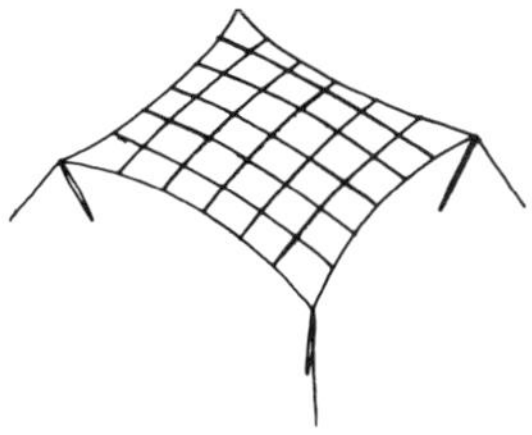

and 6

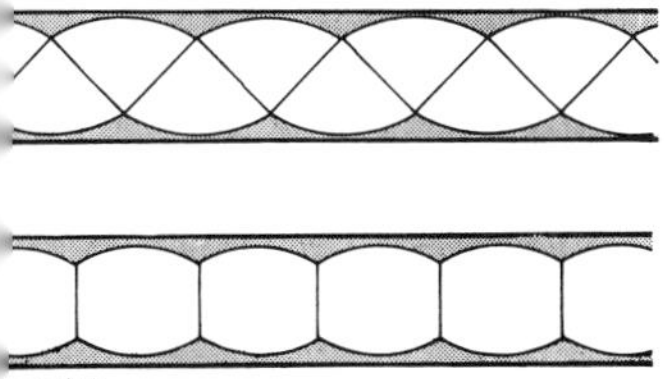

and 8

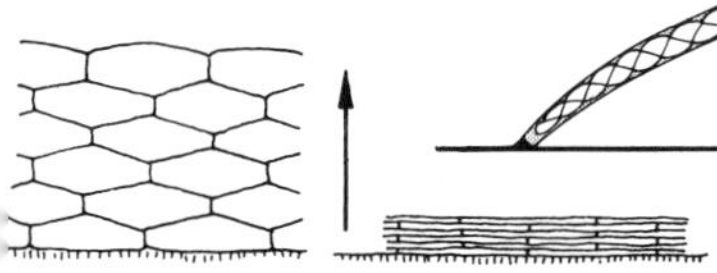

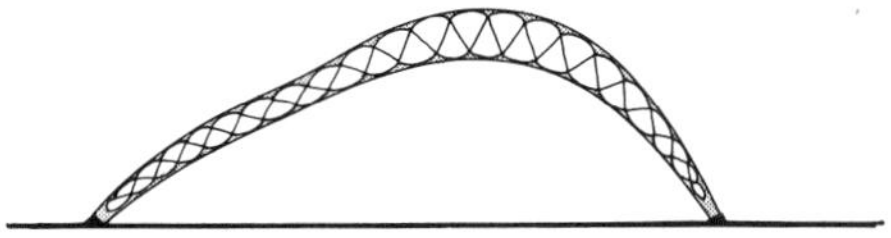

0 and 11

9

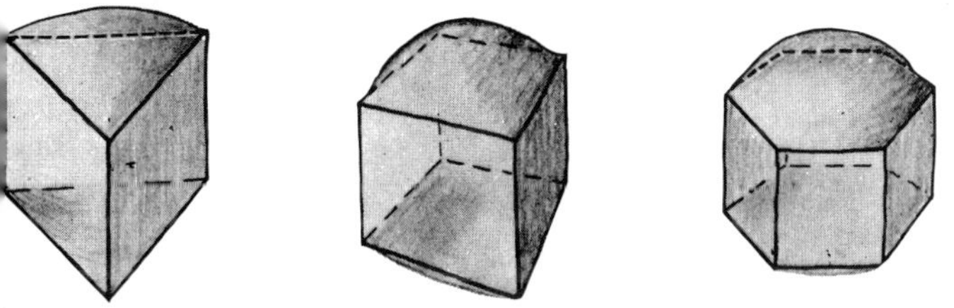

2 to 14

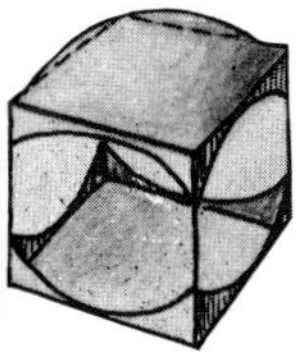

15

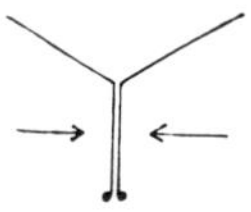

16

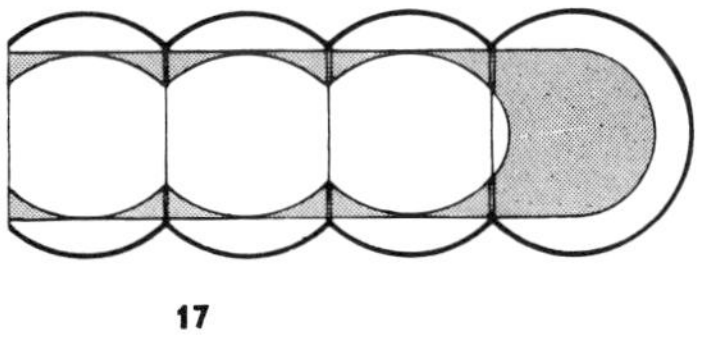

17

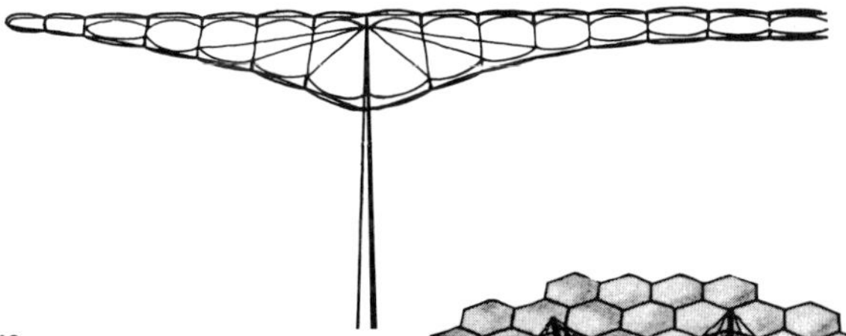

18

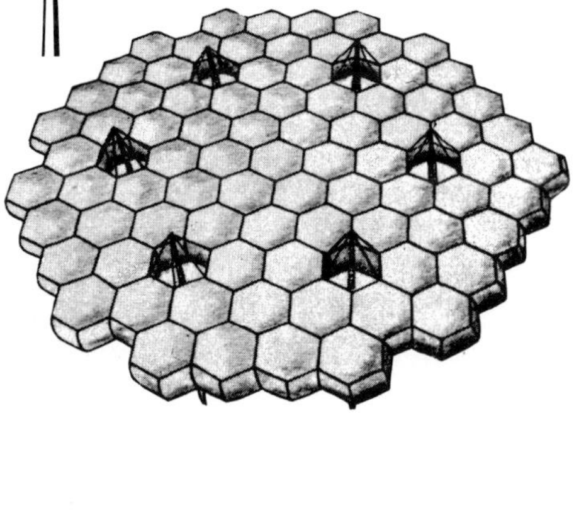

19

the roof is folded in the pneumatically untensed state by additional internal elastic elements.

In *Architectural Forum,* July 1959, Walter Bird published the design of an exhibition pavilion for the Ford Motor Company. The structure has a diameter of 90 m and is covered by a disk-shaped pneumatic roof which is obviously a cushion structure with radial partitions (Figs. 17 and 18, p. 119). Cylinders placed side by side form thc comparatively flexible lateral walls. Like most cushion structures, this one requires high internal pressure.

Domed structures of pneumatically tensed cushions* with partitions merit special attention. Since they assume a statically efficient shape (Fig. 4), the required air pressures are low. Wind suction forces can be taken up directly by the tensile resistance of the membrane. Positive loads, such as snow, necessitate a particularly high air pressure in cushion structures, unless the pressure in the interior is increased when snow loads are extreme. Such an envelope can normally be entered without air locks, but is closed when under extreme loads.

Figure 5 shows a freely accessible shell dome supported at three points, and Figs. 1 to 3 a domed shell with four footings. This is a project* for the main structure of an exhibition. Sketch 6 illustrates the additional rigidity imparted by a number of intersecting partitions to a cushion roof stretched between four cables and four points of attachment. As previously explained for structures with internal partitions, the latter form constrictions along lines so that rainwater can drain down the resulting valleys. It has been proved that bracing the interior partitions with cables is advisable, in a manner similar to that shown in Figs. 1 to 7 on p. 104 and also in Figs. 7 and 8. In this way, a large continuous space is obtained while economizing on membrane material. Furthermore, the cushion can be deformed by adjusting the cable lengths as seen in the roof cross section (Fig. 9).

The sandbag is one of the best known pneumatic structures and can be used to build walls of any dimension. A wall of joined cushions is very similar; at first it lies collapsed on the ground (Fig. 11) rising to form a rigid wall when air or a solidifying liquid is injected (Fig. 10).

Foundation elements (Figs. 12 to 14) for assembling panel-like structures can be triangular, rectangular, orthorhombic, square, or hexagonal in plan; they can have straight side walls and domed outer membrane walls. The side walls can be reduced to a minimum thus forming awning-like upper and lower parts that are connected by cables (Fig. 15). Since internal pressure forces the wall membranes together, as seen in the section through a valley joint (Fig. 16), airtight assembly of such plates presents no excessive difficulties. Figure 17 shows the edge. The plate in Fig. 19 consists of hexagonal cushions and is supported by masts via cables. Whereas pneumatic cushion structures are sensitive to highly concentrated loads, their effect can be reduced considerably by internal cable bracing as shown in Fig. 18.

1

approximately uniform water pressure at different filling levels. The discharge is at the lowest point of the container. Although such containers are subject to considerable loads when filled almost to capacity, their construction usually requires less material and work than water towers. Such containers are not merely important for water management but also for energy storage.

Containers for Liquids

The pneumatic loads of the structures dealt with hitherto were caused mainly by air pressure; however, liquids in flexible envelopes can exert similar loads. Such containers are widespread in nature, e.g., berries, tomatoes, grapes, and many others. Figure 1 shows the small juice containers of a grapefruit, greatly magnified, in which the liquid is under comparatively high pressure. While containers under gas pressure must be closed, this is not absolutely necessary for liquids. Sketch 2 shows a flexible membrane suspended from a ring and loaded by a liquid. Diagram 3 shows pressure as a function of height. It increases with depth and is proportional to the product of weight density and depth. Figure 4 shows the same container covered with a membrane on which the water pressure acts vertically upward. The container, which has an opening at the top, is closed on all sides and loaded only by pressure of the liquid, without additional tension (Fig. 5).

Additional tension can be induced by closing the container and by putting the liquid under pressure, either by pumping more liquid in or by attaching a pipe (Fig. 6). The highest point of the container is then already under pressure (Fig. 7). The pressure diagram forms a trapezoid, which can be imagined as consisting of a rectangle and a triangle. The rectangle represents a type of preloading, and the triangle corresponds to the additional load caused by the weight of the liquid between the upper and lower boundaries of the container.

The type of loading shown in Fig. 8 where a gas and a liquid are together in one container is also frequent. If the gas is under pressure, diagram 9 results. If the liquid is removed, the diagram becomes rectangular; if the gas is removed but the pressure maintained, the load is represented by diagram 7.
Figure 10 is a section through a high-pressure water tank consisting of a flexible membrane. An air cushion maintains

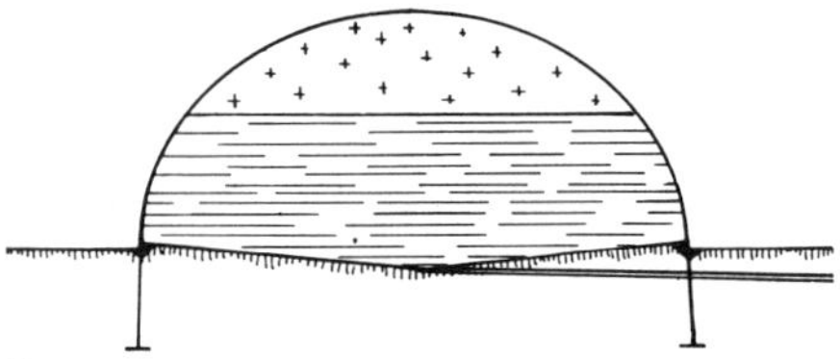
10

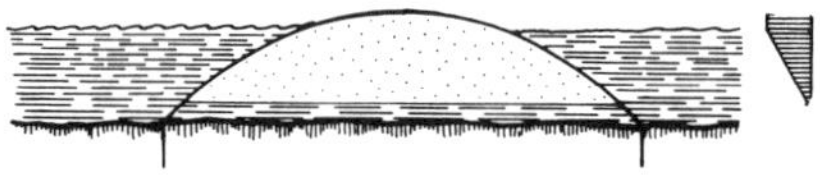
11 and 12

Figure 11 shows the inverse. A gas-filled dome is under external water pressure. In this case, water pressure on the dome, which must be counterbalanced by the internal gas pressure, increases in the downward direction. Hence, the pressure difference (Fig. 12) and, thus, the membrane tension is greatest not at the bottom but at the top. Such underwater domes could, for example, be used like caissons for laying underwater foundations.

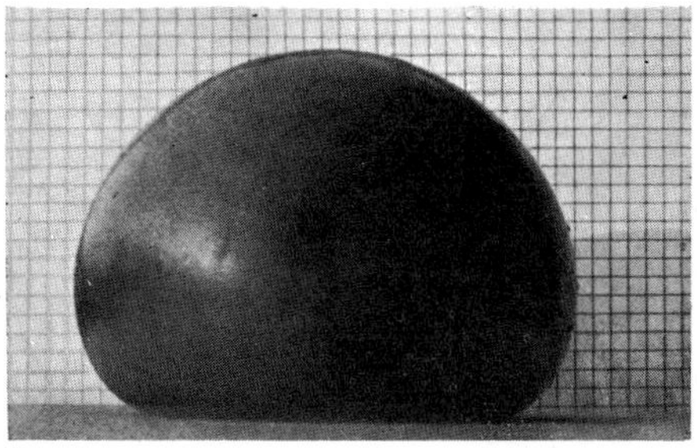
13

This process is particularly economical for large underwater constructions at shallow depths.

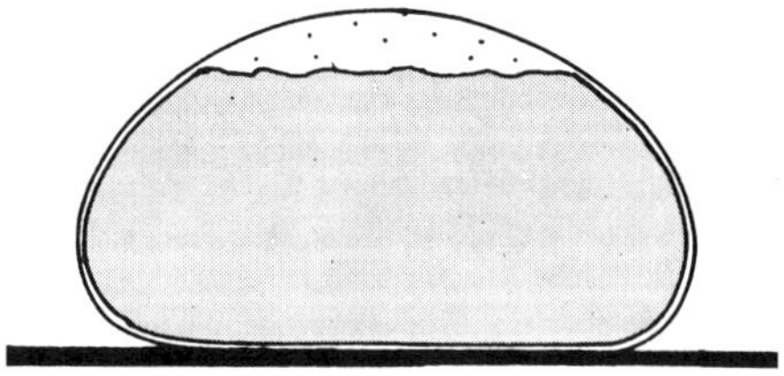
14

2 to **9**

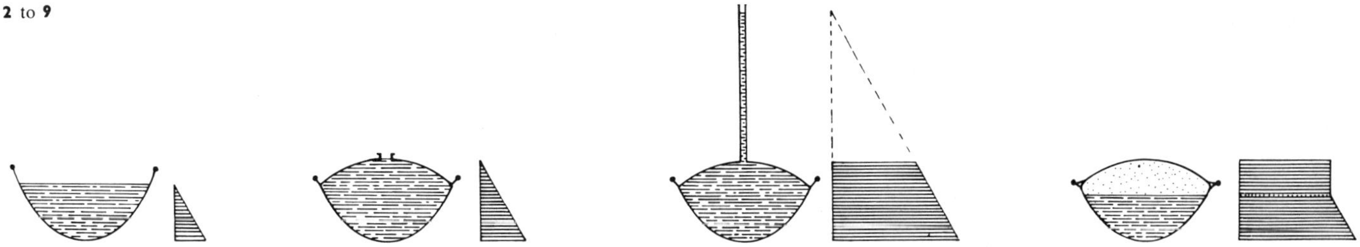

For example, the membrane can be attached to a heavy rigid ring with a sharp lower edge; alternatively, it can be pulled downward continuously with the aid of previously placed deep tension anchors.

Measuring tests (Fig. 13) using liquid-filled highly elastic rubber envelopes are important in the investigation of container shapes. The downward increase in pressure causes a droplike deformation, which is particularly visible in the photographs of a mercury drop at approximately sixfold magnification. The surface tension of the mercury has an effect similar to that of a rubber membrane, being uniform everywhere. In the very small droplet (Fig. 30) the pressure difference is very small. With decreasing diameter the shape of the drop approaches a sphere. The larger the drop (Figs. 31 to 34), the flatter its shape. Beyond a certain maximum height which it cannot exceed, it forms a large, plane surface with rounded edges.

If a flexible membrane of low deformability is constructed in the shape of such a mercury or water droplet, (which can easily be derived mathematically, or from rubber-membrane experiments [Fig. 13]) and the membrane is then filled with water, the container will slowly become inflated by water pressure, as illustrated in Figs. 15 to 19. The water first fills the container at its largest diameter and thereby induces tension in the upper part of the dome and in the bottom.

In the stages shown in Figs. 16 to 18 the container is comparatively deformable by external loads; however, when filled with liquid, the danger of wind vibration is very small. Figures 20 to 24 show such a container anchored to the ground by cables passing over the top. As the liquid level rises, the cables are loosened, so that the system is kept under control at every stage. If stabilization is to be effected by additional internal gas pressure, which would also be present in the empty state (Fig. 25), the laws governing the formation of envelopes under gas pressure must be observed (see p. 18). In that case, the container must be anchored to the ground at its edge, since otherwise the bottom membrane would curve under gas pressure and the container assume a spherical shape. However, liquids can be stored at constant or variable pressures in the lower part of ring-anchored containers, which maintain their shape (Figs. 25 to 29).

At uniform internal gas pressure (Fig. 25) the tensions in the membrane of the container differ from those induced by liquids (Fig. 29). When using membranes of low deformability the change in shape is only slight. A container constructed and filled in this way can be termed stable at every liquid level.

A decisive advantage of all flexible and collapsible containers for liquids is that the presence of gases at the various levels can be avoided. The entry of oxygen must be prevented when storing highly explosive substances.

Even in flexible containers for liquids, that

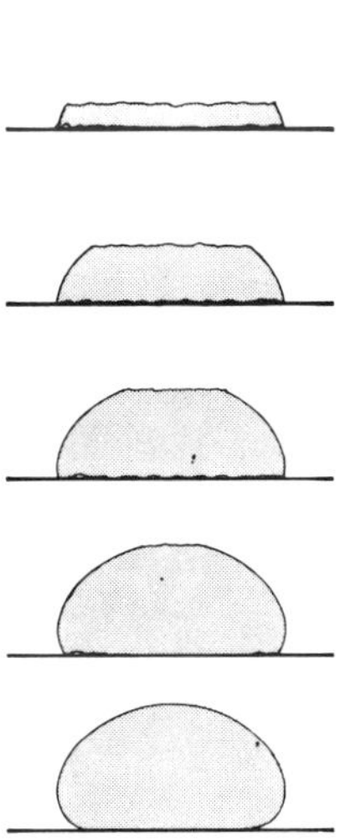

15 to **19**

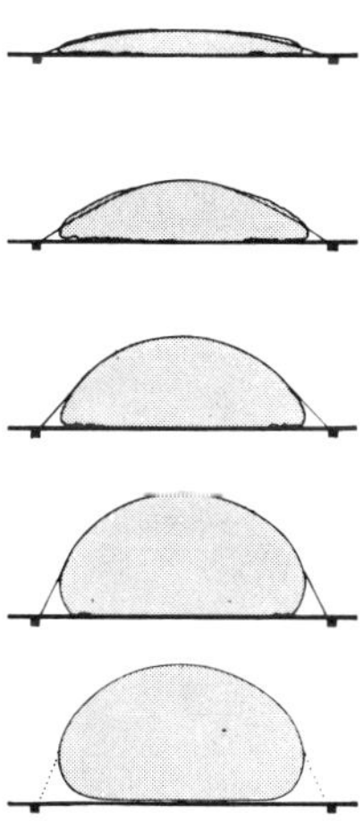

20 to **24**

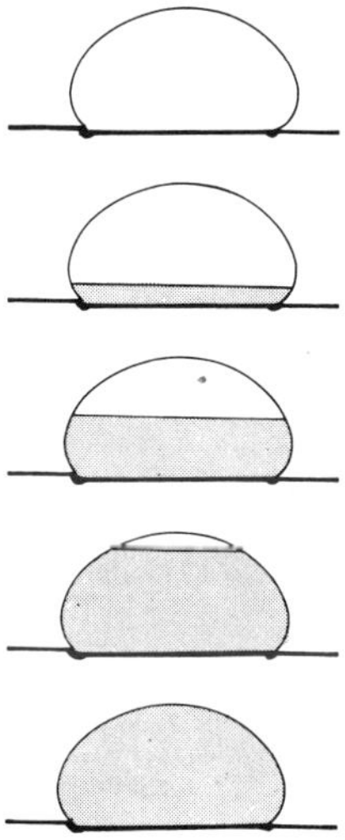

25 to **29**

▼ **30** to **34**

1

2

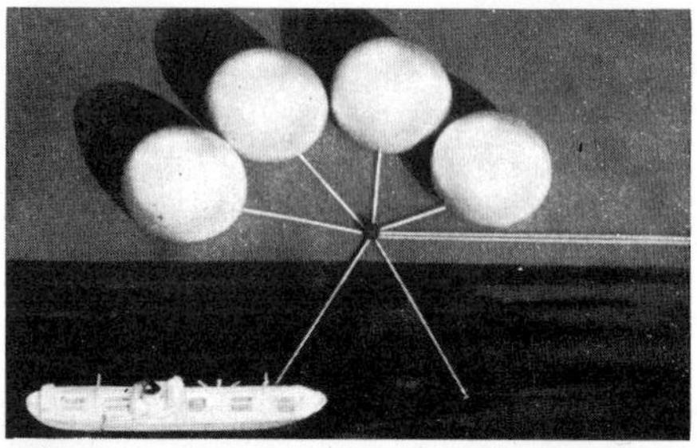

3 ▲

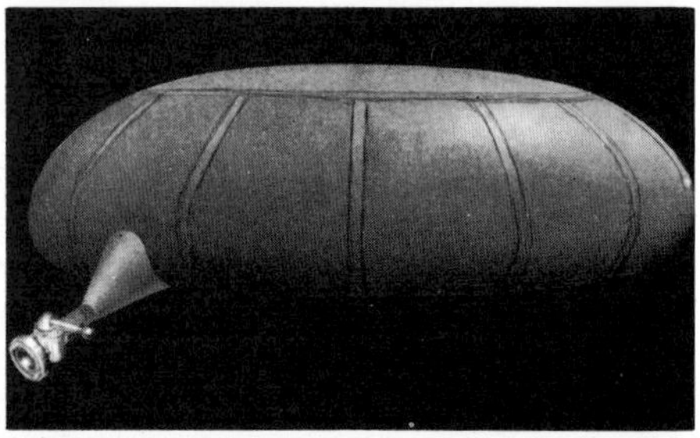

4 ▲

5 ▼

are gas-pressure stabilized as in Figs. 25 to 29, p. 123, the separation of liquid and gas can be achieved by a thin additional membrane (Fig. 14, p. 122).

Nowadays, oil storage tanks are erected near the wells or in the vicinity of ports. Such oil ports are often built out at sea to allow even the largest tankers to approach. Figure 1 shows a project* for two-tank storage installation, Figs. 2 and 3 the project of a coastal four-tank installation with a distribution center and two direct pipelines to the ships, and Fig. 4 a small water tank made by Ballonfabrik Augsburg (works photo).

The spherical containers flattened at the bottom, shown in Fig. 5 were built of thin steel sheeting by the Chicago Bridge and Iron Company.†

Figure 6 shows the stability conditions of a liquid-filled membrane shaped like a truncated cone. The pressure of the liquid, which acts at right angles to the surface of the container, induces hoop tensions which act in a horizontal direction when the axis of the container is vertical. The liquid pressure acts in an oblique upward direction, and causes tensile stresses in the container shell, which increase toward the bottom. Even if it is made completely of flexible material, such a container will right itself under the pressure of the liquid. Tension is slight at the upper edge of the membrane and increases considerably toward the bottom. The flatter the cone, the greater the forces tensing the membrane. To obtain greater rigidity at the top, a shape corresponding to Fig. 7 can be selected. Another way to increase membrane stability is to form the upper edge by means of a floating ring (Fig. 8). A conical membrane (Fig. 9) not positively anchored at its base and provided with a floor, deforms under water pressure as shown by the broken line; folds will appear along the edge of the flat bottom. The conical part of the membrane rises under water pressure.

Figures 10 to 15 illustrate different stages in the erection of a conical membrane according to Fig. 6. The edge of the conical membrane is anchored to the base plate. Considerable tensile forces act on the anchoring elements. In Figure 16 the anchors

† E. Torroja, *Logik der Form*, Munich, Callwey Verlag 1961.

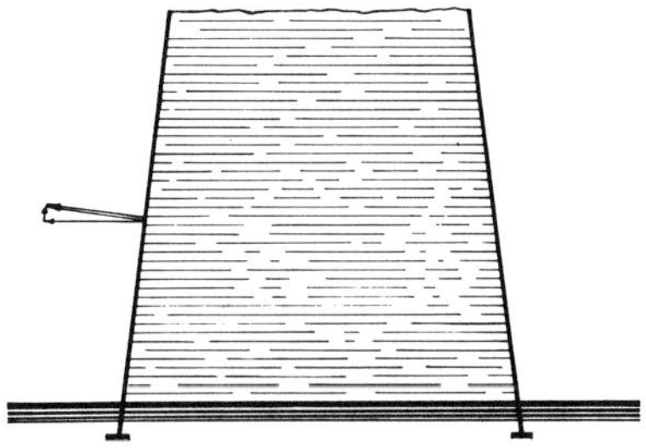

6

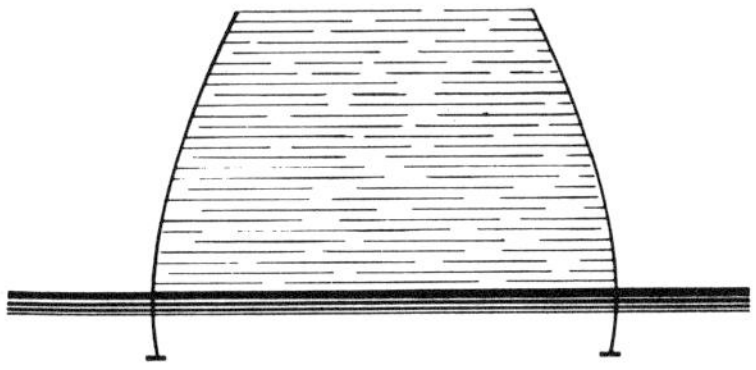

7

8

9 ▼

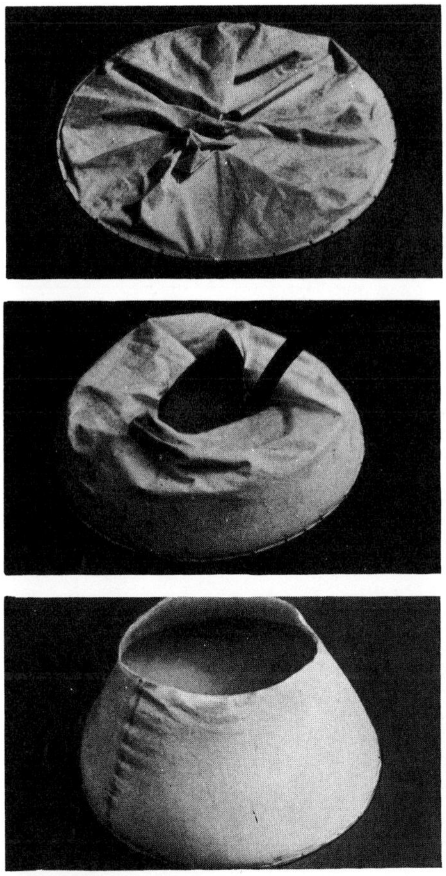

10 to 12 ▲

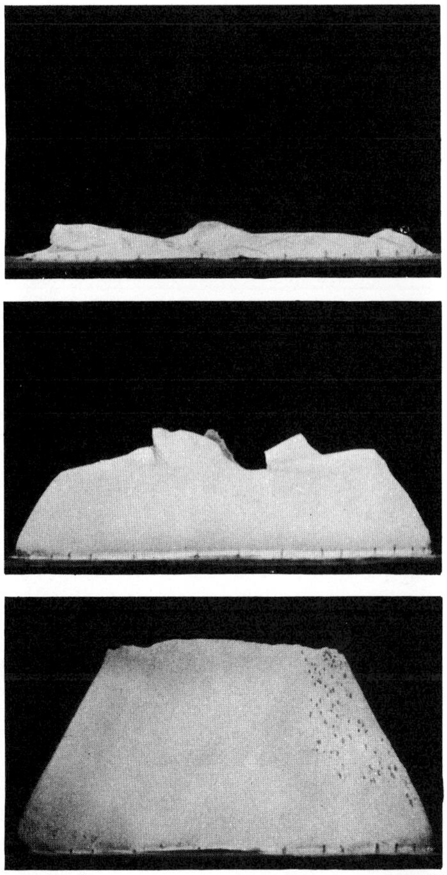

13 to 15 ▲

▼ 16

have been removed and the shape indicated in Fig. 9 results.

Containers of large diameter and low height (Fig. 7, p. 126) need not have a bottom membrane. The outward-acting tensile forces can be taken up by a circular cable; the water pressure (acting in the direction of the arrows) will ensure tightness. Ground anchors can be used instead of a circular cable (Fig. 8, p. 126).

Thin, flexible membranes of great toughness, supported and reinforced by cables, could solve many problems in container design, with applications to dams, dykes, and land reclamation. Figures 1 to 6 on p. 126 show the formation of an artificial island planned (Fig. 9 of the same page) in a wide river mouth surrounded by inhospitable jungle. A membrane is placed in shallow water on a muddy bottom that has poor supporting capacity, and is filled with water (Fig. 1, p. 126). The new water level is higher and the membrane is under tension (Fig. 2, p. 126). The container is now filled with sand brought by barges (Fig. 3, p. 126) and the water displaced. At first, the new island will settle due to the high loads acting on its base. The edge can then be hardened to form a retaining wall by injecting a concrete emulsion (grouting) through the membrane in the direction of the arrows in Fig. 4, p. 126. (Grouting is not absolutely necessary if a membrane of adequate service life is used.) A permanent settlement can then be established on the island. The foundation membrane can also anchor a surmounting pneumatic dome (Fig. 6, p. 126).

A conical membrane widened toward the top collapses under pressure of a liquid. A cylindrical membrane (Fig. 10, p. 126) is practicable if held up by a floating ring. Lately many flexible containers have been built as cylinders with floating rings. Stromeyer has gathered experience in this field.

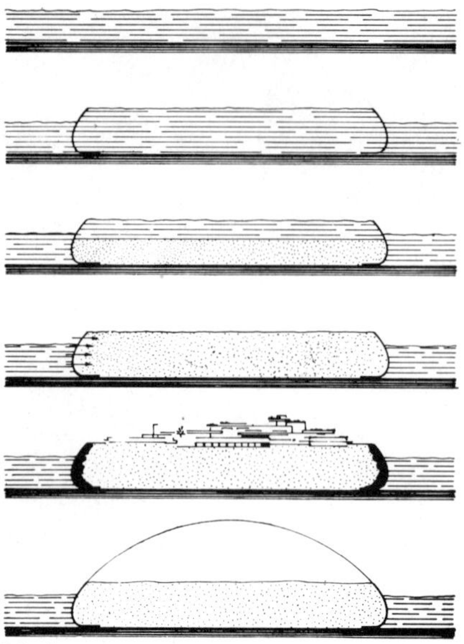

1 to 6

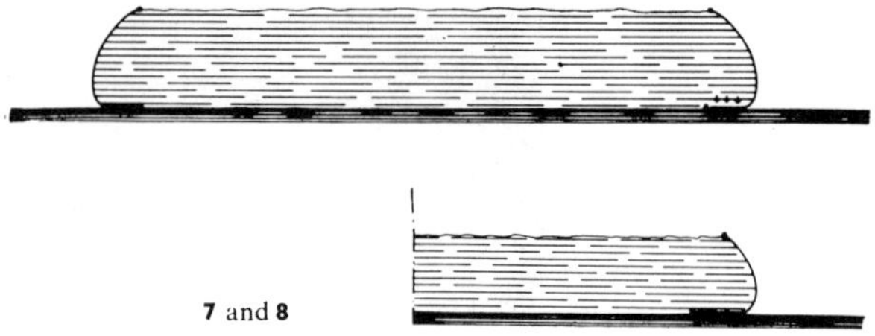

7 and 8

9

10

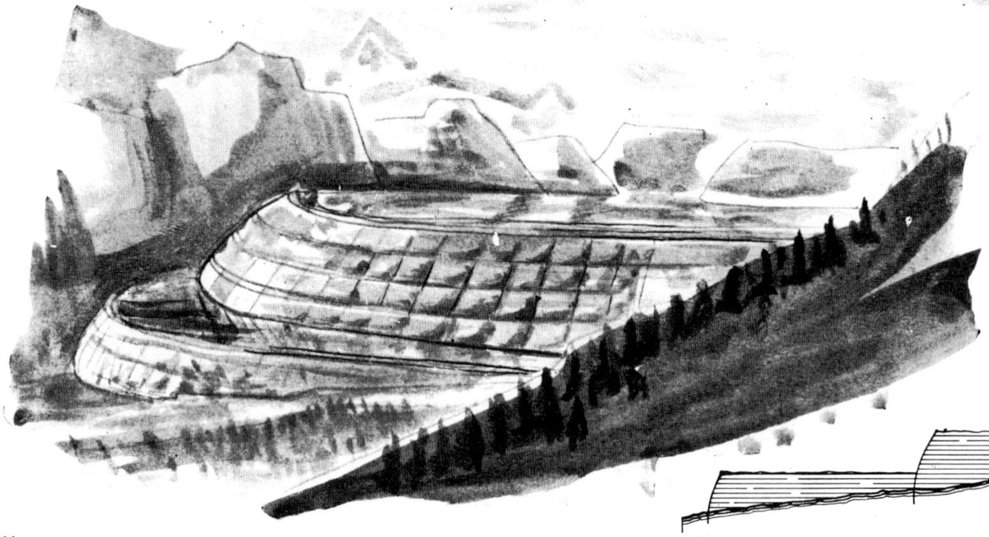

11

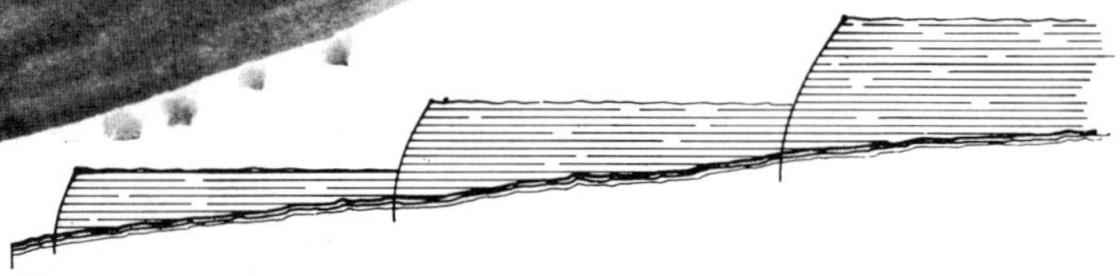

12

Container membranes with or without floating rings may be used not only for closed circular structures, but also in segments, as in the projects* for dams shown in Figs. 11 to 17. The membranes are supported by heavy cable nets because of the considerable tensile loads. If such a pneumatically tensed membrane becomes limp and changes its shape when the pressure is removed it is called a "non-rigid" structure, in contrast with the rigid structures dealt with on pp. 128 to 129.

Tension-loaded dams are highly economical and have the further advantages of being particularly immune to sliding foundations and earthquakes. Such dams are far less affected by ice and glacier pressure in high mountains or by flood-driven objects, than comparable arched retaining walls. Since it has become possible to anchor heavy cables in the foundations, and above all, to pass thin membranes into the ground to considerable depths as foundation seals, these structures have assumed great importance. Their margin of safety against deliberate destruction, such as bombing or sabotage, is far higher than is generally assumed. Even if several cables of the net are destroyed, no break will occur but only leakages which will result in a gradual emptying of the reservoir. It is also comparatively simple to build a cascade of dams, especially when the head is large (see Fig. 14). Figure 17 is a section through a cascade of two flexible dams with floating rings, which are able to retain a head approximately 20 m high. Figure 15 shows a cross section of a project to relieve an unsafe arch dam. Figure 16 is the cross section of a flexible dam with a cable net which is anchored deep in the foundations.

In the book *Das hängende Dach,* comparatively rigid dams were already envisaged spanning mountain valleys by means of saddle-shaped, prestressed cable nets bordered by a bracing cable at the crest. When the reservoir is full, the water pressure exceeds the wind pressure which acts on the empty reservoir. It is desirable to reduce the radii of curvature of the prestressed cable net, especially in

13

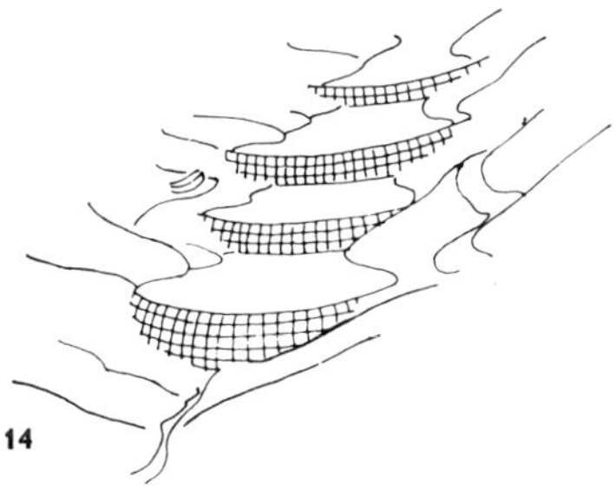

14

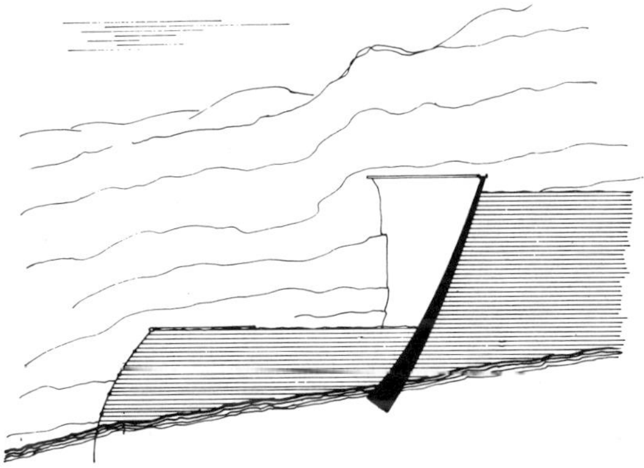

15

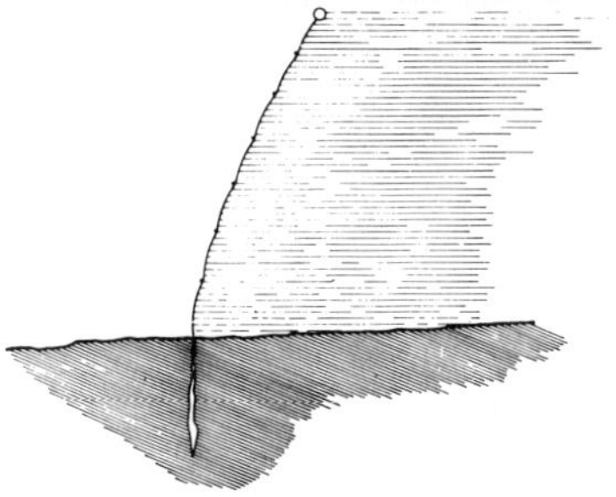

16

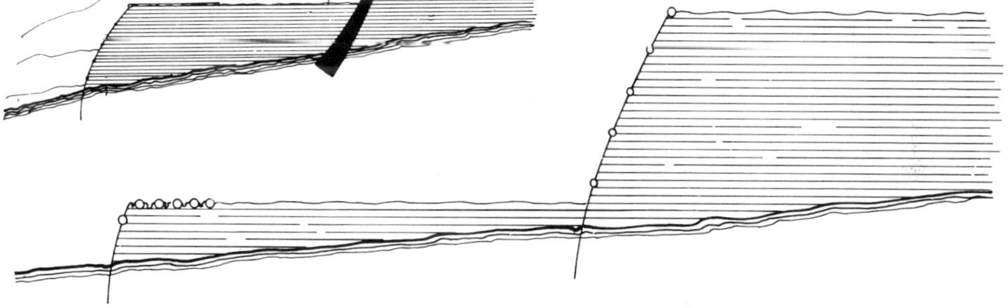

17

the direction of the water pressure. The net thus has a large curvature in the downstream direction. In the dam models shown in Figs. 1 to 5 on p. 128, this direction is horizontal, being vertical in the project* models in Figs. 6 to 11 on p. 128. A horizontal resultant of the pressure force is preferable in narrow V-shaped valleys, and a vertical resultant in wider valleys. The upper bracing cable generally ensures that the dam will be lowest at its center. Weirs can be arranged at this point (Fig. 12, p. 129). The frontal view of the dam (Fig. 13, p. 129; viewed obliquely from above in Fig. 14, p. 129) shows that the saddle shaped narrow-mesh cable net extends only up to the high water level above which it opens out into separate groups of cables. In the dam shown in Fig. 13, p. 129, the narrow-mesh cable net which takes up the water pressure forms a segment of a dome. To prevent its collapse in the empty state, the dome is braced by additional cables (Fig. 15, p. 129) which act at many points in a manner comparable to water pressure. The cable-net structures in Figs. 16 and 17, p. 129, are avalanche breakers and barriers intended to retain or divert rock and snow slides. Generally, coarse nets with little prestressing are required. Limp, untensed nets may also be of advantage.

The design of the cable net and membranes depends largely on the head and the span of the dam. Safety factors are also important. In the design of a dam membrane (Fig. 18, p. 129) large loads are taken up by a coarse-mesh net of thick parallel wire bundles, lined with a narrow-mesh cable net which, in turn, is lined with a wire net having a mesh width of approximately 15 to 20 mm. This latter supports the actual membrane, which can be of sheet metal or bituminized fabric. At high heads and large spans the main cables lie very close together. Since the cables are located on the tail-water side and the membrane on the headwater side, the state of the cables in the finished structure can be checked at all times. Heavily tinned cables in thick plastic sheaths are especially resistant to weather and water. Various types of dams can be developed, including some carrying traffic along their crest.

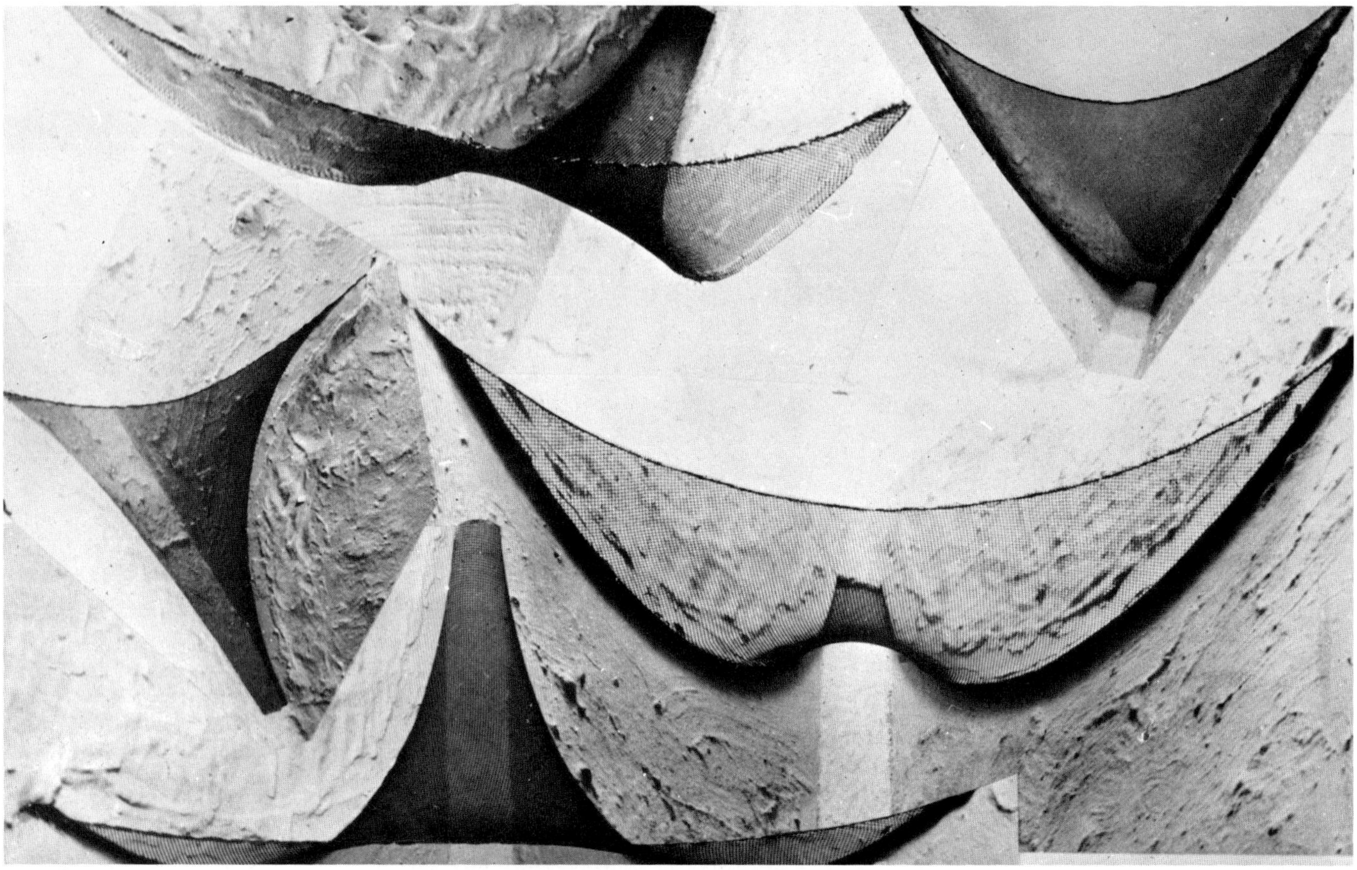

1 to 5 ▲

▼ 6 to 10

11

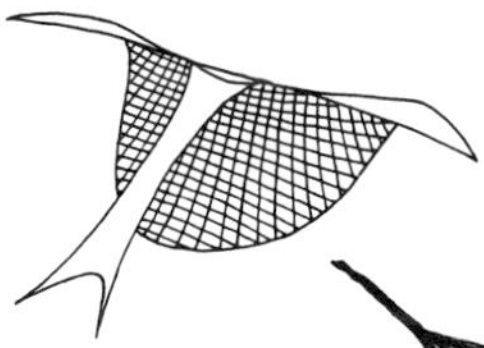

12

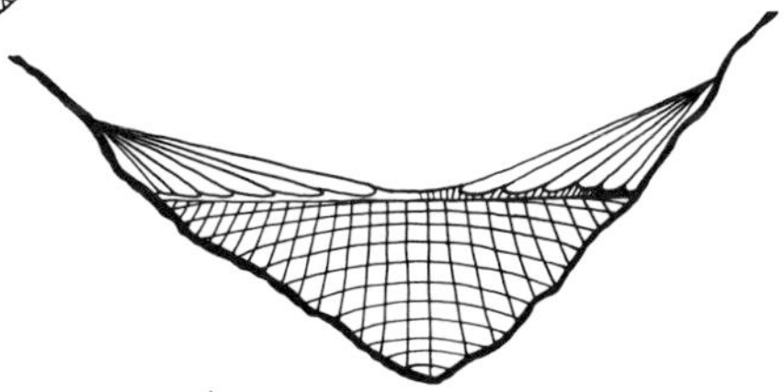

13

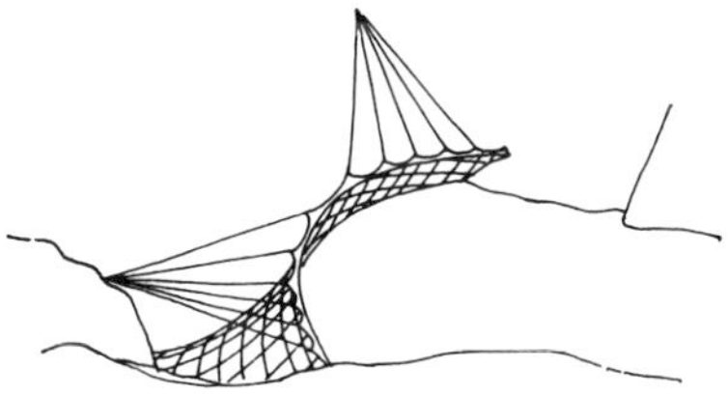

14

16

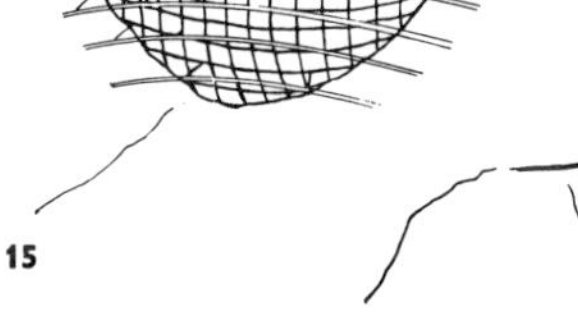

15

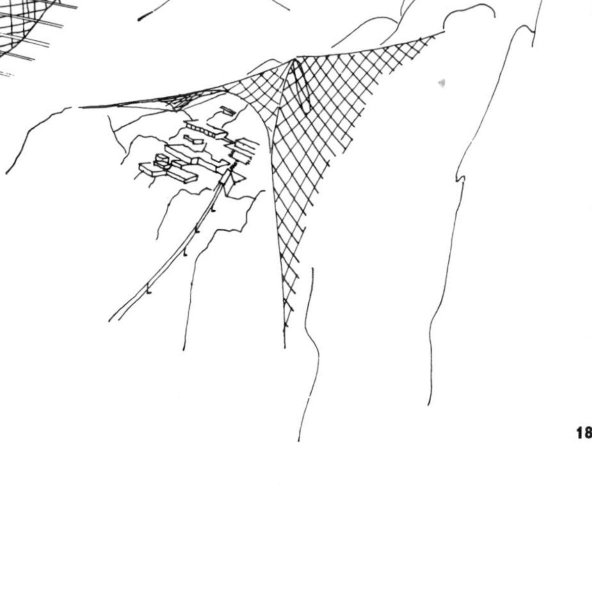

17

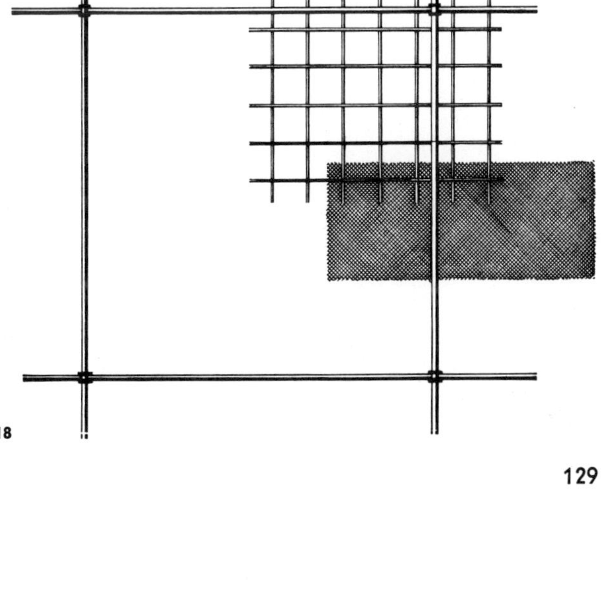

18

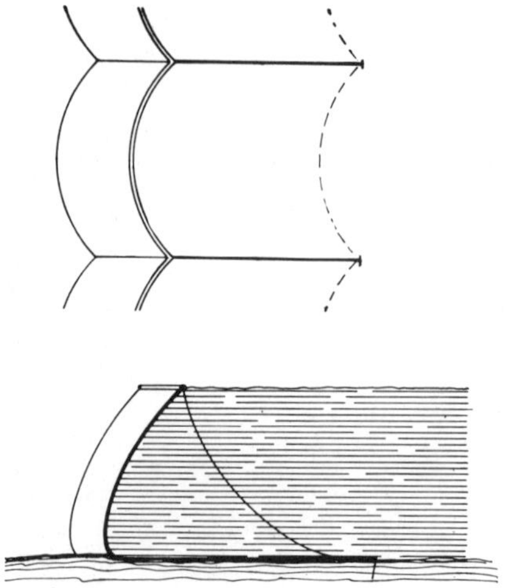

1 and 2

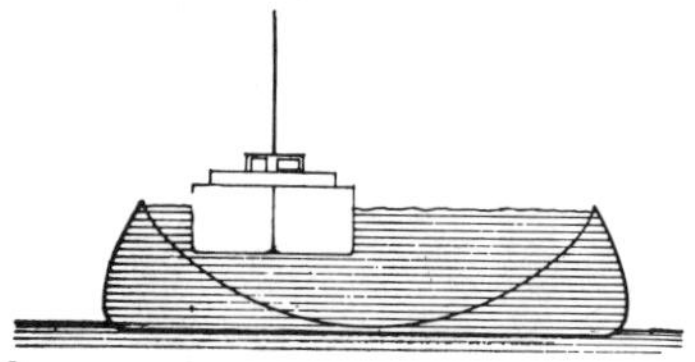

3

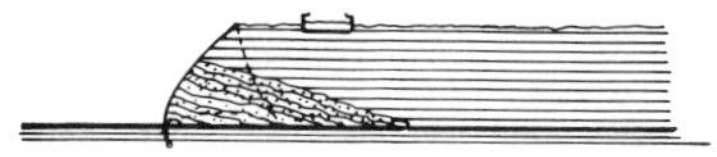

4

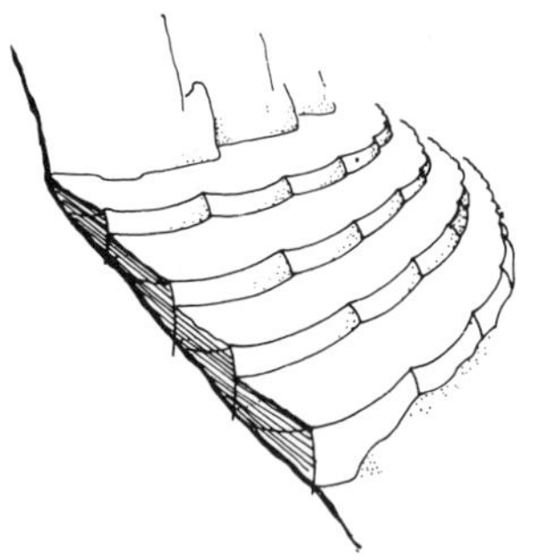

5

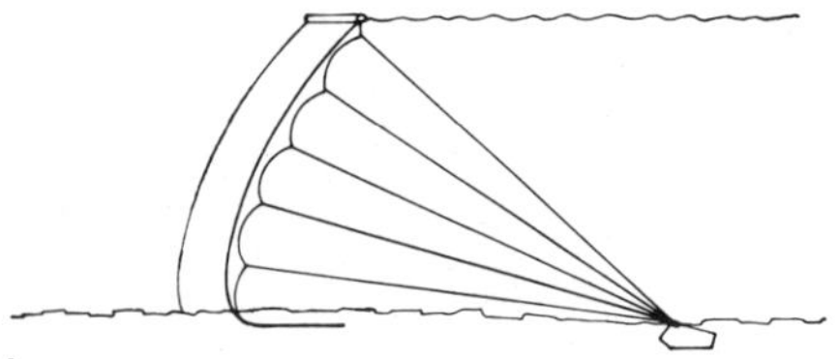

6

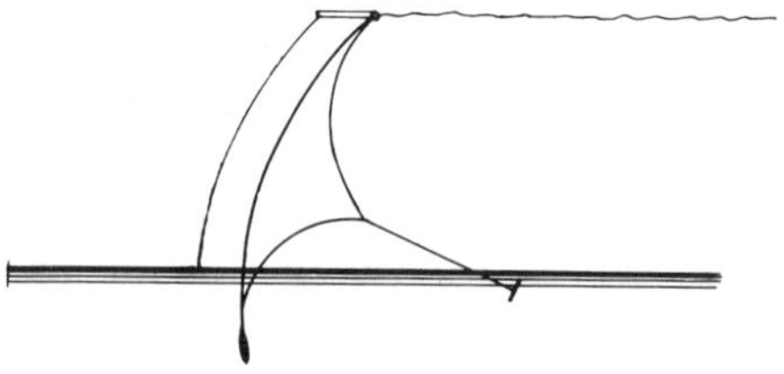

7

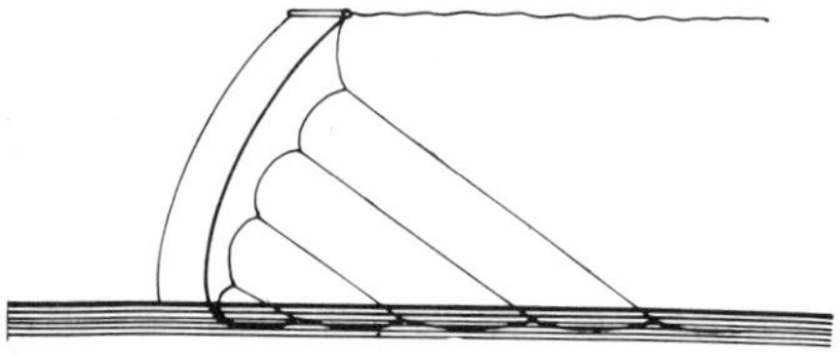

8

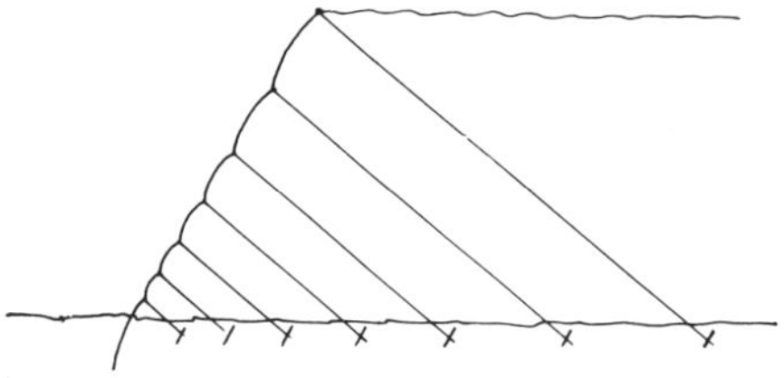

9

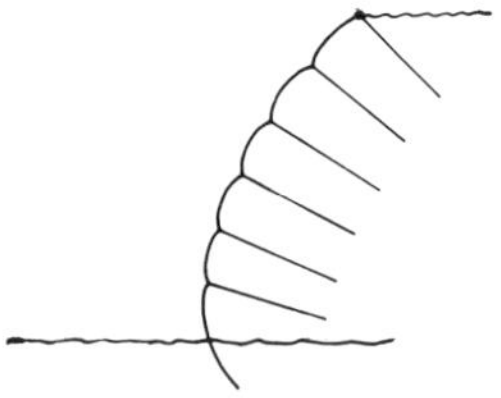

10

▼ 11

Flexible sections* of dams can be connected. This is seen in plan (Fig. 1) and section (Fig. 2). The membrane, which has a double curvature, lies on the ground, has a floating edge and cable-bordered bulkheads anchored to the foundations (Fig. 2).

The bulkheads may also consist of tension-loaded, flexible membranes. The same design was used in a project* for a raised canal (Fig. 3) in which the membranes were interconnected. In order to reduce the wall area of the bulkheads, the latter can be held by guy cables (Figs. 6 and 7) so that the remaining membrane surfaces are small.

In Figure 8 the cables are not attached to special anchors in the foundations but to a bottom membrane embedded in the latter; this may be necessary in muddy and soft ground. In the design shown in section in Figs. 9 and 10 the bulkheads have been eliminated. The cables are attached to the membrane at various points. It is thus possible, with comparatively low membrane tensions to transmit the water pressure directly to the cables.

The points of attachment of the membrane may lie closer together toward the bottom, i.e., in the region of higher water pressure.

The resulting membrane surface is related in design to pneumatic membranes tensed by air pressure and with internal drainage (see pp. 90 to 100), and presents similar problems. Dams of this type can form straight lines, leading to savings in material and shorter foundations, irrespective of whether they are long river dams or short barrages across valleys.*

The membrane in Fig. 4 is a temporary structure. To build a broad and highly resistant earth dam, rock fill is banked under water from barges to reinforce the dam base.

Figures 5 and 11 show projects* for the use of curved continuous membranes to form terraces having large surface areas.

If rigid cable-net structures are to be connected, masts or other supports are required to hold up the saddle-shaped tensed membranes or nets. This is seen in the project* for a protective wall in the sketch

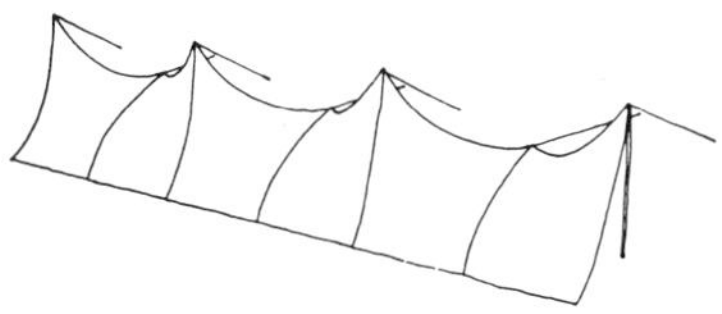
12

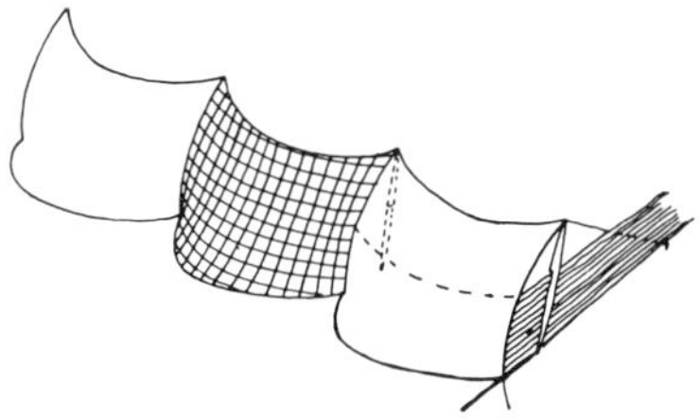
13

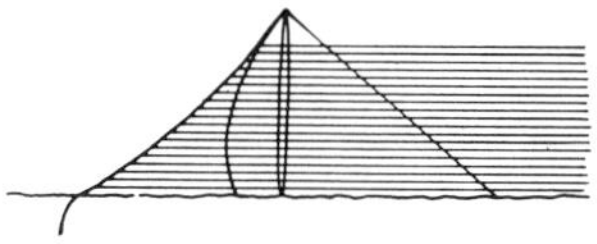
14

15

16

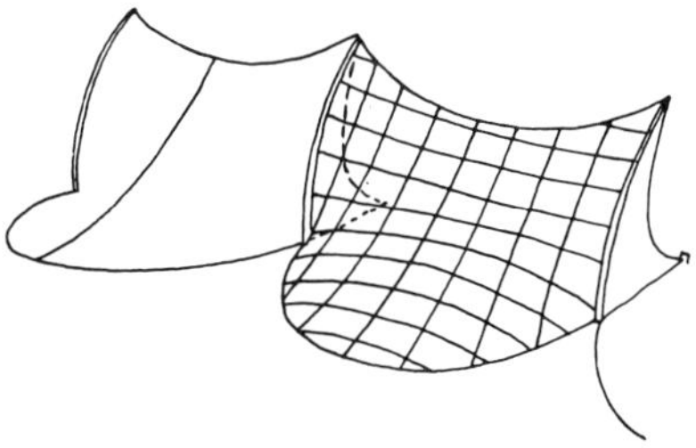
17

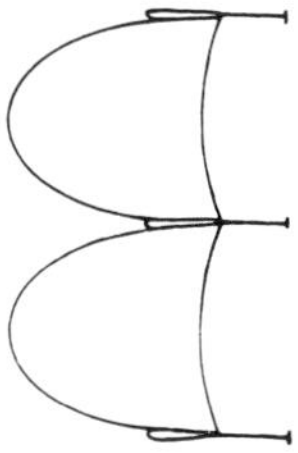
18

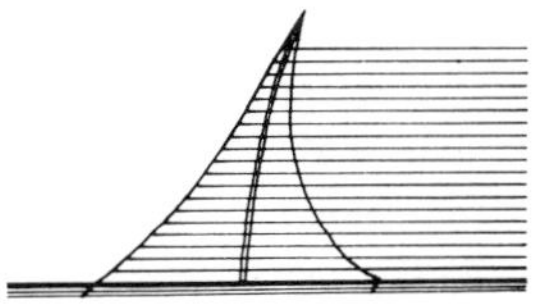
19

(Fig. 12) and photographs of the model (Figs. 15, 16 and 21; for Cologne in 1956). When using cable nets, the mesh can be left open above the water line in order to reduce wind forces. The sketch (Fig. 13) with the associated section (Fig. 14) shows another structure in which the base line is straight but curved. In this way, large curvatures can be obtained.

In all prestressed cable nets supported by masts, buckling of these structural elements, which are under considerable compressive loads, must be taken into account.

This danger can be greatly reduced if the structural elements are fitted into the cable-net system in such a way that the system itself prevents their buckling. This is shown in a sketch (Fig. 17), in the plan (Fig. 18) and the cross section (Fig. 19). The compression member or strut is slightly bent and supported in three directions, two of which are formed by the actual dam membrane and the third by a bulkhead-like partition. A similar solution is obtained when connecting saddle-shaped cable nets tensed between straight struts (Fig. 22) which are retained by a group of parallel cables on the other headwater side, as seen in section, Fig. 23.

The design shown in Fig. 20 is also similar.

In all rigid dams with compression members, the water pressure resultant should act upward, so that the compression members are only loaded when the reservoir is empty.

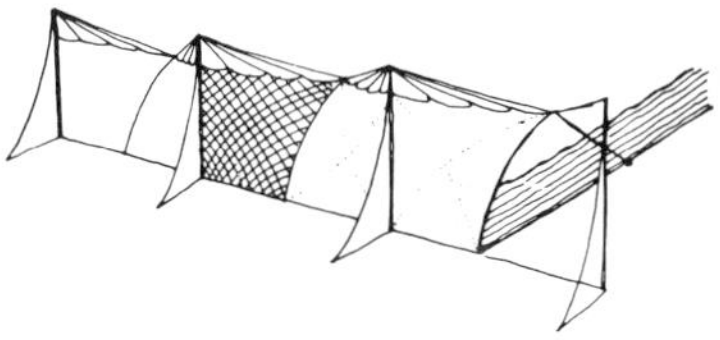
20

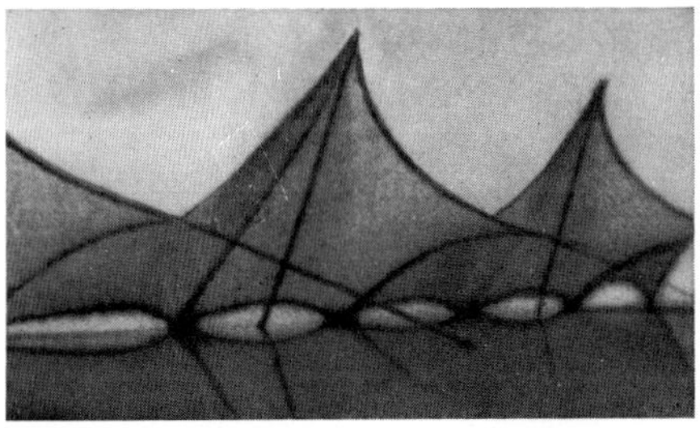
21

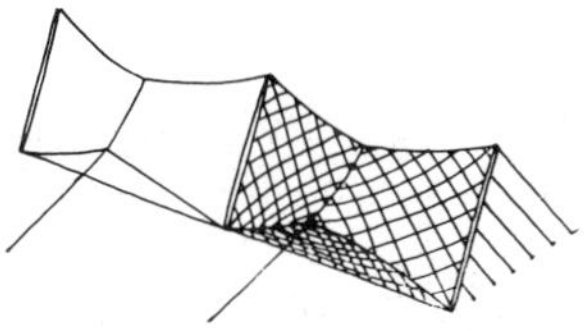
22

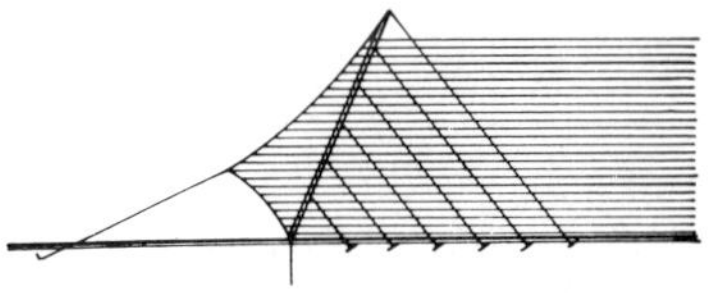
23

1

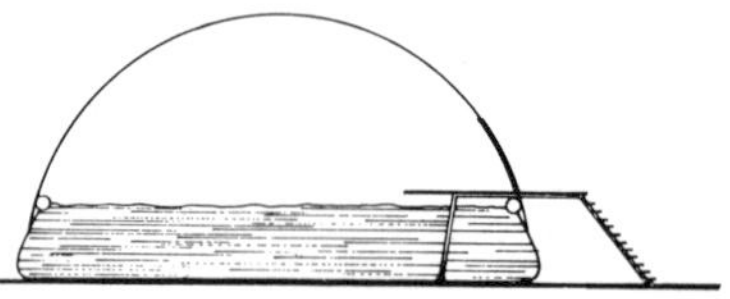

2

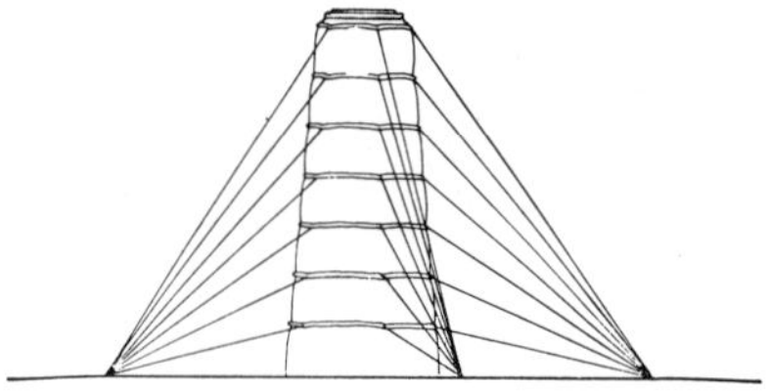

3

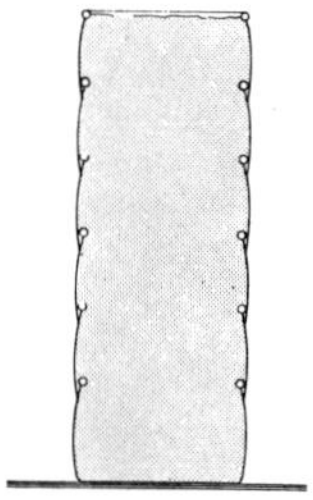

4

6

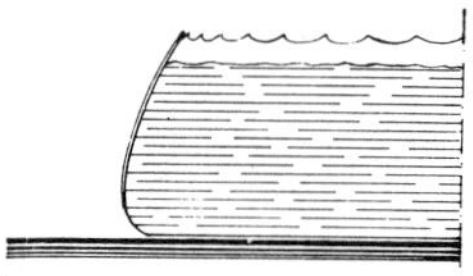

5

▼ 7

8

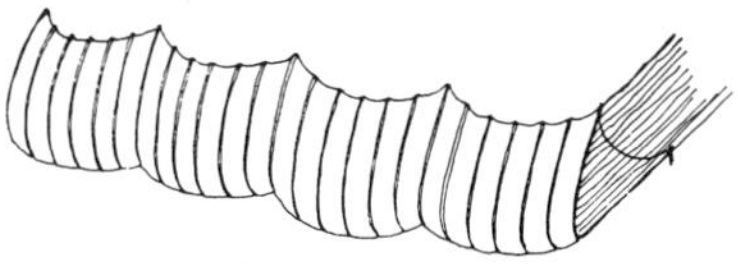

9

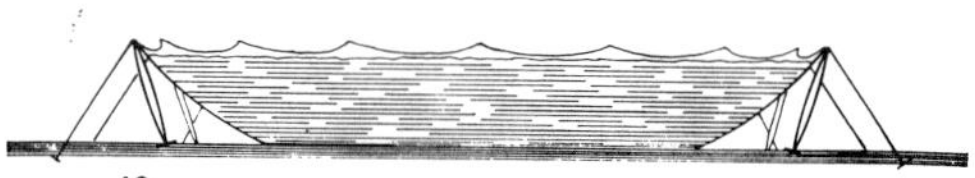

10

11

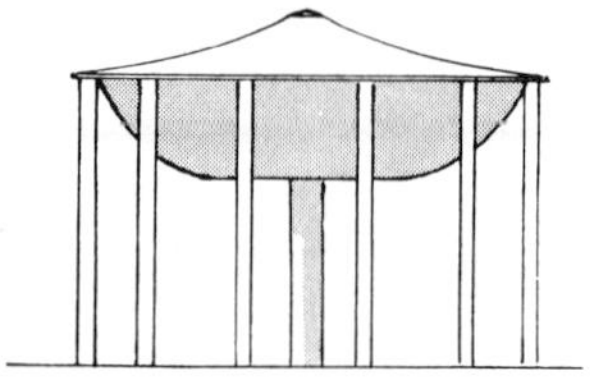

12

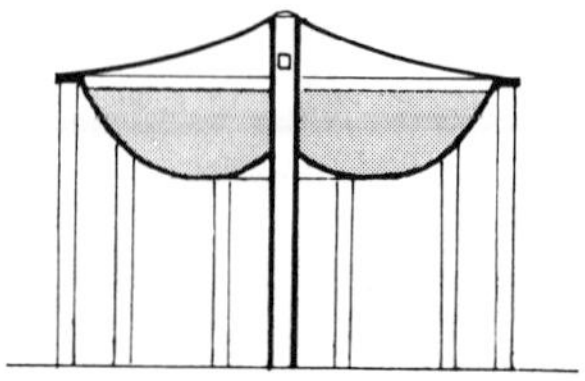

13

In the design* for a movable swimming pool the edge of the basin is held up by a floating ring. However, this requires a constant water level in the basin (Fig. 1). The basin can form the foundation for an inflated dome (Fig. 2) that is accessible through a slip-in door at the entrance bridge. Floating rings can also be used to construct almost completely cylindrical containers (Fig. 4). However, these become unstable beyond a certain height and tip over unless guyed by cables (Fig. 3); even then they cannot exceed a certain maximum height. Containers consisting of many floating rings will become erect gradually through the water pressure.

Of practical importance are water basins with sides reinforced by straight flexible rods which ensure that the upper edge of the basin is always under tension. This is best achieved by a barrel-shaped cut of the membrane and a large curvature of the originally straight rods (Figs. 8 and 5, section). The application of this design to a low barrage is illustrated in Fig. 9. Cylindrical membranes with straight lateral rods (Fig. 6; photo by Stromeyer), or supported by pneumatic rings and cylinders (Fig. 7; photo by Glanzstoff) are in extensive use.

A children's pool* (Fig. 10) was proposed in 1956 for the Horticultural Exhibition in Cologne, as well as a similar fountain made of colored tarpaulin. The pool shown in Fig. 11 (first exhibited in 1957), has a membrane resting on the ground and suspended from a rigid ring which has folding supports. The water is supplied through six nozzles in the supports. At the International Architectural Exhibition in Berlin 1957 the fountain* shown in Fig. 14 proved very popular. Its basin consists of a freely suspended membrane. The water tower* (1953) in Figs. 12 and 13 and the elevated basins in Fig. 15 and 16 are similar in principle.

In general, it is not important whether the containers are filled with water or with viscous, doughy or earthlike substances. For example, a cable net membranc can also be stretched on a ring or an angular frame. In this way structures for retaining loads such as piled grain are obtained (Fig. 17). The discharge rate can be in-

14

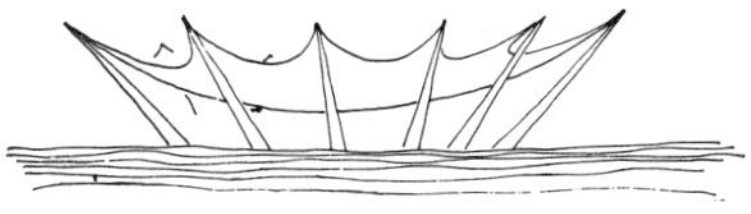

15

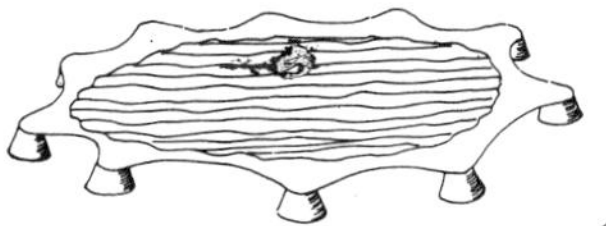

16

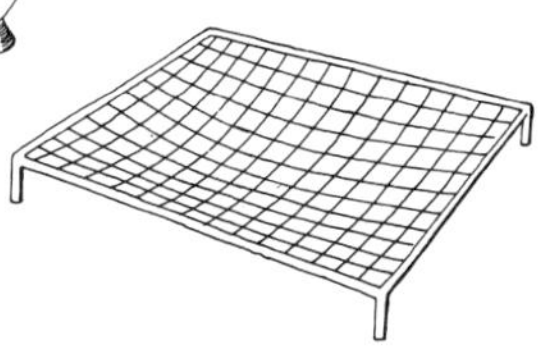

17

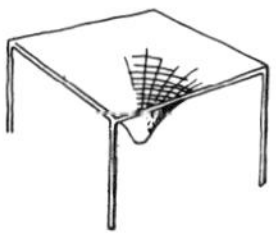

18

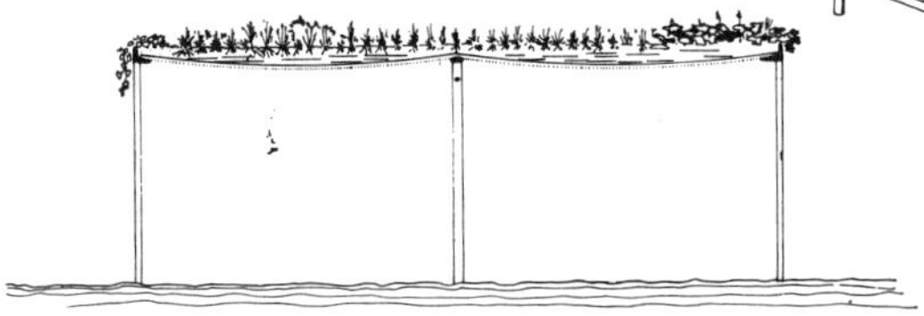

19

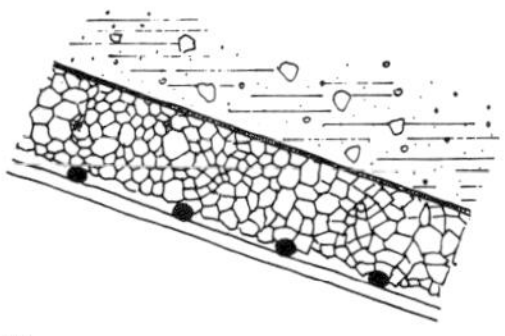

20

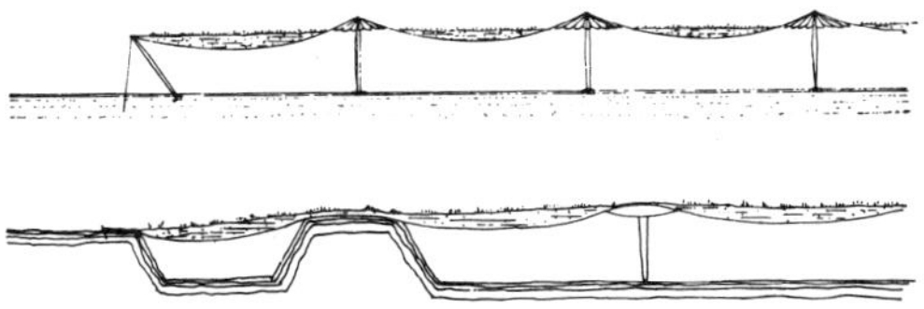

21 and 22

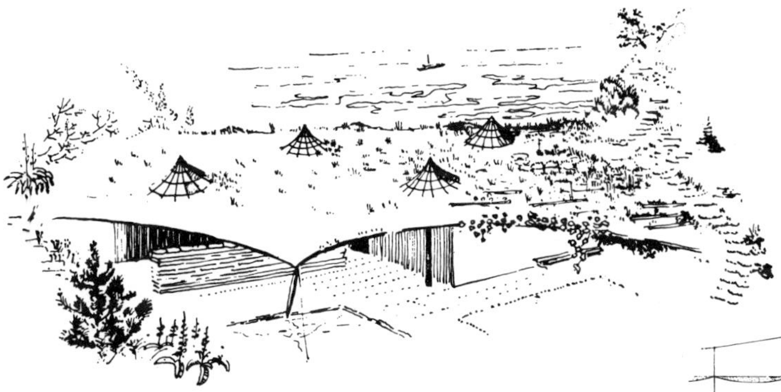

23

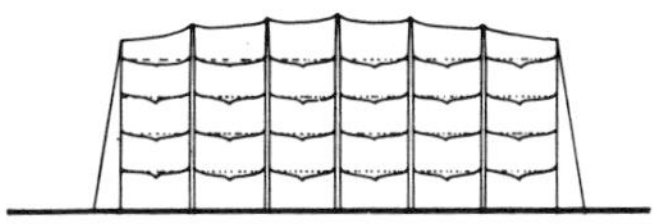

24

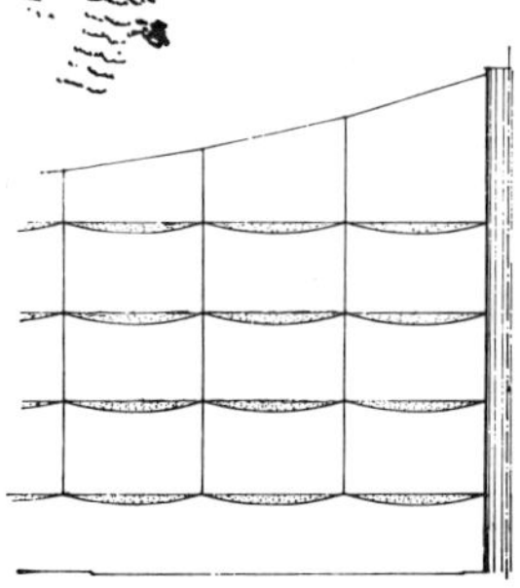

25

creased by giving a funnel shape to the membrane (Fig. 18).

The type of structure shown in Fig. 19 will undoubtedly be of increasing use in the future. A thin net, for example a mat of structural steel, stretched in a frame and insulated against heat and moisture (as shown in the detail [Fig. 20]), carries a load of earth and forms a roof on which plants can be grown. The net can also be stretched between bracing cables and supports (Fig. 21) or anchored directly to the foundations (Fig. 22), as seen in the design (Fig. 23) for a dwelling.* Above the supports, small separate cable nets with radial and circular cables were arranged to take up the higher local tensions. These small nets protrude beyond the greenery on the roof and permit the entry of light. The load on such a roof is heaviest when the earth is saturated with moisture.

The horticultural utilization of roof surfaces, fairly simple in this design, will assume increasing importance in the future. The loads are undoubtedly large, but the expenditure will be worthwhile in many cases.

The construction sketch (Fig. 24) shows a section through a warehouse for a viscous, granular material which cannot be stored in thick layers. The edge of the warehouse consists of built-in supports, the center has numerous hinged supports between which tiers of membranes with funnel-shaped discharges are stretched.

The section through a suspended house* (Fig. 25), which should be imagined to extend in all directions, is of similar design. The floors are suspended by vertical cables from a heavy supporting cable and consist of fine-mesh wire nets, whose concavities can be evened out by a slight granular fill like perlite or foam clay, so that a flat surface is formed for the flooring.

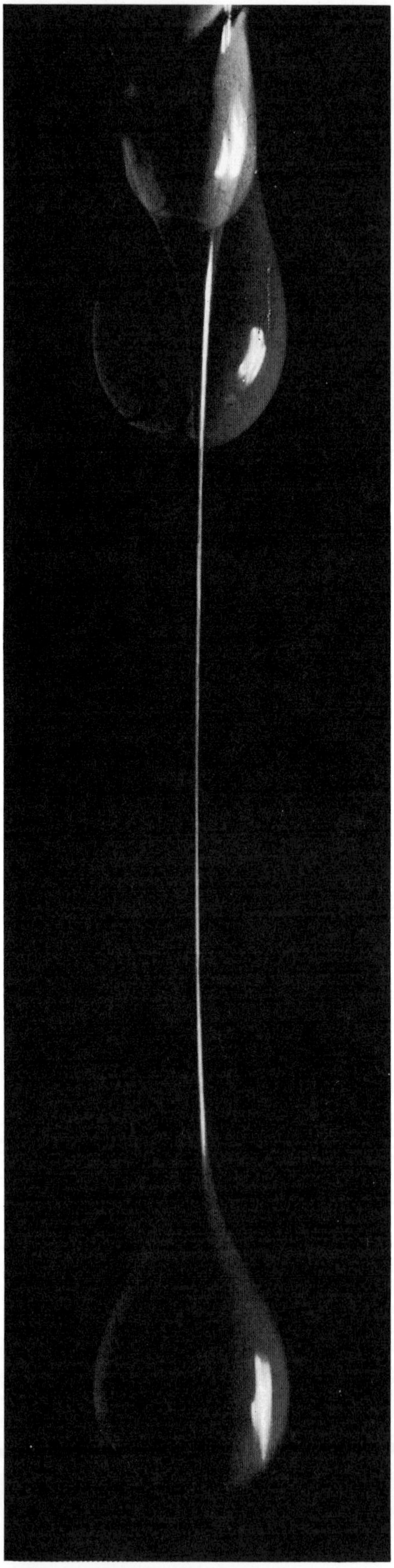

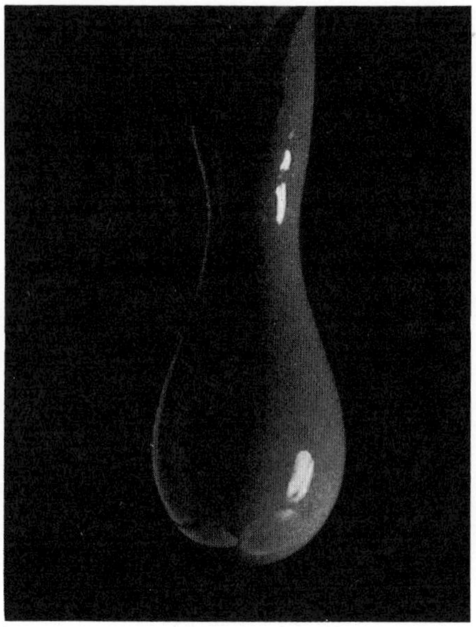

1

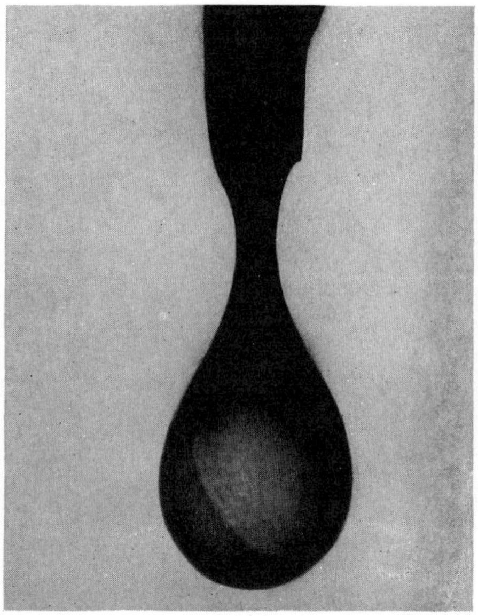

2

The previous pages dealt with freely suspended container structures filled with liquids or viscous substances and bordered by rings or attached in sheets at several places.

However, containers suspended at only one point are also important. The pressure of the liquid causes them to assume a drop-like shape.

When a liquid is supplied to the underside of a flat surface, as is often observed with porous material under water pressure, dripping occurs. At first a slight bulge of bell-shaped cross section forms. It then increases in width, a constriction appears, and dripping takes place.

The study of falling drops is useful for the design of containers. Figure 1 shows a drop of varnish at the tip of a glass tube when it has just passed the state in which surface tension prevents dripping. The surface of the liquid begins to constrict and the drop falls, as is shown for a drop of water in Fig. 2. The triple exposure of a drop in the various stages of its formation is highly instructive (Fig. 3).

◀ 3

▼ 4

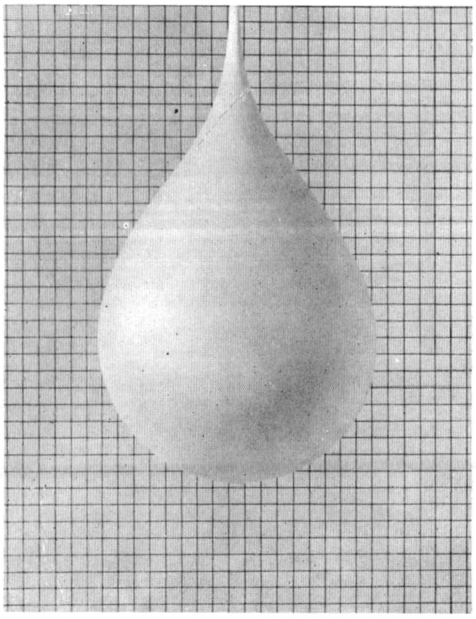

▼ 5

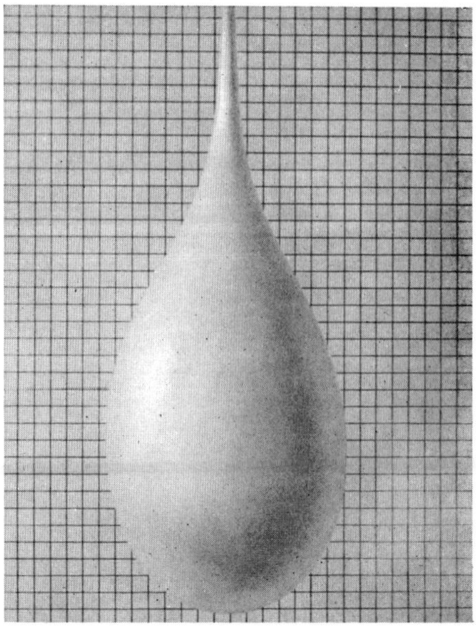

The membrane tensions of drops are equal in all directions at every point of the surface, as long as static equilibrium exists. This is no longer the case when dripping begins. The shape of the resulting drops can be determined mathematically.

The surface shape of a container having uniform normal membrane forces is generally described by the transformation-invariant equation (12.4) in the chapter on "Analysis of Membranes," p. 290.

If the surface is represented in Cartesian coordinates $[x;y;z(x,y)]$ or in cylindrical coordinates $[r;\phi;z(r,\phi)]$, then we obtain from (12.4) the differential equations (12.5c) or (12.6c) respectively, for the shape function z. In particular, the differential equation (12.15a) is obtained for the axisymmetrical case, which, when the weight g is neglected, and when $p = 0$ assumes the following form (in the case of filling by a liquid):

$$\frac{1}{r}\frac{d}{dr}\left(\frac{rz'(r)}{\sqrt{1+z'^2(v)}}\right) = -\gamma(z_0 - z)$$

(Trostel).
Of even greater practical importance are experiments with thin-walled rubber balloons.

6

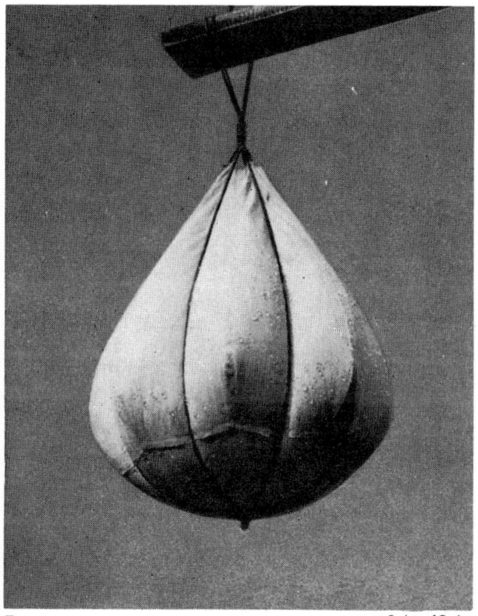

7

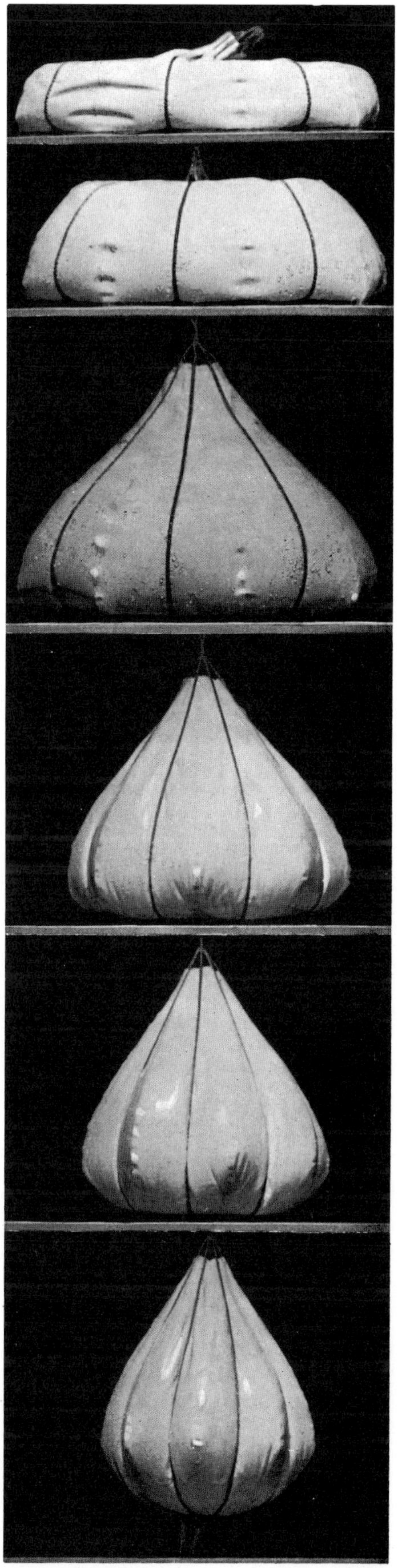

8 to 13 ▶

Figure 4 shows an initially spherical, and Fig. 5 an initially oblong balloon filled with water. The resulting shapes differ. Measurements show clearly that the tensions increase considerably toward the point of suspension. Consequently, actual containers will usually be supported by cables. Figure 6 shows a container, developed on the basis of these theories,* in its empty state and Fig. 7 shows it filled. It is important that the containers should not merely be capable of being suspended but also be able to stand upright. This is possible when the conditions stated on the previous pages are fulfilled. Figures 8 to 10 show the filling of an open container which requires no additional internal pressure and has considerable stability when filled (Fig. 10). As seen in the individual stages (Figs. 11 to 13), the container can be easily lifted without a significant change in volume. Such studies are of primary importance in the design of larger transportable containers for liquids, which are quite economical up to weights of several tons. They have a wide field of applicability, especially since they can be handled by very simple machines.
The design of transportable containers must take into account various means of transportation, e.g., trucks (Fig. 1, p. 136), ships (Fig. 2, p. 136) or cableway (Fig. 3, p. 136).

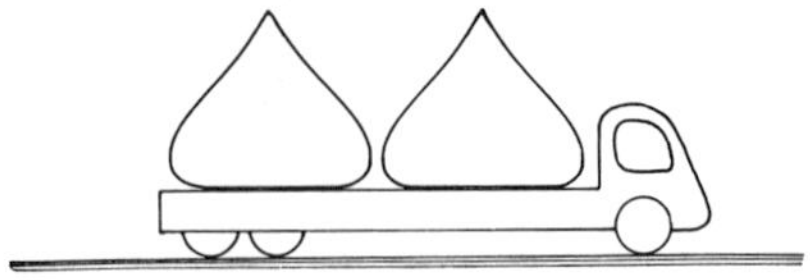
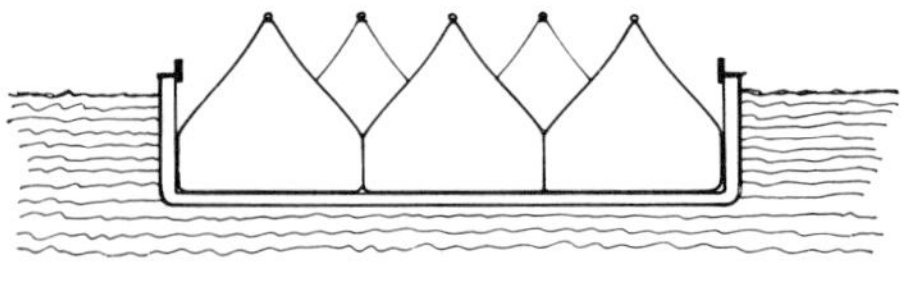
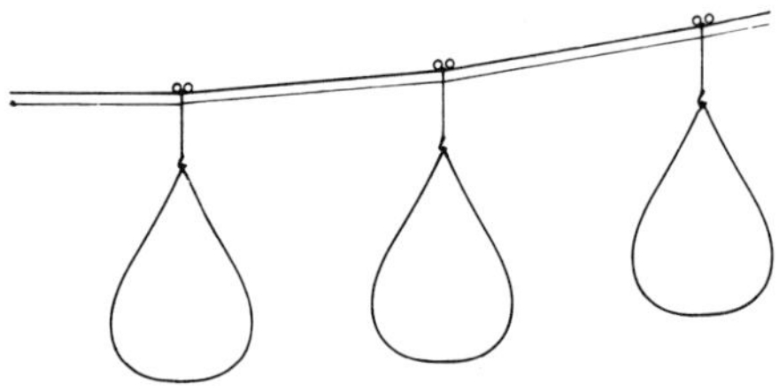

1 to **3**

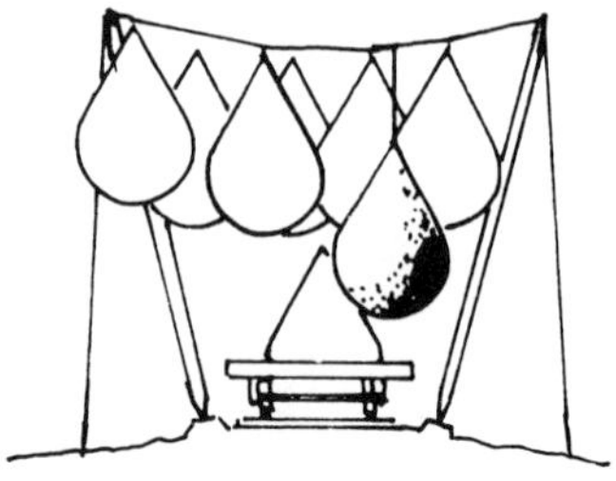
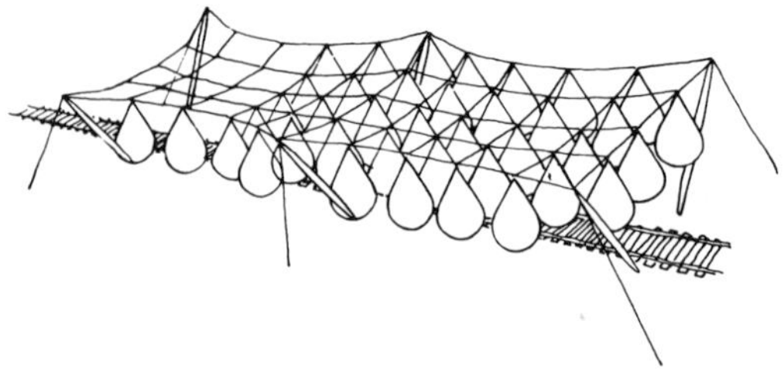
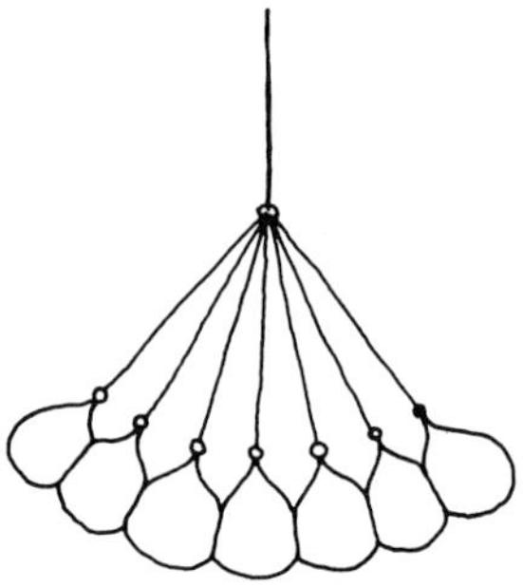

4 to **6**

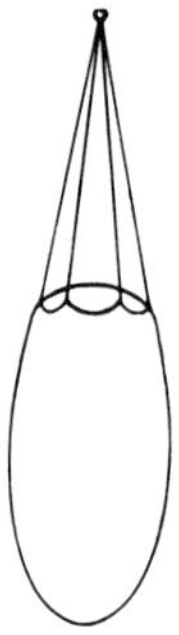
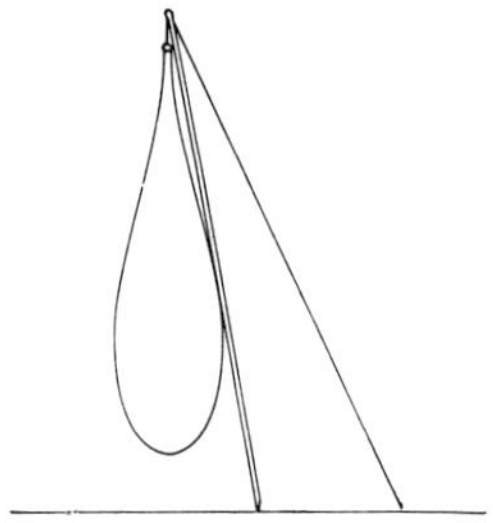
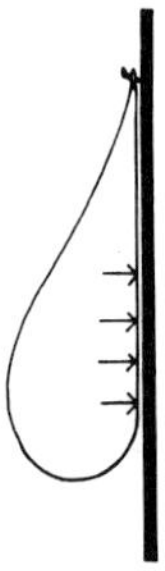

7 to **10**

11 ▼

The storage of such containers, either standing on horizontal surfaces or suspended (Figs. 4 and 5, p. 136), is also of great importance especially when this facilitates rapid handling or saves valuable ground space. If the containers are suspended from cable nets they can be lowered directly onto railway cars or trucks. Small containers can be gathered in bundles (Fig. 6). Suspension from masts (Fig. 7) could be practicable under certain conditions.

In principle, we must differentiate between containers able to remain upright when not suspended, because their bases are sufficiently wide, and those which, due to their slimness, can only be suspended or lie on the ground when filled. In slender containers the volume near the upper tip is small. This tip can be replaced by cables (Fig. 8); ellipsoidal or ovoid containers can be fitted into cable nets of similar shape. There are several basically different possibilities for the suspension of slender containers. In Figure 9 a container is suspended from a guyed rod and, in Fig. 10, from a wall; it will be observed that the container presses on the wall in the direction of the arrows. A commercial container for cement is shown in Fig. 11; photo by Stromeyer). Figure 12 shows three or four containers suspended from a suitably designed support consisting of a central vertical cable-guyed mast with small hangers at the top. If we wish to eliminate the cables, a frame-like suspension structure such as that shown in Fig. 13 must be built. In this case, storage is above railroad tracks and direct discharge into cars is possible. There are several possibilities for tight packing when storing oblong containers in trucks (Fig. 14), railcars, and ships (Figs. 15 and 16). The position of the round and pointed ends may be alternating or uniform. An interesting suggestion* is to move such containers, if their contents are lighter than water, in long chains through narrow canals (Figs. 17 and 18); this is facilitated by their streamlined shape.

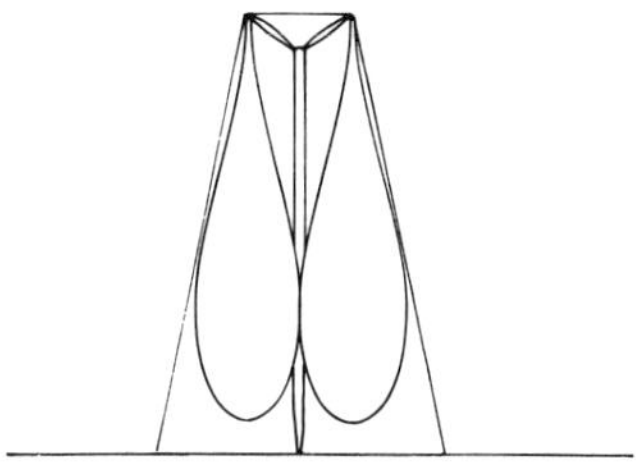

12

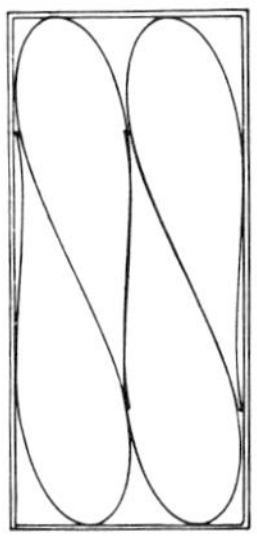

14

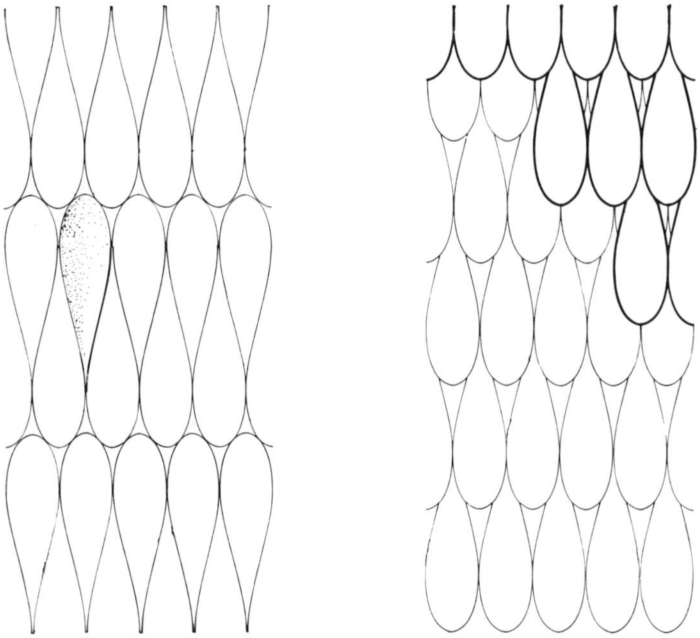

15 and 16

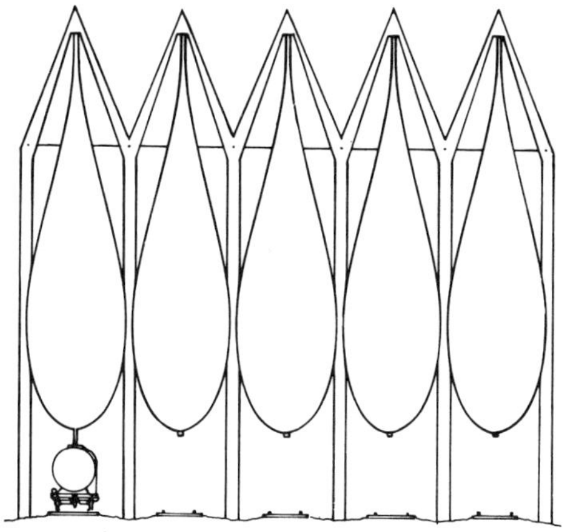

13

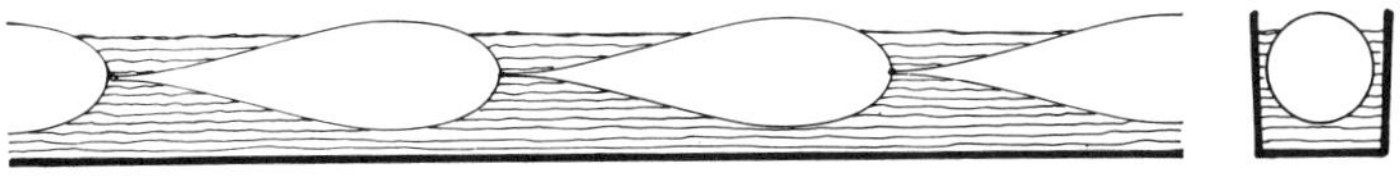

17 and 18

19 ▼

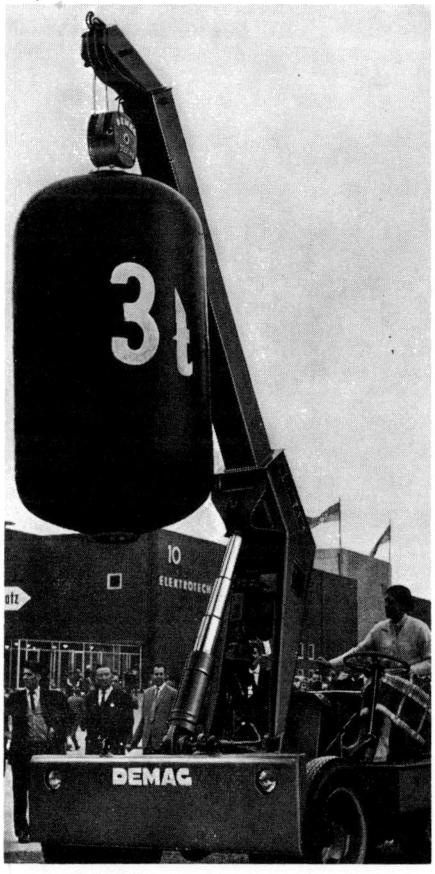

The container shown in Fig. 19 (photo by Demag) has a more cylindrical shape, which can normally be obtained only by internal bracing or by additional internal pressure.

Drop-like containers can be filled not only with liquids but also with fine granulates such as grain, flour, cement, etc. The size of movable containers is governed by the dimensions and capacity of vehicles and lifting tackle. Stationary containers, such as grain silos, should be large for greater economy.

The construction of rigid stationary containers is possible without difficulty by the use of sheet steel or fine-mesh cable or wire nets reinforced with sprayed concrete or plastics.

Supported or suspended containers can be made rigid in the following way: the container is made as a flexible membrane and filled; it is then heavily coated with plastics and fiber or wire lining. A rigid shell is formed which retains its shape when empty.

It is possible to build suspended flexible containers which retain their shape when empty, i.e., when under external gas pressure, and also containers which become limp when empty or change their form as shown in Figs. 3 to 8 on p. 139. The structure consists of a strong tubular steel mast held upright by a cable system anchored to three foundations. The shape which the membrane assumes when filled ensures discharge of the material from the lowest point. When empty (Fig. 3, p. 139) the membrane is held close to the mast by springs or rubber elements. The material is introduced through the tubular mast and inflates the membrane by its weight (Figs. 4 to 7, p. 139) until filling is completed (Fig. 8, p. 139). This is a very simple and quickly erected silo. Costs can be considerably reduced in comparison

with concrete or steel silos of equal capacity, and erection can be effected in the shortest possible time. This is of great importance during sudden accumulations of valuable bulk goods, when losses in storage must be kept to a minimum. Figures 1, 2 and 9 show the design* model from the side and from above. Figure 10 shows an experiment with a rubber membrane stretched tightly over a rod and inflated by internal pressure.

Figure 1 on p. 140 shows a membrane suspended from a rod and resting on the ground, as shown in the section (Fig. 7, p. 140) of the project.* This design could become important for sewage-water treatment.

A very simple silo structure based on a similar principle was developed by Kalle (Figs. 2 to 6, p. 140; works photo). The membrane, suspended from a rod, has a considerable storage capacity for green forage.

Lately, silos built of plastics instead of masonry or concrete are being increasingly used for the fermentation of fodder. This development was signaled by the press rammer introduced by Stromeyer. These rams are water-filled tarpaulins which compress the silage tightly.

Some special shapes of suspended containers also rate mention: containers suspended at two points are of particular advantage in cement storage, since they provide safe storage during transportation with comparatively low material cutting losses (Fig. 8, p. 140).

A unit of approximately triangular cross section, which permits several containers to be suspended from one rod, is shown in Fig. 9 on p. 140. The distension of a container by a ring is seen in Fig. 10 on the same page. A similar design is illustrated there in Fig. 11; the container is closed only up to the ring and the goods are allowed to pile up above.

Figures 10 and 11 on p. 140, are rigid containers which largely retain their form without internal load. Their outer skin is prestressed to a saddle shape. This also applies to the container with three rings, shown in Fig. 13, p. 140 and to the design in Fig. 12

2

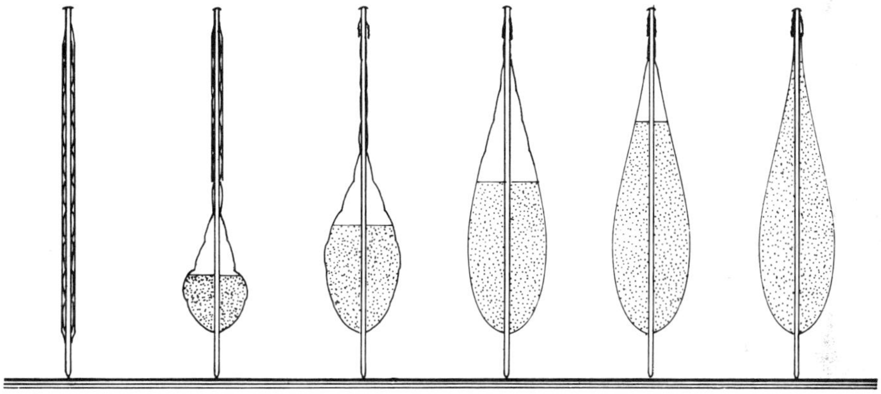

3 to 8

◀ 1 ▼ 9

▼ 10

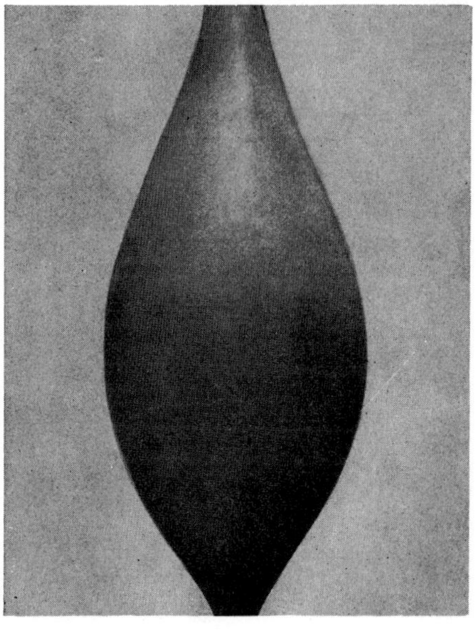

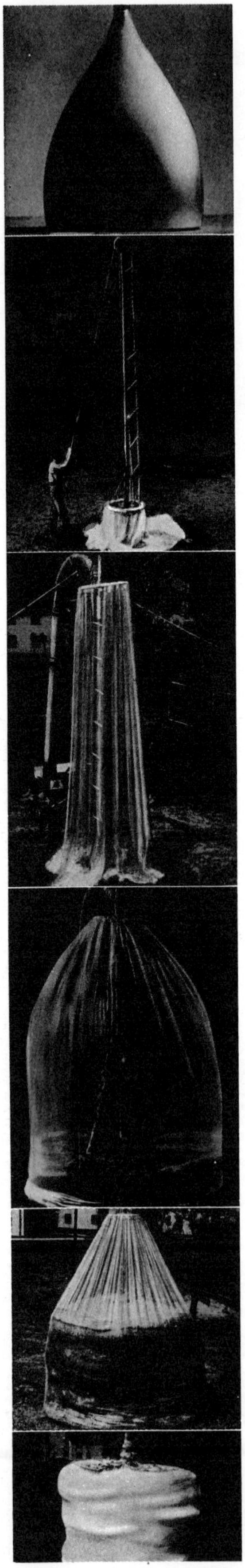

on p. 140, in which three containers attached to a rod are distended by rings at their centers. The containers prevent the tipping over of the rod or, by the introduction of partitions, its buckling. The containers shown in Figs. 14 and 15 also have central rods. The membranes are distended outward by rods to form rigid shapes. A particularly simple design for rigid containers is shown in Figs. 16 and 17. The broad shape is obtained by means of the cables guying the central rod.

By introducing interior cables or partitions, as for example by connecting the upper suspension point with the bottom, the shape of the suspended container can be altered. This is particularly important in obtaining shapes (Figs. 18 and 19) which must have high static stability when not suspended (Fig. 20). The membrane tensions can be considerably reduced by the internal connections. A very wide container which can be suspended at four points is shown in Fig. 21 from the side and in Fig. 22 in plan.

If a cylindrical membrane is folded, sealed along the sides, and suspended at two points, the shape shown in Figs. 23 and 24 is obtained. This container is particularly simple to make. However, folds can only be avoided when the material is highly elastic.

In a projected* water tower a container is suspended from a guyed mast. A vertical cross section is shown in section in Fig. 25, and a horizontal section through the container in Fig. 26. For slender, easily dismountable towers, horizontal sections as in Fig. 27 may be advisable in exceptional cases. In this design three containers can be hoisted between the guying cables. The containers must be interconnected since unequal levels induce considerable bending moments in the central mast. Figure 28 shows the complete project, Fig. 29 only the top, and Fig. 30 a model viewed obliquely from above.

In the photographs of the model (Figs. 1 to 3, p. 142), a circular, strongly prestressed rubber membrane stretched in a

◀ 1 to 6

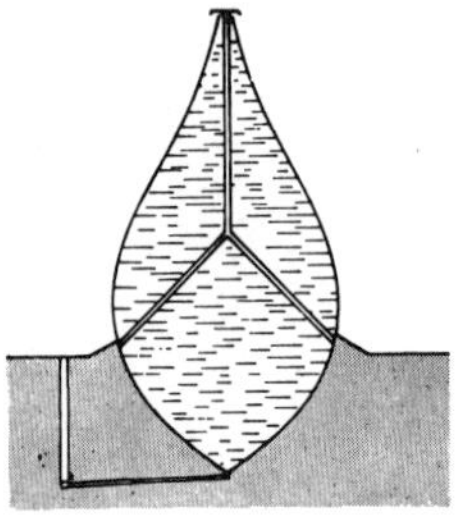

7

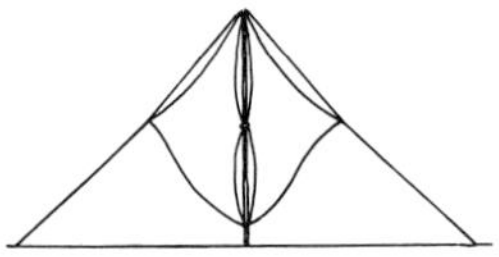

9

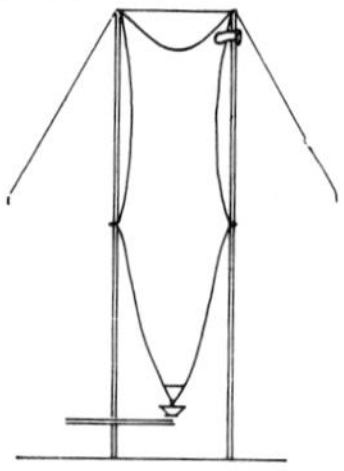

8

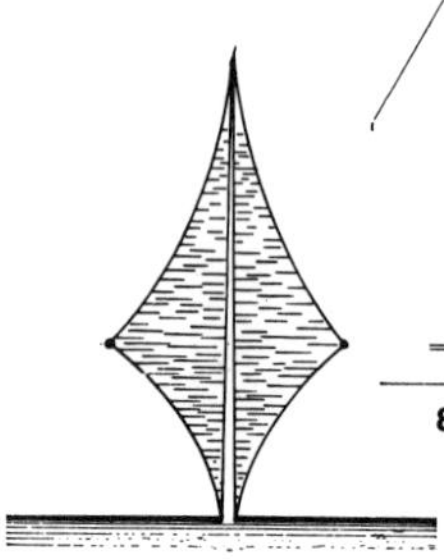

10

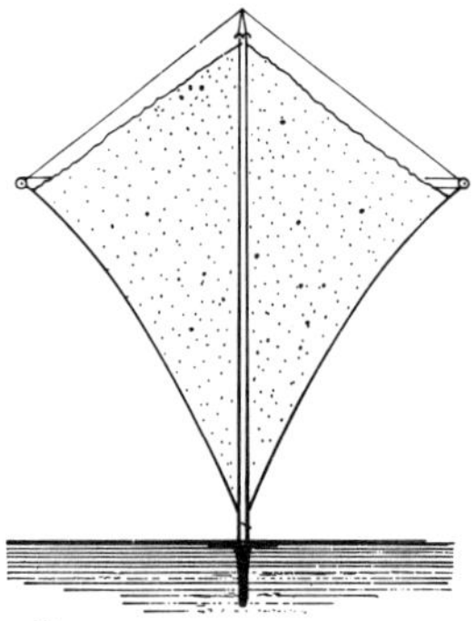

11

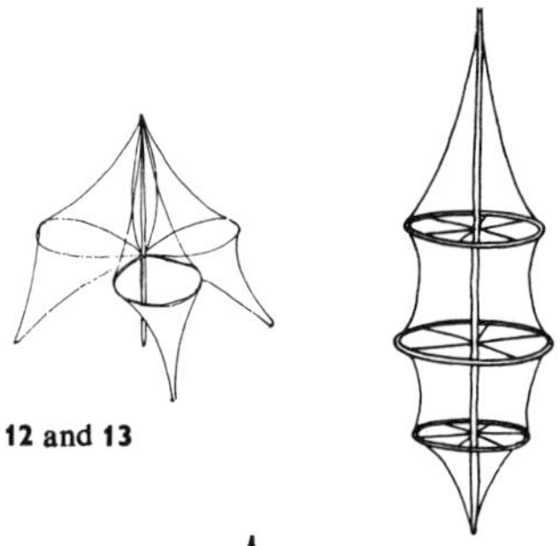

12 and 13

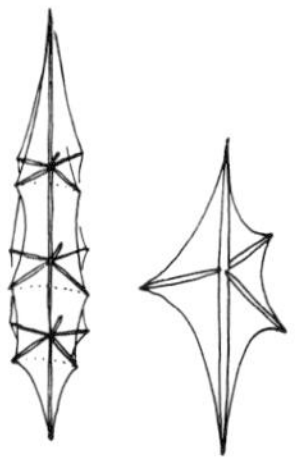

14 and 15

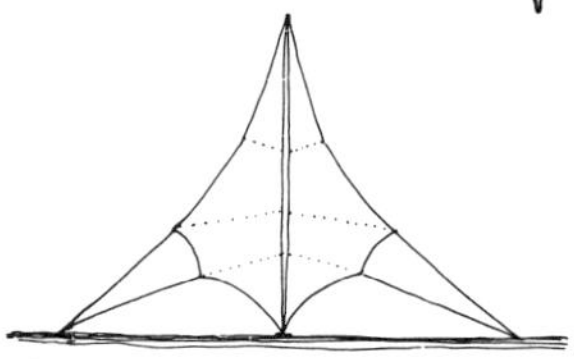

16

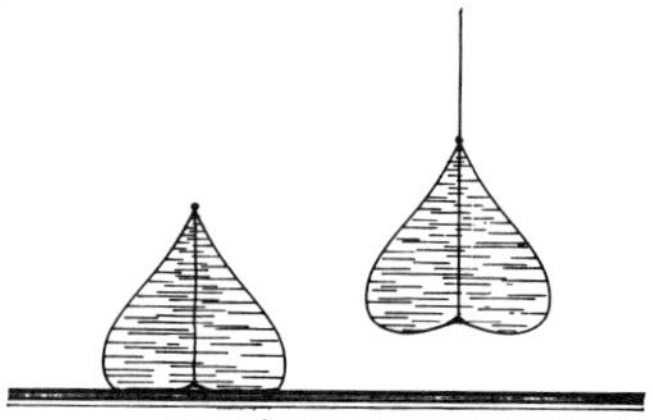

18 and 19

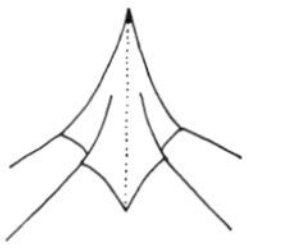

17

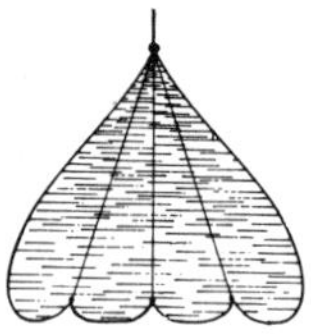

20

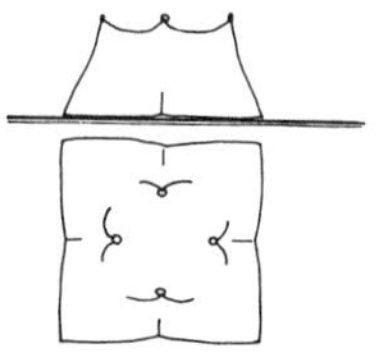

21 and 22

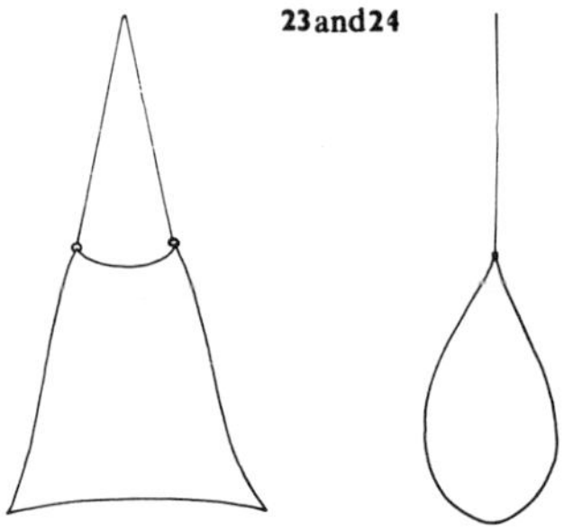

23and24

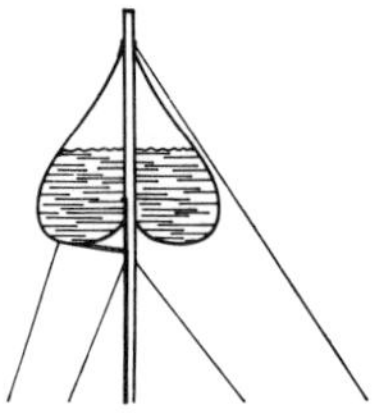

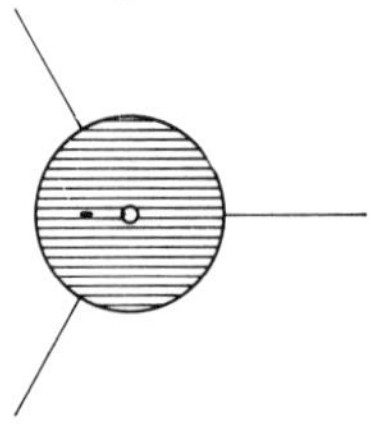

25 to 27

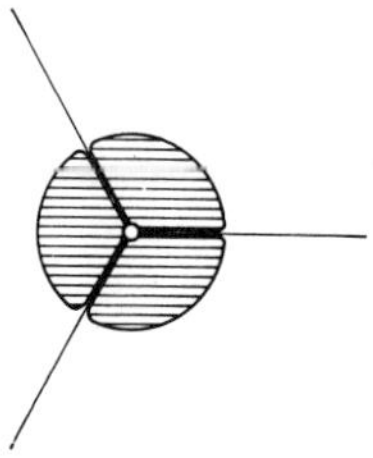

28 ▲

▼ 29

▼ 30

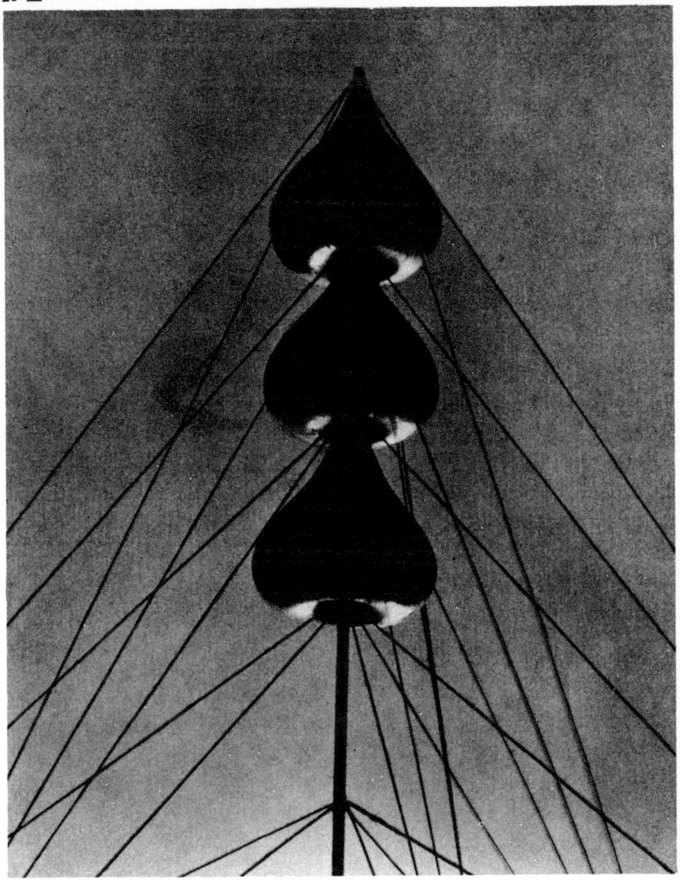

vertical frame was pressurized by a liquid and its deformations studied. An asymmetrical dome results, which can be measured by vertical shadow planes (Fig. 2) or by a background of squares (Fig. 3). The asymmetry is caused by the downward increase in internal pressure. Similar membrane shapes can also be observed in covered frames, such as floats and containers for liquids. Containers filled with light gases assume a drop-shaped form in the air, as do air containers in water; membranes stretched between frames or fixed boundaries are subject to similar laws. This opens many new fields of application. For example, the constantly increasing speed of airplanes necessitates longer landing strips for which sufficient space is rarely available in the vicinity of large cities. As a result, floating air strips are being seriously considered.

A floating surface, sufficiently rigid to support heavy modern air-

Heavy loads can be raised by injecting air into drop-shaped tanks that can be attached to them. Figure 8 shows heavy rocks being lifted, and Fig. 9 the raising of bulk material. Submerged balloons can be used to store gases under high pressure (Fig. 10), to apply the large forces necessary to extract piles, and also for load-testing of underwater tension foundations. A very special use is illustrated in Fig. 11: submerged floats form the buoyant support of a prestressed suspension bridge. Thorough investigations* showed that buoyant elements can be so securely attached even in deep waters where the sea is rough that the foundation for the compressive elements of cables or cable nets can be laid on them. The figure shows a vertical mast which transmits the positive loads of the structure to counterbalancing floats. The floats can be designed in different ways, for example with air-filled submerged balloons which have the advantage of being easily exchanged at any time. To re-

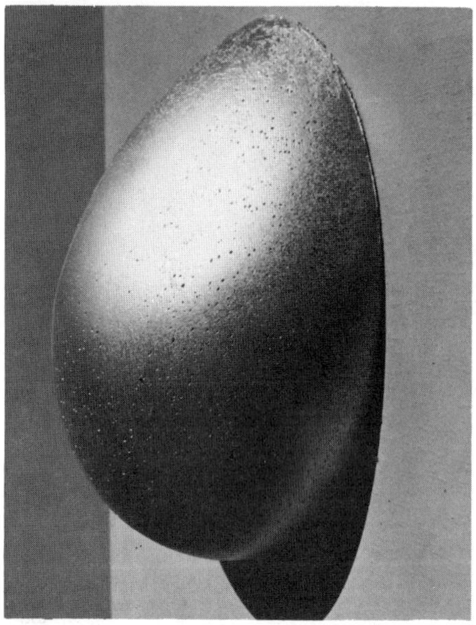

1 to **3**

planes, must be designed. The rigidity should not, however, exceed the required minimum, since otherwise the wave motion in the surrounding water would induce excessive bending moments near the edges. Figure 4 shows a comparatively rigid prestressed concrete platform supported by deep intersecting webs. The platform is closed below by a membrane which renders the structure watertight and buoyant. Figure 5 shows a quite different solution of the same problem. A lattice of uniform steel pipes is supported by drop-shaped floats. Like the design shown in Fig. 6 it is unaffected by waves. The number of compression elements of a rigid framework platform can be greatly reduced by cables that retain the submerged floats and others that support the loads above water (Fig. 7).

The use of air-filled submerged balloons for underwater construction, or for the extraction of natural resources is of great importance.

place such a balloon, the air is let out and the balloon brought to the surface. The new balloon is attached empty and then inflated. An exchange of air can take place directly if the new balloon is previously attached. Exchange without employing divers is possible if the balloons are equipped with a cable system for lowering them from above. Since the air pressure inside the balloons has merely to overcome the water pressure, membranes of wire-reinforced and plastic-saturated heavy fabrics are not excessively stressed.

Stratospheric balloons have a droplike shape at the start of their ascent. The envelope expands fully only at great heights. Figure 12 shows a Russian stratospheric balloon before ascent (photo by Shagin). Figure 13 shows a balloon being launched from the deck of the *U.S.S. Valley Forge*. The balloon is over 120 m high and filled with 283,000 m^3 helium. It was used for stratospheric research during operation "Skyhook."

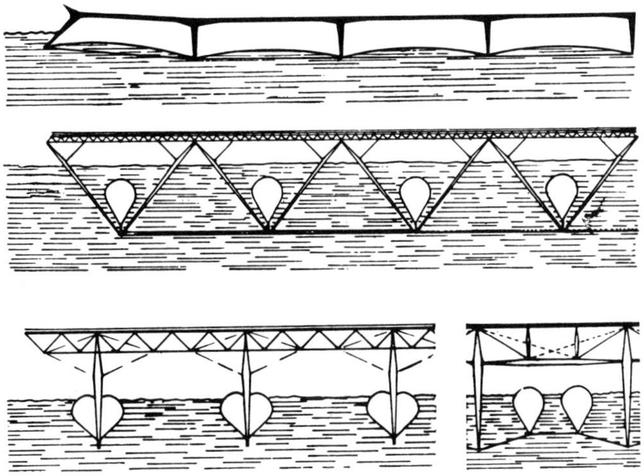

4 to 7

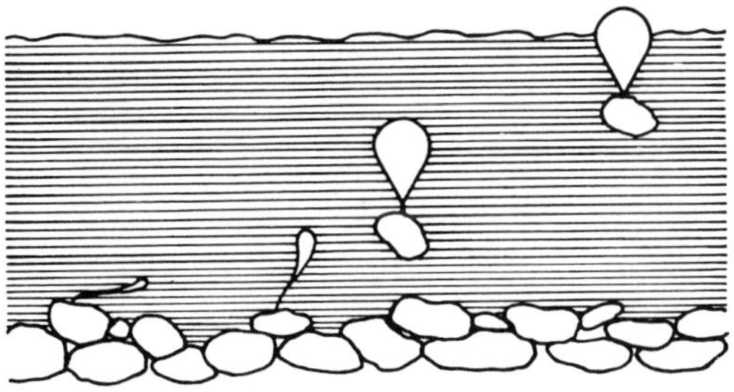

8

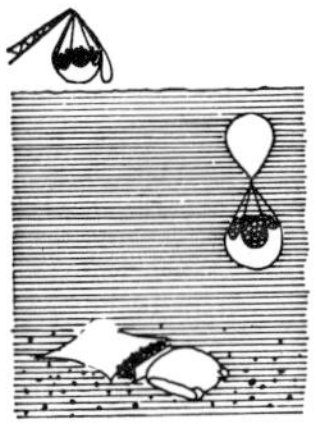

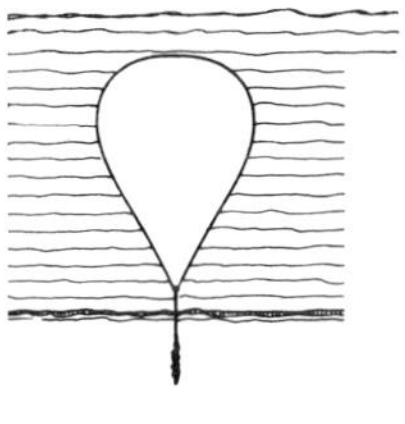

9 and 10

11 ▼

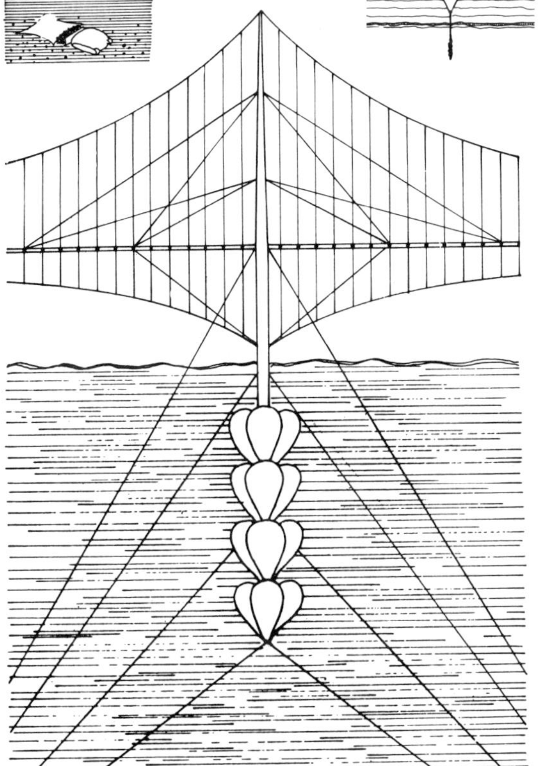

12 ▲

▼ 13

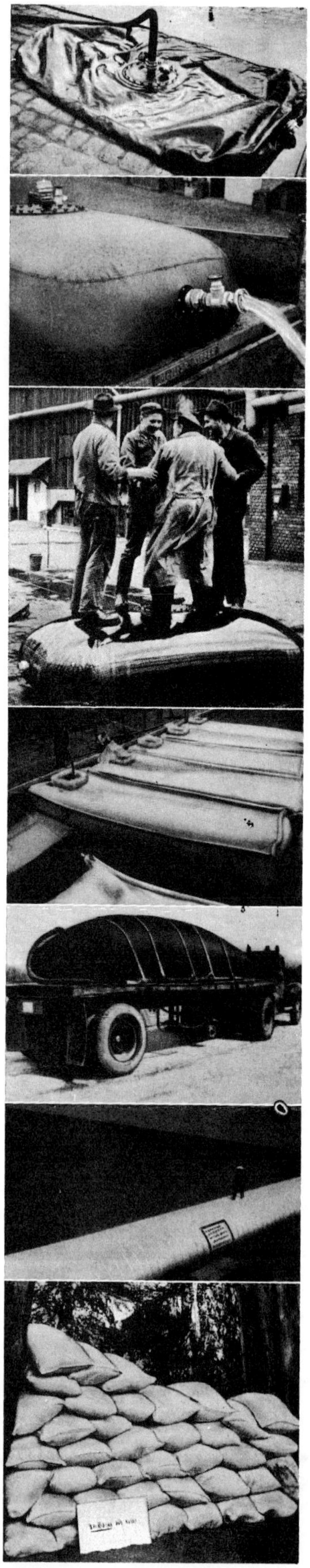

◄ 1 to 7

Hoses of uniform thickness and closed at the ends form a specially practical type of container. When filled they can be closely packed (Fig. 8). The best known container for solids in bulk or for pulverized substances is the paper bag. Its widespread use is due to its simple manufacture from a flat membrane without losses in cutting. Nowadays, large floating containers are increasingly used (Fig. 10). Long cylindrical containers can be easily stacked. The stacking height is limited however, since the bottom layer is subject to considerable loads (Fig. 9). Safe storage is very important when considerable motion is encountered during transport. Containers of highly rigid coated fabrics have proved particularly suitable for explosion-proof storage of gasoline. They allow the discharge of highly flammable substances without the introduction of air. It is also possible to make containers of multiple fabric layers with intermediate plastic sealing. This type of container is comparatively secure against damage since holes are automatically sealed by a swelling of the membrane. Development in this sphere was accelerated by the need for bullet-proof fuel tanks in airplanes during the last war. Figures 1 to 3 (works photo by Krupp) show a cushion-like container in the empty and filled state, and during a load test (Fig. 3). In 1960 plastic containers were used for wine storage after the record grape harvest in the Moselle region. They were submerged in swimming pools (Fig. 4, photo by U.P.I.). An American firm developed large containers for transportation by truck (Fig. 5; photo by U.P.I).

The Los Angeles River has been dammed for some time by a wide and long prismatic nylon hose coated with neoprene. It is secured to the base and faces of the dam and diverts a certain quantity of water to a seepage area. The internal water pressure distends the hose to a diameter of 1.55 m. If the overflow exceeds 20 cm the hose collapses automatically. It retains and diverts the high water, and is normally refilled within 24 hrs after the passage of a wave. In emergencies, the hose can be pumped to its full diameter in 25 min. Discharge is effected by a syphon in only 12 mins. Service life is estimated to be between 6 and 10 years (Fig. 6; photo from *Bauingenieur* 4/1960, see also *Engineering News Record* 162/1959). The scheme of such a dam is given in Figs. 11 and 12. Figure 14 is a section through a project* developed for emergencies in flood-threatened areas. This is a large hose of tough fabric which can be placed on endangered dykes and filled with water. The weight imparts an additional load to the dyke and increases its strength. Breaches in a dyke can be prevented in this way, even when the water tops the crest. The containers are 30 m long, have a diameter of 2 to 5 m, and can be dropped by plane; they fill automatically. The container shown in Fig. 13 consists of three parts with vertical partitions. It offers particularly high safety in storage.

Sand-filled containers can be used for different purposes in construction.† Sandbags can be used to build excellent walls (Figs. 15 and 16). Bags filled with concrete form tight interlocking walls. A wall of sandbags is not smooth on the outside (Fig. 17; photo by Glanzstoff). Nowadays, mass production enables the packing industry to manufacture boxes of sheet metal or plastics at very low cost. Figure 18 shows a wall of tin boxes that are open at the top and filled layer by layer with sand, which ensures weight and cohesion. Such walls may have very narrow joints and resistant surfaces and are easily dismantled. Due to their high weight they form an excellent acoustic barrier. Figure 19 is a section through such a wall. In Figure 20 two sandbag partitions are separated by a central heat-insulation panel. In the mountains, stone-filled wire-mesh bags are used as elastic bank reinforcements for the control of torrents (Fig. 17). They are even able to catch floating tree trunks ramming at high speeds. We mentioned that sandbags can be arranged to form arches (Fig. 21) and that they constitute excellent material for dwellings* (Figs. 22 and 23). At present such bags are made of welded plastic sheeting. They may also contain tightly packed sand and gravel (e.g., by vibration packing), and form high-strength elements by the injection of liquid cement or other adhesives.

The stresses imparted by loose and unstable soils to structural elements are often similar to those generated by liquids. In construction, therefore, pneumatic membranes are thus also important, not as closed foils but in the form of fine nets. Figure 1 on p. 146 shows a retaining wall attached to the embankment by deeply

† Report No. 6 of the Development Center for Lightweight Construction, Berlin.

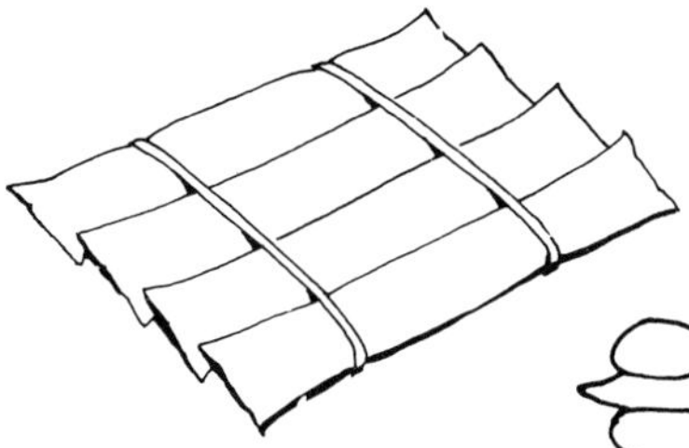
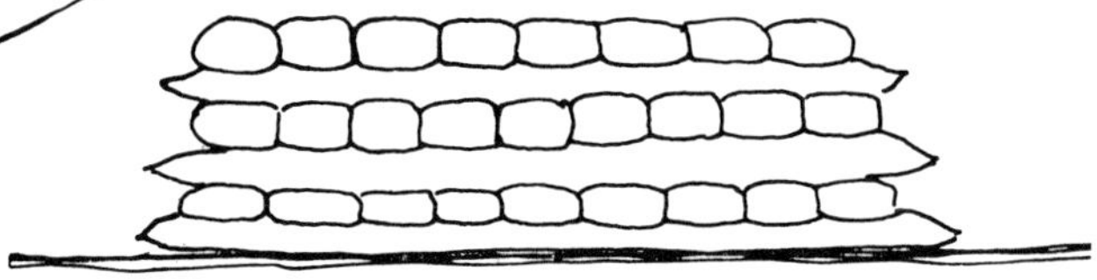

8 and 9

10

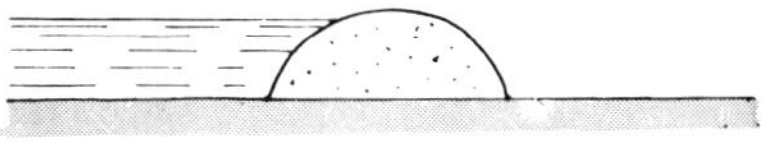

11 and 12

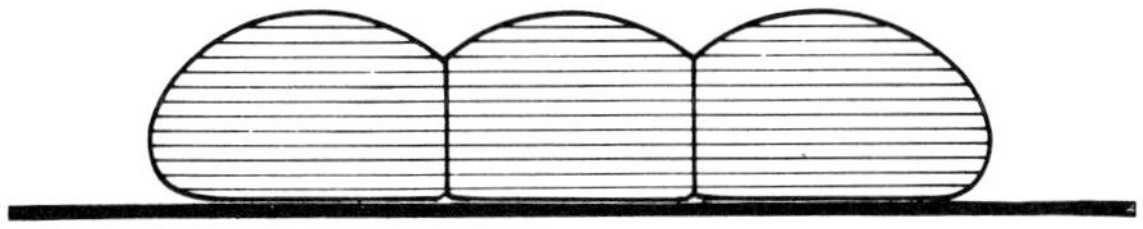

13

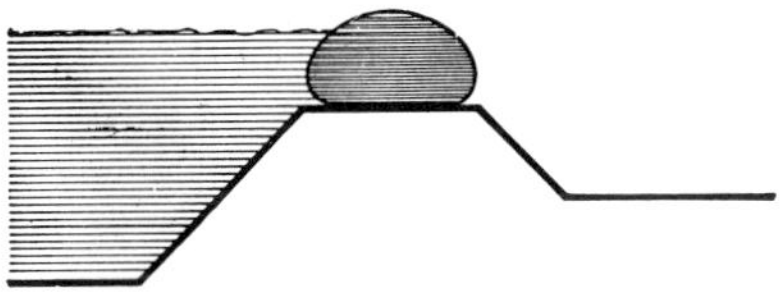
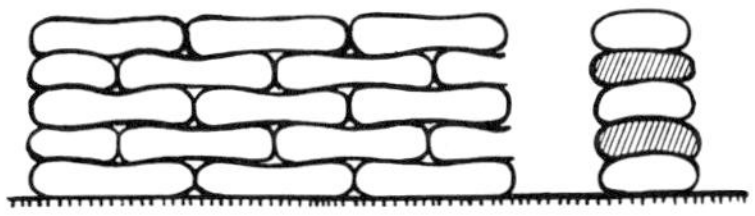

14 to 16

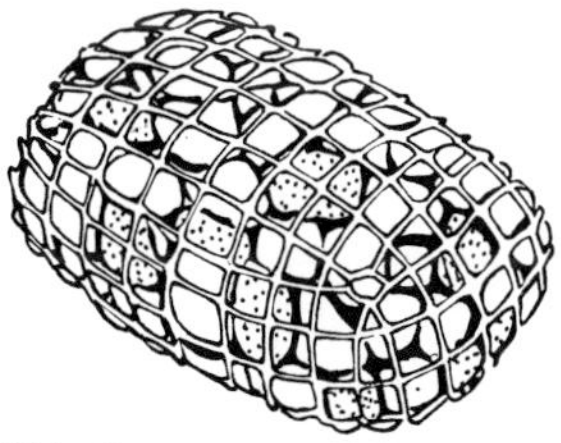
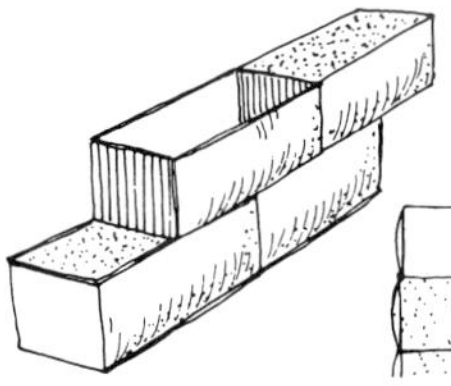

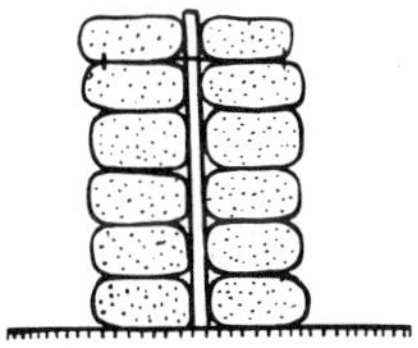

17 to 20

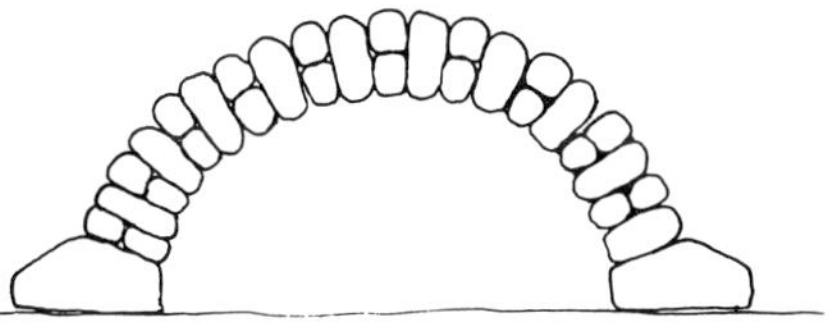
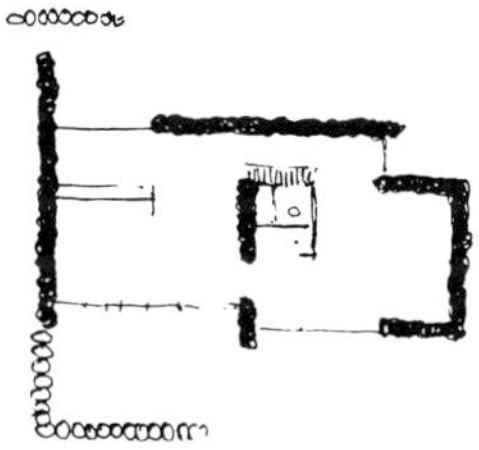

21 and 22

23 ▼

sunk anchors. The actual wall* is formed of wire fabric or heavy welded mats of structural steel (Fig. 2, p. 146). Such retaining walls can be erected with very little labor. This is made clear in Fig. 10 on p. 146. Bulldozers form the successive layers between which the anchors are inserted. Walls pervious to air or water can be erected, especially when coarse stones are packed behind the net. The construction of a compact earth wall by the same method is shown in Fig. 3 on p. 146. In the retaining wall shown in Fig. 4, p. 146, the anchors act obliquely upward. This can be of great value in vertical retaining walls. Even overhangs which protect mountain roads against rock fall and avalanches can be secured by these methods if suitable anchors are driven into the mountain (Fig. 5, p. 146).

The excavation for foundations in soft soils in the presence of groundwater is particularly difficult. At first, two membranes are introduced (see p. 312) and excavation begins (Fig. 6, p. 146); pressing-in of the membrane (Fig. 7, p. 146) is prevented by tension anchors. The soil in the center can be excavated or pumped out if it is sufficiently soft (Fig. 8, p. 146). Excavations beneath existing buildings can be carried out in a similar way. The surface of the pit is formed by a net pressed against or even into the ground by tension anchors (Fig. 9, p. 146). The pit is enlarged by excavating the soil between the meshes. The net is anchored to piles arranged over the original surface of the ground. The tension anchors penetrate through the cellar of the building. Figure 11 on p. 146 shows various stages of the excavation of a very deep foundation in the presence of groundwater under high pressure. Uniformly spaced tension anchors were passed through eyelets in a water- and pressure-proof membrane. With their aid the membrane is forced against the bottom of the pit. Between the tension anchors the membrane has circular openings closed by screw-on plates through which soil and groundwater can be pumped out. The scraping tool shown in the center can be of great assistance in this process. When the membrane is properly anchored and well tensed, the ground is prestressed and compacted; this enables heavy foundation loads, applied later to the pit bottom, to be taken up.

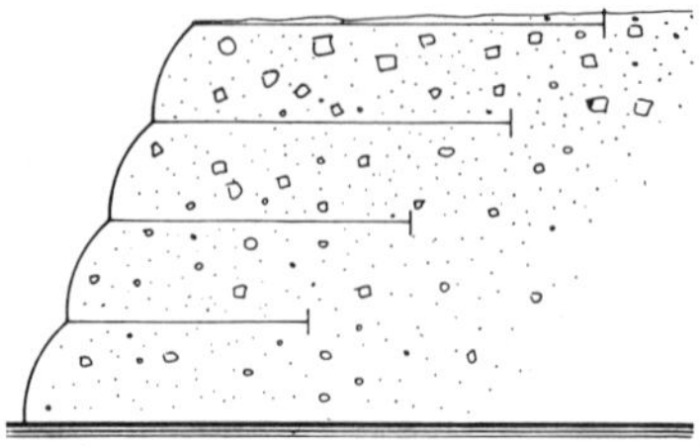

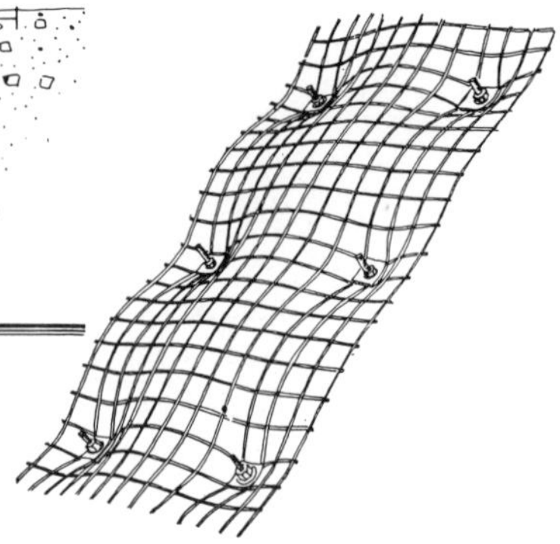

1 and 2

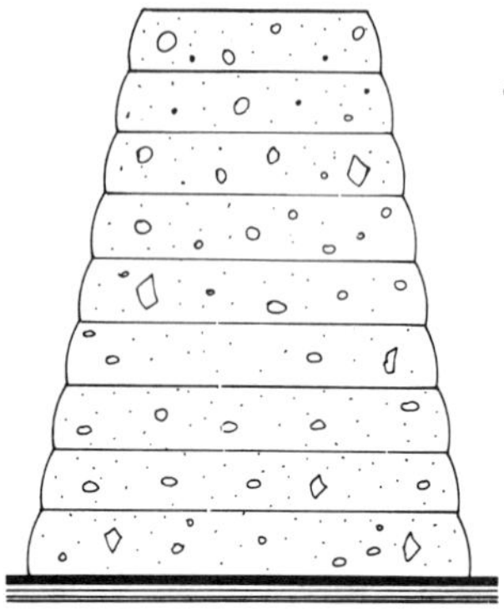

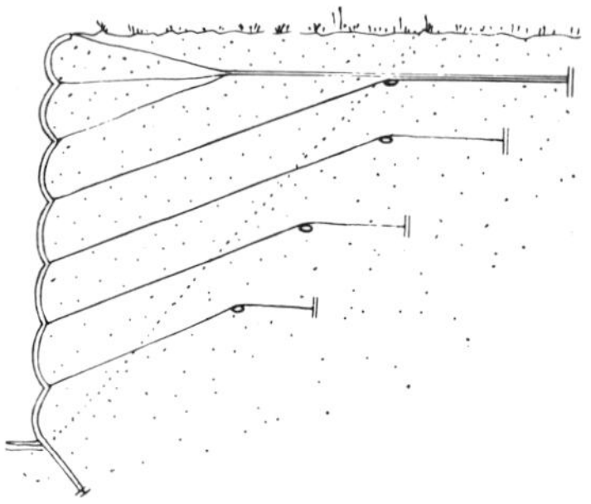

3 and 4

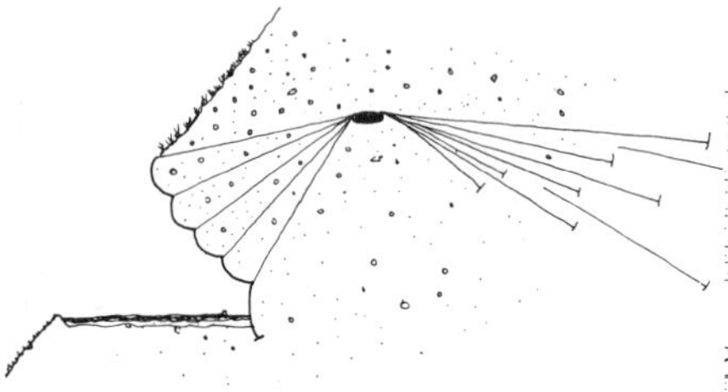

5

6 to 8 ▶

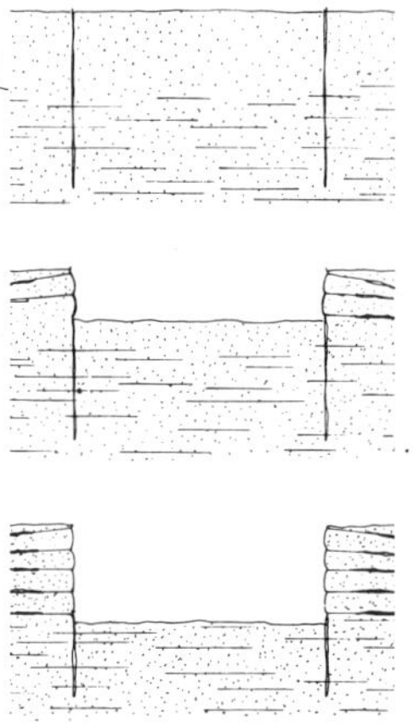

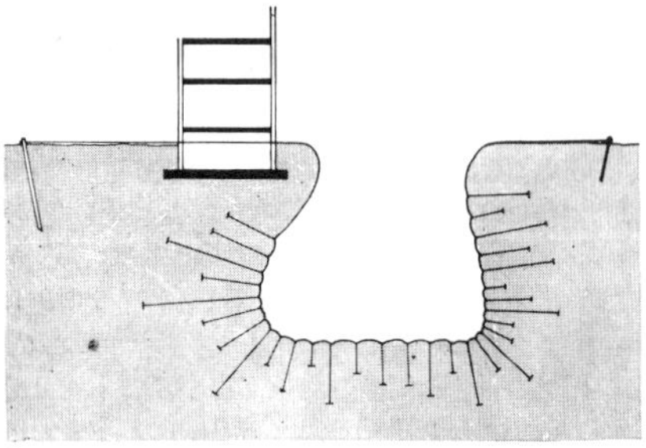

9

11 ▼

10 ▶

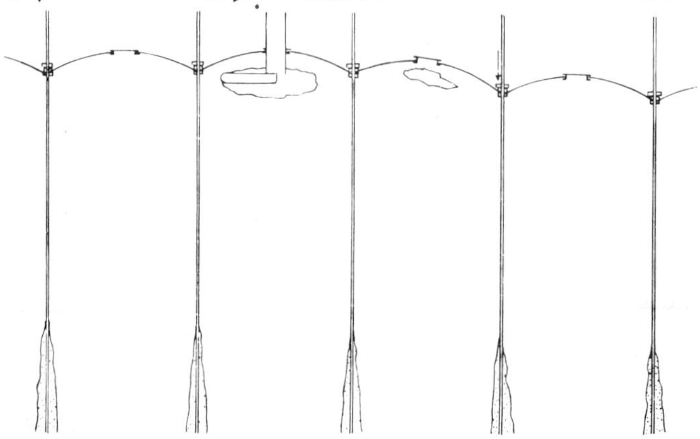

Composite Structures

Pneumatically tensed membranes can also be combined with other structural elements such as columns, cables, shells, etc.

For example, Fig. 12 shows the cross section of a strut whose core is an unbendable elastic rod surrounded by a fusiform pneumatic envelope. If the pneumatic envelope were connected to the rod only at the ends of the latter, inflation would cause a large compressive force to act on the rod, leading to its buckling. This method might be used to test struts. The strut can be effectively secured against buckling if the pneumatic body is subdivided into transverse (Fig. 13) or longitudinal chambers (Fig. 14). The hollow space can also be filled with foam (Fig. 15) which must exert pressure on the membrane to make it take up the load. Figure 16 is a section through a reinforcement of horizontal disks as suggested in Fig. 13. Figure 17 is a section through a fusiform pneumatic body to the outside of which semicircular struts (e.g., of wood) are attached. Figure 22 makes this design clear; Fig. 18 shows such a body, inflated to rigidity from an initially folded and easily transportable shape. Very light struts can be made. A further development arrived at in 1953 by Klepperwerke is also of interest: an air hose has on two sides flat leaf-shaped reinforcements of a rigid elastic substance such as plastics, metal, or plywood (Fig. 19) so that a rigid tube (Fig. 20) is obtained after inflation. Figure 23 is a section through such a structural element. Suitable folds in the individual parts permit not only prismatic, but also fusiform shapes* (Fig. 21) to be obtained.

Internal pressure imparts a higher buckling strength to such flexible shells.

Figure 25 illustrates the bracing of a pneumatically tensed rod by vertical plane membranes. Cable nets may be used instead. Figure 24 shows a cushion structure braced by struts so as to form a rigid girder. Figure 26 shows the reinforcement of a hexagonal compression-ring hose. Figure 1, p. 148 shows a strut reinforced by a cable net and distended in the center by an inflatable balloon. In Figure 2, p. 148, hose rings of different outside diameters surround a strut, tensing an outer membrane or cable net so as to reinforce the strut. The strut shown in Fig. 4, p. 148, is itself a pneumatic structure. Figure 3, p. 148, shows a rigid T-girder of the sandwich type which was described on p. 114. An additional triangular reinforcement supports the girder flange. Figure 5, p. 148 shows a pneumatic, quickly erectable antenna or observation tower consisting of several chambers. The tower (Fig. 27; photo of model*), erects itself automatically if all cables are first attached to the three or five anchoring points, and the individual chambers are then inflated separately, beginning with the bottom one.

A pneumatic hose with lateral protrusions (Fig. 6, p. 148) is tensed by additional cables and forms an arch or part of a cylindrical shell structure. A prismatic shell is shown in Fig. 7, p. 148; it consists of a

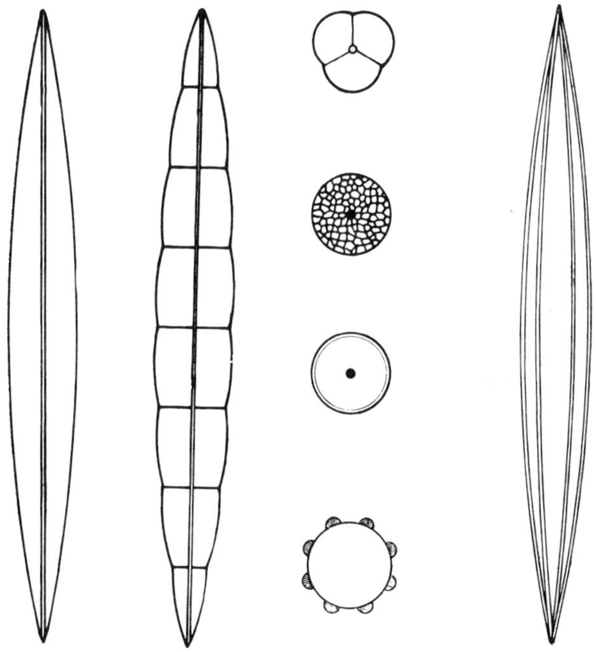

12 to 18

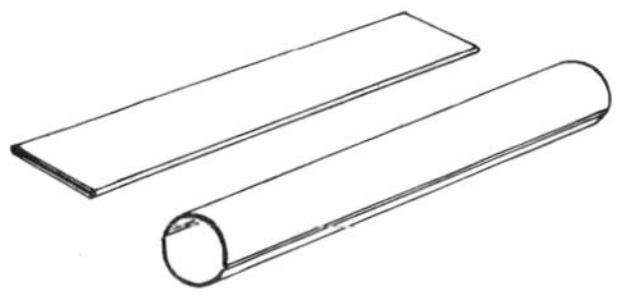

19 and 20

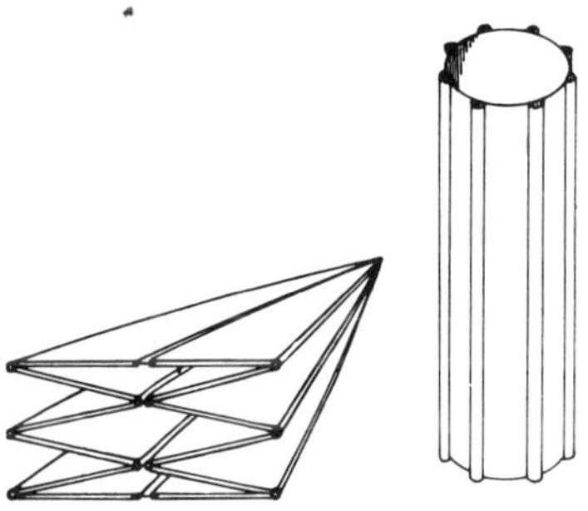

21 and 22

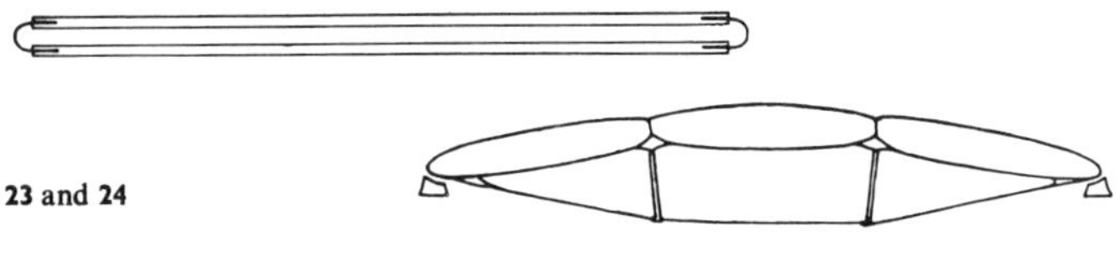

23 and 24

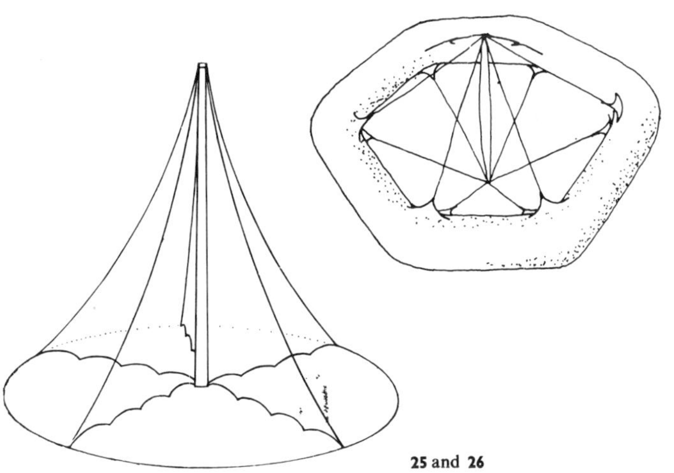

25 and 26

27 ▲

▼ 28

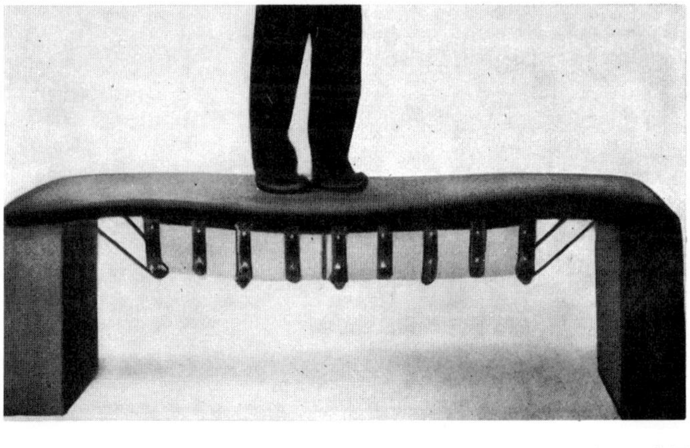

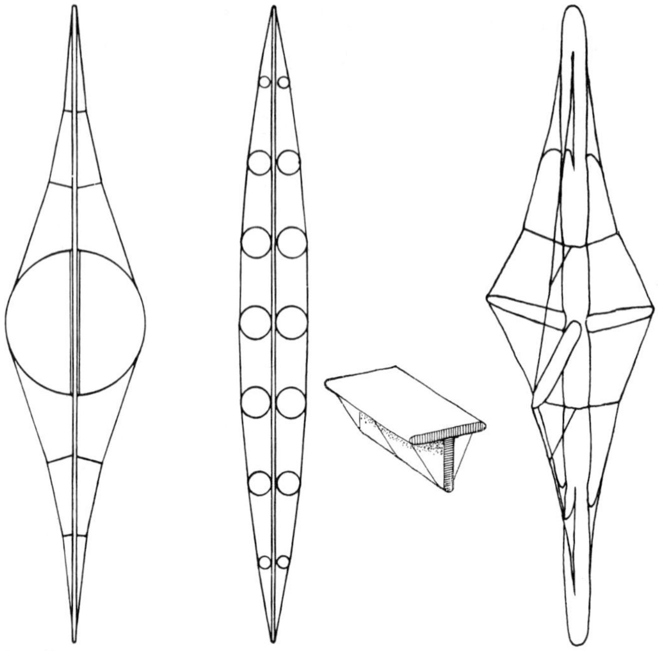

1 to 4

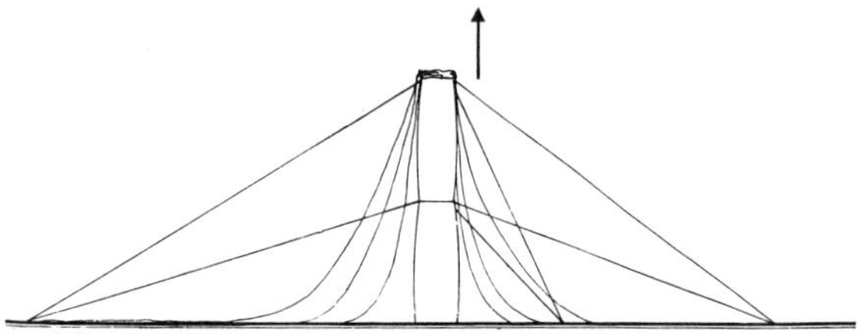

5

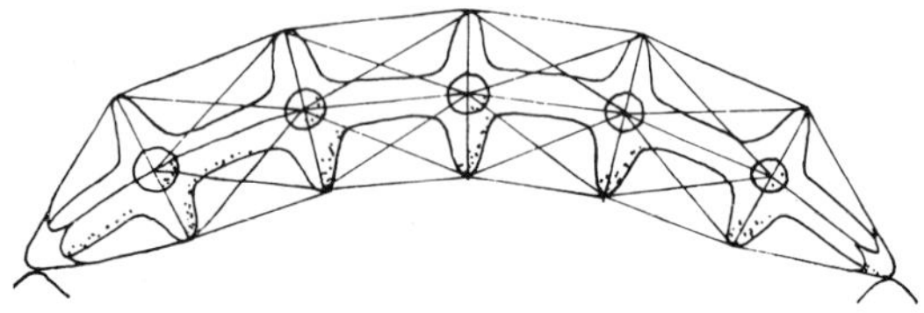

6

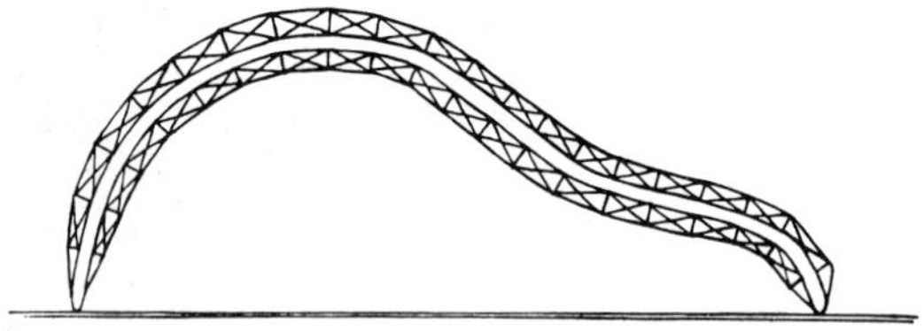

7

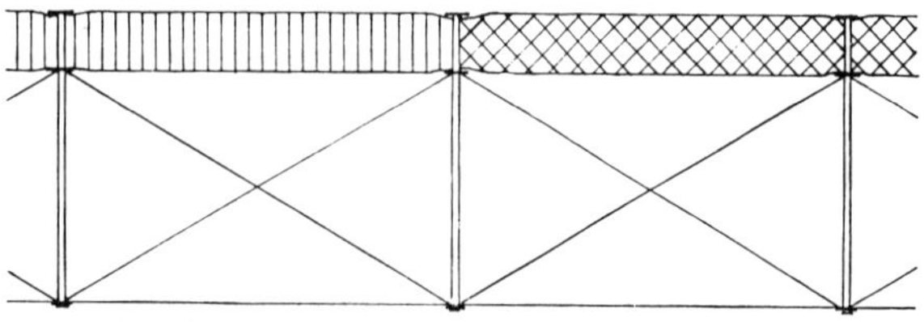

8

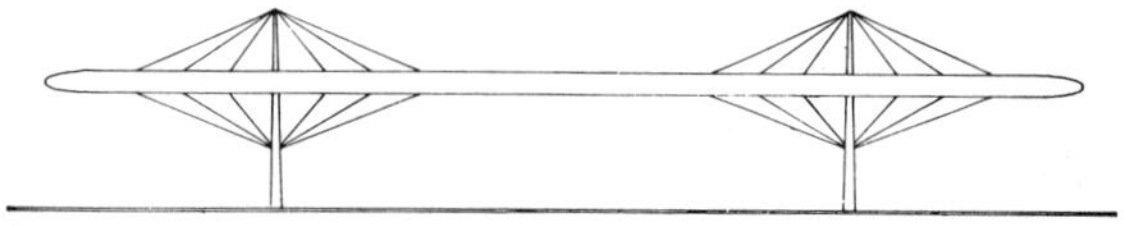

9

cushion-like inflatable sandwich element and is tensed by small external struts and a cable net. Figure 8 shows a braced sandwich panel, the left half representing the element developed by the Wingfoot Corporation. Figure 9 is a section of a building with a pneumatically tensed sandwich roof attached to the supports by cables and thus secured against wind suction and snow pressure. A braced inflated mat under load (Fig. 28, p. 147) was shown in the April 1957 issue of *Architectural Forum.*

It cannot be predicted how widely used braced pneumatic sandwich panels will be in the future. Their components are very intricate and can only be manufactured economically in mass production. Nevertheless, there are undeniably extensive fields for their application.

An envelope consisting of braced pneumatic sandwich panels was developed in about 1956 in the U.S.A. (Fig. 14; photo from *Architectural Forum*) as weather protection during repairs to the jet engines of the B-36.

The body structure of animals and human beings is a composite of rigid and compression-resistant members (bones, skeleton), surrounded by numerous tension elements such as sinews and and membranes and forming highly braced and reinforced struts. The lengths of the bracing can be adjusted by muscular action which permits activation of the entire system. The muscles are parcels of tissues tightly enclosed by membranes. Since the tissues, whose individual cells are under blood pressure, exert a load on the enveloping membranes similar to that induced by a gas or liquid, it is not surprising that all tissue elements enclosed by membranes constitute pneumatically formable shapes, i.e., the obvious relationship of all pneumatic structures to these natural shapes is not accidental but inherent in the structure (Fig. 10). Figure 11 shows the structure of a muscle, Fig. 13 the structural action of muscles and sinews, and Fig. 12 the muscles and sinews surrounding the bones of the foot.

Despite the advanced state of medical knowledge and the gradually increasing understanding of the basic relationships between "technical" and "living" structures, the fundamentals of the universal laws governing the structure of animal and human bodies are not yet clear. Braced skeletal structures and pneumatically tensed membranes are still not understood well enough for us to be able to explain the efficiency and refinement of living structures. The beauty of natural shapes and the incredibly advanced development of the relationships between all parts astonish us repeatedly, and bring us in awe of the forces and effects which may never be fully explained.

In the following we shall discuss composite structures combining pneumatic envelopes with prestressed skins which are not themselves under pneumatic tension. Shapes can be obtained in which both the pneumatically tensed envelope and the pneumatically untensed membranes form minimum surfaces. An example is the soap bubble between twelve plane membranes in a cubic frame (Fig. 20, p. 149) and the enlarged soap bubble (Fig. 21, p. 149).

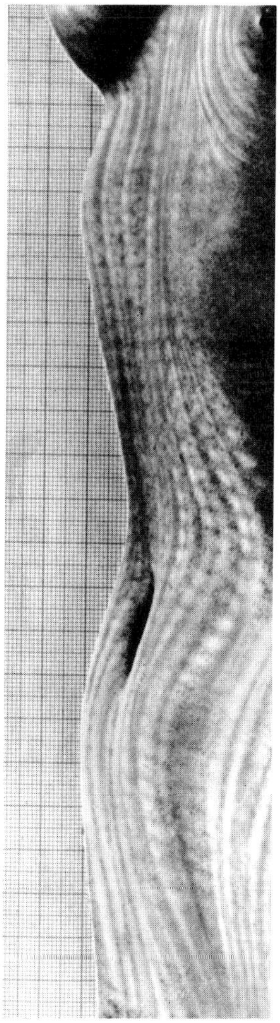

10

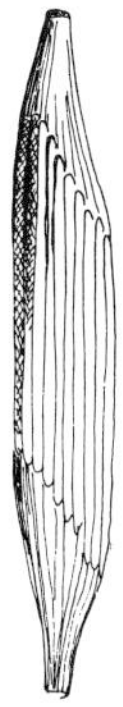

11 ▶

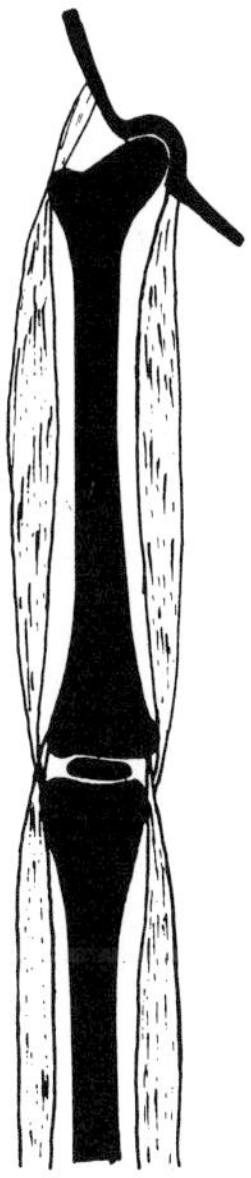

12 and 13

14

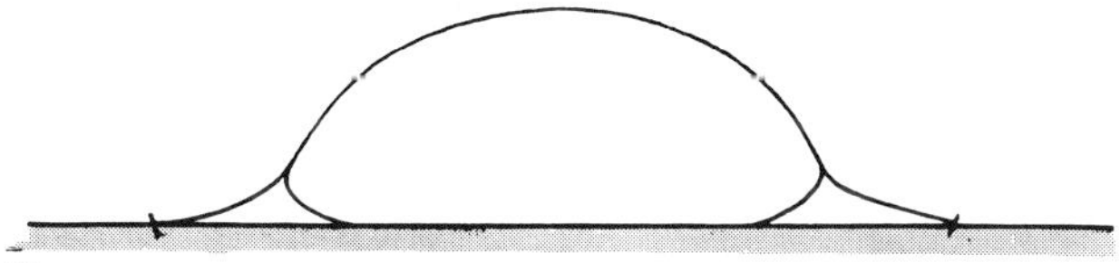

15

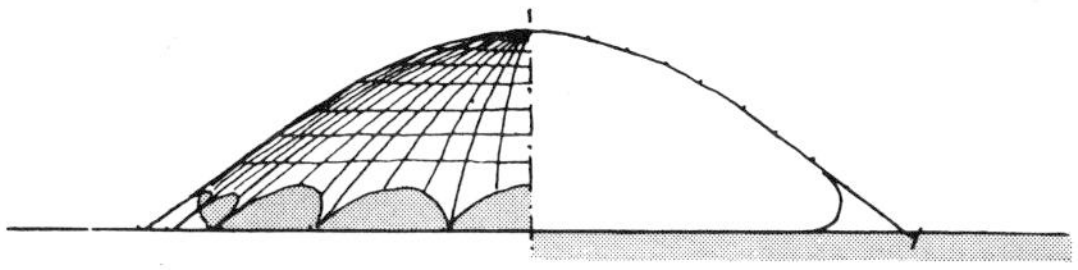

16 and 17

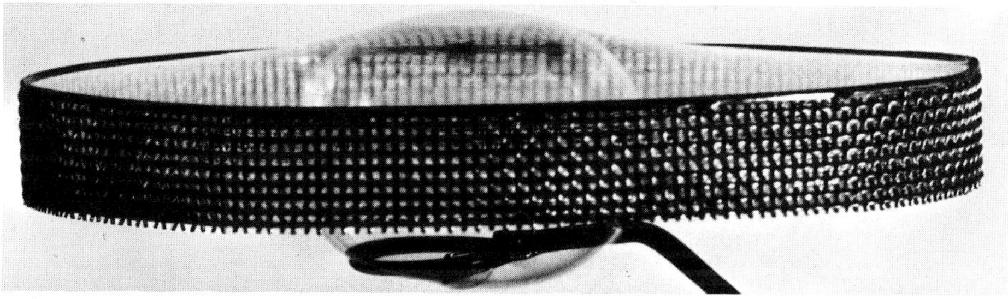

18 ▲

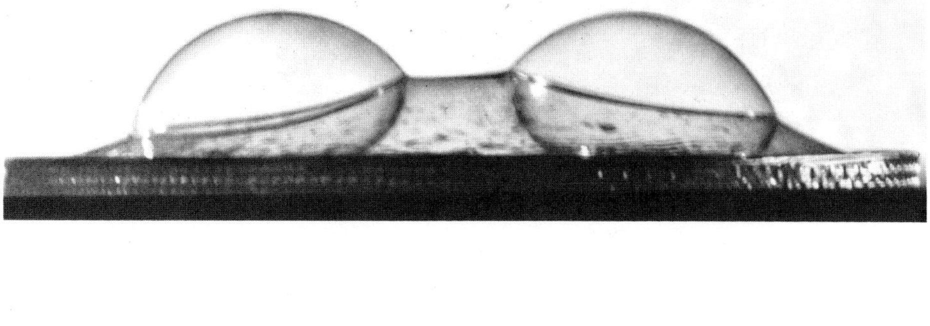

▼ 19

20 ▲

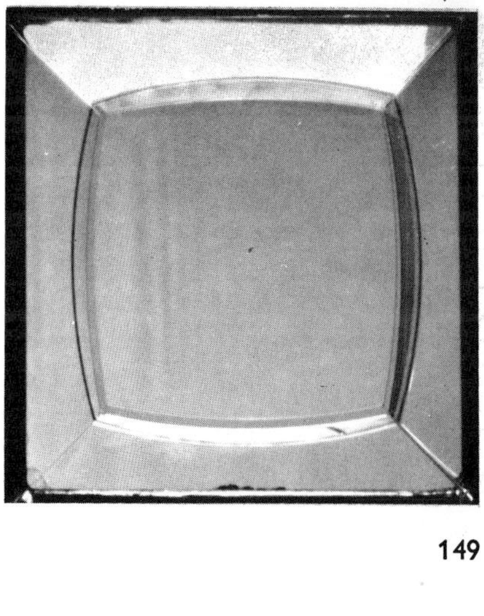

▼ 21

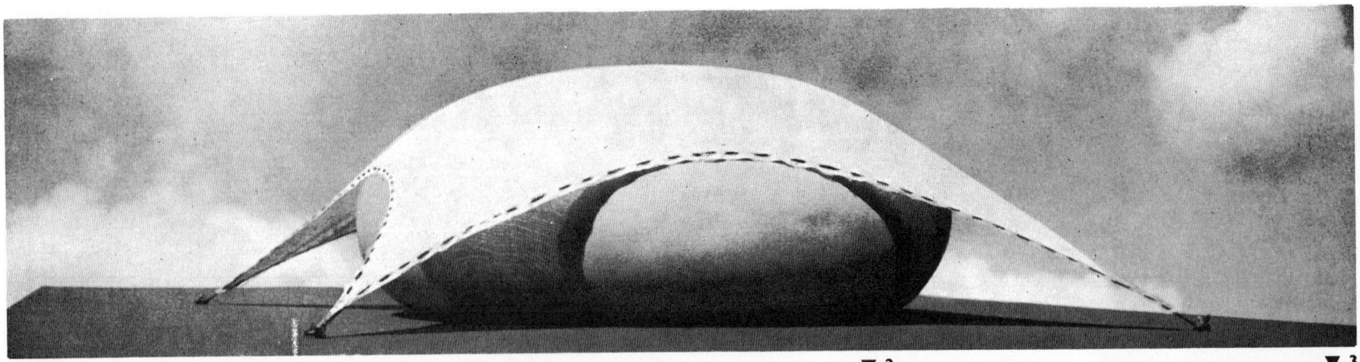

1 ▲

▼ 2

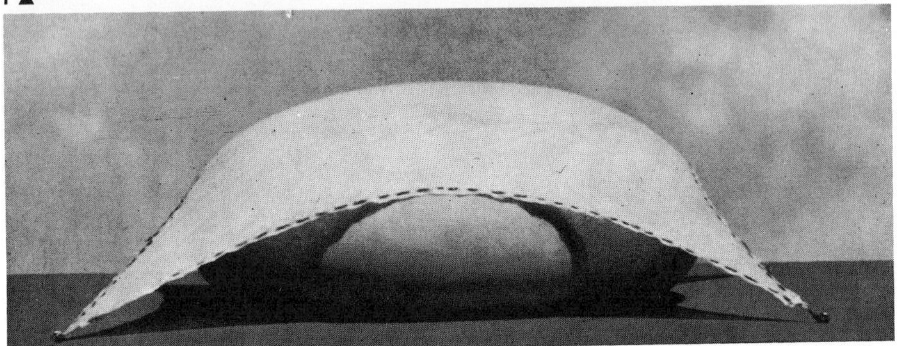

▼ 3

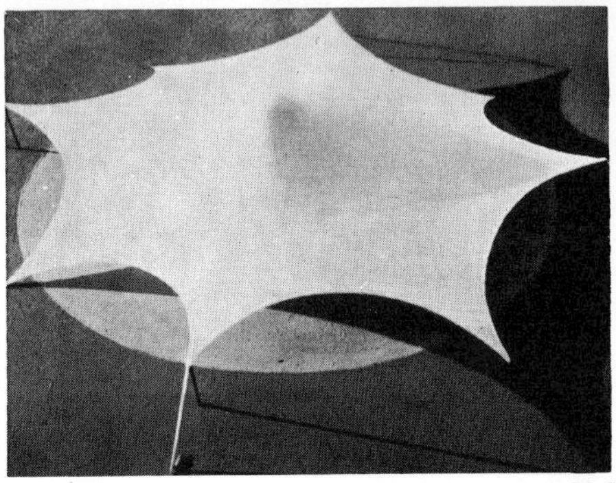

4 ▼

▼ 5

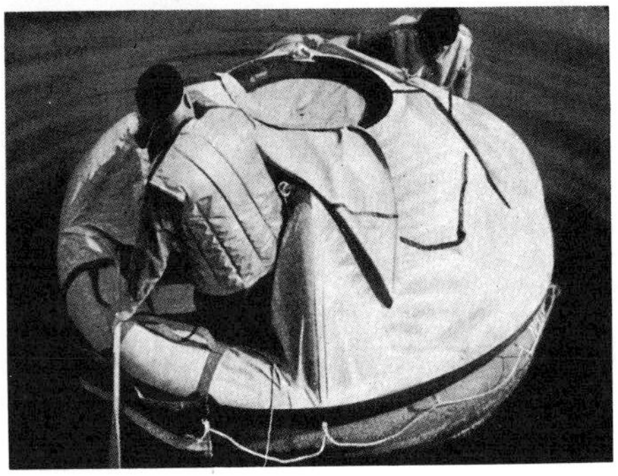

▼ 6

The system arranges itself in such a way that only three membranes meet along a line. In the cross section at right angles to the line of contact these membranes form angles of 120°. A membrane stretched in a ring (Fig. 18, p. 149), was pressed upward by a soap bubble, creating a bulging film inside the ring. The pressure exerted by this film flattens the bubble. It was also possible to support a soap film spanning the same ring, by smaller bubbles at two points, as seen from the side in Fig. 19, p. 149. In this case, the two smaller soap bubbles penetrate the main film. Each bubble is distended by the forces in the pneumatically untensed membrane, so that the conditions for the angle are also fulfilled in this case. These supports impart a considerable spatial curvature to the pneumatically untensed soap film. An interesting shape of great rigidity results.

The section, Fig. 15, p. 149 (see also the sketch, Fig. 16 on the same page) shows how a pneumatically tensed envelope is anchored to the ground by an untensed lateral continuation of the membrane which causes the main envelope to become wide and flat. This can be done similarly by a cable net (Fig. 17, p. 149). On the left is a view of the structure; on the right, a section through cable net and envelope. The envelope is closed on all sides and, unlike the net, not anchored to the foundations.

The photographs of a project* model (Figs. 1 and 2) show how a pneumatically tensed sphere is retained by a membrane simultaneously constituting a protection against light and covering the entrances. Sketch 8 shows a similar design which is related to the soap-bubble experiment in Fig. 18, p. 149. A central pneumatically tensed envelope supports a prestressed membrane. This design is important when the central envelope must give special protection while the outer membrane covers the entrances, e.g., to protect them against radiation. Containers for liquids and gas balloons under high pressure can be protected and reinforced by such membranes.

In a project* for an extraterrestrial structure the central envelope (Fig. 1, p. 26) is protected by a triple skin to provide the necessary safety for the crew (Fig. 9).

The section (Fig. 8) clarifies the basic principle of central support

7

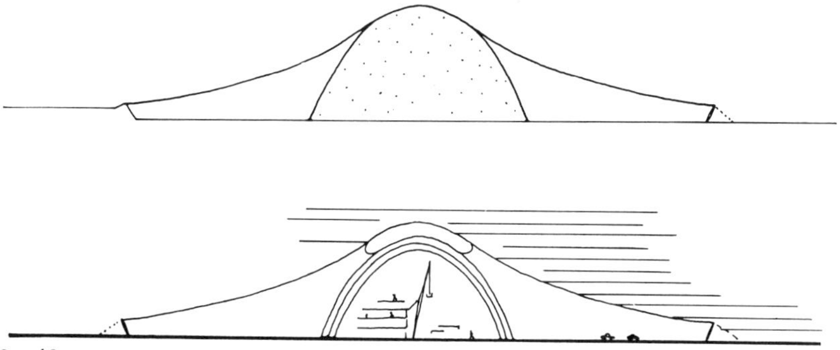
8 and 9

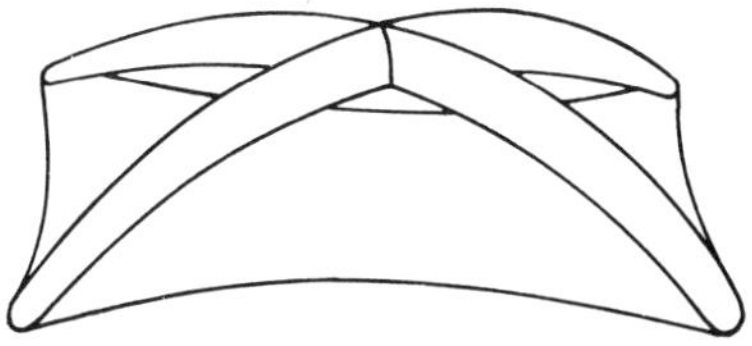
10

▼ 11

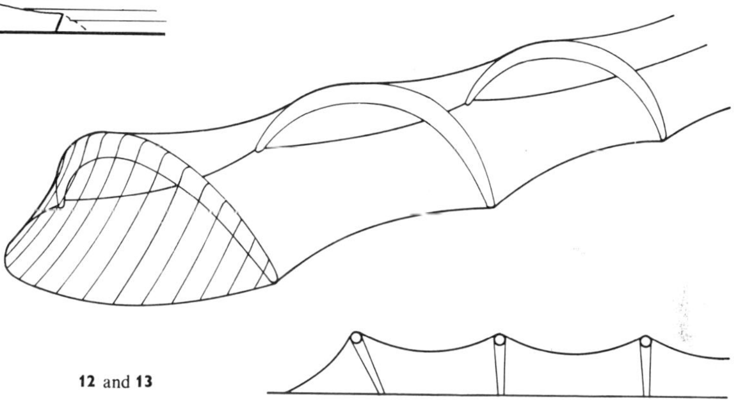
12 and 13

for a prestressed doubly curved membrane by a pneumatically tensed ellipsoidal skin. The design is illustrated by photographs (Fig. 3 and Fig. 7) of the model of a similar project.*

Combinations of pneumatically tensed torii with membranes deserve particular attention. Inflated arching hoses can support all the various cable-net and membrane shapes in compression-resistant arches.

We are familiar with spatially curved membranes and cable nets between rings which do not lie in one plane. Several such rings may intersect.

We are also familiar with membranes and cable nets between vertical arches and between inclined or intersecting arches. The number of combinations possible by the use of inflatable hoses has not even been remotely exhausted.

For example, a British firm designed a tent (Fig. 4; photo from *Bauwelt* 28/1956), with thick air-inflated arches tensing a membrane. The life raft in Fig. 5 (photo by Glanzstoff) has a bottom membrane stretched in a large and heavy buoyant ring and a roof consisting of a central smaller ring and four lateral arches, also supported by pneumatically tensed hoses. The effect of arches with membranes is illustrated in sketch (Fig. 12); parallel arches one behind the other support a saddle-shaped membrane; this is made clear in longitudinal section (Fig. 13). It is possible to shape the membrane in such a way that it becomes stretched between the arches without folds. The arches may also intersect (Fig. 10) as in the Stromeyer garage roof (Fig. 6; works photos), and in the Stromeyer camping tent, one of the first and most common structures of this type (Fig. 11). The combination of pneumatically tensed elements with prestressed cable nets or membranes is not limited to balloons or fusiform bodies for central supports or to the use of arches. It is also possible to construct rigid frames out of straight cylindrical skins under pneumatic tension, as well as wall-like supporting structures able to carry prestressed cable nets or membranes and also support freely suspended, i.e., nonprestressed tension-loaded structures.

Combinations not under Constant Pneumatic Tension

1 and 2

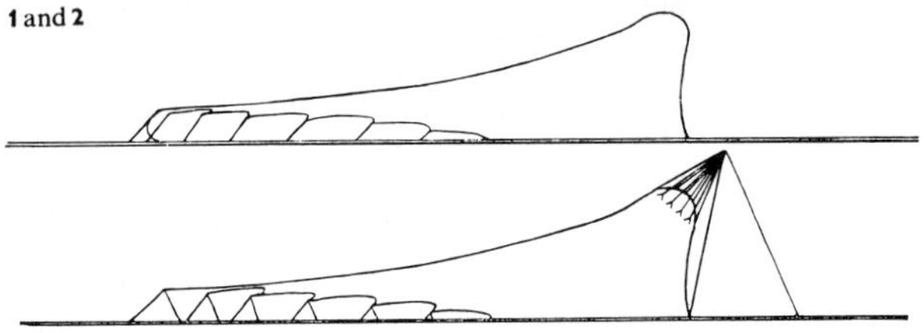

3 and 4

5 ▲

▼ 6

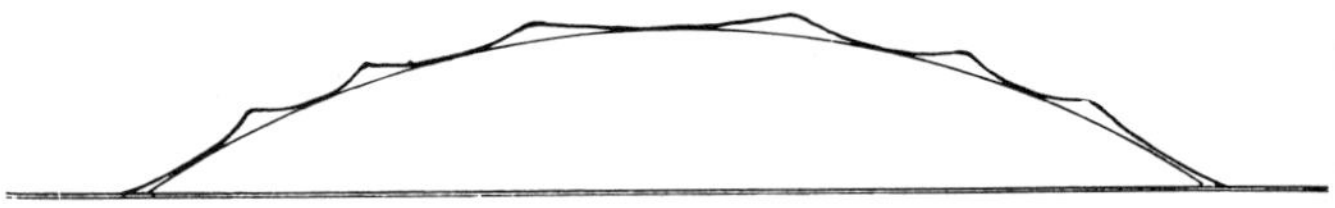

7

8

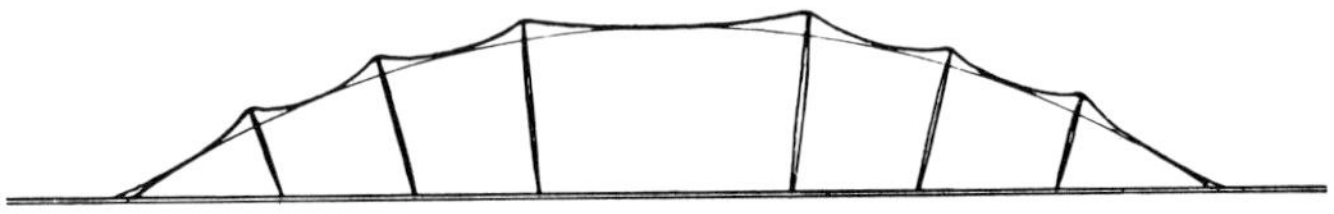

9

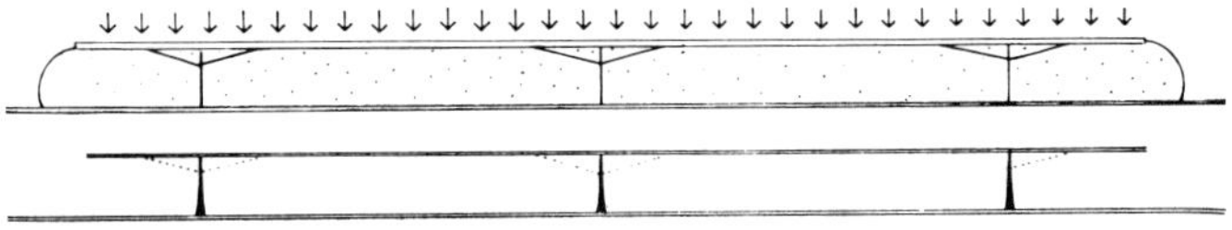

10 and 11

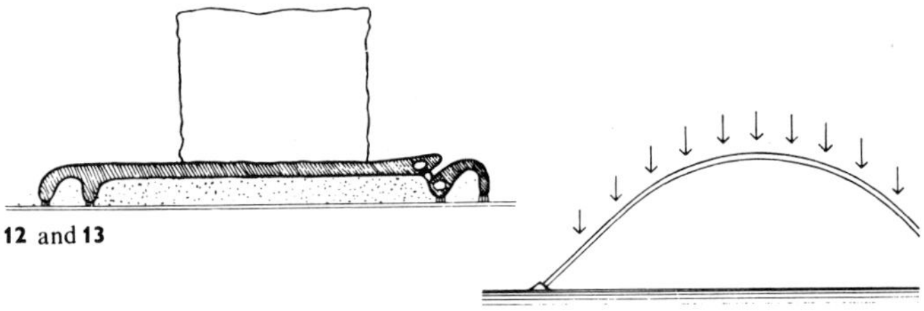

12 and 13

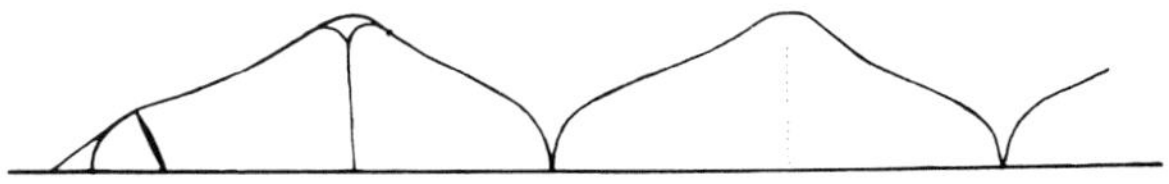

14

Membranes not under Constant Pneumatic Tension

The designs shown on this page are characterized by the fact that they may form both pneumatically tensed structures and pneumatically untensed prestressed membranes. If we consider this superficially, the combination of two different structural principles would appear unnecessary; however, its fundamental significance becomes clear upon closer examination.

For example, a pointed tent (Fig. 1) open on all sides during the summer, can be designed as a prestressed membrane forming a large sunroof accessible from all sides.

In winter the central support would carry considerable snow loads. Furthermore, a heatable closed area becomes necessary. If the envelope is closed at the sides (Fig. 2) and pressurized, the central support becomes unnecessary, since, as previously explained, this type of roof is pneumatically formable and can support snow loads when under internal pressure.

Consequently, high adaptability to the seasons is obtained by very simple means and it is no longer necessary to take measures against snow loads during periods in which they do not occur.

When transformation into pneumatically tensed membranes is simple, summer structures need not be designed for snow loads. The resulting economies can be considerable.

According to the previously stated laws of formation for pneumatic structures, domed or cylindrical shapes with sections as in Fig. 7 collapse when the internal pressure is released. Collapse can be prevented by external cables, as shown in the section, (Fig. 8) and side view (Fig. 6), or by internal supports (Fig. 9). The cables or

15 ▲

▼ 18

16 ▲

▼ 17

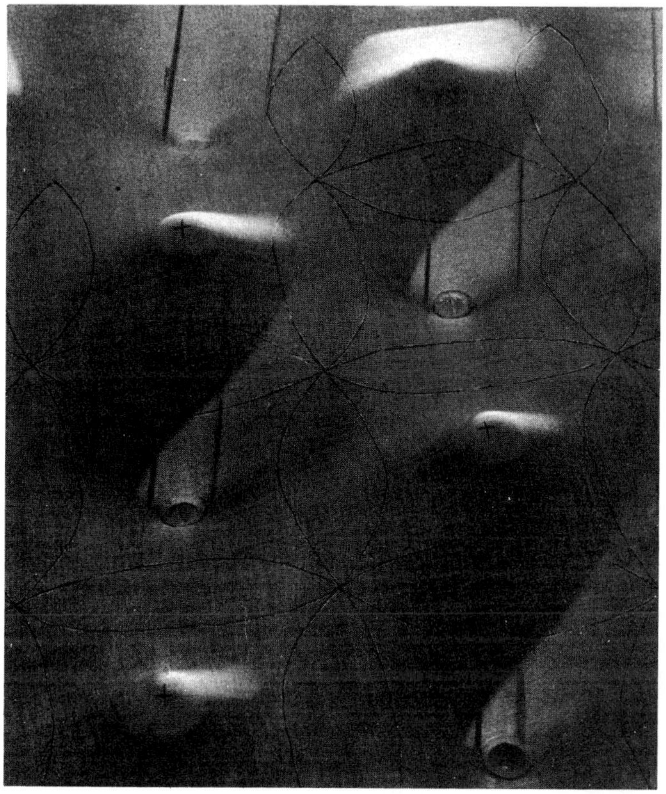

supports can be quite thin, since they merely take up the dead weight of the membrane and the small forces due to its prestressing.

Wind suction effects unloading and internal pressure takes up snow loads.

Widely differing shapes are possible, as seen in the project for the peaked membrane supported only by air pressure (Fig. 3) or by struts (Figs. 4 and 5).

It is also possible to design a thin roof panel whose positive loads (see arrows in Fig. 10) can—especially when the panel is soft and elastic—be taken up by internal pressure. The structure may be closed at the sides, though neither this nor pressurization are essential in the absence of positive loads (Fig. 11).

Similarly, in vehicles designed to carry great weights (Fig. 12), an air cushion is arranged under the load. Flaps and several chambers reduce air leakage. The loads are taken up directly by the compressed air; a powerful blower maintains pressure continuously. Figure 13 shows a section through a shell structure in which excessive positive loads can be counter-balanced by increasing the internal pressure.

Figure 14 shows a membrane with peaks and valleys, supported on the left by struts and on the right by internal pressure.

Such a shape, of which Fig. 18 shows part of the roof, and Fig. 17 a side view, can form both an open summer roof and a pneumatically reinforced winter structure. The hump membrane (Fig. 15), corresponding to Fig. 9, can also be closed in winter and the supports removed. Figure 16 shows a hump membrane with internal struts which can also be supported pneumatically in the same way.

Sails

Sails are the oldest pneumatic structures. A sail is a membrane tensed by differences in air pressure on either side. Every sailor or yachtsman knows that a properly cut sail should be free of folds and tensed as uniformly as possible.

The force of the wind is used to propel the ship, and it is even possible to sail obliquely into the wind. The sail is set in such a way that suction acts on the lee side and pressure on the wind side. The resulting pressure difference depends on the velocity of the wind relative to that of the ship.

The force of the wind acting on the sail must be transmitted to the ship. The sail is subjected to membrane tensions. When the tensile strength of the material is surpassed, the sail tears. The membrane tensions are transmitted from the sail, via rigging and masts, to the hull.

The shape of a sail is largely determined by its boundaries. A sail can be spanned in a rigid frame of rectangular (Fig. 1) or triangular shape (Fig. 2). A frame can also be stretched only on two sides in a rigid element, such as a mast or boom, and bordered by a rope (Fig. 3). The sail in Fig. 4 is bounded on three sides by rigid parts whereas the fourth side is formed by a rope. The shape shown in Fig. 5, which is characteristic for jibs, is bordered by ropes on all sides. Four-cornered shapes (Fig. 6) are also known, in addition to triangular ones. Parachute sails (Fig. 7) stayed at least at two points are increasingly coming into use.

At present, the best known type is the spinnaker, which is usually stayed at three points. Battens can be inserted to enlarge the surface of the sail (Fig. 8). This also distends the outer edge of the sail and affects its aerodynamic profile.

Another type of sail (Fig. 9) is the awning of a truck which is designed so that it is molded by the wind while in motion; this reduces the aerodynamic resistance of the vehicle. Several flexible battens maintain the shape when the vehicle is stationary. Photographers Frank and Keith Beken are noted for their sail photographs. We refer to the excellent book *Zauberwelt der Segel.*

In the schooner *Westward* (Fig. 11) the sails form a nearly closed outline and act like staggered air foils. This fast yacht had an overall length of 41 m and a total spread of 1,250 m^2.

A typical example of correct aerodynamic design is the rigging of an "Old Timer" like that of the Portuguese training ship *Sagres* (Fig. 10). Figure 12 shows the rigging of a barge. Photograph 14 depicts the typical membrane shapes of the jibs between jib boom and foremast (photo by Meincke).

The seagoing yacht *Niravana* is a 6-m boat with a spread of 43 m^2 (Fig. 13; photo by Ullstein-F.D. Becke). The large balloon shape of the spinnaker is easily recognized.

High capacity sails can be made by using large surfaces of tightly woven materials that can be quickly attached to light and foldable frames. The shape of the sails can even be adjusted later.

A sail is a highly mobile structure requiring constant attention. At present, wind power is not used very much for ship propulsion and sailing has become a sport. Sail design is based on experience and observation and has been constantly improved.

A sail is often "ironed out" by being hoisted when wet and sailed dry. This is done to remove folds and uneven areas and obtain uniform membrane tensions.

Sailmaking is a great art and sails without folds, in which the fabric spreads uniformly without peak-stress areas, are rarely seen. Nowadays the engine has replaced wind power, but the sail itself remains as a simple membrane structure to take up aerodynamic forces economically.

The sail influenced the beginnings of aviation. New applications have been found for it in the field of astronautics. For example, gigantic gliders are planned as membranes spanned between pneumatically tensed cylinders in order to effect gradual re-entry into the atmosphere.

The parachute, which was based on the invention of Montgolfier, is still the most valuable rescue device. Its shape is closely related to that of the spinnaker, whose latest forms are undoubtedly influenced by parachutes. There are many types of specialized parachutes.

A parachute should be light, easily foldable, and highly elastic. The shock sustained when it opens is a special problem. The sudden opening of the envelope increases the air resistance and exerts a powerful braking action on the falling body. Parachutes have been designed with openings and slots; some parachutes can be guided with comparative ease by pulling on the lines; this tilts the parachute and ensures a sideward descent. The parachute can thus be considered an independent "aircraft."

The manufacture of parachute fabric requires particular care. The envelope is composed of individual webs that have a diagonal weft to prevent tearing at the seams, so that a parachute which is split by the opening shock does not endanger the jumper by collapsing.

Three photographs of the Kohnkewerke show a parachute with triangular canopy (Fig. 1, p. 156), a triangular parachute with a slot (Fig. 2, p. 156) and an ordinary round parachute (Fig. 3, p. 156). The latter is still fully open after landing, and the parachutist must use his skill to make it collapse.

Windmills with sails have been known for ages, often in a very primitive form. The aerodynamic shape of sails is usually superior to that of the rigid arms in most windmills (Fig. 4, p. 156 photo by Kuhne). The bag (Fig. 6, p. 157), which indicates wind direction on

1 to 3

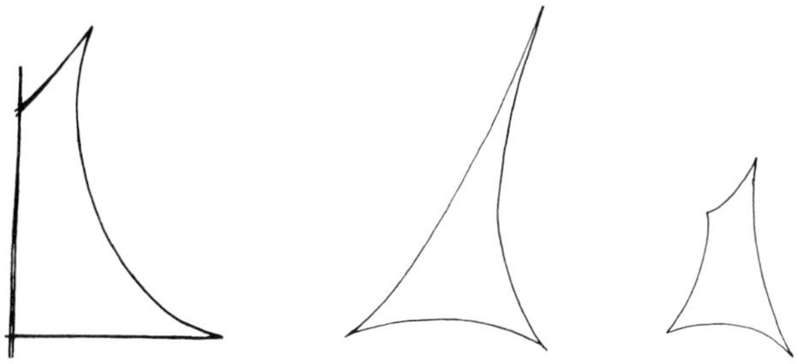

4 to 6

7

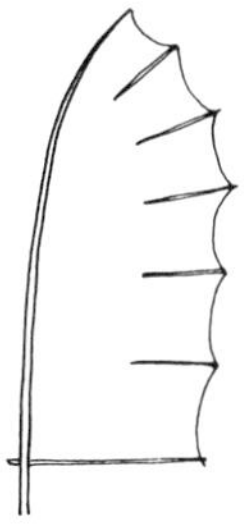

8

9

10

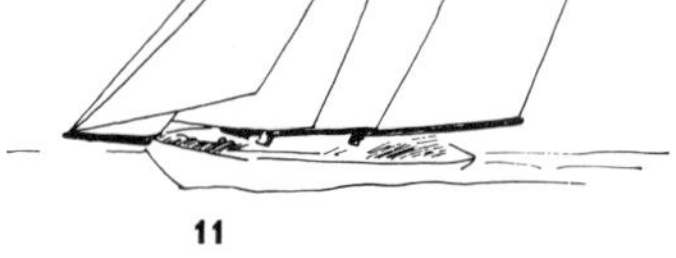

11

12

13 ▲

▼ 14

1

2

air-fields, is another well-known type of sail. This is a conical hose without a point, and the wind enters through the larger opening. Windbags remain comparatively steady in the wind without fluttering.

True sail shapes have hardly ever been used intentionally as structural forms; it is difficult to turn buildings into the wind like sails so that they become properly loaded by the latter without vibrations. Nevertheless, the study of sail shapes is of considerable importance in construction.

Roofs of large, awning-covered halls, often have wooden frameworks measuring 60 m across and up to 100 m in length. The wind makes these roofs bulge upward like balloons as in the large tent at the 1958 Hannover Fair (Fig. 5).

Wind suction causes a difference in pressure and thus bulges the membrane. An awning, nailed to its frame when flat, can only take up wind forces after deformation. The pneumatically induced sail-like deformations must be taken into account if the stability of such structures is to be determined.

Since wind direction and velocity are subject to continuous fluctuations, the areas of positive and negative pressure on the roof vary continuously. Consequently, such roofs cannot be kept under constant tension like the sails of ships. They may bulge up suddenly, be pressed down immediately after onto the framework and bulge downward. Strong shocks rock the structure and may loosen the connections with ensuing collapse.

The long service life of such halls under permanent and high mechanical stress is amazing. However, these stresses have several times caused collapse.

3

4

5

The awnings which cover small market stalls (Fig. 7) are often inflated by the wind like a spinnaker. At times the shape remains comparatively steady, even when wind velocity and direction fluctuate. This is due to the approximately uniform resistance offered to the wind by the stall on all sides. However, considerable membrane forces act upon the corners.
The photograph in Fig. 10 was also taken at the 1958 Hannover Fair during strong wind gusts. In one of the pavilions articles of "beautiful" design were shown. The structure was a rigid wooden grid shaped like a cylindrical barrel and covered by a thin sheet of plastic. This sheet was lifted almost in its entirety from the wooden structure by wind action and freely stretched between the supports, as seen in section (Fig. 8). A maximum clearance of 50 to 70 cm was observed between the sheet and the structure. The sheet acted like a true pneumatically tensed membrane, taking up all the forces. The heavy wooden structure was relieved of all loads. Figure 10 clearly shows the lifting of the sheet along the upper edge of the grid.

The study of sails is of considerable assistance in the design of structures that, for the most part, have to take up wind forces only. The envelopes should form streamlined sail shapes for any direction of the wind; their collapse in the absence of wind can be prevented by light auxiliary supports. Figure 9 shows a sail stretched between five points* and held in shape by a light suspension structure, which prestresses it by forces acting upward. When wind forces act, prestressing is reduced. All wind forces are transmitted first directly to the membrane and then via the edge to the anchoring points.

6

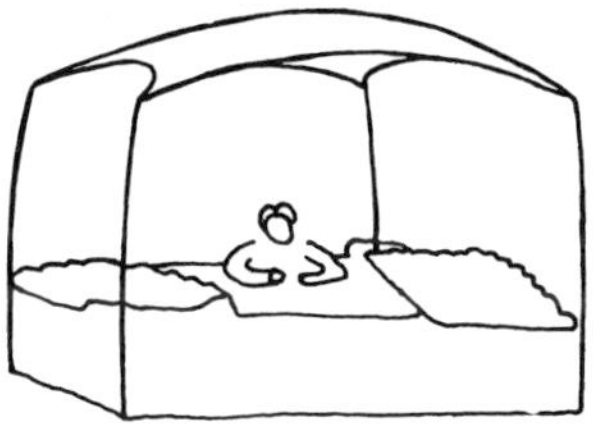
7

8

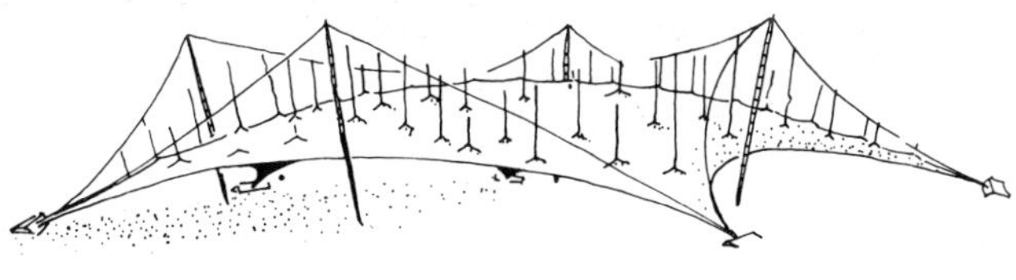
9

10
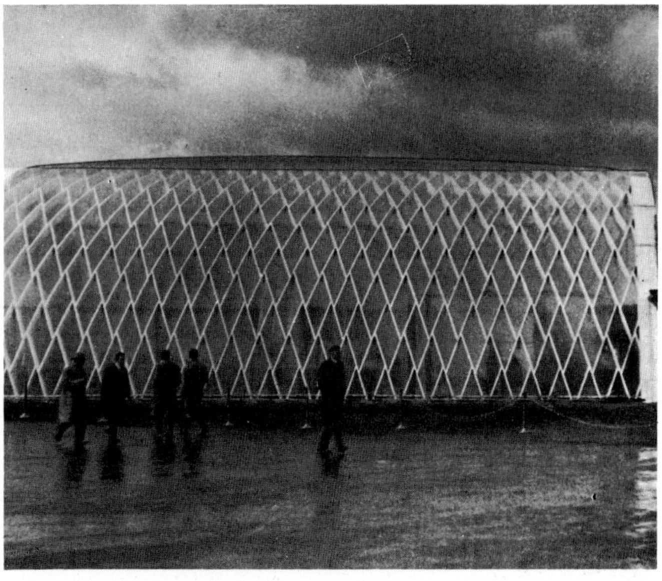

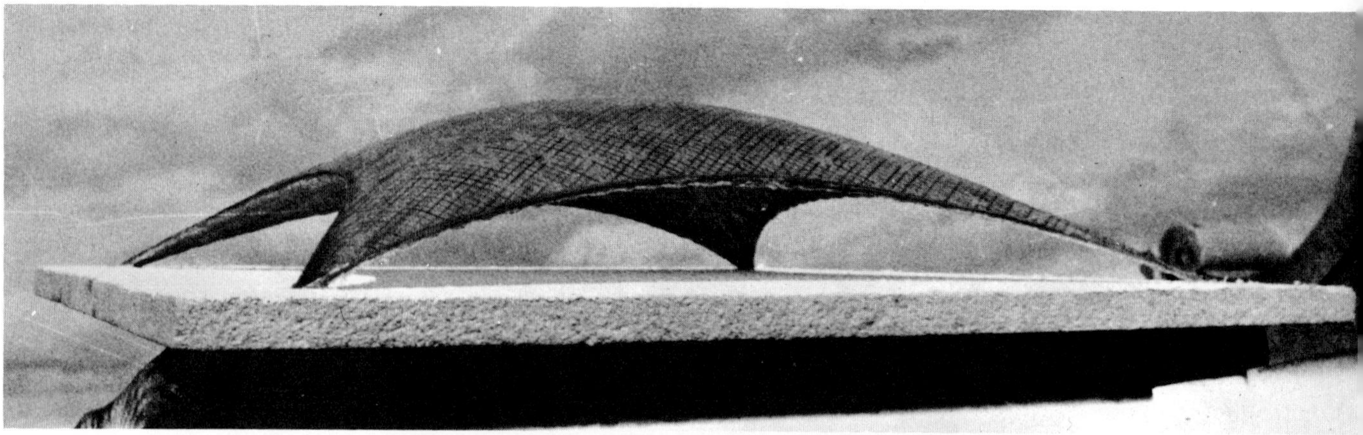

1 ▲

Sail Shells

Sail shells are thin bending- and compression-resistant structures that are shaped like a sail and subject to tensile stresses when wind-loaded, in which case they must be able to support their own weight. Experiments showed that such shapes are efficient under uniformly distributed positive loads, as for example, during prolonged snowfall. Assymmetrical loads, which occur only under the combined action of wind and snow, are most dangerous; however, when the dome is flat snow will rarely settle on it.

Unfortunately, basic research into these problems has not progressed very far.

A series of experiments* was undertaken between 1946-50 to determine the shape of sail shells, since they form a particularly resistant type of vault. These were the sub-

▼ 2

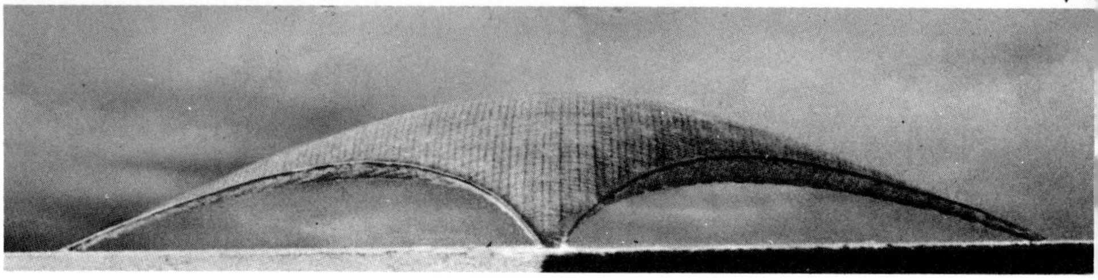

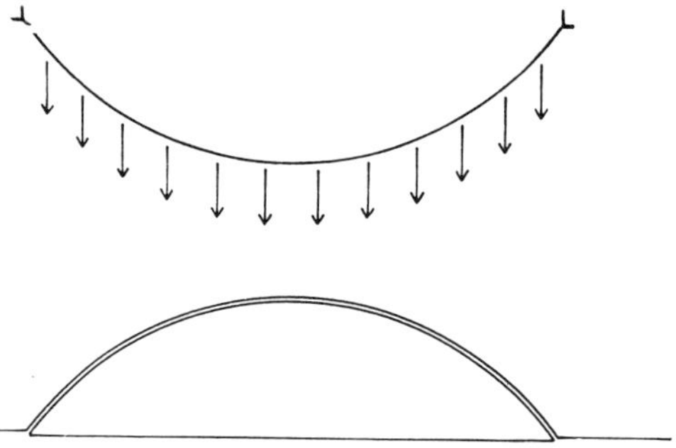

3 and 4

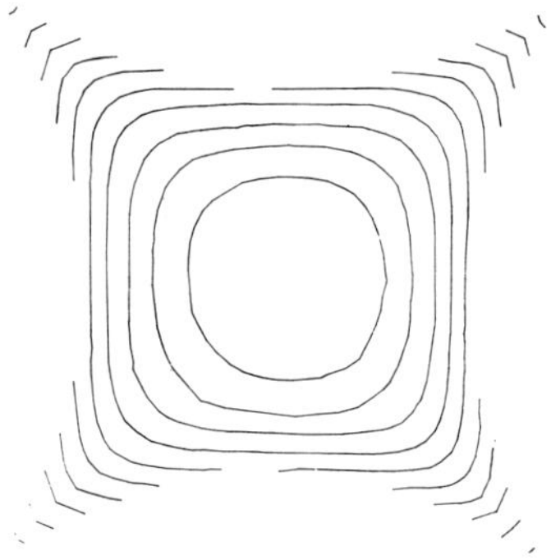

5

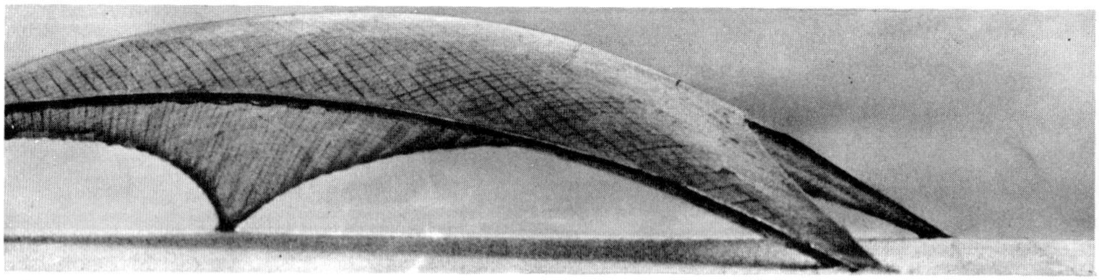

6 ▲

▼ 7

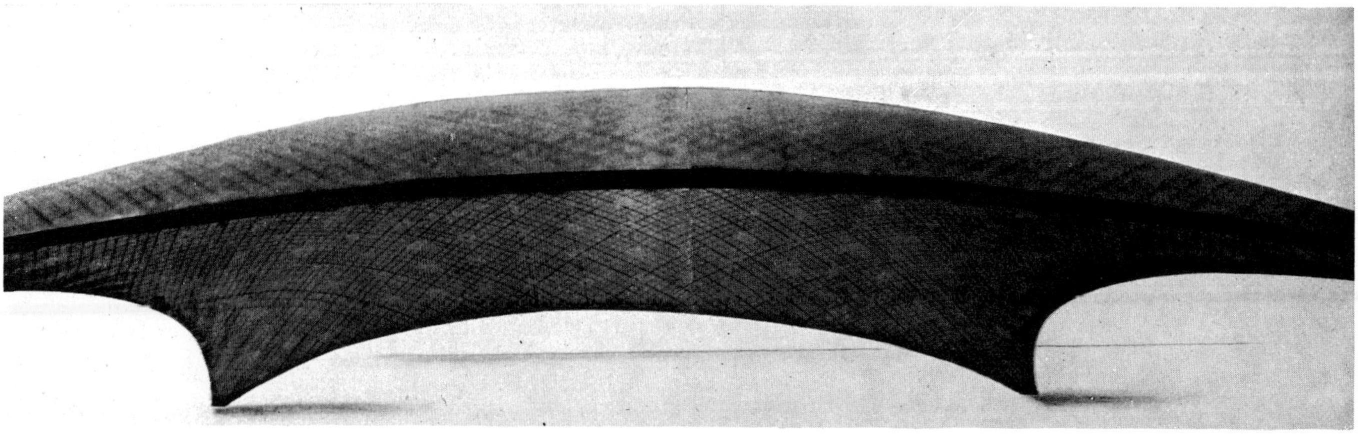

ect of conversations and lectures n the U.S.A. in 1950 which were not without influence on subsequent design. In 1951, lectures on this subject were held at the Technical University of Berlin. The experiments shown on these pages were carried out in 1958, (at a graduate seminar of the School of Architecture of Washington University in St. Louis) by Salomon, Scott and Stoecker, under the supervision of the author. First, a rubber membrane with four corners connected by curved bracing cables was stretched in a plane and—as made clear in the section (Fig. 3)—loaded with evenly distributed weights. The membrane was then "frozen" in plaster, one half of which was removed, and the fixed shape made rigid with polyester resin reinforced with glass fiber. A highly rigid test model (Figs. 1, 2, 6 and 7) resulted, on which contour lines were drawn to make its shape clear (Fig. 5). It is interesting to note that the edges of the membrane, which formed arches under compressive loads in the inverted state, exhibited only simple curvature; thus the edges lay in planes.

A further experiment was carried out with a hexagonal membrane of similar design. Figure 8 shows the load test viewed from one side, and Fig. 9 from one of the corners.

Figure 12 shows the measured contour lines. The small stars in one sixth of the membrane indicate the points of application of the weights.

The shell was to form a river pavilion (Fig. 15) for a scout camp near the Mississippi. It was designed so that it could be nailed together from individual plywood components to an exactly prescribed shape.

Various shapes can be developed. Figure 10 shows the side view and Figure 11 the plan of a sail shell with three corners; Figure 13 a high-domed shell having five corners, and Fig. 14 a shallower shell with many small lateral arches. Such shells

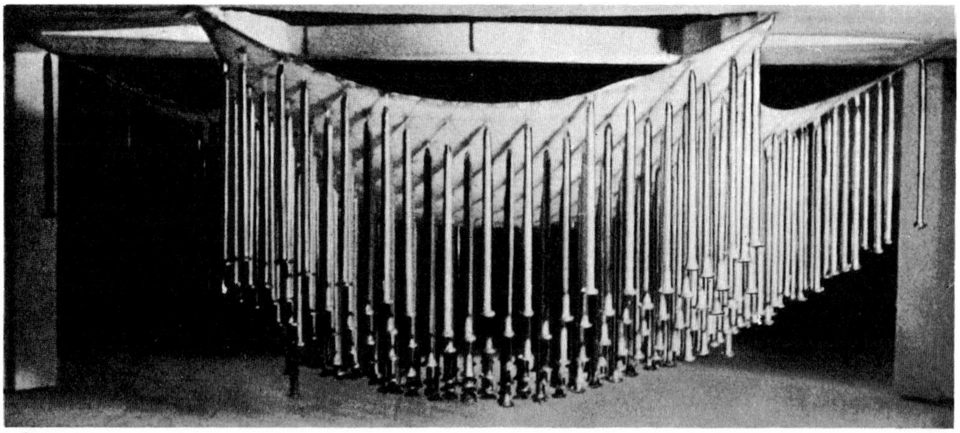

8 ▲

9 ▼

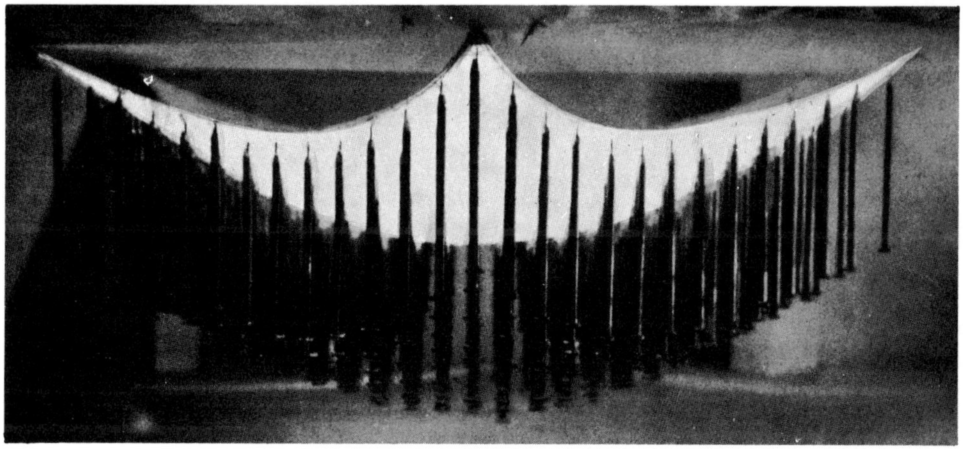

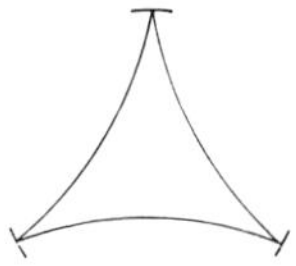

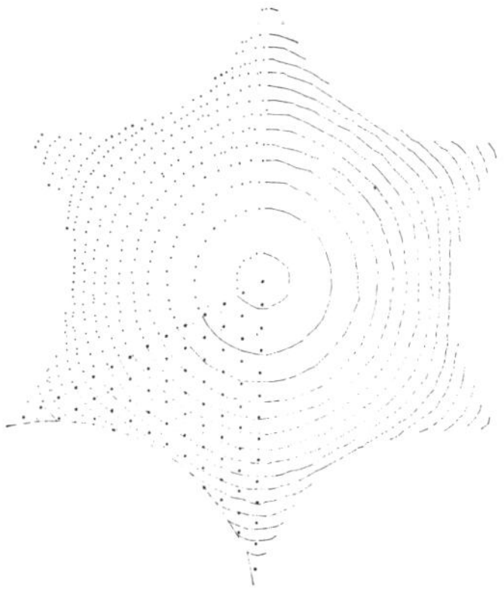

10 and 11

12

13 and 14

▼ 15

1

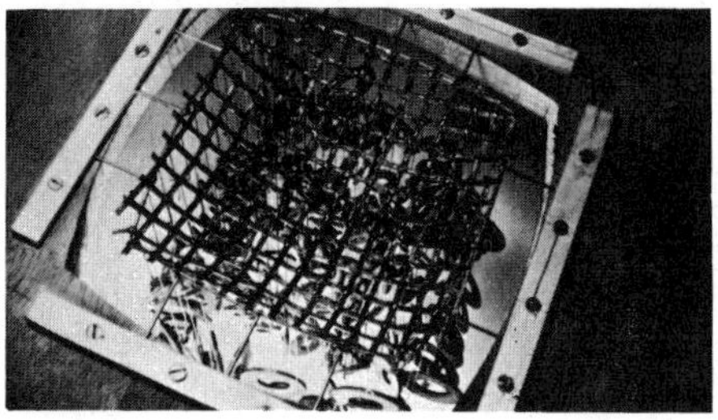

2

3

5 ▶

4 ▼

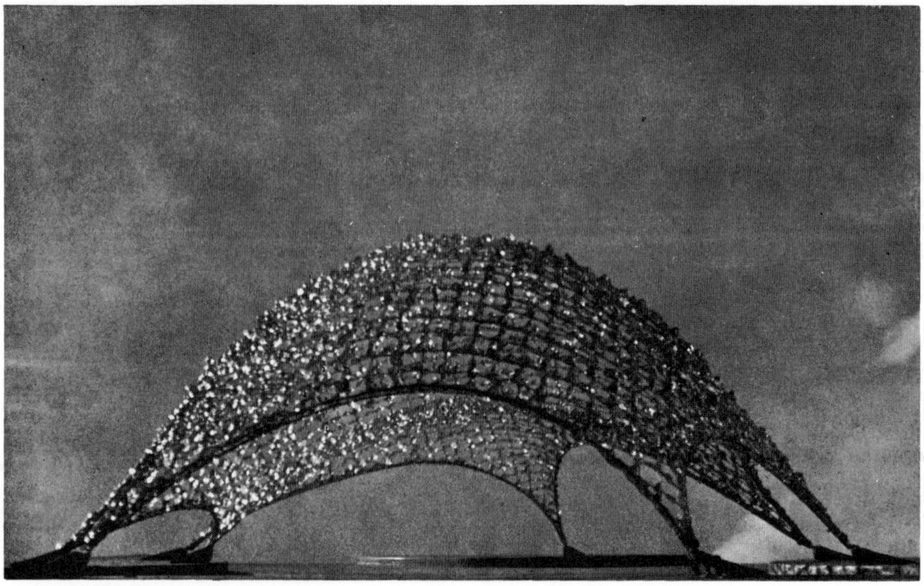

◀ 7

8 ▲

9 ▼

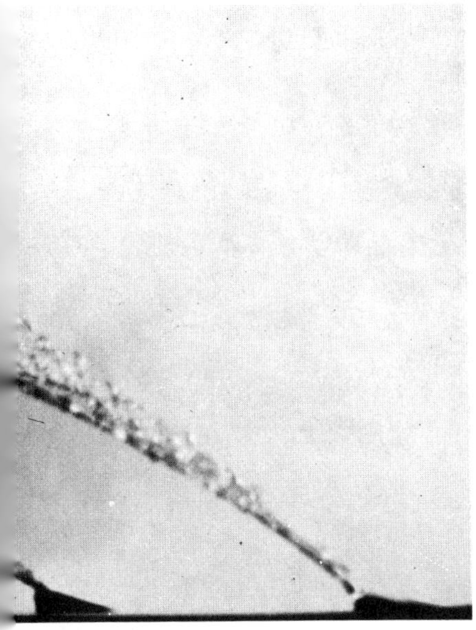

6 ▲

10 ▼

need not be bordered by arches, but can be brought down all the way to the abutments.

The St. Louis architect, John Koch, a graduate of Washington University, investigated other types of sail shells at the Development Center for Lightweight Construction in Berlin, during 1960/61. This type of shell is important for the development of efficient shell frames and their simplified manufacture. Figures 2 to 6 show the experimental stages in the construction of a dome of laths and plywood strips with the valuable assistance of Westag Sperrholzwerke. An originally square grid was deformed to a shell by displacing the corners. The shape was determined in a load test. The shell was reinforced by pouring polyester resin around the wood. In larger structures the wooden members are joined by bolts which are tightened after the shell has been formed.

This fixes the angles and makes the shell rigid. In actual construction, the framework is laid out on the ground and the shell is raised by cables to its intended shape; alternatively, a pneumatic membrane beneath the structure is inflated. In order to resist wind forces such a shell should have a pneumatic shape, i.e., that of a sail. In contrast, the best shape to resist snow pressure is determined from load tests. The two shapes are usually so similar that differences are insignificant. This proves the high efficiency of the system.

To illustrate some obvious possibilities, a highly asymmetrical model was constructed consisting of a fully mobile cable net between edge cables. This net was uniformly loaded, rigidified with polyester resin and inverted. It then formed a continuous but asymmetrical shell with a saddle between two peaks (Fig. 1 and Figs. 7 to 10).

Another sail shell of special interest consisted of a cable skeleton with square mesh (which, if inverted, could be composed of wooden laths or intersecting steel pipes) tensed in a

11

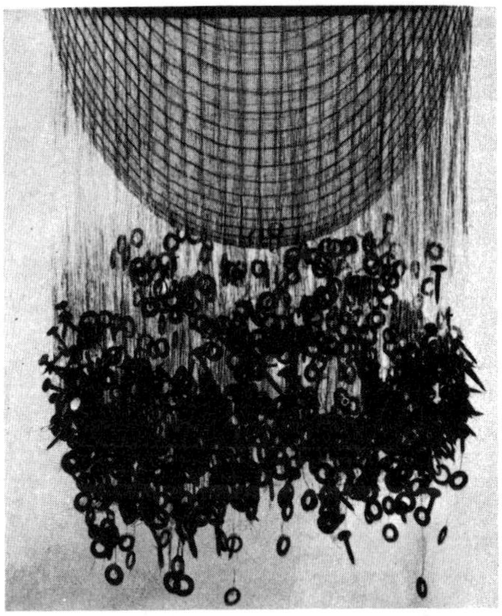

12

13 ▲

▼ 14

11

1

2 ▲

▼ 3

4 and 5

6

7 ▲

▼ 8

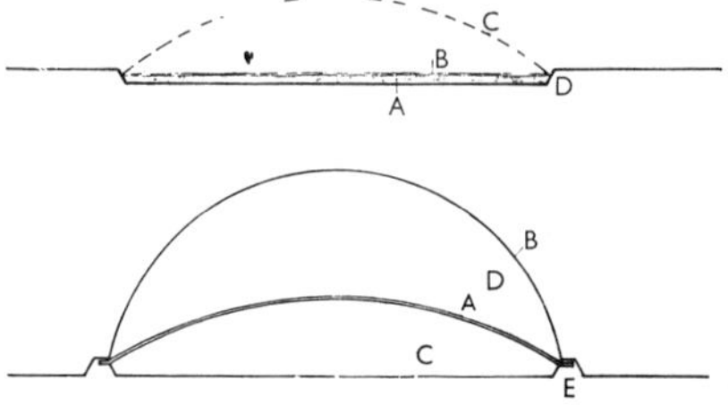

9 and 10

12

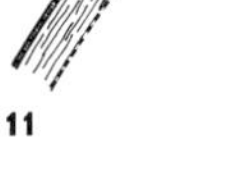

11

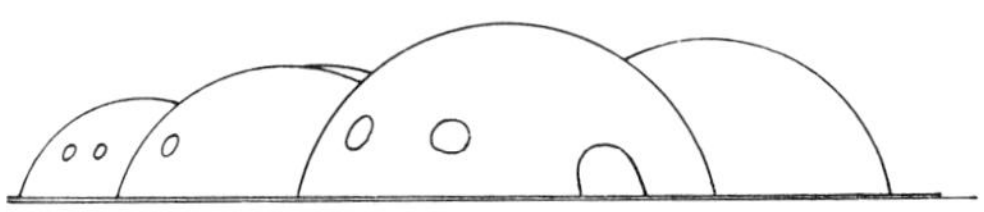

13

circular ring. All elements were of the same length. Spatial curvature was again obtained by displacing the corners. Figure 11, p. 161 is a view obliquely from above of the weight-loaded model, and seen from the side in Fig. 12, p. 161, it forms a deeply sagging catenoid. The originally square mesh assumes a strongly orthorhombic shape at four points near the circular base (Fig. 13, p. 161). The experiment was intended to determine the shape of a comparatively high dome subject to uniform compression. However, such a high shape (Fig. 14, p. 161) is subject to widely differing wind loads and not even approximately uniform wind suction. Nevertheless, the rigidity of these shapes considerably exceeds that of hemispheres. They are absolutely necessary if fairly great heights are to be obtained with simply constructed shells.

Stiffened Pneumatic Structures

Stiffened pneumatic structures are true pneumatic membranes stiffened in the tensed state to act as rigid shells without internal pressure. Valuable pioneering in this field was done by Wallace Neff of Los Angeles. He erected many buildings by a method in which concrete is sprayed on a rubber-like balloon that has wire reinforcements. The details are made clear in Figs. 1 to 3 (photo by Noyes), showing a project by architect Elliot Noyes. The process was already known in the mid-thirties and used with varying success. A major problem are fissures which develop in the concrete shells during hardening, since the latter are very soft and deform while the concrete is sprayed. Furthermore, it is nearly impossible to maintain uniform internal pressure, since this varies with the smallest change in temperature. A very simple method for constructing a suspended or vaulted shell was already outlined in *Das hängende Dach.*

A sheet-metal skin stretched in a frame can be permanently deformed by internal pressure (Figs. 4 and 5). Herbert H. Stevens, proposed pneumatically tensed buildings that have a sheet-metal skin (Fig. 6; photo by Stevens) although he wished to maintain the internal pressure, which is necessary only to a limited degree. For example, ribs* made of wooden or sheet-metal plates can be attached to a sheet-metal skin. Upon inflation they become deformed

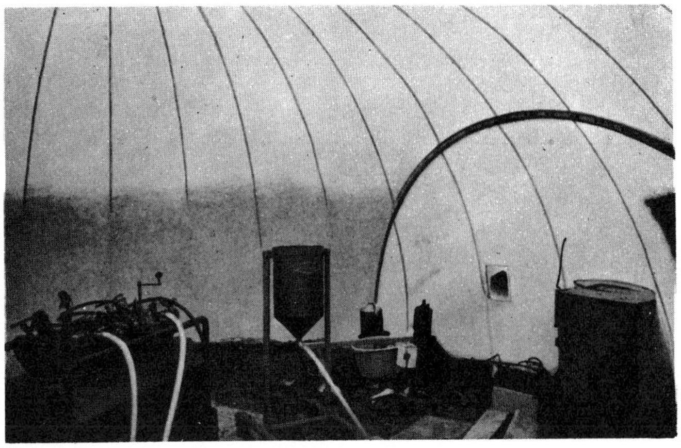
15

16

17

18 ▲

▼ 19

14

1

2 ▲ ▼ 3

with the skin and can then be bolted together to form rigid elements, i.e., a grid dome.

By inserting a pneumatic balloon (Fig. 7) Rudolph Doernach of Stuttgart deformed a sheet-metal skin, (insulated and stiffened with laminated synthetic resin foam) into a shell of predominantly simple curvature (Fig. 8). The double curvature at the center, however, is sufficient to ensure considerable rigidity. Small buildings can be easily constructed in this way. Doernach published a detailed report in the *Deutsche Bauzeitung* 7/1961.

Inflating domes like soap bubbles and allowing them to rigidify is a particularly attractive idea. In Germany, Günther Günschel† investigated this problem, as did certain American engineers of General Electric.†† However, there are basic difficulties when liquids must form very large bubbles and harden in the inflated state; these problems are familiar to a certain degree from experiences with glass and plastic balloons.

One method (Fig. 9, p. 162) has already been applied to the manufacture of membranes for model planes: membrane-forming plastic is poured on water and inflated to a dome by injecting air from below. The resulting dome can be either under constant pneumatic tension or form a shell. A similar process* is shown in Fig. 10 p. 162. A panel (A) made from a thermoplastic substance, e.g., polyacrylic acid ester, is stretched between abutments. To determine the final shape and to make the process independent of external influences, the site is covered with a pneumatic membrane of low deformability, e.g., heavy fabric (B). Hot air at 120° to 150° C is then injected on both sides of the plastic panel and the pressure in the chamber (C) raised so that the slowly softening panel curves upward. The hot air is pumped from chamber (D) to chamber (C) until the panel is pressed against the form (B) and assumes its final shape. The membrane (B) can be left as weather protection or removed if transparency is desired. The process can be controlled at every stage.

Two other quite simple processes* were developed in 1956 during the preparation of several designs for the 1957 International Architectural Exhibition in Berlin. Unfortunately, they were not implemented. A pneumatically tensed membrane can be stiffened from the inside by cold-hardening plastics, e.g., polyester resin. Stiffening is increased (Fig. 11, p. 162) if an insulating layer (B) of plastic foam or staple fiber is injected beneath the membrane (A) and provided with a sandwich-panel reinforcement (C) which should also resist diffusion of water. Pneumatic envelopes can be stiffened very simply in this way. The original membrane then forms the outer skin of the structure. At any given weight, sandwich shells have a much higher rigidity than concrete shells.

In 1962 an experimental structure* was erected in Essen at the DEUBAU. W. Mühlau was plastics consultant, aided by the firms

† *Europäisches Bauforum* 1/1961.

†† *Architectural Forum* 3/1959.

4

5

6

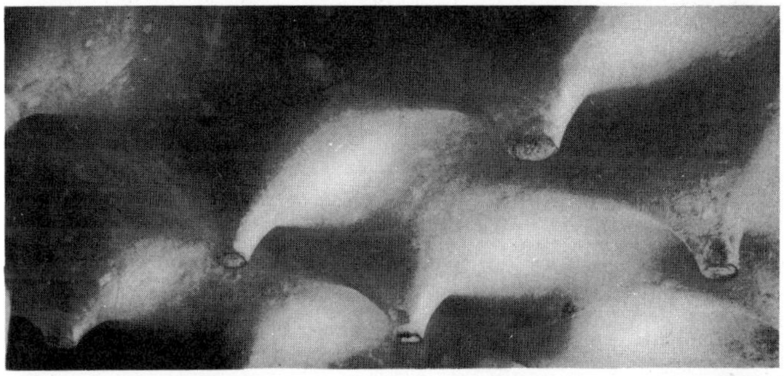

7

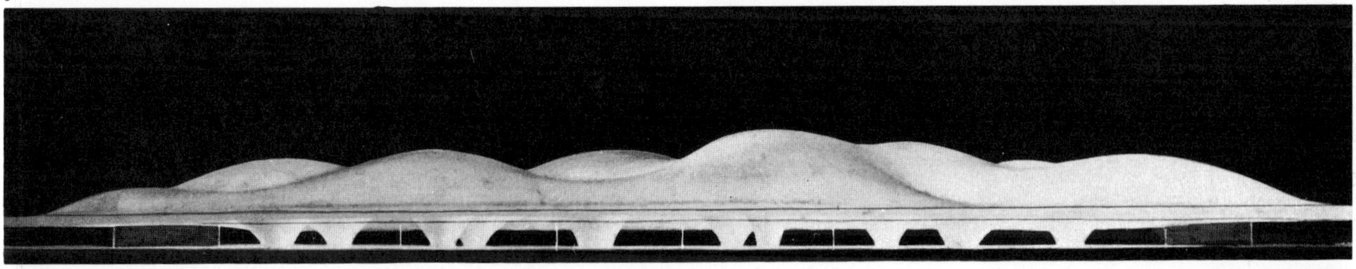

8 ▲

▼ 9

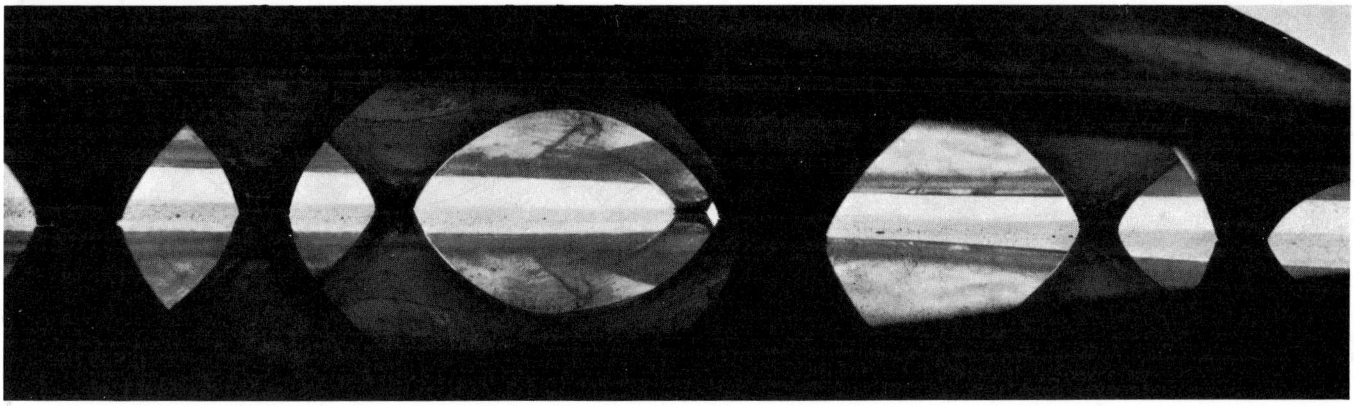

1

2

3 ▲

▼ 4

of BASF and Stromeyer. Gewetex glass fiber with polyester was sprayed on as a coating and perlite combined with polyester formed the central thermal-insulation layer. Inflation was carried out in cold weather and rain (Fig. 14, p. 163). Under these unfavorable conditions and using a Zippel sprayer, the plastic coating was applied in the heated interior at an internal pressure of 50 to 60 mm of water column. After hardening, the blower was switched off and a large opening cut into the structure; there is also a skylight of transparent resin (Figs. 15 to 19, p. 163).

A similar method, based more on manual labor, is to glue small hardfoam panels in one or more layers to the underside of a pneumatic membrane (Fig. 12, p. 162). Windows and entrances cut out of such shells should be round (Fig. 13, p. 162) in order to keep the membrane tension as uniform as possible and avoid stress concentrations at corners.

Figures 1 to 3 on p. 164 show a project* for a dome on a mountain top which was to be stiffened in a similar way. It is distinguished by its round pneumatic shape from the surrounding terraced chambers built against the mountainside along the approach road.

Pneumatically tensed membranes with internal drainage are particularly suited for stiffening, as can be seen in the photographs of the model (Figs. 4 to 9, p. 165). In this case, a large pneumatically formed model was stiffened by polyester resin reinforced with glass fiber. The interior is seen in Fig. 4 on p. 165; an external view of the structure* in daytime appears in Fig. 5; a part view of the interior in Fig. 6, and the ceiling in Fig. 7. A view of the transparent building by night is given in Fig. 8 and a view of the inside through an outer window in Fig. 8. Application of the glass-fiber webs and spraying cause a certain irregular transparency which distinguishes the structure.

Richard Buckminster Fuller, whose exceptional achievements in the field of dome construction can only receive brief mention here, used big nylon balloons coated with synthetic rubber (Hypalon) to assemble large aluminum domes without scaffolding or lifting gear. A 1,540 m^2 dome was completed in 22 hrs. In Figure 1 (photos by Der Kunststoffberater 10/1960) the approximately 15-m-high balloons are being inflated for a test; a few hours after the start of construction the upper part of the dome is already completely assembled and lies on the still uninflated balloon (Fig. 2). The elements of the dome are assembled along the edge until connection to the foundations of the completed structure can be made (Figs. 3 and 4).†

† R. Marks, *The Dymaxion World of Buckminster Fuller,* New York, Reinhold Publishing Corp.

Doors and Windows

Pneumatic envelopes can receive light by having transparent or translucent skins, or by inserting well-rounded windows into opaque membranes. Doors should be designed with care. The simplest type of entrance is the so-called "slip pocket": two membranes overlap, the inner one being forced against the outer by internal pressure (Fig. 5). A person can slip between the two membranes (Figs. 6 and 7) and thus enter or leave.

Ordinary doors can only be used if the effect of the air pressure is overcome. In structures with a moderate internal pressure a door with central pivots can be fitted, as shown in Fig. 8 in elevation and in Fig. 9 in plan. Such a door can be actuated irrespective of air pressure. When the door is not pivoted centrally (Fig. 10), the air pressure must be counterbalanced by springs or weights. The most widely known type is the revolving door (Fig. 11; photo by Birdwell), shown here as an entrance to a dwelling consisting of several pneumatically tensed domes said to have been designed by Frank Lloyd Wright. The advantage of a revolving door is that resistance to rotation does not noticeably increase even when the internal pressure is quite high. Such a door can be negotiated without hindrance. Sketch 14 shows the plan of a four-leaf door, and sketch 15 an eight-leaf door of considerably greater capacity, providing better traffic flow. Simple slip doors (Fig. 13) can be installed, like those used by Walter Bird in his roofed swimming pool in California; or, air locks can be used. These served to introduce large objects into the five-domed exhibition structure designed by Walter Bird, shown in Fig. 3, p. 35. Another possible design for airlocks is depicted in Figs. 17 and 18 which show a dome with two light external membrane structures supported by one or several rings; these form double openings. Every air lock requires a two-door system in which only one door is open at any time in order to avoid loss of pressure. However, in practice it proved possible to arrange fairly large openings in pneumatically tensed and pressurized membranes which can be used without air locks, when the air supply is adequate, to permit the direct entry and exit of trucks, etc., especially when no additional loads are induced at the same time by, e.g., wind or snow. A special emergency exit was developed* (Fig. 16) consisting of four door leaves with central pivots: each leaf is pressure-compensated, but can only be opened outward in the direction of the arrow. The openings can be several meters wide.

5 to 7 ▶

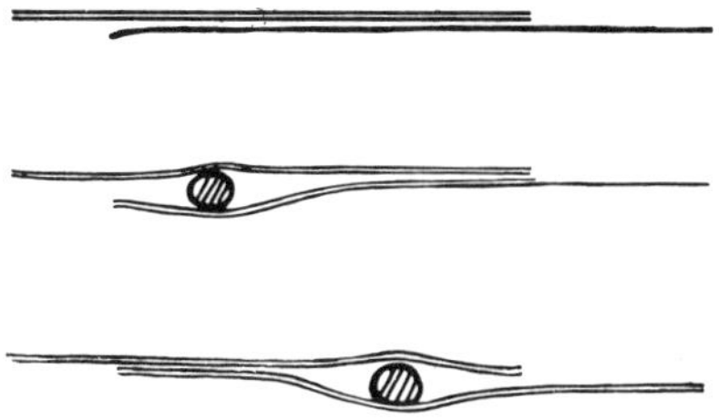

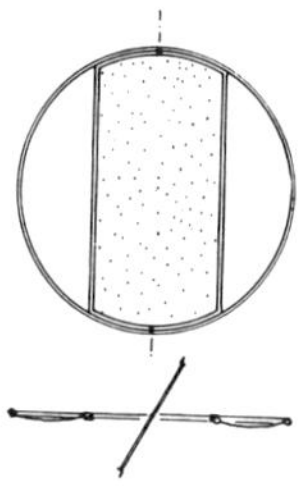

8 and 9

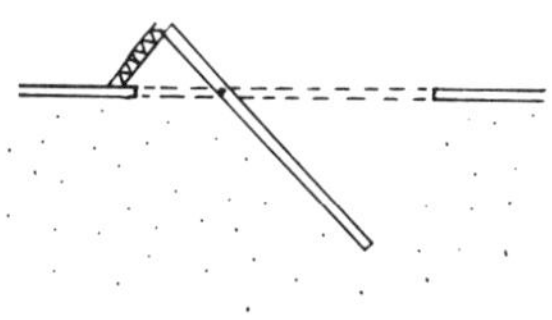

10

11

12

▼ 13

Pressurization

The type of pump used varies with the type of pneumatic structure. Small structures with pressurized chambers require hand-operated piston pumps, foot-operated membrane pumps, or bellows; larger structures require engine-driven pumps, primarily high-capacity vane-type turbine blowers (Fig. 12; photo from *Architectural Forum*), suitable for large buildings with low internal pressure. The performance required from such blowers depends largely on the airtightness of the membrane. Membranes for enclosed cushion structures are best made of tightly sealed skins. This is neither necessary nor desirable for pressurized domes in

14 and 15

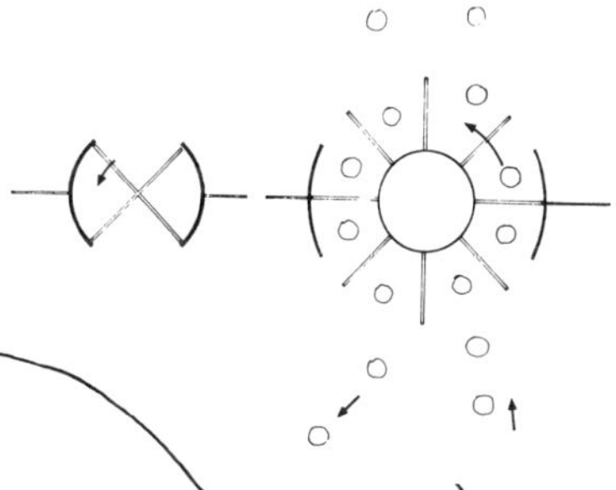

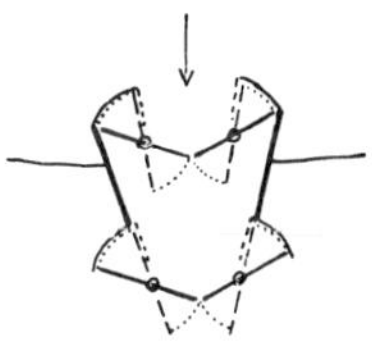

16

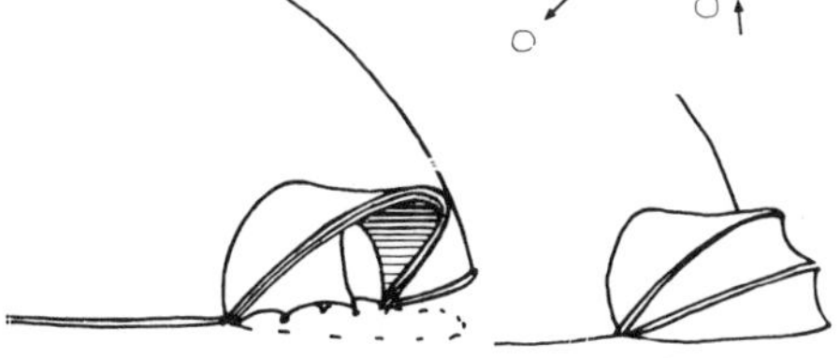

17 and 18

which human beings move, since domes enclosed on all sides permit so little air to enter from the outside that additional vents must often be fitted. Thorough ventilation of domes is definitely possible. A certain permeability of the membrane may sometimes be an advantage. It prevents condensation on the inside of the membrane when the air supply is heated, since the air layers on the inside of the dome cannot be cooled to the dew point if they are continuously forced; this was known to Lanchester. It also eliminates strong drafts created by descending cool air. In any case, heating, ventilation, and pressurization should be combined, and automatically regulated.

Structural Materials

Several types of membrane were discussed when describing the different pneumatic structures. We conclude with a brief summary commencing with the light and ending with the heavy membranes.

The lightest and most flexible membrane is of rubber. It does not even need a special cut in order to form a pneumatic shape and is so highly elastic that it can be inflated over various outlines and formed to any shape by additional forces. However, its rigidity is low.

Plastic foils are of greater practical importance. When glued together or welded, they can form pneumatic structures. Long service life and resistance to wear and tear must be ensured. Polyester foil and P.V.C. take pride of place, together with high- and low-pressure polyethylene. Cheap foils exchanged after a short time (e.g., one year) are often more economical because cleaning costs are eliminated. The tensile strength of foils lies between 3 and 20 kg/mm^2. Since aging is largely caused by ultra-violet radiation, absorbent layers of soot or vaporized metals, or linings of aluminum foil can substantially increase the service life of such foils. There are also foam foils of greater thickness for better heat insulation. Foils have a very high resistance to gas diffusion. The same holds true for sheet metals, which are also suitable for pneumatic structures, especially when they are soft enough to retain their pneumatic shape under internal pressure. Grid foils are a combination of foils and fabrics: net-like threads are embedded in the foil usually with a mesh width of 3 to 20 mm. The threads may be of natural, metallic, mineral, or synthetic materials. The mesh is closed with the same plastics that are used for the foil. In terms of durability commercially available grid foils are inferior to fabric, but superior to plain foils. Resistance to tearing is considerable. They will be particularly useful in the future for greenhouses.

Fabrics are generally coated with plastics in order to increase their resistance to gaseous diffusion. Natural fibers such as cotton, linen, or hemp can be used. Glass fiber is outstanding among mineral substances. Synthetic fibers of the polyamide type (perlon, nylon) can only be used when they are adequately protected against the effects of light, which can be accomplished by coloring the plastic coating.

At present, the most suitable fibers belong to the polyvinyl group (PC, PVC, and Rhovil), which combine high weather resistance with fire-resistant properties. Polyacryl nitriles (Pan, Dralon, Redon, Dolan) have the highest weather resistance. Polyesters like Diolene and Trevira have very high tensile strength but their weather resistance is still inferior to that of polyacryl nitriles.

Natural fibers are aged by bacteria and fungi, and other fibers by water vapor and light, especially ultraviolet radiation. A common fabric strength is 150 kg/5 cm strip width in either direction (= 3,000 kg/m). The fabrics are coated with plastics, primarily polyacryl acid ester (Plexigum), polyurethane, PVC, rubber, synthetic rubber (Opanol), polyisobutylene (Neoprene), polyester, bitumen paraffins, etc. Coatings can have any color or consist of vaporized aluminum or precious metals. Coatings of mica or quartz particles are still translucent but impart higher protection against ultraviolet radiation. An ultra-violet absorbent can also be applied in thin layers.

Membranes can be reinforced with steel-wire mesh or nets or supported by heavy steel cables until adequate strength is attained. The strength required is highest for dams where loads of 10^4 to 10^5 kg/m can occur in the membrane.

Structures with a membrane surface area larger than 600-800 m^2 are difficult to assemble and are best made in several parts. These can be joined by airtight lap seams.

Pneumatic structures of variable shape* are also possible, especially when using cable nets closed with large overlapping awnings.

Conclusion

Tension-loaded pneumatic structures are in the early stages of intense development. This book is therefore only a first attempt to survey a new branch of technology.

The diffusion of scientific information, not to mention publication of a book, can hardly keep pace with the rapid development of new ideas.

We hope that the unfinished will prove more stimulating than the the complete.

CALCULATION OF MEMBRANES

INTRODUCTION

Since a membrane can only sustain tensile stresses, it must in general be prestretched. This can be effected by tensile forces acting on the membrane edges, or, when a space is completely enclosed, by pressurizing the latter. It is well known that membranes that are stretched by internal pressure can carry large loads (pneumatic tires). This property is now being increasingly utilized in civil engineering as well. The required internal pressures in pneumatic (i.e., pressure-stabilized) envelopes are quite low (a few cm of water column) and are readily tolerated by the human body, so that the enclosed useful space may be pressurized directly.

Besides such directly pressurized spaces (envelopes), pneumatic elements can also be used as structural members (beams, struts, arches, cushions, etc., see p. 160). In these cases the smaller cross sections will generally necessitate higher stabilizing pressures.

The static analysis of pneumatic or other prestretched structures comprises two main problems:

1. Determination of the necessary inflation pressure, or other prestretching forces.
2. Establishment of the maximum tensile stresses arising in the system at the given pressure-load application (or other prestretching force). These determine the maximum size of the supporting structure.

The inflation pressure, or other prestretching force, is obtained under the assumption that no compressive stresses appear at any point of the membrane under the combined effect of external loading and internal pressure (or other prestretching forces). This means that the minimum principal stress must still be tensile. This condition is a guarantee against formation of (fairly large) folds, as confirmed by experiment. Usually, smaller folds are formed near the membrane edges, but these do not affect the stability, being caused by local accommodation of the membrane to the shape of the constraining members. Folds that strain the material unduly should be avoided by using some movable constraining members (e.g., draw-lines) which can be adapted to the deformation of the membrane edge. Formation of such folds can also be reduced by modifying the membrane stiffness or the curvature at the edges.

In order to calculate the required inflation pressure or other stretching forces, as well as the maximum stresses, we must first determine the sectional loads. We may use here the ordinary theory of shells, provided the material is only slightly deformable so that the loads can be considered to act on the undeformed system. It is far more difficult to determine the state of stress in highly deformed membranes, which in their initial shape are incapable of supporting any load. In this case the membrane undergoes finite deformations until an equilibrium shape is reached. Since the differential equations which have to be solved in order to determine the exact final shape are generally nonlinear, we resort to approximations based on the related variational problem.

Following an exposition of the required fundamentals in geometry in Section 1, the subsequent 9 sections deal with the theory of slightly deformable membranes whose initial shapes, obtained through cutting, are admissible in the sense of making equilibrium possible. After a general treatment of arbitrary shapes we consider axisymmetrical membranes in Section 3 whose sectional loads are given for the most important actual cases of loading: inflation pressure, dead weight, snow deposits, and wind. Certain simple shapes (sphere, cone, circular torus, circular cylinder) are examined, as well as composite axisymmetrical ones, notably the important case of a semi-cylinder with quarter-spherical endpieces. Pneumatic supporting members (struts, arches) are discussed in Sections 9 and 10. It is demonstrated that in the average the results of the beam theory are generally applicable, so that slender tubes can be analyzed in the familiar manner. Through a torsion experiment the folding condition was verified by comparison with the relevant formulas. An investigation of the stability of pneumatic round tubular columns showed the buckling load to be independent of inflation pressure. This causes pneumatic columns to be very compact in general, since the Euler loads are very small due to the slight bending stiffness. Stability against bending-collapse is generally higher, however.

Investigation of tubular arches by means of a generalized approximation theory based on the Galerkin method or the principle of virtual displacements yielded, among other things, simple relationships for the buckling stability of arbitrary plane arches. It follows from these relationships that arches are far more stable than straight rods.

Section 11 surveys the theory of large ("finite") membrane deformations and indicates the possibility of approximate solution by the Ritz method. One particularly interesting result is that in certain cases, the internal pressure, irrespective of the breaking strength of the material, may not exceed a limiting value without causing failure of the system.

In the last section soap films are discussed, which are of interest to engineers in connection with the problem of constant-tension membranes. Iterative methods are used here with a system of linear differential equations to investigate soap-film surfaces.

Recommended reading on supporting surface structures: Girkmann, K., *Flächentragwerke*, Springer, Vienna. 1956 (4th ed.); Flügge, W., *Stresses in Shells*, Springer, 1960; Wlassow, W.S., *Allgemeine Schalentheorie und ihre Anwendung in der Technik*, Akademie-Verlag, Berlin 1958. On finite deformations, see the contributions of Kappus, Deuker, and Truesdell in *ZAMM*, Vol. 19, No. 5; Vol. 23, Nos. 2,3; Vol. 36, Nos. 3,4; also Green, A. E., and W. Zerna, *Theoretical Elasticity*, Oxford 1954; Green, A. E., and J. E. Adkins, *Large Elastic Deformations*, Oxford 1960.

1 GEOMETRIC FUNDAMENTALS

1.1 Direction vectors, line and surface elements

A surface can be described by a position vector

$$\mathfrak{r} = \mathfrak{r}(\alpha, \beta) \tag{1.1}$$

which depends on two scalar parameters α, β. On this surface the two families of parametric curves (the "α-curves" $\mathfrak{r}(\alpha, \beta_c)$, along which $\beta =$ const and the "β-curves" $\mathfrak{r}(\alpha_c, \beta)$, along which $\alpha =$ const) form a generally nonorthogonal network. In order to

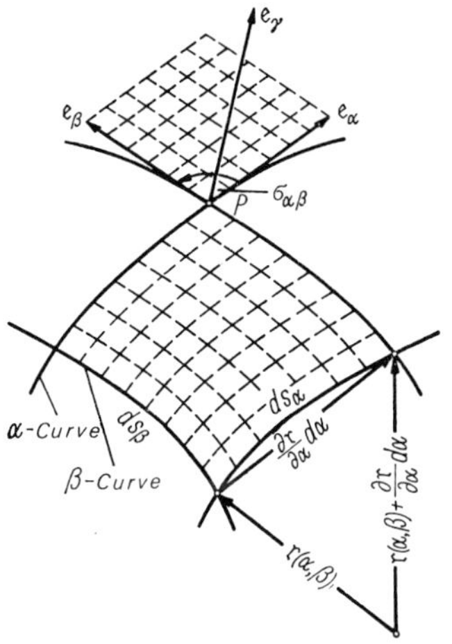

Figure 1.1

specify the orientation of the tangent plane at the surface point P, we construct the unit tangent vectors to the parametric curves at P (Figure 1.1); these are defined by

$$\mathfrak{e}_\alpha = \frac{\dfrac{\partial \mathfrak{r}}{\partial \alpha}}{\left|\dfrac{\partial \mathfrak{r}}{\partial \alpha}\right|} = \frac{\mathfrak{r}_\alpha}{|\mathfrak{r}_\alpha|} = \frac{\mathfrak{r}_\alpha}{\sqrt{g_{\alpha\alpha}}} \quad \text{and}$$

$$\mathfrak{e}_\beta = \frac{\dfrac{\partial \mathfrak{r}}{\partial \beta}}{\left|\dfrac{\partial \mathfrak{r}}{\partial \beta}\right|} = \frac{\mathfrak{r}_\beta}{|\mathfrak{r}_\beta|} = \frac{\mathfrak{r}_\beta}{\sqrt{g_{\beta\beta}}} \tag{1.2a, b}$$

Introducing the line elements corresponding to the increments

$$d s_\alpha = \left|\frac{\partial \mathfrak{r}}{\partial \alpha}\right| d\alpha = |\mathfrak{r}_\alpha|\, d\alpha = \sqrt{g_{\alpha\alpha}}\, d\alpha \quad \text{and}$$

$$d s_\beta = \left|\frac{\partial \mathfrak{r}}{\partial \beta}\right| d\beta = |\mathfrak{r}_\beta|\, d\beta = \sqrt{g_{\beta\beta}}\, d\beta \tag{1.3a, b}$$

we can also define the unit tangents as follows:

$$\mathfrak{e}_\alpha = \frac{\partial \mathfrak{r}}{\partial s_\alpha} \quad \text{and} \quad \mathfrak{e}_\beta = \frac{\partial \mathfrak{r}}{\partial s_\beta} \tag{1.4a, b}$$

The orientation of the tangent plane is specified by the unit normal at the point of tangency P, which, in terms of $\mathfrak{e}_\alpha$, $\mathfrak{e}_\beta$ is

$$\mathfrak{e}_\gamma = \frac{\mathfrak{e}_\alpha \times \mathfrak{e}_\beta}{|\mathfrak{e}_\alpha \times \mathfrak{e}_\beta|} = \frac{\mathfrak{e}_\alpha \times \mathfrak{e}_\beta}{\sin \sigma_{\alpha\beta}} \tag{1.4c}$$

Here $\sigma_{\alpha\beta}$ is the angle formed by the positive directions of the α- and β- curves (mesh angle) which is also given by

$$\cos \sigma_{\alpha\beta} = \mathfrak{e}_\alpha\, \mathfrak{e}_\beta = \frac{\mathfrak{r}_\alpha\, \mathfrak{r}_\beta}{|\mathfrak{r}_\alpha|\,|\mathfrak{r}_\beta|} = \frac{g_{\alpha\beta}}{\sqrt{g_{\alpha\alpha}}\sqrt{g_{\beta\beta}}} \tag{1.5a}$$

so that by substituting

$$\sin \sigma_{\alpha\beta} = \sqrt{1 - \cos^2 \sigma_{\alpha\beta}} = \frac{\sqrt{g_{\alpha\alpha}\, g_{\beta\beta} - g_{\alpha\beta}^2}}{\sqrt{g_{\alpha\alpha}}\sqrt{g_{\beta\beta}}} \tag{1.5b}$$

in (1.4c) we can also express the normal in the form

$$\begin{aligned} \mathfrak{e}_\gamma &= \frac{\sqrt{g_{\alpha\alpha}}\sqrt{g_{\beta\beta}}}{\sqrt{g_{\alpha\alpha}\, g_{\beta\beta} - g_{\alpha\beta}^2}}\, \mathfrak{e}_\alpha \times \mathfrak{e}_\beta = \\ &= \frac{\mathfrak{r}_\alpha \times \mathfrak{r}_\beta}{\sqrt{\mathfrak{r}_\alpha^2\, \mathfrak{r}_\beta^2 - (\mathfrak{r}_\alpha\, \mathfrak{r}_\beta)^2}} = \frac{\mathfrak{r}_\alpha \times \mathfrak{r}_\beta}{|\mathfrak{r}_\alpha \times \mathfrak{r}_\beta|} \end{aligned} \tag{1.6}$$

The surface element corresponding to the increments $d\alpha, d\beta$ is

$$\begin{aligned} dF &= \left|\frac{\partial \mathfrak{r}}{\partial \alpha} d\alpha \times \frac{\partial \mathfrak{r}}{\partial \beta} d\beta\right| = |\mathfrak{r}_\alpha \times \mathfrak{r}_\beta|\, d\alpha\, d\beta = \\ &= \sqrt{g_{\alpha\alpha}\, g_{\beta\beta} - g_{\alpha\beta}^2}\, d\alpha\, d\beta\,. \end{aligned} \tag{1.7}$$

The three fundamental first-order Gaussian invariants

$$g_{\alpha\alpha} = \mathfrak{r}_\alpha^2\,, \quad g_{\beta\beta} = \mathfrak{r}_\beta^2\,, \quad g_{\alpha\beta} = \mathfrak{r}_\alpha\, \mathfrak{r}_\beta \tag{1.8}$$

constitute the metric tensor of the surface. We can interpret $\mathfrak{r}(\alpha, \beta)$ as a mapping (distortion) of the (α, β)-plane onto the surface $\mathfrak{r}(\alpha, \beta)$. Since we will express the vector quantities appearing in the membrane theory in terms of their $(\mathfrak{e}_\alpha, \mathfrak{e}_\beta, \mathfrak{e}_\gamma)$ -components, we shall need the representation in the $(\mathfrak{e}_\alpha, \mathfrak{e}_\beta, \mathfrak{e}_\gamma)$-system of the

1.2 Derivative of a Vector Along a Parametric Curve.

Here the components of the vector

$$\mathfrak{v} = v_\alpha\, \mathfrak{e}_\alpha + v_\beta\, \mathfrak{e}_\beta + v_\gamma\, \mathfrak{e}_\gamma = \sum_{k = \alpha, \beta, \gamma} v_k\, \mathfrak{e}_k \tag{1.9}$$

are taken along the (intrinsic) coordinate axes $(\mathfrak{e}_\alpha, \mathfrak{e}_\beta, \mathfrak{e}_\gamma)$. Since the basis vectors change their direction as a function of the arc-length, not only the scalar components of the vectors, but also the basis vectors themselves, have to be differentiated. The known rule for differentiating products gives

$$\begin{aligned} \frac{\partial \mathfrak{v}}{\partial s_i} &= \frac{\partial}{\partial s_i}\left(\sum_{k = \alpha, \beta, \gamma} v_k\, \mathfrak{e}_k\right) = \sum_{k = \alpha, \beta, \gamma} \frac{\partial v_k}{\partial s_i}\, \mathfrak{e}_k + \\ &+ \sum_{k = \alpha, \beta, \gamma} v_k \frac{\partial \mathfrak{e}_k}{\partial s_i}\,. \end{aligned} \tag{1.10}$$

The terms of the first sum represent the formal differentiation of the scalar components while disregarding the change of orientation of the basis vectors. We denote this part by the symbol $\mathfrak{d}\, \mathfrak{v}/\mathfrak{d}\, s_i$. The remaining three terms of the second sum are due to the possible rotation of the basic trihedron. Accordingly, they can be expressed through vector-products of the unit vectors $\mathfrak{e}_k$ and their respective angular displacements $\overline{\omega}^{(ki)}$ per unit length of arc s_i, or else through scălar products of the unit vectors and suitably defined tensors $\mathfrak{R}^{(i)}$. We thus obtain the differentiation rule

$$\frac{\partial \mathfrak{v}}{\partial s_i} = \frac{\mathfrak{d}\,\mathfrak{v}}{\mathfrak{d}\,s_i} + \sum_{k=\alpha,\beta,\gamma} v_k\,(\overline{\omega}^{(ki)} \times \mathfrak{e}_k) = \frac{\mathfrak{d}\,\mathfrak{v}}{\mathfrak{d}\,s_i} + \mathfrak{v}\,\mathfrak{R}^{(i)}\,. \tag{1.11}$$

In order to interpret (1.11), consider two neighboring positions on the parametric curve s_i together with the corresponding basic trihedra (Figure 1.2). Since the basis vectors do not change in magnitude, their increments $(\partial\,\mathfrak{e}_k/\partial\,s_i)\,d\,s_i$ in passing from the first to the second position are solely due to the change of orientation of the basic trihedron along s_i. We should keep in mind that the individual basis vectors may undergo different rotations.*

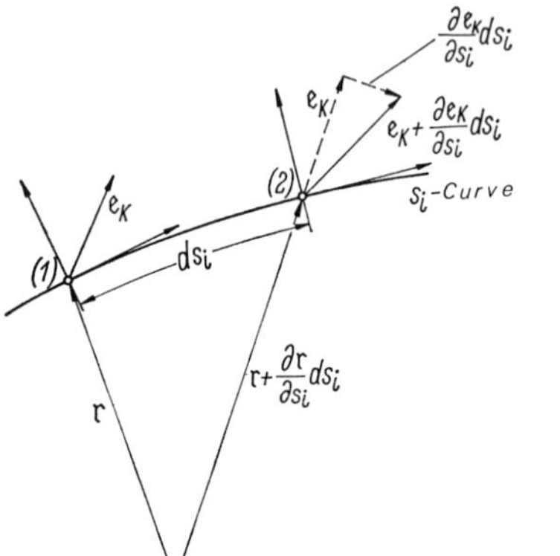

Figure 1.2

Let the basis vector s_i undergo the rotation

$$\overline{\omega}^{(ki)} = \omega_\alpha{}^{(ki)}\,\mathfrak{e}_\alpha + \omega_\beta{}^{(ki)}\,\mathfrak{e}_\beta + \omega_\gamma{}^{(ki)}\,\mathfrak{e}_\gamma\,,$$

when displaced a unit distance along the s_i curve $(\Delta\,s_i = 1)$; in passing from position 1 to position 2 (Figure 1.2) $\mathfrak{e}_k$ rotates through the angle $\overline{\omega}^{(ki)}\,d\,s_i$, and we obtain for its increment

$$\frac{\partial\,\mathfrak{e}_k}{\partial\,s_i}\,d\,s_i = \overline{\omega}^{(ki)}\,d\,s_i \times \mathfrak{e}_k \quad \text{i. e.,} \quad \frac{\partial\,\mathfrak{e}_k}{\partial\,s_i} = \overline{\omega}^{(ki)} \times \mathfrak{e}_k\,, \tag{1.12}$$

We have thus obtained (1.11) from (1.10). Arranging in the proper order of $(\mathfrak{e}_\alpha, \mathfrak{e}_\beta, \mathfrak{e}_\gamma)$-components, and noting that [by (1.4c)]

$$\begin{aligned} \mathfrak{e}_\alpha \times \mathfrak{e}_\gamma &= (\mathfrak{e}_\alpha \cos\sigma_{\alpha\beta} - \mathfrak{e}_\beta)/\sin\sigma_{\alpha\beta} \\ \mathfrak{e}_\beta \times \mathfrak{e}_\gamma &= (\mathfrak{e}_\alpha - \mathfrak{e}_\beta \cos\sigma_{\alpha\beta})/\sin\sigma_{\alpha\beta} \end{aligned} \tag{1.12a}$$

we obtain

$$\begin{aligned} \frac{\partial\,\mathfrak{v}}{\partial\,s_i} = \Bigg(&\frac{\partial\,v_\alpha}{\partial\,s_i} - \frac{v_\alpha\,\omega_\gamma{}^{(\alpha i)}\cos\sigma_{\alpha\beta} + v_\beta\,\omega_\gamma{}^{(\beta i)}}{\sin\sigma_{\alpha\beta}} + \\ &+ \frac{v_\gamma}{\sin\sigma_{\alpha\beta}}\,(\omega_\alpha{}^{(\gamma i)}\cos\sigma_{\alpha\beta} + \omega_\beta{}^{(\gamma i)})\Bigg)\,\mathfrak{e}_\alpha \\ + \Bigg(&\frac{\partial\,v_\beta}{\partial\,s_i} + \frac{v_\beta\,\omega_\gamma{}^{(\beta i)}\cos\sigma_{\alpha\beta} + v_\alpha\,\omega_\gamma{}^{(\alpha i)}}{\sin\sigma_{\alpha\beta}} - \\ &- \frac{v_\gamma}{\sin\sigma_{\alpha\beta}}\,(\omega_\beta{}^{(\gamma i)}\cos\sigma_{\alpha\beta} + \omega_\alpha{}^{(\gamma i)})\Bigg)\,\mathfrak{e}_\beta \\ + \Bigg(&\frac{\partial\,v_\gamma}{\partial\,s_i} - (v_\alpha\,\omega_\beta{}^{(\alpha i)} - v_\beta\,\omega_\alpha{}^{(\beta i)})\sin\sigma_{\alpha\beta}\Bigg)\,\mathfrak{e}_\gamma \end{aligned} \tag{1.13}$$

* Only in nets with constant mesh angle $\sigma_{\alpha\beta}$ (e.g., orthogonal nets), where the relative positions of the basis vectors are fixed (rigid trihedron) do the latter all rotate through the same angle with respect to the unit length of the parametric curve. This rotation is then the (common) rotation angle of the trihedron $(\overline{\omega}^{(ki)} = \overline{\omega}^{(i)})$.

The representation by a rotation tensor is obtained by expressing the vector components v_k in the second term of (1.11) through the triple product $[\mathfrak{e}_\alpha\,\mathfrak{e}_\beta\,\mathfrak{e}_\gamma] = \sin\sigma_{\alpha\beta}$,

$$v_\alpha = \frac{\mathfrak{v}\,(\mathfrak{e}_\beta \times \mathfrak{e}_\gamma)}{\sin\sigma_{\alpha\beta}}\,,\quad v_\beta = \frac{\mathfrak{v}\,(\mathfrak{e}_\gamma \times \mathfrak{e}_\alpha)}{\sin\sigma_{\alpha\beta}}\,,\quad v_\gamma = \frac{\mathfrak{v}\,(\mathfrak{e}_\alpha \times \mathfrak{e}_\beta)}{\sin\sigma_{\alpha\beta}}$$

whence

$$\begin{aligned} \sum_{k=\alpha,\beta,\gamma} v_k\,(\overline{\omega}^{(ki)} \times \mathfrak{e}_k) &= \frac{\mathfrak{v}\,(\mathfrak{e}_\beta \times \mathfrak{e}_\gamma)}{\sin\sigma_{\alpha\beta}}\,(\overline{\omega}^{(\alpha i)} \times \mathfrak{e}_\alpha) + \\ &+ \frac{\mathfrak{v}\,(\mathfrak{e}_\gamma \times \mathfrak{e}_\alpha)}{\sin\sigma_{\alpha\beta}}\,(\overline{\omega}^{(\beta i)} \times \mathfrak{e}_\beta) + \frac{\mathfrak{v}\,(\mathfrak{e}_\alpha \times \mathfrak{e}_\beta)}{\sin\sigma_{\alpha\beta}}\,(\overline{\omega}^{(\gamma i)} \times \mathfrak{e}_\gamma)\,, \end{aligned}$$

or in dyadic-product notation*

$$\begin{aligned} \sum_{k=\alpha,\beta,\gamma} v_k\,(\overline{\omega}^{(ki)} \times \mathfrak{e}_k) &= \frac{\mathfrak{v}}{\sin\sigma_{\alpha\beta}}\,\big((\mathfrak{e}_\beta \times \mathfrak{e}_\gamma) \otimes (\overline{\omega}^{(\alpha i)} \times \mathfrak{e}_\alpha) + \\ &+ (\mathfrak{e}_\gamma \times \mathfrak{e}_\alpha) \otimes (\overline{\omega}^{(\beta i)} \times \mathfrak{e}_\beta) + (\mathfrak{e}_\alpha \times \mathfrak{e}_\beta) \otimes (\overline{\omega}^{(\gamma i)} \times \mathfrak{e}_\gamma)\big) = \mathfrak{v}\,\mathfrak{R}^{(i)} \end{aligned}$$

which verifies the second representation of (1.11).

We now return to the components of the rotation vectors in (1.13), which remain unknown. We will express them in terms of the fundamental surface parameters. There are $2{\cdot}3 = 6$ rotation vectors altogether, but it appears from (1.13), where no components $\omega_\nu{}^{(\nu i)}$ occur, that only two components of each concern us. Moreover, of these, five are of equal magnitude which leaves altogether 7 different numerical values. To calculate them we write down (1.12) for every value of i and k. We obtain for $\Delta\,s_\alpha = 1$,

$$\left.\begin{aligned} \omega_\beta{}^{(\alpha\alpha)} &= \frac{1}{\sin\sigma_{\alpha\beta}}\,\mathfrak{e}_\alpha\,\frac{\partial\,\mathfrak{e}_\gamma}{\partial\,s_\alpha} = -\frac{1}{\sin\sigma_{\alpha\beta}}\,\mathfrak{e}_\gamma\,\frac{\partial\,\mathfrak{e}_\alpha}{\partial\,s_\alpha} = \\ &\quad - \sqrt{\frac{g_{\beta\beta}}{g_{\alpha\alpha}}}\,\frac{[\mathfrak{r}_\alpha\,\mathfrak{r}_\beta\,\mathfrak{r}_{\alpha\alpha}]}{g_{\alpha\alpha}\,g_{\beta\beta} - g_{\alpha\beta}{}^2}\,, \\ \omega_\gamma{}^{(\alpha\alpha)} &= \frac{1}{\sin\sigma_{\alpha\beta}}\,\mathfrak{e}_\beta\,\frac{\partial\,\mathfrak{e}_\alpha}{\partial\,s_\alpha} = \frac{1}{\sqrt{g_{\alpha\alpha}}\,\sqrt{g_{\alpha\alpha}\,g_{\beta\beta} - g_{\alpha\beta}{}^2}} \times \\ &\quad \times \left(\frac{\partial\,g_{\alpha\beta}}{\partial\,\alpha} - \frac{g_{\alpha\beta}}{2\,g_{\alpha\alpha}}\,\frac{\partial\,g_{\alpha\alpha}}{\partial\,\alpha} - \frac{1}{2}\,\frac{\partial\,g_{\alpha\alpha}}{\partial\,\beta}\right), \\ \omega_\alpha{}^{(\beta\alpha)} &= -\frac{1}{\sin\sigma_{\alpha\beta}}\,\mathfrak{e}_\beta\,\frac{\partial\,\mathfrak{e}_\gamma}{\partial\,s_\alpha} = \\ &= \frac{1}{\sin\sigma_{\alpha\beta}}\,\mathfrak{e}_\gamma\,\frac{\partial\,\mathfrak{e}_\beta}{\partial\,s_\alpha} = \frac{[\mathfrak{r}_\alpha\,\mathfrak{r}_\beta\,\mathfrak{r}_{\alpha\beta}]}{g_{\alpha\alpha}\,g_{\beta\beta} - g_{\alpha\beta}{}^2}\,, \\ \omega_\gamma{}^{(\beta\alpha)} &= -\frac{1}{\sin\sigma_{\alpha\beta}}\,\mathfrak{e}_\alpha\,\frac{\partial\,\mathfrak{e}_\beta}{\partial\,s_\alpha} = \\ &= -\frac{\dfrac{\partial\,g_{\alpha\alpha}}{\partial\,\beta} - \dfrac{g_{\alpha\beta}}{g_{\beta\beta}}\,\dfrac{\partial\,g_{\beta\beta}}{\partial\,\alpha}}{2\,\sqrt{g_{\alpha\alpha}}\,\sqrt{g_{\alpha\alpha}\,g_{\beta\beta} - g_{\alpha\beta}{}^2}}\,, \\ \omega_\alpha{}^{(\gamma\alpha)} &= -\frac{1}{\sin\sigma_{\alpha\beta}}\,\mathfrak{e}_\beta\,\frac{\partial\,\mathfrak{e}_\gamma}{\partial\,s_\alpha} = \omega_\alpha{}^{(\beta\alpha)}\,, \\ \omega_\beta{}^{(\gamma\alpha)} &= \frac{1}{\sin\sigma_{\alpha\beta}}\,\mathfrak{e}_\alpha\,\frac{\partial\,\mathfrak{e}_\gamma}{\partial\,s_\alpha} = \omega_\beta{}^{(\alpha\alpha)} \end{aligned}\right\} \tag{1.14a}$$

* Dyadic multiplication, denoted here by $\otimes$, is defined by $(\mathfrak{a}\,\mathfrak{b})\,\mathfrak{c} = \mathfrak{a}\,(\mathfrak{b} \otimes \mathfrak{c})$

and correspondingly for $\Delta s_\beta = 1$,

$$\begin{aligned}
\omega_\beta^{(\alpha\beta)} &= \frac{1}{\sin\sigma_{\alpha\beta}}\, e_\alpha \frac{\partial e_\gamma}{\partial s_\beta} = -\frac{1}{\sin\sigma_{\alpha\beta}}\, e_\gamma \frac{\partial e_\alpha}{\partial s_\beta} = \\
&= -\frac{[r_\alpha\, r_\beta\, r_{\alpha\beta}]}{g_{\alpha\alpha} g_{\beta\beta} - g_{\alpha\beta}^2} = -\,\omega_\alpha^{(\beta\alpha)}\,, \\
\omega_\gamma^{(\alpha\beta)} &= \frac{1}{\sin\sigma_{\alpha\beta}}\, e_\beta \frac{\partial e_\alpha}{\partial s_\beta} = \frac{\dfrac{\partial g_{\beta\beta}}{\partial\alpha} - \dfrac{g_{\alpha\beta}}{g_{\alpha\alpha}} \dfrac{\partial g_{\alpha\alpha}}{\partial\beta}}{2\sqrt{g_{\beta\beta}}\sqrt{g_{\alpha\alpha} g_{\beta\beta} - g_{\alpha\beta}^2}}\,, \\
\omega_\alpha^{(\beta\beta)} &= -\frac{1}{\sin\sigma_{\alpha\beta}}\, e_\beta \frac{\partial e_\gamma}{\partial s_\beta} = \frac{1}{\sin\sigma_{\alpha\beta}}\, e_\gamma \frac{\partial e_\beta}{\partial s_\beta} = \\
&= \sqrt{\frac{g_{\alpha\alpha}}{g_{\beta\beta}}}\, \frac{[r_\alpha\, r_\beta\, r_{\beta\beta}]}{g_{\alpha\alpha} g_{\beta\beta} - g_{\alpha\beta}^2}\,, \\
\omega_\gamma^{(\beta\beta)} &= -\frac{1}{\sin\sigma_{\alpha\beta}}\, e_\alpha \frac{\partial e_\beta}{\partial s_\beta} = -\frac{1}{\sqrt{g_{\beta\beta}}\sqrt{g_{\alpha\alpha} g_{\beta\beta} - g_{\alpha\beta}^2}} \times \\
&\quad \times \left(\frac{\partial g_{\alpha\beta}}{\partial\beta} - \frac{g_{\alpha\beta}}{2 g_{\beta\beta}} \frac{\partial g_{\beta\beta}}{\partial\beta} - \frac{1}{2}\frac{\partial g_{\beta\beta}}{\partial\alpha}\right), \\
\omega_\alpha^{(\gamma\beta)} &= -\frac{1}{\sin\sigma_{\alpha\beta}}\, e_\beta \frac{\partial e_\gamma}{\partial s_\beta} = \omega_\alpha^{(\beta\beta)}\,, \\
\omega_\beta^{(\gamma\beta)} &= \frac{1}{\sin\sigma_{\alpha\beta}}\, e_\alpha \frac{\partial e_\gamma}{\partial s_\beta} = \omega_\beta^{(\alpha\beta)}\,.
\end{aligned} \tag{1.14b}$$

In particular,

$$\begin{aligned}
\omega_\gamma^{(\beta\alpha)} - \omega_\gamma^{(\alpha\alpha)} &= -\frac{1}{\sin\sigma_{\alpha\beta}}\, e_\alpha \frac{\partial e_\beta}{\partial s_\alpha} - \frac{1}{\sin\sigma_{\alpha\beta}}\, e_\beta \frac{\partial e_\alpha}{\partial s_\alpha} = \\
&= -\frac{1}{\sin\sigma_{\alpha\beta}} \frac{\partial}{\partial s_\alpha}(e_\alpha e_\beta) = -\frac{1}{\sin\sigma_{\alpha\beta}} \frac{\partial}{\partial s_\alpha}(\cos\sigma_{\alpha\beta}) = \frac{\partial\sigma_{\alpha\beta}}{\partial s_\alpha}\,, \\
\omega_\gamma^{(\beta\beta)} - \omega_\gamma^{(\alpha\beta)} &= -\frac{1}{\sin\sigma_{\alpha\beta}}\, e_\alpha \frac{\partial e_\beta}{\partial s_\beta} - \frac{1}{\sin\sigma_{\alpha\beta}}\, e_\beta \frac{\partial e_\alpha}{\partial s_\beta} = \\
&= -\frac{1}{\sin\sigma_{\alpha\beta}} \frac{\partial}{\partial s_\beta}(e_\alpha e_\beta) = -\frac{1}{\sin\sigma_{\alpha\beta}} \frac{\partial}{\partial s_\beta}(\cos\sigma_{\alpha\beta}) = \frac{\partial\sigma_{\alpha\beta}}{\partial s_\beta}
\end{aligned}$$

The rotation vectors $\bar\omega^{(ki)}$ characterize the

1.3 Curvature and Torsion

of the surface. Consider a (space-) curve lying on the surface which

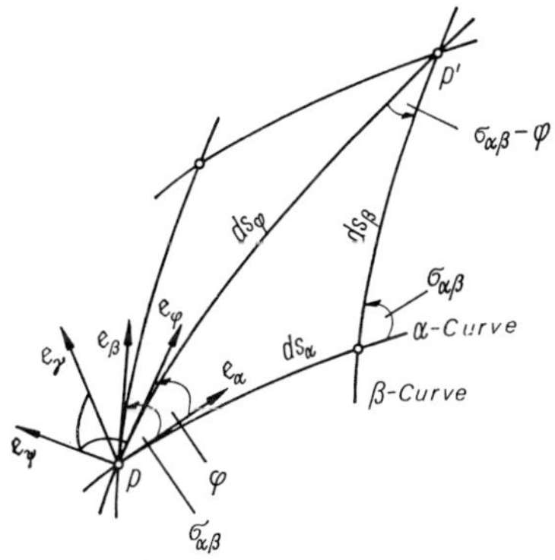

Figure 1.3

at the point P is inclined to the e_α-direction at an angle φ (Figure 1.3). The tangent vector to the curve is given by

$$e_\varphi = \frac{d\,r}{d\,s_\varphi} = \frac{\partial r}{\partial s_\alpha}\frac{d\,s_\alpha}{d\,s_\varphi} + \frac{\partial r}{\partial s_\beta}\frac{d\,s_\beta}{d\,s_\varphi} = e_\alpha \frac{d\,s_\alpha}{d\,s_\varphi} + e_\beta \frac{d\,s_\beta}{d\,s_\varphi}$$

and since by the sine rule (Figure 1.3)

$$d\,s_\alpha = d\,s_\varphi \frac{\sin(\sigma_{\alpha\beta} - \varphi)}{\sin\sigma_{\alpha\beta}} \quad \text{and} \quad d\,s_\beta = d\,s_\varphi \frac{\sin\varphi}{\sin\sigma_{\alpha\beta}} \tag{1.15a}$$

we obtain finally

$$e_\varphi = \frac{e_\alpha \sin(\sigma_{\alpha\beta} - \varphi) + e_\beta \sin\varphi}{\sin\sigma_{\alpha\beta}}\,. \tag{1.15b}$$

This tangent vector is perpendicular to the surface normal e_γ, whose derivative along the curve considered is

$$\begin{aligned}
\frac{d\,e_\gamma}{d\,s_\varphi} &= \frac{\partial e_\gamma}{\partial s_\alpha}\frac{d\,s_\alpha}{d\,s_\varphi} + \frac{\partial e_\gamma}{\partial s_\beta}\frac{d\,s_\beta}{d\,s_\varphi} = \\
&= \frac{\sin(\sigma_{\alpha\beta} - \varphi)}{\sin\sigma_{\alpha\beta}}\frac{\partial e_\gamma}{\partial s_\alpha} + \frac{\sin\varphi}{\sin\sigma_{\alpha\beta}}\frac{\partial e_\gamma}{\partial s_\beta}
\end{aligned} \tag{1.15c}$$

which shows that the vectors e_φ, e_γ, and

$$e_\psi = e_\gamma \times e_\varphi = -\frac{e_\alpha \cos(\sigma_{\alpha\beta} - \varphi) - e_\beta \cos\varphi}{\sin\sigma_{\alpha\beta}} \tag{1.15d}$$

form an orthogonal triad at each point of the curve. Introducing (as in Sec. 1.2) the vector $\bar\omega\,(\varphi)$ to describe the rotation of this triad along the unit length of the curve ($\Delta s_\varphi = 1$), we have

$$\frac{d\,e_\gamma}{d\,s_\varphi} = \bar\omega\,(\varphi) \times e_\gamma\,;$$

vector multiplication by e_γ yields

$$\begin{aligned}
e_\gamma \times \frac{d\,e_\gamma}{d\,s_\varphi} &= \bar\omega\,(\varphi) - e_\gamma\,\omega_\gamma(\varphi) = \\
&= e_\gamma \times \left(\frac{\sin(\sigma_{\alpha\beta} - \varphi)}{\sin\sigma_{\alpha\beta}}\frac{\partial e_\gamma}{\partial s_\alpha} + \frac{\sin\varphi}{\sin\sigma_{\alpha\beta}}\frac{\partial e_\gamma}{\partial s_\beta}\right).
\end{aligned} \tag{1.16a}$$

Scalar multiplication by the tangent e_φ yields the component of rotation in the tangential direction, i.e., the geodesic torsion

$$T\,(\varphi) = \bar\omega\,(\varphi)\, e_\varphi = \left(e_\gamma \times \frac{d\,e_\gamma}{d\,s_\varphi}\right) e_\varphi = -\,e_\psi \frac{d\,e_\gamma}{d\,s_\varphi}\,. \tag{1.16b}$$

Substitution of (1.15c, d) finally yields, by virtue of (1.14),

$$\begin{aligned}
T\,(\varphi) &= -\,e_\psi \frac{d\,e_\gamma}{d\,s_\varphi} = (\omega_\beta^{(\alpha\alpha)} \cos\sigma_{\alpha\beta} + \omega_\alpha^{(\beta\alpha)}) \cos 2\varphi\, + \\
&+ \left(\frac{\omega_\beta^{(\alpha\alpha)} + \omega_\alpha^{(\beta\beta)}}{2\sin\sigma_{\alpha\beta}} - \frac{\cos\sigma_{\alpha\beta}}{\sin\sigma_{\alpha\beta}}(\omega_\beta^{(\alpha\alpha)} \cos\sigma_{\alpha\beta} + \omega_\alpha^{(\beta\alpha)})\right) \sin 2\varphi\,.
\end{aligned} \tag{1.16c}$$

If we, however, perform a scalar multiplication of (1.16a) by $e_\psi = e_\gamma \times e_\varphi$, we obtain the rotation component perpendicular to the plane defined by the vectors e_γ and e_φ. This component is the curvature $K_n\,(\varphi)$ of this normal section of the surface at point P,

$$K_n\,(\varphi) = \bar\omega\,(\varphi)\, e_\psi = \left(e_\gamma \times \frac{d\,e_\gamma}{d\,s_\varphi}\right) e_\psi = e_\varphi \frac{d\,e_\gamma}{d\,s_\varphi}\,. \tag{1.16d}$$

In view of (1.15b, c) and (1.14) we finally obtain

$$\begin{aligned}
K_n\,(\varphi) &= e_\varphi \frac{d\,e_\gamma}{d\,s_\varphi} = \left(\frac{\omega_\beta^{(\alpha\alpha)} - \omega_\alpha^{(\beta\beta)}}{2\sin\sigma_{\alpha\beta}} + \omega_\alpha^{(\beta\alpha)} \frac{\cos\sigma_{\alpha\beta}}{\sin\sigma_{\alpha\beta}}\right) + \\
&+ \left(\frac{\omega_\beta^{(\alpha\alpha)} + \omega_\alpha^{(\beta\beta)}}{2\sin\sigma_{\alpha\beta}} - \frac{\cos\sigma_{\alpha\beta}}{\sin\sigma_{\alpha\beta}}(\omega_\beta^{(\alpha\alpha)} \cos\sigma_{\alpha\beta} + \omega_\alpha^{(\beta\alpha)})\right) \cos 2\varphi\, - \\
&- (\omega_\beta^{(\alpha\alpha)} \cos\sigma_{\alpha\beta} + \omega_\alpha^{(\beta\alpha)}) \sin 2\varphi\,,
\end{aligned} \tag{1.16e}$$

Writing

$$H = \frac{\omega_\beta{}^{(\alpha\alpha)} - \omega_\alpha{}^{(\beta\beta)}}{2 \sin \sigma_{\alpha\beta}} + \omega_\alpha{}^{(\beta\alpha)} \frac{\cos \sigma_{\alpha\beta}}{\sin \sigma_{\alpha\beta}},$$

$$r_1 = \frac{\omega_\alpha{}^{(\beta\beta)} + \omega_\beta{}^{(\alpha\alpha)}}{2 \sin \sigma_{\alpha\beta}} - \frac{\cos \sigma_{\alpha\beta}}{\sin \sigma_{\alpha\beta}} \times \tag{1.17a}$$

$$\times (\omega_\beta{}^{(\alpha\alpha)} \cos \sigma_{\alpha\beta} + \omega_\alpha{}^{(\beta\alpha)}), \; r_2 = \omega_\beta{}^{(\alpha\alpha)} \cos \sigma_{\alpha\beta} + \omega_\alpha{}^{(\beta\alpha)}$$

we obtain from (1.16c, e),

$$(K_n(\varphi) - H)^2 + T^2(\varphi) = r_1{}^2 + r_2{}^2 = R^2, \tag{1.17b}$$

which is the equation of a circle (Figure 1.4). Hence we deduce, first, that there exist two mutually perpendicular directions φ_{01} and

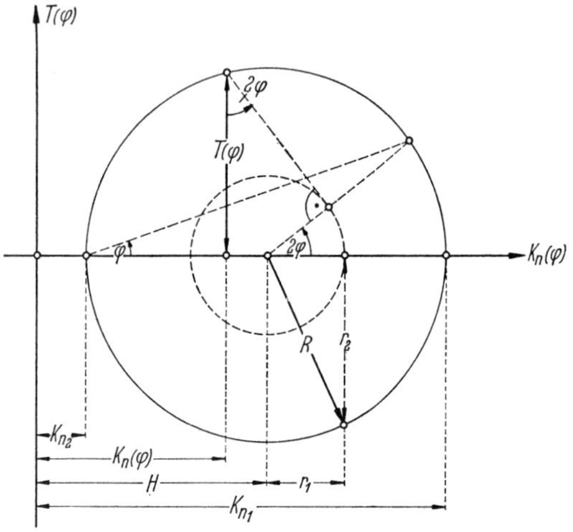

Figure 1.4

φ_{02} of extremal normal-section curvature and vanishing geodesic torsion (principal curvature directions), and second, that at a given point the sum of the curvatures of two mutually perpendicular normal sections is constant. The quantity

$$H = \frac{1}{2}(K_n(\varphi) + K_n(\varphi + \pi/2)) =$$

$$= \frac{\omega_\beta{}^{(\alpha\alpha)} - \omega_\alpha{}^{(\beta\beta)}}{2 \sin \sigma_{\alpha\beta}} + \omega_\alpha{}^{(\beta\alpha)} \frac{\cos \sigma_{\alpha\beta}}{\sin \sigma_{\alpha\beta}} = \frac{1}{2} \nabla \mathfrak{e}_\gamma, \tag{1.18a}$$

where ∇ denotes the differential operator

$$\nabla = \frac{1}{\sin^2 \sigma_{\alpha\beta}} \left(\mathfrak{e}_\alpha \left(\frac{\partial}{\partial s_\alpha} - \cos \sigma_{\alpha\beta} \frac{\partial}{\partial s_\beta} \right) + \mathfrak{e}_\beta \left(\frac{\partial}{\partial s_\beta} - \cos \sigma_{\alpha\beta} \frac{\partial}{\partial s_\alpha} \right) \right), \tag{1.18b}$$

is termed the mean curvature, while

$$K = K_n(\varphi) K_n(\varphi + \pi/2) - T^2(\varphi) = H^2 - R^2 \tag{1.18c}$$

is termed the Gaussian curvature at point P. This point is called elliptic, if $K_{n\,\min} = K_{n2} = H - R > 0$ i.e., $K > 0$, so that all normal sections have positive curvature. Their centers of curvature then all lie on that side of the surface from which the normal points away. The surface point is called parabolic if $H - R = 0$ (and thus $K = 0$), in which case there exists one direction of vanishing curvature. If the circle is intersected by the T-axis, e.g., when $H - R < 0$, and $H + R > 0$ (i.e., $K < 0$), the normal-section curvatures vary in sign. The centers of curvature then lie on either side of the surface. At such points, which are called hyperbolic, there always exist two normal sections of vanishing curvature. The structure of the formulas (1.16e, c) as regards their dependence on the direction angle shows that the curvature and torsion of a surface can be described by a tensor, called the principal surface tensor $\mathfrak{K}$.

This is seen immediately from (1.15c) when writing for the trigonometrical numerators*

$$\sin(\sigma_{\alpha\beta} - \varphi) = [\mathfrak{e}_\varphi \mathfrak{e}_\beta \mathfrak{e}_\gamma] = \mathfrak{e}_\varphi (\mathfrak{e}_\beta \times \mathfrak{e}_\gamma) = \mathfrak{e}_\varphi \frac{\mathfrak{e}_\alpha - \mathfrak{e}_\beta \cos \sigma_{\alpha\beta}}{\sin \sigma_{\alpha\beta}},$$

$$\sin \varphi = [\mathfrak{e}_\alpha \mathfrak{e}_\varphi \mathfrak{e}_\gamma] = \mathfrak{e}_\varphi (\mathfrak{e}_\gamma \times \mathfrak{e}_\alpha) = \mathfrak{e}_\varphi \frac{\mathfrak{e}_\beta - \mathfrak{e}_\alpha \cos \sigma_{\alpha\beta}}{\sin \sigma_{\alpha\beta}}$$

and applying the ∇-operator (1.18b) and the definition of the dyadic product to obtain

$$\frac{d\,\mathfrak{e}_\gamma}{d\,s_\varphi} = (\mathfrak{e}_\varphi \nabla)\, \mathfrak{e}_\gamma = \mathfrak{e}_\varphi (\nabla \otimes \mathfrak{e}_\gamma) = \mathfrak{e}_\varphi \mathfrak{K} \tag{1.18d}$$

The normal section curvature $K_n(\varphi)$ and the geodesic torsion $T(\varphi)$ are now obtained from (1.16b, d) in the form

$$K_n(\varphi) = \mathfrak{e}_\varphi \frac{d\,\mathfrak{e}_\gamma}{d\,s_\varphi} = \mathfrak{e}_\varphi (\mathfrak{e}_\varphi \mathfrak{K}), \quad T(\varphi) = -\mathfrak{e}_\psi \frac{d\,\mathfrak{e}_\gamma}{d\,s_\varphi} = -\mathfrak{e}_\psi (\mathfrak{e}_\varphi \mathfrak{K}),$$

where $\mathfrak{e}_\psi = \mathfrak{e}_\gamma \times \mathfrak{e}_\varphi$.

If the geodesic torsion vanishes along a parametric curve, then this is a line of principal curvature. From (1.16c) we accordingly find

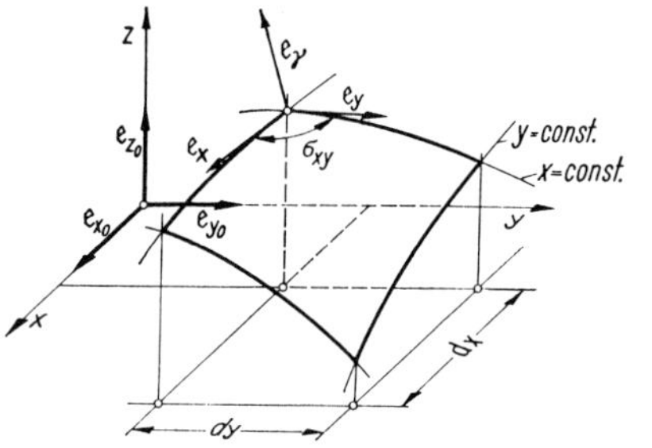

Figure 1.5

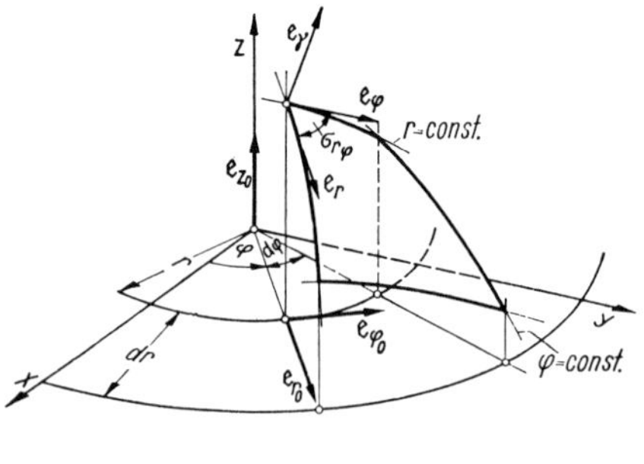

Figure 1.6

as a necessary condition for the α-curves to be lines of principal curvature:

$$T(0) = \omega_\beta{}^{(\alpha\alpha)} \cos \sigma_{\alpha\beta} + \omega_\alpha{}^{(\beta\alpha)} = 0. \tag{1.18e}$$

Example: Let us find the surface parameters when the surface is given in the forms $z = z(x, y)$ and $z = z(r, \varphi)$ (Figures 1.5, 1.6). In the first case the position vector in the Cartesian $(\mathfrak{e}_{x0}, \mathfrak{e}_{y0}, \mathfrak{e}_{z0})$ system is

$$\mathfrak{r}(x, y) = x\,\mathfrak{e}_{x0} + y\,\mathfrak{e}_{y0} + z(x, y)\,\mathfrak{e}_{z0}$$

* The square brackets indicate triple products. The following steps make use of (1.12a).

from which, setting $\alpha = x$ and $\beta = y$, we obtain

$$\begin{aligned}
&\mathfrak{r}_x = \mathfrak{e}_{x0} + z_x \mathfrak{e}_{z0}, \quad \mathfrak{r}_{xx} = z_{xx} \mathfrak{e}_{z0}, \quad \mathfrak{r}_y = \mathfrak{e}_{y0} + z_y \mathfrak{e}_{z0}, \\
&\quad \mathfrak{r}_{yy} = z_{yy} \mathfrak{e}_{z0}, \quad \mathfrak{r}_{xy} = z_{xy} \mathfrak{e}_{z0} \\
&g_{xx} = 1 + z_x^2, \quad g_{yy} = 1 + z_y^2, \quad g_{xy} = z_x z_y, \\
&\quad g_{xx} g_{yy} - g_{xy}^2 = 1 + z_x^2 + z_y^2, \\
&\sin \sigma_{xy} = \frac{\sqrt{1 + z_x^2 + z_y^2}}{\sqrt{(1 + z_x^2)(1 + z_y^2)}}, \\
&\quad \cos \sigma_{xy} = \frac{z_x z_y}{\sqrt{(1 + z_x^2)(1 + z_y^2)}}, \\
&\omega_x^{(yx)} = -\omega_y^{(xy)} = \frac{z_{xy}}{1 + z_x^2 + z_y^2}, \\
&\quad \omega_y^{(xx)} = -\sqrt{\frac{1 + z_y^2}{1 + z_x^2}} \frac{z_{xx}}{1 + z_x^2 + z_y^2}, \\
&\omega_x^{(yy)} = \sqrt{\frac{1 + z_x^2}{1 + z_y^2}} \frac{z_{yy}}{1 + z_x^2 + z_y^2}, \\
&H = -\frac{(1 + z_y^2) z_{xx} + (1 + z_x^2) z_{yy} - 2 z_x z_y z_{xy}}{2 \sqrt{1 + z_x^2 + z_y^2}^{\,3}}.
\end{aligned} \tag{1.19}$$

In the case of polar coordinates $z\,(r, \varphi)$ the position vector is given in the form

$$\mathfrak{r}\,(r, \varphi) = r\, \mathfrak{e}_{r0} + z\,(r, \varphi)\, \mathfrak{e}_{z0}$$

Setting $\alpha = r$ and $\beta = \varphi$, and noting that $\partial \mathfrak{e}_{r0}/\partial \varphi = \mathfrak{e}_{\varphi 0}$ and $\partial \mathfrak{e}_{\varphi 0}/\partial \varphi = -\mathfrak{e}_{r0}$ (the basis vectors $\mathfrak{e}_{r0}$ and $\mathfrak{e}_{\varphi 0}$ change their orientations along the parametric curves $r = \text{const}$), we obtain

$$\begin{aligned}
&\mathfrak{r}_r = \mathfrak{e}_{r0} + z_r \mathfrak{e}_{z0}, \quad \mathfrak{r}_{rr} = z_{rr} \mathfrak{e}_{z0}, \quad \mathfrak{r}_\varphi = r\, \mathfrak{e}_{\varphi 0} + z_\varphi \mathfrak{e}_{z0}, \\
&\mathfrak{r}_{\varphi\varphi} = -r\, \mathfrak{e}_{r0} + z_{\varphi\varphi} \mathfrak{e}_{z0}, \quad \mathfrak{r}_{r\varphi} = \mathfrak{e}_{\varphi 0} + z_{r\varphi} \mathfrak{e}_{z0}, \\
&g_{rr} = 1 + z_r^2, \quad g_{\varphi\varphi} = r^2 + z_\varphi^2, \quad g_{r\varphi} = z_r z_\varphi, \\
&g_{rr} g_{\varphi\varphi} - g_{r\varphi}^2 = r^2 \left(1 + z_r^2 + \frac{z_\varphi^2}{r^2}\right), \\
&\cos \sigma_{r\varphi} = \frac{z_r z_\varphi / r}{\sqrt{(1 + z_r^2)(1 + z_\varphi^2/r^2)}}, \\
&\quad \sin \sigma_{r\varphi} = \frac{\sqrt{1 + z_r^2 + z_\varphi^2/r^2}}{\sqrt{(1 + z_r^2)(1 + z_\varphi^2/r^2)}}, \\
&\omega_r^{(\varphi r)} = -\omega_\varphi^{(r\varphi)} = \frac{(z_\varphi/r)_r}{1 + z_r^2 + z_\varphi^2/r^2}, \\
&\omega_\varphi^{(rr)} = -\sqrt{\frac{1 + z_\varphi^2/r^2}{1 + z_r^2}} \frac{z_{rr}}{1 + z_r^2 + z_\varphi^2/r^2}, \\
&\omega_r^{(\varphi\varphi)} = \sqrt{\frac{1 + z_r^2}{1 + z_\varphi^2/r^2}} \frac{(z_r/r) + (z_{\varphi\varphi}/r^2)}{1 + z_r^2 + z_\varphi^2/r^2}, \\
&H = -\frac{\left(1 + \dfrac{z_\varphi^2}{r^2}\right) z_{rr} + (1 + z_r^2)\left(\dfrac{z_r}{r} + \dfrac{z_{\varphi\varphi}}{r^2}\right) - 2 z_r \dfrac{z_\varphi}{r} \left(\dfrac{z_\varphi}{r}\right)_r}{2 \sqrt{1 + z_r^2 + (z_\varphi/r)^2}^{\,3}}.
\end{aligned} \tag{1.20}$$

The formulas are considerably simplified for orthogonal networks, where $\sigma_{\alpha\beta} = \pi/2$, and thus $g_{\alpha\beta} = \mathfrak{r}_\alpha \mathfrak{r}_\beta = \cos \sigma_{\alpha\beta} = 0$, $\sin \sigma_{\alpha\beta} = 1$. We then obtain from (1.14) and (1.18a) the components of the two rotation vectors $\overline{\omega}^{(\alpha)}$ and $\overline{\omega}^{(\beta)}$, both referring to the entire trihedral system, and the mean curvature

$$\begin{aligned}
&\omega_\alpha^{(\alpha)} = -\omega_\beta^{(\beta)} = T_{\alpha\beta} = \frac{[\mathfrak{r}_\alpha \mathfrak{r}_\beta \mathfrak{r}_{\alpha\beta}]}{g_{\alpha\alpha} g_{\beta\beta}}, \quad \omega_\beta^{(\alpha)} = K_{n\alpha} = -\frac{[\mathfrak{r}_\alpha \mathfrak{r}_\beta \mathfrak{r}_{\alpha\alpha}]}{g_{\alpha\alpha} \sqrt{g_{\alpha\alpha} g_{\beta\beta}}}, \\
&\quad \omega_\gamma^{(\alpha)} = G_\alpha = -\frac{1}{\sqrt{g_{\alpha\alpha} g_{\beta\beta}}} \frac{\partial (\sqrt{g_{\alpha\alpha}})}{\partial \beta}, \\
&\omega_\alpha^{(\beta)} = -K_{n\beta} = \frac{[\mathfrak{r}_\alpha \mathfrak{r}_\beta \mathfrak{r}_{\beta\beta}]}{g_{\beta\beta} \sqrt{g_{\alpha\alpha} g_{\beta\beta}}}, \quad \omega_\gamma^{(\beta)} = -G_\beta = \frac{1}{\sqrt{g_{\alpha\alpha} g_{\beta\beta}}} \frac{\partial (\sqrt{g_{\beta\beta}})}{\partial \alpha}, \\
&\quad H = \frac{\omega_\beta^{(\alpha)} - \omega_\alpha^{(\beta)}}{2} = \frac{K_{n\alpha} + K_{n\beta}}{2}.
\end{aligned} \tag{1.21}$$

2 FUNDAMENTALS OF THE MEMBRANE THEORY OF SMALL DEFORMATIONS

2.1 General remarks on stresses and sectional loads

If the negligible bending resistance of members is discounted, there results a reduction of the number of stress components and sectional loads. Along the sections $\alpha = \text{const}$, $\beta = \text{const}$ there act only the so-called membrane forces, which are sectional forces whose lines of action lie in the tangent plane at the point concerned. The sectional stresses are in general composed of normal and shearing stresses, so that in the membrane there exists a biaxial state of stress. The membrane elements, however, cannot support compressive loads, so that the normal stresses must be positive (tensile) in any direction. The necessary condition for this is that *the principal stresses be positive everywhere* (see Sec. 2.3). *This is, as confirmed experimentally, also the necessary condition for the load to be carried without folds being formed. It is the fundamental relationship from which the minimum inflation pressure needed to stabilize the system is determined for pneumatic members, and from which the required prestretching forces for other types of membranes can be worked out.*

The membrane stresses proper will henceforth be replaced by membrane forces (sectional loads), defined as the statically equivalent loads per unit length of section. Assuming a uniform stress distribution across the membrane thickness h, the relationship between the membrane forces $\mathfrak{n}$ and the sectional stresses $\mathfrak{s}$ is $\mathfrak{n} = h\,\mathfrak{s}$, and the folding condition may therefore also be expressed in terms of the membrane forces:

A membrane will not form folds if the principal membrane forces are positive.

2.2 Equilibrium Conditions

The membrane forces in the system $(\mathfrak{e}_\alpha, \mathfrak{e}_\beta, \mathfrak{e}_\gamma)$ are

$$\mathfrak{n}_\alpha = n_\alpha\,\mathfrak{e}_\alpha + n_{\alpha\beta}\,\mathfrak{e}_\beta\,, \quad \mathfrak{n}_\beta = n_{\beta\alpha}\,\mathfrak{e}_\alpha + n_\beta\,\mathfrak{e}_\beta \tag{2.1ab}$$

Equilibrium conditions are imposed on every surface element

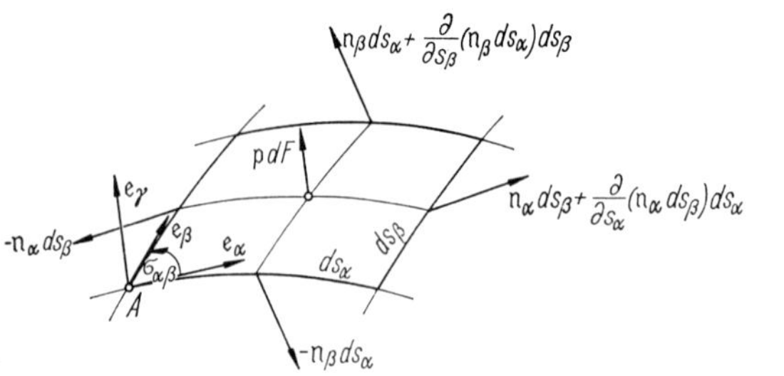

Figure 2.1

$d F = d s_\alpha\, d s_\beta \sin\sigma_{\alpha\beta}$, bounded by pairs of neighboring parametric curves (Figure 2.1). The sectional loads on the membrane must form an equilibrium system together with the surface load (per unit area) defined by

$$\mathfrak{p} = p_\alpha\,\mathfrak{e}_\alpha + p_\beta\,\mathfrak{e}_\beta + p_\gamma\,\mathfrak{e}_\gamma \tag{2.2}$$

We accordingly obtain from Figure 2.1 the following equilibrium condition:

$$\frac{\partial}{\partial s_\alpha}(\mathfrak{n}_\alpha\, d s_\beta)\, d s_\alpha + \frac{\partial}{\partial s_\beta}(\mathfrak{n}_\beta\, d s_\alpha)\, d s_\beta + \mathfrak{p}\, d s_\alpha\, d s_\beta \sin\sigma_{\alpha\beta} = 0\,.$$

The equilibrium condition for the moments about the vertex A are

$$\left(d s_\alpha\,\mathfrak{e}_\alpha + \frac{d s_\beta}{2}\,\mathfrak{e}_\beta\right) \times \left(\mathfrak{n}_\alpha d s_\beta + \frac{\partial}{\partial s_\alpha}(\mathfrak{n}_\alpha\, d s_\beta)\, d s_\alpha\right) -$$
$$- \frac{d s_\beta}{2}\,\mathfrak{e}_\beta \times \mathfrak{n}_\alpha\, d s_\beta + \left(\frac{d s_\alpha}{2}\,\mathfrak{e}_\alpha + d s_\beta\,\mathfrak{e}_\beta\right) \times$$
$$\times \left(\mathfrak{n}_\beta\, d s_\alpha + \frac{\partial}{\partial s_\beta}(\mathfrak{n}_\beta\, d s_\alpha)\, d s_\beta\right) - \frac{d s_\alpha}{2}\,\mathfrak{e}_\alpha \times \mathfrak{n}_\beta\, d s_\alpha +$$
$$+ \left(\frac{d s_\alpha}{2}\,\mathfrak{e}_\alpha + \frac{d s_\beta}{2}\,\mathfrak{e}_\beta\right) \times \mathfrak{p}\, d s_\alpha\, d s_\beta \sin\sigma_{\alpha\beta} = 0$$

By neglecting all higher-order terms and making use of (1.3a, b), (1.4c), (1.5b), and (2.1a, b) we obtain the conditions in the simplified form

$$\left.\begin{aligned} &\frac{\partial}{\partial\alpha}\left(\sqrt{g_{\beta\beta}}\;\mathfrak{n}_\alpha\right) + \frac{\partial}{\partial\beta}\left(\sqrt{g_{\alpha\alpha}}\;\mathfrak{n}_\beta\right) + \mathfrak{p}\sqrt{g_{\alpha\alpha}\,g_{\beta\beta} - g_{\alpha\beta}{}^2} = 0\,, \\ &\mathfrak{e}_\alpha \times \mathfrak{n}_\alpha + \mathfrak{e}_\beta \times \mathfrak{n}_\beta = \mathfrak{e}_\gamma \sin\sigma_{\alpha\beta}\,(n_{\alpha\beta} - n_{\beta\alpha}) = 0 \end{aligned}\right\} \tag{2.3a, b}$$

where (2.3b) in particular expresses the equality of the shear components

$$n_{\alpha\beta} = n_{\beta\alpha}\,. \tag{2.3c}$$

Using (1.13), we obtain from (2.3a)

$$\frac{\partial}{\partial\alpha}\left(\sqrt{g_{\beta\beta}}\;n_\alpha\right) + \frac{\partial}{\partial\beta}\left(\sqrt{g_{\alpha\alpha}}\,n_{\alpha\beta}\right) -$$
$$- \frac{n_\alpha\,\omega_\gamma{}^{(\alpha\alpha)}\cos\sigma_{\alpha\beta} + n_\beta\,\omega_\gamma{}^{(\beta\beta)} + n_{\alpha\beta}\,(\omega_\gamma{}^{(\beta\alpha)} + \omega_\gamma{}^{(\alpha\beta)}\cos\sigma_{\alpha\beta})}{\sqrt{g_{\alpha\alpha}\,g_{\beta\beta} - g_{\alpha\beta}{}^2}} +$$
$$+ p_\alpha\sqrt{g_{\alpha\alpha}\,g_{\beta\beta} - g_{\alpha\beta}{}^2} = 0\,,$$
$$\frac{\partial}{\partial\alpha}\left(\sqrt{g_{\beta\beta}}\,n_{\alpha\beta}\right) + \frac{\partial}{\partial\beta}\left(\sqrt{g_{\alpha\alpha}}\;n_\beta\right) +$$
$$+ \frac{n_\alpha\,\omega_\gamma{}^{(\alpha\alpha)} + n_\beta\,\omega_\gamma{}^{(\beta\beta)}\cos\sigma_{\alpha\beta} + n_{\alpha\beta}\,(\omega_\gamma{}^{(\beta\alpha)}\cos\sigma_{\alpha\beta} + \omega_\gamma{}^{(\alpha\beta)})}{\sqrt{g_{\alpha\alpha}\,g_{\beta\beta} - g_{\alpha\beta}{}^2}} +$$
$$+ p_\beta\sqrt{g_{\alpha\alpha}\,g_{\beta\beta} - g_{\alpha\beta}{}^2} = 0\,,$$
$$2\,n_{\alpha\beta}\,\omega_\alpha{}^{(\beta\alpha)} - n_\alpha\,\omega_\beta{}^{(\alpha\alpha)} + n_\beta\,\omega_\alpha{}^{(\beta\beta)} + p_\gamma = 0 \tag{2.4a-c}$$

(in the last equation we made use of $\omega_\alpha{}^{(\beta\alpha)} = -\,\omega_\beta{}^{(\alpha\beta)}$ and $n_{\alpha\beta} = n_{\beta\alpha}$.) This system of equations generally suffices to determine the three remaining unknown sectional-load components n_α, n_β, and $n_{\alpha\beta} = n_{\beta\alpha}$, provided that the surface parameters are known. If we assume that the loaded surface is only slightly deformed, we obtain a first approximation for the sectional loads by inserting the (given) parameters of the undeformed surface. The results are proportional to the load, but may differ appreciably from the true sectional loads near the edges (cf. also Sec. 7.5.2), because the linearized theory used fails to satisfy the boundary conditions in the general case. Besides the cases in which the effect of applying the exact theory on sectional loads and strains is felt only near the edges (and explains the edge folding), there also exist problems in which the undeformed surface cannot be in equilibrium when loaded by finite sectional forces. Deformations (generally large) then occur, which greatly affect the sectional forces throughout the membrane. In Sec. 11 we will briefly discuss the general case of large deformations, in which the surface parameters must also be considered as unknowns, being functions of the sectional loads through stress-strain and strain-displacement relationships. For orthogonal networks the relationships are considerably simplified. Expressing the rotation components $\omega_\gamma^{(\alpha)}$ and $\omega_\gamma^{(\beta)}$ in terms of the fundamental tensor g_{ik} according to (1.21), we obtain

$$\left.\begin{aligned}
&\frac{\partial}{\partial\alpha}\left(\sqrt{g_{\beta\beta}}\,n_\alpha\right)+\frac{1}{\sqrt{g_{\alpha\alpha}}}\frac{\partial}{\partial\beta}(g_{\alpha\alpha}\,n_{\alpha\beta})-n_\beta\frac{\partial\left(\sqrt{g_{\beta\beta}}\right)}{\partial\alpha}+\\
&\quad+p_\alpha\sqrt{g_{\alpha\alpha}\,g_{\beta\beta}}=0\,,\\
&\frac{1}{\sqrt{g_{\beta\beta}}}\frac{\partial}{\partial\alpha}(g_{\beta\beta}\,n_{\alpha\beta})+\frac{\partial}{\partial\beta}\left(\sqrt{g_{\alpha\alpha}}\,n_\beta\right)-n_\alpha\frac{\partial\left(\sqrt{g_{\alpha\alpha}}\right)}{\partial\beta}+\\
&\quad+p_\beta\sqrt{g_{\alpha\alpha}\,g_{\beta\beta}}=0\,,\\
&\quad 2\,T_{\alpha\beta}\,n_{\alpha\beta}-K_{n\alpha}\,n_\alpha-K_{n\beta}\,n_\beta+p_\gamma=0\,.
\end{aligned}\right\}\quad(2.5a\text{-}c)$$

If the membrane surface is given in the form $z = z(x, y)$ (see also (1.19) and Figure 1.5), it is often expedient to resolve the equilibrium condition (2.3a) into components along the fixed directions ($\mathfrak{e}_{x0}$, $\mathfrak{e}_{y0}$, $\mathfrak{e}_{z0}$) instead of resolving in the sense of (2.4a-c) along the unit vectors

$$\begin{aligned}
&\mathfrak{e}_x=\frac{\mathfrak{r}_x}{\sqrt{g_{xx}}}=\frac{\mathfrak{e}_{x0}+z_x\,\mathfrak{e}_{z0}}{\sqrt{1+z_x^2}}\,,\quad \mathfrak{e}_y=\frac{\mathfrak{r}_y}{\sqrt{g_{yy}}}=\frac{\mathfrak{e}_{y0}+z_y\,\mathfrak{e}_{z0}}{\sqrt{1+z_y^2}}\,,\\
&\mathfrak{e}_\gamma=\frac{\mathfrak{e}_x\times\mathfrak{e}_y}{\sin\sigma_{xy}}=\frac{\mathfrak{e}_{z0}-z_x\,\mathfrak{e}_{x0}-z_y\,\mathfrak{e}_{y0}}{\sqrt{1+z_x^2+z_y^2}}
\end{aligned}\qquad(2.6a\text{-}c)$$

To this end we resolve the membrane sectional loads for $x = \text{const}$ and $y = \text{const}$ into components of the nonrotating basic system

$$\begin{aligned}
\mathfrak{n}_x&=n_x\,\mathfrak{e}_x+n_{xy}\,\mathfrak{e}_y=\frac{n_x}{\sqrt{1+z_x^2}}\,\mathfrak{e}_{x0}+\\
&\quad+\frac{n_{xy}}{\sqrt{1+z_y^2}}\,\mathfrak{e}_{y0}+\left(\frac{n_x\,z_x}{\sqrt{1+z_x^2}}+\frac{n_{xy}\,z_y}{\sqrt{1+z_y^2}}\right)\mathfrak{e}_{z0}\,,\\
\mathfrak{n}_y&=n_{xy}\,\mathfrak{e}_x+n_y\,\mathfrak{e}_y=\frac{n_{xy}}{\sqrt{1+z_x^2}}\,\mathfrak{e}_{x0}+\\
&\quad+\frac{n_y}{\sqrt{1+z_y^2}}\,\mathfrak{e}_{y0}+\left(\frac{n_{xy}\,z_x}{\sqrt{1+z_x^2}}+\frac{n_y\,z_y}{\sqrt{1+z_y^2}}\right)\mathfrak{e}_{z0}
\end{aligned}$$

and insert these in (2.3a), expressing also the load in ($\mathfrak{e}_{x0}$, $\mathfrak{e}_{y0}$, $\mathfrak{e}_{z0}$) components in the form

$$\mathfrak{p}=p_x\,\mathfrak{e}_{x0}+p_y\,\mathfrak{e}_{y0}+p_z\,\mathfrak{e}_{z0}\,.$$

Since the basic vectors are in this case constant, only the scalar factors are differentiated in (2.3a). The equations for the components can be written down directly:

$$\begin{aligned}
\mathfrak{e}_{x0}:\ &\frac{\partial}{\partial x}\left(\sqrt{\frac{1+z_y^2}{1+z_x^2}}\,n_x\right)+\frac{\partial\,n_{xy}}{\partial y}+p_x\sqrt{1+z_x^2+z_y^2}=0\,,\\
\mathfrak{e}_{y0}:\ &\frac{\partial\,n_{xy}}{\partial x}+\frac{\partial}{\partial y}\left(\sqrt{\frac{1+z_x^2}{1+z_y^2}}\,n_y\right)+p_y\sqrt{1+z_x^2+z_y^2}=0\,,\\
\mathfrak{e}_{z0}:\ &\frac{\partial}{\partial x}\left(z_x\sqrt{\frac{1+z_y^2}{1+z_x^2}}\,n_x\right)+\frac{\partial}{\partial y}\left(z_y\sqrt{\frac{1+z_x^2}{1+z_y^2}}\,n_y\right)+\\
&+\frac{\partial}{\partial x}(z_y\,n_{xy})+\frac{\partial}{\partial y}(z_x\,n_{xy})+p_z\sqrt{1+z_x^2+z_y^2}=0\,.
\end{aligned}\qquad(2.7a\text{-}c)$$

Differentiating the terms in parentheses in the last equation, we obtain

$$\begin{aligned}
&z_{xx}\left(\sqrt{\frac{1+z_y^2}{1+z_x^2}}\,n_x\right)+z_{yy}\left(\sqrt{\frac{1+z_x^2}{1+z_y^2}}\,n_y\right)+2\,z_{xy}\,n_{xy}+\\
&\quad+z_x\left[\frac{\partial}{\partial x}\left(\sqrt{\frac{1+z_y^2}{1+z_x^2}}\,n_x\right)+\frac{\partial\,n_{xy}}{\partial y}\right]+z_y\left[\frac{\partial\,n_{xy}}{\partial x}+\right.\\
&\quad\left.+\frac{\partial}{\partial y}\left(\sqrt{\frac{1+z_x^2}{1+z_y^2}}\,n_y\right)\right]+p_z\sqrt{1+z_x^2+z_y^2}=0\,,
\end{aligned}$$

whence, from the first two equilibrium conditions,

$$\begin{aligned}
&z_{xx}\left(\sqrt{\frac{1+z_y^2}{1+z_x^2}}\,n_x\right)+z_{yy}\left(\sqrt{\frac{1+z_x^2}{1+z_y^2}}\,n_y\right)+\\
&\quad+2\,z_{xy}\,n_{xy}=-\sqrt{1+z_x^2+z_y^2}\,(p_z-z_x\,p_x-z_y\,p_y)\,.
\end{aligned}\qquad(2.7d)$$

For

$$p_x\sqrt{1+z_x^2+z_y^2}=\bar{p}_{x0}=\text{const}\,,\quad p_y\sqrt{1+z_x^2+z_y^2}=\bar{p}_{y0}=\text{const}$$

the equilibrium problem expressed by (2.7a, b, d) can be reduced to the determination of the stress function $F(x, y)$, defined in terms of its partial derivatives in the form

$$\begin{aligned}
&\sqrt{\frac{1+z_y^2}{1+z_x^2}}\,n_x=F_{yy}\,,\quad\sqrt{\frac{1+z_x^2}{1+z_y^2}}\,n_y=F_{xx}\,,\\
&\quad n_{xy}=-F_{xy}-\bar{p}_{x0}\,y-\bar{p}_{y0}\,x
\end{aligned}\qquad(2.8a\text{-}c)$$

Whereas this function satisfies the first two equilibrium conditions (2.7a, b) identically, the third equation (2.7d) yields

$$\begin{aligned}
&F_{xx}\,z_{yy}+F_{yy}\,z_{xx}-2\,F_{xy}\,z_{xy}=-\,p_z\sqrt{1+z_x^2+z_y^2}+\\
&\quad+\bar{p}_{x0}\,(z_x+2\,y\,z_{xy})+\bar{p}_{y0}\,(z_y+2\,x\,z_{xy})\,,
\end{aligned}\qquad(2.8d)$$

whose solution, satisfying the boundary conditions, defines by (2.8a-c) the state of stress in the membrane.

When the membrane surface is given in polar coordinates as $z = z(r, \varphi)$ or $\mathfrak{r}(r, \varphi) = r\,\mathfrak{e}_{r0} + z(r, \varphi)\,\mathfrak{e}_{z0}$ (Figure 1.6), the corresponding form of the equilibrium conditions is obtained by resolving the sectional loads $\mathfrak{n}_r$ and $\mathfrak{n}_\varphi$, acting along the parametric curves r=const and φ=const, into components in the cylindrical coordinate system ($\mathfrak{e}_{r0}$, $\mathfrak{e}_{\varphi 0}$, $\mathfrak{e}_{z0}$):

$$\begin{aligned}
\mathfrak{n}_r&=n_r\,\mathfrak{e}_r+n_{r\varphi}\,\mathfrak{e}_\varphi=\frac{n_r\,\mathfrak{e}_{r0}}{\sqrt{1+z_r^2}}+\frac{n_{r\varphi}\,\mathfrak{e}_{\varphi 0}}{\sqrt{1+(z_\varphi/r)^2}}+\\
&\quad+\left(\frac{n_r\,z_r}{\sqrt{1+z_r^2}}+\frac{n_{r\varphi}\,(z_\varphi/r)}{\sqrt{1+(z_\varphi/r)^2}}\right)\mathfrak{e}_{z0}\,,\\
\mathfrak{n}_\varphi&=n_{r\varphi}\,\mathfrak{e}_r+n_\varphi\,\mathfrak{e}_\varphi=\frac{n_{r\varphi}\,\mathfrak{e}_{r0}}{\sqrt{1+z_r^2}}+\frac{n_\varphi\,\mathfrak{e}_{\varphi 0}}{\sqrt{1+(z_\varphi/r)^2}}+\\
&\quad+\left(\frac{n_{r\varphi}\,z_r}{\sqrt{1+z_r^2}}+\frac{n_\varphi\,(z_\varphi/r)}{\sqrt{1+(z_\varphi/r)^2}}\right)\mathfrak{e}_{z0}
\end{aligned}$$

Inserting these in the equilibrium condition (2.3a), and expressing the load by

$$\mathfrak{p}=p_r\,\mathfrak{e}_{r0}+p_\varphi\,\mathfrak{e}_{\varphi 0}+p_z\,\mathfrak{e}_{z0}$$

we finally obtain, by virtue of $\frac{\partial\,\mathfrak{e}_{r0}}{\partial\varphi}=\mathfrak{e}_{\varphi 0}$ and $\frac{\partial\,\mathfrak{e}_{\varphi 0}}{\partial\varphi}=-\,\mathfrak{e}_{r0}$, the equations for the components

$$\frac{\partial}{\partial r}\left(\sqrt{\frac{1+(z_\varphi/r)^2}{1+z_r^2}}\, r\, n_r\right) - \sqrt{\frac{1+z_r^2}{1+(z_\varphi/r)^2}}\, n_\varphi + \\ + \frac{\partial n_{r\varphi}}{\partial \varphi} + p_r\, r \sqrt{1+z_r^2+(z_\varphi/r)^2} = 0\,,$$

$$\frac{1}{r}\frac{\partial}{\partial r}(r^2\, n_{r\varphi}) + \frac{\partial}{\partial \varphi}\left(\sqrt{\frac{1+z_r^2}{1+(z_\varphi/r)^2}}\, n_\varphi\right) + \\ + p_\varphi\, r \sqrt{1+z_r^2+(z_\varphi/r)^2} = 0\,, \tag{2.9a-c}$$

$$\frac{\partial}{\partial r}\left(\sqrt{\frac{1+(z_\varphi/r)^2}{1+z_r^2}}\, r\, n_r\, z_r\right) + \frac{\partial}{\partial \varphi}\left(\sqrt{\frac{1+z_r^2}{1+(z_\varphi/r)^2}}\, n_\varphi\, \frac{z_\varphi}{r}\right) + \\ + \frac{\partial}{\partial r}(n_{r\varphi}\, z_\varphi) + \frac{\partial}{\partial \varphi}(n_{r\varphi}\, z_r) + p_z\, r \sqrt{1+z_r^2+(z_\varphi/r)^2} = 0\,.$$

Again differentiating the terms in parentheses in the last equation and applying the first two equilibrium conditions, we obtain

$$n_r \sqrt{\frac{1+(z_\varphi/r)^2}{1+z_r^2}}\, z_{rr} + n_\varphi \sqrt{\frac{1+z_r^2}{1+(z_\varphi/r)^2}}\left(\frac{z_r}{r}+\frac{z_{\varphi\varphi}}{r^2}\right) + \\ + 2\, n_{r\varphi}\left(\frac{z_\varphi}{r}\right)_r = -\left(p_z - z_r\, p_r - \frac{z_\varphi}{r}\, p_\varphi\right)\sqrt{1+z_r^2+(z_\varphi/r)^2}\,. \tag{2.9d}$$

For the case $p_r = p_\varphi = 0$ the stress function $F\,(r,\,\varphi)$ is defined by its partial derivatives in the form

$$\sqrt{\frac{1+(z_\varphi/r)^2}{1+z_r^2}}\, n_r = \frac{F_r}{r} + \frac{F_{\varphi\varphi}}{r^2}\,, \\ \sqrt{\frac{1+z_r^2}{1+(z_\varphi/r)^2}}\, n_\varphi = F_{rr}\,, \quad n_{r\varphi} = -\left(\frac{F_\varphi}{r}\right)_r \tag{2.10a-c}$$

which again ensures identical fulfilment of the first two conditions (2.9a, b). Substitution in the last condition (2.9d) results in the differential equation for the stress function

$$z_{rr}\left(\frac{F_r}{r}+\frac{F_{\varphi\varphi}}{r^2}\right) + \left(\frac{z_r}{r}+\frac{z_{\varphi\varphi}}{r^2}\right)F_{rr} - 2\left(\frac{z_\varphi}{r}\right)_r\left(\frac{F_\varphi}{r}\right)_r = \\ = -\, p_z \sqrt{1+z_r^2+(z_\varphi/r)^2}\,. \tag{2.10d}$$

2.3 Principal Stresses, Conditions for Folding

Specifying the state of stress by the membrane forces along parametric curves would generally be arbitrary, because larger loads might be acting along differently oriented section elements (Figure 2.2). We are thus led to examine the totality of membrane loads acting on all section elements $d\,s_\psi$ of arbitrary orientation.

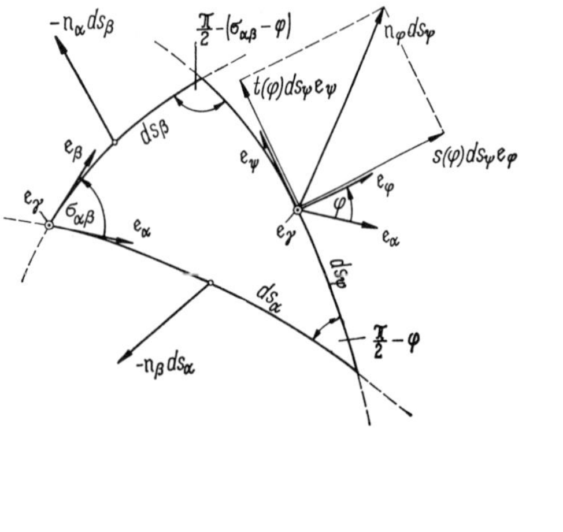

Figure 2.2

These can always be expressed in terms of the loads $\mathfrak{n}_\alpha$ and $\mathfrak{n}_\beta$ acting on the elements of the parametric curves $d\,s_\alpha$ and $d\,s_\beta$. The force-equilibrium condition for any element is:

$$\mathfrak{n}_\varphi\, d\,s_\psi - \mathfrak{n}_\alpha\, d\,s_\beta - \mathfrak{n}_\beta\, d\,s_\alpha = 0\,.$$

From the sine rule

$$d\,s_\alpha = d\,s_\psi \frac{\sin\left(\frac{\pi}{2} - (\sigma_{\alpha\beta}-\varphi)\right)}{\sin\sigma_{\alpha\beta}} = d\,s_\psi \frac{\cos(\sigma_{\alpha\beta}-\varphi)}{\sin\sigma_{\alpha\beta}}$$

$$d\,s_\beta = d\,s_\psi \frac{\sin\left(\frac{\pi}{2}-\varphi\right)}{\sin\sigma_{\alpha\beta}} = d\,s_\psi \frac{\cos\varphi}{\sin\sigma_{\alpha\beta}}$$

and hence

$$\mathfrak{n}_\varphi = \mathfrak{n}_\beta \frac{\cos(\sigma_{\alpha\beta}-\varphi)}{\sin\sigma_{\alpha\beta}} + \mathfrak{n}_\alpha \frac{\cos\varphi}{\sin\sigma_{\alpha\beta}}\,. \tag{2.11a}$$

Resolving $\mathfrak{n}_\varphi$ into a normal component $s\,(\varphi)\,e_\varphi$ and a tangential component $t\,(\varphi)\,e_\psi$ relative to the section element $d\,s_\psi$,

$$\mathfrak{n}_\varphi = s\,(\varphi)\,e_\varphi + t\,(\varphi)\,e_\psi\,,$$

where $s\,(\varphi)$ and $t\,(\varphi)$ denote, respectively, the normal and shearing forces in the membrane, we obtain by scalar multiplication of (2.11a) by e_φ and e_ψ in turn

$$\mathfrak{n}_\varphi\, e_\varphi = s\,(\varphi) = \frac{\cos(\sigma_{\alpha\beta}-\varphi)}{\sin\sigma_{\alpha\beta}}\,\mathfrak{n}_\beta\, e_\varphi + \frac{\cos\varphi}{\sin\sigma_{\alpha\beta}}\,\mathfrak{n}_\alpha\, e_\varphi\,,$$

$$\mathfrak{n}_\varphi\, e_\psi = t\,(\varphi) = \frac{\cos(\sigma_{\alpha\beta}-\varphi)}{\sin\sigma_{\alpha\beta}}\,\mathfrak{n}_\beta\, e_\psi + \frac{\cos\varphi}{\sin\sigma_{\alpha\beta}}\,\mathfrak{n}_\alpha\, e_\psi\,.$$

Inspection of Figure 2.2 shows that

$$e_\alpha\, e_\varphi = \cos\varphi\,,\quad e_\beta\, e_\varphi = \cos(\sigma_{\alpha\beta}-\varphi)\,,\quad e_\alpha\, e_\psi = \cos\left(\varphi+\frac{\pi}{2}\right) = -\sin\varphi\,,$$

$$e_\beta\, e_\psi = \cos\left(\frac{\pi}{2}+\varphi-\sigma_{\alpha\beta}\right) = \sin(\sigma_{\alpha\beta}-\varphi)$$

Substitution of these relationships finally yields

$$s\,(\varphi) = n_\beta \frac{\cos^2(\sigma_{\alpha\beta}-\varphi)}{\sin\sigma_{\alpha\beta}} + n_\alpha \frac{\cos^2\varphi}{\sin\sigma_{\alpha\beta}} + \\ + 2\, n_{\alpha\beta} \frac{\cos\varphi\,\cos(\sigma_{\alpha\beta}-\varphi)}{\sin\sigma_{\alpha\beta}} = \\ = \left(\frac{n_\alpha+n_\beta}{2\sin\sigma_{\alpha\beta}} + n_{\alpha\beta}\frac{\cos\sigma_{\alpha\beta}}{\sin\sigma_{\alpha\beta}}\right) + \\ + \left(\frac{n_\alpha-n_\beta}{2\sin\sigma_{\alpha\beta}} + \frac{\cos\sigma_{\alpha\beta}}{\sin\sigma_{\alpha\beta}}(n_\beta\cos\sigma_{\alpha\beta}+n_{\alpha\beta})\right)\cos 2\,\varphi + \\ + (n_\beta\cos\sigma_{\alpha\beta}+n_{\alpha\beta})\sin 2\,\varphi\,,$$

$$t\,(\varphi) = n_\beta \frac{\sin(\sigma_{\alpha\beta}-\varphi)\cos(\sigma_{\alpha\beta}-\varphi)}{\sin\sigma_{\alpha\beta}} - n_\alpha \frac{\sin\varphi\cos\varphi}{\sin\sigma_{\alpha\beta}} + \\ + n_{\alpha\beta} \frac{\sin(\sigma_{\alpha\beta}-\varphi)\cos\varphi - \cos(\sigma_{\alpha\beta}-\varphi)\sin\varphi}{\sin\sigma_{\alpha\beta}} = \\ = -\left(\frac{n_\alpha-n_\beta}{2\sin\sigma_{\alpha\beta}} + \frac{\cos\sigma_{\alpha\beta}}{\sin\sigma_{\alpha\beta}}(n_\beta\cos\sigma_{\alpha\beta}+n_{\alpha\beta})\right)\sin 2\,\varphi + \\ + (n_\beta\cos\sigma_{\alpha\beta}+n_{\alpha\beta})\cos 2\,\varphi\,. \tag{2.11b,c}$$

Comparison of (2.11b,c) with (1.16e,c), respectively, reveals their complete analogy. The associated normal and shearing forces

$s(\varphi)$ and $t(\varphi)$ are thus the coordinates of a point on a circle, known as Mohr's stress-circle, whose center lies on the positive s-axis at a distance

$$n_m = \frac{n_\alpha + n_\beta}{2 \sin \sigma_{\alpha\beta}} + n_{\alpha\beta} \frac{\cos \sigma_{\alpha\beta}}{\sin \sigma_{\alpha\beta}} \tag{2.12a}$$

from the origin. Putting

$$r_1 = \frac{n_\alpha - n_\beta}{2 \sin \sigma_{\alpha\beta}} + \frac{\cos \sigma_{\alpha\beta}}{\sin \sigma_{\alpha\beta}} (n_\beta \cos \sigma_{\alpha\beta} + n_{\alpha\beta}) ,$$

$$r_2 = n_\beta \cos \sigma_{\alpha\beta} + n_{\alpha\beta} , \tag{2.12b}$$

the radius of the circle is given by

$$R = \sqrt{r_1^2 + r_2^2} . \tag{2.12c}$$

The normal-force extrema

$$n_{1,2} = n_m \pm R \tag{2.13a}$$

act in section elements forming an angle

$$\varphi_{01} = \frac{1}{2} \operatorname{arc\,tg} \left(\frac{r_2}{r_1} \right) =$$

$$= \frac{1}{2} \operatorname{arc\,tg} \left[2 \sin \sigma_{\alpha\beta} \frac{n_\beta \cos \sigma_{\alpha\beta} + n_{\alpha\beta}}{n_\alpha - n_\beta + 2 \cos \sigma_{\alpha\beta} (n_\beta \cos \sigma_{\alpha\beta} + n_{\alpha\beta})} \right] ,$$

$$\varphi_{02} = \varphi_{01} + \frac{\pi}{2} \tag{2.13b}$$

with the $\mathfrak{e}_\alpha$-direction; in these section elements the shearing force vanishes. We denote by n_1 and n_2 the principal (normal) membrane forces, and accordingly obtain the no-folding condition in the form

$$n_2 = n_{\min} = n_m - R \geqq 0 . \tag{2.14}$$

If the principal membrane forces are expressed in terms of the sectional loads across orthogonal parametric curves ($g_{\alpha\beta} = 0$, $\sigma_{\alpha\beta} = \pi/2$) the components of these loads along orthogonal sections become the normal and shearing forces acting on the membrane. We obtain

$$n_{1,2} = \frac{1}{2} \left[n_\alpha + n_\beta \pm \sqrt{(n_\alpha - n_\beta)^2 + 4 n_{\alpha\beta}^2} \right] \tag{2.15a}$$

while the no-folding condition is written

$$2 n_{\min} = n_\alpha + n_\beta - \sqrt{(n_\alpha - n_\beta)^2 + 4 n_{\alpha\beta}^2} \geqq 0 \tag{2.15b}$$

or alternately as

$$n_\alpha n_\beta - n_{\alpha\beta}^2 \geqq 0 , \quad n_\alpha \geqq 0 , \quad n_\beta \geqq 0 \tag{2.15c}$$

The respective analogy between (2.11b,c) and (1.16e,c) again shows that the local state of stress can be described by a tensor, known as the membrane force tensor $\mathfrak{N}$. This is also evident from (2.11a), which by virtue of $\cos \varphi = \mathfrak{e}_\varphi \mathfrak{e}_\alpha$ and $\cos (\sigma_{\alpha\beta} - \varphi) = \mathfrak{e}_\varphi \mathfrak{e}_\beta$ can be written in the form

$$\mathfrak{n}_\varphi = (\mathfrak{e}_\varphi \mathfrak{e}_\alpha) \frac{\mathfrak{n}_\alpha}{\sin \sigma_{\alpha\beta}} + (\mathfrak{e}_\varphi \mathfrak{e}_\beta) \frac{\mathfrak{n}_\beta}{\sin \sigma_{\alpha\beta}} ,$$

or in dyadic-product notation (see footnote on p. 172 for definition)

$$\mathfrak{n}_\varphi = \mathfrak{e}_\varphi \left(\frac{\mathfrak{e}_\alpha \otimes \mathfrak{n}_\alpha}{\sin \sigma_{\alpha\beta}} + \frac{\mathfrak{e}_\beta \otimes \mathfrak{n}_\beta}{\sin \sigma_{\alpha\beta}} \right) = \mathfrak{e}_\varphi \mathfrak{N} \tag{2.16a}$$

The use of tensor notation considerably simplifies the formulation of the equilibrium problem; after some manipulations the equilibrium condition (2.3a) is obtained in the simple form

$$\nabla \mathfrak{N} + \mathfrak{p} = 0 \tag{2.16b}$$

where we have used the differential operator (1.18b).

2.4 The Deformation Condition

Sectional loads cause the membrane elements to become strained, and consequently the membrane surface undergoes a displacement. We can derive the relationships governing these displacements (which establish their dependence on the sectional loads) if we know the strain-displacement relationships and the stress-strain relationship of the material.

2.4.1 *State of strain, strain-displacement relationships*

The deformations (dilatations, distortions) of a membrane element relevant to the specification of the state of stress can in every case be characterized by three dimensionless quantities, these being the components of the (symmetrical) strain tensor $\mathfrak{D}$. If the position vector of the deformed membrane surface is $\bar{\mathfrak{r}}(\alpha, \beta)$ and the displacement vector is $\mathfrak{v}(\alpha, \beta)$ then

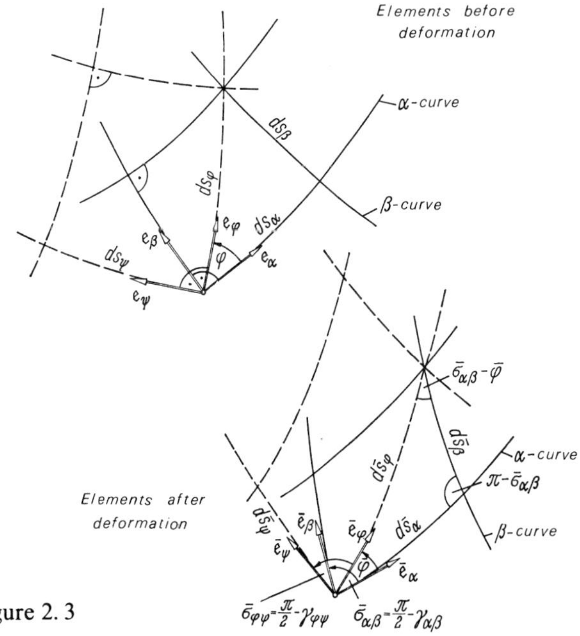

Figure 2. 3

$$\bar{\mathfrak{r}}(\alpha, \beta) = \mathfrak{r}(\alpha, \beta) + \mathfrak{v}(\alpha, \beta) . \tag{2.17}$$

A line element $d\mathfrak{s}_\varphi = \mathfrak{e}_\varphi\, d s_\varphi$ on the undeformed membrane surface $\mathfrak{r}(\alpha, \beta)$ is after deformation transformed into $d\bar{\mathfrak{s}}_\varphi = \bar{\mathfrak{e}}_\varphi\, d \bar{s}_\varphi$ (Figure 2.3), where, by virtue of (1.18d)

$$d\bar{\mathfrak{s}}_\varphi = d\mathfrak{s}_\varphi + d\mathfrak{v} = \mathfrak{e}_\varphi\, d s_\varphi + \frac{d\mathfrak{v}}{d s_\varphi} d s_\varphi =$$

$$= d s_\varphi \big(\mathfrak{e}_\varphi + \mathfrak{e}_\varphi (\nabla \otimes \mathfrak{v})\big) = d s_\varphi \big(\mathfrak{e}_\varphi \mathfrak{E} + \mathfrak{e}_\varphi (\nabla \otimes \mathfrak{v})\big) =$$

$$= d s_\varphi\, \mathfrak{e}_\varphi (\mathfrak{E} + \nabla \otimes \mathfrak{v}) = d\mathfrak{s}_\varphi (\mathfrak{E} + \mathfrak{B}) . \tag{2.18a}$$

Here $\mathfrak{E}$ is the unit tensor, while

$$\mathfrak{B} = \nabla \otimes \mathfrak{v} \text{ is} \tag{2.18b}$$

the so-called displacement dyad. We now form

$$\left.\begin{aligned} d\bar{\mathfrak{s}}_\varphi^2 &= d\bar{s}_\varphi^2 = d s_\varphi^2 \left[\mathfrak{e}_\varphi (\mathfrak{E} + \mathfrak{B})\right]^2, \\ d\bar{\mathfrak{s}}_\varphi\, d\bar{\mathfrak{s}}_\psi &= d s_\varphi\, d s_\psi \left[\mathfrak{e}_\psi (\mathfrak{E} + \mathfrak{B})\right]\left[\mathfrak{e}_\varphi (\mathfrak{E} + \mathfrak{B})\right], \end{aligned}\right\} \tag{2.19a, b}$$

taking into consideration that

$$(\mathfrak{a}\, \mathfrak{T}_1)(\mathfrak{b}\, \mathfrak{T}_2) = \mathfrak{a}\left[\mathfrak{b}\,(\mathfrak{T}_2\, \mathfrak{T}_1^t)\right] = \mathfrak{b}\left[\mathfrak{a}\,(\mathfrak{T}_1\, \mathfrak{T}_2^t)\right] \tag{2.19c}$$

where $\mathfrak{a}$ and $\mathfrak{b}$ are vectors, $\mathfrak{T}_1, \mathfrak{T}_2$, second-order tensors, and $\mathfrak{T}^t$ denotes the transposition of $\mathfrak{T}$. Thus

$$\left.\begin{aligned} &\left[\mathfrak{e}_\varphi (\mathfrak{E} + \mathfrak{B})\right]\left[\mathfrak{e}_\varphi (\mathfrak{E} + \mathfrak{B})\right] = \mathfrak{e}_\varphi (\mathfrak{e}_\varphi\, \mathfrak{W}) \\ &\text{and} \\ &\left[\mathfrak{e}_\psi (\mathfrak{E} + \mathfrak{B})\right]\left[\mathfrak{e}_\varphi (\mathfrak{E} + \mathfrak{B})\right] = \mathfrak{e}_\psi (\mathfrak{e}_\varphi\, \mathfrak{W}), \end{aligned}\right\} \tag{2.19d}$$

where

$$\begin{aligned} \mathfrak{W} &= (\mathfrak{E} + \mathfrak{B})(\mathfrak{E} + \mathfrak{B})^t = (\mathfrak{E} + \mathfrak{B})(\mathfrak{E} + \mathfrak{B}^t) = \\ &= \mathfrak{E} + \mathfrak{E}\,(\mathfrak{B} + \mathfrak{B}^t) + \mathfrak{B}\,\mathfrak{B}^t = \mathfrak{E} + \mathfrak{B} + \\ &+ \mathfrak{B}^t + \mathfrak{B}\,\mathfrak{B}^t = \mathfrak{E} + 2\,\mathfrak{D} \end{aligned} \tag{2.19e}$$

while

$$\begin{aligned} \mathfrak{D} &= \frac{1}{2}(\mathfrak{B} + \mathfrak{B}^t + \mathfrak{B}\,\mathfrak{B}^t) = \\ &= \frac{1}{2}\left[\nabla \otimes \mathfrak{v} + \overset{\downarrow}{\mathfrak{v}} \otimes \overset{\downarrow}{\nabla} + (\nabla \otimes \mathfrak{v})(\mathfrak{v} \otimes \nabla)\right] \end{aligned} \tag{2.20a}$$

is the strain tensor. Hence from (2.19a, b)

$$\begin{aligned} d\bar{\mathfrak{s}}_\varphi^2 &= d\bar{s}_\varphi^2 = d s_\varphi^2\, \mathfrak{e}_\varphi (\mathfrak{e}_\varphi\, \mathfrak{W}) = d s_\varphi^2\, \mathfrak{e}_\varphi \left[\mathfrak{e}_\varphi (\mathfrak{E} + 2\,\mathfrak{D})\right] = \\ &= d s_\varphi^2 \left[1 + 2\, \mathfrak{e}_\varphi (\mathfrak{e}_\varphi\, \mathfrak{D})\right] = d\mathfrak{s}_\varphi^2 + 2\, d\mathfrak{s}_\varphi (d\mathfrak{s}_\varphi\, \mathfrak{D}), \\ d\bar{\mathfrak{s}}_\varphi\, d\bar{\mathfrak{s}}_\psi &= d s_\varphi\, d s_\psi\, \mathfrak{e}_\psi (\mathfrak{e}_\varphi\, \mathfrak{W}) = d s_\varphi\, d s_\psi\, \mathfrak{e}_\psi \left[\mathfrak{e}_\varphi (\mathfrak{E} + 2\,\mathfrak{D})\right] = \\ &= d s_\varphi\, d s_\psi \left[\mathfrak{e}_\psi\, \mathfrak{e}_\varphi + 2\, \mathfrak{e}_\psi (\mathfrak{e}_\varphi\, \mathfrak{D})\right] = d\mathfrak{s}_\varphi\, d\mathfrak{s}_\psi + \\ &+ 2\, d s_\varphi\, d s_\psi\, \mathfrak{e}_\psi (\mathfrak{e}_\varphi\, \mathfrak{D}) = d\mathfrak{s}_\varphi\, d\mathfrak{s}_\psi + 2\, d\mathfrak{s}_\psi (d\mathfrak{s}_\varphi\, \mathfrak{D}) \end{aligned}$$

and

$$\left.\begin{aligned} d_{\varphi\varphi} &= \frac{1}{2}\left[\left(\frac{d\bar{s}_\varphi}{d s_\varphi}\right)^2 - 1\right] = \mathfrak{e}_\varphi (\mathfrak{e}_\varphi\, \mathfrak{D}), \\ d_{\varphi\psi} &= \frac{1}{2}\, \frac{d\bar{\mathfrak{s}}_\varphi\, d\bar{\mathfrak{s}}_\psi - d\mathfrak{s}_\varphi\, d\mathfrak{s}_\psi}{d s_\varphi\, d s_\psi} = \mathfrak{e}_\psi (\mathfrak{e}_\varphi\, \mathfrak{D}). \end{aligned}\right\} \tag{2.20b}$$

In order to interpret the strain components d_{ik} in terms of the usual concepts of extension and shear angle we first introduce the extension of the line element $d\mathfrak{s}_\varphi$:

$$\frac{d\bar{s}_\varphi - d s_\varphi}{d s_\varphi} = \frac{d\bar{s}_\varphi}{d s_\varphi} - 1 = \varepsilon_\varphi\,. \tag{2.21a}$$

We then obtain from (2.20b)

$$\left.\begin{aligned} d_{\varphi\varphi} &= \mathfrak{e}_\varphi (\mathfrak{e}_\varphi\, \mathfrak{D}) = \frac{1}{2}\left((1 + \varepsilon_\varphi)^2 - 1\right) = \\ &= \varepsilon_\varphi + \frac{\varepsilon_\varphi^2}{2} = \varepsilon_\varphi \left(1 + \frac{\varepsilon_\varphi}{2}\right) \\ &\text{or} \\ \varepsilon_\varphi &= \sqrt{1 + 2\, d_{\varphi\varphi}} - 1 = \sqrt{1 + 2\, \mathfrak{e}_\varphi (\mathfrak{e}_\varphi\, \mathfrak{D})} - 1\,. \end{aligned}\right\} \tag{2.21b}$$

If $\sigma_{\varphi\psi}$ is the angle between two line elements $d\mathfrak{s}_\psi$ and $d\mathfrak{s}_\varphi$ before the deformation, which after deformation becomes $\bar{\sigma}_{\varphi\psi} = \sigma_{\varphi\psi} - \gamma_{\varphi\psi}$ where

$$\gamma_{\varphi\psi} = \sigma_{\varphi\psi} - \bar{\sigma}_{\varphi\psi} \tag{2.21c}$$

is the increment of the angle (which may be negative) then

$$\begin{aligned} d_{\varphi\psi} &= \mathfrak{e}_\psi (\mathfrak{e}_\varphi\, \mathfrak{D}) = \frac{1}{2}\, \frac{d\bar{s}_\varphi\, d\bar{s}_\psi \cos\bar{\sigma}_{\varphi\psi} - d s_\varphi\, d s_\psi \cos\sigma_{\varphi\psi}}{d s_\varphi\, d s_\psi} = \\ &= \frac{1}{2}\left[(1 + \varepsilon_\varphi)(1 + \varepsilon_\psi)\cos(\sigma_{\varphi\psi} - \gamma_{\varphi\psi}) - \cos\sigma_{\varphi\psi}\right]. \end{aligned} \tag{2.21d}$$

In particular, if the line elements were initially orthogonal ($\sigma_{\varphi\psi} = \pi/2$; see Figure 2.3)

$$\left.\begin{aligned} d_{\varphi\psi} &= \mathfrak{e}_\psi (\mathfrak{e}_\varphi\, \mathfrak{D}) = \frac{1}{2}(1 + \varepsilon_\varphi)(1 + \varepsilon_\psi)\sin\gamma_{\varphi\psi} \\ &\text{or} \\ \sin\gamma_{\varphi\psi} &= \frac{2\, d_{\varphi\psi}}{(1 + \varepsilon_\varphi)(1 + \varepsilon_\psi)} = \frac{2\, \mathfrak{e}_\psi (\mathfrak{e}_\varphi\, \mathfrak{D})}{(1 + \varepsilon_\varphi)(1 + \varepsilon_\psi)}, \\ \mathfrak{e}_\psi &= \mathfrak{e}_\gamma \times \mathfrak{e}_\varphi\,. \end{aligned}\right\} \tag{2.21e}$$

Of the 8 components d_{ik} of the strain tensor

$$\begin{aligned} \mathfrak{D} &= \frac{1}{2}\left(\nabla \otimes \mathfrak{v} + \overset{\downarrow}{\mathfrak{v}} \otimes \overset{\downarrow}{\nabla} + (\nabla \otimes \mathfrak{v})(\mathfrak{v} \otimes \nabla)\right) = \\ &= \sum_{i,k = \alpha,\beta,\gamma} d_{ik}\, \mathfrak{e}_i \otimes \mathfrak{e}_k = \begin{pmatrix} d_{\alpha\alpha} & d_{\alpha\beta} & d_{\alpha\gamma} \\ d_{\beta\alpha} & d_{\beta\beta} & d_{\beta\gamma} \\ d_{\gamma\alpha} & d_{\gamma\beta} & 0 \end{pmatrix} \end{aligned}$$

the $d_{i\gamma} = d_{\gamma i}$ $(i = \alpha, \beta)$ can be shown to represent rotations causing the surface element to become warped out of its plane and are irrelevant to the state of stress of the membrane. The symmetric minor

$$\mathfrak{D}_1 = \sum_{i,k = \alpha,\beta} d_{ik}\, \mathfrak{e}_i \otimes \mathfrak{e}_k = \begin{pmatrix} d_{\alpha\alpha} & d_{\alpha\beta} \\ d_{\beta\alpha} & d_{\beta\beta} \end{pmatrix} \tag{2.22a}$$

describes the strain of the surface element in its plane. This is also seen directly from (2.21b, e) where, by virtue of $\mathfrak{e}_\varphi\, \mathfrak{e}_\gamma = 0$,

$$\left.\begin{aligned} \varepsilon_\varphi &= \sqrt{1 + 2\, \mathfrak{e}_\varphi (\mathfrak{e}_\varphi\, \mathfrak{D}_1)} - 1 \\ \text{or}\quad d_{\varphi\varphi} &= \varepsilon_\varphi \left(1 + \frac{\varepsilon_\varphi}{2}\right) = \mathfrak{e}_\varphi (\mathfrak{e}_\varphi\, \mathfrak{D}_1), \\ \sin\gamma_{\varphi\psi} &= \frac{2\, \mathfrak{e}_\psi (\mathfrak{e}_\varphi\, \mathfrak{D}_1)}{(1 + \varepsilon_\varphi)(1 + \varepsilon_\psi)} \\ \text{or}\quad d_{\varphi\psi} &= \frac{1}{2}(1 + \varepsilon_\varphi)(1 + \varepsilon_\psi)\sin\gamma_{\varphi\psi} = \mathfrak{e}_\psi (\mathfrak{e}_\varphi\, \mathfrak{D}_1) \end{aligned}\right\} \tag{2.22b, c}$$

If we consider only the orthogonal coordinates ($\sigma_{\alpha\beta} = \pi/2$) we have

$$\nabla = \mathfrak{e}_\alpha \frac{\partial}{\partial s_\alpha} + \mathfrak{e}_\beta \frac{\partial}{\partial s_\beta} = \sum_{i = \alpha,\beta} \mathfrak{e}_i \frac{\partial}{\partial s_i}$$

[cf. (1.18b)] and thus

$$\begin{aligned} \mathfrak{D} = \frac{1}{2}\Bigg[&\sum_{i = \alpha,\beta} \mathfrak{e}_i \otimes \frac{\partial \mathfrak{v}}{\partial s_i} + \sum_{i = \alpha,\beta} \frac{\partial \mathfrak{v}}{\partial s_i} \otimes \mathfrak{e}_i + \\ &+ \left(\sum_{i = \alpha,\beta} \mathfrak{e}_i \otimes \frac{\partial \mathfrak{v}}{\partial s_i}\right)\left(\sum_{j = \alpha,\beta} \frac{\partial \mathfrak{v}}{\partial s_j} \otimes \mathfrak{e}_j\right)\Bigg], \end{aligned}$$

whence finally (since $\partial/\partial s_\gamma = 0$)

$$\begin{aligned} d_{ik} &= \mathfrak{e}_k (\mathfrak{e}_i\, \mathfrak{D}) = \\ &= \frac{1}{2}\left[\mathfrak{e}_i \frac{\partial \mathfrak{v}}{\partial s_k} + \mathfrak{e}_k \frac{\partial \mathfrak{v}}{\partial s_i} + \frac{\partial \mathfrak{v}}{\partial s_i}\, \frac{\partial \mathfrak{v}}{\partial s_k}\right]_{i,k = \alpha,\beta,\gamma}, \end{aligned} \tag{2.23}$$

in which we have made use of

$$\mathfrak{e}_k\left\{\mathfrak{e}_i \sum_{i,j=\alpha,\beta}\left(\mathfrak{e}_i \otimes \frac{\partial \mathfrak{v}}{\partial s_i}\right)\left(\frac{\partial \mathfrak{v}}{\partial s_j} \otimes \mathfrak{e}_j\right)\right\} = \frac{\partial \mathfrak{v}}{\partial s_i}\,\frac{\partial \mathfrak{v}}{\partial s_k}$$

which may be verified by applying the equality $(\mathfrak{a} \otimes \mathfrak{b})\,(\mathfrak{c} \otimes \mathfrak{d}) = (\mathfrak{a} \otimes \mathfrak{d})\,(\mathfrak{b}\,\mathfrak{c})$. The components of the minor $\mathfrak{D}_1$, which are of particular interest, thus depend on the displacement derivatives:

$$\left.\begin{aligned} d_{\alpha\alpha} &= \mathfrak{e}_\alpha\,(\mathfrak{e}_\alpha\,\mathfrak{D}) = \varepsilon_\alpha\left(1+\frac{\varepsilon_\alpha}{2}\right) = \mathfrak{e}_\alpha\frac{\partial \mathfrak{v}}{\partial s_\alpha} + \frac{1}{2}\left(\frac{\partial \mathfrak{v}}{\partial s_\alpha}\right)^2, \\ d_{\beta\beta} &= \mathfrak{e}_\beta\,(\mathfrak{e}_\beta\,\mathfrak{D}) = \varepsilon_\beta\left(1+\frac{\varepsilon_\beta}{2}\right) = \mathfrak{e}_\beta\frac{\partial \mathfrak{v}}{\partial s_\beta} + \frac{1}{2}\left(\frac{\partial \mathfrak{v}}{\partial s_\beta}\right)^2, \\ d_{\alpha\beta} &= \mathfrak{e}_\beta\,(\mathfrak{e}_\alpha\,\mathfrak{D}) = \frac{1}{2}\,(1+\varepsilon_\alpha)\,(1+\varepsilon_\beta)\sin\gamma_{\alpha\beta} = \\ &= \frac{1}{2}\left(\mathfrak{e}_\alpha\frac{\partial \mathfrak{v}}{\partial s_\beta} + \mathfrak{e}_\beta\frac{\partial \mathfrak{v}}{\partial s_\alpha} + \frac{\partial \mathfrak{v}}{\partial s_\alpha}\,\frac{\partial \mathfrak{v}}{\partial s_\beta}\right), \end{aligned}\right\} \quad (2.23a)$$

from which we obtain the extensions and the sine of the shear angle:

$$\left.\begin{aligned} \varepsilon_\alpha &= \sqrt{1+2\,d_{\alpha\alpha}} - 1 = \sqrt{1 + 2\,\mathfrak{e}_\alpha\frac{\partial \mathfrak{v}}{\partial s_\alpha} + \left(\frac{\partial \mathfrak{v}}{\partial s_\alpha}\right)^2} - 1, \\ \varepsilon_\beta &= \sqrt{1+2\,d_{\beta\beta}} - 1 = \sqrt{1 + 2\,\mathfrak{e}_\beta\frac{\partial \mathfrak{v}}{\partial s_\beta} + \left(\frac{\partial \mathfrak{v}}{\partial s_\beta}\right)^2} - 1, \\ \sin\gamma_{\alpha\beta} &- \frac{2\,d_{\alpha\beta}}{(1+\varepsilon_\alpha)\,(1+\varepsilon_\beta)} = \frac{1}{(1+\varepsilon_\alpha)\,(1+\varepsilon_\beta)} \times \\ &\times \left[\mathfrak{e}_\alpha\frac{\partial \mathfrak{v}}{\partial s_\beta} + \mathfrak{e}_\beta\frac{\partial \mathfrak{v}}{\partial s_\alpha} + \frac{\partial \mathfrak{v}}{\partial s_\alpha}\,\frac{\partial \mathfrak{v}}{\partial s_\beta}\right]. \end{aligned}\right\} \quad (2.23b)$$

Putting in (2.22b, c)

$$\mathfrak{e}_\varphi = \mathfrak{e}_\alpha\cos\varphi + \mathfrak{e}_\beta\sin\varphi\,,$$

$$\mathfrak{e}_\psi = \mathfrak{e}_\alpha\cos\psi + \mathfrak{e}_\beta\sin\psi = -\,\mathfrak{e}_\alpha\sin\varphi + \mathfrak{e}_\beta\cos\varphi\,, \quad (\psi = \varphi + \pi/2)$$

we obtain

$$\left.\begin{aligned} d_{\varphi\varphi} &= \frac{d_{\alpha\alpha}+d_{\beta\beta}}{2} + \frac{d_{\alpha\alpha}-d_{\beta\beta}}{2}\cos 2\,\varphi + d_{\alpha\beta}\sin 2\,\varphi\,, \\ d_{\varphi\psi} &= -\,\frac{d_{\alpha\alpha}-d_{\beta\beta}}{2}\sin 2\,\varphi + d_{\alpha\beta}\cos 2\,\varphi\,. \end{aligned}\right\} \quad (2.24a)$$

The extension and shearing strain $d_{\varphi\varphi}$ and $d_{\varphi\psi}$ of an arbitrary, initially right-angled, surface element $d\,s_\varphi\,d\,s_\psi$ satisfy

$$\left(d_{\varphi\varphi} - \frac{d_{\alpha\alpha}+d_{\beta\beta}}{2}\right)^2 + d_{\varphi\psi}{}^2 = \left(\frac{d_{\alpha\alpha}-d_{\beta\beta}}{2}\right)^2 + d_{\alpha\beta}{}^2 = R^2 \quad (2.24b)$$

and can accordingly be represented as the abscissas and ordinates of the points on a circle whose center lies on the positive abscissa axis ($d_{\varphi\varphi}$) at a distance $(d_{\alpha\alpha}+d_{\beta\beta})/2$ from the origin (cf. Mohr's circle in Sec. 2.3). We conclude that at every surface point there exist two line elements

$$\varphi_{01} = \frac{1}{2}\,\mathrm{arc\,tg}\left(\frac{2\,d_{\alpha\beta}}{d_{\alpha\alpha}-d_{\beta\beta}}\right), \quad \varphi_{02} = \varphi_{01} + \pi/2 \quad (2.24c)$$

which are initially orthogonal and inclined to the initial $\mathfrak{e}_\alpha$-direction at the angles

$$\begin{aligned} d\,\mathfrak{s}_1 &= d\,s_1\,\mathfrak{e}_1 = d\,s_1\,(\mathfrak{e}_\alpha\cos\varphi_{01} + \mathfrak{e}_\beta\sin\varphi_{01}) \\ d\,\mathfrak{s}_2 &= d\,s_2\,\mathfrak{e}_2 = d\,s_2\,(\mathfrak{e}_\alpha\cos\varphi_{02} + \mathfrak{e}_\beta\sin\varphi_{02}) \end{aligned} \quad (2.24d)$$

and remain orthogonal also after deformation. These line elements undergo the maximum and minimum extensions

$$d_{1,2} = \frac{d_{\alpha\alpha}+d_{\beta\beta}}{2} \pm \sqrt{\left(\frac{d_{\alpha\alpha}-d_{\beta\beta}}{2}\right)^2 + d_{\alpha\beta}{}^2} \quad (2.24e)$$

and lie along the local principal axes of strain. The angle $\bar{\varphi}_{01}$, which the first principal strain axis forms with the $\bar{\mathfrak{e}}_\alpha$-direction after deformation can be determined from Figure 2.4, which shows a triangular surface element whose sides are $d\,s_1$, $d\,s_2$, and

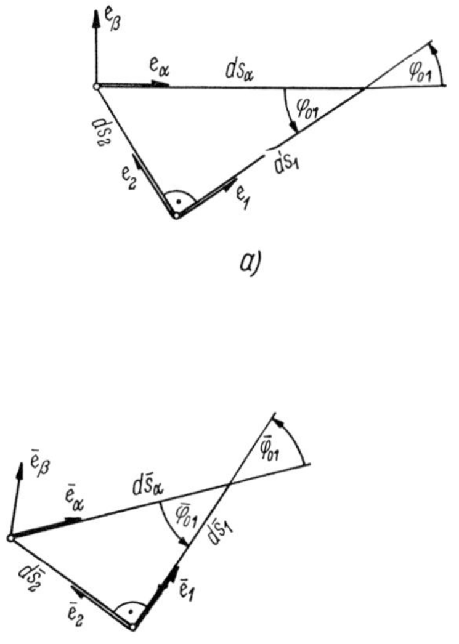

Figure 2.4a and b

$d\,s_\alpha$ before deformation (Figure 2.4a) and become $d\,\bar{s}_1$, $d\,\bar{s}_2$, and $d\,\bar{s}_\alpha$ after deformation (Figure 2.4b). From $d\,\bar{s} = (1+\varepsilon)\,d\,s$ we obtain

$$\left.\begin{aligned} \cos\bar{\varphi}_{01} &= \frac{d\,\bar{s}_1}{d\,\bar{s}_\alpha} = \frac{1+\varepsilon_1}{1+\varepsilon_\alpha}\,\frac{d\,s_1}{d\,s_\alpha} = \frac{1+\varepsilon_1}{1+\varepsilon_\alpha}\cos\varphi_{01}\,, \\ \sin\bar{\varphi}_{01} &= \frac{d\,\bar{s}_2}{d\,\bar{s}_\alpha} = \frac{1+\varepsilon_2}{1+\varepsilon_\alpha}\,\frac{d\,s_2}{d\,s_\alpha} = \frac{1+\varepsilon_2}{1+\varepsilon_\alpha}\sin\varphi_{01}\,. \end{aligned}\right. \quad (2.24f)$$

From (2.24a, e) we obtain

$$D_{\mathrm{I}} = d_1 + d_2 = d_{\alpha\alpha} + d_{\beta\beta} = d_{\varphi\varphi} + d_{\psi\psi}$$

so that

$$\begin{aligned} &\varepsilon_1\left(1+\frac{\varepsilon_1}{2}\right) + \varepsilon_2\left(1+\frac{\varepsilon_2}{2}\right) = \\ &= \varepsilon_\alpha\left(1+\frac{\varepsilon_\alpha}{2}\right) + \varepsilon_\beta\left(1+\frac{\varepsilon_\beta}{2}\right) = \varepsilon_\varphi\left(1+\frac{\varepsilon_\varphi}{2}\right) + \varepsilon_\psi\left(1+\frac{\varepsilon_\psi}{2}\right) \end{aligned}$$

and

$$\begin{aligned} &(1+\varepsilon_1)^2 + (1+\varepsilon_2)^2 = \\ &= (1+\varepsilon_\alpha)^2 + (1+\varepsilon_\beta)^2 = (1+\varepsilon_\varphi)^2 + (1+\varepsilon_\psi)^2 \end{aligned} \quad (2.24g)$$

as well as

$$D_{\mathrm{II}} = d_1\,d_2 = d_{\alpha\alpha}\,d_{\beta\beta} - d_{\alpha\beta}{}^2 = d_{\varphi\varphi}\,d_{\psi\psi} - d_{\varphi\psi}{}^2$$

so that

$$\begin{aligned} \varepsilon_1\,\varepsilon_2\left(1+\frac{\varepsilon_1}{2}\right)\left(1+\frac{\varepsilon_2}{2}\right) &= \varepsilon_\alpha\,\varepsilon_\beta\left(1+\frac{\varepsilon_\alpha}{2}\right)\left(1+\frac{\varepsilon_\beta}{2}\right) - \\ &- \left[\frac{1}{2}\,(1+\varepsilon_\alpha)\,(1+\varepsilon_\beta)\sin\gamma_{\alpha\beta}\right]^2 = \\ &= \varepsilon_\varphi\,\varepsilon_\psi\left(1+\frac{\varepsilon_\varphi}{2}\right)\left(1+\frac{\varepsilon_\psi}{2}\right) - \left[\frac{1}{2}\,(1+\varepsilon_\varphi)\,(1+\varepsilon_\psi)\sin\gamma_{\varphi\psi}\right]^2 \end{aligned}$$

and

$$(1+\varepsilon_1)(1+\varepsilon_2) = \sqrt{1+2D_{\mathrm{I}}+4D_{\mathrm{II}}} = (1+\varepsilon_\alpha)(1+\varepsilon_\beta)\cos\gamma_{\alpha\beta} =$$
$$= (1+\varepsilon_\varphi)(1+\varepsilon_\psi)\cos\gamma_{\varphi\psi} = (1+\varepsilon_\alpha)(1+\varepsilon_\beta)\sin\bar{\sigma}_{\alpha\beta} =$$
$$= (1+\varepsilon_\varphi)(1+\varepsilon_\psi)\sin\bar{\sigma}_{\varphi\psi} \qquad (2.24h)$$

Since the values of these sums are independent of direction we call D_{I} and D_{II} the first and second invariants of the strain tensor. For small deformations we obtain for the components d_{ik} of the strain tensor $\mathfrak{D}_1$, by neglecting all nonlinear displacement terms,

$$d_{ik} \approx \frac{1}{2}\left(\mathfrak{e}_i \frac{\partial \mathfrak{v}}{\partial s_k} + \mathfrak{e}_k \frac{\partial \mathfrak{v}}{\partial s_i}\right), \quad i, k = \alpha, \beta\,. \qquad (2.25a)$$

Since we can assume in this case that extensions and shear angles are small compared to unity, we can relate the components d_{ik} of the strain tensor to the extensions and shear angles by the simple expressions

$$d_{ik} \approx \frac{1}{2}\gamma_{ik}\,, \quad d_{ii} \approx \varepsilon_i \qquad (2.25b)$$

Taking into account (1.13), and again putting $\sigma_{\alpha\beta} = \pi/2$ we finally obtain

$$\left.\begin{aligned}
d_{\alpha\alpha} &= \varepsilon_\alpha = \mathfrak{e}_\alpha \frac{\partial \mathfrak{v}}{\partial s_\alpha} = \frac{\partial v_\alpha}{\partial s_\alpha} + \omega_\beta^{(\alpha)} v_\gamma - \omega_\gamma^{(\alpha)} v_\beta\,,\\
d_{\beta\beta} &= \varepsilon_\beta = \mathfrak{e}_\beta \frac{\partial \mathfrak{v}}{\partial s_\beta} = \frac{\partial v_\beta}{\partial s_\beta} + \omega_\gamma^{(\beta)} v_\alpha - \omega_\alpha^{(\beta)} v_\gamma\,,\\
d_{\alpha\beta} &= \frac{1}{2}\gamma_{\alpha\beta} = \frac{1}{2}\left(\mathfrak{e}_\alpha \frac{\partial \mathfrak{v}}{\partial s_\beta} + \mathfrak{e}_\beta \frac{\partial \mathfrak{v}}{\partial s_\alpha}\right) =\\
&= \frac{1}{2}\left(\frac{\partial v_\alpha}{\partial s_\beta} + \frac{\partial v_\beta}{\partial s_\alpha} + \omega_\gamma^{(\alpha)} v_\alpha - \omega_\gamma^{(\beta)} v_\beta - 2\,\omega_\alpha^{(\alpha)} v_\gamma\right)
\end{aligned}\right\} \qquad (2.25c)$$

We note that the displacement tensor can also be defined as half the difference between the metric tensors before and after deformation.

2.4.2 *Stress-strain Relationships for Orthogonal Anisotropic Linearly-elastic Membranes*

Materials used for membranes differ in their behavior under load. Metal skins, skins of plastic foil and nonwoven materials can be considered as isotropic materials, while the commonly used textiles (generally coated) exhibit orthogonal anisotropy, with small rigidity in shear $D_{\alpha\beta}$ as compared to their rigidities in tension D_α and D_β. Particularly with light textiles the rigidity in shear, which increases slightly with longitudinal force and internal pressure is extremely small (less than 1/15 of the rigidity in tension). Such textiles resemble cable nets in their behavior under load ($D_{\alpha\beta} = 0$). The rupture diagram, obtained from groups of four tests* of monoaxial loading on a lightly coated light textile has the typical shape shown in Figure 2.5. The curves rise gradually: warp and weft are extended (changes in relative position); apparently no large forces are needed for this. At the end of this stretching period, which is shorter for the warp than for the weft since the former is initially under larger tension than the latter, actual extension of the textile begins, being almost linearly, or slightly more than linearly, dependent on the section loads. In biaxial tests, where warp and weft are tensioned simultaneously, the stretching period is less. Small displacements can be considered to depend linearly, large

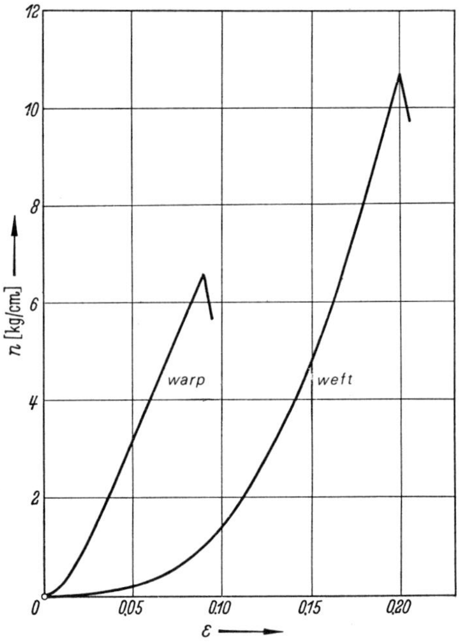

Figure 2.5

displacements slightly more than linearly, on the section loads. In the region of small displacements the stress-strain relationships for orthogonal anisotropic linearly-elastic materials will be sufficiently accurate: the components of the strain tensor $\mathfrak{D}_1$ will depend linearly on those of the membrane force tensor. Since normal forces acting along the axes of anisotropy of the membrane cause only extensions, while shearing forces cause only shear, we obtain the stress-strain relationship

$$\varepsilon_\alpha = \frac{n_\alpha}{D_\alpha} - \frac{\nu_\beta}{D_\beta} n_\beta\,, \quad \varepsilon_\beta = \frac{n_\beta}{D_\beta} - \frac{\nu_\alpha}{D_\alpha} n_\alpha\,, \quad \gamma_{\alpha\beta} = \frac{n_{\alpha\beta}}{D_{\alpha\beta}}\,, \qquad (2.26a)$$

the moduli of elasticity D_i and Poisson's ratios ν_i are (according to Maxwell and Betti's reciprocity theorem) interrelated as follows:

$$\frac{\nu_\alpha}{D_\alpha} = \frac{\nu_\beta}{D_\beta}\,. \qquad (2.26b)$$

Combining the stress-strain relationship (2.26a) with the strain-displacement relationships (2.25c), we obtain the

2.4.3 *Section-load—Displacement Relationships*

* The tensile tests were performed by Messrs. Stromeyer on a 5 cm wide and 30 cm long strip. Tests to determine the rigidity in shear (torsion tests on slender tubes, see Fig. 79, 9-11) were carried out at the Light Structures Development Center.

$$\left.\begin{aligned}
&\frac{\partial v_\alpha}{\partial s_\alpha} + \omega_\beta{}^{(\alpha)} v_\gamma - \omega_\gamma{}^{(\alpha)} v_\beta = \varepsilon_\alpha = \frac{n_\alpha}{D_\alpha} - \frac{\nu_\beta}{D_\beta} n_\beta\,,\\
&\frac{\partial v_\beta}{\partial s_\beta} + \omega_\gamma{}^{(\beta)} v_\alpha - \omega_\alpha{}^{(\beta)} v_\gamma = \varepsilon_\beta = \frac{n_\beta}{D_\beta} - \frac{\nu_\alpha}{D_\alpha} n_\alpha\,,\\
&\frac{\partial v_\alpha}{\partial s_\beta} + \frac{\partial v_\beta}{\partial s_\alpha} + \omega_\gamma{}^{(\alpha)} v_\alpha - \omega_\gamma{}^{(\beta)} v_\beta - 2\,\omega_\alpha{}^{(\alpha)} v_\gamma =\\
&\qquad = \gamma_{\alpha\beta} = \frac{n_{\alpha\beta}}{D_{\alpha\beta}}
\end{aligned}\right\} \qquad (2.27)$$

from which we obtain the displacements of the membrane surface by integrating and taking into account the boundary conditions; the required sectional loads are obtained from the equilibrium conditions.

2.5 Membranes Stretched by Edge Cables

Besides determining the sectional load as shown above, it is of interest to know what kinds of membrane surface are applicable in principle, and how the edge cables have to be arranged. Obviously, certain relationships have to be satisfied to ensure that the sectional loads acting in a membrane can be taken up by the edge cables. We consider therefore an edge element of the membrane surface with associated element of the edge cable (Figure 2.6). Let $\mathfrak{t}$ be the unit tangent vector of the edge curve and $\mathfrak{e}_{\gamma(R)}$ the unit normal vector to the surface at the edge. Since the membrane can only transmit to the edge cable sectional loads acting in its tangent plane, the load on the edge cable per unit length will be (neglecting the cable weight)

$$\mathfrak{q}(s) = q_t(s)\,\mathfrak{t} + q_n(s)\,(\mathfrak{e}_{\gamma(R)} \times \mathfrak{t}) \qquad (2.28)$$

To obtain the equilibrium condition for the cable element, we introduce the vector of the cable force $\mathfrak{S} = S\,\mathfrak{t}$ where S is the magnitude of the cable force.
Using the Frenet formula

$$\frac{d\mathfrak{t}}{ds} = \varkappa\,\mathfrak{n} = \frac{\mathfrak{n}}{R} \qquad (2.29)$$

we obtain

$$\begin{aligned}\frac{d\mathfrak{S}}{ds} &= \frac{d}{ds}(S\,\mathfrak{t}) = \frac{dS}{ds}\mathfrak{t} + S\,\frac{\mathfrak{n}}{R} =\\ &= -\,\mathfrak{q}(s) = -\left(q_t(s)\,\mathfrak{t} + q_n(s)\,(\mathfrak{e}_{\gamma(R)} \times \mathfrak{t})\right)\end{aligned} \qquad (2.30)$$

where $R = \varkappa^{-1}$ is the radius of curvature of the cable and $\mathfrak{n}$ the unit normal vector to it, perpendicular to $\mathfrak{t}$. Scalar multiplication of (2.30) by $\mathfrak{t}$ yields

$$\frac{dS}{ds} = -\,q_t(s)\,, \qquad (2.31a)$$

whence

$$\frac{S}{R}\,\mathfrak{n} + q_n\,(\mathfrak{e}_{\gamma(R)} \times \mathfrak{t}) = 0\,. \qquad (2.31b)$$

For $S \neq 0$ and $q_n \neq 0$ this is only possible when $\mathfrak{n}$ and $\mathfrak{e}_{\gamma(R)} \times \mathfrak{t}$ are parallel, i.e,

$$\mathfrak{n} \times (\mathfrak{e}_{\gamma(R)} \times \mathfrak{t}) = \mathfrak{e}_{\gamma(R)}\,(\mathfrak{n}\,\mathfrak{t}) - \mathfrak{t}\,(\mathfrak{n}\,\mathfrak{e}_{\gamma(R)}) = -\,\mathfrak{t}\,(\mathfrak{n}\,\mathfrak{e}_{\gamma(R)}) = 0$$

or $\qquad \mathfrak{n}\,\mathfrak{e}_{\gamma(R)} = 0 \qquad (2.31c)$

Thus, $\mathfrak{n}$ must be perpendicular to $\mathfrak{e}_{\gamma(R)}$. This means that the tangent plane to the membrane, defined by $\mathfrak{e}_{\gamma(R)}$ must be identical with the plane defined by $\mathfrak{t}$ and $\mathfrak{n}$. The binormal $\mathfrak{b} = \mathfrak{t} \times \mathfrak{n}$ to the edge cable and the surface normal $\mathfrak{e}_{\gamma(R)}$ are parallel.
Since $\mathfrak{e}_{\gamma(R)} \times \mathfrak{t} = -\,\mathfrak{n}$ (Figure 2.6) we obtain from (2.31b)

$$S = q_n\,R\,. \qquad (2.31d)$$

Whereas (2.31a) and (2.31d) interrelate the membrane-edge and the cable forces, and determine the radius of curvature R of the cable when the membrane edge loads q_n and q_t are given, (2.31c) gives the solution to the geometrical problem formulated above. This

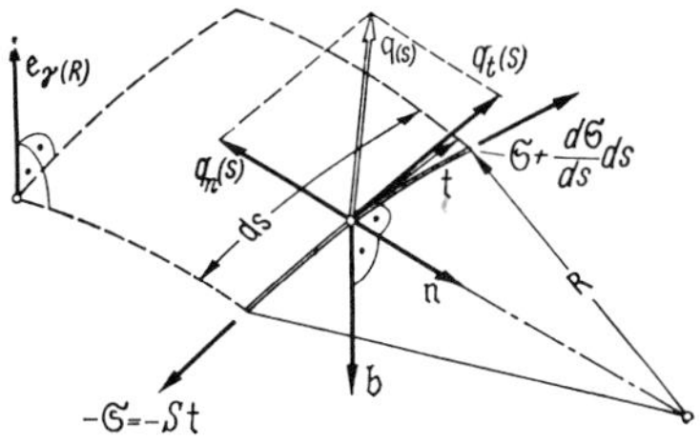

Figure 2.6

becomes clearer if we differentiate the conditions at the membrane edge

$$\mathfrak{t}\,\mathfrak{e}_{\gamma(R)} = 0\,, \quad \mathfrak{n}\,\mathfrak{e}_{\gamma(R)} = 0$$

along the edge curve:

$$\frac{d}{ds}(\mathfrak{t}\,\mathfrak{e}_{\gamma(R)}) = \frac{d\mathfrak{t}}{ds}\,\mathfrak{e}_{\gamma(R)} + \mathfrak{t}\,\frac{d\,\mathfrak{e}_{\gamma(R)}}{ds} = 0\,,$$

$$\frac{d}{ds}(\mathfrak{n}\,\mathfrak{e}_{\gamma(R)}) = \frac{d\mathfrak{n}}{ds}\,\mathfrak{e}_{\gamma(R)} + \mathfrak{n}\,\frac{d\,\mathfrak{e}_{\gamma(R)}}{ds} = 0\,.$$

By (1.16c) and (1.16d), where $\mathfrak{t}$ has been substituted for $\mathfrak{e}_\varphi$ and $-\,\mathfrak{n}$ for $\mathfrak{e}_\psi$,

$$\mathfrak{t}\,\frac{d\,\mathfrak{e}_{\gamma(R)}}{ds} = K_n(s)\,, \quad \mathfrak{n}\,\frac{d\,\mathfrak{e}_{\gamma(R)}}{ds} = T(s)\,.$$

This defines the normal curvature of a normal section containing the edge curve and the torsion of the surface along the edge curve.
In addition (2.29) holds. From the second Frenet formula

$$\frac{d\mathfrak{n}}{ds} = -\,\frac{\mathfrak{t}}{R} + \tau\,\mathfrak{b} \qquad (2.32)$$

where τ is the torsion of the edge curve,* we obtain, taking into account $\mathfrak{t}\,\mathfrak{e}_{\gamma(R)} = 0$, $\mathfrak{n}\,\mathfrak{e}_{\gamma(R)} = 0$, $\mathfrak{b}\,\mathfrak{e}_{\gamma(R)} = -\,1$**

---

* τ is the angle of rotation of the triad ($\mathfrak{t}$, $\mathfrak{n}$, $\mathfrak{b} = \mathfrak{t} \times \mathfrak{n}$) about the direction of the tangent when proceeding along the spatial curve over a distance $\Delta s = 1$.

** If $\mathfrak{n}\,\mathfrak{e}_{\gamma(R)} = -\cos\sigma(\mathfrak{n}, \mathfrak{e}_\gamma) \neq 0$, we obtain by Meusnier's theorem from the first differential equation

$$K_n(s) = \frac{1}{R_n(s)} = \varkappa\cos\sigma(\mathfrak{n}, \mathfrak{e}_\gamma) = \frac{\cos\sigma(\mathfrak{n}, \mathfrak{e}_\gamma)}{R(s)} \quad \text{and}$$

$$R(s) = R_n(s)\cos\sigma(\mathfrak{n}, \mathfrak{e}_\gamma)\,.$$

The radius of curvature of a surface curve is equal to the product of the radius of curvature of the normal section having the same tangent vector with the cosine of the angle between the surface normal and the normal to the surface curve.
Observation to (2.33a): Since $K_n(s) = 0$, we obtain from (1.18c): $K(s) = -T^2(s)$.

$$K_n(s) = 0\,, \quad T(s) = \sqrt{-K(s)} = \tau(s)\,, \tag{2.33a, b}$$

The first equation states, exactly as (2.31c), that the curvature of the normal section of the membrane must vanish along the edge curve. Since this is possible only for parabolic and hyperbolic points, we conclude that the membrane surface must have parabolic or hyperbolic character at least along the edge. Since the torsion of the edge curve can assume real values only for $K \leqq 0$, this follows also directly from (2.33b). If two cables meet at a corner, then the curvature of the normal section must vanish along both tangent vectors $\mathfrak{t}_a$ and $\mathfrak{t}_b$ (Figure 2.7) defined by the directions of the cables at the corner. This means that the corner is in every case a hyperbolic point.

Figure 2.7

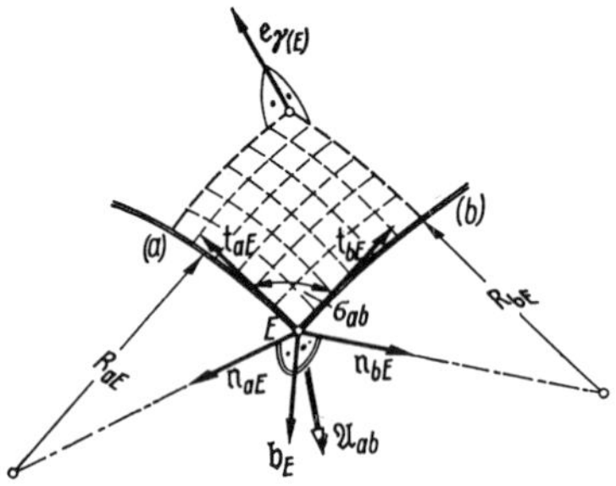

In summary, we learn that the membrane-edge curves satisfying the conditions of an edge-cable boundary must be so-called asymptotic curves of the membrane surface, their directions being defined according to (1.16e) by

$$K_n(\varphi) = H + r_1 \cos 2\varphi - r_2 \sin 2\varphi = 0$$

or

$$\sin 2\varphi = \frac{H r_2}{r_1^2 + r_2^2}\left[1 \pm \sqrt{1 + \frac{(r_1^2 - H^2)(r_1^2 + r_2^2)}{H^2 r_2^2}}\right] \tag{2.34}$$

In addition, (2.31a, d) must be satisfied.

It is of interest to note that the hyperbolic paraboloid $z = C\,x\,y$ does not satisfy the conditions of a membrane surface stretched by cables, since in this case the curves along which the normal curvature vanishes are straight lines which do not provide a possible shape for cables.

Let us consider once more the corner where the cables meet. The tangent plane to the surface at the corner must be identical with the planes defined by tangent vectors and normals of both edge curves (a) and (b) Hence, these planes coincide at the corner (E), both edge curves having the same binormal ($\mathfrak{b}_{aE} = \mathfrak{b}_{bE} = \mathfrak{b}_E$). The reaction on the ropes is determined from the equilibrium conditions at the corner

$$\mathfrak{A}_{ab} = -(S_{aE}\,\mathfrak{t}_{aE} + S_{bE}\,\mathfrak{t}_{bE})\,. \tag{2.35}$$

In the particular case when the membrane surface is a minimum surface, i.e., for vanishing mean curvature H, the above statements reduce to the following: the curvatures of the normal sections must vanish at the edge points also in the direction perpendicular to the edge curve. At the same time, the surface torsion of the membrane becomes a maximum at the edge when proceeding along the edge curve, being equal in magnitude to the principal curvatures of the normal sections inclined to the edge curve at angles of 45° and 135°. At the meeting point of two cables the principal tensor vanishes completely for a minimum surface unless the mesh angle σ_{ab} is a right angle. In these cases the torsion of the edge cables vanishes at the corner. All this can be deduced from Figure 1.4, taking into account that for $H = 0$ the center of the circle lies at the origin.

We shall now consider some particular examples of small deformations.

3 AXISYMMETRICAL MEMBRANES

3.1. General Observations

According to Figure 3.1, we introducc as orthogonal parametric curves the meridians $\varphi = \text{const}$ and the latitude circles $\vartheta = \text{const}$, where ϑ is the angle of inclination of the surface normal to the axis of symmetry of the membrane. The direction vectors are then

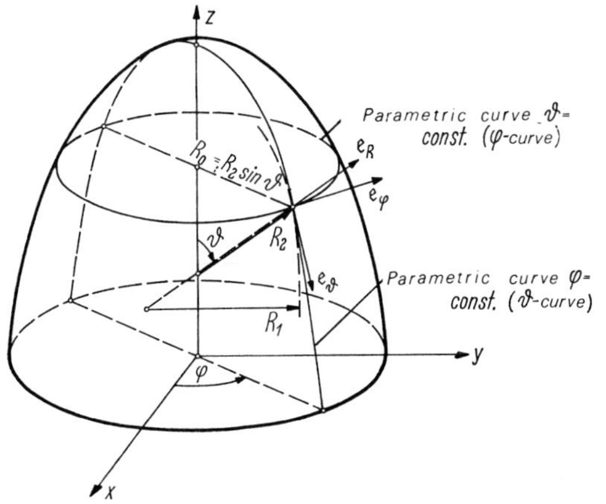

Figure 3.1

expressed in components of a Cartesian coordinate system as follows:

$$\left.\begin{aligned} \mathfrak{e}_\alpha &= \mathfrak{e}_\vartheta = \{\cos\vartheta\cos\varphi\,;\ \cos\vartheta\sin\varphi\,;\ -\sin\vartheta\}\,, \\ \mathfrak{e}_\beta &= \mathfrak{e}_\varphi = \{-\sin\varphi\,;\ \cos\varphi\,;\ 0\}\,,\quad \mathfrak{e}_\alpha\,\mathfrak{e}_\beta = 0\,, \\ \mathfrak{e}_\gamma &= \mathfrak{e}_R = \mathfrak{e}_\vartheta\times\mathfrak{e}_\varphi = \{\sin\vartheta\cos\varphi\,;\ \sin\vartheta\sin\varphi\,;\ \cos\vartheta\} \end{aligned}\right\} \quad (3.1)$$

Let $R_1 = R_1(\vartheta)$ be a radius of curvature lying in a plane of principal curvature* $\varphi = \text{const}$, and denote the radius of transverse curvature by $R_2(\vartheta)$. Then (Figure 3.2) we have

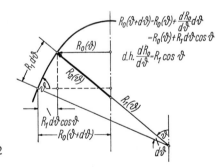

Figure 3.2

$$R_0 = R_2\sin\vartheta\,,\quad \frac{d\,R_0}{d\,\vartheta} = \frac{d}{d\,\vartheta}(R_2\sin\vartheta) = R_1\cos\vartheta \quad (3.2)$$

where $R_0(\vartheta)$ is thc radius of the latitude circle. Furthermore

$$d\,s_\vartheta = R_1(\vartheta)\,d\,\vartheta\,,\ d\,s_\varphi = R_0(\vartheta)\,d\,\varphi = R_2(\vartheta)\sin\vartheta\,d\,\varphi\,, \quad (3.3a)$$

Since by (1.3) $d\,s_\alpha = \sqrt{g_{\alpha\alpha}}\,d\,\alpha$ and $d\,s_\beta = \sqrt{g_{\beta\beta}}\,d\,\beta$, we obtain by substituting $\alpha = \vartheta$ and $\beta = \varphi$:

$$\sqrt{g_{\alpha\alpha}} = R_1(\vartheta)\,,\quad \sqrt{g_{\beta\beta}} = R_0(\vartheta) = R_2(\vartheta)\sin\vartheta\,. \quad (3.3b)$$

We can then determine the components of the rotation vectors in the basic system remembering that

$$\frac{\partial\,\mathfrak{e}_\gamma}{\partial\,s_\alpha} = \frac{\partial\,\mathfrak{e}_R}{\partial\,s_\vartheta} = \frac{1}{R_1}\frac{\partial\,\mathfrak{e}_R}{\partial\,\vartheta} = \frac{1}{R_1}\{\cos\vartheta\cos\varphi\,;\ \cos\vartheta\sin\varphi\,;\ -\sin\vartheta\}$$

$$\frac{\partial\,\mathfrak{e}_\gamma}{\partial\,s_\beta} = \frac{\partial\,\mathfrak{e}_R}{\partial\,s_\varphi} = \frac{1}{R_2\sin\vartheta}\frac{\partial\,\mathfrak{e}_R}{\partial\,\varphi} = \frac{1}{R_2\sin\vartheta}\times$$
$$\times\{-\sin\vartheta\sin\varphi\,;\ \sin\vartheta\cos\varphi\,;\ 0\}$$

and using (1.21):

$$\left.\begin{aligned} &\omega_\alpha^{(\alpha)} = -\,\omega_\beta^{(\beta)} = \omega_\vartheta^{(\vartheta)} = -\,\omega_\varphi^{(\varphi)} = 0\,, \\ &\omega_\beta^{(\alpha)} = \omega_\varphi^{(\vartheta)} = \frac{1}{R_1}\,,\quad \omega_\gamma^{(\alpha)} = \omega_R^{(\vartheta)} = 0\,, \\ &\omega_\alpha^{(\beta)} = \omega_\vartheta^{(\varphi)} = -\frac{1}{R_2}\,,\quad \omega_\gamma^{(\beta)} = \omega_R^{(\varphi)} = \frac{1}{R_2}\operatorname{ctg}\vartheta\,. \end{aligned}\right\} \quad (3.3c)$$

The vectors of the membrane displacements $\mathfrak{v}$ and the surface load $\mathfrak{p}$ are represented in the following form:

$$\mathfrak{v} = v_\vartheta\,\mathfrak{e}_\vartheta + v_\varphi\,\mathfrak{e}_\varphi + v_R\,\mathfrak{e}_R\,,\quad \mathfrak{p} = p_\vartheta\,\mathfrak{e}_\vartheta + p_\varphi\,\mathfrak{e}_\varphi + p_R\,\mathfrak{e}_R \quad (3.4)$$

3.2 Solution of the Equilibrium Problem

The equilibrium conditions for the membrane forces are by (2.5 a-c), (3.3)

$$\left.\begin{aligned} &\frac{\partial}{\partial\,\vartheta}(R_2\sin\vartheta\,n_\vartheta) + \frac{\partial}{\partial\,\varphi}(R_1\,n_{\vartheta\varphi}) - R_1\cos\vartheta\,n_\varphi + \\ &\qquad + R_1\,R_2\sin\vartheta\,p_\vartheta = 0\,, \\ &\frac{\partial}{\partial\,\vartheta}(R_2\sin\vartheta\,n_{\vartheta\varphi}) + \frac{\partial}{\partial\,\varphi}(R_1\,n_\varphi) + R_1\cos\vartheta\,n_{\vartheta\varphi} + \\ &\qquad + R_1\,R_2\sin\vartheta\,p_\varphi = 0\,, \\ &\frac{n_\vartheta}{R_1} + \frac{n_\varphi}{R_2} = p_R\,. \end{aligned}\right\} \quad (3.5\text{a-c})$$

To solve this system we eliminate the membrane force n_φ by means of (3.5c):

$$n_\varphi = R_2\,p_R - \frac{R_2}{R_1}\,n_\vartheta \quad (3.6a)$$

Inserting this value into (3.5a) and (3.5b) we obtain*

$$\left.\begin{aligned} &\frac{1}{\sin\vartheta}\frac{\partial}{\partial\,\vartheta}(R_2\sin^2\vartheta\,n_\vartheta) + \frac{\partial}{\partial\,\varphi}(R_1\,n_{\vartheta\varphi}) = \\ &\qquad = R_1\,R_2\,(p_R\cos\vartheta - p_\vartheta\sin\vartheta)\,, \\ &\frac{1}{R_2\sin\vartheta}\frac{\partial}{\partial\,\vartheta}\left((R_2\sin\vartheta)^2\,n_{\varphi\vartheta}\right) - \frac{\partial}{\partial\,\varphi}(R_2\,n_\vartheta) = \\ &\qquad = -\,R_1\,R_2\left(\frac{\partial\,p_R}{\partial\,\varphi} + p_\varphi\sin\vartheta\right) \end{aligned}\right\} \quad (3.6\text{b,c})$$

The equilibrium problem of the axisymmetrical membrane can, as

* Since (1.18e) is satisfied, the parametric curves are curves of principal curvature.

* We also made use here of (3.2).

in the case of a certain antimetrical loading, be reduced to a single integration. This provides a relatively simple solution for the cases in which the loads determine the membrane dimensions.

3.2.1 *Axisymmetrical Loading*

In this case all magnitudes depend only on ϑ, and we obtain from (3.6b, c) after integration

$$n_\vartheta(\vartheta) = \frac{1}{R_2 \sin^2\vartheta}\left[\int\limits_{\chi=0}^{\vartheta} R_1(\chi)\, R_2(\chi) \sin\chi \left(p_R(\chi)\cos\chi - \right.\right.$$

$$\left.\left. - p_\vartheta(\chi)\sin\chi\right) d\chi + C_1\right], \qquad (3.7a,b)$$

$$n_{\vartheta\varphi}(\vartheta) = -\frac{1}{R_2{}^2 \sin^2\vartheta}\left[\int\limits_{\chi=0}^{\vartheta} p_\varphi(\chi)\, R_1(\chi)\, R_2{}^2(\chi)\sin^2\chi\, d\chi + C_2\right],$$

The integration constants C_1 and C_2 are obtained from the equilibrium conditions for the forces and the moments about the axis of symmetry, by considering a "cap" cut off by a section $z =$ const:

$$C_1 = \frac{P_{z0}}{2\pi}, \quad C_2 = \frac{M_{z0}}{2\pi} \qquad (3.7c)$$

Here P_{z0} and M_{z0} denote, respectively, an axial force acting at the apex $\vartheta = 0$ and a torque acting about the z-axis. Such singular

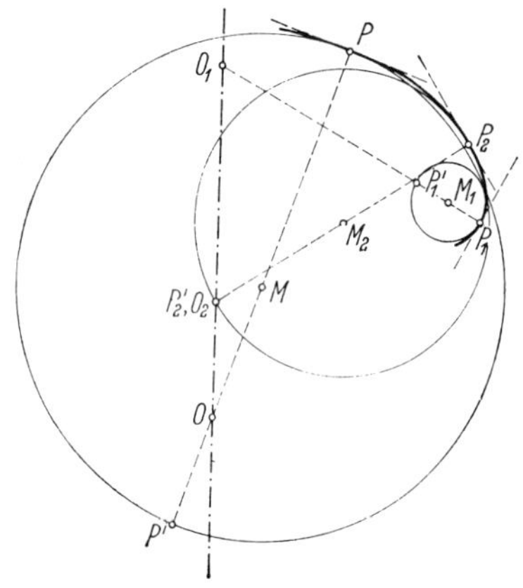

Figure 3.3

concentrated loads cause infinite sectional loads at the point of action, and should therefore, as far as possible, be avoided in membrane structures. We note that (3.7a, b) can be written in simplified form

$$n_\vartheta(\vartheta) = \frac{P_z(\vartheta)}{F(\vartheta)\sin\vartheta}, \quad n_{\vartheta\varphi}(\vartheta) = -\frac{M_z(\vartheta)}{W_p(\vartheta)} \qquad (3.7d)$$

where $P_z(\vartheta)$ and $M_z(\vartheta)$ are the external loads acting on the cap cut off at height $z(\vartheta)$, and

$$F(\vartheta) = 2\pi R_0(\vartheta), \quad W_p(\vartheta) = 2\pi R_0{}^2(\vartheta) \qquad (3.7e)$$

are, respectively, the circumference and the polar modulus of section of the latitude circle of the section. We have thus arrived at a formal identity with the expressions for the longitudinal tensile and torsional shearing stresses known from the elementary theory of a thin-walled rod having a variable circular section. This permits us to consider the axisymmetrical envelope as a rod, the axis of symmetry being the rod axis. We shall see that this is true also in the case of a simple antimetrical load. The second membrane force n_φ is obtained directly from (3.6a). We shall now consider some cases of symmetrical loading.

a) Loading by internal pressure p

We obtain from (3.7) and (3.6a) for $p_\vartheta = p_\varphi = 0$, $p_R = p$

$$n_{\vartheta p} = \frac{p}{R_2\sin^2\vartheta}\int\limits_{\chi=0}^{\vartheta} R_2\sin\chi \cdot R_1\cos\chi\, d\chi =$$

$$= \frac{p}{R_2\sin^2\vartheta}\int\limits_{\chi=0}^{\vartheta} R_2\sin\chi \frac{d}{d\chi}(R_2\sin\chi)\, d\chi =$$

$$= \frac{p}{2R_2\sin^2\vartheta}\int\limits_{\chi=0}^{\vartheta} \frac{d}{d\chi}(R_2\sin\chi)^2\, d\chi = \frac{p\,R_2}{2}, \qquad (3.8a,b)$$

$$n_{\varphi p} = R_2\, p - \frac{R_2}{R_1} n_{\vartheta p} = p\, R_2\left[1 - \frac{R_2}{2R_1}\right].$$

We conclude from (3.8a, b) that despite the internal pressure, $n_{\varphi p} < 0$ is possible, so that folds may appear in the meridianal direction. The admissible shapes (which must sustain the internal pressure without appearance of folds) must therefore satisfy the inequality

$$2R_1 > R_2 \qquad (3.8c)$$

The following simple rule ensures fulfilment of this condition (Figure 3.3): Draw the normal to the meridian at a point P to intersect the axis of symmetry at 0. The point 0 must always lie inside the circle of curvature which touches the meridian at P. Point P_1 in Figure 3.3 is under tangential compressive stresses, since $\overline{P_1P_1'} < \overline{P_1 0_1}$; at $P_2, n_{\varphi p} = 0$, since here $\overline{P_2P_2'} = \overline{P_2 0_2}$; all points above P_2 are under tangential tensile stresses since for them $\overline{PP'} > \overline{P0}$.

We obtain the meridan $z_0 = z_0(r)$ of the axisymmetrical surface, in which the internal pressure causes all tangential stresses n_φ to vanish, from

$$2R_1 - R_2 = 0,$$

i.e., since

$$R_1 = -(1 + z'^2)^{3/2}/z'', \quad R_2 = r/\sin\vartheta = -r\sqrt{1+z'^2}/z',$$

where the primes denote differentiation with respect to r, we obtain

$$r\, z_0'' - 2z_0'(1 + z_0'^2) = 0,$$

for which the solution consists of elliptic integrals.

As an example, let us consider the stresses due to internal pressure in an elliptical axisymmetrical membrane (Figure 3.4). Since

$$R_1 = \frac{1}{ab^4}\sqrt{[b^4 + (a^2 - b^2)z^2]^3},$$

$$R_2 = \frac{a}{b^2}\sqrt{b^4 + (a^2 - b^2)z^2}$$

we obtain for the sectional loads in the membrane

$$n_\vartheta = \frac{pa}{2b^2}\sqrt{b^4 + (a^2 - b^2)z^2},$$

$$n_\varphi = \frac{pa}{b^2}\sqrt{b^4 + (a^2 - b^2)z^2}\left[1 - \frac{a^2b^2}{2[b^4 + (a^2 - b^2)z^2]}\right]. \qquad (3.8d)$$

Therefore

$$2\,\frac{R_1}{R_2} = 2\,\frac{b^4 + (a^2 - b^2)\,z^2}{a^2\,b^2} > 1$$

is the necessary condition that n_φ be always positive, i.e., that no folds appear along the meridians. This is always true for $b > a$ (cigar-shaped membrane). The maximum stresses appear at $z = 0$, i.e., on the circumference of the section which divides the cigar into

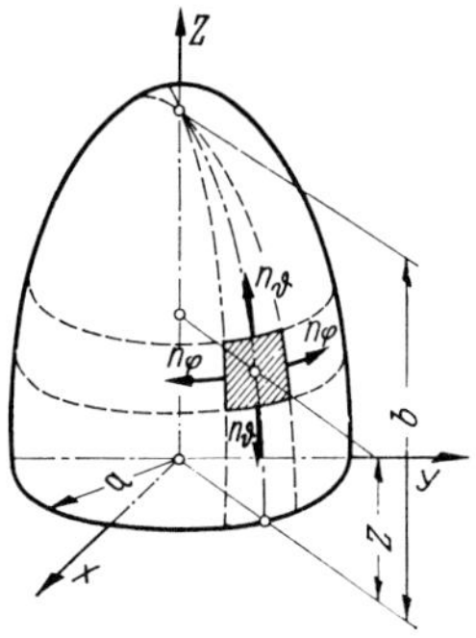

Figure 3.4

two halves:

$$n_{\vartheta\,\max} = \frac{p\,a}{2}\,, \quad n_{\varphi\,\max} = p\,a\left[1 - \frac{1}{2}\left(\frac{a}{b}\right)^2\right]. \tag{3.8e}$$

Because $n_{\varphi\max} > n_{\vartheta\max}$, the maximum tangential load determines the dimensions of the membrane.

When $b < a$ (lens-shaped membrane), folds are only absent when $b > a/\sqrt{2} = 0.7071\,a$. For $b = 0.7071\,a$, the tangential stresses vanish in the section which divides the membrane into halves, and folds appear. A lens-shaped membrane should therefore not be used as a pneumatic structure.

b. Loading by dead weight g

Let the dead weight be $g = \gamma\,h$ per unit surface area (γ = specific weight of membrane material, h = membrane thickness). Then, by Figure 3.5:

$$p_\vartheta = g \sin\vartheta\,, \quad p_\varphi = 0\,, \quad p_R = -\,g\cos\vartheta\,, \tag{3.9}$$

and we obtain from (3.7) and (3.6a)

$$n_{\vartheta g} = -\frac{g}{R_2 \sin^2\vartheta}\int_{\chi=0}^{\vartheta} R_1(\chi)\,R_2(\chi)\sin\chi\,d\chi\,,$$

$$n_{\varphi g} = -\,g\,R_2\cos\vartheta - \frac{R_2}{R_1}\,n_{\vartheta g}\,. \tag{3.10a, b}$$

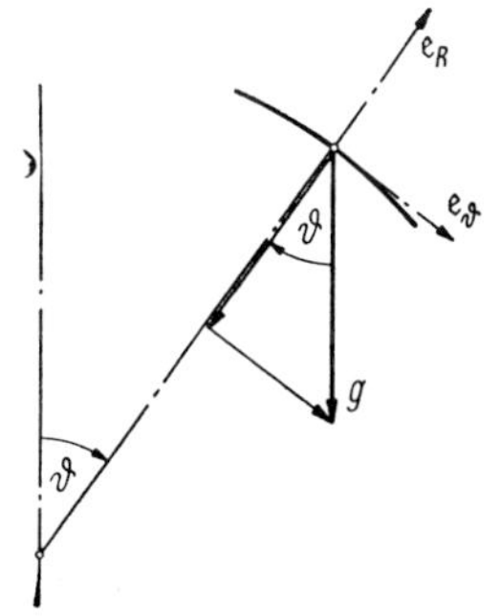

Figure 3.5

c. Symmetrical snow load

Approximating the standard snow-load distribution according to DIN 1055, p. 5, by a vertical load per unit ground area

$$p_{zs}' = s \cdot \cos\vartheta\,, \quad 0 \leqq \vartheta \leqq \frac{\pi}{2} \tag{3.11a}$$

where s = 75 kg/m^2, we obtain the vertical snow load per unit surface area of the membrane:

$$p_s = p_{zs}'\cos\vartheta = s \cdot \cos^2\vartheta\,, \qquad 0 \leqq \vartheta \leqq \frac{\pi}{2}\,, \tag{3.11b}$$

in which the components are

$$p_\vartheta = p_s \sin\vartheta = s \cdot \sin\vartheta\cos^2\vartheta\,, \quad p_\varphi = 0\,,$$

$$p_R = -\,p_s\cos\vartheta = -\,s\cos^3\vartheta\,, \qquad 0 \leqq \vartheta \leqq \frac{\pi}{2} \tag{3.11c, d}$$

We have to distinguish between two cases, depending on the angle ϑ_0, which is half the angle subtended by the membrane. For $\vartheta_0 \leqq \pi/2$ the snow acts on the entire membrane.

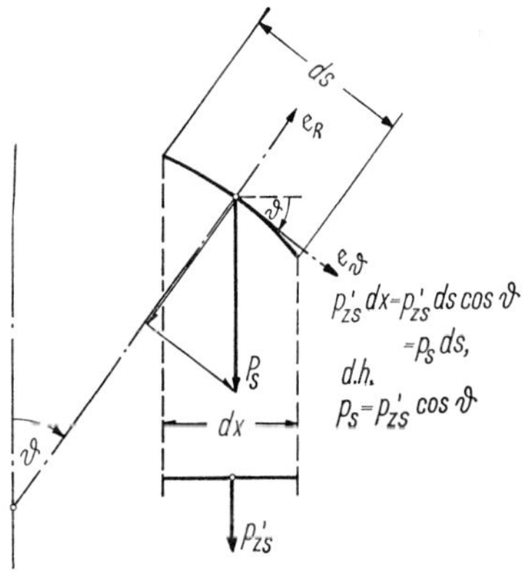

Figure 3.6

Substituting (3.11c, d) in (3.7) and (3.6a), we obtain

$$n_{\vartheta_{s1}} = -\frac{s}{R_2\sin^2\vartheta}\int_{\chi=0}^{\vartheta} R_1(\chi)\,R_2(\chi)\sin\chi\cos^2\chi\,d\chi\,,$$

$$n_{\varphi_{s1}} = -\,s\,R_2\cos^3\vartheta - \frac{R_2}{R_1}\,n_{\vartheta_{s1}}\,, \quad \vartheta \leqq \vartheta_0 \leqq \frac{\pi}{2} \tag{3.12a, b}$$

for $\vartheta_0 > \pi/2$, the snow acts only on the upper part of the load $0 \leqq \vartheta \leqq \pi/2$, so that (3.12a, b) applies only to this region. For ($\vartheta > \pi/2$) the snow load does not affect the dome, so that in this region $p_\vartheta = p_\varphi = p_R = 0$. We then obtain from (3.7), since the integrand differs from zero only for $0 \leqq \vartheta \leqq \pi/2$:

$$n_{\vartheta_{s1}} = -\frac{s}{R_2\sin^2\vartheta}\int_0^{\pi/2} R_1(\chi)\,R_2(\chi)\sin\chi\cos^2\chi\,d\chi =$$

$$= \frac{n_{\vartheta_{s1}}\left(\frac{\pi}{2}\right)R_2\left(\frac{\pi}{2}\right)}{R_2(\vartheta)\sin^2\vartheta}\,, \quad \frac{\pi}{2} \leqq \vartheta \leqq \vartheta_0 \tag{3.13a}$$

By (3.6a), putting $p_R = 0$:

$$n_{\varphi_{s1}} = -\frac{R_2}{R_1} n_{\vartheta_{s1}}, \quad \frac{\pi}{2} \leq \vartheta \leq \vartheta_0 \tag{3.13b}$$

d. Loading due to snow accumulation as in Figure 3.7

In contrast to the previous example, the snow load given by

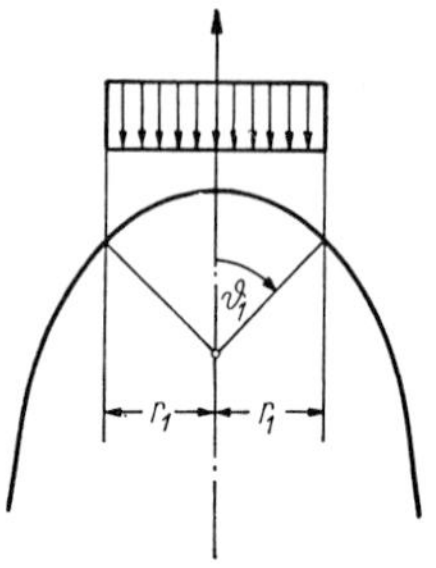

Figure 3.7

(3.11,cd) acts only in the region $0 \leq \vartheta \leq \vartheta_1$. Accordingly

$$\left.\begin{aligned} n_{\vartheta_{s2}} &= -\frac{s}{R_2 \sin^2 \vartheta} \int\limits_{\chi=0}^{\vartheta} R_1(\chi) R_2(\chi) \sin\chi \cos^2\chi \, d\chi, \\ n_{\varphi_{s2}} &= -s R_2 \cos^3 \vartheta - \frac{R_2}{R_1} n_{\vartheta_{s2}}, \end{aligned}\right\} \quad 0 \leq \vartheta \leq \vartheta_1 \tag{3.14a, b}$$

and

$$\left.\begin{aligned} n_{\vartheta_{s2}} &= -\frac{s}{R_2 \sin^2 \vartheta} \int\limits_{\chi=0}^{\vartheta_1} R_1(\chi) R_2(\chi) \sin\chi \cos^2\chi \, d\chi = \\ &= \frac{n_{\vartheta_{s2}}(\vartheta_1) \cdot R_2(\vartheta_1) \sin^2 \vartheta_1}{R_2(\vartheta) \sin^2 \vartheta}, \\ n_{\varphi_{s2}} &= -\frac{R_2}{R_1} n_{\vartheta_{s2}}. \end{aligned}\right\} \quad \vartheta \geq \vartheta_1 \tag{3.14c, d}$$

3.2.2 *Simple Antimetrical Loading*

When the load is given in the form

$$\begin{aligned} \mathfrak{p}(\vartheta, \varphi) &= p_\vartheta(\vartheta, \varphi) \, \mathfrak{e}_\vartheta + p_\varphi(\vartheta, \varphi) \, \mathfrak{e}_\varphi + p_R(\vartheta, \varphi) \, \mathfrak{e}_R = \\ &= \bar{p}_\vartheta(\vartheta) \cos\varphi \, \mathfrak{e}_\vartheta + \bar{p}_\varphi(\vartheta) \sin\varphi \, \mathfrak{e}_\varphi + \bar{p}_R(\vartheta) \cos\varphi \, \mathfrak{e}_R \end{aligned} \tag{3.15a}$$

we can solve the equilibrium problem by putting

$$\begin{aligned} n_\vartheta(\vartheta, \varphi) &= f_\vartheta(\vartheta) \cos\varphi, \quad n_\varphi(\vartheta, \varphi) = f_\varphi(\vartheta) \cos\varphi, \\ n_{\vartheta\varphi}(\vartheta, \varphi) &= f_{\vartheta\varphi}(\vartheta) \sin\varphi. \end{aligned} \tag{3.15b}$$

This can be proved by substituting (3.15a, b) in (3.6), which then reduces to a system of ordinary differential equations for the function $f(\vartheta)$.
By the assumption (3.15) we express the fact that a load, antimetrical with respect to the (y, z) plane, gives rise to membrane forces n_φ and n_ϑ, also antimetrical with respect to the (y, z) plane, and shearing forces $n_{\vartheta\varphi}$, symmetrical with respect to this plane. We shall replace the differential equation with integral expressions for the determination of the sectional loads.

These are obtained from the equilibrium conditions applied to appropriately cut-out parts of the membrane. Let us cut the membrane by a horizontal plane $z = z(\vartheta)$ (Figure 3.8). Normal and

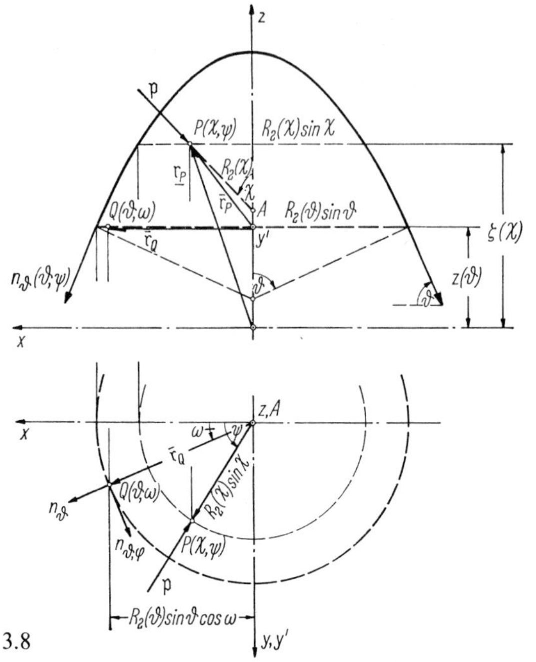

Figure 3.8

shearing forces n_ϑ and $n_{\vartheta\varphi}$ will then act at the boundary of the cut-off cap. We can obtain n_ϑ directly by equating to zero the sum of the moments about the y'-axis which is parallel to the y axis. When n_ϑ is known, we obtain the shearing force $n_{\vartheta\varphi}$ by equating to zero the sum of all forces acting in the x-direction. The other normal force n_φ is then found from (3.6a).
We first determine the resultant of the external load acting on the cap, as well as the moment due to it about the intersection A of the y'-axis and the axis of symmetry (z-axis).
The load acting at the surface point $P(\chi, \psi)$ is

$$\begin{aligned} \mathfrak{p}(\chi, \psi) &= (\mathfrak{e}_x \mathfrak{p}) \, \mathfrak{e}_x + (\mathfrak{e}_y \mathfrak{p}) \, \mathfrak{e}_y + (\mathfrak{e}_z \mathfrak{p}) \, \mathfrak{e}_z = \\ &= [(\bar{p}_\vartheta(\chi) \cos\chi + \bar{p}_R(\chi) \sin\chi) \cos^2\psi - \bar{p}_\varphi(\chi) \sin^2\psi] \, \mathfrak{e}_x + \\ &+ [\bar{p}_\vartheta(\chi) \cos\chi + \bar{p}_\varphi(\chi) + \bar{p}_R(\chi) \sin\chi] \sin\psi \cos\psi \, \mathfrak{e}_y + \\ &+ [-\bar{p}_\vartheta(\chi) \sin\chi + \bar{p}_R(\chi) \cos\chi] \cos\psi \, \mathfrak{e}_z \end{aligned} \tag{3.16a}$$

The associated surface element is

$$dF(\chi, \psi) = R_1(\chi) R_2(\chi) \sin\chi \, d\chi \, d\psi \tag{3.16b}$$

The elementary force acting at $P(\chi, \psi)$ is

$$d\mathfrak{P}_p = \mathfrak{p} \, dF, \tag{3.16c}$$

Integrating over the surface of the cut-off cap, we obtain the resultant of the external load acting on the cap:

$$\mathfrak{P}_p(\vartheta) = \int\limits_{\psi=0}^{2\pi} \int\limits_{\chi=0}^{\vartheta} d\mathfrak{P}_p = \int\limits_{\psi=0}^{2\pi} \int\limits_{\chi=0}^{\vartheta} \mathfrak{p}(\chi, \psi) \, dF. \tag{3.16d}$$

Substituting (3.16a, b) for $\mathfrak{p}$ and dF, noting that

$$\int_{\psi=0}^{2\pi} \sin\psi\cos\psi\, d\psi = \int_0^{2\pi} \cos\psi\, d\psi = 0\,, \qquad \int_{\psi=0}^{2\pi} \sin^2\psi\, d\psi = \int_0^{2\pi} \cos^2\psi\, d\psi = \pi \tag{3.17}$$

and integrating over ψ, we obtain

$$\mathfrak{P}_p(\vartheta) = \mathfrak{e}_x \pi \int_{\chi=0}^{\vartheta} (\bar{p}_\vartheta \cos\chi - \bar{p}_\varphi + \bar{p}_R \sin\chi)\, R_1 R_2 \sin\chi\, d\chi = \mathfrak{e}_x Q_{px}(\vartheta)\,. \tag{3.18}$$

The resultant has therefore only a component in the x-direction. Since the load defined by (3.15a) is symmetrical with respect to the x, z plane, the resultant (3.18) lies in this plane. Only moments about the y'-axis are thus possible, when we consider point A. The position vector of point $P(\chi, \psi)$ in relation to point A is

$$\bar{\mathfrak{r}}_P(\chi, \psi, \vartheta) = \mathfrak{r}_P(\chi, \psi) - z(\vartheta)\,\mathfrak{e}_z = R_2(\chi)\sin\chi\,(\mathfrak{e}_x\cos\psi + \mathfrak{e}_y\sin\psi) + [\zeta(\chi) - z(\vartheta)]\,\mathfrak{e}_z \tag{3.19a}$$

The moment about point A due to the elementary force $d\,\mathfrak{P}_p$ is

$$d\,\mathfrak{M}_{Ap} = \bar{\mathfrak{r}}_p \times d\,\mathfrak{P}_p$$

and its component about the y'-axis

$$d\,M_{Apy'} = \mathfrak{e}_y\, d\,\mathfrak{M}_{Ap} = [\mathfrak{e}_y\, \bar{\mathfrak{r}}_P\, d\,\mathfrak{P}_p] = [\mathfrak{e}_y\, \bar{\mathfrak{r}}_P\, \mathfrak{p}]\, dF = (-\bar{r}_{Px}\, p_z + \bar{r}_{Pz}\, p_x)\, dF \tag{3.19b}$$

where the square brackets denote a scalar triple product. Integrating over the surface of the cut-off cap, we obtain the moment due to the external load

$$M_{py}(\vartheta) = \int_{\psi=0}^{2\pi} \int_{\chi=0}^{\vartheta} d\,M_{Apy'}\,. \tag{3.19c}$$

Substituting (3.19a) and (3.19a, b), integrating over ψ, and taking account of (3.17), we obtain

$$M_{py}(\vartheta) = \pi \Big[\int_{\chi=0}^{\vartheta} (\bar{p}_\vartheta \sin\chi - \bar{p}_R \cos\chi)\, R_1 R_2^2 \sin^2\chi\, d\chi + \int_{\chi=0}^{\vartheta} (\bar{p}_\vartheta\cos\chi - \bar{p}_\varphi + \bar{p}_R \sin\chi)\,[\zeta(\chi) - z(\vartheta)]\, R_1 R_2 \sin\chi\, d\chi \Big]. \tag{3.20}$$

To obtain the force acting on the cap and the moments about point A due to the sectional loads, we consider point $Q(\vartheta, \omega)$ lying on the latitude circle at height $z(\vartheta)$.
The line element is

$$d\,s_\omega = R_2(\vartheta)\sin\vartheta\, d\omega \tag{3.21a}$$

The membrane loads are

$$n_\vartheta(\vartheta, \omega) = f_\vartheta(\vartheta)\cos\omega\,, \quad n_{\vartheta\varphi}(\vartheta, \omega) = f_{\vartheta\varphi}(\vartheta)\sin\omega$$

The corresponding elementary force is

$$\begin{aligned} d\,\mathfrak{P}_n &= (n_\vartheta(\vartheta,\omega)\,\mathfrak{e}_\vartheta(\vartheta,\omega) + n_{\vartheta\varphi}(\vartheta,\omega)\,\mathfrak{e}_\varphi(\vartheta,\omega))\, d\,s_\omega = \\ &= (f_\vartheta(\vartheta)\cos\vartheta\cos^2\omega - f_{\vartheta\varphi}(\vartheta)\sin^2\omega)\, R_2(\vartheta)\sin\vartheta\, d\omega\, \mathfrak{e}_x + \\ &+ (f_\vartheta(\vartheta)\cos\vartheta + f_{\vartheta\varphi}(\vartheta))\, R_2(\vartheta)\sin\vartheta\sin\omega\cos\omega\, d\omega\, \mathfrak{e}_y - \\ &- f_\vartheta(\vartheta)\, R_2(\vartheta)\sin^2\vartheta\cos\omega\, \mathfrak{e}_z \end{aligned} \tag{3.21b}$$

Integrating along the circumference of the section and taking account of (3.17), we obtain the resultant sectional load

$$\mathfrak{P}_n(\vartheta) = \int_{\omega=0}^{2\pi} d\,\mathfrak{P}_n = \pi\big(f_\vartheta(\vartheta)\cos\vartheta - f_{\vartheta\varphi}(\vartheta)\big)\, R_2 \sin\vartheta\, \mathfrak{e}_x\,, \tag{3.21c}$$

which must also lie in the x, z plane, since the sectional loads acting on the cap are symmetrical with respect to this plane. The moment due to these loads must therefore act about the y' axis. The position vector of point $Q(\vartheta, \omega)$ with respect to A is

$$\bar{\mathfrak{r}}_Q(\vartheta, \omega) = R_2(\vartheta)\sin\vartheta\,(\mathfrak{e}_x\cos\omega + \mathfrak{e}_y\sin\omega)\,. \tag{3.22a}$$

The elementary moment due to the sectional load is therefore

$$d\,\mathfrak{M}_{An} = \bar{\mathfrak{r}}_Q \times d\,\mathfrak{P}_n$$

and its component about the y'-axis

$$d\,M_{Any'} = \mathfrak{e}_y\, d\,\mathfrak{M}_{An} = [\mathfrak{e}_y\, \bar{\mathfrak{r}}_Q\, d\,\mathfrak{P}_n] = (-\bar{r}_{Qx}\, d\,P_{nz} + \bar{r}_{QZ}\, d\,P_{nx}) = -\bar{r}_{Qx}\, d\,P_{nz}\,. \tag{3.22b}$$

Substituting (3.21b) and (3.22a), integrating along the circumference of the section, and taking into account (3.17), we obtain

$$M_{ny}(\vartheta) = \int_{\omega=0}^{2\pi} d\,M_{Any'} = \pi f_\vartheta(\vartheta)\, R_2^2(\vartheta)\sin^3\vartheta = \frac{f_\vartheta}{R_2}\,\bar{J}_y \tag{3.23a}$$

where

$$\bar{J}_y(\vartheta) = \pi R_2^3(\vartheta)\sin^3\vartheta = \pi R_0^3(\vartheta) \tag{3.23b}$$

is the moment of inertia of the latitude circle about the y'-axis.
We have thus determined all loads acting on the cap. The equilibrium condition for the moments is

$$\Sigma M_{Ay'} = 0 = M_{py}(\vartheta) + M_{ny}(\vartheta)\,.$$

Substituting from (3.23a)

$$f_\vartheta(\vartheta) = -\frac{M_{py}(\vartheta)}{\bar{J}_y(\vartheta)}\, R_2(\vartheta) \tag{3.24a}$$

and writing

$$x = R_0(\vartheta)\cos\varphi = R_2(\vartheta)\sin\vartheta\cos\varphi \tag{3.24b}$$

for the distance from the y'-axis of a point on the latitude circle, we obtain, in accordance with (3.15b)

$$n_\vartheta(\vartheta, x) = -\frac{M_{py}(\vartheta)}{\bar{J}_y(\vartheta)}\frac{R_2\sin\vartheta}{\sin\vartheta}\cos\varphi = -\frac{1}{\sin\vartheta}\frac{M_{py}(\vartheta)}{\bar{J}_y(\vartheta)}\, x\,. \tag{3.24c}$$

This expression is in complete agreement with the corresponding expression for the normal bending stresses, known from the elementary theory of the bending of a thin-walled beam having a variable circular cross section. The equilibrium condition for the forces

$$\Sigma\,\mathfrak{P} = \mathfrak{P}_p(\vartheta) + \mathfrak{P}_n(\vartheta) = 0$$

yields

$$f_{\vartheta\varphi}(\vartheta) = f_\vartheta(\vartheta)\cos\vartheta + \frac{Q_{px}(\vartheta)}{\pi R_2(\vartheta)\sin\vartheta} \tag{3.25a}$$

from which we obtain, in accordance with (3.15b),

$$n_{\vartheta\varphi} = f_{\vartheta\varphi}(\vartheta)\sin\varphi = \left(f_\vartheta\cos\vartheta + \frac{Q_{px}}{\pi R_2\sin\vartheta}\right)\sin\varphi\,. \tag{3.25b}$$

A reduction to the simple expressions (3.24) and (3.25) is impossible in the general case when the load is given by

$$\mathfrak{p} = \mathfrak{p}_k = \bar{p}_{\vartheta k}(\vartheta)\cos k\varphi\,\mathfrak{e}_\vartheta + \bar{p}_{\varphi k}(\vartheta)\sin k\varphi\,\mathfrak{e}_\varphi + \bar{p}_{Rk}(\vartheta)\cos k\varphi\,\mathfrak{e}_R\,, \quad k = 2, 3 \ldots \tag{3.26a}$$

since the sectional loads are then given in the form

$$n_{\vartheta k} = f_{\vartheta k}(\vartheta)\cos k\varphi\,, \quad n_{\vartheta\varphi k} = f_{\vartheta\varphi k}(\vartheta)\sin k\varphi\,, \quad n_{\varphi k} = f_{\varphi k}(\vartheta)\cos k\varphi \tag{3.26b}$$

in which case the linear law (3.24c) no longer applies. However, when expanding the expression for the load in a trigonometrical series, the amplitudes $\bar{p}_k(\vartheta)$ decrease rapidly with increasing k and (3.7d, e), (3.24), and (3.25) can be applied also to more general cases, where the loading is neither axisymmetrical nor simply antimetrical. Good approximations are obtained by resolving the load into axisymmetrical and antimetrical parts and applying the above formulas. In particular, the meridianal forces are computed according to the theory of the bending of beams by considering the membrane as a rod extending in the direction of the axis of symmetry.

The exact solution for an arbitrary load, expanded according to (3.26a) in trigonometrical series, leads to a system of linear differential equations of the second order, which can only in certain cases be integrated in closed form (e.g., for spherical and parabolical membranes). We therefore restrict ourselves to cases of simple antimetrical loading, and shall attempt to approximate one-sided snow loads and winds by means of antimetrical and axisymmetrical loads.

a) One-sided snow load

As a first approximation we put (cf. 3.11c, d)

$$p_\vartheta = \frac{s}{2}\sin\vartheta\cos^2\vartheta\,(1+\cos\varphi)\,,\quad p_\varphi = 0\,,\qquad 0 \leqq \vartheta \leqq \pi/2$$

$$p_R = -\frac{s}{2}\cos^3\vartheta\,(1+\cos\varphi)$$

The part

$$p_\vartheta^{(1)} = \frac{s}{2}\sin\vartheta\cos^2\vartheta\,,\quad p_R^{(1)} = -\frac{s}{2}\cos^3\vartheta\,,\quad p_\varphi^{(1)} = 0$$

is axisymmetrical, giving rise to sectional loads $n_{\vartheta s1}/2$ and $n_{\varphi s1}/2$ whereas the part

$$p_\vartheta = \frac{s}{2}\sin\vartheta\cos^2\vartheta\cos\varphi\,,\quad p_R = -\frac{s}{2}\cos^3\vartheta\cos\varphi\,,\quad p_\varphi = 0$$

is simply antimetrical with respect to the y, z plane.
Putting in (3.18) and (3.20)

$$\bar{p}_\vartheta = \frac{s}{2}\sin\vartheta\cos^2\vartheta\,,\quad \bar{p}_R = -\frac{s}{2}\cos^3\vartheta\,,\quad \bar{p}_\varphi = 0$$

we obtain

$$Q_{px}(\vartheta) = 0\,,\quad M_{py}(\vartheta) = \pi\frac{s}{2}\int_0^\vartheta R_1 R_2^2 \sin^2\chi\cos^2\chi\,d\chi\,,$$

or, taking into account (3.23b), (3.24a), and (3.25a)

$$f_\vartheta = -\frac{s}{2R_2^2\sin^3\vartheta}\int_0^\vartheta R_1 R_2^2\sin^2\chi\cos^2\chi\,d\chi\,, \tag{3.27}$$

$$f_{\vartheta\varphi} = f_\vartheta\cos\vartheta\,.$$

These expressions define, in accordance with (3.15b) and (3.6a), the sectional loads due to the antimetrical part of the snow load. To these we must add the symmetrical parts $n_{\vartheta s1}/2$ and $n_{\varphi s1}/2$. We then obtain as a final result

$$n_{\vartheta s3} = -\frac{s}{2R_2(\vartheta)\sin^2\vartheta}\left(\int_{\chi=0}^{\vartheta} R_1(\chi)R_2(\chi)\sin\chi\cos^2\chi\,d\chi + \right.$$

$$\left. + \frac{\cos\varphi}{R_2(\vartheta)\sin\vartheta}\int_{\chi=0}^{\vartheta} R_1(\chi)R_2^2(\chi)\sin^2\chi\cos^2\chi\,d\chi\right),$$

$$n_{\vartheta\varphi s3} = -\frac{s\cdot\sin\varphi\cos\vartheta}{2R_2^2(\vartheta)\sin^3\vartheta}\int_{\chi=0}^{\vartheta} R_1(\chi)R_2^2(\chi)\sin^2\chi\cos^2\chi\,d\chi\,,\qquad \boxed{0 \leqq \vartheta \leqq \frac{\pi}{2}}\,,$$

$$n_{\varphi s3} = -\frac{sR_2}{2}\cos^3\vartheta\,(1+\cos\varphi) - \frac{R_2}{R_1}n_{\vartheta s3}\,. \tag{3.28a-c}$$

For $\vartheta_0 > \pi/2$, the snow load acts only on the upper part of the dome. For the lower part we then have:

$$\left.\begin{aligned} n_{\vartheta s3} &= -\frac{s}{2R_2(\vartheta)\sin^2\vartheta}\left(\int_0^{\pi/2} R_1R_2\sin\chi\cos^2\chi\,d\chi + \frac{\cos\varphi}{R_2(\vartheta)\sin\vartheta}\int_0^{\pi/2} R_1R_2^2\sin^2\chi\cos^2\chi\,d\chi\right),\\ n_{\vartheta\varphi s3} &= -\frac{s\cdot\sin\varphi\cos\vartheta}{2R_2^2(\vartheta)\sin^3\vartheta}\int_0^{\pi/2} R_1R_2^2\sin^2\chi\cos^2\chi\,d\chi\,,\qquad \boxed{\frac{\pi}{2} \leqq \vartheta \leqq \vartheta_0}\,.\\ n_{\varphi s3} &= -\frac{R_2}{R_1}n_{\vartheta s3} \end{aligned}\right\} \tag{3.28d-f}$$

b. Wind load

Let the wind pressure acting along the surface normal be w, so that

$$p_\vartheta = p_\varphi = 0\,,\quad p_R = -w\,.$$

We assume that the winds blow from the direction of the negative x-axis, and that as first approximation the wind pressure is given by

$$w = w_0 + w_1\sin\vartheta\cos\varphi \tag{3.29a}$$

where w_0 and w_1 are constants.
The constant part w_0, which constitutes an axisymmetrical load, has been discussed in 3.21.
The part

$$p_R = -w_1\sin\vartheta\cos\varphi \tag{3.29b}$$

is antimetrical with respect to the y, z plane and symmetrical with respect to the x, z plane. The corresponding sectional loads

$$\bar{p}_\vartheta = \bar{p}_\varphi = 0\,,\quad \bar{p}_R = -w_1\sin\vartheta$$

are obtained from (3.24) and (3.25). In this case

$$Q_{px} = -\pi w_1\int_{\chi=0}^{\vartheta} R_1R_2\sin^3\chi\,d\chi$$

$$M_{py} = -\pi w_1\int_{\chi=0}^{\vartheta}\left[\zeta(\chi) - z(\vartheta) - R_2(\chi)\cos\chi\right]R_1R_2\sin^3\chi\,d\chi$$

so that we find from (3.23b), (3.24a), and (3.25a):

$$f_{\vartheta_{w1}} = \frac{w_1}{R_2^2(\vartheta)\sin^3\vartheta} \int_{\chi=0}^{\vartheta} [\zeta(\chi) - z(\vartheta) - R_2(\chi)\cos\chi]\, R_1 R_2 \sin^3\chi \, d\chi \, , \qquad (3.30a)$$

$$f_{\vartheta\varphi_{w1}} = \frac{w_1}{R_2(\vartheta)\sin\vartheta}\left[\frac{\cos\vartheta}{R_2(\vartheta)\sin^2\vartheta}\int_{\chi=0}^{\vartheta}[\zeta(\chi) - z(\vartheta) - R_2(\chi)\cos\chi]\, R_1 R_2 \sin^3\chi\, d\chi - \int_{\chi=0}^{\vartheta} R_1 R_2 \sin^3\chi\, d\chi\right],$$

In accordance with (3.6a) and (3.15b) the sectional loads are

$$n_{\vartheta_{w1}} = f_{\vartheta_{w1}}\cos\varphi\, , \quad n_{\vartheta\varphi_{w1}} = f_{\vartheta\varphi_{w1}}\sin\varphi\, ,$$
$$n_{\varphi_{w1}} = -\, w_1 R_2 \sin\vartheta\cos\varphi - \frac{R_2}{R_1} n_{\vartheta_{w1}} \qquad (3.30b)$$

3.2.3 *Edge Loads Along a Parametric Curve* $\vartheta = \vartheta_c$

These must be analyzed as shown in section 6 for compound axisymmetrical shapes. We restrict our considerations to axisymmetrical and simply antimetrical edge loads (with respect to the y, z plane) (Figure 3.9):

$$n_\vartheta(\vartheta_c, \varphi) = Z(\varphi) = Z_0 + Z_1\cos\varphi\, ,$$
$$n_{\vartheta\varphi}(\vartheta_c, \varphi) = T(\varphi) = T_0 + T_1\sin\varphi\, , \qquad (3.31a)$$

These result in forces acting at A_c:

$$P_z(\vartheta_c) = \int_{\varphi=0}^{2\pi} Z(\varphi)\sin\vartheta_c R_2(\vartheta_c)\sin\vartheta_c\, d\varphi - 2\pi Z_0 R_2(\vartheta_c)\sin^2\vartheta_c\, ,$$

$$Q_x(\vartheta_c) = \int_{\varphi=0}^{2\pi}(-Z(\varphi)\cos\vartheta_c\cos\varphi + T(\varphi)\sin\varphi)\, R_2(\vartheta_c)\sin\vartheta_c\, d\varphi = -\,\pi(Z_1\cos\vartheta_c - T_1)\, R_2(\vartheta_c)\sin\vartheta_c\, ,$$

and in a torque about the axis of symmetry:

$$M_z(\vartheta_c) = -\int_{\varphi=0}^{2\pi} T(\varphi)\, R_2^2(\vartheta_c)\sin^2\vartheta_c\, d\varphi = 2\pi T_0 R_2^2(\vartheta_c)\sin^2\vartheta_c$$

as well as in a moment about A_c, i.e., for reasons of symmetry about the y-axis:

$$M_y(\vartheta_c) = -\int_{\varphi=0}^{2\pi} Z(\varphi)\sin\vartheta_c R_2^2(\vartheta_c)\sin^2\vartheta_c\cos\varphi\, d\varphi = -\,\pi Z_1 R_2^2(\vartheta_c)\sin^3\vartheta_c$$

In this case we can apply the simple formulas of 3.2.2. In a horizontal section $z = z(\vartheta)$ we obtain the "beam-section load"

$$P_z(\vartheta) = P_z(\vartheta_c)\, , \quad Q_x(\vartheta) = Q_x(\vartheta_c)\, , \quad M_z(\vartheta) = M_z(\vartheta_c)\, ,$$
$$M_y(\vartheta) = M_y(\vartheta_c) + Q_x(\vartheta_c)\,[z(\vartheta_c) - z(\vartheta)]$$

from which we determine the axisymmetrical parts of the sectional loads by (3.6a) and (3.7d):

$$n_{\vartheta 0} = Z_0\frac{R_2(\vartheta_c)\sin^2\vartheta_c}{R_2(\vartheta)\sin^2\vartheta}\, , \quad n_{\vartheta\varphi 0} = T_0\frac{R_2^2(\vartheta_c)\sin^2\vartheta_c}{R_2^2(\vartheta)\sin^2\vartheta}\, ,$$
$$n_{\varphi 0} = -\frac{R_2(\vartheta)}{R_1(\vartheta)} n_{\vartheta 0} \qquad (3.31b)$$

The antimetrical parts of the sectional loads are by (3.23b), (3.24), and (3.25)

$$f_{\vartheta 1} = \frac{R_2(\vartheta_c)\sin\vartheta_c}{R_2^2(\vartheta)\sin^3\vartheta}\left[Z_1 R_2(\vartheta_c)\sin^2\vartheta_c + (Z_1\cos\vartheta_c - T_1)\,(z(\vartheta_c) - z(\vartheta))\right]$$

$$f_{\vartheta\varphi 1} = f_{\vartheta 1}\cos\vartheta - (Z_1\cos\vartheta_c - T_1)\frac{R_2(\vartheta_c)\sin\vartheta_c}{R_2(\vartheta)\sin\vartheta} \qquad (3.31c)$$

and

$$n_{\vartheta 1} = f_{\vartheta 1}\cos\varphi\, , \quad n_{\vartheta\varphi 1} = f_{\vartheta\varphi 1}\sin\varphi\, , \quad n_{\varphi 1} = -\frac{R_2(\vartheta)}{R_1(\vartheta)} n_{\vartheta 1}$$

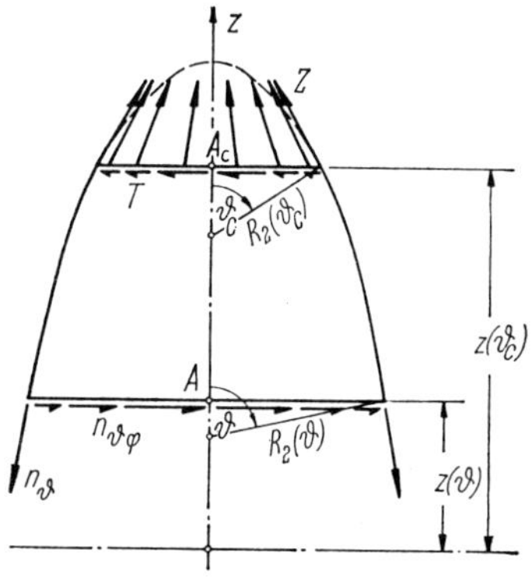

Figure 3.9

3.3 The Deformation

of an axisymmetrical membrane is obtained from (2.27), taking into account (3.3). We obtain the following system of equations:

$$\frac{1}{R_1}\frac{\partial v_\vartheta}{\partial\vartheta} + \frac{v_R}{R_1} = \frac{n_\vartheta}{D_\vartheta} - \frac{\nu_\varphi}{D_\varphi} n_\varphi\, ,$$
$$\frac{1}{R_2\sin\vartheta}\frac{\partial v_\varphi}{\partial\varphi} + \frac{\operatorname{ctg}\vartheta}{R_2} v_\vartheta + \frac{v_R}{R_2} = \frac{n_\varphi}{D_\varphi} - \frac{\nu_\vartheta}{D_\vartheta} n_\vartheta\, , \qquad (3.32\text{ a-c})$$
$$\frac{1}{R_2\sin\vartheta}\frac{\partial v_\vartheta}{\partial\varphi} + \frac{1}{R_1}\frac{\partial v_\varphi}{\partial\vartheta} - \frac{\operatorname{ctg}\vartheta}{R_2} v_\varphi = \frac{n_{\vartheta\varphi}}{D_{\vartheta\varphi}}\, ,$$

Solving (3.32a) for v_R:

$$v_R = R_1\left(\frac{n_\vartheta}{D_\vartheta} - \frac{\nu_\varphi}{D_\varphi} n_\varphi\right) - \frac{\partial v_\vartheta}{\partial\vartheta}\, , \qquad (3.33a)$$

and substituting in (3.32b), we obtain the following two equations:

$$\frac{\sin\vartheta}{R_2}\frac{\partial}{\partial\vartheta}\left(\frac{v_\vartheta}{\sin\vartheta}\right) - \frac{1}{R_2\sin\vartheta}\frac{\partial v_\varphi}{\partial\varphi} = \frac{n_\vartheta}{D_\vartheta}\left(\frac{R_1}{R_2} + \nu_\vartheta\right) - \frac{n_\varphi}{D_\varphi}\left(1 + \nu_\varphi\frac{R_1}{R_2}\right),$$
$$\frac{1}{R_2\sin\vartheta}\frac{\partial v_\vartheta}{\partial\varphi} + \frac{R_2}{R_1}\sin\vartheta\frac{\partial}{\partial\vartheta}\left(\frac{v_\varphi}{R_2\sin\vartheta}\right) = \frac{n_{\varphi\vartheta}}{D_{\varphi\vartheta}}\, , \qquad (3.33\text{b,c})$$

3.3.1 *Axisymmetrical Deformations*

caused by axisymmetrical loading, are characterized by the fact that all displacements are independent of φ. Integrating (3.33b, c), we obtain

$$v_\vartheta = \left\{C + \int \frac{1}{\sin\vartheta}\left[\frac{n_\vartheta}{D_\vartheta}(R_1 + \nu_\vartheta R_2) - \frac{n_\varphi}{D_\varphi}(\nu_\varphi R_1 + R_2)\right] d\vartheta\right\}\sin\vartheta = \sin\vartheta\left\{C + \int \frac{R_1\varepsilon_\vartheta - R_2\varepsilon_\varphi}{\sin\vartheta}\, d\vartheta\right\}, \tag{(3.34a)}$$

$$v_\varphi = R_2\sin\vartheta\left\{D + \int \frac{n_{\varphi\vartheta}}{D_{\varphi\vartheta}}\,\frac{R_1\, d\vartheta}{R_2\sin\vartheta}\right\} = R_2\sin\vartheta\left\{D + \int \frac{R_1\gamma_{\varphi\vartheta}}{R_2\sin\vartheta}\, d\vartheta\right\}, \tag{3.34b}$$

where C and D are still undetermined constants [and (2.26a) has been taken into account]. Hence finally, by (3.33a):

$$v_R = R_2\left(\frac{n_\varphi}{D_\varphi} - \frac{\nu_\vartheta}{D_\vartheta}n_\vartheta\right) - \cos\vartheta\left\{C + \int \frac{1}{\sin\vartheta}\left[\frac{n_\vartheta}{D_\vartheta}(R_1 + \nu_\vartheta R_2) - \frac{n_\varphi}{D_\varphi}(\nu_\varphi R_1 + R_2)\right] d\vartheta\right\} = R_2\,\varepsilon_\varphi - v_\vartheta \operatorname{ctg}\vartheta\,. \tag{3.34c}$$

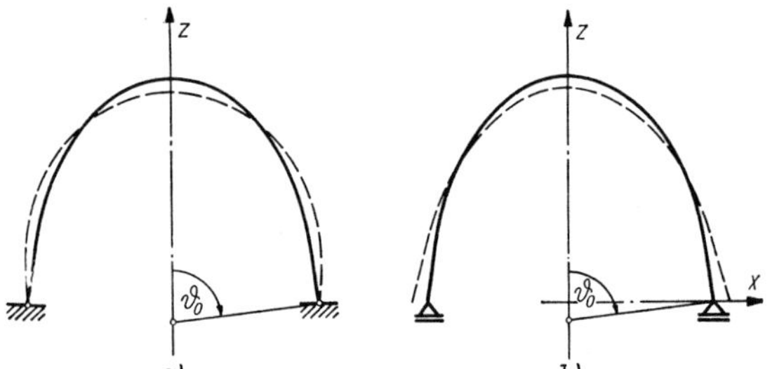

Figure 3.10 a and b

If we assume that the edge $\vartheta = \vartheta_0$ cannot move in the tangential direction, we can determine D from $v_\varphi(\vartheta_0) = 0$, so that

$$v_\varphi(\vartheta) = -R_2\sin\vartheta\int_{\chi=\vartheta}^{\vartheta_0}\frac{R_1\gamma_{\varphi\vartheta}}{R_2\sin\chi}\, d\chi = -R_2\sin\vartheta\int_{\chi=\vartheta}^{\vartheta_0}\frac{n_{\vartheta\varphi}}{D_{\vartheta\varphi}}\,\frac{R_1\, d\chi}{R_2\sin\chi}\,.$$

To find the two remaining displacement components, we consider the boundary conditions for the membrane shown in Figure 3.10a, where

$$v_R\big|_{\vartheta=\vartheta_0} = 0\,; \quad v_\vartheta\big|_{\vartheta=\vartheta_0} = 0\,,$$

Since we have to assume $\varepsilon_\varphi\big|_{\vartheta=\vartheta_0} \neq 0$, we cannot satisfy both conditions with the single constant C. This is the same difficulty which, in the theory of shells, requires application of the theory of bending. However, the fact that in bending a membrane possesses no rigidity makes it impossible to compensate for the discontinuity of the membrane deformations at the edge by corresponding bending deformations. In general, therefore, the boundary conditions cannot be satisfied by applying the linear theory, as was already mentioned in Section 2.2. However, it is found (e.g., in Section 7.5.2, where a circular pipe is analyzed) that by means of the linear theory the state of stress (i.e., the state of strain) is determined almost exactly for most of the membrane, the refinement due to the exact theory (in which the dimensions of the surface area also have to be considered initially unknown) being significant only in a small region near the edge.

In this region the displacements determined by the linear theory have to be fitted to the given boundary conditions. In general this leads to large displacements near the edge and causes folding in this region. This can be prevented by supporting the edge suitably (e.g., by cables), so that membrane displacements are permitted which cannot accommodate themselves to the boundary conditions postulated by the linear theory, and represent a self-contained deformation of the membrane. In the case considered we shall replace the fixed support by a cable adjusting itself to the extensions of the membrane edge $\varepsilon_\varphi\big|_{\vartheta=\vartheta_0}$. If we thus permit radial displacements of the membrane edge (Figure 3.10b), we determine the integration constant C from the condition

$$v_z\big|_{\vartheta=\vartheta_0} = \left[v_R\cos\vartheta - v_\vartheta\sin\vartheta\right]_{\vartheta=\vartheta_0} = 0 \tag{3.34d}$$

Substituting (3.34a, c), we obtain

$$C = R_2(\vartheta_0)\cos\vartheta_0\left[\frac{n_\varphi(\vartheta_0)}{D_\varphi} - \frac{\nu_\vartheta}{D_\vartheta}n_\vartheta(\vartheta_0)\right] - \left[\int \frac{1}{\sin\vartheta}\left[\frac{n_\vartheta}{D_\vartheta}(R_1 + \nu_\vartheta R_2) - \frac{n_\varphi}{D_\varphi}(\nu_\varphi R_1 + R_2)\right] d\vartheta\right]_{\vartheta=\vartheta_0},$$

so that finally, for a membrane supported as in Figure 3.10b,

$$\left.\begin{aligned} v_\vartheta &= \sin\vartheta\left\{R_2(\vartheta_0)\cos\vartheta_0\left[\frac{n_\varphi(\vartheta_0)}{D_\varphi} - \frac{\nu_\vartheta}{D_\vartheta}n_\vartheta(\vartheta_0)\right] - \int_\vartheta^{\vartheta_0}\frac{1}{\sin\chi}\left[\frac{n_\vartheta}{D_\vartheta}(R_1 + \nu_\vartheta R_2) - \frac{n_\varphi}{D_\varphi}(\nu_\varphi R_1 + R_2)\right] d\chi\right\},\\ v_R &= R_2(\vartheta)\left\{\frac{n_\varphi(\vartheta)}{D_\varphi} - \frac{\nu_\vartheta}{D_\vartheta}n_\vartheta(\vartheta)\right\} - v_\vartheta\operatorname{ctg}\vartheta\,. \end{aligned}\right\} \tag{3.35a, b}$$

The circumferential extension at the support and the horizontal displacement of the support are respectively

$$\left.\begin{aligned} \varepsilon_\varphi(\vartheta_0) &= \frac{n_\varphi(\vartheta_0)}{D_\varphi} - \frac{\nu_\vartheta}{D_\vartheta}n_\vartheta(\vartheta_0)\,,\\ v_H(\vartheta_0) &= v_\vartheta(\vartheta_0)\cos\vartheta_0 + v_R(\vartheta_0)\sin\vartheta_0 =\\ &= \left[v_R(\vartheta_0) + v_\vartheta(\vartheta_0)\operatorname{ctg}\vartheta_0\right]\sin\vartheta_0 =\\ &= R_2(\vartheta_0)\sin\vartheta_0\left[\frac{n_\varphi(\vartheta_0)}{D_\varphi} - \frac{\nu_\vartheta}{D_\vartheta}n_\vartheta(\vartheta_0)\right]. \end{aligned}\right\} \tag{3.35c, d}$$

3.3.2 *Deformations Due to Antimetrical Loading*

Putting $n_\vartheta(\vartheta, \varphi) = f_\vartheta(\vartheta)\cos\varphi$, $n_\varphi(\vartheta, \varphi) = f_\varphi(\vartheta)\cos\varphi$, $n_{\vartheta\varphi}(\vartheta, \varphi) = f_{\vartheta\varphi}(\vartheta)\sin\varphi$ we obtain from (3.32a-c):

$$\frac{\partial v_\vartheta}{\partial \vartheta} + v_R = R_1 \bar{\varepsilon}_\vartheta \cos\varphi\,, \quad \bar{\varepsilon}_\vartheta(\vartheta) = \frac{f_\vartheta}{D_\vartheta} - \frac{\nu_\varphi}{D_\varphi} f_\varphi\,,$$
$$\frac{\partial v_\varphi}{\partial \varphi} + v_\vartheta \cos\vartheta + v_R \sin\vartheta = R_2 \sin\vartheta \cdot \bar{\varepsilon}_\varphi \cos\varphi\,,$$
$$\bar{\varepsilon}_\varphi(\vartheta) = \frac{f_\varphi}{D_\varphi} - \frac{\nu_\vartheta}{D_\vartheta} f_\vartheta\,, \tag{3.36a–c}$$
$$\frac{\partial v_\vartheta}{\partial \varphi} + \frac{R_2 \sin\vartheta}{R_1}\frac{\partial v_\varphi}{\partial \vartheta} - \cos\vartheta\, v_\varphi = R_2 \sin\vartheta\, \bar{\gamma}_{\vartheta\varphi} \sin\varphi\,,$$
$$\bar{\gamma}_{\vartheta\varphi}(\vartheta) = \frac{f_{\vartheta\varphi}}{D_{\vartheta\varphi}}$$

Expressing v_ϑ and v_R through the vertical and horizontal displacement components v_z and v_H,

$$v_\vartheta = -v_z \sin\vartheta + v_H \cos\vartheta\,, \quad v_R = v_z \cos\vartheta + v_H \sin\vartheta \tag{3.37a, b}$$

and substituting in (3.36a-c), we obtain

$$\cos\vartheta \frac{\partial v_H}{\partial \vartheta} - \sin\vartheta \frac{\partial v_z}{\partial \vartheta} = R_1 \bar{\varepsilon}_\vartheta \cos\varphi\,,$$
$$v_H + \frac{\partial v_\varphi}{\partial \varphi} = R_2 \sin\vartheta\, \bar{\varepsilon}_\varphi \cos\varphi\,, \tag{3.38a-c}$$
$$-\sin\vartheta \frac{\partial v_z}{\partial \varphi} + \cos\vartheta \frac{\partial v_H}{\partial \varphi} + \frac{R_2 \sin\vartheta}{R_1}\frac{\partial v_\varphi}{\partial \vartheta} - \cos\vartheta\, v_\varphi = R_2 \sin\vartheta\, \bar{\gamma}_{\vartheta\varphi} \sin\varphi\,.$$

Putting

$$v_H(\vartheta, \varphi) = V_H(\vartheta)\cos\varphi\,, \quad v_z(\vartheta, \varphi) = V_z(\vartheta)\cos\varphi\,, \quad v_\varphi(\vartheta, \varphi) = V_\varphi(\vartheta)\sin\varphi \tag{3.39a-c}$$

we obtain the ordinary differential equations

$$\cos\vartheta \frac{d V_H}{d\vartheta} - \sin\vartheta \frac{d V_z}{d\vartheta} = R_1 \bar{\varepsilon}_\vartheta\,,$$
$$V_H + V_\varphi = R_2 \sin\vartheta\, \bar{\varepsilon}_\varphi\,, \tag{3.40a-c}$$
$$\cos\vartheta\, V_H - \sin\vartheta\, V_z - \frac{R_2}{R_1}\sin\vartheta \frac{d V_\varphi}{d\vartheta} + \cos\vartheta\, V_\varphi = -R_2 \sin\vartheta\, \bar{\gamma}_{\vartheta\varphi}\,.$$

Our assumption (3.39), which expresses the appearance of antimetrical deformations v_z and v_H in the (y, z) plane and of symmetrical deformations v_φ, due to loading antimetrical with respect to the (y, z) plane, thus leads to no contradiction.
We then find from (3.40b)

$$V_\varphi = -V_H + R_2 \sin\vartheta\, \bar{\varepsilon}_\varphi\,. \tag{3.41a}$$

Substitution in (3.40c) yields

$$-\sin\vartheta\, V_z + \frac{R_2}{R_1}\sin\vartheta \frac{d V_H}{d\vartheta} - \frac{R_2}{R_1}\sin\vartheta \frac{d}{d\vartheta}(R_2 \sin\vartheta\, \bar{\varepsilon}_\varphi) + R_2 \sin\vartheta \cos\vartheta\, \bar{\varepsilon}_\varphi = -R_2 \sin\vartheta\, \bar{\gamma}_{\vartheta\varphi}\,,$$

whence, solving for V_z and taking into account (3.2), we obtain

$$V_z = \frac{R_2}{R_1}\frac{d V_H}{d\vartheta} + R_2 \bar{\gamma}_{\vartheta\varphi} - \frac{R_2^2 \sin\vartheta}{R_1}\frac{d \bar{\varepsilon}_\varphi}{d\vartheta} \tag{3.41b}$$

We have thus expressed the vertical displacements V_z and circumferential displacements V_φ through the radial horizontal displacements V_H, for which we obtain a differential equation of the second order by inserting (3.41b) into (3.40a):

$$\cos\vartheta \frac{d V_H}{d\vartheta} - \sin\vartheta \frac{d}{d\vartheta}\left(\frac{R_2}{R_1}\frac{d V_H}{d\vartheta}\right) = R_1 \bar{\varepsilon}_\vartheta + \sin\vartheta \frac{d}{d\vartheta}\left[R_2 \bar{\gamma}_{\vartheta\varphi} - \frac{R_2^2 \sin\vartheta}{R_1}\frac{d \bar{\varepsilon}_\varphi}{d\vartheta}\right]. \tag{3.41c}$$

Since by (3.2)

$$\sin\vartheta \frac{d}{d\vartheta}\left(\frac{R_2}{R_1}\frac{d V_H}{d\vartheta}\right) - \cos\vartheta \frac{d V_H}{d\vartheta} = \sin\vartheta\left[\frac{d}{d\vartheta}\left(\frac{R_2}{R_1}\frac{d V_H}{d\vartheta}\right) - \frac{R_1 \cos\vartheta}{R_2 \sin\vartheta}\left(\frac{R_2}{R_1}\frac{d V_H}{d\vartheta}\right)\right] =$$
$$= \sin\vartheta \cdot R_2 \sin\vartheta \frac{d}{d\vartheta}\left[\frac{R_2}{R_1}\frac{d V_H}{d\vartheta}\frac{1}{R_2 \sin\vartheta}\right] = R_2 \sin^2\vartheta \frac{d}{d\vartheta}\left[\frac{1}{R_1 \sin\vartheta}\frac{d V_H}{d\vartheta}\right],$$

we can rewrite (3.41c) as follows:

$$\frac{d}{d\vartheta}\left[\frac{1}{R_1 \sin\vartheta}\frac{d V_H}{d\vartheta}\right] = -\frac{R_1 \bar{\varepsilon}_\vartheta}{R_2 \sin^2\vartheta} + \frac{1}{R_2 \sin\vartheta}\frac{d}{d\vartheta}\left[\frac{R_2^2 \sin\vartheta}{R_1}\frac{d \bar{\varepsilon}_\varphi}{d\vartheta} - R_2 \bar{\gamma}_{\vartheta\varphi}\right]. \tag{3.42a}$$

This permits repeated integration. We first obtain, C_1 being the integration constant,

$$\frac{1}{R_1 \sin\vartheta}\frac{d V_H}{d\vartheta} = C_1 + \frac{R_2}{R_1}\frac{d \bar{\varepsilon}_\varphi}{d\vartheta} - \frac{\bar{\gamma}_{\vartheta\varphi}}{\sin\vartheta} + \int \frac{\cos\vartheta}{\sin\vartheta}\frac{d\bar{\varepsilon}_\varphi}{d\vartheta} d\vartheta - \int \frac{R_1 \cos\vartheta}{R_2 \sin\vartheta}\frac{\bar{\gamma}_{\vartheta\varphi}}{\sin\vartheta} d\vartheta - \int \frac{R_1 \bar{\varepsilon}_\vartheta}{R_2 \sin^2\vartheta} d\vartheta \tag{3.42b}$$

and thus, by (3.41b),

$$V_z = R_2 \sin\vartheta\left[C_1 + \int \frac{\cos\vartheta}{\sin\vartheta}\frac{d\bar{\varepsilon}_\varphi}{d\vartheta} d\vartheta - \int \frac{R_1 \cos\vartheta}{R_2 \sin\vartheta}\frac{\bar{\gamma}_{\vartheta\varphi}}{\sin\vartheta} d\vartheta - \int \frac{R_1 \bar{\varepsilon}_\vartheta}{R_2 \sin^2\vartheta} d\vartheta\right]. \tag{3.42c}$$

We determine C_1 from the boundary condition $V_z(\vartheta_0) = 0$:

$$C_1 = -\left[\int \frac{\cos\vartheta}{\sin\vartheta}\frac{d\bar{\varepsilon}_\varphi}{d\vartheta} d\vartheta - \int \frac{R_1 \cos\vartheta}{R_2 \sin\vartheta}\frac{\bar{\gamma}_{\vartheta\varphi}}{\sin\vartheta} d\vartheta - \int \frac{R_1 \bar{\varepsilon}_\vartheta}{R_2 \sin^2\vartheta} d\vartheta\right]_{\vartheta = \vartheta_0}$$

so that we finally obtain the axial displacement

$$V_z = -R_2 \sin\vartheta \times \int_\vartheta^{\vartheta_0}\left[\frac{\cos\chi}{\sin\chi}\frac{d\bar{\varepsilon}_\varphi}{d\chi} - \frac{R_1 \cos\chi}{R_2 \sin\chi}\frac{\bar{\gamma}_{\vartheta\varphi}}{\sin\chi} - \frac{R_1 \bar{\varepsilon}_\vartheta}{R_2 \sin^2\chi}\right] d\chi\,. \tag{3.43a}$$

Solving (3.41b) for $d V_H/d\vartheta$ and integrating, yields

$$V_H = C_2 + \int \frac{R_1}{R_2}\left(V_z - R_2 \bar{\gamma}_{\vartheta\varphi} + \frac{R_2^2 \sin\vartheta}{R_1}\frac{d \bar{\varepsilon}_\varphi}{d\vartheta}\right) d\vartheta\,,$$

Substituting this in (3.41a), we obtain the circumferential displacements

$$V_\varphi = -C_2 - \int \frac{R_1}{R_2}\left(V_z - R_2 \bar{\gamma}_{\vartheta\varphi} + \frac{R_2^2 \sin\vartheta}{R_1}\frac{d \bar{\varepsilon}_\varphi}{d\vartheta}\right) d\vartheta + R_2 \sin\vartheta\, \bar{\varepsilon}_\varphi\,.$$

In order to determine C_2 we assume that no circumferential displacements of the edge occur, i.e., $V_\varphi(\vartheta_0) = 0$.
We then obtain

$$C_2 = \left[R_2 \bar{\varepsilon}_\varphi \sin\vartheta - \int \frac{R_1}{R_2} \left(\bar{V}_z - R_2 \bar{\gamma}_{\vartheta\varphi} + \frac{R_2{}^2 \sin\vartheta}{R_1} \frac{d\bar{\varepsilon}_\varphi}{d\vartheta} \right) d\vartheta \right]_{\vartheta = \vartheta_0}$$

so that finally

$$V_H = R_2(\vartheta_0) \sin\vartheta_0 \, \bar{\varepsilon}_\varphi(\vartheta_0) - \int_{\vartheta}^{\vartheta_0} \frac{R_1}{R_2} \left(\bar{V}_z - R_2 \bar{\gamma}_{\vartheta\varphi} + \frac{R_2{}^2 \sin\chi}{R_1} \frac{d\bar{\varepsilon}_\varphi}{d\chi} \right) d\chi ,$$

$$V_H(\vartheta_0) = R_2(\vartheta_0) \sin\vartheta_0 \, \bar{\varepsilon}_\varphi(\vartheta_0) ,$$

$$v_H(\vartheta_0, \varphi) = R_2(\vartheta_0) \sin\vartheta_0 \left[\frac{f_\varphi}{D_\varphi} - \frac{\nu_\vartheta}{D_\vartheta} f_\vartheta \right] \cos\varphi , \tag{3.43b}$$

and

$$V_\varphi = R_2 \sin\vartheta \, \bar{\varepsilon}_\varphi - R_2(\vartheta_0) \sin\vartheta_0 \, \bar{\varepsilon}_\varphi(\vartheta_0) + \int_{\vartheta}^{\vartheta_0} \frac{R_1}{R_2} \left(\bar{V}_z - R_2 \bar{\gamma}_{\vartheta\varphi} + \frac{R_2{}^2 \sin\chi}{R_1} \frac{d\bar{\varepsilon}_\varphi}{d\chi} \right) d\chi , \tag{3.43c}$$

We have thus obtained the deformations due to antimetrical loading with respect to the (y, z) plane, in the sense of Sections 3.2.2 and 3.2.3. In fact, C_2 could also have been obtained from a boundary condition for V_H. However, circumferential displacements of the membrane edge would then occur. This proves again that the displacements of the membrane edge, as determined by the linear theory, cannot satisfy arbitrary boundary conditions for all three displacement components. We shall now consider particular cases of axisymmetrical membranes.

4 THE SPHERICAL MEMBRANE

When $R_1 = R_2 = R$, the general equations of Section 3 reduce to the relationships for a sphere.

4.1 Sectional Loads

4.1.1 *Loading by Internal Pressure*

We obtain from (3.8a, b)

$$n_{\varphi p} = n_{\vartheta p} = \frac{p\,R}{2}\,. \qquad (4.1a, b)$$

4.1.2 *Loading by Dead Weight* (Figure 4.1)

We obtain from (3.10a, b)

$$\left.\begin{aligned} n_{\vartheta g} &= -\,g\,R\,\frac{1-\cos\vartheta}{\sin^2\vartheta} = -\,\frac{g\,R}{2\cos^2\dfrac{\vartheta}{2}} = g\,R\,a_g(\vartheta)\,,\\ n_{\varphi g} &= g\,R\left(\frac{1-\cos\vartheta}{\sin^2\vartheta} - \cos\vartheta\right) =\\ &= g\,R\left(\frac{1}{2\cos^2\dfrac{\vartheta}{2}} - \cos\vartheta\right) = g\,R\,c_g(\vartheta)\,. \end{aligned}\right\} \qquad (4.2a, b)$$

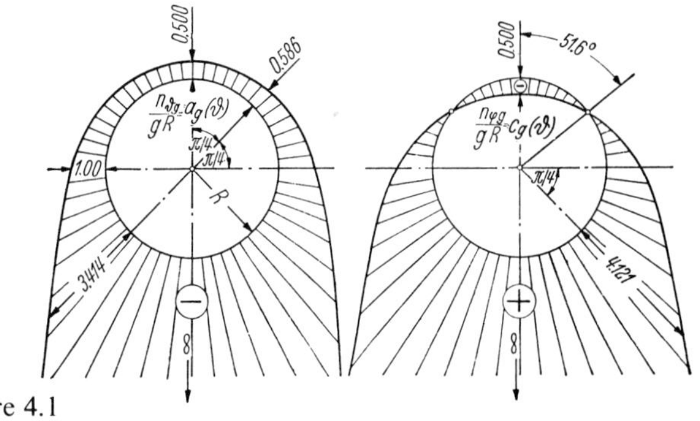

Figure 4.1

4.1.3 *Symmetrical Snow Load* (Figure 4.2)

We obtain from (3.12a, b) or (3.13a, b), respectively,

$$n_{\vartheta_{s_1}} = \left\{\begin{array}{l} -\dfrac{s\,R}{3}\,\dfrac{1-\cos^3\vartheta}{\sin^2\vartheta}\,,\ 0 \leqq \vartheta \leqq \pi/2\\ -\dfrac{s\,R}{3}\,\dfrac{1}{\sin^2\vartheta}\,,\ \pi/2 \leqq \vartheta \leqq \vartheta_0 \end{array}\right\} = s\,R\,a_{s_1}(\vartheta)$$

$$n_{\varphi_{s_1}} = \left\{\begin{array}{l} \dfrac{s\,R}{3}\left(\dfrac{1-\cos^3\vartheta}{\sin^2\vartheta} - 3\cos^3\vartheta\right),\\ 0 \leqq \vartheta \leqq \pi/2\,,\\ \dfrac{s\,R}{3}\,\dfrac{1}{\sin^2\vartheta}\,,\ \pi/2 \leqq \vartheta \leqq \vartheta_0 \end{array}\right\} = s\,R\,c_{s_1}(\vartheta) \qquad (4.3a, b)$$

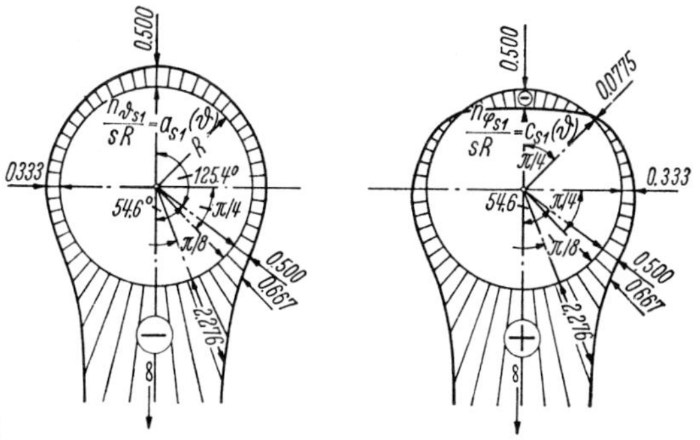

Figure 4.2

4.1.4 *One-sided Snow Load* (Figure 4.3)

We obtain from (3.28)

$$n_{\vartheta_{s3}} = \left\{\begin{array}{l} -\dfrac{s\,R}{6}\left(\dfrac{1-\cos^3\vartheta}{\sin^2\vartheta} + \dfrac{3}{32}\,\times\right.\\ \left.\times\,\dfrac{4\,\vartheta - \sin 4\,\vartheta}{\sin^3\vartheta}\cos\varphi\right),\\ 0 \leqq \vartheta \leqq \pi/2\,,\\ -\dfrac{s\,R}{6\sin^2\vartheta}\left(1 + \dfrac{3\,\pi}{16}\,\dfrac{\cos\varphi}{\sin\vartheta}\right),\\ \pi/2 \leqq \vartheta \leqq \vartheta_0 \end{array}\right\} = \frac{s\,R}{2}\,[a_{s1}(\vartheta) + a_{s3}(\vartheta)\cos\varphi]\,,$$

$$n_{\vartheta\varphi_{s3}} = \left\{\begin{array}{l} -\dfrac{s\,R}{64}\,\dfrac{\cos\vartheta\,(4\,\vartheta - \sin 4\,\vartheta)}{\sin^3\vartheta}\,\times\\ \times\,\sin\varphi\,,\quad 0 \leqq \vartheta \leqq \pi/2\,,\\ -\dfrac{s\,R\,\pi}{32}\,\dfrac{\cos\vartheta}{\sin^3\vartheta}\,\sin\varphi\,,\\ \pi/2 \leqq \vartheta \leqq \vartheta_0 \end{array}\right\} = \frac{s\,R}{2}\,b_{s3}(\vartheta)\sin\varphi\,,$$

$$n_{\varphi_{s3}} = \left\{\begin{array}{l} \dfrac{s\,R}{6}\left(\dfrac{1-\cos^3\vartheta}{\sin^2\vartheta} - 3\cos^3\vartheta\right) +\\ +\,\dfrac{s\,R}{2}\left(\dfrac{1}{32}\,\dfrac{4\,\vartheta - \sin 4\,\vartheta}{\sin^3\vartheta}\,-\right.\\ \left.-\,\cos^3\vartheta\right)\cos\varphi\,,\\ 0 \leqq \vartheta \leqq \pi/2\,,\\ \dfrac{s\,R}{6\sin^2\vartheta}\left(1 + \dfrac{3\,\pi}{16}\,\dfrac{\cos\varphi}{\sin\vartheta}\right),\\ \pi/2 \leqq \vartheta \leqq \vartheta_0 \end{array}\right\} = \frac{s\,R}{2}\,[c_{s1}(\vartheta) + c_{s3}(\vartheta)\cos\varphi]\,. \qquad (4.4a\text{-}c)$$

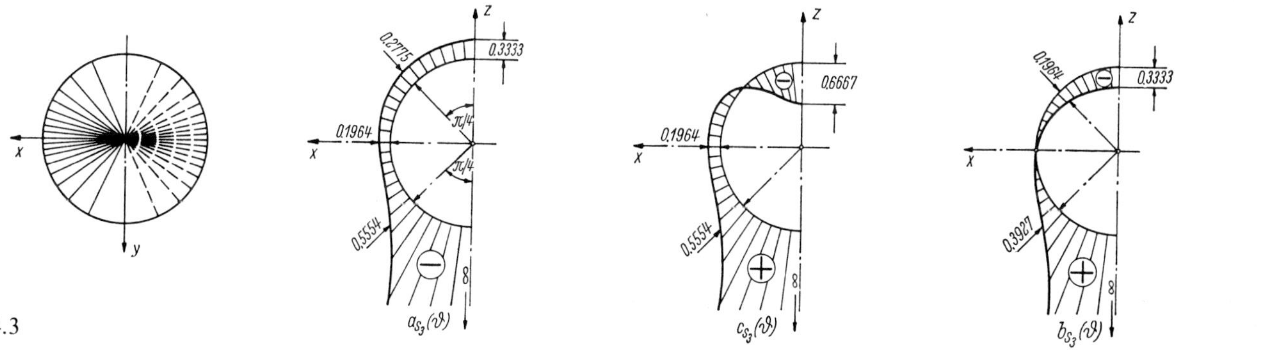

Figure 4.3

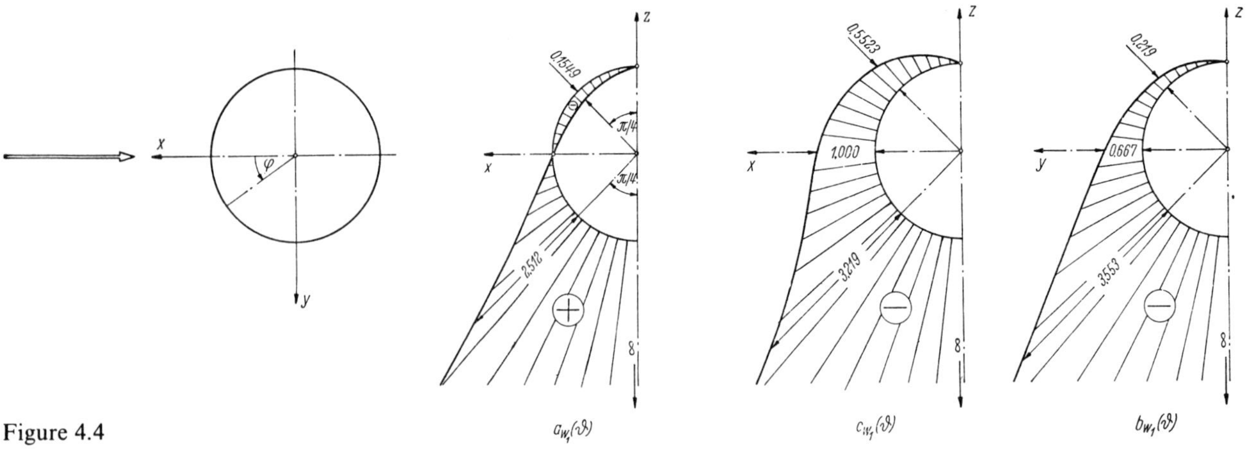

Figure 4.4

ϑ	Dead weight		Symmetrical snow load		Antimetrical part of snow load			Antimetrical part of wind load		
	$a_g(\vartheta)$	$c_g(\vartheta)$	$a_{s1}(\vartheta)$	$c_{s1}(\vartheta)$	$a_{s3}(\vartheta)$	$b_{s3}(\vartheta)$	$c_{s3}(\vartheta)$	$a_{w1}(\vartheta)$	$b_{w1}(\vartheta)$	$c_{w1}(\vartheta)$
0	– 0.500	– 0.500	– 0.5000	– 0.5000	– 0.3333	– 0.3333	– 0.6667	0	0	0
10	– 0.504	– 0.481	– 0.4968	– 0.4583	– 0.3323	– 0.3272	– 0.6228	– 0.0379	– 0.0385	– 0.1260
20	– 0.516	– 0.424	– 0.4851	– 0.3447	– 0.3214	– 0.3020	– 0.5084	– 0.0846	– 0.0900	– 0.2577
30	– 0.536	– 0.330	– 0.4674	– 0.1821	– 0.3071	– 0.2659	– 0.3424	– 0.1192	– 0.1376	– 0.3812
40	– 0.566	– 0.200	– 0.4441	– 0.0054	– 0.2883	– 0.2208	– 0.1612	– 0.1456	– 0.1901	– 0.4973
45	– 0.586	– 0.121	– 0.4310	0.0775	– 0.2775	– 0.1964	– 0.0758	– 0.1549	– 0.2190	– 0.5523
50	– 0.609	– 0.034	– 0.4172	0.1516	– 0.2664	– 0.1712	0.0008	– 0.1608	– 0.2501	– 0.6053
60	– 0.667	0.167	– 0.3889	0.2639	– 0.2432	– 0.1216	0.1182	– 0.1604	– 0.3207	– 0.7056
70	– 0.745	0.403	– 0.3624	0.3224	– 0.2211	– 0.0756	0.1811	– 0.1393	– 0.4073	– 0.8004
80	– 0.852	0.678	– 0.3419	0.3367	– 0.2038	– 0.0354	0.1986	– 0.0899	– 0.5181	– 0.8948
90	– 1.000	1.000	– 0.3333	0.3333	– 0.1964	0	0.1964	0	– 0.6667	– 1.0000
100	– 1.210	1.384	– 0.3437	0.3437	– 0.2056	0.0357	0.2056	0.1524	– 0.8779	– 1.1372
110	– 1.520	1.862	– 0.3775	0.3775	– 0.2366	0.0809	0.2366	0.4102	– 1.1994	– 1.3499
120	– 2.000	2.500	– 0.4445	0.4445	– 0.3023	0.1512	0.3023	0.8661	– 1.7321	– 1.7320
130	– 2.800	3.443	– 0.5681	0.5681	– 0.4368	0.2808	0.4368	1.7459	– 2.7161	– 2.5118
135	– 3.414	4.121	– 0.6667	0.6667	– 0.5554	0.3927	0.5554	2.5122	– 3.5528	– 3.2190
140	– 4.275	5.041	– 0.8067	0.8067	– 0.7392	0.5662	0.7392	3.6996	– 4.8298	– 4.3427
150	– 7.465	8.331	– 1.3333	1.3333	– 1.5707	1.3602	1.5707	9.1186	– 10.5296	– 9.6185
160	– 16.589	17.529	– 2.8498	2.8498	– 4.9085	4.6125	4.9085	31.2403	– 33.2450	– 31.5827
170	– 65.789	66.774	– 11.0619	11.0619	– 37.7500	37.1762	37.7500	252.4686	– 256.3654	– 252.6388
180°	– ∞	∞	– ∞	∞	– ∞	∞	∞	∞	– ∞	– ∞

Table 1

4.1.5 *Wind Load According to Section* 3.2.2b (Figure 4.4)

The symmetrical part according to (4.1a, b) is

$$n_{\vartheta w0} = n_{\varphi w0} = -\, w_0\, R/2\,, \tag{4.5a, b}$$

while from (3.30) we obtain, since $\zeta(\chi) - z(\vartheta) = R(\cos\chi - \cos\vartheta)$

$$\left.\begin{aligned}
n_{\vartheta w1} &= w_1\, R \left(-\frac{2}{3} + \cos\vartheta - \frac{1}{3}\cos^3\vartheta\right)\frac{\cos\vartheta\cos\varphi}{\sin^3\vartheta} = \\
&= w_1\, R\, a_{w1}(\vartheta)\cos\varphi\,, \\
n_{\vartheta\varphi_{w1}} &= w_1\, R\left(-\frac{2}{3} + \cos\vartheta - \frac{1}{3}\cos^3\vartheta\right)\frac{\sin\varphi}{\sin^3\vartheta} = \\
&= w_1\, R\, b_{w1}(\vartheta)\sin\varphi\,, \\
n_{\varphi_{w1}} &= w_1\, R\left(\frac{2}{3}\cos\vartheta - \sin^2\vartheta - \frac{2}{3}\cos^4\vartheta\right)\frac{\cos\varphi}{\sin^3\vartheta} = \\
&= w_1\, R\, c_{w1}(\vartheta)\cos\varphi\,.
\end{aligned}\right\} \tag{4.6a-c}$$

4.1.6 *Table for Computing Sectional Loads*

The functions

$$\left.\begin{aligned}
a_g(\vartheta) &= -\frac{1}{2\cos^2\frac{\vartheta}{2}}\,, \quad c_g(\vartheta) = \frac{1}{2\cos^2\frac{\vartheta}{2}} - \cos\vartheta\,, \\
a_{s1}(\vartheta) &= \left\{\begin{aligned} &-\frac{1-\cos^3\vartheta}{3\sin^2\vartheta}\,, && 0 \leqq \vartheta \leqq \pi/2 \\ &-\frac{1}{3\sin^2\vartheta}\,, && \pi/2 \leqq \vartheta \leqq \vartheta_0 \end{aligned}\right\}, \\
c_{s1}(\vartheta) &= \left\{\begin{aligned} &\frac{1-\cos^3\vartheta}{3\sin^2\vartheta} - \cos^3\vartheta\,, && 0 \leqq \vartheta \leqq \pi/2 \\ &\frac{1}{3\sin^2\vartheta}\,, && \pi/2 \leqq \vartheta \leqq \vartheta_0 \end{aligned}\right\}, \\
a_{s3}(\vartheta) &= \left\{\begin{aligned} &-\frac{4\vartheta - \sin 4\vartheta}{32\sin^3\vartheta}\,, && 0 \leqq \vartheta \leqq \pi/2 \\ &-\frac{\pi}{16\sin^3\vartheta}\,, && \pi/2 \leqq \vartheta \leqq \vartheta_0 \end{aligned}\right\}, \\
b_{s3}(\vartheta) &= \left\{\begin{aligned} &-\frac{4\vartheta - \sin 4\vartheta}{32\sin^3\vartheta}\cos\vartheta\,, && 0 \leqq \vartheta \leqq \pi/2 \\ &-\frac{\pi\cos\vartheta}{16\sin^3\vartheta}\,, && \pi/2 \leqq \vartheta \leqq \vartheta_0 \end{aligned}\right\}, \\
c_{s3}(\vartheta) &= \left\{\begin{aligned} &\frac{4\vartheta - \sin 4\vartheta}{32\sin^3\vartheta} - \cos^3\vartheta\,, && 0 \leqq \vartheta \leqq \pi/2 \\ &\frac{\pi}{16\sin^3\vartheta}\,, && \pi/2 \leqq \vartheta \leqq \vartheta_0 \end{aligned}\right\}, \\
a_{w1}(\vartheta) &= \left(-\frac{2}{3} + \cos\vartheta - \frac{1}{3}\cos^3\vartheta\right)\frac{\cos\vartheta}{\sin^3\vartheta}\,, \\
b_{w1}(\vartheta) &= \left(-\frac{2}{3} + \cos\vartheta - \frac{1}{3}\cos^3\vartheta\right)\frac{1}{\sin^3\vartheta}\,, \\
c_{w1}(\vartheta) &= \left(\frac{2}{3}\cos\vartheta - \sin^2\vartheta - \frac{2}{3}\cos^4\vartheta\right)\frac{1}{\sin^3\vartheta}
\end{aligned}\right\} \tag{4.7}$$

are given in Table 1 for different values of ϑ.

4.2 Deformations

4.2.1 *Axisymmetrical States*

We obtain from (3.35) for $R_1 = R_2 = R$

$$\left.\begin{aligned}
v_\vartheta &= R\sin\vartheta\left\{\cos\vartheta_0\left[\frac{n_\varphi(\vartheta_0)}{D_\varphi} - \frac{\nu_\vartheta}{D_\vartheta}\, n_\vartheta(\vartheta_0)\right] - \right. \\
&\qquad \left. -\int_\vartheta^{\vartheta_0}\frac{1}{\sin\chi}\left[\frac{n_\vartheta(1+\nu_\vartheta)}{D_\vartheta} - \frac{n_\varphi(1+\nu_\varphi)}{D_\varphi}\right] d\chi\right\}, \\
v_R &= R\left[\frac{n_\varphi}{D_\varphi} - \frac{\nu_\vartheta}{D_\vartheta}\, n_\vartheta\right] - v_\vartheta\,\mathrm{ctg}\,\vartheta\,, \\
v_H(\vartheta_0) &= R\sin\vartheta_0\left[\frac{n_\varphi(\vartheta_0)}{D_\varphi} - \frac{\nu_\vartheta}{D_\vartheta}\, n_\vartheta(\vartheta_0)\right].
\end{aligned}\right\} \tag{4.8a-c}$$

Of greatest interest are the radial horizontal displacements which have to be permitted at the lower edge in order to prevent folds. These are, respectively:

$$\left.\begin{aligned}
&\text{a) due to internal pressure [cf. (4.1a, b)]} \\
&v_{Hp}(\vartheta_0) = \frac{p\,R^2}{2}\sin\vartheta_0\left(\frac{1}{D_\varphi} - \frac{\nu_\vartheta}{D_\vartheta}\right), \\
&\text{b) due to dead weight [cf. (4.2a, b)]} \\
&v_{Hg}(\vartheta_0) = g\,R^2\sin\vartheta_0\left(\frac{c_g(\vartheta_0)}{D_\varphi} - \frac{\nu_\vartheta}{D_\vartheta}\, a_g(\vartheta_0)\right), \\
&\text{c) due to a symmetrical snow load [cf. (4.3a, b)]} \\
&v_{H_{s1}}(\vartheta_0) = s\,R^2\sin\vartheta_0\left(\frac{c_{s1}(\vartheta_0)}{D_\varphi} - \frac{\nu_\vartheta}{D_\vartheta}\, a_{s1}(\vartheta_0)\right).
\end{aligned}\right\} \tag{4.9a-c}$$

4.2.2 *Antimetrical States*

We obtain from (3.43) for $R_1 = R_2 = R$

$$V_z = -\,R\sin\vartheta\int_\vartheta^{\vartheta_0}\left(\mathrm{ctg}\,\chi\,\frac{d\varepsilon_\varphi}{d\chi} - \mathrm{ctg}\,\chi\,\frac{\gamma_{\vartheta\varphi}}{\sin\chi} - \frac{\varepsilon_\vartheta}{\sin^2\chi}\right) d\chi \tag{4.10a}$$

If no circumferential displacements are permitted at the lower edge, then

$$V_H = R\left[\bar\varepsilon_\varphi(\vartheta_0)\sin\vartheta_0 - \int_\vartheta^{\vartheta_0}\left(\frac{V_z}{R} - \bar\gamma_{\vartheta\varphi} + \sin\chi\,\frac{d\,\bar\varepsilon_\varphi}{d\chi}\right) d\chi\right], \tag{4.10b}$$

$$v_H(\vartheta_0, \varphi) = R\sin\vartheta_0\left[\frac{f_\varphi(\vartheta_0)}{D_\varphi} - \frac{\nu_\vartheta}{D_\vartheta}\, f_\vartheta(\vartheta_0)\right]\cos\varphi\,,$$

$$V_\varphi = R\left[\bar\varepsilon_\varphi\sin\vartheta - \bar\varepsilon_\varphi(\vartheta_0)\sin\vartheta_0 + \right.$$

$$\left. + \int_\vartheta^{\vartheta_0}\left(\frac{V_z}{R} - \bar\gamma_{\vartheta\varphi} + \sin\chi\,\frac{d\,\bar\varepsilon_\varphi}{d\chi}\right) d\chi\right]. \tag{4.10c}$$

Accordingly, at the lower edge we obtain

a) for a one-sided snow load [cf. (4.4)]

$$v_{Hs_3}(\vartheta_0, \varphi) = \frac{s R^2}{2} \sin \vartheta_0 \left[\left(\frac{c_{s1}(\vartheta_0)}{D_\varphi} - \frac{\nu_\vartheta}{D_\vartheta} a_{s1}(\vartheta_0) \right) + \right.$$

$$\left. + \left(\frac{c_{s3}(\vartheta_0)}{D_\varphi} - \frac{\nu_\vartheta}{D_\vartheta} a_{s3}(\vartheta_0) \right) \cos \varphi \right],$$

b) for a wind load [cf. (4.5), (4.6)]

$$v_{Hw}(\vartheta_0, \varphi) = - \frac{w_0 R^2}{2} \sin \vartheta_0 \left(\frac{1}{D_\varphi} - \frac{\nu_\vartheta}{D_\vartheta} \right) +$$

$$+ w_1 R^2 \sin \vartheta_0 \left(\frac{c_{w1}(\vartheta_0)}{D_\varphi} - \frac{\nu_\vartheta}{D_\vartheta} a_{w1}(\vartheta_0) \right) \cos \varphi . \qquad \text{(4.11 a, b)}$$

4.3 Determining the Required Internal Pressure

4.3.1 *Internal Pressure for Load Due Solely to Dead Weight. Maximum Span*

Since the loads „g" and „p" are axisymmetrical ($n_{\vartheta\varphi} \equiv 0$), the membrane forces n_ϑ and n_φ are principal forces. According to (2.15c) we must have

$$n_\vartheta \geqq 0 , \quad n_\varphi \geqq 0 , \quad n_\vartheta n_\varphi \geqq 0 \qquad (4.12)$$

Since the third inequality in (4.12) is always satisfied if the first two are true, it suffices to ensure that both n_ϑ and n_φ are positive. Since

$$n_\vartheta = n_{\vartheta p} + n_{\vartheta g} = \frac{p R}{2} + g R a_g(\vartheta) ,$$

$$n_\varphi = n_{\varphi p} + n_{\varphi g} = \frac{p R}{2} + g R c_g(\vartheta) \qquad (4.12a)$$

and $a_g(\vartheta) \leqq c_g(\vartheta)$, the first two inequalities (4.12) are satisfied if

$$n_\vartheta = n_{\vartheta p} + n_{\vartheta g} = \frac{p R}{2} + g R a_g(\vartheta) \geqq 0 .$$

Thus, if the meridianal stresses are positive, only tensile stresses arise in the system. From (4.7) we obtain as a necessary condition for the internal pressure

$$\min n_\vartheta = \min \left[\frac{p R}{2} - \frac{g R}{2 \cos^2 \frac{\vartheta}{2}} \right] = \frac{p R}{2} - \frac{g R}{2 \cos^2 \frac{\vartheta_0}{2}} \geqq 0 ,$$

or

$$p = p_g \geqq \frac{g}{\cos^2 \frac{\vartheta_0}{2}} . \qquad (4.13)$$

The internal pressure is thus independent of the radius of the sphere but depends on the angle ϑ_0, becoming higher the more the spherical membrane resembles a perfect sphere. It is also evident from Figures 4.1 through 4.4 that the compressive forces in the membrane (in the case of wind or one-sided snow loads, also the shearing forces) increase rapidly with ϑ. It was already stated that the tensile forces due to the internal pressure must always exceed the compressive forces. There exist, however, regions in the membrane where the external load causes tensile forces in certain directions. (In the case considered, the dead weight causes circumferential tensile stresses for $\vartheta = 51.6°$, see Figure 4.1). When these are added to the forces due to the internal pressure, and the permissible maximum stresses for the material taken into account, we obtain an unworkable value for the radius of the sphere if ϑ_0 is appreciably larger than $\pi/2$. This is shown by the following calculation.

The minimum internal pressure according to (4.13) leads to the following membrane forces:

$$n_{\vartheta g + pg} = \frac{p_g R}{2} + g R a_g(\vartheta) \geqq \frac{g R}{2} \left[\frac{1}{\cos^2 \frac{\vartheta_0}{2}} - \frac{1}{\cos^2 \frac{\vartheta}{2}} \right],$$

$$n_{\varphi g + pg} = \frac{p_g R}{2} + g R c_g(\vartheta) \geqq \frac{g R}{2} \left[\frac{1}{\cos^2 \frac{\vartheta_0}{2}} + \frac{1}{\cos^2 \frac{\vartheta}{2}} - 2 \cos \vartheta \right].$$

Since $c_g \geqq a_g$, the circumferential forces always exceed the meridianal forces, being largest at the lower membrane edge $\vartheta = \vartheta_0$ (see also Figure 4.1):

$$\max n_{\varphi g + pg} \geqq g R \left[\frac{1}{\cos^2 \frac{\vartheta_0}{2}} - \cos \vartheta_0 \right].$$

The maximum possible radius of the sphere is obtained in the limiting case, in which the internal pressure is the minimum required to maintain the lower edge unstressed in the meridianal direction, so that the last inequality becomes an equality:

$$g R \left[\frac{1}{\cos^2 \frac{\vartheta_0}{2}} - \cos \vartheta_0 \right] = n_{\text{perm}}$$

Here n_{perm} is the maximum permissible membrane force per unit length of section. We thus obtain

$$R_{\max} = \frac{n_{\text{perm}}}{g \left[\frac{1}{\cos^2 \frac{\vartheta_0}{2}} - \cos \vartheta_0 \right]} . \qquad (4.14)$$

If we put $n_{\text{perm}} = n_{\text{tear}} = 30$ kg/cm (a value attainable in new fabric) and $g = 1$ kg/m², the theoretical maximum radius of the spherical membrane is found to be

$$R_{\max}(\vartheta_0) = \frac{3000}{\frac{1}{\cos^2 \frac{\vartheta_0}{2}} - \cos \vartheta_0} \; [\text{m}] .$$

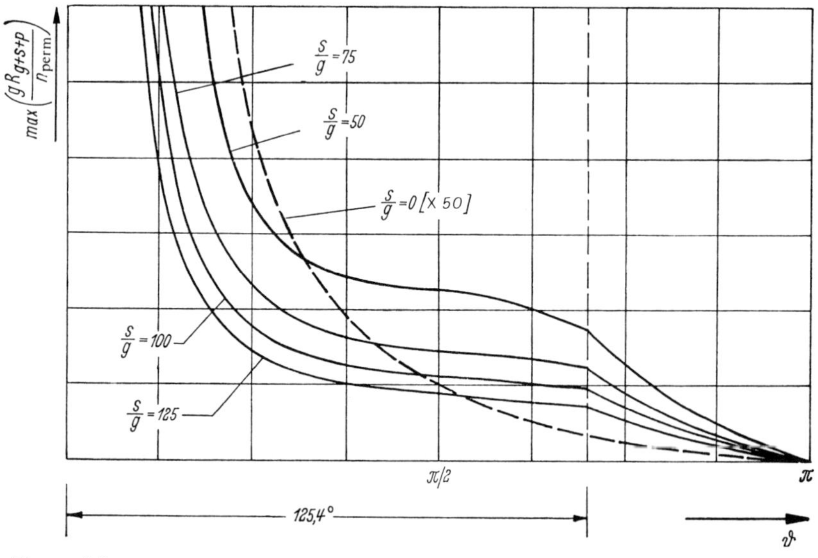

Figure 4.5

For $\vartheta_0 = \pi/2$ we obtain $R_{max}(\pi/2) = 1500$ m, for smaller angles subtended by the membrane the radius becomes still larger. For $\vartheta_0 \to 0$ we obtain $R_{max} \to \infty$, the corresponding inflation pressure being $p_g = g$; this is the case of a plane membrane whose weight is counterbalanced by the "internal" pressure acting from underneath. Larger values of ϑ_0 lead to a marked reduction in the maximum radius. Thus, $R_{max}(3\pi/4) = 398$ m. Of course, the internal pressures required in practice are higher, and the attainable radii less. This is due to the fact that, on the one hand, snow and wind loads, whose influence is many times larger than that of the dead weight, were neglected, while, on the other hand, the permissible tensile stresses have to be kept considerably below the ultimate stress for new fabric, taking into account the aging of the material.

4.3.2 *Dead Weight and Symmetrical Snow Load*

In this case also, the membrane forces n_ϑ and n_φ represent the principal forces. Since the tensile forces $n_{\vartheta p}$ and $n_{\varphi p}$, due to the internal pressure, are equal everywhere, and the meridianal compressive forces representing "g" + "s" always exceed the corresponding circumferential compressive forces, it suffices to counterbalance the largest compressive forces n_ϑ. We then obtain only tensile forces in the system. From section 4.1 (cf. in particular Figure 4.2)

$$\min n_{\vartheta_{p+g+s}} \geqq \frac{pR}{2} - \frac{gR}{2\cos^2\frac{\vartheta_0}{2}} - \frac{sR}{2} \quad \text{for } \vartheta_0 \leqq 125.4°,$$

$$\min n_{\vartheta_{p+g+s}} = \frac{pR}{2} - \frac{gR}{2\cos^2\frac{\vartheta_0}{2}} - \frac{sR}{3\sin^2\vartheta_0} \quad \text{for } \vartheta_0 \geqq 125.4°$$

We thus obtain the inflation pressure for $\min n_\vartheta \geqq 0$

$$\left.\begin{aligned} p_{g+s} &\geqq s + \frac{g}{\cos^2\frac{\vartheta_0}{2}} = s + p_g \quad \text{for } \vartheta_0 \leqq 125.4° \\ p_{g+s} &\geqq \frac{2}{3}\,\frac{s}{\sin^2\vartheta_0} + \frac{g}{\cos^2\frac{\vartheta_0}{2}} \quad \text{for } \vartheta_0 \geqq 125.4°. \end{aligned}\right\} \quad (4.15\text{a, b})$$

The maximum tensile forces in the membrane are the circumferential forces n_φ at the lower membrane edge. We thus obtain from (4.1b), (4.2b), and (4.3b) at the minimum inflation pressure according to (4.15a, b):

$$\max n_{\varphi_{g+s+p}} \geqq \left\{\begin{aligned} & gR\left[\frac{1}{\cos^2\frac{\vartheta_0}{2}} - \cos\vartheta_0\right] + sR\left[\frac{1}{2} + \frac{1-\cos^3\vartheta_0}{3\sin^2\vartheta_0} - \cos^3\vartheta_0\right], \quad \vartheta_0 \leqq \pi/2, \\ & gR\left[\frac{1}{\cos^2\frac{\vartheta_0}{2}} - \cos\vartheta_0\right] + sR\left[\frac{1}{2} + \frac{1}{3\sin^2\vartheta_0}\right], \quad \frac{\pi}{2} \leqq \vartheta_0 \leqq 125.4°, \\ & gR\left[\frac{1}{\cos^2\frac{\vartheta_0}{2}} - \cos\vartheta_0\right] + sR\,\frac{2}{3\sin^2\vartheta_0}, \quad \vartheta_0 \geqq 125.4° \end{aligned}\right\} \quad (4.16)$$

We can then determine the maximum possible radius of the sphere from the condition $\max n_\varphi \leqq n_{perm}$ (Figure 4.5)

$$\max\left(\frac{g R_{g+s+p}}{n_{perm}}\right) = \left\{\begin{aligned} & \left[\frac{1}{\cos^2\frac{\vartheta_0}{2}} - \cos\vartheta_0 + \frac{s}{g}\left(\frac{1}{2} + \frac{1-\cos^3\vartheta_0}{3\sin^2\vartheta_0} - \cos^3\vartheta_0\right)\right]^{-1}, \quad \vartheta_0 \leqq \pi/2, \\ & \left[\frac{1}{\cos^2\frac{\vartheta_0}{2}} - \cos\vartheta_0 + \frac{s}{g}\left(\frac{1}{2} + \frac{1}{3\sin^2\vartheta_0}\right)\right]^{-1}, \quad \frac{\pi}{2} \leqq \vartheta_0 \leqq 125.4°, \\ & \left[\frac{1}{\cos^2\frac{\vartheta_0}{2}} - \cos\vartheta_0 + \frac{s}{g}\,\frac{2}{3\sin^2\vartheta_0}\right]^{-1}. \quad \vartheta_0 \geqq 125.4° \end{aligned}\right\} \quad (4.17)$$

The values obtained for the maximum radius (cf. Table 2) are appreciably les than those obtained in Subsection 4.3.1. In the example considered above ($g = 1$ kg/m², $s = 75$ kg/m², thus $s/g = 75$) we find for $n_{perm} = n_{tear}/3 = 10$ kg/cm or $n_{perm}/g = 10 \cdot 10^4$ cm $= 1000$ m

$$\left.\begin{aligned} &\text{a) for } \vartheta_0 = \pi/4: R_{g+s+p} \leqq 1000 \cdot 0.02284 = 22.84\,\text{m} \\ &\text{b) for } \vartheta_0 = \pi/2: R_{g+s+p} \leqq 1000 \cdot 0.01550 = 15.50\,\text{m} \\ &\text{c) for } \vartheta_0 = 3\pi/4: R_{g+s+p} \leqq 1000 \cdot 0.0093 = 9.30\,\text{m} \end{aligned}\right\} \quad (4.15\text{a})$$

The corresponding minimum inflation pressures are

$$\left.\begin{aligned} &\text{a) for } \vartheta_0 = \pi/4: p_{g+s} \geqq 10^{-4} \cdot 76.17\,\text{atm} \\ &\text{b) for } \vartheta_0 = \pi/2: p_{g+s} \geqq 10^{-4} \cdot 77\,\text{atm} \\ &\text{c) for } \vartheta_0 = 3\pi/4: p_{g+s} \geqq 10^{-4} \cdot 106.83\,\text{atm} \end{aligned}\right\} \quad (4.15\text{b})$$

If, however, we take into account only the snow load, thus neglecting the dead weight, we obtain the following values for $\max R$ and $\min p$ from the data of the last two columns in Table 2 when $n_{perm}/s = 10/75 \cdot 10^{-4} = 1333$ cm $= 13.33$ m

$$\left.\begin{aligned} &\text{a) for } \vartheta_0 = \pi/4: R_{s+p} \leqq 13.33 \cdot 1.7316 = 23.08\,\text{m}, \\ &\qquad p_s \geqq 75 \cdot 10^{-4} \cdot 1\,\text{atm} \\ &\text{b) for } \vartheta_0 = \pi/2: R_{s+p} \leqq 13.33 \cdot 1.20 = 16.00\,\text{m}, \\ &\qquad p_s \geqq 75 \cdot 10^{-4} \cdot 1\,\text{atm} \\ &\text{c) for } \vartheta_0 = 3\pi/4: R_{s+p} \leqq 13.33 \cdot 0.75 = 10.00\,\text{m}, \\ &\qquad p_s \geqq 75 \cdot 10^{-4} \cdot 1.33 = 100 \cdot 10^{-4}\,\text{atm} \end{aligned}\right\} \quad (4.15\text{c})$$

Comparison with the values given in (4.15a, b) shows that the differences in general are negligible. This is due to the fact that in comparison with the snow load, which has to be estimated, the dead weight of the membrane is very small, e.g.: $g = 1$ kg/m² would be considered a large value.

4.3.3 *One-sided Snow Load and Internal Pressure*

Neglecting the dead weight of the membrane, which can be considered negligible, as shown in the last subsection, we obtain

ϑ_0	Values of max $\left[\frac{g\,R_{g+s+p}}{n_{\text{perm}}}\right]$					Values of min $[p_{g+s}/g]$					max $\left[\frac{s\,R_{p+s}}{n_{\text{perm}}}\right]$	min $\left[\frac{p_s}{s}\right]$
	$\frac{s}{g}=125$	$\frac{s}{g}=100$	$\frac{s}{g}=75$	$\frac{s}{g}=50$	$\frac{s}{g}=0$	$\frac{s}{g}=125$	$\frac{s}{g}=100$	$\frac{s}{g}=75$	$\frac{s}{g}=50$	$\frac{s}{g}=0$		
0	∞	∞	∞	∞	∞	126	101	76	51	1	∞	1.000
$\pi/8$	0.04136	0.05164	0.06871	0.10266	8.65052	126.04	101.04	76.04	51.04	1.0395	5.1948	1.000
$\pi/4$	0.01376	0.01718	0.02284	0.03408	2.15332	126.17	101.17	76.17	51.17	1.1715	1.7316	1.000
$3\,\pi/8$	0.00974	0.01215	0.01613	0.02399	0.94011	126.45	101.45	76.45	51.45	1.4464	1.2306	1.000
$\pi/2$	0.00942	0.01172	0.01550	0.02290	0.5000	127	102	77	52	2	1.2	1.000
$5\,\pi/8$	0.00870	0.01079	0.01420	0.02077	0.27604	128.24	103.24	78.24	53.24	3.2407	1.1230	1.000
125.4°	0.00764	0.00946	0.01241	0.01802	0.18747	129.75	104.75	79.75	54.75	4.7549	1	1.000
$3\,\pi/4$	0.00574	0.00710	0.00930	0.01348	0.13272	173.49	144.71	106.83	73.49	6.8278	0.75	1.3333
$7\,\pi/8$	0.00168	0.00207	0.00271	0.00392	0.03674	595.25	481.46	367.67	253.88	26.2950	0.2197	4.5516
π	0	0	0	0	0	∞	∞	∞	∞	∞	0	∞

Table 2

$$\left.\begin{aligned}
n_\vartheta &= \frac{p\,R}{2} + \frac{s\,R}{2}\left[a_{s1}(\vartheta) + a_{s3}(\vartheta)\cos\varphi\right] = \\
&= \frac{s\,R}{2}\left[\frac{p}{s} + a_{s1} + a_{s3}\cos\varphi\right], \\
n_{\vartheta\varphi} &= \frac{s\,R}{2}\, b_{s3}(\vartheta)\sin\varphi\,, \\
n_\varphi &= \frac{p\,R}{2} + \frac{s\,R}{2}\left[c_{s1}(\vartheta) + c_{s3}(\vartheta)\cos\varphi\right] = \\
&= \frac{s\,R}{2}\left[\frac{p}{s} + c_{s1} + c_{s3}\cos\varphi\right].
\end{aligned}\right\} \qquad (4.16\text{a-c})$$

Taking into account that

$$a_{s1} + c_{s1} = a_{s3} + c_{s3} = A(\vartheta) = \begin{cases} -\cos^3\vartheta & \text{for } \vartheta \leqq \pi/2 \\ 0 & \text{for } \vartheta \geqq \pi/2 \end{cases}$$

and writing

$$B^2 = (a_{s1} - c_{s1})^2 + 4\,b_{s3}^2\,, \quad C = (a_{s1} - c_{s1})(a_{s3} - c_{s3})\,,$$
$$D^2 = (a_{s3} - c_{s3})^2 - 4\,b_{s3}^2$$

we obtain the principal membrane forces from (2.15a) for $\alpha = \vartheta$ and $\beta = \varphi$

$$\begin{aligned}
n_{1,2} &= \frac{1}{2}\left[n_\vartheta + n_\varphi \pm \sqrt{(n_\vartheta - n_\varphi)^2 + 4\,n_{\vartheta\varphi}^2}\,\right] = \\
&= \frac{s\,R}{4}\left[2\frac{p}{s} + a_{s1} + c_{s1} + (a_{s3} + c_{s3})\cos\varphi \pm \right. \\
&\left. \pm \sqrt{[a_{s1} - c_{s1} + (a_{s3} - c_{s3})\cos\varphi]^2 + 4\,b_{s3}^2\sin^2\varphi}\,\right] = \qquad (4.17) \\
&= \frac{s\,R}{4}\left[2\frac{p}{s} + A\,(1 + \cos\varphi) \pm \right. \\
&\left. \pm \sqrt{B^2 + 2\,C\cos\varphi + D^2\cos^2\varphi}\,\right]
\end{aligned}$$

In order to find the condition necessary for the absence of folds [min $n_2 \geqq 0$] and to show that the maximum permissible stress [max $n_1 \leqq n_{\text{perm}}$] has not been exceeded, we have first to obtain the extreme values of (4.17). From

$$\frac{\partial\, n_{1,2}}{\partial\,\varphi} = -\sin\varphi\left[A \pm \frac{C + D^2\cos\varphi}{\sqrt{B^2 + 2\,C\cos\varphi + D^2\cos^2\varphi}}\right] = \frac{s\,R}{4} = 0$$

we obtain

$$\sin\varphi = 0 \quad \text{or} \quad \varphi_1 = 0\,, \quad \varphi_2 = \pi \qquad (4.18\text{a, b})$$

By equating the term inside the square brackets to zero, we obtain additional extrema at $\varphi_{3,4}$:

$$A^2\,(B^2 + 2\,C\cos\varphi + D^2\cos^2\varphi) = (C + D^2\cos\varphi)^2$$

or

$$\cos^2\varphi + 2\frac{C}{D^2}\cos\varphi + \frac{A^2\,B^2 - C^2}{D^2\,(A^2 - D^2)} = 0\,,$$

or finally

$$\cos\varphi_{3,4} = -\frac{C}{D^2}\left[1 \pm \frac{A}{C}\sqrt{\frac{C^2 - D^2\,B^2}{A^2 - D^2}}\right] = -\frac{C}{D^2}\left[1 \pm \frac{A}{C}\sqrt{F(\vartheta)}\right].$$

For $\pi/2 \leqq \vartheta \leqq \vartheta_0$ no other extrema besides those at φ_1 and φ_2 (i.e., also no additional principal-force extrema) exist, since, with $A = 0$, we obtain

$$\left|\cos\varphi_{3,4}\right| = \left|-\frac{C}{D^2}\right| = \left|\frac{a_{s1}\,a_{s3}}{b_{s3}^2 - a_{s3}^2}\right| = \left|-\frac{1}{3\,\pi\sin\vartheta}\right| > 1\,.$$

However, numerical computation of

$$F(\vartheta) = 4\,b_{s3}^2\,\frac{a_{s1}^2 - a_{s3}^2 - A\,(a_{s1} - a_{s3}) + b_{s3}^2}{a_{s3}\,c_{s3} + b_{s3}^2}\,,$$

(cf. Table 3) shows that when $\left|\cos\varphi_{3,4}\right| \leqq 1$, an extreme at φ_3 exists only for $0 \leqq \vartheta \leqq 53.75°$, while an extreme at φ_4 exists only for $0 \leqq \vartheta \leqq 34.79°$.

ϑ^0	0	10	20	30	40	45	50	60	70	80	90
$F(\vartheta)$	0.1111	0.1177	0.1252	0.1459	0.1901	0.2408	0.3721	− 0.3757	− 0.0055	− 0.0097	0

Table 3

The corresponding membarane forces are, by (4.17)

$$n_{1,2}\left(\vartheta, \varphi_3(\vartheta)\right) = \frac{sR}{2}\left\{\begin{matrix} \frac{p}{s} + U_{\mathrm{I}}(\vartheta) \\ \frac{p}{s} + U_{\mathrm{II}}(\vartheta) \end{matrix}\right\}, \tag{4.19a}$$

$$n_{1,2}\left(\vartheta, \varphi_4(\vartheta)\right) = \frac{sR}{2}\left\{\begin{matrix} \frac{p}{s} + P_{\mathrm{I}}(\vartheta) \\ \frac{p}{s} + P_{\mathrm{II}}(\vartheta) \end{matrix}\right\}, \tag{4.19b}$$

where

$$U_{\mathrm{I,II}} = \frac{1}{2}\left[A(1+\cos\varphi_3) \pm \sqrt{B^2 + 2C\cos\varphi_3 + D^2\cos^2\varphi_3}\,\right],$$

$$P_{\mathrm{I,II}} = \frac{1}{2}\left[A(1+\cos\varphi_4) \pm \sqrt{B^2 + 2C\cos\varphi_4 + D^2\cos^2\varphi_4}\,\right] \tag{4.19c, d}$$

A few values are given in Table 4.

For the extrema at $\varphi_1 = 0$ and $\varphi_2 = \pi$ we obtain the principal membrane forces

ϑ_0	$U_{\mathrm{I}}(\vartheta)$	$U_{\mathrm{II}}(\vartheta)$	$P_{\mathrm{I}}(\vartheta)$	$P_{\mathrm{II}}(\vartheta)$
0	0.1667	− 0.1667	− 0.8333	− 1.1667
10	0.1647	− 0.1784	− 0.7456	− 1.0887
20	0.1644	− 0.1894	− 0.5743	− 0.9281
30	0.1640	− 0.2180	− 0.4083	− 0.7903
34.79			− 0.3522	− 0.7553
40	0.1695	− 0.2715		
45	0.1789	− 0.3118		
50	0.2012	− 0.4087		
53.75	0.2506	− 0.6644		

Table 4

$$n_{1,2}(\vartheta, \varphi_1) = \frac{sR}{2}\left\{\begin{matrix} p/s + a_{s1} + a_{s3} \\ p/s + c_{s1} + c_{s3} \end{matrix}\right\} = \left\{\begin{matrix} n_\vartheta(\vartheta, \varphi_1) \\ n_\varphi(\vartheta, \varphi_1) \end{matrix}\right\}, \tag{4.20a, b}$$

$$n_{1,2}(\vartheta, \varphi_2) = \frac{sR}{2}\left\{\begin{matrix} p/s + a_{s1} - a_{s3} \\ p/s + c_{s1} - c_{s3} \end{matrix}\right\} = \left\{\begin{matrix} n_\vartheta(\vartheta, \varphi_2) \\ n_\varphi(\vartheta, \varphi_2) \end{matrix}\right\} \tag{4.21a, b}$$

Figure 4.6 shows $a_{s1} + a_{s3}$, $c_{s1} + c_{s3}$, $a_{s1} - a_{s3}$, $c_{s1} - c_{s3}$, U_{I}, U_{II}, P_{I} and P_{II} as functions of ϑ. It can be seen that for domes in which $\vartheta_0 \geqq 134°$, the compressive membrane forces due to snow loads are largest at the peak of the dome in the circumferential direction. For domes in which ϑ_0 is larger, the compressive membrane forces are higher at the lower edge of the membrane in the meridianal direction. We thus obtain the minimum inflation pressure, which for $0 \leqq \vartheta_0 \leqq 134°$ has to counterbalance the largest circumferential compressive forces at the dome peak, while for $\vartheta_0 \gtreqless 134°$ it has to counterbalance the largest meridianal compressive forces at the lower edge of the membrane at $\varphi_1 = 0$.

$$\frac{p_{\min}}{s} \geqq -\left\{\begin{matrix} c_{s1}(0) + c_{s3}(0) \\ a_{s1}(\vartheta) + a_{s3}(\vartheta) \end{matrix}\right\} = \left\{\begin{matrix} 1{,}1667 & \text{for } 0 \leqq \vartheta_0 \leqq 134° \\ -\left[a_{s1}(\vartheta) + a_{s3}(\vartheta)\right] & \text{for } \vartheta_0 \geqq 134° \end{matrix}\right\}. \tag{4.22a, b}$$

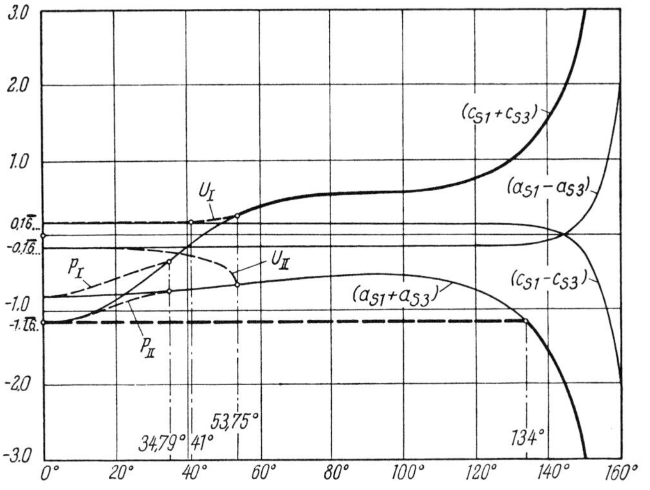

Figure 4.6

Figure 4.6 shows that the compressive membrane forces at $\varphi_{3,4}(\vartheta)$ nowhere determine the inflation pressure.

The largest tensile forces due to snow loads are, for $\vartheta_0 \leqq 41°$, the circumferential forces at $\varphi_2 = \pi$ (on the side opposite the snow accumulation). They are nearly equal to those corresponding to $U_{\mathrm{I}}(\varphi_3(\vartheta))$, and can be considered constant (cf. Figure 4.6). Thus, for $\vartheta_0 \leqq 41°$, snow load and internal pressure cause the following maximum membrane force:

$$n_{\max} = \frac{sR}{2}\left[\frac{p}{s} + c_{s1}(0) - c_{s3}(0)\right] = \frac{sR}{2}\left[\frac{p}{s} + 0.16667\right], \tag{4.23a}$$

$$0 \leqq \vartheta_0 \leqq 41°.$$

There follows a transition range $41° \leqq \vartheta_0 \leqq 53.75°$, in which the largest tensile forces are due to the snow load at $(\vartheta_0, \varphi_3(\vartheta_0))$, so that

$$n_{\max} = \frac{sR}{2}\left(\frac{p}{s} + U_{\mathrm{I}}(\vartheta_0)\right), \quad 41° \leqq \vartheta_0 \leqq 53.75° \tag{4.23b}$$

For $\vartheta_0 = 53.75°$, the circumferential tensile forces at the lower membrane edge become predominant at the side on which the snow has accumulated $(\varphi_1 = 0)$, whence

$$n_{\max} = \frac{sR}{2}\left[\frac{p}{s} + c_{s1}(\vartheta_0) + c_{s3}(\vartheta_0)\right], \quad \vartheta_0 \geqq 53.75° \tag{4.23c}$$

Since $n_{\max} \leqq n_{\mathrm{perm}}$, the maximum possible radius of the sphere is, in the presence of snow load and internal pressure,

$$\frac{sR}{n_{\mathrm{perm}}} \leqq 2\left\{\begin{matrix} \left[\frac{p}{s} + 0.1667\right]^{-1}, & 0 \leqq \vartheta_0 \leqq 41° \\ \left[\frac{p}{s} + U_{\mathrm{I}}(\vartheta_0)\right]^{-1}, & 41° \leqq \vartheta_0 \leqq 53.75° \\ \left[\frac{p}{s} + c_{s1}(\vartheta_0) + c_{s3}(\vartheta_0)\right]^{-1}, & \vartheta_0 \geqq 53.75°. \end{matrix}\right. \tag{4.24}$$

ϑ^0	100°	110°	120°	130°	135°	140°	150°	160°	170°	180°
$\cos\varphi_3$	0.9387	0.7352	0.5344	0.3565	0.2807	0.2154	0.1138	0.0480	0.0113	0

Table 5

Inserting the value for the minimum inflation pressure from (4.22a, b) we obtain Figure 4.7

We see that the assumed one-sided snow load exerts an influence only in domes for which $\vartheta_0 \leqq 53.75°$. The values obtained for domes in which $\vartheta_0 \geqq 53.75°$ approximate those corresponding to a symmetrical snow load.

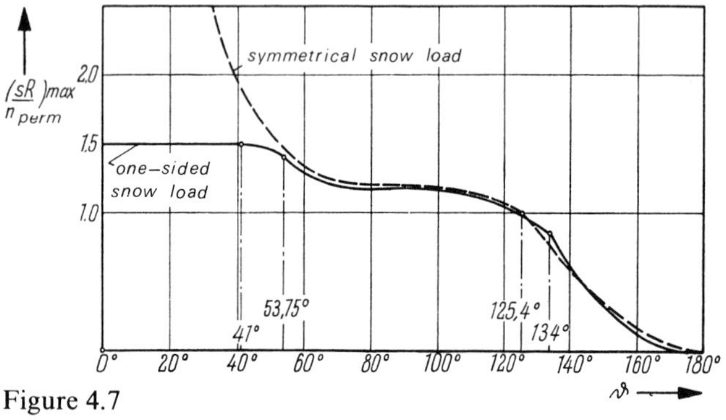

Figure 4.7

4.3.4 *Wind Load and Internal Pressure*

The membrane forces in this case are

$$\left.\begin{aligned} n_\vartheta &= \frac{R}{2}(p - w_0 + 2\, w_1\, a_{w1}(\vartheta)\cos\varphi)\,,\\ n_{\vartheta\varphi} &= \frac{R}{2}\cdot 2\, w_1\, b_{w1}(\vartheta)\sin\varphi\,,\\ n_\varphi &= \frac{R}{2}(p - w_0 + 2\, w_1\, c_{w1}(\vartheta)\cos\varphi)\,,\end{aligned}\right\} \qquad (4.25\text{a-c})$$

Hence the principal membrane forces are

$$\begin{aligned} n_{1,2} &= \frac{R}{4}\Big[2(p - w_0) + 2\, w_1 (a_{w1} + c_{w1})\cos\varphi \pm \\ &\pm \sqrt{4\, w_1^2 (a_{w1} - c_{w1})^2 \cos^2\varphi + 4\cdot 4\, w_1^2\, b_{w1}^2 \sin^2\varphi}\,\Big] \\ &= \frac{R}{2}\Big[p - w_0 + w_1(a_{w1} + c_{w1})\cos\varphi \pm \\ &\pm w_1 \sqrt{4\, b_{w1}^2 + [(a_{w1} - c_{w1})^2 - 4 b_{w1}^2]\cos^2\varphi}\,\Big]\end{aligned} \qquad (4.26)$$

From

$$\frac{\partial n_{1,2}}{\partial\varphi} = -\, w_1 \sin\varphi \left[a_{w1} + c_{w1} \pm \pm \frac{[(a_{w1} - c_{w1})^2 - 4\, b_{w1}^2]\cos\varphi}{\sqrt{4\, b_{w1}^2 + [(a_{w1} - c_{w1})^2 - 4\, b_{w1}^2]\cos^2\varphi}}\right]\frac{R}{2} = 0$$

we obtain the extrema

$$\sin\varphi = 0\,,\quad \text{i.e.,}\quad \varphi_1 = 0\,,\quad \varphi_2 = \pi \qquad (4.27\text{a, b})$$

Furthermore, equating the expression inside the square brackets to zero,

$$(a_{w1} + c_{w1})^2\{4\, b_{w1}^2 + [(a_{w1} - c_{w1})^2 - 4\, b_{w1}^2]\cos^2\varphi\} = \\ = [(a_{w1} - c_{w1})^2 - 4\, b_{w1}^2]^2\cos^2\varphi\,,$$

we obtain

$$\cos\varphi_3 = \pm\frac{b_{w1}(a_{w1} + c_{w1})}{\sqrt{(a_{w1}\, c_{w1} + b_{w1}^2)(4\, b_{w1}^2 - (a_{w1} - c_{w1})^2)}} = \\ = \pm f(\vartheta) \qquad (4.27\text{c})$$

Numerical computation of (4.27c) yields always $|\cos\varphi_3| > 1$. for $0 \leqq \vartheta \leqq \pi/2$. Hence, no extreme of principal membrane forces exists, except at $\varphi_1 = 0$ and $\varphi_2 = \pi$, in the upper semisphere. The values of $|\cos\varphi_3|$ for $\vartheta \geqq \pi/2$ are given in Table 5.

For $\varphi_1 = 0$ and $\varphi_2 = \pi$ we obtain

$$n_{1,2}(\vartheta, \varphi_1) = \frac{R}{2}\left\{\begin{matrix} p - w_0 + 2\, w_1\, a_{w1}(\vartheta) \\ p - w_0 + 2\, w_1\, c_{w1}(\vartheta)\end{matrix}\right\} = \left\{\begin{matrix} n_\vartheta(\vartheta, \varphi_1) \\ n_\varphi(\vartheta, \varphi_1)\end{matrix}\right.,$$

$$n_{1,2}(\vartheta, \varphi_2) = \frac{R}{2}\left\{\begin{matrix} p - w_0 - 2\, w_1\, a_{w1}(\vartheta) \\ p - w_0 - 2\, w_1\, c_{w1}(\vartheta)\end{matrix}\right\} = \left\{\begin{matrix} n_\vartheta(\vartheta, \varphi_2) \\ n_\varphi(\vartheta, \varphi_2)\end{matrix}\right.,$$

Hence, by virtue of (cf. Table 1) $c_{w1} < a_{w1}$, $c_{w1} < 0$

$$\left.\begin{aligned} n_{2\,\min} &= \frac{R}{2}\{p - w_0 + 2\, w_1\, c_{w1}(\vartheta_0)\} = n_\varphi(\vartheta_0, \varphi_1) \\ n_{1\,\max} &= \frac{R}{2}\{p - w_0 - 2\, w_1\, c_{w1}(\vartheta_0)\} = n_\varphi(\vartheta_0, \varphi_2)\end{aligned}\right| \qquad (4.28\text{a, b})$$

The extremes of the principal membrane forces at φ_3, where $\cos\varphi_3 = = \pm f(\vartheta)$, have to be found numerically in order to decide whether the values given by (4.28a, b) determine the minimum inflation pressure or the maximum permissible tensile stress. Insertion of (4.27c) into (4.26) yields the principal membrane forces for φ_3, which may represent additional extrema, apart from those given by (4.28a, b). Thus

$$n_{1,2} = \pm\left|\begin{matrix} w_1 \dfrac{4\, b_{w1}(a_{w1}\, c_{w1} + b_{w1}^2)}{\sqrt{(a_{w1}\, c_{w1} + b_{w1}^2)(4\, b_{w1}^2 - (a_{w1} - c_{w1})^2)}} \\ w_1 \dfrac{2\, b_{w1}(a_{w1}^2 + c_{w1}^2 - 2\, b_{w1}^2)}{\sqrt{(a_{w1}\, c_{w1} + b_{w1}^2)(4\, b_{w1}^2 - (a_{w1} - c_{w1})^2)}}\end{matrix}\right|\frac{R}{2} + \\ + (p - w_0)\frac{R}{2} = \frac{R}{2}\left(p - w_0 \pm \left\{\begin{matrix}\Psi(\vartheta) \\ \Phi(\vartheta)\end{matrix}\right\} w_1\right).$$

Figure 4.8 gives $\Phi(\vartheta)$, $\Psi(\vartheta)$, and $2\, c_{w1}(\vartheta)$ as functions of ϑ. We can see that the extremes of the principal forces at φ_1 and φ_2 are decisive only for $\vartheta_0 \leqq 90°$. For $\vartheta \geqq 90°$, the internal pressure and the maximum tensile stress are determined by $\Psi(\vartheta)$, while $\Phi(\vartheta)$ has no influence whatsoever. Putting

$$F(\vartheta) = \left\{\begin{matrix} 2\,|\, c_{w1}(\vartheta)\,|\,, & 0 \leqq \vartheta \lesssim \pi/2 \\ |\,\Psi(\vartheta)\,|\,, & \pi/2 \lesssim \vartheta\end{matrix}\right\} \qquad (4.28\text{c})$$

we finally obtain $n_{2\,\min}$ and $n_{1\,\max}$:

$$\left.\begin{aligned} n_{2\,\min} &= \frac{R}{2}\left(p - w_0 - w_1 F(\vartheta_0)\right), \\ n_{1\,\max} &= \frac{R}{2}\left(p - w_0 + w_1 F(\vartheta_0)\right).\end{aligned}\right| \qquad (4.29\text{a, b})$$

ϑ^0	0	10	20	30	40	45	50	60	70	80
$F(\vartheta)$	0	0.2520	0.5154	0.7624	0.9946	1.1046	1.2106	1.4112	1.6008	1.7896
ϑ^0	90	100	110	120	130	135	140	150	160	170
$F(\vartheta)$	2.0000	2.2778	2.7689	3.7030	5.5706	7.2058	9.7295	21.0865	66.4995	512.6922

Table 6

The required internal pressure is found from the condition $n_{2\,\min} \geqq 0$

$$p_{\min} \geqq w_0 + w_1 F(\vartheta_0)\,, \qquad (4.30a)$$

while the maximum possible radius is obtained from (4.30a) and the condition $n_{1\,\max} \leqq n_{\text{perm}}$

$$\frac{w_1 R_{\max}}{n_{\text{perm}}} \leqq \frac{1}{F(\vartheta_0)} \qquad (4.30b)$$

The function $F(\vartheta)$ is given in Table 6 $[F(\pi) \to \infty]$.

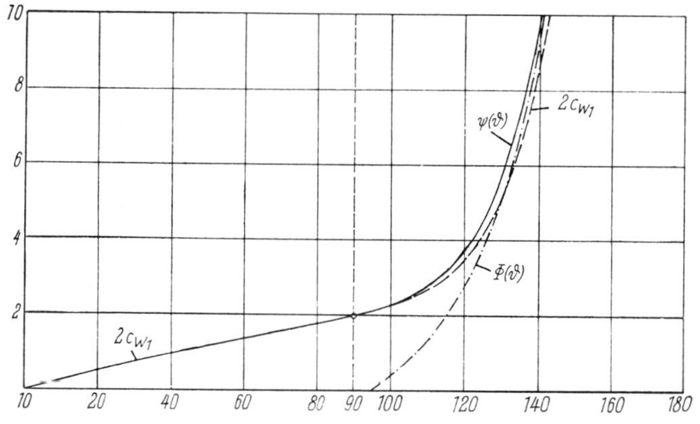

Figure 4.8

4.3.5 *General Loading*

The various components of a general load cause maximum stresses at different points of the membrane. If the relationships for φ and ϑ are too complicated, the principal membrane forces have to be computed separately for each point. However, the internal pressure p causes a constant (hydrostatic) membrane force $n = p\,R/2$ at every point of a spherical membrane. The resulting principal forces can thus be obtained by adding the principal forces due to the external load and the membrane force $n = p\,R/2$. The procedure for determining the required internal pressure and the maximum tensile forces in the system is as follows:
We first determine from the external load $[n_\vartheta^{(a)}, n_{\vartheta\varphi}^{(a)}, n_\varphi^{(a)}]$ the principal membrane forces at the different points

$$n_{1,2}^{(a)} = \frac{1}{2}\left[(n_\vartheta^{(a)} + n_\varphi^{(a)}) \pm \sqrt{(n_\vartheta^{(a)} - n_\varphi^{(a)})^2 + 4\, n_{\vartheta\varphi}^{(a)\,2}}\,\right] \qquad (4.31)$$

From these we obtain the curves of equal principal membrane forces $n_1^{(a)}$ and $n_2^{(a)}$. This enables us to find the location and magnitude of the extrema of the principal tensile and compressive forces $n_1^{(a)}{}_{\max}$ and $n_2^{(a)}{}_{\min}$, due to the external load. The required inflation pressure p is then obtained from

$$n_{2\,\min\,\text{tot}} = n_2^{(a)}{}_{\min} + \frac{p\,R}{2} \geqq 0 \quad \text{as}$$

$$p \geqq -\frac{2\,n_2^{(a)}{}_{\min}}{R} = -2\,\bar{n}_2^{(a)}{}_{\min}\,, \qquad (4.32a)$$

$$p \geqq -\frac{2\,n_2^{(a)}{}_{\min}}{} = -2\,\bar{n}_2^{(a)}{}_{\min}\,,$$

where $\bar{n} = n/R$. From

$$n_{1\,\max\,\text{tot}} = n_1^{(a)}{}_{\max} + \frac{p\,R}{2} = R\left[\frac{p}{2} + \bar{n}_1^{(a)}{}_{\max}\right] \leqq n_{\text{perm}}$$

we obtain the maximum possible radius of the sphere:

$$\frac{R_{\max}}{n_{\text{perm}}} \leqq \left[\frac{p}{2} + \bar{n}_1^{(a)}{}_{\max}\right]^{-1} \leqq \left[\bar{n}_1^{(a)}{}_{\max} - \bar{n}_2^{(a)}{}_{\min}\right]^{-1}. \qquad (4.32b)$$

4.3.6 *Edge Loads on a Quarter Sphere*

The general equilibrium conditions (3.6) yield, in the absence of surface loading of the sphere, $(R_1 = R_2 = R)$:

$$\left.\begin{aligned} & n_\varphi + n_\vartheta = 0\,, \\ & \frac{1}{\sin\vartheta}\frac{\partial}{\partial\vartheta}(n_\vartheta \sin^2\vartheta) + \frac{\partial n_{\vartheta\varphi}}{\partial\varphi} = 0\,, \\ & \frac{1}{\sin\vartheta}\frac{\partial}{\partial\vartheta}(n_{\vartheta\varphi}\sin^2\vartheta) - \frac{\partial n_\vartheta}{\partial\varphi} = 0\,. \end{aligned}\right\} \qquad (4.33a\text{-}c)$$

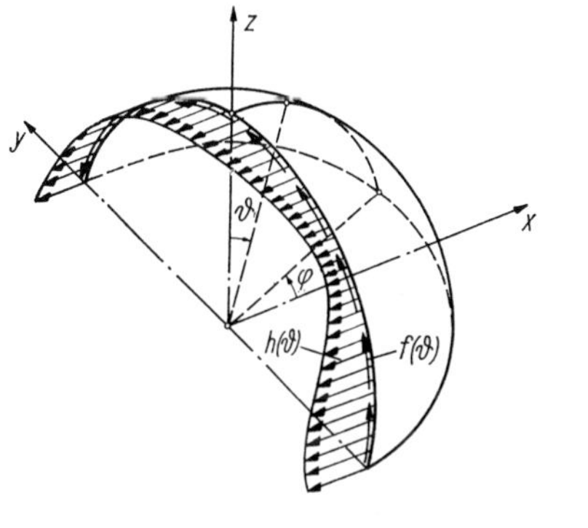

Figure 4.9

Substituting from (4.33b)

$$\frac{\partial n_{\vartheta\varphi}}{\partial\varphi} = -\frac{1}{\sin\vartheta}\frac{\partial}{\partial\vartheta}(n_\vartheta\sin^2\vartheta) \qquad (4.33d)$$

in (4.33c), previously differentiated with respect to φ, we obtain

$$\sin\vartheta\frac{\partial}{\partial\vartheta}\left[\sin\vartheta\frac{\partial}{\partial\vartheta}(n_\vartheta\sin^2\vartheta)\right] + \frac{\partial^2}{\partial\varphi^2}(n_\vartheta\sin^2\vartheta) = 0\,, \qquad (4.34a)$$

The substitution

$$n_\vartheta\sin^2\vartheta = N_\vartheta \qquad (4.34b)$$

yields

$$\sin\vartheta\frac{\partial}{\partial\vartheta}\left[\sin\vartheta\frac{\partial N_\vartheta}{\partial\vartheta}\right]+\frac{\partial^2 N_\vartheta}{\partial\varphi^2}=0 \tag{4.34c}$$

We select

$$\xi=\ln \operatorname{tg}\frac{\vartheta}{2} \tag{4.34d}$$

as the independent variable, so that

$$N_\vartheta=N_\vartheta(\xi,\varphi) \tag{4.34e}$$

and

$$\frac{\partial N_\vartheta}{\partial\vartheta}=\frac{\partial N_\vartheta}{\partial\xi}\frac{d\xi}{d\vartheta}=\frac{\partial N_\vartheta}{\partial\xi}\frac{1}{\sin\vartheta},\qquad \text{i.e.}\quad \sin\vartheta\frac{\partial N_\vartheta}{\partial\vartheta}=\frac{\partial N_\vartheta}{\partial\xi}. \tag{4.34f}$$

We can thus rewrite (4.34c) as follows:

$$\frac{\partial^2 N_\vartheta}{\partial\xi^2}+\frac{\partial^2 N_\vartheta}{\partial\varphi^2}=\Delta N_\vartheta=0;\quad \Delta=\frac{\partial^2}{\partial\xi^2}+\frac{\partial^2}{\partial\varphi^2}. \tag{4.35}$$

From (4.33a) we also obtain for $N_\varphi=n_\varphi\sin^2\vartheta$

$$\Delta N_\varphi=0, \tag{4.36}$$

whereas (4.33d) yields

$$\frac{\partial}{\partial\varphi}(n_{\vartheta\varphi}\sin^2\vartheta)=-\sin\vartheta\frac{\partial}{\partial\vartheta}(n_\vartheta\sin^2\vartheta),$$

or, putting $N_{\vartheta\varphi}=n_{\vartheta\varphi}\sin^2\vartheta$,

$$\frac{\partial N_{\vartheta\varphi}}{\partial\varphi}=-\frac{\partial N_\vartheta}{\partial\xi}=\frac{\partial N_\varphi}{\partial\xi}. \tag{4.37}$$

We obtain the solutions of (4.35) through (4.37) in the form of products if we write

$$N_\varphi=-N_\vartheta=\sum_{k=0}^{\infty}(N_{\varphi k}(\vartheta)\cos k\varphi+\bar N_{\varphi k}(\vartheta)\sin k\varphi) \tag{4.38a}$$

for which (4.37) leads to

$$N_{\vartheta\varphi}=C+\sum_{k=0}^{\infty}\left(\frac{dN_{\varphi k}}{d\xi}\sin k\varphi-\frac{d\bar N_{\varphi k}}{d\xi}\cos k\varphi\right)\frac{1}{k}, \tag{4.38b}$$

where C is a constant*.

Substituting (4.38a) in (4.35) or (4.36) yields

$$\sum_{k=0}^{\infty}\left[\left(\frac{d^2N_{\varphi k}}{d\xi^2}-k^2N_{\varphi k}\right)\cos k\varphi+\left(\frac{d^2\bar N_{\varphi k}}{d\xi^2}-k^2\bar N_{\varphi k}\right)\sin k\varphi\right]=0.$$

(Since φ is arbitrary, this requires that the coefficient of each term in $\sin k\varphi$ and $\cos k\varphi$ vanish separately):

$$\frac{d^2N_{\varphi k}}{d\xi^2}-k^2N_{\varphi k}=0,\quad \frac{d^2\bar N_{\varphi k}}{d\xi^2}-k^2\bar N_{\varphi k}=0,\quad k=0\ldots\infty$$

The general solution is thus

$$N_{\varphi k}=C_{1k}e^{k\xi}+C_{2k}e^{-k\xi},\quad \bar N_{\varphi k}=\bar C_{1k}e^{k\xi}+\bar C_{2k}e^{-k\xi}.$$

We then obtain from (4.38a, b)

$$\left.\begin{aligned}N_\varphi=-N_\vartheta&=\sum_{k=0}^{\infty}\big[(C_{1k}e^{k\xi}+C_{2k}e^{-k\xi})\cos k\varphi+\\&\quad+(\bar C_{1k}e^{k\xi}+\bar C_{2k}e^{-k\xi})\sin k\varphi\big],\\ N_{\vartheta\varphi}&=C+\sum_{k=0}^{\infty}\big[(C_{1k}e^{k\xi}-C_{2k}e^{-k\xi})\sin k\varphi-\\&\quad-(\bar C_{1k}e^{k\xi}-\bar C_{2k}e^{-k\xi})\cos k\varphi\big].\end{aligned}\right\} \tag{4.39a, b}$$

Since

$$e^{k\xi}=e^{k\ln\operatorname{tg}\frac{\vartheta}{2}}=e^{\ln\left(\operatorname{tg}\frac{\vartheta}{2}\right)^k}=\operatorname{tg}^k\frac{\vartheta}{2};$$

$$e^{-k\xi}=\frac{1}{e^{k\xi}}=\frac{1}{\operatorname{tg}^k\frac{\vartheta}{2}}=\operatorname{ctg}^k\frac{\vartheta}{2}$$

we have, finally

$$\left.\begin{aligned}N_\varphi=-N_\vartheta&=\sum_{k=0}^{\infty}\left[\left(C_{1k}\operatorname{tg}^k\frac{\vartheta}{2}+C_{2k}\operatorname{ctg}^k\frac{\vartheta}{2}\right)\cos k\varphi+\right.\\&\quad\left.+\left(\bar C_{1k}\operatorname{tg}^k\frac{\vartheta}{2}+\bar C_{2k}\operatorname{ctg}^k\frac{\vartheta}{2}\right)\sin k\varphi\right],\\ N_{\vartheta\varphi}&=C+\sum_{k=0}^{\infty}\left[\left(C_{1k}\operatorname{tg}^k\frac{\vartheta}{2}-C_{2k}\operatorname{ctg}^k\frac{\vartheta}{2}\right)\sin k\varphi-\right.\\&\quad\left.-\left(\bar C_{1k}\operatorname{tg}^k\frac{\vartheta}{2}-\bar C_{2k}\operatorname{ctg}^k\frac{\vartheta}{2}\right)\cos k\varphi\right],\end{aligned}\right\} \tag{4.40a, b}$$

so that the sectional loads are

$$n_\varphi=-n_\vartheta=\frac{1}{\sin^2\vartheta}\sum_{k=0}^{\infty}\left[\left(C_{1k}\operatorname{tg}^k\frac{\vartheta}{2}+C_{2k}\operatorname{ctg}^k\frac{\vartheta}{2}\right)\cos k\varphi+\left(\bar C_{1k}\operatorname{tg}^k\frac{\vartheta}{2}+\bar C_{2k}\operatorname{ctg}^k\frac{\vartheta}{2}\right)\sin k\varphi\right],$$

$$n_{\vartheta\varphi}=\frac{1}{\sin^2\vartheta}\left\{C+\sum_{k=0}^{\infty}\left[\left(C_{1k}\operatorname{tg}^k\frac{\vartheta}{2}-C_{2k}\operatorname{ctg}^k\frac{\vartheta}{2}\right)\sin k\varphi-\left(\bar C_{1k}\operatorname{tg}^k\frac{\vartheta}{2}-\bar C_{2k}\operatorname{ctg}^k\frac{\vartheta}{2}\right)\cos k\varphi\right]\right\}. \tag{4.41a, b}$$

If we assume that the sectional loads at the peak $(\vartheta=0)$ are finite, all C_{2k} and $\bar C_{2k}$ must vanish. The same is true for $C_{10}, C_{11}, \bar C_{10}, \bar C_{11}$, and C. Writing $C_{1k}=C_k, \bar C_{1k}=\bar C_k$, we obtain

$$\left.\begin{aligned}N_\varphi=-N_\vartheta&=\sum_{k=2}^{\infty}e^{k\xi}(C_k\cos k\varphi+\bar C_k\sin k\varphi)=\\&=\sum_{k=2}^{\infty}\operatorname{tg}^k\frac{\vartheta}{2}(C_k\cos k\varphi+\bar C_k\sin k\varphi),\\ N_{\vartheta\varphi}&=\sum_{k=2}^{\infty}e^{k\xi}(C_k\sin k\varphi-\bar C_k\cos k\varphi)=\\&=\sum_{k=2}^{\infty}\operatorname{tg}^k\frac{\vartheta}{2}(C_k\sin k\varphi-\bar C_k\cos k\varphi),\end{aligned}\right\} \tag{4.42a, b}$$

thus

$$n_\varphi=-n_\vartheta=\frac{1}{\sin^2\vartheta}\sum_{k=2}^{\infty}\operatorname{tg}^k\frac{\vartheta}{2}(C_k\cos k\varphi+\bar C_k\sin k\varphi),$$

$$n_{\vartheta\varphi}=\frac{1}{\sin^2\vartheta}\sum_{k=2}^{\infty}\operatorname{tg}^k\frac{\vartheta}{2}(C_k\sin k\varphi-\bar C_k\cos k\varphi). \tag{4.43a, b}$$

The constants C_k and $\bar C_k$ are determined from the boundary conditions, i.e., from the edge loads along the sections $\varphi=\pi/2$ and

* This constant takes into account the shearing stresses due to a concentrated torque M_z acting at the dome peak $\vartheta=0$ (cf. 3.7b).

$\varphi = -\pi/2$. If the edge loads are symmetrical with respect to the (x, z) plane, the sectional loads n_φ and n_ϑ must also be symmetrical with respect to this plane, in which case all constants $\overline{C}_k$ must vanish. Correspondingly, when the load is antimetrical with respect to the (x, z) plane, all constants C_k vanish. We shall now consider certain particular cases:

a) Only shearing forces acting along the edge $\varphi = \pm\pi/2$

a1) Shearing forces antimetrical with respect to the (x, z) plane. This state of stress causes membrane forces n_φ and n_ϑ which are symmetrical with respect to the (x, z) plane. Hence all $\overline{C}_k$ must vanish. We then obtain from (4.43a,b):

$$n_\varphi = -n_\vartheta = \frac{1}{\sin^2\vartheta}\sum_{k=2}^{\infty} C_k \operatorname{tg}^k \frac{\vartheta}{2} \cos k\varphi\,,$$

$$n_{\vartheta\varphi} = \frac{1}{\sin^2\vartheta}\sum_{k=2}^{\infty} C_k \operatorname{tg}^k \frac{\vartheta}{2} \sin k\varphi\,, \qquad (4.44\text{a, b})$$

where the constants are determined from the boundary conditions

$$n_\varphi\Big|_{\varphi=\pm\pi/2} = 0\,,\quad n_{\vartheta\varphi}\Big|_{\varphi=\pi/2} = f(\vartheta)\,,\quad n_{\vartheta\varphi}\Big|_{\varphi=-\pi/2} = -f(\vartheta). \qquad (4.44\text{c})$$

Hence, for all even values of $k, C_k = 0$, so that

$$n_\varphi = -n_\vartheta = \frac{1}{\sin^2\vartheta}\sum_{n=1}^{\infty} C_{2n+1} \operatorname{tg}^{(2n+1)} \frac{\vartheta}{2} \cos(2n+1)\varphi\,,$$

$$n_{\vartheta\varphi} = \frac{1}{\sin^2\vartheta}\sum_{n=1}^{\infty} C_{2n+1} \operatorname{tg}^{(2n+1)} \frac{\vartheta}{2} \sin(2n+1)\varphi\,. \qquad (4.44\text{d,e})$$

The constants C_{2n+1} can be found from

$$n_{\vartheta\varphi}\Big|_{\varphi=\pi/2} = \frac{1}{\sin^2\vartheta}\sum_{n=1}^{\infty}(-1)^n C_{2n+1} \operatorname{tg}^{(2n+1)}\frac{\vartheta}{2} = f(\vartheta) \quad \text{or}$$

$$\sum_{n=1}^{\infty}(-1)^n C_{2n+1} \operatorname{tg}^{(2n+1)}\frac{\vartheta}{2} = f(\vartheta)\sin^2\vartheta$$

by the method of least squares. Writing

$$F = \int_{\vartheta=0}^{\pi/2}\left[f(\vartheta)\sin^2\vartheta - \sum_{n=1}^{\infty}(-1)^n C_{2n+1} \operatorname{tg}^{(2n+1)}\frac{\vartheta}{2}\right]^2 d\vartheta = \min$$

and setting $\partial F/\partial C_{2k+1} = 0$, we obtain the system of linear equations

$$\sum_{i=1}^{\infty} C_{2i+1}\,\delta_{2i+1,2k+1} = f_{2k+1}\,,\quad k = 1\ldots\infty \qquad (4.45\text{a})$$

where

$$f_{2k+1} = (-1)^k \int_0^{\pi/2} f(\vartheta)\sin^2\vartheta \operatorname{tg}^{(2k+1)}\frac{\vartheta}{2}\, d\vartheta\,,$$

$$\delta_{2i+1,2k+1} = (-1)^{i+k}\int_0^{\pi/2} \operatorname{tg}^{2(i+k+1)}\frac{\vartheta}{2}\, d\vartheta\,. \qquad (4.45\text{b, c})$$

Since $\delta_{\nu\mu} \neq 0$ we obtain an infinite system of linear equations in each of which all unknowns appear. We must therefore equate all constants to zero for $i > i_0$, and consider only the first i_0 equations. We could, of course, perform an orthogonalization of the equations, e.g., by the method of Schmidt. This would, however, lead to complicated expressions for the solving functions (4.44d, e), and will therefore not be done.

a2) Shearing forces symmetrical with respect to (x, z) plane. In this case all C_k in (4.43a, b) must vanish. We then obtain

$$n_\varphi = -n_\vartheta = \frac{1}{\sin^2\vartheta}\sum_{k=2}^{\infty} \overline{C}_k \operatorname{tg}^k \frac{\vartheta}{2} \sin k\varphi\,,$$

$$n_{\vartheta\varphi} = -\frac{1}{\sin^2\vartheta}\sum_{k=2}^{\infty} \overline{C}_k \operatorname{tg}^k \frac{\vartheta}{2} \cos k\varphi\,. \qquad (4.46\text{a,b})$$

In order that the boundary conditions

$$n_\varphi\Big|_{\varphi=\pm\pi/2} = 0\,,\quad n_{\vartheta\varphi}\Big|_{\varphi=\pm\pi/2} = f(\vartheta)$$

be satisfied, the $\overline{C}_k$ must vanish for all odd values of k. Hence

$$n_\varphi = -n_\vartheta = \frac{1}{\sin^2\vartheta}\sum_{n=1}^{\infty} \overline{C}_{2n} \operatorname{tg}^{2n} \frac{\vartheta}{2} \sin 2n\varphi\,,$$

$$n_{\vartheta\varphi} = -\frac{1}{\sin^2\vartheta}\sum_{n=1}^{\infty} \overline{C}_{2n} \operatorname{tg}^{2n} \frac{\vartheta}{2} \cos 2n\varphi \qquad (4.46\text{c, d})$$

The constants $\overline{C}_{2n}$ are determined from

$$n_{\vartheta\varphi}\Big|_{\varphi=\pm\pi/2} = -\frac{1}{\sin^2\vartheta}\sum_{n=1}^{\infty}(-1)^n \overline{C}_{2n} \operatorname{tg}^{2n}\frac{\vartheta}{2} = f(\vartheta) \quad \text{or}$$

$$-\sum_{n=1}^{\infty}(-1)^n \overline{C}_{2n} \operatorname{tg}^{2n}\frac{\vartheta}{2} = f(\vartheta)\sin^2\vartheta$$

by writing

$$F = \int_0^{\pi/2}\left[f(\vartheta)\sin^2\vartheta + \sum_{n=1}^{\infty}(-1)^n \overline{C}_{2n} \operatorname{tg}^{2n}\frac{\vartheta}{2}\right]^2 d\vartheta = \min\,.$$

Setting $\partial F/\partial \overline{C}_{2k} = 0$ and writing

$$\bar{f}_{2k} = (-1)^{k+1}\int_0^{\pi/2} f(\vartheta)\sin^2\vartheta \operatorname{tg}^{2k}\frac{\vartheta}{2}\, d\vartheta\,,$$

$$\delta_{2i,2k} = (-1)^{i+k}\int_0^{\pi/2} \operatorname{tg}^{2(i+k)}\frac{\vartheta}{2}\, d\vartheta \qquad (4.47\text{a, b})$$

we finally obtain equations of the form

$$\sum_{i=1}^{\infty} \overline{C}_{2i}\,\delta_{2i,2k} = \bar{f}_{2k}\,,\quad k = 1\ldots\infty \qquad (4.47\text{c})$$

b) Only normal forces acting along the edge $\varphi = \pm\pi/2$

b1) Normal forces symmetrical with respect to the (x, z) plane. In this case, the loading is again symmetrical with respect to the (x, z) plane. The solution is similar to (4.44a, b). The boundary conditions

$$n_{\vartheta\varphi}\Big|_{\varphi=\pm\pi/2} = 0\,,\quad n_\varphi\Big|_{\varphi=\pm\pi/2} = h(\vartheta)$$

require that all C_k vanish for odd values of k, so that

$$n_\varphi = -n_\vartheta = \frac{1}{\sin^2\vartheta}\sum_{n=1}^{\infty} C_{2n} \operatorname{tg}^{2n} \frac{\vartheta}{2} \cos 2n\varphi\,,$$

$$n_{\vartheta\varphi} = \frac{1}{\sin^2\vartheta}\sum_{n=1}^{\infty} C_{2n} \operatorname{tg}^{2n} \sin 2n\varphi\,. \qquad (4.48\text{a, b})$$

Since

ϑ^0	0	10	20	30	40	45	50	60	70	80	90
$\mathrm{tg}^2 \frac{\vartheta}{2} \Big/ \sin^2 \vartheta$	0.2500	0.2539	0.2658	0.2872	0.3206	0.3431	0.3706	0.4444	0.5553	0.7260	1.000
$\mathrm{tg}^3 \frac{\vartheta}{2} \Big/ \sin^2 \vartheta$	0.0000	0.0222	0.0469	0.0770	0.1167	0.1421	0.1728	0.2566	0.3888	0.6092	1.000
$\mathrm{tg}^4 \frac{\vartheta}{2} \Big/ \sin^2 \vartheta$	0.0000	0.0019	0.0083	0.0206	0.0425	0.0589	0.0806	0.1482	0.2722	0.5112	1.000
$\mathrm{tg}^5 \frac{\vartheta}{2} \Big/ \sin^2 \vartheta$	0.0000	0.0002	0.0015	0.0055	0.0155	0.0244	0.0376	0.0855	0.1906	0.4289	1.000

Table 7 ·

$$n_\varphi\Big|_{\varphi=\pm\pi/2} = \frac{1}{\sin^2\vartheta}\sum_{n=1}^{\infty}(-1)^n C_{2n}\,\mathrm{tg}^{2n}\frac{\vartheta}{2} = h(\vartheta)$$

the error integral, which has to be minimized, becomes

$$F = \int_0^{\pi/2}\left[h(\vartheta)\sin^2\vartheta - \sum_{n=1}^{\infty}(-1)^n C_{2n}\,\mathrm{tg}^{2n}\frac{\vartheta}{2}\right]^2 d\vartheta$$

so that, setting $\partial F/\partial C_{2k} = 0$ and writing

$$h_{2k} = (-1)^k\int_0^{\pi/2} h(\vartheta)\sin^2\vartheta\,\mathrm{tg}^{2k}\frac{\vartheta}{2}\,d\vartheta\,,$$

$$\delta_{2i,2k} = (-1)^{i+k}\int_0^{\pi/2}\mathrm{tg}^{2(i+k)}\frac{\vartheta}{2}\,d\vartheta \qquad (4.48\text{c, d})$$

we obtain the system of linear equations

$$\sum_{i=1}^{\infty} C_{2i}\,\delta_{2i,2k} = h_{2k}\,, \quad k = 1\ldots\infty\,. \qquad (4.48\text{e})$$

b2) Normal forces antimetrical with respect to the (x, z) plane.

In this case the sectional loads are antimetrical with respect to the (x, z)plane; hence, the solution is similar to (4.46a, b). The boundary conditions are

$$n_{\vartheta\varphi}\Big|_{\varphi=\pm\pi/2} = 0\,,\quad n_\varphi\Big|_{\varphi=\pi/2} = h(\vartheta)\,,\quad n_\varphi\Big|_{\varphi=-\pi/2} = -h(\vartheta)\,.$$

Therefore, the $\bar{C}_k$ must vanish for all even values of k. We thus obtain

$$n_\varphi = -n_\vartheta = \frac{1}{\sin^2\vartheta}\sum_{n=1}^{\infty}\bar{C}_{2n+1}\,\mathrm{tg}^{2n+1}\frac{\vartheta}{2}\sin(2n+1)\varphi\,,$$

$$n_{\vartheta\varphi} = -\frac{1}{\sin^2\vartheta}\sum_{n=1}^{\infty}\bar{C}_{2n+1}\,\mathrm{tg}^{2n+1}\frac{\vartheta}{2}\cos(2n+1)\varphi\,. \qquad (4.49\text{a, b})$$

The boundary condition

$$n_\varphi\Big|_{\varphi=\pi/2} = \frac{1}{\sin^2\vartheta}\sum_{n=1}^{\infty}(-1)^n\bar{C}_{2n+1}\,\mathrm{tg}^{2n+1}\frac{\vartheta}{2} = h(\vartheta)$$

yields the error integral

$$F = \int_0^{\pi/2}\left[h(\vartheta)\sin^2\vartheta - \sum_{n=1}^{\infty}(-1)^n\bar{C}_{2n+1}\,\mathrm{tg}^{2n+1}\frac{\vartheta}{2}\right]^2 d\vartheta\,,$$

which has to be minimized. Setting $\partial F/\partial\bar{C}_{2k+1}$ and writing

$$\bar{h}_{2k+1} = (-1)^k\int_0^{\pi/2} h(\vartheta)\sin^2\vartheta\,\mathrm{tg}^{2k+1}\frac{\vartheta}{2}\,d\vartheta\,,$$

$$\delta_{2i+1,\,2k+1} = (-1)^{i+k}\int_0^{\pi/2}\mathrm{tg}^{2(i+k+1)}\frac{\vartheta}{2}\,d\vartheta \qquad (4.49\text{c, d})$$

we obtain the system of linear equations

$$\sum_{i=1}^{\infty}\bar{C}_{2i+1}\,\delta_{2i+1,\,2k+1} = \bar{h}_{2k+1}\,,\quad k = 1\ldots\infty\,. \qquad (4.49\text{e})$$

Table 7 gives some values of $\dfrac{\mathrm{tg}^k\frac{\vartheta}{2}}{\sin^2\vartheta}$.

Furthermore we have

$$\delta_{22} = \int_0^{\pi/2}\mathrm{tg}^4\frac{\vartheta}{2}\,d\vartheta = \frac{\pi}{2} - \frac{4}{3} = 0.237463\,,$$

$$\delta_{24} = \delta_{42} = -\int_0^{\pi/2}\mathrm{tg}^6\frac{\vartheta}{2}\,d\vartheta = \frac{26}{15} - \frac{\pi}{2} = -0.162537\,,$$

$$\delta_{44} = \int_0^{\pi/2}\mathrm{tg}^8\frac{\vartheta}{2}\,d\vartheta = \frac{\pi}{2} - \frac{152}{105} = 0.123177\,,$$

$$\delta_{33} = -\delta_{24} = \frac{26}{15} - \frac{\pi}{2} = 0.162537\,,$$

$$\delta_{35} = -\delta_{44} = -0.123177\,,$$

$$\delta_{55} = \int_0^{\pi/2}\mathrm{tg}^{10}\frac{\vartheta}{2}\,d\vartheta = \frac{526}{315} - \frac{\pi}{2} = 0.099045\,.$$

as well as

$$\beta_{22} = \frac{\delta_{44}}{\delta_{22}\,\delta_{44} - \delta_{24}^2} = 43.4993\,;$$

$$\beta_{24} = \beta_{42} = -\frac{\delta_{24}}{\delta_{22}\,\delta_{44} - \delta_{24}^2} = 57.3991\,;$$

$$\beta_{44} = \frac{\delta_{22}}{\delta_{22}\,\delta_{44} - \delta_{24}^2} = 83.8588;$$

$$\beta_{33} = \frac{\delta_{55}}{\delta_{33}\delta_{55} - \delta_{35}^2} = 106.9716\,;$$

$$\beta_{35} = \beta_{53} = -\frac{\delta_{35}}{\delta_{33}\delta_{55} - \delta_{35}^2} = 133.0349\,;$$

$$\beta_{55} = \frac{\delta_{33}}{\delta_{33}\delta_{55} - \delta_{35}^2} = 175.5449\,. \qquad (4.50)$$

If (4.45a), (4.47c), (4.48e) and (4.49e) are considered as approximations, each of which contains two terms of a series, then the β given by (4.50) represent the elements of the reciprocal matrix of the system considered. We thus obtain for the constants in the corresponding cases

a1) $C_3 = \beta_{33}\,f_3 + \beta_{35}\,f_5\,;\quad C_5 = \beta_{35}\,f_3 + \beta_{55}\,f_5\,,$

a2) $\bar{C}_2 = \beta_{22}\,\bar{f}_2 + \beta_{24}\,\bar{f}_4\,;\quad \bar{C}_4 = \beta_{24}\,\bar{f}_2 + \beta_{44}\,\bar{f}_4\,,$

b1) $C_2 = \beta_{22}\,h_2 + \beta_{24}\,h_4\,;\quad C_4 = \beta_{24}\,h_2 + \beta_{44}\,h_4\,,$

b2) $\bar{C}_3 = \beta_{33}\,\bar{h}_3 + \beta_{35}\,\bar{h}_5\,;\quad \bar{C}_5 = \beta_{35}\,\bar{h}_3 + \beta_{55}\,\bar{h}_5\,.$ (4.51a-d)

5 CONICAL MEMBRANES

The particularly simple shape of the conical membrane enables us to express the sectional loads and deformations in explicit form.

5.1 Sectional Loads

From Figure 5.1 we obtain

$$\left.\begin{aligned} &\vartheta = \text{const} = \frac{\pi}{2} - \alpha\,, \quad R_0 = \zeta \operatorname{tg} \alpha\,, \\ &R_2 = R_0/\cos\alpha = \zeta \frac{\sin\alpha}{\cos^2\alpha}\,, \\ &R_1 = \infty \quad \text{and} \quad d\,s_\vartheta = R_1(\vartheta)\,d\,\vartheta = \frac{d\,\zeta}{\cos\alpha} \end{aligned}\right\} \qquad (5.1)$$

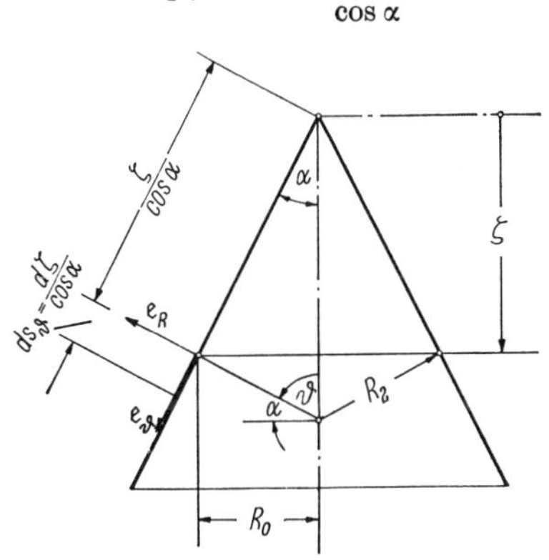

Figure 5.1

Dividing (3.6b, c) by R_1 and noting that $R_1\,d\,\vartheta = d\,\zeta/\cos\alpha$, we obtain from the general equilibrium conditions (3.6a-c):

$$\left.\begin{aligned} &n_\varphi = \zeta \frac{\sin\alpha}{\cos^2\alpha}\,p_R, \\ &\sin\alpha \frac{\partial}{\partial\zeta}(\zeta\, n_\vartheta) + \frac{\partial n_{\vartheta\varphi}}{\partial\varphi} = \zeta\,(p_R \operatorname{tg}^2\alpha - p_\vartheta \operatorname{tg}\alpha)\,, \\ &\frac{\partial}{\partial\zeta}(\zeta^2\, n_{\vartheta\varphi}) = -\,\zeta^2\left(\frac{p_\varphi}{\cos\alpha} + \frac{\partial\, p_R/\partial\,\varphi}{\cos^2\alpha}\right). \end{aligned}\right\} \qquad (5.2\text{a-c})$$

Integrating (5.2c), we obtain

$$n_{\vartheta\varphi} = \frac{1}{\zeta^2}\left[C_1(\varphi) - \int \zeta^2\left(\frac{p_\varphi}{\cos\alpha} + \frac{\partial\, p_R/\partial\,\varphi}{\cos^2\alpha}\right)d\,\zeta\right],$$

where $C_1(\varphi)$ is a constant which has to be determined. If we exclude concentrated loads at the apex of the cone and assume that both p_φ and $\partial\, p_R/\partial\,\varphi$ remain finite there, we must set $C_1(\varphi) = 0$ in order to obtain finite shearing forces at the apex. Hence, these shearing forces vanish at the apex under the stated conditions, which are always fulfilled. Thus,

$$n_{\vartheta\varphi} = -\frac{1}{\zeta^2}\int \zeta^2\left(\frac{p_\varphi}{\cos\alpha} + \frac{\partial\, p_R/\partial\,\varphi}{\cos^2\alpha}\right)d\,\zeta\,, \qquad (5.2\text{d})$$

Integrating (5.2b), we obtain the meridianal force

$$n_\vartheta = \frac{1}{\zeta\sin\alpha}\left\{C_2(\varphi) + \int \zeta\,(p_R \operatorname{tg}^2\alpha - p_\vartheta \operatorname{tg}\alpha)\,d\,\zeta - \int \frac{\partial\, n_{\vartheta\varphi}}{\partial\,\varphi}\,d\,\zeta\right\}.$$

If we assume finite surface loads at the apex of the cone, the integration constant $C_2(\varphi)$ must be zero in order that the meridianal forces at the apex remain finite. Substituting (5.2d), we obtain finally

$$n_\vartheta = \frac{1}{\zeta\sin\alpha}\left\{\int \zeta\,(p_R \operatorname{tg}^2\alpha - p_\vartheta \operatorname{tg}\alpha)\,d\,\zeta + \int \frac{1}{\zeta^2}\left[\int \zeta^2\left(\frac{\partial\, p_\varphi/\partial\,\varphi}{\cos\alpha} + \frac{\partial^2 p_R/\partial\,\varphi^2}{\cos^2\alpha}\right)d\,\zeta\right]d\,\zeta\right\}. \qquad (5.2\text{e})$$

We shall now consider certain particular cases of loading.

5.1.1 *Loading Due to Internal Pressure* p

Putting $p_R = p$, $p_\varphi = p_\vartheta = 0$, we obtain from (5.2a), (5.2d) and (5.2e)

$$n_{\vartheta p} = p\,\zeta\frac{\sin\alpha}{2\cos^2\alpha}\,, \quad n_{\varphi p} = p\,\zeta\frac{\sin\alpha}{\cos^2\alpha} = 2\,n_{\vartheta p}\,, \quad n_{\vartheta\varphi_p} = 0\,, \qquad (5.3\text{a, b})$$

We could have obtained this result directly from (3.8a, b) by taking into account (5.1).

5.1.2 *Loading Due to Dead Weight* g

Putting $p_\vartheta = g\cos\alpha$, $p_R = -\,g\sin\alpha$, $p_\varphi = 0$ we obtain from (5.2a), (5.2d) and (5.2e)

$$n_{\vartheta g} = -\,g\,\zeta\frac{1}{2\cos^2\alpha}\,, \quad n_{\varphi g} = -\,g\,\zeta \operatorname{tg}^2\alpha\,, \quad n_{\vartheta\varphi_g} = 0\,. \qquad (5.4\text{a, b})$$

This could also have been obtained directly from (3.10a, b).

5.1.3 *Symmetrical Snow Load* s

Putting $p_\vartheta = s\cdot\cos\alpha\sin^2\alpha$, $p_R = -\,s\cdot\sin^3\alpha$, $p_\varphi = 0$ (cf. 3.11 c, d) we obtain from (5.2a), (5.2d) and (5.2e)

$$n_{\vartheta s_1} = -\,s\,\zeta\frac{\operatorname{tg}^2\alpha}{2}\,, \quad n_{\varphi s_1} = -\,s\,\zeta\frac{\sin^4\alpha}{\cos^2\alpha}\,, \quad n_{\vartheta\varphi_{s_1}} = 0\,, \qquad (5.5\text{a, b})$$

which follows also directly from (3.12a, b)

5.1.4 *One-sided Snow Load*

Writing, as in Subsection 3.2.2a

$$p_{\vartheta s} = \frac{s}{2}\sin\vartheta\cos^2\vartheta\,(1 + \cos\varphi) = \frac{s}{2}\cos\alpha\sin^2\alpha\,(1 + \cos\varphi)\,,$$

$$p_{Rs} = -\,\frac{s}{2}\cos^3\vartheta\,(1 + \cos\varphi) = -\,\frac{s}{2}\sin^3\alpha\,(1 + \cos\varphi)$$

we obtain from (5.2a), (5.2d) and (5.2e), or directly from (3.28a-c)

$$\begin{aligned} n_{\vartheta s_3} &= -\,s\,\zeta\frac{\operatorname{tg}^2\alpha}{2}\left(\frac{1}{2} + \frac{1}{3}\cos\varphi\right), \\ n_{\varphi s_3} &= -\,s\,\zeta\frac{\sin^4\alpha}{\cos^2\alpha}\,\frac{1}{2}\,(1 + \cos\varphi)\,, \\ n_{\vartheta\varphi_{s_3}} &= -\,s\,\zeta\frac{\sin^3\alpha}{6\cos^2\alpha}\sin\varphi\,. \end{aligned} \qquad (5.6\text{a-c})$$

5.1.5 *Wind Load*

Assuming (cf. 3.29b)

$$p_{\vartheta w} = 0\,, \quad p_{\varphi w} = 0\,, \quad p_{Rw} = -\,w_0 - w_1\sin\vartheta\cos\varphi = -\,w_0 - w_1\cos\alpha\cos\varphi$$

we obtain first the symmetrical part (w_0)

$$n_{\vartheta w_0} = -\, w_0\,\zeta\,\frac{\sin\alpha}{2\cos^2\alpha}\,,\quad n_{\varphi w_0} = -\, w_0\,\zeta\,\frac{\sin\alpha}{\cos^2\alpha}\,; \qquad (5.7a)$$

$$\left[n_{\vartheta\varphi_{w0}} = 0\right].$$

The antimetrical part (w_1) is according to (5.2a), (5.2d) and (5.2e)

$$n_{\vartheta w_1} = w_1\,\zeta\,\frac{1}{6}\,(\operatorname{ctg}\alpha - 2\operatorname{tg}\alpha)\cos\varphi\,,$$

$$n_{\varphi w_1} = -\, w_1\,\zeta\,\operatorname{tg}\alpha\cos\varphi\,,\quad n_{\vartheta\varphi_{w1}} = -\, w_1\,\zeta\,\frac{\sin\varphi}{3\cos\alpha} \qquad (5.7b)$$

Hence, combining (5.7a) and (5.7b),

$$\left.\begin{aligned} n_{\vartheta w} &= \zeta\left[-\,w_0\,\frac{\sin\alpha}{2\cos^2\alpha} + \frac{w_1}{6}\,(\operatorname{ctg}\alpha - 2\operatorname{tg}\alpha)\cos\varphi\right],\\ n_{\vartheta\varphi_w} &= -\, w_1\,\zeta\,\frac{\sin\varphi}{3\cos\alpha}\,,\\ n_{\varphi w} &= -\,\zeta\left[w_0\,\frac{\sin\alpha}{\cos^2\alpha} + w_1\operatorname{tg}\alpha\cos\varphi\right]. \end{aligned}\right\} \qquad (5.7\text{c-e})$$

5.2 Required Inflation Pressure and Maximum Stresses

The formulas obtained in Section 5.1 show that the sectional loads vary linearly with the distance ζ from the apex of the cone. The highest compressive stresses due to the external load, which have to be counterbalanced by the inflation pressure, as well as the maximum tensile stresses, appear therefore at the lower edge of the membrane $\zeta = h$, where h is the height of the cone.

5.2.1 *Dead Weight, Symmetrical Snow Load, and Inflation Pressure. Ultimate Strength*

We obtain from Section 5.1

$$\left.\begin{aligned} n_{\vartheta\,\text{extr}} &= h\left[p\,\frac{\sin\alpha}{2\cos^2\alpha} - \frac{g}{2\cos^2\alpha} - \frac{s}{2}\operatorname{tg}^2\alpha\right],\\ n_{\varphi\,\text{extr}} &= h\left[p\,\frac{\sin\alpha}{\cos^2\alpha} - g\operatorname{tg}^2\alpha - s\,\frac{\sin^4\alpha}{\cos^2\alpha}\right]. \end{aligned}\right\} \qquad (5.8\text{a, b})$$

Since due to the symmetrical loading all shearing forces $n_{\vartheta\varphi}$ vanish, (5.8a, b) defines the principal membrane forces. Hence, condition (2.15c) for the absence of folds $n_{\vartheta\,\text{extr}} \geqq 0$ and $n_{\varphi\,\text{extr}} \geqq 0$ becomes

$$p\,\frac{\sin\alpha}{2\cos^2\alpha} - \frac{g}{2\cos^2\alpha} - \frac{s}{2}\operatorname{tg}^2\alpha \geqq 0 \quad \text{and}$$

$$p\,\frac{\sin\alpha}{\cos^2\alpha} - g\operatorname{tg}^2\alpha - s\,\frac{\sin^4\alpha}{\cos^2\alpha} \geqq 0$$

whence

$$p \geqq \frac{g}{\sin\alpha} + s\cdot\sin\alpha \quad \text{and}$$

$$p \geqq g\sin\alpha + s\cdot\sin^3\alpha = \sin^2\alpha\left(\frac{g}{\sin\alpha} + s\cdot\sin\alpha\right).$$

The minimum inflation pressure is thus

$$p \geqq \frac{g}{\sin\alpha} + s\cdot\sin\alpha\,. \qquad (5.9)$$

We then have

$$n_{\vartheta\,\text{extr}} \geqq 0\,,\quad n_{\varphi\,\text{extr}} \geqq h\,[g + s\cdot\sin^2\alpha]\,,$$

where the sign of equality applies to the minimum pressure. The maximum tensile stresses thus appear at the lower membrane edge in the circumferential direction. The condition $n_{\varphi\,\text{extr}} \leqq n_{\text{perm}}$ yields (Figure 5.2)

$$\frac{g\,h}{n_{\text{perm}}} \leqq \left[1 + \frac{s}{g}\sin^2\alpha\right]^{-1}. \qquad (5.10)$$

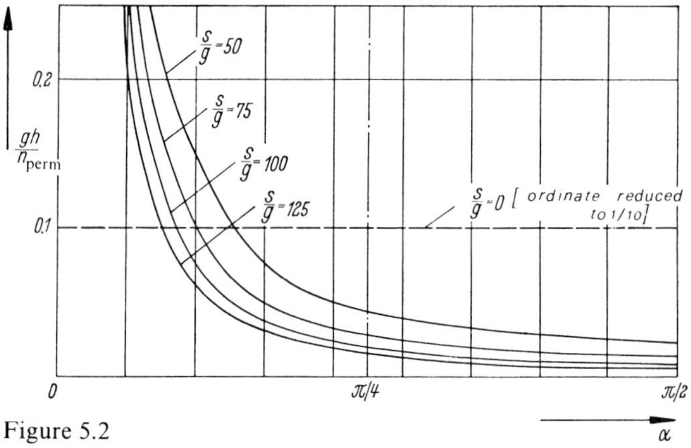

Figure 5.2

For $s = 0$ we obtain the theoretical maximum height for the case in which only the dead weight has to be counterbalanced (by the internal pressure). Putting $n_{\text{perm}} = n_{\text{tear}}$, we find

$$h \leqq \frac{n_{\text{tear}}}{g} = \frac{30\ [\text{kg/cm}]}{10^{-4}\ [\text{kg/cm}^2]} = 3\cdot 10^5\ \text{cm} = 3\ \text{km}\,,$$

which is independent of the cone angle α.

The practically attainable values are many times smaller since we cannot stress the material to its ultimate strength and must also take snow and wind loads into account. In this case, the dimensions of the cone will depend strongly on α (cf. 5.10). The maximum height decreases rapidly with increasing cone angle (cf. Figure 5.2). Thus, for $\alpha = 20°$ $[s/g = 75]$ $n_{\text{perm}} = 10$ kg/cm, $g = 1$ kg/m^2, we have

$$\frac{g\,h}{n_{\text{perm}}} = 0.1023\,,\quad h = 0.1023\,\frac{n_{\text{perm}}}{g} = 102.3\ \text{m}\,,$$

whereas for $\alpha = 45°$ (all other magnitudes being equal)

$$\frac{g\,h}{n_{\text{perm}}} = 0.026\,,\quad h = 0.026\,\frac{n_{\text{perm}}}{g} = 26\ \text{m}$$

Figure 5.2 shows that, for small cone angles, the proper weight has only little influence in comparison to the snow load.

5.2.2 *General Analysis of Loading*

The formulas of Section 5.1 enable us to express the sectional loads at the lower membrane edge in the generalized form

$$n_\vartheta = h\,[A_\vartheta + B_\vartheta\cos\varphi]\,,\quad n_{\vartheta\varphi} = h\,B_{\vartheta\varphi}\sin\varphi,$$
$$n_\varphi = h\,[A_\varphi + B_\varphi\cos\varphi] \qquad (5.11)$$

For instance, taking into account dead weight, a symmetrical snow load, wind, and inflation pressure, we obtain

$$A_\vartheta = \frac{p \sin\alpha}{2\cos^2\alpha} - \frac{g}{2\cos^2\alpha} - \frac{s}{2}\operatorname{tg}^2\alpha - \frac{w_0 \sin\alpha}{2\cos^2\alpha},$$

$$A_\varphi = \frac{p\sin\alpha}{\cos^2\alpha} - g\operatorname{tg}^2\alpha - s\frac{\sin^4\alpha}{\cos^2\alpha} - \frac{w_0\sin\alpha}{\cos^2\alpha}, \tag{5.12}$$

$$B_\vartheta = \frac{w_1}{6}(\operatorname{ctg}\alpha - 2\operatorname{tg}\alpha), \quad B_\varphi = -w_1\operatorname{tg}\alpha, \quad B_{\vartheta\varphi} = -\frac{w_1}{3\cos\alpha}.$$

Whereas the shearing forces $n_{\vartheta\varphi}$ attain their extrema at $\varphi = \pm\pi/2$, the meridianal and circumferential forces have their extreme values at $\varphi = 0$ and $\varphi = \pi$. The points at which the highest tensile and compressive forces appear can thus be found by extremizing the relevant expressions.

The principal membrane forces are (cf. 2.15a)

$$n_{1,2} = \frac{h}{2}\Big[(A_\vartheta + A_\varphi) + (B_\vartheta + B_\varphi)\cos\varphi \pm \pm\sqrt{[(A_\vartheta - A_\varphi) + (B_\vartheta - B_\varphi)\cos\varphi]^2 + 4B_{\vartheta\varphi}^2\sin^2\varphi}\,\Big]$$

$$= \frac{h}{2}\Big[(A_\vartheta + A_\varphi) + (B_\vartheta + B_\varphi)\cos\varphi \pm \pm\sqrt{[(A_\vartheta - A_\varphi)^2 + 4B_{\vartheta\varphi}^2] + 2(A_\vartheta - A_\varphi)(B_\vartheta - B_\varphi)\times \times\cos\varphi + [(B_\vartheta - B_\varphi)^2 - 4B_{\vartheta\varphi}^2]\cos^2\varphi}\,\Big]. \tag{5.13}$$

Their extrema are found from

$$\frac{\partial n_{1,2}}{\partial\varphi} = 0 = -\sin\varphi\left\{B_\vartheta + B_\varphi \pm \pm\frac{(A_\vartheta - A_\varphi)(B_\vartheta - B_\varphi) + [(B_\vartheta - B_\varphi)^2 - 4B_{\vartheta\varphi}^2]\cos\varphi}{\sqrt{[(A_\vartheta - A_\varphi)^2 + 4B_{\vartheta\varphi}^2] + 2(A_\vartheta - A_\varphi)(B_\vartheta - B_\varphi)\times\cos\varphi + [(B_\vartheta - B_\varphi)^2 - 4B_{\vartheta\varphi}^2]\cos^2\varphi}}\right\}$$

to be at

$$\varphi_1 = 0, \quad \varphi_2 = \pi. \tag{5.14a, b}$$

Furthermore, equating the expression inside the brackets to zero, we obtain

$$\cos\varphi_3 = -\frac{C}{D^2}\left[1 \pm \frac{A}{C}\sqrt{\frac{C^2 - D^2B^2}{A^2 - D^2}}\right], \tag{5.14c}$$

where

$$A = B_\vartheta + B_\varphi, \quad C = (A_\vartheta - A_\varphi)(B_\vartheta - B_\varphi), \quad B^2 = (A_\vartheta - A_\varphi)^2 + 4B_{\vartheta\varphi}^2, \quad D^2 = (B_\vartheta - B_\varphi)^2 - 4B_{\vartheta\varphi}^2. \tag{5.14d}$$

The extrema of the principal membrane forces are thus

$$n_{1,2}(\varphi_1) = \frac{h}{2}\left[(A_\vartheta + B_\vartheta) + (A_\varphi + B_\varphi) \pm \pm\big((A_\vartheta + B_\vartheta) - (A_\varphi + B_\varphi)\big)\right] = \begin{cases} h(A_\vartheta + B_\vartheta) = n_\vartheta(\varphi_1), \\ h(A_\varphi + B_\varphi) = n_\varphi(\varphi_1), \end{cases} \tag{5.15a, b}$$

$$n_{1,2}(\varphi_2) = \frac{h}{2}\left[(A_\vartheta - B_\vartheta) + (A_\varphi - B_\varphi) \pm \pm\big((A_\vartheta - B_\vartheta) - (A_\varphi - B_\varphi)\big)\right] = \begin{cases} h(A_\vartheta - B_\vartheta) = n_\vartheta(\varphi_2), \\ h(A_\varphi - B_\varphi) = n_\varphi(\varphi_2), \end{cases} \tag{5.15c, d}$$

$$n_{1,2}(\varphi_3) = \frac{h}{2}\left[(A_\vartheta + A_\varphi) + A\cos\varphi_3 \pm \pm\sqrt{B^2 + 2C\cos\varphi_3 + D^2\cos^2\varphi_3}\,\right] = \frac{h}{2}\left[A_\vartheta + A_\varphi - \frac{AC}{D^2} \pm \left(\frac{A^2}{D^2} \pm 1\right)\sqrt{\frac{C^2 - D^2B^2}{A^2 - D^2}}\right]$$

$$n_{1,2}(\varphi_3) = h\left\{\frac{(B_\vartheta - B_\varphi)(A_\varphi B_\vartheta - A_\vartheta B_\varphi) - 2B_{\vartheta\varphi}^2(A_\vartheta + A_\varphi)}{(B_\vartheta - B_\varphi)^2 - 4B_{\vartheta\varphi}^2} \pm \pm\frac{B_{\vartheta\varphi}\begin{Bmatrix} B_\vartheta^2 + B_\varphi^2 - 2B_{\vartheta\varphi}^2 \\ 2(B_\vartheta B_\varphi + B_{\vartheta\varphi}^2)\end{Bmatrix}\sqrt{\dfrac{(A_\vartheta - A_\varphi)^2 - (B_\vartheta - B_\varphi)^2 + 4B_{\vartheta\varphi}^2}{B_\vartheta B_\varphi + B_{\vartheta\varphi}^2}}}{(B_\vartheta - B_\varphi)^2 - 4B_{\vartheta\varphi}^2}\right\}. \tag{5.15e}$$

These expressions have to satisfy the condition (2.15b,c) ensuring the absence of folds. Whereas the first four equations (5.15a-d)

$$A_\vartheta + B_\vartheta \geqq 0, \quad A_\vartheta - B_\vartheta \geqq 0, \quad A_\varphi + B_\varphi \geqq 0, \quad A_\varphi - B_\varphi \geqq 0,$$

yield linear relationships for the determination of the inflation pressure, (5.15e) leads to complicated equations which can generally only be solved by numerical methods. The highest value obtained from the various expressions determines the inflation pressure. Inserting it into (5.15) we find the maximum tensile force, which, compared with the permissible value n_{perm}, determines the maximum height h.

5.3 Deformations

Inserting (5.1) into (3.32a-c), we obtain

$$\cos\alpha\frac{\partial v_\vartheta}{\partial\zeta} = \frac{n_\vartheta}{D_\vartheta} - \frac{\nu_\varphi}{D_\vartheta}n_\varphi,$$

$$\frac{1}{\zeta\operatorname{tg}\alpha}\frac{\partial v_\varphi}{\partial\varphi} + \frac{1}{\zeta}v_\vartheta\cos\alpha + \frac{v_R}{\zeta}\frac{\cos^2\alpha}{\sin\alpha} = \frac{n_\varphi}{D_\varphi} - \frac{\nu_\vartheta}{D_\vartheta}n_\vartheta,$$

$$\frac{1}{\zeta\operatorname{tg}\alpha}\frac{\partial v_\vartheta}{\partial\varphi} + \cos\alpha\frac{\partial v_\varphi}{\partial\zeta} - \cos\alpha\frac{v_\varphi}{\zeta} = \frac{n_{\vartheta\varphi}}{D_{\vartheta\varphi}}. \tag{5.16a-c}$$

Integrating (5.16a), we obtain the meridianal displacements

$$v_\vartheta = \frac{1}{\cos\alpha}\left[C_1(\varphi) + \int\left(\frac{n_\vartheta}{D_\vartheta} - \frac{\nu_\varphi}{D_\varphi}n_\varphi\right)d\zeta\right]. \tag{5.17a}$$

Inserting this into (5.16c), we obtain the differential equation for the circumferential displacements

$$\cos\alpha\left(\frac{\partial v_\varphi}{\partial\zeta} - \frac{v_\varphi}{\zeta}\right) = \zeta\cos\alpha\frac{\partial}{\partial\zeta}\left(\frac{v_\varphi}{\zeta}\right) = \frac{n_{\vartheta\varphi}}{D_{\vartheta\varphi}} - \frac{1}{\zeta\operatorname{tg}\alpha}\frac{\partial v_\vartheta}{\partial\varphi} = \frac{n_{\vartheta\varphi}}{D_{\vartheta\varphi}} - \frac{1}{\zeta\sin\alpha}\left[\frac{dC_1}{d\varphi} + \int\left(\frac{\partial n_\vartheta/\partial\varphi}{D_\vartheta} - \frac{\nu_\varphi}{D_\varphi}\frac{\partial n_\varphi}{\partial\varphi}\right)d\zeta\right]$$

for which the solution is

$$v_\varphi = \frac{\zeta}{\cos\alpha}\left[C_2(\varphi) + \int\frac{1}{\zeta}\left\{\frac{n_{\vartheta\varphi}}{D_{\vartheta\varphi}} - \frac{1}{\zeta\sin\alpha}\left[\frac{dC_1}{d\varphi} + \int\left(\frac{\partial n_\vartheta/\partial\varphi}{D_\vartheta} - \frac{\nu_\varphi}{D_\varphi}\frac{\partial n_\varphi}{\partial\varphi}\right)d\zeta\right]\right\}d\zeta\right]. \tag{5.17b}$$

From (5.16b) we obtain the normal displacements

$$v_R = \zeta\frac{\sin\alpha}{\cos^2\alpha}\left(\frac{n_\varphi}{D_\varphi} - \frac{\nu_\vartheta}{D_\vartheta}n_\vartheta\right) - \frac{1}{\cos\alpha}\frac{\partial v_\varphi}{\partial\varphi} - v_\vartheta\operatorname{tg}\alpha. \tag{5.17c}$$

Just as in the case of a spherical membrane, we cannot completely satisfy the boundary conditions here either, since the three displacement components can only be determined by the two functions

$C_1(\varphi)$ and $C_2(\varphi)$. If, e.g., we prevent circumferential displacements at the lower edge, then we must permit horizontal radial displacements in order to obviate small folds near the supports. Assuming a horizontal displacement

$$v_H = v_R \cos\alpha + v_\vartheta \sin\alpha = \cos\alpha\,(v_R + v_\vartheta \operatorname{tg}\alpha) = \\ = \zeta \operatorname{tg}\alpha \left(\frac{n_\varphi}{D_\varphi} - \frac{\nu_\vartheta}{D_\vartheta} n_\vartheta\right) - \frac{\partial v_\varphi}{\partial \varphi} \tag{5.18a}$$

and a vertical displacement

$$v_z = v_R \sin\alpha - v_\vartheta \cos\alpha = \sin\alpha\,(v_R - v_\vartheta \operatorname{ctg}\alpha) = \\ = \zeta \operatorname{tg}^2\alpha \left(\frac{n_\varphi}{D_\varphi} - \frac{\nu_\vartheta}{D_\vartheta} n_\vartheta\right) - \operatorname{tg}\alpha \frac{\partial v_\varphi}{\partial \varphi} - \frac{v_\vartheta}{\cos\alpha} \tag{5.18b}$$

we obtain the boundary conditions at the lower edge $\zeta = h$:

$$v_z\big|_{\zeta=h,\varphi} = 0\,, \quad v_\varphi\big|_{\zeta=h,\varphi} = 0\,, \quad \text{i.e., also} \quad \frac{\partial v_\varphi}{\partial \varphi}\bigg|_{\zeta=h,\varphi} = 0. \tag{5.19a-c}$$

Inserting (5.18b) into (5.19a) and taking account of (5.19c), we find

$$C_1(\varphi) = h \sin^2\alpha \left[\frac{n_\varphi}{D_\varphi} - \frac{\nu_\vartheta}{D_\vartheta} n_\vartheta\right]_{\zeta=h} - \\ - \int \left(\frac{n_\vartheta}{D_\vartheta} - \frac{\nu_\varphi}{D_\varphi} n_\varphi\right) d\zeta\,\Big|_{\zeta=h}. \tag{5.20a}$$

Inserting (5.17b) into (5.19b) yields

$$C_2(\varphi) = -\int \frac{1}{\zeta}\left\{\frac{n_{\vartheta\varphi}}{D_{\vartheta\varphi}} - \frac{1}{\zeta \sin\alpha}\left[\frac{d C_1}{d\varphi} + \right.\right. \\ \left.\left. + \int \left(\frac{\partial n_\vartheta/\partial\varphi}{D_\vartheta} - \frac{\nu_\varphi}{D_\varphi}\frac{\partial n_\varphi}{\partial \varphi}\right) d\zeta\right]\right\} d\zeta\,\Big|_{\zeta=h}.$$

Taking into account (5.20a) leads to

$$C_2(\varphi) = -\int \frac{1}{\zeta}\left\{\frac{n_{\vartheta\varphi}}{D_{\vartheta\varphi}} + \frac{1}{\zeta \sin\alpha}\int_\zeta^h \left(\frac{\partial n_\vartheta/\partial\varphi}{D_\vartheta} - \right.\right. \\ \left.\left. - \frac{\nu_\varphi}{D_\varphi}\frac{\partial n_\varphi}{\partial\varphi}\right) d\zeta - \frac{h}{\zeta}\sin\alpha \frac{\partial}{\partial\varphi}\left(\frac{n_\varphi}{D_\varphi} - \frac{\nu_\vartheta}{D_\vartheta} n_\vartheta\right)_{\zeta=h}\right\} d\zeta\,\Big|_{\zeta=h}. \tag{5.20b}$$

The displacements are now completely determined. We thus have, by (5.17) through (5.20),

$$v_\vartheta = h \frac{\sin^2\alpha}{\cos\alpha}\left[\frac{n_\varphi}{D_\varphi} - \frac{\nu_\vartheta}{D_\vartheta} n_\vartheta\right]_{\zeta=h} - \frac{1}{\cos\alpha}\int_\zeta^h \left(\frac{n_\vartheta}{D_\vartheta} - \frac{\nu_\varphi}{D_\varphi} n_\varphi\right) d\zeta\,,$$

$$v_\varphi = h \operatorname{tg}\alpha \frac{\partial}{\partial\varphi}\left[\frac{n_\varphi}{D_\varphi} - \frac{\nu_\vartheta}{D_\vartheta} n_\vartheta\right]_{\zeta=h} \cdot \left(1 - \frac{\zeta}{h}\right) - \\ - \frac{\zeta}{\cos\alpha}\int_\zeta^h \frac{1}{\zeta}\left\{\frac{n_{\vartheta\varphi}}{D_{\vartheta\varphi}} + \frac{1}{\zeta\sin\alpha}\int_\zeta^h \left(\frac{\partial n_\vartheta/\partial\varphi}{D_\vartheta} - \frac{\nu_\varphi}{D_\varphi}\frac{\partial n_\varphi}{\partial\varphi}\right) d\zeta\right\} d\zeta\,,$$

$$v_R = \zeta \frac{\sin\alpha}{\cos^2\alpha}\left(\frac{n_\varphi}{D_\varphi} - \frac{\nu_\vartheta}{D_\vartheta} n_\vartheta\right) - \frac{1}{\cos\alpha}\frac{\partial v_\varphi}{\partial\varphi} - v_\vartheta \operatorname{tg}\alpha\,, \tag{5.21a-c}$$

the horizontal radial displacement at the lower edge being

$$v_H(h) = h \operatorname{tg}\alpha \left(\frac{n_\varphi}{D_\varphi} - \frac{\nu_\vartheta}{D_\vartheta} n_\vartheta\right). \tag{5.21d}$$

Introducing the generalized expressions

$$n_\vartheta = \zeta\,(A_\vartheta + B_\vartheta \cos\varphi)\,, \quad n_{\vartheta\varphi} = \zeta\, B_{\vartheta\varphi} \sin\varphi\,, \\ n_\varphi = \zeta\,(A_\varphi + B_\varphi \cos\varphi)\,, \tag{5.22}$$

where A and B are constants determined by the load (cf. 5.12) and writing

$$\bar\varepsilon_{\vartheta A} = \frac{A_\vartheta}{D_\vartheta} - \frac{\nu_\varphi}{D_\varphi} A_\varphi\,, \quad \bar\varepsilon_{\vartheta B} = \frac{B_\vartheta}{D_\vartheta} - \frac{\nu_\varphi}{D_\varphi} B_\varphi\,, \quad \bar\gamma_{\vartheta\varphi B} = \frac{B_{\vartheta\varphi}}{D_{\vartheta\varphi}}\,, \\ \bar\varepsilon_{\varphi A} = \frac{A_\varphi}{D_\varphi} - \frac{\nu_\vartheta}{D_\vartheta} A_\vartheta\,, \quad \bar\varepsilon_{\varphi B} = \frac{B_\varphi}{D_\varphi} - \frac{\nu_\vartheta}{D_\vartheta} B_\vartheta\,, \tag{5.23}$$

we obtain for the displacements

$$v_\vartheta = h^2\left[\frac{\sin^2\alpha}{\cos\alpha}(\bar\varepsilon_{\varphi A} + \bar\varepsilon_{\varphi B}\cos\varphi) - \right. \\ \left. - \frac{1}{2\cos\alpha}\left[1 - \left(\frac{\zeta}{h}\right)^2\right](\bar\varepsilon_{\vartheta A} + \bar\varepsilon_{\vartheta B}\cos\varphi)\right],$$

$$v_\varphi = -h^2 \sin\varphi\left[\bar\varepsilon_{\varphi B} \operatorname{tg}\alpha\left(1 - \frac{\zeta}{h}\right) + \frac{\bar\gamma_{\vartheta\varphi B}}{\cos\alpha}\frac{\zeta}{h}\left(1 - \frac{\zeta}{h}\right) - \right. \\ \left. - \frac{\bar\varepsilon_{\vartheta B}}{\sin 2\alpha}\left(1 - 2\frac{\zeta}{h} + \left(\frac{\zeta}{h}\right)^2\right)\right],$$

$$v_R = \zeta^2 \frac{\sin\alpha}{\cos^2\alpha}(\bar\varepsilon_{\varphi A} + \bar\varepsilon_{\varphi B}\cos\varphi) - \frac{1}{\cos\alpha}\frac{\partial v_\varphi}{\partial\varphi} - v_\vartheta \operatorname{tg}\alpha\,,$$

$$v_H(h) = h^2 \operatorname{tg}\alpha\,(\bar\varepsilon_{\varphi A} + \bar\varepsilon_{\varphi B}\cos\varphi)\,. \tag{5.24a-d}$$

5.4 The Truncated Cone Free of Forces at the Top

When no forces act at the upper edge $\zeta = \zeta_0$ (Figure 5.3), the boundary conditions are

$$n_\vartheta\big|_{\zeta=\zeta_0} = 0\,, \quad n_{\vartheta\varphi}\big|_{\zeta=\zeta_0} = 0\,.$$

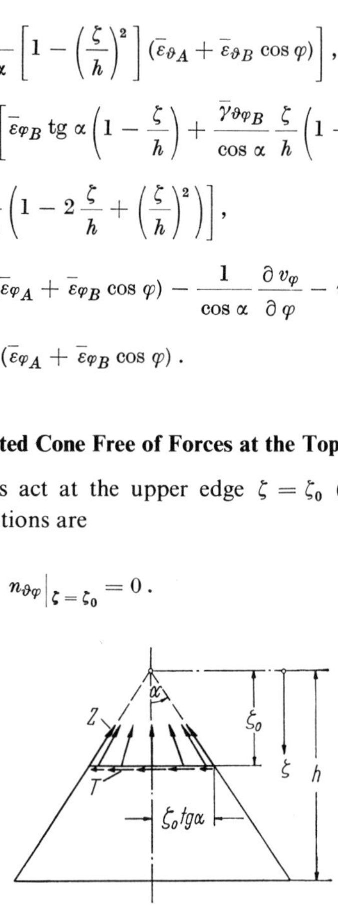

Figure 5.3

We then obtain from (5.2e, d)

$$n_\vartheta = \frac{1}{\zeta\sin\alpha}\left\{\int_{\zeta_0}^{\zeta} \zeta\,(p_R \operatorname{tg}^2\alpha - p_\vartheta \operatorname{tg}\alpha)\, d\zeta + \right. \\ \left. + \int_{\zeta_0}^{\zeta} \frac{1}{\zeta^2}\left[\int_{\zeta_0}^{\zeta} \zeta^2\left(\frac{\partial p_\varphi/\partial\varphi}{\cos\alpha} + \frac{\partial^2 p_R/\partial\varphi^2}{\cos^2\alpha}\right) d\zeta\right] d\zeta\right\}, \\ n_{\vartheta\varphi} = -\frac{1}{\zeta^2}\int_{\zeta_0}^{\zeta} \zeta^2\left(\frac{p_\varphi}{\cos\alpha} + \frac{\partial p_R/\partial\varphi}{\cos^2\alpha}\right) d\zeta\,, \tag{5.25a, b}$$

while (5.2a) remains unchanged

$$n_\varphi = \zeta \frac{\sin\alpha}{\cos^2\alpha} p_R \tag{5.25c}$$

For the various cases of loading discussed in Section 5.1, we find

5.4.1 *Loading by Internal Pressure* $[p_\vartheta = p_\varphi = 0,\ p_R = p]$

$$n_{\vartheta p} = \frac{p\sin\alpha}{2\cos^2\alpha}\left(\zeta - \frac{\zeta_0^2}{\zeta}\right),\quad n_{\vartheta\varphi p} = 0\,,\quad n_{\varphi p} = \frac{p\sin\alpha}{\cos^2\alpha}\zeta\,. \tag{5.26}$$

5.4.2 *Loading by Dead Weight* $[p_\vartheta = g\cos\alpha,\ p_\varphi = 0,\ p_R = -g\sin\alpha]$

$$n_{\vartheta g} = -\frac{g}{2\cos^2\alpha}\left(\zeta - \frac{\zeta_0^2}{\zeta}\right),\quad n_{\vartheta\varphi g} = 0\,,\quad n_{\varphi g} = -g\,\zeta\,\mathrm{tg}^2\alpha\,. \tag{5.27}$$

5.4.3 *Symmetrical Snow Load* $[p_\vartheta = s\cos\alpha\sin^2\alpha,\ p_\varphi = 0,\ p_R = -s\sin^3\alpha]$

$$n_{\vartheta s_1} = -s\frac{\mathrm{tg}^2\alpha}{2}\left(\zeta - \frac{\zeta_0^2}{\zeta}\right),\quad n_{\vartheta\varphi s_1} = 0\,,\quad n_{\varphi s_1} = -s\frac{\sin^4\alpha}{\cos^2\alpha}\zeta\,. \tag{5.28}$$

5.4.4 *One-sided Snow Load* $[p_\vartheta = (s/2)\cos\alpha\sin^2\alpha\,(1+\cos\varphi),\ p_\varphi = 0,\ p_R = -(s/2)\sin^3\alpha\,(1+\cos\varphi)]$

$$\left.\begin{aligned} n_{\vartheta s_3} &= -\frac{s}{2}\mathrm{tg}^2\alpha\left[\frac{1}{2}\left(\zeta - \frac{\zeta_0^2}{\zeta}\right) + \frac{\cos\varphi}{3}\left(\zeta - \frac{\zeta_0^3}{\zeta^2}\right)\right] \\ n_{\vartheta\varphi s_3} &= -\frac{s\cdot\sin^3\alpha}{6\cos^2\alpha}\left(\zeta - \frac{\zeta_0^3}{\zeta^2}\right)\sin\varphi\,, \\ n_{\varphi s_3} &= -\frac{s\cdot\sin^4\alpha}{2\cos^2\alpha}\zeta\,(1+\cos\varphi)\,. \end{aligned}\right\} \tag{5.29}$$

5.4.5 *Wind Load* $[p_\vartheta = p_\varphi = 0,\ p_R = -w_0 - w_1\cos\alpha\cos\varphi]$

$$n_{\vartheta w_0} = -\frac{w_0\sin\alpha}{2\cos^2\alpha}\left(\zeta - \frac{\zeta_0^2}{\zeta}\right),\quad n_{\vartheta\varphi w_0} = 0\,,\quad n_{\varphi w_0} = -w_0\zeta\frac{\sin\alpha}{\cos^2\alpha}\,, \tag{5.30a}$$

$$\begin{aligned} n_{\vartheta w_1} = \frac{w_1\cos\varphi}{6}&\left[\zeta\left(1 - \frac{\zeta_0^2}{\zeta^2}\right)(\mathrm{ctg}\,\alpha - 2\,\mathrm{tg}\,\alpha) - \right. \\ &\left. - \frac{2\zeta_0}{\sin\alpha\cos\alpha}\frac{\zeta_0}{\zeta}\left(1 - \frac{\zeta_0}{\zeta}\right)\right], \end{aligned} \tag{5.30b}$$

$$n_{\vartheta\varphi_{w_1}} = -\frac{w_1}{3\cos\alpha}\left(\zeta - \frac{\zeta_0^3}{\zeta^2}\right)\sin\varphi\,,\quad n_{\varphi w_1} = -w_1\,\mathrm{tg}\,\alpha\,\zeta\cos\varphi\,.$$

5.4.6 *A Truncated Cone Filled with Liquid to the Upper Edge*

For $p_\vartheta = p_\varphi = 0, p_R = \gamma(\zeta - \zeta_0)$, where γ = specific weight of the fluid, we obtain from (5.25a-c): $n_{\vartheta\varphi} = 0$ and

$$\begin{aligned} n_\vartheta &= \gamma\frac{\sin\alpha}{\cos^2\alpha}\frac{1}{\zeta}\left(\frac{\zeta^3}{3} + \frac{\zeta_0^3}{6} - \frac{\zeta_0\zeta^2}{2}\right) = \\ &= \gamma\,\zeta_0^2\frac{\sin\alpha}{\cos^2\alpha}\frac{\left(2 + \frac{1}{\eta}\right)(\eta-1)^2}{6} \geqq 0\,,\ \eta = \frac{\zeta}{\zeta_0} \geqq 1\,, \end{aligned}$$

$$n_\varphi = \gamma\frac{\sin\alpha}{\cos^2\alpha}\zeta(\zeta - \zeta_0) = \gamma\,\zeta_0^2\frac{\sin\alpha}{\cos^2\alpha}\eta\,(\eta - 1) \geqq 0.$$

The stresses are thus positive throughout the membrane, and increase in the downward direction. A truncated cone, free of forces at the top and increasing in diameter in the downward direction, can thus hold a liquid without folds being formed. A necessary condition for this is, however, that the lower edge is secured in such a way that tensile forces

$$n_\vartheta(h) = \frac{\gamma h^2}{6}\frac{\sin\alpha}{\cos^2\alpha}\left(2 + \left(\frac{\zeta_0}{h}\right)^3 - 3\frac{\zeta_0}{h}\right)$$

can be carried. Since

$$\frac{\eta}{\left(2+\frac{1}{\eta}\right)\frac{(\eta-1)}{6}} = \frac{6\eta^2}{(2\eta+1)(\eta-1)} = \frac{6\eta^2}{2\eta^2 - \eta - 1} > 1$$

the circumferential stresses always exceed the meridianal stresses. Putting

$$n_{\varphi\max} = \gamma\frac{\sin\alpha}{\cos^2\alpha}h\,(h - \zeta_0) \leqq n_{\text{perm}}$$

we obtain for the maximum level of the liquid $t = h - \zeta_0$

$$t \leqq \frac{\zeta_0}{2}\left[\sqrt{1 + \frac{4\,n_{\text{perm}}\cos^2\alpha}{\gamma\,\zeta_0^2\sin\alpha}} - 1\right].$$

If the membrane is closed at the bottom by a plate, the latter is acted upon by shearing forces transmitted to it from the mantle of the cone. These are, per unit of circumference, equal to

$$q = n_\vartheta(h)\cos\alpha = \frac{\gamma h^2}{6}\,\mathrm{tg}\,\alpha\left[2 + \left(\frac{\zeta_0}{h}\right)^3 - 3\frac{\zeta_0}{h}\right]$$

Together with the hydrostatic pressure, they cause bending of the plate. The horizontal components of the tensile forces acting in the mantle of the cone cause constant compressive forces in the plate, which are equal to

$$n_\vartheta^{(Pl)} = n_\varphi^{(Pl)} = -n_\vartheta(h)\sin\alpha = -\frac{\gamma h^2}{6}\mathrm{tg}^2\alpha\left[2 + \left(\frac{\zeta_0}{h}\right)^3 - 3\frac{\zeta_0}{h}\right].$$

5.5 A Truncated Cone Loaded at the Upper Edge

Setting $p_R = p_\vartheta = p_\varphi = 0$, we obtain from the general formulas of Section 5.1

$$n_\varphi = 0,\quad n_{\vartheta\varphi} = \frac{C_1(\varphi)}{\zeta^2}\,,\quad n_\vartheta = \frac{1}{\zeta\sin\alpha}\left[C_2(\varphi) + \frac{1}{\zeta}\frac{dC_1}{d\varphi}\right]. \tag{5.31}$$

The functions $C_1(\varphi)$ and $C_2(\varphi)$ are determined from the boundary conditions specifying the loads acting at the upper edge. Denoting the meridianal tensile forces acting (per unit length of circumference) at the upper edge by $Z(\varphi)$ and the shearing forces by $T(\varphi)$ (Figure 5.3), the boundary conditions become

$$n_{\vartheta\varphi}\big|_{\zeta_0} = \frac{C_1(\varphi)}{\zeta_0^2} = T(\varphi)\,,\quad n_\vartheta\big|_{\zeta_0} = \frac{1}{\zeta_0\sin\alpha}\left[C_2(\varphi) + \frac{1}{\zeta_0}\frac{dC_1}{d\varphi}\right] = Z(\varphi)\,,$$

whence

$$C_1(\varphi) = \zeta_0^2\,T(\varphi)\,,\quad C_2(\varphi) = \zeta_0\left[Z(\varphi)\sin\alpha - \frac{dT}{d\varphi}\right]. \tag{5.32a, b}$$

Inserting (5.32) into (5.31), we obtain the sectional loads

$$\left.\begin{aligned} n_\varphi &= 0\,,\quad n_{\vartheta\varphi} = T(\varphi)\left(\frac{\zeta_0}{\zeta}\right)^2, \\ n_\vartheta &= Z(\varphi)\left(\frac{\zeta_0}{\zeta}\right) - \frac{1}{\sin\alpha}\left(1 - \frac{\zeta_0}{\zeta}\right)\frac{\zeta_0}{\zeta}\frac{dT}{d\varphi}\,. \end{aligned}\right\} \tag{5.33}$$

5.6 A Truncated Cone with Spherical Cap (Figure 5.4)

It was shown in Section 5.1 that no forces can act on the apex of a cone $\zeta = 0$. Buckling of the apex is therefore likely to occur. To prevent this, it is advisable to round off the peak of the cone by replacing the perfect cone by a truncated one with spherical cap.

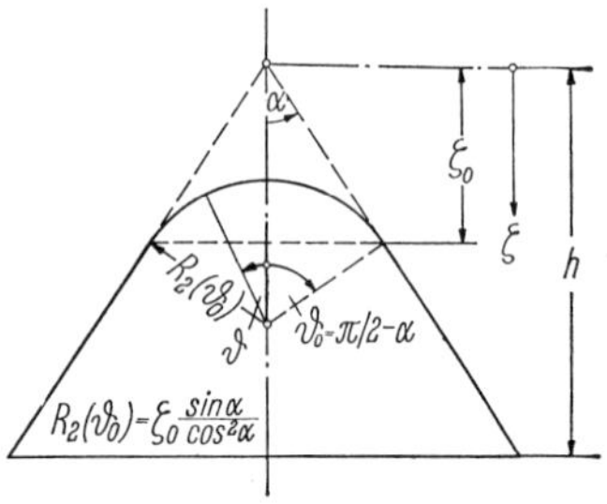

Figure 5.4

The sectional loads do not vanish at the peak of such a cap. We can easily analyze this system even for an arbitrary shape of the cap by making use of the formulas given in Sections 3 and 4, and Sections 5.4 and 5.3. We first determine the sectional loads in the cap, in particular at its lower edge $\vartheta = \vartheta_0 = (\pi/2) - \alpha$, which form the edge loads of the truncated cone

$$Z = n_\vartheta\big|_{\vartheta = (\pi/2) - \alpha}\,, \qquad T = n_{\vartheta\varphi}\big|_{\vartheta = (\pi/2) - \alpha}\,. \tag{5.34}$$

The sectional loads of the truncated cone are then obtained as shown in Sections 5.4 and 5.5 by inserting Z and T according to (5.34). A fundamental difficulty then arises: applying the membrane theory of small deformations, it is generally impossible to obtain continuous circumferential forces n_φ at the juncture between spherical cap and truncated cone. Thus, at the juncture, the circumferential extensions are also usually discontinuous, the only exception being when the principal curvature of the cap $1/R_1$ vanishes at the juncture.
We then obtain from (3.6a)

$$n_\varphi(\vartheta_0) = R_2(\vartheta_0)\, p_R(\vartheta_0) = \zeta_0 \frac{\sin\alpha}{\cos^2\alpha}\, p_R\,,$$

which is equal to the value given by (5.25c) for the upper edge of the truncated cone. According to Section 5.5, no additional circumferential forces are caused by the edge loads. If the condition of continuity for the principal curvature $1/R_1$ at the juncture is not satisfied, the circumferential extensions will in general differ at the juncture, causing the appearance of small folds (i.e., additional stresses). In this case we can only prevent incompatibilities by selecting different rigidities for the two shapes in such a way that for the usual cases of loading the circumferential extensions become continuous. We obtain from (3.6a)*

$$n_\varphi = R_2\, p_R - \frac{R_2}{R_1}\, n_\vartheta \leqq R_2\, p_R\,.$$

The circumferential membrane forces at the upper edge of the truncated cone thus always exceed those of the cap unless the curvature is continuous at the joint. This means that the rigidity in tension D_φ of the truncated cone at its upper edge must exceed the rigidity in tension of the spherical cap at the joint. We can achieve this by using a softer material for the cap; alternatively, we can increase (preferably stepwise) the rigidity of the truncated cone at its upper edge by pasting material onto it. We shall now consider various cases of loading for the system of a spherical cap —truncated cone.

* The condition for the absence of folds requires that $n_\vartheta \geqq 0$, $n_\varphi \geqq 0$ and thus $p_R \geqq 0$.

5.6.1 *Loading by Internal Pressure*

We obtain from Section 4 for the spherical cap

$$n_{\vartheta p} = n_{\varphi p} = \frac{pR}{2} = \frac{p\,\zeta_0 \sin\alpha}{2\cos^2\alpha}\,, \qquad n_{\vartheta\varphi_p} = 0\,. \tag{5.35a}$$

Therefore,

$$Z_p = n_{\vartheta p}(\vartheta_0) = \frac{p\,\zeta_0\sin\alpha}{2\cos^2\alpha}\,,$$
$$n_{\varphi_p}(\vartheta_0) = \frac{p\,\zeta_0\sin\alpha}{2\cos^2\alpha}\,, \qquad T_p(\vartheta_0) = 0\,. \tag{5.35b}$$

For the truncated cone we obtain from Sections 5.4 and 5.5

$$n_{\vartheta p} = \frac{p\sin\alpha}{2\cos^2\alpha}\left(\zeta - \frac{\zeta_0^2}{\zeta}\right) + \frac{p\,\zeta_0\sin\alpha}{2\cos^2\alpha}\left(\frac{\zeta_0}{\zeta}\right) = \frac{p\sin\alpha}{2\cos^2\alpha}\,\zeta\,,$$
$$n_{\varphi p} = \frac{p\sin\alpha}{\cos^2\alpha}\,\zeta\,, \qquad n_{\vartheta\varphi p} = 0\,. \tag{5.35c}$$

Thus, in this case also the meridianal forces acting in the truncated cone are equal to those which would act in a perfect cone (for the circumferential forces this follows from (5.2a) and (5.25c)).

5.6.2 *Loading by Dead Weight*

For the spherical cap we obtain from Section 4 by writing $R = \zeta_0 \sin\alpha/\cos^2\alpha$ and $2\cos^2\vartheta/2 = 1 + \cos\vartheta$:

$$n_{\vartheta g} = -\frac{g\,\zeta_0\sin\alpha}{\cos^2\alpha}\,\frac{1}{1+\cos\vartheta}\,,$$
$$n_{\varphi_g} = \frac{g\,\zeta_0\sin\alpha}{\cos^2\alpha}\left(\frac{1}{1+\cos\vartheta} - \cos\vartheta\right), \qquad n_{\vartheta\varphi_g} = 0\,. \tag{5.36a}$$

Putting $\vartheta_0 = (\pi/2) - \alpha$, we have

$$Z_g = n_{\vartheta_g}(\vartheta_0) = -\frac{g\,\zeta_0\sin\alpha}{\cos^2\alpha\,(1+\sin\alpha)}\,,$$
$$n_{\varphi_g}(\vartheta_0) = \frac{g\,\zeta_0\sin\alpha}{\cos^2\alpha}\left(\frac{1}{1+\sin\alpha} - \sin\alpha\right), \quad T_g(\vartheta_0) = 0\,, \tag{5.36b}$$

Hence, for the truncated cone we obtain in accordance with Sections 5.4 and 5.5

$$n_{\vartheta_g} = -\frac{g}{2\cos^2\alpha}\left(\zeta - \frac{\zeta_0^2}{\zeta}\right) - \frac{g\,\zeta_0\sin\alpha}{\cos^2\alpha\,(1+\sin\alpha)}\left(\frac{\zeta_0}{\zeta}\right) =$$
$$= -\frac{g\,\zeta}{2\cos^2\alpha}\left[1 - \frac{1-\sin\alpha}{1+\sin\alpha}\left(\frac{\zeta_0}{\zeta}\right)^2\right], \tag{5.36c}$$
$$n_{\varphi_g} = -g\,\zeta\,\mathrm{tg}^2\alpha\,, \qquad n_{\vartheta\varphi_g} = 0$$

The meridianal forces are thus slightly less than in a perfect cone. However, for small spherical caps this difference is negligible by virtue of $(\zeta_0/h)^2 \ll 1$, in particular at the lower edge where the meridianal forces are largest.

5.6.3 *Symmetrical Snow Load*

We obtain from (4.3a, b)

$$n_{\vartheta s_1} = -s\,\frac{\zeta_0 \sin\alpha}{3\cos^2\alpha}\,\frac{1-\cos^3\vartheta}{\sin^2\vartheta}\,,$$

$$n_{\varphi s_1} = s\,\frac{\zeta_0\sin\alpha}{3\cos^2\alpha}\left(\frac{1-\cos^3\vartheta}{\sin^2\vartheta} - 3\cos^3\vartheta\right),\quad n_{\vartheta\varphi s_1} = 0\,. \tag{5.37a}$$

Hence,

$$Z_{s1} = n_{\vartheta s1}(\vartheta_0) = -\frac{s\,\zeta_0\,(1-\sin^3\alpha)\sin\alpha}{3\cos^4\alpha}\,,$$

$$n_{\varphi s1}(\vartheta_0) = \frac{s\zeta_0\sin\alpha}{3\cos^2\alpha}\left(\frac{1-\sin^3\alpha}{\cos^2\alpha} - 3\sin^3\alpha\right),\quad T_{s1} = 0\,. \tag{5.37b}$$

For the truncated cone we find, according to Sections 5.4 and 5.5

$$n_{\vartheta s_1} = -\frac{s}{2}\,\mathrm{tg}^2\alpha\left(\zeta - \frac{\zeta_0^2}{\zeta}\right) - \frac{s\,\zeta_0\sin\alpha\,(1-\sin^3\alpha)}{3\cos^4\alpha}\left(\frac{\zeta_0}{\zeta}\right) =$$

$$= -\frac{s}{2}\,\mathrm{tg}^2\alpha\,\zeta\left[1 + \left(\frac{2}{3}\,\frac{1-\sin^3\alpha}{\sin\alpha\cos^2\alpha} - 1\right)\left(\frac{\zeta_0}{\zeta}\right)^2\right], \tag{5.37c}$$

$$n_{\varphi s_1} = -\frac{s\cdot\sin^4\alpha}{\cos^2\alpha}\,\zeta\,,\quad n_{\vartheta\varphi s_1} = 0\,.$$

The meridianal compressive forces in this case exceed those arising in a perfect cone. They attain a minimum at

$$\zeta_{\min} = \zeta_0\sqrt{\frac{2}{3}\,\frac{1-\sin^3\alpha}{\sin\alpha\cos^2\alpha} - 1}$$

For $\zeta > \zeta_{\min}$ the compressive forces increase again. At

$$\zeta_1 = \left(\frac{2}{3}\,\frac{1-\sin^3\alpha}{\sin\alpha\cos^2\alpha} - 1\right)\zeta_0$$

they attain the value at the upper edge of the truncated cone $\zeta = \zeta_0$. For $h \geqq \zeta_1$ we thus obtain the largest compressive forces at the lower edge of the cone.

5.6.4 *One-sided Snow Load*

For the spherical cap we find from (4.4a-c)

$$n_{\vartheta s3} = \frac{s\,\zeta_0\sin\alpha}{2\cos^2\alpha}\,[a_{s1}(\vartheta) + a_{s3}(\vartheta)\cos\varphi] =$$

$$= -\frac{s\,\zeta_0\sin\alpha}{6\cos^2\alpha}\left[\frac{1-\cos^3\vartheta}{\sin^2\vartheta} + \frac{3}{32}\,\frac{4\vartheta - \sin 4\vartheta}{\sin^3\vartheta}\cos\varphi\right],$$

$$n_{\vartheta\varphi s3} = \frac{s\,\zeta_0\sin\alpha}{2\cos^2\alpha}\,b_{s3}(\vartheta)\sin\varphi =$$

$$= -\frac{s\,\zeta_0\sin\alpha}{64\cos^2\alpha}\,\frac{\cos\vartheta\,(4\vartheta - \sin 4\vartheta)}{\sin^3\vartheta}\sin\varphi\,, \tag{5.38a}$$

$$n_{\varphi s3} = \frac{s\,\zeta_0\sin\alpha}{2\cos^2\alpha}\,[c_{s1}(\vartheta) + c_{s3}(\vartheta)\cos\varphi] =$$

$$= \frac{s\,\zeta_0\sin\alpha}{6\cos^2\alpha}\left(\frac{1-\cos^3\vartheta}{\sin^2\vartheta} - 3\cos^3\vartheta\right) +$$

$$+ \frac{s\,\zeta_0\sin\alpha}{2\cos^2\alpha}\left(\frac{1}{32}\,\frac{4\vartheta - \sin 4\vartheta}{\sin^3\vartheta} - \cos^3\vartheta\right)\cos\varphi\,.$$

Hence,

$$Z_{s3} = n_{\vartheta s3}(\vartheta_0) = -\frac{s\,\zeta_0\sin\alpha}{6\cos^4\alpha}\,(1-\sin^3\alpha) -$$

$$-\frac{s\,\zeta_0\sin\alpha}{64\cos^5\alpha}\,(2\pi - 4\alpha + \sin 4\alpha)\cos\varphi\,,$$

$$T_{s3} = n_{\vartheta\varphi s3}(\vartheta_0) = -\frac{s\zeta_0\sin^2\alpha}{64\cos^5\alpha}\,(2\pi - 4\alpha + \sin 4\alpha)\sin\varphi\,, \tag{5.38b}$$

$$n_{\varphi s3}(\vartheta_0) = \frac{s\,\zeta_0\sin\alpha}{6\cos^2\alpha}\left(\frac{1-\sin^3\alpha}{\cos^2\alpha} - 3\sin^3\alpha\right) +$$

$$+ \frac{s\,\zeta_0\sin\alpha}{2\cos^2\alpha}\left(\frac{1}{32}\,\frac{2\pi - 4\alpha + \sin 4\alpha}{\cos^3\alpha} - \sin^3\alpha\right)\cos\varphi\,.$$

According to Sections 5.4 and 5.5 we obtain the sectional loads of the truncated cone

$$n_{\vartheta s3} = -\frac{(s/2)}{2}\,\zeta\,\mathrm{tg}^2\alpha\left[1 + \left(\frac{2}{3}\,\frac{1-\sin^3\alpha}{\sin\alpha\cos^2\alpha} - 1\right)\left(\frac{\zeta_0}{\zeta}\right)^2\right] -$$

$$-\frac{s\zeta}{6}\,\mathrm{tg}^2\alpha\cos\varphi\left[1 + \left(\frac{3}{32}\,\frac{2\pi - 4\alpha + \sin 4\alpha}{\sin\alpha\cos^3\alpha} - 1\right)\left(\frac{\zeta_0}{\zeta}\right)^3\right],$$

$$n_{\vartheta\varphi s3} = -\frac{s\sin^3\alpha}{6\cos^2\alpha}\,\zeta\sin\varphi\left[1 + \left(\frac{3}{32}\,\frac{2\pi - 4\alpha + \sin 4\alpha}{\sin\alpha\cos^3\alpha} - 1\right)\left(\frac{\zeta_0}{\zeta}\right)^3\right],$$

$$n_{\varphi s3} = -\frac{s\sin^4\alpha}{2\cos^2\alpha}\,\zeta\,(1 + \cos\varphi)\,. \tag{5.38c}$$

Again, these values exceed those obtained for the perfect cone. Those terms in the expressions for the meridianal and shearing forces which depend on φ, at first decrease with increasing ζ, attaining extrema at

$$\zeta_{\min} = \zeta_0\sqrt[3]{2\left(\frac{3}{32}\,\frac{2\pi - 4\alpha + \sin 4\alpha}{\sin\alpha\cos^3\alpha} - 1\right)}\,,$$ for instance,

$$\min\left|n_{\vartheta\varphi s3}\right| = \frac{3}{2}\,\frac{s\sin^3\alpha}{6\cos^2\alpha}\,\zeta_{\min}\sin\varphi\,,$$

For $\zeta > \zeta_{\min}$, these forces increase again until, for

$$\zeta_1 = \frac{1}{2}\left[(B-1) + \sqrt{(B-1)(B+3)}\right],$$

$$B = \frac{3}{32}\,\frac{2\pi - 4\alpha + \sin 4\alpha}{\sin\alpha\cos^3\alpha}$$

they again attain their respective values as they existed at the upper edge of the truncated cone. Thus, for $h \geqq \zeta_1$, the shearing forces, as well as those terms in the expression for the meridianal forces which depend on φ, are largest at the lower edge of the cone. A comparison of the formulas of subsections 5.6.3 and 5.6.4 with those of Section 5.1 shows that for small spherical caps $[\zeta_0/h \ll 1]$ the membrane forces approximate those obtained for a perfect cone.

5.6.6 *Wind Load*

Considering only the antimetrical part, we obtain from (4.6a-c) for the spherical cap

$$n_{\vartheta w1} = w_1\,\frac{\zeta_0\sin\alpha}{\cos^2\alpha}\,a_{w1}(\vartheta)\cos\varphi\,,\quad n_{\vartheta\varphi w1} = w_1\,\frac{\zeta_0\sin\alpha}{\cos^2\alpha}\,b_{w1}(\vartheta)\sin\varphi\,,$$

$$n_{\vartheta w1} = w_1\,\frac{\zeta_0\sin\alpha}{\cos^2\alpha}\,c_{w1}(\vartheta)\cos\varphi\,, \tag{5.39a}$$

Hence

$$Z_{w1} = n_{\vartheta w1}(\vartheta_0) = w_1 \frac{\zeta_0 \sin\alpha}{\cos^2\alpha} a_{w1}\left(\frac{\pi}{2} - \alpha\right)\cos\varphi\,,$$

$$T_{w1} = n_{\vartheta\varphi_{w1}}(\vartheta_0) = w_1 \frac{\zeta_0 \sin\alpha}{\cos^2\alpha} b_{w1}\left(\frac{\pi}{2} - \alpha\right)\sin\varphi\,, \qquad (5.39b)$$

The sectional loads of the truncated cone are thus

$$n_{\vartheta w1} = n_{\vartheta w1}{}^{(KS)} + Z_{w1}\left(\frac{\zeta_0}{\zeta}\right) - \frac{1}{\sin\alpha}\left(1 - \frac{\zeta_0}{\zeta}\right)\frac{\zeta_0}{\zeta}\frac{d T_{w1}}{d\varphi}\,,$$

$$n_{\vartheta\varphi_{w1}} = n_{\vartheta\varphi_{w1}}{}^{(KS)} + T_{w1}(\varphi)\left(\frac{\zeta_0}{\zeta}\right)^2, \quad n_{\varphi_{w1}} = n_{\varphi_{w1}}{}^{(KS)} \qquad (5.39c)$$

where $n^{(KS)}$ denotes the sectional loads of the truncated cone, given by (5.30).

5.6.7 *Equalization of Circumferential Extensions*

We return to the problem of determining the rigidities so that the circumferential extensions at the joint between truncated cone and spherical cap be continuous. The necessary condition is obviously

$$\varepsilon_\varphi{}^{(Ku)}(\vartheta_0) = \frac{n_\varphi{}^{(Ku)}(\vartheta_0)}{D_\varphi{}^{(Ku)}} - \frac{\nu_\vartheta{}^{(Ku)}}{D_\vartheta{}^{(Ku)}} n_\vartheta{}^{(Ku)}(\vartheta_0) =$$

$$= \varepsilon_\varphi{}^{(Ke)}(\zeta_0) = \frac{n_\varphi{}^{(Ke)}(\zeta_0)}{D_\varphi{}^{(Ke)}} - \frac{\nu_\vartheta{}^{(Ke)}}{D_\vartheta{}^{(Ke)}} n_\vartheta{}^{(Ke)}(\zeta_0)\,, \qquad (5.40a)$$

where the superscripts (Ku) and (Ke) refer, respectively, to the spherical cap and the truncated cone. Assuming identical materials, i.e., equal Poisson ratios ν_ϑ, as well as $D_\vartheta{}^{(Ku)} = D_\vartheta{}^{(Ke)}$, and taking account of the condition at the joint $n_\vartheta{}^{(Ku)} = n_\vartheta{}^{(Ke)} = Z$, we obtain the simple relationship'

$$\frac{n_\varphi{}^{(Ku)}(\vartheta_0)}{D_\varphi{}^{(Ku)}} = \frac{n_\varphi{}^{(Ke)}(\zeta_0)}{D_\varphi{}^{(Ke)}} \quad \text{or}$$

$$D_\varphi{}^{(Ke)} = \frac{n_\varphi{}^{(Ke)}(\zeta_0)}{n_\varphi{}^{(Ku)}(\vartheta_0)} D_\varphi{}^{(Ku)} > D_\varphi{}^{(Ku)} \qquad (5.40b)$$

from which the ratio of the circumferential rigidities can be found directly if the sectional loads are known. We can increase the circumferential rigidity of the upper cone edge without increasing the meridianal rigidity by arranging strips at the edge in the circumferential direction. These should only be fixed to the membrane along discrete latitude circles. If care is taken that these strips remain slack in the meridianal direction, no meridianal forces will be taken up by them, so that the meridianal rigidity remains unchanged. If the rigidity ratio obtained from (5.40b) differs greatly from unity (this corresponds to a considerable reinforcement of the upper cone edge) the rigidity should be increased stepwise by means of circumferential strips. As an example, we shall determine the rigidity ratio necessary for the equalization of the circumferential extensions when loading is due to dead weight and internal pressure.

From subsections 5.6.1 and 5.6.2 we find

$$n_{\vartheta g+p}{}^{(Ku)} = \frac{\zeta_0 \sin\alpha}{\cos^2\alpha}\left(\frac{p}{2} - \frac{g}{1+\cos\vartheta}\right),$$

$$n_{\varphi g+p}{}^{(Ku)} = \frac{\zeta_0 \sin\alpha}{\cos^2\alpha}\left[\frac{p}{2} + g\left(\frac{1}{1+\cos\vartheta} - \cos\vartheta\right)\right],$$

$$n_{\vartheta g+p}{}^{(Ke)} = \frac{\zeta_0 \sin\alpha}{\cos^2\alpha}\left\{\frac{p}{2}\frac{\zeta}{\zeta_0} - \frac{g}{2\sin\alpha}\frac{\zeta}{\zeta_0}\left[1 - \frac{1-\sin\alpha}{1+\sin\alpha}\left(\frac{\zeta_0}{\zeta}\right)^2\right]\right\},$$

$$n_{\varphi g+p}{}^{(Ke)} = \frac{\zeta \sin\alpha}{\cos^2\alpha}(p - g\sin\alpha)$$

whence we obtain from (5.40b)

$$D_\varphi{}^{(Ke)} = 2\frac{(p - g\sin\alpha)\, D_\varphi{}^{(Ku)}}{p + 2g\left(\dfrac{1}{1+\cos\vartheta_0} - \cos\vartheta_0\right)} =$$

$$= 2\frac{p - g\sin\alpha}{p + 2g\left(\dfrac{1}{1+\sin\alpha} - \sin\alpha\right)} D_\varphi{}^{(Ku)} = \Phi\left(\frac{p}{g}, \alpha\right) D_\varphi{}^{(Ku)}\,.$$

p/g \ α	0°	10°	20°	30°	40°	45°	90°
2	1.000	1.095	1.180	1.386	1.406	1.486	2
5	1.430	1.518	1.603	1.744	1.765	1.811	2
10	1.667	1.733	1.790	1.866	1.886	1.908	2
50	1.925	1.945	1.956	1.975	1.977	1.986	2
∞	2	2	2	2	2	2	2

Table 8

Table 8 gives some values of $\Phi(p/g, \alpha)$ for various values of p/g and α. We see that the rigidity ratio varies between 1.7 and 2.0 for higher values of p/g (internal pressure relatively large compared to dead weight), which are required for stabilizing the system, taking into account the possibility of sudden wind gusts. In general, satisfactory results will be obtained when the rigidity at the upper cone edge is taken equal to $1.9\, D_\varphi{}^{(Ku)}$. This means that for the equalization of the circumferential extensions, only the internal pressure has to be taken into account.

6 COMBINED SHAPES OF AXISYMMETRICAL MEMBRANES

6.1 General Observations

In Section 5.6 we discussed one combined shape. If we apply the condition of equalization for circumferential extensions only to constant loads, and disregard it with respect to varying loads, then, by selecting the rigidity ratio accordingly, we can combine various axisymmetrical shapes, since the continuity condition for the radius of principal curvature can then be discarded. The tangent planes at the joint need not coincide if circumferential tension cables

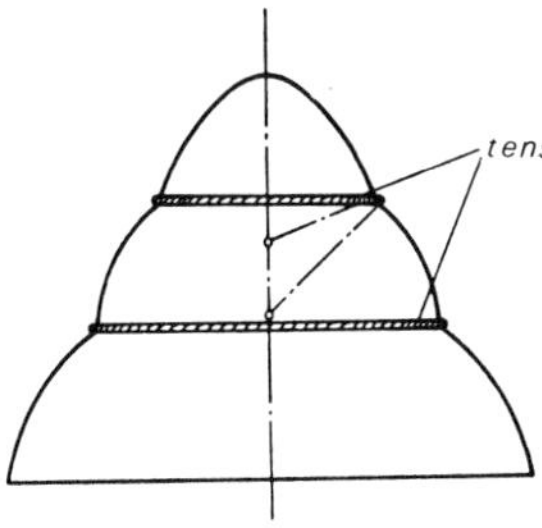

Figure 6.1

take up those components of the transmitted forces which do not lie in the respective tangent planes (Figure 6.1).
If we consider a narrow membrane element, cut out of the joint in the meridianal direction (Figure 6.2), then the equilibrium conditions for this element are as follows (notations as in Figure 6.2)

$$\left.\begin{aligned} &Z_k^{(u)} \cos \vartheta_k^{(u)} + q_{kH} - Z_{k+1}^{(0)} \cos \vartheta_{k+1}^{(0)} = 0\,, \\ &Z_k^{(u)} \sin \vartheta_k^{(u)} - Z_{k+1}^{(0)} \sin \vartheta_{k+1}^{(0)} - q_{kz} = 0\,, \\ &T_k^{(u)} + q_{k\varphi} - T_{k+1}^{(0)} = 0\,, \end{aligned}\right\} \qquad (6.1\text{a-c})$$

where $q_{kz} = g_k^{(s)}$ is the weight per unit length of the tension cable. This follows directly from the equilibrium conditions applied to the vertical forces acting on the cable element (Figure 6.2). When $Z_K^{(u)}$, being the meridianal force acting on the supports of the upper (k-th) partial membrane, is known, we obtain directly from (6.1b) the force acting on the upper edge of the ($k+1$)th partial membrane

$$Z_{k+1}^{(0)} = Z_k^{(u)} \frac{\sin \vartheta_k^{(u)}}{\sin \vartheta_{k+1}^{(0)}} - \frac{q_{kz}}{\sin \vartheta_{k+1}^{(0)}}\,. \qquad (6.2\text{a})$$

The radial force transmitted to the (k-th) tension cable is found from (6.1a) by inserting into this (6.2a):

$$q_{kH} = Z_{k+1}^{(0)} \cos \vartheta_{k+1}^{(0)} - Z_k^{(u)} \cos \vartheta_k^{(u)} =$$

$$= Z_k^{(u)} \frac{\sin (\vartheta_k^{(u)} - \vartheta_{k+1}^{(0)})}{\sin \vartheta_{k+1}^{(0)}} - q_{kz} \operatorname{ctg} \vartheta_{k+1}^{(0)}\,. \qquad (6.2\text{b})$$

If we connect the cable to the membrane in such a way that no relative circumferential displacements between cable and membrane are possible, then forces $q_{k\varphi}$ acting in the direction of the cable axis can be transmitted from membrane to cable. These forces, as well as the cable forces S proper, are determined from the equilibrium conditions for the cable element shown in Figure 6.2. We obtain for the tangential and normal directions

$$\frac{dS}{ds} ds + q_{k\varphi}\, ds = 0\,, \quad S\, d\varphi - q_{kH}\, ds = 0\,.$$

Putting $ds = R_{0k}\, d\varphi$, i.e., assuming that the cable curve retains approximately the shape of a circle after deformation, which is permissible due to the smallness of the latter, we find

$$S = R_{0k}\, q_{kH} = Z_k^{(u)} R_{0k} \frac{\sin (\vartheta_k^{(u)} - \vartheta_{k+1}^{(0)})}{\sin \vartheta_{k+1}^{(0)}} - q_{kz} R_{0k} \operatorname{ctg} \vartheta_{k+1}^{(0)},$$

$$q_{k\varphi} = -\frac{1}{R_{0k}} \frac{dS}{d\varphi} = -\frac{\sin (\vartheta_k^{(u)} - \vartheta_{k+1}^{(0)})}{\sin \vartheta_{k+1}^{(0)}} \frac{dZ_k^{(u)}}{d\varphi}\,. \qquad (6.3\text{a, b})$$

We thus have to show that

$$\max S = R_{0k} \frac{\sin (\vartheta_k^{(u)} - \vartheta_{k+1}^{(0)})}{\sin \vartheta_{k+1}^{(0)}} Z_{k\,\max}^{(u)} - $$

$$- q_{kz} R_{0k} \operatorname{ctg} \vartheta_{k+1}^{(0)} \leq S_{\text{perm}} \qquad (6.4\text{a})$$

and that the connections between membrane and cable, or the friction between them, can transmit a force

$$\max |q_{k\varphi}| = \max \left| \frac{dZ_k^{(u)}}{d\varphi} \right| \frac{\sin (\vartheta_k^{(u)} - \vartheta_{k+1}^{(0)})}{\sin \vartheta_{k+1}^{(0)}} \qquad (6.4\text{b})$$

per unit cable length.
In order to prevent small folds, the circumferential extensions at

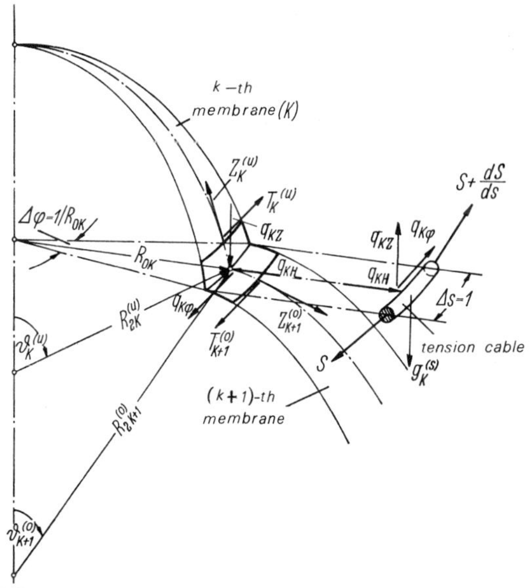

Figure 6.2

the joint, due to the constant loads, should be equal for the k-th and ($k+1$)-th membrane and for the cable. This requirement leads to the following equation by taking (6.2a) and (6.3a) into account and neglecting the cable weight $q_{kz} = g_k^{(s)}$:

$$\varepsilon_{\varphi k}^{(u)} = \frac{n_{\varphi k}^{(u)}}{D_{\varphi k}^{(u)}} - \frac{\nu_{\vartheta k}}{D_{\vartheta k}^{(u)}} Z_k^{(u)} = \varepsilon_{\varphi k+1}^{(0)} = \frac{n_{\varphi k+1}^{(0)}}{D_{\varphi k+1}^{(0)}} -$$

$$- \frac{\nu_{\vartheta k+1}^{(0)}}{D_{\vartheta k+1}^{(0)}} Z_k^{(u)} \frac{\sin \vartheta_k^{(u)}}{\sin \vartheta_{k+1}^{(0)}} = \varepsilon_s =$$

$$= \frac{Z_k^{(u)}}{E_s F_s} R_{0k} \frac{\sin (\vartheta_k^{(u)} - \vartheta_{k+1}^{(0)})}{\sin \vartheta_{k+1}^{(0)}}\,,$$

where E_s = Modulus of elasticity of the cable;
F_s = Cross-sectional area of the cable

whence, for $D_{\vartheta k}{}^{(u)} = D_{\vartheta k+1}{}^{(0)} = D_\vartheta$, $\nu_{\vartheta k} = \nu_{\vartheta k+1} = \nu_\vartheta$, we obtain

$$D_{\varphi k}{}^{(u)} = \frac{D_{\varphi k+1}{}^{(0)}}{\dfrac{n_{\varphi k+1}{}^{(0)}}{n_{\varphi k}{}^{(u)}} - D_{\varphi k+1}{}^{(0)} \dfrac{\nu_\vartheta}{D_\vartheta\, n_{\varphi k}{}^{(u)}} \dfrac{Z_k{}^{(u)} \sin \vartheta_k{}^{(u)} - \sin \vartheta_{k+1}{}^{(0)}}{\sin \vartheta_{k+1}{}^{(0)}}} \tag{6.5a}$$

$$E_s F_s = \frac{Z_k{}^{(u)} R_{0k} \dfrac{\sin(\vartheta_k{}^{(u)} - \vartheta_{k+1}{}^{(0)})}{\sin \vartheta_{k+1}{}^{(0)}}}{\dfrac{n_{\varphi k+1}{}^{(0)}}{D_{\varphi k+1}{}^{(0)}} - \dfrac{\nu_\vartheta}{D_\vartheta} Z_k{}^{(u)} \dfrac{\sin \vartheta_k{}^{(u)}}{\sin \vartheta_{k+1}{}^{(0)}}} \tag{6.5b}$$

If we restrict ourselves to equalizing the circumferential extensions due to the internal pressure, we obtain from the formulas (3.8a, b), which are valid in this case also,

$$D_{\varphi k}{}^{(u)} = D_{\varphi k+1}{}^{(0)} \left[\frac{\sin \vartheta_k{}^{(u)}}{\sin \vartheta_{k+1}{}^{(0)}} \, \frac{1 - \dfrac{R_{2\,k+1}{}^{(0)}}{2 R_{1\,k+1}{}^{(0)}}}{1 - \dfrac{R_{2\,k}{}^{(u)}}{2 R_{1\,k}{}^{(u)}}} - \right.$$

$$\left. - \nu_\vartheta \frac{D_{\varphi k+1}{}^{(0)}}{D_\vartheta} \, \frac{\sin \vartheta_k{}^{(u)} - \sin \vartheta_{k+1}{}^{(0)}}{\left(2 - \dfrac{R_{2\,k}{}^{(u)}}{R_{1\,k}{}^{(u)}}\right) \sin \vartheta_{k+1}{}^{(0)}} \right]^{-1} \tag{6.6a}$$

and

$$E_s F_s = \frac{D_{\varphi k+1}{}^{(0)} R_{2\,k}{}^{(u)} \sin(\vartheta_k{}^{(u)} - \vartheta_{k+1}{}^{(0)})}{2 - \dfrac{R_{2\,k+1}{}^{(0)}}{R_{1\,k+1}{}^{(0)}} - \nu_\vartheta \dfrac{D_{\varphi k+1}{}^{(0)}}{D_\vartheta}} \,. \tag{6.6b}$$

We can obtain the sectional loads of combined shapes by a method similar to that used in Section 5.6. We still require general relationships for the sectional loads of axisymmetrical membranes, free of forces at the upper edge, due to loading by dead weight, snow, and wind. These have to be added to the sectional loads due to the edge loads Z and T. We obtain these formulas from the corresponding expressions, given in Subsections 3.2.1 and 3.2.2 for the closed membrane, by setting as the lower limit of integration $\chi = \vartheta_c$ instead of $\chi = 0$, where $\chi = \vartheta_c$ is half the angle subtended by the membrane at the upper edge. We can, however, analyze combined forms directly by means of the relationships obtained in Subsections 3.2.1 and 3.2.2.

6.2 Example

Let us consider the system shown in Figure 6.3 consisting of two spherical membranes and assumed to be loaded by dead weight

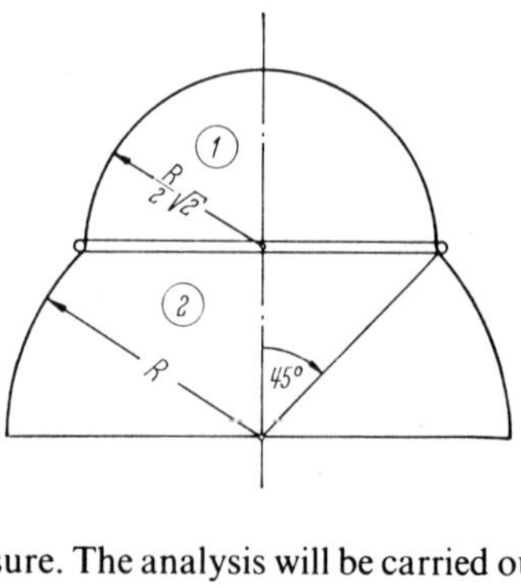

Figure 6.3

and internal pressure. The analysis will be carried out by the method of superposition according to Section 5.6. For the upper membrane we obtain from (4.1) and (4.2) the sectional loads

$$n_\vartheta{}^{(1)} = \frac{R}{2} \sqrt{2} \left(\frac{p}{2} - \frac{g}{1 + \cos \vartheta} \right),$$

$$n_\varphi{}^{(1)} = \frac{R}{2} \sqrt{2} \left[\frac{p}{2} + g \left(\frac{1}{1 + \cos \vartheta} - \cos \vartheta \right) \right].$$

Thus, at the lower edge of the upper membrane (1) the meridianal force is

$$Z_1{}^{(u)} = n_\vartheta{}^{(1)} (\pi/2) = \frac{R}{2} \sqrt{2} \left(\frac{p}{2} - g \right).$$

If we neglect the cable weight and write $\vartheta_1{}^{(u)} = \pi/2$, $\vartheta_2{}^{(0)} = \pi/4$, $R_{01} = R \sin 45^\circ = R \sqrt{2}/2$,
we find from (6.2a) and (6.3a) the meridianal force acting at the upper edge of the lower membrane (2):

$$Z_2{}^{(0)} = Z_1{}^{(u)} \frac{1}{\sqrt{2}/2} = \sqrt{2}\, Z_1{}^{(u)} = R \left(\frac{p}{2} - g \right)$$

The cable force is

$$S = Z_1{}^{(u)} \frac{R}{2} \sqrt{2} \cdot \frac{\sqrt{2}/2}{\sqrt{2}/2} = \frac{R}{2} \sqrt{2}\, Z_1{}^{(u)} = \frac{R^2}{2} \left(\frac{p}{2} - g \right).$$

The sectional loads of the lower membrane, due to the edge load $Z_2{}^{(0)}$, are by (3.31b) (the case considered is axisymmetrical) for $Z_0 = Z_2{}^{(0)}$, $R_2(\vartheta_c) = R_2(\vartheta) = R$, $\vartheta_c = \vartheta_1{}^{(0)} = 45^\circ$ found to be

$$n_{\vartheta Z}{}^{(2)} = - n_{\varphi Z}{}^{(2)} = Z_2{}^{(0)} \frac{1}{2 \sin^2 \vartheta} = \frac{R}{2} \left(\frac{p}{2} - g \right) \frac{1}{\sin^2 \vartheta}.$$

To these have to be added the sectional loads due to the dead weight and internal pressure, arising when the lower membrane is free of forces at its upper edge. For $R_1 = R_2 = R$, $p_R = p - g \cos \vartheta$, $p_\vartheta = g \sin \vartheta$, we obtain from (3.7a), integrating between the limits $\chi = \vartheta_1{}^{(0)} = 45^\circ$ and $\chi = \vartheta$,

$$n'_\vartheta{}^{(2)} = \frac{R}{\sin^2 \vartheta} \int_{\chi = \vartheta_1{}^{(0)}}^{\vartheta} \sin \chi \, (p_R \cos \chi - p_\vartheta \sin \chi)\, d\chi =$$

$$= \frac{pR}{2} \left[1 - \frac{1}{2 \sin^2 \vartheta} \right] - g R \frac{\dfrac{\sqrt{2}}{2} - \cos \vartheta}{\sin^2 \vartheta}$$

whence, by (3.6a), we obtain

$$n'_\varphi{}^{(2)} = R p_R - n'_\vartheta{}^{(2)} = \frac{pR}{2} \left[1 + \frac{1}{2 \sin^2 \vartheta} \right] +$$

$$+ g R \left[\frac{\dfrac{\sqrt{2}}{2} - \cos \vartheta}{\sin^2 \vartheta} - \cos \vartheta \right].$$

Adding, the sectional loads of the lower membrane (2) are found to be

$$n_\vartheta{}^{(2)} = n_{\vartheta Z}{}^{(2)} + n'_\vartheta{}^{(2)} = \frac{pR}{2} - \frac{gR}{2 \sin^2 \vartheta} \left[1 + \sqrt{2} - 2 \cos \vartheta \right],$$

$$n_\varphi{}^{(2)} = n_{\varphi Z}{}^{(2)} + n'_\varphi{}^{(2)} = \frac{pR}{2} + \frac{gR}{2 \sin^2 \vartheta} \left[1 + \sqrt{2} - 2 \cos \vartheta \right] -$$

$$- g R \cos \vartheta \,.$$

We can obtain the sectional loads and tension-cable forces in the same manner also for nonaxisymmetrical cases.

7 CIRCULAR CYLINDRICAL MEMBRANES

7.1 General Observations

In this case also we can obtain an explicit solution for the sectional loads and deformations due to arbitrary external loads. Introducing the position vector, defined by the coordinates (Figure 7.1)

$$\mathfrak{r} = \mathfrak{r}(x, \vartheta) = \{x;\, y;\, z\} = \{x;\, R \sin\vartheta;\, R\cos\vartheta\}$$

and putting $\alpha = x$ and $\beta = \vartheta$, we have

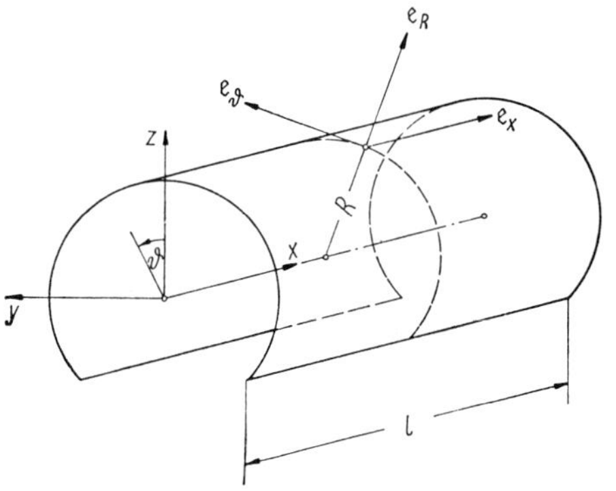

Figure 7.1

$$\mathfrak{r}_\alpha = \mathfrak{r}_x = \{1; 0; 0\}\,, \quad |\mathfrak{r}_\alpha| = \sqrt{g_{\alpha\alpha}} = 1\,,$$
$$\mathfrak{r}_\beta = \mathfrak{r}_\vartheta = R\,\{0; \cos\vartheta; -\sin\vartheta\}\,, \quad |\mathfrak{r}_\beta| = \sqrt{g_{\beta\beta}} = R$$

and

$$\mathfrak{r}_{\alpha\alpha} = \mathfrak{r}_{xx} = 0\,, \quad \mathfrak{r}_{\alpha\beta} = \mathfrak{r}_{x\vartheta} = 0\,, \quad \mathfrak{r}_{\beta\beta} = \mathfrak{r}_{\vartheta\vartheta} = -R\,\{0; \sin\vartheta; \cos\vartheta\}\,,$$
$$\mathfrak{r}_\alpha\, \mathfrak{r}_\beta = g_{\alpha\beta} = 0\,.$$

Accordingly, we obtain from (1.21)

$$\omega_\alpha{}^{(\alpha)} = \omega_x{}^{(x)} = -\,\omega_\beta{}^{(\beta)} = -\,\omega_\vartheta{}^{(\vartheta)} = 0\,,$$
$$\omega_\beta{}^{(\alpha)} = \omega_\vartheta{}^{(x)} = 0\,, \quad \omega_\gamma{}^{(\alpha)} = \omega_R{}^{(x)} = 0\,,$$
$$\omega_\alpha{}^{(\beta)} = \omega_x{}^{(\vartheta)} = \frac{[\mathfrak{r}_\alpha\, \mathfrak{r}_\beta\, \mathfrak{r}_{\beta\beta}]}{g_{\beta\beta}\sqrt{g_{\alpha\alpha}\, g_{\beta\beta}}} = -\frac{R^2}{R^3} = -\frac{1}{R}\,, \quad \omega_\gamma{}^{(\beta)} = \omega_R{}^{(\vartheta)} = 0\,.$$

The general equilibrium conditions (2.5) then reduce to

$$\left.\begin{aligned} R\frac{\partial n_x}{\partial x} + \frac{\partial n_{x\vartheta}}{\partial \vartheta} + R\, p_x &= 0\,,\\ R\frac{\partial n_{x\vartheta}}{\partial x} + \frac{\partial n_\vartheta}{\partial \vartheta} + R\, p_\vartheta &= 0\,,\\ -\frac{n_\vartheta}{R} + p_R &= 0 \end{aligned}\right\} \qquad (7.1\text{a-c})$$

where p_x, p_ϑ, and p_R are the load components, referred to the axes of the local system $\mathfrak{e}_x$, $\mathfrak{e}_\vartheta$, $\mathfrak{e}_R$ (Figure 7.1).
We then obtain from (2.27)

$$\left.\begin{aligned} \frac{\partial v_x}{\partial x} &= \varepsilon_x = \frac{n_x}{D_x} - \frac{\nu_\vartheta}{D_\vartheta}\, n_\vartheta\,,\\ \frac{1}{R}\left[\frac{\partial v_\vartheta}{\partial \vartheta} + v_R\right] &= \varepsilon_\vartheta = \frac{n_\vartheta}{D_\vartheta} - \frac{\nu_x}{D_x}\, n_x\,,\\ \frac{1}{R}\frac{\partial v_x}{\partial \vartheta} + \frac{\partial v_\vartheta}{\partial x} &= \gamma_{x\vartheta} = \frac{n_{x\vartheta}}{D_{x\vartheta}}\,, \end{aligned}\right\} \qquad (7.2\text{a-c})$$

where v_x, v_ϑ, v_R are the components of the displacement vector referred to the axes of the local system.

7.2 Solution of the Equilibrium Problem

Since by (7.1c)

$$n_\vartheta = R\, p_R \qquad (7.3\text{a})$$

we obtain from (7.1b) by substituting (7.3a) and integrating

$$n_{x\vartheta} = C_1(\vartheta) - \int\left(p_\vartheta + \frac{\partial p_R}{\partial \vartheta}\right) d\,x\,. \qquad (7.3\text{b})$$

We then obtain from (7.1a) by integrating once more

$$n_x = C_2(\vartheta) - \frac{x}{R}\frac{d\,C_1}{d\,\vartheta} + \int\left\{-\,p_x + \frac{1}{R}\int\left(\frac{\partial p_\vartheta}{\partial \vartheta} + \frac{\partial^2 p_R}{\partial \vartheta^2}\right) d\,x\right\} d\,x\,. \qquad (7.3\text{c})$$

If the load does not depend on x and if $p_x = 0$, we have

$$\begin{aligned} n_\vartheta = R\, p_R\,, \quad n_{x\vartheta} &= C_1(\vartheta) - x\left(p_\vartheta + \frac{d\,p_R}{d\,\vartheta}\right),\\ n_x &= C_2(\vartheta) - \frac{x}{R}\frac{d\,C_1}{d\,\vartheta} + \frac{x^2}{2\,R}\left(\frac{d\,p_\vartheta}{d\,\vartheta} + \frac{d^2\,p_R}{d\,\vartheta^2}\right), \end{aligned} \qquad (7.4\text{a-c})$$

where $C_1(\vartheta)$ and $C_2(\vartheta)$ are constants to be determined. If loading and support are symmetrical with respect to the plane $x = l/2$, the condition of symmetry $n_{x\vartheta}|_{x = l/2} = 0$ yields

$$C_1(\vartheta) = \frac{l}{2}\left(p_\vartheta + \frac{d\,p_R}{d\,\vartheta}\right),$$

whence

$$\begin{aligned} n_\vartheta = R\, p_R\,, \quad n_{x\vartheta} &= \left(p_\vartheta + \frac{d\,p_R}{d\,\vartheta}\right)\frac{l}{2}\left[1 - 2\,\frac{x}{l}\right],\\ n_x &= C_2(\vartheta) - \left(\frac{d\,p_\vartheta}{d\,\vartheta} + \frac{d^2\,p_R}{d\,\vartheta^2}\right)\frac{l^2}{2\,R}\left[\frac{x}{l} - \left(\frac{x}{l}\right)^2\right]. \end{aligned} \qquad (7.5\text{a-c})$$

We shall now consider different cases of loading.

7.2.1 *Loading by Internal Pressure*

For $p_R = p$, $p_\vartheta = p_x = 0$ we obtain from (7.5a-c)

$$n_{\vartheta p} = p\,R\,, \quad n_{x\vartheta p} = 0\,, \quad n_{xp} = C_{2p}(\vartheta)\,. \qquad (7.6)$$

7.2.2 *Loading by Dead Weight*

For $p_\vartheta = g \sin\vartheta$, $p_R = -\,g\cos\vartheta$, $p_x = 0$ we obtain from (7.5a-c)

$$\begin{aligned} n_{\vartheta g} = -\,g\,R\cos\vartheta\,, \quad n_{x\vartheta g} &= g\,l\sin\vartheta\left[1 - 2\,\frac{x}{l}\right],\\ n_x &= C_{2g}(\vartheta) - \frac{g\,l^2}{R}\cos\vartheta\left[\frac{x}{l} - \left(\frac{x}{l}\right)^2\right]. \end{aligned} \qquad (7.7)$$

7.2.3 *Symmetrical Snow Load*

For $p_\vartheta = s\cos^2\vartheta\sin\vartheta$, $p_R = -\,s\cos^3\vartheta$, $p_x = 0$ $[\,|\vartheta| \leq \pi/2]$ we obtain from (7.5a-c)

$$\begin{aligned} n_{\vartheta_{s1}} = -\,s\,R\cos^3\vartheta\,, \quad n_{x\vartheta_{s1}} &= 2\,s\,l\cos^2\vartheta\sin\vartheta\left[1 - 2\,\frac{x}{l}\right],\\ n_{x_{s1}} &= C_{2s_1}(\vartheta) - 2\,s\,\frac{l^2}{R}\cos\vartheta\,(\cos^2\vartheta - 2\sin^2\vartheta)\,\times\\ &\times\left[\frac{x}{l} - \left(\frac{x}{l}\right)^2\right]; \quad |\vartheta| \leq \frac{\pi}{2}\,. \end{aligned} \qquad (7.8)$$

For $|\vartheta| \geqq \frac{\pi}{2}$, we have $p_R = p_\vartheta = 0$,
thus $n_{\vartheta s_1} = n_{x\vartheta s_1} = 0$, $n_{x s_1} = \overline{C}_{2 s_1}(\vartheta)$.

7.2.4 *One-sided Snow Load*

On the assumption $\mathfrak{p} = -\frac{s}{2}\cos^2\vartheta\,(1+\sin\vartheta)\,\mathfrak{e}_z$ $[\,|\vartheta| \leqq \pi/2]$, thus

$$p_\vartheta = \frac{s}{2}\cos^2\vartheta\sin\vartheta\,(1+\sin\vartheta)\,, \quad p_R = -\frac{s}{2}\cos^3\vartheta\,(1+\sin\vartheta)\,,$$

we obtain from (7.5a-c)

$$n_{\vartheta s_3} = -\frac{s\,R}{2}\cos^3\vartheta\,(1+\sin\vartheta)\,,$$

$$n_{x\vartheta s_3} = s\,l\cos^2\vartheta\left[\sin\vartheta\,(1+\sin\vartheta) - \frac{1}{4}\cos^2\vartheta\right]\left[1 - 2\frac{x}{l}\right],$$

$$n_{x s_3} = C_{2 s_3}(\vartheta) - \frac{s\,l^2}{R}\cos\vartheta\left[(1+\sin\vartheta)(\cos^2\vartheta - \right.$$

$$\left. -2\sin^2\vartheta) + 2\cos^2\vartheta\sin\vartheta\right]\left[\frac{x}{l} - \left(\frac{x}{l}\right)^2\right], \quad |\vartheta| \leqq \frac{\pi}{2}. \tag{7.9}$$

For $|\vartheta| \geqq \frac{\pi}{2}$, we have again $n_{\vartheta s_3} = n_{x\vartheta s_3} = 0$, $n_{x s_3} = \overline{C}_{2 s_3}(\vartheta)$.

7.2.5 *Wind Load (Wind Direction Perpendicular to Longitudinal Axis)*

Assuming as a first approximation that $p_R = -w_0 - w_1\sin\vartheta$, we obtain from (7.5a-c)

$$n_{\vartheta w} = -w_0\,R - w_1\,R\sin\vartheta\,, \quad n_{x\vartheta w} = -\frac{w_1\,l}{2}\cos\vartheta\left(1 - 2\frac{x}{l}\right),$$

$$n_{x w} = C_{2w}(\vartheta) - \frac{w_1\,l^2}{2\,R}\sin\vartheta\left[\frac{x}{l} - \left(\frac{x}{l}\right)^2\right]. \tag{7.10}$$

7.3 Deformations

Integrating (7.2a), we obtain

$$v_x = \int \varepsilon_x\,d\,x + C_3(\vartheta) = C_3(\vartheta) + \int\left[\frac{n_x}{D_x} - \frac{\nu_\vartheta}{D_\vartheta}\,n_\vartheta\right]d\,x\,, \tag{7.11a}$$

hence, from (7.2c),

$$v_\vartheta = \int\left[\gamma_{x\vartheta} - \frac{1}{R}\frac{\partial\,v_x}{\partial\,\vartheta}\right]d\,x + C_4(\vartheta) =$$

$$= C_4(\vartheta) - \frac{x}{R}\frac{d\,C_3}{d\,\vartheta} + \int\left[\gamma_{x\vartheta} - \frac{1}{R}\int\frac{\partial\,\varepsilon_x}{\partial\,\vartheta}\,d\,x\right]d\,x =$$

$$= C_4(\vartheta) - \frac{x}{R}\frac{d\,C_3}{d\,\vartheta} + \tag{7.11b}$$

$$+ \int\left[\frac{n_{x\vartheta}}{D_{x\vartheta}} - \frac{1}{R}\int\left(\frac{\partial\,n_x/\partial\,\vartheta}{D_x} - \frac{\nu_\vartheta}{D_\vartheta}\frac{\partial\,n_\vartheta}{\partial\,\vartheta}\right)d\,x\right]d\,x$$

and from (7.2b)

$$v_R = R\,\varepsilon_\vartheta - \frac{\partial\,v_\vartheta}{\partial\,\vartheta} = R\,\varepsilon_\vartheta - \frac{d\,C_4}{d\,\vartheta} + \frac{x}{R}\frac{d^2\,C_3}{d\,\vartheta^2} -$$

$$- \int\left[\frac{\partial\,\gamma_{x\vartheta}}{\partial\,\vartheta} - \frac{1}{R}\int\frac{\partial^2\,\varepsilon_x}{\partial\,\vartheta^2}\,d\,x\right]d\,x = R\left[\frac{n_\vartheta}{D_\vartheta} - \right.$$

$$\left. - \frac{\nu_x}{D_x}\,n_x\right] - \int\left[\frac{\partial\,n_{x\vartheta}/\partial\,\vartheta}{D_{x\vartheta}} - \frac{1}{R}\int\left(\frac{\partial^2 n_x/\partial\,\vartheta^2}{D_x} - \right.\right. \tag{7.11c}$$

$$\left.\left. - \frac{\nu_\vartheta}{D_\vartheta}\frac{\partial^2\,n_\vartheta}{\partial\,\vartheta^2}\right)d\,x\right]d\,x - \frac{d\,C_4}{d\,\vartheta} + \frac{x}{R}\frac{d^2\,C_3}{d\,\vartheta^2}\,.$$

The arbitrary functions arising during integration can be determined from the boundary conditions. Since they are solely functions of ϑ, only boundary conditions along the curves $x = \text{const}$ can be satisfied. The general solution for small deformations cannot, therefore, be subjected to boundary conditions along the edges $\vartheta = \text{const}$. We thus cannot prevent small folds at the edges of a longitudinally supported membrane, since we cannot select the integration constants in such a way as to make even the vertical displacement components vanish along the support edges $(\vartheta = +\vartheta_0)$. The available "integration functions" do not even permit satisfaction of general boundary conditions at the edges $x = \text{const}$, where small folds can only be prevented if (similarly to axisymmetrical membranes) the unavoidable edge deformations of the membrane are taken up by flexible supports (e.g., adjustable cables). We can also vary the rigidity ratio at the edges.

7.4 Semicircular Cylinder with Adjoining Quarter Spheres

(Figure 7.2)

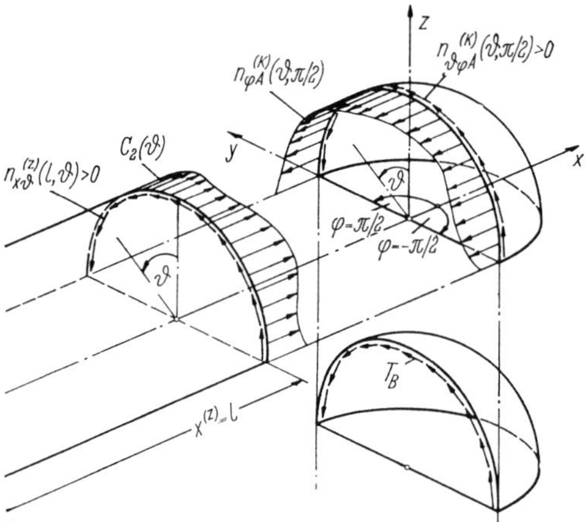

Figure 7.2

7.4.1 *General Observations*

For a given load, we determine first

1) the sectional loads of the quarter-spheres according to Section 4.1, assuming these, for the time being, to act also within the quarter-spheres. (They are denoted by $n_{\vartheta A}{}^{(K)}$, $n_{\varphi A}{}^{(K)}$, $n_{\vartheta\varphi A}{}^{(K)}$);
2) the sectional loads of the semicylinder according to Section 7.1. In accordance with the assumptions, which led to the formulas in Subsections 7.2.1 through 7.2.5 (symmetry with respect to the normal bisecting the axis of the cylinder) only the axial force $n_x{}^{(Z)}$ can be selected arbitrarily by means of the function $C_2(\vartheta)$. These sectional loads are denoted by $n_\vartheta{}^{(Z)}$, $n_{x\vartheta}{}^{(Z)}$, and $n_x{}^{(Z)} = n_{xA}{}^{(Z)} + C_2(\vartheta)$.

At the cylinder end $x^{(Z)} = l$ the sectional loads of the cylinder are

1) the normal force $n_x{}^{(Z)} = C_2(\vartheta)$;
2) the shearing force $n_{x\vartheta}{}^{(Z)}(l, \vartheta)$.

At the edge of the quarter-sphere, the sectional loads are

1) the normal force $n_{\varphi A}{}^{(K)}(\vartheta, \varphi = \pm\pi/2)$
2) the shearing force $n_{\vartheta\varphi A}{}^{(K)}(\vartheta, \varphi = \pm\pi/2)$. These are determined according to Section 4.1.

Since the shearing forces $n_{x\vartheta}{}^{(Z)}(l, \vartheta)$ at the cylinder edge, obtained according to Subsections 7.2.1 through 7.2.5, contain no arbitrary functions [$C_1(\varphi)$ is determined by the conditions of symmetry], and thus represent the final values, we have to introduce an additional shearing force at the edge of the quarter-sphere in order to make $n_{\vartheta\varphi A}{}^{(K)}(\vartheta, \pm\pi/2)$ equal to the shearing forces acting at the cylinder edge. The condition $n_{\varphi\vartheta}{}^{(K)}(\vartheta, \pm\pi/2) = - n_{x\vartheta}{}^{(Z)}(l, \vartheta)$ leads to the expression

$$T_B = -\left[n_{x\vartheta}{}^{(Z)}(l, \vartheta) + n_{\vartheta\varphi A}{}^{(K)}\left(\vartheta, \pm\frac{\pi}{2}\right)\right] = f(\vartheta) \tag{7.12a}$$

for this additional force. The corresponding sectional loads are, according to Subsection 4.3.6a, $n_{\vartheta B}{}^{(K)} = - n_{\varphi B}{}^{(K)}$ and $n_{\vartheta\varphi B}{}^{(K)}$, which are found by solving systems (4.45) or (4.47). Putting $C_2(\vartheta) = n_{\varphi A}{}^{(K)}(\vartheta, \pm\pi/2)$, we would be able to satisfy the boundary conditions at the juncture with regard to normal and shearing forces. However, this determination of $C_2(\vartheta)$ is in some way arbitrary; in fact, we can determine $C_2(\vartheta)$ by postulating the continuity of the deformations. Complete fulfilment of all conditions, which might be formulated for the deformations at the juncture, is not possible within the scope of the membrane theory. Only a single deformation condition can be satisfied through the selection of $C_2(\vartheta)$, and we cannot decide which deformation this should be. If, for instance, we postulate the continuity of the circumferential extensions $\varepsilon_\vartheta{}^{(Z)}(l, \vartheta)$ at the joint between cylinder and quarter sphere (this condition includes two deformation components), i.e., $\varepsilon_\vartheta{}^{(Z)}(l, \vartheta) = \varepsilon_\vartheta{}^{(K)}(\vartheta, \pm\pi/2)$, we obtain $C_2(\vartheta) = 0$ if $D_\vartheta{}^{(K)} = D_\vartheta{}^{(Z)}$. (This means that the circumferential sectional loads $n_{\varphi A}{}^{(K)}$ have to be made to vanish by introducing additional normal edge loads). The result thus obtained is certainly incorrect. Considering only loading by internal pressure, and passing from the semicylinder with quarter spheres to a full cylinder with adjoining hemispheres, we obtain the following equilibrium condition for the semisphere, referred to the direction of the cylinder axis: $C_2(\vartheta) = n_x{}^{(Z)}(l, \vartheta) = pR/2$. We obtain the same result by putting $C_2(\vartheta) = n_{\varphi A}{}^{(K)}(\vartheta, \pm\pi/2)$ [$= pR/2$]. We therefore write

$$C_2(\vartheta) = n_{\varphi A}{}^{(K)}(\vartheta, \pm\pi/2), \tag{7.12b}$$

thus completely determining the state of stress in the cylindrical membrane. The resultant sectional loads are obtained by superposition of states "A" and "B." We shall only consider the first two terms of each series representing the sectional loads corresponding to state "B."

7.4.2 *Loading by Internal Pressure p*

We obtain from (4.1a, b)

$$n_{\vartheta A}{}^{(K)} = n_{\varphi A}{}^{(K)} = pR/2, \quad n_{\vartheta\varphi A}{}^{(K)} = 0,$$
$$\text{hence } C_{2p}(\vartheta) = n_{\varphi A}{}^{(K)}\left(\vartheta, \pm\frac{\pi}{2}\right) = p\frac{R}{2}, \tag{7.13}$$

thus, for the semicylinder, by (7.6)

$$n_\vartheta{}^{(Z)} = pR, \quad n_{x\vartheta}{}^{(Z)} = 0, \quad n_x{}^{(Z)} = C_{2p} = pR/2. \tag{7.14a-c}$$

Since no shearing forces are in this case transmitted by the semicylinder to the quarter-spheres, no state of stress "B" exists, and state "A" represents the total sectional loads of the sphere.

7.4.3 *Loading by Dead Weight*

We first obtain from (4.2a, b)

$$n_{\vartheta A}{}^{(K)} = -\frac{gR}{1+\cos\vartheta}, \quad n_{\varphi A}{}^{(K)} = gR\left(\frac{1}{1+\cos\vartheta} - \cos\vartheta\right),$$
$$n_{\vartheta\varphi A}{}^{(K)} = 0, \text{thus } C_{2g}(\vartheta) = gR\left(\frac{1}{1+\cos\vartheta} - \cos\vartheta\right). \tag{(7.15a-d)}$$

The sectional loads of the semicylinder are thus by (7.7)

$$n_\vartheta{}^{(Z)} = -gR\cos\vartheta, \quad n_{x\vartheta}{}^{(Z)} = gl\sin\vartheta\left[1 - 2\frac{x}{l}\right], \tag{7.16}$$
$$n_x{}^{(Z)} = gR\left[\frac{1}{1+\cos\vartheta} - \cos\vartheta - \left(\frac{l}{R}\right)^2\left(\frac{x}{l} - \frac{x^2}{l^2}\right)\cos\vartheta\right].$$

The additional shearing forces at the edge of the quarter sphere (see Figure 7.2) are according to (7.12a)

$$T_B = -n_{x\vartheta}{}^{(Z)}(l, \vartheta) = gl\sin\vartheta = f(\vartheta) \tag{7.17a}$$

which are antimetrical with respect to the (x, z) plane. We have thus to solve the system (4.45). Taking only the first two terms of the series, we obtain

$$f_3 = -\int_0^{\pi/2} gl\sin^3\vartheta\,\mathrm{tg}^3\frac{\vartheta}{2}\,d\vartheta = -16gl\int_0^{\pi/4}\sin^6 u\,du =$$
$$= -\frac{gl}{6}(7.5\pi - 22) = -0.260324\,gl,$$
$$f_5 = \int_0^{\pi/2} gl\sin^3\vartheta\,\mathrm{tg}^5\frac{\vartheta}{2}\,d\vartheta = 16gl\int_0^{\pi/4}\frac{\sin^8 u}{\cos^2 u}\,du =$$
$$= gl\left[2 - \frac{7}{6}(7.5\pi - 22)\right] = 0.177732\,gl$$

whence by (4.51a)*

$$C_3 = [-106.9716\cdot 0.260324 + 133.0349\cdot 0.177732]\,gl =$$
$$= -4.2027\,gl,$$
$$C_5 = [-133.0349\cdot 0.260324 + 175.5449\cdot 0.177732]\,gl = \tag{7.17b-c}$$
$$= -3.4322\,gl.$$

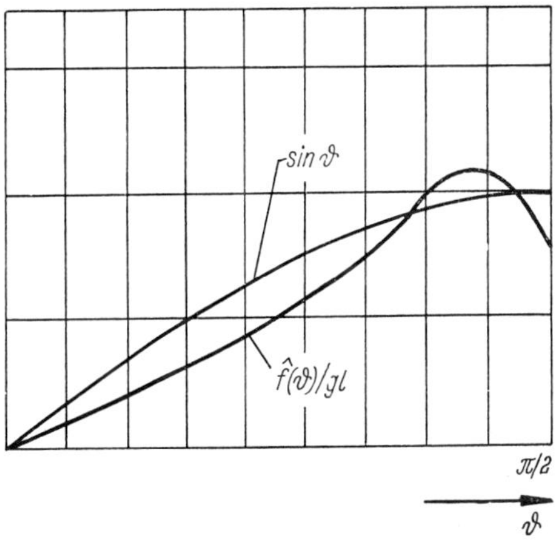

Figure 7.3

* The accuracy of this approximation can be estimated with the aid of Figure 7.3 which shows the function $\sin\vartheta$, which has to be approximated, together with $\hat{f}(\vartheta)/gl = [(-1)^1 C_3\,\mathrm{tg}^3\,\vartheta/2 + (-1)^2 C_5\,\mathrm{tg}^5\,\vartheta/2]/gl$

With these values we obtain from (4.44d, e)

$$n_{\varphi_B}{}^{(K)} = -n_{\vartheta_B}{}^{(K)} \approx \frac{1}{\sin^2\vartheta}\left[C_3 \operatorname{tg}^3\frac{\vartheta}{2}\cos 3\varphi + C_5 \operatorname{tg}^5\frac{\vartheta}{2}\cos 5\varphi\right] = -\frac{g\,l}{\sin^2\vartheta}\left[4.2027\operatorname{tg}^3\frac{\vartheta}{2}\cos 3\varphi + 3.4322\operatorname{tg}^5\frac{\vartheta}{2}\cos 5\varphi\right]$$

$$n_{\vartheta\varphi_B}{}^{(K)} \approx \frac{1}{\sin^2\vartheta}\left[C_3 \operatorname{tg}^3\frac{\vartheta}{2}\sin 3\varphi + C_5 \operatorname{tg}^5\frac{\vartheta}{2}\sin 5\varphi\right] = -\frac{g\,l}{\sin^2\vartheta}\left[4.2027\operatorname{tg}^3\frac{\vartheta}{2}\sin 3\varphi + 3.4322\operatorname{tg}^5\frac{\vartheta}{2}\sin 5\varphi\right].$$

The resultant sectional loads of the quarter spheres are thus

$$n_\vartheta{}^{(K)} \approx n_{\vartheta_A}{}^{(K)} + n_{\vartheta_B}{}^{(K)} = -g\,R\left[\frac{1}{1+\cos\vartheta} - \frac{l}{R}\left(4.2027\frac{\operatorname{tg}^3\frac{\vartheta}{2}}{\sin^2\vartheta}\cos 3\varphi + 3.4322\frac{\operatorname{tg}^5\frac{\vartheta}{2}}{\sin^2\vartheta}\cos 5\varphi\right)\right],$$

$$n_\varphi{}^{(K)} \approx g\,R\left[\frac{1}{1+\cos\vartheta} - \cos\vartheta - \frac{l}{R}\left(4.2027\frac{\operatorname{tg}^3\frac{\vartheta}{2}}{\sin^2\vartheta}\cos 3\varphi + 3.4322\frac{\operatorname{tg}^5\frac{\vartheta}{2}}{\sin^2\vartheta}\cos 5\varphi\right)\right], \quad (7.18a\text{-}c)$$

$$n_{\vartheta\varphi}{}^{(K)} \approx -\frac{g\,l}{\sin^2\vartheta}\left[4.2027\operatorname{tg}^3\frac{\vartheta}{2}\sin 3\varphi + 3.4322\operatorname{tg}^5\frac{\vartheta}{2}\sin 5\varphi\right].$$

7.4.4 *Symmetrical Snow Load*

For the quarter spheres we find from (4.3)

$$n_{\vartheta_A}{}^{(K)} = -\frac{s\,R}{3}\,\frac{1-\cos^3\vartheta}{\sin^2\vartheta}, \quad n_{\vartheta\varphi_A}{}^{(K)} = 0,$$

$$n_{\varphi_A}{}^{(K)} = \frac{s\,R}{3}\left[\frac{1-\cos^3\vartheta}{\sin^2\vartheta} - 3\cos^3\vartheta\right], \quad (7.19a\text{-}d)$$

$$\text{hence } C_{2s1}(\vartheta) = \frac{s\,R}{3}\left[\frac{1-\cos^3\vartheta}{\sin^2\vartheta} - 3\cos^3\vartheta\right].$$

The sectional loads of the semicylinder are thus according to (7.8)

$$n_\vartheta{}^{(Z)} = -s\,R\cos^3\vartheta, \quad n_{x\vartheta}{}^{(Z)} = 2\,s\,l\cos^2\vartheta\sin\vartheta\left(1 - 2\frac{x}{l}\right),$$

$$n_x{}^{(Z)} = s\,R\left[\frac{1-\cos^3\vartheta}{3\sin^2\vartheta} - \cos^3\vartheta - 2\left(\frac{l}{R}\right)^2\cos\vartheta\,(\cos^2\vartheta - 2\sin^2\vartheta)\left(\frac{x}{l} - \frac{x^2}{l^2}\right)\right]. \quad (7.20a\text{-}c)$$

The shearing forces at the edge of the quarter spheres are

$$T_B{}^{(\vartheta)} = -n_{x\vartheta}{}^{(Z)}(l,\vartheta) = 2\,s\,l\sin\vartheta\cos^2\vartheta = -T_B(-\vartheta). \quad (7.21a)$$

Hence

$$f_3 = -2\,s\,l\int_0^{\pi/2}\cos^2\vartheta\sin^3\vartheta\operatorname{tg}^3\vartheta/2\,d\vartheta = -2\,s\,l\left[16\int_0^{\pi/4}\sin^6 u\,du - 64\int_0^{\pi/4}\sin^8 u\,du + 64\int_0^{\pi/4}\sin^{10} u\,du\right] =$$

$$= -s\,l\left[\frac{1}{6}(7.5\,\pi - 22)\frac{13}{10} - \frac{3}{10}\right] = -0.038421\,s\,l,$$

$$f_5 = 2\,s\,l\int_0^{\pi/2}\cos^2\vartheta\sin^3\vartheta\operatorname{tg}^5\frac{\vartheta}{2}\,d\vartheta = 2\,s\,l\left[16\int_0^{\pi/4}\frac{\sin^8 u}{\cos^2 u}\,du - 64\int_0^{\pi/4}\sin^{10} u\,du\right] = s\,l\left[-\frac{1}{6}(7.5\,\pi - 22)\frac{203}{10} + \frac{53}{10}\right] =$$

$$= 0.015423\,s\,l$$

whence according to (4.15a)

$$C_3 = -2.0582\,s\,l, \quad C_5 = -2.4039\,s\,l. \quad (7.21b,c)$$

The sectional loads corresponding to state "*B*" are thus

$$\left.\begin{aligned} n_{\varphi_B}{}^{(K)} &= -n_{\vartheta_B}{}^{(K)} \approx -\frac{s\,l}{\sin^2\vartheta}\left[2.0582\operatorname{tg}^3\frac{\vartheta}{2}\cos 3\varphi + 2.4039\operatorname{tg}^5\frac{\vartheta}{2}\cos 5\varphi\right], \\ n_{\vartheta\varphi_B}{}^{(K)} &\approx -\frac{s\,l}{\sin^2\vartheta}\left[2.0582\operatorname{tg}^3\frac{\vartheta}{2}\sin 3\varphi + 2.4039\operatorname{tg}^5\frac{\vartheta}{2}\sin 5\varphi\right], \end{aligned}\right\} \quad (7.22a,b)$$

which have to be added to those corresponding to state "*A*."

7.4.5 *One-sided Snow Load*

Assuming a one-sided snow load ($y>0$), and replacing φ by $\varphi - \pi/2$ in (4.4), we find

$$n_{\vartheta_A}{}^{(K)} = \frac{s\,R}{2}\left[a_{s1}(\vartheta) + a_{s3}(\vartheta)\sin\varphi\right],$$

$$n_{\vartheta\varphi_A}{}^{(K)} = -\frac{s\,R}{2}\,b_{s3}(\vartheta)\cos\varphi,$$

$$n_{\varphi_A}{}^{(K)} = \frac{s\,R}{2}\left[c_{s1}(\vartheta) + c_{s3}(\vartheta)\sin\varphi\right], \quad (7.23a\text{-}d)$$

hence

$$C_{2s3}(\vartheta) = \frac{s\,R}{2}\left\{\begin{aligned} &c_{s1}(\vartheta) + c_{s3}(\vartheta) \text{ for } \varphi = \frac{\pi}{2}, \text{ thus } \vartheta^{(Z)} \geqq 0, \\ &c_{s1}(\vartheta) - c_{s3}(\vartheta) \text{ for } \varphi = -\frac{\pi}{2}, \text{ thus } \vartheta^{(Z)} \leqq 0 \end{aligned}\right\}.$$

The sectional loads of the semicylinder are according to (7.9)

$$n_\vartheta{}^{(Z)} = -\frac{s\,R}{2}\cos^3\vartheta\,(1+\sin\vartheta),$$

$$n_{x\vartheta}{}^{(Z)} = s\,l\cos^2\vartheta\left[\sin\vartheta\,(1+\sin\vartheta) - \frac{1}{4}\cos^2\vartheta\right]\left(1 - 2\frac{x}{l}\right),$$

$$n_x{}^{(Z)} = \frac{s\,R}{2}\left[\left\{\begin{aligned} c_{s1}(\vartheta) + c_{s3}(\vartheta) \text{ for } \vartheta \geqq 0 \\ c_{s1}(\vartheta) - c_{s3}(\vartheta) \text{ for } \vartheta \leqq 0 \end{aligned}\right\} - 2\left(\frac{l}{R}\right)^2\cos\vartheta\left[(1+\sin\vartheta)(\cos^2\vartheta - 2\sin^2\vartheta) + 2\cos^2\vartheta\sin^2\vartheta\right]\left(\frac{x}{l} - \frac{x^2}{l^2}\right)\right]. \quad (7.24a\text{-}c)$$

The state of stress "*A*" causes no shearing forces at the edges of the quarter spheres [$\varphi = \pm\pi/2$], so that

$$T_B = -n_{x\vartheta}{}^{(Z)}(l,\vartheta) = s\,l\left(\cos^2\vartheta\sin^2\vartheta - \frac{1}{4}\cos^4\vartheta\right) + s\,l\cos^2\vartheta\sin\vartheta. \quad (7.25a)$$

The second (antimetrical) term is equal to half the value given by (7.21a). We obtain, similarly to (7.21b, c)

$$C_3 = -1.0291\, s\, l\,, \quad C_5 = -1.2020\, s\, l\,. \tag{7.25b, c}$$

The first term

$$\widehat{T}_B = s\, l\left(\cos^2\vartheta \sin^2\vartheta - \frac{1}{4}\cos^4\vartheta\right) = s\, l\left(\cos^2\vartheta - \frac{5}{4}\cos^4\vartheta\right) \tag{7.25d}$$

corresponds to a symmetrical shearing force and should thus be represented by a series expression in terms of even k according to Subsection 4.3.6a 2. Taking only the first two terms, we have

$$\bar{f}_2 = s\, l \int_0^{\pi/2} \left(\cos^2\vartheta - \frac{5}{4}\cos^4\vartheta\right)\sin^2\vartheta\, \mathrm{tg}^2\frac{\vartheta}{2}\, d\,\vartheta = 0.024534\, s\, l\,,$$

$$\bar{f}_4 = -\, s\, l \int_0^{\pi/2} \left(\cos^2\vartheta - \frac{5}{4}\cos^4\vartheta\right)\sin^2\vartheta\, \mathrm{tg}^4\frac{\vartheta}{2}\, d\,\vartheta = -\,0.009834\, s\, l\,,$$

whence, according to (4.51b),

$$\bar{C}_2 = 0.5027\, s\, l\,, \quad \bar{C}_4 = 0.5836\, s\, l\,. \tag{7.25e, f}$$

The additional sectional loads, caused by state of stress "B", are thus according to (4.44d, e) and (4.46c, d)

$$\left.\begin{aligned} n_{\varphi_B}{}^{(K)} = -\, n_{\vartheta_B}{}^{(K)} \approx s\, l \Big[& 0.5027\, \mathrm{tg}^2\frac{\vartheta}{2}\sin 2\varphi - \\ & -1.0291\, \mathrm{tg}^3\frac{\vartheta}{2}\cos 3\varphi + 0.5836\, \mathrm{tg}^4\frac{\vartheta}{2}\sin 4\varphi - \\ & -1.2020\, \mathrm{tg}^5\frac{\vartheta}{2}\cos 5\varphi\Big]\frac{1}{\sin^2\vartheta}\,, \\ n_{\vartheta\varphi_B}{}^{(K)} \approx s\, l \Big[& -0.5027\, \mathrm{tg}^2\frac{\vartheta}{2}\cos 2\varphi - \\ & -1.0291\, \mathrm{tg}^3\frac{\vartheta}{2}\sin 3\varphi - 0.5836\, \mathrm{tg}^4\frac{\vartheta}{2}\cos 4\varphi - \\ & -1.2020\, \mathrm{tg}^5\frac{\vartheta}{2}\sin 5\varphi\Big]\frac{1}{\sin^2\vartheta}\,. \end{aligned}\right\} \tag{7.26a, b}$$

7.4.6 *Wind Load (Wind Blowing from Negative y-Direction)*

Replacing φ by $\varphi - \pi/2$ again in (4.6) (these formulas correspond to a wind blowing from the negative x-direction), we obtain the sectional loads of the quarter spheres as

$$\left.\begin{aligned} n_{\vartheta_A}{}^{(K)} &= -\, w_0\frac{R}{2} + w_1\, R\, a_{w1}{}^{(\vartheta)}\sin\varphi\,, \\ n_{\vartheta\varphi_A}{}^{(K)} &= -\, w_1\, R\, b_{w1}(\vartheta)\cos\varphi\,, \\ n_{\vartheta_A}{}^{(K)} &= -\, w_0\frac{R}{2} + w_1\, R\, c_{w1}(\vartheta)\sin\varphi\,. \end{aligned}\right\} \tag{7.27a, b}$$

Thus, the normal forces

$$C_{2w}(\vartheta) = n_{\varphi_A}{}^{(K)}\left(\vartheta, \pm\frac{\pi}{2}\right) = -\, w_0\frac{R}{2} + \\ + w_1\, R\begin{Bmatrix} c_{w1}(\vartheta) & \text{for} \quad \varphi = \dfrac{\pi}{2}, & \text{thus } \vartheta^{(Z)} \geq 0\,, \\ -\, c_{w1}(\vartheta) & \text{for } \varphi = -\dfrac{\pi}{2}, & \text{thus } \vartheta^{(Z)} \leq 0 \end{Bmatrix}$$

are transmitted by the quarter spheres to the cylinder, for which we obtain the sectional loads from (7.10)

$$\left.\begin{aligned} n_\vartheta{}^{(Z)} &= -\, w_0\, R - w_1\, R\sin\vartheta\,, \\ n_{x\vartheta}{}^{(Z)} &= -\,\frac{w_1\, l}{2}\cos\vartheta\left(1 - 2\frac{x}{l}\right), \\ n_x{}^{(Z)} &= -\, w_0\frac{R}{2} + w_1\, R\left[\begin{Bmatrix} c_{w1}(\vartheta) & \text{for } \vartheta \geq 0 \\ -\, c_{w1}(\vartheta) & \text{for } \vartheta \leq 0 \end{Bmatrix} - \right. \\ & \left. -\,\frac{1}{2}\left(\frac{l}{R}\right)^2 \sin\vartheta\left[\frac{x}{l} - \left(\frac{x}{l}\right)^2\right]\right]. \end{aligned}\right\} \tag{7.28a, b}$$

The additional (symmetrical) shearing forces at the joint between cylinder and quarter spheres are

$$T_B(\vartheta) = -\, n_{x\vartheta}{}^{(Z)}(l, \vartheta) = -\,\frac{w_1\, l}{2}\cos\vartheta = T_B(-\,\vartheta)\,.$$

We then obtain

$$\bar{f}_2 = \frac{w_1\, l}{2}\int_0^{\pi/2}\cos\vartheta\sin^2\vartheta\, \mathrm{tg}^2\frac{\vartheta}{2}\, d\,\vartheta = 0.047936\, w_1\, l\,,$$

$$\bar{f}_4 = \frac{w_1\, l}{2}\int_0^{\pi/2}\cos\vartheta\sin^2\vartheta\, \mathrm{tg}^4\frac{\vartheta}{2}\, d\,\vartheta = 0.020654\, w_1\, l\,,$$

whence, according to (4.15b),

$$\bar{C}_2 = -\,0.8997\, w_1\, l\,, \quad \bar{C}_4 = -\,1.0195\, w_1\, l$$

so that the sectional loads caused by state of stress "B" are

$$\left.\begin{aligned} n_{\varphi_B}{}^{(K)} = -\, n_{\vartheta_B}{}^{(K)} \approx & - \\ & -\frac{w_1\, l}{\sin^2\vartheta}\Big[+0.8997\, \mathrm{tg}^2\frac{\vartheta}{2}\sin 2\varphi + \\ & +1.0195\, \mathrm{tg}^4\frac{\vartheta}{2}\sin 4\varphi\Big], \\ n_{\vartheta\varphi_B}{}^{(K)} \approx & \frac{w_1\, l}{\sin^2\vartheta}\Big[0.8997\, \mathrm{tg}^2\frac{\vartheta}{2}\cos 2\varphi + \\ & +1.0195\, \mathrm{tg}^4\frac{\vartheta}{2}\cos 4\varphi\Big]. \end{aligned}\right\} \tag{7.29a, b}$$

We can analyze different cases of loading in the same manner.

7.4.7 *Observations Regarding the Choice of Dimensions*

The problems of determining the inflation pressure and the maximum tensile stresses require separate analysis of the various parts constituting the system. Whereas for the quarter spheres we might proceed according to Subsection 4.3.5, we cannot, for the cylinder, consider the stresses due to internal pressure and to external loads separately since the tensor of the membrane forces due to inflation pressure is not spherical for the cylinder. Should extremalization be excessively difficult due to a complicated dependence of the sectional loads on ϑ, we must calculate the principal stresses point for point, assuming different values for the inflation pressure.

7.5 The Circular Tube

7.5.1 *State of Stress*

A perfect circular tube is a system which can take up loads only at the edges $x = \text{const}$. We thus (even when the tubes are not slender) obtain a rod-shaped structure. This becomes apparent also from the analysis. We first determine the total loads acting at a cross section $x = \text{const}$. (normal and shearing forces, bending and twisting moments) by integrating the expressions for the sectional loads $n_{x\vartheta}$ and n_x over the membrane circumference. Let

$$q_x(x) = \int_0^{2\pi} p_x R\, d\vartheta, \quad q_y(x) = \int_0^{2\pi} (p_\vartheta \cos\vartheta + p_R \sin\vartheta)\, R\, d\vartheta = \int_0^{2\pi} \left(p_\vartheta + \frac{\partial p_R}{\partial \vartheta}\right) R \cos\vartheta\, d\vartheta,$$

$$q_z(x) = \int_0^{2\pi} (-\,p_\vartheta \sin\vartheta + p_R \cos\vartheta)\, R\, d\vartheta = -\int_0^{2\pi} \left(p_\vartheta + \frac{\partial p_R}{\partial \vartheta}\right) R \sin\vartheta\, d\vartheta \tag{7.30a-c}$$

denote the loads per unit tube length, acting in the directions of the corresponding axes, while

$$m_x(x) = -\int_0^{2\pi} p_\vartheta R^2\, d\vartheta = -\int_0^{2\pi} \left(p_\vartheta + \frac{\partial p_R}{\partial \vartheta}\right) R^2\, d\vartheta\,,$$

$$m_y(x) = \int_0^{2\pi} p_x R \cos\vartheta\, R\, d\vartheta, \quad m_z(x) = -\int_0^{2\pi} p_x R \sin\vartheta\, R\, d\vartheta \tag{7.30d-f}$$

denotes the corresponding moment components per unit tube length. Rewriting (7.3) in the form

$$n_\vartheta = R\, p_R\,, \quad n_{x\vartheta} = n_{x\vartheta 0}(\vartheta) - \int_{x=0}^{x} \left(p_\vartheta + \frac{\partial p_R}{\partial \vartheta}\right) dx\,, \tag{7.31a-c}$$

$$n_x = n_{x0}(\vartheta) - \int_{x=0}^{x} \left\{p_x + \frac{1}{R}\frac{\partial n_{x\vartheta}}{\partial \vartheta}\right\} dx = n_{x0}(\vartheta) - \frac{x}{R}\frac{d\, n_{x\vartheta 0}}{d\vartheta} + \int_{x=0}^{x} \left\{-\,p_x + \frac{1}{R}\int_{x=0}^{x} \frac{\partial}{\partial \vartheta}\left(p_\vartheta + \frac{\partial p_R}{\partial \vartheta}\right) dx\right\} dx$$

where $n_{x\vartheta 0}(\vartheta)$ and $n_{x0}(\vartheta)$ denote the corresponding values for $x = 0$, we obtain

a) the shearing force acting in the z-direction

$$Q_z(x) = -\int_0^{2\pi} n_{x\vartheta} \sin\vartheta\, R\, d\vartheta = -R\int_0^{2\pi} n_{x\vartheta 0} \sin\vartheta\, d\vartheta + R\int_{x=0}^{x}\left[\int_0^{2\pi}\left(p_\vartheta + \frac{\partial p_R}{\partial \vartheta}\right)\sin\vartheta\, d\vartheta\right] dx = Q_{z0} - \int_{x=0}^{x} q_z(x)\, dx\,, \tag{7.32a}$$

b) the shearing force acting in the y-direction

$$Q_y(x) = \int_0^{2\pi} n_{x\vartheta} \cos\vartheta\, R\, d\vartheta = R\int_0^{2\pi} n_{x\vartheta 0} \cos\vartheta\, d\vartheta - R\int_{x=0}^{x}\left[\int_0^{2\pi}\left(p_\vartheta + \frac{\partial p_R}{\partial \vartheta}\right)\cos\vartheta\, d\vartheta\right] dx = Q_{y0} - \int_{x=0}^{x} q_y(x)\, dx\,, \tag{7.32b}$$

c) the normal (longitudinal) force

$$Q_x(x) = \int_0^{2\pi} n_x R\, d\vartheta = R\int_0^{2\pi} n_{x0}(\vartheta)\, d\vartheta - R\int_{x=0}^{x}\left[\int_0^{2\pi} p_x\, d\vartheta\right] dx - R\,\frac{1}{R}\int_{x=0}^{x}\left[\int_0^{2\pi}\frac{\partial n_{x\vartheta}}{\partial \vartheta}\, d\vartheta\right] dx = Q_{x0} - \int_{x=0}^{x} q_x(x)\, dx\,, \tag{7.32c}$$

d) the twisting moment (torque)

$$M_x(x) = -\int_0^{2\pi} R\, n_{x\vartheta} R\, d\vartheta = -R^2\int_0^{2\pi} n_{x\vartheta 0}(\vartheta)\, d\vartheta + R^2\int_{x=0}^{x}\left[\int_0^{2\pi}\left(p_\vartheta + \frac{\partial p_R}{\partial \vartheta}\right) d\vartheta\right] dx = M_{x0} - \int_{x=0}^{x} m_x(x)\, dx\,, \tag{7.32d}$$

e) the bending moment about the y-axis

$$\begin{aligned} M_y(x) &= \int_0^{2\pi} n_x R \cos\vartheta\, R\, d\vartheta = R^2\int_0^{2\pi} n_{x0}(\vartheta)\cos\vartheta\, d\vartheta - R^2\int_0^{x}\left[\int_0^{2\pi} p_x \cos\vartheta\, d\vartheta\right] dx - R^2\,\frac{1}{R}\int_0^{x}\left[\int_0^{2\pi}\frac{\partial n_{x\vartheta}}{\partial \vartheta}\cos\vartheta\, d\vartheta\right] dx = \\ &= M_{y0} - \int_0^{x} m_y(x)\, dx - R\int_0^{x}\left[\int_0^{2\pi} n_{x\vartheta}\sin\vartheta\, d\vartheta\right] dx = \\ &= M_{y0} + \int_0^{x} Q_z(x)\, dx - \int_0^{x} m_y(x)\, dx\,, \end{aligned} \tag{7.32e}$$

f) the bending moment about the z-axis

$$\begin{aligned} M_z(x) &= -\int_0^{2\pi} n_x R \sin\vartheta\, R\, d\vartheta = -R^2\int_0^{2\pi} n_{x0}(\vartheta)\sin\vartheta\, d\vartheta + R^2\int_0^{x}\left[\int_0^{2\pi} p_x \sin\vartheta\, d\vartheta\right] dx + R^2\,\frac{1}{R}\int_0^{x}\left[\int_0^{2\pi}\frac{\partial n_{x\vartheta}}{\partial \vartheta}\sin\vartheta\, d\vartheta\right] dx = \\ &= M_{z0} - \int_0^{x} m_z(x)\, dx + R\int_0^{x}\left[-\int_0^{2\pi} n_{x\vartheta}\cos\vartheta\, d\vartheta\right] dx = \\ &= M_{z0} - \int_0^{x} Q_y(x)\, dx - \int_0^{x} m_z(x)\, dx\,, \end{aligned} \tag{7.32f}$$

where

$$\left.\begin{aligned} Q_{x0} &= R\int_0^{2\pi} n_{x0}(\vartheta)\,d\vartheta\,, \quad Q_{y0} = R\int_0^{2\pi} n_{x\vartheta 0}(\vartheta)\cos\vartheta\,d\vartheta\,,\\ Q_{z0} &= -R\int_0^{2\pi} n_{x\vartheta 0}(\vartheta)\sin\vartheta\,d\vartheta\,,\\ M_{x0} &= -R^2\int_0^{2\pi} n_{x\vartheta 0}(\vartheta)\,d\vartheta\,, \quad M_{y0} = R^2\int_0^{2\pi} n_{x0}(\vartheta)\cos\vartheta\,d\vartheta\,,\\ M_{z0} &= -R^2\int_0^{2\pi} n_{x0}(\vartheta)\sin\vartheta\,d\vartheta \end{aligned}\right\} \qquad (7.33\text{a-f})$$

are the respective values of forces and moments for the tube end $x = 0$. The relationships coincide with those obtained from the general equilibrium conditions for a tubular beam. We shall only consider loads which are either axisymmetrical or symmetrical with respect to the (x, z) plane. The loads per unit surface can then be represented as follows:

$$\begin{aligned} p_\vartheta &= \bar{p}_{\vartheta 0}(x) + \sum_{k=1}^{\infty} \bar{p}_{\vartheta k}(x)\sin k\vartheta\,, \quad \bar{p}_{\vartheta 0} = \frac{1}{2\pi}\int_0^{2\pi} p_\vartheta\,d\vartheta\,,\\ \bar{p}_{\vartheta k} &= \frac{1}{\pi}\int_0^{2\pi} p_\vartheta \sin k\vartheta\,d\vartheta\,,\\ p_x &= \bar{p}_{x0}(x) + \sum_{k=1}^{\infty} \bar{p}_{xk}(x)\cos k\vartheta\,, \quad \bar{p}_{x0} = \frac{1}{2\pi}\int_0^{2\pi} p_x\,d\vartheta\,,\\ \bar{p}_{xk} &= \frac{1}{\pi}\int_0^{2\pi} p_x\cos k\vartheta\,d\vartheta\,,\\ p_R &= \bar{p}_{R0}(x) + \sum_{k=1}^{\infty} \bar{p}_{Rk}(x)\cos k\vartheta\,, \quad \bar{p}_{R0} = \frac{1}{2\pi}\int_0^{2\pi} p_R\,d\vartheta\,,\\ \bar{p}_{Rk} &= \frac{1}{\pi}\int_0^{2\pi} p_R\cos k\vartheta\,d\vartheta \end{aligned} \qquad (7.34)$$

so that the loads per unit tube length become

$$\begin{aligned} q_x(x) &= R\int_0^{2\pi} p_x\,d\vartheta = 2\pi R\,\bar{p}_{x0}\,,\\ q_z(x) &= -R\int_0^{2\pi}\left(p_\vartheta + \frac{\partial p_R}{\partial\vartheta}\right)\sin\vartheta\,d\vartheta = -\pi R\,(\bar{p}_{\vartheta 1} - \bar{p}_{R1})\,,\\ m_x(x) &= -R^2\int_0^{2\pi} p_\vartheta\,d\vartheta = -2\pi R^2\,\bar{p}_{\vartheta 0}\,,\\ m_y(x) &= R^2\int_0^{2\pi} p_x\cos\vartheta\,d\vartheta = \pi R^2\,\bar{p}_{x1} \end{aligned} \qquad (7.35)$$

The sectional loads at the tube edge $x = 0$ must also be given in the form

$$\begin{aligned} n_{x\vartheta 0}(\vartheta) &= \bar{n}_{x\vartheta 0}^{(0)} + \sum_{k=1}^{\infty} \bar{n}_{x\vartheta 0}^{(k)}\sin k\vartheta\,, \quad \bar{n}_{x\vartheta 0}^{(0)} = \frac{1}{2\pi}\int_0^{2\pi} n_{x\vartheta 0}\,d\vartheta\,,\\ \bar{n}_{x\vartheta 0}^{(k)} &= \frac{1}{\pi}\int_0^{2\pi} n_{x\vartheta 0}\sin k\vartheta\,d\vartheta\,,\\ n_{x0}(\vartheta) &= \bar{n}_{x0}^{(0)} + \sum_{k=1}^{\infty} \bar{n}_{x0}^{(k)}\cos k\vartheta\,, \quad \bar{n}_{x0}^{(0)} = \frac{1}{2\pi}\int_0^{2\pi} n_{x0}\,d\vartheta\,,\\ \bar{n}_{x0}^{(k)} &= \frac{1}{\pi}\int_0^{2\pi} n_{x0}\cos k\vartheta\,d\vartheta \end{aligned} \qquad (7.36)$$

whence we obtain the total forces and moments acting at the tube section $x = 0$:

$$\begin{aligned} Q_{x0} &= R\int_0^{2\pi} n_{x0}\,d\vartheta = 2\pi R\,\bar{n}_{x0}^{(0)}\,,\\ Q_{z0} &= -R\int_0^{2\pi} n_{x\vartheta 0}\sin\vartheta\,d\vartheta = -\pi R\,\bar{n}_{x\vartheta 0}^{(1)}\,,\\ M_{x0} &= -R^2\int_0^{2\pi} n_{x\vartheta 0}\,d\vartheta = -2\pi R^2\,\bar{n}_{x\vartheta 0}^{(0)}\,,\\ M_{y0} &= R^2\int_0^{2\pi} n_{x0}\cos\vartheta\,d\vartheta = \pi R^2\,\bar{n}_{x0}^{(1)} \end{aligned} \qquad (7.37)$$

The only nonzero forces and moments are thus Q_x, Q_z, M_x, and M_y . The terms corresponding to $k \geqq 2$ do not affect the tube loads, as is evident from (7.35) and (7.37), and are therefore in equilibrium along the circumference.

Substituting (7.34) and (7.36) in (7.31a-c), we obtain

$$n_\vartheta = R\,p_R\,, \qquad (7.38\text{a})$$

$$\begin{aligned} n_{x\vartheta} = {} & \left(\bar{n}_{x\vartheta 0}^{(0)} - \int_0^x \bar{p}_{x\vartheta 0}\,dx\right) + \sin\vartheta\left(\bar{n}_{x\vartheta 0}^{(1)} - \int_0^x (\bar{p}_{\vartheta 1} - \bar{p}_{R1})\,dx\right) +\\ & + \sum_{k=2}^{\infty} \sin k\vartheta\left[\bar{n}_{x\vartheta 0}^{(k)} - \int_0^x (\bar{p}_{\vartheta k} - k\,\bar{p}_{Rk})\,dx\right], \end{aligned}$$

whence, according to (7.35) and (7.37)

$$\begin{aligned} n_{x\vartheta} = {} & -\frac{M_{x0} - \int_0^x m_x\,dx}{2\pi R^2} - \frac{\sin\vartheta}{\pi R}\left(Q_{z0} - \int_0^x q_z\,dx\right) +\\ & + \sum_{k=2}^{\infty} \sin k\vartheta\left[\bar{n}_{x\vartheta 0}^{(k)} - \int_0^x (\bar{p}_{\vartheta k} - k\,\bar{p}_{Rk})\,dx\right]. \end{aligned}$$

Substituting (7.32a, d), we obtain

$$\begin{aligned} n_{x\vartheta} = {} & \underline{-\frac{M_x(x)}{2\pi R^2} - \frac{Q_z(x)}{\pi R}\sin\vartheta} +\\ & + \sum_{k=2}^{\infty} \sin k\vartheta\left[\bar{n}_{x\vartheta 0}^{(k)} - \int_0^x (\bar{p}_{\vartheta k} - k\,\bar{p}_{Rk})\,dx\right] = n_{x\vartheta\,\text{rod}} + \Delta n_{x\vartheta}, \end{aligned} \qquad (7.38\text{b})$$

and, correspondingly,

$$\begin{aligned} n_x = {} & \left(\bar{n}_{x0}^{(0)} - \int_0^x \bar{p}_{x0}\,dx\right) + \cos\vartheta\left(\bar{n}_{x0}^{(1)} - \int_0^x \bar{p}_{x1}\,dx\right) +\\ & + \sum_{k=2}^{\infty} \cos k\vartheta\left(\bar{n}_{x0}^{(k)} - \int_0^x \bar{p}_{xk}\,dx\right) - \frac{1}{R}\int_0^x \frac{\partial n_{x\vartheta}}{\partial\vartheta}\,dx =\\ = {} & \frac{1}{2\pi R}\left(Q_{x0} - \int_0^x q_x\,dx\right) + \frac{\cos\vartheta}{\pi R^2}\left(M_{y0} - \int_0^x m_y\,dx + \int_0^x Q_z\,dx\right) +\\ & + \sum_{k=2}^{\infty} \cos k\vartheta\left[\bar{n}_{x0}^{(k)} - k\frac{x}{R}\bar{n}_{x\vartheta 0}^{(k)} - \int_0^x \left\{\bar{p}_{xk} - \frac{k}{R}\int_0^x (\bar{p}_{\vartheta k} - k\bar{p}_{Rk})\,dx\right\}dx\right]\\ = {} & \underline{\frac{Q_x(x)}{2\pi R} + \frac{M_y(x)}{\pi R^2}\cos\vartheta} +\\ & + \sum_{k=2}^{\infty} \cos k\vartheta\left[\bar{n}_{x0}^{(k)} - k\frac{x}{R}\bar{n}_{x\vartheta 0}^{(k)} - \int_0^x \left\{\bar{p}_{xk} - \frac{k}{R}\int_0^x (\bar{p}_{\vartheta k} - k\bar{p}_{Rk})\,dx\right\}dx\right]\\ = {} & n_{x\,\text{rod}} + \Delta n_x\,. \end{aligned} \qquad (7.38\text{c})$$

The underlined terms correspond to those obtained from the theory of the bending of beams

$$\sigma_x h = n_x = h\left(\frac{Q_x(x)}{F} + \frac{M_y(x)}{J_y} z\right)$$
$$\tau_{x\vartheta} h = n_{x\vartheta} = -h\left(\frac{M_x(x)}{2F_m h} + \frac{Q_z(x) S}{J_y b}\right) \tag{7.39}$$

where h is the wall thickness of the tube, $F = 2\pi R h$ is the cross-sectional area of the tube wall, $J_y \approx \pi R^3 h$ is the moment of inertia with respect to the y-axis, $F_m = \pi R^2$ is the mean section of the tube, $z = R\cos\vartheta$, $b = 2h$, and $S \approx 2\int_{\chi=0}^{\vartheta} h R \, d\chi \, R\cos\chi = 2R^2 h \sin\vartheta$ is the static moment of the tube-wall section. The remaining terms

$$\Delta n_{x\vartheta} = \sum_{k=2}^{\infty} \sin k\vartheta \left[\bar{n}_{x\vartheta 0}{}^{(k)} - \int_0^x (\bar{p}_{\vartheta k} - k\bar{p}_{Rk})\, dx\right] =$$
$$= \frac{1}{\pi}\sum_{k=2}^{\infty} \sin k\vartheta \int_{\vartheta=0}^{2\pi}\left[n_{x\vartheta 0} - \int_{x=0}^{x}\left(p_\vartheta + \frac{\partial p_R}{\partial\vartheta}\right) dx\right] \sin k\vartheta \, d\vartheta =$$
$$= \frac{1}{\pi}\sum_{k=2}^{\infty} \sin k\vartheta \int_0^{2\pi} n_{x\vartheta} \sin k\vartheta \, d\vartheta \tag{7.40a}$$

and

$$\Delta n_x =$$
$$= \sum_{k=2}^{\infty} \cos k\vartheta \left[\bar{n}_{x0}{}^{(k)} - k\frac{x}{R}\bar{n}_{x\vartheta 0}{}^{(k)} - \int_0^x \left\{\bar{p}_{xk} - \frac{k}{R}\int_0^x (\bar{p}_{\vartheta k} - k\bar{p}_{Rk})\, dx\right\} dx\right]$$
$$= \frac{1}{\pi}\sum_{k=2}^{\infty} \cos k\vartheta \int_{\vartheta=0}^{2\pi}\left[n_{x0} - \frac{x}{R}\frac{d n_{x\vartheta 0}}{d\vartheta} - \int_0^x\left\{p_x - \frac{1}{R}\int_0^x \frac{\partial}{\partial\vartheta}\left(p_\vartheta + \frac{\partial p_R}{\partial\vartheta}\right) dx\right\} dx\right] \times$$
$$\times \cos k\vartheta \, d\vartheta = \frac{1}{\pi}\sum_{k=2}^{\infty} \cos k\vartheta \int_0^{2\pi} n_x \cos k\vartheta \, d\vartheta \tag{7.40b}$$

form the deviations from the stress distribution given by the formulas for the bending of beams. Since

$$\int_0^{2\pi} \sin k\vartheta \, d\vartheta = \int_0^{2\pi} \cos k\vartheta \, d\vartheta = 0,$$
$$\int_0^{2\pi} \sin k\vartheta \sin\vartheta \, d\vartheta = \int_0^{2\pi} \cos k\vartheta \cos\vartheta \, d\vartheta = 0 \text{ for } k \geqq 2$$

these deviations form equilibrium systems for each cross section $x = \text{const}$. From (7.40a, b) we can determine which nonslender tubes satisfy the stress distribution according to the theory of the bending of beams.

The necessary conditions for this are

$$n_{x\vartheta 0} = \bar{n}_{x\vartheta 0}{}^{(0)} + \bar{n}_{x\vartheta 0}{}^{(1)} \sin\vartheta = -\frac{M_{x0}}{2\pi R^2} - \frac{Q_{z0}}{\pi R}\sin\vartheta$$
$$n_{x0} = \bar{n}_{x0}{}^{(0)} + \bar{n}_{x0}{}^{(1)} \cos\vartheta = \frac{Q_{x0}}{2\pi R} + \frac{M_{y0}}{\pi R^2}\cos\vartheta$$

and

$$p_x = \bar{p}_{x0} + \bar{p}_{x1}\cos\vartheta$$
$$p_\vartheta + \frac{\partial p_R}{\partial\vartheta} = G_0(x) + G_1(x)\sin\vartheta \tag{7.41a, b}$$

This means that the edge loads must be transmitted to the tube as follows: Torques M_{x0} and normal forces Q_{x0} must be uniformly distributed over the circumference. The shearing force Q_{z0} and the bending moments M_{y0} must cause stresses respectively proportional to $y = R\sin\vartheta$ and $z = R\cos\vartheta$.

We see from (7.41b) that the required sectional-load distribution takes place when loading is due to internal pressure $[p_\vartheta = p_x = 0,\ p_R = p]$ and wind $[p_\vartheta = p_x = 0,\ p_R = -w_0 - w_0\cos\vartheta$, wind blowing from the direction of the negative y-axis]. For vertical loads we obtain

$$p_\vartheta = -p_z\sin\vartheta, \quad p_R = p_z\cos\vartheta,$$

hence

$$p_\vartheta + \frac{\partial p_R}{\partial\vartheta} = \frac{1}{\cos\vartheta}\frac{\partial}{\partial\vartheta}(p_z\cos^2\vartheta) = G_0(x) + G_1(x)\sin\vartheta,$$

whence the stress distribution must be

$$p_z(x, \vartheta) = G_0(x)\frac{\sin\vartheta}{\cos^2\vartheta} + \frac{G_1(x)}{2}\operatorname{tg}^2\vartheta + \frac{K(x)}{\cos^2\vartheta} \tag{7.42}$$

We can form linear combinations of these results. For instance, by putting $G_0 = 0$, $G_1 = -2K$ in (7.42), we find $p_z = K(x)$. Setting $K(x) = -g$, we obtain the stress distribution due to dead weight. The same distribution is obtained for inclined tubes. Let α be the angle of inclination toward the horizontal. The loads per unit surface area are then $p_x = -g\sin\alpha$, $p_z = -g\cos\alpha$, hence

$p_z = -g\cos\alpha$, thus

$$\bar{p}_{x0} = -g\sin\alpha, \quad K = -g\cos\alpha. \tag{7.43}$$

7.5.2 *Deformations*

The deformations of the tube are obtained by inserting (7.38) into (7.11):

$$v_x = C_3(\vartheta) + \int\left(\frac{Q_x}{2\pi R D_x} + \frac{M_y\cos\vartheta}{\pi R^2 D_x}\right) dx +$$
$$+ \int\left(\frac{\Delta n_x}{D_x} - \frac{\nu_\vartheta}{D_\vartheta} n_\vartheta\right) dx, \tag{7.44a}$$

$$v_\vartheta = C_4(\vartheta) - \frac{x}{R}\frac{dC_3}{d\vartheta} + \int\left[-\frac{M_x}{2\pi R^2 D_{x\vartheta}} - \right.$$
$$\left. - \frac{Q_z\sin\vartheta}{\pi R D_{x\vartheta}} + \int\frac{M_y\sin\vartheta}{\pi R^3 D_x} dx\right] dx + \tag{7.44b}$$
$$+ \int\left[\frac{\Delta n_{x\vartheta}}{D_{x\vartheta}} - \frac{1}{R}\int\left(\frac{1}{D_x}\frac{\partial(\Delta n_x)}{\partial\vartheta} - \frac{\nu_\vartheta}{D_\vartheta}\frac{\partial n_\vartheta}{\partial\vartheta}\right) dx\right] dx,$$

$$v_R = -\frac{dC_4}{d\vartheta} + \frac{x}{R}\frac{d^2 C_3}{d\vartheta^2} - \nu_x R\left(\frac{Q_x}{2\pi R D_x} + \frac{M_y\cos\vartheta}{\pi R^3 D_x}\right) +$$
$$+ \int\left[\frac{Q_z\cos\vartheta}{\pi R D_{x\vartheta}} - \int\frac{M_y\cos\vartheta}{\pi R^3 D_x} dx\right] dx +$$
$$+ R\left(\frac{n_\vartheta}{D_\vartheta} - \frac{\nu_x}{D_x}\Delta n_x\right) - \int\left[\frac{1}{D_{x\vartheta}}\frac{\partial(\Delta n_{x\vartheta})}{\partial\vartheta} - \right. \tag{7.44c}$$
$$\left. - \frac{1}{R}\int\left(\frac{1}{D_x}\frac{\partial^2(\Delta n_x)}{\partial\vartheta^2} - \frac{\nu_\vartheta}{D_\vartheta}\frac{\partial^2 n_\vartheta}{\partial\vartheta^2}\right) dx\right] dx,$$

and

$$v_z = v_R \cos\vartheta - v_\vartheta \sin\vartheta = -\cos^2\vartheta \frac{d}{d\vartheta}\left[\frac{1}{\cos\vartheta}\left(C_4 - \frac{x}{R}\frac{dC_3}{d\vartheta}\right)\right] -$$
$$- v_x R\cos\vartheta\left(\frac{Q_x}{2\pi R D_x} + \frac{M_y \cos\vartheta}{\pi R^2 D_x}\right) +$$
$$+ \int\left[\frac{Q_z}{\pi R D_{x\vartheta}} - \int \frac{M_y\, dx}{\pi R^3 D_x}\right] dx + \int \frac{M_x \sin\vartheta}{2\pi R^2 D_{x\vartheta}}\, dx +$$
$$+ R\cos\vartheta\left(\frac{n_\vartheta}{D_\vartheta} - \frac{v_x}{D_x}\Delta n_x\right) - \cos^2\vartheta \frac{\partial}{\partial\vartheta}\left\{\frac{1}{\cos\vartheta}\int\left[\frac{\Delta n_{x\vartheta}}{D_{x\vartheta}} -\right.\right.$$
$$\left.\left. - \frac{1}{R}\frac{\partial}{\partial\vartheta}\int\left(\frac{\Delta n_x}{D_x} - \frac{v_\vartheta}{D_\vartheta} n_\vartheta\right) dx\right] dx\right\}, \qquad (7.44d)$$

$$v_y = v_R \sin\vartheta + v_\vartheta \cos\vartheta = -\sin^2\vartheta \frac{d}{d\vartheta}\left[\frac{1}{\sin\vartheta}\left(C_4 - \frac{x}{R}\frac{dC_3}{d\vartheta}\right)\right] -$$
$$- v_x R\sin\vartheta\left(\frac{Q_x}{2\pi R D_x} + \frac{M_y \cos\vartheta}{\pi R^2 D_x}\right) - \int \frac{M_x \cos\vartheta}{2\pi R^2 D_{x\vartheta}}\, dx +$$
$$+ R\sin\vartheta\left(\frac{n_\vartheta}{D_\vartheta} - \frac{v_x}{D_x}\Delta n_x\right) - \sin^2\vartheta \frac{\partial}{\partial\vartheta}\left\{\frac{1}{\sin\vartheta}\int\left[\frac{\Delta n_{x\vartheta}}{D_{x\vartheta}} -\right.\right.$$
$$\left.\left. - \frac{1}{R}\frac{\partial}{\partial\vartheta}\int\left(\frac{\Delta n_x}{D_x} - \frac{v_\vartheta}{D_\vartheta} n_\vartheta\right) dx\right] dx\right\}. \qquad (7.44e)$$

The integration functions are determined by the generalized boundary conditions:
Let the axial displacement at the edge $x = x_c$ be

$$v_x(x_c, \vartheta) = u_c + \beta_{yc} z + \varphi_{cx}(\vartheta), \quad \varphi_{cx}\left(\pm\frac{\pi}{2}\right) = 0, \quad z = R\cos\vartheta$$

The first two terms correspond to a rigid-body displacement at $x = x_c$ (axial translatory displacement u_c, rotation about y-axis $= \beta_{yc}$), with a superimposed warping of the cross-section $= \varphi_{cx}(\vartheta)$. Accordingly,

$$C_3(\vartheta) = u_c + \beta_{yc} z + \varphi_{cx}(\vartheta) - \int\left(\frac{Q_x}{E_x F} + \frac{M_y z}{E_x J_y}\right) dx\Big|_{x=x_c} -$$
$$- \int\left(\frac{\Delta n_x}{D_x} - \frac{v_\vartheta}{D_\vartheta} n_\vartheta\right) dx\Big|_{x=x_c} \qquad (7.45)$$

where $E_x = D_x/h$, $F = 2\pi R h$, $J_y = \pi R^3 h$

whence finally,

$$v_x = \varphi_{cx}(\vartheta) + \int_{x_c}^{x}\left(\frac{\Delta n_x}{D_x} - \frac{v_\vartheta}{D_\vartheta} n_\vartheta\right) dx +$$
$$+ \left(u_c + \int_{x_c}^{x}\frac{Q_x\, dx}{E_x F}\right) + z\left(\beta_{yc} + \int_{x_c}^{x}\frac{M_y\, dx}{E_x J_y}\right) = \qquad (7.46a)$$
$$= \varphi_{cx}(\vartheta) + \int_{x_c}^{x}\left(\frac{\Delta n_x}{D_x} - \frac{v_\vartheta}{D_\vartheta} n_\vartheta\right) dx + u(x) + z\,\beta_y(x),$$

where $u(x)$ and $\beta_y(x)$ satisfy the differential equations

$$\frac{du}{dx} = \frac{Q_x}{E_x F}, \quad \frac{d\beta_y}{dx} = \frac{M_y}{E_x J_y} \qquad (7.46b)$$

and the boundary conditions

$$u(x_c) = u_c, \quad \beta_y(x_c) = \beta_{yc} \qquad (7.46c)$$

and thus represent the deformations of a beam due to bending and normal loads (Bernoulli's hypothesis).
Expressing v_ϑ in generalized form

$$v_\vartheta(x_c, \vartheta) = -R\,\Theta_c - w_c \sin\vartheta + \varphi_{c\vartheta}(\vartheta)$$

where the first two terms again correspond to a rigid-body displacement of the end section (rotation about the positive x-axis $= \Theta_c$, translatory displacement in direction of the positive z-axis $= w_c$), we obtain from (7.44b)

$$C_4(\vartheta) = -R\,\Theta_c - w_c\sin\vartheta + \varphi_{c\vartheta}(\vartheta) + \frac{x_c}{R}\frac{dC_3}{d\vartheta} +$$
$$+ R\int\frac{M_x\, dx}{G_{x\vartheta} J_p}\Big|_{x_c} + \int\frac{\alpha Q_z \sin\vartheta}{G_{x\vartheta} F}\, dx\Big|_{x_c} -$$
$$- \int\left[\int\frac{M_y \sin\vartheta}{E_x J_y}\, dx\right] dx\Big|_{x_c} - \int\left[\frac{\Delta n_{x\vartheta}}{D_{x\vartheta}} - \right. \qquad (7.47a)$$
$$\left. - \frac{1}{R}\int\left(\frac{1}{D_x}\frac{\partial(\Delta n_x)}{\partial\vartheta} - \frac{v_\vartheta}{D_\vartheta}\frac{\partial n_\vartheta}{\partial\vartheta}\right) dx\right] dx\Big|_{x_c},$$

$$G_{x\vartheta} = D_{x\vartheta}/h, \quad \alpha = \frac{|\text{extr. } \tau_{x\vartheta Q_z}|}{Q_z/F} = 2,$$

Substituting for C_3 from (7.45), and transforming the double integrals by partial integration

$$\int_{x_c}^{x}\left[\int f(x)\, dx\right] dx = \int_{x_c}^{x}\left[\frac{d}{dx}(x)\int f(x)\, dx\right] dx = \left[x\int f(x)\, dx\right]_{x_c}^{x} -$$
$$- \int_{x_c}^{x} x f(x)\, dx = (x - x_c)\left[\int f(x)\, dx\right]_{x_c} + \int_{\bar{x}=x_c}^{x}(x - \bar{x})\, f(\bar{x})\, d\bar{x}$$

we obtain

$$v_\vartheta = \varphi_{c\vartheta}(\vartheta) - \frac{x - x_c}{R}\frac{d\varphi_{cx}}{d\vartheta} + \int_{\bar{x}=x_c}^{x}\left[\frac{\Delta n_{x\vartheta}}{D_{x\vartheta}} - \right.$$
$$\left. - \frac{x - \bar{x}}{R}\left(\frac{1}{D_x}\frac{\partial(\Delta n_x)}{\partial\vartheta} - \frac{v_\vartheta}{D_\vartheta}\frac{\partial n_\vartheta}{\partial\vartheta}\right)\right] d\bar{x} - \qquad (7.47b)$$
$$- R\,\Theta(x) - w(x)\sin\vartheta = -R\,\Theta(x) - w(x)\sin\vartheta + \Delta v_\vartheta$$

where

$$\Theta(x) = \Theta_c + \int_{x_c}^{x}\frac{M_x(\bar{x})\, d\bar{x}}{G_{x\vartheta} J_p}, \qquad (7.47c)$$

$$w(x) = w_c - \beta_{yc}(x - x_c) -$$
$$- \int_{\bar{x}=x_c}^{x}\frac{(x - \bar{x})}{E_x J_y} M_y(\bar{x})\, d\bar{x} + \int_{\bar{x}=x_c}^{x}\frac{\alpha Q_z(\bar{x})\, d\bar{x}}{G_{x\vartheta} F}, \qquad (7.47d)$$

which satisfy the boundary conditions

$$\Theta(x_c) = \Theta_c, \quad w(x_c) = w_c, \quad \frac{dw}{dx}\Big|_{x_c} = -\beta_{yc} + \frac{\alpha Q_z(x_c)}{G_{x\vartheta} F} \qquad (7.47e)$$

and the differential equations

$$\frac{d\Theta}{dx} = \frac{M_x}{G_{x\vartheta} J_p}, \quad \frac{d}{dx}\left(\frac{dw}{dx} - \frac{\alpha Q_z}{G_{x\vartheta} F}\right) = -\frac{M_y}{E_x J_y}, \qquad (7.47f)$$

These expressions correspond, in the theory of the bending of beams, to the torsional deformations of an annular cross section and to the bending deflections, if the deformations due to the shearing forces are (approximately) taken into account.

We finally obtain the radial displacements from (7.44c)

$$v_R = -\frac{\partial v_\vartheta}{\partial \vartheta} + R\,\varepsilon_\vartheta = -\frac{\partial v_\vartheta}{\partial \vartheta} + R\left(\frac{n_\vartheta}{D_\vartheta} - \frac{\nu_x}{D_x} n_x\right) =$$

$$= w(x)\cos\vartheta - \nu_x R\left(\frac{d u}{d x} + z\frac{d \beta_y}{d x}\right) -$$

$$-\frac{d\varphi_{c\vartheta}}{d\vartheta} + \frac{x - x_c}{R}\frac{d^2 \varphi_{cx}}{d\vartheta^2} - \frac{\partial}{\partial\vartheta}\int\limits_{\bar{x}=x_c}^{x}\left[\frac{\Delta n_{x\vartheta}}{D_{x\vartheta}} - \right. \tag{7.48}$$

$$\left. - \frac{x - \bar{x}}{R}\frac{\partial}{\partial\vartheta}\left(\frac{\Delta n_x}{D_x} - \frac{\nu_\vartheta}{D_\vartheta} n_\vartheta\right)\right] d\bar{x} + R\left(\frac{n_\vartheta}{D_\vartheta} - \frac{\nu_x}{D_x}\Delta n_x\right) =$$

$$= w(x)\cos\vartheta - \nu_x R\left(\frac{d u}{d x} + z\frac{d \beta_y}{d x}\right) + \Delta v_R$$

while (7.44d, e) yields

$$v_z = w(x) + y\,\Theta(x) - \nu_x z\left(\frac{d u}{d x} + z\frac{d \beta_y}{d x}\right) +$$

$$+ \Delta v_R \cos\vartheta - \Delta v_\vartheta \sin\vartheta\,,$$

$$v_y = -z\,\Theta(x) - \nu_x y\left(\frac{d u}{d x} + z\frac{d \beta_y}{d x}\right) +$$

$$+ \Delta v_R \sin\vartheta + \Delta v_\vartheta \cos\vartheta\,. \tag{7.49a, b}$$

We shall apply these results to a membrane shaped like a circular cylinder and closed at both ends by rigid disks. The disk located at the end $x_c = x_0 = 0$ exhibits rigid-body displacements $u_0, w_0, \beta_{y0}, \Theta_0$, which means that the warping functions $\varphi_{cx}(\vartheta)$ and $\varphi_{c\vartheta}(\vartheta)$ must vanish there. Since at the end $x = l$ closing is also effected by a rigid disk, there, too, only rigid-body displacements are possible. Disregarding radial displacements, we obtain from (7.46a) and (7.47b)

$$\int\limits_0^l\left(\frac{\Delta n_x}{D_x} - \frac{\nu_\vartheta}{D_\vartheta}\Delta n_\vartheta\right) d x = 0\,,$$

$$\int\limits_0^l\left[\frac{\Delta n_{x\vartheta}}{D_{x\vartheta}} - \frac{l - x}{R}\frac{\partial}{\partial\vartheta}\left(\frac{\Delta n_x}{D_x} - \frac{\nu_\vartheta}{D_\vartheta}\Delta n_\vartheta\right)\right] d x = 0 \tag{7.50a, b}$$

where

$$\Delta n_\vartheta = R\sum_{k=2}^{\infty}\bar{p}_{Rk}(x)\cos k\vartheta = \frac{R}{\pi}\sum_{k=2}^{\infty}\cos k\vartheta\int\limits_0^{2\pi} p_R \cos k\vartheta\, d\vartheta \tag{7.51a}$$

is the part of the circumferential sectional loads

$$n_\vartheta = R\,p_R = R\,\bar{p}_{R0}(x) + z\,\bar{p}_{R1}(x) + \Delta n_\vartheta \tag{7.51b}$$

which does not depend linearly on $z = R\cos\vartheta$.
The displacements at $x = l$ are thus

$$v_x(\vartheta, l) = \left[u(l) - \frac{\nu_\vartheta}{D_\vartheta} R\int\limits_0^l \bar{p}_{R0}\, d x\right] + z\left[\beta_y(l) - \frac{\nu_\vartheta}{D_\vartheta}\int\limits_0^l \bar{p}_{R1}\, d x\right],$$

$$v_\vartheta(\vartheta, l) = -R\,\Theta(l) - \sin\vartheta\left[w(l) + \frac{\nu_\vartheta}{D_\vartheta}\int\limits_0^l (l - x)\,\bar{p}_{R1}\, d x\right]. \tag{7.52a, b}$$

They, in fact, represent a rigid-body displacement of the section $x = l$ if radial displacements are neglected. This displacement is composed only of the deformations (u, w, β_y, Θ) known from the theory of the bending of beams, and of those parts of the first two terms of the expansion of n_ϑ, which correspond to the transverse extension.

We return to the consideration of the conditions (7.50a, b) necessary for the rigid-body displacement of the two tube ends. If these conditions are satisfied separately for each value of k, we obtain, taking into account (7.51) and (7.40a, b) a system of linear equations for the edge-load amplitudes $\bar{n}_{x0}^{(k)}$ and $\bar{n}_{x\vartheta 0}^{(k)}$. Denoting

$$\delta_{1k} = \frac{1}{\pi}\int\limits_{\xi=0}^{1}\int\limits_{\vartheta=0}^{2\pi}\left\{\int\limits_0^{\xi}\left[p_x\frac{R}{l} - \int\limits_0^{\xi}\frac{\partial}{\partial\vartheta}\left(p_\vartheta + \frac{\partial p_R}{\partial\vartheta}\right) d\xi\right] d\xi - \right.$$

$$\left. - \nu_\vartheta\frac{D_x}{D_\vartheta}\left(\frac{R}{l}\right)^2 p_R\right\}\cos k\vartheta\, d\vartheta\, d\xi\,, \tag{7.53a, b}$$

$$\delta_{2k} = \frac{2}{\pi k}\int\limits_{\xi=0}^{1}\int\limits_{\vartheta=0}^{2\pi}\left\{(1 - \xi)\int\limits_0^{\xi}\left[\int\limits_0^{\xi}\frac{\partial^2}{\partial\vartheta^2}\left(p_\vartheta + \frac{\partial p_R}{\partial\vartheta}\right) d\xi - \frac{R}{l}\frac{\partial p_x}{\partial\xi}\right] d\xi + \right.$$

$$\left. + \left(\frac{R}{l}\right)^2\left[\frac{D_x}{D_{x\vartheta}}\int\limits_0^{\xi}\left(p_\vartheta + \frac{\partial p_R}{\partial\vartheta}\right) d\xi - \nu_\vartheta\frac{D_x}{D_\vartheta}(1 - \xi)\frac{\partial p_R}{\partial\vartheta}\right]\right\} \times$$

$$\times \sin k\vartheta\, d\xi\, d\vartheta\,,$$

where $\xi = x/l$, we have

$$\bar{n}_{x0}^{(k)} = -l\,\frac{\dfrac{l}{R}\left[2\,\delta_{1k}\left(1 - \dfrac{6}{k^2}\dfrac{D_x}{D_{x\vartheta}}\left(\dfrac{R}{l}\right)^2\right) - 3\,\delta_{2k}\right]}{1 + \dfrac{12}{k^2}\dfrac{D_x}{D_{x\vartheta}}\left(\dfrac{R}{l}\right)^2}\,, \tag{7.53c}$$

$$n_{x\vartheta 0}^{(k)} = -l\,\frac{6}{k}\,\frac{\delta_{1k} - \delta_{2k}}{1 + \dfrac{12}{k^2}\dfrac{D_x}{D_{x\vartheta}}\left(\dfrac{R}{l}\right)^2}\,, \quad k = 2 \ldots \infty\,.$$

The radial displacements at the edges are, since the derivative according to ϑ of (7.50b) is, of course, also equal to zero,

$$v_R(0, \vartheta) = \underline{w(0)\cos\vartheta} + R\left[\frac{n_\vartheta}{D_\vartheta} - \frac{\nu_x}{D_x}\Delta n_x - \nu_x\left(\frac{d u}{d x} + z\frac{d \beta_y}{d x}\right)\right]_{x=0}$$

$$= \underline{w(0)\cos\vartheta} + R\left[\frac{n_\vartheta}{D_\vartheta} - \frac{\nu_x}{D_x} n_x\right] = \underline{w(0)\cos\vartheta} + R\,\varepsilon_\vartheta(0, \vartheta)\,,$$

$$v_R(l, \vartheta) = \underline{\cos\vartheta\left[w(l) + \frac{\nu_\vartheta}{D_\vartheta}\int\limits_0^l (l - x)\,\bar{p}_{R1}\, d x\right]} + R\,\varepsilon_\vartheta(l, \vartheta)\,. \tag{7.54}$$

The underlined terms again correspond to a rigid-body displacement of the end sections. The other terms correspond to a centric dilatation of the cross section due to the circumferential forces and to the influence of the normal forces n_x on the transverse extension. These terms can no longer be made to satisfy the boundary conditions within the scope of the linear theory. The deviation from the results obtained by the exact theory (in which the sectional loads are calculated for the deformed system) is, however, only significant near the edges. The dimensions of this perturbation zone are of the order of magnitude of the tube radius; they are thus, particularly in the case of slender tubes, considerably smaller than the tube length. Under these conditions the edge deformations, which have been determined from the linear theory and do not satisfy all boundary conditions, have to adapt themselves to the prescribed edge deformations only within a very restricted zone. This causes large changes in deformation near the edges, leading to (small) folds in this region. (This has been verified experimentally.) This becomes clearer if we consider the simple case of a tubular membrane, stretched between two rigid disks and acted upon by an axial load Q_{x0} and the internal pressure p (Figure 7.4)

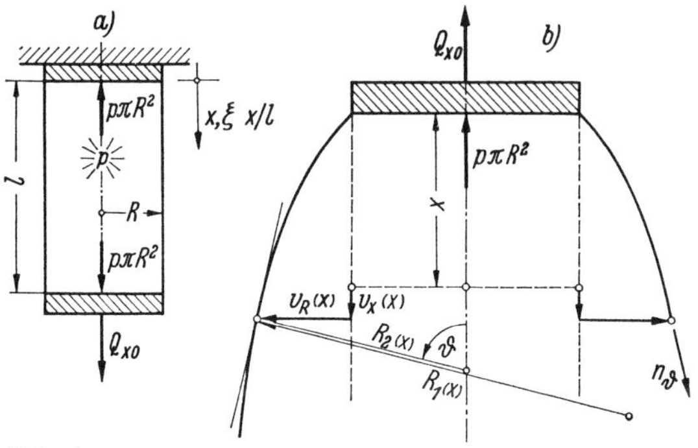

Figure 7.4a, b

The formulas of the linear theory (superscript "0") are

$$n_x^{(0)} = n_{x0}^{(0)} = \frac{Q_{x0}}{2\pi R.} + \frac{p\,R}{2}, \quad n_\varphi^{(0)} = n_{\varphi 0}^{(0)} = p\,R\,. \qquad (7.55\text{a, b})$$

(In contrast to the foregoing, we denote the circumferential forces here by n_φ.) .

The components of the axisymmetrical state of deformation are

$$v_x^{(0)} = \varepsilon_{x0}^{(0)}\,x = x\left(\frac{n_{x0}^{(0)}}{D_x} - \frac{\nu_\varphi}{D_\varphi}\,n_{\varphi 0}^{(0)}\right),$$

$$v_R^{(0)} = R\,\varepsilon_\varphi^{(0)} = R\,\varepsilon_{\varphi 0}^{(0)} = R\left(\frac{n_{\varphi 0}^{(0)}}{D_\varphi} - \frac{\nu_x}{D_x}\,n_{x0}^{(0)}\right), \qquad (7.55\text{c, d})$$

The radial displacements do not satisfy the condition $v_R^{(0)}(0) = v_R^{(0)}(l) = 0$. According to the exact theory we should therefore consider the deformed circular tube as an axisymmetrical shell having radii of curvature $R_1(x)$ and $R_2(x)$ which have to be determined (Figure 7.4b). Setting $p_\vartheta = p_\varphi = 0$, $p_R = p$, we obtain from (3.6a) and (3.7)

$$n_\vartheta = \frac{Q_{x0} + p\,\pi\,R_2^{\,2}}{2\,\pi\,R_2\sin^2\vartheta}, \quad n_\varphi = p\,R_2 - \frac{R_2}{R_1}\,n_\vartheta \qquad (7.56\text{a, b})$$

Substituting these expressions in the stress-deformation relationships

$$\varepsilon_\vartheta = \frac{n_\vartheta}{D_x} - \frac{\nu_\varphi}{D_\varphi}\,n_\varphi, \quad \varepsilon_\varphi = \frac{n_\varphi}{D_\varphi} - \frac{\nu_x}{D_x}\,n_\vartheta \qquad (7.56\text{c, d})$$

we obtain the equations describing the displacements, after expressing the extensions and radii of curvature through the components of the displacement vector.

In order to simplify the problem we shall try to linearize it as far as possible. Writing $R_2(x) \approx R$, $\sin^2\vartheta \approx 1$ and

$$R_1(x) \approx -\left[\frac{d^2 v_R}{d\,x^2}\right]^{-1} = -\frac{1}{v_R''(x)},$$

where v_R is the radial displacement, we obtain from (7.56a, b)

$$n_\vartheta \approx \frac{Q_{x0} + p\,\pi\,R^2}{2\,\pi\,R} = n_{x0}^{(0)},$$

$$n_\varphi \approx p\,R + n_{x0}^{(0)}\,R\,v_R'' = n_{\varphi 0}^{(0)} + n_{x0}^{(0)}\,R\,v_R''. \qquad (7.57\text{a, b})$$

The deformations are by (7.56c, d)

$$\varepsilon_\varphi = \frac{v_R}{R} = \frac{n_{\varphi 0}^{(0)}}{D_\varphi} - \frac{\nu_x}{D_x}\,n_{x0}^{(0)} + \frac{n_{x0}^{(0)}\,R\,v_R''}{D_\varphi} =$$

$$= \varepsilon_{\varphi 0}^{(0)} + \frac{R\,n_{x0}^{(0)}}{D_\varphi}\,v_R'', \qquad (7.57\text{c, d})$$

$$\varepsilon_\vartheta = \sqrt{(1 + v_x'^2) + v_R'^2} - 1 \approx \frac{d\,v_x}{d\,x} = \varepsilon_{x0}^{(0)} - \frac{\nu_\varphi}{D_\varphi}\,n_{x0}^{(0)}\,R\,v_R''.$$

We can rewrite (7.57c) as follows:

$$\frac{d^2 v_R}{d\,\xi^2} - \lambda^2\,v_R = -\,l\,\varepsilon_{\varphi 0}^{(0)}\,\frac{l}{R}\,\frac{D_\varphi}{n_{x0}^{(0)}}, \quad \lambda = \frac{l}{R}\sqrt{\frac{D_\varphi}{n_{x0}^{(0)}}},$$

$$\xi = x/l\,. \qquad (7.58\text{a})$$

Integrating, we obtain

$$v_R = R\,\varepsilon_{\varphi 0}^{(0)} + C_1\,e^{\lambda\xi} + C_2\,e^{-\lambda\xi}.$$

The integration constants are found from the boundary conditions $v_R = 0$ at $\xi = 0$ and $\xi = 1$:

$$C_1 = -\,R\,\varepsilon_{\varphi 0}^{(0)}\,\frac{1 - e^{-\lambda}}{e^\lambda - e^{-\lambda}}, \quad C_2 = -\,R\,\varepsilon_{\varphi 0}^{(0)}\,\frac{e^\lambda - 1}{e^\lambda - e^{-\lambda}}.$$

Thus, finally

$$v_R = R\,\varepsilon_{\varphi 0}^{(0)}\left[1 - \frac{(1 - e^{-\lambda})\,e^{\lambda\xi} + (e^\lambda - 1)\,e^{-\lambda\xi}}{e^\lambda - e^{-\lambda}}\right]. \qquad (7.58\text{b})$$

If we now consider slender tubes ($R/l \ll 1$, thus $\lambda \gg 1$), we have $e^\lambda \gg 1 \gg e^{-\lambda}$, thus approximately

$$v_R = R\,\varepsilon_{\varphi 0}^{(0)}\left[1 - e^{-\lambda\xi} - e^{-\lambda(1-\xi)}\right].$$

In the neighborhood of $\xi = 0$,

$$v_R \approx R\,\varepsilon_{\varphi 0}^{(0)}\left[1 - e^{-\lambda\xi}\right]. \qquad (7.58\text{c})$$

We see that already at small distances from the edge, the radial displacements approach those given by the linear theory. If we define the boundary of the zone of edge perturbations as the distance x_0 at which the radial deformations are equal to 90% of those given by the linear theory, we obtain from

$$v_R(\xi_0) = 0.9\,R\,\varepsilon_{\varphi 0}^{(0)} = R\,\varepsilon_{\varphi 0}^{(0)}\,(1 - e^{-\lambda\xi_0})$$

the relationship

$$\frac{x_0}{l} = 2.3026\,\frac{R}{l}\sqrt{\frac{n_{x0}^{(0)}}{D_\varphi}} \quad \text{or} \quad x_0 = 2.3026\,R\sqrt{\frac{n_{x0}^{(0)}}{D_\varphi}}. \qquad (7.59)$$

Since $n_{x0}^{(0)}$ may not exceed the maximum membrane force, i.e.,

$$\left(\frac{n_{x0}^{(0)}}{D_\varphi}\right)_{\max} \approx \frac{1}{12}\ \text{to}\ \frac{1}{10}$$

we obtain for the boundary of the perturbation zone the estimate

$$x_0 \leqq (0.65 \text{ to } 0.75)\, R\,, \tag{7.60}$$

Integrating (7.57d) for the boundary condition $v_x(0) = 0$, and making use of (7.58c), we obtain

$$v_x = x\, \varepsilon_{x0}{}^{(0)} - \frac{\nu_\varphi}{D_\varphi}\, n_{x0}{}^{(0)}\, R\, \big(v_R'(x) - v_R'(0)\big) =$$

$$= l\left[\xi\, \varepsilon_{x0}{}^{(0)} + \frac{R}{l}\, \nu_\varphi\, \varepsilon_{\varphi 0}{}^{(0)} \sqrt{\frac{n_{x0}{}^{(0)}}{D_\varphi}}\, (1 - e^{-\lambda\xi})\right].$$

For $R/l \ll 1$ we obtain immediately the result of the linear theory. The circumferential sectional loads in the neighborhood of $\xi = 0$ are thus, by (7.57b) and (7.58c) approximately equal to [cf. (7.56d)]

$$n_\varphi \approx n_{\varphi 0}{}^{(0)} + n_{x0}{}^{(0)}\, R\, v_R''(x) \approx n_{\varphi 0}{}^{(0)}\, (1 - e^{-\lambda\xi}) + \nu_x \frac{D_\varphi}{D_x}\, n_{x0}{}^{(0)}\, e^{-\lambda\xi}\,. \tag{7.61}$$

Due to the rigid end disks, no transverse contraction is possible at the edge, where the circumferential sectional loads are

$$n_\varphi(0) = \nu_x \frac{D_\varphi}{D_x}\, n_{x0}{}^{(0)}\;.$$

Toward the boundary of the perturbation zone these sectional loads increase until they attain the values given by the linear theory. These large changes in stresses and deformations are the cause of small folds near the edges.

8 THE CIRCULAR TOROIDAL MEMBRANE

8.1 General Observations

According to Figure 8.1

$$\mathfrak{r}(\vartheta, \varphi) = \{x(\vartheta, \varphi); y(\vartheta, \varphi); z(\vartheta, \varphi)\} =$$
$$= \{(R + r \sin \vartheta) \cos \varphi; (R + r \sin \vartheta) \sin \varphi; r \cos \vartheta\}.$$

Hence, putting $\alpha = \vartheta$, $\beta = \varphi$

$$\mathfrak{r}_\vartheta = \mathfrak{r}_\alpha = r \{\cos \vartheta \cos \varphi; \cos \vartheta \sin \varphi; -\sin \vartheta\},$$
$$|\mathfrak{r}_\alpha| = \sqrt{g_{\alpha\alpha}} = |\mathfrak{r}_\vartheta| = r, \quad g_{\alpha\beta} = \mathfrak{r}_\alpha \mathfrak{r}_\beta = 0$$
$$\mathfrak{r}_\beta = \mathfrak{r}_\varphi = (R + r \sin \vartheta) \{-\sin \varphi; \cos \varphi; 0\},$$
$$|\mathfrak{r}_\beta| = \sqrt{g_{\beta\beta}} = |\mathfrak{r}_\varphi| = R + r \sin \vartheta,$$
$$\mathfrak{r}_{\alpha\alpha} = \mathfrak{r}_{\vartheta\vartheta} = -r \{\sin \vartheta \cos \varphi; \sin \vartheta \sin \varphi; \cos \vartheta\},$$
$$\mathfrak{r}_{\alpha\beta} = \mathfrak{r}_{\vartheta\varphi} = r \cos \vartheta \{-\sin \varphi; \cos \varphi; 0\},$$
$$\mathfrak{r}_{\beta\beta} = \mathfrak{r}_{\varphi\varphi} = -(R + r \sin \vartheta) \{\cos \varphi; \sin \varphi; 0\}.$$

Since the parametric curves form an orthogonal net, we obtain from (1.21)

$$\omega_\alpha^{(\alpha)} = \omega_\vartheta^{(\vartheta)} = -\omega_\beta^{(\beta)} = -\omega_\varphi^{(\varphi)} = 0,$$
$$\omega_\beta^{(\alpha)} = \omega_\varphi^{(\vartheta)} = -\frac{[\mathfrak{r}_\alpha \mathfrak{r}_\beta \mathfrak{r}_{\alpha\alpha}]}{g_{\alpha\alpha} \sqrt{g_{\alpha\alpha} g_{\beta\beta}}} = \frac{1}{r}, \qquad \omega_\gamma^{(\alpha)} = 0,$$
$$\omega_\alpha^{(\beta)} = \omega_\vartheta^{(\varphi)} = \frac{[\mathfrak{r}_\alpha \mathfrak{r}_\beta \mathfrak{r}_{\beta\beta}]}{g_{\beta\beta} \sqrt{g_{\alpha\alpha} g_{\beta\beta}}} = -\frac{\sin \vartheta}{R + r \sin \vartheta},$$
$$\omega_\gamma^{(\beta)} = \frac{1}{\sqrt{g_{\alpha\alpha} g_{\beta\beta}}} \frac{\partial (\sqrt{g_{\beta\beta}})}{\partial \alpha} = \frac{\cos \vartheta}{R + r \sin \vartheta}.$$

8.2 Equilibrium Conditions

Using the results of Section 8.1, we obtain from the equilibrium conditions (2.5a-c), valid for orthogonal nets

$$\left.\begin{aligned}
&\frac{\partial}{\partial \vartheta} [(R + r \sin \vartheta) n_\vartheta] + \frac{\partial}{\partial \varphi} [r n_{\vartheta\varphi}] - \\
&\quad - r (R + r \sin \vartheta) \left[\frac{\cos \vartheta}{R + r \sin \vartheta} n_\varphi - p_\vartheta\right] = 0, \\
&\frac{\partial}{\partial \vartheta} [(R + r \sin \vartheta) n_{\vartheta\varphi}] + \frac{\partial}{\partial \varphi} [r n_\varphi] + \\
&\quad + r (R + r \sin \vartheta) \left[\frac{\cos \vartheta}{R + r \sin \vartheta} n_{\vartheta\varphi} + p_\varphi\right] = 0, \\
&\frac{n_\vartheta}{r} + \frac{\sin \vartheta}{R + r \sin \vartheta} n_\varphi = p_r.
\end{aligned}\right\} \tag{8.1a-c}$$

Solving (8.1c) for the meridianal forces

$$n_\vartheta = r \left(p_r - \frac{\sin \vartheta}{R + r \sin \vartheta} n_\varphi\right) \tag{8.2a}$$

and substituting in (8.1a), we obtain the system of differential equations

$$\left.\begin{aligned}
&\frac{\partial}{\partial \vartheta} (n_\varphi \sin^2 \vartheta) - \frac{\partial}{\partial \varphi} (n_{\vartheta\varphi} \sin \vartheta) = \\
&\quad = \sin \vartheta \left[p_\vartheta (R + r \sin \vartheta) + \frac{\partial}{\partial \vartheta} \left(p_r (R + r \sin \vartheta)\right)\right], \\
&\frac{\partial}{\partial \vartheta} \left(n_{\vartheta\varphi} (R + r \sin \vartheta)^2\right) + \frac{\partial}{\partial \varphi} \left(n_\varphi r (R + r \sin \vartheta)\right) = \\
&\quad = -p_\varphi r (R + r \sin \vartheta)^2.
\end{aligned}\right\} \tag{8.2b, c}$$

8.2.1 *Axisymmetrical Problems*

In the axisymmetrical case all magnitudes depend solely on ϑ, so that (8.2b, c) can be integrated directly. Setting $p_\varphi = 0$, we obtain

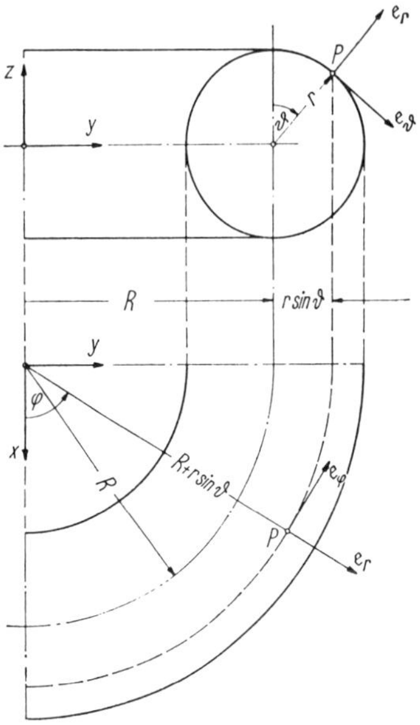

Figure 8.1

$$n_{\vartheta\varphi} = \frac{C_1}{(R + r \sin \vartheta)^2}, \tag{8.3a, b}$$
$$n_\varphi = \frac{C_2}{\sin^2 \vartheta} + \frac{1}{\sin^2 \vartheta} \int \sin \vartheta \left[p_\vartheta (R + r \sin \vartheta) + \right.$$
$$\left. + \frac{d}{d \vartheta} \left(p_r (R + r \sin \vartheta)\right)\right] d \vartheta =$$
$$= \frac{C_2}{\sin^2 \vartheta} + p_r \frac{R + r \sin \vartheta}{\sin \vartheta} + \frac{1}{\sin^2 \vartheta} \int (R +$$
$$+ r \sin \vartheta) (p_\vartheta \sin \vartheta - p_r \cos \vartheta) \, d \vartheta,$$

Thus (8.2a) yields

$$n_\vartheta = -\frac{r \sin \vartheta}{R + r \sin \vartheta} \left(n_\varphi - p_r \frac{R + r \sin \vartheta}{\sin \vartheta}\right) = -$$
$$- \frac{r}{\sin \vartheta (R + r \sin \vartheta)} [C_2 + \int (R + r \sin \vartheta) \times \tag{8.3c}$$
$$\times (p_\vartheta \sin \vartheta - p_r \cos \vartheta) \, d \vartheta].$$

For reasons of symmetry we put $C_1 = 0$, i.e., $n_{\vartheta\varphi} = 0$. The constant C_2 can be determined by considering the equilibrium conditions, with respect to the vertical forces, of a membrane annulus bounded by the curves $\vartheta = 0$ and $\vartheta = \vartheta$. We find

$$C_2 = -\left[\int (R + r \sin \vartheta) (p_\vartheta \sin \vartheta - p_r \cos \vartheta) \, d \vartheta\right]_{\vartheta = 0},$$

so that in the case considered

$$n_\vartheta = -\frac{r}{\sin \vartheta (R + r \sin \vartheta)} \int_0^\vartheta (R + r \sin \chi) (p_\vartheta \sin \chi - p_r \cos \chi) \, d \chi, \tag{8.4a}$$

$$n_{\varphi} = \frac{R + r \sin \vartheta}{\sin \vartheta} p_r + \frac{1}{\sin^2 \vartheta} \int_0^{\vartheta} (R + r \sin \chi)(p_{\vartheta} \sin \chi - p_r \cos \chi)\, d\chi . \tag{8.4b}$$

We shall now examine some particular cases of loading:

a) By internal pressure:

Setting $p_{\vartheta} = 0$, $p_r = p$, $\varkappa = r/R$ we obtain from (8.4)

$$n_{\vartheta p} = \frac{p\, r}{2} \frac{2 + \varkappa \sin \vartheta}{1 + \varkappa \sin \vartheta}, \quad n_{\varphi p} = \frac{p\, r}{2}. \tag{8.5a, b}$$

b) By dead weight:

For $p_{\vartheta} = g \sin \vartheta$, $p_r = -g \cos \vartheta$ we obtain from (8.4)

$$\begin{aligned} n_{\vartheta g} &= -g\, r \frac{\vartheta + \varkappa (1 - \cos \vartheta)}{\sin \vartheta (1 + \varkappa \sin \vartheta)}, \\ n_{\varphi g} &= g\, r \frac{1 + \varkappa \sin \vartheta}{\varkappa \sin \vartheta} \left[\frac{\vartheta + \varkappa (1 - \cos \vartheta)}{\sin \vartheta (1 + \varkappa \sin \vartheta)} - \cos \vartheta \right]. \end{aligned} \tag{8.6a, b}$$

c) By a symmetrical snow load:

For (cf. 3.11c, d) $p_{\vartheta} = s \sin \vartheta \cos^2 \vartheta$, $p_R = - s \cos^3 \vartheta$, $0 \leqq \vartheta \leqq \pi/2$ we obtain from (8.4)

$$n_{\vartheta s1} = - s\, r \frac{3 (2\vartheta + \sin 2\vartheta) + 4 \varkappa (1 - \cos^3 \vartheta)}{12 \sin \vartheta (1 + \varkappa \sin \vartheta)} = s\, r\, \bar{a}_{s1}(\vartheta), \quad 0 \leqq \vartheta \leqq \frac{\pi}{2},$$

$$n_{\vartheta s1} = - s\, r \frac{3\pi + 4\varkappa}{12 \sin \vartheta (1 + \varkappa \sin \vartheta)} = s\, r\, \bar{a}_{s1}(\vartheta), \quad \vartheta \geqq \frac{\pi}{2},$$

$$n_{\varphi s1} = - s\, r \frac{1 + \varkappa \sin \vartheta}{\varkappa \sin \vartheta} \left(\bar{a}_{s1}(\vartheta) + \cos^3 \vartheta \right), \quad 0 \leqq \vartheta \leqq \frac{\pi}{2},$$

$$n_{\varphi s1} = - \frac{R + r \sin \vartheta}{r \sin \vartheta} n_{\vartheta s1} = s\, r \frac{3\pi + 4\varkappa}{12 \varkappa \sin^2 \vartheta}, \quad \vartheta \geqq \frac{\pi}{2} \tag{8.7}$$

Analysis of the deformations by means of (3.35), which has to be carried out separately for $0 \leqq \vartheta \leqq \vartheta_0$ and $-\vartheta_0 \leqq \vartheta \leqq 0$ when the membrane extends between the latitude circles $\vartheta = \vartheta_0$ and $\vartheta = -\vartheta_0$, shows discontinuities along the circle $\vartheta = 0$. In particular, the displacements may have singularities there. This means that the deformations determined from the sectional loads according to the theory of small deformations are geometrically incompatible.* Near the circle $\vartheta = 0$ we shall have larger deformations, so that the sectional loads will deviate significantly from those calculated for the undeformed system.

8.2.2 *Loading, Antimetrical with Respect to the* (y, z) *Plane*

Let the load be defined by

$$p_{\vartheta}(\vartheta, \varphi) = \bar{p}_{\vartheta}(\vartheta) \cos \varphi, \quad p_r(\vartheta, \varphi) = \bar{p}_r(\vartheta) \cos \varphi \tag{8.8}$$

We can then solve (8.2) by writing

$$\begin{aligned} n_{\vartheta}(\vartheta, \varphi) &= f_{\vartheta}(\vartheta) \cos \varphi, \quad n_{\vartheta\varphi}(\vartheta, \varphi) = f_{\vartheta\varphi}(\vartheta) \sin \varphi, \\ n_{\varphi}(\vartheta, \varphi) &= f_{\varphi}(\vartheta) \cos \varphi \end{aligned} \tag{8.9a-c}$$

Indeed, substitution of (8.8) and (8.9) in (8.2) yields a system of ordinary differential equations, so that assumption (8.9) is justified. The solution of this system is similar to that of the general case of axisymmetrical membranes in that we consider the equilibrium conditions of suitably cut-out, finite membrane parts. Cutting out a membrane annulus along the parametric curves $\vartheta = 0$ and $\vartheta = \vartheta$ (Figure 8.2), we obtain at the edges the sectional loads

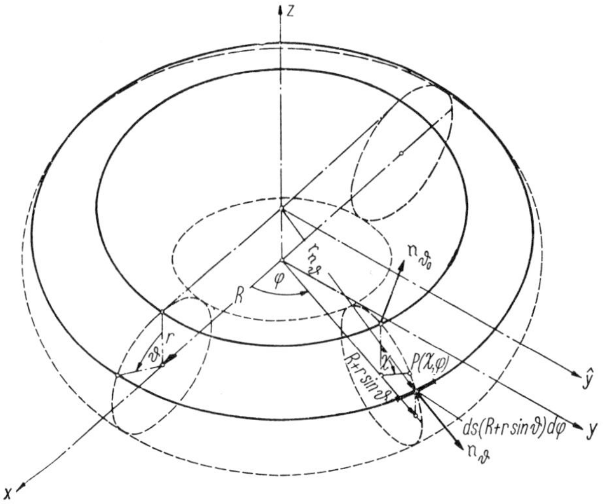

Figure 8.2

$$\begin{aligned} \mathfrak{n}_{\vartheta 0} &= - n_{\vartheta}(0, \varphi)\, \mathfrak{e}_{\vartheta}(0, \varphi) - n_{\vartheta\varphi}(0, \varphi)\, \mathfrak{e}_{\varphi}(0, \varphi) = \\ &= - [f_{\vartheta}(0) \cos \varphi\, \mathfrak{e}_{\vartheta}(0, \varphi) + f_{\vartheta\varphi}(0) \sin \varphi\, \mathfrak{e}_{\varphi}(0, \varphi)] \; (\text{edge } \vartheta = 0) \end{aligned} \tag{8.10a}$$

and

$$\begin{aligned} \mathfrak{n}_{\vartheta} &= n_{\vartheta}(\vartheta, \varphi)\, \mathfrak{e}_{\vartheta}(\vartheta, \varphi) + n_{\vartheta\varphi}(\vartheta, \varphi)\, \mathfrak{e}_{\varphi}(\vartheta, \varphi) = \\ &= f_{\vartheta}(\vartheta) \cos \varphi\, \mathfrak{e}_{\vartheta} + f_{\vartheta\varphi}(\vartheta) \sin \varphi\, \mathfrak{e}_{\varphi} \; (\text{edge } \vartheta = \vartheta) \end{aligned} \tag{8.10b}$$

The unit vectors are expressed in Cartesian coordinates (x, y, z) as follows:

$$\left. \begin{aligned} \mathfrak{e}_{\vartheta} &= \frac{\mathfrak{r}_{\vartheta}}{|\mathfrak{r}_{\vartheta}|} = \{\cos \vartheta \cos \varphi;\ \cos \vartheta \sin \varphi;\ -\sin \vartheta\}, \\ \mathfrak{e}_{\varphi} &= \frac{\mathfrak{r}_{\varphi}}{|\mathfrak{r}_{\varphi}|} = \{-\sin \varphi;\ \cos \varphi;\ 0\}, \\ \mathfrak{e}_r &= \mathfrak{e}_{\vartheta} \times \mathfrak{e}_{\varphi} = \{\sin \vartheta \cos \varphi;\ \sin \vartheta \sin \varphi;\ \cos \vartheta\} \end{aligned} \right\} \tag{8.11a-c}$$

The edge loads, expressed in Cartesian coordinates, are

$$\begin{aligned} \mathfrak{n}_{\vartheta 0} &= - \{f_{\vartheta}(0) \cos^2 \varphi - f_{\vartheta\varphi}(0) \sin^2 \varphi;\ \sin \varphi \cos \varphi\, (f_{\vartheta}(0) + f_{\vartheta\varphi}(0));\ 0\}, \\ \mathfrak{n}_{\vartheta} &= \{f_{\vartheta}(\vartheta) \cos \vartheta \cos^2 \varphi - f_{\vartheta\varphi}(\vartheta) \sin^2 \varphi; \\ &\quad \sin \varphi \cos \varphi\, (f_{\vartheta}(\vartheta) \cos \vartheta + f_{\vartheta\varphi}(\vartheta));\ - f_{\vartheta}(\vartheta) \sin \vartheta \cos \varphi\}. \end{aligned} \tag{8.12a, b}$$

The vector of the surface load acting at a point $P(\chi, \varphi)$ $[0 \leqq \chi \leqq \vartheta]$ of the cut-out annulus is

$$\begin{aligned} \mathfrak{p}(\chi, \varphi) &= p_{\vartheta}(\chi, \varphi)\, \mathfrak{e}_{\vartheta}(\chi, \varphi) + p_r(\chi, \varphi)\, \mathfrak{e}_r(\chi, \varphi) = \\ &= \bar{p}_{\vartheta}(\chi) \cos \varphi\, \mathfrak{e}_{\vartheta}(\chi, \varphi) + \bar{p}_r(\chi) \cos \varphi\, \mathfrak{e}_r(\chi, \varphi), \end{aligned}$$

or, expressing the unit vectors in components of the system (x, y, z)

$$\begin{aligned} \mathfrak{p}(\chi, \varphi) = \{&(\bar{p}_{\vartheta}(\chi) \cos \chi + \bar{p}_r \sin \chi) \cos^2 \varphi; \\ &(\bar{p}_{\vartheta}(\chi) \cos \chi + \bar{p}_r(\chi) \sin \chi) \sin \varphi \cos \varphi; \\ &(- \bar{p}_{\vartheta}(\chi) \sin \chi + \bar{p}_r(\chi) \cos \chi) \cos \varphi\}. \end{aligned} \tag{8.13}$$

* See also W. Flügge's book mentioned at the beginning.

We consider the equilibrium conditions for the membrane annulus with respect to the moments about $\hat{y}$-axis (Figure 8.2), lying parallel to the y-axis and intersecting the z-axis at $z = r$. In addition, we apply the condition $\Sigma K_x = 0$. The position vector from the intersection of the $\hat{y}$- and z-axes to a point lying on the edge $\vartheta = \vartheta$ is

$$\mathfrak{r}_{\mathfrak{n}_\vartheta} = \{(R + r \sin\vartheta)\cos\varphi; (R + r\sin\vartheta)\sin\varphi; -r(1-\cos\vartheta)\}$$

The moment of the sectional loads, acting at the edge $\vartheta = \vartheta$, about the $\hat{y}$-axis is thus

$$M_{\hat{y},\mathfrak{n}_\vartheta} = \int_{\varphi=0}^{2\pi} [\mathfrak{r}_{\mathfrak{n}_\vartheta}\,\mathfrak{n}_\vartheta\,\mathfrak{e}_y](R + r\sin\vartheta)\,d\varphi,$$

where the square brackets denote the triple product

$$[\mathfrak{r}_{\mathfrak{n}_\vartheta}\,\mathfrak{n}_\vartheta\,\mathfrak{e}_y] = f_\vartheta(\vartheta)\big(R\sin\vartheta + r(1-\cos\vartheta)\big)\cos^2\varphi + f_{\vartheta\varphi}(\vartheta)\,r(1-\cos\vartheta)\sin^2\varphi\,.$$

Integrating over φ, we obtain by virtue of

$$\int_0^{2\pi}\sin^2\varphi\,d\varphi = \int_0^{2\pi}\cos^2\varphi\,d\varphi = \pi:$$

$$M_{\hat{y},\mathfrak{n}_\vartheta} = \pi(R + r\sin\vartheta)\big[f_\vartheta(\vartheta)\big(R\sin\vartheta + r(1-\cos\vartheta)\big) + f_{\vartheta\varphi}(\vartheta)\,r(1-\cos\vartheta)\big]\,. \tag{8.14a}$$

Since the $\hat{y}$-axis lies in the same plane ($z = r$) as the parametric curve $\vartheta = 0$, the sectional loads $\mathfrak{n}_{\vartheta 0}$ acting in this plane can cause no moment about the $\hat{y}$-axis. The only moments are those caused by the surface loads. The position vector of a point $P(\chi, \varphi)$ is

$$\mathfrak{r}_\mathfrak{p}(\chi,\varphi) = \{(R + r\sin\chi)\cos\varphi; (R + r\sin\chi)\sin\varphi; -r(1-\cos\chi)\}.$$

The moment due to the surface load at this point is

$$M_{\hat{y},\mathfrak{p}} = \int_{\varphi=0}^{2\pi}\int_{\chi=0}^{\vartheta}[\mathfrak{r}_\mathfrak{p}\,\mathfrak{p}\,\mathfrak{e}_y](R + r\sin\chi)\,d\varphi\cdot r\,d\chi\,,$$

where

$$[\mathfrak{r}_\mathfrak{p}\,\mathfrak{p}\,\mathfrak{e}_y] = \cos^2\varphi\,\big(p_\vartheta\big[R\sin\chi + r(1-\cos\chi)\big] - p_r(R\cos\chi + r\sin\chi)\big)\,.$$

Integrating over φ, we obtain

$$M_{\hat{y},\mathfrak{p}} = \pi r\int_{\chi=0}^{\vartheta}(R + r\sin\chi)\big(\bar{p}_\vartheta\big[R\sin\chi + r(1-\cos\chi)\big] - \bar{p}_r(R\cos\chi + r\sin\chi)\big)\,d\chi = \pi r A(\vartheta)\,. \tag{8.14b}$$

Inserting (8.14a, b) into the condition $\Sigma M_{\hat{y}}=0$ i.e., $M_{\hat{y},\mathfrak{n}_\vartheta}+M_{\hat{y},\mathfrak{p}}=0$ we obtain

$$f_\vartheta(\vartheta)\big(R\sin\vartheta + r(1-\cos\vartheta)\big) + f_{\vartheta\varphi}(\vartheta)\,r(1-\cos\vartheta) = -\frac{r}{R + r\sin\vartheta}\int_{\chi=0}^{\vartheta}(R + r\sin\chi)\big(\bar{p}_\vartheta\big[R\sin\chi + r(1-\cos\chi)\big] - \bar{p}_r(R\cos\chi + r\sin\chi)\big)\,d\chi\,. \tag{8.15}$$

The forces due to the sectional and surface loads acting in the x-direction are respectively

$$K_{x,\mathfrak{n}_\vartheta} = \int_{\varphi=0}^{2\pi}(\mathfrak{n}_\vartheta\,\mathfrak{e}_x)(R + r\sin\vartheta)\,d\varphi = \pi(R + r\sin\vartheta)\big(f_\vartheta(\vartheta)\cos\vartheta - f_{\vartheta\varphi}(\vartheta)\big)\,, \tag{8.16a}$$

$$K_{x,\mathfrak{n}_{\vartheta 0}} = -\pi R\big(f_\vartheta(0) - f_{\vartheta\varphi}(0)\big)\,, \tag{8.16b-c}$$

$$K_{x,\mathfrak{p}} = \int_{\varphi=0}^{2\pi}\int_{\chi=0}^{\vartheta}(\mathfrak{p}\,\mathfrak{e}_x)(R + r\sin\chi)\,d\varphi\,r\,d\chi = \pi r\int_{\chi=0}^{\vartheta}(R + r\sin\chi)\big(\bar{p}_\vartheta(\chi)\cos\chi + \bar{p}_r(\chi)\sin\chi\big)\,d\chi = \pi r B(\vartheta)\,.$$

Thus, the equilibrium condition $\Sigma K_x = 0 = K_{x,\mathfrak{n}_\vartheta} + K_{x,\mathfrak{n}_{\vartheta 0}} + K_{x,\mathfrak{p}}$ yields finally

$$f_\vartheta(\vartheta)\cos\vartheta - f_{\vartheta\varphi}(\vartheta) = \frac{1}{R + r\sin\vartheta}\Big[R\big(f_\vartheta(0) - f_{\vartheta\varphi}(0)\big) - r\int_{\chi=0}^{\vartheta}(R + r\sin\chi)(\bar{p}_\vartheta\cos\chi + \bar{p}_r\sin\chi)\,d\chi\Big]\,. \tag{8.17}$$

We can now determine $f_\vartheta(\vartheta)$ and $f_{\vartheta\varphi}(\vartheta)$ from (8.15) and (8.17). Writing

$$f_\vartheta(0) - f_{\vartheta\varphi}(0) = n_0 \tag{8.18a}$$

we obtain

$$f_\vartheta(\vartheta) = -\frac{r[A + (Br - Rn_0)(1-\cos\vartheta)]}{\sin\vartheta\,(R + r\sin\vartheta)^2}\,,$$

$$f_{\vartheta\varphi}(\vartheta) = -\frac{rA\cos\vartheta - (Br - Rn_0)[R\sin\vartheta + r(1-\cos\vartheta)]}{\sin\vartheta\,(R + r\sin\vartheta)^2}\,. \tag{8.18b,c}$$

The third unknown is found from (8.1c)

$$f_\varphi(\vartheta) = -\frac{R + r\sin\vartheta}{r\sin\vartheta}f_\vartheta + \frac{R + r\sin\vartheta}{\sin\vartheta}\bar{p}_r = \frac{R + r\sin\vartheta}{\sin\vartheta}\bar{p}_r + \frac{A + (Br - Rn_0)(1-\cos\vartheta)}{\sin^2\vartheta\,(R + r\sin\vartheta)}\,. \tag{8.18d}$$

Passing to the limit, we obtain from (8.18b) or (8.18c)

$$f_\vartheta(0) = r\bar{p}_r(0)\,,\quad\text{thus}\quad n_\vartheta(0,\varphi) = r\,p_r(0,\varphi)\,, \tag{8.19a}$$

This result could have been obtained directly from (8.1c), assuming that $n_\varphi(0,\varphi)$ remains finite.

For loads, symmetrical with respect to the (x, y) plane, $[\bar{p}_\vartheta(\vartheta) = -\bar{p}_\vartheta(\pi-\vartheta), \bar{p}_r(\vartheta) = \bar{p}_r(\pi-\vartheta)]$ the condition of symmetry $f_{\vartheta\varphi}(\pi/2) = 0$ leads to $n_0 = r\,B(\pi/2)/R$

$$f_{\vartheta\varphi}(0) = f_\vartheta(0) - n_0 = r\bar{p}_r(0) - \frac{r}{R}B\left(\frac{\pi}{2}\right) = r\bar{p}_r(0) - \frac{r}{2R}B(\pi) \tag{8.19b}$$

By virtue of $\{A + r[B(\vartheta) - B(\pi/2)](1-\cos\vartheta)\}_{\vartheta=\pi} = 0$ we have $f_\vartheta(\pi) = r\bar{p}_r(\pi) = r\bar{p}_r(0) = f_\vartheta(0), f_{\vartheta\varphi}(\pi) = -f_{\vartheta\varphi}(0)$ as can be verified by passing to the limit in (8.18b,c). The direction of the force K_x resulting from the load acting on the joint face $0 \leqq \vartheta \leqq \pi$ coincides in this case with the direction of the x-axis. From the equilibrium conditions we find that for fully toroidal membranes it counterbalances the resultant of the surface loads acting on the joint face $\pi \leqq \vartheta \leqq 2\pi$.

For loads, antimetrical with respect to the (x,y) plane $[\bar{p}_\vartheta(\vartheta) = \bar{p}_\vartheta(\pi-\vartheta),\ \bar{p}_r(\vartheta) = -\bar{p}_r(\pi-\vartheta)]$ the condition $f_\vartheta(\pi/2) = 0$ leades to another relationship for the determination of $f_{\vartheta\varphi}(0)$. In this case, the load acting on the joint face $0 \leqq \vartheta \leqq \pi$ causes only a moment about the y-axis which, for fully toroidal membranes, has to be counter-balanced by the moment due to the load acting on the joint face $\pi \leqq \vartheta \leqq 2\pi$. We conclude our observations by referring to the statements in Subsection 8.2.1 concerning the accuracy of the values obtained for the sectional loads along the circles $\vartheta = 0$ and $\vartheta = \pi$, calculated for the undeformed system.

9 SLENDER CIRCULAR TUBES, CLOSED AT BOTH ENDS, USED AS GIRDERS

Until now we have discussed single-walled shapes in which the inner space is used to stabilize the system by means of the inflation pressure. We shall now deal with pneumatic structures used as girders, columns, and arches, i.e., closed shapes stabilized by internal pressure in which the enclosed usable space need not be pressurized.

9.1 Loading by Internal Pressure

Taking into account that the forces on the end covers are equal to $p \pi R^2$, we obtain from (7.6)

$$n_{\vartheta p} = p R, \quad n_{xp} = p \pi R^2 / 2 \pi R = p R/2, \quad n_{x\vartheta} = 0. \tag{9.1}$$

9.2 Generalized Loading. Reduction to the Theory of the Bending of Beams

In the case of slender structures or thin-walled structures of large surface area we can replace the three-dimensional theory of the elastic continuum by the theory of rods, plates, and shells. The simplified assumptions regarding the deformations greatly reduce the amount of calculations necessary. We can show by means of energy considerations that, e.g., for a rod, the results of the general theory pass over into those of the theory of beams.* This is done by proving that the elastic potential of a beam, considered as a spatial system, converges towards the elastic potential of a rod if its cross section is taken to be concentrated at its centroid. We cannot determine directly to what degree this procedure, used for a singly-connected cross section, can also be applied to thin-walled tubes. At least, in the case in which the distribution of the membrane forces in nonslender tubes obeys the linear law (7.39), we can show that for $R/l \ll 1$ the deformations of the tube pass into those given by the beam theory. This is done by applying the displacement equations of Subsection 7.5.2. Putting $\Delta n_x = 0$, we obtain from (7.46a)

$$\frac{\partial v_x}{\partial x} = \frac{d u}{d x} + z \frac{d \beta_y}{d x} - \frac{v_\vartheta}{D_\vartheta} n_\vartheta = \frac{Q_x}{2 \pi R D_x} + \frac{M_y z}{\pi R^3 D_x} - \frac{v_\vartheta}{D_\vartheta} n_\vartheta .$$

Taking into account that, for a generalized loading (p_ϑ, p_x, p_R), $n_\vartheta \sim p R$ and (except near a free edge) $Q_x \sim p R l$ and $M_y \sim p R l^2$ we see that when $R/l \ll 1$ the influence of higher order circumferential forces becomes small.**

We then have

$$\frac{\partial v_x}{\partial x} = \varepsilon_x (x, z) \approx \frac{d u}{d x} + z \frac{d \beta_y}{d x}, \tag{9.2a}$$

which expresses Bernoulli's hypothesis of the beam theory: The displacement of an element of the tube consists of an extension, uniform over the section $x = \text{const}$, amounting to

$$\varepsilon_x (x, 0) = \left(\frac{\partial v_x}{d x}\right)_{z=0} = \frac{d u}{d x} = \frac{Q_x}{2 \pi R D_x} = \frac{Q_x}{E_x F}, \tag{9.2b}$$

this being also the extension of the tube axis, and of a rigid-body rotation about the y-axis of one section in relation to the adjoining section, amounting to

$$\frac{d \beta_y}{d x} = \frac{\partial^2 v_x}{\partial x \partial z} = \frac{M_y}{\pi R^3 D_x} = \frac{M_y}{E_x J_y}. \tag{9.2c}$$

The tube ends have to be closed by rigid disks. These may be either solid plates or rings, rigid in comparison with the membrane, over which circular membranes are stretched. The warping $\varphi_{cx}(\vartheta), \varphi_{c\vartheta}(\vartheta)$ of the section, which is independent of x, is therefore equal to zero. Assuming that, except near any free ends, the sectional loads have the orders of magnitude

$$M_x \sim p R^2 l, \quad n_\vartheta \sim p R, \quad M_y \sim p R l^2$$

i.e.,

$$R \Theta \sim \int_{x_c}^{x} \frac{M_x d x}{2 \pi R^2 D_{x\vartheta}} \sim p l^2, \quad \int_{x_c}^{x} \frac{x - \bar{x}}{R D_\vartheta} \frac{\partial n_\vartheta}{\partial \vartheta} d \bar{x} \sim p l^2,$$

$$w \sim \int \left[\int \frac{M_y d x}{\pi R^3 D_x} \right] d x \sim p l^2 \left(\frac{l}{R}\right)^2$$

we obtain from (7.47b) for $\Delta n_x = \Delta n_{x\vartheta} = 0$:

$$v_\vartheta \approx - w (x) \sin \vartheta . \tag{9.3}$$

Since for $R/l \ll 1$ we have in general, except at points of support where $w = 0$,

$$R \left(\frac{d u}{d x} + z \frac{d \beta_y}{d x}\right) \ll w$$

we obtain from (7.48)

$$v_R \approx w (x) \cos \vartheta . \tag{9.4}$$

With the above assumptions regarding the order of magnitude of the sectional loads, the radial and circumferential displacements are thus solely determined by the bending deflections w given by the beam theory, which predominate over all other effects* (This is true when all components of the surface load have the same order of magnitude).

In the general case of nonvanishing additional membrane loads Δn, we can, when considering a slender tube, only obtain the mean deformations given by the rod theory. Making the same assumptions as before regarding the order of magnitude of the sectional loads, and taking into account that $\varphi_{cx} = \varphi_{c\vartheta} = 0$ as well as that

$$\int_0^{2\pi} \Delta n_x d\vartheta = \int_0^{2\pi} \Delta n_x \begin{Bmatrix} \sin \vartheta \\ \cos \vartheta \end{Bmatrix} d \vartheta = \int_0^{2\pi} \Delta n_{x\vartheta} \begin{Bmatrix} \sin \vartheta \\ \cos \vartheta \end{Bmatrix} d \vartheta = 0$$

we obtain from (7.46a) for $R/l \ll 1$

$$v_x^{(m)} = \frac{1}{2 \pi} \int_0^{2\pi} v_x d \vartheta = u (x) - \frac{v_\vartheta}{2 \pi D_\vartheta} \int_0^{2\pi} \int_{x_c}^{x} n_\vartheta d \vartheta d x \approx u (x), \tag{9.5a}$$

---

* For more details, see: K. André, *Mathematische Begründung der Theorie des Balkens*, Dissertation, Berlin 1959.

* ** We except the case of loading solely by inflation pressure, which has to be discussed separately. In this case $M_y = 0$, and the extensions due to the circumferential forces pR are of the order of magnitude of those due to $Q_x = \pi R^2 p$. We shall discuss here only external loads causing moments and longitudinal (normal) forces.

* This does not hold if the order of magnitude of the sectional loads is different. If, e.g., torque predominates ($M_y = Q_z = Q_x = n_\vartheta \to 0$), we have $v_\vartheta \approx - R \Theta (x)$, $v_R \approx 0$. etc.

$$J_y \beta_y^{(m)} = \int_{(F)} z v_x \, dF = R h \int_0^{2\pi} z v_x \, d\vartheta =$$

$$= J_y \beta_y - \nu_\vartheta \frac{R^2 h}{D_\vartheta} \int_0^{2\pi} \int_{x_C}^{x} n_\vartheta \cos\vartheta \, dx \, d\vartheta \approx J_y \beta_y . \tag{9.5b}$$

From (7.47b) we obtain

$$\Theta^{(m)} = -\frac{1}{2\pi} \int_0^{2\pi} \frac{v_\vartheta}{R} \, d\vartheta = \Theta , \tag{9.6}$$

while (7.49a) yields for $R/l \ll 1$

$$v_z^{(m)} = \frac{1}{2\pi} \int_0^{2\pi} v_z \, d\vartheta = w - \frac{\nu_x}{2} \frac{d\beta_y}{dx} +$$

$$+ \frac{R}{2\pi D_\vartheta} \int_0^{2\pi} \left[n_\vartheta + 2 \nu_\vartheta \int_{x_C}^{x} \frac{x - \bar{x}}{R^2} n_\vartheta \, d\bar{x} \right] \cos\vartheta \, d\vartheta \approx w . \tag{9.7}$$

We thus obtain for the mean deformations the differential equations of the beam theory

$$\frac{d v_x^{(m)}}{dx} = \frac{du}{dx} = \frac{Q_x}{E_x F}, \qquad \frac{d\beta_y^{(m)}}{dx} = \frac{d\beta_y}{dx} = \frac{M_y}{E_x J_y},$$

$$\frac{d\Theta^{(m)}}{dx} = \frac{d\Theta}{dx} = \frac{M_x}{G_{x\vartheta} J_p}, \tag{9.8}$$

$$\frac{d^2 v_z^{(m)}}{dx^2} = \frac{d^2 w}{dx^2} = -\frac{M_y}{E_x J_y} + \frac{d}{dx}\left(\frac{\alpha Q_z}{G_{x\vartheta} F}\right).$$

With rigid end disks, the additional forces Δn are exactly zero for loads acting only at the edges and for surface loads given by the first two terms of (7.34). This follows directly from (7.53a-c) and (7.40a, b). It follows from this that, in the general case, the forces determined according to the beam theory are of greater order of magnitude than the additional loads. This is due to the fact that the higher harmonics ($k \geq 2$) generally have small amplitudes, and that additional load-transmitting members (apart from the rigid end disks), rigid in comparison with the membrane, greatly reduce the stresses caused by the additonal loads. To make this clear, we consider the case of a load, independent of x (p_R, p_ϑ) (we assume $p_x = 0$), acting on a slender tubular girder ($R/l \ll 1$). Assuming the load components and their derivatives according to ϑ to be of equal order of magnitude, we obtain from (7.53a, b) neglecting all terms containing $(R/l)^2$ and integrating over $\xi = x/l$

$$\delta_{1k} \approx -\frac{1}{6\pi} \int_0^{2\pi} \frac{d}{d\vartheta} \left(p_\vartheta + \frac{d p_R}{d\vartheta} \right) \cos k\vartheta \, d\vartheta , \tag{9.9}$$

$$\delta_{2k} \approx \frac{1}{12\pi k} \int_0^{2\pi} \frac{d^2}{d\vartheta^2} \left(p_\vartheta + \frac{d p_R}{d\vartheta} \right) \sin k\vartheta \, d\vartheta =$$

$$= -\frac{1}{12\pi} \int_0^{2\pi} \frac{d}{d\vartheta} \left(p_\vartheta + \frac{d p_R}{d\vartheta} \right) \cos k\vartheta \, d\vartheta . \tag{9.10}$$

Thus, by (7.53c)

$$\bar{n}_{x0}^{(k)} \approx -l \frac{l}{R} (2\delta_{1k} - 3\delta_{2k}) =$$

$$= l \left(\frac{l}{R} \right) \frac{1}{12\pi} \int_0^{2\pi} \frac{d}{d\vartheta} \left(p_\vartheta + \frac{d p_R}{d\vartheta} \right) \cos k\vartheta \, d\vartheta , \tag{9.11}$$

$$\bar{n}_{x\vartheta 0}^{(k)} \approx -l \frac{6}{k} (\delta_{1k} - \delta_{2k}) =$$

$$= \frac{l}{2\pi k} \int_0^{2\pi} \frac{d}{d\vartheta} \left(p_\vartheta + \frac{d p_R}{d\vartheta} \right) \cos k\vartheta \, d\vartheta = \tag{9.12}$$

$$= \frac{l}{2\pi} \int_0^{2\pi} \left(p_\vartheta + \frac{d p_R}{d\vartheta} \right) \sin k\vartheta \, d\vartheta ,$$

whence, by (7.40a, b), the additional loads are finally found to be

$$\Delta n_x = \frac{l}{12} \left(\frac{l}{R} \right) [1 - 6(\xi - \xi^2)] \sum_{k=2}^{\infty} \cos k\vartheta \times$$

$$\times \left(\frac{1}{\pi} \int_0^{2\pi} \frac{d}{d\vartheta} \left(p_\vartheta + \frac{d p_R}{d\vartheta} \right) \cos k\vartheta \, d\vartheta \right) = f_1(\xi) g_1(\vartheta),$$

$$\Delta n_{x\vartheta} = \frac{l}{2} (1 - 2\xi) \sum_{k=2}^{\infty} \sin k\vartheta \left(\frac{1}{\pi} \int_0^{2\pi} \left(p_\vartheta + \frac{d p_R}{d\vartheta} \right) \sin k\vartheta \, d\vartheta \right) =$$

$$= f_2(\xi) g_2(\vartheta) . \tag{9.13a, b}$$

They are given in Figure 9.1. If we arrange a further rigid disk

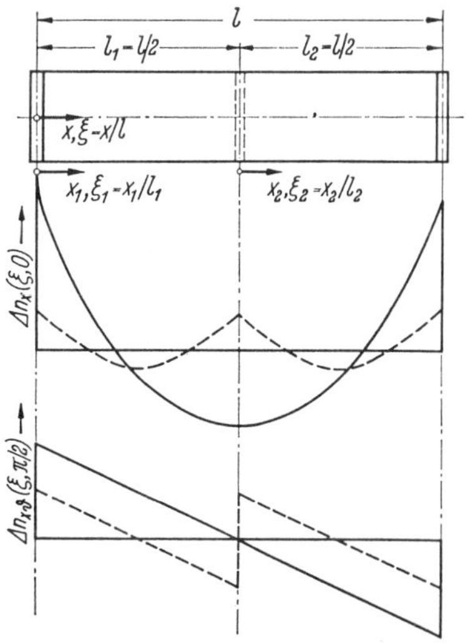

Figure 9.1

in the center of the tube $x = l/2$, we have to formulate the integration conditions separately for the regions

$0 \leq x_1 = x \leq l_1 = l/2$

and

$l/2 \leq x \leq l$ or $0 \leq x_2 \leq l_2 = l/2$

This means that in equations (9.13), which are valid both in region I ($0 \leq x_1 \leq l_1 = l/2$) and II ($0 \leq x_2 \leq l_2 = l/2$), we have to replace l by $l_1 = l_2 = l/2$ respectively. This already reduces the additional forces Δn_x to one-quarter and $\Delta n_{x\vartheta}$ to one-half. (This is shown in broken lines in Figure 9.1.) If two rigid intermediate members are inserted, e.g., at $x = l/3$ and $x = 2\,l/3$ Δn_x reduces to one-ninth of the original value, $\Delta n_{x\vartheta}$ to one-third, etc. In conclusion we can state the following with respect to slender tubes. Except in the case of loading solely by inflation pressure, we can consider the results, as regards membrane forces and deformation, given by the beam theory to be exact (except for small perturbation zones at the edges) when the loads are transmitted to the membrane by members rigid in comparison to the former, or when the surface loads are given by the first two terms in (7.34). If several load-transmitting members rigid in comparison with the membrane, are included in the system considered, the beam theory will yield a satisfactory approximation also when the external loads are arbitrary. If such members are not provided, the deformations will correspond to those given by the beam theory only in the mean, when the loads are arbitrary. This has to be remembered in the ensuing discussion, as well as in the analysis given in Part 10.

9.3 Torsion Experiment

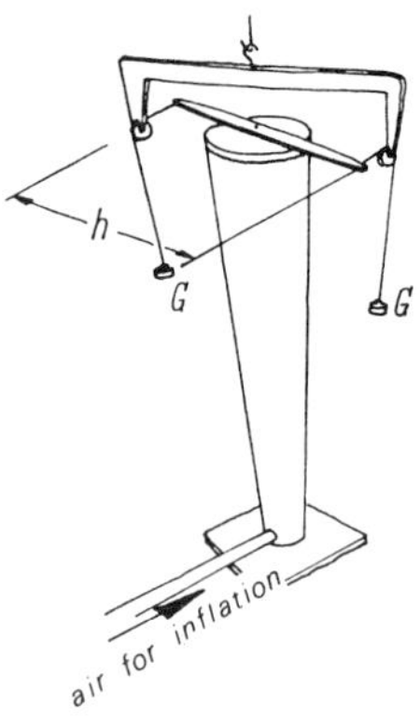

Figure 9.2

In order to confirm the conditions necessary for the absence of folds, which determine the minimum inflation pressure, experiments were performed in the Light-Structures Development Center with tubular membranes, shaped like circular cylinders and consisting of tarpaulins. In order to obtain the simplest possible relationship between the inflation pressure and the external load, a tube was built-in rigidly at its lower end and acted upon by a torque M_t at its upper end (Figure 9.2). Neglecting the small influence of the dead weight, the state of stress in the tube is then characterized by shearing stresses

$$n_{x\vartheta} = -\frac{M_t}{2\pi R^2} \tag{9.14a}$$

obtained from (7.38b) by setting $Q_z = 0$, and by normal forces caused by the internal pressure:

$$n_\vartheta = p\,R > 0\,, \quad n_x = p\,R/2 > 0 \tag{9.14b,c}$$

The condition for the absence of folds

$$n_x\,n_\vartheta - n_{x\vartheta}^2 \geqq 0\,,$$

then yields the minimum inflation pressure

$$p \geqq \frac{M_t}{\sqrt{2}\,\pi\,R^3}\,. \tag{9.15a}$$

The torque was obtained by cable forces acting eccentrically on the upper reinforced edge; both cables were tensioned by equal weights G. Care was taken during the experiment to have the cable forces act perpendicularly to the transmitting strut, so that the distance between the lines of action of the cable forces $S = G$ was always maintained constant and equal to the distance $h = 20$ cm between the connections to the transmitting strut. The radius of the tube was $R = 3.35$ cm. Inserting these values into (9.15a) yields

$$p \geqq \frac{G \cdot h}{\sqrt{2}\,\pi\,R^3} = \frac{20\,G}{\sqrt{2}\,\pi\,(3.35)^3} = 0.1197\,G \tag{9.15b}$$

where p is given in g/cm², i.e., in cm water column, when G is given in grams. The inside of the tube was pressurized by reversing the action of a vacuum cleaner. The pressures were read off a water-filled manometric tube. Denoting the difference in levels in the manometric tube by x (in mm), we obtain from (9.15b)

$$x\,[\text{mm}] = 10.0 \cdot x\,[\text{cm}] = 1.197\,G\,[g]\,. \tag{9.15c}$$

The experiment was carried out as follows: The torque was applied when the inflation pressure was high. By means of a regulating system, the pressure was slowly reduced, until folds appeared in the membrane. The pressure existing at this instant should correspond to the value x in (9.15c). Only folds in the central region of the membrane were taken into account, since near the tube ends it was expected that folds would appear because transverse extension of the tube was prevented by the rigid end members. Taking these latter folds into consideration would have falsified the results. The following table permits a comparison between experimental and theoretical values, the latter obtained from (9.15c).

G [g]	x [mm w.c.] measured	x [mm w.c.] acc. to (9.15c)
190	200	227
290	350	347
490	580	586

The agreement is thus quite satisfactory. The experiments also yielded approximately constant angles of inclination of the folds, in conformity with the result obtained from the equations describing a biaxial state of stress. This inclination to a line parallel to the tube axis is obtained from

$$\operatorname{tg} 2\alpha = \frac{2\,n_{x\vartheta}}{n_x - n_\vartheta} =$$

$$= -\frac{2\,\dfrac{M_t}{2\pi R^2}}{\dfrac{p\,R}{2} - p\,R} = \frac{2\,M_t}{p\,\pi\,R^3} \xrightarrow{p = \frac{M_t}{\sqrt{2}\,\pi\,R^3}} 2\sqrt{2}\,, \tag{9.16}$$

and defines the direction of the principal force n_1, since the minimum principal force n_2 normal to it just vanishes at this instant. The value given by (9.16) is indeed independent of the magnitude of the load.

9.4 General Analysis of Slender Tubes

9.4.1 *Bending Stresses on a Tubular Girder*

Internal pressure causes sectional loads

$$n_{\vartheta p} = p\,R\,, \quad n_{xp} = p\,R/2$$

while external loads cause sectional loads [cf. (7.38)]

$$n_{\vartheta a} = R p_{Ra}\,, \quad n_{x\vartheta a} = -\frac{Q_z(x)}{\pi R}\sin\vartheta\,, \quad n_{xa} = \frac{M_y(x)}{\pi R^2}\cos\vartheta\,. \tag{9.17}$$

In a first approximation we neglect the sectional loads $n_{\vartheta a}$ and $n_{x\vartheta a}$ which for $R/l \ll 1$ are much smaller than n_{xa}. In this case the principal stresses lie in the x-direction, and we obtain as a condition for the absence of folds

$$\min n_x = \frac{pR}{2} + \left[\frac{M_y(x)}{\pi R^2}\cos\vartheta\right]_{\min} \xrightarrow{\cos\vartheta = \pm 1} \frac{pR}{2} - \frac{|\text{extr.}\,M_y|}{\pi R^2} \geqq 0\,,$$

whence

$$p \geqq \frac{2\,|\text{extr.}\,M_y|}{\pi R^3}\,. \tag{9.18a}$$

The maximum tensile stress appears in the same section as the minimum stress given by (9.18a), but on the opposite side. It lies also in the x-direction and is given by

$$\max n_x = \frac{|\text{extr.}\,M_y|}{\pi R^2} + \frac{pR}{2} \leqq pR\,. \tag{9.18b}$$

Since, for reasons of safety, the inflation pressure must always exceed the value determined from (9.18a), the maximum tensile force n_x is always less than the principal (tensile) sectional load $n_\vartheta = pR$ acting in the circumferential direction.
This latter therefore determines the maximum stress.

9.4.2 *Bending with Axial Force*

In contrast to ordinary beams, the problem of eccentric loading of pneumatic girders merits our close attention.
This is true even for fairly small axial compressive forces. One reason for this is that the center loads of such structures are in any case very small, so that even comparatively small compressive forces may cause the buckling load to attain critical values. Another reason is that the compressive loading stresses, due to the external load, rise because the moments exerted by the axial forces increase during deformation. This causes a rapid reduction of the pretensioning due to the inflation pressure, leading to immediate collapse through folding if the tension vanishes. We shall first discuss pure buckling, showing that the critical load is independent of the inflation pressure.

a) Buckling of a cylindrical tube in the presence of internal pressure.

We consider a tube element in its position after buckling, determining the deformations according to Bernoulli's hypothesis (Figure 9.3). The fibers, which originally were of uniform length ds, now assume lengths

$$ds(\vartheta) = ds - R\cos\vartheta\frac{d\varphi}{ds}ds = ds\left(1 - R\frac{d\varphi}{ds}\cos\vartheta\right). \tag{9.19}$$

The internal-pressure forces acting on the membrane element thus no longer constitute an equilibrium system, but have a resultant in the direction of the normal $\mathfrak{n}$, of magnitude

$$\begin{aligned} dP_{\mathfrak{n}} &= -\int_{\vartheta=0}^{2\pi} pR\,d\vartheta\,ds(\vartheta)\cdot\cos\vartheta = \\ &= -pR\,ds\int_{\vartheta=0}^{2\pi}\left(1 - R\frac{d\varphi}{ds}\cos\vartheta\right)\cos\vartheta\,d\vartheta = \\ &= \pi R^2 p\frac{d\varphi}{ds}ds\,, \end{aligned} \tag{9.20}$$

which must be in equilibrium with the sectional loads. The equilibrium conditions for the tube element thus become

$$\frac{d\bar N}{ds}ds + p\pi R^2\frac{d\varphi}{ds}ds\sin\varphi = 0\,, \tag{9.21}$$

$$\frac{d\bar Q}{ds}ds + p\pi R^2\frac{d\varphi}{ds}ds\cos\varphi = 0\,,$$

$$\frac{dM}{ds}ds - \bar Q\,ds\cos\varphi - \bar N\,ds\sin\varphi + p\pi R^2\frac{d\varphi}{ds}ds\frac{ds}{2} = 0\,.$$

In the third equation, if we neglect the small higher-order term containing the internal pressure, we obtain

$$\left.\begin{aligned} \frac{d\bar N}{ds} &= -p\pi R^2\sin\varphi\frac{d\varphi}{ds} = p\pi R^2\frac{d}{ds}(\cos\varphi)\,, \\ \frac{d\bar Q}{ds} &= -p\pi R^2\cos\varphi\frac{d\varphi}{ds} = -p\pi R^2\frac{d}{ds}(\sin\varphi)\,, \\ \frac{dM}{ds} &= \bar Q\cos\varphi + \bar N\sin\varphi\,. \end{aligned}\right\} \tag{9.22a-c}$$

Integration of (9.22a, b) yields

$$\bar N = C_1 + p\pi R^2\cos\varphi\,, \quad \bar Q = C_2 - p\pi R^2\sin\varphi\,.$$

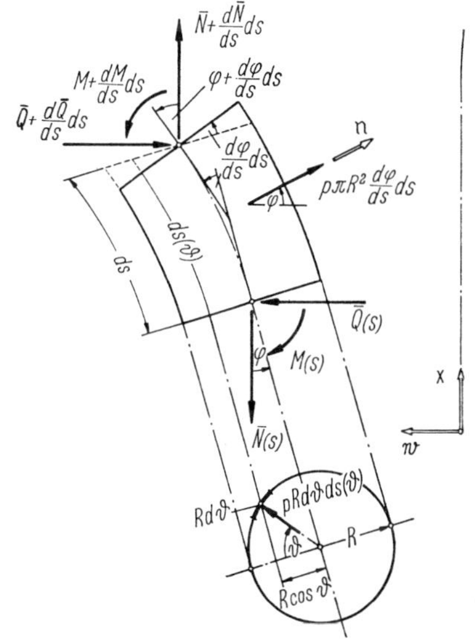

Figure 9.3

The integration constants are found from the boundary conditions for the sectional loads. Denoting the shearing force acting on the tube at the edge $x = 0$ and due, e.g., to a support, by Q_0, we obtain the equilibrium condition for the edge element of the tube (Figure 9.4), taking into account that the force exerted by the internal pressure on the end cover equals $p\,\pi\,R^2$:

$$\overline{N}(0)\left[= C_1 + p\,\pi\,R^2\cos\varphi_0\right] = -P + p\,\pi\,R^2\cos\varphi_0\,,$$
$$\overline{Q}(0)\left[= C_2 - p\,\pi\,R^2\sin\varphi_0\right] = Q_0 - p\,\pi\,R^2\sin\varphi_0\,, \qquad (9.23)$$

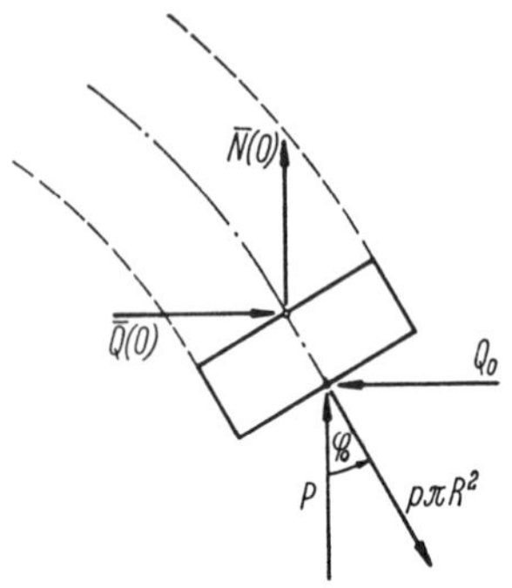

Figure 9.4

whence $C_1 = -P$ and $C_2 = Q_0$ We thus have, finally,

$$\overline{N} = -P + p\,\pi\,R^2\cos\varphi\,,\quad \overline{Q} = Q_0 - p\,\pi\,R^2\sin\varphi\,, \qquad (9.24a, b)$$

whence, by (9.22c)

$$\frac{dM}{ds} = Q_0\cos\varphi - P\sin\varphi\,, \qquad (9.25)$$

Integrating and taking into account that $\cos\varphi = dx/ds$, $\sin\varphi = dw/ds$ we obtain

$$M = M_0 + Q_0\,x - P\,w \qquad (9.26)$$

where M_0 is the bending moment at $x = 0$. This equation, which is of importance in the problem of buckling, no longer contains the internal pressure. It is identical with the expression obtained when considering buckling of a tubular girder not stabilized by internal pressure. (The constants M_0 and Q_0 cannot depend on the internal pressure, since they are determined from the geometrical boundary conditions which do not include the inflation pressure). Combining (9.26) with the differential equation of the beam

$$M = EJ\,\frac{d\varphi}{ds} = D_x\,\pi\,R^3\,\frac{d\varphi}{ds} \qquad (9.27)$$

which is more exact than the linearized equation (7.46b), corresponds fully to the procedure adopted for ordinary (nonpneumatic) girders. This proves that the buckling load is independent of the inflation pressure. We shall, however, continue our analysis. We obtain from (9.26) and (9.27):

$$\frac{dM}{ds} = Q_0\cos\varphi - P\sin\varphi = EJ\,\frac{d^2\varphi}{ds^2}$$

or

$$EJ\,\frac{d\varphi}{ds}\,\frac{d^2\varphi}{ds^2} = \frac{EJ}{2}\,\frac{d}{ds}\left(\frac{d\varphi}{ds}\right)^2 = Q_0\cos\varphi\,\frac{d\varphi}{ds} - P\sin\varphi\,\frac{d\varphi}{ds} =$$
$$= \frac{d}{ds}\,(Q_0\sin\varphi + P\cos\varphi)\,.$$

Integrating we have

$$\left(\frac{d\varphi}{ds}\right)^2 = \frac{2}{EJ}\,(Q_0\sin\varphi + P\cos\varphi) + C_3\,,$$

where C_3 is a constant.

We consider a column, rigidly built in at $s = 0$, on which a load P acts at the free end $s = l$. In this case $Q_0 = 0$. From

$$M(l) = 0 \quad\text{or}\quad \left(\frac{d\varphi}{ds}\right)^2_l = \frac{2\,P\cos\varphi_l}{EJ} + C_3 = 0 \quad\text{we obtain}$$

$$C_3 = -\frac{2\,P\cos\varphi_l}{EJ}\,,$$

so that

$$\frac{d\varphi}{ds} = \sqrt{\frac{2\,P}{EJ}\,(\cos\varphi - \cos\varphi_l)} = \frac{M}{EJ}\,. \qquad (9.28a)$$

Separation of variables and integration yields

$$\sqrt{\frac{EJ}{2\,P}}\int_0^{\varphi}\frac{d\varphi}{\sqrt{\cos\varphi - \cos\varphi_l}} = s + C_4\,. \qquad (9.28b)$$

The boundary condition $\varphi = 0$ at $s = 0$ (built-in end), leads to

$$C_4 = 0\,, \qquad (9.28c)$$

so that finally

$$s = \sqrt{\frac{EJ}{2P}}\int_0^{\varphi}\frac{d\varphi}{\sqrt{\cos\varphi - \cos\varphi_l}} =$$
$$= \sqrt{\frac{EJ}{4P}}\int_0^{\varphi}\frac{d\varphi}{\sqrt{\sin^2\dfrac{\varphi_l}{2} - \sin^2\dfrac{\varphi}{2}}}\,. \qquad (9.29)$$

We substitute in the integrand

$$\sin\frac{\varphi}{2} = \sin\frac{\varphi_l}{2}\sin\vartheta,\quad d\varphi = 2\sin\frac{\varphi_l}{2}\,\frac{\cos\vartheta\,d\vartheta}{\cos\dfrac{\varphi}{2}} =$$
$$= 2\sin\frac{\varphi_l}{2}\,\frac{\cos\vartheta\,d\vartheta}{\sqrt{1 - \sin^2\dfrac{\varphi_l}{2}\sin^2\vartheta}} = 2\varkappa\,\frac{\cos\vartheta\,d\vartheta}{\sqrt{1 - \varkappa^2\sin^2\vartheta}}\,,$$

$$\varkappa^2 = \sin^2\frac{\varphi_l}{2} \leq 1\,,$$

and transform the limits of integration:

$$\vartheta_1 = \vartheta\,|_{\varphi=0} = 0 \quad\text{to}\quad \vartheta_2 = \vartheta\,|_{\varphi=\varphi} = \arcsin\left(\frac{\sin\dfrac{\varphi}{2}}{\sin\dfrac{\varphi_l}{2}}\right).$$

Integrating, we obtain

$$\int_0^{\varphi}\frac{d\varphi}{\sqrt{\varkappa^2 - \sin^2\dfrac{\varphi}{2}}} = 2\int_{\vartheta=0}^{\vartheta_2 = \arcsin\left[\frac{\sin\frac{\varphi}{2}}{\varkappa}\right]}\frac{d\vartheta}{\sqrt{1^2 - \varkappa^2\sin\vartheta}} = 2\,F\,[\vartheta_2(\varphi), \varkappa]\,,$$

which is an elliptic integral of the first kind. We thus obtain from (9.29)

$$s(\varphi) = \sqrt{\frac{EJ}{P}}\, F\,[\vartheta_2(\varphi), \varkappa]\,, \tag{9.30a}$$

whence we find at the free end $s = l$, where $\varphi = \varphi_l$

$$l = s(\varphi_l) = \sqrt{\frac{EJ}{P}}\, F\left(\frac{\pi}{2}, \varkappa\right) = \sqrt{\frac{EJ}{P}}\, K(\varkappa) \tag{9.30b}$$

Solving for P yields the relationship between the axial load and the angle φ_l:

$$P(\varphi_l) = \frac{EJ}{l^2} K^2(\varkappa)\,, \quad \varkappa = \sin\frac{\varphi_l}{2}\,. \tag{9.30c}$$

We can obtain the values of $K(\varkappa)$ from tables (e.g., Hütte, Berlin 1959), which are plotted in Figure 9.5, from which we see that for $\frac{Pl^2}{EJ} \leqq \frac{\pi^2}{4}$ no buckling of the column is statically possible. Only for $P_{kr}^{(B)} = \frac{\pi^2}{4}\frac{EJ}{l^2}$ * do equilibrium positions exist for

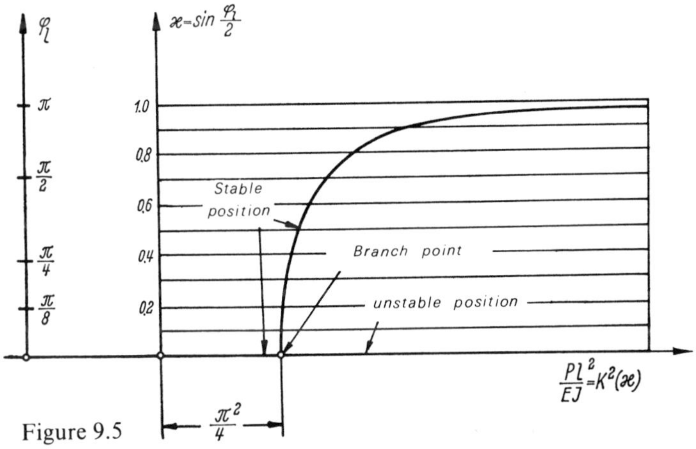

Figure 9.5

the bent system. These are, in general, assumed by the system, since for $P \geqq P_{kr}^{(B)}$ the straight position is unstable.

The load characterizing the branch point,

$$P_{kr}^{(B)} = \frac{\pi^2}{4}\frac{EJ}{l^2} = \frac{\pi^2}{4}\frac{E_x h \pi R^3}{l^2} = \frac{D_x}{4}\frac{\pi^3 R^3}{l^2}$$

is the critical buckling load (Euler load), which is independent of the inflation pressure. We note that this is true for all stability problems of the tubular girder (including static stability). We confirmed the fact that the buckling load is independent of the inflation pressure by experiments carried out in the Light-Structures Development Center. The following table gives the buckling loads for different methods of support. It also shows the first eigenvalues $\lambda_1^{(B)} = \lambda_{kr}^{(B)}$ and the so-called "reduced lengths" through which the buckling loads can be expressed in the form

$$P_{kr}^{(B)} = \lambda_{kr}^{(B)2}\frac{EJ}{l^2} = \frac{\pi^2 EJ}{(l\,\pi/\lambda_{kr}^{(B)})^2} = \frac{\pi^2 EJ}{l_r^{(B)2}} = D_x\frac{\pi^3 R^3}{l_r^{(B)2}} \tag{9.30d}$$

* The superscript (B) signifies that the result has been obtained from (9.27) which has been derived for pure bending. The influence of shearing forces will be discussed later.

Method of support	$\lambda_{kr}^{(B)}$	$l_r^{(B)} = l\frac{\pi}{\lambda_{kr}^{(B)}}$	$P_{kr}^{(B)} = \frac{D_x \pi^3 R^3}{l_r^{(B)2}}$
a 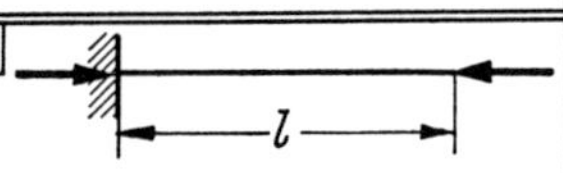	$\frac{\pi}{2}$	$2l$	$\frac{1}{4}\;\frac{D_x \pi^3 R^3}{l^2}$
b 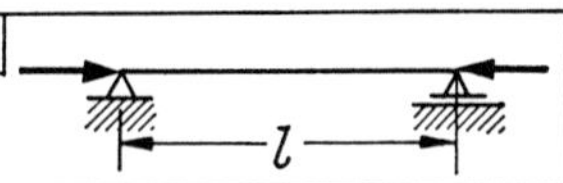	π	l	$\frac{D_x \pi^3 R^3}{l^2}$
c 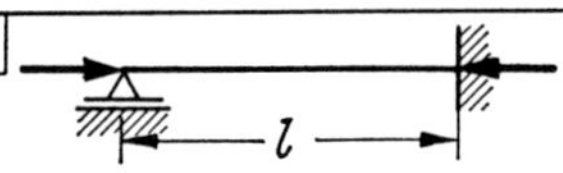	4.493 $\approx \pi/0.7$	$0.7l$	$2.04\;\frac{D_x \pi^3 R^3}{l^2}$
d 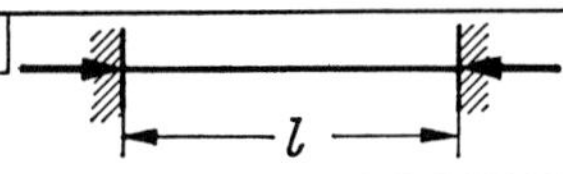	2π	$l/2$	$4\;\frac{D_x \pi^3 R^3}{l^2}$

However, for small slenderness ratios, when the modulus of elasticity in shear $G_{x\vartheta}$ $(D_{x\vartheta})$ is small in comparison with the modulus of elasticity in tension E_x (D_x), the influence of shear deformation becomes appreciable. We shall analyze this influence with the aid of the linearized equations (7.46b) and (7.47f), which enable us to determine the critical loads and approximately also the shape of the buckling line. The buckling loads are found by solving the boundary-value or eigenvalue problem, from which we obtain in every case an infinite number of eigenvalues λ_k, the smallest of which $\lambda_1 = \lambda_{kr}$ determines the load characterizing the branch point on the stability diagram. Considering as positive, in contrast to Section 7.5, bending moments and angles of rotation about the negative y-axis, as well as transverse forces in the direction of the negative z-(w-), axis we obtain from (7.46b) and (7.47)* the relationship

$$\frac{d\beta}{dx} = \frac{d}{dx}\left(\frac{dw}{dx} + \frac{\alpha Q}{G_{x\vartheta} F}\right) = \frac{M}{E_x J}\,. \tag{9.31a}$$

Neglecting the moments m_y due to distributed loads, we obtain in accordance with (7.32e)

$$Q = dM/dx = M'. \tag{9.31b}$$

Substituting of (9.31b) in (9.31a) yields

$$\beta = \frac{dw}{dx} + \frac{\alpha Q}{G_{x\vartheta} F} = \frac{d}{dx}\left(w + \frac{\alpha M}{G_{x\vartheta} F}\right), \tag{9.31c, d}$$

$$\frac{d^2 w}{dx^2} = \frac{M}{E_x J} - \frac{\alpha}{G_{x\vartheta} F}\frac{dQ}{dx} = \frac{M}{E_x J} - \frac{\alpha}{G_{x\vartheta} F}\frac{d^2 M}{dx^2}\,.$$

Introducing the edge loads M_0 and Q_0, we obtain for the buckling of a rod (cf. (9.26))

$$M = M_0 + Q_0 x - P w(x)$$

$$Q \approx Q_0 - P w'\,,$$

whence, from (9.31c, d)

$$\beta = \frac{\alpha Q_0}{G_{x\vartheta} F} + \left(1 - \frac{\alpha P}{G_{x\vartheta} F}\right) w'\,. \tag{9.32a}$$

Writing $\xi = x/l$, we obtain the equation for the displacements

$$\frac{d^2 w}{d\xi^2} + \lambda^2 w = \left(\frac{M_0}{P} + \frac{Q_0}{P} x\right)\lambda^2 \tag{9.32b}$$

* Henceforth we shall omit subscripts, writing β_y $(=\beta)$, M_y $(=M)$, Q_z $(=Q)$ J_y $(=J)$

where

$$\lambda^2 = \frac{P\,l^2/E_x J}{1 - \frac{\alpha P}{G_{x\vartheta} F}} \qquad \text{or} \qquad P = \frac{\lambda^2 E_x J/l^2}{1 + \lambda^2 \alpha \frac{E_x}{G_{x\vartheta}} \frac{J}{F l^2}} \,. \tag{9.32c}$$

The solution of (9.32a, b) is

$$w = \frac{M_0}{P} + \frac{Q_0}{P} x + C_1 \cos \lambda \xi + C_2 \sin \lambda \xi \,, \tag{9.32d}$$

$$\beta = \frac{\alpha Q_0}{G_{x\vartheta} F} + \left(1 - \frac{\alpha P}{G_{x\vartheta} F}\right) w' =$$

$$= \frac{Q_0}{P} + \frac{\lambda}{l}\left(1 - \frac{\alpha P}{G_{x\vartheta} F}\right)\left(- C_1 \sin \lambda \xi + C_2 \cos \lambda \xi\right) =$$

$$= \frac{Q_0}{P} + \frac{\frac{\lambda}{l}\left(- C_1 \sin \lambda \xi + C_2 \cos \lambda \xi\right)}{1 + \lambda^2 \alpha \frac{E_x}{G_{x\vartheta}} \frac{J}{F l^2}} \,. \tag{9.32e}$$

For a further analysis we must consider the boundary-value problem. We shall do this for the four cases of Euler loads given in the table:

a) Putting $M_0 = P w(1)$, $Q_0 = 0$, $w(0) = 0$ and $\beta(0) = 0$ we obtain $C_1 = w(1)$, $C_2 = 0$, as well as the equation for the eigenvalues

$$\cos \lambda = 0 \tag{9.33a}$$

for which the solutions are

$$\lambda = \lambda_k = (2k - 1)\pi/2 \,, \quad k = 1 \ldots \infty \,. \tag{9.33b}$$

The corresponding elastic lines (eigenfunctions) are

$$e_k(\xi) = 1 - \cos (2k - 1)\frac{\pi}{2}\xi \,, \quad k = 1 \ldots \infty \,, \quad \max e_1 = 1 \,. \tag{9.33c}$$

b) Putting $M_0 = Q_0 = 0$ and $w(0) = w(1) = 0$ we obtain from (9.32d): $C_1 = 0$. The equation for the eigenvalues is

$$\sin \lambda = 0 \tag{9.34a}$$

for which the solutions are

$$\lambda = \lambda_k = k\pi \,, \quad k = 1 \ldots \infty \,, \tag{9.34b}$$

the corresponding eigenfunctions being

$$e_k(\xi) = \sin k \pi \xi \,, \quad k = 1 \ldots \infty \,, \quad \max e_k = 1 \,. \tag{9.34c}$$

c) In this case the boundary conditions are $M_0 = w(0) = w(1) = \beta(1) = 0$. We obtain $C_1 = 0$,

$$C_2 = - \frac{Q_0 l}{P \sin \lambda} = - \frac{Q_0 l}{P \lambda \cos \lambda}\left(1 + \lambda^2 \alpha \frac{E_x}{G_{x\vartheta}} \frac{J}{F l^2}\right);$$

the equation for the eigenvalues is

$$\operatorname{tg} \lambda = \left(1 - \frac{\alpha P}{G_{x\vartheta} F}\right)\lambda = \frac{\lambda}{1 + \lambda^2 \alpha \frac{E_x}{G_{x\vartheta}} \frac{J}{F l^2}} \,, \tag{9.35a}$$

which can only be solved numerically. Thus, for $\lambda^2 \alpha \frac{E_x}{G_{x\vartheta}} \frac{J}{F l^2} \ll 1$ (taking only bending deformations into account) we obtain as solutions of the equation $\operatorname{tg} \lambda = \lambda$

$$\lambda_1 = 4.493, \quad \lambda_2 = 7.725, \quad \lambda_3 = 10.904, \quad \lambda_4 = 14.066,$$

$$\lim_{n \to \infty} \lambda_n = \frac{2n + 1}{2}\pi \,. \tag{9.35b}$$

The corresponding eigenfunctions are obtained from (9.32d) as

$$e_k(\xi) = \frac{\lambda_k \xi - \frac{\sin \lambda_k \xi}{\cos \lambda_k \varrho_k}}{\left(\lambda_k \xi - \frac{\sin \lambda_k \xi}{\cos \lambda_k \varrho_k}\right)_{\text{extr.}}} \,, \quad k = 1 \ldots \infty \,, \quad \max e_k = 1 \,, \tag{9.35c}$$

where

$$\cos \lambda_k \varrho_k = \frac{\cos \lambda_k}{1 + \lambda_k^2 \alpha \frac{E_x}{G_{x\vartheta}} \frac{J}{F l^2}} \,. \tag{9.35d}$$

In particular, the first eigenfunction is

$$e_1(\xi) = e(\lambda_1 \xi) = e(\lambda_{kr} \xi) = \frac{\lambda_{kr} \xi - \frac{\sin \lambda_{kr} \xi}{\cos \lambda_{kr} \varrho_1}}{2\pi + \operatorname{tg} \lambda_{kr} \varrho_1 - \lambda_{kr} \varrho_1} \,. \tag{9.35e}$$

Neglecting the shear deformations, i.e., putting $\varrho_1 = 1$ and $\operatorname{tg} \lambda_{kr} = \lambda_{kr}$, we obtain

$$e(\lambda_{kr} \xi) = \frac{1}{2\pi}\left(\lambda_{kr} \xi - \frac{\sin \lambda_{kr} \xi}{\cos \lambda_{kr}}\right) . \tag{9.35f}$$

d) The boundary conditions $w(0) = \beta(0) = 0$ yield $C_1 = -M_0/P$ and $C_2 = -\frac{Q_0 l}{P \lambda}\left(1 + \lambda^2 \alpha \frac{E_x}{G_{x\vartheta}} \frac{J}{F l^2}\right)$, whence

$$w = \frac{M_0}{P}\left(1 - \cos \lambda \xi\right) + \frac{Q_0 l}{P \lambda}\left[\lambda \xi - \left(1 + \lambda^2 \alpha \frac{E_x}{G_{x\vartheta}} \frac{J}{F l^2}\right) \sin \lambda \xi\right],$$

$$\beta = \frac{M_0 \lambda}{P l} \frac{\sin \lambda \xi}{1 + \lambda^2 \alpha \frac{E_x}{G_{x\vartheta}} \frac{J}{F l^2}} + \frac{Q_0}{P}(1 - \cos \lambda \xi) \,. \tag{9.36a}$$

The boundary conditions $w(1) = \beta(1) = 0$ then yield

$$\frac{M_0}{P}\left(1 - \cos \lambda\right) + \frac{Q_0 l}{P \lambda}\left[\lambda - \left(1 + \lambda^2 \alpha \frac{E_x}{G_{x\vartheta}} \frac{J}{F l^2}\right) \sin \lambda\right] = 0 \,,$$

$$\frac{M_0}{P} \frac{\sin \lambda}{1 + \lambda^2 \alpha \frac{E_x}{G_{x\vartheta}} \frac{J}{F l^2}} + \frac{Q_0 l}{P \lambda}(1 - \cos \lambda) = 0 \,.$$

Assuming $M_0/P \neq 0$, $Q_0 l/(P\lambda) \neq 0$, the determinant of their coefficients must vanish. This yields the following equation for the eigenvalues

$$2 \sin \frac{\lambda}{2}\left[\left(1 + \lambda^2 \alpha \frac{E_x}{G_{x\vartheta}} \frac{J}{F l^2}\right) \sin \frac{\lambda}{2} - \frac{\lambda}{2} \cos \frac{\lambda}{2}\right] = 0 \tag{9.36b}$$

which can be satisfied,

1) for symmetrical buckling ($Q_0 = 0$) by

$$\lambda = \lambda_k^{(s)} = 2k\pi \,, \quad k = 1 \ldots \infty \,, \tag{9.36c}$$

the corresponding eigenfunctions being by (9.36a)

$$e_k^{(s)}(\xi) = \frac{1}{2}(1 - \cos 2k\pi\xi) \,, \quad k = 1 \ldots \infty \,, \quad \max e_k^{(s)} = 1 \,, \tag{9.36d}$$

2) for antimetrical buckling ($Q_0 = -2 M_0/l \neq 0$) by the eigenvalues satisfying the equation

$$\operatorname{tg} \frac{\lambda^{(a)}}{2} = \frac{\lambda^{(a)}/2}{1 + \lambda^{(a)2} \alpha \frac{E_x}{G_{x\vartheta}} \frac{J}{F l^2}} \tag{9.36e}$$

Neglecting the shear deformations, we obtain values twice those given by (9.35b). The corresponding buckling line is, according to (9.36a), given by

$$w_k^{(a)} = \frac{M_0}{P}\left[(1-2\,\xi) + \frac{\sin\lambda\left(\xi-\frac{1}{2}\right)}{\sin\frac{\lambda}{2}}\right] = \tag{9.36f}$$

$$= -\frac{2\,M_0}{P\,\lambda}\left[\lambda\left(\xi-\frac{1}{2}\right) - \left(1+\lambda^2\,\alpha\,\frac{E_x}{G_{x\vartheta}}\,\frac{J}{F\,l^2}\right)\frac{\sin\lambda\left(\xi-\frac{1}{2}\right)}{\cos\frac{\lambda}{2}}\right]$$

The first antimetrical eigenvalue is thus

$$e_1^{(a)} = e^{(a)}\,(\lambda_{kr}\,\xi) = -\frac{\lambda_{kr}^{(a)}\left(\xi-\frac{1}{2}\right) - \dfrac{\sin\lambda_{kr}^{(a)}\left(\xi-\frac{1}{2}\right)}{\cos\frac{\lambda_{kr}^{(a)}\,\mu_1}{2}}}{2\,\pi + \operatorname{tg}\frac{\lambda_{kr}^{(a)}\,\mu_1}{2} - \frac{\lambda_{kr}^{(a)}\,\mu_1}{2}} =$$

$$= \frac{\dfrac{\lambda_{kr}^{(a)}}{2}\,(1-2\,\xi) - \dfrac{\sin\frac{\lambda_{kr}^{(a)}}{2}\,(1-2\,\xi)}{\cos\frac{\lambda_{kr}^{(a)}}{2}\,\mu_1}}{2\,\pi + \operatorname{tg}\frac{\lambda_{kr}^{(a)}}{2}\,\mu_1 - \frac{\lambda_{kr}^{(a)}}{2}\,\mu_1}\,, \tag{9.36g}$$

$\max e_1^{(a)} = 1\,,$ where

$$\cos\lambda_{kr}^{(a)}\,\frac{\mu_1}{2} = \frac{\cos\frac{\lambda_{kr}^{(a)}}{2}}{1+\lambda_{kr}^{(a)2}\,\alpha\,\frac{E_x}{G_{x\vartheta}}\,\frac{J}{F\,l^2}} \tag{9.36h}$$

Taking into account only the deformations due to pure bending, we have $\operatorname{tg}\frac{\lambda_{kr}^{(a)}}{2} = \frac{\lambda_{kr}^{(a)}}{2}$ and $\mu_1 = 1$, hence

$$e_1^{(a)} = \frac{1}{2\,\pi}\left[\frac{\lambda_{kr}^{(a)}}{2}\,(1-2\,\xi) - \frac{\sin\frac{\lambda_{kr}^{(a)}}{2}\,(1-2\,\xi)}{\cos\frac{\lambda_{kr}^{(a)}}{2}}\right] =$$

$$= \frac{\lambda_{kr}^{(a)}}{4\,\pi}\left[1-2\,\xi - \frac{\sin\frac{\lambda_{kr}^{(a)}}{2}\,(1-2\,\xi)}{\sin\frac{\lambda_{kr}^{(a)}}{2}}\right]. \tag{9.36i}$$

Summarizing these results, we obtain, for $E_x J = D_x\,\pi\,R^3$, $G_{x\vartheta} F = D_{x\vartheta}\,2\,\pi\,R$, and $\alpha = 2$, the critical load from (9.32c), when the shear deformations are taken into account, as

$$P_{kr} = \frac{\lambda_{kr}^2\,E_x\,J/l^2}{1+\lambda_{kr}^2\,\alpha\,\frac{E_x}{G_{x\vartheta}}\,\frac{J}{F\,l^2}} = \frac{\pi^3\,D_x\,R^3}{l_r^2} \tag{9.37a}$$

with

$$l_r = l\,\frac{\pi}{\lambda_{kr}}\sqrt{1+\pi^2\,\frac{D_x}{D_{x\vartheta}}\left(\frac{R}{l\,\frac{\pi}{\lambda_{kr}}}\right)^2}\,. \tag{9.37b}$$

In the statically determined cases (a) and (b) the eigenvalues are identical with those which would have been obtained by taking into account only the bending deformations. The same is true in the statically undetermined case (d) if we consider symmetrical buckling (which is decisive in this case). In these three cases we obtain for $\lambda_{kr} = \lambda_{kr}^{(B)}$, hence $l\,\frac{\pi}{\lambda_{kr}} = l\,\frac{\pi}{\lambda_{kr}^{(B)}}$, the reduced length

$$l_r = l_r^{(B)}\sqrt{1+\pi^2\,\frac{D_x}{D_{x\vartheta}}\left(\frac{R}{l_r^{(B)}}\right)^2}\,. \tag{9.37c}$$

The statically undetermined case (c) cannot be similarly reduced to the expressions obtained for pure bending.

Since pneumatic columns are easily bent, and it is hardly possible to prevent initial bending during production, it is advisable to keep the axial loads considerably below the values given by (9.37). The reason for this is that the additional deformations, caused by initial bending, increase rapidly when the axial loads approach the Euler loads.

We obtain the minimum safety margin against buckling by requiring that, given the initial bending, the resulting maximum deformations should not exceed a certain limiting value. Let us denote by $\eta_0 = \eta_0\,(x) = f_0\,\bar{\eta}_0\,(x)$ $[\bar{\eta}_{0\,\max} = 1]$ the ordinates, due to initial bending of the unconstrained rod. In this condition no moments act on the rod; only the sectional loads $n_x = p\,R/2$ and $n_\vartheta = p\,R$, due to the inflation pressure, act on it. When this rod is erected so that it is supported in a statically undetermined manner, constraining stresses due to bending moments appear in it. These stresses must be linear functions of x. This is seen immediately by considering a rod, fixed at both ends, which was initially bent. Were the

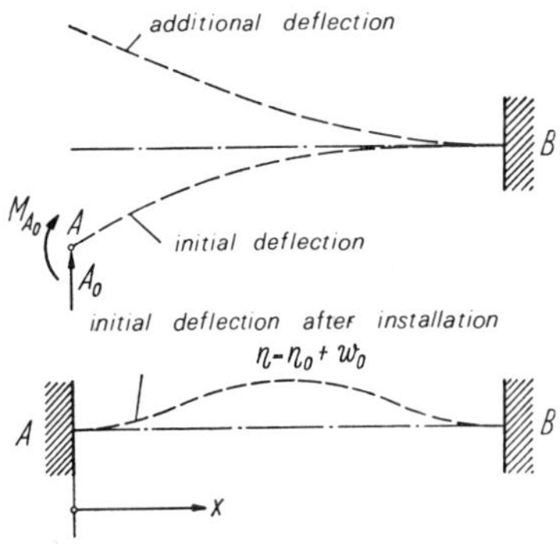

Figure 9.6

rod built-in only on the right (B), the initial bending $\eta_0\,(x)$ would be present. However, the boundary conditions for a rod, built-in also at A, would not be satisfied there. This gives rise to the presence of statically undetermined loads of magnitudes A_0 and M_{A0} after installation. The bending moments and shearing forces acting on the system are thus

$$M_0\,(x) = M_{A0} + A_0\,x\,, \quad Q_0\,(x) = A_0\,.$$

The additional sectional loads thus caused give rise to additional deformations $w_0(x)$, $\beta_0(x)$, which can be determined in accordance with (9.31c, d) from the linearized equations

$$\frac{d^2 w_0}{dx^2} = \frac{M_0(x)}{EJ} - \frac{\alpha}{GF}\frac{dQ_0}{dx} = \frac{1}{EJ}[M_{A0} + A_0 x],$$

$$\beta_0(x) = \frac{dw_0}{dx} + \frac{\alpha Q_0(x)}{GF} = \frac{dw_0}{dx} + \frac{\alpha A_0}{GF}.$$

We see from this that additional deformations $w_0(x)$, caused by $M_0(x)$ and $Q_0(x)$, can at the most represent parabolas of the third degree. The total resulting deformations can therefore be expressed in the form

$$\eta(x) = \eta_0(x) + w_0(x) = = \eta_0(x) + C_{00} + C_{10}x + \frac{M_{A0}}{2EJ}x^2 + \frac{A_0}{6EJ}x^3 \quad (9.38a)$$

$$\beta_\eta = \beta_{\eta 0} + \beta_{w0} = \eta_0' + \beta_0(x) = \eta_0' + w_0' + \frac{\alpha A_0}{GF} = = \eta_0' + C_{10} + \frac{M_{A0}}{EJ}x + A_0\left(\frac{x^2}{2EJ} + \frac{\alpha}{GF}\right). \quad (9.38b)$$

The four integration constants C_{00}, C_{10}, M_{A0}, and A_0 enable us to subject the resulting deformations $[\eta(x), \beta_\eta(x)]$ to the existing boundary conditions for arbitrary intial-bending functions $\eta_0(x)$. We shall now consider the system wherein the predeformation during installation is described by $\eta = \eta(x)$ and $\beta_\eta = \beta_\eta(x)$, under the action of an axial load P causing additional deformations w and β. The total deformations are thus

$$W = w + \eta = w + \eta_0 + w_0, \quad \mathcal{B} = \beta + \beta_\eta. \quad (9.39a)$$

The total edge loads are then

$$M(x) = M_A + Ax - P(W(x) - W_A), \quad Q(x) = \frac{dM}{dx} = A - PW', \quad (9.39b)$$

where W_A is the displacement of the edge.
Since the initial ordinate $\eta_0(x)$ referred to an unconstrained state, we obtain from (9.31a)

$$\frac{d}{dx}(\mathcal{B} - \beta_0) = (\mathcal{B} - \eta_0')' = \frac{d}{dx}\left[\frac{d}{dx}(W - \eta_0) + \frac{\alpha Q}{GF}\right] = = \left(1 - \frac{\alpha P}{GF}\right)W'' - \eta_0'' = \frac{M}{EJ} = = \frac{M_A + Ax - P[W(x) - W_A]}{EJ}, \quad (9.39c)$$

whence

$$\mathcal{B}' = \left(1 - \frac{\alpha P}{GF}\right)W'', \quad (9.39d)$$

$$\left(1 - \frac{\alpha P}{GF}\right)W'' + \frac{P}{EJ}W = \eta_0'' + \frac{M_A + Ax - PW_A}{EJ}. \quad (9.39e)$$

Differentiating twice, we obtain

$$\left(1 - \frac{\alpha P}{GF}\right)\frac{d^4 W}{dx^4} + \frac{P}{EJ}\frac{d^2 W}{dx^2} = \frac{d^4 \eta_0}{dx^4}. \quad (9.39f)$$

Introducing the new variable $\xi = x/l$ and writing

$$\lambda^2 = \frac{Pl^2/EJ}{1 - \frac{\alpha P}{GF}} \quad (9.40a)$$

we have finally

$$\frac{d^4 W}{d\xi^4} + \lambda^2\frac{d^2 W}{d\xi^2} = \frac{1}{1 - \frac{\alpha P}{GF}}\frac{d^4\eta_0}{d\xi^4} = \frac{1}{1 - \frac{\alpha P}{GF}}\frac{d^4}{d\xi^4}\left[\eta - \left(C_{00} + C_{10}l\xi + \frac{M_{A0}l^2}{2EJ}\xi^2 + \frac{A_0 l^3}{6EJ}\xi^3\right)\right] = = \frac{1}{1 - \frac{\alpha P}{GF}}\frac{d^4\eta}{d\xi^4}. \quad (9.40b)$$

We can easily find the solution of this differential equation from the solution of the homogeneous equation if we assume that the prebending function $\eta(\xi)$ is given in the form

$$\eta = f e(\lambda_{kr}\xi), \quad (\eta_{\max} = f, \quad e_{\max} = 1). \quad (9.40c)$$

Here $e(\lambda_{kr}\xi)$ is the first eigenfunction of the system, which approximately defines the shape of the buckling line for a given axial load P_{kr}, and thus represents a solution of (9.32b), satisfying all boundary conditions. It then also satisfies the homogeneous differential equation

$$\frac{d^4 e}{d\xi^4} + \lambda_{kr}^2\frac{d^2 e}{d\xi^2} = 0, \quad (9.40d)$$

obtained by twice differentiating (9.32b). Substituting (9.40c) in (9.40b) and taking into account (9.40d), we obtain the simple relationship

$$\frac{d^4 W}{d\xi^4} + \lambda^2\frac{d^2 W}{d\xi^2} = \frac{1}{1 - \frac{\alpha P}{GF}}\frac{d^4\eta}{d\xi^4} = \frac{f}{1 - \frac{\alpha P}{GF}}\frac{d^4 e}{d\xi^4} = = -\frac{f\lambda_{kr}^2}{1 - \frac{\alpha P}{GF}}\frac{d^2 e}{d\xi^2}. \quad (9.41a)$$

The solution of this equation, satisfying the boundary conditions is

$$W = Ce(\lambda_{kr}\xi). \quad (9.41b)$$

Substituting in (9.41a) and equating the coefficients of $(d^2 e/d\xi^2)$, we find [again using (9.40d)]

$$C = \frac{f}{1 - \frac{\alpha P}{GF}}\frac{\lambda_{kr}^2}{\lambda_{kr}^2 - \lambda^2} = \frac{f}{1 - \frac{\alpha P}{GF}}\frac{\dfrac{P_{kr}l^2/EJ}{1 - \frac{\alpha P_{kr}}{GF}}}{\dfrac{P_{kr}l^2/EJ}{1 - \frac{\alpha P_{kr}}{GF}} - \dfrac{Pl^2/EJ}{1 - \frac{\alpha P}{GF}}} = = f\frac{\nu}{\nu - 1}, \quad (9.41c)$$

where

$$\nu = P_{kr}/P \quad (9.41d)$$

defines the safety margin against buckling of the system. We thus obtain, in accordance with (9.41b), the total deflection

$$W = \frac{\nu}{\nu - 1}fe(\lambda_{kr}\xi) - \frac{\nu}{\nu - 1}\eta. \quad (9.41e)$$

We now require the safety margin against buckling to be such that the total deflection W exceed by not more than 50% the initial deflection η, present before the axial load was applied. We then obtain from (9.41e) the safety margin as

$$\boxed{\nu = \frac{\dfrac{W}{\eta}}{\dfrac{W}{\eta} - 1} \geqq \frac{1.5}{0.5} = 3} \tag{9.42}$$

In addition, the deflections $W = w + \eta$ lead to bending moments by the axial load P. The compressive stresses thus induced must be compensated by the inflation pressure. We thus have to determine the moments from (9.39c)

$$M = EJ \frac{d^2}{dx^2}\left[\left(1 - \frac{\alpha P}{GF}\right) W - \eta_0\right] = \frac{EJ}{l^2}\left[\frac{\nu}{\nu - 1}\left(1 - \frac{\alpha P}{GF}\right)\frac{d^2\eta}{d\xi^2} -\right.$$

$$\left. - \frac{d^2\eta_0}{d\xi^2}\right] = \frac{EJ}{l^2}\left[\frac{\nu}{\nu-1}\left(1 - \frac{\alpha P}{GF}\right)\frac{d^2\eta}{d\xi^2} - \right.$$

$$\left. - \frac{d^2}{d\xi^2}\left(\eta - C_{00} - C_{10}\, l\, \xi - \frac{M_{A0}\, l^2}{2EJ}\xi^2 - \frac{A_0\, l^3}{6EJ}\xi^3\right)\right] =$$

$$= \frac{EJ}{l^2}\left[\frac{\nu}{\nu-1}\left(1 - \frac{\alpha P}{GF}\right) - 1\right]\frac{d^2\eta}{d\xi^2} + M_{A0} + A_0\, l\, \xi =$$

$$= \frac{EJ}{l^2} f\left[\frac{\nu}{\nu-1}\left(1 - \frac{\alpha P}{GF}\right) - 1\right]\frac{d^2 e}{d\xi^2} + M_{A0} + A_0\, l\, \xi =$$

$$= \frac{EJ}{l^2} f \lambda_{kr}^2\left[\frac{\nu}{\nu-1}\left(1 - \frac{\alpha P}{GF}\right) - 1\right]\frac{d^2 e}{d(\lambda_{kr}\xi)^2} +$$

$$+ M_{A0} + A_0\, l\, \xi = \frac{P_{kr} f}{\nu - 1}\frac{d^2 e}{d(\lambda_{kr}\xi)^2} + M_{A0} + A_0\, l\, \xi \tag{9.43}$$

The first eigenfunctions are, according to (9.33) through (9.36):

a) for a girder built-in at $x = 0$ $(\xi = 0)$ and free at $x =$ $(\xi = 1)$

$$e = 1 - \cos\frac{\pi}{2}\xi\,, \quad \lambda_{kr} = \frac{\pi}{2}\,, \quad \frac{d^2 e}{d(\lambda_{kr}\xi)^2} = \cos\frac{\pi}{2}\xi\,, \tag{9.44a}$$

b) for a girder hinged at $x = 0$ $(\xi = 0)$ and $x = l$ $(\xi = 1)$

$$e = \sin\pi\xi\,, \quad \lambda_{kr} = \pi\,, \quad \frac{d^2 e}{d(\lambda_{kr}\xi)^2} = -\sin\pi\xi\,, \tag{9.44b}$$

c) for a girder hinged at $x = 0$ $(\xi = 0)$ and built-in at $x = l$ $(\xi = 1)$

$$\frac{d^2 e}{d(\lambda_{kr}\xi)^2} = \frac{\sin\lambda_{kr}\xi}{(2\pi + \operatorname{tg}\lambda_{kr}\varrho_1 - \lambda_{kr}\varrho_1)\cos\lambda_{kr}\varrho_1}\,, \tag{9.44c}$$

whence, neglecting the deformations due to shearing force, and putting $\varrho_1 = 1$ and $\operatorname{tg}\lambda_{kr} = \lambda_{kr} = 4.493$, we obtain

$$\frac{d^2 e}{d(\lambda_{kr}\xi)^2} = \frac{\sin\lambda_{kr}\xi}{2\pi\cos\lambda_{kr}} = -\frac{\sqrt{1+\lambda_{kr}^2}}{2\pi}\sin\lambda_{kr}\xi = -0.732\sin\lambda_{kr}\xi\,, \tag{9.44d}$$

d) for a girder built-in at $x = 0$ $(\xi = 0)$ and $x = l$ $(\xi = 1)$

$$e = e^{(s)} = 0.5\,(1 - \cos 2\pi\xi)\,,$$

$$\lambda_{kr}^{(s)} = 2\pi\,, \quad \frac{d^2 e}{d(\lambda_{kr}\xi)^2} = \cos 2\pi\xi\,. \tag{9.44e}$$

(symmetrical buckling).

On the basis of the equilibrium conditions, no stresses due to constraints are caused by the initial deformations in the statically determined cases (a) and (b). Hence $A_0 = M_{A0} = 0$. This is also evident from (9.38), since in these cases only two boundary conditions are required to determine uniquely the initial deflections η and section rotations β_η. For this the constants C_{00} and C_{10} suffice. We then have

$$M = \frac{P_{kr}}{\nu - 1}\left\{\begin{array}{c} f^{(a)}\cos\dfrac{\pi}{2}\xi \\ -f^{(b)}\sin\pi\xi \end{array}\right\} = \frac{\nu}{\nu - 1}P\left\{\begin{array}{c} f^{(a)}\cos\dfrac{\pi}{2}\xi \\ -f^{(b)}\sin\pi\xi \end{array}\right\},$$

thus

$$|\,\text{extr.}\, M\,| = \frac{\nu}{\nu - 1}\left\{\begin{array}{c} P f^{(a)} \\ P f^{(b)} \end{array}\right\}. \tag{9.45a, b}$$

It should be noted that for a girder, hinged at both ends, the maximum initial deflection $f = \eta_{\max}$ denotes the deflection of the centre point, whereas for a girder built-in at one end, it denotes the deflection of the free end. Thus f is greater in case (a) than in case (b). This is immediately seen from (9.38) by using as a first approximation for the initial deflection of the unconstrained girder $\eta_0(x) = f^{(a)}\xi^2$. This function satisfies the boundary conditions $\eta_0(0) = \eta_0'(0) = 0$. Thus, for a girder fixed at one end, where $C_{00} = C_{10}\ 0, \eta = f^{(a)}\xi^2$. In case (b) we obtain from (9.38) $\eta(x) = f^{(a)}\xi^2 + C_{00} + C_{10}\, l\, \xi$. The boundary conditions $\eta(0) = \eta(1) = 0$ yield $C_{00} = 0$, $C_{10}\, l = -f^{(a)}$, whence

$$\eta(\xi) = -f^{(a)}(\xi - \xi^2)\,; \quad |\,\eta_{\max}\,| = \frac{f^{(a)}}{4} = f^{(b)} \tag{9.45c}$$

The maximum initial deflections in case (b) are therefore one fourth of those in case (a). The initial deflections of the unconstrained girder are greatly reduced in the statically undetermined cases. This does not mean, however, that in these cases the total moments are much smaller than in the statically determined cases. It is true that the increase of the moments of the axial forces caused by the additional deformations W is much less than in the statically determined cases. On the other hand, additional moments $M_0(x)$ arise due to the constraints caused during installation; these moments are of the order of magnitude of those given by (9.45a). This is clearly evident from case (c). Since in this case the girder is hinged at $\xi = 0$, we have $M_{A0} = 0$. Using the approximation $\eta_0(\xi) = -f^{(a)}\xi^2$ for the initial deflections of the unconstrained girder, we obtain from (9.38)

$$\eta(\xi) = -f^{(a)}\xi^2 + C_{00} + C_{10}\, l\, \xi + \frac{A_0\, l^3}{6EJ}\xi^3\,,$$

$$\beta_\eta = -2\frac{f^{(a)}}{l}\xi + C_{10} + A_0\left(\frac{l^2}{2EJ}\xi^2 + \frac{\alpha}{GF}\right).$$

The integration constants are found from the boundary conditions $\eta(0) = \eta(1) = \beta_\eta(1) = 0$:

$$C_{00} = 0\,, \; C_{10}\, l = f^{(a)} - \frac{f^{(a)}/2}{1 + 3\alpha\dfrac{E}{G}\dfrac{J}{F l^2}} = f^{(a)} - \frac{f^{(a)}/2}{1 + 3\dfrac{D_x}{D_{x\vartheta}}\left(\dfrac{R}{l}\right)^2}\,,$$

$$A_0 = \frac{3EJ}{l^3}\frac{f^{(a)}}{1 + 3\alpha\dfrac{E}{G}\dfrac{J}{F l^2}} = \frac{3EJ}{l^3}\frac{f^{(a)}}{1 + 3\dfrac{D_x}{D_{x\vartheta}}\left(\dfrac{R}{l}\right)^2}\,.$$

Thus, finally,

$$\eta(\xi) = f^{(a)}\left\{\xi - \xi^2 - \frac{\xi - \xi^3}{2\left[1 + 3\dfrac{D_x}{D_{x\vartheta}}\left(\dfrac{R}{l}\right)^2\right]}\right\}.$$

Neglecting the influence of the shear deformations, we obtain

$$\eta(\xi) = \frac{f^{(a)}}{2}(\xi - 2\xi^2 + \xi^3), \quad \eta_{\max} = \frac{f^{(a)}}{13.5} = f^{(c)}. \tag{9.46a}$$

This means that after installation the initial deflections of the unconstrained beam are reduced to one-fourteenth. If we use the eigenvalues according to (9.35f) or (9.44d) instead of the approximation (9.46a), we obtain from (9.43) the approximation

$$\begin{aligned} M &= \frac{P_{kr} f^{(a)}/13.5}{\nu - 1}\left(-0.732 \sin \lambda_{kr}\xi\right) + \frac{3EJ}{l^2} f^{(a)}\xi = \\ &= P f^{(a)}\left\{-\frac{0.732}{13.5}\frac{\nu}{\nu - 1}\sin\lambda_{kr}\xi + \frac{3}{\lambda_{kr}^2}\nu\xi\right\} = \\ &= P f^{(a)}\left\{-0.0540\frac{\nu}{\nu - 1}\sin\lambda_{kr}\xi + 0.1485\,\nu\xi\right\}. \end{aligned} \tag{9.46b}$$

The largest bending moment acts at the built-in end $\xi = 1$. (It exceeds the relative maximum for intermediate values of ξ). Its value is

$$\max M = P f^{(a)}\left\{0.0526\frac{\nu}{\nu - 1} + 0.1485\,\nu\right\}. \tag{9.46c}$$

The first term is due to the increased moments caused by the initial deflection. Comparison with (9.45a) shows that this term amounts to only one-twentieth of the respective value for the cantilever beam, a result that could have been expected. Against this reduction we now have, in the second term, the moment due to the constraints appearing during installation which greatly exceeds the value of the first term: its order of magnitude is that of the moment given by (9.45a). We complete our discussion by considering also case (d), assuming again $\eta_0(\xi) = -f^{(a)}\xi^2$. The boundary conditions $\eta(0) = \eta(1) = \beta_\eta(0) = \beta_\eta(1) = 0$ yield

$$C_{00} = C_{10} = A_0 = 0, \quad M_{A0} = \frac{2EJ}{l^2} f^{(a)}.$$

We then obtain from (9.38): $\eta = 0$. Although this result is not exact, it nevertheless proves that after installation the initial deflection becomes very small. The resulting moments will therefore be almost solely caused by the constraints appearing during the mounting of the initially deformed system. We thus have approximately

$$M(x) = \frac{2EJ}{l^2} f^{(a)} = \frac{1}{2\pi^2}\nu P f^{(a)}. \tag{9.47}$$

We now assume a 10% standard deviation in length, caused by production errors: $f^{(a)} = 0.1\,l$. This comparatively large value also provides a margin of safety against momentary transverse impacts. In addition to considering a safety factor against buckling, we have to take into account the following moments when determining the inflation pressure:

case (a) $\max M = P f^{(a)}\dfrac{\nu}{\nu - 1} = 0.1\,Pl\dfrac{\nu}{\nu - 1}$,

case (b) $\max M = P f^{(b)}\dfrac{\nu}{\nu - 1} = 0.025\,Pl\dfrac{\nu}{\nu - 1}$,

case (c) $\max M = P f^{(a)}\,0.0526\dfrac{\nu}{\nu - 1} + \dfrac{3EJ}{l^2}f^{(a)} = 0.005\,Pl\dfrac{\nu}{\nu - 1} + 0.3\dfrac{EJ}{l}$,

case d) $\max M = \dfrac{2EJ}{l^2}f^{(a)} = 0.2\dfrac{EJ}{l}$.

These values are largest for the smallest permissible safety margin against buckling $\nu = 3$. We then have

a) $\max M = 0.15\,Pl$, b) $\max M = 0.0375\,Pl$,

c) $\max M = 0.008\,Pl + 0.3\dfrac{EJ}{l}$, d) $\max M = 0.2\dfrac{EJ}{l}$.

Writing $E \cdot J = E_x \cdot \pi R^3 h = E_x h \pi R^3 = D_x \pi R^3$ we obtain the maximum compressive sectional loads n_x caused by the axial forces

$$\min n_{xP} = -\left[\frac{P}{2\pi R} + \frac{\max M}{\pi R^2}\right] = -\frac{P}{2\pi R}\left[1 + \frac{2\max M}{PR}\right],$$

i.e.,

a) $\min n_{xP} = -\dfrac{P}{2\pi R}\left(1 + 0.3\dfrac{l}{R}\right)$,

b) $\min n_{xP} = -\dfrac{P}{2\pi R}\left(1 + 0.075\dfrac{l}{R}\right)$,

c) $\min n_{xP} = -\dfrac{P}{2\pi R}\left(1 + 0.016\dfrac{l}{R}\right) - 0.3\,D_x\left(\dfrac{R}{l}\right)$,

d) $\min n_{xP} = -0.2\,D_x\left(\dfrac{R}{l}\right) - \dfrac{P}{2\pi R}$.

The minimum inflation pressure is found from

$$\min n_x = \frac{pR}{2} + \min n_{xP} \geqq 0 \quad \text{or} \quad p \geqq -\frac{2\min n_{xP}}{R}$$

to be

$$\begin{aligned} &\text{a) } p \geqq \frac{P}{\pi R^2}\left(1 + 0.3\frac{l}{R}\right), \quad \text{b) } p \geqq \frac{P}{\pi R^2}\left(1 + 0.075\frac{l}{R}\right), \\ &\text{c) } p \geqq \frac{P}{\pi R^2}\left(1 + 0.016\frac{l}{R}\right) + 0.6\frac{D_x}{l}, \\ &\text{d) } p \geqq 0.4\frac{D_x}{l} + \frac{P}{\pi R^2}. \end{aligned} \tag{9.48a}$$

The maximum tensile forces acting on the membrane are again the circumferential loads $n_\vartheta = pR$. We thus have to show that $pR \leqq n_{\text{perm}}$. For the minimum inflation pressures given by (9.48a) we obtain

$$\begin{aligned} &\text{a) } \frac{P}{\pi R}\left(1 + 0.3\frac{l}{R}\right) \leqq n_{\text{perm}}, \\ &\text{b) } \frac{P}{\pi R}\left(1 + 0.075\frac{l}{R}\right) \leqq n_{\text{perm}}, \\ &\text{c) } \frac{P}{\pi R}\left(1 + 0.016\frac{l}{R}\right) + 0.6\,D_x\frac{R}{l} \leqq n_{\text{perm}}, \\ &\text{d) } 0.4\,D_x\frac{R}{l} + \frac{P}{\pi R} \leqq n_{\text{perm}}. \end{aligned} \tag{9.48b}$$

To ensure against buckling, we must have

$$P \leqq \frac{P_{kr}}{\nu} = \frac{\pi^2 E J}{\nu\, l_r^2} = \frac{\pi^3 D_x R^3}{\nu\, l_r^2} \quad . \tag{9.49a}$$

Fulfilment of (9.48) and (9.49a) is sufficient to prove the structure as adequate. In conclusion, we consider a column, hinged at both both ends $(l_r \approx l_r^{(B)} = l)$. We shall calculate the maximum permissible axial loads, first by assuming a safety factor of 3 against buckling, i.e.

$$P \leqq P_1 = \frac{\pi^3}{3} D_x \frac{R^3}{l^2}$$

and then, by requiring the maximum tensile force n_ϑ to be less than n_{perm}, using

$$P \leqq P_2 = \frac{\pi R\, n_{\mathrm{perm}}}{1 + 0.075 \dfrac{l}{R}} .$$

Putting $P_1 \leqq P_2$, i.e.

$$\frac{\pi^2}{3} D_x \left(\frac{R}{l}\right)^2 \leqq \frac{n_{\mathrm{perm}}}{1 + 0.075 \dfrac{l}{R}}$$

we can determine the limiting slenderness ratio for which the permissible tensile load, and not the buckling load, is decisive.
We obtain

$$\left(\frac{R}{l}\right)^2 \left[1 + 0.075 \frac{l}{R}\right] \leqq \frac{3\, n_{\mathrm{perm}}}{\pi^2 D}$$

for which the solution is

$$\frac{R}{l} \leqq \sqrt{\left(\frac{0.075}{2}\right)^2 + \frac{3}{\pi^2} \frac{n_{\mathrm{perm}}}{D_x}} - \frac{0.075}{2} \approx \frac{1}{\pi} \sqrt{\frac{3\, n_{\mathrm{perm}}}{D_x}} .$$

For $n_{\mathrm{perm}} = n_{\mathrm{tear}}/3 = 10\,\mathrm{kg/cm}$, $D_x = 130\,\mathrm{kg/cm}$ (these values were obtained experimentally by the firm of Stromeyer) we obtain $(R/l) \leqq 0.48$, $(l/R) \geqq 2.08$. With columns hinged at both ends, buckling stability is always decisive when the slenderness ratio exceeds 2.08. For columns fixed at one end, the limiting value of (l/R) is even smaller. In addition, the influence of shear deformations, not taken into account in the above calculations, becomes significant at these small slenderness ratios. This means that the strength of the material cannot be fully utilized in practice. The tensile stresses induced by the inflation pressure always remain far below the maximum permissible values, since low internal pressure can be maintained by virtue of the reduced axial loads permitted for reasons of stability. Conditions are slightly better in the case of statically undetermined structures. Nevertheless pneumatic columns have to be very thick in order to be stable. This is illustrated by the following example, which also shows the general procedure for the buckling analysis of pneumatic columns: it is required to determine the dimensions of a column, hinged at both ends, of length $l = 3\,\mathrm{m}$, acted upon by an axial load $P = 200$.

1) Assuming a safety factor of 3 against buckling, we obtain from (9.37a) for $\lambda_{kr} = \pi$ and $\nu = 3$:

$$P \leqq \frac{\pi^3 D_x R^3}{\nu\, l^2 \left[1 + \pi^2 \dfrac{D_x}{D_{x\vartheta}} \left(\dfrac{R}{l}\right)^2\right]} \quad \text{or}$$

$$\frac{R}{l} \geqq \sqrt[3]{\frac{\nu P}{\pi^3 D_x l}} \sqrt[3]{1 + \pi^2 \frac{D_x}{D_{x\vartheta}} \left(\frac{R}{l}\right)^2} = f\left(\frac{R}{l}\right) . \tag{9.49b}$$

We determine the required tube radius by iteration: proceeding from the first approximation $\left(\dfrac{R}{l}\right)_0 = \sqrt[3]{\dfrac{\nu P}{\pi^3 D_x l}}$, obtained by taking into account only deformations due to pure bending, we establish improved approximations

$$\left(\frac{R}{l}\right)_1 = f\left[\left(\frac{R}{l}\right)_0\right], \quad \left(\frac{R}{l}\right)_2 = f\left[\left(\frac{R}{l}\right)_1\right]$$

until satisfactory accuracy is attained, the difference between consecutive values being sufficiently small. For the values given, and assuming $D_x/D_{x\vartheta} = 10$, we obtain the consecutive approximations

$$\left(\frac{R}{l}\right)_0 \geqq 0.0791; \left(\frac{R}{l}\right)_1 \geqq 0.0928; \left(\frac{R}{l}\right)_2 \geqq 0.097; \left(\frac{R}{l}\right)_3 \geqq 0.0983;$$

$$\left(\frac{R}{l}\right)_4 \geqq 0.0987; \left(\frac{R}{l}\right)_5 \geqq 0.0989 = 1.251 \left(\frac{R}{l}\right)_0 \approx 0.1,$$

The marked influence of the shear deformation on the buckling stability is apparent from these results (a 25% increase in the radius!). We thus obtain $R = 0.1\, l = 30\,\mathrm{cm}$.

2) The required inflation pressure is found from (9.48a)

$$p \geqq \frac{P}{\pi R^2} \left[1 + 0.075 \left(\frac{l}{R}\right)\right] = 0.124\,\mathrm{kg/cm^2} = 0.124\,\mathrm{atm} .$$

3) The maximum circumferential sectional loads are

$$n_\vartheta = R\, p = 0.124 \cdot 30 = 3.72\,\mathrm{kg/cm} < n_{\mathrm{perm}} = 10\,\mathrm{kg/cm} .$$

For an axial load of only 200 kg, we have thus obtained a length-diameter ratio of 300/60 = 5, which indicates a very thick column.

b) Bending with axial force.

b1) General solution.

In contrast to the deformations caused by transverse loads, the initial deflections η can be neglected here. We thus have (Fig. 9.7)

$$M(x) = M_A + A\, x - \int_{v=0}^{x} q(v)\,(x - v)\, d v - P\, w(x), \tag{9.50}$$

$$Q(x) = M'(x) = A - \int_{v=0}^{x} q(v)\, d v - P\, w'(x) \quad .$$

The linearized equations (9.31c, d) yield

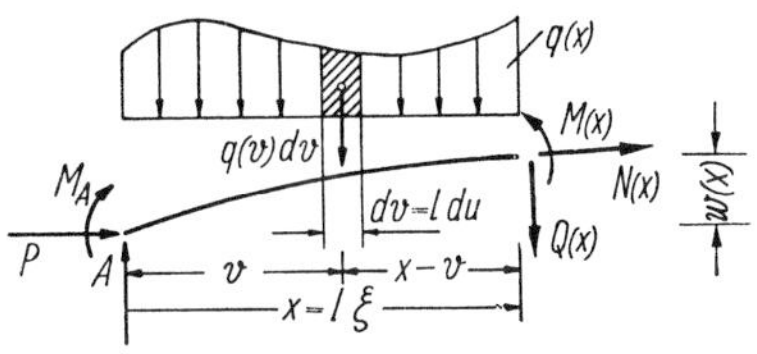

Figure 9.7

$$\beta = \frac{d w}{d x} + \frac{\alpha Q}{G F} = \left(1 - \frac{\alpha P}{G F}\right) w' + \frac{\alpha}{G F}\left(A - \int_{v=0}^{x} q(v)\, d v\right) =$$

$$= \left(1 - \frac{\alpha P}{G F}\right) \frac{1}{l} \frac{d w}{d \xi} + \frac{\alpha}{G F}\left(A - l \int_{u=0}^{\xi} q(u)\, d u\right) , \tag{9.51a}$$

$$\frac{d^2 w}{d x^2} = \frac{1}{l^2}\frac{d^2 w}{d \xi^2} = \frac{M}{EJ} - \frac{\alpha}{GF}\frac{d Q}{d x} = \\ = \frac{1}{EJ}\left[M_A + A l \xi - l^2 \int_{u=0}^{\xi} q(u)(\xi - u)\, d u - P w\right] - \\ - \frac{\alpha}{GF}\left(-q(\xi) - \frac{P}{l^2}\frac{d^2 w}{d \xi^2}\right). \tag{9.51b}$$

We resolve the edge loads A and M_A into components (A_q, M_{Aq}), induced by the transverse load q and components $M_A{}^*$, A^*, due to the axial load:

$$M_A = M_A{}^* + M_{Aq}, \quad A = A^* + A_q \tag{9.52a}$$

The loads acting at section x, due only to the transverse load, are

$$M_q(x) = M_{Aq} + A_q x - \int_{v=0}^{x} q(v)(x - v)\, d v, \tag{9.52b}$$

$$Q_q(x) = A_q - \int_{v=0}^{x} q(v)\, d v.$$

The loads are, in the general case, statically undetermined. Writing

$$\lambda^2 = \frac{P l^2/EJ}{1 - \dfrac{\alpha P}{GF}} \tag{9.53a}$$

we obtain from (9.51) the relationships

$$\beta = \left(1 - \frac{\alpha P}{GF}\right)\frac{1}{l}\frac{d w}{d \xi} + \frac{\alpha}{GF}(A^* + Q_q), \tag{9.53b,c}$$

$$\frac{d^2 w}{d \xi^2} + \lambda^2 w = \frac{\lambda^2}{P}\left[M_A{}^* + A^* l \xi + M_q(\xi) - \frac{\alpha E J}{G F l}\frac{d Q_q}{d \xi}\right],$$

where $q = -d Q_q/d x$. The general solution consists of the complementary function (i.e., the solution of the homogeneous equation) and a particular integral (of the inhomogeneous equation) which can be determined by the method of variation of the constants. The complete solution of (9.53b,c) is thus

$$w = \frac{M_A{}^*}{P} + \frac{A^*}{P} l \xi + C_1 \cos \lambda \xi + C_2 \sin \lambda \xi + \\ + \frac{\lambda}{P}\int_{u=0}^{\xi} \sin \lambda(\xi - u)\, \Psi_q(u)\, d u, \tag{9.54a,b}$$

$$\beta = \frac{A^*}{P} + \frac{\alpha Q_q}{GF} + \frac{\lambda}{l}\left(1 - \frac{\alpha P}{GF}\right) \times \\ \times \left[-C_1 \sin \lambda \xi + C_2 \cos \lambda \xi + \frac{\lambda}{P}\int_{u=0}^{\xi} \Psi_q(u) \cos \lambda(\xi - u)\, d u\right],$$

where

$$\Psi_q(\xi) = M_q(\xi) - \frac{\alpha E J}{G F l}\frac{d Q_q}{d \xi} \tag{9.54d}$$

The integration constants C_1 and C_2, as well as $M_A{}^*$ and A^*, are determined from the specific boundary conditions. The bending moments are then found to be

$$M(\xi) = EJ\frac{d \beta}{d x} = \frac{EJ}{l}\frac{d \beta}{d \xi} = -P(C_1 \cos \lambda \xi + \\ + C_2 \sin \lambda \xi) + M_q(\xi) - \lambda \int_0^{\xi} \Psi_q(u) \sin \lambda(\xi - u)\, d u. \tag{9.54d}$$

We shall now consider some particular cases:

a) Cantilever beam built-in at $x = 0$ $(\xi = 0)$:

The additional edge load due to the axial force P is $M_A{}^* = P w_B = = P w(1)$. This moment is caused by the point of application of P (free end B) being displaced. We then obtain from $M_A{}^* = P w(1)$ and $A^* = 0$:

$$w(\xi) = w(1) + C_1 \cos \lambda \xi + C_2 \sin \lambda \xi + \\ + \frac{\lambda}{P}\int_{u=0}^{\xi} \Psi_q(u) \sin \lambda(\xi - u)\, d u, \tag{9.55a,b}$$

$$\beta(\xi) = \frac{\alpha Q_q}{GF} + \frac{\lambda}{l}\left(1 - \frac{\alpha P}{GF}\right) \times \\ \times \left[-C_1 \sin \lambda \xi + C_2 \cos \lambda \xi + \frac{\lambda}{P}\int_{u=0}^{\xi} \Psi_q(u) \cos \lambda(\xi - u)\, d u\right],$$

where M_q and Q_q denote the loads in section ξ due to the transverse load acting on the cantilever. The boundary conditions are $w(0) = 0$, $\beta(0) = 0$, whence

$$C_1 = -w(1), \quad C_2 = -\frac{\alpha Q_q(0)\, l}{\lambda(GF - \alpha P)}.$$

We then find

$$w(\xi) = w(1)[1 - \cos \lambda \xi] + \frac{\lambda}{P}\int_{u=0}^{\xi} M_q(u) \sin \lambda(\xi - u)\, du - \\ - \frac{\alpha l/GF}{1 - \dfrac{\alpha P}{GF}}\int_{u=0}^{\xi} Q_q(u) \cos \lambda(\xi - u)\, d u. \tag{9.55c}$$

We obtain for $\xi = 1$:

$$w(1) = \frac{1}{\cos \lambda}\left\{\frac{\lambda}{P}\int_{u=0}^{1} M_q(u) \sin \lambda(1 - u)\, d u - \\ - \frac{\alpha l/GF}{1 - \dfrac{\alpha P}{GF}}\int_0^1 Q_q(u) \cos \lambda(1 - u)\, d u\right\}, \tag{9.55d}$$

so that, finally

$$w(\xi) = \frac{1 - \cos \lambda \xi}{\cos \lambda}\left\{\frac{\lambda}{P}\int_0^1 M_q(u) \sin \lambda(1 - u)\, d u - \\ - \frac{\alpha l/GF}{1 - \dfrac{\alpha P}{GF}}\int_0^1 Q_q(u) \cos \lambda(1 - u)\, d u + \\ + \frac{\lambda}{P}\int_0^{\xi} M_q(u) \sin \lambda(\xi - u)\, d u\right\}. \tag{9.55e}$$

By (9.54d),

$$M(\xi) = M_q(\xi) + \lambda \left\{ \frac{\cos \lambda \xi}{\cos \lambda} \int_0^1 M_q(u) \sin \lambda (1-u)\, du - \int_0^\xi M_q(u) \sin \lambda (\xi - u)\, du \right\} - l \frac{\alpha P/GF}{1 - \frac{\alpha P}{GF}} \left\{ \frac{\cos \lambda \xi}{\cos \lambda} \int_0^1 Q_q(u) \cos \lambda (1-u)\, du - \int_0^\xi Q_q(u) \cos \lambda (\xi - u)\, du \right\}. \tag{9.55f}$$

b) Rod hinged at both ends.

The axial loads cause no additional support reactions, so that $M_A^* = A^* = 0$. The constants C_1 and C_2 are obtained from the boundary conditions $w(0) = w(1) = 0$:

$$C_1 = 0, \quad C_2 = -\frac{\lambda}{P \sin \lambda} \int_0^1 \Psi_q(u) \sin \lambda (1-u)\, du$$

whence

$$w(\xi) = -\frac{\lambda}{P} \left[\frac{\sin \lambda \xi}{\sin \lambda} \int_0^1 \Psi_q(u) \sin \lambda (1-u)\, du - \int_0^\xi \Psi_q(u) \sin \lambda (\xi - u)\, du \right]. \tag{9.56a}$$

The bending moments are thus

$$M(\xi) = M_q(\xi) + \lambda \left\{ \frac{\sin \lambda \xi}{\sin \lambda} \int_0^1 \Psi_q(u) \sin \lambda (1-u)\, du - \int_0^\xi \Psi_q(u) \sin \lambda (\xi - u)\, du \right\}. \tag{9.56b}$$

Here Q_q and M_q are, respectively, the shearing force and bending moment due to the transverse load.

c) Rod hinged at $x = 0\ (\xi = 0)$ and built-in at $x = l\ (\xi = 1)$. Due to the absence of edge moments at $A(x = 0)$ we have $M_A^* = 0$. We obtain from (9.54)

$$w = \frac{A^*}{P} l \xi + C_1 \cos \lambda \xi + C_2 \sin \lambda \xi + \frac{\lambda}{P} \int_0^\xi \sin \lambda (\xi - u)\, \Psi_q(u)\, du,$$

$$\beta = \frac{A^*}{P} + \frac{\alpha Q_q}{GF} + \frac{\lambda}{l} \left(1 - \frac{\alpha P}{GF}\right) \left[- C_1 \sin \lambda \xi + C_2 \cos \lambda \xi + \frac{\lambda}{P} \int_0^\xi \Psi_q(u) \cos \lambda (\xi - u)\, du \right]. \tag{9.57a}$$

The constants A^*, C_1, and C_2 are determined from the boundary conditions $w(0) = w(1) = \beta(1) = 0$, writing $\zeta = \frac{\alpha P}{GF}$:

$$C_1 = 0, \quad \frac{A^* l}{P} = \frac{\frac{\lambda^2}{P} (1 - \zeta) \int_0^1 M_q(u) \sin \lambda u\, du + \frac{\lambda l}{P} \zeta \int_0^1 Q_q(u) \cos \lambda u\, du}{(1 - \zeta) \lambda \cos \lambda - \sin \lambda},$$

$$C_2 + \frac{Q(0) \lambda \alpha EJ}{PGFl} = \frac{\frac{\lambda}{P} \int_0^1 M_q [\sin \lambda (1-u) - \lambda (1 - \zeta) \cos \lambda (1-u)]\, du}{(1 - \zeta) \lambda \cos \lambda - \sin \lambda} - \frac{l}{P} \frac{\zeta \int_0^1 Q_q \left[\lambda \sin \lambda (1-u) + \frac{\cos \lambda (1-u)}{1 - \zeta} \right] du}{(1 - \zeta) \lambda \cos \lambda - \sin \lambda}$$

whence the deformations are found:

$$w = \frac{\lambda}{P} \left\{ \lambda \xi \frac{(1 - \zeta) \int_0^1 M_q(u) \sin \lambda u\, du}{(1 - \zeta) \lambda \cos \lambda - \sin \lambda} - \sin \lambda \xi \frac{\int_0^1 M_q(u) [\sin \lambda (1-u) - \lambda (1 - \zeta) \cos \lambda (1-u)]\, du}{(1 - \zeta) \lambda \cos \lambda - \sin \lambda} + \int_0^\xi M_q(u) \sin \lambda (\xi - u)\, du \right\} + l \frac{\zeta}{P} \left\{ \lambda \xi \frac{\int_0^1 Q_q(u) \cos \lambda u\, du}{(1 - \zeta) \lambda \cos \lambda - \sin \lambda} - \sin \lambda \xi \frac{\int_0^1 Q_q(u) \left[\lambda \sin \lambda (1-u) + \frac{\cos \lambda (1-u)}{1 - \zeta} \right] du}{(1 - \zeta) \lambda \cos \lambda - \sin \lambda} - \frac{1}{1 - \zeta} \int_0^\xi Q_q(u) \cos \lambda (\xi - u)\, du \right\} \tag{9.57b}$$

The bending moments are

$$M(\xi) = M_q(\xi) - \lambda \left\{ \sin \lambda \xi \int_0^1 \frac{\sin \lambda (1-u) - \lambda (1 - \zeta) \cos \lambda (1-u)}{(1 - \zeta) \lambda \cos \lambda - \sin \lambda} M_q(u)\, du + \int_0^\xi M_q(u) \sin \lambda (\xi - u)\, du \right\} - \zeta l \left\{ \sin \lambda \xi \int_0^1 \frac{\lambda \sin \lambda (1-u) + \frac{\cos \lambda (1-u)}{1 - \zeta}}{(1 - \zeta) \lambda \cos \lambda - \sin \lambda} Q_q(u)\, du - \frac{1}{1 - \zeta} \int_0^\xi Q_q(u) \cos \lambda (\xi - u)\, du \right\}. \tag{9.57c}$$

Here, M_q and Q_q are respectively the bending moment and the shearing force due to the transverse load acting on the statically once-undetermined system.

d) Rod built-in at both ends.

The boundary conditions $w(0) = w(1) = \beta(0) = \beta(1) = 0$ yield A^*, $M_A{}^*$, C_1 and C_2 :

$$C_1 = -\frac{M_A{}^*}{P} =$$

$$= \frac{\lambda}{P}\int_0^1 \frac{\sin\lambda(1-u) - \lambda(1-\zeta)\cos\lambda(1-u) + \sin\lambda u}{2(1-\cos\lambda) - (1-\zeta)\lambda\sin\lambda} M_q(u)\,du -$$

$$-\frac{l}{P}\frac{\zeta}{1-\zeta}\int_0^1 \frac{\cos\lambda(1-u) + \lambda(1-\zeta)\sin\lambda(1-u) - \cos\lambda u}{2(1-\cos\lambda) - (1-\zeta)\lambda\sin\lambda} Q_q(u)\,du,$$

$$(1-\zeta)\left(C_2 + \frac{\lambda\,\alpha\,E\,J\,Q_q(0)}{P\,G\,F\,l}\right) = -\frac{A^*\,l}{P\,\lambda} = -$$

$$-\frac{\lambda}{P}(1-\zeta)\int_0^1 \frac{\cos\lambda u - \cos\lambda(1-u)}{2(1-\cos\lambda) - (1-\zeta)\lambda\sin\lambda} M_q(u)\,du +$$

$$+\frac{l}{P}\zeta\int_0^1 \frac{[\sin\lambda(1-u) + \sin\lambda u]\,Q_q(u)}{2(1-\cos\lambda) - (1-\zeta)\lambda\sin\lambda}\,du\,.$$

The deflections are thus

$$w(\xi) = \frac{\lambda}{P}\Bigg\{(1-\cos\lambda\xi)\times$$

$$\times\int_0^1 \frac{\lambda(1-\zeta)\cos\lambda(1-u) - \sin\lambda(1-u) - \sin\lambda u}{2(1-\cos\lambda) - (1-\zeta)\lambda\sin\lambda} M_q(u)\,du -$$

$$-[(1-\zeta)\lambda\xi - \sin\lambda\xi]\int_0^1 \frac{[\cos\lambda(1-u) - \cos\lambda u]\,M_q(u)}{2(1-\cos\lambda) - (1-\zeta)\lambda\sin\lambda}\,du +$$

$$+\int_0^\xi M_q(u)\sin\lambda(\xi-u)\,du\Bigg\} + \frac{l}{P}\frac{\zeta}{1-\zeta}\Bigg\{(1-\cos\lambda\xi)\times$$

$$\times\int_0^1 \frac{\cos\lambda(1-u) + \lambda(1-\zeta)\sin\lambda(1-u) - \cos\lambda u}{2(1-\cos\lambda) - (1-\zeta)\lambda\sin\lambda} Q_q(u)\,du -$$

$$-[(1-\zeta)\lambda\xi - \sin\lambda\xi]\int_0^1 \frac{[\sin\lambda(1-u) + \sin\lambda u]\,Q_q(u)}{2(1-\cos\lambda) - (1-\zeta)\lambda\sin\lambda}\,du -$$

$$-\int_0^\xi Q_q(u)\cos\lambda(\xi-u)\,du\Bigg\} \tag{9.58a}$$

while the bending moments are

$$M(\xi) = M_q(\xi) - \lambda\Bigg\{\cos\lambda\xi\times$$

$$\times\int_0^1 \frac{\sin\lambda(1-u) + \sin\lambda u - \lambda(1-\zeta)\cos\lambda(1-u)}{2(1-\cos\lambda) - (1-\zeta)\lambda\sin\lambda} M_q(u)\,du -$$

$$-\sin\lambda\xi\int_0^1 \frac{\cos\lambda u - \cos\lambda(1-u)}{2(1-\cos\lambda) - (1-\zeta)\lambda\sin\lambda} M_q(u)\,du +$$

$$+\int_0^\xi M_q(u)\sin\lambda(\xi-u)\,du\Bigg\} + l\frac{\zeta}{1-\zeta}\Bigg\{\cos\lambda\xi\times$$

$$\times\int_0^1 \frac{\cos\lambda(1-u) - \cos\lambda u + \lambda(1-\zeta)\sin\lambda(1-u)}{2(1-\cos\lambda) - (1-\zeta)\lambda\sin\lambda} Q_q(u)\,du -$$

$$-\sin\lambda\xi\int_0^1 \frac{[\sin\lambda u + \sin\lambda(1-u)]\,Q_q(u)}{2(1-\cos\lambda) - (1-\zeta)\lambda\sin\lambda}\,du +$$

$$+\int_0^\xi Q_q(u)\cos\lambda(\xi-u)\,du\Bigg\}\,. \tag{9.58b}$$

When M_q and Q_q, and thus Ψ_q, are polynomials (this is mostly the case) it it is advisable to use Dischinger's solution of (9.53c)

$$w = C_1\cos\lambda\xi + C_2\sin\lambda\xi +$$

$$+\frac{1}{P}\left[M_A{}^* + A^*\,l\,\xi + \sum_{k=0}^{\infty}\frac{(-1)^k}{\lambda^{2k}}\frac{d^{2k}\Psi_q}{d\,\xi^{2k}}\right] \tag{9.59}$$

The validity of (9.59) is proved by writing

$$w = \sum_{k=0}^{\infty} A_k\frac{d^{2k}\Psi_q}{d\,\xi^{2k}}$$

for a particular solution of (9.53c), and then determining the coefficients A_k. We obtain particularly simple relationships if we assume the bending moments M_q to be proportional to the second derivative according to ξ of the first eigenfunctions e, so that the shearing forces Q_q become proportional to the third derivative:

$$M_q(\xi) = K\frac{d^2 e}{d\,\xi^2}, \quad Q_q(\xi) = \frac{d\,M_q}{d\,x} = \frac{1}{l}\frac{d\,M_q}{d\,\xi} = \frac{K}{l}\frac{d^3 e}{d\,\xi^3} \tag{9.60a}$$

where K is a constant. We then have, using (9.40d)

$$\frac{d^2 M_q}{d\,\xi^2} = K\frac{d^4 e}{d\,\xi^4} = -K\lambda_{kr}{}^2\frac{d^2 e}{d\,\xi^2},$$

$$\frac{d^3 Q_q}{d\,\xi^3} = \frac{d^3}{d\,\xi^3}\left(\frac{d\,M_q}{d\,x}\right) = \frac{1}{l}\frac{d^4 M_q}{d\,\xi^4} = \frac{K}{l}\frac{d^6 e}{d\,\xi^6} = \frac{K}{l}\lambda_{kr}{}^4\frac{d^2 e}{d\,\xi^2}\,.$$

Differentiating (9.53c) twice according to ξ and putting $\zeta = \alpha\,P/(G\,F)$, $\zeta_{kr} = \alpha\,P_{kr}/(G\,F) = (P_{kr}/P)\cdot\alpha\,P/(G\,F) = \nu\,\zeta$ we obtain

$$\frac{d^4 w}{d\,\xi^4} + \lambda^2\frac{d^2 w}{d\,\xi^2} = \frac{\lambda^2}{P}\left(\frac{d^2 M_q}{d\,\xi^2} - \frac{\alpha\,E\,J}{G\,F\,l}\frac{d^3 Q}{d\,\xi^3}\right) =$$

$$= -\frac{\lambda^2\lambda_{kr}{}^2}{P}K\left(1 + \frac{\alpha\,E\,J}{G\,F\,l^2}\lambda_{kr}{}^2\right)\frac{d^2 e}{d\,\xi^2} = -\frac{K\,\lambda^2\,\lambda_{kr}{}^2}{P(1-\zeta_{kr})}\frac{d^2 e}{d\,\xi^2}\,.$$

Writing $w = C\,e(\xi)$ which satisfies the boundary conditions and dividing by $d^2 e/d\,\xi^2$, we then obtain

$$C = \frac{\lambda_{kr}{}^2}{\lambda_{kr}{}^2 - \lambda^2}\frac{K\,\lambda^2}{P(1-\zeta_{kr})} = K\frac{\lambda^2}{P}\frac{1-\zeta}{1-\zeta_{kr}}\frac{\lambda_{kr}{}^2}{(1-\zeta)(\lambda_{kr}{}^2 - \lambda^2)} =$$

$$= K\frac{\lambda^2}{P}\frac{1-\zeta}{1-\nu\zeta}\frac{\nu}{\nu-1},$$

[cf. (9.41c)], whence

$$w(\xi) = \frac{\nu}{\nu-1}\frac{1-\zeta}{1-\nu\zeta}K\frac{\lambda^2}{P}e(\xi)\,. \tag{9.60b}$$

The bending moments are then obtained from (9.31a) and (9.53b)

$$M(\xi) = EJ\frac{d\beta}{dx} = \frac{EJ}{l}\frac{d\beta}{d\xi} = \frac{EJ}{l^2}(1-\zeta)\frac{d^2 w}{d\xi^2} + \frac{\alpha EJ}{GFl}\frac{dQ_q}{d\xi} =$$

$$= \frac{EJ}{l^2}(1-\zeta)K\frac{\lambda^2}{P}\frac{1-\zeta}{1-\nu\zeta}\frac{\nu}{\nu-1}\frac{d^2 e}{d\xi^2} + \frac{\alpha EJ}{GFl^2}K\frac{d^4 e}{d\xi^2}$$

$$= K\frac{1-\zeta}{1-\nu\zeta}\frac{\nu}{\nu-1}\frac{d^2 e}{d\xi^2} - K\frac{\lambda_{kr}{}^2\alpha EJ}{GFl^2}\frac{d^2 e}{d\xi^2} =$$

$$= \frac{K}{1-\nu\zeta}\left[\frac{\nu(1-\zeta)}{\nu-1} - \nu\zeta\right]\frac{d^2 e}{d\xi^2} =$$

$$= \frac{\nu}{\nu-1}K\frac{d^2 e}{d\xi^2} = \frac{\nu}{\nu-1}M_q(\xi)\,. \tag{9.60c}$$

These simple relationships are usually applicable even when the initial bending-moment diagram (neglecting the influence of axial loads) deviates markedly from the assumed shape.* The influence of the axial loads is clearly evident: even when a safety factor of 3 is assumed against buckling, there is, by virtue of $M(\xi) = [3/(3-1)]\,M_q(\xi) = 1.5\,M_q(\xi)$, a 50% increase in the bending moments due to the action of the axial force.

We conclude by summarizing the procedure employed to determine the necessary safety factor against buckling and the maximum compressive loads:

1) Safety against buckling: when the axial force P is given, we obtain a safety factor of ν if the tube radius is determined according to (9.37a)

$$R \geqq R_1 = \frac{1}{\pi}\sqrt[3]{\frac{\nu P l_r{}^2}{D_x}}\,. \tag{9.61a}$$

2) Determination of the required internal pressure and of the maximum stresses. The maximum compressive loads in the membrane, due to the axial load P and $\max M$, are

$$\min n_{x_{P+q}} = -\left[\frac{P}{2\pi R} + \frac{\max M}{\pi R^2}\right].$$

We then obtain from $n_x = p\,R/2 + \min n_{x_{p+q}} \geqq 0$ the required internal pressure

$$p \geqq p_{\min} = \frac{P}{\pi R^2} + \frac{2\max M}{\pi R^3} \tag{9.61b}$$

and the maximum tensile loads in the circumferential direction $n_\vartheta = R\,p$. Since, for safety reasons, the internal pressure must exceed the minimum value ($p = \omega\, p_{\min}$, where ω is a safety factor), we obtain the tube radius from $n_\vartheta = R\,\omega\, p_{\min} \leqq n_{\text{perm}}$ taking into account the permissible tensile loads:

$$R \geqq R_2 = \frac{P\omega}{2\pi n_{\text{perm}}} + \sqrt{\left(\frac{P\omega}{2\pi n_{\text{perm}}}\right)^2 + \frac{2\max M\cdot\omega}{\pi n_{\text{perm}}}}\,. \tag{9.61c}$$

Of the two values given by (9.61a) and (9.61c) we have to select the larger. Since, l_r usually depends on R, and $\max M$ on ν, i.e., also on the tube radius, the correct result can only be obtained from (9.61a, c) by iteration.

Example: A tube, hinged at both ends, of length $l =$ 3m, has to be designed to withstand a distributed transverse load $q_0 =$ 25.0 kg/m and an axial compressive force $P = 100$ kg. A safety factor of 3 is required against buckling. Writing

* If the bending moments M_q are due to a uniformly distributed load $q(x) = q_0$, then (9.60c) is always sufficiently accurate.

$$l_r = l\sqrt{1 + \pi^2\frac{D_x}{D_{x\vartheta}}\left(\frac{R}{l}\right)^2}$$

we obtain from (9.49b) and (9.61a)

$$\left(\frac{R}{l}\right) \geqq \frac{R_1}{l} = \sqrt[3]{\frac{3P}{\pi^3 D_x l}}\sqrt[3]{1 + \pi^2\frac{D_x}{D_{x\vartheta}}\left(\frac{R_1}{l}\right)^2}\,. \tag{9.62a}$$

For $D_x = 130$ kg/cm and $D_x/D_{x\vartheta} = 10$ we obtain after a few iterations

$$R_1 = 0.072\,l = 21.6 \text{ cm}\,. \tag{9.62b}$$

Neglecting shear deformations, we would have obtained $R_1 =$ 18.85 cm. The maximum bending moment due to the transverse load is $\max M_q = q\,l^2/8 = 28.10$ kg m. The maximum bending moment, taking account of the axial load, follows then from (9.60c) for $\nu = 3$:

$$\max M \approx \max M_q\frac{\nu}{\nu-1} \approx \frac{3}{2}\cdot 28.10 = 42.2 \text{ kg m}\,. \tag{9.62c}$$

We then obtain from (9.61c) for $\omega = 1.5$ and $n_{\text{perm}} = 10$ kg/cm:

$$R_2 = \frac{100\cdot 1.5}{2\pi\cdot 10} + \sqrt{\left(\frac{100\cdot 1.5}{2\pi\cdot 10}\right)^2 + \frac{84.4\cdot 1.5\cdot 100}{\pi\cdot 10}} = 22.6 \text{ cm}\,.$$

This value is larger than R_1. The safety factor against buckling is thus greater than 3:

$$\nu = \frac{\pi^3 D_x R^3}{P l^2\left[1 + \pi^2\frac{D_x}{D_{x\vartheta}}\left(\frac{R}{l}\right)^2\right]} = 3.35\,.$$

This means, however, that the maximum bending moment is less than the value given by (9.62c). This, in turn, reduces the value of R_2 further. We therefore assume $\nu = 3.25$ for determining $\max M$ .This yields

$$\max M \approx \frac{3.25}{2.25}\,28.1 = 40.6 \text{ kg m}$$

whence, by (9.61c)

$$R_2 = \frac{100\cdot 1.5}{2\pi\cdot 10} + \sqrt{\left(\frac{100\cdot 1.5}{2\pi\cdot 10}\right)^2 + \frac{2\cdot 40.\ \cdot 1.5\cdot 100}{\pi\cdot 10}} \approx 22.3 \text{ cm}\,.$$

If we determine the safety factor against buckling, using this value of R_2, we obtain

$$\nu = 3.23 \approx 3.25\,.$$

The required tube radius is thus $R = R_2 =$ 22.3 cm. The inflation pressure is found from (9.61b) to be

$$p = \omega\, p_{\min} = \omega\left[\frac{P}{\pi R^2} + \frac{2\max M}{\pi R^3}\right] =$$

$$= 1.5\left[\frac{100}{\pi(22.3)^2} + \frac{2\cdot 4060}{\pi(22.3)^3}\right] = 0.447 \text{ kg/cm}^2 = 0.447 \text{ atm.}$$

9.4.3 *Static Stability*

If the load is uniformly distributed along the edge, or if its resultant acts only at the lower half of the tube, no problem of static stability arises. Whenever static instability is liable to cause displacements of the point of action of forces in the direction in which the latter are acting, we have to consider also the static stability of the system, unless overturning can be prevented by suitable anchoring. Since the internal pressure has no stabilizing effect in this case, we can apply the results obtained for ordinary rods. We shall consider the most unfavorable case (Figure 9.8) in which

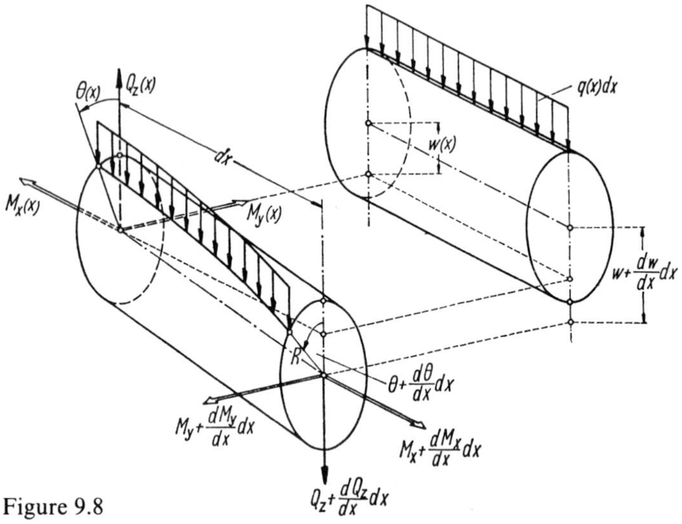

Figure 9.8

the load is distributed along a line at the vertex of the tube. The condition of equilibrium with respect to the torsional moments is

$$\frac{d\,M_x}{d\,x}\,d\,x + q\,(x)\,d\,x \cdot R \sin\Theta = 0\,,$$

$$\frac{d\,M_x}{d\,x} + q\,(x)\,R\sin\Theta = 0\,. \tag{9.63a}$$

We combine this relationship with the expression obtained from (7.47f), namely

$$M_x\,(x) = G_{x\vartheta}\,J_p\,\frac{d\,\Theta}{d\,x} = 2\,\pi\,R^3\,D_{x\vartheta}\,\frac{d\,\Theta}{d\,x}\,, \tag{9.63b}$$

and obtain

$$\frac{d^2\,\Theta}{d\,x^2} + \frac{q\,(x)}{2\,\pi\,R^2\,D_{x\vartheta}}\sin\Theta = 0\,. \tag{9.63c}$$

Writing $\sin\Theta \approx \Theta$, this leads to

$$\frac{d^2\,\Theta}{d\,x^2} + \frac{q\,(x)}{2\,\pi\,R^2\,D_{x\vartheta}}\,\Theta\,(x) = 0\,. \tag{9.63d}$$

For the particular case of a uniformly distributed load $q\,(x) = q_0$, we have for $\xi = x/l$:

$$\frac{d^2\,\Theta}{d\,\xi^2} + \frac{q_0\,l^2}{2\,\pi\,R^2\,D_{x\vartheta}}\,\Theta\,(x) = 0 \tag{9.64}$$

for which the solution is

$$\Theta\,(\xi) = C_1\cos\lambda\,\xi + C_2\sin\lambda\,\xi\,,\qquad \lambda = \frac{l}{R}\sqrt{\frac{q_0}{2\,\pi\,D_{x\vartheta}}}\,. \tag{9.65}$$

To determine the integration constants and the first eigenvalue (the critical overturning load) we must establish the boundary conditions. We consider the following cases:

a) Tube supported irrotatably (e.g., built-in, supported in a fork bearing): $\Theta = 0$.

b) Tube end freely rotatable: $M_x = 0$, i.e., $d\,\Theta/d\,x = 0$.

1) Tube built-in at $x = 0\ (\xi = 0)$ and free at $x = l\ (\xi = 1)$: The boundary conditions $\Theta\,(0) = 0$, $\Theta'\,(1) = 0$ yield $C_1 = 0$. Assuming $C_2 \neq 0$, i.e., the possibility of overturning, we obtain

$$\cos\lambda = 0\,,\qquad \text{i.e.,}\qquad \lambda = \lambda_n = \frac{2\,n - 1}{2}\,\pi\,.$$

The smallest value $\lambda_{kr} = \lambda_1 = \pi/2$ corresponds to the distributed load

$$q_{0\,kr} = 2\,\pi\,D_{x\vartheta}\left(\frac{R}{l}\right)^2\lambda_{kr}{}^2 = \frac{\pi^3}{2}\,D_{x\vartheta}\left(\frac{R}{l}\right)^2, \tag{9.66}$$

which determines the static stability.

2) Tube supported irrotatably at both ends: the boundary conditions $\Theta\,(0) = 0$, $\Theta\,(1) = 0$ yield $C_1 = 0$, and, assuming again $C_2 \neq 0$

$$\sin\lambda = 0 \qquad \text{i.e.,}\qquad \lambda = \lambda_n = n\,\pi\,.$$

The smallest value $\lambda_{kr} = \lambda_1 = \pi$ corresponds to a distributed load

$$q_{0\,kr} = 2\,\pi^3\,D_{x\vartheta}\left(\frac{R}{l}\right)^2. \tag{9.67}$$

which is four times the value obtained for the girder fixed at one end. For a first approximation $D_{x\vartheta} = D_x/10 \approx 10$ **kg/cm** we obtain from (9.66)

$$q_{0\,kr} \approx 155\left(\frac{R}{l}\right)^2 [\text{kg/cm}]\,.$$

For $R/l = 1/10 = 0.1$ this yields $q_{0\,kr} = 1.55$ kg/cm. For pneumatic girders such loads must be considered to be very high; hence, the static stability need not in general be taken into account when dimensioning such structures. When, however, the rigidity in shear is very small, static stability should also be considered.

10 SLIGHTLY CURVED TUBES (TUBULAR ARCHES)

10.1 General Observations

If the curvature of the tube axis is sufficiently small, we can obtain satisfactory approximations for the stresses and deformations by applying the results obtained for straight tubular girders. In particular the deformations of slender tube arches coincide in the mean, and under certain conditions even exactly, with those obtained by the theory of slightly curved rods. We can thus apply the entire theory of the statics of rods to the problem under consideration. Before entering into details of the theory of tube arches we shall prove, using the equilibrium conditions, that the membrane loads of the tube arch can be obtained from the equilibrium conditions for straight tubes when the curvature of the arch is slight. This means that there is, in fact, a transition to the results obtained for straight tubes.

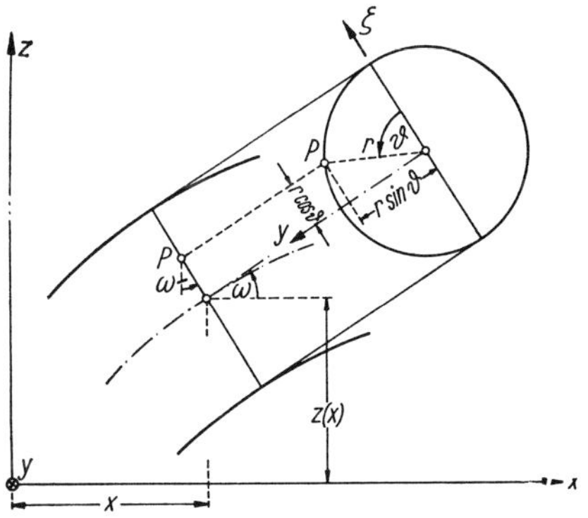

Figure 10.1

We consider a toroid in which the axis is an arbitrary curve $z = z(x)$. We then have

$\operatorname{tg} \omega = z'(x)$, $\sin \omega = z'/\sqrt{1+z'^2}$, $\cos \omega = 1/\sqrt{1+z'^2}$ (Fig.10.1)

whence $\mathfrak{r}_P = \{x_P; y_P; z_P\} =$

$$= \{x - r\cos\vartheta \sin\omega\,;\, r\sin\vartheta\,;\, z(x) + r\cos\vartheta\cos\omega\} = \left\{x - \frac{r\cos\vartheta\, z'}{\sqrt{1+z'^2}}\,;\, r\sin\vartheta\,;\, z + \frac{r\cos\vartheta}{\sqrt{1+z'^2}}\right\} = \mathfrak{r}(x,\vartheta), \tag{10.1}$$

Putting $\alpha = x$ $\beta = \vartheta$, and

$\varkappa = \dfrac{z''}{[1+z'^2]^{3/2}}$, we obtain

$$\mathfrak{r}_\alpha = \mathfrak{r}_x = (1 - \varkappa r\cos\vartheta)\{1; 0; z'\},$$

$$|\mathfrak{r}_\alpha| = \sqrt{g_{\alpha\alpha}} = (1 - \varkappa r\cos\vartheta)\sqrt{1+z'^2},$$

$$\mathfrak{r}_{\alpha\alpha} = \mathfrak{r}_{xx} = \{-\varkappa' r\cos\vartheta\,; 0\,; z'' - r(\varkappa' z' + \varkappa z'')\cos\vartheta\},$$

$$\mathfrak{r}_{\alpha\beta} = \mathfrak{r}_{\beta\alpha} = \mathfrak{r}_{x\vartheta} = \varkappa r\sin\vartheta\,\{1; 0; z'\},$$

$$\mathfrak{r}_\beta = \mathfrak{r}_\vartheta = \left\{\frac{r\sin\vartheta\, z'}{\sqrt{1+z'^2}}\,;\, r\cos\vartheta\,;\, -\frac{r\sin\vartheta}{\sqrt{1+z'^2}}\right\},$$

$$|\mathfrak{r}_\beta| = \sqrt{g_{\beta\beta}} = r\,, \quad \mathfrak{r}_\alpha \mathfrak{r}_\beta = g_{\alpha\beta} = 0\,,$$

$$\mathfrak{r}_{\beta\beta} = \mathfrak{r}_{\vartheta\vartheta} = \left\{\frac{r\cos\vartheta\, z'}{\sqrt{1+z'^2}}\,;\, -r\sin\vartheta\,;\, -\frac{r\cos\vartheta}{\sqrt{1+z'^2}}\right\},$$

whence, by (1.21)

$$\omega_\alpha{}^{(\alpha)} = -\,\omega_\beta{}^{(\beta)} = 0\,, \quad \omega_\beta{}^{(\alpha)} = -\frac{1}{r}\,\frac{\varkappa r\cos\vartheta}{1 - \varkappa r\cos\vartheta}\,,$$

$$\omega_\gamma{}^{(\alpha)} = -\frac{1}{r}\,\frac{\varkappa r\sin\vartheta}{1 - \varkappa r\cos\vartheta}\,, \quad \omega_\alpha{}^{(\beta)} = -\frac{1}{r}\,, \quad \omega_\gamma{}^{(\beta)} = 0\,.$$

The equilibrium conditions (2.5) yield

$$\begin{aligned}
&\frac{\partial}{\partial x}(r\,n_x) + \frac{1}{(1-\varkappa r\cos\vartheta)\sqrt{1+z'^2}}\,\frac{\partial}{\partial\vartheta}\left[(1-\varkappa r\cos\vartheta)^2 \times\right.\\
&\qquad \left.\times\,(1+z'^2)\,n_{x\vartheta}\right] + p_x\, r\,(1-\varkappa r\cos\vartheta)\sqrt{1+z'^2} = 0\,,\\
&\frac{\partial}{\partial x}(r\,n_{x\vartheta}) + \frac{\partial}{\partial\vartheta}\left[(1-\varkappa r\cos\vartheta)\sqrt{1+z'^2}\,n_\vartheta\right] - \\
&\qquad -\,\varkappa r\sin\vartheta\sqrt{1+z'^2}\,n_x + p_\vartheta\, r\,(1-\varkappa r\cos\vartheta)\sqrt{1+z'^2} = 0\,,\\
&\frac{\varkappa r\cos\vartheta}{1-\varkappa r\cos\vartheta}\,\frac{n_x}{r} - \frac{n_\vartheta}{r} + p_r = 0\,.
\end{aligned} \tag{10.2a-c}$$

For $\varkappa r \ll 1$ and $d\,s = \sqrt{1+z'^2}\,d\,x$ we obtain the system of equations

$$r\,\frac{\partial n_x}{\partial s} + \frac{\partial n_{x\vartheta}}{\partial\vartheta} + r\,p_x = 0\,,$$

$$r\,\frac{\partial n_{x\vartheta}}{\partial s} + \frac{\partial n_\vartheta}{\partial\vartheta} + r\,p_\vartheta = 0\,, \quad n_\vartheta = r\,p_r$$

which is identical to the equilibrium conditions for a straight tube [cf. (7.1)] if we remember that the coordinate x, measured along the axis of the straight tube, is now replaced by the arch length

$s = \int\limits_0^x \sqrt{1+z'^2}\,d\,x$ measured along the center line of the tube.

Let us consider in particular the case of loading by internal pressure. We put $p_x = p_\vartheta = 0$ and $p_r = p$ in (10.2). The sectional loads are then found to be

$$n_x = \frac{p\,r}{2}\,, \quad n_{x\vartheta} = 0\,, \quad n_\vartheta = \frac{p\,r}{2}\,\frac{2-\varkappa r\cos\vartheta}{1-\varkappa r\cos\vartheta}\,. \tag{10.3a-c}$$

For small curvatures $(\varkappa r \ll 1)$ we obtain

$$n_x = \frac{p\,r}{2}\,, \quad n_{x\vartheta} = 0\,, \quad n_\vartheta \approx p\,r\,, \tag{10.4a-c}$$

which is identical to the results for a straight tube. Just as for the rod, the marked flexibility of the system requires as far as possible the application of the exact theory of arches, which takes into account the deformations when determining the sectional loads. An exact analysis will not, however, lead to solvable relationships. We have, therefore, to restrict ourselves to approximations obtained by linearizing the exact equations or by energy considerations.

10.2 Displacement Relationships for a Plane Arch

10.2.1 *General Observations*

The available relationships are:

a) the equilibrium conditions;

b) the load—deformation laws;

c) the relationships between displacements and deformations.

With the aid of (c) we can determine from (b) the sectional loads as functions of the displacements. Inserting the result into (a), we obtain the displacement equations for the problem concerned. In the following three subsections we shall discuss the relationships referred to under (a)-(c); in Subsection 10.2.5 the results will be used to formulate the displacement equations.

10.2.2 *Geometry of the Arch* (Figure 10.2)

We define the undeformed axis of the arch by $\mathfrak{r} = \mathfrak{r}(t)$, where t is a scalar parameter. The corresponding arc element $d\,s$, and the

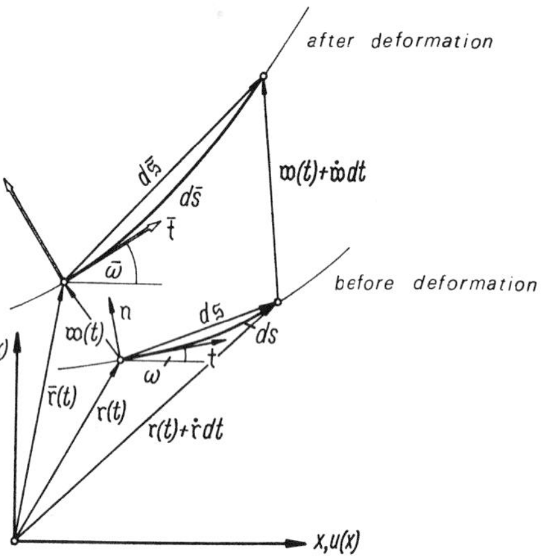

Figure 10.2

tangent vector $d\mathfrak{t}$ to the arc, are, respectively,

$$d\,s = |\,\dot{\mathfrak{r}}\,|\,dt = \sqrt{\dot{\mathfrak{r}}^2}\,d\,t\,, \quad \mathfrak{t} = \frac{\dot{\mathfrak{r}}}{|\,\dot{\mathfrak{r}}\,|} = \mathfrak{r}'\,, \tag{10.5a, b}$$

where differentiation with respect to t and s are denoted by a dot and a prime respectively. The Frenet formulas for the plane arch are

$$\frac{d\,\mathfrak{t}}{d\,s} = \mathfrak{t}' = \varkappa\,\mathfrak{n}\,, \quad \frac{d\,\mathfrak{n}}{d\,s} = \mathfrak{n}' = -\,\varkappa\,\mathfrak{t} \tag{10.5c, d}$$

where $\mathfrak{n}$ is the unit (principal) normal vector, pointing toward the center of curvature. Since

$$\mathfrak{n} = \frac{\dot{\mathfrak{t}}}{|\,\dot{\mathfrak{t}}\,|} = \frac{\dot{\mathfrak{r}}^2\,\ddot{\mathfrak{r}} - \dot{\mathfrak{r}}\,(\dot{\mathfrak{r}}\,\ddot{\mathfrak{r}})}{\sqrt{\dot{\mathfrak{r}}^2}\,\sqrt{\dot{\mathfrak{r}}^2\,\ddot{\mathfrak{r}}^2 - (\dot{\mathfrak{r}}\,\ddot{\mathfrak{r}})^2}} = \frac{\mathfrak{t}'}{|\,\mathfrak{t}'\,|} = \frac{\mathfrak{t}'}{\sqrt{\mathfrak{t}'^2}} = \frac{\mathfrak{r}''}{\sqrt{\mathfrak{r}''^2}} \tag{10.5e}$$

the curvature of the arc is

$$\varkappa = \sqrt{\mathfrak{t}'^2} = \sqrt{\mathfrak{r}''^2} = \frac{1}{\sqrt{\dot{\mathfrak{r}}^2}}\sqrt{\dot{\mathfrak{t}}^2} = \frac{1}{\sqrt{\dot{\mathfrak{r}}^2}^{\,3}}\sqrt{\dot{\mathfrak{r}}^2\,\ddot{\mathfrak{r}}^2 - (\dot{\mathfrak{r}}\,\ddot{\mathfrak{r}})^2}\;. \tag{10.5f}$$

Denoting the displacement vector by $\mathfrak{w}$, we can describe the arc after deformation by

$$\bar{\mathfrak{r}}\,(t) = \mathfrak{r} + \mathfrak{w}\,. \tag{10.6a}$$

The arc element corresponding to an increment dt is then

$$d\,\bar{s} = |\,\dot{\bar{\mathfrak{r}}}\,|\,dt = \sqrt{(\dot{\mathfrak{r}} + \dot{\mathfrak{w}})^2}\,d\,t = \tag{10.6b}$$

$$= \sqrt{\dot{\mathfrak{r}}^2}\,d\,t\,\sqrt{1 + 2\,\frac{\dot{\mathfrak{r}}\,\dot{\mathfrak{w}}}{\dot{\mathfrak{r}}^2} + \frac{\dot{\mathfrak{w}}^2}{\dot{\mathfrak{r}}^2}} = d\,s\,\sqrt{1 + 2\,\frac{\dot{\mathfrak{r}}\,\dot{\mathfrak{w}}}{\dot{\mathfrak{r}}^2} + \frac{\dot{\mathfrak{w}}^2}{\dot{\mathfrak{r}}^2}}\;.$$

The extension of the arc element is therefore

$$\varepsilon = \frac{d\,\bar{s} - d\,s}{d\,s} = \sqrt{1 + 2\,\frac{\dot{\mathfrak{r}}\,\dot{\mathfrak{w}}}{\dot{\mathfrak{r}}^2} + \frac{\dot{\mathfrak{w}}^2}{\dot{\mathfrak{r}}^2}} - 1 = \tag{10.6c}$$

$$= \sqrt{1 + 2\,\mathfrak{r}'\,\mathfrak{w}' + \mathfrak{w}'^2} - 1\;.$$

The tangent and normal vectors of the deformed arc are correspondingly

$$\bar{\mathfrak{t}} = \frac{d\,\bar{\mathfrak{r}}}{d\,\bar{s}} = \frac{1}{1+\varepsilon}\,\frac{d\,\bar{\mathfrak{r}}}{d\,s} = \frac{\mathfrak{r}' + \mathfrak{w}'}{1+\varepsilon} = \frac{\dot{\mathfrak{r}} + \dot{\mathfrak{w}}}{\sqrt{(\dot{\mathfrak{r}} + \dot{\mathfrak{w}})^2}}\,, \tag{10.6d, e}$$

$$\bar{\mathfrak{n}} = \frac{\dfrac{d\,\bar{\mathfrak{t}}}{d\,\bar{s}}}{\left|\dfrac{d\,\bar{\mathfrak{t}}}{d\,\bar{s}}\right|} = \frac{\dfrac{d\,\bar{\mathfrak{t}}}{d\,s}}{\left|\dfrac{d\,\bar{\mathfrak{t}}}{d\,s}\right|} = \frac{\bar{\mathfrak{t}}'}{\sqrt{\bar{\mathfrak{t}}'^2}}\;.$$

The curvature of the deformed arc is thus, according to the Frenet formula,

$$\frac{d\,\bar{\mathfrak{t}}}{d\,\bar{s}} = \frac{1}{1+\varepsilon}\,\frac{d\,\bar{\mathfrak{t}}}{d\,s} = \frac{1}{1+\varepsilon}\,\bar{\mathfrak{t}}' = \bar{\varkappa}\,\bar{\mathfrak{n}} = \bar{\varkappa}\,\frac{\bar{\mathfrak{t}}'}{\sqrt{\bar{\mathfrak{t}}'^2}}\,,$$

or directly from (10.5f) by replacing in it $\mathfrak{r}$ by $\bar{\mathfrak{r}} = \mathfrak{r} + \mathfrak{w}$,

$$\bar{\varkappa} = \frac{1}{1+\varepsilon}\,\sqrt{\bar{\mathfrak{t}}'^2} = \tag{10.6f}$$

$$= \frac{1}{\sqrt{(\dot{\mathfrak{r}} + \dot{\mathfrak{w}})^2}^{\,3}}\,\sqrt{(\dot{\mathfrak{r}} + \dot{\mathfrak{w}})^2\,(\ddot{\mathfrak{r}} + \ddot{\mathfrak{w}})^2 - \left[(\dot{\mathfrak{r}} + \dot{\mathfrak{w}})\,(\ddot{\mathfrak{r}} + \ddot{\mathfrak{w}})\right]^2}\;.$$

If the angle between the tangent to the arc and the x-axis before deformation is denoted by ω, and the angle of bending by $\Delta\omega$, then the angle between the tangent and the x-axis after deformation is $\bar{\omega} = \omega + \Delta\,\omega$. The bending angle is obtained from $d\,\mathfrak{s}\,d\,\bar{\mathfrak{s}} = |\,d\,\mathfrak{s}\,|\;|\,d\,\bar{\mathfrak{s}}\,|\,\cos\Delta\,\omega = d\,s^2\,(1+\varepsilon)\cos\Delta\,\omega$ in the form

$$\left.\begin{aligned}
\cos\Delta\,\omega &= \frac{d\,\mathfrak{s}\,d\,\bar{\mathfrak{s}}}{d\,s^2\,(1+\varepsilon)} = \frac{\mathfrak{t}\,d\,s\,\bar{\mathfrak{t}}\,d\,s\,(1+\varepsilon)}{d\,s^2\,(1+\varepsilon)} = \mathfrak{t}\,\bar{\mathfrak{t}} = \\
&= \frac{\mathfrak{r}'\,(\mathfrak{r}' + \mathfrak{w}')}{1+\varepsilon} = \frac{\dot{\mathfrak{r}}}{\sqrt{\dot{\mathfrak{r}}^2}}\,\frac{\dot{\mathfrak{r}} + \dot{\mathfrak{w}}}{\sqrt{(\dot{\mathfrak{r}} + \dot{\mathfrak{w}})^2}}\,, \\
\sin\Delta\,\omega &= \sqrt{1 - \cos^2\Delta\,\omega} = \\
&= \sqrt{\frac{\mathfrak{r}'^2\,\mathfrak{w}'^2 - (\mathfrak{r}'\,\mathfrak{w}')^2}{(1+\varepsilon)^2}} = \frac{1}{\sqrt{\dot{\mathfrak{r}}^2}}\,\sqrt{\frac{\dot{\mathfrak{r}}^2\,\dot{\mathfrak{w}}^2 - (\dot{\mathfrak{r}}\,\dot{\mathfrak{w}})^2}{(\dot{\mathfrak{r}} + \dot{\mathfrak{w}})^2}}\,.
\end{aligned}\right\} \tag{10.6g}$$

If we select as parameter the coordinate x ,

$$\mathfrak{r} = \mathfrak{r}\,(x) = x\,\mathfrak{e}_x + z\,(x)\,\mathfrak{e}_z = \{x;\,z\,(x)\}$$

and express the displacement vector in components of the x, z system

$$\mathfrak{w} = \mathfrak{w}\,(x) = u\,(x)\,\mathfrak{e}_x + v\,(x)\,\mathfrak{e}_z = \{u\,(x);\,v\,(x)\}$$

we have, denoting differentiation with respect to x by a prime,

$$\dot{\mathfrak{r}} = \mathfrak{r}_x = \{1;\,z'\}\,,\ \dot{\mathfrak{r}}^2 = \mathfrak{r}_x^2 = 1 + z'^2\,,\ \dot{\mathfrak{w}} = \mathfrak{w}_x = \{u'\,(x)\,;\,v'\,(x)\}\,,$$

$$\dot{\mathfrak{w}}^2 = u'^2 + v'^2\,,\quad \dot{\mathfrak{r}}\,\dot{\mathfrak{w}} = u' + z'\,v'\,.$$

The extension is thus

$$\varepsilon = \sqrt{1 + \frac{2}{1+z'^2}\left[u' + z'\,v' + \frac{1}{2}\,(u'^2 + v'^2)\right]} - 1 = \tag{10.7a}$$

$$= \frac{1}{\sqrt{1+z'^2}}\,\sqrt{(1+u')^2 + (z'+v')^2} - 1\,,$$

also,

$$\dot{\mathfrak{r}} + \dot{\mathfrak{w}} = \mathfrak{r}_x + \mathfrak{w}_x = \{1 + u'; z' + v'\},$$

$$(\dot{\mathfrak{r}} + \dot{\mathfrak{w}})^2 = (1 + u')^2 + (z' + v')^2,$$

$$\ddot{\mathfrak{r}} + \ddot{\mathfrak{w}} = \mathfrak{r}_{xx} + \mathfrak{w}_{xx} = \{u''; z'' + v''\},$$

$$(\ddot{\mathfrak{r}} + \ddot{\mathfrak{w}})^2 = u''^2 + (z'' + v'')^2,$$

$$(\dot{\mathfrak{r}} + \dot{\mathfrak{w}})(\ddot{\mathfrak{r}} + \ddot{\mathfrak{w}}) = u''(1 + u') + (z' + v')(z'' + v'').$$

The curvatures are thus

$$\varkappa = \frac{z''}{[1 + z'^2]^{3/2}}, \quad \bar{\varkappa} = \frac{(1 + u')(z'' + v'') - u''(z' + v')}{[(1 + u')^2 + (z' + v')^2]^{3/2}} = \frac{(1 + u')(z'' + v'') - u''(z' + v')}{[1 + z'^2]^{3/2}(1 + \varepsilon)^3}, \tag{10.7b}$$

their difference being

$$\bar{\varkappa} - \varkappa = \frac{1}{[1 + z'^2]^{3/2}}\left[\frac{(1 + u')(z'' + v'') - u''(z' + v')}{(1 + \varepsilon)^3} - z''\right]. \tag{10.7c}$$

10.2.3 *Sectional Load—Deformation Relationships* (Figure 10.3)

We use Bernoulli's hypothesis and Hooke's law. The results of Section 9.2 are then exact for certain types of loading, being valid

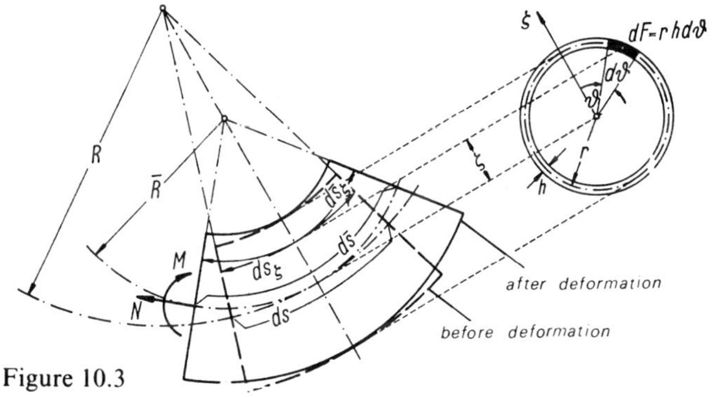

Figure 10.3

in the mean for arbitrary loads. By Bernoulli's hypothesis, neglecting shear deformations, we can assume that an arc element ds becomes deformed as shown in Figure 10.3. A fiber, located at distance ζ from the middle surface and having the length

$$ds_\zeta = ds\left(1 - \frac{\zeta}{R}\right) = ds\,(1 - \varkappa\zeta), \quad \varkappa = 1/R \tag{10.8a}$$

is, after deformation, extended to length

$$d\bar{s}_\zeta = d\bar{s}\left(1 - \frac{\zeta}{\bar{R}}\right) = d\bar{s}\,(1 - \bar{\varkappa}\zeta) = ds\,(1 + \varepsilon)(1 - \bar{\varkappa}\zeta) \tag{10.8b}$$

where $\varepsilon = (d\bar{s} - ds)/ds$ denotes the extension of the fibers $\zeta = 0$.

The extension of an arbitrary fiber is thus

$$\varepsilon_s(\zeta) = \frac{d\bar{s}_\zeta - ds_\zeta}{ds_\zeta} = \frac{(1 + \varepsilon)(1 - \bar{\varkappa}\zeta) - (1 - \varkappa\zeta)}{1 - \varkappa\zeta} = (1 + \varepsilon)\frac{1 - \bar{\varkappa}\zeta}{1 - \varkappa\zeta} - 1 \tag{10.8c}$$

being expressed through the extension ε of the center fiber and the curvatures $\varkappa$ and $\bar{\varkappa}$. Applying Hooke's law, we obtain

$$\sigma_s(\zeta) = E\,\varepsilon_s(\zeta) = E\left[(1 + \varepsilon)\frac{1 - \bar{\varkappa}\zeta}{1 - \varkappa\zeta} - 1\right]. \tag{10.8d}$$

Summing the normal loads over the section to form the normal force N and the bending moment M, we obtain

$$N = \int_{(F)} \sigma\,dF = E\left[(1 + \varepsilon)\int_{(F)} \frac{1 - \bar{\varkappa}\zeta}{1 - \varkappa\zeta}\,dF - F\right],$$

$$M = -\int_{(F)} \sigma\zeta\,dF = -E\left[(1 + \varepsilon)\int_{(F)} \frac{\zeta(1 - \bar{\varkappa}\zeta)}{1 - \varkappa\zeta}\,dF - \int_{(F)} \zeta\,dF\right]. \tag{10.9a, b}$$

Writing

$$F = 2\pi r h, \quad \int_{(F)} \zeta\,dF = 0, \quad \int_{(F)} \frac{\zeta^2\,dF}{1 - \varkappa\zeta} = \frac{1}{\varkappa}\int_{(F)}\left(\frac{\zeta}{1 - \varkappa\zeta} - \zeta\right)dF =$$

$$= \frac{1}{\varkappa}\int_{(F)} \frac{\zeta\,dF}{1 - \varkappa\zeta} = \frac{1}{\varkappa^2}\int_{(F)}\left(\frac{1}{1 - \varkappa\zeta} - 1\right)dF = \frac{1}{\varkappa^2}\left(\int_{(F)} \frac{dF}{1 - \varkappa\zeta} - F\right),$$

$$\int_{(F)} \frac{dF}{1 - \varkappa\zeta} = rh\int_0^{2\pi} \frac{d\vartheta}{1 - \varkappa r\cos\vartheta} = rh\frac{2\pi}{\sqrt{1 - \varkappa^2 r^2}} = \frac{F}{\sqrt{1 - \varkappa^2 r^2}}$$

the final result is

$$N = EF\left\{(1 + \varepsilon)\left[\frac{1}{\sqrt{1 - \varkappa^2 r^2}} - \frac{\bar{\varkappa}}{\varkappa}\left(\frac{1}{\sqrt{1 - \varkappa^2 r^2}} - 1\right)\right] - 1\right\},$$

$$M = \frac{EF}{\varkappa}(1 + \varepsilon)\left(\frac{1}{\sqrt{1 - \varkappa^2 r^2}} - 1\right)\left(\frac{\bar{\varkappa}}{\varkappa} - 1\right). \tag{10.9c, d}$$

Since we consider only the case of small initial curvatures ($\varkappa r = r/R \ll 1$), we can write

$$\frac{1}{\sqrt{1 - \varkappa^2 r^2}} \approx 1 + \frac{1}{2}\varkappa^2 r^2$$

which, inserted into (10.9c, d), yields

$$N = EF\left\{\varepsilon + (1 + \varepsilon)\varkappa\frac{r^2}{2}(\varkappa - \bar{\varkappa})\right\} = D_x\bar{F}\varepsilon - D_x\bar{J}\varkappa(1 + \varepsilon)(\bar{\varkappa} - \varkappa) = D_x\bar{F}\varepsilon - \varkappa M,$$

$$M = EF(1 + \varepsilon)\frac{r^2}{2}(\bar{\varkappa} - \varkappa) = D_x\bar{J}(1 + \varepsilon)(\bar{\varkappa} - \varkappa), \tag{10.10a, b}$$

where

$$D_x = Eh, \quad \bar{F} = 2\pi r, \quad \bar{J} = \bar{F}\frac{r^2}{2} = \pi r^3 \tag{10.10c}$$

10.2.4 *Equilibrium Conditions* (Figure 10.4)

Denoting the load acting on a unit length of the deformed arc by $\bar{\mathfrak{p}}$, we obtain from Figure 10.4 the equilibrium conditions for the forces:

$$\frac{d}{d\bar{s}}(N\bar{\mathfrak{t}})\,d\bar{s} - \frac{d}{d\bar{s}}(Q\bar{\mathfrak{n}})\,d\bar{s} + \bar{\mathfrak{p}}\,d\bar{s} = 0 \tag{10.11a}$$

and for the moments:

$$\frac{dM}{d\bar{s}}d\bar{s} - Q\,d\bar{s} = 0 \quad \text{or}, \quad Q = \frac{dM}{d\bar{s}} \tag{10.11b}$$

Eliminating Q between (10.11a) and (10.11b), and noting that $d\bar{s} = (1+\varepsilon)\,ds$, we obtain

$$\frac{d}{ds}(N\bar{\mathfrak{t}}) - \frac{d}{ds}\left[\frac{dM}{d\bar{s}}\bar{\mathfrak{n}}\right] + \bar{\mathfrak{p}}(1+\varepsilon) = 0\,. \qquad (10.11c)$$

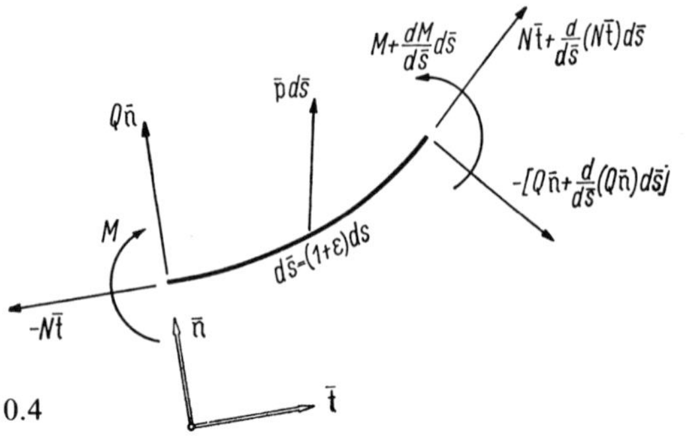

Figure 10.4

Integration of this equation yields the constant vector $\mathfrak{A}$, which defines the reaction at the left end of the arc (Figure 10.5):

$$N\bar{\mathfrak{t}} - \frac{dM}{d\bar{s}}\bar{\mathfrak{n}} + \int_{s=0}^{s}\bar{\mathfrak{p}}(1+\varepsilon)\,ds + \mathfrak{A} = 0\,, \qquad (10.11d)$$

This is the equilibrium condition for the part of the arch between the support and the section s. Scalar multiplication by $\bar{\mathfrak{t}}$ and $\bar{\mathfrak{n}}$ yields, respectively, the components

$$N = -\left(\mathfrak{A} + \int_{s=0}^{s}\bar{\mathfrak{p}}(1+\varepsilon)\,ds\right)\bar{\mathfrak{t}} \qquad (10.11e)$$

$$\frac{dM}{d\bar{s}}(=Q) = \left(\mathfrak{A} + \int_{s=0}^{s}\bar{\mathfrak{p}}(1+\varepsilon)\,ds\right)\bar{\mathfrak{n}}\,. \qquad (10.11f)$$

Integrating (10.11f) we obtain

$$M = M_A + \int_{\bar{s}=0}^{\bar{s}}\left(\mathfrak{A} + \int_{s=0}^{s}\bar{\mathfrak{p}}(1+\varepsilon)\,ds\right)\bar{\mathfrak{n}}\,d\bar{s} = M_A + \int_{\bar{s}=0}^{\bar{s}}\mathfrak{B}\,\bar{\mathfrak{n}}\,d\bar{s}\,,$$

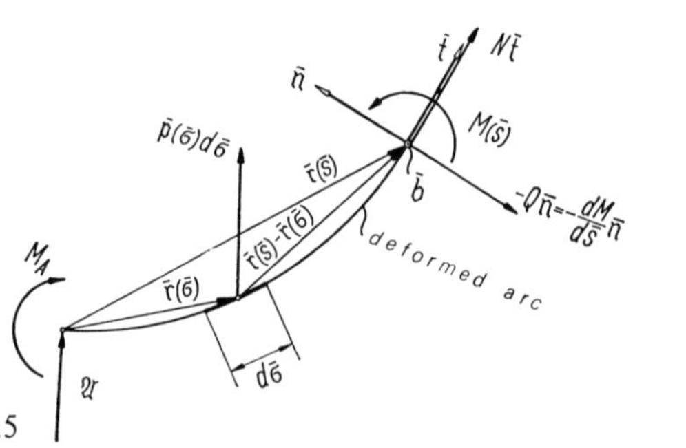

Figure 10.5

where M_A is a constant, defining the bending moment at the the built-in end. We define the unit binormal vector $\bar{\mathfrak{b}}$ of the deformed arc by

$\bar{\mathfrak{b}} = \bar{\mathfrak{t}} \times \bar{\mathfrak{n}}$ (hence also $\bar{\mathfrak{b}} \times \bar{\mathfrak{t}} = \bar{\mathfrak{n}}$);

we then obtain

$$\mathfrak{B}\,\bar{\mathfrak{n}}\,d\bar{s} = \mathfrak{B}(\bar{\mathfrak{b}} \times \bar{\mathfrak{t}})\,d\bar{s} = \bar{\mathfrak{b}}(\bar{\mathfrak{t}}\,d\bar{s} \times \mathfrak{B}) = \bar{\mathfrak{b}}(d\bar{\mathfrak{s}} \times \mathfrak{B}) = \bar{\mathfrak{b}}(d\bar{\mathfrak{r}} \times \mathfrak{B})\,.$$

Since for a plane arc (i.e., lying in the x, z-plane), $\bar{\mathfrak{b}} = \text{const} = -\mathfrak{e}_y$ we have

$$M = M_A + \bar{\mathfrak{b}}\int_{\bar{s}=0}^{\bar{s}} d\bar{\mathfrak{r}} \times \left(\mathfrak{A} + \int_{\bar{s}=0}^{\bar{s}}\bar{\mathfrak{p}}\,d\bar{s}\right) =$$

$$= M_A + \bar{\mathfrak{b}}\left[\bar{\mathfrak{r}} \times \mathfrak{A} + \int_{\bar{s}=0}^{\bar{s}} d\bar{\mathfrak{r}} \times \left(\int_{\bar{s}=0}^{\bar{s}}\bar{\mathfrak{p}}\,d\bar{s}\right)\right].$$

The integral can be simplified as follows:

$$\int_{\bar{s}=0}^{\bar{s}} d\bar{\mathfrak{r}} \times \left(\int_{\bar{s}=0}^{\bar{s}}\bar{\mathfrak{p}}\,d\bar{s}\right) = \int_{\bar{s}=0}^{\bar{s}}\frac{d\bar{\mathfrak{r}}}{d\bar{s}} \times \left(\int_{\bar{s}=0}^{\bar{s}}\bar{\mathfrak{p}}\,d\bar{s}\right)d\bar{s} =$$

$$= \bar{\mathfrak{r}}(\bar{s}) \times \int_{\bar{\sigma}=0}^{\bar{s}}\bar{\mathfrak{p}}(\bar{\sigma})\,d\bar{\sigma} - \int_{\bar{\sigma}=0}^{\bar{s}}\bar{\mathfrak{r}}(\bar{\sigma}) \times \bar{\mathfrak{p}}(\bar{\sigma})\,d\bar{\sigma} =$$

$$= \int_{\bar{\sigma}=0}^{\bar{s}}\left[\bar{\mathfrak{r}}(\bar{s}) - \bar{\mathfrak{r}}(\bar{\sigma})\right] \times \bar{\mathfrak{p}}(\bar{\sigma})\,d\bar{\sigma} =$$

$$= \int_{\sigma=0}^{s}\left[\mathfrak{r}(s) - \mathfrak{r}(\sigma) + \mathfrak{w}(s) - \mathfrak{w}(\sigma)\right] \times \bar{\mathfrak{p}}(1+\varepsilon)\,d\sigma\,.$$

The moment is thus finally

$$M = M_A + \bar{\mathfrak{b}}\left[\bar{\mathfrak{r}} \times \mathfrak{A} + \int_{\bar{\sigma}=0}^{\bar{s}}\left[\bar{\mathfrak{r}}(\bar{s}) - \bar{\mathfrak{r}}(\bar{\sigma})\right] \times \bar{\mathfrak{p}}(\bar{\sigma})\,d\bar{\sigma}\right]. \qquad (10.11g)$$

We could have obtained this result directly from Figure 10.5 by considering the equilibrium conditions with respect to moments at section $\bar{s}$. Except for loads due to the pressure of liquids or gases, $\bar{\mathfrak{p}}$ depends directly on ε: $\bar{\mathfrak{p}}(1+\varepsilon) = \mathfrak{p} = \text{const}$. An example is the dead weight: if the latter is g per unit length, we have, before deformation, $dG = g \cdot ds$. During deformation the length of the element becomes $d\bar{s} = ds(1+\varepsilon)$, but its weight remains the same; hence,

$dG = g \cdot ds = \bar{g}(1+\varepsilon)\,ds$, thus $\bar{g}(1+\varepsilon) = g$.

10.2.5 *Equilibrium Equations for the Arch*

We express the sectional loads in (10.11c) and the equivalent integral equations through the deformations in accordance with the sectional load—deformation relationships (10.10a, b). In their turn, the deformations are then expressed through the displacements in accordance with (10.7a, c). The tangent and normal vectors are expressed as functions of the displacements, using (10.6d e). Thus, from (10.11e) and (10.11g), taking into account (10.10), we obtain

$$N = D_x\bar{F}\left(\sqrt{1+2\mathfrak{r}'\mathfrak{w}'+\mathfrak{w}'^2} - 1\right) - \sqrt{\mathfrak{r}''^2}\Big[M_A + \bar{\mathfrak{b}}\Big((\mathfrak{r}+\mathfrak{w}) \times \mathfrak{A} +$$

$$+ \int_{\sigma=0}^{s}\left[\mathfrak{r}(s) - \mathfrak{r}(\sigma) + \mathfrak{w}(s) - \mathfrak{w}(\sigma)\right] \times$$

$$\times\, \bar{\mathfrak{p}}(\sigma)\sqrt{1+2\mathfrak{r}'\mathfrak{w}'+\mathfrak{w}'^2}\,d\sigma\Big)\Big] = -\Big(\mathfrak{A} +$$

$$+ \int_{\sigma=0}^{s}\bar{\mathfrak{p}}(\sigma)\sqrt{1+2\mathfrak{r}'\mathfrak{w}'+\mathfrak{w}'^2}\,d\sigma\Big)\left(\frac{\mathfrak{r}'+\mathfrak{w}'}{\sqrt{1+2\mathfrak{r}'\mathfrak{w}'+\mathfrak{w}'^2}}\right), \qquad (10.12a)$$

$$M = D_x \bar{J} \left[\sqrt{\left(\frac{\mathfrak{r}' + \mathfrak{w}'}{\sqrt{1 + 2\,\mathfrak{r}'\,\mathfrak{w}' + \mathfrak{w}'^2}} \right)'^2} - \right.$$

$$\left. - \sqrt{1 + 2\mathfrak{r}'\,\mathfrak{w}' + \mathfrak{w}'^2}\, \sqrt{\mathfrak{r}''^2} \right] = M_A + \mathfrak{b}\Big[(\mathfrak{r} + \mathfrak{w}) \times \mathfrak{A} +$$

$$+ \int_{\sigma=0}^{s} [\mathfrak{r}(s) - \mathfrak{r}(\sigma) + \mathfrak{w}(s) - \mathfrak{w}(\sigma)] \times$$

$$\times\, \bar{\mathfrak{p}}(\sigma) \sqrt{1 + 2\,\mathfrak{r}'\,\mathfrak{w}' + \mathfrak{w}'^2}\, d\sigma \Big]. \qquad (10.12b)$$

10.2.6 *The Unextended Arch*

For very large rigidities in tension $D_x \bar{F}$, (10.10a) yields $\varepsilon = 0$. We then obtain from (10.7a) $(1 + u')^2 + (z' + v')^2 = 1 + z'^2$, hence $u' = \sqrt{1 - 2\,z'\,v' - v'^2} - 1$

$$u'' = - \frac{(z' + v')\,v'' + z''\,v'}{\sqrt{1 - 2\,z'\,v' - v'^2}}, \qquad (10.13a, b)$$

We have thus found a simple relationship between the vertical and horizontal displacement components. From (10.7c) we obtain the change in curvature

$$\bar{\varkappa} - \varkappa = \frac{1}{[1 + z'^2]^{3/2}} \left[\frac{v''\,(1 + z'^2) + z''\,(1 - z'\,v')}{\sqrt{1 - 2\,z'\,v' - v'^2}} - z'' \right]. \qquad (10.13c)$$

Equating (10.10b) with (10.11g), using $\mathfrak{A} = A_x\,\mathfrak{e}_x + A_z\,\mathfrak{e}_z$, $\mathfrak{p} = \bar{\mathfrak{p}}\,(1 + \varepsilon) = p_x\,\mathfrak{e}_x + p_z\,\mathfrak{e}_z$ and $d\,s = \sqrt{1 + z'^2}\,d\,x$ we obtain

$$M = M_A + A_z(x + u) - A_x(z + v) + \int_{\bar{x}=0}^{x} \Big[p_z\big(x - \bar{x} + u(x) - u(\bar{x})\big) -$$

$$- p_x\big(z(x) - z(\bar{x}) + v(x) - v(\bar{x})\big) \Big] \sqrt{1 + z'^2}\, d\,\bar{x} =$$

$$= \frac{D_x \bar{J}}{[1 + z'^2]^{3/2}} \left[\frac{v''\,(1 + z'^2) + z''\,(1 - z'\,v')}{\sqrt{1 - 2\,z'\,v' - v'^2}} - z'' \right]. \qquad (10.13d)$$

Differentiating (10.13d) with respect to x and using (10.13a) we obtain the following differential equation containing solely the vertical displacement component v:

$$\left\{ \frac{D_x \bar{J}}{[1 + z'^2]^{3/2}} \left[\frac{v''\,(1 + z'^2) + z''\,(1 - z'\,v')}{\sqrt{1 - 2\,z'\,v' - v'^2}} - z'' \right] \right\}' =$$

$$= \left(A_z + \int_{\bar{x}=0}^{x} p_z \sqrt{1 + z'^2}\, d\,\bar{x} \right) \sqrt{1 - 2\,z'\,v' - v'^2} - \qquad (10.13e)$$

$$- \left(A_x + \int_{\bar{x}=0}^{x} p_x \sqrt{1 + z'^2}\, d\,\bar{x} \right) (z' + v').$$

The solution of the system of equations (10.13a, e) contains six integration constants, including A_x and A_z. These suffice to satisfy the boundary conditions. However, the nonlinearity of the differential equations makes their solution almost impossible. Linearization can only be applied in the case of small deformations, though even then an explicit solution can be obtained only for very shallow arches.* This, however, presents no interest in our case. In order to obtain an approximate solution, even in the theory of small deformations, we have to replace the differential equations by equivalent integral equations: these can be obtained by the method of Galerkin, or by the principle of virtual displacements. Before discussing this, we shall summarize the differential equations of the linearized theory.

* F. Dischinger, Elastic and Plastic Deformations of Reinforced-concrete Structures, in particular Arched Bridges. Reprint from *Der Bauingenieur* 1937, 1939.

10.3 Linearized Equations of a Plane Arch

If we expand (10.7a) and (10.7c) (the displacement derivatives being small in comparison with unity), retaining only the constant and linear terms, we obtain

$$\varepsilon \approx \left(1 + \frac{1}{2} \cdot \frac{2}{1 + z'^2} (u' + z'\,v') \right) - 1 = \frac{u' + z'\,v'}{1 + z'^2}, \qquad (10.14a)$$

$$\bar{\varkappa} - \varkappa \approx \frac{1}{[1 + z'^2]^{3/2}} \Big\{ \big[(1 + u')\,(z'' + v'') - u''\,(z' + v') \big] [1 - 3\,\varepsilon] - z'' \Big\}$$

$$\approx \frac{1}{[1 + z'^2]^{3/2}} \Big\{ \big[(1 + u')\,z'' + v'' - u''\,z' \big] [1 - 3\,\varepsilon] - z'' \Big\}$$

$$\approx \frac{1}{[1 + z'^2]^{3/2}} \Big\{ (1 + u')\,z'' + v'' - u''\,z' - 3\,\varepsilon\,z'' - z'' \Big\} =$$

$$= \frac{1}{[1 + z'^2]^{3/2}} \left[v'' - z'^2 \left(\frac{u'}{z'} \right)' - 3\,\varepsilon\,z'' \right].$$

Since, by (10.14a)

$$\frac{u'}{z'} = \frac{1 + z'^2}{z'}\,\varepsilon - v', \quad \text{i.e.,} \quad \left(\frac{u'}{z'} \right)' = \left(\frac{1 + z'^2}{z'}\,\varepsilon \right)' - v''$$

we have

$$\bar{\varkappa} - \varkappa = \frac{1}{\sqrt{1 + z'^2}} \big[v'' - (\varepsilon\,z')' \big] - \varkappa\,\varepsilon =$$

$$= \frac{1}{\sqrt{1 + z'^2}} \left[v'' - \left(\frac{z'\,(u' + z'\,v')}{1 + z'^2} \right)' \right] - \frac{z''\,(u' + z'\,v')}{[1 + z'^2]^{5/2}}. \qquad (10.14b)$$

We can also linearize the relationships between sectional load and deformations if the latter are small. For $\varepsilon \ll 1$, we obtain from (10.10a, b)

$$N = D_x \bar{F}\,\varepsilon - \varkappa\,M, \qquad M = D_x \bar{J}\,(\bar{\varkappa} - \varkappa). \qquad (10.15a, b)$$

We shall now linearize the equilibrium conditions (10.11c, g). First, we have

$$\bar{\mathfrak{t}} = \frac{1}{1 + \varepsilon} \left(\frac{d\,\mathfrak{r}}{d\,s} + \frac{d\,\mathfrak{w}}{d\,s} \right) \approx (1 - \varepsilon) \left(\frac{d\,\mathfrak{r}}{d\,s} + \frac{d\,\mathfrak{w}}{d\,s} \right) \approx (1 - \varepsilon) \frac{d\,\mathfrak{r}}{d\,s} +$$

$$+ \frac{d\,\mathfrak{w}}{d\,s} = \frac{1}{\sqrt{1 + z'^2}} \left[\left(1 - \frac{u' + z'\,v'}{1 + z'^2} \right) \frac{d\,\mathfrak{r}}{d\,x} + \frac{d\,\mathfrak{w}}{d\,x} \right] =$$

$$= \frac{1}{\sqrt{1 + z'^2}} \left[\left(1 - \frac{u' + z'\,v'}{1 + z'^2} \right) \{1;\, z'\} + \{u';\, v'\} \right] =$$

$$= \left\{ \frac{1}{\sqrt{1 + z'^2}} - \frac{z'\,(v' - z'\,u')}{\sqrt{1 + z'^2}^{\,3}};\ \frac{z'}{\sqrt{1 + z'^2}} + \frac{v' - z'\,u'}{\sqrt{1 + z'^2}^{\,3}} \right\}.$$

We then obtain from (10.11e)

$$N = -\left(\{A_x;\, A_z\} + \int_{\bar{x}=0}^{x} \{\bar{p}_x;\, \bar{p}_z\} \left(1 + \frac{u' + z'\,v'}{1 + z'^2} \right) \sqrt{1 + z'^2}\, d\,\bar{x} \right) \bar{\mathfrak{t}} \approx$$

$$\approx - \left(A_x + \int_{\bar{x}=0}^{x} \bar{p}_x \sqrt{1 + z'^2}\, d\,\bar{x} \right) \left(\frac{1}{\sqrt{1 + z'^2}} - \frac{z'\,(v' - z'\,u')}{\sqrt{1 + z'^2}^{\,3}} \right) -$$

$$- \left(A_z + \int_{\bar{x}=0}^{x} \bar{p}_z \sqrt{1 + z'^2}\, d\,\bar{x} \right) \left(\frac{z'}{\sqrt{1 + z'^2}} + \frac{v' - z'\,u'}{\sqrt{1 + z'^2}^{\,3}} \right) -$$

$$- \frac{1}{\sqrt{1 + z'^2}} \int_{\bar{x}=0}^{x} \frac{u'(\bar{x}) + z'(\bar{x})\,v'(\bar{x})}{\sqrt{1 + z'^2(\bar{x})}} \big(\bar{p}_x(\bar{x}) + z'(x)\,\bar{p}_z(\bar{x}) \big)\, d\,\bar{x}. \qquad (10.15c)$$

The linearized equation for the moments is found from (10.11g):

$$M = M_A + \big(A_z(x+u) - A_x(z+v)\big) + \int_{\bar{x}=0}^{x} \Big[\bar{p}_z\big(x - \bar{x} + u(x) - u(\bar{x})\big) - \bar{p}_x\big(z(x) - z(\bar{x}) + v(x) - v(\bar{x})\big)\Big]\left(1 + \frac{u' + z'v'}{1+z'^2}\right)\sqrt{1+z'^2}\, d\bar{x} \approx$$

$$\approx M_A + \big(A_z(x+u) - A_x(z+v)\big) + \int_{\bar{x}=0}^{x} \Big[\bar{p}_z\big(x - \bar{x} + u(x) - u(\bar{x})\big) - \bar{p}_x\big(z(x) - z(\bar{x}) + v(x) - v(\bar{x})\big)\Big]\sqrt{1+z'^2(\bar{x})}\, d\bar{x} + \int_{\bar{x}=0}^{x} \frac{u'(\bar{x}) + z'(\bar{x})\, v'(\bar{x})}{\sqrt{1+z'^2(\bar{x})}} \Big[\bar{p}_z(\bar{x})(x-\bar{x}) - \bar{p}_x(\bar{x})\big(z(x) - z(\bar{x})\big)\Big] d\bar{x}\,. \tag{10.15d}$$

Inserting (10.15a, b) into (10.15c, d) and taking account of (10.14 a, b) yields the linearized equations for the displacements.

10.3.1 *The Unextended Arch*

We obtain from (10.14a) for $\varepsilon = 0$

$$u' = -z'v'\,. \tag{10.16a}$$

The change in curvature is then

$$\bar{\varkappa} - \varkappa = \frac{v''}{\sqrt{1+z'^2}}\,. \tag{10.16b}$$

Inserting these values into (10.15b, d), we obtain

$$M = D_x J \frac{v''}{\sqrt{1+z'^2}} = M_A + \big[A_z(x+u) - A_x(z+v)\big] + \int_{\bar{x}=0}^{x} \Big\{\bar{p}_z\big(x - \bar{x} + u(x) - u(\bar{x})\big) - \bar{p}_x\big(z(x) - z(\bar{x}) + v(x) - v(\bar{x})\big)\Big\}\sqrt{1+z'^2(\bar{x})}\, d\bar{x}\,.$$

Differentiating this equation with respect to x and taking into account (10.16a) we obtain a differential equation of the third order containing only the derivatives of the vertical displacements:

$$\left(D_x J \frac{v''}{\sqrt{1+z'^2}}\right)' = \left(A_z + \int_{\bar{x}=0}^{x} \bar{p}_z \sqrt{1+z'^2(\bar{x})}\, d\bar{x}\right)(1 - z'v') - \left(A_x + \int_{\bar{x}=0}^{x} \bar{p}_x \sqrt{1+z'^2(\bar{x})}\, d\bar{x}\right)(z' + v')\,. \tag{10.16c}$$

If the distributed load is vertical: $\bar{p}_z = -q(x)\big/\sqrt{1+z'^2}$ where $q(x)$ is the load per unit length of the horizontal projection of the arc, we have $\bar{p}_x = 0$. If $A_x = H$ denotes the horizontal reaction at the end, we obtain

$$\left(D_x J \frac{v''}{\sqrt{1+z'^2}}\right)' = \left(A_z - \int_{\bar{x}=0}^{x} q\, d\bar{x}\right)(1 - z'v') - H(z' + v')\,. \tag{10.17a}$$

For further simplification we now multiply (10.17a) by $(1 + z'v')$ (by virtue of $z'v' \ll 1$ this is equivalent to dividing by $(1 - z'v')$). Neglecting all nonlinear terms in the displacement derivatives and differentiating again, we obtain

$$\left(D_x J \frac{v''}{\sqrt{1+z'^2}}\right)'' + H\big((1+z'^2)\, v'\big)' = -(H z'' + q)\,. \tag{10.17b}$$

The statically undetermined moments $\hat{M}$ are, by the first-order theory, given by

$$\hat{M} = \hat{M}_A + \hat{A}\, x - \hat{H}\, z - \int_{\bar{x}=0}^{x} q\,(x - \bar{x})\, d\bar{x}\,,$$

$$\text{i.e.,}\quad \hat{M}'' = -(\hat{H} z'' + q)\,, \tag{10.17c}$$

where $\hat{M}_A$, $\hat{A}$ and $\hat{H}$ are the support reactions, determined in the usual way according to the first-order theory (the statically undetermined problem). Writing $\Delta H = H - \hat{H}$, we can reduce (10.17b) to the form

$$\left(D_x J \frac{v''}{\sqrt{1+z'^2}}\right)'' + H\big[(1+z'^2)\, v'\big]' = \hat{M}'' - \Delta H\, z''\,. \tag{10.17d}$$

Integrating (10.16a) yields

$$u(x) = C - \int_{\bar{x}=0}^{x} z'v'\, d\bar{x}\,.$$

Since the points of support are horizontally fixed, we have $C = 0$ and

$$\int_0^l z'v'\, dx = 0\,. \tag{10.18}$$

Accordingly, in addition to the four boundary conditions formulated for v (two at each end), we have also to take account of (10.18). These five conditions can be satisfied by the four constants obtained when integrating (10.17d), and by H.

10.3.2 *Approximate Solution for the Unextended Arch by Means of Galerkin's Method. Buckling of Arches*

For an arbitrary function $f(x)$, (10.17d) becomes equivalent to

$$\int_0^l \left\{\left[D_x J \frac{v''}{\sqrt{1+z'^2}}\right]'' + H\big[(1+z'^2)\, v'\big]' - \hat{M}'' + \Delta H\, z''\right\} \times f(x)\, dx = 0\,. \tag{10.19a}$$

If we now require that $f(x)$ satisfy the boundary conditions for the displacement v, including (10.18), we can write

$$\left.\begin{aligned}
&\int_0^l \left(D_x J \frac{v''}{\sqrt{1+z'^2}}\right)'' f\, dx = \left[\left(D_x J \frac{v''}{\sqrt{1+z'^2}}\right)' f\right]_{x=0}^{l} - \left[D_x J \frac{v''}{\sqrt{1+z'^2}} f'\right]_{x=0}^{l} + \int_0^l D_x J \frac{v'' f''}{\sqrt{1+z'^2}}\, dx = \int_0^l D_x J \frac{v'' f''}{\sqrt{1+z'^2}}\, dx,\\
&\int_0^l \big[(1+z'^2)\, v'\big]' f\, dx = \big[(1+z'^2)\, v' f\big]_{x=0}^{l} - \int_0^l (1+z'^2)\, v' f'\, dx = -\int_0^l (1+z'^2)\, v' f'\, dx\,,\\
&\int_0^l z'' f\, dx = \big[z' f\big]_{x=0}^{l} - \int_0^l z' f'\, dx = -\int_0^l z' f'\, dx = 0
\end{aligned}\right\} \tag{10.19b}$$

The reason for this is that, on the one hand, the immovability of the supports leads to $v(0) = v(l) = 0$, hence also $f(0) = f(l) = 0$ while on the other hand, the boundary terms

$$\left[D_x J \frac{v''}{\sqrt{1+z'^2}} f'\right]_0^l = \big[M f'\big]_0^l$$

must vanish, since, at the edge, either $M = 0$ (hinged support) or $v' = 0$, thus $f' = 0$ (built-in end).* Using (10.19b), we obtain from (10.19a)

$$\int_0^l D_x \bar{J} \frac{v'' f''}{\sqrt{1+z'^2}} d x - H \int_0^l (1 + z'^2)\, v' f' d x - \int_0^l \hat{M}'' f\, d x = 0, \tag{10.19c}$$

on which we base our approximations. We express the unknown displacement v in the form

$$v = \sum_{k=1}^{n} C_k v_k, \tag{10.20a}$$

where the constants C_k have to be determined, while the v_k satisfy all boundary conditions (including (10.18)). Inserting (10.20a) into (10.19c) and putting $f = v_i$, we obtain the system of equations

$$\sum_{k=1}^{n} C_k (\alpha_{ik} - H \beta_{ik}) = \gamma_i \Big|_{i=1\ldots n} \tag{10.20b}$$

where

$$\alpha_{ik} = \alpha_{ki} = \int_0^l D_x \bar{J} \frac{v_i'' v_k''}{\sqrt{1+z'^2}} d x, \quad \beta_{ik} = \beta_{ki} = \int_0^l (1 + z'^2)\, v_i' v_k' d x, \quad \gamma_i = \int_0^l \hat{M}'' v_i d x = -\int_0^l q\, v_i d x. \tag{10.20c}$$

If we select systems of orthogonal functions satisfying the conditions

$$\int_0^l D_x \bar{J} \frac{v_i'' v_k''}{\sqrt{1+z'^2}} d x = 0, \quad \int_0^l (1 + z'^2)\, v_i' v_k' d x = 0 \tag{10.20d}$$

$[i \neq k]$, we can obtain the constants C_k directly from

$$C_k = \frac{\gamma_k}{\alpha_{kk} - H \beta_{kk}} = \frac{\gamma_k}{H \beta_{kk}} \frac{1}{\dfrac{\alpha_{kk}}{H \beta_{kk}} - 1} \Bigg|_{k=1\ldots n} \tag{10.20e}$$

For

$$H = H_k = \frac{\alpha_{kk}}{\beta_{kk}} = \frac{\int_0^l D_x \bar{J} \dfrac{v_k''^2}{\sqrt{1+z'^2}} d x}{\int_0^l (1 + z'^2)\, v_k'^2 d x} \tag{10.21}$$

the C_k, and thus displacements, become infinitely large if $\hat{M} \neq 0$. In the linearized theory this denotes the beginning of instability. Thus, when the displacement v is approximated by v_k, (10.21) yields an equation for the approximate determination of the horizontal end reactions H_k, causing buckling of the arch in the form described by v_k. Of these reactions, only the smallest $H_1 = H_{kr}$ is of interest in practice. The respective elastic line corresponds to the least work in bending, and exhibits thus, within the region of the arch, the smallest number of zero points. Since we assumed that no extension of the arch takes place, this elastic line has one zero point. For symmetrical arches, the line is antimetrical. The initial horizontal reaction is approximately

$$H_1 = H_{kr} = \frac{\alpha_{11}}{\beta_{11}} = \frac{\int_0^l D_x \bar{J} \dfrac{v_1''^2}{\sqrt{1+z'^2}} d x}{\int_0^l (1 + z'^2)\, v_1'^2 d x}, \tag{10.22}$$

where v_1 is a function which satisfies all boundary conditions (including (10.18)) and possesses only one zero point in the region of the arch.

Writing

$$\nu_k = \frac{H_k}{H} = \frac{\alpha_{kk}}{H \beta_{kk}} \tag{10.23a}$$

we obtain from (10.20e)

$$C_k = \frac{\gamma_k}{H \beta_{kk}} \frac{1}{\nu_k - 1}. \tag{10.23b}$$

The displacements are thus

$$v(x) = \sum_{k=1}^{n} C_k v_k = \sum_{k=1}^{n} \frac{\gamma_k}{H \beta_{kk}} \frac{v_k(x)}{\nu_k - 1}, \tag{10.23c}$$

the moments being

$$M(x) = \frac{D_x \bar{J} v''}{\sqrt{1+z'^2}} = \sum_{k=1}^{n} \frac{D_x \bar{J} \gamma_k}{H \beta_{kk}} \frac{1}{\nu_k - 1} \frac{v_k''}{\sqrt{1+z'^2}}. \tag{10.23d}$$

If the moments $\hat{M}$ can be expressed in the form

$$\hat{M}(x) = \sum_{k=1}^{n} \hat{M}_k(x) = \sum_{k=1}^{n} A_k \left(D_x \bar{J} \frac{v_k''}{\sqrt{1+z'^2}} \right) = \sum_{k=1}^{n} A_k m_k(x), \tag{10.24a}$$

i.e., in a series of the bending moments corresponding to the functions v_k, we obtain particularly simple expressions for moments and displacements. By virtue of the orthogonality of the functions v_i we have

$$\gamma_i = \int_0^l \hat{M}'' v_i d x = \sum_{k=1}^{n} A_k \int_0^l \left(\frac{D_x \bar{J}}{\sqrt{1+z'^2}} v_k'' \right)'' v_i d x = \sum_{k=1}^{n} A_k \int_0^l D_x \bar{J} \frac{v_i'' v_k''}{\sqrt{1+z'^2}} d x = A_i \int_0^l D_x \bar{J} \frac{v_i''^2}{\sqrt{1+z'^2}} d x = A_i \alpha_{ii}, \tag{10.24b}$$

whence, by (10.23b) $C_i = A_i \dfrac{\nu_i}{\nu_i - 1}$.

We then obtain from (10.23c, d)

$$v(x) = \sum_{k=1}^{n} A_k \frac{\nu_k}{\nu_k - 1} v_k(x), \tag{10.24c}$$

$$M(x) = D_x \bar{J} \frac{v''}{\sqrt{1+z'^2}} = \sum_{k=1}^{n} A_k \left(\frac{D_x \bar{J}}{\sqrt{1+z'^2}} v_k'' \right) \frac{\nu_k}{\nu_k - 1} = \sum_{k=1}^{n} \hat{M}_k \frac{\nu_k}{\nu_k - 1}. \tag{10.24d}$$

---

* We neglect resiliently built-in ends or additional concentrated moments which might act at a hinged support.

Since the ratios $\nu_k = H_k/H$ increase rapidly with k, only the first terms of (10.24a) are significantly increased because of the deformations. As a first approximation we can therefore write the ratios ν_k in the form

$$\nu_k = \frac{H_k}{H} \approx \frac{H_k}{\hat{H}} = \hat{\nu}_k$$

where $\hat{H}$ is the horizontal reaction determined from the first-order theory. For a more accurate determination of H (and thus of ν_k), we can use (10.19a), putting $f(x) = 1$. Substituting in (10.17d) $\Delta H = H - \hat{H}$, we obtain

$$\left(\frac{D_x \bar{J}}{\sqrt{1+z'^2}}\, v''\right)'' + H\left[z' + (1+z'^2)\, v'\right]' = \hat{M}'' + \hat{H} z''$$

which is equivalent to

$$\int_0^l \left(D_x \bar{J}\frac{v''}{\sqrt{1+z'^2}}\right)'' d x + H \int_0^l \left[z' + (1+z'^2)\, v'\right]' d x = $$

$$= \int_0^l (\hat{M}'' + \hat{H} z'')\, d x \;.$$

In view of the expected smallness of the displacements we can write

$$\int_0^l \left[z' + (1+z'^2)\, v'\right]' d x \approx \int_0^l z''\, d x \,.$$

Substituting $D_x \bar{J} \dfrac{v''}{\sqrt{1+z'^2}} = M$

we obtain as an approximation

$$(H - \hat{H}) \int_0^l z''\, d x = \Delta H \int_0^l z''\, d x = - \int_0^l (M - \hat{M})''\, d x,$$

$$\Delta H = - \frac{\int_0^l (M - \hat{M})''\, d x}{\int_0^l z''\, d x} = - \frac{(M - \hat{M})'_l - (M - \hat{M})'_0}{z'(l) - z'(0)} =$$

whence, taking into account (10.24a, d), we find

$$= - \sum_{k=1}^{n} \frac{\hat{M}'_k(l) - \hat{M}'_k(0)}{(\nu_k - 1)\,[z'(l) - z'(0)]} \,. \qquad (10.24e)$$

This corresponds to an averaging of (10.17d) over the span of the arch.

With the exception of (10.24e), the approximate results become exact if we introduce the eigenfunction e_i of the system instead of the function v_i. These eigenfunctions are the solutions, satisfying all boundary conditions, of the linearized differential equation of arch buckling. This latter is obtained for $\hat{M} = 0$ from (10.17d) in the form

$$\left(D_x \bar{J}\frac{v''}{\sqrt{1+z'^2}}\right)'' + H\left[(1+z'^2)\, v'\right]' = - \Delta H z'' \,.$$

If we distinguish between buckling with and without change in horizontal reaction, we obtain for $\Delta H = 0$ the homogeneous differential equation

$$\left(D_x \bar{J}\frac{v''}{\sqrt{1+z'^2}}\right)'' + H\left[(1+z'^2)\, v'\right]' = 0 \,.$$

On the other hand, putting $v = \dfrac{\Delta H}{H}\tilde{v}$, we obtain for the case of buckling with change in the horizonatal reaction

$$\left(D_x \bar{J}\frac{\tilde{v}''}{\sqrt{1+z'^2}}\right)'' + H\left[z' + (1+z'^2)\, \tilde{v}'\right]' = 0 \,.$$

In analogy to the buckling of a rod, the five homogeneous boundary conditions yield five integration constants (including H) differing from zero only for certain values $H = H_k$. The eigenfunctions $v_k = e_k^{(a)}$, $\tilde{v}_k = e_k^{(s)}$ corresponding to these eigenvalues therefore satisfy the equations*

$$\left(D_x \bar{J}\frac{e_k^{(a)''}}{\sqrt{1+z'^2}}\right)'' + H_k^{(a)}\left[(1+z'^2)\, e_k^{(a)'}\right]' = 0$$

$$\text{or} \quad \left(D_x \bar{J}\frac{e_k^{(s)''}}{\sqrt{1+z'^2}}\right)'' + H_k^{(s)}\left[z' + (1+z'^2)\, e_k^{(s)'}\right]' = 0 \,. \qquad (10.25\text{a, b})$$

For

$$\left(D_x \bar{J}\frac{e_i^{(a)''}}{\sqrt{1+z'^2}}\right)'' + H_i^{(a)}\left[(1+z'^2)\, e_i^{(a)'}\right]' = 0 \quad \text{or}$$

$$\left(D_x \bar{J}\frac{e_i^{(s)''}}{\sqrt{1+z'^2}}\right)'' + H_i^{(s)}\left[z' + (1+z'^2)\, e_i^{(s)'}\right]' = 0 \qquad (10.26\text{a, b})$$

we obtain by multiplying (10.25a, b) by $e_i^{(a)}$ and $e_i^{(s)}$, respectively, as well as (10.26a, b) by $e_k^{(a)}$ and $e_k^{(s)}$, respectively, and integrating over x between the limits 0 and l, taking into account all boundary conditions for v (i.e., also for e_i and e_k), for both cases of buckling

$$\int_0^l \frac{D_x \bar{J}}{\sqrt{1+z'^2}}\, e_i''\, e_k''\, d x - H_k \int_0^l (1+z'^2)\, e_i'\, e_k'\, d x = 0 \,,$$

$$\int_0^l \frac{D_x \bar{J}}{\sqrt{1+z'^2}}\, e_i''\, e_k''\, d x - H_i \int_0^l (1+z'^2)\, e_i'\, e_k'\, d x = 0 \,, \qquad (10.27\text{a, b})$$

(where the superscripts have now been discarded). Therefore

$$\int_0^l \frac{D_x \bar{J}}{\sqrt{1+z'^2}}\, e_i''\, e_k''\, d x = 0 \,, \quad \int_0^l (1+z'^2)\, e_i'\, e_k'\, d x = 0 \,. \qquad (10.27\text{c})$$

This proves the orthogonality of the eigenfunctions, for which the corresponding eigenvalues can be obtained from, e.g., (10.27a) for $i = k$:

$$H_k = \frac{\int_0^l \frac{D_x \bar{J}}{\sqrt{1+z'^2}}\, e_k''^2\, d x}{\int_0^l (1+z'^2)\, e_k'^2\, d x} \,. \qquad (10.27\text{d})$$

Writing down the moments in the form

$$\hat{M}(x) = \sum_{k=1}^{n} \bar{A}_k^{(s)}\left(\frac{D_x \bar{J}\, e_k^{(s)''}}{\sqrt{1+z'^2}}\right) + \bar{A}_k^{(a)}\left(\frac{D_x \bar{J}\, e_k^{(a)''}}{\sqrt{1+z'^2}}\right) =$$

$$= \sum_{k=1}^{n} \bar{A}_k^{(s)}\, m_k^{(s)}(x) + \bar{A}_k^{(a)}\, m_k^{(a)}(x) = \sum_{k=1}^{n} \hat{M}_k^{(s)} + \hat{M}_k^{(a)} \qquad (10.27\text{e})$$

* The superscripts (s) and (a) indicate that for symmetrical arches, buckling without change in horizontal reaction leads to an antimetrical shape after buckling, while buckling with change in horizontal reaction leads to a symmetrical shape.

we can obtain a solution of (10.17d), satisfying all boundary conditions, in the form

$$v(x) = \sum_{k=1}^{n} \bar{C}_k^{(s)} e_k^{(s)}(x) + \bar{C}_k^{(a)} e_k^{(a)}(x) \qquad (10.27f)$$

We can show this by inserting (10.27e, f) into (10.17d), which, taking (10.25a, b) into account, leads to

$$\sum_{k=1}^{n}\left[\bar{C}_k^{(s)}\left(1-\frac{H}{H_k^{(s)}}\right)-\bar{A}_k^{(s)}\right]\left(\frac{D_x \bar{J}\, e_k^{(s)''}}{\sqrt{1+z'^2}}\right)'' +$$

$$+\left[\bar{C}_k^{(a)}\left(1-\frac{H}{H_k^{(a)}}\right)-\bar{A}_k^{(a)}\right]\left(\frac{D_x \bar{J}\, e_k^{(a)''}}{\sqrt{1+z'^2}}\right)'' +$$

$$+H\left(\frac{\Delta H}{H}-\sum_{k=1}^{n}\bar{C}_k^{(s)}\right)z''=0 .$$

This equation can be satisfied by

$$\bar{C}_k^{(s)}=\bar{A}_k^{(s)}\frac{\nu_k^{(s)}}{\nu_k^{(s)}-1}, \quad \bar{C}_k^{(a)}=\bar{A}_k^{(a)}\frac{\nu_k^{(a)}}{\nu_k^{(a)}-1},$$

$$\text{where } \bar{C}_k=\bar{A}_k\frac{\nu_k}{\nu_k-1} \qquad (10.27g)$$

(cf. (10.24b))

$$\frac{\Delta H}{H}=\sum_{k=1}^{n}\bar{C}_k^{(s)}=\sum_{k=1}^{n}\bar{A}_k^{(s)}\frac{\nu_k^{(s)}}{\nu_k^{(s)}-1} . \qquad (10.27h)$$

We can then rewrite (10.27f) as follows:

$$v(x)=\sum_{k=1}^{n}\frac{\bar{A}_k\,\nu_k}{\nu_k-1}e_k(x), \quad M(x)=\frac{D_x \bar{J}}{\sqrt{1+z'^2}}v''=\sum_{k=1}^{n}\hat{M}_k\frac{\nu_k}{\nu_k-1}$$

(cf. (10.24c, d)). We use (10.27h), which, with the exception of (10.24e), has no equivalent in the approximation theory, to determine the horizontal reaction H. We see that with symmetrical arches only the symmetrical parts of the load cause a change in the horizontal reaction.

10.3.3 *Buckling Loads of the Symmetrical Plane Arch*

Before dealing with practical calculations for plane arches acted upon by arbitrary loads, we shall discuss pure buckling of arches. We determine the critical horizontal reaction with the aid of (10.21) or (10.22), in which, for simplicity of computation, we approximate the function $\varphi = 1/\sqrt{1+z'^2}$ in the integrand of the numerator by a polynomial:

$$\varphi=\frac{1}{\sqrt{1+z'^2}}\approx C_0+C_1x+C_2x^2+C_3x^3+C_4x^4 \qquad (10.28a)$$

We determine the unknown constants C_k by means of the boundary conditions valid for the actual function φ, namely

$$\varphi(0)=\varphi(l)=\frac{1}{\sqrt{1+z_0'^2}}, \; \varphi\left(\frac{l}{2}\right)=1^{*)},$$

$$\varphi'(0)=-\varphi'(l)=-z_0'\frac{z_0''}{[1+z_0'^2]^{3/2}}=-\frac{z_0'}{R_0} .$$

Therefore,

$$C_0=\frac{1}{\sqrt{1+z_0'^2}}, \; C_1 l=-z_0'\frac{l}{R_0},$$

$$C_2 l^2=16(1-C_0)-5C_1 l=16\left(1-\frac{1}{\sqrt{1+z_0'^2}}\right)+5z_0'\frac{l}{R_0},$$

$$C_3 l^3=-32(1-C_0)+8C_1 l=-32\left(1-\frac{1}{\sqrt{1+z_0'^2}}\right)-8z_0'\frac{l}{R_0},$$

$$C_4 l^4=16(1-C_0)-4C_1 l=16\left(1-\frac{1}{\sqrt{1+z_0'^2}}\right)+4z_0'\frac{l}{R_0} .$$

Writing $\xi = x/l$, we obtain

$$\varphi(\xi)=\frac{1}{\sqrt{1+z_0'^2}}+16\left(1-\frac{1}{\sqrt{1+z_0'^2}}\right)(\xi-\xi^2)^2- \qquad (10.28b)$$

$$-z_0'\frac{z_0''\,l}{[1+z_0'^2]^{3/2}}\left[(\xi-\xi^2)-4(\xi-\xi^2)^2\right].$$

We then have by (10.21) for a constant moment of inertia

$$H_k=\frac{D_x\bar{J}}{l^2}\frac{\int_0^1\varphi(\xi)\left(\frac{d^2v_k}{d\xi^2}\right)^2d\xi}{\int_0^1\left[1+\frac{1}{l^2}\left(\frac{dz}{d\xi}\right)^2\right]\left(\frac{dv_k}{d\xi}\right)^2d\xi} \qquad (10.29)$$

Let us consider the parabolic arch

$$z(\xi)=4f(\xi-\xi^2), \; \frac{dz}{d\xi}=4f(1-2\xi), \; \frac{1}{l}\frac{dz}{d\xi}\bigg|_0=$$

$$=\frac{1}{l}\frac{dz_0}{d\xi}=\frac{4f}{l}=\alpha, \; \frac{1}{l^2}\frac{d^2z}{d\xi^2}\bigg|_0=z_0''=-\frac{8f}{l^2}=-\frac{2}{l}\alpha, \qquad (10.30)$$

$$\varphi(\xi)=\frac{1}{\sqrt{1+\alpha^2}}+16\left(1-\frac{1}{\sqrt{1+\alpha^2}}\right)(\xi-\xi^2)^2+$$

$$+\frac{2\alpha^2}{[1+\alpha^2]^{3/2}}\left[(\xi-\xi^2)-4(\xi-\xi^2)^2\right],$$

We shall determine the critical horizontal reactions for antimetrical and symmetrical buckling when the arch is either hinged or rigidly built-in at both ends .

a) Buckling load of the parabolic arch, hinged at both ends.

a1) Antimetrical buckling.

The function

$$v_a(\xi)=v_1(\xi)=\sin 2\pi\xi$$

satisfies the boundary conditions for the arch hinged at both ends: $v(0)=v(l)=0$, $M(0)=M(l)=0$, i.e., $v''(0)=v''(l)$ as well as $\int_0^l z'v'\,dx=-\int_0^l zv''\,dx=0$. Insertion into (10.29) yields

$$H_{kr}^{(a)}=H_1=\frac{4\pi^2D_x\bar{J}}{l^2}\times$$

$$\times\frac{\int_0^1\varphi(\xi)\sin^2 2\pi\xi\,d\xi}{\int_0^1[1+\alpha^2(1-2\xi)^2]\cos^2 2\pi\xi\,d\xi}=H_{0kr}^{(a)}\Phi_a(\alpha), \qquad (10.31a)$$

where $H_{0kr}^{(a)}=4\pi^2D_x\bar{J}/l^2$ is the critical load for an infinitely shallow arch, and $\Phi_a(\alpha)$ is, after evaluation of the integral, found to be*

$$\Phi_a(\alpha)=$$

$$\frac{1+2\left(\sqrt{1+\alpha^2}-1\right)\left(\frac{4}{15}+\frac{3}{4\pi^4}\right)+\frac{\alpha^2}{1+\alpha^2}\left(\frac{1}{15}+\frac{1}{4\pi^2}-\frac{3}{4\pi^4}\right)}{\left[1+\alpha^2\left(\frac{1}{3}+\frac{1}{2\pi^2}\right)\right]\sqrt{1+\alpha^2}}$$

$$=\frac{1+0.5486\left(\sqrt{1+\alpha^2}-1\right)+0.0843\frac{\alpha^2}{1+\alpha^2}}{(1+0.3841\alpha^2)\sqrt{1+\alpha^2}} . \qquad (10.31b)$$

*For symmetrical arches, we have $z'(l/2)=0$!

* See p. 258.

f/l	0	0.1	0.2	0.3	0.4	0.5	0.6	0.7	0.8	0.9	1.0	according to
$\alpha = 4f/l$	0	0.4	0.8	1.2	1.6	2.0	2.4	2.8	3.2	3.6	4.0	eq.
$\Phi_a(\alpha)$	1.000	0.918	0.745	0.562	0.412	0.308	0.234	0.181	0.143	0.116	0.095	(10.31 b)
$\hat{\Phi}_a(\alpha)$	1.000	0.943	0.803	0.645	0.502	0.394	0.311	0.250	0.203	0.167	0.140	(10.31 c)
$\hat{\Phi}_a(\alpha)$	1.000	0.919	0.802	0.637	0.493	0.381	—	—	—	—	—	(10.31 d)

The above table gives some values of $\Phi_a(\alpha)$. The second line gives values of

$$\hat{\Phi}_a(\alpha) = \frac{1}{1+\alpha^2\left(\frac{1}{3}+\frac{1}{2\pi^2}\right)} = \frac{1}{1+0{,}3841\,\alpha^2} \qquad (10.31c)$$

presented for the sake of comparison with known results. They are obtained from (10.21) for the same function v_k, assuming the moments of inertia to obey the law $\bar{J} = \bar{J}_c\sqrt{1+z'^2} = \bar{J}_c/\cos\omega$. Line 3 gives Dischinger's results (cf. his paper referred to before), expressed in the form

$$\hat{\Phi}_a(\alpha) = \frac{1}{1+0.385\,\alpha^2\,\dfrac{1+0.432\,\alpha^2}{1+0.393\,\alpha^2}} \qquad (10.31d)$$

The differences are, as evident from (10.31c, d), insignificant.

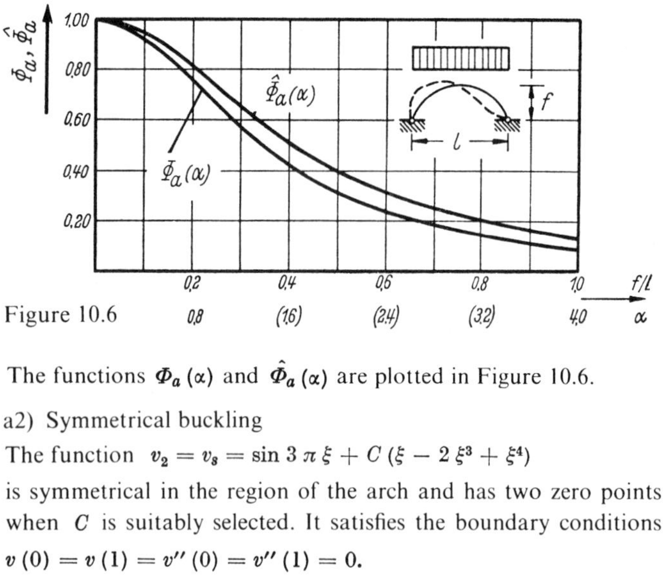

Figure 10.6

The functions $\Phi_a(\alpha)$ and $\hat{\Phi}_a(\alpha)$ are plotted in Figure 10.6.

a2) Symmetrical buckling

The function $v_2 = v_s = \sin 3\pi\xi + C(\xi - 2\xi^3 + \xi^4)$ is symmetrical in the region of the arch and has two zero points when C is suitably selected. It satisfies the boundary conditions $v(0) = v(1) = v''(0) = v''(1) = 0$.

The condition $\int_0^1 z'\,v'(\xi)\,d\xi = -\int_0^1 z''(\xi)\,v(\xi)\,d\xi = 0$, [1]

reduces in this case to $\int_0^1 v(\xi)\,d\xi = 0$

by virtue of $z'' = \text{const}$. This yields $C = -10/(3\pi)$. The function

$$v(\xi) = \sin 3\pi\xi - \frac{10}{3\pi}(\xi - 2\xi^3 + \xi^4) \qquad (10.32a)$$

thus satisfies all conditions formulated for v. From

$$v'(\xi) = \frac{dv}{d\xi} = 3\pi\left[\cos 3\pi\xi - \frac{10}{9\pi^2}(1 - 6\xi^2 + 4\xi^3)\right],$$

$$v''(\xi) = \frac{d^2v}{d\xi^2} = -9\pi^2\left[\sin 3\pi\xi - \frac{40}{9\pi^3}(\xi - \xi^2)\right],$$

we obtain the critical horizontal reaction for $\bar{J} = \text{const}$ in accordance with (10.29):

$$H_{kr}^{(s)} = H_2 = \frac{9\pi^2 D_x \bar{J}}{l^2} \times$$

$$\times \frac{\int_0^1 \varphi(\xi)\left[\sin 3\pi\xi - \frac{40}{9\pi^3}(\xi - \xi^2)\right]^2 d\xi}{\int_0^1 [1+\alpha^2(1-2\xi)^2]\left[\cos 3\pi\xi - \frac{10}{9\pi^2}(1 - 6\xi^2 + 4\xi^3)\right]^2 d\xi}$$

After integration and some calculations we obtain

$$H_{kr}^{(s)} = 0.989\cdot 9\pi^2\frac{D_x\bar{J}}{l^2} \times$$

$$\times \frac{1+0.5538\left(\sqrt{1+\alpha^2}-1\right)+0.0734\,\dfrac{\alpha^2}{1+\alpha^2}}{(1+0.3022\,\alpha^2)\sqrt{1+\alpha^2}} = H_{0kr}^{(s)}\,\Phi_s(\alpha), \qquad (10.32b)$$

where $H_{0kr}^{(s)} = 0.989\cdot 9\,\pi^2 D_x\bar{J}/l^2 = 87.86\,D_x\bar{J}/l^2$

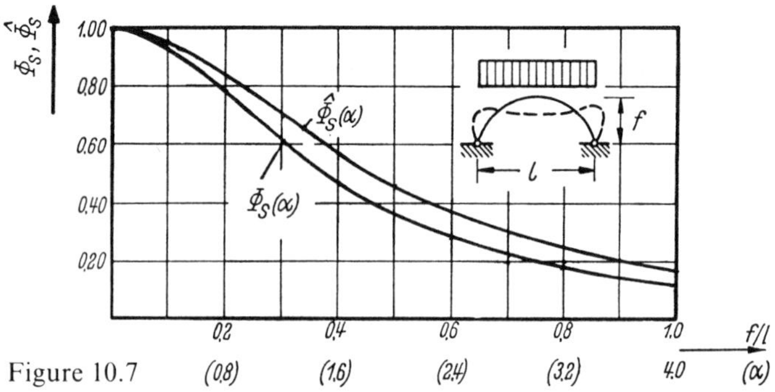

Figure 10.7

again denotes the critical horizontal reaction for very shallow arches $(\alpha \to 0)$. If the moments of inertia are assumed to obey the law $\bar{J} = \bar{J}_c/\cos\omega$, we obtain

$$H_{kr}^{(s)} = 0.989\cdot 9\pi^2\frac{D_x\bar{J}_c}{l^2}\,\frac{1}{1+0.3022\,\alpha^2} = \hat{H}_{kr0}^{(s)}\,\hat{\Phi}_s(\alpha), \qquad (10.32c)$$

where $\hat{H}_{0kr}^{(s)} = 87.86\,D_x\bar{J}_c/l^2$. The accuracy of this approximation can be shown for $\alpha = 0$. Dischinger's result for this case is $\hat{H}_{kr}^{(s)} = 87.84\,D_x\bar{J}_c/l^2$. Values of $\Phi_s(\alpha)$ and $\hat{\Phi}_s(\alpha)$ have been tabulated for some values of α, and are plotted in Figure 10.7.

---

* We have $\int_0^1 \sin^2 2\pi\xi\,d\xi = \int_0^1 \cos^2 2\pi\xi\,d\xi = \frac{1}{2}$, $\int_0^1 (\xi - \xi^2)\sin^2 2\pi\xi$ $= \frac{1}{12} + \frac{1}{16\pi^2}$, $\int_0^1 (\xi - \xi^2)^2 \sin^2 2\pi\xi\,d\xi = \frac{1}{60} + \frac{3}{64\pi^4}$, $\int_0^1 (1-2\xi)^2 \times$ $\times \cos^2 2\pi\xi\,d\xi = \frac{1}{6} + \frac{1}{4\pi^2}$.

f/l	0	0.1	0.2	0.3	0.4	0.5	0.6	0.7	0.8	0.9	1.0
$\alpha = 4\,f/l$	0	0.4	0.8	1.2	1.6	2.0	2.4	2.8	3.2	3.6	4.0
$\Phi_s(\alpha)$	1.000	0.932	0.775	0.604	0.461	0.353	0.274	0.215	0.173	0.141	0.116
$\hat{\Phi}_s(\alpha)$	1.000	0.954	0.838	0.697	0.564	0.453	0.365	0.297	0.244	0.203	0.171

b) Buckling loads of a parabolic arch built-in at both ends

b1) Antimetrical buckling.

We introduce the antimetrical function (cf. 9.36i))

$$v_a = v_1 = 1 - 2\xi + \frac{\sin\lambda\,(2\xi - 1)}{\sin\lambda} \tag{10.33a}$$

which satisfies the boundary conditions
$v(0) = v'(0) = v(l) = v'(l) = 0$

and the condition $\int_0^l z'\,v'\,d\,x = 0$ when $\lambda = 4.4934$ is the first solution of the equation $\operatorname{tg}\lambda = \lambda$. The critical arch thrust for antimetrical buckling is thus for $J = \text{const}$:

$$H_{kr}^{(a)} = H_1 = \frac{4\,\lambda^2\,D_x\,\bar{J}}{l^2} \times$$

$$\times \frac{\int_0^1 \varphi(\xi)\,\frac{\sin^2\lambda\,(2\xi - 1)}{\sin^2\lambda}\,d\,\xi}{\int_0^1 [1 + \alpha^2(1 - 2\xi)^2]\left[-\frac{1}{\lambda} + \frac{\cos\lambda\,(2\xi - 1)}{\sin\lambda}\right]^2 d\,\xi}\,. \tag{10.33b}$$

Since

$$\int_0^1 \frac{\sin^2\lambda\,(2\xi - 1)}{\sin^2\lambda}\,d\,\xi = \frac{1}{2}\,,$$

$$\int_0^1 (\xi - \xi^2)\,\frac{\sin^2\lambda\,(2\xi - 1)}{\sin^2\lambda}\,d\,\xi = \frac{1 + 4\lambda^2}{48\,\lambda^2} = 0.0845\,,$$

$$\int_0^1 (\xi - \xi^2)^2\,\frac{\sin^2\lambda\,(2\xi - 1)}{\sin^2\lambda}\,d\,\xi = \frac{16\,\lambda^2\,(1 + \lambda^2) + 15}{960\,\lambda^4} = 0.01755\,,$$

$$\int_0^1 \left[-\frac{1}{\lambda} + \frac{\cos\lambda\,(2\xi - 1)}{\sin\lambda}\right]^2 d\,\xi = \frac{1}{2}\,,$$

$$\int_0^1 (1 - 2\xi)^2\left[-\frac{1}{\lambda} + \frac{\cos\lambda\,(2\xi - 1)}{\sin\lambda}\right]^2 d\,\xi = \frac{2\,\lambda^2 - 15}{12\,\lambda^2} = 0.1046\,;$$

we have

$$H_{kr}^{(a)} = H_1 \approx$$

$$\approx 4\,\lambda^2\,\frac{D_x\bar{J}}{l^2}\,\frac{1 + 0.5615\left(\sqrt{1 + \alpha^2} - 1\right) + 0.0572\,\frac{\alpha^2}{1 + \alpha^2}}{(1 + 0.2096\,\alpha^2)\sqrt{1 + \alpha^2}} =$$

$$= H_{kr\,0}^{(a)}\,\Phi_a(\alpha) \tag{10.33c}$$

where $H_{kr\,0}^{(a)} = 4\,\lambda^2\,D_x\,\bar{J}/l^2 = 80.76\,D_x\,\bar{J}/l^2$
For $\bar{J} = J_c/\cos\omega$ we obtain

$$H_{kr}^{(a)} = 4\,\lambda^2\,\frac{D_x J_c}{l^2}\,\frac{1}{1 + 0.2096\,\alpha^2} = \hat{H}_{kr\,0}^{(a)}\,\hat{\Phi}_a(\alpha)\,;$$

$$\hat{\Phi}_a(\alpha) = \frac{1}{1 + 0.2096\,\alpha^2}\,, \tag{10.33d}$$

whereas the result given by Dischinger is

$$\hat{\Phi}_a(\alpha) = \frac{1}{1 + 0.215\,\frac{1 + 0.2605\,\alpha^2}{1 + 0.2285\,\alpha^2}}\,, \tag{10.33e}$$

the same symbols being used. The following table gives some values

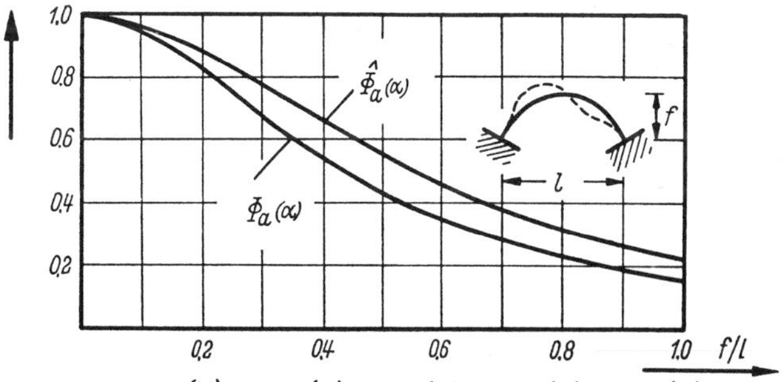

Figure 10.8 (0.8) (1.6) (2.4) (3.2) (4.0) (α)

of $\Phi_a(\alpha)$ and $\hat{\Phi}_a(\alpha)$. The last line shows, for the sake of comparison, Dischinger's results. The differences are insignificant. The functions Φ_a and $\hat{\Phi}_a$ are plotted in Figure 10.8.

f/l	0	0.1	0.2	0.3	0.4	0.5	0.6	0.7	0.8	0.9	1.0	according
$\alpha = 4\,f/l$	0	0.4	0.8	1.2	1.6	2.0	2.4	2.8	3.2	3.6	4.0	to eq.
$\Phi_a(\alpha)$	1.000	0.936	0.815	0.666	0.533	0.426	0.358	0.277	0.227	0.188	0.158	(10.33c)
$\hat{\Phi}_a(\alpha)$	1.000	0.968	0.883	0.768	0.651	0.544	0.453	0.379	0.319	0.269	0.230	(10.33d)
$\hat{\Phi}_a(\alpha)$	1.000	0.971	0.877	0.758	0.633	0.518	—	—	—	—	—	(10.33e)

f/l	0	0.1	0.2	0.3	0.4	0.5	0.6	0.7	0.8	0.9	1.0
$\alpha = 4\,f/l$	0	0.4	0.8	1.2	1.6	2.0	2.4	2.8	3.2	3.6	4.0
$\Phi_s\,(\alpha)$	1.000	0.9298	0.7706	0.6019	0.4613	0.3542	0.2751	0.2169	0.1738	0.1415	0.1168
$\hat{\Phi}_s\,(\alpha)$	1.000	0.9624	0.8648	0.7397	0.6151	0.5057	0.4153	0.3429	0.2855	0.2400	0.2036

b2) Symmetrical buckling

We introduce the symmetrical function

$$v_2 = v_s = \frac{1}{2}(1 - \cos 2\pi\xi) + C(\xi - \xi^2)^2 = \sin^2 \pi\xi + C(\xi - \xi^2)^2 \qquad (10.34a)$$

which satisfies the boundary conditions

$v(0) = v'(0) = v(l) = v'(l) = 0.$

The condition $\int_0^l z'\,v'\,d\,x = 0$ or $\int_0^1 v\,d\,\xi = 0$

yields $C = -15$. The function

$$v_2 = v_s = \frac{1}{2}(1 - \cos 2\pi\xi) - 15(\xi - \xi^2)^2 = \sin^2 \pi\xi - 15(\xi - \xi^2)^2 \qquad (10.34b)$$

thus satisfies all conditions postulated for constant moment of inertia. The critical arch thrust is thus, approximately

$$H_2 = H_{kr}^{(s)} = \frac{\int_0^1 \varphi(\xi)\{2\pi^2\cos 2\pi\xi - 30[(1-2\xi)^2 - 2(\xi-\xi^2)]\}^2 d\xi}{\int_0^1 [1+\alpha^2(1-2\xi)^2][\pi\sin 2\pi\xi - 30(1-2\xi)(\xi-\xi^2)]^2 d\xi}\,\frac{D_x\bar{J}}{l^2}. \qquad (10.34c)$$

Evaluation of the integrals in numerator and denominator yields

$$H_{kr}^{(s)} = 145.8\,\frac{D_x\bar{J}}{l^2}\,\frac{1 + 0.419\left(\sqrt{1+\alpha^2} - 1\right) + 0.0604\,\frac{\alpha^2}{1+\alpha^2}}{(1 + 0.2444\,\alpha^2)\sqrt{1+\alpha^2}} = H_{kr\,0}^{(s)}\,\Phi_s(\alpha), \qquad (10.34d)$$

where $H_{kr\,0}^{(s)} = 145.8\,\frac{D_x\bar{J}}{l^2}$.

For $\bar{J} = J_c/\cos\omega$ we obtain

$$H_{kr}^{(s)} = 145.8\,\frac{D_x J_c}{l^2}\,\frac{1}{1 + 0.2444\,\alpha^2} = \hat{H}_{kr\,0}^{(s)}\,\hat{\Phi}_s(\alpha). \qquad (10.34e)$$

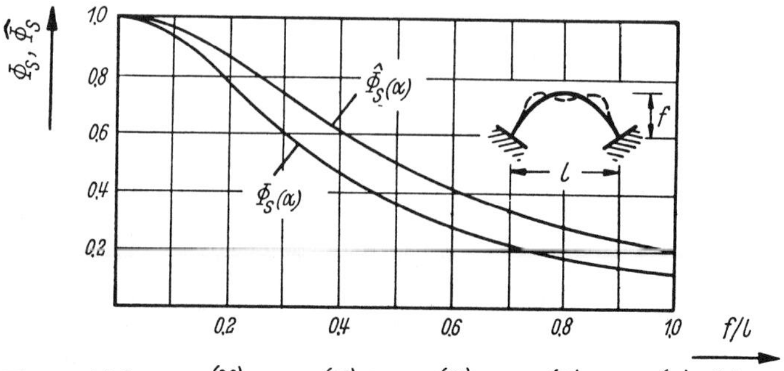

Figure 10.9

The functions Φ_s and $\hat{\Phi}_s$ are given in the above table for some values of α, and are plotted in Figure 10.9.

c) Summary

We conclude from (a) and (b) that the critical case is always antimetrical buckling. The critical arch thrusts $H_{kr}^{(a)}$ decrease rapidly with increasing ratio $\alpha = 4\,f/l$. This does not, however, mean that a steep arch is, for reasons of stability, capable of carrying only smaller loads than a shallow arch: for a given load the arch thrusts also decrease when α increases. Consider the load acting along the line of pressure of a parabolic arch given by

$\hat{M}'' = \hat{H}\,z'' + q = 0$, i.e., $q = -\hat{H}\,z'' = \hat{H}\,\frac{8f}{l^2} = q_0$.

In this case we have

$$\hat{H} = \frac{q_0\,l^2}{8f} = \frac{q_0\,l}{2}\,\frac{1}{\alpha}.$$

Writing $\hat{H} = \frac{q_0\,l}{2}\cdot\frac{1}{\alpha} = H_{kr}'^{(a)} = H_{kr\,0}^{(a)}\,\Phi_a(\alpha)$

we obtain the critical load acting along the line of pressure of the parabolic arch as

$$q_{0\,kr} = \frac{2\,H_{kr\,0}^{(a)}}{l}\,\alpha\,\Phi_a(\alpha) = \frac{2\,H_{kr\,0}^{(a)}}{l}\,\Psi_a(\alpha). \qquad (10.35)$$

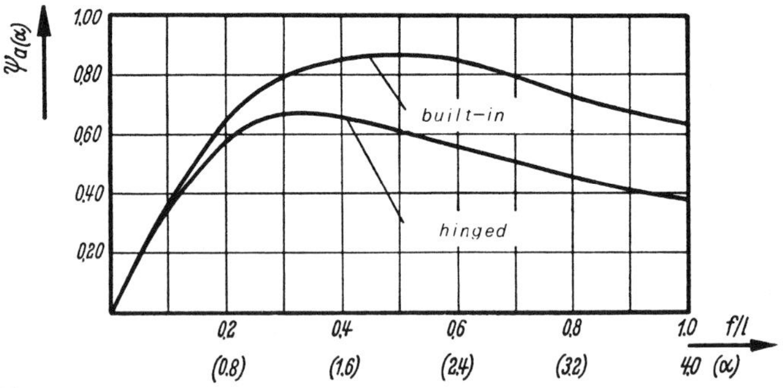

Figure 10.10

The functions $\Psi_a(\alpha) = \alpha\,\Phi_a(\alpha)$ are plotted in Figure 10.10 for arches hinged and built-in at both ends. The functions are tabulated below.

Stability is thus greatest for $0.3 \leqq f/l \leqq 0.6$.

We shall now determine the slenderness ratio l/r above which stability is decisive for a loaded arch, assuming a factor of safety against buckling of 3. We first determine the maximum compressive force, induced in the arch by the external load, which occurs where the inclination of the arch is greatest. Its value is

f/l	0	0.1	0.2	0.3	0.4	0.5	0.6	0.7	0.8	0.9	1.0
$\alpha = 4\,f/l$	0	0.4	0.8	1.2	1.6	2.0	2.4	2.8	3.2	3.6	4.0
$\Psi_a(\alpha)$ hinged	0	0.367	0.596	0.675	0.658	0.616	0.561	0.507	0.458	0.418	0.380
$\Psi_a(\alpha)$ built-in	0	0.374	0.653	0.800	0.854	0.852	0.858	0.776	0.726	0.676	0.632

$$\min N = -\hat{H}/\cos\omega_{\min} = -\hat{H}\left(\sqrt{1+z'^2}\right)_{\max} = -\hat{H}\sqrt{1+\alpha^2} = -\frac{q_0\,l}{2}\frac{\sqrt{1+\alpha^2}}{\alpha}.$$

We obtain the minimum inflation pressure from the condition that the sectional loads must be positive:

$$\min n_x = \frac{p\,r}{2} + \frac{\min N}{F} = \frac{p\,r}{2} + \frac{\min N}{2\,\pi\,r} = \frac{p\,r}{2} - \frac{q_0\,l}{4\,\pi\,r}\frac{\sqrt{1+\alpha^2}}{\alpha} \geqq 0\,.$$

Hence

$$p \geqq p_{\min} = \frac{q_0\,l}{2\pi r^2}\frac{\sqrt{1+\alpha^2}}{\alpha}\,.$$

Introducing the safety factor ϱ, the circumferential sectional loads are then

$$\max n_\vartheta = r\,p = r\,\varrho\,p_{\min} = \frac{q_0\,l\,\varrho}{2\,\pi\,r}\frac{\sqrt{1+\alpha^2}}{\alpha}\,.$$

The condition $n_\vartheta \leqq n_{\text{perm}}$ then leads to

$$q_0 \leqq q_{01} = 2\,\frac{\pi}{\varrho}\,n_{\text{perm}}\frac{\alpha}{\sqrt{1+\alpha^2}}\frac{r}{l}$$

On the other hand, the stability conditions require that

$$q_0 \leqq q_{02} = \frac{q_{0kr}}{3} = \frac{2}{3}\frac{H_{kr\,0}{}^{(a)}}{l}\,\alpha\,\Phi_a(\alpha) = \frac{2}{3}\,\zeta^2\,\frac{D_x\,J}{l^3}\,\alpha\,\Phi_a(\alpha) = \frac{2\,\zeta^2\,\pi}{3}\,\alpha\,\Phi_a(\alpha)\,D_x\left(\frac{r}{l}\right)^3$$

where $\zeta^2 = 4\,\pi^2 = 39.45$ for the arch hinged at both ends and $\zeta^2 = 4\,\lambda^2 = 80.76$ for the arch built-in at both ends. The condition $q_{02} \leqq q_{01}$ yields the slenderness ratio above which the stability conditions are decisive:

$$\frac{r}{l} \leqq \frac{r_{kr}}{l} = \frac{1}{\zeta}\sqrt{\frac{3\,n_{\text{perm}}}{\varrho\,D_x}}\,g(\alpha)\,;\; g(\alpha) = \frac{1}{\sqrt{\Phi_a(\alpha)\sqrt{1+\alpha^2}}}\,. \tag{10.36}$$

We consider an arch hinged at both ends ($\zeta = 2\,\pi$). We obtain for $n_{\text{perm}} = n_{\text{tear}}/3 = 30/3 = 10$ kg/cm, $D_x = 130$ kg/cm, $\varrho = 1.5$, and the maximum value $g = 1.598$ corresponding to $\alpha = 4$:

$$\left(\frac{r_{kr}}{l}\right)_{\max} = \frac{1}{2\,\pi}\sqrt{\frac{3\cdot 10}{1.5\cdot 130}}\cdot 1.598 = 0.0998 \approx \frac{1}{10}\,.$$

Since, in the general case, loads do not act solely along the line of pressure, stability considerations will not be decisive even for $\frac{r}{l} < \frac{1}{10}$. Arches are thus far more suitable for pneumatic supports than columns. This is true despite the fact that, as shown above, stability is of importance also for arches, and taking into account that we neglected the influence of shear deformations.

10.3.4. *Practical Analysis of Unextended Plane Symmetrical Arches*

We consider only the first two terms of (10.24d), since only an increase of the first terms of the expansion of $\hat{M}$ affects them significantly. With symmetrical arches these are the simply antimetrical and simply symmetrical parts of the moment, induced by loads which are respectively antimetrical with one zero point in the region of the arch, or symmetrical with no zero point in the region of the arch:

$$\hat{M} \approx \hat{M}_1 + \hat{M}_2 \approx \hat{M}_a + \hat{M}_s\,. \tag{10.37a}$$

Examples of $\hat{M}_s$ are moments due to dead weight or a symmetrical snow load; of $\hat{M}_a$, moments due to the antimetrical part of a one-sided snow load, obtained by resolving the latter into symmetrical and antimetrical parts, the amplitude of each being half the amplitude of the combined load. Using (10.37a), we obtain from (10.24d) the following approximation:

$$M(x) \approx \hat{M}_a(x)\frac{\nu_a}{\nu_a - 1} + \hat{M}_s(x)\frac{\nu_s}{\nu_s - 1}, \tag{10.37b}$$

where

$$\nu_a = \nu_1 = \frac{H_1}{H} = \frac{H_{kr}{}^{(a)}}{H}, \quad \nu_s = \nu_2 = \frac{H_2}{H} = \frac{H_{kr}{}^{(s)}}{H} \tag{10.37c}$$

denote respectively the safety factors against antimetrical and symmetrical buckling. The arch thrust H is determined approximately from (10.24e). By virtue of $\hat{M}_a'(0) = \hat{M}_a'(l)$, the antimetrical part of the moments does not affect the result. Since $\hat{H} = \hat{H}_s$ (according to the first-order theory, arch thrusts can only be caused by symmetrical loads), we obtain

f/l	0	0.1	0.2	0.3	0.4	0.5	0.6	0.7	0.8	0.9	1.0
$\alpha = 4\,f/l$	0	0.4	0.8	1.2	1.6	2.0	2.4	2.8	3.2	3.6	4.0
$g(\alpha)$ hinged	1.000	1.005	1.017	1.067	1.135	1.204	1.283	1.365	1.445	1.517	1.598
$g(\alpha)$ built-in	1.000	0.996	0.978	0.978	0.998	1.026	1.036	1.100	1.146	1.193	1.238

$$\Delta H = H - \hat{H} = H - \hat{H}_s = -\frac{1}{\nu_s - 1}\frac{\hat{M}_s'(0)}{z'(0)} =$$

$$= -\frac{H_{kr}^{(s)}}{\nu_s - 1}\frac{\hat{M}_s'(0)}{H_{kr}^{(s)} z'(0)} = \frac{H_{kr}^{(s)}}{\nu_s - 1}\delta, \quad \delta = -\frac{\hat{M}_s'(0)}{H_{kr}^{(s)} z'(0)}.$$

Writing $\dfrac{H}{H_{kr}^{(s)}} = \dfrac{1}{\nu_s}$ and $\dfrac{\hat{H}}{H_{kr}^{(s)}} = \dfrac{1}{\hat{\nu}_s}$

this becomes

$$\nu_s = \frac{1}{2}[\hat{\nu}_s + 1 - \hat{\nu}_s\delta] + \sqrt{\frac{1}{4}[\hat{\nu}_s + 1 - \hat{\nu}_s\delta]^2 - \hat{\nu}_s} =$$

$$= \frac{1}{2}(\hat{\nu}_s + 1 - \hat{\nu}_s\delta) + \tag{10.37d}$$

$$+ \sqrt{\left(\frac{\hat{\nu}_s - 1}{2}\right)^2 - \frac{\hat{\nu}_s\delta}{4}[2(\hat{\nu}_s + 1) - \hat{\nu}_s\delta]}.$$

If $|\delta| \ll 1$, we can expand the radical in a series, discarding all nonlinear terms in δ:

$$\nu_s \approx \frac{\hat{\nu}_s + 1}{2} - \frac{\hat{\nu}_s\delta}{2} + \left[\frac{\hat{\nu}_s - 1}{2} + \frac{1}{2\cdot\frac{\hat{\nu}_s - 1}{2}}\left(-\frac{\hat{\nu}_s\delta}{4}\right)\cdot 2(\hat{\nu}_s + 1)\right] = \tag{10.37e}$$

$$= \hat{\nu}_s\left[1 - \delta\frac{\hat{\nu}_s}{\hat{\nu}_s - 1}\right].$$

We consider, as an example, a parabolic arch, hinged at both ends and acted upon by a load, taking into account the deformations caused by the axial forces. The procedure is as follows:

1) The system is analyzed, as usual, according to the first-order theory. In the case considered, the arch thrust

$H_0 = q_0 l^2/(8f) = \dfrac{q_0 l}{2}\dfrac{1}{\alpha}$ is reduced by

$$H_e = H_0 \frac{\int_0^l ds}{\frac{F}{J}\int_0^l z^2\, ds + \int_0^l \cos^2\omega\, ds} =$$

$$= H_0 \frac{\int_0^1 \sqrt{1 + \alpha^2(1 - 2\xi)^2}\, d\xi}{16 f^2 \frac{F}{J}\int_0^1 (\xi - \xi^2)^2 \sqrt{1 + \alpha^2(1 - 2\xi)^2}\, d\xi + \int_0^1 \frac{d\xi}{\sqrt{1 + \alpha^2(1 - 2\xi)^2}}}$$

The moments determined by the first-order theory are $\hat{M} = \hat{M}_s' = H_e z$.

2) The value of δ is determined. In our case,

$$\delta = -\frac{\hat{M}_s'(0)}{H_{kr}^{(s)} z'(0)} = -\frac{H_e}{H_{kr}^{(s)}}.$$

In the case of steep arches we have, by virtue of $16 f^2 F/J = 32 \times (f/r)^2 \gg 1, H_e \ll H_0$ also $|\delta| = H_e/H_{kr}^{(s)} \ll 1$,

so that

3) the determination of H or ν_s and ν_a yields

$$\nu_s = \hat{\nu}_s\left[1 + \frac{H_e}{H_{kr}^{(s)}}\frac{\hat{\nu}_s}{\hat{\nu}_s - 1}\right]$$

from (10.37e). Here $\hat{\nu}_s = \dfrac{H_{kr}^{(s)}}{\hat{H}} = \dfrac{H_{kr}^{(s)}}{H_0 - H_e}$.

This also yields

$$\nu_a = \frac{H_{kr}^{(a)}}{H} = \frac{H_{kr}^{(a)}}{H_{kr}^{(s)}}\frac{H_{kr}^{(s)}}{H} = \frac{H_{kr}^{(a)}}{H_{kr}^{(s)}}\nu_s.$$

4) The moments are finally obtained: $(\hat{M}_a = 0)$

$$M(x) \approx \hat{M}_s\frac{\nu_s}{\nu_s - 1} = H_e z\frac{\nu_s}{\nu_s - 1}.$$

If we include moments $\hat{M}_a$, determined by the first-order theory, we obtain

$$M(x) \approx H_e z\frac{\nu_s}{\nu_s - 1} + \hat{M}_a\frac{\nu_a}{\nu_a - 1}.$$

(The values of H, and thus of ν_a and ν_s do not change, since the value of δ is not affected by $\hat{M}_a$). For a safety factor against buckling $\nu_a = 3$, the antimetrical parts of the moments increase by 50% in comparison with the results obtained by the first-order theory. Thus, the value of $\nu_a = 3$ is recommended as minimum, just as it is for rods.

We shall now present a theoretical basis for the approximate solution given above, using the principle of virtual displacements.

10.4 The Variational Principle Applied to the Plane Arch

10.4.1 *General Observations*

The existence of a variational problem characterizing the elastic stresses or strains of an arch is verified by the principle of virtual displacements, which states that for equilibrium to exist, the deformations $\mathfrak{w} = \mathfrak{w}_0$ must extremize the so-called elastic potential $\Pi = W - A$, where W is the deformation energy and A the work done by the external forces. The statements

$$\Pi|_{\mathfrak{w} = \mathfrak{w}_0} = (W - A)_{\mathfrak{w} = \mathfrak{w}_0} = \text{Extr.}$$

$$\text{or} \quad \delta_{\mathfrak{w}}\Pi|_{\mathfrak{w} = \mathfrak{w}_0} = 0 \tag{10.38a, b}$$

are equivalent to the differential equations of the arch. This is seen immediately if we form the variational derivative as defined by (10.38b), i.e., set up the Eulerian differential equations of the problem (10.38a). For the case of buckling of an arch we can make a different, more specific, statement, referring to the second variation: stable equilibrium exists, if the initial position is again assumed after a small perturbation. This is seen clearly in the example of a straight rod, loaded by a force $P < P_{kr}$, which is slightly deflected in a direction perpendicular to its axis. The rod assumes again its initial position, after the deflections have been attenuated through the (always present) damping. The time taken for the return to the initial position increases with the axial load. In the limiting case $P = P_{kr}$ the rod no longer returns to the initial position: the deflection remains. This shows that for $P = P_{kr}$ the initial (straight) position is not a stable equilibrium position: there exists a position, near the initial one, which can also be an equilibrium position. In this case the straight position corresponds to a neutral equilibrium, in which small perturbations lead to other equilibrium positions. Thus, the kind of equilibrium depends on the load. We can define the beginning of instability in a certain position $\mathfrak{w}_0$ by stating that a position $\mathfrak{w}_0 + \Delta\,\mathfrak{w}$ infinitely close to the former is also an equilibrium position. Thus, in accordance with (10.38b), we have

$$\delta_{\mathfrak{w}}\,\Pi\,\big|_{\mathfrak{w}=\mathfrak{w}_0} = 0\,, \quad \delta_{\mathfrak{w}}\,\Pi\,\big|_{\mathfrak{w}=\mathfrak{w}_0+\Delta\mathfrak{w}} = 0\,,$$

i.e.,

$$\delta_{\mathfrak{w}}\,\Pi\,\big|_{\mathfrak{w}_0+\Delta\mathfrak{w}} - \delta_{\mathfrak{w}}\,\Pi\,\big|_{\mathfrak{w}_0} = 0 \quad \text{or} \quad \delta^2_{\mathfrak{w}}\,\Pi\,\big|_{\mathfrak{w}=\mathfrak{w}_0} = 0\,, \quad (10.38c)$$

The beginning of instability of an equilibrium position is therefore defined by the vanishing of the second variation of the elastic potential Π.

We shall first express the potential Π as a function of the displacements, thus verifying the differential equations of the arch in accordance with (10.38a). By simplifying the relationships between deformations and displacements we shall obtain the approximate solutions presented above, applying the method of Ritz.

10.4.2 *Expressing Π as a Function of Displacements*

a) The deformation energy W

We first determine the specific deformation energy W_s (per unit length $\Delta\,s = 1$) of the undeformed arch. Writing [cf. (10.8a)] $d\,V = d\,F\,\Delta\,s_\zeta\big|_{\Delta s=1} = (1 - \varkappa\,\zeta)\,d\,F$ we have

$$W_s = \frac{1}{2}\int\limits_{[V]}\frac{\sigma_s^2(\zeta)}{E}\,d\,V = \frac{E}{2}\int\limits_{[V]}\varepsilon_s^2(\zeta)\,d\,V = \frac{E}{2}\int\limits_{[F]}\varepsilon_s^2(\zeta)\,(1-\varkappa\,\zeta)\,d\,F.$$

Inserting (10.8c), we obtain

$$W_s = \frac{E}{2}\int\limits_{[F]}\left[(1+\varepsilon)^2\frac{(1-\bar{\varkappa}\,\zeta)^2}{1-\varkappa\,\zeta} - 2(1+\varepsilon)(1-\bar{\varkappa}\zeta) + (1-\varkappa\zeta)\right]dF =$$

$$= \frac{E}{2}\left\{(1+\varepsilon)^2\left[\frac{F}{\sqrt{1-\varkappa^2 r^2}} - 2\frac{\bar{\varkappa}}{\varkappa}F\left(\frac{1}{\sqrt{1-\varkappa^2 r^2}} - 1\right) + \right.\right.$$

$$\left.\left. + \frac{\bar{\varkappa}^2}{\varkappa^2}F\left(\frac{1}{\sqrt{1-\varkappa^2 r^2}} - 1\right)\right] - 2\,(1+\varepsilon)\,F + F\right\}.$$

For small initial curvatures, where

$$\frac{F}{\sqrt{1-\varkappa^2 r^2}} \approx F\left(1 + \frac{\varkappa^2 r^2}{2}\right) = F + \varkappa^2\frac{F\,r^2}{2} = F + \varkappa^2 J\,,$$

$$\frac{1}{\sqrt{1-\varkappa^2 r^2}} - 1 \approx \left(1 + \frac{\varkappa^2 r^2}{2}\right) - 1 = \frac{\varkappa^2 r^2}{2}$$

we have

$$W_s = \frac{E}{2}\{(1+\varepsilon)^2\,[F + \varkappa^2 J - 2\,\bar{\varkappa}\,\varkappa\,J + \bar{\varkappa}^2 J] -$$

$$- 2\,(1+\varepsilon)\,F + F\} = \frac{E}{2}\{F\,\varepsilon^2 + J\,(1+\varepsilon)^2\,(\bar{\varkappa}-\varkappa)^2\} \quad (10.39a)$$

$$= \frac{D_x}{2}\{\bar{F}\,\varepsilon^2 + \bar{J}(1+\varepsilon)^2\,(\bar{\varkappa}-\varkappa)^2\}.$$

Expressing the deformations ε and $(\bar{\varkappa}-\varkappa)$ through the displacements in accordance with (10.6) and (10.7), we determine W_s as a function of the displacements. Integrating over the length of the arch, we obtain the total deformation energy

$$W = \int\limits_0^L W_s\,d\,s = \frac{D_x}{2}\int\limits_0^L\{\bar{F}\,\varepsilon^2 + \bar{J}\,(1+\varepsilon)^2\,(\bar{\varkappa}-\varkappa)^2\}\,d\,s =$$

$$= \frac{D_x}{2}\int\limits_0^L\left\{\bar{F}\left[\sqrt{1 + \frac{2}{1+z'^2}\left[u' + z'\,v' + \frac{1}{2}\,(u'^2 + v'^2)\right]} - 1\right]^2 + \right.$$

$$+ \frac{\bar{J}}{(1+z'^2)^3}\left[1 + \frac{2}{1+z'^2}\left[u' + z'\,v' + \frac{1}{2}\,(u'^2 + v'^2)\right]\right] \times \quad (10.39b)$$

$$\left. \times \left[\frac{(1+u')\,(z''+v'') - u''\,(z'+v')}{\sqrt{1 + \frac{2}{1+z'^2}\left[u' + z'\,v' + \frac{1}{2}\,(u'^2+v'^2)\right]}^{\,3}} - z''\right]^2\right\}d\,s\,.$$

Expressing the displacements through the sectional loads in accordance with (10.10) we obtain

$$W = \int\limits_0^L\frac{1}{2\,D_x}\left\{\frac{N^2}{\bar{F}} + 2\,\varkappa\,\frac{M\,N}{\bar{F}} + \frac{M^2}{\bar{J}}\left(1 + \frac{\varkappa^2 r^2}{2}\right)\right\}d\,s \approx$$

$$\approx \frac{1}{2\,D_x}\int\limits_0^L\left\{\frac{N^2}{\bar{F}} + \frac{M^2}{\bar{J}} + 2\,\varkappa\,\frac{M\,N}{\bar{F}}\right\}d\,s\,. \quad (10.39c)$$

b) Work done by external forces

We denote by $\bar{\mathfrak{p}}\,(\tilde{\mathfrak{w}})$ the load per unit length, acting on the (deformed) arch at an intermediate state of deformation $\tilde{\mathfrak{w}}$. The work done by the external forces is then

$$A = \int\limits_{s=0}^{L}\left[\int\limits_{\tilde{\mathfrak{w}}=0}^{\mathfrak{w}}\bar{\mathfrak{p}}\,(\tilde{\mathfrak{w}})\,(1+\tilde{\varepsilon})\,d\,\tilde{\mathfrak{w}}\right]d\,s \quad (10.40a)$$

The variation of the external work with respect to the displacements

$$\delta_{\mathfrak{w}}\,A = \int\limits_{s=0}^{L}\bar{\mathfrak{p}}\,(\mathfrak{w})\,(1+\varepsilon)\,\delta\,\mathfrak{w}\,d\,s = \delta_{\mathfrak{w}}\int\limits_{s=0}^{L}\left[\overset{\downarrow}{\bar{\mathfrak{p}}\,(\mathfrak{w})\,(1+\varepsilon)}\,\mathfrak{w}\right]d\,s \quad (10.40b)$$

is identical with the variational derivative of the work done if the final load $\bar{\mathfrak{p}}(\mathfrak{w})(1+\varepsilon)\,d\,s$ were to be moved instantly through the final deformation.

10.4.3 *The Variational Principle Applied to the Arch*

This principle is defined as follows in accordance with (10.38b) with the aid of (10.39b) and (10.40a):

$$\delta_{\mathfrak{w}}\int\limits_{s=0}^{L}\left\{\frac{D_x\,\bar{F}}{2}\,\varepsilon^2 + \frac{D_x\,\bar{J}}{2}\,(1+\varepsilon)^2\,(\bar{\varkappa}-\varkappa)^2 - \right.$$

$$\left. - \int\limits_{\tilde{\mathfrak{w}}=0}^{\mathfrak{w}}\bar{\mathfrak{p}}\,(\tilde{\mathfrak{w}})\,(1+\tilde{\varepsilon})\,d\,\tilde{\mathfrak{w}}\right\}ds\,\Bigg|_{\mathfrak{w}=\mathfrak{w}_0} = 0 \quad (10.41a)$$

or, in a simpler form,

$$\delta_{\mathfrak{w}}\int\limits_0^L\left\{\frac{D_x\,\bar{F}}{2}\,\varepsilon^2 + \frac{D_x\,\bar{J}}{2}\,(1+\varepsilon)^2\,(\bar{\varkappa}-\varkappa)^2 - \right.$$

$$\left. - \overset{\downarrow}{\bar{\mathfrak{p}}\,(1+\varepsilon)}\,\mathfrak{w}\right\}d\,s\,\Bigg|_{\mathfrak{w}=\mathfrak{w}_0} = 0 \quad (10.41b)$$

where the arrow indicates that in the load term only the displacement is varied. If we exclude loads due to the pressure of liquids or gases, we have $\bar{\mathfrak{p}}\,(1+\varepsilon)=\mathfrak{p}$, whence

$$\delta_{\mathfrak{w}}\int_0^L\left[\frac{D_xF}{2}\,\varepsilon^2+\frac{D_xJ}{2}(1+\varepsilon)^2(\bar{\varkappa}-\varkappa)^2-\mathfrak{p}\overset{\downarrow}{\mathfrak{w}}\right]ds\Bigg|_{\mathfrak{w}=\mathfrak{w}_0}=0. \quad (10.41c)$$

10.4.4 *The Eulerian Equations of the Problem*

Variational differentiation of (10.41b) yields

$$\int_0^L\{D_xF\,\varepsilon\,\delta_{\mathfrak{w}}\,\varepsilon+D_xJ\,(1+\varepsilon)\,(\bar{\varkappa}-\varkappa)\,\delta_{\mathfrak{w}}\,[(1+\varepsilon)\,(\bar{\varkappa}-\varkappa)]-$$
$$-\bar{\mathfrak{p}}\,(1+\varepsilon)\,\delta\,\mathfrak{w}\}\,ds=0.$$

In order to clarify the reduction of this expression to the equilibrium conditions for the arch, we insert the expressions for the sectional loads given by (10.10):

$$\delta_{\mathfrak{w}}\,\Pi=\int_0^L\{(N+\varkappa M)\,\delta_{\mathfrak{w}}\,\varepsilon+M\,\delta_{\mathfrak{w}}\,[(1+\varepsilon)\,(\bar{\varkappa}-\varkappa)]-$$
$$-\bar{\mathfrak{p}}\,(1+\varepsilon)\,\delta\,\mathfrak{w}\}\,ds=$$
$$=\int_0^L\{N\,\delta_{\mathfrak{w}}\,\varepsilon+\varkappa\,M\,\delta_{\mathfrak{w}}\,\varepsilon+M\,[(\bar{\varkappa}-\varkappa)\,\delta_{\mathfrak{w}}\,\varepsilon+$$
$$+(1+\varepsilon)\,\delta_{\mathfrak{w}}\bar{\varkappa}]-\bar{\mathfrak{p}}\,(1+\varepsilon)\,\delta\,\mathfrak{w}\}\,ds=$$
$$=\int_0^L\{N\,\delta_{\mathfrak{w}}\,\varepsilon+M\,[\bar{\varkappa}\,\delta_{\mathfrak{w}}\,\varepsilon+(1+\varepsilon)\,\delta_{\mathfrak{w}}\bar{\varkappa}]-$$
$$-\bar{\mathfrak{p}}\,(1+\varepsilon)\,\delta\,\mathfrak{w}\}\,ds=0$$

or

$$\delta_{\mathfrak{w}}\,\Pi=\int_0^L\{N\,\delta_{\mathfrak{w}}\,\varepsilon+M\,\delta_{\mathfrak{w}}\,[(1+\varepsilon)\bar{\varkappa}]-\bar{\mathfrak{p}}\,(1+\varepsilon)\,\delta\,\mathfrak{w}\}\,ds=0. \quad (10.42)$$

Taking into account (10.6d), we obtain from (10.6c):

$$\delta_{\mathfrak{w}}\,\varepsilon=\frac{2\left[\dfrac{\dot{\mathfrak{r}}\,\delta\,\dot{\mathfrak{w}}}{\dot{\mathfrak{r}}^2}+\dfrac{\dot{\mathfrak{w}}\,\delta\,\dot{\mathfrak{w}}}{\dot{\mathfrak{r}}^2}\right]}{2\sqrt{1+2\dfrac{\dot{\mathfrak{r}}\,\dot{\mathfrak{w}}}{\dot{\mathfrak{r}}^2}+\dfrac{\dot{\mathfrak{w}}^2}{\dot{\mathfrak{r}}^2}}}=\frac{(\dot{\mathfrak{r}}+\dot{\mathfrak{w}})\;\;\delta\,\dot{\mathfrak{w}}}{\sqrt{(\dot{\mathfrak{r}}+\dot{\mathfrak{w}})^2}\,\sqrt{\dot{\mathfrak{r}}^2}}=\bar{\mathfrak{t}}\,\delta\,\mathfrak{w}', \quad (10.43a)$$

where the prime again denotes differentiation with respect to the arc length s and from (10.6f)

$$\delta_{\mathfrak{w}}\,[(1+\varepsilon)\,\bar{\varkappa}]=\delta_{\mathfrak{w}}\left(\sqrt{\bar{\mathfrak{t}}'^2}\right)=\frac{\bar{\mathfrak{t}}'\,\delta_{\mathfrak{w}}\,\bar{\mathfrak{t}}'}{\sqrt{\bar{\mathfrak{t}}'^2}}=\frac{\bar{\mathfrak{t}}'\,\delta_{\mathfrak{w}}\,\bar{\mathfrak{t}}'}{(1+\varepsilon)\,\bar{\varkappa}}.$$

According to the Frenet formulas

$$\bar{\mathfrak{t}}'=\frac{d\,\bar{\mathfrak{t}}}{d\,s}=(1+\varepsilon)\,\frac{d\,\bar{\mathfrak{t}}}{d\,\bar{s}}=(1+\varepsilon)\,\bar{\varkappa}\,\bar{\mathfrak{n}}$$

where $\bar{\mathfrak{n}}$ is the normal vector of the deformed arc. Using this expression, we obtain

$$\delta_{\mathfrak{w}}\,[(1+\varepsilon)\,\bar{\varkappa}]=\bar{\mathfrak{n}}\,\delta_{\mathfrak{w}}\,\bar{\mathfrak{t}}'=\bar{\mathfrak{n}}\,\delta_{\mathfrak{w}}\left(\frac{d\,\bar{\mathfrak{t}}}{d\,s}\right)=\bar{\mathfrak{n}}\,\frac{d}{d\,s}(\delta_{\mathfrak{w}}\,\bar{\mathfrak{t}})=$$
$$=\frac{d}{d\,s}\left[\bar{\mathfrak{n}}\,(\delta_{\mathfrak{w}}\,\bar{\mathfrak{t}})\right]-\frac{d\,\bar{\mathfrak{n}}}{d\,s}\,\delta_{\mathfrak{w}}\,\bar{\mathfrak{t}}.$$

According to the Frenet formulas for plane arches,

$$\frac{d\,\bar{\mathfrak{n}}}{d\,s}=(1+\varepsilon)\,\frac{d\,\bar{\mathfrak{n}}}{d\,\bar{s}}=-\,\bar{\varkappa}\,(1+\varepsilon)\,\bar{\mathfrak{t}}.$$

On the other hand,

$$\bar{\mathfrak{t}}=\frac{\dot{\mathfrak{r}}+\dot{\mathfrak{w}}}{\sqrt{(\dot{\mathfrak{r}}+\dot{\mathfrak{w}})^2}}=\frac{\mathfrak{r}'+\mathfrak{w}'}{1+\varepsilon}$$

$$\delta_{\mathfrak{w}}\,\bar{\mathfrak{t}}=\frac{\delta\,\mathfrak{w}'}{1+\varepsilon}-\frac{(\mathfrak{r}'+\mathfrak{w}')}{(1+\varepsilon)^2}\,\delta_{\mathfrak{w}}\,\varepsilon=\frac{\delta\,\mathfrak{w}'}{1+\varepsilon}-\frac{\bar{\mathfrak{t}}}{1+\varepsilon}\,\delta_{\mathfrak{w}}\,\varepsilon,$$

whence, taking into account (10.43a), we obtain

$$\delta_{\mathfrak{w}}\,\bar{\mathfrak{t}}=\frac{\delta\,\mathfrak{w}'}{1+\varepsilon}-\frac{\bar{\mathfrak{t}}}{1+\varepsilon}\,(\bar{\mathfrak{t}}\,\delta\,\mathfrak{w}')=\frac{1}{1+\varepsilon}\,[\delta\,\mathfrak{w}'-\bar{\mathfrak{t}}\,(\bar{\mathfrak{t}}\,\delta\,\mathfrak{w}')]=$$
$$=\frac{1}{1+\varepsilon}\,\bar{\mathfrak{t}}\times(\delta\,\mathfrak{w}'\times\bar{\mathfrak{t}}).$$

Thus, finally, writing $\bar{\mathfrak{n}}\times\bar{\mathfrak{t}}=-\,\bar{\mathfrak{b}}$ where $\bar{\mathfrak{b}}$ is the binormal vector of the deformed arc, we obtain

$$\delta_{\mathfrak{w}}\,[(1+\varepsilon)\,\bar{\varkappa}]=\frac{d}{d\,s}\left[-\,\frac{\bar{\mathfrak{b}}}{1+\varepsilon}\,(\delta\,\mathfrak{w}'\times\bar{\mathfrak{t}})\right]$$

which, by virtue of $\bar{\mathfrak{t}}\times\bar{\mathfrak{b}}=-\,\bar{\mathfrak{n}}$ becomes

$$\delta_{\mathfrak{w}}\,[(1+\varepsilon)\,\bar{\varkappa}]=\frac{d}{d\,s}\left[\frac{\delta\,\mathfrak{w}'\,\bar{\mathfrak{n}}}{1+\varepsilon}\right]. \quad (10.43b)$$

Inserting the displacement variations given by (10.43a, b) into (10.42), we obtain the extremum problem

$$\int_0^L\left\{N\,\bar{\mathfrak{t}}\,\delta\,\mathfrak{w}'+M\,\frac{d}{d\,s}\left[\frac{\delta\,\mathfrak{w}'\,\bar{\mathfrak{n}}}{1+\varepsilon}\right]-\bar{\mathfrak{p}}\,(1+\varepsilon)\,\delta\,\mathfrak{w}\right\}\,ds=0 \quad (10.43c)$$

which is independent of the stress-strain law. Partial integration of the first two terms yields

$$\left[N\,\bar{\mathfrak{t}}\,\delta\,\mathfrak{w}\right]_0^L-\left[\frac{d\,M}{d\,s}\,\frac{\delta\,\mathfrak{w}}{1+\varepsilon}\,\bar{\mathfrak{n}}\right]_0^L+\left[M\,\frac{\delta\,\mathfrak{w}'}{1+\varepsilon}\,\bar{\mathfrak{n}}\right]_0^L-$$
$$-\int_0^L\left\{\frac{d}{d\,s}\,(N\,\bar{\mathfrak{t}})-\frac{d}{d\,s}\left[\frac{1}{1+\varepsilon}\,\frac{d\,M}{d\,s}\,\bar{\mathfrak{n}}\right]+\bar{\mathfrak{p}}\,(1+\varepsilon)\right\}\,\delta\,\mathfrak{w}\,ds=0.$$

Since the displacement variations must be compatible, the immovability of the supports yields $\delta\,\mathfrak{w}|_0=\delta\,\mathfrak{w}|_L=0$, so that the first two boundary terms vanish. From $\dfrac{\delta\,\mathfrak{w}'}{1+\varepsilon}\,\bar{\mathfrak{n}}=\dfrac{d}{d\,\bar{s}}\,(\delta\,\mathfrak{w})\cdot\bar{\mathfrak{n}}=\delta\,\varphi$ where $\delta\,\varphi$ is the angle of inclination of the varied bending line $\delta\,\mathfrak{w}$, in relation to the deformed arc, we find that the third term represents the product of edge moment and edge-rotation variation. This term is also zero, since either the edge moments (hinged supports)* or the edge rotations of the (compatible) displacement variations (built-in arch) must vanish. Hence

$$\int_0^L\left\{\frac{d}{d\,s}\,(N\,\bar{\mathfrak{t}})-\frac{d}{d\,s}\left[\frac{d\,M}{d\,\bar{s}}\,\bar{\mathfrak{n}}\right]+\bar{\mathfrak{p}}\,(1+\varepsilon)\right\}\,\delta\,\mathfrak{w}\,ds=0.$$

Since the displacement variations are arbitrary, we have

$$\frac{d}{d\,s}\,(N\,\bar{\mathfrak{t}})-\frac{d}{d\,s}\left[\frac{d\,M}{d\,\bar{s}}\,\bar{\mathfrak{n}}\right]+\bar{\mathfrak{p}}\,(1+\varepsilon)=0 \quad (10.44)$$

which is identical with (10.11c), obtained from the equilibrium conditions.

* See footnote on p. 255.

10.4.5 *The Variational Principle Applied to the Unextended Arch*
For $\varepsilon = 0$ we obtain from (10.13a)

$$u' = \frac{d\,u}{d\,x} = \sqrt{1 - 2\,z'\,v' - v'^2} - 1\,.$$

Integration yields

$$u = C + \int_0^x \left(\sqrt{1 - 2\,z'\,v' - v'^2} - 1\right) d\,x\,.$$

By virtue of the immovability of the supports $[u\,(0) = u\,(l) = 0]$ we have $C = 0$ and

$$\int_0^l \left(\sqrt{1 - 2\,z'\,v' - v'^2} - 1\right) d\,x = 0\,. \tag{10.45a}$$

Using (10.13c) and noting that $d\,s = \sqrt{1 + z'^2}\,d\,x$ we then obtain from (10.41c),

$$\Pi = \int_{x=0}^{l} \left\{ \frac{D_x \bar{J}}{2\,[1 + z'^2]^{5/2}} \left[\frac{v''\,(1 + z'^2) + z''\,(1 - z'\,v')}{\sqrt{1 - 2\,z'\,v' - v'^2}} - z'' \right]^2 - \left[p_x \int_0^x \left(\sqrt{1 - 2\,z'\,v' - v'^2} - 1\right) d\,x + p_z\,v \right] \sqrt{1 + z'^2} \right\} d\,x = \text{Extr.} \tag{10.45b}$$

In this case Π depends solely on the vertical displacements. When these are varied, we have to take into account not only the boundary conditions for v but also (10.45a). Introducing the Lagrange multiplier λ, we have the isoperimetric problem

$$\delta_{v,\lambda}\,\bar{\Pi} = 0\,;$$

$$\bar{\Pi} = \int_0^l \left\{ \frac{D_x \bar{J}}{2\,[1 + z'^2]^{5/2}} \left[\frac{v''\,(1 + z'^2) + z''\,(1 - z'\,v')}{\sqrt{1 - 2\,z'\,v' - v'^2}} - z'' \right]^2 + \left(\int_0^x p_x \sqrt{1 + z'^2}\,d\,x \right) \left(\sqrt{1 - 2\,z'\,v' - v'^2} - 1 \right) - p_z\,v\,\sqrt{1 + z'^2} + \lambda \left[\sqrt{1 - 2\,z'\,v' - v'^2} - 1 \right] \right\} d\,x. \tag{10.45c}$$

Here, partial integration, taking into account (10.45a), yielded

$$- \int_0^l p_x \sqrt{1 + z'^2} \left(\int_0^x \left(\sqrt{1 - 2\,z'\,v' - v'^2} - 1\right) d\,x \right) d\,x =$$

$$= - \int_0^l \frac{d}{d\,x} \left(\int_0^x p_x \sqrt{1 + z'^2}\,d\,x \right) \left(\int_0^x \left(\sqrt{1 - 2\,z'\,v' - v'^2} - 1\right) d\,x \right) d\,x =$$

$$= \int_0^l \left(\sqrt{1 - 2\,z'\,v' - v'^2} - 1\right) \left(\int_0^x p_x \sqrt{1 + z'^2}\,d\,x \right) d\,x\,.$$

The physical meaning of λ becomes clear from the Euler-Lagrange differential equation of the problem, obtained after variation with respect to v. From

$$\Phi = \frac{D_x \bar{J}}{2\,[1 + z'^2]^{5/2}} \left[\frac{v''\,(1 + z'^2) + z''\,(1 - z'\,v')}{\sqrt{1 - 2\,z'\,v' - v'^2}} - z'' \right]^2 + \left(\lambda + \int_0^x p_x \sqrt{1 + z'^2}\,d\,x \right) \left(\sqrt{1 - 2\,z'\,v' - v'^2} - 1 \right) - p_z \sqrt{1 + z'^2}\,v$$

we have

$$\frac{\partial \Phi}{\partial v''} = \frac{D_x \bar{J}}{[1 + z'^2]^{3/2}} \, \frac{\left[\dfrac{v''\,(1 + z'^2) + z''\,(1 - z'\,v')}{\sqrt{1 - 2\,z'\,v' - v'^2}} - z'' \right]}{\sqrt{1 - 2\,z'\,v' - v'^2}} =$$

$$= \frac{D_x \bar{J}\,(\bar{\varkappa} - \varkappa)}{\sqrt{1 - 2\,z'\,v' - v'^2}} = \frac{M}{\sqrt{1 - 2\,z'\,v' - v'^2}}\,,$$

$$\frac{\partial \Phi}{\partial v'} = \frac{D_x \bar{J}}{[1 + z'^2]^{3/2}} \left[\frac{v''\,(1 + z'^2) + z''\,(1 - z'\,v')}{\sqrt{1 - 2\,z'\,v' - v'^2}} - z'' \right] \times$$

$$\times \frac{1}{1 + z'^2} \, \frac{\partial}{\partial v'} \left[\frac{v''\,(1 + z'^2) + z''\,(1 - z'\,v')}{\sqrt{1 - 2\,z'\,v' - v'^2}} \right] -$$

$$- \left[\lambda + \int_0^x p_x \sqrt{1 + z'^2}\,d\,x \right] \frac{z' + v'}{\sqrt{1 - 2\,z'\,v' - v'^2}} =$$

$$= \frac{M}{1 + z'^2} \, \frac{\partial}{\partial v'} \left[\frac{v''\,(1 + z'^2) + z''\,(1 - z'\,v')}{\sqrt{1 - 2\,z'\,v' - v'^2}} \right] -$$

$$- \left[\lambda + \int_0^x p_x \sqrt{1 + z'^2}\,d\,x \right] \frac{z' + v'}{\sqrt{1 - 2\,z'\,v' - v'^2}} =$$

$$= M \cdot \frac{v''\,z' + z''\,v' + v''\,v'}{\sqrt{1 - 2\,z'\,v' - v'^2}^{\,3}} -$$

$$- \left[\lambda + \int_0^x p_x \sqrt{1 + z'^2}\,d\,x \right] \frac{z' + v'}{\sqrt{1 - 2\,z'\,v' - v'^2}} =$$

$$= M \frac{d}{d\,x} \left[\frac{1}{\sqrt{1 - 2\,z'\,v' - v'^2}} \right] -$$

$$- \left[\lambda + \int_0^x p_x \sqrt{1 + z'^2}\,d\,x \right] \frac{z' + v'}{\sqrt{1 - 2\,z'\,v' - v'^2}}\,,$$

$$\frac{\partial \Phi}{\partial v} = - p_z \sqrt{1 + z'^2}\,.$$

The Euler-Lagrange differential equation

$$\frac{\partial \Phi}{\partial v} - \frac{d}{d\,x} \left(\frac{\partial \Phi}{\partial v'} \right) + \frac{d^2}{d\,x^2} \left(\frac{\partial \Phi}{\partial v''} \right) = 0$$

then yields

$$\frac{d^2}{d\,x^2} \left[\frac{M}{\sqrt{1 - 2\,z'\,v' - v'^2}} \right] - \frac{d}{d\,x} \left[M \frac{d}{d\,x} \left(\frac{1}{\sqrt{1 - 2\,z'\,v' - v'^2}} \right) \right] + \frac{d}{d\,x} \left[\frac{\left(\lambda + \int_0^x p_x \sqrt{1 + z'^2}\,d\,x \right) (z' + v')}{\sqrt{1 - 2\,z'\,v' - v'^2}} \right] - p_z \sqrt{1 + z'^2} = 0$$

or

$$\frac{d}{d\,x} \left[\frac{1}{\sqrt{1 - 2\,z'\,v' - v'^2}} \, \frac{d\,M}{d\,x} \right] + \frac{d}{d\,x} \left[\frac{\left(\lambda + \int_0^x p_x \sqrt{1 + z'^2}\,d\,x \right) (z' + v')}{\sqrt{1 - 2\,z'\,v' - v'^2}} \right] - p_z \sqrt{1 + z'^2} = 0\,. \tag{10.46a}$$

For the arc element shown in Figure 10.11 we obtain the equilibrium condition

$$\frac{d\,Q_x}{d\,x} + p_x \sqrt{1 + z'^2} = 0 \quad \text{or}$$

$$Q_x = - \left(A_x + \int_0^x p_x \sqrt{1 + z'^2}\,d\,x \right), \tag{10.46b}$$

where A_x is the horizontal reaction at the left end of the arch $(x = 0)$, as well as

$$\frac{dQ_z}{dx} - p_z\sqrt{1+z'^2} = 0 \quad \text{or} \quad \frac{dQ_z}{dx} = p_z\sqrt{1+z'^2} \tag{10.46c}$$

and

$$\frac{dM}{dx} - Q_z(1+u') - Q_x(z'+v') = 0 . \tag{10.46d}$$

Dividing (10.46d) by $1 + u' = \sqrt{1 - 2z'v' - v'^2}$

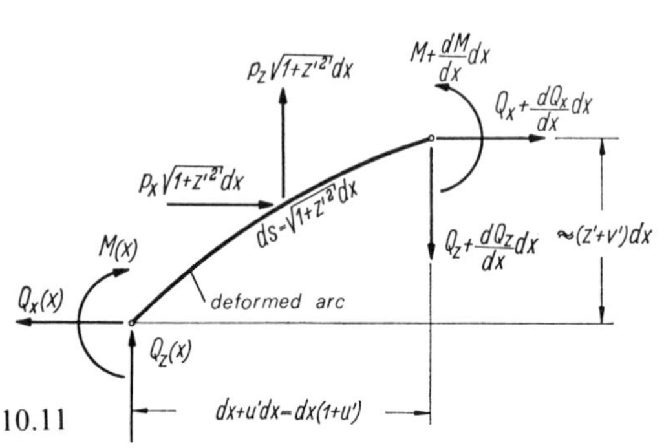

Figure 10.11

and again differentiating with respect to x, we obtain, taking into account (10.46b, c),

$$\frac{d}{dx}\left[\frac{1}{\sqrt{1-2z'v'-v'^2}}\,\frac{dM}{dx}\right] + \tag{10.46e}$$

$$+\frac{d}{dx}\left[\frac{\left(A_x + \int\limits_0^x p_x\sqrt{1+z'^2}\,dx\right)(z'+v')}{\sqrt{1-2z'v'-v'^2}}\right] - p_z\sqrt{1+z'^2} = 0 .$$

Comparison with (10.46a) then shows that $\lambda = A_x$, i.e., the Lagrange multiplier is identical with the horizontal reaction at the left end of the arch.

The variational problem of the unextended arch can thus be stated as follows: $\delta_{v,\,A_x}\Pi = 0$;

$$\Pi = \int\limits_0^l \left\{\frac{D_x\bar{J}}{2\,[1+z'^2]^{5/2}}\left[\frac{v''(1+z'^2)+z''(1-z'v')}{\sqrt{1-2z'v'-v'^2}} - z''\right]^2 - \right. \tag{10.47}$$

$$- p_z v\sqrt{1+z'^2} +$$

$$\left. + \left(A_x + \int\limits_0^x p_x\sqrt{1+z'^2}\,dx\right)\left(\sqrt{1-2z'v'-v'^2} - 1\right)\right\} dx .$$

For vertical loads, i.e., $p_x = 0$, and $p_z = -\dfrac{q(x)}{\sqrt{1+z'^2}}$ where $q(x)$ is the vertical load (directed downward) per unit length of the horizontal projection of the arch and $A_x = H$ (horizontal arch thrust), we have

$\delta_{v,\,H}\Pi = 0$;

$$\Pi = \int\limits_0^l \left\{\frac{D_x\bar{J}}{2\,[1+z'^2]^{5/2}}\left[\frac{v''(1+z'^2)+z''(1-z'v')}{\sqrt{1-2z'v'-v'^2}} - z''\right]^2 + \right. \tag{10.48}$$

$$\left. + H\left(\sqrt{1-2z'v'-v'^2} - 1\right) + qv\right\} dx .$$

10.4.6 *The Variational Problem of the Linearized Equations of the Arch*

The variational problem corresponding to the linearized displacement equations can at most contain quadratic terms in the displacement derivatives. Hence, in the first term of (10.41b) (the extension term), ε^2 has to be found by squaring that part of the extension (obtained from the first-order theory) which is linear in the displacement derivatives. Thus, by (10.14a)

$$\varepsilon^2 = \left(\frac{u' + z'v'}{1+z'^2}\right)^2 . \tag{10.49a}$$

The curvature term is also formed only by the linear parts of the curvature:

$$(\bar{\varkappa} - \varkappa)^2 = \left\{\frac{1}{\sqrt{1+z'^2}}\left[v'' - (\varepsilon z')'\right] - \varkappa\,\varepsilon\right\}^2 = \tag{10.49b}$$

$$= \left\{\frac{1}{\sqrt{1+z'^2}}\left[v'' - \left(\frac{z'(u'+z'v')}{1+z'^2}\right)'\right] - \frac{z''(u'+z'v')}{[1+z'^2]^{5/2}}\right\}^2 .$$

In addition we have to put

$$(1+\varepsilon)^2 \approx 1 \tag{10.49c}$$

in order to obtain terms of second-order smallness. Thus, the variational problem is

$$\delta_{u,v}\int\limits_{x=0}^{l}\left[\frac{D_x\bar{F}}{2}\left(\frac{u'+z'v'}{1+z'^2}\right)^2 + \frac{D_x\bar{J}}{2}\left\{\frac{1}{\sqrt{1+z'^2}}\left[v'' - \right.\right.\right. \tag{10.50}$$

$$\left.\left. - \left(\frac{z'(u'+z'v')}{1+z'^2}\right)'\right] - \frac{z''(u'+z'v')}{(1+z'^2)^{5/2}}\right\}^2 -$$

$$\left. - p_x u - p_z v\right]\sqrt{1+z'^2}\,dx = 0 .$$

We obtain the variational problem for the unextended arch by discarding in (10.47) all terms of higher order than the second in the displacement derivatives. Writing

$$\frac{1}{\sqrt{1+z'^2}^{\,3}}\left[\frac{v''(1+z'^2)+z''(1-z'v')}{\sqrt{1-2z'v'-v'^2}} - z''\right] = \tag{10.51a}$$

$$= \bar{\varkappa} - \varkappa \approx \frac{v''}{\sqrt{1+z'^2}}$$

and

$$\sqrt{1-2z'v'-v'^2} - 1 \approx \left[1 + \frac{1}{2}(-2z'v' - v'^2) + \right. \tag{10.51b}$$

$$\left. + \frac{1}{2!}\,\frac{1}{2}\left(-\frac{1}{2}\right)(2z'v' + v'^2)^2\right] - 1 \approx -z'v' - \frac{1+z'^2}{2}v'^2$$

we obtain

$$\delta_{v,\,A_x}\Pi = 0\,;\quad \Pi = \int\limits_{x=0}^{l}\left\{\frac{D_x\bar{J}}{2\sqrt{1+z'^2}}\,v''^2 - p_z v\sqrt{1+z'^2} - \right. \tag{10.52a}$$

$$\left. - \left(A_x + \int\limits_0^x p_x\sqrt{1+z'^2}\,dx\right)\left(z'v' + \frac{1+z'^2}{2}v'^2\right)\right\} dx ,$$

which, for vertical loads, reduces to

$$\delta_{v,\,H}\Pi = 0\,;\quad \Pi = \int\limits_{x=0}^{l}\left\{\frac{D_x\bar{J}}{2\sqrt{1+z'^2}}\,v''^2 - \right. \tag{10.52b}$$

$$\left. - H\left(z'v' + \frac{1+z'^2}{2}v'^2\right) + qv\right\} dx .$$

10.4.7 *Applying the Method of Ritz*

This method of solving variational problems approximately consists of selecting special functions, e.g., for the problem (10.52b)

$$v(x) = \sum_{k=1}^{n} C_k v_k(x) \tag{10.53}$$

where the $v_k(x)$ satisfy, as far as possible, all boundary conditions, and the C_k are constants which have to be determined. After integration we can express $\bar{\Pi}(C_1 \ldots C_n)$ as a function of the constants C_k. We then replace the exact fulfilment of the variational problem for $\bar{\Pi}(C_1 \ldots C_n)$ by the requirement that $\partial \bar{\Pi} / \partial C_i = 0|_{i=1 \cdots n}$. These extremum conditions serve for the determination of the C_k. Inserting (10.53) into (10.52b), and using symbols (10.20c), we obtain from $\partial \bar{\Pi} / \partial C_i = 0|_{i=1 \cdots n}$, the system (10.20b). This verifies the connection between the approximate method, used in Subsection 10.3.2, with the principle of virtual displacements. The method of Ritz can also be applied, when deformations due to axial forces are taken into account. In this case we would have to start from (10.50) where both u and v would have to be expressed through functions satisfying the boundary conditions:

$$u(x) \approx \sum_{k=1}^{n} C_k^{(u)} u_k(x), \quad v(x) \approx \sum_{k=1}^{n} C_k^{(v)} v_k(x).$$

The constants are again obtained from $\partial \Pi / C_k^{(u)} = 0|_{k=1 \cdots n}$ and $\partial \Pi / \partial C_k^{(v)} = 0|_{k=1 \cdots n}$. Analysis of shallow arches shows that the influence of ε on the critical arch load is insignificant.

11 PRINCIPLES OF THE THEORY OF LARGE MEMBRANE DEFORMATIONS

11.1 Introduction

When we consider the problem of forcing an initially plane membrane out of its plane, we arrive at the conclusion that the relationships of the linearized theory, in which we neglected the deformations when determining the sectional loads, are no longer adequate, since the undeformed membrane is not capable of withstanding the inflation pressure acting normal to its plane. Equilibrium can only be attained when, due to the deformations, the membrane becomes curved, so that the sectional loads have components normal to the plane of the undeformed membrane. The state of stress thus depends markedly on the final shape of the membrane. This shape is, however, unknown, as are the sectional loads. When the equilibrium state of a system has to be determined in the final position which depends on the deformations, we have to apply the theory of large or finite deformations, in contrast with the usually assumed infinitesimal deformations. We cannot then linearize the displacement-deformation relationships, which is only permissible for small deformations, but have to apply the actual nonlinear displacement-deformation relationships. This leads, in the general case, to nonlinear displacement equations.

As was shown in the analysis of the finite nonlinear deformations of an arch, we cannot generally obtain an exact solution of the differential equations for the displacements. We have, therefore, to use equivalent integral equations (variational problem), which can be evaluated approximately according to the method of Ritz. In Section 11.3 we establish the extremum problem, which can also be derived directly by means of the principle of virtual displacements, by proceeding from the equilibrium conditions for the deformed membrane. We shall verify this procedure in Sections 11.4 and 11.5, where we shall also determine the accuracy of the approximations, obtained by simple applications of the method of Ritz, in comparison with the exact solutions, for a sphere or a small rectangular membrane forced out of its plane. These latter solutions can be presented in a simple form. We shall thereafter consider circular and square membranes, forced out of their planes, and compare the theoretical with experimental results.

These investigations, carried out for various stress-strain relationships, show the inherent nonlinearity of the problem. This is evident from the systems of nonlinear equations, obtained for the constants introduced when applying the method of Ritz (Sections 11.5,6,7). Their solution is exceedingly tedious, so that in practice the number of functions introduced must be restricted to two. This is, however, in many cases sufficient to solve a problem with satisfactory accuracy. We shall first discuss the

11.2 General Fundamentals

proceeding from an initially arbitrary surface $\mathfrak{r}(\alpha, \beta)$ definable by orthogonal parametric curves ($\mathfrak{r}_\alpha \mathfrak{r}_\beta = g_{\alpha\beta} = \cos \sigma_{\alpha\beta} = 0$). The available equations are

a) the equilibrium conditions of the membrane;

b) the sectional load-deformation relationships;

c) the relationships between deformations and displacements.

We can obtain the differential equations of the problem, i.e., the displacement equations of the membrane, in a manner similar to that for the arch, by expressing first the sectional loads through the displacements, using (b) and (c), and inserting the results into the equilibrium conditions. Lack of space prevents us from demonstrating this last step here. In any case, we shall not proceed from the (nonlinear) displacement equations when carrying out calculations in practice. Section 11.2, therefore, contains only general statements on geometry, equilibrium, and stress-strain relationships.

11.2.1 *Geometrical Fundamentals*

These have already been discussed in Section 2.4: as a result of the deformations $\mathfrak{v}(\alpha, \beta)$, the undeformed membrane, defined by $\mathfrak{r}(\alpha, \beta)$, becomes deformed to the surface

$$\bar{\mathfrak{r}}(\alpha, \beta) = \mathfrak{r}(\alpha, \beta) + \mathfrak{v}(\alpha, \beta).$$

The deformations of the surface elements and of the net of parametric curves forming these elements are described by the deformation tensor (2.22a), through which we were able to prove the existence of so-called principal directions:

There exist always on the undeformed surface two orthogonal families of curves which remain orthogonal also after deformation (curves of principal extension). Since

$$d\,\bar{s}_\varphi = (1 + \varepsilon_\varphi)\, d\, s_\varphi$$

and thus

$$d\,\bar{\mathfrak{s}}_\varphi = \bar{\mathfrak{e}}_\varphi\, d\,\bar{s}_\varphi = \bar{\mathfrak{e}}_\varphi (1 + \varepsilon_\varphi)\, d\, s_\varphi\,,$$

it follows from (2.18a) that a unit vector $\mathfrak{e}_\varphi$, fixed to the undeformed surface, is transformed after deformation into the unit vector

$$\bar{\mathfrak{e}}_\varphi = \frac{\mathfrak{e}_\varphi (\mathfrak{E} + \mathfrak{B})}{1 + \varepsilon_\varphi} = \frac{\mathfrak{e}_\varphi + (\mathfrak{e}_\varphi \nabla)\, \mathfrak{v}}{1 + \varepsilon_\varphi} = \frac{\mathfrak{e}_\varphi + \partial\, \mathfrak{v}/\partial\, s_\varphi}{1 + \varepsilon_\varphi} = \frac{\partial\, \bar{\mathfrak{r}}}{\partial\, \bar{s}_\varphi}\,. \tag{11.1a}$$

In particular, the unit tangent vectors to the deformed parametric curves are

$$\bar{\mathfrak{e}}_\alpha = \frac{\partial\, \bar{\mathfrak{r}}}{\partial\, \bar{s}_\alpha} = \frac{\mathfrak{e}_\alpha + \partial\, \mathfrak{v}/\partial\, s_\alpha}{1 + \varepsilon_\alpha} = \frac{\mathfrak{e}_\alpha (\mathfrak{E} + \mathfrak{B})}{1 + \varepsilon_\alpha}\,,$$
$$\bar{\mathfrak{e}}_\beta = \frac{\partial\, \bar{\mathfrak{r}}}{\partial\, \bar{s}_\beta} = \frac{\mathfrak{e}_\beta + \partial\, \mathfrak{v}/\partial\, s_\beta}{1 + \varepsilon_\beta} = \frac{\mathfrak{e}_\beta (\mathfrak{E} + \mathfrak{B})}{1 + \varepsilon_\beta}\,. \tag{11b,c}$$

To apply the principle of virtual displacements, we need the displacement variations of the deformations. Taking into account (11.1), we obtained from (2.23a)

$$\delta_\mathfrak{v}\, d_{\alpha\alpha} = \delta_\mathfrak{v} \left(\varepsilon_\alpha + \frac{{\varepsilon_\alpha}^2}{2}\right) = (1 + \varepsilon_\alpha)\, \delta_\mathfrak{v}\, \varepsilon_\alpha$$

or

$$\delta_{\mathfrak{v}} \varepsilon_\alpha = \frac{\delta_{\mathfrak{v}} d_{\alpha\alpha}}{1+\varepsilon_\alpha} = \frac{1}{1+\varepsilon_\alpha} \delta_{\mathfrak{v}} \left[\mathfrak{e}_\alpha \frac{\partial \mathfrak{v}}{\partial s_\alpha} + \frac{1}{2} \left(\frac{\partial \mathfrak{v}}{\partial s_\alpha} \right)^2 \right] =$$
$$= \frac{1}{1+\varepsilon_\alpha} \left(\mathfrak{e}_\alpha \delta_{\mathfrak{v}} \frac{\partial \mathfrak{v}}{\partial s_\alpha} + \frac{\partial \mathfrak{v}}{\partial s_\alpha} \delta_{\mathfrak{v}} \frac{\partial \mathfrak{v}}{\partial s_\alpha} \right) =$$
$$= \frac{\mathfrak{e}_\alpha + \partial \mathfrak{v}/\partial s_\alpha}{1+\varepsilon_\alpha} \delta_{\mathfrak{v}} \left(\frac{\partial \mathfrak{v}}{\partial s_\alpha} \right) = \bar{\mathfrak{e}}_\alpha \delta_{\mathfrak{v}} \left(\frac{\partial \mathfrak{v}}{\partial s_\alpha} \right) = \tag{11.2a}$$
$$= \bar{\mathfrak{e}}_\alpha \frac{\partial (\delta \mathfrak{v})}{\partial s_\alpha} = \bar{\mathfrak{e}}_\alpha \delta_{\mathfrak{v}} \left(\frac{\partial \bar{\mathfrak{r}}}{\partial s_\alpha} \right)$$

and correspondingly

$$\delta_{\mathfrak{v}} \varepsilon_\beta = \frac{\delta_{\mathfrak{v}} d_{\beta\beta}}{1+\varepsilon_\beta} = \bar{\mathfrak{e}}_\beta \frac{\partial (\delta \mathfrak{v})}{\partial s_\beta} = \bar{\mathfrak{e}}_\beta \delta_{\mathfrak{v}} \left(\frac{\partial \bar{\mathfrak{r}}}{\partial s_\beta} \right) \tag{11.2b}$$

as well as

$$\delta_{\mathfrak{v}} (2\, d_{\alpha\beta}) = \delta_{\mathfrak{v}} \left[(1+\varepsilon_\alpha)(1+\varepsilon_\beta) \sin \gamma_{\alpha\beta} \right] = \delta_{\mathfrak{v}} \left[\mathfrak{e}_\alpha \frac{\partial \mathfrak{v}}{\partial s_\beta} + \right.$$
$$\left. + \mathfrak{e}_\beta \frac{\partial \mathfrak{v}}{\partial s_\alpha} + \frac{\partial \mathfrak{v}}{\partial s_\alpha} \frac{\partial \mathfrak{v}}{\partial s_\beta} \right] = \mathfrak{e}_\alpha \delta_{\mathfrak{v}} \frac{\partial \mathfrak{v}}{\partial s_\beta} +$$
$$+ \mathfrak{e}_\beta \delta_{\mathfrak{v}} \frac{\partial \mathfrak{v}}{\partial s_\alpha} + \frac{\partial \mathfrak{v}}{\partial s_\alpha} \delta_{\mathfrak{v}} \frac{\partial \mathfrak{v}}{\partial s_\beta} + \frac{\partial \mathfrak{v}}{\partial s_\beta} \delta_{\mathfrak{v}} \frac{\partial \mathfrak{v}}{\partial s_\alpha} = \tag{11.2c}$$
$$= \left(\mathfrak{e}_\alpha + \frac{\partial \mathfrak{v}}{\partial s_\alpha} \right) \delta_{\mathfrak{v}} \left(\frac{\partial \mathfrak{v}}{\partial s_\beta} \right) + \left(\mathfrak{e}_\beta + \frac{\partial \mathfrak{v}}{\partial s_\beta} \right) \delta_{\mathfrak{v}} \left(\frac{\partial \mathfrak{v}}{\partial s_\alpha} \right) =$$
$$= (1+\varepsilon_\alpha)\, \bar{\mathfrak{e}}_\alpha \frac{\partial (\delta \mathfrak{v})}{\partial s_\beta} + (1+\varepsilon_\beta)\, \bar{\mathfrak{e}}_\beta \frac{\partial (\delta \mathfrak{v})}{\partial s_\alpha} .$$

11.2.2 *State of Stress, Equilibrium Conditions*

It was stated in Section 2.2 that the sectional loads can be determined from the equilibrium conditions only when the surface characteristics are known. If we assume large deformations, which may attain an order of magnitude of the dimensions of the undeformed surface, we must use the exact characteristics corresponding to the deformed surface. (These will be denoted by a light bar.) We then obtain from (2.3a, b) for the sectional loads*

$$\bar{\mathfrak{n}}_\alpha = \bar{n}_\alpha \bar{\mathfrak{e}}_\alpha + \bar{n}_{\alpha\beta} \bar{\mathfrak{e}}_\beta , \quad \bar{\mathfrak{n}}_\beta = \bar{n}_{\beta\alpha} \bar{\mathfrak{e}}_\alpha + \bar{n}_\beta \bar{\mathfrak{e}}_\beta \tag{11.3}$$

acting along the deformed parametric curves the equilibrium conditions

$$\frac{\partial}{\partial \alpha} \left(\sqrt{\bar{g}_{\beta\beta}}\, \bar{\mathfrak{n}}_\alpha \right) + \frac{\partial}{\partial \beta} \left(\sqrt{\bar{g}_{\alpha\alpha}}\, \bar{\mathfrak{n}}_\beta \right) + \bar{\mathfrak{p}} \sqrt{\bar{g}_{\alpha\alpha} \bar{g}_{\beta\beta} - \bar{g}_{\alpha\beta}{}^2} = 0 ,$$
$$\bar{n}_{\alpha\beta} = \bar{n}_{\beta\alpha} , \tag{11.4a, b}$$

where

$$\bar{\mathfrak{p}} = \bar{p}_\alpha \bar{\mathfrak{e}}_\alpha + \bar{p}_\beta \bar{\mathfrak{e}}_\beta + \bar{p}_\gamma \bar{\mathfrak{e}}_\gamma \tag{11.4c}$$

is the load acting on the deformed surface. Since, by virtue of (2.23b) we have

$$\bar{g}_{\alpha\alpha} = \bar{\mathfrak{r}}_\alpha{}^2 = \left(\frac{\partial \bar{\mathfrak{r}}}{\partial \alpha} \right)^2 = g_{\alpha\alpha} \left(\frac{\partial \bar{\mathfrak{r}}}{\partial s_\alpha} \right)^2 = g_{\alpha\alpha} \left(\mathfrak{e}_\alpha + \frac{\partial \mathfrak{v}}{\partial s_\alpha} \right)^2 = g_{\alpha\alpha} (1+\varepsilon_\alpha)^2 ,$$
$$\bar{g}_{\beta\beta} = \bar{\mathfrak{r}}_\beta{}^2 = g_{\beta\beta} (1+\varepsilon_\beta)^2 \tag{11.5a, b}$$

and

$$\sqrt{\bar{g}_{\alpha\alpha} \bar{g}_{\beta\beta} - \bar{g}_{\alpha\beta}{}^2} = \sqrt{\bar{\mathfrak{r}}_\alpha{}^2 \bar{\mathfrak{r}}_\beta{}^2 - (\bar{\mathfrak{r}}_\alpha \bar{\mathfrak{r}}_\beta)^2} =$$
$$= \sqrt{\bar{\mathfrak{r}}_\alpha{}^2 \bar{\mathfrak{r}}_\beta{}^2 - \bar{\mathfrak{r}}_\alpha{}^2 \bar{\mathfrak{r}}_\beta{}^2 \cos^2 \bar{\sigma}_{\alpha\beta}} = \sqrt{\bar{\mathfrak{r}}_\alpha{}^2} \sqrt{\bar{\mathfrak{r}}_\beta{}^2} \sin \bar{\sigma}_{\alpha\beta} = \tag{11.5c}$$
$$= \sqrt{g_{\alpha\alpha} g_{\beta\beta}}\, (1+\varepsilon_\alpha)(1+\varepsilon_\beta) \sin \bar{\sigma}_{\alpha\beta}$$

we can rewrite (11.4a) as follows, using the values of the surface deformation:

$$\frac{\partial}{\partial \alpha} \left[\sqrt{g_{\beta\beta}}\, (1+\varepsilon_\beta)\, \bar{\mathfrak{n}}_\alpha \right] + \frac{\partial}{\partial \beta} \left[\sqrt{g_{\alpha\alpha}}\, (1+\varepsilon_\alpha)\, \bar{\mathfrak{n}}_\beta \right] +$$
$$+ \bar{\mathfrak{p}} \sqrt{g_{\alpha\alpha} g_{\beta\beta}}\, (1+\varepsilon_\alpha)(1+\varepsilon_\beta) \sin \bar{\sigma}_{\alpha\beta} = 0 \tag{11.6}$$

By virtue of $d\,\bar{s}_i = (1+\varepsilon_i)\, d\,s_i = \sqrt{g_{ii}}\, (1+\varepsilon_i)\, d\,i$, $(i = \alpha, \beta)$ this can be obtained directly from the equilibrium conditions of the deformed membrane element (Figure 11.1). The state of

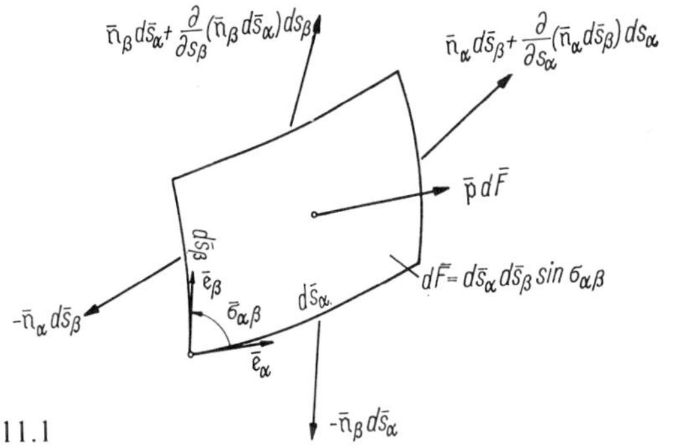

Figure 11.1

stress of the deformed membrane surface can also be described in several ways by a tensor. We define in analogy to (2.16a) a membrane-load tensor

$$\bar{\mathfrak{N}} = \frac{\bar{\mathfrak{e}}_\alpha \otimes \bar{\mathfrak{n}}_\alpha + \bar{\mathfrak{e}}_\beta \otimes \bar{\mathfrak{n}}_\beta}{\sin \bar{\sigma}_{\alpha\beta}} . \tag{11.7a}$$

The vector of the sectional load $\bar{\mathfrak{n}}_\varphi$ acting on a section element $d\,\bar{\mathfrak{s}}_\varphi = d\,\bar{s}_\varphi\, \bar{\mathfrak{e}}_\varphi$ is obtained with the aid of the unit normal vector

$$\bar{\mathfrak{e}}_{\varphi n} = \bar{\mathfrak{e}}_\varphi \times \bar{\mathfrak{e}}_\gamma \tag{11.7b}$$

to the line element $d\,\bar{\mathfrak{s}}_\varphi$ in the form

$$\bar{\mathfrak{n}}_\varphi = \bar{\mathfrak{e}}_{\varphi n} \bar{\mathfrak{N}} . \tag{11.7c}$$

The normal and shearing forces acting on the membrane are thus

$$\bar{s}_\varphi = \bar{\mathfrak{e}}_{\varphi n} (\bar{\mathfrak{e}}_{\varphi n} \bar{\mathfrak{N}}) , \quad \bar{t}_\varphi = \bar{\mathfrak{e}}_\varphi (\bar{\mathfrak{e}}_{\varphi n} \bar{\mathfrak{N}}) . \tag{11.7d, e}$$

It is more advisable to use a tensor related to the undeformed basic system $(\mathfrak{e}_\alpha, \mathfrak{e}_\beta, \mathfrak{e}_\gamma)$. We obtain from (11.1b, c)*

$$\bar{\mathfrak{e}}_i \otimes \bar{\mathfrak{e}}_k = \frac{\mathfrak{e}_i (\mathfrak{E} + \mathfrak{V})}{1+\varepsilon_i} \otimes \frac{\mathfrak{e}_k (\mathfrak{E} + \mathfrak{V})}{1+\varepsilon_k} = \frac{(\mathfrak{E} + \mathfrak{V})^t (\mathfrak{e}_i \otimes \mathfrak{e}_k) (\mathfrak{E} + \mathfrak{V})}{(1+\varepsilon_i)(1+\varepsilon_k)} .$$

Substitution in (11.7a) yields

$$\bar{\mathfrak{N}} = \frac{1}{K} (\mathfrak{E} + \mathfrak{V})^t \tilde{\mathfrak{N}} (\mathfrak{E} + \mathfrak{V}) , \tag{11.8a}$$

* where the components in the $(\bar{\mathfrak{e}}_\alpha, \bar{\mathfrak{e}}_\beta)$ system are, in the general case, neither normal nor shearing forces. The reason for this is that the deformed basic system $(\bar{\mathfrak{e}}_\alpha, \bar{\mathfrak{e}}_\beta, \bar{\mathfrak{e}}_\gamma)$ is not necessarily orthogonal even if the parametric curves were initially orthogonal, unless the latter are curves of principal extension.

* If $\mathfrak{a}$ and $\mathfrak{b}$ are vectors, and $\mathfrak{T}_1$ and $\mathfrak{T}_2$ tensors of the second order than we have $(\mathfrak{a}\, \mathfrak{T}_1) \otimes (\mathfrak{b}\, \mathfrak{T}_2) = \mathfrak{T}_1{}^t (\mathfrak{a} \otimes \mathfrak{b})\, \mathfrak{T}_2$.

where $\widetilde{\mathfrak{N}}$ is the symmetrical tensor

$$\widetilde{\mathfrak{N}} = \sum_{i,k=\alpha,\beta} \widetilde{n}_{ik}\, \mathfrak{e}_i \otimes \mathfrak{e}_k = \bar{n}_\alpha \frac{1+\varepsilon_\beta}{1+\varepsilon_\alpha}\, \mathfrak{e}_\alpha \otimes \mathfrak{e}_\alpha +$$

$$+ \bar{n}_\beta \frac{1+\varepsilon_\alpha}{1+\varepsilon_\beta}\, \mathfrak{e}_\beta \otimes \mathfrak{e}_\beta + \bar{n}_{\alpha\beta}\,(\mathfrak{e}_\alpha \otimes \mathfrak{e}_\beta + \mathfrak{e}_\beta \otimes \mathfrak{e}_\alpha) =$$

$$= \begin{pmatrix} \widetilde{n}_{\alpha\alpha} & \widetilde{n}_{\alpha\beta} \\ \widetilde{n}_{\alpha\beta} & \widetilde{n}_{\beta\beta} \end{pmatrix} = \begin{pmatrix} \bar{n}_\alpha \dfrac{1+\varepsilon_\beta}{1+\varepsilon_\alpha} & \bar{n}_{\alpha\beta} \\ \bar{n}_{\alpha\beta} & \bar{n}_\beta \dfrac{1+\varepsilon_\alpha}{1+\varepsilon_\beta} \end{pmatrix}, \tag{11.8b}$$

while, using the first and second invariants of the deformation tensor (cf. (2.24g, h)) we obtain

$$K = (1+\varepsilon_\alpha)(1+\varepsilon_\beta)\sin\bar{\sigma}_{\alpha\beta} = \sqrt{1 + 2D_{\mathrm{I}} + 4D_{\mathrm{II}}} =$$

$$= \sqrt{(1+2d_{\alpha\alpha})(1+2d_{\beta\beta}) - 4d_{\alpha\beta}^2} = \tag{11.8c}$$

$$= \sqrt{(1+2d_{\varphi\varphi})(1+2d_{\psi\psi}) - 4d_{\varphi\psi}^2}\,.$$

We express the unit normal vector $\bar{\mathfrak{e}}_{\varphi n}$ to the deformed line element $d\bar{\mathfrak{s}}_\varphi$ through the unit vectors $\mathfrak{e}_\varphi$ and $\mathfrak{e}_\psi$ $(=\mathfrak{e}_\gamma \times \mathfrak{e}_\varphi)$, which, before deformation, are, respectively, the tangent and normal vectors to the undeformed line element $d\mathfrak{s}_\varphi = \mathfrak{e}_\varphi\, d s_\varphi$. Using (11.1), we obtain

$$\bar{\mathfrak{e}}_{\varphi n} = \bar{\mathfrak{e}}_\psi \times \bar{\mathfrak{e}}_\gamma = \bar{\mathfrak{e}}_\psi \times \frac{\bar{\mathfrak{e}}_\varphi \times \bar{\mathfrak{e}}_\psi}{\sin\bar{\sigma}_{\varphi\psi}} = \frac{\bar{\mathfrak{e}}_\varphi - \bar{\mathfrak{e}}_\psi(\bar{\mathfrak{e}}_\varphi \bar{\mathfrak{e}}_\psi)}{\sin\bar{\sigma}_{\varphi\psi}} =$$

$$= \frac{\bar{\mathfrak{e}}_\varphi - \bar{\mathfrak{e}}_\psi\cos\bar{\sigma}_{\varphi\psi}}{\sin\bar{\sigma}_{\varphi\psi}} = \frac{\dfrac{\mathfrak{e}_\varphi}{1+\varepsilon_\varphi} - \dfrac{\mathfrak{e}_\psi}{1+\varepsilon_\psi}\cos\bar{\sigma}_{\varphi\psi}}{\sin\bar{\sigma}_{\varphi\psi}}\,(\mathfrak{E}+\mathfrak{V}) =$$

$$= \frac{\mathfrak{e}_\varphi(1+\varepsilon_\psi)^2 - \mathfrak{e}_\psi(1+\varepsilon_\varphi)(1+\varepsilon_\psi)\cos\bar{\sigma}_{\varphi\psi}}{(1+\varepsilon_\varphi)(1+\varepsilon_\psi)^2\sin\bar{\sigma}_{\varphi\psi}}\,(\mathfrak{E}+\mathfrak{V}) =$$

$$= \frac{\mathfrak{e}_\varphi(1+2d_{\psi\psi}) - 2d_{\varphi\psi}\,\mathfrak{e}_\psi}{K(1+\varepsilon_\psi)}\,(\mathfrak{E}+\mathfrak{V}). \tag{11.8d}$$

Substitution of (11.8a-d) in (11.7c) yields [cf. (2.19e)]

$$\bar{\mathfrak{n}}_\varphi = \frac{\mathfrak{e}_\varphi(1+2d_{\psi\psi}) - 2d_{\varphi\psi}\,\mathfrak{e}_\psi}{K^2(1+\varepsilon_\psi)}\,(\mathfrak{E}+\mathfrak{V})(\mathfrak{E}+\mathfrak{V})^t\,\widetilde{\mathfrak{N}}\,(\mathfrak{E}+\mathfrak{V}) =$$

$$= \frac{\mathfrak{e}_\varphi(1+2d_{\psi\psi}) - 2d_{\varphi\psi}\,\mathfrak{e}_\psi}{K^2(1+\varepsilon_\psi)}\,(\mathfrak{E}+2\mathfrak{D})\,\widetilde{\mathfrak{N}}\,(\mathfrak{E}+\mathfrak{V})\,. \tag{11.8e}$$

Since

$$\mathfrak{e}_\varphi(\mathfrak{E}+2\mathfrak{D}) = (1+2d_{\varphi\varphi})\,\mathfrak{e}_\varphi + 2d_{\varphi\psi}\,\mathfrak{e}_\psi$$

$$\mathfrak{e}_\psi(\mathfrak{E}+2\mathfrak{D}) = 2d_{\varphi\psi}\,\mathfrak{e}_\varphi + (1+2d_{\psi\psi})\,\mathfrak{e}_\psi \tag{11.8f}$$

we have

$$\frac{\mathfrak{e}_\varphi(1+2d_{\psi\psi}) - 2d_{\varphi\psi}\,\mathfrak{e}_\psi}{K^2(1+\varepsilon_\psi)}\,(\mathfrak{E}+2\mathfrak{D}) =$$

$$= \frac{(1+2d_{\psi\psi})[(1+2d_{\varphi\varphi})\,\mathfrak{e}_\varphi + 2d_{\varphi\psi}\,\mathfrak{e}_\psi] - 2d_{\varphi\psi}[2d_{\varphi\psi}\,\mathfrak{e}_\varphi + (1+2d_{\psi\psi})\,\mathfrak{e}_\psi]}{K^2(1+\varepsilon_\psi)}$$

$$= \frac{\mathfrak{e}_\varphi[(1+2d_{\varphi\varphi})(1+2d_{\psi\psi}) - 4d_{\varphi\psi}^2]}{K^2(1+\varepsilon_\psi)} = \frac{\mathfrak{e}_\varphi K^2}{K^2(1+\varepsilon_\psi)} = \frac{\mathfrak{e}_\varphi}{1+\varepsilon_\psi}\,.$$

Inserting this result into (11.8e), we obtain

$$\bar{\mathfrak{n}}_\varphi(1+\varepsilon_\psi) = \mathfrak{e}_\varphi[\widetilde{\mathfrak{N}}(\mathfrak{E}+\mathfrak{V})] = \mathfrak{e}_\varphi\,\widetilde{\mathfrak{N}}\,(\mathfrak{E}+\mathfrak{V})\,, \tag{11.9}$$

This relationship can be verified by considering the equilibrium of a deformed triangular element in the same way as in Section 2.3.

Resolving the vector of the membrane force acting on the section element $d\bar{\mathfrak{s}}_\varphi$ given by

$$\bar{\mathfrak{n}}_\varphi = \bar{n}_\varphi\,\bar{\mathfrak{e}}_\varphi + \bar{n}_{\varphi\psi}\,\bar{\mathfrak{e}}_\psi \tag{11.10a}$$

along the directions which the initially orthogonal vectors $\mathfrak{e}_\varphi$ and $\mathfrak{e}_\psi = \mathfrak{e}_\gamma \times \mathfrak{e}_\varphi$ assume after deformation, we obtain by scalar multiplication of (11.10a) with the vector products $\bar{\mathfrak{e}}_\psi \times \bar{\mathfrak{e}}_\gamma$ and $\bar{\mathfrak{e}}_\gamma \times \bar{\mathfrak{e}}_\varphi$ respectively

$$\bar{n}_\varphi = \frac{\bar{\mathfrak{n}}_\varphi(\bar{\mathfrak{e}}_\psi \times \bar{\mathfrak{e}}_\gamma)}{\bar{\mathfrak{e}}_\varphi(\bar{\mathfrak{e}}_\psi \times \bar{\mathfrak{e}}_\gamma)}\,, \qquad \bar{n}_{\varphi\psi} = \frac{\bar{\mathfrak{n}}_\varphi(\bar{\mathfrak{e}}_\gamma \times \bar{\mathfrak{e}}_\varphi)}{\bar{\mathfrak{e}}_\psi(\bar{\mathfrak{e}}_\gamma \times \bar{\mathfrak{e}}_\varphi)}\,. \tag{11.10b}$$

Since by (11.8d)

$$\bar{\mathfrak{e}}_\psi \times \bar{\mathfrak{e}}_\gamma = \bar{\mathfrak{e}}_{\varphi n} = \frac{\mathfrak{e}_\varphi(1+2d_{\psi\psi}) - 2d_{\varphi\psi}\,\mathfrak{e}_\psi}{K(1+\varepsilon_\psi)}\,(\mathfrak{E}+\mathfrak{V})$$

we have*

$$\bar{\mathfrak{e}}_\varphi(\bar{\mathfrak{e}}_\psi \times \bar{\mathfrak{e}}_\gamma) = \bar{\mathfrak{e}}_\psi(\bar{\mathfrak{e}}_\gamma \times \bar{\mathfrak{e}}_\varphi) = \frac{\mathfrak{e}_\varphi(\mathfrak{E}+\mathfrak{V})}{1+\varepsilon_\varphi}\,\cdot$$

$$\cdot\,\frac{\mathfrak{e}_\varphi(1+2d_{\psi\psi}) - 2d_{\varphi\psi}\,\mathfrak{e}_\psi}{K(1+\varepsilon_\psi)}\,(\mathfrak{E}+\mathfrak{V}) =$$

$$= \frac{(1+2d_{\psi\psi})[\mathfrak{e}_\varphi(\mathfrak{E}+\mathfrak{V})][\mathfrak{e}_\varphi(\mathfrak{E}+\mathfrak{V})] - 2d_{\varphi\psi}[\mathfrak{e}_\varphi(\mathfrak{E}+\mathfrak{V})][\mathfrak{e}_\psi(\mathfrak{E}+\mathfrak{V})]}{K(1+\varepsilon_\varphi)(1+\varepsilon_\psi)}$$

$$= \frac{[(1+2d_{\psi\psi})\,\mathfrak{e}_\varphi - 2d_{\varphi\psi}\,\mathfrak{e}_\psi][\mathfrak{e}_\varphi(\mathfrak{E}+2\mathfrak{D})]}{K(1+\varepsilon_\varphi)(1+\varepsilon_\psi)} =$$

$$= \frac{(1+2d_{\psi\psi})(1+2d_{\varphi\varphi}) - 4d_{\varphi\psi}^2}{K(1+\varepsilon_\varphi)(1+\varepsilon_\psi)} = \frac{K}{(1+\varepsilon_\varphi)(1+\varepsilon_\psi)}$$

and

$$\bar{\mathfrak{e}}_\gamma \times \bar{\mathfrak{e}}_\varphi = -\,\bar{\mathfrak{e}}_\varphi \times \bar{\mathfrak{e}}_\gamma = -\,\bar{\mathfrak{e}}_\varphi \times \frac{\bar{\mathfrak{e}}_\varphi \times \bar{\mathfrak{e}}_\psi}{\sin\bar{\sigma}_{\varphi\psi}} =$$

$$= -\,\frac{\bar{\mathfrak{e}}_\varphi\cos\bar{\sigma}_{\varphi\psi} - \bar{\mathfrak{e}}_\psi}{\sin\bar{\sigma}_{\varphi\psi}} = \frac{\dfrac{\mathfrak{e}_\psi}{1+\varepsilon_\psi} - \dfrac{\mathfrak{e}_\varphi}{1+\varepsilon_\varphi}\cos\bar{\sigma}_{\varphi\psi}}{\sin\bar{\sigma}_{\varphi\psi}}\,(\mathfrak{E}+\mathfrak{V}) =$$

$$= \frac{\mathfrak{e}_\psi(1+\varepsilon_\varphi)^2 - (1+\varepsilon_\varphi)(1+\varepsilon_\psi)\cos\bar{\sigma}_{\varphi\psi}\,\mathfrak{e}_\varphi}{(1+\varepsilon_\varphi)^2(1+\varepsilon_\psi)\sin\bar{\sigma}_{\varphi\psi}}\,(\mathfrak{E}+\mathfrak{V}) =$$

$$= \frac{\mathfrak{e}_\psi(1+2d_{\varphi\varphi}) - 2d_{\varphi\psi}\,\mathfrak{e}_\varphi}{K(1+\varepsilon_\varphi)}\,(\mathfrak{E}+\mathfrak{V}).$$

We then obtain from (11.10b)

$$\bar{n}_\varphi = \bar{\mathfrak{n}}_\varphi\,\frac{1+\varepsilon_\varphi}{K^2}\Big[(1+2d_{\psi\psi})\,\mathfrak{e}_\varphi - 2d_{\varphi\psi}\,\mathfrak{e}_\psi)(\mathfrak{E}+\mathfrak{V})\Big],$$

$$\bar{n}_{\varphi\psi} = \bar{\mathfrak{n}}_\varphi\,\frac{1+\varepsilon_\psi}{K^2}\Big[(-\,2d_{\varphi\psi}\,\mathfrak{e}_\varphi + (1+2d_{\varphi\varphi})\,\mathfrak{e}_\psi)(\mathfrak{E}+\mathfrak{V})\Big],$$

whence, by (11.9)

$$\bar{n}_\varphi = \frac{1}{K^2}\,\frac{1+\varepsilon_\varphi}{1+\varepsilon_\psi}\Big[\mathfrak{e}_\varphi\,\widetilde{\mathfrak{N}}(\mathfrak{E}+\mathfrak{V})\Big]\Big[\big((1+2d_{\psi\psi})\,\mathfrak{e}_\varphi - 2d_{\varphi\psi}\,\mathfrak{e}_\psi\big)(\mathfrak{E}+\mathfrak{V})\Big],$$

$$\bar{n}_{\varphi\psi} = \frac{1}{K^2}\Big[\mathfrak{e}_\varphi\,\widetilde{\mathfrak{N}}\,(\mathfrak{E}+\mathfrak{V})\Big]\Big[\big(-\,2d_{\varphi\psi}\,\mathfrak{e}_\varphi + (1+2d_{\varphi\varphi})\,\mathfrak{e}_\psi\big)(\mathfrak{E}+\mathfrak{V})\Big].$$

Using (2.19c), these expressions become

$$\frac{1+\varepsilon_\psi}{1+\varepsilon_\varphi}\,\bar{n}_\varphi = \frac{1}{K^2}\Big\{(1+2d_{\psi\psi})\,\mathfrak{e}_\varphi\Big[\mathfrak{e}_\varphi(\mathfrak{E}+\mathfrak{V})\big(\widetilde{\mathfrak{N}}(\mathfrak{E}+\mathfrak{V})\big)^t\Big] -$$

$$-\,2d_{\varphi\psi}\,\mathfrak{e}_\varphi\Big[\mathfrak{e}_\psi(\mathfrak{E}+\mathfrak{V})\big(\widetilde{\mathfrak{N}}(\mathfrak{E}+\mathfrak{V})\big)^t\Big]\Big\}\,,$$

$$\bar{n}_{\varphi\psi} = \frac{1}{K^2}\Big\{-\,2d_{\varphi\psi}\,\mathfrak{e}_\varphi\Big[\mathfrak{e}_\varphi(\mathfrak{E}+\mathfrak{V})\big(\widetilde{\mathfrak{N}}(\mathfrak{E}+\mathfrak{V})\big)^t\Big] +$$

$$+\,(1+2d_{\varphi\varphi})\,\mathfrak{e}_\varphi\Big[\mathfrak{e}_\psi(\mathfrak{E}+\mathfrak{V})\big(\widetilde{\mathfrak{N}}(\mathfrak{E}+\mathfrak{V})\big)^t\Big]\Big\}.$$

* See (2.19c)

Since

$$\left(\tilde{\mathfrak{N}}\,(\mathfrak{E}+\mathfrak{B})\right)^t = (\mathfrak{E}+\mathfrak{B})^t\,\tilde{\mathfrak{N}}^t = (\mathfrak{E}+\mathfrak{B})^t\,\tilde{\mathfrak{N}}\,,$$

thus

$$(\mathfrak{E}+\mathfrak{B})\left(\tilde{\mathfrak{N}}\,(\mathfrak{E}+\mathfrak{B})\right)^t = (\mathfrak{E}+\mathfrak{B})\,(\mathfrak{E}+\mathfrak{B})^t\,\tilde{\mathfrak{N}} = (\mathfrak{E}+2\,\mathfrak{D})\,\tilde{\mathfrak{N}}$$

we have

$$\frac{1+\varepsilon_\psi}{1+\varepsilon_\varphi}\,\bar{n}_\varphi = \frac{e_\varphi}{K^2}\left\{\left[(1+2\,d_{\psi\psi})\,\mathfrak{e}_\varphi - 2\,d_{\varphi\psi}\,\mathfrak{e}_\psi\right](\mathfrak{E}+2\,\mathfrak{D})\,\tilde{\mathfrak{N}}\right\},$$

$$\bar{n}_{\varphi\psi} = \frac{e_\varphi}{K^2}\left\{\left[-\,2\,d_{\varphi\psi}\,\mathfrak{e}_\varphi + (1+2\,d_{\varphi\varphi})\,\mathfrak{e}_\psi\right](\mathfrak{E}+2\,\mathfrak{D})\,\tilde{\mathfrak{N}}\right\}.$$

Making use of (11.8f), we then obtain

$$\frac{1+\varepsilon_\psi}{1+\varepsilon_\varphi}\,\bar{n}_\varphi = \tilde{n}_\varphi = \mathfrak{e}_\varphi\,(\mathfrak{e}_\varphi\,\tilde{\mathfrak{N}}),\qquad \bar{n}_{\varphi\psi} = \tilde{n}_{\varphi\psi} = \mathfrak{e}_\varphi\,(\mathfrak{e}_\psi\,\tilde{\mathfrak{N}}) = \mathfrak{e}_\psi\,(\mathfrak{e}_\varphi\,\tilde{\mathfrak{N}})\,. \tag{11.11}$$

We have thus expressed the components of the vector of the sectional loads of the deformed membrane as functions of the direction vectors of the undeformed system.

11.2.3 *Load-strain Relationships*

By virtue of the complicated nonlinear form of the equations obtained, the selection of a suitable load-strain relationship is of utmost importance, since it enables us to simplify considerably the equations and the variational problem for the membrane. The ordinary Hooke's law, which for the principal directions (axes of anisotropy) takes the form

$$\varepsilon_1 = \frac{\bar{n}_1}{D_1} - \frac{\nu_2}{D_2}\,\bar{n}_2\,,\quad \varepsilon_2 = \frac{\bar{n}_2}{D_2} - \frac{\nu_1}{D_1}\,\bar{n}_1 \quad \text{or}$$

$$\bar{n}_1 = \frac{D_1}{1-\nu_1\,\nu_2}\,(\varepsilon_1+\nu_2\,\varepsilon_2)\,,\quad \bar{n}_2 = \frac{D_2}{1-\nu_1\,\nu_2}\,(\varepsilon_2+\nu_1\,\varepsilon_1) \tag{11.12}$$

is less suitable than other nonlinear laws, as will be shown below.

a) The generalized Kappus law represents a nonlinear extension of Hooke's Law in the region of large deformations. Like the latter, it formally relates the components of a tensor $\tilde{\mathfrak{N}}$ to those of the deformation tensor $\mathfrak{D}_1$ in the form

$$d_{\alpha\alpha} = \frac{\tilde{n}_{\alpha\alpha}}{D_\alpha} - \frac{\nu_\beta}{D_\beta}\,\tilde{n}_{\beta\beta}\,,\quad d_{\beta\beta} = \frac{\tilde{n}_{\beta\beta}}{D_\beta} - \frac{\nu_\alpha}{D_\alpha}\,\tilde{n}_{\alpha\alpha}\,,\quad 2\,d_{\alpha\beta} = \frac{\tilde{n}_{\alpha\beta}}{D_{\alpha\beta}} \tag{11.13a}$$

or

$$\tilde{n}_{\alpha\alpha} = \frac{D_\alpha\,(d_{\alpha\alpha}+\nu_\beta\,d_{\beta\beta})}{1-\nu_\alpha\,\nu_\beta}\,,\quad \tilde{n}_{\beta\beta} = \frac{D_\beta\,(d_{\beta\beta}+\nu_\alpha\,d_{\alpha\alpha})}{1-\nu_\alpha\,\nu_\beta}\,,\qquad \tilde{n}_{\alpha\beta} = 2\,D_{\alpha\beta}\,d_{\alpha\beta} \tag{11.13b}$$

In the isotropic case $D_\alpha = D_\beta = D,\ \nu_\alpha = \nu_\beta = \nu\,,D_{\alpha\beta} = \dfrac{D}{2\,(1+\nu)}$ so that we obtain the tensor equation

$$\mathfrak{D}_1 = \frac{1+\nu}{D}\left[\tilde{\mathfrak{N}} - \frac{\nu}{1+\nu}\,(\tilde{\mathfrak{N}}\,..\,\bar{\mathfrak{E}})\,\bar{\mathfrak{E}}\right] \tag{11.13c}$$

or

$$\tilde{\mathfrak{N}} = \frac{D}{1+\nu}\left[\mathfrak{D}_1 + \frac{\nu}{1-\nu}\,(\mathfrak{D}_1\,..\,\bar{\mathfrak{E}})\,\bar{\mathfrak{E}}\right], \tag{11.13d}$$

where $\bar{\mathfrak{E}} = \mathfrak{e}_\alpha\otimes\mathfrak{e}_\alpha + \mathfrak{e}_\beta\otimes\mathfrak{e}_\beta = \mathfrak{E} - \mathfrak{e}_\gamma\otimes\mathfrak{e}_\gamma$ while $(\tilde{\mathfrak{N}}\,..\,\bar{\mathfrak{E}}) = \tilde{n}_{\alpha\alpha} + \tilde{n}_{\beta\beta} = Sp\,(\tilde{\mathfrak{N}})$ or $(\mathfrak{D}_1..\bar{\mathfrak{E}}) = d_{\alpha\alpha} + d_{\beta\beta} = Sp\,(\mathfrak{D}_1)$ are respectively the traces (first invariants) of the tensors of the sectional load and of the deformation $\mathfrak{D}_1$ *

Putting $\bar{n}_\alpha = \bar{n}_1,\ \bar{n}_\beta = \bar{n}_2 = 0,\ \bar{n}_{\alpha\beta} = 0$, i.e., $\tilde{n}_\beta = \tilde{n}_{\alpha\beta} = 0$ we obtain

$$d_2 = \varepsilon_2\left(1+\frac{\varepsilon_2}{2}\right) = -\,\nu_1\,d_1 = -\,\nu_1\,\varepsilon_1\left(1+\frac{\varepsilon_1}{2}\right),$$

$$\text{i.e.,}\quad \varepsilon_2 = -1+\sqrt{1-2\,\nu_1\,\varepsilon_1\left(1+\frac{\varepsilon_1}{2}\right)},$$

or the equivalent monoaxial law

$$\bar{n}_1 = D_1\,\frac{d_1\,(1+\varepsilon_1)}{\sqrt{1-2\,\nu_1\,\varepsilon_1\left(1+\dfrac{\varepsilon_1}{2}\right)}} = D_1\,\frac{\varepsilon_1\,(1+\varepsilon_1)\left(1+\dfrac{\varepsilon_1}{2}\right)}{\sqrt{1-2\,\nu_1\,\varepsilon_1\left(1+\dfrac{\varepsilon_1}{2}\right)}}\,. \tag{11.13e}$$

Multiplying (11.13e) by $(1+\varepsilon_2)$, we obtain

$$\bar{n}_1\,(1+\varepsilon_2) = n_1{}' = D_1\,\varepsilon_1\,(1+\varepsilon_1)\left(1+\frac{\varepsilon_1}{2}\right).$$

We have

$$n_1{}' = \bar{n}_1\,(1+\varepsilon_2) = \frac{\bar{n}_1\,(1+\varepsilon_2)\,b_0}{b_0} = \frac{\bar{n}_1\,b}{b_0} = \frac{P}{b_0}\,,$$

$$b = b_0\,(1+\varepsilon_2)\,,\quad \bar{n}_1\,b = P\,.$$

Here b_0 denotes the initial width of a strip extending in the α-direction, and b its instantaneous width. Thus, according to Kappus' law, the sectional loads n' as referred to the initial state of the surface, are nonlinearly related to the extensions.

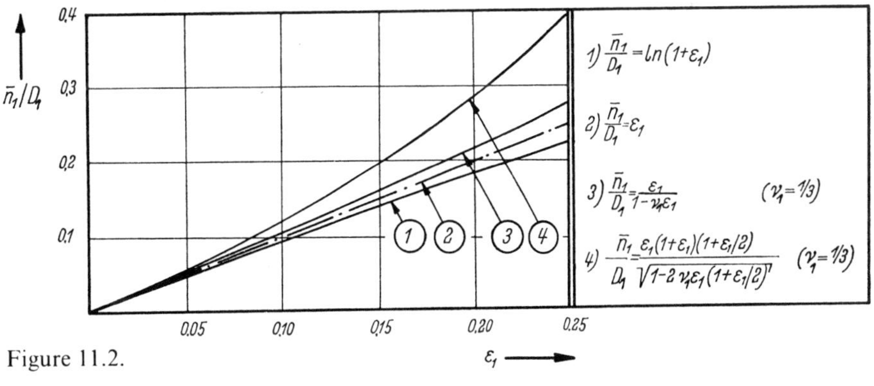

Figure 11.2.

b) A linear relationship between the sectional loads, as referred to the initial state of the surface, and the corresponding extensions can be written in the form

$$n_1{}' = \bar{n}_1\,(1+\varepsilon_2) = D_1\,\varepsilon_1\,. \tag{11.14a}$$

Its two-dimensional generalization (referred to the principal directions, which are the axes of anisotropy) is

* The double-scalar product of two tensors $\mathfrak{T}_1 = \sum t_{ik}{}^{(1)}\,\mathfrak{e}_i\otimes\mathfrak{e}_k$ and $\mathfrak{T}_2 = \sum t_{ik}{}^{(2)}\,\mathfrak{e}_i\otimes\mathfrak{e}_k$ is defined by $\mathfrak{T}_1\,..\,\mathfrak{T}_2 = \sum t_{ik}{}^{(1)}\,t_{ki}{}^{(2)}$.

$$\varepsilon_1 = \frac{n_1'}{D_1} - \frac{\nu_2}{D_2} n_2' = \frac{\bar{n}_1 (1+\varepsilon_2)}{D_1} - \frac{\nu_2}{D_2} \bar{n}_2 (1+\varepsilon_1),$$

$$\varepsilon_2 = \frac{n_2'}{D_2} - \frac{\nu_1}{D_1} n_1' \qquad (11.14b)$$

or

$$n_1' = (1+\varepsilon_2)\bar{n}_1 = \frac{D_1}{1-\nu_1\nu_2}(\varepsilon_1 + \nu_2\varepsilon_2),$$

$$n_2' = (1+\varepsilon_1)\bar{n}_2 = \frac{D_2}{1-\nu_1\nu_2}(\varepsilon_2 + \nu_1\varepsilon_1). \qquad (11.14c)$$

This relationship is, of course, nonlinear with respect to the actual sectional loads $\bar{n}$. For $n_2' = 0$ i.e., $\varepsilon_2 = -\nu_1\varepsilon_1$ we obtain from (11.14b) the monoaxial law (see Figure 11.2)

$$\bar{n}_1 = \frac{n_1'}{1+\varepsilon_2} = \frac{D_1\varepsilon_1}{1+\varepsilon_2} = \frac{D_1\varepsilon_1}{1-\nu_1\varepsilon_1} > D_1\varepsilon_1. \qquad (11.14d)$$

c) Also nonlinear is the following load-strain relationship which uses the concept of logarithmic extension, due to *Röntgen, Ludwik,* and *Henky*. For small extensions it becomes, like the laws (a) and (b), Hooke's law. We assume that the increments of the actual sectional loads are proportional to the increments of the extensions, as referred to the instantaneous lengths. If the instantaneous edge lengths of a rectangular membrane are l_1 and l_2, the membrane loads acting at this instant being $\bar{n}_1$ and $\bar{n}_2$, uniformly distributed along the edges, then

$$d\bar{n}_1 = \frac{\partial \bar{n}_1}{\partial l_1} d l_1 + \frac{\partial \bar{n}_1}{\partial l_2} d l_2 \quad \text{and} \quad d\bar{n}_2 = \frac{\partial \bar{n}_2}{\partial l_1} d l_1 + \frac{\partial \bar{n}_2}{\partial l_2} d l_2$$

If Hooke's law applies, we obtain for the extension increments

$$\left.\begin{aligned} d\bar{\varepsilon}_1 &= \frac{d l_1}{l_1} = \frac{d\bar{n}_1}{D_1} - \frac{\nu_2}{D_2} d\bar{n}_2, \\ d\bar{\varepsilon}_2 &= \frac{d l_2}{l_2} = \frac{d\bar{n}_2}{D_2} - \frac{\nu_1}{D_1} d\bar{n}_1 \end{aligned}\right\} \qquad (11.15a.$$

or

$$\left.\begin{aligned} d\bar{n}_1 &= \frac{\partial \bar{n}_1}{\partial l_1} d l_1 + \frac{\partial \bar{n}_1}{\partial l_2} d l_2 = \frac{D_1}{1-\nu_1\nu_2}\left(\frac{dl_1}{l_1} + \nu_2\frac{dl_2}{l_2}\right), \\ d\bar{n}_2 &= \frac{\partial \bar{n}_2}{\partial l_1} d l_1 + \frac{\partial \bar{n}_2}{\partial l_2} d l_2 = \frac{D_2}{1-\nu_1\nu_2}\left(\frac{dl_2}{l_2} + \nu_1\frac{dl_1}{l_1}\right). \end{aligned}\right\}$$

Equating in the first equation (11.15b) the coefficients l_1 and $d\,l_2$, respectively, we find

$$\frac{\partial \bar{n}_1}{\partial l_1} = \frac{D_1}{1-\nu_1\nu_2}\frac{1}{l_1}, \quad \frac{\partial \bar{n}_1}{\partial l_2} = \nu_2\frac{D_1}{1-\nu_1\nu_2}\frac{1}{l_2}.$$

Integrating, taking into account the condition $\bar{n}_1(l_{10}, l_{20}) = 0$ where l_{10} and l_{20} are the initial edge lengths of the unstressed membrane, we obtain

$$\bar{n}_1 = \frac{D_1}{1-\nu_1\nu_2}\left(\ln\frac{l_1}{l_{10}} + \nu_2\ln\frac{l_2}{l_{20}}\right). \qquad (11.15c)$$

Similarly, the second equation (11.15b) yields

$$\bar{n}_2 = \frac{D_2}{1-\nu_1\nu_2}\left(\ln\frac{l_2}{l_{20}} + \nu_1\ln\frac{l_1}{l_{10}}\right). \qquad (11.15d)$$

Writing

$$\frac{l_1}{l_{10}} = \frac{l_{10}+\Delta l_1}{l_{10}} = 1 + \frac{\Delta l_1}{l_{10}} = 1+\varepsilon_1,$$

$$\frac{l_2}{l_{20}} = \frac{l_{20}+\Delta l_2}{l_{20}} = 1 + \frac{\Delta l_2}{l_{20}} = 1+\varepsilon_2, \qquad (11.16a)$$

where ε_1 and ε_2 are, as usual, the extensions referred to the initial lengths, we obtain finally

$$\left.\begin{aligned} \bar{n}_1 &= \frac{D_1}{1-\nu_1\nu_2}\left[\ln(1+\varepsilon_1) + \nu_2\ln(1+\varepsilon_2)\right], \\ \bar{n}_2 &= \frac{D_2}{1-\nu_1\nu_2}\left[\ln(1+\varepsilon_2) + \nu_1\ln(1+\varepsilon_1)\right]. \end{aligned}\right\} \qquad (11.16b)$$

Solving for the deformations, we find

$$\ln(1+\varepsilon_1) = \bar{\varepsilon}_1 = \ln\frac{l_1}{l_{10}} = \frac{\bar{n}_1}{D_1} - \frac{\nu_2}{D_2}\bar{n}_2,$$

$$\ln(1+\varepsilon_2) = \bar{\varepsilon}_2 = \ln\frac{l_2}{l_{20}} = \frac{\bar{n}_2}{D_2} - \frac{\nu_1}{D_1}\bar{n}_1. \qquad (11.16c)$$

For $\bar{n}_2 = 0$, i.e., $(1+\varepsilon_2) = -\nu_1\ln(1+\varepsilon_1)$ we obtain the monoaxial law

$$\bar{n}_1 = D_1\ln(1+\varepsilon_1) < D_1\varepsilon_1. \qquad (11.16d)$$

11.3 The Variational Problem of the Membrane Theory

11.3.1 *The Fundamental Equations of the Principle of Virtual Displacements*

We verify the integral equation equivalent to the equilibrium conditions by multiplying (11.6) with the arbitrary displacement variation $\delta\mathfrak{v}$ and integrating over the entire undeformed membrane. We then obtain

$$\int_{\beta_0}^{\alpha_1 \beta_1}\!\!\int \Big[\frac{\partial}{\partial\alpha}\left(\sqrt{g_{\beta\beta}}(1+\varepsilon_\beta)\,\mathfrak{n}_\alpha\right) + \frac{\partial}{\partial\beta}\left(\sqrt{g_{\alpha\alpha}}(1+\varepsilon_\alpha)\,\mathfrak{n}_\beta\right) + \qquad (11.17a)$$

$$+\bar{\mathfrak{p}}(1+\varepsilon_\alpha)(1+\varepsilon_\beta)\sqrt{g_{\alpha\alpha}g_{\beta\beta}}\sin\bar{\sigma}_{\alpha\beta}\Big]\,\delta\mathfrak{v}\,d\alpha\,d\beta = 0.$$

Partial integration yields

$$\int_{\alpha_0}^{\alpha_1}\left[\sqrt{g_{\alpha\alpha}}(1+\varepsilon_\alpha)\,\mathfrak{n}_\beta\,\delta\mathfrak{v}\right]_{\beta_0}^{\beta_1} d\alpha + \int_{\beta_0}^{\beta_1}\left[\sqrt{g_{\beta\beta}}(1+\varepsilon_\beta)\,\mathfrak{n}_\alpha\,\delta\mathfrak{v}\right]_{\alpha_0}^{\alpha_1} d\beta -$$

$$-\int_{\alpha_0}^{\alpha_1}\!\!\int_{\beta_0}^{\beta_1}\Big[\sqrt{g_{\beta\beta}}(1+\varepsilon_\beta)\,\mathfrak{n}_\alpha\frac{\partial\,\delta\mathfrak{v}}{\partial\alpha} + \sqrt{g_{\alpha\alpha}}(1+\varepsilon_\alpha)\,\mathfrak{n}_\beta\frac{\partial\,\delta\mathfrak{v}}{\partial\beta} -$$

$$-\bar{\mathfrak{p}}(1+\varepsilon_\alpha)(1+\varepsilon_\beta)\sqrt{g_{\alpha\alpha}g_{\beta\beta}}\sin\bar{\sigma}_{\alpha\beta}\,\delta\mathfrak{v}\Big]\,d\alpha\,d\beta = 0,$$

where $\alpha = \alpha_0$, $\alpha = \alpha_1$, $\beta = \beta_0$, and $\beta = \beta_1$, defines the immovable edges of the underformed membrane. We assume the geometrical compatibility of the displacement variations, i.e., the vanishing of the latter along the edges. The line integrals at the edges are thus equal to zero. Putting

$$\frac{\partial\,\delta\mathfrak{v}}{\partial\alpha} = \sqrt{g_{\alpha\alpha}}\frac{\partial\,\delta\mathfrak{v}}{\sqrt{g_{\alpha\alpha}}\,\partial\alpha} = \sqrt{g_{\alpha\alpha}}\frac{\partial\,\delta\mathfrak{v}}{\partial s_\alpha}, \quad \frac{\partial\,\delta\mathfrak{v}}{\partial\beta} = \sqrt{g_{\beta\beta}}\frac{\partial\,\delta\mathfrak{v}}{\partial s_\beta} \qquad (11.17b)$$

and remembering that $\sqrt{g_{\alpha\alpha}g_{\beta\beta}}\,d\alpha\,d\beta = d s_\alpha\,d s_\beta = dF$

is the area of the surface element of the undeformed membrane, we obtain

$$\iint\limits_{(F)} \left[\bar{n}_\alpha (1+\varepsilon_\beta) \frac{\partial \delta \mathfrak{v}}{\partial s_\alpha} + \bar{n}_\beta (1+\varepsilon_\alpha) \frac{\partial \delta \mathfrak{v}}{\partial s_\beta} - - \bar{\mathfrak{p}} (1+\varepsilon_\alpha)(1+\varepsilon_\beta) \sin \bar{\sigma}_{\alpha\beta}\, \delta \mathfrak{v} \right] dF = 0$$

or, resolving the components of the sectional loads according to (11.3)

$$\iint\limits_{(F)} \left[(1+\varepsilon_\beta)\, \bar{n}_\alpha\, \bar{\mathfrak{e}}_\alpha \frac{\partial \delta \mathfrak{v}}{\partial s_\alpha} + (1+\varepsilon_\alpha)\, \bar{n}_\beta\, \bar{\mathfrak{e}}_\beta \frac{\partial \delta \mathfrak{v}}{\partial s_\beta} + + \left((1+\varepsilon_\beta)\, \bar{\mathfrak{e}}_\beta \frac{\partial \delta \mathfrak{v}}{\partial s_\alpha} + (1+\varepsilon_\alpha)\, \bar{\mathfrak{e}}_\alpha \frac{\partial \delta \mathfrak{v}}{\partial s_\beta} \right) \bar{n}_{\alpha\beta} - - \bar{\mathfrak{p}} (1+\varepsilon_\alpha)(1+\varepsilon_\beta) \sin \bar{\sigma}_{\alpha\beta}\, \delta \mathfrak{v} \right] dF = 0 .$$

Replacing, according to (11.2) the derivatives of the displacement variations by the displacement variations themselves, we obtain

$$\iint\limits_{(F)} [\bar{n}_\alpha (1+\varepsilon_\beta)\, \delta_\mathfrak{v}\, \varepsilon_\alpha + \bar{n}_\beta (1+\varepsilon_\alpha)\, \delta_\mathfrak{v}\, \varepsilon_\beta + + \bar{n}_{\alpha\beta}\, \delta_\mathfrak{v} \left((1+\varepsilon_\alpha)(1+\varepsilon_\beta) \sin \gamma_{\alpha\beta} \right) - - \bar{\mathfrak{p}} (1+\varepsilon_\alpha)(1+\varepsilon_\beta) \sin \bar{\sigma}_{\alpha\beta}\, \delta \mathfrak{v}]\, dF = 0 \qquad (11.18)$$

or

$$\iint\limits_{(F)} \left[\bar{n}_\alpha \frac{1+\varepsilon_\beta}{1+\varepsilon_\alpha} \delta_\mathfrak{v}\, d_{\alpha\alpha} + \bar{n}_\beta \frac{1+\varepsilon_\alpha}{1+\varepsilon_\beta} \delta_\mathfrak{v}\, d_{\beta\beta} + 2\, \bar{n}_{\alpha\beta}\, \delta_\mathfrak{v}\, d_{\alpha\beta} - - \bar{\mathfrak{p}} (1+\varepsilon_\alpha)(1+\varepsilon_\beta) \sin \bar{\sigma}_{\alpha\beta}\, \delta \mathfrak{v} \right] dF = 0 . \qquad (11.19a)$$

Hence,

$$\iint\limits_{(F)} \{ \tilde{n}_{\alpha\alpha}\, \delta_\mathfrak{v}\, d_{\alpha\alpha} + \tilde{n}_{\beta\beta}\, \delta_\mathfrak{v}\, d_{\beta\beta} + 2\, \tilde{n}_{\alpha\beta}\, \delta_\mathfrak{v}\, d_{\alpha\beta} - - \bar{\mathfrak{p}} (1+\varepsilon_\alpha)(1+\varepsilon_\beta) \sin \bar{\sigma}_{\alpha\beta}\, \delta \mathfrak{v} \}\, dF = 0 . \qquad (11.19b)$$

We write

$$\frac{\delta_\mathfrak{v}\, \varepsilon_\alpha}{1+\varepsilon_\alpha} = \delta_\mathfrak{v} [\ln (1+\varepsilon_\alpha)] = \delta_\mathfrak{v}\, \bar{\varepsilon}_\alpha , \qquad \frac{\delta_\mathfrak{v}\, \varepsilon_\beta}{1+\varepsilon_\beta} = \delta_\mathfrak{v} [\ln (1+\varepsilon_\beta)] = \delta_\mathfrak{v}\, \bar{\varepsilon}_\beta \qquad (11.20a)$$

$$\frac{\delta_\mathfrak{v}\, d_{\alpha\beta}}{(1+\varepsilon_\alpha)(1+\varepsilon_\beta) \sin \bar{\sigma}_{\alpha\beta}} = \frac{1}{2} \frac{\delta_\mathfrak{v} [(1+\varepsilon_\alpha)(1+\varepsilon_\beta) \cos \bar{\sigma}_{\alpha\beta}]}{(1+\varepsilon_\alpha)(1+\varepsilon_\beta) \sin \bar{\sigma}_{\alpha\beta}} = = \frac{\operatorname{ctg} \bar{\sigma}_{\alpha\beta}}{2} \delta_\mathfrak{v} (\bar{\varepsilon}_\alpha + \bar{\varepsilon}_\beta) + \frac{1}{2} \delta_\mathfrak{v}\, \gamma_{\alpha\beta} . \qquad (11'20b)$$

Denoting in (11.18) the common factor

$$dF (1+\varepsilon_\alpha)(1+\varepsilon_\beta) \sin \bar{\sigma}_{\alpha\beta} = d\bar{F} \qquad (11.20c)$$

which represents the area of the deformed surface element, we obtain

$$\iint\limits_{(F)} \left\{ \frac{\bar{n}_\alpha + \bar{n}_{\alpha\beta} \cos \bar{\sigma}_{\alpha\beta}}{\sin \bar{\sigma}_{\alpha\beta}} \delta_\mathfrak{v}\, \bar{\varepsilon}_\alpha + \frac{\bar{n}_\beta + \bar{n}_{\alpha\beta} \cos \bar{\sigma}_{\alpha\beta}}{\sin \bar{\sigma}_{\alpha\beta}} \delta_\mathfrak{v}\, \bar{\varepsilon}_\beta + + \bar{n}_{\alpha\beta}\, \delta_\mathfrak{v}\, \gamma_{\alpha\beta} - \bar{\mathfrak{p}}\, \delta \mathfrak{v} \right\} d\bar{F} = 0 . \qquad (11.20d)$$

Introducing the sectional loads and deformations referred to the principal directions, (11.18) reduces to

$$\iint\limits_{(F)} [\bar{n}_1 (1+\varepsilon_2)\, \delta_\mathfrak{v}\, \varepsilon_1 + \bar{n}_2 (1+\varepsilon_1)\, \delta_\mathfrak{v}\, \varepsilon_2 - - \bar{\mathfrak{p}} (1+\varepsilon_1)(1+\varepsilon_2)\, \delta \mathfrak{v}]\, dF = 0 \qquad (11.18a)$$

which yields

$$\iint\limits_{(F)} [\tilde{n}_1\, \delta_\mathfrak{v}\, d_1 + \tilde{n}_2\, \delta_\mathfrak{v}\, d_2 - \bar{\mathfrak{p}} (1+\varepsilon_1)(1+\varepsilon_2)\, \delta \mathfrak{v}]\, dF = 0 \qquad (11.19c)$$

and

$$\iint\limits_{(\bar{F})} \{ \bar{n}_1\, \delta_\mathfrak{v}\, \bar{\varepsilon}_1 + \bar{n}_2\, \delta_\mathfrak{v}\, \bar{\varepsilon}_2 - \bar{\mathfrak{p}}\, \delta \mathfrak{v} \}\, d\bar{F} = 0 . \qquad (11.20e)$$

Frictionless fabric surfaces and cable nets constitute an important special case of orthogonal and anistropic membranes. Let the positioning of the threads in the unstressed membrane define the parametric curves $\beta = \text{const}$ (α-curves) and $\alpha = \text{const}$ (β-curves). In this case we have $\bar{n}_{\alpha\beta} = 0$, so that the variational problem is

$$\iint\limits_{(F)} [\bar{n}_\alpha (1+\varepsilon_\beta)\, \delta_\mathfrak{v}\, \varepsilon_\alpha + \bar{n}_\beta (1+\varepsilon_\alpha)\, \delta_\mathfrak{v}\, \varepsilon_\beta - - \bar{\mathfrak{p}} (1+\varepsilon_\alpha)(1+\varepsilon_\beta) \sin \bar{\sigma}_{\alpha\beta}\, \delta \mathfrak{v}]\, dF = 0 . \qquad (11.21)$$

From this we derive directly the case of a cable net with finite distances between the cables. Let the fabric consist of strips, extending along the discrete parametric curves $\beta = \beta_i$ ($\alpha^{(i)}$-curves) and $\alpha = \alpha_k$ ($\beta^{(k)}$-curves), whose widths b_i and b_k tend to zero. We denote by

$$S^{(i)}(\alpha) = [\bar{n}_\alpha (1+\varepsilon_\beta)\, d s_\beta]_{\alpha, \beta_i} = [\bar{n}_\alpha (1+\varepsilon_\beta)]_{\alpha, \beta_i} b_i$$

$$S^{(k)}(\beta) = [\bar{n}_\beta (1+\varepsilon_\alpha)\, d s_\alpha]_{\alpha_k, \beta} = [\bar{n}_\beta (1+\varepsilon_\alpha)]_{\alpha_k, \beta} b_k$$

the cable loads, and by

$$\bar{\mathfrak{q}}^{(i)}(\alpha) = [\bar{\mathfrak{p}} (1+\varepsilon_\beta) \sin \bar{\sigma}_{\alpha\beta}\, d s_\beta]_{\alpha, \beta_i} = [\bar{\mathfrak{p}} (1+\varepsilon_\beta) \sin \bar{\sigma}_{\alpha\beta}]_{\alpha, \beta_i} b_i ,$$

$$\bar{\mathfrak{q}}^{(k)}(\beta) = [\bar{\mathfrak{p}} (1+\varepsilon_\alpha) \sin \bar{\sigma}_{\alpha\beta}\, d s_\alpha]_{\alpha_k, \beta} = [\bar{\mathfrak{p}} (1+\varepsilon_\alpha) \sin \bar{\sigma}_{\alpha\beta}]_{\alpha_k, \beta} b_k$$

the distributed external loads acting on the cable elements. These magnitudes are assumed to be finite. Integrating (11.21) we obtain

$$\sum_{i=1}^{n} \int_{\alpha_1}^{\alpha_m} [S^{(i)}(\alpha)\, \delta_\mathfrak{v}\, \varepsilon_\alpha^{(i)} - \bar{\mathfrak{q}}^{(i)}(\alpha) (1+\varepsilon_\alpha^{(i)})\, \delta \mathfrak{v}^{(i)}(\alpha)]\, d s_\alpha^{(i)} + + \sum_{k=1}^{m} \int_{\beta_1}^{\beta_n} [S^{(k)}(\beta)\, \delta_\mathfrak{v}\, \varepsilon_\beta^{(k)} - \bar{\mathfrak{q}}^{(k)}(\beta) (1+\varepsilon_\beta^{(k)})\, \delta \mathfrak{v}^{(k)}(\beta)]\, d s_\beta^{(k)} = 0 . \qquad (11.22a)$$

The summation is extended over all n $\alpha^{(i)}$-cables and m $\beta^{(k)}$-cables ($i = 1 \ldots n$, $k = 1 \ldots m$). A concentrated load acting, e.g., at the cable junctions, can also be represented in this way. Let this load $\mathfrak{P}_{ik}$ act at the point corresponding to $\alpha = \alpha_k$, and $\beta = \beta_i$. We then have

$$(1+\varepsilon_\alpha^{(i)})\, \bar{\mathfrak{q}}^{(i)}(\alpha) = \begin{cases} 0 & \text{for } \alpha_1 \leqq \alpha < (\alpha_k - \zeta) \text{ and } \alpha_k + \zeta < \alpha \leqq \alpha_m \\ \dfrac{\mathfrak{P}_{ik}}{2\zeta \sqrt{g_{\alpha\alpha}^{(i)}}} & \text{for } \alpha_k - \zeta \leqq \alpha \leqq \alpha_k + \zeta \end{cases}$$

where $\zeta \to 0$.

These singularities can be excluded from the integration, so that

$$\sum_{i=1}^{n} \int_{\alpha_1}^{\alpha_m} [S^{(i)}(\alpha)\, \delta_\mathfrak{v}\, \varepsilon_\alpha^{(i)} - \bar{\mathfrak{q}}^{(i)}(\alpha) (1+\varepsilon_\alpha^{(i)})\, \delta \mathfrak{v}^{(i)}(\alpha)]\, d s_\alpha^{(i)} + + \sum_{k=1}^{m} \int_{\beta_1}^{\beta_n} [S^{(k)}(\beta)\, \delta_\mathfrak{v}\, \varepsilon_\beta^{(k)} - \bar{\mathfrak{q}}^{(k)}(\beta) (1+\varepsilon_\beta^{(k)})\, \delta \mathfrak{v}^{(k)}(\beta)]\, d s_\beta^{(k)} - - \sum_{i=1}^{n} \sum_{k=1}^{m} \mathfrak{P}_{ik}\, \delta \mathfrak{v}_{ik} = 0 . \qquad (11.22b)$$

Integration is best carried out separately for each region lying between two junction points. We then obtain finally

$$\sum_{i=1}^{n}\sum_{k=1}^{m-1}\int_{\alpha k}^{\alpha k+1}\left[S^{(i)}(\alpha)\,\delta_{\mathfrak{v}}\,\varepsilon_\alpha^{(i)} - \bar{\mathfrak{q}}^{(i)}(\alpha)\left(1+\varepsilon_\alpha^{(i)}(\alpha)\right)\delta\,\mathfrak{v}^{(i)}(\alpha)\right]d\,s_\alpha^{(i)} +$$
$$+\sum_{i=1}^{n-1}\sum_{k=1}^{m}\int_{\beta i}^{\beta i+1}\left[S^{(k)}(\beta)\,\delta_{\mathfrak{v}}\,\varepsilon_\beta^{(k)} - \bar{\mathfrak{q}}^{(k)}(\beta)\left(1+\varepsilon_\beta^{(k)}(\beta)\right)\delta\,\mathfrak{v}^{(k)}(\beta)\right]d\,s_\beta^{(k)} -$$
$$-\sum_{i=1}^{n}\sum_{k=1}^{m}\mathfrak{P}_{ik}\,\delta\,\mathfrak{v}_{ik} = 0\,. \tag{11.22c}$$

The correctness of the extremum problem (11.22c) is verified by expressing the deformation variations through the displacement variations with the aid of (11.2a, b). Writing $\delta_{\mathfrak{v}}\,\varepsilon_\alpha = \bar{\mathfrak{e}}_\alpha \dfrac{\partial\,\delta\,\mathfrak{v}}{\partial\,s_\alpha}$ and $\delta_{\mathfrak{v}}\,\varepsilon_\beta = \bar{\mathfrak{e}}_\beta \dfrac{\partial\,\delta\,\mathfrak{v}}{\partial\,s_\beta}$ we obtain through partial integration of the first terms of each integrand

$$\sum_{i=1}^{n}\sum_{k=1}^{m-1}\left[S^{(i)}\bar{\mathfrak{e}}_\alpha^{(i)}\,\delta\,\mathfrak{v}^{(i)}(\alpha)\right]_{\alpha k+0}^{\alpha k+1-0} +$$
$$+\sum_{i=1}^{n-1}\sum_{k=1}^{m}\left[S^{(k)}\bar{\mathfrak{e}}_\beta^{(k)}\,\delta\,\mathfrak{v}^{(k)}(\beta)\right]_{\beta i+0}^{\beta i+1-0} - \sum_{i=1}^{n}\sum_{k=1}^{m}\mathfrak{P}_{ik}\,\delta\,\mathfrak{v}_{ik} -$$
$$-\sum_{i=1}^{n}\sum_{k=1}^{m-1}\int_{\alpha k}^{\alpha k+1}\left[\frac{d}{d\,s_\alpha}\left(S^{(i)}\,\bar{\mathfrak{e}}_\alpha^{(i)}\right) + \bar{\mathfrak{q}}^{(i)}\left(1+\varepsilon_\alpha^{(i)}\right)\right]\delta\,\mathfrak{v}^{(i)}(\alpha)\,d\,s_\alpha^{(i)} -$$
$$-\sum_{i=1}^{n-1}\sum_{k=1}^{m}\int_{\beta i}^{\beta i+1}\left[\frac{d}{d\,s_\beta}\left(S^{(i)}\,\mathfrak{e}_\beta^{(k)}\right) + \bar{\mathfrak{q}}^{(k)}\left(1+\varepsilon_\beta^{(k)}\right)\right]\delta\,\mathfrak{v}^{(k)}(\beta)\,d\,s_\beta^{(k)} = 0$$

Since the displacement variations are arbitrary, we must have

$$\begin{aligned}&\frac{d}{d\,s_\alpha}\left(S^{(i)}\,\bar{\mathfrak{e}}_\alpha^{(i)}\right) + \bar{\mathfrak{q}}^{(i)}\left(1+\varepsilon_\alpha^{(i)}\right) = 0\,, \quad i = 1\ldots n\,,\\ &\frac{d}{d\,s_\beta}\left(S^{(k)}\,\bar{\mathfrak{e}}_\beta^{(k)}\right) + \bar{\mathfrak{q}}^{(k)}\left(1+\varepsilon_\beta^{(k)}\right) = 0\,, \quad k = 1\ldots m.\end{aligned} \tag{11.23a}$$

These are, however, the equilibrium conditions for the cable elements lying between the junction points. The summation terms can be written in the form

$$-\sum_{i=2}^{n-1}\sum_{k=2}^{m-1}\left[\left(S^{(i)}\,\bar{\mathfrak{e}}_\alpha^{(i)}\right)_{\alpha k+0} - \left(S^{(i)}\,\bar{\mathfrak{e}}_\alpha^{(i)}\right)_{\alpha k-0} +\right.$$
$$\left.+\left(S^{(k)}\,\bar{\mathfrak{e}}_\beta^{(k)}\right)_{\beta i+0} - \left(S^{(k)}\,\bar{\mathfrak{e}}_\beta^{(k)}\right)_{\beta i-0} + \mathfrak{P}_{ik}\right]\delta\,\mathfrak{v}_{ik}\,.$$

Similar expressions can be found for the junction points lying on the edges, if we put $\delta\,\mathfrak{v}^{(i)}(\alpha_k+0) = \delta\,\mathfrak{v}^{(i)}(\alpha_k-0) = \delta\,\mathfrak{v}^{(k)}(\beta_i-0) = \delta\,\mathfrak{v}^{(k)}(\beta_i+0) = \delta\,\mathfrak{v}_{ik}$. Since the displacements $\delta\,\mathfrak{v}_{ik}$ are arbitrary, we obtain

$$\begin{aligned}&\left(S^{(i)}\,\bar{\mathfrak{e}}_\alpha^{(i)}\right)_{\alpha k+0} - \left(S^{(i)}\,\bar{\mathfrak{e}}_\alpha^{(i)}\right)_{\alpha k-0} +\\ &\quad+\left(S^{(k)}\,\bar{\mathfrak{e}}_\beta^{(k)}\right)_{\beta i+0} - \left(S^{(k)}\,\bar{\mathfrak{e}}_\beta^{(k)}\right)_{\beta i-0} + \mathfrak{P}_{ik} = 0\,,\\ &\quad i = 2\ldots n-1\,,\; k = 2\ldots m-1\,.\end{aligned} \tag{11.23b}$$

These are the equilibrium conditions for the junction points. The problem of cable nets will be considered in the second volume. We now consider once more (11.18) through (11.20). For numerical computations we have to express the sectional loads through the displacements and deformations, applying the load-strain relationships given in Subsection 11.2.3. We shall only consider isotropic materials for which

$$\left(\nu_\alpha = \nu_\beta = \nu_1 = \nu_2 = \nu,\; D_\alpha = D_\beta = D_1 = D_2 = D,\; D_{\alpha\beta} = \frac{D}{2(1+\nu)}\right).$$

11.3.2 *The Variational Problem when Hooke's Law Applies* (11.12)

Inserting (11.12) into (11.18a) yields

$$\begin{aligned}\iint_{(F)}\Big\{&\frac{D}{1-\nu^2}\left[(\varepsilon_1+\nu\,\varepsilon_2)(1+\varepsilon_2)\,\delta_{\mathfrak{v}}\,\varepsilon_1 +\right.\\ &\left.+(\varepsilon_2+\nu\,\varepsilon_1)(1+\varepsilon_1)\,\delta_{\mathfrak{v}}\,\varepsilon_2\right] -\\ &-\bar{\mathfrak{p}}\,(1+\varepsilon_1)\,(1+\varepsilon_2)\,\delta\,\mathfrak{v}\Big\}\,d\,F = 0\,.\end{aligned} \tag{11.24a}$$

We separate the deformation-energy terms as follows:

$$\begin{aligned}&(\varepsilon_1+\nu\,\varepsilon_2)(1+\varepsilon_2)\,\delta_{\mathfrak{v}}\,\varepsilon_1 + (\varepsilon_2+\nu\,\varepsilon_1)(1+\varepsilon_1)\,\delta_{\mathfrak{v}}\,\varepsilon_2 =\\ &= \left[(\varepsilon_1+\nu\,\varepsilon_2)\,\delta_{\mathfrak{v}}\,\varepsilon_1 + (\varepsilon_2+\nu\,\varepsilon_1)\,\delta_{\mathfrak{v}}\,\varepsilon_2\right] +\\ &+\left[\varepsilon_2\,(\varepsilon_1+\nu\,\varepsilon_2)\,\delta_{\mathfrak{v}}\,\varepsilon_1 + \varepsilon_1\,(\varepsilon_2+\nu\,\varepsilon_1)\,\delta_{\mathfrak{v}}\,\varepsilon_2\right] =\\ &= \delta_{\mathfrak{v}}\,W_1 + \delta_{\mathfrak{v}}\,\overline{W}_2\,.\end{aligned}$$

The first term in the last expression represents the complete variation of the energy

$$W_1 = \frac{1}{2}\,(\varepsilon_1^2 + \varepsilon_2^2 + 2\,\nu\,\varepsilon_1\,\varepsilon_2). \tag{11.24b}$$

The second term

$$\delta_{\mathfrak{v}}\,\overline{W}_2 = \varepsilon_2\,(\varepsilon_1+\nu\,\varepsilon_2)\,\delta_{\mathfrak{v}}\,\varepsilon_1 + \varepsilon_1\,(\varepsilon_2+\nu\,\varepsilon_1)\,\delta_{\mathfrak{v}}\,\varepsilon_2$$

cannot, by virtue of

$$\frac{\partial}{\partial\,\varepsilon_2}\left[\varepsilon_2\,(\varepsilon_1+\nu\,\varepsilon_2)\right] = \varepsilon_1 + 2\,\nu\,\varepsilon_2 \neq \frac{\partial}{\partial\,\varepsilon_1}\left[\varepsilon_1\,(\varepsilon_2+\nu\,\varepsilon_1)\right] = \varepsilon_2 + 2\,\nu\,\varepsilon_1$$

be expressed as the complete variation of a corresponding energy term. Introducing the integrating factor $\overline{M}$ and writing

$$\overline{M}\,\delta_{\mathfrak{v}}\,\overline{W}_2 = \delta_{\mathfrak{v}}\,W_2 = \overline{M}\,\varepsilon_2\,(\varepsilon_1+\nu\,\varepsilon_2)\,\delta_{\mathfrak{v}}\,\varepsilon_1 + \overline{M}\,\varepsilon_1\,(\varepsilon_2+\nu\,\varepsilon_1)\,\delta_{\mathfrak{v}}\,\varepsilon_2$$

we obtain the complete variation of the function W_2 if $\overline{M}$ satisfies the partial differential equation

$$\frac{\partial}{\partial\,\varepsilon_2}\left[\overline{M}\,\varepsilon_2\,(\varepsilon_1+\nu\,\varepsilon_2)\right] = \frac{\partial}{\partial\,\varepsilon_1}\left[\overline{M}\,\varepsilon_1\,(\varepsilon_2+\nu\,\varepsilon_1)\right].$$

Putting

$$\varepsilon_1\,(\varepsilon_2+\nu\,\varepsilon_1)\,\frac{\partial\,\overline{M}}{\partial\,\varepsilon_1} - \varepsilon_2\,(\varepsilon_1+\nu\,\varepsilon_2)\,\frac{\partial\,\overline{M}}{\partial\,\varepsilon_2} - \overline{M}\,(1-2\,\nu)\,(\varepsilon_1-\varepsilon_2) = 0$$

yields

$$\varepsilon_1^{m}\,\varepsilon_2^{n+1}\,(m - n\,\nu + 1 - 2\,\nu) - \varepsilon_1^{m+1}\,\varepsilon_2^{n}\,(n - m\,\nu + 1 - 2\,\nu) = 0\,,$$

whence $m = n = -\dfrac{1-2\,\nu}{1-\nu}$.

Putting $C = 1$, we find that

$$\overline{M} = (\varepsilon_1\,\varepsilon_2)^{-\frac{1-2\nu}{1-\nu}} = M^{-1}\,,\quad M = (\varepsilon_1\,\varepsilon_2)^{\frac{1-2\nu}{1-\nu}} \tag{11.24c}$$

whence

$$\begin{aligned}\delta_{\mathfrak{v}}\,W_2 &= \frac{\partial\,W_2}{\partial\,\varepsilon_1}\,\delta_{\mathfrak{v}}\,\varepsilon_1 + \frac{\partial\,W_2}{\partial\,\varepsilon_2}\,\delta_{\mathfrak{v}}\,\varepsilon_2 = (\varepsilon_1\,\varepsilon_2)^{-\frac{1-2\nu}{1-\nu}}\,\varepsilon_2\,(\varepsilon_1+\nu\,\varepsilon_2)\,\delta_{\mathfrak{v}}\,\varepsilon_1\\ &+ (\varepsilon_1\,\varepsilon_2)^{-\frac{1-2\nu}{1-\nu}}\,\varepsilon_1\,(\varepsilon_2+\nu\,\varepsilon_1)\,\delta_{\mathfrak{v}}\,\varepsilon_2\,.\end{aligned}$$

Equating coefficients of $\delta_{\mathfrak{v}}\,\varepsilon_1$ and $\delta_{\mathfrak{v}}\,\varepsilon_2$, we obtain

$$\frac{\partial W_2}{\partial \varepsilon_1} = (\varepsilon_1\,\varepsilon_2)^{-\frac{1-2\nu}{1-\nu}}\,\varepsilon_2\,(\varepsilon_1 + \nu\,\varepsilon_2)\,,$$

$$\frac{\partial W_2}{\partial \varepsilon_2} = (\varepsilon_1\,\varepsilon_2)^{-\frac{1-2\nu}{1-\nu}}\,\varepsilon_1\,(\varepsilon_2 + \nu\,\varepsilon_1)\,.$$

Integration yields

$$W_2 = (1-\nu)\left[\varepsilon_1^{\frac{1}{1-\nu}}\,\varepsilon_2^{\frac{\nu}{1-\nu}} + \varepsilon_2^{\frac{1}{1-\nu}}\,\varepsilon_1^{\frac{\nu}{1-\nu}}\right]. \tag{11.24d}$$

The deformation-energy component is thus

$$\delta_{\mathfrak{v}}\,W_1 + \delta_{\mathfrak{v}}\,\overline{W}_2 = \delta_{\mathfrak{v}}\,W_1 + \overline{M}^{-1}\,\delta_{\mathfrak{v}}\,\overline{W}_2 = \delta_{\mathfrak{v}} W_1 + M\,\delta_{\mathfrak{v}}\,W_2 = \\ = \delta_{\mathfrak{v}}\,(\overset{\downarrow}{W_1} + M\,\overset{\downarrow}{W_2})\,.$$

The arrows indicate that the displacement variations extend only over the energy components W_1 and W_2. Hence

$$\delta_{\mathfrak{v}} \iint\limits_{(F)} \left\{\frac{D}{1-\nu^2}\,(\overset{\downarrow}{W_1} + M\,\overset{\downarrow}{W_2}) - \bar{\mathfrak{p}}\,(1+\varepsilon_1)\,(1+\varepsilon_2)\,\overset{\downarrow}{\mathfrak{v}}\right\} d\,F = 0\,. \tag{11.24e}$$

For $\nu = 1/2$, we have $M = 1$, $W_1 = (\varepsilon_1^2 + \varepsilon_2^2 + \varepsilon_1\,\varepsilon_2)/2$, $W_2 = (\varepsilon_1^2\,\varepsilon_2 + \varepsilon_1\,\varepsilon_2^2)/2$, so that

$$\delta_{\mathfrak{v}} \iint\limits_{(F)} \left\{\frac{2}{3}\,\overbrace{D\,(\varepsilon_1^2 + \varepsilon_2^2 + \varepsilon_1\,\varepsilon_2 + \varepsilon_1^2\,\varepsilon_2 + \varepsilon_1\,\varepsilon_2^2)}^{\downarrow} - \\ - \bar{\mathfrak{p}}\,(1+\varepsilon_1)\,(1+\varepsilon_2)\,\overset{\downarrow}{\mathfrak{v}}\right\} d\,F = 0\,. \tag{11.24f}$$

11.3.4 *The Variational Problem when* (11.14) *is Valid*

Inserting (11.14) into (11.18a), we obtain

$$\iint\limits_{(F)} \left\{\frac{D}{1-\nu^2}\left[(\varepsilon_1 + \nu\,\varepsilon_2)\,\delta_{\mathfrak{v}}\,\varepsilon_1 + (\varepsilon_2 + \nu\,\varepsilon_1)\,\delta_{\mathfrak{v}}\,\varepsilon_2\right] - \\ - \bar{\mathfrak{p}}\,(1+\varepsilon_1)\,(1+\varepsilon_2)\,\delta\,\mathfrak{v}\right\} d\,F = 0 \tag{11.25a}$$

or

$$\delta_{\mathfrak{v}} \iint\limits_{(F)} \left\{\frac{D}{1-\nu^2}\,\overbrace{\frac{1}{2}\,(\varepsilon_1^2 + \varepsilon_2^2 + 2\,\nu\,\varepsilon_1\,\varepsilon_2)}^{\downarrow} - \\ - \bar{\mathfrak{p}}\,(1+\varepsilon_1)\,(1+\varepsilon_2)\,\overset{\downarrow}{\mathfrak{v}}\right\} d\,F = \tag{11.25b}$$

$$= \delta_{\mathfrak{v}} \iint\limits_{(F)} \left\{\frac{D}{1-\nu^2}\,\overset{\downarrow}{W_1} - \bar{\mathfrak{p}}\,(1+\varepsilon_1)\,(1+\varepsilon_2)\,\overset{\downarrow}{\mathfrak{v}}\right\} d\,F = 0\,.$$

11.3.5 *The Variational Problem when* (11.16) *is Valid*

Inserting (11.16) into (11.20e) and putting $\bar{\varepsilon}_i = \ln(1+\varepsilon_i)$, we obtain

$$\iint\limits_{(F)} \left\{\frac{D}{1-\nu^2}\left[(\bar{\varepsilon}_1 + \nu\,\bar{\varepsilon}_2)\,\delta_{\mathfrak{v}}\,\bar{\varepsilon}_1 + (\bar{\varepsilon}_2 + \nu\,\bar{\varepsilon}_1)\,\delta_{\mathfrak{v}}\,\bar{\varepsilon}_2\right] - \bar{\mathfrak{p}}\,\delta\,\mathfrak{v}\right\} d\,\bar{F} = 0$$

or

$$\iint\limits_{(\bar{F})} \delta_{\mathfrak{v}} \left\{\frac{D}{2\,(1-\nu^2)}\,\overbrace{(\bar{\varepsilon}_1^2 + \bar{\varepsilon}_2^2 + 2\,\nu\,\bar{\varepsilon}_1\,\bar{\varepsilon}_2)}^{\downarrow} - \bar{\mathfrak{p}}\,\overset{\downarrow}{\mathfrak{v}}\right\} d\,\bar{F} = 0\,. \tag{11.26a}$$

In contrast to both preceding variational problems, we obtain in this case a simple representation by means of the sectional loads if the latter are used to express the deformations in accordance with (11.16):

$$\iint\limits_{(\bar{F})} \delta_{\mathfrak{v}} \left\{\frac{1}{2\,D}\,\overbrace{(\bar{n}_1^2 + \bar{n}_2^2 - 2\,\nu\,\bar{n}_1\,\bar{n}_2)}^{\downarrow} - \bar{\mathfrak{p}}\,\overset{\downarrow}{\mathfrak{v}}\right\} d\,\bar{F} = 0\,. \tag{11.26b}$$

By virtue of $\bar{\mathfrak{r}} = \mathfrak{r} + \mathfrak{v}$, a variation with respect to $\mathfrak{v}$ is, at the same time, a variation with respect to $\bar{\mathfrak{r}}$. Hence

$$\iint\limits_{(\bar{F})} \delta_{\bar{\mathfrak{r}}} \left\{\frac{1}{2\,D}\,\overbrace{(\bar{n}_1^2 + \bar{n}_2^2 - 2\,\nu\,\bar{n}_1\,\bar{n}_2)}^{\downarrow} - \bar{\mathfrak{p}}\,\overset{\downarrow}{\bar{\mathfrak{r}}}\right\} d\,\bar{F} = 0\,. \tag{11.26c}$$

11.3.6 *The Variational Problem when Kappus' Law Applies*

Inserting (11.13) into (11.19b), we obtain

$$\delta_{\mathfrak{v}} \iint\limits_{(F)} \left\{\frac{D}{2\,(1-\nu^2)}\,\overbrace{\left[d_{\alpha\alpha}^2 + d_{\beta\beta}^2 + 2\,\nu\,d_{\alpha\alpha}\,d_{\beta\beta} + 2\,(1-\nu)\,d_{\alpha\beta}^2\right]}^{\downarrow} - \\ - \bar{\mathfrak{p}}\,(1+\varepsilon_\alpha)\,(1+\varepsilon_\beta)\,\sin\bar{\sigma}_{\alpha\beta}\,\overset{\downarrow}{\mathfrak{v}}\right\} d\,F = 0\,. \tag{11.27a}$$

Expressing the deformations through the displacements in accordance with (2.23a), this becomes

$$\delta_{\mathfrak{v}} \iint\limits_{(F)} \left\{\frac{D}{2\,(1-\nu^2)}\left[\left(\mathfrak{e}_\alpha\,\frac{\partial\,\mathfrak{v}}{\partial\,s_\alpha} + \frac{1}{2}\left(\frac{\partial\,\mathfrak{v}}{\partial\,s_\alpha}\right)^2\right)^2 + \right.\right. \\ + \left(\mathfrak{e}_\beta\,\frac{\partial\,\mathfrak{v}}{\partial\,s_\beta} + \frac{1}{2}\left(\frac{\partial\,\mathfrak{v}}{\partial\,s_\beta}\right)^2\right)^2 + 2\,\nu\left(\mathfrak{e}_\alpha\,\frac{\partial\,\mathfrak{v}}{\partial\,s_\alpha} + \right. \\ + \left.\frac{1}{2}\left(\frac{\partial\,\mathfrak{v}}{\partial\,s_\alpha}\right)^2\right)\left(\mathfrak{e}_\beta\,\frac{\partial\,\mathfrak{v}}{\partial\,s_\beta} + \frac{1}{2}\left(\frac{\partial\,\mathfrak{v}}{\partial\,s_\beta}\right)^2\right) + \\ + \left.\frac{1-\nu}{2}\left(\mathfrak{e}_\alpha\,\frac{\partial\,\mathfrak{v}}{\partial\,s_\beta} + \mathfrak{e}_\beta\,\frac{\partial\,\mathfrak{v}}{\partial\,s_\alpha} + \left(\frac{\partial\,\mathfrak{v}}{\partial\,s_\alpha}\right)\left(\frac{\partial\,\mathfrak{v}}{\partial\,s_\beta}\right)\right)^2\right] - \\ \left. - \underline{\bar{\mathfrak{p}}\,(1+\varepsilon_\alpha)\,(1+\varepsilon_\beta)\,\sin\bar{\sigma}_{\alpha\beta}}\,\mathfrak{v}\right\} d\,F = 0\,, \tag{11.27b}$$

where the underlined term should not be varied.

In the following examples we shall only consider deformations due to the internal pressure p. In this case, the load term can be simplified. Introducing the unit vectors [cf. (11.1)]

$$\bar{\mathfrak{e}}_\alpha = \frac{1}{1+\varepsilon_\alpha}\left(\frac{\partial\,\mathfrak{r}}{\partial\,s_\alpha} + \frac{\partial\,\mathfrak{v}}{\partial\,s_\alpha}\right) = \frac{1}{1+\varepsilon_\alpha}\left(\mathfrak{e}_\alpha + \frac{\partial\,\mathfrak{v}}{\partial\,s_\alpha}\right),$$

$$\bar{\mathfrak{e}}_\beta = \frac{1}{1+\varepsilon_\beta}\left(\mathfrak{e}_\beta + \frac{\partial\,\mathfrak{v}}{\partial\,s_\beta}\right)$$

we obtain the unit vector $\bar{\mathfrak{e}}_\gamma$ of the normal to the deformed surface:

$$\bar{\mathfrak{e}}_\gamma = \frac{\bar{\mathfrak{e}}_\alpha \times \bar{\mathfrak{e}}_\beta}{|\bar{\mathfrak{e}}_\alpha \times \bar{\mathfrak{e}}_\beta|} = \frac{\bar{\mathfrak{e}}_\alpha \times \bar{\mathfrak{e}}_\beta}{\sin\bar{\sigma}_{\alpha\beta}} = \frac{\left(\mathfrak{e}_\alpha + \frac{\partial\,\mathfrak{v}}{\partial\,s_\alpha}\right) \times \left(\mathfrak{e}_\beta + \frac{\partial\,\mathfrak{v}}{\partial\,s_\beta}\right)}{(1+\varepsilon_\alpha)\,(1+\varepsilon_\beta)\,\sin\bar{\sigma}_{\alpha\beta}}\,.$$

The surface-load vector is therefore

$$\bar{\mathfrak{p}} = p\,\bar{\mathfrak{e}}_\gamma = \frac{p\left(\mathfrak{e}_\alpha + \frac{\partial\,\mathfrak{v}}{\partial\,s_\alpha}\right) \times \left(\mathfrak{e}_\beta + \frac{\partial\,\mathfrak{v}}{\partial\,s_\beta}\right)}{(1+\varepsilon_\alpha)\,(1+\varepsilon_\beta)\,\sin\bar{\sigma}_{\alpha\beta}}\,.$$

We thus have

$$\bar{\mathfrak{p}}\,(1+\varepsilon_\alpha)\,(1+\varepsilon_\beta)\sin\bar{\sigma}_{\alpha\beta} = p\left(\mathfrak{e}_\alpha + \frac{\partial \mathfrak{v}}{\partial s_\alpha}\right)\times\left(\mathfrak{e}_\beta + \frac{\partial \mathfrak{v}}{\partial s_\beta}\right) = \bar{\mathfrak{p}}\,(1+\varepsilon_1)\,(1+\varepsilon_2) = p\left(\mathfrak{e}_1 + \frac{\partial \mathfrak{v}}{\partial s_1}\right)\times\left(\mathfrak{e}_2 + \frac{\partial \mathfrak{v}}{\partial s_2}\right) \quad (11.28)$$

Before proceeding to the discussion of approximate solutions obtained by the method of Ritz, we shall compare the results obtained by this method with the exact solutions obtained for certain problems. In the following section we shall first consider an initially spherical membrane loaded by internal pressure, the final shape being also spherical. The exact solution will be verified by variational methods; when applying the method of Ritz we shall proceed from the assumption that the final shape is in fact spherical. The second example deals with the central region of a very long initially plane membrane (oblong rectangle). We find from the equilibrium conditions and the displacement equations that the final shape of the membrane is that of a circular cylinder. The exact results will be used to verify the results obtained by the method of Ritz. This will be done by representing the displacements in the form of simple polynomials or trigonometrical functions.

11.4 The Initially Spherical Membrane Loaded by Internal Pressure

11.4.1 *Solution with the Aid of the Relevant Differential Equations*

For

$$\mathfrak{r} = R_0\,(\sin\vartheta\cos\varphi\,\mathfrak{e}_x + \sin\vartheta\sin\varphi\,\mathfrak{e}_y + \cos\vartheta\,\mathfrak{e}_z)\,,$$

where R_0 = initial radius of sphere; φ = polar angle, measured in x, y -plane from the positive direction of the x-axis; ϑ = angle of latitude, measured from the positive direction of the z-axis; (cf. Figure 3.1, in which the same symbols are used in the general case of an axisymmetrical membrane), we have

$$\sqrt{g_{\alpha\alpha}} = |\mathfrak{r}_\alpha| = |\mathfrak{r}_\vartheta| = R_0\,,\quad \sqrt{g_{\beta\beta}} = |\mathfrak{r}_\beta| = |\mathfrak{r}_\varphi| = R_0\sin\vartheta\,,$$

$$\mathfrak{e}_\alpha = \mathfrak{e}_\vartheta = \frac{\mathfrak{r}_\vartheta}{|\mathfrak{r}_\vartheta|} = \cos\vartheta\cos\varphi\,\mathfrak{e}_x + \cos\vartheta\sin\varphi\,\mathfrak{e}_y - \sin\vartheta\,\mathfrak{e}_z\,,$$

$$\mathfrak{e}_\beta = \mathfrak{e}_\varphi = \frac{\mathfrak{r}_\varphi}{|\mathfrak{r}_\varphi|} = -\sin\varphi\,\mathfrak{e}_x + \cos\varphi\,\mathfrak{e}_y\,,$$

$$\mathfrak{e}_\gamma = \mathfrak{e}_R = \mathfrak{e}_\alpha\times\mathfrak{e}_\beta = \sin\vartheta\cos\varphi\,\mathfrak{e}_x + \sin\vartheta\sin\varphi\,\mathfrak{e}_y + \cos\vartheta\,\mathfrak{e}_z\,.$$

The state of deformation is spherical-symmetrical; the deformation vector is thus $\mathfrak{v} = v_R\,\mathfrak{e}_R = (R - R_0)\,\mathfrak{e}_R$ where R is the radius after deformation. We then obtain from (2.23b)* (since the parametric curves are lines of principal extension)

$$\varepsilon_\alpha = \varepsilon_\vartheta = \varepsilon_1 = \sqrt{1 + 2\,\mathfrak{e}_\vartheta\frac{\partial\mathfrak{v}}{\partial s_\vartheta} + \left(\frac{\partial\mathfrak{v}}{\partial s_\vartheta}\right)^2} - 1 = \frac{v_R}{R_0} = \frac{R - R_0}{R_0} = \frac{R}{R_0} - 1 = \varepsilon_\beta = \varepsilon_\varphi = \varepsilon_2 = \sqrt{1 + 2\,\mathfrak{e}_\varphi\frac{\partial\mathfrak{v}}{\partial s_\varphi} + \left(\frac{\partial\mathfrak{v}}{\partial s_\varphi}\right)^2} = \varepsilon\,.$$

* We have $\dfrac{\partial\,\mathfrak{e}_R}{\partial s_\vartheta} = \dfrac{\mathfrak{e}_\vartheta}{R_0}\,,\quad \dfrac{\partial\,\mathfrak{e}_R}{\partial s_\varphi} = \dfrac{\mathfrak{e}_\varphi}{R_0}\,.$

The equality of the extensions, which are independent of ϑ and φ, thus leads to constant uniform sectional loads $\bar{n}_1 = \bar{n}_2 = \bar{n}_\vartheta = \bar{n}_\varphi = \bar{n}$. The equilibrium conditions (11.6) for $\alpha = \vartheta,\ \beta = \varphi,\ \sqrt{g_{\alpha\alpha}} = \sqrt{\mathfrak{r}_\vartheta^2} = R_0,\ \sqrt{g_{\beta\beta}} = \sqrt{\mathfrak{r}_\varphi^2} = R_0\times\sin\vartheta,$ $(1+\varepsilon)\,R_0 = R,\ \bar{\sigma}_{\alpha\beta} = \pi/2$ und $\bar{\mathfrak{p}} = p\,\bar{\mathfrak{e}}_\gamma$ can be written in the form

$$\frac{\partial}{\partial\vartheta}(R\sin\vartheta\,\bar{n}\,\bar{\mathfrak{e}}_\vartheta) + \frac{\partial}{\partial\varphi}(R\,\bar{n}\,\bar{\mathfrak{e}}_\varphi) + p\,R^2\sin\vartheta\,\bar{\mathfrak{e}}_\gamma = 0\,.$$

Taking into account that $\mathfrak{V} = \nabla\otimes\mathfrak{v} = \left(\mathfrak{e}_\vartheta\dfrac{\partial}{\partial s_\vartheta} + \mathfrak{e}_\varphi\dfrac{\partial}{\partial s_\varphi}\right)\otimes(v_R\,\mathfrak{e}_R) = \dfrac{v_R}{R_0}(\mathfrak{e}_\vartheta\otimes\mathfrak{e}_\vartheta + \mathfrak{e}_\varphi\otimes\mathfrak{e}_\varphi) = \dfrac{v_R}{R_0}\bar{\mathfrak{E}} = \varepsilon\,\mathfrak{E}$, so that by (11.1) we have $\mathfrak{e}_\varphi = \bar{\mathfrak{e}}_\varphi,\ \mathfrak{e}_\gamma = \bar{\mathfrak{e}}_\gamma = \mathfrak{e}_R$ as well as

$$\frac{\partial\,\mathfrak{e}_\vartheta}{\partial\vartheta} = -\,\mathfrak{e}_\gamma\,,\qquad \frac{\partial\,\mathfrak{e}_\varphi}{\partial\varphi} = -\cos\vartheta\,\mathfrak{e}_\vartheta - \sin\vartheta\,\mathfrak{e}_\gamma$$

we finally obtain $\bar{n} = p\,R/2$. Using the load-strain laws, we now find the relationships between the final radius of the sphere and the load.

a) When Hooke's law applies,

$$\bar{n}_1 = \bar{n}_2 = \bar{n} = \frac{p\,R}{2} = \frac{D}{1-\nu^2}(\varepsilon_1 + \nu\,\varepsilon_2) = \frac{D}{1-\nu}\varepsilon = \frac{D}{1-\nu}\left(\frac{R}{R_0} - 1\right)$$

or

$$\frac{p\,R_0\,(1-\nu)}{2\,D} = \varkappa = 1 - \frac{R_0}{R}\,;\quad \frac{R}{R_0} = \frac{1}{1-\varkappa}\,;\qquad \frac{\bar{n}\,(1-\nu)}{D} = \frac{R}{R_0} - 1 = \frac{\varkappa}{1-\varkappa}\,. \quad (11.29)$$

b) When (11.14) is valid (the relationship is here nonlinear since $\varepsilon > 0$),

$$\bar{n}_1 = \bar{n}_2 = \bar{n} = \frac{p\,R}{2} = \frac{D}{1-\nu^2}\,\frac{1}{1+\varepsilon}(\varepsilon_1 + \nu\,\varepsilon_2) = \frac{D}{1-\nu}\,\frac{\varepsilon}{1+\varepsilon} = \frac{D}{1-\nu}\left(1 - \frac{R_0}{R}\right)$$

or

$$\frac{p\,R_0\,(1-\nu)}{2\,D} = \varkappa = \frac{R_0}{R} - \left(\frac{R_0}{R}\right)^2;\quad \frac{R_0}{R} = \frac{1}{2}\left(1 \pm \sqrt{1 - 4\,\varkappa}\right);\qquad \frac{\bar{n}\,(1-\nu)}{D} = 1 - \frac{R_0}{R} = 1 - \frac{1}{2}\left(1 \pm \sqrt{1 - 4\,\varkappa}\right). \quad (11.30)$$

c) When Kappus' law applies,

$$\bar{n}_1 = \bar{n}_2 = \bar{n} = \frac{p\,R}{2} = \frac{D}{1-\nu^2}(d_1 + \nu\,d_2) = \frac{D}{1-\nu}\,d = \frac{D}{1-\nu}\,\varepsilon\left(1 + \frac{\varepsilon}{2}\right) = \frac{D}{1-\nu}\cdot\frac{1}{2}\left[\left(\frac{R}{R_0}\right)^2 - 1\right]$$

or

$$\frac{p\,R_0\,(1-\nu)}{2\,D} = \varkappa = \frac{1}{2}\left(\frac{R}{R_0} - \frac{R_0}{R}\right);\quad \frac{R}{R_0} = \varkappa + \sqrt{1 + \varkappa^2}\,;\quad \frac{\bar{n}\,(1-\nu)}{D} = \frac{1}{2}\left[\left(\frac{R}{R_0}\right)^2 - 1\right] = \varkappa^2 + \varkappa\sqrt{1 + \varkappa^2}\,. \quad (11.31)$$

d) When (11.16) is valid,

$$\bar{n}_1 = \bar{n}_2 = \bar{n} = \frac{p\,R}{2} = \frac{D}{1-\nu^2}\left[\ln\left(1+\varepsilon_1\right) + \nu \ln\left(1+\varepsilon_2\right)\right] =$$

$$= \frac{D}{1-\nu}\ln\left(1+\varepsilon\right) = \frac{D}{1-\nu}\ln\frac{R}{R_0}$$

or

$$\frac{p\,R_0\,(1-\nu)}{2\,D} = \varkappa = \frac{R_0}{R}\ln\frac{R}{R_0}\,; \quad \frac{\bar{n}\,(1-\nu)}{D} = \ln\frac{R}{R_0}\,. \qquad (11.32)$$

Figure (11.3) shows R/R_0 and $\bar{n}\,(1-\nu)/D$ as functions of $\varkappa = p\,R_0\,(1-\nu)/(2\,D)$. By virtue of $\bar{n}_{\max} = n_{\text{tear}} \approx 0.25\,D$, only the range $0 \leq \bar{n}\,(1-\nu)/D \lessapprox 0.25$ is of practical interest. This corresponds approximately to the range $0 \leq \varkappa < 0.20$ within which the relationships between sectional loads and internal pressure depend less on the choice of the load-strain law than the relationships between deformations and internal pressure. We can thus select the load-strain relationship which yields the simplest expressions.

It should be noted that, with the exception of Kappus' law, all other load-strain relationships postulate failure of the spherical membrane at finite internal pressures, irrespective of the ultimate strength of the material. According to Hooke's law, for $\varkappa = 1$, i.e., $p = p_{kr} = \dfrac{2\,D}{R_0\,(1-\nu)}$, the radius of the sphere becomes infinite. If we apply (11.16) or (11.14), the maximum values of $\varkappa$ are, respectively, $\varkappa = 1/e = 1/2.7182 = 0.368$ and $\varkappa = 0.25$, thus $p_{kr} = \dfrac{2\,D}{R_0\,(1-\nu)\,e}$ and $p_{kr} = \dfrac{D}{2\,R_0\,(1-\nu)}$. Larger ratios than, respectively, $R/R_0 = 2$ and $R/R_0 = e$ can only be obtained when the internal pressure is again reduced. Thus, for each value of $\varkappa$ (i.e., of the internal pressure) there exist two possible values for the radius; this can be confirmed experimentally.

We shall now verify these results by considering the variational problem of the membrane, using the exact solution for the displacements.

11.4.2 *Solution by Means of the Variational Problem of the Membrane Theory*

a) Material obeying Hooke's law.

We have

$$W_1 = \frac{1}{2}\left(\varepsilon_1^2 + \varepsilon_2^2 + 2\,\nu\,\varepsilon_1\,\varepsilon_2\right) = (1+\nu)\,\varepsilon^2 = (1+\nu)\left(\frac{R}{R_0} - 1\right)^2,$$

$$M = \left(\varepsilon_1\,\varepsilon_2\right)^{\frac{1-2\nu}{1-\nu}} = \varepsilon^{\frac{2(1-2\nu)}{1-\nu}} = \left(\frac{R}{R_0} - 1\right)^{\frac{2(1-2\nu)}{1-\nu}},$$

$$W_2 = (1-\nu)\left[\varepsilon_1^{\frac{1}{1-\nu}}\,\varepsilon_2^{\frac{\nu}{1-\nu}} + \varepsilon_2^{\frac{1}{1-\nu}}\,\varepsilon_1^{\frac{\nu}{1-\nu}}\right] =$$

$$= 2\,(1-\nu)\,\varepsilon^{\frac{1+\nu}{1-\nu}} = 2\,(1-\nu)\left(\frac{R}{R_0} - 1\right)^{\frac{1+\nu}{1-\nu}},$$

$$\mathfrak{p}\,(1+\varepsilon_1)\,(1+\varepsilon_2)\,\overset{\downarrow}{\mathfrak{v}} = p\,\mathfrak{e}_\gamma\,(1+\varepsilon)^2\,\overset{\downarrow}{v}_R\,\mathfrak{e}_\gamma = p\,(1+\varepsilon)^2\,\overset{\downarrow}{v}_R =$$

$$= p\left(\frac{R}{R_0}\right)^2 (\overset{\downarrow}{R} - R_0) = p\,R_0\left(\frac{R}{R_0}\right)^2\left(\frac{\overset{\downarrow}{R}}{R_0} - 1\right),$$

whence, in accordance with (11.24e)

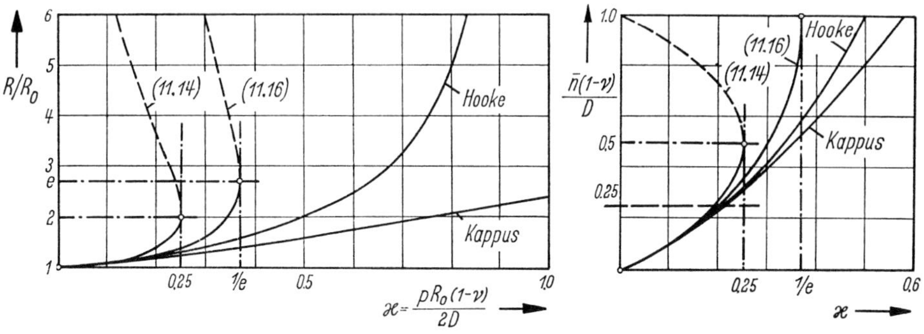

Figure 11.3

$$\delta_R\,\Pi = \delta_R \iint_{(F)} \left\{\frac{D}{1-\nu^2}\left[(1+\nu)\left(\frac{\overset{\downarrow}{R}}{R_0} - 1\right)^2 + \right.\right.$$

$$\left. + \left(\frac{R}{R_0} - 1\right)^{\frac{2(1-2\nu)}{1-\nu}} \cdot 2\,(1-\nu)\left(\frac{\overset{\downarrow}{R}}{R_0} - 1\right)^{\frac{1+\nu}{1-\nu}}\right] -$$

$$\left. - p\,R_0\left(\frac{R}{R_0}\right)^2\left(\frac{\overset{\downarrow}{R}}{R_0} - 1\right)\right\} R_0^2 \sin\vartheta\, d\,\varphi\, d\,\vartheta = 0\,.$$

The expression inside the braces is independent of ϑ and φ, so that integration can be carried out directly. Dividing by $4\,\pi\,R_0^2$, we obtain

$$\delta_R\,\Pi = \frac{\partial\,\Pi}{\partial\,R}\,\delta\,R = 0\,; \quad \Pi = \frac{D}{1-\nu^2}\left[(1+\nu)\left(\frac{\overset{\downarrow}{R}}{R_0} - 1\right)^2 + \right.$$

$$\left. + 2\,(1-\nu)\left(\frac{R}{R_0} - 1\right)^{\frac{2(1-2\nu)}{1-\nu}}\left(\frac{\overset{\downarrow}{R}}{R_0} - 1\right)^{\frac{1+\nu}{1-\nu}}\right] -$$

$$- p\,R_0\left(\frac{R}{R_0}\right)^2\left(\frac{\overset{\downarrow}{R}}{R_0} - 1\right),$$

where only those terms indicated by an arrow are to be differentiated. The result is

$$\left\{\frac{D}{1-\nu^2}\left[2\,(1+\nu)\left(\frac{R}{R_0} - 1\right)\frac{1}{R_0} + 2\,(1-\nu)\left(\frac{R}{R_0} - 1\right)^{\frac{2(1-2\nu)}{1-\nu}} \cdot\right.\right.$$

$$\left.\left. \cdot\,\frac{1+\nu}{1-\nu}\left(\frac{R}{R_0} - 1\right)^{\left(\frac{1+\nu}{1-\nu} - 1\right)} \cdot \frac{1}{R_0}\right] - p\left(\frac{R}{R_0}\right)^2\right\}\delta\,R = 0\,.$$

Since $\delta\,R$ is arbitrary, the expression inside the braces must vanish. This leads to (11.29).

b) Material obeying (11.14). In this case (11.25b) yields

$$\delta_R \Pi = \delta_R \iint\limits_{(F)} \left\{ \frac{D}{1-\nu^2} \left[(1+\nu) \left(\frac{\overset{\downarrow}{R}}{R_0} - 1 \right)^2 \right] - \right.$$

$$\left. - p R_0 \left(\frac{R}{R_0} \right)^2 \left(\frac{\overset{\downarrow}{R}}{R_0} - 1 \right) \right\} R_0^2 \sin \vartheta \, d\varphi \, d\vartheta = 0 .$$

Integrating, dividing by $4\pi R_0^2$, and varying, we obtain

$$\delta_R \Pi = \frac{\partial \Pi}{\partial R} \delta R = \left\{ \frac{2D}{1-\nu} \left(\frac{R}{R_0} - 1 \right) \frac{1}{R_0} - p \left(\frac{R}{R_0} \right)^2 \right\} \delta R = 0 .$$

Equating the term inside the braces to zero leads to (11.30).

c) Material obeying Kappus' law. For

$d_1 = d_2 = \frac{1}{2} \left[\left(\frac{R}{R_0} \right)^2 - 1 \right]$ we obtain from (11.27a)

$$\delta_R \Pi = \delta_R \iint\limits_{(F)} \left\{ \frac{D}{2(1-\nu^2)} \left[2(1+\nu) \frac{1}{4} \left(\left(\frac{\overset{\downarrow}{R}}{R_0} \right)^2 - 1 \right)^2 \right] - \right.$$

$$\left. - p R_0 \left(\frac{R}{R_0} \right)^2 \left(\frac{\overset{\downarrow}{R}}{R_0} - 1 \right) \right\} R_0^2 \sin \vartheta \, d\varphi \, d\vartheta = 0 .$$

Integrating, dividing by $4\pi R_0^2$, and varying yields

$$\delta_R \Pi = \frac{\partial \Pi}{\partial R} \delta R = \left\{ \frac{D}{1-\nu} \left(\left(\frac{R}{R_0} \right)^2 - 1 \right) \frac{R}{R_0^2} - p \left(\frac{R}{R_0} \right)^2 \right\} \delta R = 0.$$

Equating the term inside the braces to zero leads to (11.31).

d) Material obeying (11.16).
In this case (11.26a) yields

$$\delta_R \Pi = \iint\limits_{(F)} \delta_R \left\{ \frac{D}{2(1-\nu^2)} \left[2(1+\nu) \left(\ln \frac{\overset{\downarrow}{R}}{R_0} \right)^2 \right] - \right.$$

$$\left. - p \left(\frac{\overset{\downarrow}{R}}{R_0} - 1 \right) R_0 \right\} R^2 \sin \vartheta \, d\varphi \, d\vartheta =$$

$$= 4\pi R^2 \delta_R \left\{ \frac{D}{1-\nu} \left(\ln \frac{\overset{\downarrow}{R}}{R_0} \right)^2 - p R_0 \left(\frac{\overset{\downarrow}{R}}{R_0} - 1 \right) \right\} =$$

$$= 4\pi R^2 \left\{ \frac{2D}{1-\nu} \left(\ln \frac{R}{R_0} \right) \cdot \frac{1}{R} - p \right\} \delta R = 0 .$$

Equating the term inside the braces to zero leads to (11.32).

11.5 The Central Region of an Initially Plane Rectangular Membrane

11.5.1 *Solution with the Aid of Differential Equations*

Using Cartesian coordinates, we can describe the undeformed plane rectangular surface, whose edge lengths are a and b, by $\mathfrak{r} = x\,\mathfrak{e}_x + y\,\mathfrak{e}_y$, $0 \leq x \leq a$, $0 \leq y \leq b$.
When $a \ll b$, the parametric curves $x = \text{const.}$ and $y = \text{const.}$ are the lines of principal extension in the central region ($y \approx b/2$). We have in this case a plane state of deformation in the (x, z) plane ($\varepsilon_y = \varepsilon_2 = 0$), with all magnitudes dependent only on x. The displacements are described by $\mathfrak{v} = u(x)\,\mathfrak{e}_x + w(x)\,\mathfrak{e}_z$. Furthermore,

$$\varepsilon_x = \varepsilon_1 = \sqrt{1 + 2 \frac{\partial \mathfrak{r}}{\partial x} \frac{\partial \mathfrak{v}}{\partial x} + \left(\frac{\partial \mathfrak{v}}{\partial x} \right)^2} - 1 = \sqrt{(1+u')^2 + w'^2} - 1 ,$$

$$\bar{\mathfrak{e}}_x = \frac{1}{1+\varepsilon_x} \frac{\partial}{\partial x} (\mathfrak{r} + \mathfrak{v}) = \frac{1}{1+\varepsilon_x} \frac{\partial}{\partial x} [(x+u)\,\mathfrak{e}_x + y\,\mathfrak{e}_y + w\,\mathfrak{e}_z] =$$

$$= \frac{(1+u')\,\mathfrak{e}_x + w'\,\mathfrak{e}_z}{\sqrt{(1+u')^2 + w'^2}} , \quad \bar{\mathfrak{e}}_y = \mathfrak{e}_y ,$$

$$\bar{\mathfrak{e}}_\gamma = \bar{\mathfrak{e}}_z = \frac{\bar{\mathfrak{e}}_x \times \bar{\mathfrak{e}}_y}{\sin \bar{\sigma}_{xy}} = \bar{\mathfrak{e}}_x \times \bar{\mathfrak{e}}_y = \frac{(1+u')\,\mathfrak{e}_z - w'\,\mathfrak{e}_x}{\sqrt{(1+u')^2 + w'^2}} =$$

$$= \frac{(1+u')\,\mathfrak{e}_z - w'\,\mathfrak{e}_x}{1+\varepsilon_x} .$$

Writing

$$\mathfrak{p} = p\,\bar{\mathfrak{e}}_\gamma , \quad \alpha = x , \quad \sqrt{g_{\alpha\alpha}} = \sqrt{\left(\frac{\partial \mathfrak{r}}{\partial x} \right)^2} = 1 ,$$

$$\beta = y , \quad \sqrt{g_{\beta\beta}} = \sqrt{\left(\frac{\partial \mathfrak{r}}{\partial y} \right)^2} = 1 , \quad \frac{\partial}{\partial \beta} (\ldots) = 0$$

we obtain from (11.6) the equilibrium conditions

$$\frac{d}{dx} \left[\bar{n}_x \frac{(1+u')\,\mathfrak{e}_x + w'\,\mathfrak{e}_z}{\sqrt{(1+u')^2 + w'^2}} \right] + p\,[(1+u')\,\mathfrak{e}_z - w'\,\mathfrak{e}_x] = 0 .$$

Resolved into x- and z-components, this becomes

$$\frac{d}{dx} \left(\bar{n}_x \frac{1+u'}{\sqrt{(1+u')^2 + w'^2}} \right) - p\,w' = 0 ,$$

$$\frac{d}{dx} \left(\bar{n}_x \frac{w'}{\sqrt{(1+u')^2 + w'^2}} \right) + p\,(1+u') = 0 .$$

Integration yields

$$\bar{n}_x \frac{1+u'}{\sqrt{(1+u')^2 + w'^2}} = p\,w + C_1 ,$$

$$\bar{n}_x \frac{w'}{\sqrt{(1+u')^2 + w'^2}} = -p\,(x+u) + C_2 . \qquad (11.33\text{a, b})$$

For reasons of symmetry, we must have $w' = 0$ and $u = 0$ at $x = a/2$. Hence, by (11.33b), $C_2 = p\,a/2$, and this equation becomes

$$\frac{\bar{n}_x w'}{\sqrt{(1+u')^2 + w'^2}} = p \left[\frac{a}{2} - (x+u) \right] . \qquad (11.33\text{c})$$

The final shape of the cylindrical surface can be determined directly from the equilibrium conditions. Dividing (11.33a) by (11.33c) yields

$$\frac{1+u'}{w'} = \frac{p\,w + C_1}{p \left[\frac{a}{2} - (x+u) \right]} \quad \text{or} \quad (1+u') \left[\frac{a}{2} - (x+u) \right] =$$

$$= -\frac{1}{2} \frac{d}{dx} \left[\frac{a}{2} - (x+u) \right]^2 = w\,w' + \frac{C_1}{p} w' =$$

$$= \frac{d}{dx} \left(\frac{w^2}{2} + \frac{C_1}{p} w \right) .$$

Integrating, we obtain

$$\left[(x+u) - \frac{a}{2} \right]^2 + \left[w + \frac{C_1}{p} \right]^2 = \left(\frac{C_1}{p} \right)^2 + C_3^2 = \text{const} = R^2 , \qquad (11.34\text{a})$$

where C_3^2 is a constant. After deformation, the membrane surface thus assumes the shape of a circular cylinder. Putting $C_3 = a/2$, we have

$$R = \sqrt{\left(\frac{a}{2}\right)^2 + \left(\frac{C_1}{p}\right)^2}, \tag{11.34b}$$

which satisfies the boundary conditions $u = 0$ and $w = 0$ at $x = 0$ and $x = a$ (Figure 11.4).
We then obtain from (11.33a, c)

$$\bar{n}_x = p \frac{w + \frac{C_1}{p}}{1 + u'} \sqrt{(1 + u')^2 + w'^2} = \tag{11.34c}$$

$$= p \frac{1}{w'} \left[\frac{a}{2} - (x + u)\right] \sqrt{(1 + u')^2 + w'^2} = p\, R = \text{const}.$$

We can thus determine the still unknown radius R for the various

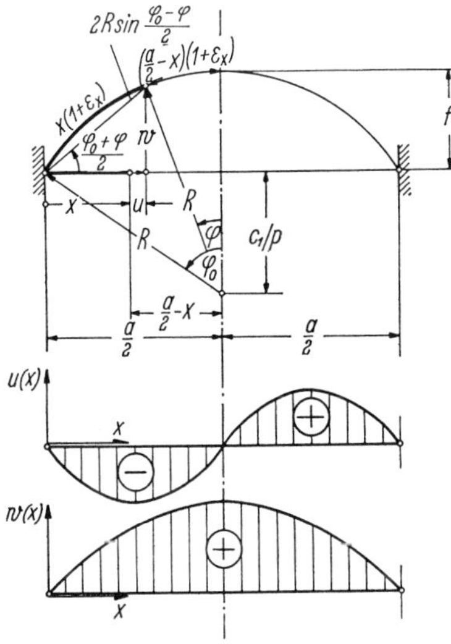

Figure 11.4

load-strain relationships. Since the membrane extensions must be constant by virtue of $\bar{n}_x = $ const, we obtain, writing $\sin \varphi_0 = a/(2\,R)$,

$$\varepsilon_x = \frac{2\,R\,\varphi_0 - a}{a} = 2\,\varphi_0 \frac{R}{a} - 1 = \frac{\varphi_0}{\sin \varphi_0} - 1 = \tag{11.35}$$

$$= \frac{2\,R}{a} \text{arc sin} \frac{a}{2\,R} - 1 = \text{const};$$

for a given load-strain relationship, we can thus find the angle φ_0 and thence R or C_1/p and the maximum deflection f.

a) Material obeying Hooke's Law.

We obtain

$$\bar{n}_x = p\,R = \frac{D}{1 - \nu^2} \varepsilon_x = \frac{D}{1 - \nu^2} \left(\frac{\varphi_0}{\sin \varphi_0} - 1\right)$$

or, writing $\varkappa = p\,a\,(1 - \nu^2)/D$ the relationship

$$\frac{p\,(1 - \nu^2)\,R}{D} = \frac{p\,a\,(1 - \nu^2)}{D} \frac{1}{2} \frac{2\,R}{a} = \frac{\varkappa}{2} \frac{1}{\sin \varphi_0} = \frac{\varphi_0}{\sin \varphi_0} - 1,$$

whence

$$\varkappa = 2\,(\varphi_0 - \sin \varphi_0) = 2 \left[\text{arc sin} \left(\frac{a}{2\,R}\right) - \frac{a}{2\,R}\right]. \tag{11.36a}$$

Furthermore

$$\frac{f}{a} = \frac{R\,(1 - \cos \varphi_0)}{a} = 2 \frac{R}{a} \sin^2 \frac{\varphi_0}{2} = \frac{\sin^2 \frac{\varphi_0}{2}}{\sin \varphi_0} = \tag{11.36b}$$

$$= \frac{1}{2} \text{tg} \frac{\varphi_0}{2} = \frac{1}{2} \text{tg} \left(\frac{1}{2} \text{arc sin} \frac{a}{2\,R}\right)$$

and

$$\frac{\bar{n}_x\,(1 - \nu^2)}{D} = \frac{p\,R\,(1 - \nu^2)}{D} = \tag{11.36c}$$

$$= \frac{p\,a\,(1 - \nu^2)}{D} \frac{1}{2} \frac{2\,R}{a} = \frac{\varkappa}{2 \sin \varphi_0}.$$

By virtue of $\varepsilon_y = \varepsilon_2 = 0$, we obtain the same relationships when (11.14) is valid.

b) Material obeying Kappus' law.

We obtain from

$$\bar{n}_x = \frac{D}{1 - \nu^2} d_{xx} (1 + \varepsilon_x) = \frac{D}{1 - \nu^2} \varepsilon_x (1 + \varepsilon_x) \left(1 + \frac{\varepsilon_x}{2}\right) =$$

$$= \frac{D}{2\,(1 - \nu^2)} \left[\left(\frac{\varphi_0}{\sin \varphi_0}\right)^2 - 1\right] \frac{\varphi_0}{\sin \varphi_0} =$$

$$= p\,R = \frac{1}{2} p\,a \frac{2\,R}{a} = \frac{p\,a}{2 \sin \varphi_0}$$

the relationship

$$\frac{p\,a\,(1 - \nu^2)}{D} = \varkappa = \varphi_0 \left[\left(\frac{\varphi_0}{\sin \varphi_0}\right)^2 - 1\right] \tag{11.37a, b}$$

or $$\frac{\bar{n}_x (1 - \nu^2)}{D} = \frac{\varkappa}{2 \sin \varphi_0} = \frac{\varphi_0}{2 \sin \varphi_0} \left[\left(\frac{\varphi_0}{\sin \varphi_0}\right)^2 - 1\right].$$

c) Material obeying (11.16).

We obtain from

$$\bar{n}_x = \frac{D}{1 - \nu^2} \ln\,(1 + \varepsilon_x) = \frac{D}{1 - \nu^2} \ln \frac{\varphi_0}{\sin \varphi_0} = p\,R =$$

$$= \frac{p\,a}{2} \frac{2\,R}{a} = \frac{p\,a}{2 \sin \varphi_0}$$

the relationship

$$\frac{p\,a\,(1 - \nu^2)}{D} = \varkappa = 2 \sin \varphi_0 \ln \frac{\varphi_0}{\sin \varphi_0} \tag{11.38a, b}$$

or $$\frac{\bar{n}_x\,(1 - \nu^2)}{D} = \frac{\varkappa}{2 \sin \varphi_0} = \ln \frac{\varphi_0}{\sin \varphi_0}.$$

Figure 11.5 shows R/a, f/a as well as $\bar{n}_x\,(1 - \nu^2)/D$ as functions of $\varkappa = \frac{p\,a\,(1 - \nu^2)}{D}$.

We see that, as mentioned earlier, in the important (in actual practice) range $0 \leq \bar{n} \lessapprox 0.25\,D$ the relationship between sectional loads and internal pressure is almost independent of the choice of the load-strain law. The deformations, however, depend to a greater degree on this choice. The theoretical behavior of the material at very high pressures is of interest. If Kappus' law applies, infinite extensions (cylinder radii) are obtained only at infinite pressure. If, however, Hooke's law applies, infinite extension can be attained for $\varkappa = 2\pi$, or $p = 2\pi D/[a(1-\nu^2)]$ i.e., at a finite pressure. When (11.16) is valid the maximum attainable pressure is only $p = 1.721\, D/[a(1-\nu^2)]$ corresponding to $R/a = 0.778$.

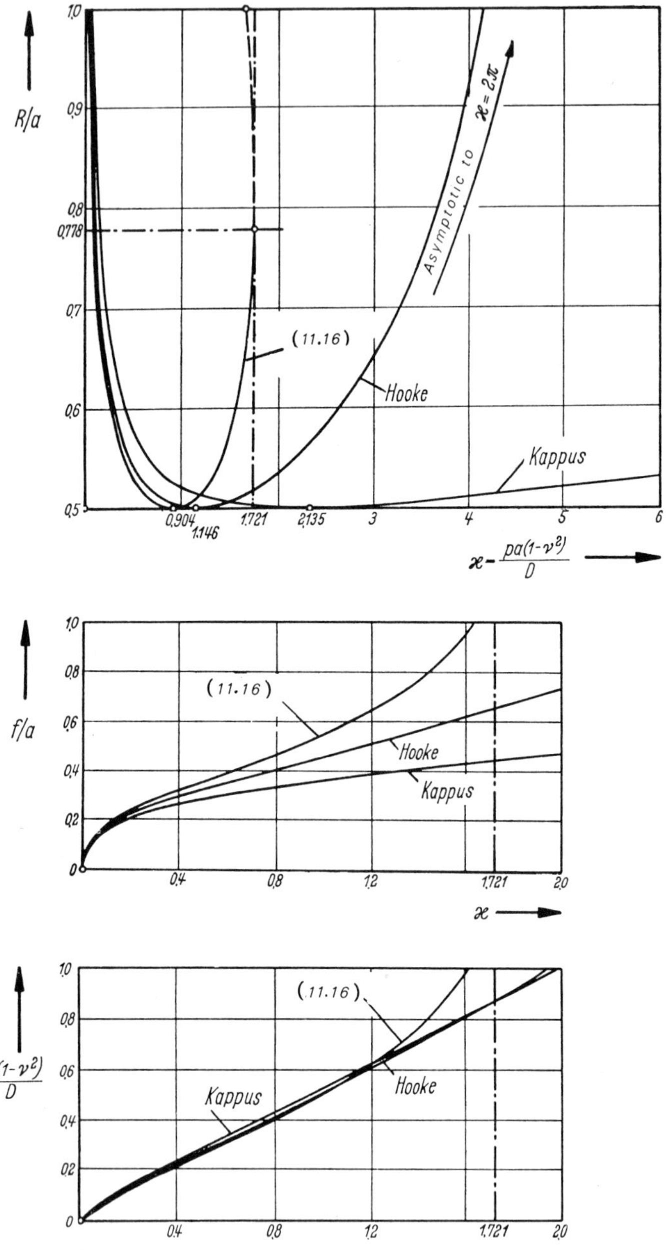

Fig. 11.5

We shall consider once more the displacements of the membrane. Introducing the angle (Figure 11.4)

$$\varphi = \varphi(x) = \frac{\left(\frac{a}{2} - x\right)(1+\varepsilon_x)}{R} =$$

$$= \frac{a}{2R}(1+\varepsilon_x)\left(1 - 2\frac{x}{a}\right) = \varphi_0\left(1 - 2\frac{x}{a}\right)$$

we obtain

$$u(x) = 2R\sin\frac{\varphi_0-\varphi}{2}\cos\frac{\varphi_0+\varphi}{2} - x = R(\sin\varphi_0 - \sin\varphi) - x,$$

whence, finally

$$u(x) = \frac{a}{2}\left[\left(1 - 2\frac{x}{a}\right) - \frac{\sin\left[\varphi_0\left(1-2\frac{x}{a}\right)\right]}{\sin\varphi_0}\right] = \qquad (11.39a)$$

$$= R\left[\left(1-2\frac{x}{a}\right)\sin\varphi_0 - \sin\left(\left(1-2\frac{x}{a}\right)\varphi_0\right)\right],$$

$$\left(\frac{u}{a}\right)_{\text{extr}} = -\frac{u(x_{\text{extr}})}{a} = \frac{u(a - x_{\text{extr}})}{a} =$$

$$= \frac{1}{2\varphi_0}\left[\arccos\left(\frac{\sin\varphi_0}{\varphi_0}\right) - \sqrt{\left(\frac{\varphi_0}{\sin\varphi_0}\right)^2 - 1}\right], \qquad (11.39b)$$

$$\frac{x_{\text{extr}}}{a} = \frac{1}{2}\left[1 - \frac{1}{\varphi_0}\arccos\left(\frac{\sin\varphi_0}{\varphi_0}\right)\right].$$

The vertical displacements are

$$w(x) = R(\cos\varphi - \cos\varphi_0) = R\left\{\cos\left[\varphi_0\left(1-2\frac{x}{a}\right)\right] - \cos\varphi_0\right\}. \qquad (11.39c)$$

They are shown (not to scale) in Figure 11.4.

11.5.2 *Approximate Solution by the Method of Ritz*

In the previous example we inserted the exact solution into the variational integrals. We then obtained again the exact solution through extremalization. We would obtain the same result in the present case. However, we shall use simple assumptions, by which the differential equations cannot be satisfied, in order to compare the results thus obtained with the exact solution. We consider a membrane for which Kappus' law holds. We then have

$$d_{xx} = d_1 = \mathfrak{e}_x\frac{\partial\mathfrak{v}}{\partial x} + \frac{1}{2}\left(\frac{\partial\mathfrak{v}}{\partial x}\right)^2 = \frac{du}{dx} + \frac{1}{2}\left[\left(\frac{du}{dx}\right)^2 + \left(\frac{dw}{dx}\right)^2\right],$$

$$d_{yy} = d_2 = 0.$$

Furthermore, by (11.28)

$$\bar{\mathfrak{p}}(1+\varepsilon_1)(1+\varepsilon_2)\overset{\downarrow}{\mathfrak{v}} = \bar{\mathfrak{p}}(1+\varepsilon_x)(1+\varepsilon_y)\overset{\downarrow}{\mathfrak{v}} =$$

$$= p\left[\left(\mathfrak{e}_x + \frac{\partial\mathfrak{v}}{\partial x}\right)\times\left(\mathfrak{e}_y + \frac{\partial\mathfrak{v}}{\partial y}\right)\right]\overset{\downarrow}{\mathfrak{v}} =$$

$$= p\left[((1+u')\,\mathfrak{e}_x + w'\,\mathfrak{e}_z)\times\mathfrak{e}_y\right]\overset{\downarrow}{\overbrace{(u\,\mathfrak{e}_x + w\,\mathfrak{e}_z)}} =$$

$$= p\left[\left(1+\frac{du}{dx}\right)\overset{\downarrow}{w} - \frac{dw}{dx}\overset{\downarrow}{u}\right].$$

Therefore, according to (11.27)* the variational problem is

$$\delta_{u,w}\Pi = \delta_{u,w}\int_{x=0}^{a}\left\{\frac{D}{2(1-\nu^2)}\overset{\downarrow}{\overbrace{\left[\frac{du}{dx} + \frac{1}{2}\left(\left(\frac{du}{dx}\right)^2 + \left(\frac{dw}{dx}\right)^2\right)\right]^2}} - \right.$$

$$\left. - p\left[\left(1+\frac{du}{dx}\right)\overset{\downarrow}{w} - \frac{dw}{dx}\overset{\downarrow}{u}\right]\right\}dx. \qquad (11.40)$$

we set

$$u(x) = C_u u_1(x), \quad w(x) = C_w w_1(x), \qquad (11.41)$$

where $u_1(x)$ and $w_1(x)$ are functions satisfying the boundary

* We integrate over an initial surface whose edge lengths are a and $\Delta y = 1$. Since all magnitudes are independent of y, we can immediately integrate over y, so that only integration over x remains.

conditions while the constants C_u and C_w have to be determined. Thus, $\Pi = \Pi(C_u, C_w)$ depends only on these constants. Setting $\partial \Pi / \partial C_u = 0$ and $\partial \Pi / \partial C_w = 0$ (this replaces the exact solution of the variational problem), where only the terms indicated by arrows are differentiated, yields

$$\left.\begin{aligned}
&\left(\frac{C_w}{a}\right)^2 \left[\int_0^1 w_1'^2 u_1' \, d\xi + \frac{C_u}{a} \int_0^1 w_1'^2 u_1'^2 \, d\xi\right] + \\
&\quad + 2\varkappa \frac{C_w}{a} \int_0^1 w_1' u_1 \, d\xi + \left(\frac{C_u}{a}\right)^3 \int_0^1 u_1'^4 \, d\xi + \\
&\quad + 3\left(\frac{C_u}{a}\right)^2 \int_0^1 u_1'^3 \, d\xi + 2 \frac{C_u}{a} \int_0^1 u_1'^2 \, d\xi = 0 , \\
&\left(\frac{C_u}{a}\right)^2 \left[\frac{C_w}{a} \int_0^1 u_1'^2 w_1'^2 \, d\xi\right] + \\
&\quad + 2 \frac{C_u}{a} \left[\frac{C_w}{a} \int_0^1 u_1' w_1'^2 \, d\xi - \varkappa \int_0^1 u_1' w_1 \, d\xi\right] + \\
&\quad + \left(\frac{C_w}{a}\right)^3 \int_0^1 w_1'^4 \, d\xi - 2\varkappa \int_0^1 w_1 \, d\xi = 0 ,
\end{aligned}\right\} \quad (11.42a, b)$$

where the primes denote differentiation with respect to $\xi = x/a$. This system of equations is best solved graphically. We first solve (11.42a) for C_w/a, so that we obtain the curve $(C_w/a) = f(C_u/a; \varkappa_0)$ for a given value of $\varkappa = \varkappa_0$. Similarly, we obtain from (11.42b) the curves $C_u/a = g(C_w/a; \varkappa_0)$ for the same value of $\varkappa = \varkappa_0$. Both curves are plotted in C_u/a, C_w/a, coordinates; their intersection defines the pair of values C_u/a, C_w/a corresponding to $\varkappa = \varkappa_0$. This procedure is repeated for various values of $\varkappa$. We give two examples:

We set

$$u_1(\xi) = -\sin 2\pi\xi, \quad w_1(\xi) = \sin \pi\xi . \qquad (11.43a, b)$$

The boundary conditions $w_1 = 0$ and $u_1 = 0$ for $\xi = 0$ and $\xi = 1$ are then satisfied; furthermore, the displacements w are symmetrical, and the displacements u, antimetrical, with respect to the perpendicular $\xi = 1/2$. Carrying out all integrations in (11.42 a, b), we obtain

$$\left(\frac{C_w}{a}\right)^2 + \frac{16}{3\pi^3} \frac{\varkappa}{1 - 2\pi \dfrac{C_u}{a}} \frac{C_w}{a} - \frac{8}{\pi} \frac{C_u}{a} \frac{1 + \dfrac{3}{2}\pi^2 \left(\dfrac{C_u}{a}\right)^2}{1 - 2\pi \dfrac{C_u}{a}} = 0,$$

$$\left(\frac{C_u}{a}\right)^2 - \frac{1}{\pi}\left[1 + \frac{8}{3\pi^3} \frac{\varkappa a}{C_w}\right] \frac{C_u}{a} + \frac{3}{8}\left[\left(\frac{C_w}{a}\right)^2 - \frac{32}{3\pi^5} \frac{\varkappa a}{C_w}\right] = 0 , \qquad (11.43c, d)$$

whence

$$\frac{C_w}{a} = \sqrt{\left[\frac{8}{3\pi^3} \frac{\varkappa}{1 - 2\pi \dfrac{C_u}{a}}\right]^2 + \frac{8}{\pi} \frac{C_u}{a} \frac{1 + \dfrac{3}{2}\pi^2 \left(\dfrac{C_u}{a}\right)^2}{1 - 2\pi \dfrac{C_u}{a}}} - \frac{8}{3\pi^3} \frac{\varkappa}{1 - 2\pi \dfrac{C_w}{a}} = f\left(\frac{C_u}{a}; \varkappa\right),$$

$$\frac{C_u}{a} = \frac{1}{2\pi}\left(1 + \frac{8}{3\pi^3} \frac{\varkappa a}{C_w}\right) - \sqrt{\frac{1}{4\pi^2}\left[1 + \frac{8}{3\pi^3} \frac{\varkappa a}{C_w}\right]^2 - \frac{3}{8}\left[\left(\frac{C_w}{a}\right)^2 - \frac{32}{3\pi^5} \frac{\varkappa a}{C_w}\right]} = g\left(\frac{C_w}{a}; \varkappa\right). \qquad (11.43e, f)$$

Setting

$$u_1(\xi) = -6\sqrt{3}(\xi - 3\xi^2 + 2\xi^3), \quad w_1(\xi) = 4(\xi - \xi^2),$$

$$|u_{1\,\mathrm{extr}}| = -u_1\left(\frac{1}{2}\left(1 - \frac{1}{\sqrt{3}}\right)\right) = u_1\left(\frac{1}{2}\left(1 + \frac{1}{\sqrt{3}}\right)\right) = 1, \quad w_{1\,\mathrm{extr}} = w_1\left(\frac{1}{2}\right) = 1, \qquad (11.44a, b)$$

whereby all conditions at the boundaries and with respect to the perpendicular $\xi = 1/2$, as enumerated above, are satisfied, we obtain after integrating

$$\frac{C_w}{a} = \left\{\left[\frac{0.0625\,\varkappa}{1 - \dfrac{33\sqrt{3}}{7} \dfrac{C_u}{a}}\right]^2 + \frac{27}{28} \cdot \frac{7}{2\sqrt{3}} \frac{C_u}{a} \times \frac{1 - \dfrac{18}{7}\sqrt{3}\dfrac{C_u}{a} + \dfrac{162}{7}\left(\dfrac{C_u}{a}\right)^2}{1 - \dfrac{33\sqrt{3}}{7}\dfrac{C_u}{a}}\right\}^{1/2} - \frac{0.0625\,\varkappa}{1 - \dfrac{33\sqrt{3}}{7} \dfrac{C_u}{a}} = f\left(\frac{C_u}{a}; \varkappa\right),$$

$$\frac{C_u}{a} = \frac{7}{33\sqrt{3}}\left(1 + 0.0625 \frac{\varkappa a}{C_w}\right) - \sqrt{\left[\frac{7}{33\sqrt{3}}\left(1 + 0.0625 \frac{\varkappa a}{C_w}\right)\right]^2 - \frac{28}{99}\left[\left(\frac{C_w}{a}\right)^2 - \frac{5}{192} \frac{\varkappa a}{C_w}\right]} = g\left(\frac{C_w}{a}; \varkappa\right). \qquad (11.44c, d)$$

A few solutions of these equations are tabulated below and plotted in Figure 11.6.

$\varkappa$	0	0.05	0.1	0.2	0.3	0.4	0.5	Equation
C_u/a	0	0.0083	0.0122	0.0195	0.0260	0.0314	0.0357	(11.43a, b)
C_w/a	0	0.1398	0.1746	0.2201	0.2526	0.2778	0.2990	
C_u/a	0	0.0093	0.0147	0.0236	0.0306	0.0370	0.0425	(11.44a, b)
C_w/a	0	0.1329	0.1672	0.2106	0.2403	0.2639	0.2833	

The broken lines correspond to (11.43) and dot- and -dashes lines to (11.44).
The full lines correspond to the exact solution according to (11.36b) and (11.39b), using (11.37a). We observe that both approximations agree well with the exact solution within the practically important range $0 = \varkappa \leqq 0.5$. We obtain slightly more accurate values by

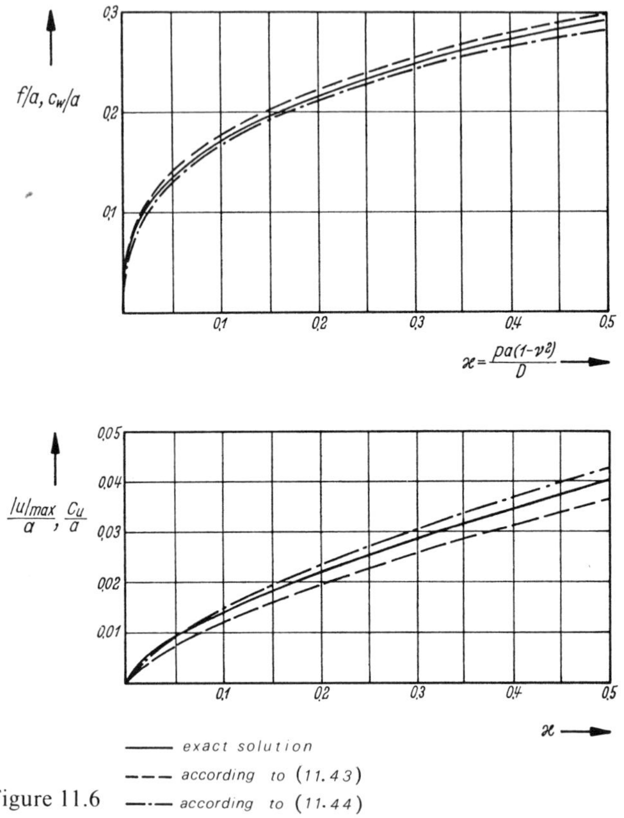

Figure 11.6

proceeding from (11.44). The reason for this is that (11.43) defines, as will be shown below, a surface whose curvature vanishes at the points of support. This is, however, impossible under actual conditions, because the load, induced by the internal pressure, can only be counterbalanced by finite sectional loads if the radius of curvature of the membrane remains finite everywhere. Therefore, the assumption (11.43) is, as regards equilibrium conditions near the supports, less correct than (11.44). Figures 11.7 and 11.8 show the displacements and sectional loads in comparison with the exact values. The sectional loads $\bar{n}_x$ are obtained, on the one hand, from the deformations, assuming Kappus' law to be valid:

$$\bar{n}_x = \frac{D}{1-\nu^2}(1+\varepsilon_x)\, d_{xx} = \frac{D}{2(1-\nu^2)}\sqrt{\left(1+\frac{du}{dx}\right)^2+\left(\frac{dw}{dx}\right)^2} \times$$

$$\times\left[\left(1+\frac{du}{dx}\right)^2+\left(\frac{dw}{dx}\right)^2-1\right] = \tag{11.45a}$$

$$= \frac{D}{2(1-\nu^2)}\sqrt{\left(1+\frac{C_u}{a}\frac{du_1}{d\xi}\right)^2+\left(\frac{C_w}{a}\right)^2\left(\frac{dw_1}{d\xi}\right)^2} \times$$

$$\times\left[\left(1+\frac{C_u}{a}\frac{du_1}{d\xi}\right)^2+\left(\frac{C_w}{a}\right)^2\left(\frac{dw_1}{d\xi}\right)^2-1\right].$$

On the other hand, the equilibrium condition for a deformed membrane element, referred to the direction normal to it, yields

$$\bar{n}_x = p\, R_1 \tag{11.45b}$$

where

$$R_1 = -\frac{\sqrt{\left(1+\frac{du}{dx}\right)^2+\left(\frac{dw}{dx}\right)^2}^{\,3}}{\left(1+\frac{du}{dx}\right)\frac{d^2w}{dx^2}-\frac{dw}{dx}\frac{d^2u}{dx^2}} = \tag{11.45c}$$

$$= -a\cdot\frac{a}{C_w}\,\frac{\sqrt{\left(1+\frac{C_u}{a}\frac{du_1}{d\xi}\right)^2+\left(\frac{C_w}{a}\right)^2\left(\frac{dw_1}{d\xi}\right)^2}^{\,3}}{\frac{d^2w_1}{d\xi^2}+\frac{C_u}{a}\left(\frac{du_1}{d\xi}\frac{d^2w_1}{d\xi^2}-\frac{d^2u_1}{d\xi^2}\frac{dw_1}{d\xi}\right)}$$

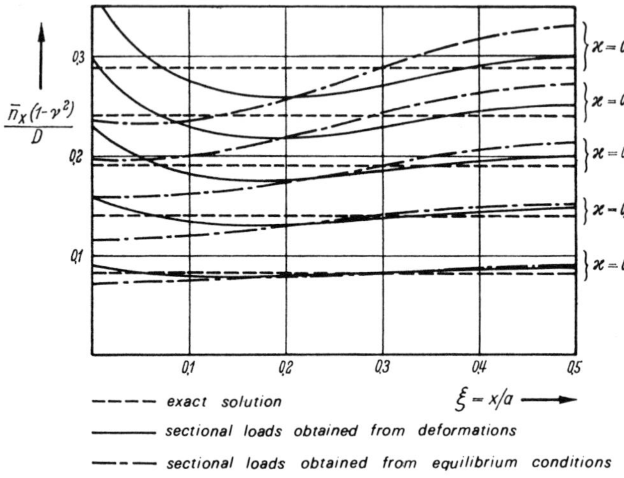

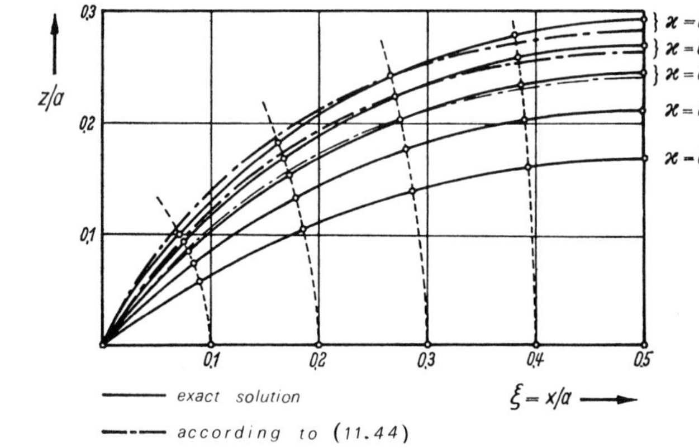

Figure 11.7

is the radius of curvature of the deformed surface. We observe that the approximations of the sectional loads are far less satisfactory than those of the displacements. The values obtained from (11.45a) are much more accurate than those obtained from (11.45b), *so that the sectional loads are best determined from the displacements.*

11.6 The Initially Plane Membrane, Immovably Supported Along Its Edges and Loaded by Internal Pressure

We shall consider here only approximations based on Kappus' law. The parametric curves are the diameters ($\varphi = \text{const}$) of the undeformed circular surface and the concentric circles ($r = \text{const}$). Using polar coordinates, we thus have

$$\mathfrak{r} = r\,(\mathfrak{e}_x \cos\varphi + \mathfrak{e}_y \sin\varphi)\,. \tag{11.46a}$$

After deformation, the parametric curves $\varphi = \text{const}$ become meridianal curves, while the curves $r = \text{const}$ form latitude

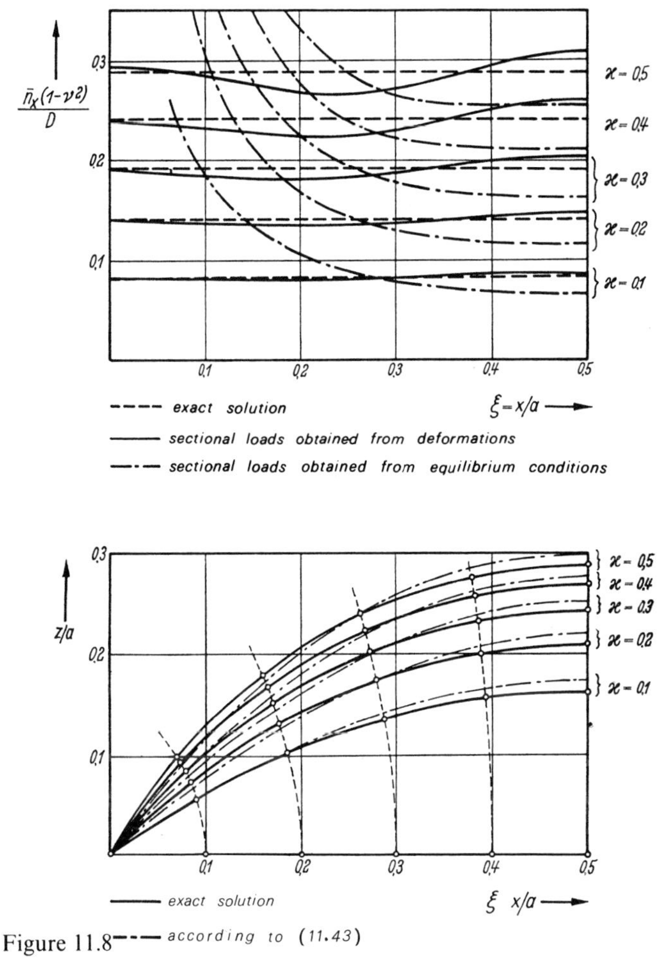

Figure 11.8

circles. We thus obtain an orthogonal net on the deformed axisymmetrical surface, so that the parametric curves constitute the lines of principal extension. Writing $\alpha = r, \beta = \varphi$, we obtain

$$\frac{\partial \mathfrak{r}}{\partial \alpha} = \frac{\partial \mathfrak{r}}{\partial r} = \mathfrak{e}_x \cos\varphi + \mathfrak{e}_y \sin\varphi\,,$$

$$\frac{\partial \mathfrak{r}}{\partial \beta} = \frac{\partial \mathfrak{r}}{\partial \varphi} = r\,(-\,\mathfrak{e}_x \sin\varphi + \mathfrak{e}_y \cos\varphi)\,,$$

$$\sqrt{g_{\alpha\alpha}} = \sqrt{\left(\frac{\partial \mathfrak{r}}{\partial \alpha}\right)^2} = 1\,,\quad \sqrt{g_{\beta\beta}} = \sqrt{\left(\frac{\partial \mathfrak{r}}{\partial \beta}\right)^2} = r\,,$$

$$d\,s_\alpha = \sqrt{g_{\alpha\alpha}}\,d\,\alpha = 1\cdot d\,r\,,\quad d\,s_\beta = \sqrt{g_{\beta\beta}}\,d\,\beta = r\,d\,\varphi\,,$$

$$d\,F = d\,s_\alpha\,d\,s_\beta = r\,d\,r\,d\,\varphi\,,\quad \mathfrak{e}_\alpha = \mathfrak{e}_r = \frac{1}{\sqrt{g_{\alpha\alpha}}}\frac{\partial \mathfrak{r}}{\partial \alpha} =$$

$$= \mathfrak{e}_x \cos\varphi + \mathfrak{e}_y \sin\varphi\,,\quad \mathfrak{e}_\beta = \mathfrak{e}_\varphi = \frac{1}{\sqrt{g_{\beta\beta}}}\frac{\partial \mathfrak{r}}{\partial \beta} =$$

$$= -\,\mathfrak{e}_x \sin\varphi + \mathfrak{e}_y \cos\varphi\,,\quad \mathfrak{e}_r \times \mathfrak{e}_\varphi = \mathfrak{e}_z\,.$$

For reasons of symmetry, the displacements are described by the vector

$$\mathfrak{v} = \mathfrak{v}\,(r) = u\,(r)\,\mathfrak{e}_r + w\,(r)\,\mathfrak{e}_z\,. \tag{11.46b}$$

Hence

$$\frac{\partial \mathfrak{v}}{\partial s_\alpha} = \frac{\partial \mathfrak{v}}{\partial r} = \frac{d\,u}{d\,r}\,\mathfrak{e}_r + \frac{d\,w}{d\,r}\,\mathfrak{e}_z\,;\quad \frac{d\,\mathfrak{v}}{d\,s_\beta} = \frac{1}{r}\frac{\partial \mathfrak{v}}{\partial \varphi} = \frac{u}{r}\,\mathfrak{e}_\varphi\,;$$

$$\left(\frac{\partial \mathfrak{v}}{\partial s_\alpha}\right)^2 = \left(\frac{d\,u}{d\,r}\right)^2 + \left(\frac{d\,w}{d\,r}\right)^2;\quad \left(\frac{\partial \mathfrak{v}}{\partial s_\beta}\right)^2 = \frac{u^2}{r^2}\,;$$

$$d_{\alpha\alpha} = \mathfrak{e}_\alpha\,\frac{\partial \mathfrak{v}}{\partial s_\alpha} + \frac{1}{2}\left(\frac{\partial \mathfrak{v}}{\partial s_\alpha}\right)^2 = \frac{d\,u}{d\,r} + \frac{1}{2}\left[\left(\frac{d\,u}{d\,r}\right)^2 + \left(\frac{d\,w}{d\,r}\right)^2\right],$$

$$d_{\beta\beta} = \mathfrak{e}_\beta\,\frac{\partial \mathfrak{v}}{\partial s_\beta} + \frac{1}{2}\left(\frac{\partial \mathfrak{v}}{\partial s_\beta}\right)^2 = \frac{u}{r} + \frac{1}{2}\frac{u^2}{r^2}\,,$$

$$\left(\mathfrak{e}_\alpha + \frac{\partial \mathfrak{v}}{\partial s_\alpha}\right) \times \left(\mathfrak{e}_\beta + \frac{\partial \mathfrak{v}}{\partial s_\beta}\right) = \left[\left(1 + \frac{d\,u}{d\,r}\right)\mathfrak{e}_r + \frac{d\,w}{d\,r}\,\mathfrak{e}_z\right] \times$$

$$\times \left(1 + \frac{u}{r}\right)\mathfrak{e}_\varphi = \left(1 + \frac{d\,u}{d\,r}\right)\left(1 + \frac{u}{r}\right)\mathfrak{e}_z - \left(1 + \frac{u}{r}\right)\frac{d\,w}{d\,r}\,\mathfrak{e}_r\,.$$

We then obtain from (11.27a) after integrating over φ from 0 to $2\,\pi$, dividing by $2\,\pi$, and using (11.28)

$$\delta_{u,w}\,\Pi = \delta_{u,w}\int_{r=0}^{a}\left\{\frac{D}{2\,(1-\nu^2)}\left[\left(\frac{d\,u}{d\,r} + \frac{1}{2}\left(\frac{d\,u}{d\,r}\right)^2 + \frac{1}{2}\left(\frac{d\,w}{d\,r}\right)^2\right)^2 + \right.\right.$$

$$+ \left(\frac{u}{r} + \frac{1}{2}\frac{u^2}{r^2}\right)^2 + 2\,\nu\left(\frac{d\,u}{d\,r} + \frac{1}{2}\left(\frac{d\,u}{d\,r}\right)^2 + \right.$$

$$\left.\left. + \frac{1}{2}\left(\frac{d\,w}{d\,r}\right)^2\right)\left(\frac{u}{r} + \frac{u^2}{2\,r^2}\right)\right] - \underline{p\left(1 + \frac{d\,u}{d\,r}\right)\left(1 + \frac{u}{r}\right)} w +$$

$$\left. + \underline{p\left(1 + \frac{u}{r}\right)\frac{d\,w}{d\,r}}\,u\right\} r\,d\,r = 0\,, \tag{11.46e}$$

where the underlined terms are not to be varied. For an approximate solution by the method of Ritz we put

$$u\,(r) = C_u\,u_1\,(r)\,,\quad w\,(r) = C_w\,w_1\,(r)\,, \tag{11.47a, b}$$

where $u_1\,(r)$ and $w_1\,(r)$ satisfy the boundary conditions, and Π depends on the still unknown constants C_u and C_w. Setting $\partial\,\Pi/\partial\,C_u = 0$ and $\partial\,\Pi/\partial\,C_w = 0$, where the terms underlined in (11.46c) are not to be differentiated, dividing by the radius a of the membrane edge, and denoting differentiation with respect to $\varrho = r/a$ by a prime, we obtain

$$\left(\frac{C_w}{a}\right)^2\left[\int_0^1 w_1'^2\left(u_1' + \nu\,\frac{u_1}{\varrho}\right)\varrho\,d\,\varrho + \frac{C_u}{a}\int_0^1 w_1'^2\left(u_1'^2 + \nu\,\frac{u_1^2}{\varrho^2}\right)\varrho\,d\,\varrho\right]$$

$$+ 2\,\varkappa\,\frac{C_w}{a}\left[\int_0^1 w_1'\,u_1\,\varrho\,d\,\varrho + \frac{C_u}{a}\int_0^1 w_1'\,u_1^2\,d\,\varrho\right] +$$

$$+ \left[\left(\frac{C_u}{a}\right)^3\int_0^1\left[u_1'^4 + \frac{u_1^4}{\varrho^4} + 2\,\nu\,\frac{u_1^2\,u_1'^2}{\varrho^2}\right]\varrho\,d\,\varrho + \right.$$

$$+ 3\left(\frac{C_u}{a}\right)^2\int_0^1\left[u_1'^3 + \frac{u_1^3}{\varrho^3} + \nu\,\frac{u_1\,u_1'}{\varrho}\left(u_1' + \frac{u_1}{\varrho}\right)\right]\varrho\,d\,\varrho +$$

$$\left. + 2\,\frac{C_u}{a}\int_0^1\left[u_1'^2 + \frac{u_1^2}{\varrho^2} + 2\,\nu\,\frac{u_1\,u_1'}{\varrho}\right]\varrho\,d\,\varrho\right] = 0\,, \tag{11.47c}$$

$$\left(\frac{C_u}{a}\right)^2\left[\int_0^1 w_1'^2\left(u_1'^2+\nu\frac{u_1^2}{\varrho^2}\right)\varrho\,d\varrho-2\frac{\varkappa a}{C_w}\int_0^1 u_1 u_1' w_1\,d\varrho\right]+$$

$$+2\frac{C_u}{a}\left[\int_0^1 w_1'^2\left(u_1'+\nu\frac{u_1}{\varrho}\right)\varrho\,d\varrho-\frac{\varkappa a}{C_w}\int_0^1 w_1\left(u_1'+\frac{u_1}{\varrho}\right)\varrho\,d\varrho\right]+$$

$$+\left[\left(\frac{C_w}{a}\right)^2\int_0^1 w_1'^4\varrho\,d\varrho-2\frac{\varkappa a}{C_w}\int_0^1 w_1\varrho\,d\varrho\right]=0, \tag{11.47d}$$

where

$$\varkappa=\frac{p\,a(1-\nu^2)}{D}. \tag{11.47e}$$

After selection of a system of functions (u_1, w_1) we can carry out the integrations indicated in (11.47c, d). We can then solve (11.47c) for C_w/a and (11.47d) for C_u/a, and plot curves $C_w/a=f(C_u/a;\varkappa)$ and $C_u/a=g(C_w/a;\varkappa)$. Their intersections yield pairs of solutions $(C_u/a, C_w/a)$ for the corresponding values of $\varkappa$. When the deformations are known, we can find

$$\varepsilon_\alpha=\varepsilon_r=\sqrt{1+2\frac{\partial\mathfrak{v}}{\partial s_\alpha}\frac{\partial\mathfrak{r}}{\partial s_\alpha}+\left(\frac{\partial\mathfrak{v}}{\partial s_\alpha}\right)^2}-1=$$

$$=\sqrt{\left(1+\frac{du}{dr}\right)^2+\left(\frac{dw}{dr}\right)^2}-1, \tag{11.48a, b}$$

$$\varepsilon_\beta=\varepsilon_\varphi=\sqrt{1+2\frac{\partial\mathfrak{v}}{\partial s_\beta}\frac{\partial\mathfrak{r}}{\partial s_\beta}+\left(\frac{\partial\mathfrak{v}}{\partial s_\beta}\right)^2}-1=\frac{u}{r}.$$

The sectional loads are then obtained from Kappus' law (11.13)

$$\frac{\bar{n}_r(1-\nu^2)}{D}=\frac{1+\varepsilon_r}{1+\varepsilon_\varphi}(d_{rr}+\nu\,d_{\varphi\varphi})=\frac{\sqrt{\left(1+\frac{du}{dr}\right)^2+\left(\frac{dw}{dr}\right)^2}}{1+\frac{u}{r}}\times$$

$$\times\left[\frac{du}{dr}+\frac{1}{2}\left(\frac{du}{dr}\right)^2+\frac{1}{2}\left(\frac{dw}{dr}\right)^2+\nu\left(\frac{u}{r}+\frac{1}{2}\frac{u^2}{r^2}\right)\right]=$$

$$=\frac{\sqrt{\left(1+\frac{C_u}{a}u'_1\right)^2+\left(\frac{C_w}{a}\right)^2 w_1'^2}}{1+\frac{C_u}{a}\frac{u_1}{\varrho}}\left[\frac{C_u}{a}u_1'+\right.$$

$$\left.+\frac{1}{2}\left(\frac{C_u}{a}\right)^2 u_1'^2+\frac{1}{2}\left(\frac{C_w}{a}\right)^2 w_1'^2+\nu\left(\frac{C_u}{a}\frac{u_1}{\varrho}+\frac{1}{2}\left(\frac{C_u}{a}\right)^2\frac{u_1^2}{\varrho^2}\right)\right],$$

$$\frac{\bar{n}_\varphi(1-\nu^2)}{D}=\frac{1+\varepsilon_\varphi}{1+\varepsilon_r}(d_{\varphi\varphi}+\nu\,d_{rr})=\frac{1+\frac{u}{r}}{\sqrt{\left(1+\frac{du}{dr}\right)^2+\left(\frac{dw}{dr}\right)^2}}\times$$

$$\times\left[\frac{u}{r}+\frac{1}{2}\frac{u^2}{r^2}+\nu\left(\frac{du}{dr}+\frac{1}{2}\left(\frac{du}{dr}\right)^2+\frac{1}{2}\left(\frac{dw}{dr}\right)^2\right)\right]=$$

$$=\frac{1+\frac{C_u}{a}\frac{u_1}{\varrho}}{\sqrt{\left(1+\frac{C_u}{a}u_1'\right)^2+\left(\frac{C_w}{a}\right)^2 w_1'^2}}\left[\frac{C_u}{a}\frac{u_1}{\varrho}+\frac{1}{2}\left(\frac{C_u}{a}\right)^2\frac{u_1^2}{\varrho^2}+\right.$$

$$\left.+\nu\left(\frac{C_u}{a}u_1'+\frac{1}{2}\left(\frac{C_u}{a}\right)^2 u_1'^2+\frac{1}{2}\left(\frac{C_w}{a}\right)^2 w_1'^2\right)\right], \tag{11.48c, d}$$

where the primes denote differentiation with respect to $\varrho=r/a$. Putting

$$u_1(\varrho)=\frac{3}{2}\sqrt{3}(\varrho-\varrho^3)=2.5981(\varrho-\varrho^3),$$

$$u_{1\,\max}=u_1\left(\frac{1}{\sqrt{3}}\right)=1, \quad w(\varrho)=1-\varrho^2, \tag{11.49a, b}$$

which satisfies the boundary conditions $u=w=0$ for $\varrho=1$ as well as the symmetry condition $w_1'(0)=0$, $u_1(0)=0$, $\left.\frac{d\bar{n}_r}{d\varrho}\right|_{\varrho=0}=\left.\frac{d\bar{n}_\varphi}{d\varrho}\right|_{\varrho=0}=0$, we obtain (from (11.47c, d)) the system of equations

$$\left(\frac{C_w}{a}\right)^2\left[1-\frac{9(9+\nu)}{4\sqrt{3}(3-\nu)}\frac{C_u}{a}\right]+\frac{\varkappa}{3-\nu}\left(1+\frac{9}{4\sqrt{3}}\frac{C_u}{a}\right)\frac{C_w}{a}-$$

$$-\frac{243(9+\nu)}{20\sqrt{3}(3-\nu)}\left(\frac{C_u}{a}\right)^3+\frac{81}{8}\left(\frac{C_u}{a}\right)^2-\frac{18}{\sqrt{3}(3-\nu)}\frac{C_u}{a}=0,$$

$$\left(\frac{C_u}{a}\right)^2\left[1-\frac{1}{2(9+\nu)}\frac{\varkappa a}{C_w}\right]-\frac{8\sqrt{3}(3-\nu)}{9(9+\nu)}\left(1+\right.$$

$$\left.+\frac{1}{2(3-\nu)}\frac{\varkappa a}{C_w}\right)\frac{C_u}{a}+\frac{4}{9(9+\nu)}\left(\frac{16}{3}\left(\frac{C_w}{a}\right)^2-\frac{\varkappa a}{C_w}\right)=0, \tag{11.49c, d}$$

which, for $\nu=1/3$, yields

$$\frac{C_w}{a}=\left\{\left[0.1875\,\varkappa\frac{1+1.299039\frac{C_u}{a}}{1-4.546633\frac{C_u}{a}}\right]^2+\right.$$

$$\left.+\frac{3.897114\frac{C_u}{a}-10.125\left(\frac{C_u}{a}\right)^2+24.551832\left(\frac{C_u}{a}\right)^3}{1-4.546633\frac{C_u}{a}}\right\}^{1/2}-$$

$$-0.1875\varkappa\frac{1+1.299039\frac{C_u}{a}}{1-4.546633\frac{C_u}{a}}=f\left(\frac{C_u}{a};\varkappa\right),$$

$$\frac{C_u}{a}=0.219943\frac{1+0.1875\frac{\varkappa a}{C_w}}{1-0.053571\frac{\varkappa a}{C_w}}- \tag{11.49e, f}$$

$$-\left\{\left[0.219943\frac{1+0.1875\frac{\varkappa a}{C_w}}{1-0.053571\frac{\varkappa a}{C_w}}\right]^2-\right.$$

$$\left.-\frac{0.253968\left(\frac{C_w}{a}\right)^2-0.047619\frac{\varkappa a}{C_w}}{1-0.053571\frac{\varkappa a}{C_w}}\right\}^{1/2}=g\left(\frac{C_w}{a};\varkappa\right).$$

A few values of the solution are tabulated below and plotted in Figure 11.9. Figure 11.10a shows the membrane displacements.

$\varkappa$	0	0.05	0.1	0.2	0.3	0.4	0.5
C_w/a	0	0.259	0.328	0.415	0.4775	0.527	0.569
C_u/a	0	0.0180	0.0293	0.0484	0.0654	0.0810	0.0959

For comparison, an experiment on a model is shown in Figure 11.10b. Figures 11.11 and 11.12 give the sectional loads determined by (11.48 c, d). It is seen that they attain their maximum at the center of the membrane, for which the value is given by

$$\frac{\bar n_{\max}(1-\nu^2)}{D} = \left[\frac{\bar n_r(1-\nu^2)}{D}\right]_{\varrho=0} = \left[\frac{\bar n_\varphi(1-\nu^2)}{D}\right]_{\varrho=0} \approx (1+\nu)\left[\frac{3}{2}\sqrt{3}\,\frac{C_u}{a}+\frac{27}{8}\left(\frac{C_u}{a}\right)^2\right]$$

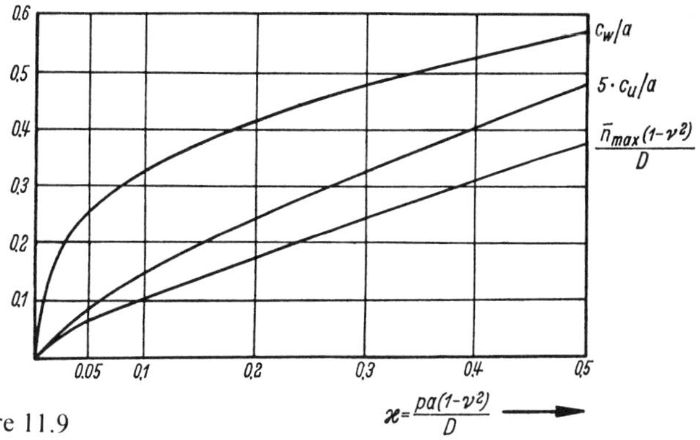

Figure 11.9

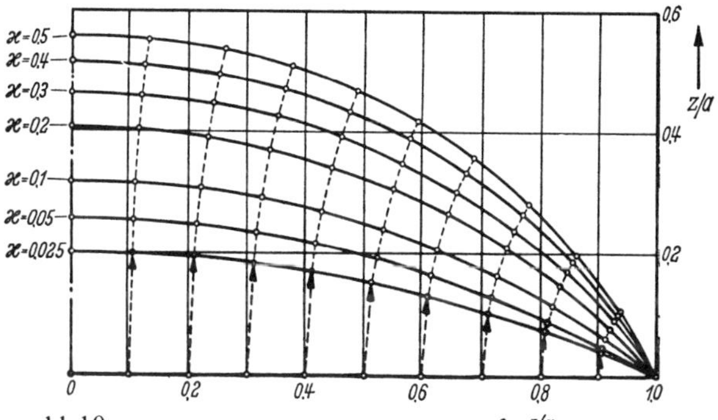

Figure 11.10,a

(cf. Figure 11.9). The broken lines in Figures 11.11 and 11.12 represent the sectional load determined from the equilibrium conditions for a membrane whose deformations are given by (11.47) and (11.49). Inserting into (11.6) the values

$\alpha = r,\ \beta=\varphi,\ \sqrt{g_{\alpha\alpha}}=1,\quad \sqrt{g_{\beta\beta}}=r$,

$$\varepsilon_\alpha=\varepsilon_r=\sqrt{\left(1+\frac{du}{dr}\right)^2+\left(\frac{dw}{dr}\right)^2}-1\,,\quad \varepsilon_\beta=\varepsilon_\varphi=\frac{u}{r}\,,$$

$$\bar{\mathfrak e}_\alpha=\bar{\mathfrak e}_r=\frac{1}{1+\varepsilon_\alpha}\left(\mathfrak e_\alpha+\frac{\partial\mathfrak v}{\partial s_\alpha}\right)=\frac{\left(1+\frac{du}{dr}\right)\mathfrak e_r+\frac{dw}{dr}\mathfrak e_z}{\sqrt{\left(1+\frac{du}{dr}\right)^2+\left(\frac{dw}{dr}\right)^2}}\,,$$

$$\bar{\mathfrak e}_\beta=\bar{\mathfrak e}_\varphi=\frac{1}{1+\varepsilon_\beta}\left(\mathfrak e_\beta+\frac{\partial\mathfrak v}{\partial s_\beta}\right)=\mathfrak e_\varphi$$

and

$$\bar{\mathfrak p}=p\,\bar{\mathfrak e}_r\times\bar{\mathfrak e}_\varphi=p\,\frac{\left(1+\frac{du}{dr}\right)\mathfrak e_z-\frac{dw}{dr}\mathfrak e_r}{\sqrt{\left(1+\frac{du}{dr}\right)^2+\left(\frac{dw}{dr}\right)^2}}$$

we obtain

$$\frac{\partial}{\partial r}\left[r\left(1+\frac{u}{r}\right)\bar n_r\,\frac{\left(1+\frac{du}{dr}\right)\mathfrak e_r+\frac{dw}{dr}\mathfrak e_z}{\sqrt{\left(1+\frac{du}{dr}\right)^2+\left(\frac{dw}{dr}\right)^2}}\right]+$$
$$+\frac{\partial}{\partial\varphi}\left[\sqrt{\left(1+\frac{du}{dr}\right)^2+\left(\frac{dw}{dr}\right)^2}\,\bar n_\varphi\,\mathfrak e_\varphi\right]+$$
$$+p\,r\left(1+\frac{u}{r}\right)\left[\left(1+\frac{du}{dr}\right)\mathfrak e_z-\frac{dw}{dr}\mathfrak e_r\right]=0\,.$$

Since all scalar magnitudes depend only on r, the last equation yields, by virtue of

$\partial\,\mathfrak e_\varphi/\partial\,\varphi=-\,\mathfrak e_r,\ \dfrac{\partial\,\mathfrak e_r}{\partial r}=\dfrac{\partial\,\mathfrak e_z}{\partial r}=0$ the relationship

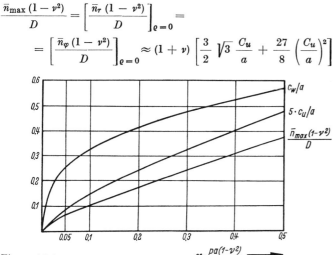

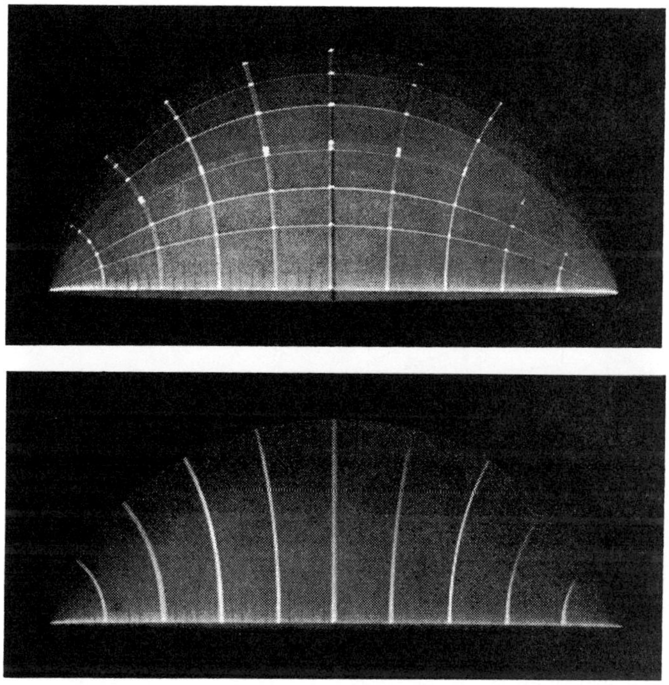

Figure 11.10b

$$\mathfrak e_r\left\{\frac{d}{dr}\left[\frac{(r+u)\left(1+\frac{du}{dr}\right)}{\sqrt{\left(1+\frac{du}{dr}\right)^2+\left(\frac{dw}{dr}\right)^2}}\,\bar n_r\right]-\right.$$
$$\left.-\,\bar n_\varphi\sqrt{\left(1+\frac{du}{dr}\right)^2+\left(\frac{dw}{dr}\right)^2}-p\,(r+u)\frac{dw}{dr}\right\}+$$
$$+\,\mathfrak e_z\left\{\frac{d}{dr}\left[\frac{(r+u)\frac{dw}{dr}}{\sqrt{\left(1+\frac{du}{dr}\right)^2+\left(\frac{dw}{dr}\right)^2}}\,\bar n_r\right]+\right.$$
$$\left.+\,p\,(r+u)\left(1+\frac{du}{dr}\right)\right\}=0\,.$$

We integrate and equate the z-component to zero. The integration constant must be zero, since n_r remains finite in the center of the membrane. The result is

$$\bar{n}_r = p\,\frac{1}{2}\left[-\frac{(r+u)\sqrt{\left(1+\frac{d\,u}{d\,r}\right)^2+\left(\frac{d\,w}{d\,r}\right)^2}}{d\,w/d\,r}\right] = p\,\frac{R_2}{2}\,, \qquad (11.49\text{g})$$

Equating the r-component to zero and taking into account (11.49g) leads to

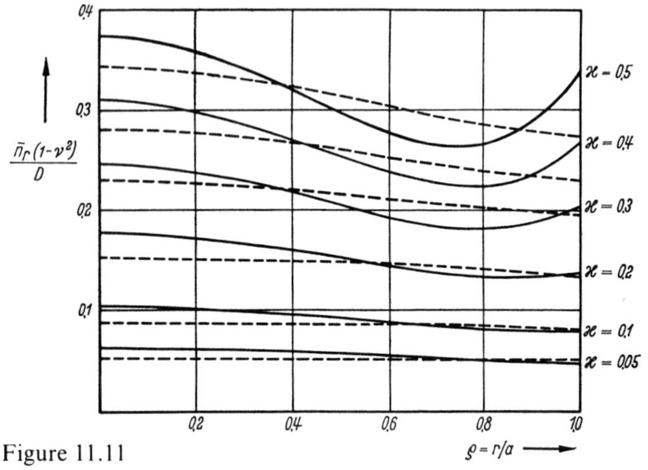

Figure 11.11

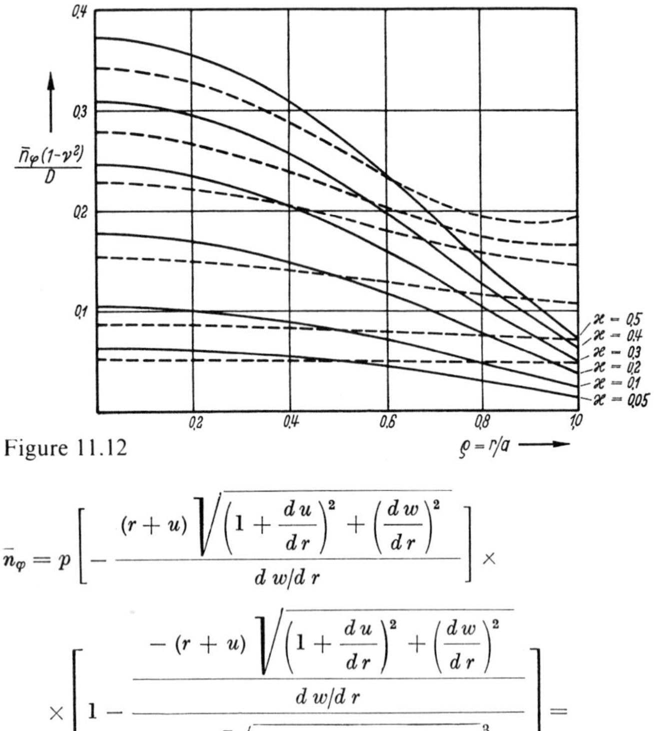

Figure 11.12

$$\bar{n}_\varphi = p\left[-\frac{(r+u)\sqrt{\left(1+\frac{d\,u}{d\,r}\right)^2+\left(\frac{d\,w}{d\,r}\right)^2}}{d\,w/d\,r}\right]\times$$

$$\times\left[1-\frac{-\dfrac{(r+u)\sqrt{\left(1+\frac{d\,u}{d\,r}\right)^2+\left(\frac{d\,w}{d\,r}\right)^2}}{d\,w/d\,r}}{2\left(-\dfrac{\sqrt{\left(1+\frac{d\,u}{d\,r}\right)^2+\left(\frac{d\,w}{d\,r}\right)^2}^{\,3}}{\left(1+\frac{d\,u}{d\,r}\right)\frac{d^2 w}{d\,r^2}-\frac{d\,w}{d\,r}\frac{d^2 u}{d\,r^2}}\right)}\right]=$$

$$= p\,R_2\left[1-\frac{R_2}{2\,R_1}\right]. \qquad (11.49\text{h})$$

It is easily shown by geometrical considerations that R_1 and R_2 are the radii of curvature as given by (3.8a, b)*.

We finally obtain from (11.49g, h)

$$\frac{\bar{n}_r\,(1-\nu^2)}{D} = \frac{p\,R_2\,(1-\nu^2)}{2\,D} = \frac{p\,a\,(1-\nu^2)}{D}\cdot\frac{1}{2}\,\frac{R_2}{a} = \frac{\varkappa}{2}\,\frac{R_2}{a}\,,$$

$$\frac{\bar{n}_\varphi\,(1-\nu^2)}{D} = \varkappa\,\frac{R_2}{a}\left[1-\frac{R_2}{2\,R_1}\right],$$

where, using the approximations (11.47a, b)

$$\frac{R_2}{a} = -\frac{1}{\dfrac{C_w}{a}\dfrac{d\,w_1}{d\,\varrho}}\left(\varrho+\frac{C_u}{a}\,u_1\right)\sqrt{\left(1+\frac{C_u}{a}\frac{d\,u_1}{d\,\varrho}\right)^2+\left(\frac{C_w}{a}\right)^2\left(\frac{d\,w_1}{d\,\varrho}\right)^2}$$

$$= -\frac{\varrho\,(1+\varepsilon_r)\,(1+\varepsilon_\varphi)}{\dfrac{C_w}{a}\dfrac{d\,w_1}{d\,\varrho}}\,,$$

$$\frac{R_1}{a} = -\frac{a}{C_w}\,\frac{\sqrt{\left(1+\frac{C_u}{a}\frac{d\,u_1}{d\,\varrho}\right)^2+\left(\frac{C_w}{a}\right)^2\left(\frac{d\,w_1}{d\,\varrho}\right)^2}^{\,3}}{\left(1+\frac{C_u}{a}\frac{d\,u_1}{d\,\varrho}\right)\frac{d^2 w_1}{d\,\varrho^2}-\left(\frac{C_u}{a}\right)\frac{d\,w_1}{d\,\varrho}\,\frac{d^2 u_1}{d\,\varrho^2}}$$

The differences are considerable, in particular for the circumferential sectional loads. The approximate curves (broken lines) are far less accurate since they are, in accordance with (11.49h), obtained after twice differentiating the displacement function, whereas only the first derivatives appear in (11.48d). An approximation is better, the greater the agreement between the values of the sectional loads determined from the deformations and from the equilibrium conditions. A better agreement than that obtained here is possible if, either the number of functions introduced in (11.47) is increased (this would, however, increase the number of cubic equations to be solved), or, if the approximations for the displacements (and thus also for the sectional loads if the corresponding relationship is given) are made to satisfy also the equilibrium conditions (and thus the displacement equations), at several points of the membrane. Inserting (11.48c, d) into (11.49g, h), we obtain the displacement equations for the axisymmetrical problem

$$\left(\frac{d\,w}{d\,r}\right)^3 + 2\left[\frac{d\,u}{d\,r}+\frac{1}{2}\left(\frac{d\,u}{d\,r}\right)^2+\nu\left(\frac{u}{r}+\frac{u^2}{2\,r^2}\right)\right]\frac{d\,w}{d\,r} +$$

$$+\varkappa\,\frac{r}{a}\left(1+\frac{u}{r}\right)^2 = 0\,,$$

$$\left(\frac{d\,w}{d\,r}\right)^4 + 2\,\varkappa\,\frac{r}{a}\left(\frac{d\,w}{d\,r}\right)^3 + 2\left[\frac{u}{r}+\frac{u^2}{2\,r^2}+\nu\left(\frac{d\,u}{d\,r}+\right.\right.$$

$$\left.\left.+\frac{1}{2}\left(\frac{d\,u}{d\,r}\right)^2\right)\right]\left(\frac{d\,w}{d\,r}\right)^2 + \varkappa\,\frac{r}{a}\left[2\left(1+\frac{d\,u}{d\,r}\right)^2+\right.$$

$$\left.+(r+u)\frac{d^2 u}{d\,r^2}\right]\frac{d\,w}{d\,r} - \varkappa\,\frac{r}{a}\,(r+u)\left(1+\frac{d\,u}{d\,r}\right)\frac{d^2 w}{d\,r^2} = 0\,.$$

The first equation yields

$$\frac{d\,u}{d\,r} = \sqrt{1-\left(\frac{d\,w}{d\,r}\right)^2-\varkappa\,\frac{r}{a}\,\frac{\left(1+\frac{u}{r}\right)^2}{d\,w/d\,r}-2\,\nu\left(\frac{u}{r}+\frac{u^2}{2\,r^2}\right)}-1\,,$$

in particular, for $r = a$ and $r = 0$, noting that $u\,(0) = u\,(a) = (d\,w/d\,r)_0 = 0$, we obtain

* We need only replace x by r to obtain R_1 as given by (11.45c).

$$\left(\frac{d u}{d r}\right)_a = \sqrt{1-\left(\frac{d w}{d r}\right)_a^2 - \frac{\varkappa}{(d w/d r)_a}} - 1,$$

$$\left(\frac{d u}{d r}\right)_0 = \sqrt{1-\frac{\varkappa}{a}\lim_{r\to 0}\left(\frac{r}{d w/d r}\right)} - 1 =$$

$$= \sqrt{1-\frac{\varkappa}{a}\frac{1}{(d^2 w/d r^2)_0}} - 1 .$$

These conditions, in addition to the boundary conditions, can be used to refine the assumptions (11.47). Similar relationships can be derived from the second equation.

A simple application of the method of Ritz is obtained by using the functional representation of the surface of a sphere, the meridianal extensions being assumed constant. We shall not enter into details, but shall consider some bursting-pressure experiments carried out by the firm of Stromeyer. A light coated textile was used. In a monoaxial tensile test (cf. Figure 2.5) the elastic constant was determined as $D \approx 70$ kg/cm (mean of 4 tests) for the more rigid direction (weft), the (lower) value of the tensile strength being $n_{\text{tear}} \approx 7$ kg/cm, referred to the initial width. The fabric was retained by a ring of radius $a = 5.75$ cm and distended by internal pressure. Althogether, 13 tests were carried out, but only in 4 did the fabric become torn at the edge. This was obviously due to nonuniformity of the structure. In 9 cases the tears appeared in the central region of the membrane, in conformity with the results obtained from Figure 11.11 and 11.12. This means that the sectional-load extrema are found in the center of the membrane. The bursting pressure, determined as the mean of all test values, was found to be 1.52 atm. Assuming $\nu = 1/3$, we then obtain

$$\varkappa = \frac{p\,a\,(1-\nu^2)}{D} = \frac{1.52 \cdot 5.75\,(1-0.111)}{70} = 0.1111,$$

and from Figure (11.9) we determine the corresponding value

$$\frac{\bar{n}_{\max}(1-\nu^2)}{D} = 0.11 \text{ or}$$

$$\bar{n}_{\max} = 0.11\frac{D}{1-\nu^2} = 0.11 \cdot \frac{70}{1-0.111} = 8.66 \text{ kg/cm}.$$

This is in good agreement* with the experimental result $n_{\text{tear}} = 7$ kg/cm, the difference being 24%. If the transverse contraction of the material is taken into account ($\varepsilon_{\text{tear}} = 0.09$) we obtain for $\nu = 1/3$

$$\bar{n}_{\text{tear}} = \frac{7}{1-0.09/3} = 7.23 \text{ kg/cm}.$$

which is in even better agreement with the theoretical value $\bar{n}_{\max} = 8.66$ kg/cm, the difference being about 20%. Very good agreement was obtained for the maximum deflections. The mean value, obtained from the experiments, was 1.883 cm, whereas Figure (11.9) gives for $\varkappa = 0.1111$

$$\frac{C_w}{a} = 0.336\,, \text{ i.e., } C_w = 0.336 \cdot a = 0.336 \cdot 5.75 = 1.93 \text{ cm}$$

the difference being about 2.5%.

* Taking into account the errors in determining the elastic constant for the actually biaxial state of stress.

11.7 The Initially Plane Rectangular Membrane

The edge lengths are a and b. The parametric curves in the undeformed state are the lines $y = \text{const}$ and $x = \text{const}$ (Cartesian coordinates). Putting

$$\mathfrak{v}(x, y) = u(x, y)\,\mathfrak{e}_x + v(x, y)\,\mathfrak{e}_y + w(x, y)\,\mathfrak{e}_z \tag{11.50a}$$

and

$$\begin{aligned}\bar{\mathfrak{p}}\,(1+\varepsilon_\alpha)(1+\varepsilon_\beta)\sin\bar{\sigma}_{\alpha\beta} &= \mathfrak{p}\,(1+\varepsilon_x)(1+\varepsilon_y)\sin\bar{\sigma}_{xy} = \\ &= p\left(\mathfrak{e}_x + \frac{\partial\mathfrak{v}}{\partial x}\right)\times\left(\mathfrak{e}_y + \frac{\partial\mathfrak{v}}{\partial y}\right) = \\ &= p\left[\left(\frac{\partial v}{\partial x}\frac{\partial w}{\partial y} - \left(1+\frac{\partial v}{\partial y}\right)\frac{\partial w}{\partial x}\right)\mathfrak{e}_x + \right. \\ &\quad + \left(\frac{\partial u}{\partial y}\frac{\partial w}{\partial x} - \left(1+\frac{\partial u}{\partial x}\right)\frac{\partial w}{\partial y}\right)\mathfrak{e}_y + \\ &\quad \left. + \left(\left(1+\frac{\partial u}{\partial x}\right)\left(1+\frac{\partial v}{\partial y}\right) - \frac{\partial u}{\partial y}\frac{\partial v}{\partial x}\right)\mathfrak{e}_z\right]\end{aligned} \tag{11.50b}$$

we obtain from (11.27b) the variational problem

$$\begin{aligned}\delta_{u,v,w}\Pi = 0\,;\ \Pi = \iint\limits_{(F)} \Bigg\{ & \frac{D}{2(1-\nu^2)}\left[\left(\frac{\partial u}{\partial x} + \frac{1}{2}\left[\left(\frac{\partial u}{\partial x}\right)^2 + \right.\right.\right. \\ & + \left(\frac{\partial v}{\partial x}\right)^2 + \left.\left(\frac{\partial w}{\partial x}\right)^2\right]\Bigg)^2 + \left(\frac{\partial v}{\partial y} + \frac{1}{2}\left[\left(\frac{\partial u}{\partial y}\right)^2 + \right.\right. \\ & + \left(\frac{\partial v}{\partial y}\right)^2 + \left.\left(\frac{\partial w}{\partial y}\right)^2\right]\Bigg)^2 + 2\,\nu\left(\frac{\partial u}{\partial x} + \right. \\ & + \frac{1}{2}\left[\left(\frac{\partial u}{\partial x}\right)^2 + \left(\frac{\partial v}{\partial x}\right)^2 + \left(\frac{\partial w}{\partial x}\right)^2\right]\Bigg)\left(\frac{\partial v}{\partial y} + \right. \\ & + \frac{1}{2}\left[\left(\frac{\partial u}{\partial y}\right)^2 + \left(\frac{\partial v}{\partial y}\right)^2 + \left(\frac{\partial w}{\partial y}\right)^2\right]\Bigg) + \\ & + \frac{1-\nu}{2}\left(\frac{\partial u}{\partial y} + \frac{\partial v}{\partial x} + \frac{\partial u}{\partial x}\frac{\partial u}{\partial y} + \frac{\partial v}{\partial x}\frac{\partial v}{\partial y} + \right. \\ & + \left.\frac{\partial w}{\partial x}\frac{\partial w}{\partial y}\right)^2\Bigg] - p\left[\underline{\left(\frac{\partial v}{\partial x}\frac{\partial w}{\partial y} - \left(1+\frac{\partial v}{\partial y}\right)\frac{\partial w}{\partial x}\right)}\,u + \right. \\ & + \underline{\left(\frac{\partial u}{\partial y}\frac{\partial w}{\partial x} - \left(1+\frac{\partial u}{\partial x}\right)\frac{\partial w}{\partial y}\right)}\,v + \\ & + \left.\underline{\left(\left(1+\frac{\partial u}{\partial x}\right)\left(1+\frac{\partial v}{\partial y}\right) - \frac{\partial u}{\partial y}\frac{\partial v}{\partial x}\right)}\,w\right]\Bigg\}\,d x\,d y\,,\end{aligned} \tag{11.50c}$$

where the underlined terms are not to be varied. Setting

$$u = C_u u_1\,;\ v = C_v v_1\,;\ w = C_w w_1 \tag{11.50d}$$

we obtain a system of three cubic equations through extremalization, putting $\partial\Pi/\partial C_u = 0$, $\partial\Pi/\partial C_v = 0$, and $\partial\Pi/\partial C_w = 0$. We shall only consider a particular problem which can be reduced to a system of two cubic equations.

11.8 The Initially Plane Square Membrane, Supported Along its Entire Edge and Loaded by Internal Pressure

The symmetry of the resulting state of deformation requires that the displacements be given by

$$u = f(x, y)\,,\quad v = f(y, x). \tag{11.51a}$$

We can therefore put $u_1(x, y) = v_1(y, x)$, $v_1(x, y) = u_1(y, x)$ and $w_1(x, y)$, approximating the displacements by

$$u(x, y) = C_1 u_1(x, y)\,;\ v(x, y) = C_1 v_1(x, y)\,;\quad w(x, y) = C_w w(x, y) \tag{11.51b}$$

where Π depends solely on C_1 and C_w. The extremum conditions $\partial\Pi/\partial(C_1/a)=0$ and $\partial\Pi/\partial(C_w/a)=0$ lead to: (the underlined terms are not to be differentiated)

$$\left(\frac{C_w}{a}\right)^2\left[\lambda_1\frac{C_1}{a}+\lambda_2\right]-2\varkappa\frac{C_w}{a}\left[\lambda_3\frac{C_1}{a}-\lambda_4\right]+ +\lambda_5\left(\frac{C_1}{a}\right)^3+3\lambda_6\left(\frac{C_1}{a}\right)^2+2\lambda_7\left(\frac{C_1}{a}\right)=0,$$

$$\left(\frac{C_1}{a}\right)^2\left[\lambda_1-2\lambda_8\frac{\varkappa a}{C_w}\right]+2\frac{C_1}{a}\left[\lambda_2-\lambda_9\frac{\varkappa a}{C_w}\right]+ +\lambda_{10}\left(\frac{C_w}{a}\right)^2-2\lambda_{11}\frac{\varkappa a}{C_w}=0, \qquad (11.52a,b)$$

where

$$\lambda_1=\int_{\xi=0}^{1}\int_{\eta=0}^{1}\left[(w_{1\xi}^2+\nu w_{1\eta}^2)(u_{1\xi}^2+v_{1\xi}^2)+(w_{1\eta}^2+\nu w_{1\xi}^2)(u_{1\eta}^2+v_{1\eta}^2)+2(1-\nu)w_{1\xi}w_{1\eta}(u_{1\xi}u_{1\eta}+v_{1\xi}v_{1\eta})\right]d\xi\,d\eta,$$

$$\lambda_2=\int_{\xi=0}^{1}\int_{\eta=0}^{1}\left[w_{1\xi}^2(u_{1\xi}+\nu v_{1\eta})+w_{1\eta}^2(v_{1\eta}+\nu u_{1\xi})+(1-\nu)w_{1\xi}w_{1\eta}(u_{1\eta}+v_{1\xi})\right]d\xi\,d\eta,$$

$$\lambda_3=\int_{\xi=0}^{1}\int_{\eta=0}^{1}\left[u_1(v_{1\xi}w_{1\eta}-v_{1\eta}w_{1\xi})+v_1(u_{1\eta}w_{1\xi}-u_{1\xi}w_{1\eta})\right]d\xi\,d\eta,$$

$$\lambda_4=\int_{\xi=0}^{1}\int_{\eta=0}^{1}(u_1w_{1\xi}+v_1w_{1\eta})\,d\xi\,d\eta,$$

$$\lambda_5=\int_{\xi=0}^{1}\int_{\eta=0}^{1}\left[(u_{1\xi}^2+v_{1\xi}^2)^2+(u_{1\eta}^2+v_{1\eta}^2)^2+2\nu(u_{1\xi}^2+v_{1\xi}^2)(u_{1\eta}^2+v_{1\eta}^2)+2(1-\nu)(u_{1\xi}u_{1\eta}+v_{1\xi}v_{1\eta})^2\right]d\xi\,d\eta,$$

$$\lambda_6=\int_{\xi=0}^{1}\int_{\eta=0}^{1}\left[u_{1\xi}(u_{1\xi}^2+v_{1\xi}^2)+v_{1\eta}(u_{1\eta}^2+v_{1\eta}^2)+\nu u_{1\xi}(u_{1\eta}^2+v_{1\eta}^2)+\nu v_{1\eta}(u_{1\xi}^2+v_{1\xi}^2)+(1-\nu)(u_{1\eta}+v_{1\xi})(u_{1\xi}u_{1\eta}+v_{1\xi}v_{1\eta})\right]d\xi\,d\eta,$$

$$\lambda_7=\int_{\xi=0}^{1}\int_{\eta=0}^{1}\left[u_{1\xi}^2+v_{1\eta}^2+2\nu u_{1\xi}v_{1\eta}+\frac{1-\nu}{2}(u_{1\eta}+v_{1\xi})^2\right]d\xi\,d\eta,$$

$$\lambda_8=\int_{\xi=0}^{1}\int_{\eta=0}^{1}\left[u_{1\xi}v_{1\eta}-u_{1\eta}v_{1\xi}\right]w_1\,d\xi\,d\eta,$$

$$\lambda_9=\int_{\xi=0}^{1}\int_{\eta=0}^{1}(v_{1\eta}+u_{1\xi})\,w_1\,d\xi\,d\eta=-\lambda_4,$$

$$\lambda_{10}=\int_{\xi=0}^{1}\int_{\eta=0}^{1}(w_{1\xi}^2+w_{1\eta}^2)^2\,d\xi\,d\eta,$$

$$\lambda_{11}=\int_{\xi=0}^{1}\int_{\eta=0}^{1}w_1\,d\xi\,d\eta,\qquad \varkappa=\frac{p\,a(1-\nu^2)}{D}. \qquad (11.52c)$$

The subscripts ξ and η denote differentiation with respect to $\xi=x/a$ and $\eta=y/a$, respectively. We put

$$u_1=-\sin 2\pi\xi\sin\pi\eta,\quad v_1=-\sin\pi\xi\sin 2\pi\eta,\quad w_1=\sin\pi\xi\sin\pi\eta. \qquad (11.53a)$$

These functions satisfy the condition of immovable edges, as well as the conditions of symmetry and antimetry of the problem concerned. Carrying out all integrations, we find

$$\lambda_1=\frac{15}{16}\pi^4\left(1+\frac{\nu}{3}\right),\quad \lambda_2=-\frac{5}{3}\pi^2(1-0{,}6\,\nu),\quad \lambda_3=\frac{3}{8}\pi^2,$$

$$\lambda_4=-\lambda_9=-\frac{4}{3},\quad \lambda_5=\frac{193}{32}\pi^4\left(1+\frac{68}{193}\nu\right),$$

$$\lambda_6=-\frac{4}{3}\pi^2(1-3\nu),\quad \lambda_7=\frac{16}{9}+\frac{9\pi^2}{4}+\nu\left(\frac{16}{9}-\frac{\pi^2}{4}\right),$$

$$\lambda_8=\frac{3}{16}\pi^2,\quad \lambda_{10}=\frac{5}{16}\pi^4,\quad \lambda_{11}=\frac{4}{\pi^2},$$

so that, for $\nu=1/3$, we obtain from (11.52a, b) the equations

$$\frac{C_w}{a}=\left\{\left[\frac{\varkappa}{\pi^2}\,\frac{1+\frac{9}{32}\pi^2\left(\frac{C_1}{a}\right)}{1-\frac{25}{32}\pi^2\left(\frac{C_1}{a}\right)}\right]^2+\frac{\frac{579}{128}\pi^2\left(1+\frac{68}{579}\right)\left(\frac{C_1}{a}\right)^3+\left(\frac{32}{9\pi^2}+\frac{13}{4}\right)\frac{C_1}{a}}{1-\frac{25}{32}\pi^2\left(\frac{C_1}{a}\right)}\right\}^{1/2}-\frac{\varkappa}{\pi^2}\,\frac{1+\frac{9}{32}\pi^2\left(\frac{C_1}{a}\right)}{1-\frac{25}{32}\pi^2\left(\frac{C_1}{a}\right)}=f\left(\frac{C_1}{a};\varkappa\right),$$

$$\frac{C_1}{a}=\frac{32}{25\pi^2}\,\frac{1+\frac{1}{\pi^2}\frac{\varkappa a}{C_w}}{1-\frac{9}{25\pi^2}\frac{\varkappa a}{C_w}}-\sqrt{\left[\frac{32}{25\pi^2}\,\frac{1+\frac{1}{\pi^2}\frac{\varkappa a}{C_w}}{1-\frac{9}{25\pi^2}\frac{\varkappa a}{C_w}}\right]^2-\frac{0.3\left(\frac{C_w}{a}\right)^2-\frac{192}{25\pi^6}\frac{\varkappa a}{C_w}}{1-\frac{9}{25\pi^2}\frac{\varkappa a}{C_w}}}=g\left(\frac{C_w}{a};\varkappa\right) \qquad (11.53b,c)$$

A few solutions are tabulated below.

$\varkappa$	0	0.05	0.1	0.2	0.3	0.4	0.5
C_1/a	0	0.0043	0.0071	0.0118	0.0162	0.0203	0.0242
C_w/a	0	0.1215	0.1540	0.1950	0.2250	0.2490	0.2690

From (2.23a) we obtain

$$\left.\begin{aligned}
d_{xx} &= \mathfrak{e}_x \frac{\partial \mathfrak{v}}{\partial x} + \frac{1}{2}\left(\frac{\partial \mathfrak{v}}{\partial x}\right)^2 = \frac{\partial u}{\partial x} + \frac{1}{2}\left[\left(\frac{\partial u}{\partial x}\right)^2 + \right. \\
&\quad \left. + \left(\frac{\partial v}{\partial x}\right)^2 + \left(\frac{\partial w}{\partial x}\right)^2\right] = \frac{C_1}{a} u_{1\xi} + \\
&\quad + \frac{1}{2}\left[\left(\frac{C_1}{a}\right)^2 (u_{1\xi}^2 + v_{1\xi}^2) + \left(\frac{C_w}{a}\right)^2 w_{1\xi}^2\right], \\
d_{yy} &= \mathfrak{e}_x \frac{\partial \mathfrak{v}}{\partial y} + \frac{1}{2}\left(\frac{\partial \mathfrak{v}}{\partial y}\right)^2 = \frac{\partial v}{\partial y} + \frac{1}{2}\left[\left(\frac{\partial u}{\partial y}\right)^2 + \right. \\
&\quad \left. + \left(\frac{\partial v}{\partial y}\right)^2 + \left(\frac{\partial w}{\partial y}\right)^2\right] = \frac{C_1}{a} v_{1\eta} + \\
&\quad + \frac{1}{2}\left[\left(\frac{C_1}{a}\right)^2 (u_{1\eta}^2 + v_{1\eta}^2) + \left(\frac{C_w}{a}\right)^2 w_{1\eta}^2\right], \\
2\, d_{xy} &= \mathfrak{e}_x \frac{\partial \mathfrak{v}}{\partial y} + \mathfrak{e}_y \frac{\partial \mathfrak{v}}{\partial x} + \left(\frac{\partial \mathfrak{v}}{\partial x}\right)\left(\frac{\partial \mathfrak{v}}{\partial y}\right) = \frac{\partial u}{\partial y} + \\
&\quad + \frac{\partial v}{\partial x} + \left[\left(\frac{\partial u}{\partial x}\right)\left(\frac{\partial u}{\partial y}\right) + \left(\frac{\partial v}{\partial x}\right)\left(\frac{\partial v}{\partial y}\right) + \right. \\
&\quad \left. + \left(\frac{\partial w}{\partial x}\right)\left(\frac{\partial w}{\partial y}\right)\right] = \frac{C_1}{a}(u_{1\eta} + v_{1\xi}) + \\
&\quad + \left(\frac{C_1}{a}\right)^2 (u_{1\xi}\, u_{1\eta} + v_{1\xi}\, v_{1\eta}) + \left(\frac{C_w}{a}\right)^2 w_{1\xi}\, w_{1\eta}.
\end{aligned}\right\} \quad (11.54\text{a-c})$$

The principal extensions are according to (2.24e)

$$\begin{aligned}
d_{1,2} &= \frac{1}{2}\left[d_{xx} + d_{yy} \pm \sqrt{(d_{xx} - d_{yy})^2 + 4\, d_{xy}^2}\right], \\
1 + \varepsilon_{1,2} &= \sqrt{1 + 2\, d_{1,2}}\,.
\end{aligned} \qquad (11.54\text{d, e})$$

The principal normal sectional loads are thus by (11.13)

$$\begin{aligned}
\bar{n}_{1,2} &= \frac{D}{1 - \nu^2}\,\frac{1 + \varepsilon_{1,2}}{1 + \varepsilon_{2,1}}\,(d_{1,2} + \nu\, d_{2,1}) = \\
&= \frac{D}{1 - \nu^2}\,\frac{\sqrt{1 + 2\, d_{1,2}}}{\sqrt{1 + 2\, d_{2,1}}}\,(d_{1,2} + \nu\, d_{2,1}).
\end{aligned} \qquad (11.54\text{f})$$

The orientation of the principal directions, referred to the deformed x-direction, is described in accordance with (2.24f) by

$$\operatorname{tg} \bar{\varphi}_0 = \frac{1 + \varepsilon_2}{1 + \varepsilon_1} \operatorname{tg} \varphi_0 = \frac{\sqrt{1 + 2 d_2}}{\sqrt{1 + 2 d_1}} \operatorname{tg} \varphi_0 \qquad (11.54\text{g})$$

where, by (2.24c),

$$\operatorname{tg} 2\varphi_0 = \frac{2\, d_{xy}}{d_{xx} - d_{yy}}. \qquad (11.54\text{h})$$

These laborious computations were performed for $\varkappa = 0.3$. The results are plotted in Figures 11.13a-c. Figure 11.13a shows the principal directions, i.e., the trajectories of the principal sectional loads. Figure 11.13b shows curves of equal extremum principal sectional loads.

The diagram of the trajectories leads to the conclusion that the load-carrying behavior of the square membrane is similar to that of the circular membrane. The influence of the square shape increases as the edges are approached. The sectional loads are mainly directed parallel and normal to the edges in the neighborhood of the latter. The calculations show that compressive stresses should appear in the hatched zones at the corners. This is impossible in reality. The approximation (11.53a) therefore becomes invalid in these zones, and different functions have to be selected. Figure 11.13c represents a contour map of the membrane surface (cf. Figure 60, ref. 1).

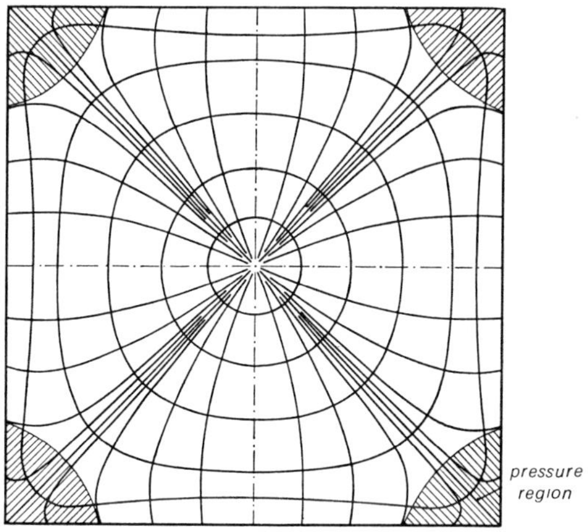

Figure 11.13a

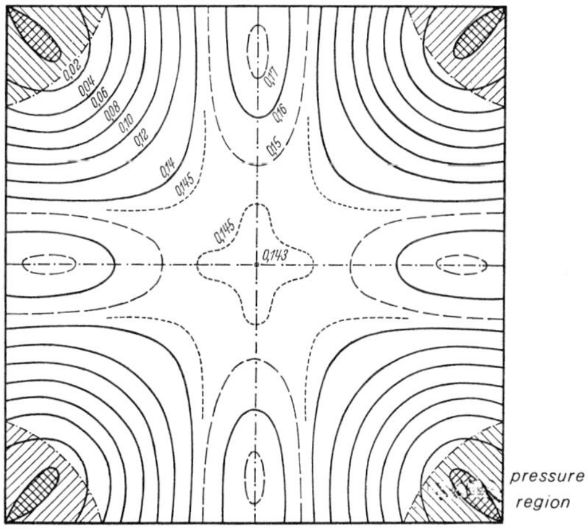

Figure 11.13b

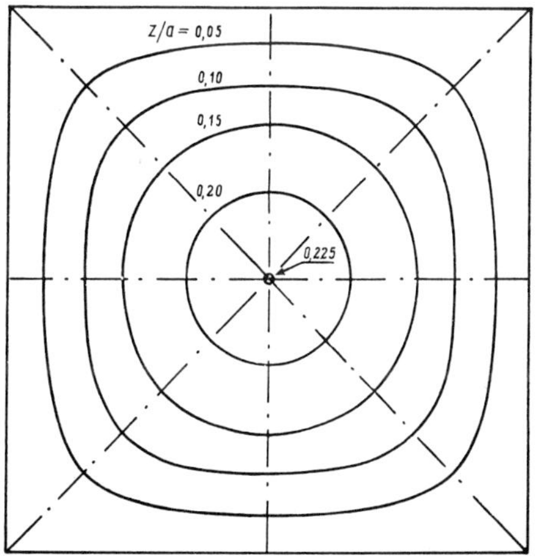

Figure 11.13c

12 SOAP FILMS

12.1 General Observations

Soap films differ from all other membranes that have been discussed till now in that they cannot transmit shearing forces. The biaxial state of stress of a soap film is therefore defined by a spherical tensor, in analogy to the state of stress induced by hydrostatic pressure, since the absence of shearing stresses causes the normal stresses to be equal in all directions. In spite of this peculiarity, analysis of soap films has proved to be important in the design of membrane structures, which is closely related to the problem of equally stressed membranes.

The condition stipulating vanishing shearing stresses considerably simplifies the problem of membrane analysis, since the number of magnitudes defining a certain state is reduced to two. These are the sectional load n (generally variable, though equal in all directions at a given point), and the final shape of the surface (e.g., $z = z(x, y)$). These unknowns can be determined from the equilibrium conditions for a membrane element, which, for $n_\alpha = n_\beta = n$ and $n_{\alpha\beta} = 0$, are obtained from (2.5a-c) in the simple form

$$\frac{1}{\sqrt{g_{\alpha\alpha}}}\frac{\partial n}{\partial \alpha} = \frac{\partial n}{\partial s_\alpha} = -p_\alpha\,; \qquad \frac{1}{\sqrt{g_{\beta\beta}}}\frac{\partial n}{\partial \beta} = \frac{\partial n}{\partial s_\beta} = -p_\beta\,;$$

$$n\,(K_{n\alpha} + K_{n\beta}) = p_\gamma. \qquad (12.1a\text{-}c)$$

12.2 The Differential Equation of the Problem

We shall only consider loading by dead weight, internal pressure, and hydrostatic pressure. For the last two cases mentioned,

$p_\alpha = p_\beta = 0,\ p_\gamma = \pm\,(p + \gamma\,(z_0 - z))$

where p is the internal pressure, and γ the specific weight of the liquid causing the hydrostatic pressure.*

If the dead weight per unit surface is constant ($= g$), then

$$\mathfrak{p} = p_\alpha\, e_\alpha + p_\beta\, e_\beta + p_\gamma\, e_\gamma = -\,g\, e_z =$$

$$= -\,g\,[(e_z\, e_\alpha)\, e_\alpha + (e_z\, e_\beta)\, e_\beta + (e_z\, e_\gamma)\, e_\gamma].$$

If z is measured from a horizontal plane, we have

$$e_z\, e_\alpha = \frac{\partial z}{\partial s_\alpha}, \quad e_z\, e_\beta = \frac{\partial z}{\partial s_\beta},$$

so that (12.1a, b) yield

$$\frac{\partial n}{\partial s_\alpha} = g\,\frac{\partial z}{\partial s_\alpha}, \quad \frac{\partial n}{\partial s_\beta} = g\,\frac{\partial z}{\partial s_\beta},$$

Integrating, we obtain

$$n = n_0 + g\,z \qquad (12.2)$$

where n_0 is a constant. Taking into account (1.21), which leads to

$$K_{n\alpha} + K_{n\beta} = \omega_\beta^{(\alpha)} - \omega_\alpha^{(\beta)} = 2\,H = \frac{1}{R_1} + \frac{1}{R_2}, \qquad (12.3)$$

i.e., twice the mean curvature of the surface, we obtain from (12.1c) the differential equation

$$2\,(n_0 + g\,z)\,H = \pm\,(p + \gamma\,(z_0 - z)) - g\,(e_z\, e_\gamma)\,. \qquad (12.4)$$

If $g = \gamma = 0$, we obtain for loading by internal pressure

$H = \pm\, p/(2\,n_0) = \text{const.}$

The membrane surface thus has a constant mean curvature. In particular, for $p = 0$ we obtain $H = 0$; thus *an unstressed soap film always assumes the shape of a minimum surface.*

For practical calculations we cannot use the representation (12.4) which is invariant with respect to coordinate transformations. Introducing Cartesian coordinates, we represent the surface in the form $z = z\,(x, y)$. The tangent vectors are*

$$e_x = \frac{e_{x0} + z_x\, e_z}{\sqrt{1 + z_x^2}}, \quad e_y = \frac{e_{y0} + z_y\, e_z}{\sqrt{1 + z_y^2}}$$

The unit vector e_γ of the surface normal to the parametric curves cut in the surface by planes $y = \text{const}$ and $x = \text{const}$ is

$$e_\gamma = \frac{e_{x0} \times e_{y0}}{|\,e_{x0} \times e_{y0}\,|} = \frac{e_z - z_x\, e_{x0} - z_y\, e_{y0}}{\sqrt{1 + z_x^2 + z_y^2}}.$$

Hence

$$e_z\, e_\gamma = \frac{1}{\sqrt{1 + z_x^2 + z_y^2}}. \qquad (12.5a)$$

The mean curvature can, in accordance with (1.19), be represented in the form

$$H = -\,\frac{\Delta z + L(z)}{2\,\sqrt{1 + z_x^2 + z_y^2}^{\,3}} \text{ where } \Delta z = z_{xx} + z_{yy}, \qquad (12.5b)$$

$$L(z) = z_x^2\, z_{yy} - 2\, z_x\, z_y\, z_{xy} + z_y^2\, z_{xx}.$$

We then obtain from (12.4) the differential equation

$$(n_0 + g\,z)\,\frac{\Delta z + L(z)}{\sqrt{1 + z_x^2 + z_y^2}^{\,3}} = \mp\,(p + \gamma\,(z_0 - z)) + \frac{g}{\sqrt{1 + z_x^2 + z_y^2}}. \qquad (12.5c)$$

For small deflections, when ($z_x^2 \ll 1,\ z_y^2 \ll 1,\ g\,z \ll n_0,\ \gamma\,(z_0 - z) \ll p$), the quadratic terms can be discarded, and we obtain the well-known expression

$$\Delta z = -\,\frac{p - g}{n_0} \qquad (12.5d)$$

for a membrane, prestressed to n_0 and loaded by its dead weight and the internal pressure (in which case the sign of p should be negative), valid when the deflections are small. Introducing cylindrical coordinates (r, φ, z), we have $\mathfrak{r} = r\, e_{r0} + z\,(r, \varphi)\, e_z$, i.e., the unit vectors**

$$e_r = \frac{\mathfrak{r}_r}{|\mathfrak{r}_r|} = \frac{e_{r0} + z_r\, e_z}{\sqrt{1 + z_r^2}},$$

$$e_\varphi = \frac{\mathfrak{r}_\varphi}{|\mathfrak{r}_\varphi|} = \frac{r\, e_{\varphi 0} + z_\varphi\, e_z}{\sqrt{r^2 + z_\varphi^2}} = \frac{e_{\varphi 0} + \frac{z_\varphi}{r}\, e_z}{\sqrt{1 + \left(\frac{z_\varphi}{r}\right)^2}},$$

* If we consider p to be variable, we can also describe the wind load by it. The selection of the sign depends upon whether the surface normal is directed inward or outward. The positive sign corresponds to the latter case.

* The subscripts of z denote differentiation with respect to x or y.

** The subscripts of z denote differentiation with respect to r and φ.

which represent the tangent vectors to the curves cut in the membrane by surfaces φ = const and r=const. The unit vector of the surface normal is

$$e_\gamma = \frac{e_r \times e_\varphi}{|e_r \times e_\varphi|} = \frac{e_z - z_r e_{r0} - \frac{z_\varphi}{r} e_{\varphi 0}}{\sqrt{1 + z_r^2 + \left(\frac{z_\varphi}{r}\right)^2}}$$

whence

$$e_z e_\gamma = \frac{1}{\sqrt{1 + z_r^2 + \left(\frac{z_\varphi}{r}\right)^2}}. \tag{12.6a}$$

The mean curvature is, in accordance with (1.20),

$$H = -\frac{\Delta z + L(z)}{2\sqrt{1 + z_r^2 + \left(\frac{z_\varphi}{r}\right)^2}^3} \text{ where } \Delta z = z_{rr} + \frac{z_r}{r} + \frac{z_{\varphi\varphi}}{r^2},$$
$$L(z) = \frac{z_\varphi^2}{r^2}\left(z_{rr} + 2\frac{z_r}{r}\right) + \frac{z_r^3}{r} + \frac{z_r}{r^2}(z_r z_{\varphi\varphi} - 2 z_\varphi z_{r\varphi}). \tag{12.6b}$$

We then obtain from (12.4)

$$(n_0 + g z)\frac{\Delta z + L(z)}{\sqrt{1 + z_r^2 + \left(\frac{z_\varphi}{r}\right)^2}^3} = \mp \left(p + \gamma (z_0 - z)\right) + \frac{g}{\sqrt{1 + z_r^2 + \left(\frac{z_\varphi}{r}\right)^2}}. \tag{12.6c}$$

12.3 Observations Regarding the Solution of the Soap-film Equation

Apart from a few special cases for which exact solutions can be obtained (see the last two examples in 12.4), the problem can only be solved approximately by iterations. The examples show, however, that a single iteration provides, in general, satisfactory accuracy. We rewrite (12.5c) in the form

$$\Delta z = \frac{\sqrt{1 + z_x^2 + z_y^2}^3}{n_0 + g z}\left[\mp \left(p + \gamma (z_0 - z)\right) + \frac{g}{\sqrt{1 + z_x^2 + z_y^2}}\right] - L(z) = \bar{L}(z), \tag{12.7a}$$

Neglecting, as a first approximation all second-degree terms of z on the right side, and putting $n_0 + g z \approx n_0$, we obtain a first approximation $z^{(0)}$ as a solution of the linear differential equation

$$\Delta z^{(0)} = \frac{1}{n_0}\left[\mp \left(p + \gamma (z_0 - z)\right) + g\right], \tag{12.7b}$$

which is the equation of the slightly curved prestressed membrane. Inserting this solution, which satisfies the boundary conditions, into the right side of (12.7a), we obtain an improved approximation $z^{(1)}$ from the differential equation

$$\Delta z^{(1)} = \bar{L}(z^{(0)}) \tag{12.7c}$$

which is also linear. Repeated iterations lead to

$$\Delta z^{(n)} = \bar{L}(z^{(n-1)}). \tag{12.7d}$$

Instead of obtaining successively improved approximations $z^{(n)}$, it may be preferable to find only the differences (corrections) $f^{(n)} = z^{(n)} - z^{(n-1)}$ when the values of z are prescribed along a spatial boundary curve. If the first approximation $z^{(0)}$ satisfies the boundary conditions for z, we obtain homogeneous boundary conditions for the differences, as in the case of a membrane supported along a plane curve. In accordance with (12.7c, d), the differences satisfy the differential equations

$$\Delta f^{(1)} = \Delta (z^{(1)} - z^{(0)}) = \bar{L}(z^{(0)}) - \frac{1}{n_0}\left[\mp \left(p + \gamma (z_0 - z)\right) + g\right],$$
$$\Delta f^{(n)} = \Delta (z^{(n)} - z^{(n-1)}) = \bar{L}(z^{(n-1)}) - \bar{L}(z^{(n-2)}) \tag{12.7e}$$

In the general case of irregular boundary curves we shall look for an approximate solution instead of the exact solution of (12.7b-e). We shall then use relaxation methods or the method of Ritz, considering the variational problem equivalent to the differential equations. Replacing differentials by differences, we obtain

$$\left.\frac{\partial z}{\partial x}\right|_{i,k} = \frac{z_{i+1,k} - z_{i-1,k}}{2\Delta a}, \quad \left.\frac{\partial z}{\partial y}\right|_{i,k} = \frac{z_{i,k+1} - z_{i,k-1}}{2\Delta a},$$
$$\left.\frac{\partial^2 z}{\partial x^2}\right|_{i,k} = \frac{z_{i+1,k} - 2 z_{i,k} + z_{i-1,k}}{(\Delta a)^2},$$
$$\left.\frac{\partial^2 z}{\partial y^2}\right|_{i,k} = \frac{z_{i,k+1} - 2 z_{i,k} - z_{i,k-1}}{(\Delta a)^2}, \tag{12.8a}$$
$$\left.\Delta z\right|_{i,k} = \frac{z_{i+1,k} + z_{i,k+1} + z_{i-1,k} + z_{i,k-1} - 4 z_{i,k}}{(\Delta a)^2},$$

where Δa is the mesh width of a square net formed by the coordinates x = const and y = const, at whose lattice points (i, k) we need to know the surface ordinates $z_{i,k}$ approximately. Instead of (12.7d), we then obtain for each internal lattice point (i, k) the difference equation

$$z_{i+1,k}^{(n)} + z_{i,k+1}^{(n)} + z_{i-1,k}^{(n)} + z_{i,k-1}^{(n)} - 4 z_{i,k}^{(n)} = R_{i,k}^{(n)}$$
$$\text{where } R_{i,k}^{(n)} = (\Delta a)^2 \left[\bar{L}(z^{(n-1)})\right]_{i,k}. \tag{12.8b}$$

The resulting system of linear equations, whose reciprocal matrix remains the same for all iterations (n), enables us to determine the displacements of all internal points.

Applying the method of Ritz, we consider the variational problem equivalent to (12.4). Using the relationships found in Subsection 11.3.1, we insert the equations obtained from the condition of vanishing shearing stresses [cf. 11.3]

$$\bar{n}_\alpha \cos \bar{\sigma}_{\alpha\beta} + \bar{n}_{\alpha\beta} = 0, \quad \bar{n}_\beta \cos \bar{\sigma}_{\alpha\beta} + \bar{n}_{\alpha\beta} = 0$$

i.e., $\bar{n}_\alpha = \bar{n}_\beta = -\bar{n}_{\alpha\beta}/\cos \bar{\sigma}_{\alpha\beta}$ and $\bar{n}_\alpha \sin \bar{\sigma}_{\alpha\beta} = \bar{n}_\beta \sin \bar{\sigma}_{\alpha\beta} = n$.

or

$$\bar{n}_\alpha = \bar{n}_\beta = n/\sin \bar{\sigma}_{\alpha\beta}, \quad \bar{n}_{\alpha\beta} = -n \cos \bar{\sigma}_{\alpha\beta}/\sin \bar{\sigma}_{\alpha\beta}. \tag{12.9a}$$

Since

$$(\bar{n}_\alpha + \bar{n}_{\alpha\beta} \cos \bar{\sigma}_{\alpha\beta})/\sin \bar{\sigma}_{\alpha\beta} = (\bar{n}_\beta + \bar{n}_{\alpha\beta} \cos \bar{\sigma}_{\alpha\beta})/\sin \bar{\sigma}_{\alpha\beta} = n \ ,$$

$$\left(\delta_{\mathfrak{v}} \bar{\varepsilon}_\alpha + \delta_{\mathfrak{v}} \bar{\varepsilon}_\beta - \frac{\cos \bar{\sigma}_{\alpha\beta}}{\sin \bar{\sigma}_{\alpha\beta}} \delta_{\mathfrak{v}} \gamma_{\alpha\beta}\right) d\bar{F} = \delta_{\mathfrak{v}} \left[(1+\varepsilon_\alpha)(1+\varepsilon_\beta) \sin \bar{\sigma}_{\alpha\beta} \, dF\right] =$$

$$= \delta_{\mathfrak{v}} \, d\bar{F} = \delta_{\bar{\mathfrak{r}}} \, d\bar{F} = \delta \, d\bar{F}$$

and

$\delta \mathfrak{v} = (\bar{\mathfrak{r}} - \mathfrak{r}) = \delta \bar{\mathfrak{r}}$ we obtain from (11.20d) the extremum problem

$$\iint_{(\bar{F})} (n \, \delta \, d\bar{F} - \bar{\mathfrak{p}} \, \delta \bar{\mathfrak{r}} \, d\bar{F}) = 0 \, . \tag{12.9b}$$

The load vector is given by

$$\bar{\mathfrak{p}} = \pm \left[p + \gamma (z_0 - z)\right] \bar{\mathfrak{e}}_\gamma - g \, \mathfrak{e}_z = \pm \, p(z) \, \bar{\mathfrak{e}}_\gamma - g \, \mathfrak{e}_z \, .$$

Taking into account (12.2) and writing $\mathfrak{e}_z \delta \bar{\mathfrak{r}} = \delta z$, we obtain

$$n_0 \, \delta \bar{F} + g \, \delta \int_{(\bar{F})} (\overset{\downarrow}{z} \, d\bar{F}) \mp \int_{(\bar{F})} p(z) \, \bar{\mathfrak{e}}_\gamma \, \delta \bar{\mathfrak{r}} \, d\bar{F} = 0 \, . \tag{12.9c}$$

Introducing the variables t_α and t_β, the membrane surface can be defined by $z = z\,(t_\alpha, t_\beta)$. Writing

$$\bar{\mathfrak{r}} = x\,(t_\alpha, t_\beta)\, \mathfrak{e}_{x0} + y\,(t_\alpha, t_\beta)\, \mathfrak{e}_{y0} + z\,(t_\alpha, t_\beta)\, \mathfrak{e}_z = \mathfrak{r}_0\,(t_\alpha, t_\beta) + z\,(t_\alpha, t_\beta)\, \mathfrak{e}_z,$$

we obtain $\delta \bar{\mathfrak{r}} = \delta z \, \mathfrak{e}_z$. For orthogonal grid lines ($\mathfrak{r}_{0t_\alpha} \mathfrak{r}_{0t_\beta} = 0$) we have

$$\operatorname{grad} z = \frac{\mathfrak{r}_{0t_\alpha}}{\mathfrak{r}_{0t_\alpha}{}^2} \frac{\partial z}{\partial t_\alpha} + \frac{\mathfrak{r}_{0t_\beta}}{\mathfrak{r}_{0t_\beta}{}^2} \frac{\partial z}{\partial t_\beta} \, .$$

The surface element in the (x, y)-plane, corresponding to the increments $d t_\alpha$, and $d t_\beta$, is $d F_0 = |\, \mathfrak{r}_{0t_\alpha} \times \mathfrak{r}_{0t_\beta} | \, d t_\alpha \, d t_\beta$.

We thus obtain

$$d\bar{F} = \sqrt{1 + (\operatorname{grad} z)^2} \, dF_0 \quad \text{and} \quad \bar{\mathfrak{e}}_\gamma \, \delta \bar{\mathfrak{r}} \, d\bar{F} = \delta z \, dF_0 \, .$$

The extreme problem equivalent to (12.4), is thus

$$\delta_z \iint_{(F_0)} \left[n_0 \sqrt{1 + (\operatorname{grad} z)^2} + g \, \overbrace{\left(z \sqrt{1 + (\operatorname{grad} z)^2}\right)}^{\downarrow} \mp p(z) \, \overset{\downarrow}{z}\right] dF_0 = 0 \, . \tag{12.9d}$$

In particular, for $p = g = 0$, (12.9c) leads to

$n_0 \, \delta F = 0$ or $F = \text{Extr.} = \text{Min.}$:

In the absence of shearing stresses the unloaded membrane therefore assumes a shape having the least surface area possible for the prescribed boundaries (minimum surface).

12.4 Examples of Minimum Surfaces

12.4.1 *The Unloaded Soap Film, Maintained Between Four Inclined Straight Lines Projecting as a Rectangle*

In this case, $p = g = \gamma = 0$. We obtain from (12.5c)

$$\Delta z = - L(z) \, . \tag{12.10}$$

According to (12.7b) the first approximation $z^{(0)}$ has to satisfy the equation

$$\Delta z^{(0)} = \frac{\partial^2 z^{(0)}}{\partial x^2} + \frac{\partial^2 z^{(0)}}{\partial y^2} = 0 \tag{12.11a}$$

and the boundary conditions (Figure 12.1)

$$z^{(0)}\left(\frac{a}{2}, y\right) = h \frac{y}{b}, \ z^{(0)}\left(-\frac{a}{2}, y\right) = -h \frac{y}{b},$$
$$z^{(0)}\left(x, \frac{b}{2}\right) = h \frac{x}{a}, \ z^{(0)}\left(x, -\frac{b}{2}\right) = -h \frac{x}{a} \, . \tag{12.11b}$$

The solution is the hyperbolic paraboloid

$$z^{(0)}(x, y) = 2h \frac{x}{a} \frac{y}{b} \, , \tag{12.11c}$$

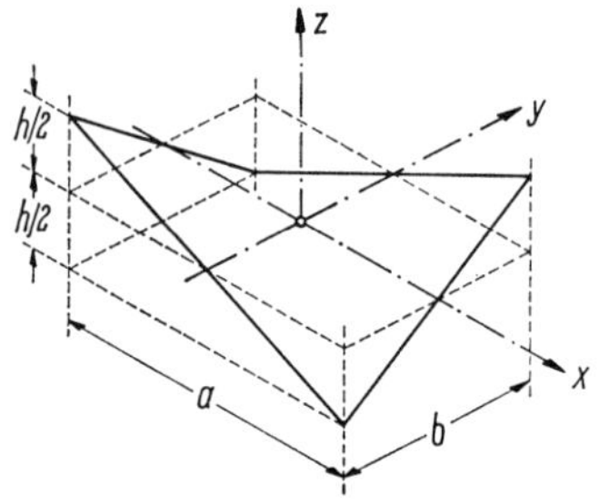

Figure 12.1

as can be shown by substitution in (12.11a, b). The first correction $f^{(1)}$ is given, in accordance with (12.7e), by

$$\Delta f^{(1)} = \bar{L}(z^{(0)}) = - L(z^{(0)}) = - [z_x{}^{(0)2} z_{yy}{}^{(0)} -$$
$$- 2 z_x{}^{(0)} z_y{}^{(0)} z_{xy}{}^{(0)} + z_y{}^{(0)2} z_{xx}{}^{(0)}] = 16 \frac{h^3}{a^2 b^2} \frac{x}{a} \frac{y}{b} \, , \tag{12.12a}$$

the homogeneous boundary conditions being

$$f^{(1)}\left(\frac{a}{2}, y\right) = f^{(1)}\left(-\frac{a}{2}, y\right) = f^{(1)}\left(x, \frac{b}{2}\right) =$$
$$= f^{(1)}\left(x, -\frac{b}{2}\right) = 0 \, . \tag{12.12b}$$

In the physical sense this reduces to the problem of determining the deformed surface of a membrane, supported in a rectangular plane frame and acted upon by a load $- L(z^{(0)}) = 16 \dfrac{h^3}{a^2 b^2} \dfrac{x}{a} \dfrac{y}{b}$.

The solution can be obtained by expansions in Fourier series. By virtue of the antimetry of the problem with respect to the x and y-axis, and taking into account the boundary conditions (12.12b), we assume a solution in the form

$$f^{(1)} = \sum_{i=1}^{\infty} \sum_{k=1}^{\infty} C_{ik}{}^{(1)} \sin i \, 2\pi \frac{x}{a} \sin k \, 2\pi \frac{y}{b} \tag{12.13a}$$

where the constants $C_{ik}{}^{(1)}$ have to be determined. Expanding the right side of (12.12a) in a series of trigonometric products

$$- L(z^{(0)}) = 16 \frac{h^3}{a^2 b^2} \frac{x}{a} \frac{y}{b} =$$
$$= - \sum_{i=1}^{\infty} \sum_{k=1}^{\infty} A_{ik}{}^{(0)} \sin i \, 2\pi \frac{x}{a} \sin k \, 2\pi \frac{y}{b} \tag{12.13b}$$

and substituting (12.13a) in the left side of (12.12a), we obtain

$$\sum_{i=1}^{\infty} \sum_{k=1}^{\infty} \left\{4\pi^2 C_{ik}{}^{(1)} \left(\frac{i^2}{a^2} + \frac{k^2}{b^2}\right) - A_{ik}{}^{(0)}\right\} \sin i \, 2\pi \frac{x}{a} \sin k \, 2\pi \frac{y}{b} = 0 \, .$$

This yields for each term (i, k)

$$C_{ik}^{(1)} = \frac{A_{ik}^{(0)}}{4\pi^2\left(\dfrac{i^2}{a^2} + \dfrac{k^2}{b^2}\right)} \tag{12.13c}$$

By virtue of the orthogonality relationships

$$\int\limits_{x=-a/2}^{+a/2}\int\limits_{y=-b/2}^{+b/2} \sin j\,2\pi\frac{x}{a}\sin i\,2\pi\frac{x}{a}\sin k\,2\pi\frac{y}{b}\sin m\,2\pi\frac{y}{b}\,dx\,dy =$$

$$= \begin{cases} \dfrac{ab}{4} \text{ for } i = j \text{ and } k = m \\ 0 \text{ for } i \neq j \text{ and } k \neq m \end{cases}$$

we obtain, minimalizing the error by the method of least squares,

$$A_{ik}^{(0)} = \frac{4}{ab}\int\limits_{x=-a/2}^{+a/2}\int\limits_{y=-b/2}^{+b/2} L(z^{(0)})\sin i\,2\pi\frac{x}{a}\sin k\,2\pi\frac{y}{b}\,dx\,dy. \tag{12.13d}$$

The solution of (12.12a), satisfying the boundary conditions (12.12b), is thus

$$f^{(1)}(x, y) = \frac{1}{\pi^2 ab}\sum_{i=1}^{\infty}\sum_{k=1}^{\infty}\frac{\sin i\,2\pi\dfrac{x}{a}\sin k\,2\pi\dfrac{y}{b}}{\left(\dfrac{i^2}{a^2}+\dfrac{k^2}{b^2}\right)} \times \tag{12.13e}$$

$$\times \int\limits_{x=-a/2}^{+a/2}\int\limits_{y=-b/2}^{+b/2} L(z^{(0)})\sin i\,2\pi\frac{x}{a}\sin k\,2\pi\frac{y}{b}\,dx\,dy\,.$$

Inserting $L(z^{(0)}) = -16\dfrac{h^3}{a^2b^2}\dfrac{x}{a}\dfrac{y}{b}$ and integrating, we finally obtain

$$f^{(1)}(x, y) = -h\frac{4}{\pi^4}\left(\frac{h}{a}\right)^2\sum_{i=1}^{\infty}\sum_{k=1}^{\infty}\frac{(-1)^{i+k}\sin i\,2\pi\dfrac{x}{a}\sin k\,2\pi\dfrac{y}{b}}{ik\left[\dfrac{b^2}{a^2}i^2+k^2\right]}, \tag{12.13f}$$

and particularly for a square plan $a = b$, we have

$$f^{(1)}(x, y) = -h\frac{4}{\pi^4}\left(\frac{h}{a}\right)^2\sum_{i=1}^{\infty}\sum_{k=1}^{\infty}\frac{(-1)^{i+k}\sin i\,2\pi\dfrac{x}{a}\sin k\,2\pi\dfrac{y}{a}}{ik\,(i^2+k^2)}\,. \tag{12.13g}$$

The convergence of this series is satisfactory, since the maximum values of the terms $(i = 2,\ k = 1)$ and $(i = 1,\ k = 2)$, are, for $a \approx b$, only about 20% of the first term. The maximum value of the term $(i = 2,\ k = 2)$ is, at most, only 6% of the first term. It will therefore be sufficient to use only the first three terms (1,1) (1,2), and (2,1) of (12.13f, g). In order to compare the values of the first correction and of the first approximation, we consider, for the sake of simplicity, only the first term of the series. We have

$$\left|\frac{f^{(1)}}{h}\right|_{\max} \approx \frac{4}{\pi^4}\left(\frac{h}{a}\right)^2\frac{1}{\dfrac{b^2}{a^2}+1} = 0.0411\left(\frac{h}{a}\right)^2\frac{1}{1+\left(\dfrac{b}{a}\right)^2}$$

whereas the maximum value of the first approximation is given by $\left|\dfrac{z^{(0)}}{h}\right|_{\max} = \dfrac{1}{2}$. Thus, the correction is very small even for large values h/a. If we require that the maximum value of the first cortion be less than $\dfrac{\mu}{100} = 3\%$ of the maximum value of the first approximation, we obtain from

$$\frac{4}{\pi^2}\left(\frac{h}{a}\right)^2\frac{1}{1+\left(\dfrac{b}{a}\right)^2} \leq \frac{\mu}{100}\cdot 0.5 = \frac{\mu}{200}$$

the limiting ratio between height and edge length

$$\frac{h}{a} \leq \sqrt{\frac{\mu\pi^4}{800}}\sqrt{1+\left(\frac{b}{a}\right)^2} =$$

$$= \sqrt{\frac{3\pi^4}{800}}\sqrt{1+\left(\frac{b}{a}\right)^2} \approx 0.6\sqrt{1+\left(\frac{b}{a}\right)^2}\,. \tag{12.13h}$$

In these cases the first approximation (hyperbolic paraboloid) is sufficiently accurate. For $b/a = 1$ we obtain the limiting ratio

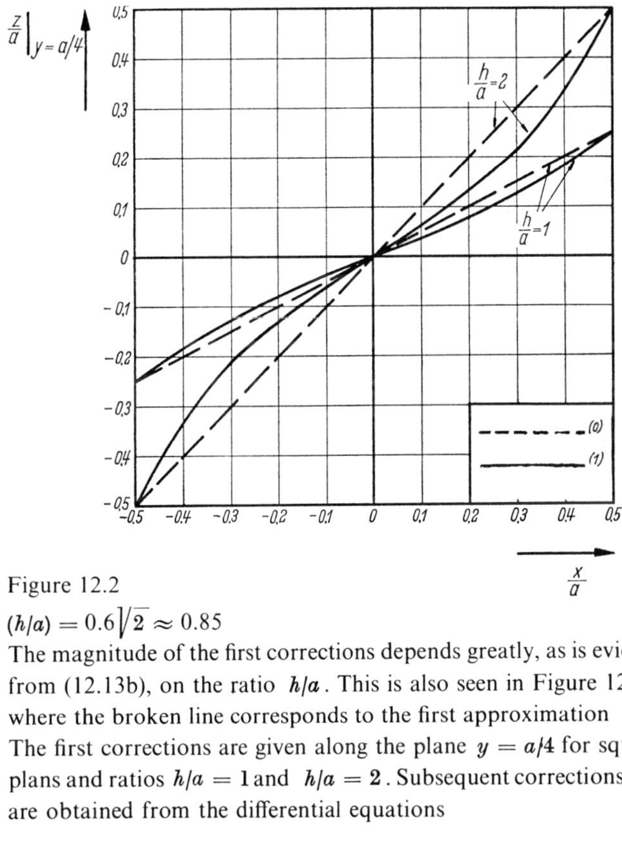

Figure 12.2

$(h/a) = 0.6\sqrt{2} \approx 0.85$

The magnitude of the first corrections depends greatly, as is evident from (12.13b), on the ratio h/a. This is also seen in Figure 12.12, where the broken line corresponds to the first approximation $z^{(0)}$. The first corrections are given along the plane $y = a/4$ for square plans and ratios $h/a = 1$ and $h/a = 2$. Subsequent corrections $f^{(n)}$ are obtained from the differential equations

$$\Delta f^{(n)} = \Delta(z^{(n)} - z^{(n-1)}) = -L(z^{(n-1)}) + L(z^{(n-2)})$$

taking into account the boundary conditions (12.12b). We can however, immediately use the solution (12.13e) if we replace $L(z^{(0)})$ by $L(z^{(n-1)}) - L(z^{(n-2)})$.

We conclude by observing that for a square plan $(a = b)$ and a ratio

$$h/a = 2\ln\frac{1}{\cos\dfrac{\sqrt{2}}{2}} \approx 0.55$$

the Scherk-Plateau minimum surface

$$z = a \ln \frac{\cos(y/a)}{\cos(x/a)} \tag{12.14}$$

provides a satisfactory approximation, since z/a varies almost linearly along the straight edges (cf. Figure 12.3) .

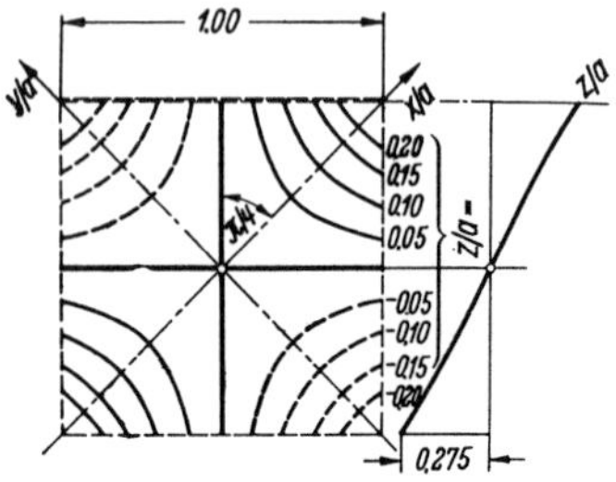

Figure 12.3

12.4.2 *The Axisymmetrical Problem*

For

$$z_\varphi = z_{\varphi\varphi} = 0\,, \quad \Delta z = z_{rr} + \frac{z_r}{r} = z'' + \frac{z'}{r}\,, \quad L(z) = \frac{1}{r} z_r^3 = \frac{1}{r} z'^3\,,$$

$$\frac{\Delta z + L(z)}{\sqrt{1+z'^2}^{\,3}} = \frac{z'' + \frac{z'}{r} + \frac{z'^3}{r}}{\sqrt{1+z'^2}^{\,3}} = \frac{r z'' + z'(1+z'^2)}{r\sqrt{1+z'^2}^{\,3}} = \frac{1}{r}\frac{d}{dr}\left(\frac{r z'}{\sqrt{1+z'^2}}\right)$$

we obtain from (12.6c) the equation

$$(n_0 + g z)\frac{1}{r}\frac{d}{dr}\left(\frac{r z'}{\sqrt{1+z'^2}}\right) = \mp\left(p + \gamma(z_0 - z)\right) + \frac{g}{\sqrt{1+z'^2}}\,. \tag{12.15a}$$

Setting $g = \gamma = 0$, the load induced by the internal pressure (the sign of p must be negative) is then

$$\frac{1}{r}\frac{d}{dr}\left(\frac{r z'}{\sqrt{1+z'^2}}\right) = -\frac{p}{n_0}\,. \tag{12.15b}$$

Integration yields

$$\frac{z'}{\sqrt{1+z'^2}} = -\frac{p r}{2 n_0} + \frac{C_1}{r} \tag{12.15c}$$

or

$$z' = \pm \frac{C_1 - \frac{p}{2 n_0} r^2}{\sqrt{r^2 - \left(C_1 - \frac{p}{2 n_0} r^2\right)^2}}\,,$$

where C_1 is a constant. Integrating once more, we obtain

$$z = C_2 \pm \int \frac{\left(C_1 - \frac{p}{2 n_0} r^2\right) dr}{\sqrt{r^2 - \left(C_1 - \frac{p}{2 n_0} r^2\right)^2}}\,.$$

If the membrane is immovably supported along a circle of radius r_a , the boundary condition becomes $z(r_a) = 0$, whence

$$C_2 = \mp\left[\int \frac{\left(C_1 - \frac{p}{2 n_0} r^2\right) dr}{\sqrt{r^2 - \left(C_1 - \frac{p}{2 n_0} r^2\right)^2}}\right]_{r = ra}$$

We thus obtain finally

$$z = \pm \int_r^{ra} \frac{\frac{p}{2 n_0} r^2 - C_1}{\sqrt{r^2 - \left(C_1 - \frac{p}{2 n_0} r^2\right)^2}}\, dr\,. \tag{12.15d}$$

We shall consider two particular cases:

a) A closed soap film, maintained by a ring of radius $r = r_a$ and loaded by internal pressure.
For a closed axisymmetrical shape we must have $z'(0) = 0$, thus, by (12.15c), $C_1 = 0$.*

$$z = \pm \frac{p}{2 n_0}\int_r^{ra} \frac{r\,dr}{\sqrt{1 - \left(\frac{p}{2 n_0}\right)^2 r^2}} =$$

$$= \mp \frac{2 n_0}{p}\left[\sqrt{1 - \left(\frac{p}{2 n_0}\right)^2 r_a^2} - \sqrt{1 - \left(\frac{p}{2 n_0}\right)^2 \cdot r^2}\right]$$

We then obtain from (12.15d)

$$\frac{\left[z \pm \sqrt{\left(\frac{2 n_0}{p}\right)^2 - r_a^2}\right]^2}{\left(\frac{2 n_0}{p}\right)^2} + \frac{r^2}{\left(\frac{2 n_0}{p}\right)^2} = 1\,.$$

The meridianal curves of the resulting surface are therefore circular arcs of radius $R = 2 n_0/p$. Their centers lie, respectively, on the negative and positive z-axis at a distance of

$$\sqrt{\left(\frac{2 n_0}{p}\right)^2 - r_a^2} = \sqrt{R^2 - r_a^2}$$

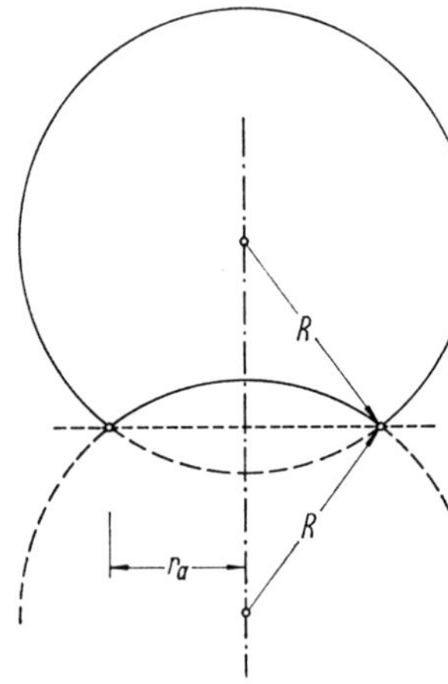

Figure 12.4

from the plane of the annulus. The two signs of the radical in the first term of the equation of the circular arc indicate that there always exist two circles, of equal radius R, which pass through the edge points (Figure 12.4). By virtue of $p = 2 n_0/R$, a definite radius corresponds to each value of p. Thus, assuming as a first approximation that n_0 is independent of the deformations, we have two possible membrane shapes of equal radius R for every value of the internal pressure p. One form is larger, the other

* This, of course, considerably restricts the number of possible solutions. See Tölke, *Rotationsschalen gleicher Festigkeit*, Z. A. M. M. 1939.

smaller, than the corresponding hemisphere. This is also evident from Figure 12.5, in which

$$\frac{f}{r_a} = \frac{R}{r_a} \mp \sqrt{\left(\frac{R}{r_a}\right)^2 - 1} = \frac{1}{\varkappa}\left[1 \mp \sqrt{1-\varkappa^2}\right], \quad \varkappa = \frac{r_a}{R} = \frac{p\, r_a}{2\, n_0}$$

has been plotted.

It is also seen that by virtue of $\varkappa_{\max} = r_a/R_{\min} = 1$, the internal

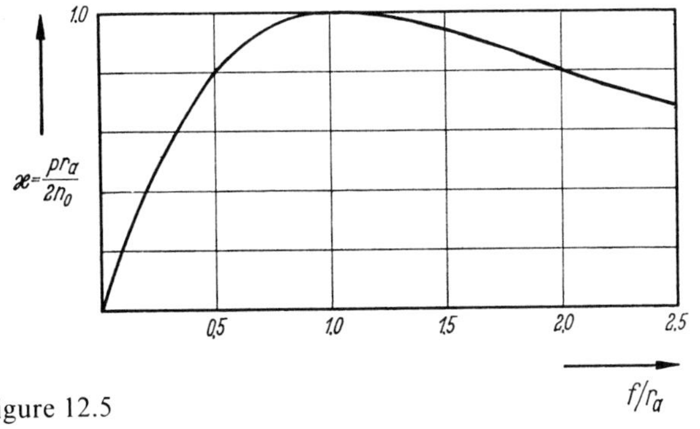

Figure 12.5

pressure cannot exceed $p_{\max} = 2\, n_0/r_a$. For constant n_0, the highest pressure is required to form a hemisphere $(f/r_a = 1)$.

b) An unloaded soap film, stretched between an outer ring of radius $r = r_a$, and a concentric inner ring of radius r_i, located at an elevation h above the outer ring.

Setting $p = 0$ in (12.15d), we obtain

$$z = C_1 \int_r^{r_a} \frac{d\,r}{\sqrt{r^2 - C_1^2}} = C_1 \left(\mathfrak{Ar}\,\mathfrak{Cof}\, \frac{r_a}{C_1} - \mathfrak{Ar}\,\mathfrak{Cof}\, \frac{r}{C_1}\right)$$

Putting $z/r_a = \zeta$, $C_1/r_a = \bar{C}_1$, $r/r_a = \varrho$, this reduces to

$$\varrho = \bar{C}_1\, \mathfrak{Cof}\left(\frac{\zeta - \bar{C}_1\, \mathfrak{Ar}\,\mathfrak{Cof}\, \frac{1}{\bar{C}_1}}{\bar{C}_1}\right) = f(\zeta, \bar{C}_1)$$

The family of curves $\varrho = f(\zeta, \bar{C}_1)$ has been plotted in Figure 12.6 for several values of the parameter $\bar{C}_1$.

We recognize that when r_i is given, the height h cannot be selected arbitrarily, since the hyperbolic-cosine curves have their minimum distance $(\varrho_{\min} = \bar{C}_1)$ from the symmetry axis at $\zeta_0 = \bar{C}_1\, \mathfrak{Ar}\,\mathfrak{Cos}\; 1/\bar{C}_1$

Putting $\bar{C}_1 = \varrho_i$, we obtain

$$\zeta_0 = \varrho_i\, \mathfrak{Ar}\,\mathfrak{Cof}\, \frac{1}{\varrho_i} = \varrho_i \ln\left(\frac{1}{\varrho_i} + \sqrt{\frac{1}{\varrho_i^2} - 1}\right) = \varrho_i \ln \frac{1 + \sqrt{1 - \varrho_i^2}}{\varrho_i}$$

or

$$h_0 = r_i \ln \frac{r_a + \sqrt{r_a^2 - r_i^2}}{r_i}$$

where n_0 is the maximum height to which a ring of radius r_i can be raised with the soap film intact. For $r_i = 0.25\, r_a$, $h = 0.5\, r_a$, i.e., $\varrho = 0.25$, $\zeta = 0.5$, we obtain $\bar{C}_1 = 0.249$, or

$$\varrho = 0.249\, \mathfrak{Cof}\left[\frac{\zeta}{0.249} - \mathfrak{Ar}\,\mathfrak{Cof}\, \frac{1}{0.249}\right]. \qquad (12.16a)$$

This curve is shown in Figure 12.6 by the broken line. The ring could have been raised slightly higher since the value given by (12.16) still lies below the curve of minimum distances also shown in Figure 12.6 by a broken line.

We shall now apply the iteration procedure, explained in Section

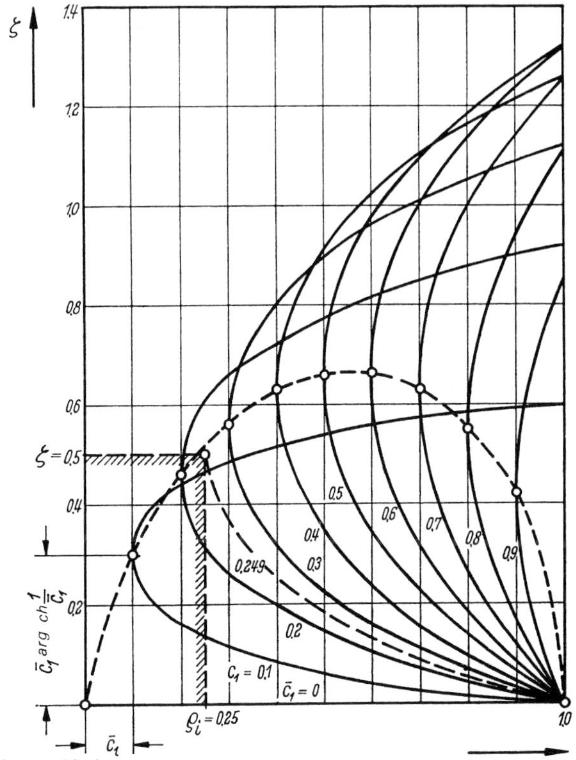

Figure 12.6

12.3, to the example considered.

For $p = g = \gamma = 0$, we determine, in accordance with (12.7b), the first approximation $z^{(0)}$ from

$$\Delta\, z^{(0)} = \left(\frac{d^2}{d\,r^2} + \frac{1}{r}\frac{d}{d\,r}\right) z^{(0)} = \frac{1}{r}\frac{d}{d\,r}\left(r\, \frac{d\, z^{(0)}}{d\,r}\right) = 0,$$

the boundary conditions being $z(r_a) = 0$, $z(r_i) = h$.

We obtain

$$z^{(0)} = h\, \frac{\ln \frac{r}{r_a}}{\ln \frac{r_i}{r_a}} \quad \text{or} \quad \zeta^{(0)} = \zeta_i \frac{\ln \varrho}{\ln \varrho_i}, \quad \zeta_i = \frac{h}{r_a}. \qquad (12.16b)$$

In accordance with (12.7e), the first correction is given by

$$\Delta\, f^{(1)} = \frac{1}{r}\frac{d}{d\,r}\left(r\, \frac{d\, f^{(1)}}{d\,r}\right) = \bar{L}(z^{(0)}) = -L(z^{(0)}) =$$

$$= -\frac{1}{r}\left(\frac{d\, z^{(0)}}{d\,r}\right)^3 = -\left(\frac{h}{\ln \varrho_i}\right)^3 \frac{1}{r^4},$$

the homogeneous boundary conditions being $f(r_i) = f(r_a) = 0$.

The general solution is

$$f^{(1)} = C_1 + C_2 \ln r - \frac{1}{4}\left(\frac{h}{\ln \varrho_i}\right)^3 \frac{1}{r^2}.$$

After satisfying the boundary conditions for the first correction, we obtain

$$\frac{f^{(1)}}{r_a} = \frac{\zeta_i^3}{4(\ln \varrho_i)^3}\left[\left(\frac{1}{\varrho_i^2} - 1\right)\frac{\ln \varrho}{\ln \varrho_i} - \left(\frac{1}{\varrho^2} - 1\right)\right], \qquad (12.16c)$$

so that the improved approximation becomes

$$\zeta^{(1)} = \zeta^{(0)} + \frac{f^{(1)}}{r_a}. \qquad (12.16d)$$

Figure 12.7 shows the exact solution ζ according to (12.16a), the first approximation $\zeta^{(0)}$ according to (12.16b), and the improved approximation according to (12.16d). Whereas the first approxima-

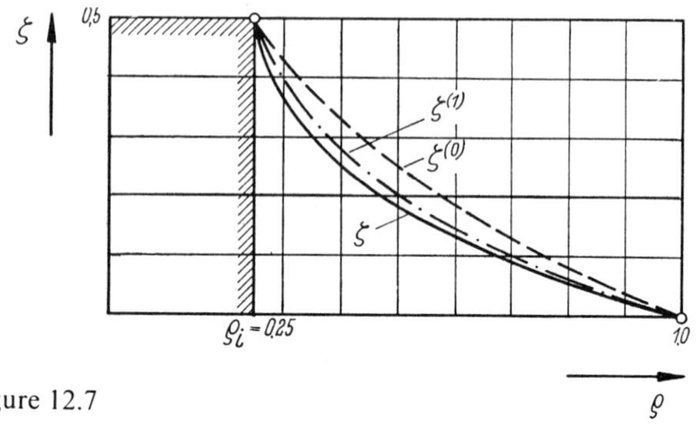

Figure 12.7

tion still differs considerably from the exact solution, the improved approximation shows very good agreement with the actual (minimum) surface, although the deformations are of the order of magnitude of the radius r_a.

We mention in conclusion that the case (12.15d) was solved by Tölke (see footnote on p. 294). He proved that, in addition to the sphere (the only shape closed on top), there are other solutions for the case of a soap film loaded by internal pressure stretched between two rings located at different heights. One solution is presented in a wave function varying periodically in the ζ-direction. Tölke's integration of (12.15d) leads to nonelementary functions. For $g = p = 0$ we obtain from (12.15a) the differential equation of a soap film loaded by hydrostatic pressure. This problem was investigated by Federhofer,* Krebitz, Flügge,** and Kottenmeier.***

The closed axisymmetrical shapes are those assumed by drops of liquid resting on a base.

The problem of minimum surfaces has been investigated by famous mathematicians (Lagrange, Legendre, Meusnier, Weierstrass, H. A. Scharz, and others). In particular, the representation given by Weierstrass shows a connection with the theory of complex functions.

12.4.3 *Observations on Membranes Pretensioned by Cables to a Uniform Sectional Load* n_0

This is an extension of the boundary-value problem of the preceding examples, in which the boundary curve itself was given (geometrical boundary problem). In the present case, the boundary problem is dynamical, since the shape of the edge-cable curves, and thus of the membrane edges, depends on the acting forces. Using the results of Section 2.5, we can, however, reduce this problem to geometrical boundary conditions. In order that the tangent plane to the membrane be identical with the osculating plane to the edge curve, we must have by (2.13c)

$$\mathfrak{n}\, \mathfrak{e}_{\gamma(R)} = 0. \qquad (12.17a)$$

Since the pretensioning of the membrane is intended to remove shearing stresses (state of normal sectional loads n_0), we obtain from (2.31a, d) for $q_t = 0$ and $q_n = n_0$

$$S = \text{const} = S_0 \quad \text{or} \quad R = \frac{S_0}{n_0} = R_0 = \text{const}. \qquad (12.17b)$$

The edge-cable curves must therefore be asymptotic lines of constant curvature.

Solving the boundary-value problem (12.17a, b) in conjunction with the requirements formulated in Section 2.5 for a cable corner which does not form a right angle, leads to the trivial result that the edge-cable curves form circular arcs only if all edge curves lie in one plane. In this case the membrane itself remains plane. In the more general problem of linking four points not lying in one plane by tension cables (Figure 12.1), circles cannot form the solution, since the corner points cannot be linked by four coplanar circular arcs. If the mesh angle of the corner point is not a right angle, we must also exclude the linear helix possessing constant curvature since its tension τ is constant, and does not therefore vanish at the corners. This problem is extremely complicated. If we discard the representation (12.17a, b), which is invariant with respect to coordinate transformations, we obtain two interdependent nonlinear differential equations. The entire problem is thus almost unsolvable mathematically. In this case, as with most minimum surface problems, it is best to use test models.

14.4.4 *Observations on Models of Minimum Surfaces*

A model of minimum surface satisfying given boundary conditions is best made by means of a rubber membrane, strongly and uniformly pretensioned in all directions when in the plane state. The pretensioning should be sufficiently high to enable us to neglect the additional extensions, i.e., stresses caused by fitting the initially plane membrane to the required boundary conditions. We then obtain a surface satisfying the boundary conditions, in which the sectional loads consist approximately of normal forces equal in magnitude in all directions. This is thus approximately the required minimum surface. In this way we can also solve the problem of a membrane pretensioned by cables. Consider, for instance, a membrane pretensioned by four edge cables, whose corner points are not coplanar (Figure 12.1). In this case, the plane rubber membrane is first strongly pretensioned equally in all directions. After this, two opposite corner points are raised. Care should be taken to avoid transmitting shearing stresses to the membrane. This can be achieved by guiding the cables along the membrane edges with as little friction as possible.

* Federhofer, K.: Über die Form des Wölbmantelbeckens, *Eisenbau* 4 (H. 10), 1913. Federhofer-Krebitz: Über die strenge Ermittlung der Form einer allseitig gleichgespannten Rotationsmembran, *Eisenbau* 5 (H. 6), 1914.

** Flügge, W.: *Statik und Dynamik der Schalen*, Springer Berlin 1934.

*** Kottenmeier, E.: *Der Stahlbehälterbau, Stahlbau*, 3 (1030).

TENSION ANCHORING IN THE FOUNDATIONS

Introduction

The following is an attempt at a brief survey of tension anchorings in foundations. Solutions to several important questions will also be proposed.

The forces acting in tension-loaded structures are frequently transmitted to the foundations.

The oldest types are mobile anchorings, e.g., for tents.

The first major problems in permanent anchoring arose in the middle of the last century, when the first large suspension bridges were built (Roebling).* The immense loads were often taken up by huge weights and transmitted to the foundations. At the beginning of the thirties Coyne used cables, deeply anchored in the bedrock, to stabilize dams. Between 1950 and 1960, advances were due to the urgent problem of anchoring quay and retaining walls.

Until now, tension anchorings in structural foundations have not been the subject of comprehensive basic research. The increasing use of tension-loaded structures has imparted great importance to this field, which, if mastered, could make many new methods used in tension-loaded structures more economical.

Tension anchoring to the foundations is particularly necessary in structures whose weight is less than the maximum likely wind force, which is generally assumed to be 40 to 120 kg/m^2 (depending on geographic location and the height of the structure); under unfavorable conditions, extreme values of 200 kg/m^2 are possible. Today, the structural weights of buildings are often considerably lower than that, even if structures other than tension-loaded ones are in question, e.g., finely meshed lattice structures, etc. Figures 1 to 6 show the wind-load resultants for structures of various shapes. In high buildings (Fig. 1) the resultant is slightly inclined. The dotted line indicates the wind pressure, referred to the surface area of the building. In lower buildings (Fig. 2) the resultant is more inclined, which is even more pronounced in domed structures (Fig. 3). High buildings (Fig. 4) tend to tip over; their foundations are in tension on the windward and under compression on the lee side. The steeply inclined wind-force resultant of a low building (Fig. 5) imparts tension to the entire foundation. Wind suction is particularly high in halls that are open on all sides (Fig. 6), in which case tension-resistant anchoring of each separate support is usually necessary.

Wind loads are not constant and they exert dynamic stresses on the foundations. Wind velocity and direction vary, especially during heavy thunderstorms, on which all calculations must be based, since they cause the highest loads.

The intrinsic properties of wind and gusts have not been thoroughly investigated. Maximum velocities may follow directly after minima, in which the velocity may be only 30% of the maximum. The fluctuation periods are between 3 and 20 sec. However, intervals are not uniform, so that the danger of resonance is not great, unless the structure itself is aerodynamically unstable. The considerable fluctuations of wind velocities cause enormous loads to be applied within a few seconds, followed by immediate unloading.

The degree to which buildings are able to absorb these shocks by their mass or elasticity, so that only part of the load is transmitted to the foundations, is not yet clear. Neither is it known what foundations in which type of soil are best suited to absorbing these dynamic stresses.

The load fluctuations which must be taken into account in tension anchorings are generally much higher than those occuring in compression foundations. There are also constant tension loads, e.g., prestressing forces, or stresses which remain uniform over long periods, such as snow loads or water retained by dams.

Ground-supported Gravity Anchors for Vertical Tension

Weights placed on the ground can support tensile loads equal to their weight. Gravity anchors are frequently used. Figure 7 is a section through the foundations of a pneumatically tensed membrane which is internally drained: a bag is suspended from a tubular steel ring and filled with water from the drainage pipe. An outlet prevents overflow. The tubular steel ring is attached to the tension-loaded drainage pipe by cables.

A hose which widens to form a water bag (Fig. 8), or containers filled with water or sand, are also suitable as gravity anchors, as are water- or sandbags (Figs. 9 and 11) suspended from a ring. Figure 13 shows an originally flat membrane, filled with sand or gravel, raised at the edge by cables, like a parachute, and connected to a tension ring.

Frequently, weights acting like springs are used to compensate for the differences in temperature and moisture content in a structure. Figure 10 shows how such weights constitute a spring when their individual parts are lifted successively.

The foundation in Fig. 12 shows how a cable anchored in the ground is tensed by a water bag. Only when the weight of the water has been overcome can the full load be taken up. Bags with water and sand also act as resilient anchoring (Fig. 9), unless they are all lifted at the same time.

The more rigidly a gravity anchor is connected to the foundations, the higher is the tensile load which can be taken up. This is demonstrated with a partly buried weight (Fig. 15). We should point out that, for example, a large thin plate (Fig. 16) resists brief loads far better than permanent loads, if the junction between the plate and the foundations is not vented. In this case, the atmospheric pressure acts as an external load. Pressure equalization through the ground is not possible during brief wind loads. This can be called "retention by suction." The action of weights,

* [I. A. Roebling, who built the Niagara Bridge in 1952-55.]

e.g., of concrete, buried in the ground (Fig. 18), is enhanced by the weight of the soil above them. Consequently, even a thin light anchor plate (Fig. 17) can take up tensile forces equal to the weight of the soil above it. There are various types of anchor plates, e.g., parachute membranes (Fig. 19), or membranes in compression rings† (Fig. 1, p. 302) which, because of their wedge shape, always cause the load to act centrally. This can also be achieved with wedge-shaped concrete blocks (Fig. 3, p. 302), which may be round or star-shaped in plan (Figs. 2 and 4, p. 302). Wedge forms are particularly suited to consolidation with the ground.

Gravity anchors, firmly consolidated with the foundations, can be sunk as shown in Figs. 5 to 9, p. 302. A trench is dug and a hose inserted to which the cables are attached; the hose is then filled with a slow-setting cement mortar. The trench is immediately covered, and the hose injected with more cement mortar under high pressure, until it becomes rigidly consolidated with the foundations.*

Some Remarks on Consolidation with the Ground

The tensile forces acting on a buried plate (Fig. 17) can exceed the combined weight of the plate and the soil above it. In general, the weight acting is not merely that of the prism above the plate but also that of the cone which is ejected in case of failure.

If the plate is deeply buried, however, the weight of the ejected cone is less decisive than the weight of the soil prism above the plate and the frictional resistance of the soil. Figure 3, p. 301, shows a cone torn from hard Molasse sandstone by an anchor (from Report No. 28 of the Research Institute for Hydrotechnical Engineering and Earthworks, Zürich). Figures 1 and 2, p. 301, show that the weight of the earth wedge played a considerable role even in gravity foundations with vertical walls. This was proved by A. C. Müller and R. Haefeli in the above-mentioned report. Widening the footing greatly increases the tensile forces which can be taken up. Tension tests with a foundation model in fat clay (Figs. 4 and 5, p. 301) first showed very fine fissures, and then the beginning of radial cracks until the soil broke with wide open radial cracks. No cone was torn out since the foundation slid smoothly from the soil.

Further experiments showed clearly that broadening the footing and, to an even greater extent, tamping concrete directly into the foundation pit, considerably increase the strength of the foundation. Tamping ensures consolidation of the concrete with the soil. Since the soil is placed under compression greater forces can be taken up.

There are two basically different types of anchor: anchor plates and friction anchors.

The size of the anchor plates required to take up a given load de-

† Suggestions and research results of the author (1953-1961) have been marked with an asterisk.

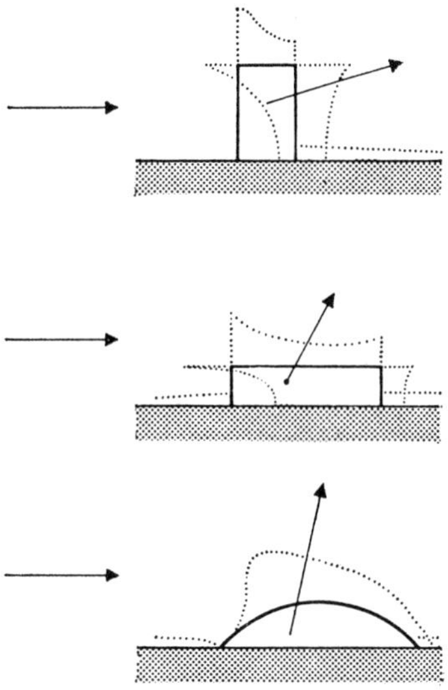

1 to 3

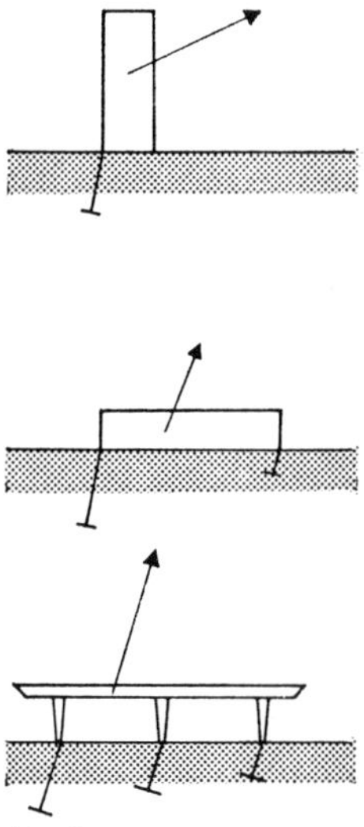

4 to 6

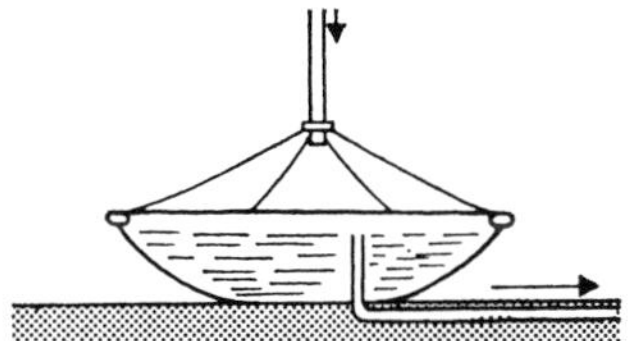

7

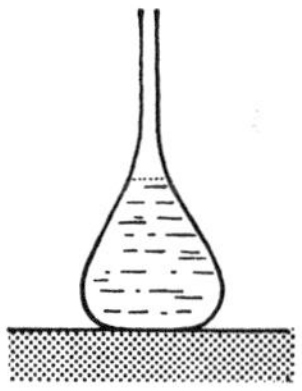

8

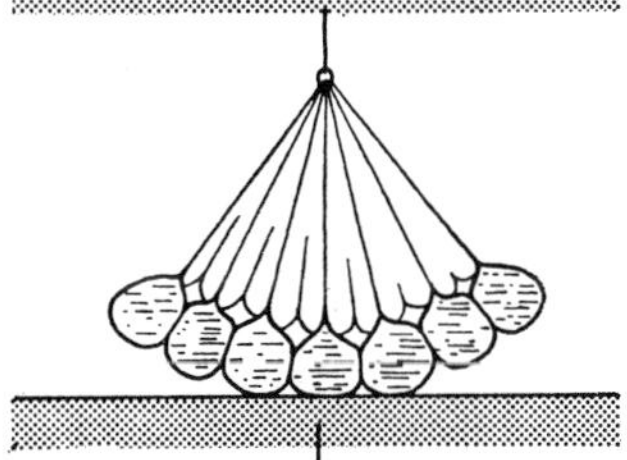

9

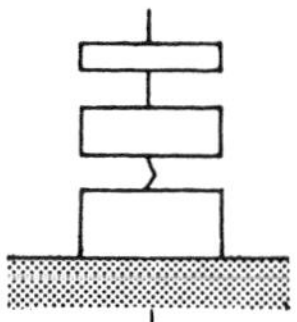

10

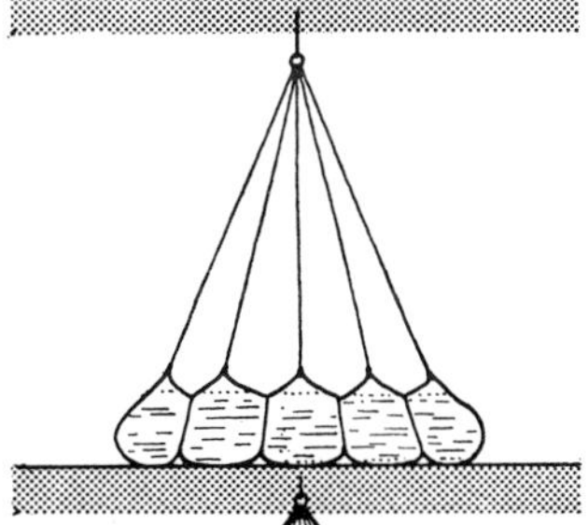

11

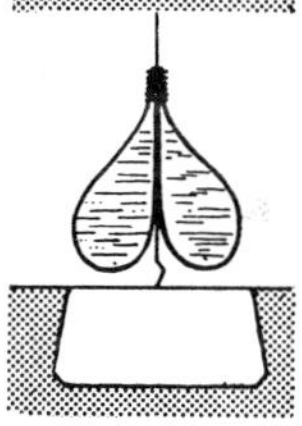

12

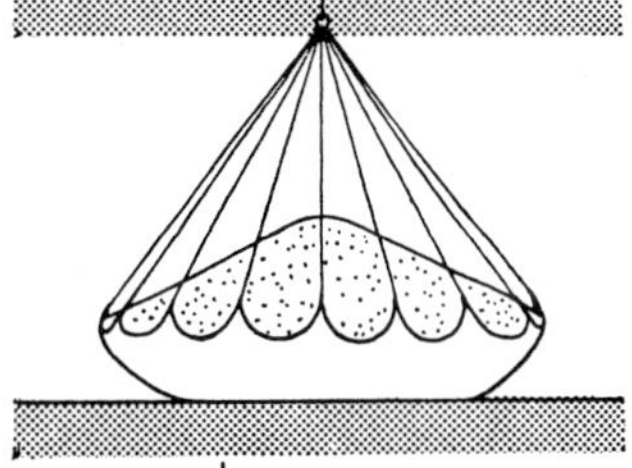

13

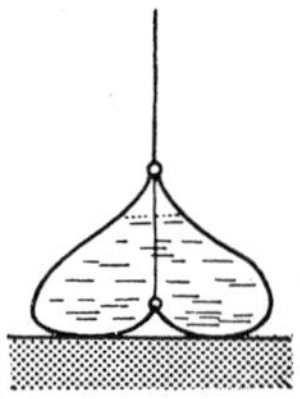

14

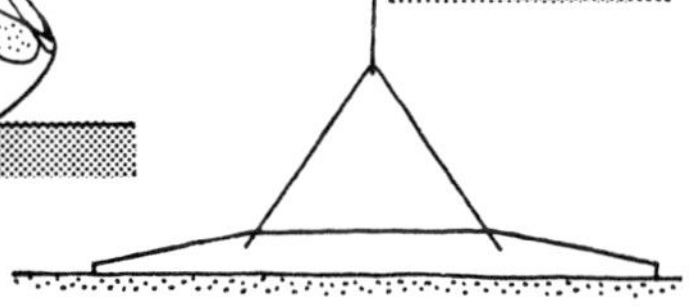

▲ 16

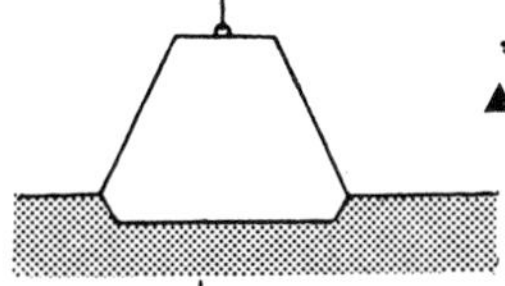

15

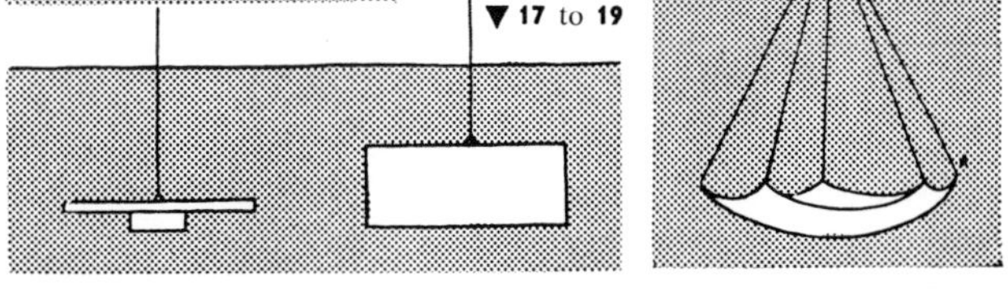

▼ 17 to 19

pends on their depth in the soil. The more deeply a plate is buried, the higher its resistance. This is, however, not always valid and depends greatly on the type of soil. The method of anchoring must be determined separately in each case.

Friction anchors should be as long as possible, have a rough surface, and be solidly entrenched. In most cases the major problem is how to bury the anchor deeply by simple means. This is not only of interest for large loads, where a relatively great technical effort is not prohibitive, but also for small loads, particularly in the case of prestressed, tension-loaded roofs, where the widely distributed membrane forces are transmitted from the roof directly to the foundations.

In the following, various methods of burying anchor plates or friction piles at great depths will be discussed.

Screw Anchors

Screw anchors are a very old type of anchor which is twisted into the soil like a carpenter's screw. Originally, screw anchors were probably used to drill holes in soft soils, the anchor being withdrawn after a few turns and the soil removed. Screw anchors make clean round holes which remain intact for fairly long periods even in soft soil.

For example, drills as shown in Fig. 6 are used mainly to prepare the foundations for small structures such as walls or tombstones, but also for floors and partitions of small detached houses standing on piles approximately 0.8 to 1.5 m deep which are tamped manually into the drilled holes with concrete.

It is known that such drills were used as permanent foundation anchors in the last century.

With all these screw anchors it is most important that the anchor penetrate the soil as smoothly as possible when being inserted. This is comparatively easy in finely granulated, cohesive, or sandy soils.

The anchors are usually attached to a torsion-resistant bar and are screwed in by hand. Machines are rarely used, since manual operation with a lever permits better control for the smooth penetration of the soil.

The screw plate of an anchor is cheap compared to the torsion-resistant bar, particularly when the anchor is inserted at great depth.

An early German patent (DRP 98037 by H. Bückling) envisaged attaching flexible tension anchors, e.g., round rods or cables, to the screw blade and cutting the whole into the soil by means of a retractable pipe which engages the screw blade with lugs, and which can be withdrawn after insertion of the anchor. Only the plate and flexible tension element remain in the ground; the latter must, of course, be protected against corrosion. Today, high-grade, heavily tinned steel cables with corrosion-proof safety jackets of bitumen or plastic are bedded in an oil bath; this guarantees long service life.

Screw anchors are extensively used in the United States (Figs. 7 to 9; photos by James R. Kearney Corp., St. Louis, Mo.). The anchors have cast-iron blades and threaded steel rods or commercial pipes which can be selected in accordance with the type of soil. In retractable anchors (Fig. 9) the shaft is permanently connected with the screw blade.

The load capacity of these commercial anchors with diameters of 10 to 35 cm, varies between 1 and 8 tons at a depth of 2 m. They are used mainly in guying masts of transmission lines.

Figures 10 to 15, p. 302, show various screw blades. The short blade (Fig. 10, p. 302), shown in plan Fig. 11, p. 302, is particularly suitable for permanent anchorings, whereas the convoluted screws (Figs. 12 to 15, p. 302) are better for temporary anchoring or drilling.

Some soils cannot be penetrated unless the anchor is withdrawn from time to time and the borehole cleared, particularly when the upper soil layers are very firm and contain much coarse gravel. In this case it may be necessary (Fig. 16, p. 302) to use the screw anchor as a drill and subsequently tamp the borehole carefully. The removed soil can be used for this purpose by tamping it in while moist (Fig. 17, p. 302). By using concrete the friction between anchor and ground is increased. A simple method to increase the ground resistance of an anchor drill is shown in Fig. 18, p. 302. After tamping the borehole with the removed soil, three or more piles are driven into the ground around the anchor. They compress the soil and increase the effective zone of the anchor.

Anchors consisting of convoluted bands or sharp profiles are very simple and have been known for a long time. They are driven in by blows and turn in the ground due to their shape. It is known that little friction exists between straight piles and the soil, especially when they are loosened by transverse blows.

Convoluted piles (Fig. 19, p. 302) have high resistance, if they can be prevented from turning out. When a pair of such piles is connected by a yoke (Fig. 20, p. 302), they can take up considerable loads, since the inclined planes of the thread cause considerable friction.

The surfaces of the flanges must be sufficiently large, and the piles must have adequate resistance to buckling while being driven. This is guaranteed by the profiles shown in Figs. 23 to 28 on p. 302.

Convoluted piles can take up greater forces when these act at slight angles to the long axis of the piles, particularly if the latter are free to rotate in the ground (Fig. 22, p. 302).

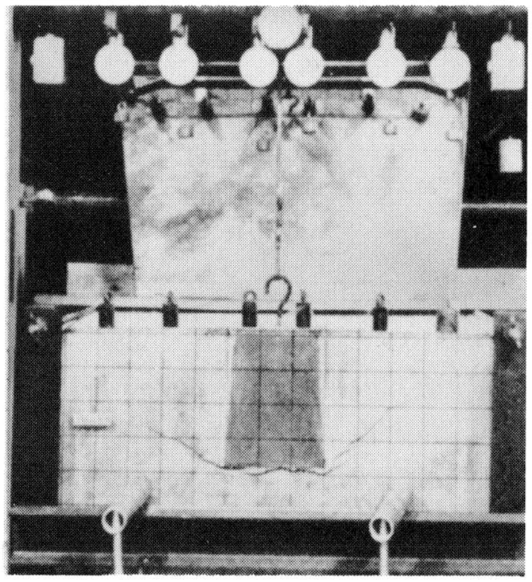

1

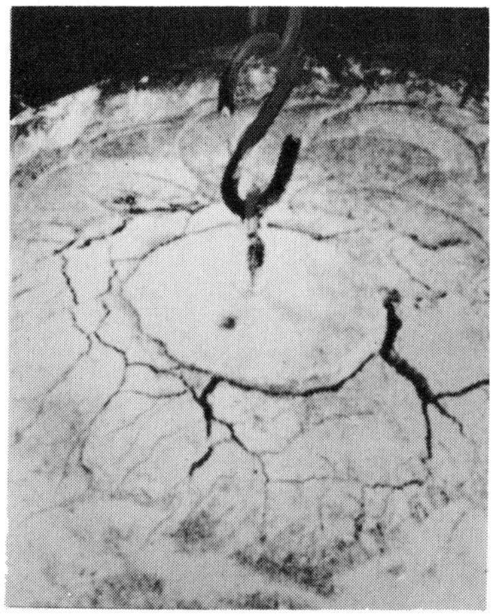

4

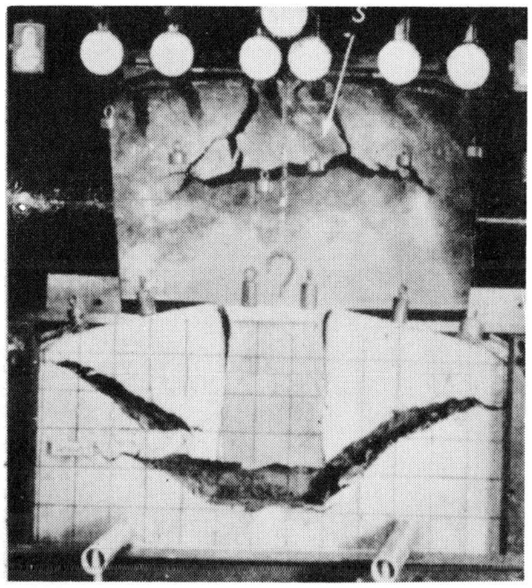

2 ▲ ▼ 3

5 ▲ ▼ 6

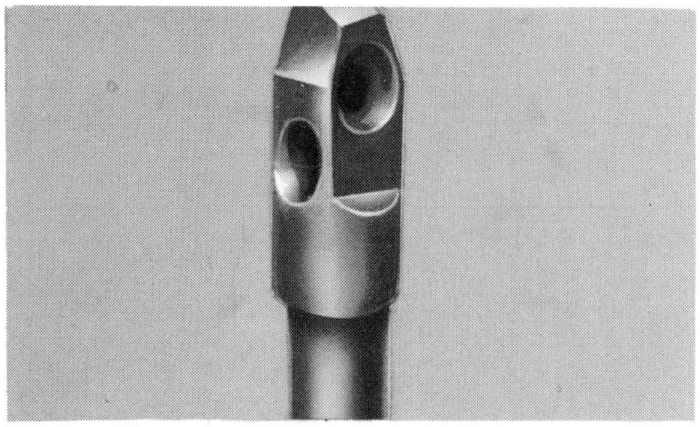

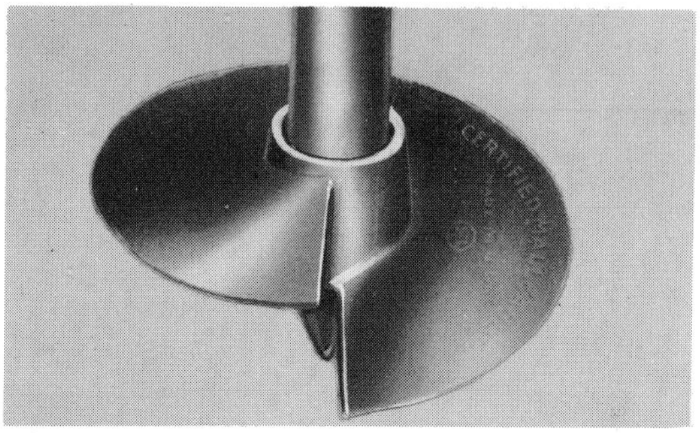

7 ▲

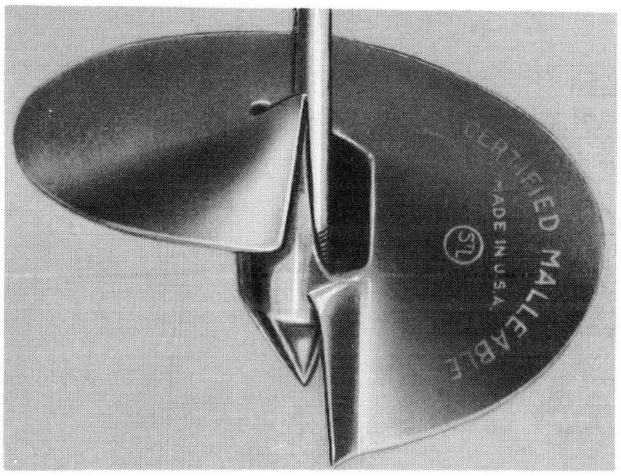

8 ▲ ▼ 9

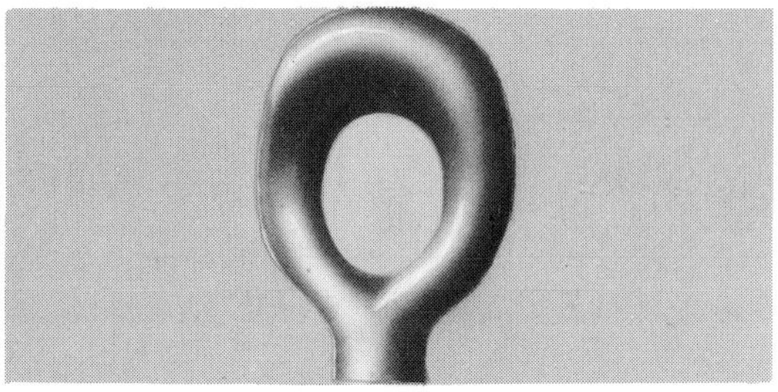

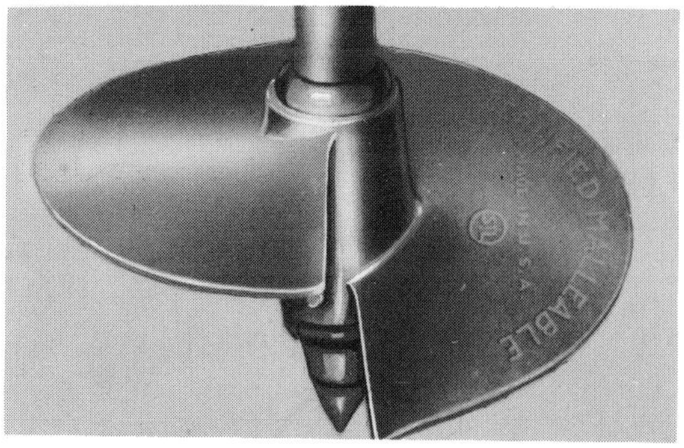

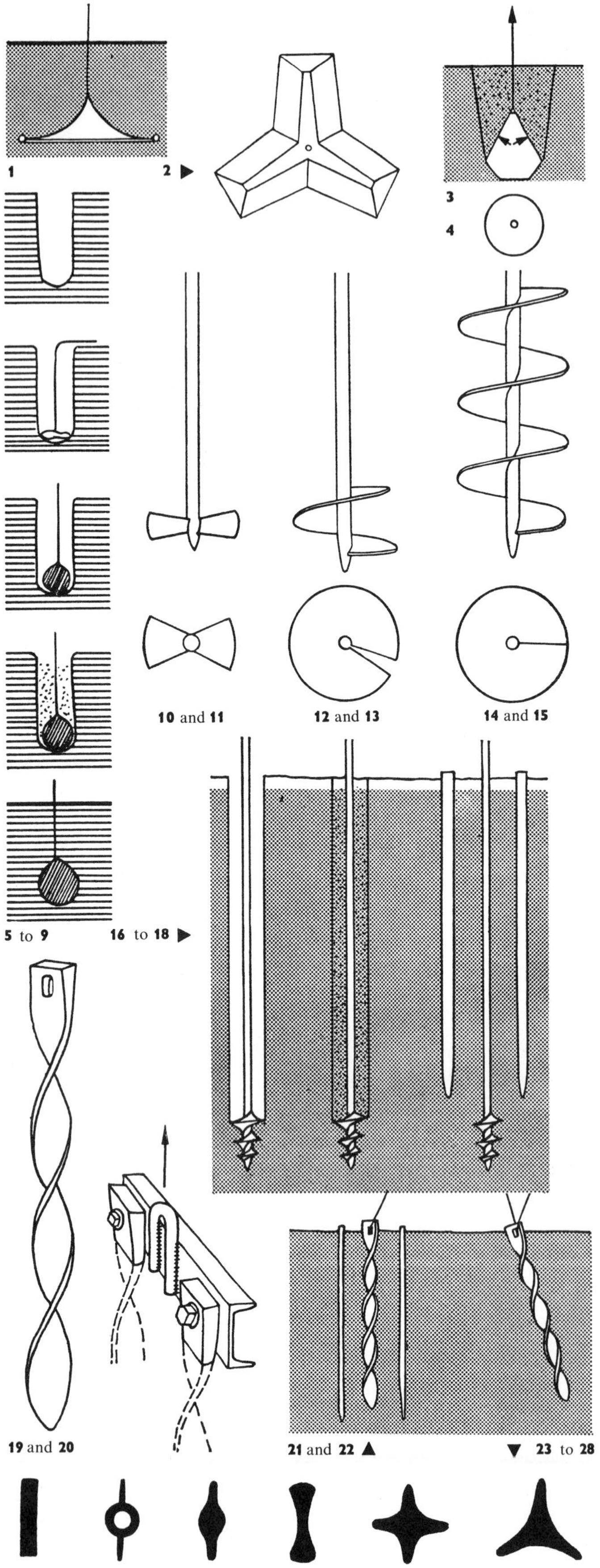

So-called "dummy piles" can also be driven in around convoluted piles (Fig. 21). They greatly increase soil packing and compression and thus the resistance of the pile.

Expanding Anchors

Expanding anchors are designed on the principle of harpoons. Slender while being driven in (Fig. 29), they spread automatically (Fig. 30) when pulled back; their resistance is therefore high. Harpoon anchors are generally "lost anchors" which can rarely be recovered undamaged, especially if they have no hinges and their surface is bent. Since considerable moments may act on the anchor plate, the tip and the zone of bending must be sufficiently strong (Fig. 33).

Expanding plates may also be attached to the shaft of a pile (Figs. 31 and 32). This may be necessary when the expanding anchor plates are not very wide. Narrow expanding plates make a slender pile, but their load-carrying capacity is small. It can be considerably increased by staggering the expanding surfaces along and around the axis.

A large number of expanding steel strips are welded to the anchor shown in Figs. 35 and 36. The various phases of the anchoring process are shown in Fig. 34.

Figures 21 to 25 on p. 305 (photos by James R. Kearney Corp., St. Louis) show a commercially available American expanding anchor that is widely used for the foundations of poles for overhead transmission lines.

To insert these anchors, a hole must first be made in the ground, using a spiral drill. The anchor is then introduced and expanded. It can be seen in Fig. 21, p. 305, that the anchor consists of an anchor plate approximately equal in diameter to the borehole, a screwed-on tension rod, and from two to four anchor plates folded above the round plate and hinged to each other. The hinge is struck by a pipe or special tool surrounding the tension rod. The anchor plates then spread and penetrate into the soil until they assume the position shown in Fig. 24, p. 305. The borehole is then filled. All components are of cast iron. Sheet metal anchors without hinges, whose anchor plates bend upwards, are also available, (Fig. 23, p. 305).

A three-plate anchor is shown in Fig. 25 on the same page. Figure 22, p. 305, shows a four-plate anchor when closed, and Fig. 23, p. 305, when expanded.

The four-plate anchor, which fits into a borehole approximately 25 cm in diameter and has an expanded surface of about 1,200 cm^2, is nominally a 9.5-ton anchor. Its resistance in sand is given as 6 tons, in sandy clay as 8 tons, and in very hard soil cover, as 15 tons.

These anchors are moderately priced and can be driven by one worker in a short time. Consequently, their cost, including assembly, is less than that of a foundation designed to take up compressive forces of equal magnitude. The low price is due to mass-production methods.

In the anchor needle* with expanding traction plates shown in Fig. 38, the plates lie close against the shaft while the anchor is being driven. They are positively connected with the shaft at their lower and upper ends. The lower connection, which consists of wires or cables and is very short, is located near the point of the needle. The upper connection is longer and leads from the end of the plate to a pipe which surrounds the anchor needle. When rammed in, the plates (dotted lines in Fig. 38) lie close to the shaft. If the pipe is pushed down, the plates expand when the needle is pulled back. This design permits the traction plates to turn downward (Fig. 39), if further displacement of the pipe in relation to the needle is possible. This type of expanding anchor can easily be recovered after use.

A similar design* (Fig. 37) uses plates of spring steel which are expanded by pushing the pipe down along the shaft; they are retractable.

For the sake of completeness, a further type of anchor needle with expanding plates deserves mention. It consists of the actual needle body formed of a strong pipe to which a tube or a bent metal plate is secured by several heavy arms (Figs. 1 and 2, p. 304). After being driven in, a pull on the anchor (Fig. 3 and 4, p. 304) causes the pressure element of the tube to be forced against the ground, thereby increasing its resistance.

Anchor needles with "lost" tips* also belong to this group. Figures 5 and 6, p. 304, show an explosive needle before and after firing. It consists of a pipe of very tough steel with a massive point which is expanded by a small explosive charge.

The anchor needle shown in Figs. 7 and 8, p. 304, is of similar design. It is expanded by compressed air, water, or cement mortar at internal pressures of 10 to 150 atmospheres. The pipe jacket near the tip is made of thin tough metal or plastic and expanded by internal pressure.

In very soft soils that show little resistance it is necessary to provide large traction surfaces at great depths.

Parachute-like anchors* are suitable in such cases. A steel tube is first driven into the ground (Fig. 9, p. 304) and the anchor then introduced (Fig. 10, p. 304). Next, the steel tube is withdrawn (Fig. 11, p. 304). If the anchor cable is now pulled (Fig. 12, p. 304) the parachute opens in the soil. When expanded it is star-shaped (Fig. 13, p. 304). The ribs of these anchors consist of highly elastic spring-steel wires; the traction surfaces consist of thin steel nets with narrow mesh or of a net with plastic fabric between the meshes. All steel parts are stainless or highly corrosion-proofed, e.g., by tough plastic jackets. Such anchors are best used below groundwater level where they are less subject to corrosion.

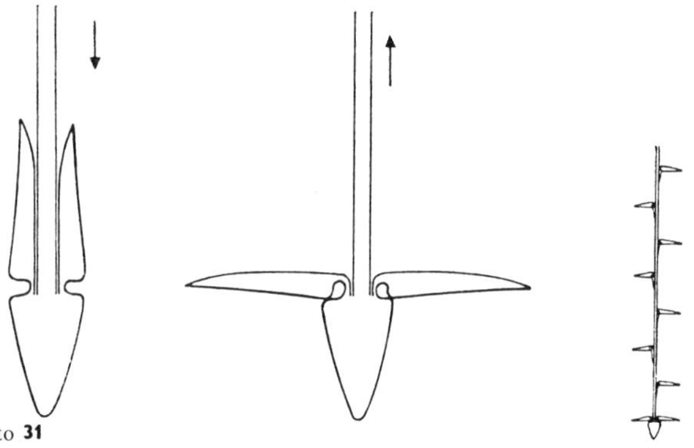

29 to 31

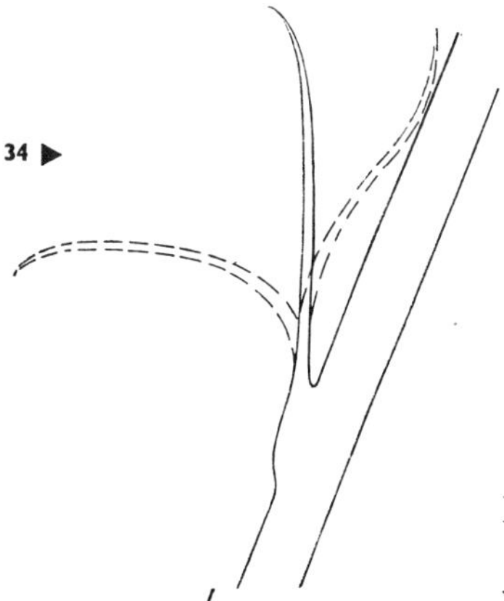

34 ▶

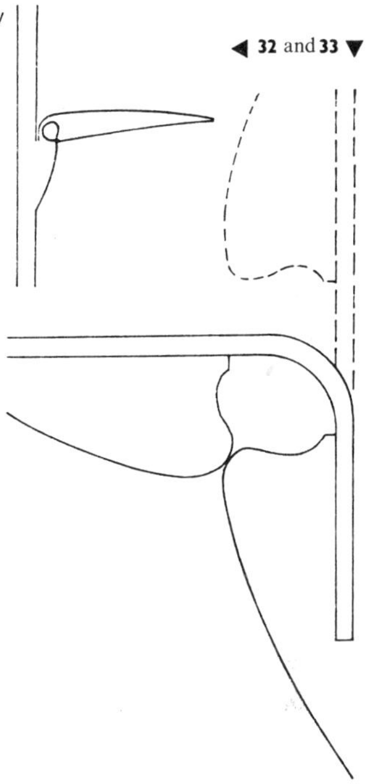

◀ 32 and 33 ▼

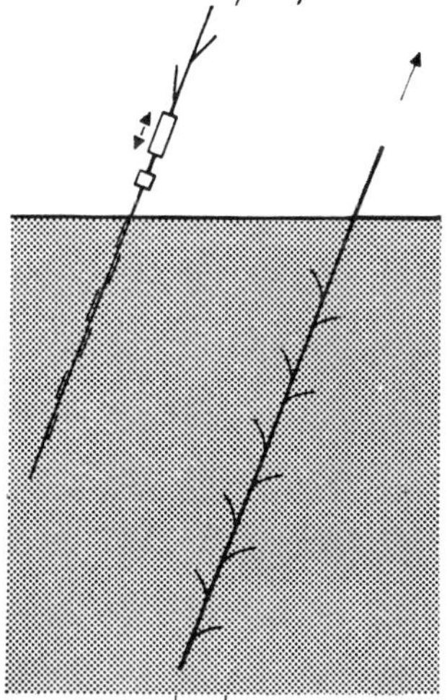

35 and 36

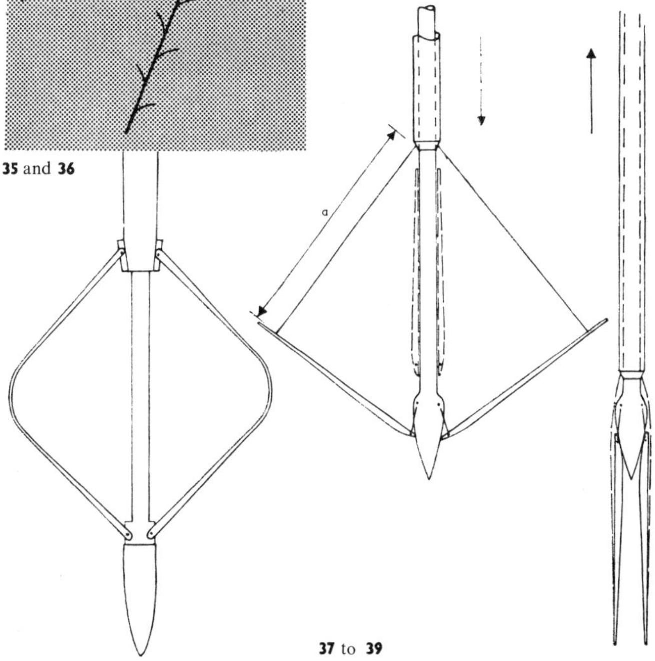

37 to 39

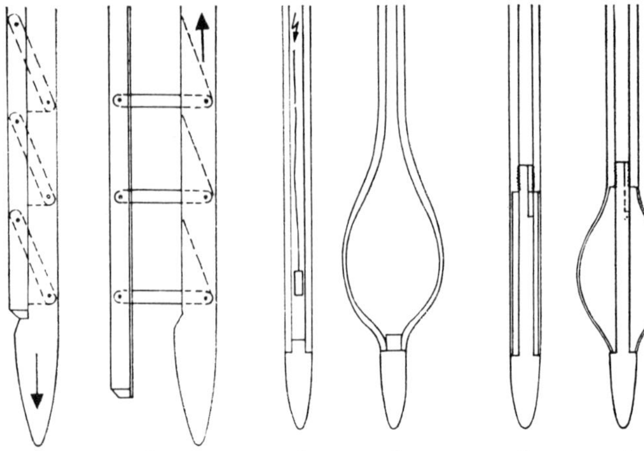

1 3 5 6 7 8

2 and 4

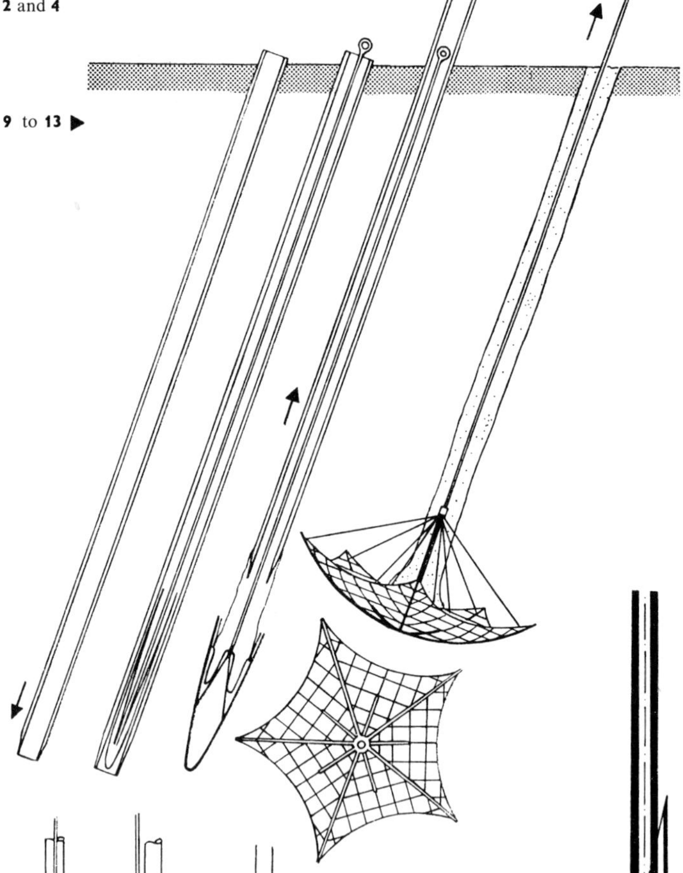

9 to 13 ▶

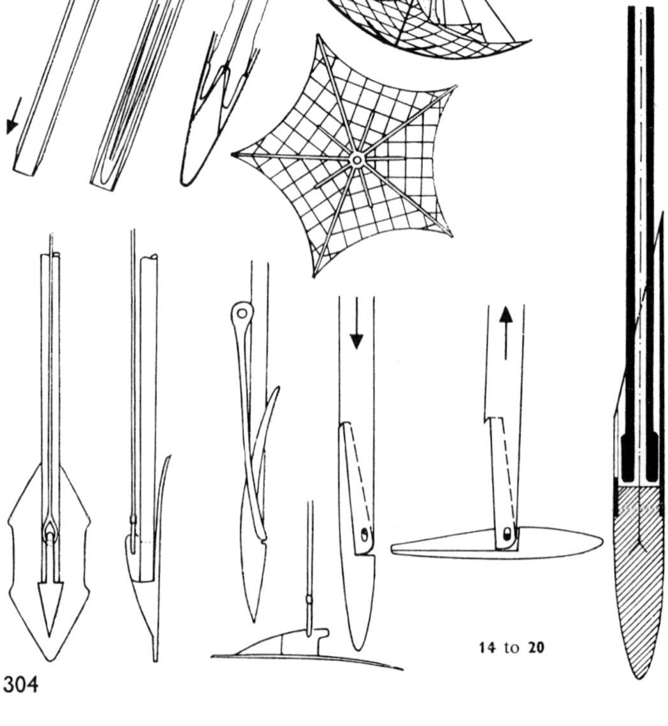

14 to 20

There are also piles with bordered footings, especially the Lorenz pile, which are similar to an expanding anchor. These devices were developed as compression piles to provide a larger support surface. Experience showed that they are also able to take up considerable tensile loads. The widening causes conical compression of the soil when the pile is pulled. This imparts a high tensile-load-carrying capacity to the piles.

Generally, a hole is drilled and the space for the footing cut out of the ground with a flat steel loop. The cavity is lined with steel. For tension anchorings a steel cable with unspliced ends is introduced. The hollow space is then tamped with concrete.

Tension pilings with deeply buried widened footings have frequently been used to guy radio masts and anchor quay walls (see C. F. Kohlbrunner, Paris: *Verankerungen im Baugrund,* from the Main Report to the Second International Congress for Bridge Building and Construction, Berlin 1936).

Folding Anchors

Folding anchors appear to have a long history. After the Development Center for Lightweight Construction in Berlin had, during 1956-8, perfected the folding anchors shown in Figs. 9 to 16, p. 307, it was discovered that a number of US patents covered such devices. Jacob Wilcox, of Ohio, U.S.A., applied for patents for such anchors in 1910 and 1916 (US patents 972306 and 1178282), and Louis Flateau of St. Louis, Mo., U.S.A., in 1917 (US patent 1232266).

These devices had anchor plates which were driven into the ground by tubes and then unfolded by means of round rods.

The first anchor invented by Jacob Wilcox is shown in the closed state while being driven in in Figs. 14 and 15, and opened in Fig. 16. The anchor is driven by means of a rod and then opened.

Figure 17 shows a later design developed by Wilcox in 1916. The action of folding anchors was demonstrated by experiments* performed at the Development Center for Lightweight Construction, Berlin.

Figures 18 and 19 show a rod attached to a folding tip which opens when the rod is pulled. The rod is rammed into the ground. The anchor tip is secured to the rod in a slot and cannot pivot until the rod is pulled. It is a known fact that plates secured at the center assume positions normal to the direction of motion both in gases and liquids as well as in plastic, earthy media.

Another type of anchor (Fig. 20) investigated by the Center is easy to make. The tip of the rod is driven in with a pipe through which a cable is drawn; this is attached to the tip. The latter has a piece of tubing as an extension. After being driven in, the pipe used for this purpose can be withdrawn and only the cable and the tip remain in the ground. When the cable is tightened the tip assumes a transverse position.

Experiments showed that because of safety considerations it is important to use two cables instead of one cable or tension element. The installation of an anchor plate with two cables is shown in Figs. 9 to 13 on p. 307. An anchor plate with rounded edges is slid into a bore hole, as seen from two sides in Figs. 9 and 10 on p. 307. When the lower cable is tightened, the upper end of the anchor plate begins to penetrate the soil (Fig. 12, p. 307) until the position of the plate is transverse. Markings at the ends of the cables allow the position of the plate in the ground to be ascertained.

An anchor plate can also be driven in directly. For this purpose a pipe was fitted over the end of an anchor plate (Figs. 14 and 15, p. 307) so that the plate formed the tip of a pile. In the two views the cables are represented by broken lines. When the anchor plate has reached the required depth the fitted pipe is removed and the cables tightened as previously described, so as to set the plate transversely.

Another type (Fig. 16, p. 307) is designed according to the same principle as the anchor plate with a single cable shown in Fig. 20.

Photos 1 to 8 on p. 306 were taken behind a glass wall and show an experiment with an anchor plate of the type shown in Figs. 14 and 15 on p. 307. In Fig. 1 on p. 306 the anchor (Figs. 26 to 28) has already been driven and the pipe withdrawn. In Fig. 2 of the same page the lower cable is being tightened. In Fig. 3 the plate begins to assume a transverse position. In Fig. 4 the transverse position is almost reached. The original borehole has filled up and a cavity has formed beneath the anchor plate. The resistance attains a maximum in a position between those shown in Figs. 4 and 5, p. 306. The anchor is loaded till the ground breaks up; this has already taken place in Fig. 5, p. 306. The sliding-out is clearly visible in Fig. 6. The anchor forces the soil out over an area corresponding to its dimensions. Upon further pulling (Figs. 7 and 8, p. 306), the soil is ejected.

Such an anchor can be easily recovered by pulling on one cable and releasing the other (Figs. 17 to 19). After the anchor has assumed the transverse position it is best to withdraw the anchor with the tip pointing upward (Fig. 19, p. 307), to ensure the lowest possible resistance of the soil.

A small and very simple instrument was developed for tightening such anchors* (Fig. 20, p. 307). It consists of an ordinary oil pressure cylinder and a spindle mounted above the borehole on two thick planks. A short crossbar connects press and spindle. The cables are turned several times around this bar and restrained by hand. Tightening either one or both cables can thus be accomplished in one motion and the tension controlled. Each anchor is not merely brought into the correct position, but its resistance in the soil is also tested.

21 to 23

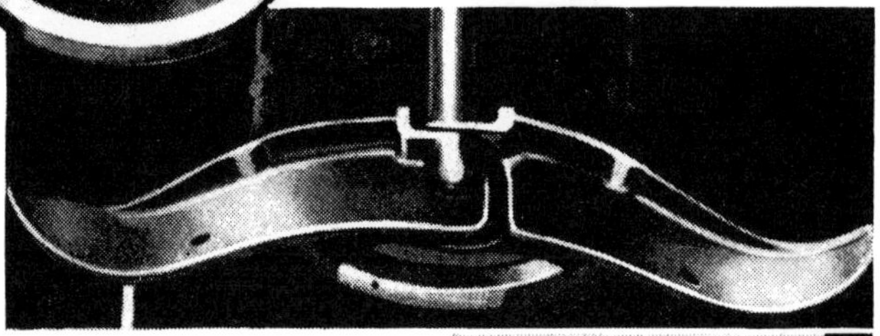

24 ▲

26 ▶

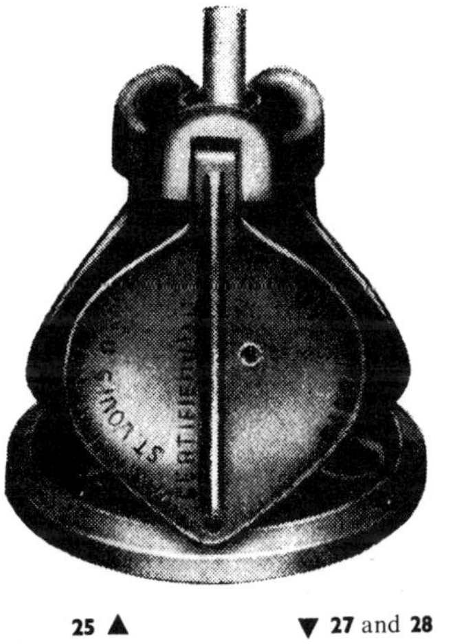

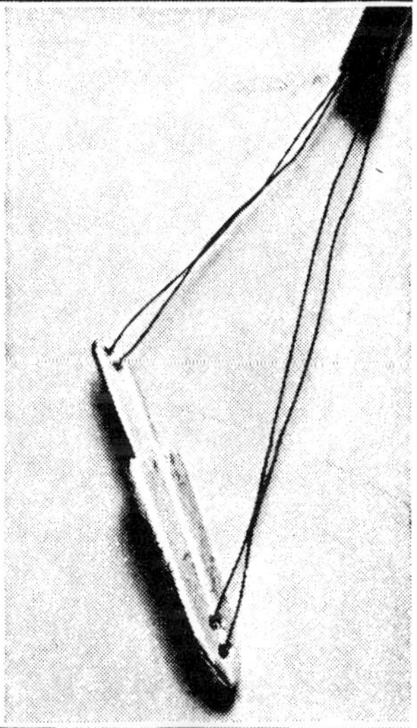

25 ▲

▼ 27 and 28

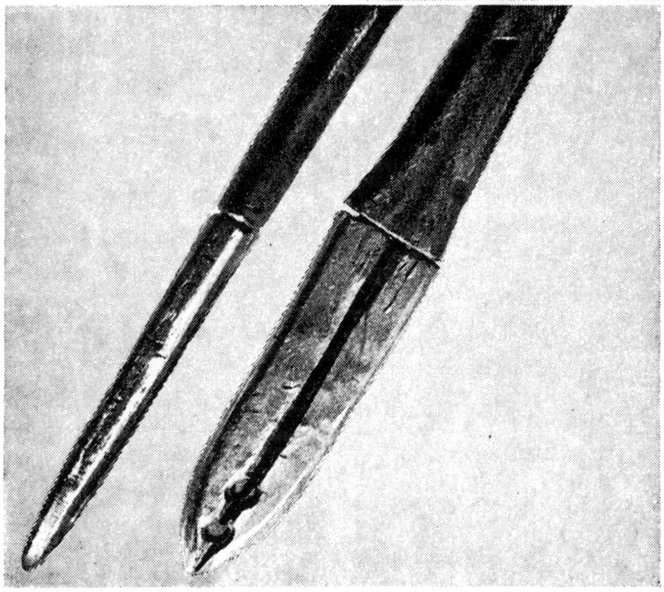

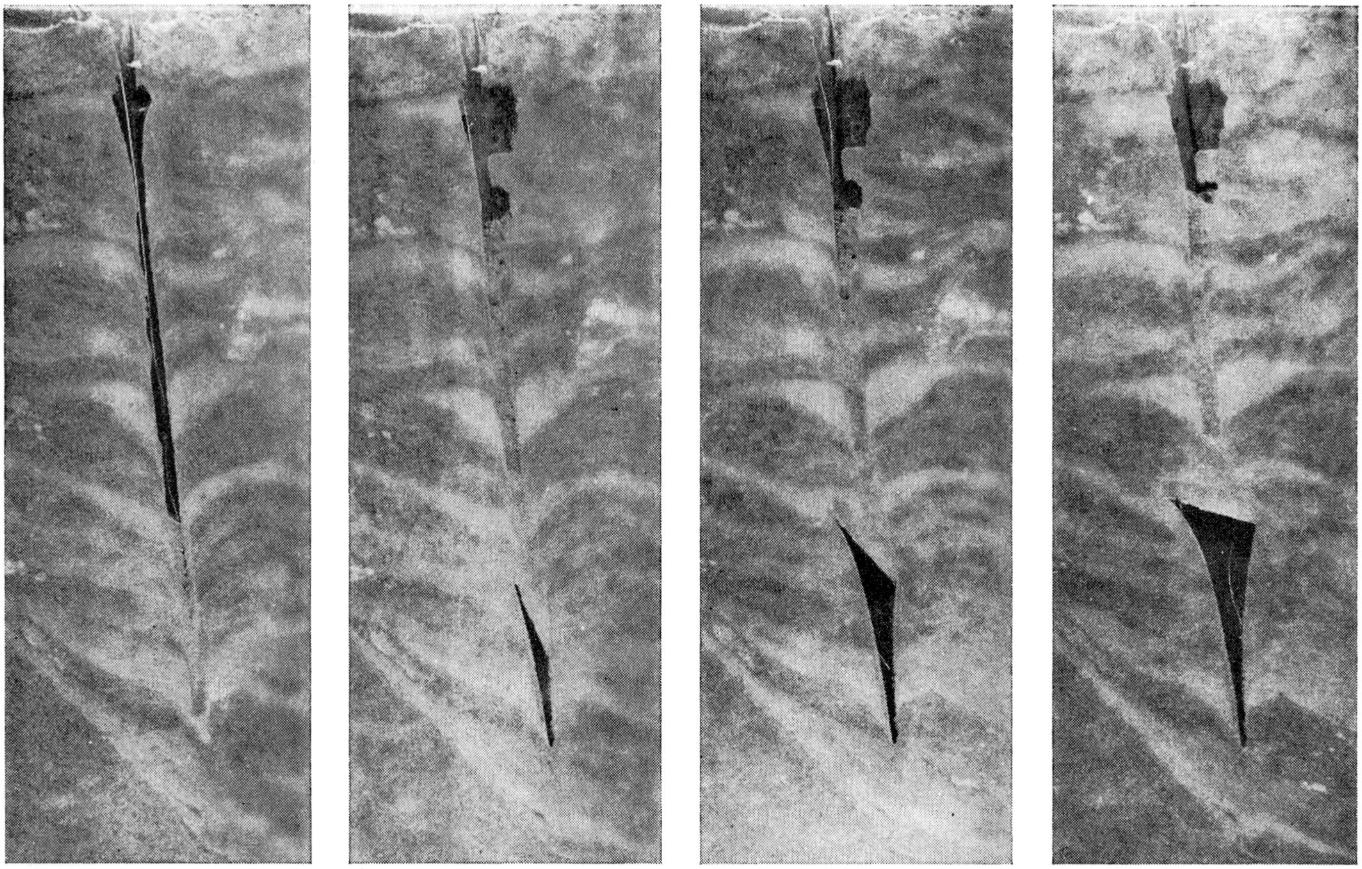

1 to **4** ▲ ▼ **5** to **8**

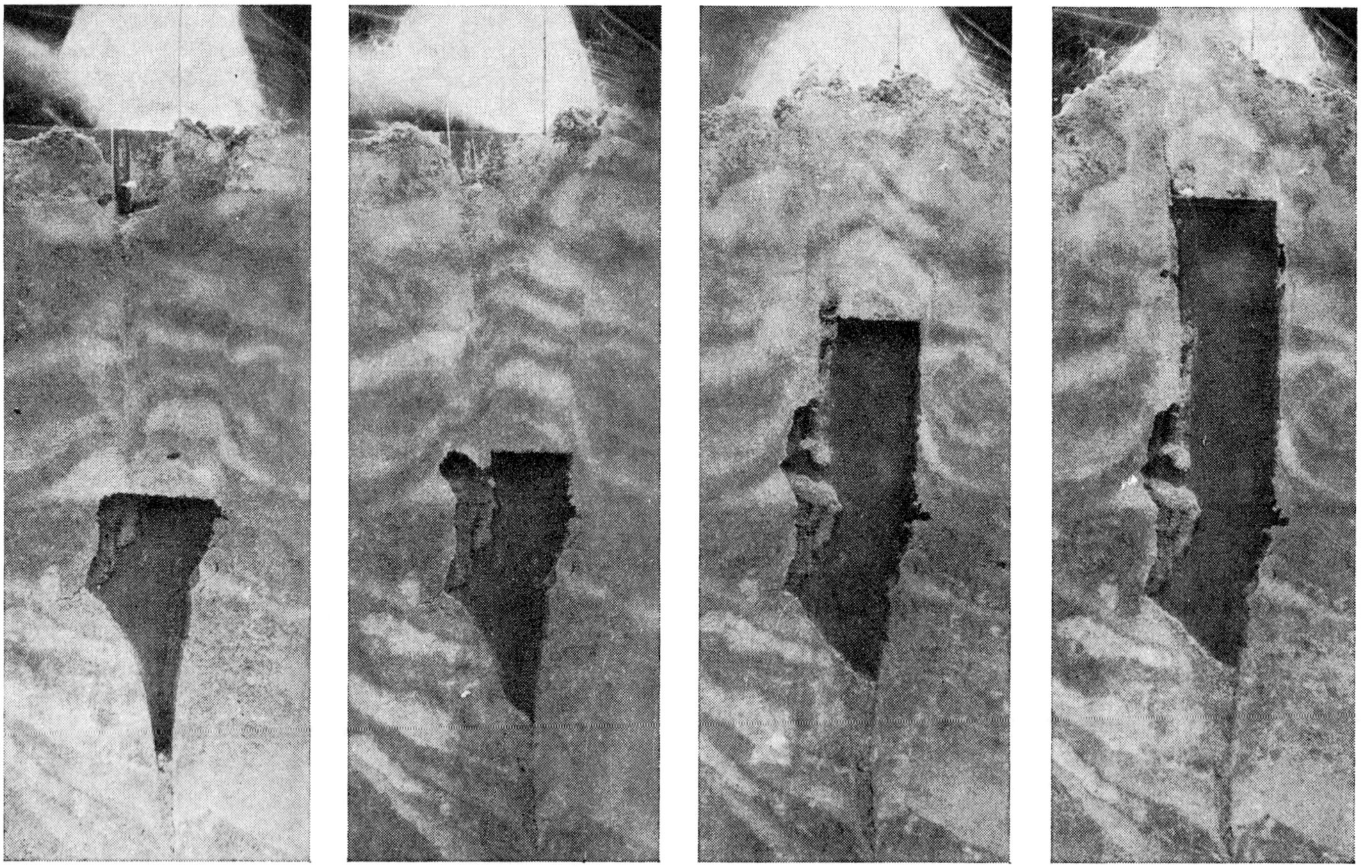

The design shown in Figs. 21 and 22 is similar. The hydraulic press is located exactly above the borehole in a crossbar frame. The surrounding foundation should be disturbed as little as possible when introducing the anchor. Any loosening of previously undisturbed soil causes a considerable reduction in its resistance.

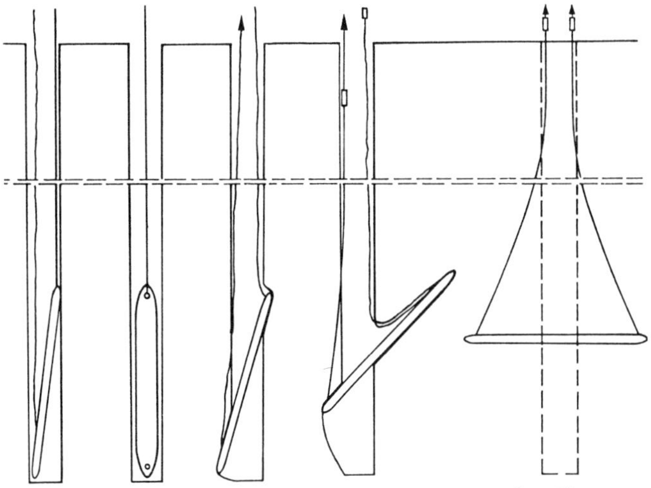

9 to 13

Tension Anchoring for Vertical Pull in Hard Ground

Solid rock is admirably suited to taking up high and even very high tensile loads. Eyebolts and threaded bolts (Figs. 2 and 3, p. 308) have been used for anchoring in solid rock for ages. A hole is made which is either wider at the bottom than at the top, or which has especially roughened sides. The steel or copper bolts are split or shaped like rag bolts. Cement mortar is used to tamp the hole. Lead was often used in the past; it was well forced in after cooling in order to fill the fissures between filler and rock after shrinkage of the metal. The best fillers are those which do not shrink but swell upon becoming solidified, e.g., plaster, which is an excellent filler for dry sites, especially covered spaces. Expanding cement has a similar effect in open-air construction.

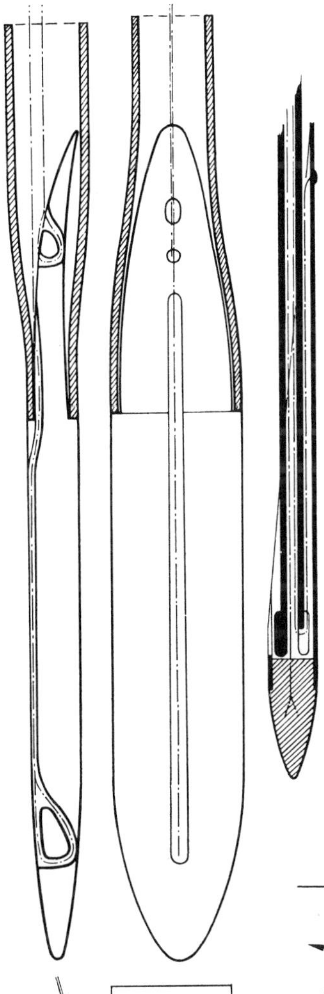

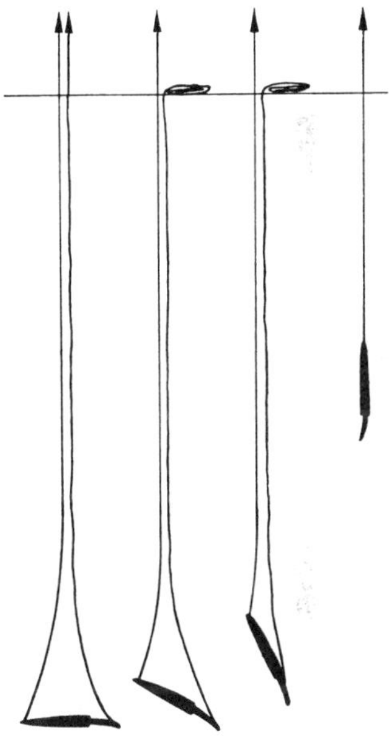

14 to 19

An old type of recoverable anchor, known as "wolf" (Fig. 1, p. 308) consists of two wedges and a center piece. The wedges are introduced separately into a swallow-tail-shaped hole in the rock and expanded by means of the center piece. This type of anchor is often employed to lift large stones used in construction. Cables passing around the stones, which often damage the smooth hewn edges and surfaces, are then unnecessary.

▼ 20

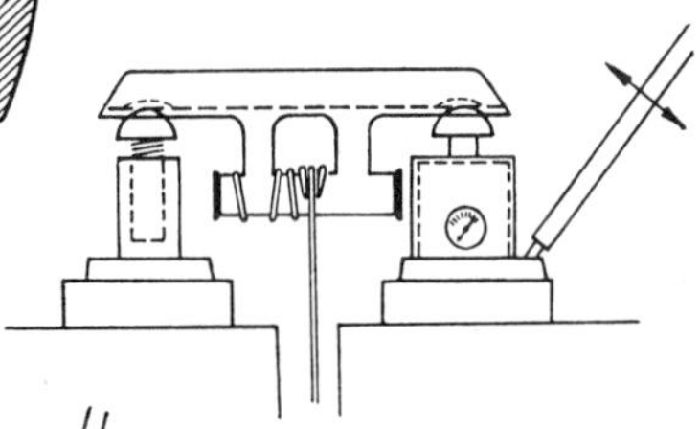

The anchoring of cables in boreholes is of great importance for structures under high tensile loads (Fig. 4, p. 308). The cable is tied off at intervals and introduced into the hole where it fans out slightly due to its own weight. The hole is then filled with cement mortar under high pressure. If the actual anchoring point of the cable is to be located at a very great depth, the upper part of the cable is covered with a substance which prevents direct contact between cable and concrete. For this purpose a jacket of bitumen seems to work best.

The highest loads known today to have been taken up by tamped cable anchors were over 1,000 tons. These anchorings were used several decades ago by M. Coyne of Paris for a high gravity dam at Oued Mékerra in Algeria. Coyne's task was to increase the height of the old dam and protect it against overturning. He drove boreholes through the old dam deep into the sandstone foundations and introduced cables consisting of 630 galvanized steel wires 5 mm in diameter (Fig. 5, p. 308). Each cable had a diameter of 15 cm, the mean diameter of the wrapped cable being 20 cm. The cables were coated with Flintkote and wrapped in sailcloth which was saturated with Flintkote, and bound fast with an aloe rope.

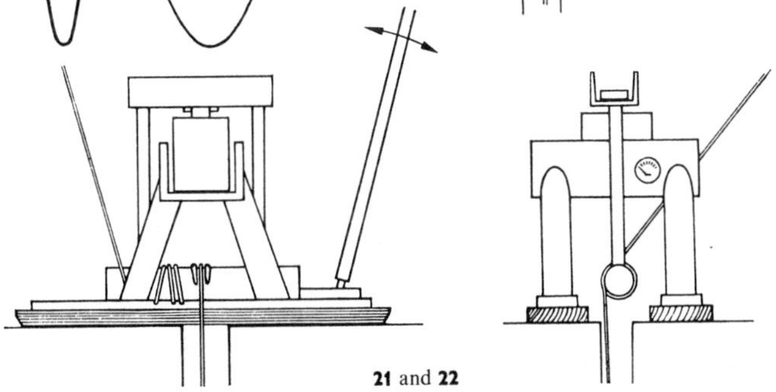

21 and 22

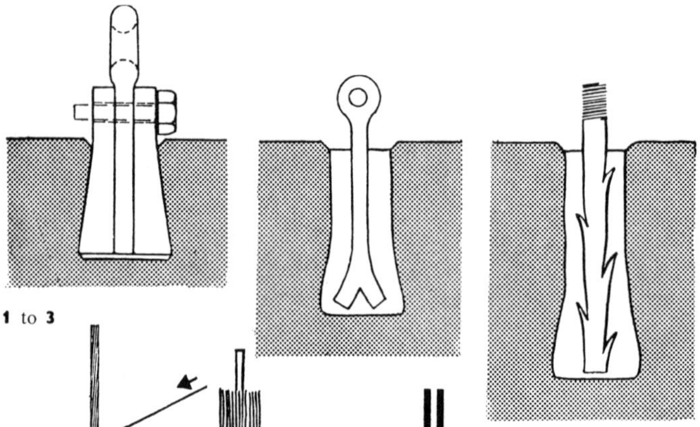

1 to **3**

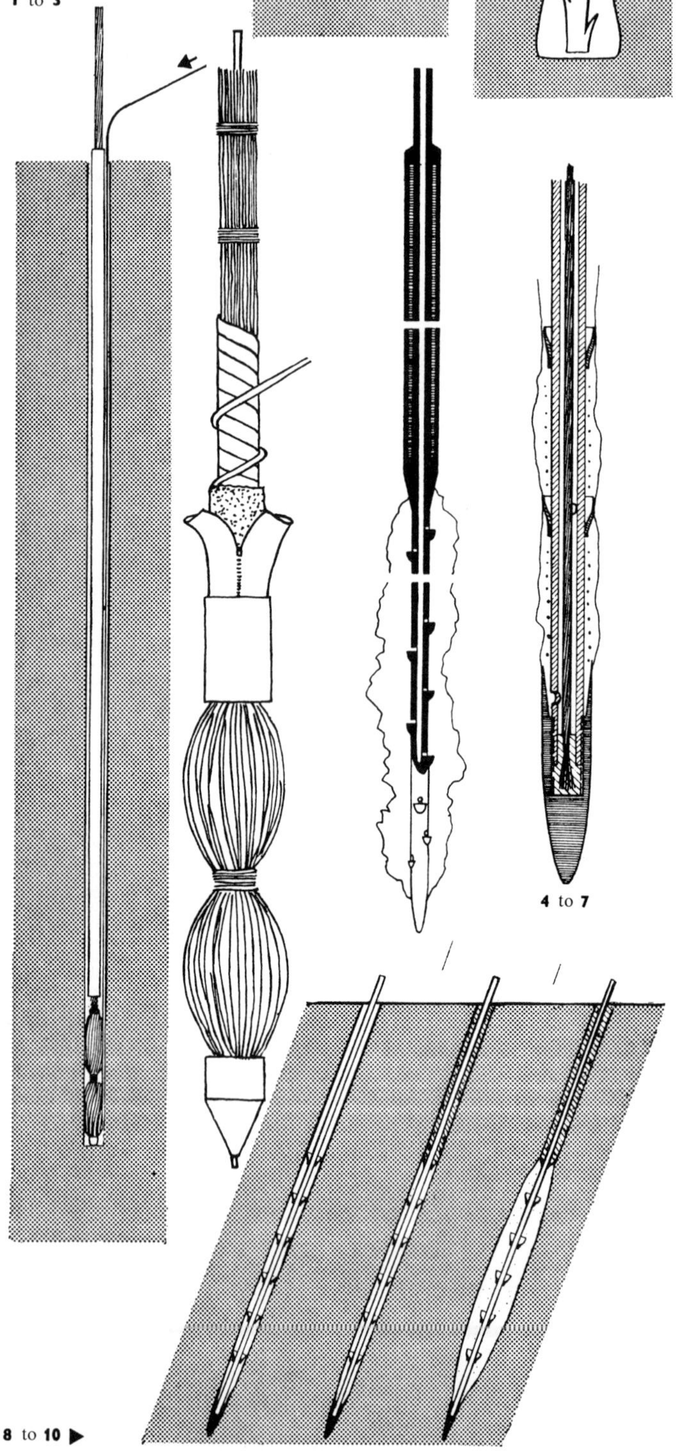

4 to **7**

8 to **10** ▶

The interstices of the aloe rope were filled with a plastic layer of fat and bitumen, all being covered with a sailcloth sheath closed by a zip fastener. The sailcloth sheath was then covered with mortar. At its lowest point the cable spread out like a fan. The injection pipe was located in the center of the cable, with its discharge opening at the lowest point. The injection mass was thus pressed upward from the bottom. M. Coyne reported on this to the Second International Congress for Bridge Building and Construction in 1936, in a lecture entitled *Anwendung der Vorspannung auf Staumauern* (published by Wilhelm Ernst & Sohn, Berlin 1938).

Cables can also be safely anchored in less solid rock. If, for example, a cable is led into a deep borehole in medium-strength granular soil, it can be grouted in the same way as in solid rock. The grouting mass must be firmly consolidated with the ground by tamping.

Methods like those which have been used for many years for pile foundations taking up compressive loads can be employed here: concrete is tamped into the drilling or ramming pipe while the latter is being withdrawn; the concrete is pressed against the foundations and forms a very rough surface. The pile cross sections will then be much larger in soft than in more solid layers. Such pressure piles, used until now for compressive loads, are reinforced with structural steel in order to provide resistance against compression and buckling. If a cable is anchored to the foot of the pile, Coyne's method can be used whereby the cable is anchored only at the foot, the remainder of the cable being prevented, by means of lubricants, from coming into direct contact with the concrete.

It is advisable to prestress the concrete of a pile by means of the cable in such a way that even at the maximum cable tension the concrete itself is not under tension and thus remains free of fissures. This is possible if the cable is everywhere in contact with the concrete. In order to tense a cable in prestressed-concrete structures, it is usually surrounded by a pipe of sheet metal or steel. When the concrete has hardened the cable is pretensioned by means of hydraulic presses, the concrete being thus precompressed; the hollow space is then filled with liquid cement. To ensure proper venting this is best done through another channel from below.

Anchor Needles

The necessity of developing a high-capacity anchoring for suspended roofs was mentioned in *Das hängende Dach* (Bauwelt Verlag, Berlin 1954) and in *Deutscher Baumarkt,* issue 26 of 24 June, 1954, *Das hängende Dach, eine Stahlbauweise*. This is of particular importance when highly stressed roofs extend directly to the foundations where large tensile forces must be taken up at many points.

This led to the development of anchor needles in which thin steel pipes, perforated at the tip, are driven into the ground. Through these pipes cement mortar or other materials which harden or petrify the soil are injected, i.e., the soil is chemically consolidated. In this way a mantle of concrete or petrified soil is formed around the anchor needle in which the roughened surface of the latter is firmly retained.

It has been proved that a flexible but highly tension-resistant needle of this type can take up considerable forces after being consolidated. The anchor needle* shown in Fig. 6 is a steel pipe with an external diameter of approximately 25 mm and a wall thickness of 8 mm. At the lower end the pipe is provided with holes 3 mm in diameter, which are protected against clogging by protruding lugs. After injection these lugs effect a stronger bond with the grouting mass. The upper part of the steel needle is widened in order to prevent extrusion of the grouting mass and to facilitate expansion of the steel in soil layers which do not carry loads.

A thin and deformable sheet-metal jacket is therefore fitted over the actual tension-loaded steel pipe and the interspace filled with bitumen. This also increases the corrosion resistance of the steel, especially in soil above ground-water level.

In another type of anchor needle* (Fig. 7), a steel pipe is attached to the hard steel tip of the needle. This pipe has an external diameter of approximately 60 mm and is used to drive the needle into the ground. In order to increase consolidation with the grouting mass and leave the borehole open, the steel pipe is wound with wire and in special cases can also be provided with spaced collars. The tension cable is led through the steel pipe and cast in the tip. After the needle is driven in (Fig. 8), the upper end of the hole is closed by tamping concrete, soil, or a special injection mass which only fills the upper end (Fig. 9). The space at the lower end of the needle is then filled at very high pressure to ensure that the ground is strongly compressed or even forced back by the injection mass (Fig. 10). Blocking the space between the needle and the ground is necessary if high pressures are to be attained at the lower end of the needle. Otherwise the injection mass or even the needle itself might be ejected upward; under certain circumstances this could occur at ballistic velocities.

When driving thin injection needles, that are between 10 to 25 m in length and have hardly any resistance to buckling, other methods must be used. Such a needle should not be driven at its end, but always directly above the foundations. Clamping jaws are attached to the needle and the latter is used as a guide for a pipe rammer (Fig. 15).

Anchor needles can also be introduced with a jet stream, especially in sandy soils. For example, thin-walled steel pipes 25 to 50 mm in diameter can be pushed into the soil by hand, under high water pressure. Frequently, the pressure of the local water supply is sufficient for this purpose. Of course, needles can also be driven in with pneumatic drills; this method is effective for joining short

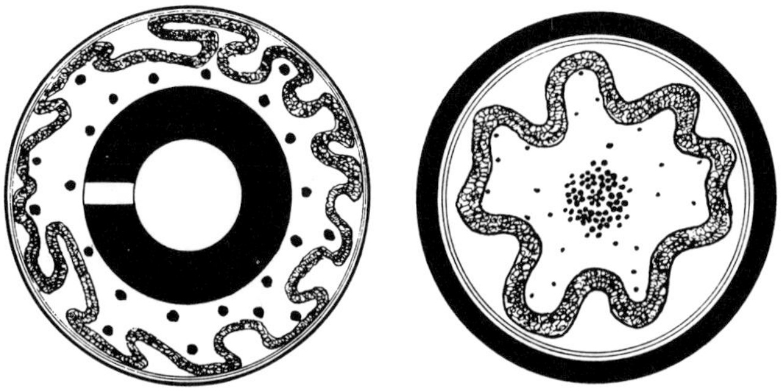

11 and **12** ▲

13 to **15** ▶

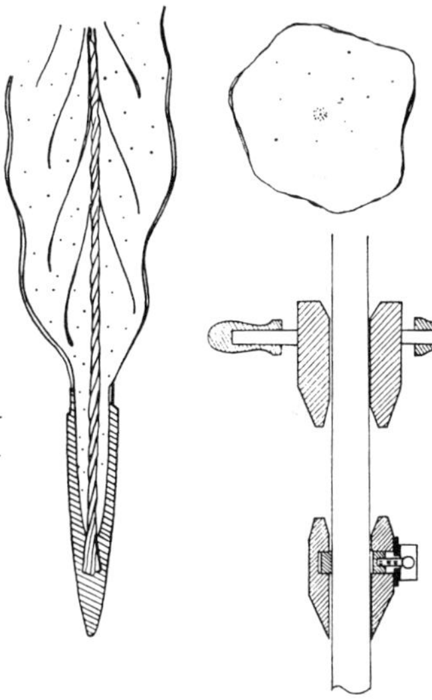

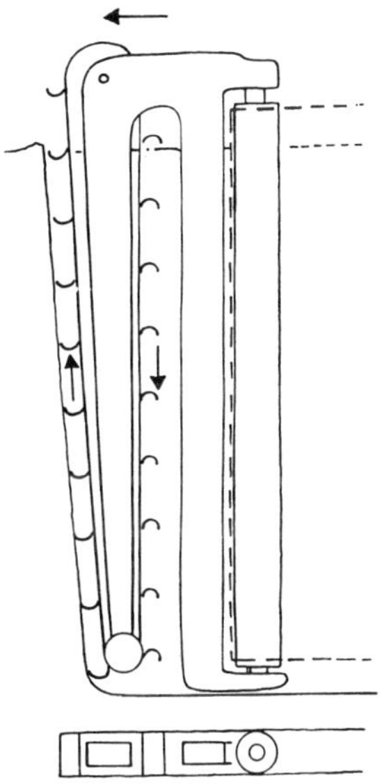

17 and **18** ▲

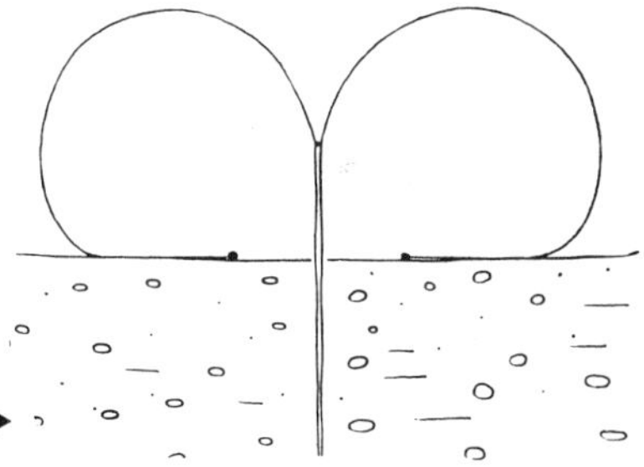

16 ▶

19 and **20** ▼

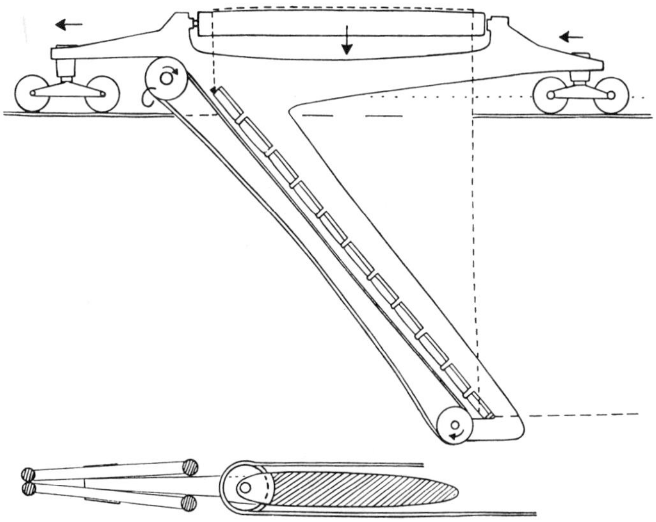

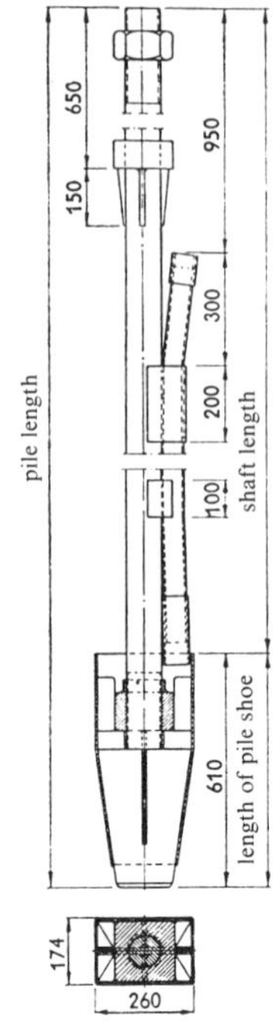

1

2 to 4

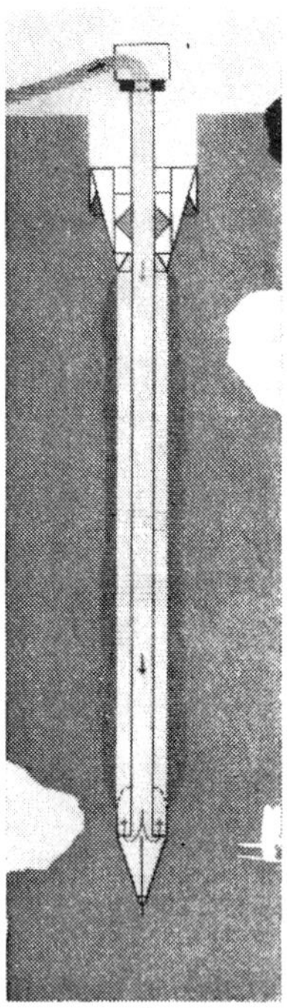

◀ 5 and 6 ▼

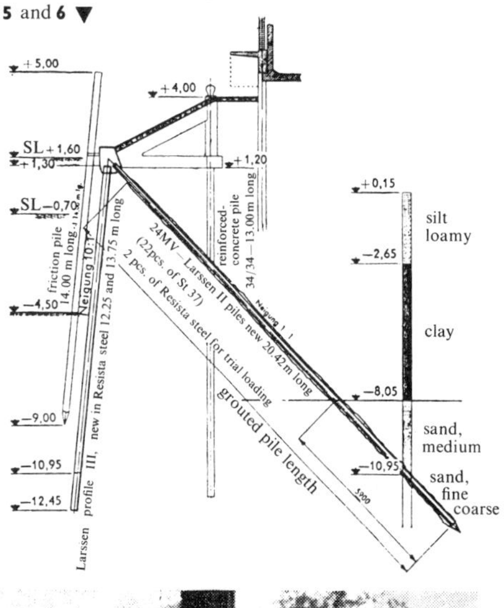

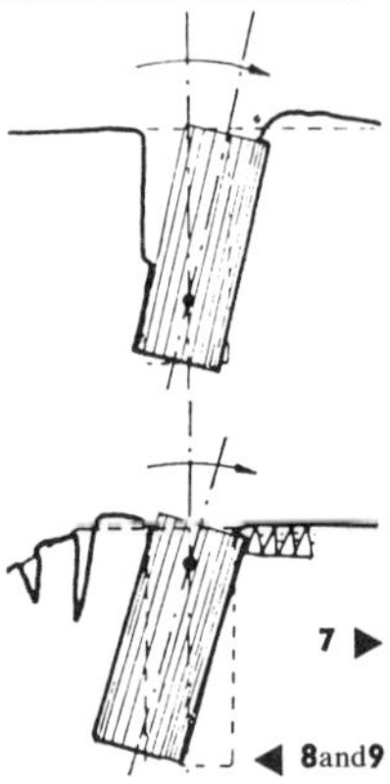

7 ▶

◀ 8and9

sections together. They can also be drilled in or, in special cases, burnt in at very high temperatures. The use of heavy auxiliary equipment can, therefore, usually be avoided.

Experiments with so-called ground rockets have been carried out in Poland (Fig. 1; from *Der Aufbau* 8/1961), in which a pointed cable tip is driven through the ground by compressed air, pulling the air hose and a tension cable with it up to distances of 30 m. This method was developed for laying underground lines beneath obstacles. These Polish experiments appear to confirm the results obtained in Berlin. It remains to be seen whether cables not supported by rigid pipes can be shot into foundations along a predetermined path.

In soils of uneven structure a grouting mass injected at strong pressure can extrude into soft layers so that consolidation with the needle remains imperfect. A special anchor needle was developed for such an eventuality*. It is surrounded by a soft sheath of plastic or rubber which expands in the soil and prevents escape of the grouting mass. Figure 11 on p. 309 is a section through such a needle. The steel pipe in the center takes up the driving force when the needle is introduced by ramming, jet pressure or pushing into the foundations; it has an injection channel at its center with perforations to the outside at various points. The steel pipe is wound with steel wire attached to the pipe itself and to the rubber hose. In the final state these wires reinforce the grouted mass like sinews. The rubber hose which surrounds the steel pipe and the wires has a larger diameter than the hole and is therefore folded. This is particularly necessary in soft soils which permit considerable expansion of the rubber hose. In solid ground folding is not required. While the pipe is being driven into the ground the hose is wrapped in paper for protection. Further protection of the paper by a thin sheath of sheet metal or plastic is often necessary. The rubber hose is firmly connected at the lower end of the anchor needle and also for two-thirds of its length to the tip of the anchor.

When the anchor needle has been driven into the soil the outer

remain in the ground. Due to the moisture in the ground the paper rapidly loses its strength; it tears when the anchor is grouted and thus permits the rubber to expand.
protective sheath is withdrawn and the paper cover allowed to
In very soft soils, or in soft layers between more solid ones, the rubber hose may expand excessively during grouting, leading to its rupture. In such cases wires or belts are placed like rings or spirals around the hose, or glued to it, so that its expansion can be restricted. When using rubber or plastic sheaths, anchor needles can be used for mobile structures in which the anchoring must be recovered undamaged. Such needles are not grouted with liquid cement or cement mortar but with water, and in special cases even with air; the water or air pressure must be checked from time to time as in automobile tires, since it ensures friction between anchor

needle and soil. Grouting masses which harden but can be softened later are of particular interest. For example, hot liquid asphalt soon hardens in the cool soil, but the mass can be softened later by electric heating. Such resistance heating of the metal elements is easy to carry out, especially when only the tip of the needle is in noninsulated contact with the ground.

Another variation is shown in section in Fig. 12 on p. 309. The strong steel pipe, with which the anchor needle is driven in, surrounds the tension cable. The cable is enveloped by a rubber hose which is itself protected by a wrapping of paper or similar material. After driving in the needle the outer steel pipe is withdrawn. A section through the tip of such a needle is shown in Fig. 13 on p. 309 after pipe withdrawal and grouting; Fig. 14 on p. 309 is a cross section. Recovery of the pipe is economical since it can be reused. Furthermore, it would corrode in the ground unless specially protected. This type of anchor needle provides simple anchoring at minimum cost.

Lately, the so-called MV pile has been coming into use. This has a tip profile of shaped steel-sheet piling, rolled section, or steel pipe with a pile shoe. When rammed in, the hole is not entirely filled by the shaft of the pile. This cavity is filled with a grouting mass injected at the pile head during ramming. The mass is supplied by a special grouting pipe. Figures 2 to 6 show details of the MV pile. Figure 4 shows the tip, Figs. 2 and 3 are a view and a cross section of a pile. MV piles have given good service in many projects over the last three years, and have been used for tensile loads up to 250 tons. For the bank revetment of the Neuhof Power Plant in Hamburg (Fig. 6) MV piles were driven to a depth of 20.5 m. Their lower parts are located in sand through 5.9 m while the upper parts are in silt and clay mud. The limiting load was 160 tons. The longest pile used to date measured 25.5 m. The surface friction of such a pile can vary from 13 to 30 t/m^2.

Figure 5 shows, schematically, a process which uses anchor needles approximately as described. We refer the reader to the pamphlet *Der MV Pfahl* (the MV Pile) by Ludwig Müller, Marburg/Lahn, and issue 5/1960 of *Baumaschine und Bautechnik;* also to *Der Bauingenieur,* issue 10/1960 and trade marks 1790793 and 1787195 (all photos by Müller of Marburg).

A special instrument was developed* for pulling out anchor needles (Fig. 16, p. 309). It consists of a flexible and highly tension-resistant membrane, pneumatically tensed by means of pumps or compressors, which engages the anchor at its center. The shape of a centrally anchored balloon is particularly suitable since the pressure reaction is widely distributed over the foundations and not concentrated around the borehole, which could cause undesirable compression of the ground around the needle.

10 and **11**

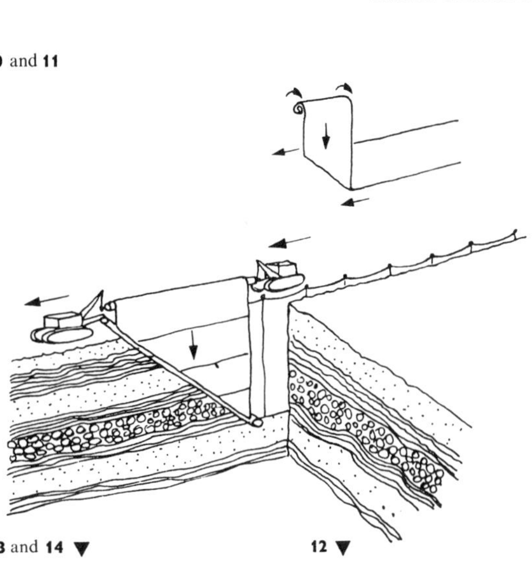

13 and **14** ▼

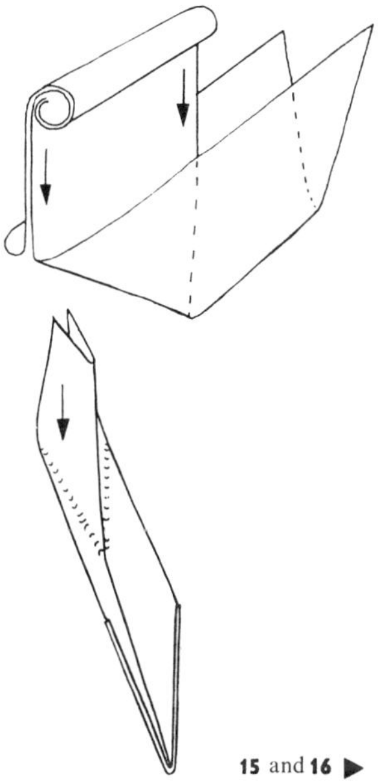

12 ▼

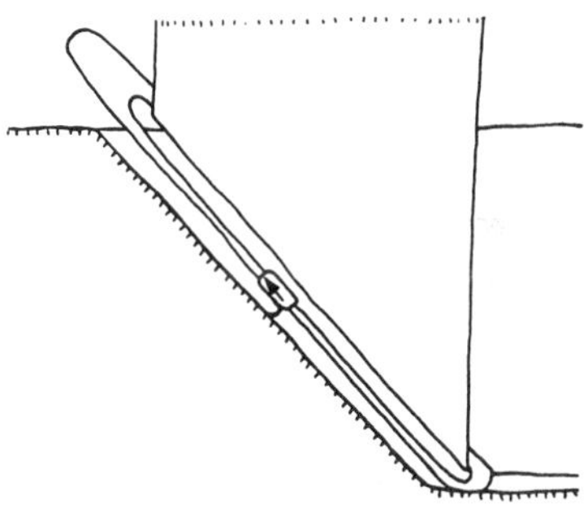

15 and **16** ▶

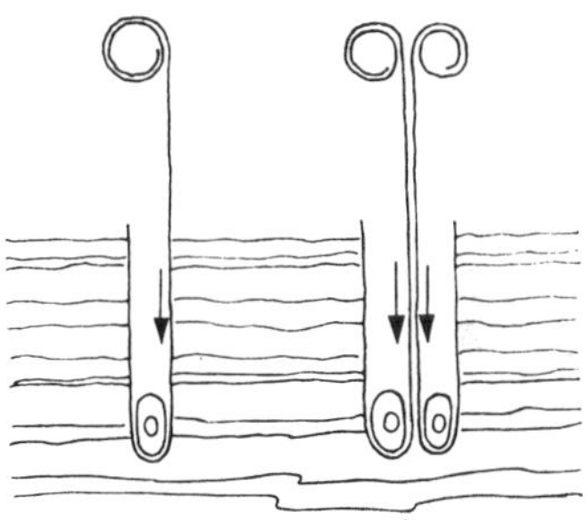

◀ **17** and **18** ▶

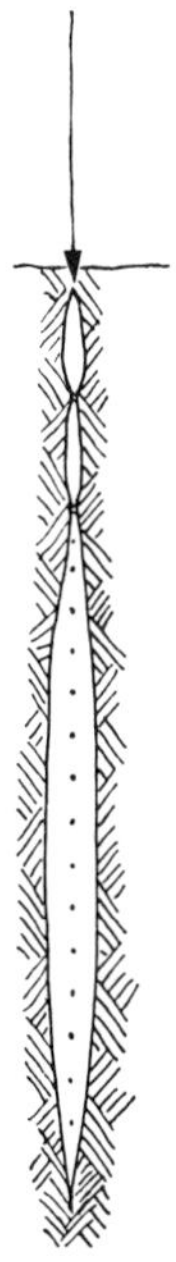

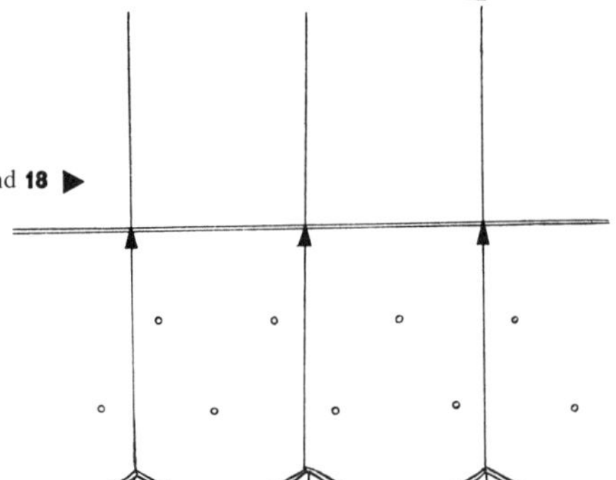

19 ▶

Membranes Buried in the Foundations

For tension-loaded dams (see p. 127) it is particularly necessary to bury tension-loaded membranes deeply in order to ensure both effective tension anchoring and imperviousness to water seepage. The stored water tends to seep through the foundation, and this must be prevented since it could undermine the dams. Consequently, the insertion of heavy membranes of wire, or of synthetic fibers coated with plastic, into narrow slits in the foundations has recently been considered.* These membranes are intended to form diaphragms without being subjected to the pressure differences usually acting on diaphragms. This is possible if the membranes are flexible. Various methods were developed to introduce the membranes into the foundations. Attempts were also made to develop double membranes to be grouted into the foundations like anchor needles, and to use them to anchor tension-loaded parts of dams or of prestressed roofs.

A trench is cut into the foundation by a narrow excavator (see vertical section in Fig. 17, p. 309 and horizontal section in Fig. 18, p. 309; the membrane is then unfurled from a vertical roll and introduced into the trench. The latter must be at least as wide as the maximum diameter of the roll with the membrane. If it is necessary to avoid excessive disturbance of the foundation, which in any case adversely affects its load-carrying capacity, and to save labor, special methods can be used to introduce a membrane into an even narrower trench.

In the method shown in Figs. 10 and 11 on p. 311 the roll travels above ground. It is therefore merely necessary to cut a slot into the earth by means of cables or very narrow excavator chains, and introduce the membrane immediately behind the cutter. A continuous watertight membrane of any length can thus be formed above ground on the roll and laid in the foundation. Sketch 19 on p. 309 makes clear the operation of such a soil cutter. The cut is made by two parallel cables. The membrane is guided around short rollers mounted on a steel arm which protrudes into the slit, as seen in cross section in Fig. 20, on p. 309. In very soft soils an exavating bucket (Fig. 12, p. 311) sliding along a rail is most appropriate.

These methods can also be used to introduce double membranes closed at their upper and lower edges, which can subsequently be filled to form a compression seal with the foundations. Figure 17 on p. 311 shows such a double membrane in cross section, while Fig. 18 is a longitudinal section. Figure 19 is the plan. The double membrane encloses a wire net which takes up the tensile loads transmitted by the cables issuing from the membrane. In order to prevent excessive bulging of the double membrane near the surface or its extrusion during the filling, the membranes are connected to each other at their upper edges, either at several points or along certain lines.

The introduction of single or double membranes into soils in which the freshly cut slit remains open presents no difficulties. This is not so with soils in which the slit closes immediately. If the membrane is turned in the foundation through an angle of 45°, the roller assumes a horizontal position. The membrane is then slid vertically into the ground. If the cut closes immediately, considerable friction can be caused during the introduction of the membrane. The introduction of one membrane is shown schematically in vertical section in Fig. 15 on p. 311. In self-closing doughy soils it will be necessary to introduce two membranes simultaneously. A thin auxiliary membrane ensures that this is done in the center of the slit, as shown in Fig. 16, p. 311. Two adjacent guide rollers are used which are supported by an arm.

A membrane can also be folded in half before being wound on the roll and then inverted while being introduced into the soil, as shown in Figs. 13 and 14 on p. 311. Such a membrane assumes a V-shape in the ground; both its upper edges protrude. Subsequent grouting is possible if the upper ends are closed.

Since it is possible to cut even fairly hard rock with cables, membranes can be introduced into various types of soil. Naturally, the prevailing circumstances must be taken into account. Should this new method prove itself, tension-loaded structures could be built very economically.

Declined Gravity Anchors

If the angle of inclination α (Fig. 1) is less than 30°, the previously described vertical tension anchorings can no longer be used. However, nearly horizontal loads can be taken up by gravity anchors, such as the square building stone (Fig. 1) where the necessary resistance is created by friction with the ground. The wedge-shaped foundation (Fig. 2) shown in the plan in Fig. 3 is already partially buried, as is the pyramidal gravity anchor in Fig. 4 which is acted upon by horizontal tension forces.

Most of the well-known suspension bridges have large gravity abutments at both cable ends which are deeply buried in the foundations and often anchored in the rock in a toothed fashion. It is essential with gravity anchors to increase friction; this can be accomplished by serrations (Fig. 5). In smaller projects a block of concrete lying on the ground can be retained by piles (Fig. 17). A variation of this is shown in Fig. 18. The weight is a stable container filled with water or sand. Anchors have been driven in along the front to increase friction (Figs. 19 and 20), whereas in Fig. 21 the anchor is centrally placed in the gravity foundations. The combination of weight and pile is very advantageous.

Buried concrete blocks (Fig. 6) are frequently used since they are easy to make. They can have many shapes (Figs. 7 to 9). The shape that will best increase the resistance of a buried block of any given weight has not yet been established. However, it is very important that such blocks be tamped directly into the foundation pit with concrete, without smoothing the lateral walls and bottom. The buried gravity anchor in Fig. 22 consists only partly of concrete, some of the weight being due to piled sand. The block of concrete shown in Fig. 23 is very economical. It is shaped like a foot. The cable tension z exerts an overturning moment of arm b, which must be counterbalanced by the restoring moment due to the dead weight of the block acting at the center of gravity s and having the arm a. Such a foot-like anchor digs into the ground with its "toe." Its load capacity is increased if the heel undercuts the ground.

The weight of a concrete block (Fig. 10) entirely buried in the ground, has added to it the weight of the soil on top. Friction with the ground is thus increased. When the direction of the tension is inclined, the front of the block is subjected to considerable compression. In soils of paste-like consistency no increase in weight due to the soil on top should be assumed, since the block must be considered as a buoyant body whose apparent loss of weight is equivalent to the volume displaced. Its resistance is then mainly determined by surface friction at its front and sides. The anchor in Fig. 11 is wedge-shaped; when the cable is tensed the anchor is driven more deeply into the ground until the resistance is adequate. A heavy inclined anchor plate (Fig. 12) is the best illustration of what is generally referred to as a buried "dead man." The vertical anchor plate shown in Fig. 13 is prevented from sliding out by its own weight. The anchor plate shown in Fig. 14 is triangular in section; its resistance is a maximum with a minimum use of concrete. A suitable shape is also shown in Fig. 15. Figure 16 shows a buried gravity anchor consisting of prefabricated concrete elements. The individual parts interlock; they are placed so as to ensure high resistance in the soil. Another type of gravity anchor* is shown in Figs. 24 and 25. It is suitable for round pneumatically tensed domes, membranes, or cable nets (Fig. 26) with round foundations and inclined surfaces, as well as for containers of liquids. First a trench (Fig. 24) is dug and the roof membrane, reinforced at its lower end by a steel cable, laid in it (Fig. 25), after which the cable is tightened, pressing the membrane against the soil. In this way greater firmness is imparted to the foundations of the structure. The pit is then filled. Several cables may be used to hold the membrane in the ground. This type of anchoring has many variants.

Piles and Anchor Plates

The pile is an ancient anchoring method used for inclined loads. When the angle α (Fig. on p. 314) is between 0 and 10°, the angle of inclination γ of the pile should be 90°. If such a pile is overloaded it either bends and comes out, or the ground breaks up and the pile slides out intact, obliquely. The angle β between the directions of the cable and the pile (Fig. 2) can be increased to approximately

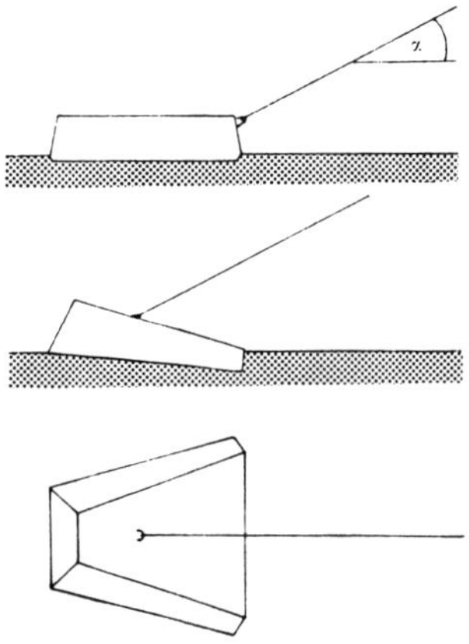

1 to 3 ▲

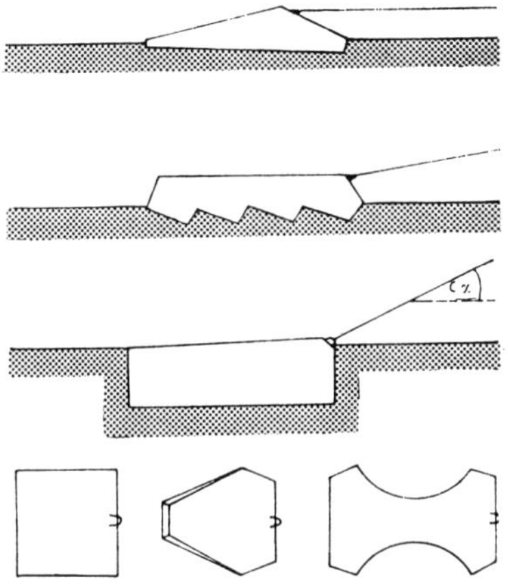

4 to 9 ▲

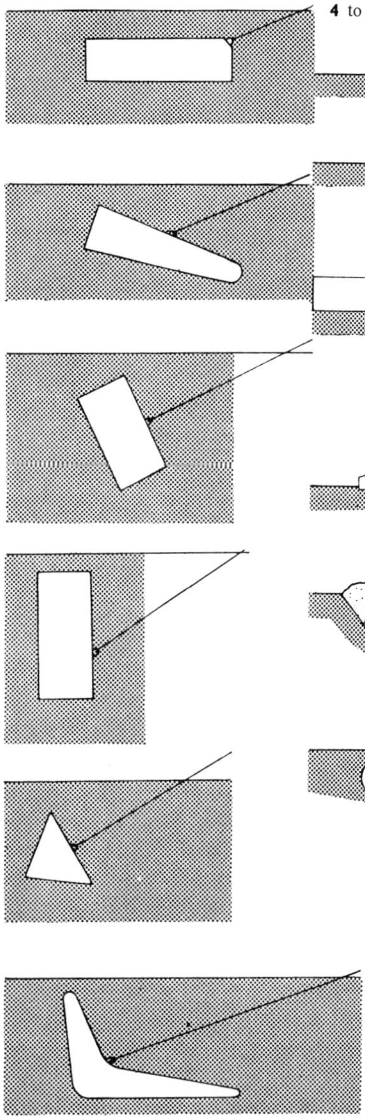

10 to 15 ▲

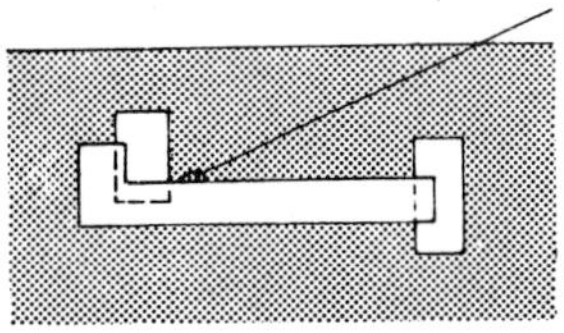

▼ 16

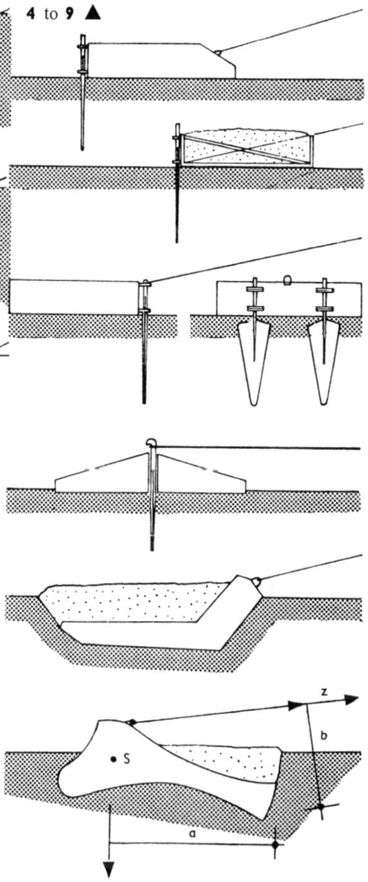

17 to 23 ▲

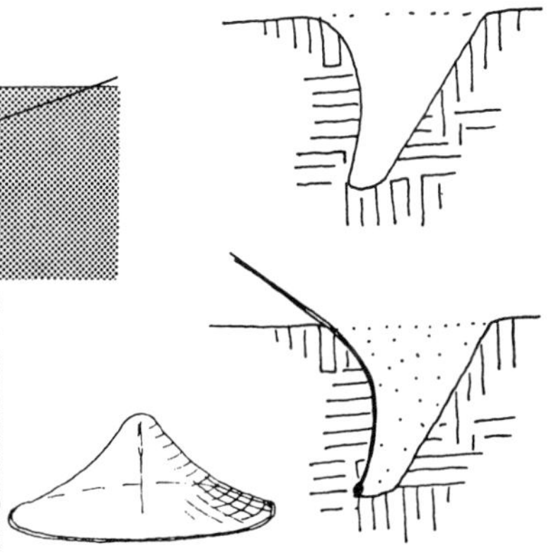

▼ 24 to 26

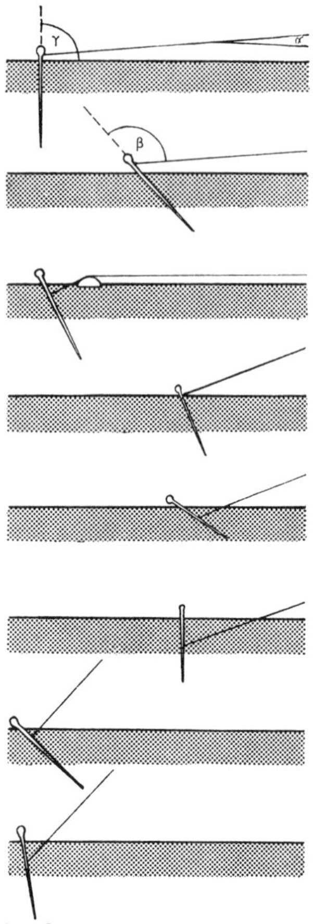

1 to 8

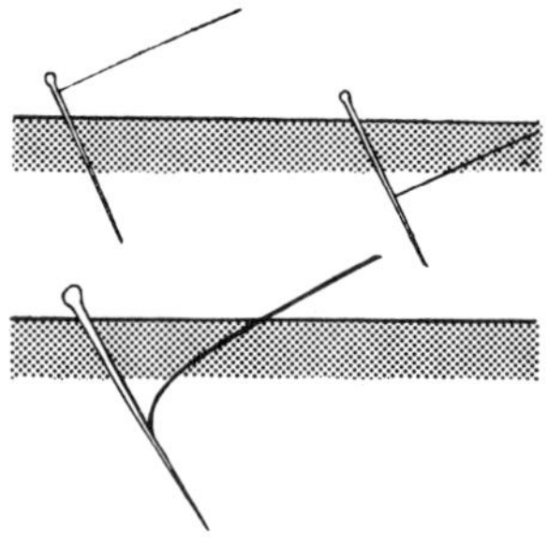

9 to 11

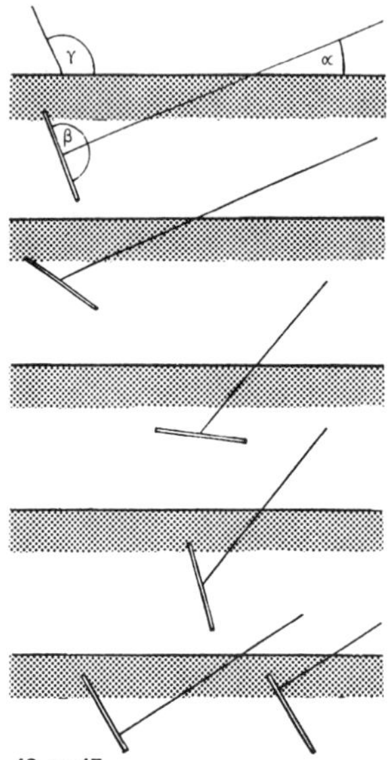

12 to 17

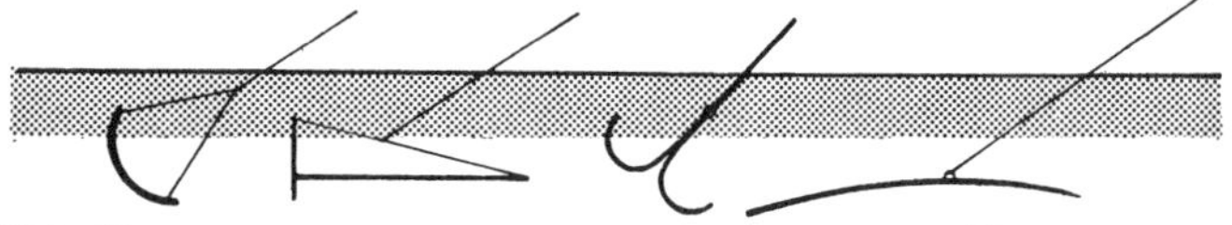

18 to 21

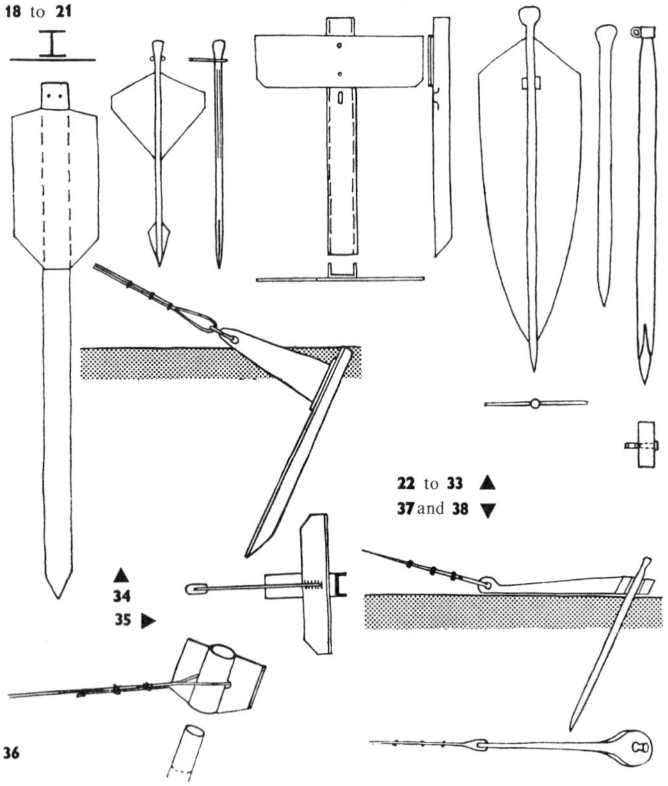

22 to 33 ▲
37 and 38 ▼
▲ 34
35 ▶
36

140°; this prevents the pile from coming out and can even cause it to be driven more deeply into the ground. However, also in this case the pile will tend to assume a vertical position and come out if the ground begins to break up. This is less likely for a pile with a pressure mound (Fig. 3) in which the point of application of the cable force is located below ground.

The same problems exist when the angle between the cable and the horizontal is between 10 and 40°. In Fig. 5 the pile lies very flat as in Fig. 2, while in Fig. 6, it is almost vertical. Either of these arrangements can be preferable depending on the conditions of the ground and the type of pile. The steeper the cable the more necessary it is to lower the point of application of the cable force. When the cable makes an angle of 40 to 65° with the horizontal, the anchor is normal to the direction of pull (Fig. 7) or almost normal to the surface of the ground (Fig. 8). If the point of application of the cable force is high (Fig. 9), a large bending moment is exerted on the anchoring pile. A low point of application (Fig. 10), as near as possible to the center of resistance, reduces the bending moments considerably.

The advantage of piles is that they can be driven in easily. A pile driven into untouched ground has a higher resistance than one which is buried. A deep position (Fig. 11) can be obtained by driving the cable in with the anchor and leading it along the anchor to the pile head. When loaded, it cuts into the ground and assumes a suitable position by itself. This method has the disadvantage that the full load can only be taken up after considerable deformation of the cable line. This is a matter of concern when forces acting in the structure are used to make the cut in the ground, but it can be obviated if, for example, two anchors are tensed against each other by an auxiliary cable until the final location of the anchoring cable in the ground has been attained.

The same applies to anchor plates which, however, can rarely be rammed in like piles and must usually be dug in. Careful sluicing and tamping of the refilled soil is a primary condition for the firmness of an anchor plate. The anchor plate is usually arranged normally to the direction of the cable (Fig. 12), but the plowshare effect (Fig. 13) of a steeper anchor (Fig. 14) can also be used. An excessively steep anchor plate (Fig. 15) tends to slide out if the friction between plate and ground is overcome. An anchor plate with a low cable connection point (Fig. 16) becomes less inclined, while an anchor plate with a high point of connection (Fig. 17) becomes steeper. There exist many designs of anchor plates as shown in Figs. 18 to 21. They exhibit either high frictional resistance or a plowshare effect. The latter is clearly observed in the anchor plate shown in Fig. 21 which penetrates deeply into the soil when the anchor is overloaded until the plate is nearly normal to the direction of the cable.

The widely used "earth nail", is a round steel peg 2 to 5 cm in diameter with a wide head and a sharp point. Wooden pegs with steel points and steel-enclosed heads are also used frequently (Fig. 32) as are wooden beams rammed into the soil as shown in plan in Fig. 33. Stromeyer's wing anchor with the cable attached at the bottom (Figs. 29 and 30), has proved useful in setting up tents. It was designed on the basis of the aforementioned considerations, and can be driven in by hand if it is no longer than 125 cm or wider than 30 cm. In medium soils anchoring forces up to approximately 3 tons can be obtained. The heavy machine-rammed broad-flange double-T section shown in Fig 23 (view) and Fig. 22 (plan) is used as an anchor pile; it can be reinforced by an anchor plate, and can take up forces up to 200 tons. The entrance roof* of the Federal Horticultural Exhibition held in Cologne in 1957 (see *Deutsche Bauzeitung* 7/1960) was retained by such piles. This roof consisted of a prestressed glass-fiber membrane stretched over an unsupported arch having a span of approximately 36 m.

The small anchor (Figs. 26, 27, 28) consists of two parts that are not firmly connected. First the U-section and then the anchor plate are driven into the soil. Finally, the cable is drawn through the eye, but care must be taken not to disturb the soil. In the anchor shown in Fig. 34 (seen from above in Fig. 35) the U-section and anchor plate form one piece. The cable is not attached below the surface but above ground to a vertical plate which is driven in together with the anchor.

Wing anchors with a large wing near the pile head and a smaller wing at the tip save steel and have given good service (Figs. 24 and 25). The angular anchor has been known for years. The load is not transmitted directly to the pile but to a rigid lever through which the pile is driven, as seen in Fig. 37 from the side and in Fig. 38 from above. Both elements are subjected to bending and must be designed accordingly. The cable is angled towards the center of gravity of the anchor surface. Wings can be driven in without difficulty along piles consisting of round steel rods or pipes (Fig. 36).

In 1957 a bent spring-steel anchor* with special properties was developed (Figs. 39 and 40). It is driven in by a rammer working closely above the ground (Fig. 41) until only the head protrudes (Fig. 42). When subjected to tension the anchor assumes an S-shape (Fig. 43) which exhibits high resistance.

Heavy anchor piles and anchor plates to which the cables are attached near the bottom must be driven in slightly behind the point where the cable penetrates into the ground. However, it is rarely possible to ram in heavy anchors without having them turn or become displaced. Since careful construction requires accurate anchoring, however, it is often advantageous to drive in a small guide anchor in order to fix the point of cable penetration. This guide anchor serves as a bench mark and is driven in when the foundations are laid out. Guide and main anchors are shown in section in Fig. 44 and in plan in Fig. 45; the frequently observed turning of the main anchor in the ground is also shown. There are various ways to manufacture simple guide anchors, e.g., of round

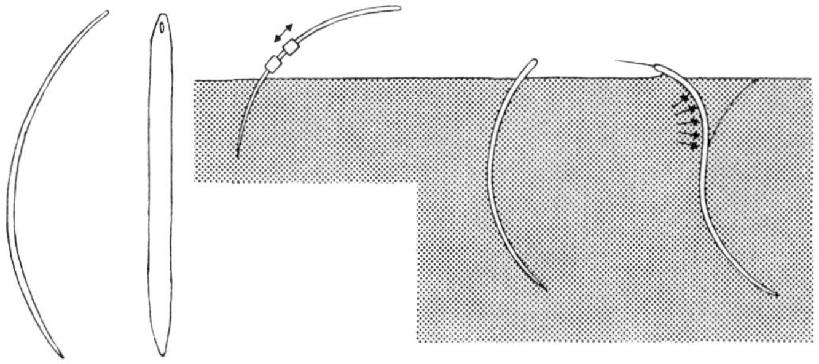

39 to 43 ▲

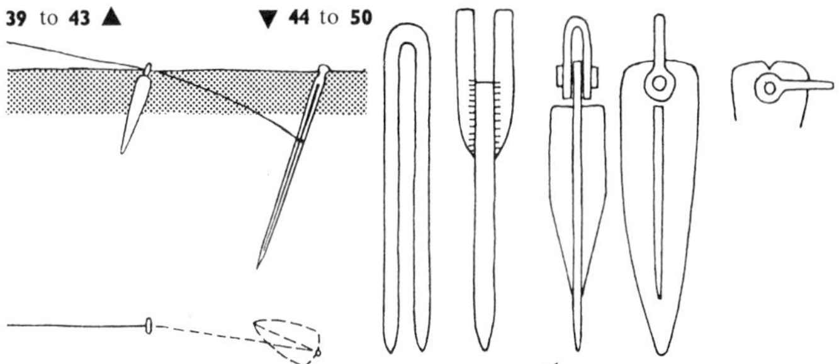

▼ 44 to 50

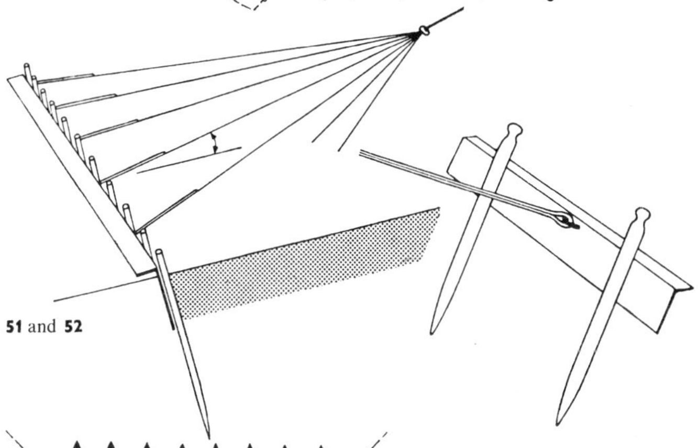

51 and 52

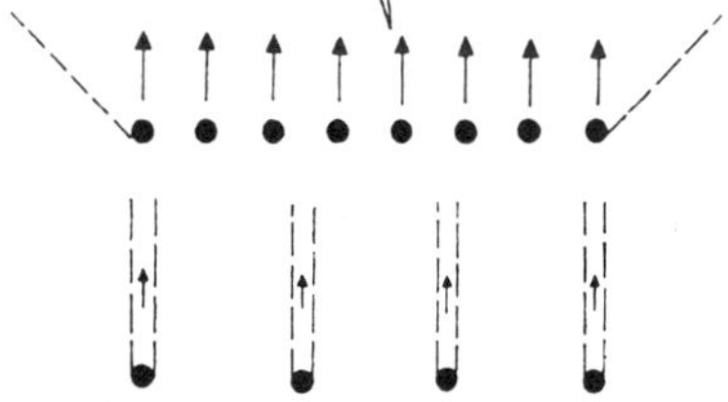

53 and 54

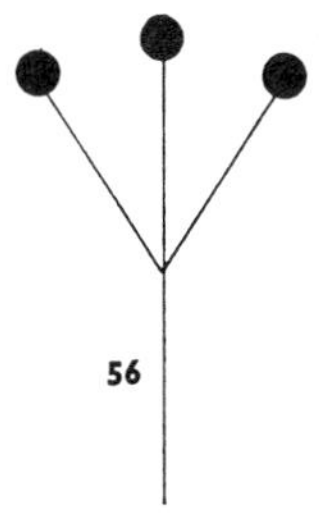

56

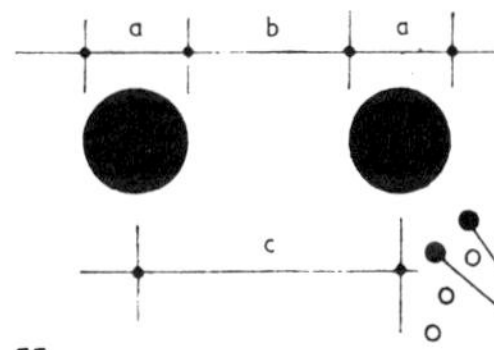

55

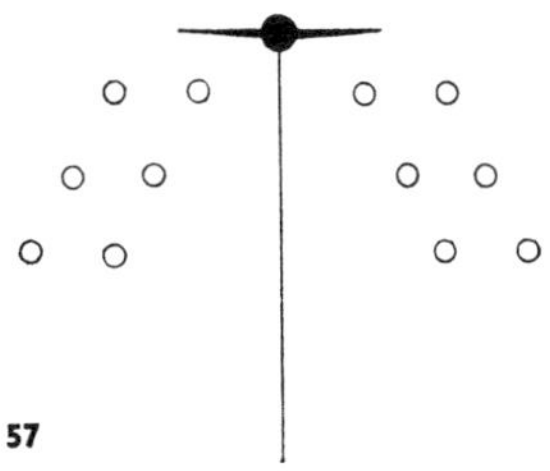

57

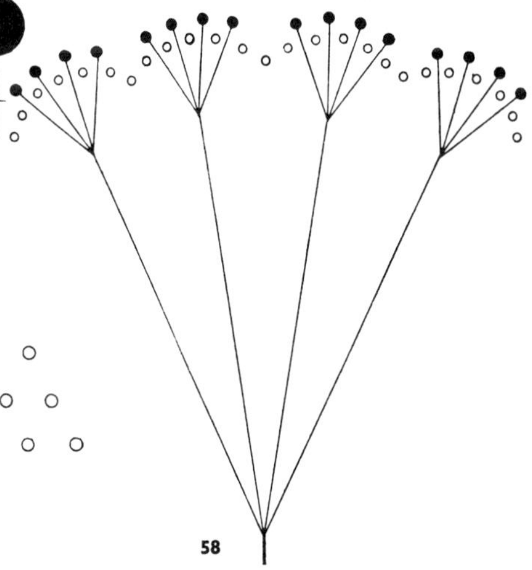

58

rods (Figs. 46 and 47), or of rolled sections (Figs. 48 and 49, p. 315) in which the attached shackle (Fig. 50, p. 315) allows the placing of a mark.

Piles driven in groups are often advantageous. Figure 52, p. 315, shows two piles connected by an angle iron. An entire pile wall anchoring a fanned-out cable by means of an angle iron is shown in Fig. 51 on p. 315. Figure 53 on p. 315 shows a line of closely spaced piles acting like an anchor plate. When the piles are overloaded, the ground breaks up approximately along the dotted line. Figure 54 on p. 315 shows the piles spaced more widely. When overloaded, each individual pile is pulled through the ground, the fissures following the dotted lines. The most economical arrangement (Fig. 55, p. 315) is determined by the ratio of the pile spacing c to the pile thickness a or to the clearance b (Buchholz: *Jahrbuch der Hafenbautechnischen Gesellschaft,* Volume, 12, 1930/1931; abstracted in *Grundbautaschenbuch,* published by Ernst & Sohn, Berlin).

It is generally not necessary to equip fanned-out cables attached to piles with turnbuckles in order to ensure a uniform force distribution to each pile, if these are spaced fairly accurately. Overloaded piles tend to yield in the ground until the cable forces have been equalized. As a rule, the cable forces become uniform at the first test loading.

When groups of piles have been driven in, the fanning-out of the cable is of particular importance. Each pile of a group can be attached to a separate cable (Fig. 56, p. 315), but it is also possible to load only a wing pile (Fig. 57, p. 315) and to drive in the remaining piles as dummies (shown as circles). These dummies consolidate the soil and increase the resistance of the directly loaded anchor. The distribution of a large tensile load (Fig. 58, p. 315) over sixteen loaded anchors reinforced by twenty-five dummy piles permits considerable horizontal forces to be taken up by light anchors driven in by hand. Such anchors were designed for the project of a mobile theater* in 1955 (see *Deutsche Bauzeitschrift* 8/1958).

Clamped Rods

Rods loaded transversely tip over unless they are restrained by the weight of the plate to which they are clamped. Plates acting as gravity anchors for clamped rods are rarely used, except for movable interior partitions. In engineering construction the overturning moments are generally transmitted directly to the foundations, e.g., by the use of vertical plates. We refer to the study of M. A. Lazard (*Annales de l'institut technique du bâtiment et des travaux publiques,* No. 85, January 1955). Lazard considered the problems of the foundations of masts for electric transmission lines and investigated existing masts. He distinguished between two types of ground failure when a clamped cylindrical foundation is overloaded: the first is the "plowshare" effect (Fig. 8, p. 310) in which the lower part of the foundation remains in the ground, while break-up occurs in the upper part. In Lazard's photo (Fig. 7, p. 310) the wedge-shaped soil fissure is clearly seen. The rope pulley with which the mast was pulled is seen in the background. When the surface is hard, e.g., in the case of masts near railroad tracks or roads, a different type of soil break-up can be observed (Fig. 9, p. 310), which can be described as "undermining" or "scooping-out." The upper part of the foundation remains in place while the soil breaks up at its bottom.

Frequently, foundations with clamped rods are loaded in several directions. Such rods must be designed accordingly. They may, for example, be formed by intersecting plates.

Slender tubular steel or wooden masts positioned in a hole drilled into medium- or poor-quality soil can take up only insignificant bending moments since the soil generally breaks up before the mast fails. A frequently used method is to dig a hole having three to four times the diameter of the mast, introduce the latter, and fill the space with tamped concrete. However, tamping rocks or coarse gravel around the mast foot and around the clamping point near ground level is simpler and usually equally effective.

A simple type of foundation was specially developed* for light buildings in which the clamped rods must be positioned very accurately. An ordinary commercial concrete or stoneware pipe is buried in the ground with the socket pointing downward; it is then tamped and the ground leveled. The support—usually a steel tube or wide-flanged rolled section—has a base plate at its lower end which can take up vertical positive or negative loads, e.g., wind suction. The support is placed inside the pipe and its base tamped with coarse gravel; the tube is then filled with sand or fine gravel and closed at ground level with coarse gravel; occasionally, the foundations can also be reinforced with a layer of cement mortar. If the support is adequately protected against corrosion, e.g., by a jute wrapping soaked in bitumen, a durable foundation is obtained, which can easily be removed without damaging the individual parts. This foundation can take up not only compression due to the proper weight of the structure and positive loads acting on it, but also tension and bending moments due to the action of the wind.

Dismountable foundations, which can take up considerable bending moments, were used at the 1955 Federal Horticultural Exhibition in Kassel in the construction of the pavilion* "The Three Mushrooms." They consisted of six steel plates which were bolted to a steel tube.

Chimneys are generally anchored to deeply buried foundation plates. However, they may be built in by means of concrete double cones, which is a more effective method in insecure ground. The central mast of the skyscraper designed by Frank Lloyd Wright for the Johnson Wax Co. was anchored with a deep point-like foundation that became wider near the top, and which has an efficient cross-sectional shape.

Only some of the various types of foundations suitable for transmitting bending moments to the building site could be mentioned here.

Bibliography

Beken, Fr. and K.: Zauberwelt der Segel. Bielefeld: Delius, Klasing & Co. 1959. 154
Boys, C.V.: Soap bubbles, their colors and the forces which mould them. Dover Publ. New York 1911/1959. 11
Buchholz: Jahrbuch der Hafenbautechnischen Gesellschaft. Bd. 12 1930/1931. 316
Conrads, U. and Sperlich, E.: Phantastische Architektur. Stuttgart: Hatje 1960. 38
Coyne, M.: Anwendung der Vorspannung auf Staumauern. Hauptbericht 2. internat. Kongress f. Brückenbau u. Hochbau 1936. Berlin: Wilhelm Ernst & Sohn 1938. 308
Dischinger, F.: Elastische und plastische Verformungen der Eisenbetontragwerke und insbesondere der Bogenbrücken, Sonderdruck aus „Der Bauingenieur". Berlin : Springer 1937 u. 1939. 253
Flügge, W.: Statik und Dynamik der Schalen. Berlin: Springer 1934. 296
—Stresses in shells. Berlin: Springer 1960. 170
Girkmann, K.: Flächentragwerke. Wien: Springer 1956. 170
Green, A.E. and Adkins, J.E.: Large Elastic Deformations and Non-Linear Continuum Mechanics. Oxford: Oxford University Press 1960. 170
—and Zerna, W.: Theoretical Elasticity. Oxford: Oxford University Press 1954. 170
Grundlagenbautaschenbuch. Berlin: Ernst & Sohn. 316
Kohlbrunner, C.F.: Verankerungen im Baugrund. Hauptbericht 2. internat. Kongress f. Brückenbau u. Hochbau 1936. Berlin: Wilhelm Ernst & Sohn 1938. 304
Marks, R.: The dymaxion world of Buckminster Fuller. New York: Reinhold Publishing Corp. 166
Otto, F.: Das hängende Dach. Berlin: Bauwelt Verlag 1954. 5, 20, 38, 308
Torroja, E.: Logik der Form. München: Callway 1961. 124
Wlassow, W.S.: Allgemeine Schalentheorie und ihre Anwendung in der Technik. Berlin: Akademie-Verlag 1958. 170

Periodicals

Acier · Stahl · Steel. Brussels 9/1960. 24
AIA Journal, Washington 4/1962.
Annales de l'institut technique du bâtiment et des travaux publiques. Paris 85/1955 316
Architectural Forum, New York 4/1957. 162
3/1959. 148, 164
Baumaschine und Bautechnik, Wiesbaden 5/1960. 311
Bauwelt, Berlin 28/1956. 151
21/1958. 23
Der Bauingenieur, Berlin 1/1960. 311
Der deutsche Baumarkt, Düsseldorf 26/1954. 308
Der Kunststoff-Berater, Frankfurt/M. 10/1960. 166
Deutsche Bauzeitschrift, Gütersloh 9/1958. 316
Deutsche Bauzeitung, Stuttgart 7/1960. 39
7/1961. 164
Eisenbau 4/1913, 5/1914. 296
Europäisches Bauforum 7/1959. 81, 117
12/1960. 11, 121
1/1961. 164
London Illustrated News, London 1844. 21, 22
Manchester Association of Civil Engineers, Manchester 1938. 44
Mitteilungen der Entwicklungsstätte für den Leichtbau, Berlin. 144
Mitteilungen der Versuchsanstalt für Wasserbau und Erdbau, Eidgen. Techn. Hochschule Zürich. 299
Der Stahlbau, Berlin 3/1930. 296
Students publications, North Carolina State College. Raleigh 5/1. 30

Patents

DRP 98037. 300
USP 972306, 1178282, 1232266. 304

Sources of Photographs

(The number preceding the slash indicates the page number; that following the slash indicates the number of the figure).
dpa Deutsche Presse-Agentur, Berlin: 33/12. dpa Deutsche Presse-Agentur, Frankfurt a.M.: 21/6. Esso-Bild, Hamburg: 70/1. Pressebildarchiv Heinz Finke, Konstanz: 106/6. Maurey Gaber, New York: 115/24, 26. Robert D. Harvey Studio, Boston: 110/7. David Hirsch, New York: 110/6, 111/8, 9. Dr. Fred Meincke, Wedel/Holst.: 155/14. Ullstein-Bilderdienst, Berlin: 22/3, 33/10, 155/13. USIS, Bad Godesberg: 143/13. All other photographs are works photos or were taken by the author.

Subject and Name Index

Tensile Structures

Volume 2

Frei Otto: Basic Concepts and Survey
of Tensile Structures

Friedrich-Karl Schleyer: Analysis of
Cables, Cable Nets, and Cable Structures

Designs by the author are marked by an asterisk in the text.

The figures are separately numbered on all double pages. If the figure is mentioned on the same double page, only the figure number is given; otherwise the page number is also given.

EDITOR'S FOREWORD

It is the purpose of this work to report about tensile structures, to record the present state of their development, and to provide a stimulus for further study. The first volume consisted first of all of a detailed and copiously illustrated text concerning pneumatic structures which for the most part are tensile, load-bearing surfaces. Its second section, by Rudolf Trostel, furnished the mathematical basis for these membranes, and I closed with a survey of tension anchoring and foundations. The second volume continues along the same path with chapters concerning basic concepts and a survey of tensile structures and an analysis of cable nets.

As does the first volume, the second also deals with independent themes which are designed for architects, engineers, and specialists in associated fields. By fitting together a variety of considerations in each volume, it is intended that a greater mutual understanding between all those who are at present concerned with structural form is to be brought about.

Although in a few places in the mathematical section there are references to the preceding general considerations, and calculation methods of certain constructions discussed in the first volume are referred to, no artificial intermeshing of the areas has been attempted, nor have I tried to match the basic concepts. The reason for this is that today's progress in communication between architects and engineers has not yet reached a sufficiently high level.

The chapter on basic concepts and survey of tensile structures is intended as an introduction into the entire field. It can be claimed with some justification, in discussing the structure of this chapter, that an introduction into the total field ought to have been put at the beginning of the first volume. In rebuttal it can be stated that the formulation of comprehensive chapters is only possible when the entire field is available in a manner that can be readily surveyed. Since during the past decades a great many fundamental discussions concerning suspension bridges have been published and between 1954-1960 many papers concerning hanging roofs have appeared, the one thing that was lacking in completing the basic fields was pneumatic structures. These were finally covered in Volume I, and in so doing a reference was established to this survey in the present volume.

The chapter concerning the mathematical cable nets by Friedrich-Karl Schleyer contains a section that can be readily understood, is designed for architects, and permits rapid calculations. This was included in response to frequently voiced demands. It is therefore hoped that this contribution will be of immediate practical use.

The area of tensile structures continues to expand rapidly. Between the publication of the first and that of the second volume a large number of structures and projects appeared. The literature (see the Bibliography) was enriched by many papers in professional journals and in books; of these I would particularly like to cite the report by Esquillan and Saillard about the ephochal Colloquium of the International Association for Concrete Structures in Paris, 1962, the publications of the Academy for Structural Sciences in Moscow, and the workshop report by Conrad Roland, which contains a survey of the material for tensile structures and a summary of many actually constructed membrane buildings that can only be briefly alluded to in the present volume in connection with the survey on tensile structures.

Since it was not possible to achieve anything like completeness, this volume again dispenses with a comprehensive list of projects and literature concerning tensile structures. Such a list, however, is now in preparation and is intended for the next volume. The publishers as well as the editor request all interested persons to advise them of any structures or projects as well as of literature references concerning tensile structures.

Special thanks are due Mr. Friedrich-Karl Schleyer for his never-ending patience in our collaboration in this volume. The publication of this volume was made possible by the understanding support brought to it by the publishers. A substantial part of the work load fell on Berne Friedrich Romberg in carrying on experiments and in designing the layouts, on my wife in preparing the text, and on all my co-workers at the Institute for Light Structure at the Technical University in Stuttgart as well as in the development workshop for light structures in Berlin, above all John Reuer, Andreas Edzard, and Günther Scherzinger.

Frei Otto

Berlin, October, 1965

SURVEY OF VOLUME 1

CONTENTS

BASIC CONCEPTS AND SURVEY OF TENSILE STRUCTURES

General Fundamentals of Constructions, Survey of the Historic Development, and Classification of Tensile Structures

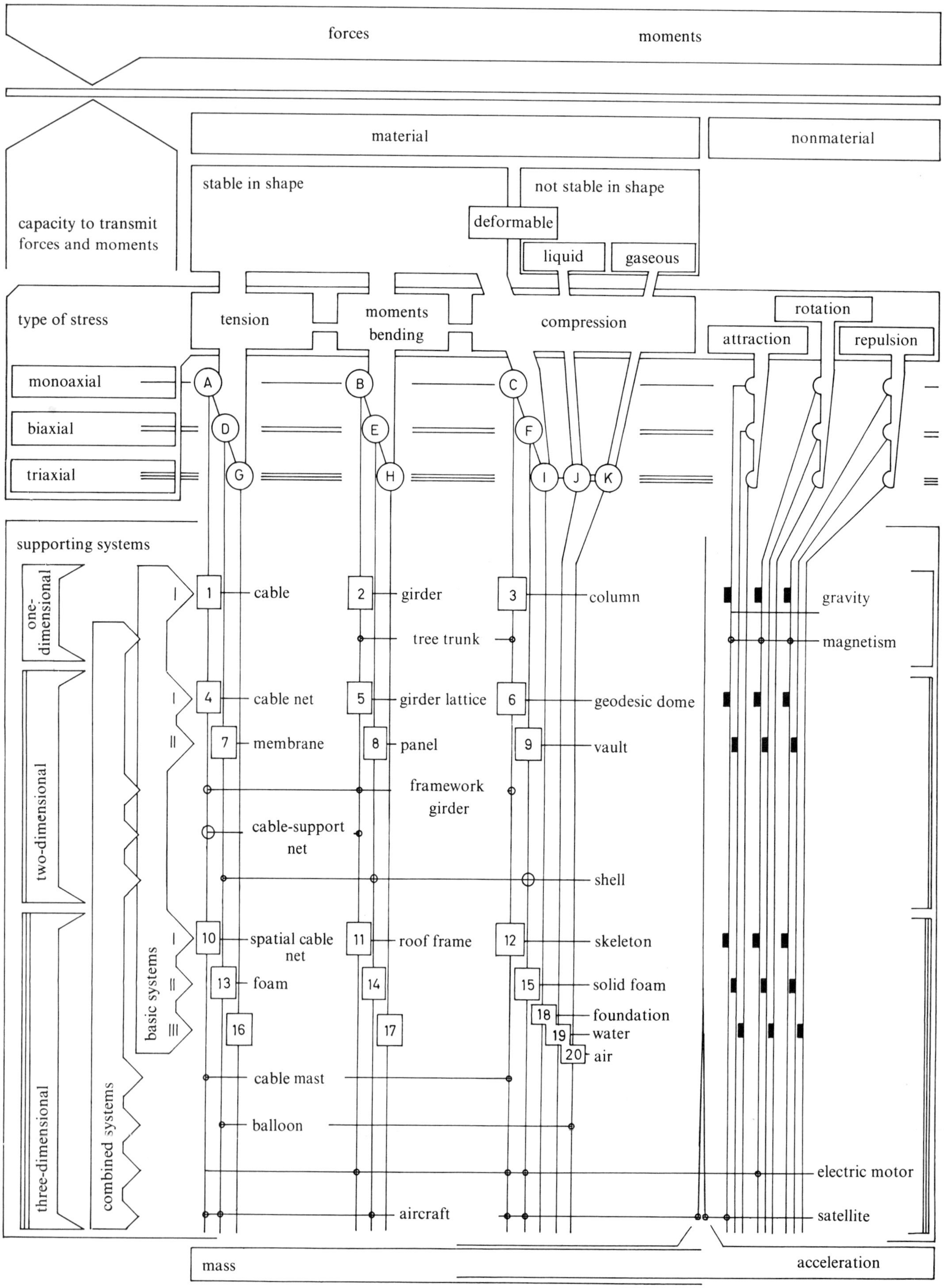
forces
moments
material
nonmaterial
capacity to transmit forces and moments
stable in shape
not stable in shape
deformable
liquid
gaseous
type of stress
tension
moments bending
compression
rotation
attraction
repulsion
monoaxial
biaxial
triaxial
A
B
C
D
E
F
G
H
I
J
K
supporting systems
one-dimensional
two-dimensional
three-dimensional
combined systems
basic systems
I
II
III
1 cable
2 girder
3 column
tree trunk
4 cable net
5 girder lattice
6 geodesic dome
7 membrane
8 panel
9 vault
framework girder
cable-support net
shell
10 spatial cable net
11 roof frame
12 skeleton
13 foam
14
15 solid foam
16
17
18 foundation
19 water
20 air
cable mast
balloon
aircraft
gravity
magnetism
electric motor
satellite
mass
acceleration

GENERAL PRINCIPLES

We propose to classify all structures according to a system, in order to form a basis for the general understanding of "structures under tensile loads." Their various aspects will then be considered.

A brief description of the development is followed by a discussion of the most important systems.

The Capacity to Transmit Forces and Moments

Forces and moments can be transmitted, e.g., from one point to another, and can act either along lines or at distances from fixed points.

A cable transmitting a force has the "capacity to transmit" tension. An engine shaft or a girder has the capacity to transmit moments. A rock or building presses upon the ground with its weight. An aircraft is supported by masses of air to which it imparts a downward acceleration. The centrifugal force acting on a natural or artificial satellite is opposed by the earth's force of gravity, which acts exactly like a cable.

Structures are "means." To construct, means, in fact, "to assemble." The word "structure," itself, means something that has been built, although it is now used in a more comprehensive sense.

The capacity to transmit forces and moments is found in the macrocosm and in the microcosm, in animate and in inanimate nature.

Structures are means employed in animate nature. Used by men, they pertain to engineering and are technical structures. In contrast, plants and animals are living structures.

All things and phenomena that have the capacity to transmit forces and moments become structures when this capacity is used by man: this applies to stones, earth, air, water, all the elements, and their effects.

Classification of Structures

Structures are means for transmitting forces and moments.
In Fig. 1 we have tried to establish a clearly understandable system. This system includes not only technical but also living structures, as well as all observed capacities of inanimate things to transmit forces and moments.

Forces and moments can be transmitted by matter; the structures, then, are material.

Transmission of forces and moments is also possible without employing matter, e.g., magnetic fields.

Until now, the resulting nonmaterial structures have had little significance in architecture.

Since antiquity, classical architecture has employed materials of stable shape. Today, liquid and gaseous materials, unstable in shape, are being used increasingly.

Many building materials are solid below, but easily deformable beyond a certain stress and temperature. They then become plastic and approach the liquid state.

Tensile, Compressive, and Bending Stresses

Forces and moments transmitted by materials affect these in different ways.

Material structures are best classified according to the type of stress acting on them. Materials can be subjected to tensile, bending and compressive stress.

Tensile stress is the utilization of the capacity of the material to resist tension.

The same applies, by analogy, to compressive stress. Tensile and compressive stresses are "force stresses."

Although bending stress may be regarded as a combination of tensile and compressive stress, this would not approximate reality in every sense.

Bending stress is a "moment stress." Moments of various kinds can be taken up by the resistance of the material to moments.

Moment stresses act in pure form in the absence of compressive or tensile stress. Torsion is also a moment stress, but shear or transverse stress is a force stress.

Different stresses frequently occur simultaneously in one component which is then subjected to mixed stresses.

Attractive forces acting outside matter correspond to tension in matter. Repulsion can be compared to compression, and rotation to torsion.

Monoaxial, Biaxial, and Triaxial Stresses

Apart from tension, moments, and compression, stresses may act simultaneously in several directions. A stress is monoaxial if it acts in one direction only, (A), (B), and (C). It is then linear. A cable is almost solely subjected to monoaxial stress (A). A girder may also be subjected to monoaxial bending (B), and a support to monoaxial compression (C). A thick vertically loaded wall is mainly subjected to monoaxial stress.

A stress is biaxial if it acts simultaneously in two directions, (D), (E), and (F). This is a surface stress.

The eardrum is subjected to biaxial tensile stress (D).

A panel may be subjected to bending on all sides, i.e., to biaxial stress, but may also be compressed (E) and (F).

The stresses along the two axes may differ in kind and magnitude. Thin hyperbolic-paraboloid shells are frequently subjected to surface tension in one direction and to surface compression in the other.

Triaxial stresses act on all sides and are therefore three-dimensional, (G), (H), and (I). Any solid substance can be stretched or compressed in all directions.

It is known that all substances can be highly stressed by compression on all sides. Liquids are practically incompressible. Gases can take up large loads and become compressed, until they are liquefied. Liquids (J) and gases (K) cannot, however, take up uni- or biaxial stresses. They also cannot take up nonuniform triaxial stresses, but only uniform triaxial compression. (Viscous liquids and plastic substances can take up nonuniform stresses for short periods only.)

Solids may be subjected to different stresses in every direction. All combinations are possible.

Mass and Acceleration

A mass can be accelerated by forces or moments. The acceleration of moving masses frequently gives rise to forces or moments that may oppose others. This may permit forces and moments to be taken up and transmitted.

Supporting Systems

Apart from the type of stress, a structure is also characterized by its supporting system. There are line, surface, and three-dimensional structures, i.e., one-, two- and three-dimensional supporting systems.

Supporting systems mainly subjected to one type of stress, e.g., tensile, bending, or compressive stress, will be called basic systems, in contrast to mixed systems, which may be subjected simultaneously to several types of stress.

One-Dimensional Supporting Systems

Such systems can also be called line supporting structures. They are large in one dimension and small in the other two. The material is concentrated along a straight, curved, or angular line. A flexible cable is such a line supporting structure. The required cross section tends to zero as the tensile strength of the material increases.

A straight or curved girder which transmits moments can also be regarded as a line supporting structure, although it must almost always have a greater height or width, and thus usually requires more material than a comparable structure under tensile load. Built-in straight or curved supports which transmit compressive forces are also line supporting structures.

A stretched cable (1), a girder subjected to bending (2), and a support under compression (3) are examples of the basic system of one-dimensional supporting structures. In contrast, a trunk supporting the weight of the entire tree, but which also transmits moments caused by wind forces as bending stresses, must be regarded as a one-dimensional mixed system.

Two-Dimensional Supporting Systems or Surface Structures

Two-dimensional supporting systems or surface structures are large in two dimensions and small in the third. The material forms a surface which may be plane, possess single or double curvature (synclastic or anticlastic), or be angular.

A surface structure may also consist of line elements that form a continuous surface. Such structures are also subjected to monoaxial stress, e.g., cable nets (4), girder lattices (5), or geodesic domes (6). These can be regarded as examples of basic systems of monoaxially-stressed surface structures with line components.

The membrane (7), panel (8), and domed vault (9) are examples of basic systems of ~~mono~~biaxially-stressed surface structures.

The membrane[1] is a stretched flexible skin that can only be subjected to tensile stress; it may be plane or curved.

[1] The definition of a flexible stretched skin as a "membrane" corresponds to the original meaning as well as to general and technical usage in nearly all branches of engineering. Exceptions are some fields of structural engineering, where the term "membrane theory" has been introduced in the analysis of shells with reference to theoretically flexible surface structures. The membrane became the symbol of flexibility. The simplified term "membrane stresses" is used instead of the exact term "surface stresses in the flexible shell," even in the case of compressive stresses which cannot arise in a true membrane forming a flexible skin. This caused confusion, particularly in recent years, when many structures were built with true membranes, differing greatly in design from shells. At the International Convention of the IASS on "Hanging Roofs" in Paris, in July 1962 (see N. Esquillan and Y. Saillard (eds.), *Hanging Roofs,* (Interscience) John Wiley, New York, 1964.) and at the International Conference on Shells (see *World Conference on Shell Structures,* Oct. 1–4, 1962, San Francisco, National Academy of Sciences, Washington, D.C., 1964), the author suggested applying the term "membrane" only to flexible stretched skins. The general membrane theory should, therefore, again become the theory of flexible surface structures. Oniashvilli states that Vlassov does not use the term "membrane theory" in Russian but refers to the "theory of moment-free shells."

A membrane can be perforated until it is reduced to a cable net. It is the simplest of all surface structures under tensile loads.

The panel or disk is a rigid plane surface structure. Panels can generally take up compression and tension, as well as moments inducing mono- and biaxial stresses.

A girder lattice or grid can be obtained by regular perforation of a panel.

Vaults are surface structures primarily subjected to compressive stresses.

The surface of a biaxially stressed vault can be perforated or replaced by rods; the stress then becomes monoaxial. We thus obtain net or rib domes.

The basic systems of surface structures, mainly subjected to either compression, bending, or tension, are distinct from mixed systems, which form the majority of all surface structures.

Folding structures are surface structures consisting of plane surfaces assembled at angles, which can be subjected to mono- or biaxial tension, compression, or bending.

Shells[2] are rigid curved surface structures.

Any curvature or angle is possible. In practice, every rigid nonplane surface is a shell (crustaceans, egg shells, shell structures).

Shells can take up compression, tension, and moments. A rigid shell surface can be subjected to mono- or biaxial stress. Vaults can also be regarded as shells, i.e., as rigid curved surface structures whose surfaces are subjected to compression only.

A frame girder can also be regarded as a two-dimensional structure, if it lies in a single plane. When the nodes are flexible, such a girder consists of rods subjected either to monoaxial tension or to monoaxial compression.

Three-Dimensional Supporting Systems

These systems are large in three dimensions and may have any shape. Massive solid bodies can take up forces and moments while subjected to mono-, bi-, or triaxial stress. They are also suitable for low-strength structural materials. Three-dimensional supporting systems fill space and retain their bulk even when perforated or provided with hollow spaces or holes, which reduce the specific volume.

Hollow spaces in supporting components can be enlarged to such a degree (particularly for the better utilization of high-grade structural materials, or for other purposes) that only thin rods or walls (one-or two-dimensional elements) remain. The total volume of the entire structure is retained; the sum of the volumes of all hollow spaces tends to this volume as the rods or walls become thinner.

A three-dimensional supporting structure behaves as such even when one- or two-dimensional elements are used as linear surface structures subjected to mono- or biaxial stresses. The term "space structures" is used for three-dimensional supporting systems of low specific volume, which can be subdivided into "geodesic structures" and "spatial structures."

Geodesic structures may consist of rigid or flexible rods meeting at nodes. "Spatial cable nets" is a term used only for flexible structural elements under tension.

A spatial cable net (10) is a three-dimensional structure under tensile load, consisting of one-dimensional elements; a roof frame (11) is similarly subjected to bending, and a skeleton structure (12) to compression.

Foam of liquids (13) can be regarded as a basic three-dimensional supporting system, in which biaxial tensile stresses act on two-dimensional components. Solid foams (e.g., glass foams) are similarly subjected to bending or compression (14 and 15). The same is true for the panel and box assemblies frequently used in tall, concrete buildings.

Three-dimensional basic supporting systems are subjected to triaxial tensile stresses (16) during contractions (welding stresses). Triaxial bending stresses (17) are comparatively rare. However, triaxial compressive stresses are known in foundations (18) which are nonuniformly stressed near the surface, and in water (19) and air (20), with uniform stress in all directions. Three-dimensional supporting systems include many mixed systems. Thus, a guyed mast is a combination of one-dimensional components, under monoaxial tension or compression, forming a spatial system. A balloon, whether used as an aircraft or as a hall on the ground, is a pneumatic structure composed of biaxially stressed two-dimensional membranes. They are supported by three-dimensional gas or air pressure acting along three axes that can take up directly the external loads acting on the balloon, which is thus structurally stressed (see Vol. 1).

Many different bending, compressive, and tensile stresses act inside the solid components of an electric motor. The torque is, however, taken up by magnetic forces.

Types of stress and supporting systems rarely occur in their pure form. The most varied combinations are known or may still be discovered.

[2] This clear and brief definition of a shell as a "rigid curved surface structure" was proposed by the author at the International Conference on Shells in San Francisco. It is partly in accordance with Dischinger's definition and Joedicke's extension thereof (see Joedicke, *Schalenbau*, Kramer-Verlag, Stuttgart, 1962.)
This brief definition of the shell is generally applicable. It does not affect the common definition of a shell, used to describe rigid containers, primarily living shell structures (e.g., oyster shells, egg shells, crustaceans), but provides a unique definition for all branches of engineering.

The line system has neither surface area nor volume. If such a system is employed as a structure, the material used must always have a finite volume, which is often very small.

Every solid material can be subjected to mono-, bi-, and triaxial stress. Theoretically, an extremely thin stretched wire can be subjected to transverse stresses along its diameter. By transmitting this force over a short path, equal to the diameter, it serves, in a small way, a structural purpose.

Building materials that may be subjected to different stresses along the three axes can be considered for all supporting systems.

Consequently, systems are not limited to specific materials, e.g., steel, wood, or concrete.

Steel, wood, or concrete constructions denote the methods and processes specific to each material when used in any supporting system. Certain supporting systems are undoubtedly most suited to some specific material. However, a fundamental division of structures consisting of solid materials is not possible.

Forces and Stresses

Tension, compression, and bending may act as forces or moments in one-dimensional components.

In two-dimensional components, they can occur as stresses acting in the surface. Surface tension is the force per unit cross section that has the dimensions of length (e.g., kp/m).

Stresses in three-dimensional components usually mean "body stresses" referred to the cross-sectional area (e.g., kp/cm^2).

The resistance of materials is usually evaluated with reference to stresses that can be taken up (body stresses). This is true also for the one- and two-dimensional components of determinable thickness.

However, the effective cross-sectional area of one- or two-dimensional components with very small cross sections is often difficult to determine, and is not always significant in evaluating the load capacity of a structure. This applies particularly to cables, fabrics, or plastic fibers that consist of large numbers of frequently noncircular microscopic filaments.

The total load taken up by a cable or rod can be determined, but not the effective cross section.

Knowledge of the effective forces and their influence on a component is of particular importance in the case of flexible line elements under tension. This influence is determined from the rupture strength (measured, e.g., in kp), extensibility (changes of length in relation to the original length), and elasticity (determined from the stress-strain diagram).

The active surface tension that must be taken up (measured, e.g., in kp/m) is important in the case of surface structures of determinable or unknown thickness, e.g., cable nets, fabrics, porous leather-like skins, etc. This also applies to ideal infinitely thin surfaces analyzed according to the theory of flexible surface structures.

The supporting surface is evaluated according to its rupture strength and its strains, measured as surface stresses. The surface stress that can be taken up is usually determined from rupture tests based on the monoaxial stress of strips (e.g., 30 cm long and 5 cm wide). Bursting-pressure tests are used for biaxial stress measurements.

The stress-strain diagram (relationship between surface stress and strain) and the surface modulus of elasticity (kp/cm) are very important. It should be noted that many new high-strength structural materials have nonlinear stress-strain diagrams, and do not, therefore, obey Hooke's law. Little is known of the behavior of structural materials under bi- and triaxial stress. Practical test methods have not yet been fully developed.

Prestressing

In principle, every structure can also be evaluated according to whether or not it is prestressed.

A structure is not prestressed if no forces or stresses act when it is not loaded.

A structure is not loaded when it transmits no forces or moments, not even its dead weight.

A structure is prestressed if forces or stresses act on it when it is not loaded (and is assumed to have no dead weight). These forces or stresses are present before any load is applied.

The term "prestressing" refers almost exclusively to structural systems. The term "internal stress" is applied to the materials themselves or to the bodies which they form. Like prestresses, they are forces and stresses that act in the absence of loads. For example, a tennis racquet or a harp is prestressed. Large forces, moments, and stresses act on strings and frame. The same applies to a block of concrete compressed by tension elements (prestressed concrete), and to a tempered glass plate whose surfaces have been prestressed by rapid cooling ("frozen" compressive stresses), its center subjected to "frozen" tensile stresses.

Materials and structures are rarely free from prestresses and internal stresses the effects of which are not always positive. Prestressing is of value if a higher load-carrying capacity is obtained through stressing when no loads act.

Flexible nonprestressed structures intended to take up tension, such as cables, cable nets, fabrics, membranes, and spatial nets, have no uniquely defined shape when not loaded. They assume their structural form only under loading.

Flexible nonprestressed structures, such as cable and membrane structures, including those intended to take up compression, such as vaults, always require an adequate load, usually imparted by weight.

Nonflexible prestressed structures may assume their basic shape when not loaded. This shape, like the prestresses, is independent of the location of the structure in space. A cable connecting two points is prestressed if, when not stressed, its length is less than the distance between the two points. The basic form of this system is a straight line.

Flexible prestressed tension-loaded surface structures may be plane or have double (saddle-like) curvature. An exception is single curvature in the monoaxial state of tension; domelike (synclastic) curvature is not possible.

THE DEVELOPMENT OF TENSION-LOADED STRUCTURES

No comprehensive survey of tension-loaded structures exists. Such a survey would be impossible today, since developments are rapid and frequently disjointed.

A comprehensive classification of tension-loaded structures and their historical and technical interrelations will become necessary in the next few years. When this is done, the development of tension-loaded structures will be seen in a different light. Knowledge of the interrelations and of the importance of the most significant works will permit their correct evaluation. Therefore we now make only some preliminary observations.

The capacity to transmit forces and moments by tension-loaded materials is found in animate and inanimate nature. With the exception of asbestos fibers, minerals cannot transmit large forces by tension. However, many rocks have measurable, though low, tensile strength. Tensile stresses in the earth occur, to a limited degree, only near the surface. They are found more frequently in animate nature. Thus, wood can be stressed from all sides, e.g., by compression, tension, or bending.

Tensile stresses occur alone, or together with bending stresses. Whereas the trunk of a tree must take up both compressive and bending stresses, bending stresses predominate in the large branches, and tensile stresses in the small ones. Flexible tension-resisting skins and sinews are necessary wherever the supporting system is movable. Compressive stresses are usually taken up by rigid components resisting compression. For example, crustaceans have tubular external pressure skeletons capable of taking up bending stresses to a certain degree, and held together and controlled by an internal tension-loaded movement system. In vertebrates the articulated pressure system (skeleton) is inside, being covered and actuated by a complex tension system of sinews, muscles, and skin. It can transmit considerable forces and moments.

Animal bodies vary greatly. They are mostly a combination of several tension-loaded systems with a compression-loaded skeleton. Mixed and bending stresses are rarer.

Living structures have highly developed systems the performance of which has rarely been attained by the best light structures built by men. Structures built by animals are generally on a much lower level. But here, too, tension-loaded components occur. Frequently, self-produced high-strength threads are woven to form useful structures, e.g., cobwebs.

Development of Tension-Loaded Structures

The first tension-loaded structures built by men were probably tentlike, made of animal skins or thin branches. The invention of knotting and weaving made possible fabric tents, fishing nets, and sails. For thousands of years nets and fabrics have been made of fibers whose strength has only recently been surpassed.

Until recently, all prestressed net and membrane structures, regarded as the acme of engineering development, could have been built in ancient times with equal perfection, using the structural materials then available.

It can be assumed that important designs of this type were known long ago. Nevertheless, the few records available on tent and net structures, in contrast to structures subjected to compression and bending, indicate that major achievements, comparable to the present state of technology, were not attained in antiquity or the Middle Ages. Tension-loaded structures are a development of the last decades. This contrasts with, e.g., the spidery Gothic vaults subjected to compression. Unfortunately, no significant progress has been made in this field since the Middle Ages, although such might have been possible.

Tents were the first surface structures under tensile loads. Their flexible skins can take up large stresses.

The basic types have scarcely changed over the centuries. The pointed tent is well known: a central mast, surrounded by a conical membrane. Another version has two masts and resembles a steep gabled roof. Early representations are known, but original tents were discovered only much later. We know of luxurious tent palaces and tent cities. Although the highest perfection in craftsmanship was attained, only simple variations of the basic shapes seem to have been used.

Ship sails, which must be included among pneumatic structures (see Vol. 1), were developed separately from tents. The stringent requirements of seafaring soon led to perfection of the design.

Fundamental improvements in sail-making became possible only through developments in aerodynamics and in the design of membranes. However, apart from yacht racing, wind power is rarely used as a source of energy today. Incentives for further development are therefore lacking. This may, however, be altered by changed circumstances.

Large circus tents appear to have acquired their well-known shape only in the last century. Usually they have four large masts along the edge of the arena, from which the center of the tent is suspended. Inclined rods support the membrane above annular rows of seats.

The large spans and high loads lead to very large membrane stresses. The fabric (linen, hemp, or cotton) is therefore reinforced at the critical points by sewn-on ropes.

In bridge building, the single cable led to double- and multicable suspension bridges with pathways following along the catenaries. The path is either placed directly on the cables or suspended underneath them. Large-span suspension bridges have been known for a long time and are still being built.

Before the introduction of steel cables, plant fibers of limited service life were used. The ropes of early suspension bridges thus required frequent replacement. Some bridges had to be renewed every year. Wrought-iron chains, known since the 7th century, though possibly existing even before, were used later for suspension bridges. Important chain suspension bridges existed in Britain.

Level roadways, suspended from the cables but not following along the catenaries, appeared in the 19th century. The roadway is separated from the main structure. The first cable suspension bridge was built around 1816. Very large spans thus became possible (Finlay, Ellet, Brunel, Telford; see E. Mock, *The Architecture of Bridges,* Museum of Modern Art, New York, 1949).

The gravity suspension bridge perfected by John Roebling retained its significance until recently and influenced the design of all large new suspension bridges. It has cables spun in place, a rigid roadway, and cable nets forming vertical surfaces connecting the suspension cables and the roadway.

Roebling's most important designs are the Ohio Bridge in Cincinnati and the Brooklyn Bridge in New York.

Figure 1, p. 15, shows the then new Brooklyn Bridge, as drawn by W. Hildebrandt in 1876 for the Library of Congress. A copy was kindly supplied to the author by David B. Steinman. See also D. B. Steinman, *Famous Bridges of the World,* Dover Publications, New York, 1953. Figure 1, p. 17, is a photograph taken by the author, and shows the structure of the cable nets consisting of vertical and inclined cables. Present-day builders and designers of large suspension bridges include Steinman, Strauss, Amman, and Leonhardt.

Recently, a new design for suspension bridges has been developed. At least three, but usually four cables form a three-dimensional prestressed system. It can be used to reinforce very light highly-stressed bridges at small deformations (p. 91).

Until now it could not be established when cables were first used to secure suspension bridges laterally and from below against lifting and twisting. Elizabeth Mock showed the Winch Bridge over the Tees (England, around 1741); John and Washington Roebling also used such cables. However, intentional and really effective prestressing of a three-dimensional cable system was introduced only recently. Following the example of bridges, roofs were also suspended from cables in the last century (Laurent 1837, Lorient Arsenal, *Engineering News Record,* Oct. 27, 1921). Such structures were designed and built until recently. Suspended roofs raise quite different problems from suspension bridges. Roofs are much lighter because of the smaller loads acting on them. Their low dead weight usually renders them much more sensitive to lifting by wind suction than heavy bridge roadways. On the other hand, recent experience seems to show that the danger of aerodynamic instability of such roofs is much smaller.

The designs of Shuchov in Nizhni Novgorod are generally regarded as the first engineering surface structures in which roof membrane and structure form one unit. These buildings had been forgotten, and were only rediscovered lately. They can be considered as tents built by the structural-steel method (see *Visyachii Pokrytie*, Russian translation of Frei Otto, *Das hängende Dach* (Hanging Roofs), appendix by I. G. Lyudkovskii, State Publishing House for Architecture and Structural Materials, Moscow, 1960.

A strong impetus was given at the beginning of the 1930's to the development of modern tension-loaded surface structures by attempts to roof large grain silos with steel sheeting of simple curvature (Albany, St. Louis, Memphis, etc.). Laffaille developed, in Paris, sheet-metal shell structures, later also tension-loaded sheet-metal roofs.

Nowicki's design for the Raleigh Arena in 1950 forms a separate phase of development. It was carried out by Severud and Deitrick in 1953.

These cable nets and membranes, arches stabilized by cable nets, edge cables and edge supports used also for nonprestressed tension-loaded surfaces, as well as undulating, prestressed, centrally supported surface structures, were surveyed for the first time in 1951–1953 by the author in his dissertation *Das hängende Dach*. A further impetus was thus given to the development of suspended roofs in the following years. Large structures were built all over the earth. Some exceptional theoretical and practical work was done by architects and engineers, among them Borges, Bird, Costas Alliana, Finsterwalder, Friemann, Hottinger, Irwin, Jawerth, Le Ricolais, Leonhardt, Lyudkovskii, Jorgensen, Horak, Maring, Mondino, Rabinovic, Rudolph, Saarinen, Sarger, Schelling, Schleyer, Severud, Stone, Stromeyer, Stubbins, Tange, Trostel, Tsuboi, Weidlinger, Yuncken, Zetlin. Some important structures are the Schwarzwald Hall in Karlsruhe, the Rio Grande do Sul Pavilion in São Paulo, the Yale Hockey Rink in New Haven, the Sydney Meyer Music Bowl in Melbourne, the Dulles Airport in Washington, D.C., the swimming pool in Wuppertal, the French and U.S. pavilions at the Brussels World's Fair, the small Westphalian Hall in Dortmund, the auditorium in Utica, and the olympic gymnasiums in Tokyo.

General development, internationally, in the field of tension-loaded surface structures has been noticeable since 1960.

Cables forming tension-loaded structural members are found in nearly all branches of engineering. Stayed masts of sailing ships are the predecessors of the highest towers built today. Since the 1920's, consideration has been given to the suspension of walk-on ceilings from masts in the construction of tall buildings (Rasch, Buckminster Fuller, Bakema, Pardo, Borisowsky, Lehmann, etc.). The development of these structures, in which all compressive forces are concentrated in a few elements, is still at the very beginning. However, in the future they will also be used in conjunction with prestressed three-dimensional cable nets (see Report No. 8 of the Development Center for Light Structures, Berlin, 1962, and *Deutsche Bauzeitschrift* 7/1962).

1

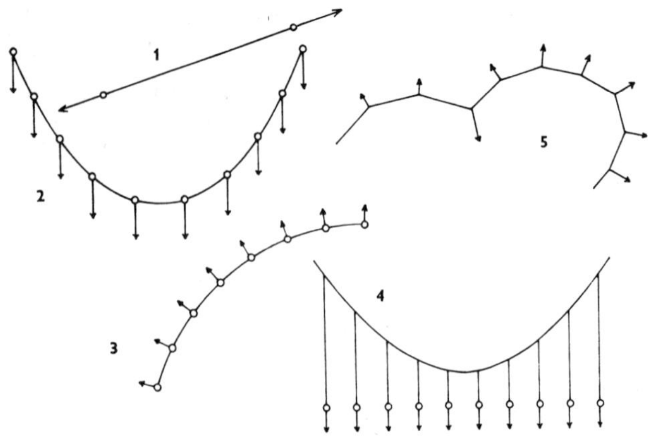

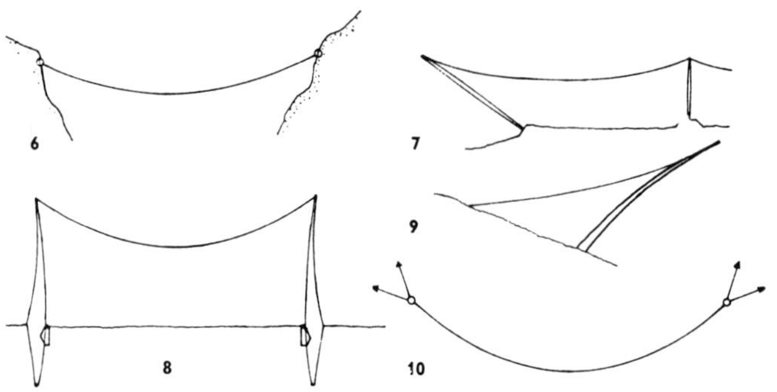

NONPRESTRESSED SYSTEMS OF TENSION-LOADED STRUCTURES

General Remarks: The chapter "Basic Structural Concepts" dealt with tension-loaded structures as a part of structures in general. They were subdivided into one-, two-, and three-dimensional supporting systems consisting of one-, two-, and three-dimensional elements subjected to mono-, bi-, and triaxial tension.

No danger of buckling, associated with compressive loads, arises in tension. Furthermore, tension-loaded structures are rarely subjected to such complicated states of stress as occur in bending. These structures are therefore easily analyzed. This applies in particular when all tension-loaded components are, in fact, capable of taking up only tension, i.e., when they are rigid neither in bending nor in compression. This can be achieved by the use of cables or flexible membranes. There is no clear demarcation between structures loaded by bending and by compression, since components rigid in compression are nearly always rigid in bending while those rigid in bending are mostly rigid also in compression and tension.

Tension-loaded structures consisting of flexible elements obey certain geometric laws, comparable only to the behavior of masonry pillars and vaults under pure compression. Flexible tension-loaded components automatically assume an equilibrium shape most suited to transmission of forces and moments.

Components subjected to bending or compression must first be given such a shape.

Shape and structure are largely one entity in a flexible tension-loaded system.

Although the variety of possible shapes is reduced when only flexible tension-resistant components are used, their number is still very large. As a rule, nonprestressed tension-loaded structures can be clearly distinguished from prestressed ones by their behavior. Tension-loaded structures may also be grouped according to other aspects.

As already stated, a supporting system is considered "nonprestressed" and "free from internal stresses" if it is stressed only under load.

The Simple Cable

A "cable" is understood to be any support element that can be loaded by tension but is very flexible, e.g., chains, bands, filaments, etc.

A cable is a linear (one-dimensional) supporting system, large in one dimension and small in the other two. When a cable ;(Fig. 1) transmits tensile forces it forms a straight line. A cable (Fig. 2) suspended between two fixed points is uniformly loaded and forms a catenary. Figures 11 and 14 show a chain of constant length suspended between two points that initially coincide and are then drawn apart horizontally in equal steps.

Figure 12 is a long-time exposure of a chain oscillating in its plane of suspension. Figure 13 shows different catenaries. If a cable is loaded uniformly at right angles to the curve formed by it, the resulting cable curve (Fig. 3) is a circle. A cable to which equal loads are applied at uniform horizontal intervals forms a parabola (Fig. 4).

Different forces (Fig. 5) either coplanar or forming a spatial system, can act on a cable. In the former case the cable lies in the plane; in the latter, the cable forms a three-dimensional curve.

When "fixed," e.g., between two mountain sides (Fig. 6), the abutments can be considered as immovable. Temperature fluctuations increase or reduce the sag of the wire due to expansion or contraction.

Cables may be attached to elements rigid in bending (Fig. 8), compression (Figs. 7 and 9), or tension (Fig. 10). Such means of attachment are displaced by the action of loads, e.g., the dead weight of the cable, or by changes in temperature. This also affects the shape of the cable.

When cables are attached to a rigid closed frame of the same material, sag and cable forces do not change when the temperature varies, since the deformations are geometrically similar. Theoretically, contraction of the frame during temperature drops equals that of the cables if they are cooled at the same rate. In practice this happens rarely.

11 ▼

◀ 12

13 ▲

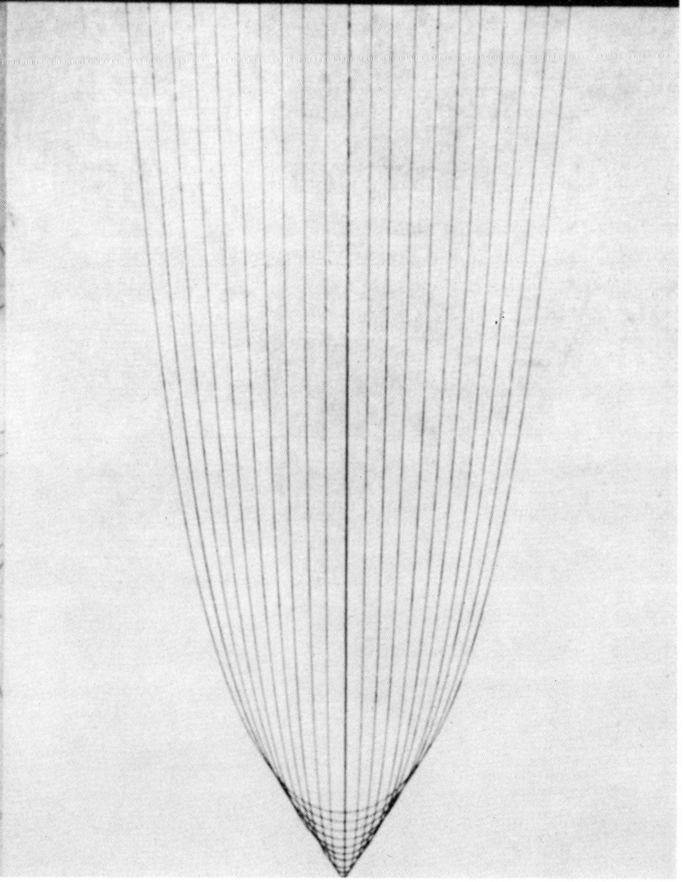

14 ▲

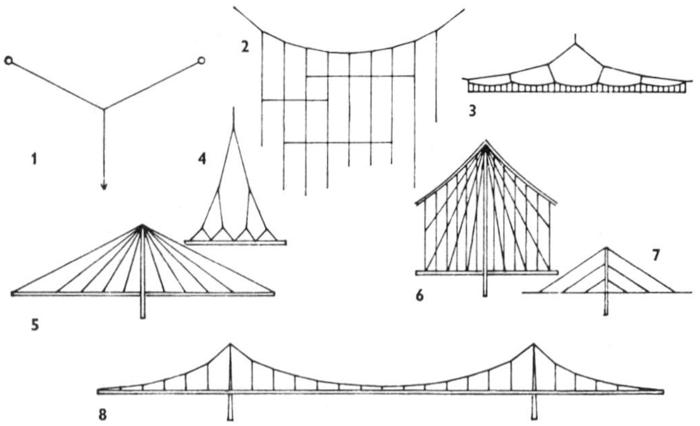
1 2 3 4 5 6 7 8

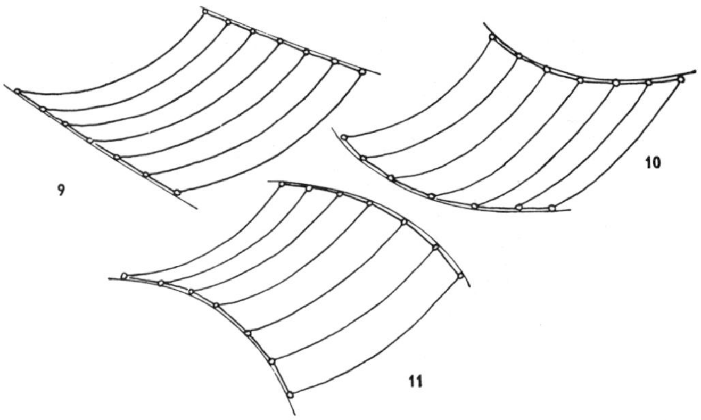
9 10 11

Cable Systems and Nets Forming Vertical Surfaces

If the load of a vertical cable is transmitted by two other cables to two fixed points, the three cables form a vertical plane. This is a frequent case (Fig. 1). A two-dimensional supporting system results.

If several vertical cables are attached to a supporting cable and interconnected, e.g., by girders or cables, a vertical plane suspended net (Fig. 2) results. The cable surfaces of a suspension bridge can also be regarded as a vertical net in which the supporting cable is passed over two pylons (Fig. 8) or over a single pylon (Fig. 5). The roadway supports can be suspended from special cables (Fig. 8) or directly (Figs. 5 and 7) if the point of suspension is directly connected with the point of force application. A system consisting of triangles results.

To ensure uniform sag of, for example, the supports of a suspended rapid-transit track under a uniformly moving load, the track can be suspended (Fig. 3) from short intermediate cables connected to the main supporting system at larger intervals. The suspension may also be branched (Fig. 4).

Since the Cincinnati and Brooklyn Bridges were built by John Roebling (Fig. 1, p. 15 and Fig. 1, p. 17), the superposition of a system of inclined cables forming triangles (Fig. 5) on a suspension system with vertical cables (Fig. 8) has become known. Such a combination (Fig. 6) is particularly rigid under distributed and concentrated moving loads.

Freely Suspended Cables that Form Surfaces

If cables of equal length (Fig. 9) are suspended at equal distances between two horizontal parallel lines, a simply curved surface is obtained whose section parallel to the cables represents a catenary while a section normal to the cables forms a horizontal line. If the suspension points move in two imaginary parallel vertical planes along curves convex downward, the suspended cables of equal length form a spatially curved surface whose longitudinal section is a catenary, while any cross section represents the generatrix. The surface is synclastically curved, forming an inverted dome (Fig. 10).

If the curve described by the suspension points is convex upward (Fig. 11), we obtain a saddle-shaped or anticlastic surface.

Synclastic and anticlastic curvatures can also be obtained with suspension points, as shown in Fig. 9, if the sag of the cables varies continuously. The surface is synclastic if the central cables have the largest sag, and anticlastic when these cables sag least.

Figures 17 to 20 show experiments with cables of equal length, suspended at equal distances between horizontal parallel lines and forming simply curved surfaces. In Figs. 21 and 22 the cable sag is varied; the test model shows both synclastic and anticlastic surfaces. The cables can be attached at the edge (Figs. 6–10, p. 18) in such a way that each individual cable is fixed; alternatively the family of

17 18 21 22

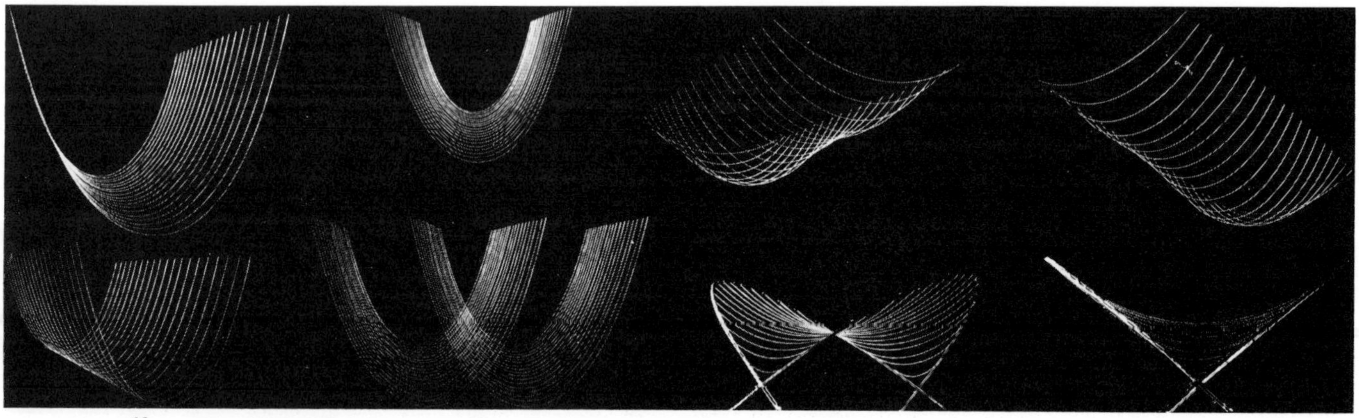
19 20 23 24

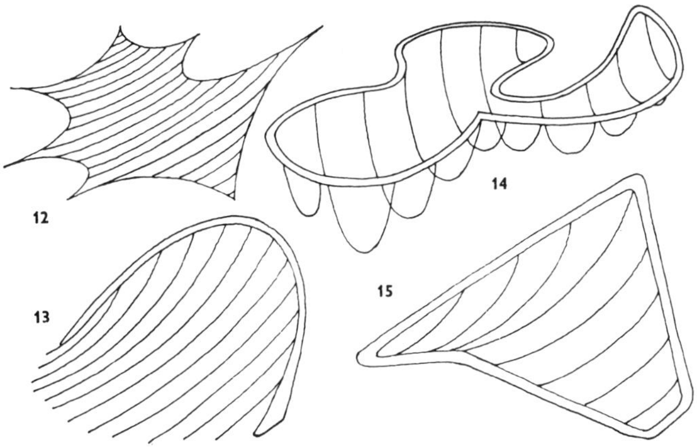

12 13 14 15

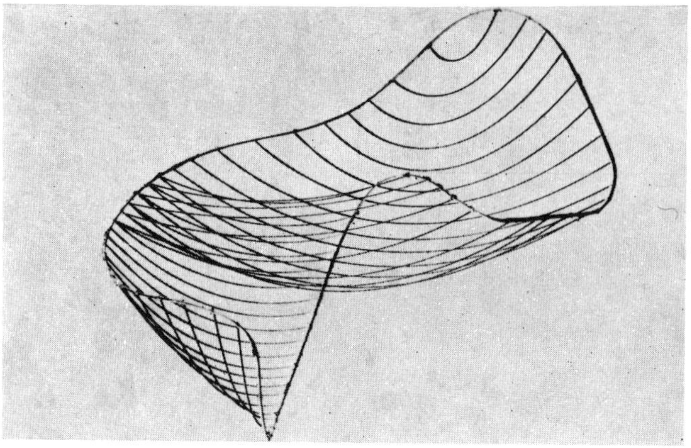

16

cables may be suspended in a closed frame capable of transmitting forces from the cables to a few points. In Fig. 12 the cables are attached to external cables forming the edge, and in Fig. 13 to one side of an arch loaded by compression. In Fig. 14 they are attached to a spatially curved closed rigid frame, and in Fig. 15 to a frame subjected to bending, and formed by straight elements.

The model in Fig. 16 was used to investigate the possibility of suspending a family of cables, forming a continuous surface, in a frame of asymmetrical shape representing a helix on one side. The distances between the cables are equal in plan, but the sag varies. This can be seen from the side views of the model (Figs. 27, 28, 30, and 31). Figure 29 was photographed obliquely from above. Figure 28 is a side view into the center of the helix. Each cable, of course, forms a catenary.

A further model experiment to investigate the basic systems was performed with a family of parallel cables suspended between two arches (Figs. 23, 24, and 26). As seen in the side view (Fig. 24), the cables are suspended in such a way that the tangents at the suspension points lie exactly in the planes of the arches. The arches, subjected to compression, coincide with the support line, and thus take up no bending moments in the initial state. However, they must be sufficiently rigid, and be secured against overturning by means of supports rigid in compression and tension, or by being fixed at the intersection of the arches. This design is applicable to suspended roofs, consisting of parallel cables and with sufficient roof weight or rigidity. The Feierabendhaus at Knappsack-Griesheim (Architect and Photograph: Hell) is an example of this basic shape (Fig. 25). The principle of such a roof suspended between two arches was first applied to the Raleigh Arena. This building represented an important stage of development; however, the low weight of the roof membrane later required additional slight prestressing of parts of the cable nets, as well as fixation of the cable nets near the arch apex in order to hold them down. Here too, the supporting cables are almost tangential to the arch plane at the suspension points, and form in this region a surface of primarily simple curvature. The stiffening effect of prestressing is of minor importance for such a surface. Although the Raleigh Arena is mentioned in connection with prestressed cable nets (pp. 56 and 57), it should be noted that prestressing is of little importance in the over-all design of this building.

Other examples of cable families attached to cables are given in Figs. 1 to 4, p. 22, which show a family of cables of single curvature, attached to two edge cables. Figure 1, p. 22, is a view of the model, and Fig. 2 is a view at an angle of 45°; Figs. 3 and 4 are side views.

Figures 5 to 18, p. 22, show the same model net at various heights of the four corner points. Surfaces result which are inclined or have single, anticlastic, or synclastic curvature. Their sections in one direction are again catenaries. This type of construction has variants only a few of which can be mentioned.

25

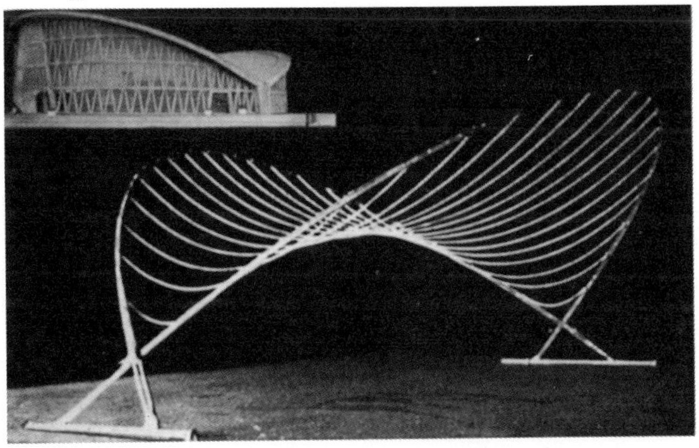

26

27 28 29

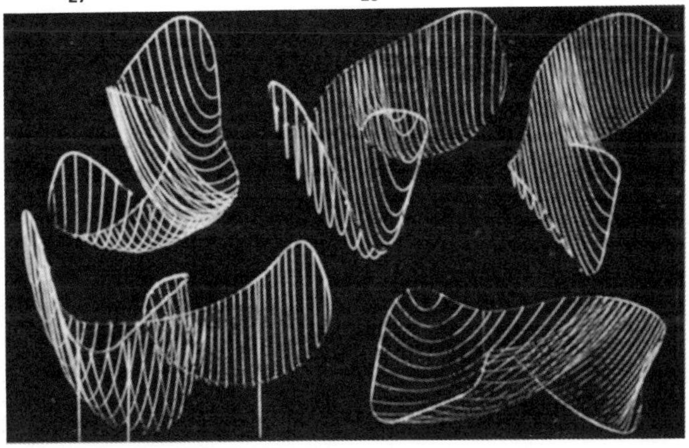

30 31

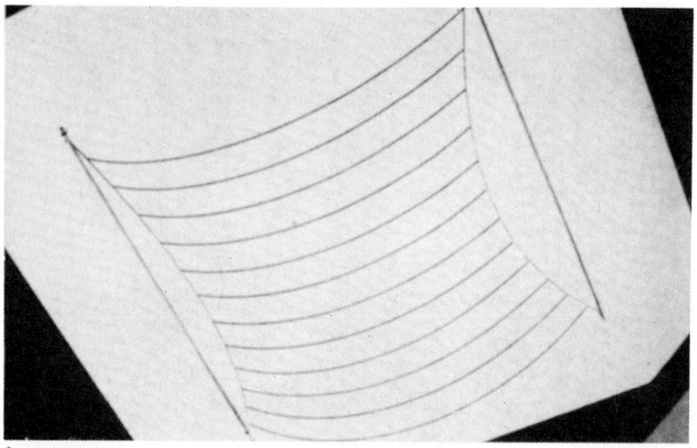

1

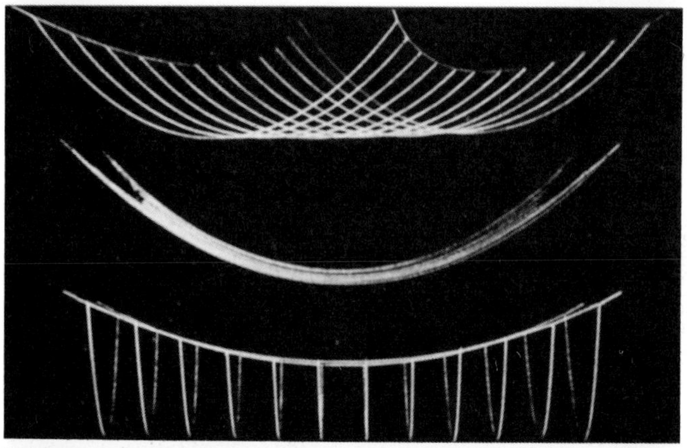

2 to 4 ▲ 5 to 7 ▼

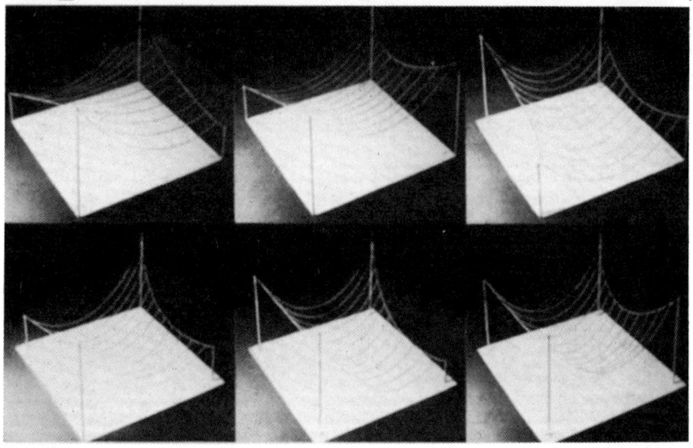

8 to 10 ▲ ▼ 11 to 18

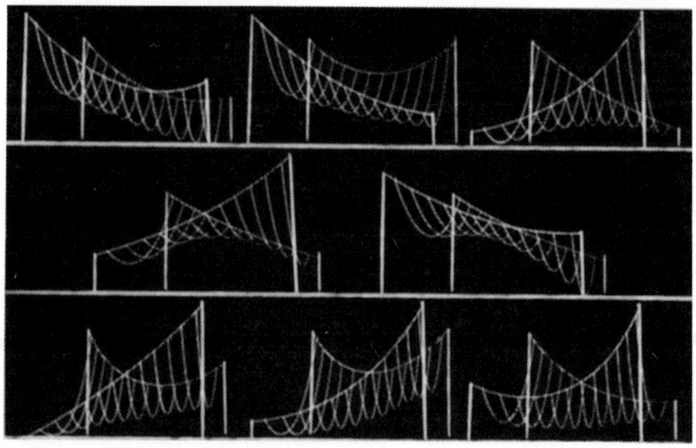

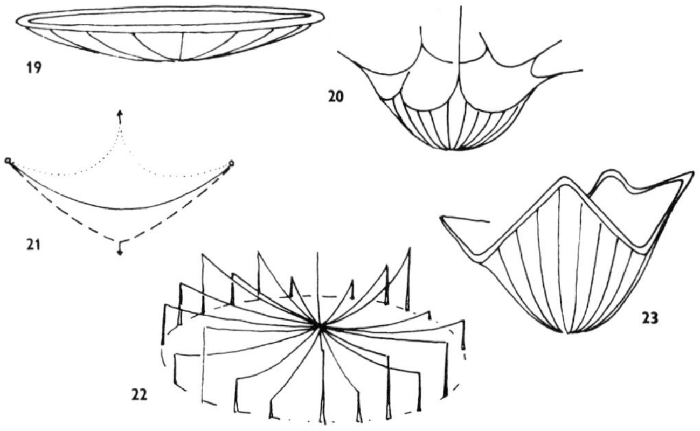

Single Cables Arranged Radially

The pictures on p. 23 show mainly models designed in October 1962 in collaboration* with students of the Masters Class at the University of California, Berkeley. They show a survey of surfaces that can be formed by single, radially arranged cables.

Thus, for example, cables suspended at equal intervals in a horizontal annular frame form a cylindrical surface (Fig. 25). If all free ends are attached at one point a catenoid (Fig. 24) results, at whose center (Fig. 26) all cables converge radially.

If the suspension plane (Fig. 28) is inclined, an asymmetrical surface results. If the center is raised by an additional cable we obtain the shapes shown in Figs. 27, 29, 30, 31, and 32; all these have in common an anticlastic curvature near the central suspension point. The outer circle may be replaced by an arbitrary curve, which can move in a plane or curved surface. The central suspension point may be replaced by circles or other closed curves.

Suspended shapes formed by cables rigid in bending can be used to derive similar structures, subjected to compression, which do not bend under uniform loads. Consequently, cable models serve also as models for arch or geodesic-shell structures (Fig. 33).

In the model shown in Figs. 34 to 36 the cables are alternately attached at 12 high and 12 low points lying in a circle. Near the suspension points the circular section of the resulting surface is wavelike since every high cable is followed by a low one.

However, the resulting shape can also be regarded as composed of two surfaces of revolution, of which the upper has a synclastic and the lower (centrally attached), an anticlastic curvature.

Figures 19 to 22 show various basic shapes of radial cable arrangements: suspension from a ring rigid in bending (Fig. 19), inside attachment of cables to outer edge cables (Fig. 20), variation of the shape of the catenaries by a force acting upward or downward at the center (Fig. 21), suspension from a curve which does not lie in one plane (Figs. 22 and 23).

Single radially arranged cables have already been used, although radial nets are more common, see, p. 29.

24
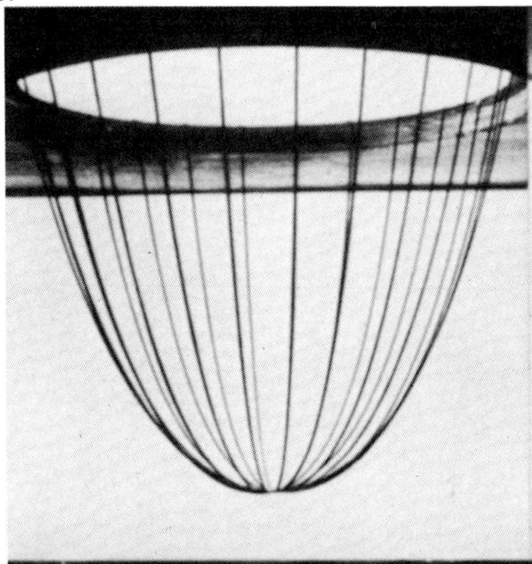
25

26

29
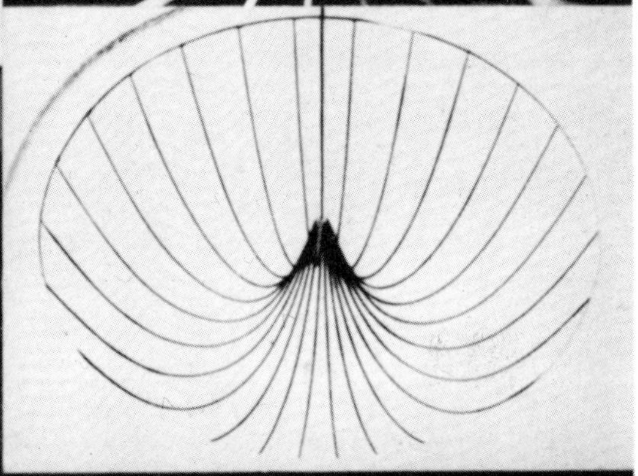
7
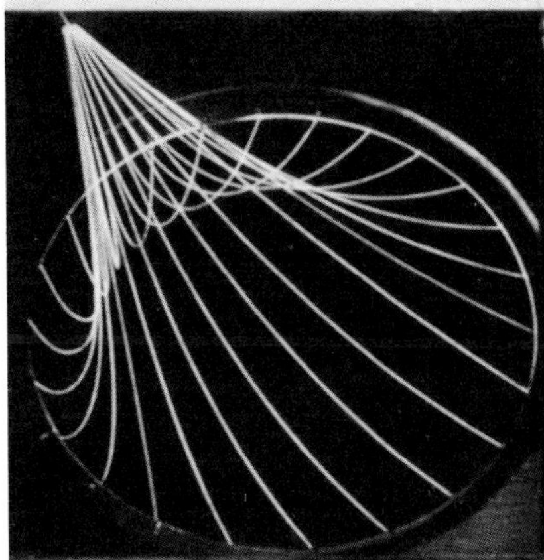
28
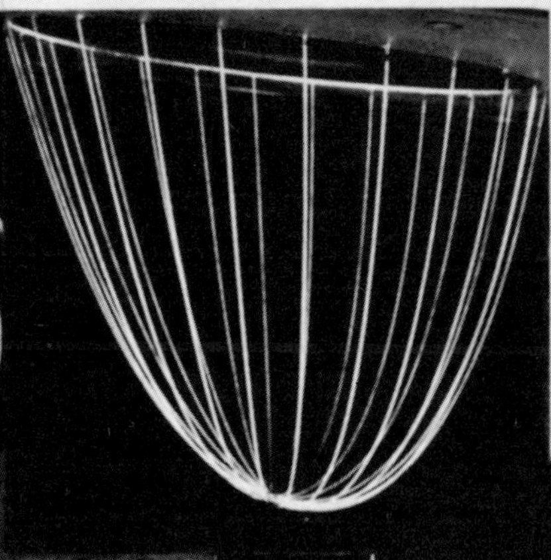
33

30
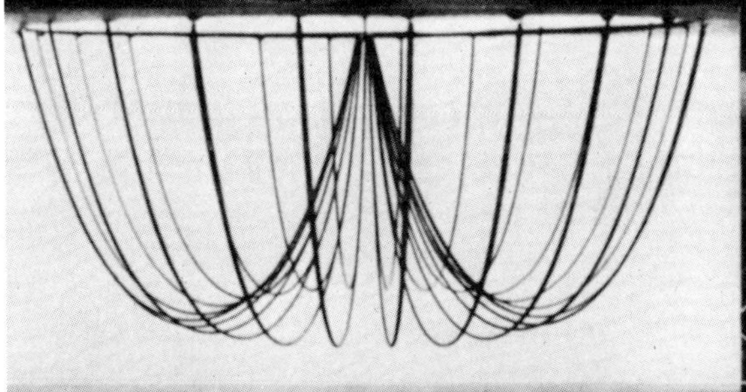
34

31
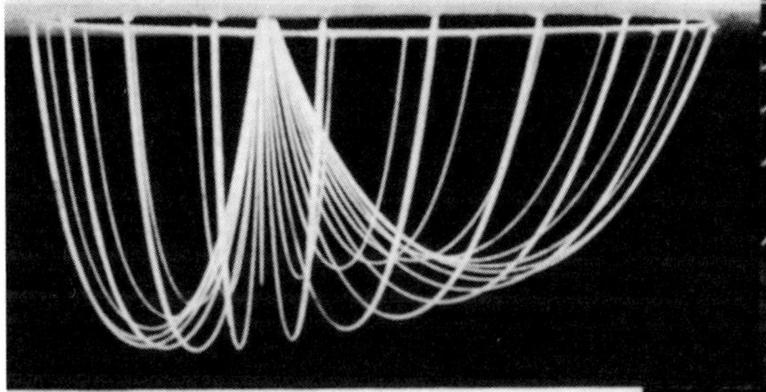
32
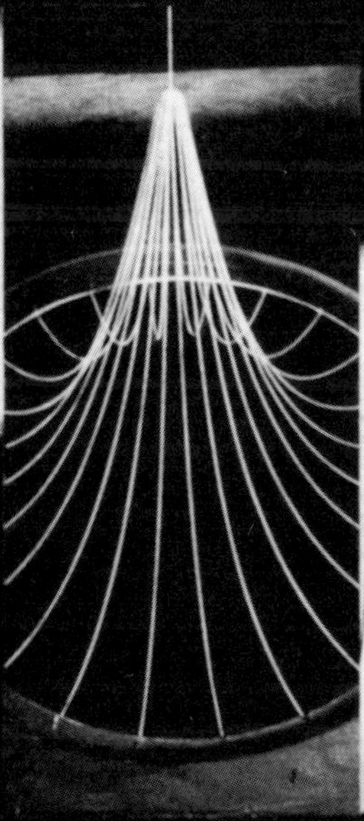
35

36

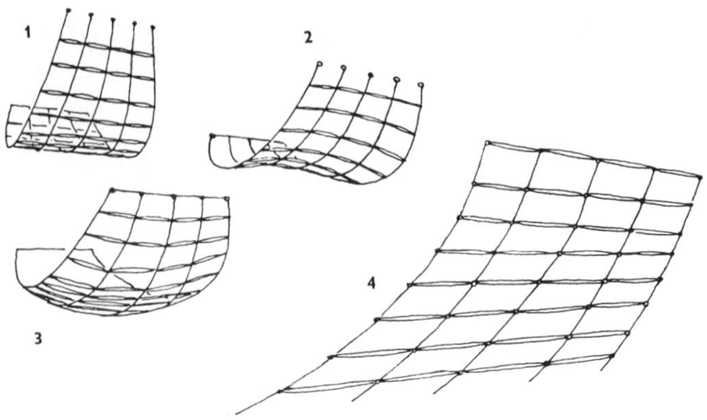

1 2 3 4

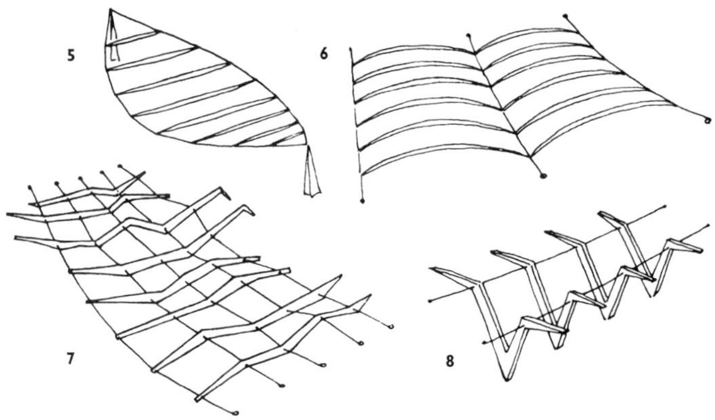

5 6 7 8

Nets of Cables and Struts

Nets of cables and struts can be designed. They have certain peculiarities determined in 1962 by model experiments in cooperation with students at M.I.T. If struts are fixed between two suspended cables (Fig. 5), the rigid struts are subjected to compression. This shape was used by Schwantzer for the 1958 Europe Pavilion in Brussels. Experiments showed that additional cables can be attached at both sides of such a system. We then obtain surfaces with single (Fig. 1) or double anticlastic (Fig. 2) or synclastic (Fig. 3) curvature. Such nets (Fig. 4) are subjected to transverse compression only if the width of the net where it is suspended is less than in the middle.

Spreads exceeding those shown in Figs. 1 to 3 are hardly possible. If attempted, interesting wavelike shapes are obtained. The smaller the mesh size, the less is the freely suspended net capable of taking up compressive forces. Folds and waves are already formed at small spreads.

Nets of Cables and Elements Rigid in Bending

The struts in the roof shown in Fig. 5 must be rigid in bending to take up roof loads. Figures 14 to 20 show a model made of cables and rigid rods, suspended in different ways. Simply curved surfaces were mainly obtained (Figs. 16, 17, and 20). The cables invariably lay in vertical planes, while sometimes the rigid rods were inclined. If the suspension points of cables of uniform length do not form parallel lines, the surface formed by the net may be anticlastic (Figs. 14, 15, 18, and 19). The different cable sags between the rods show that the cable forces are greater near the edge of the surface than in the middle. This can be prevented by shortening the central cables, which also greatly reduces the bending stresses in the rods.
If the rigid parts are arches rigid in compression (Fig. 6), they must be secured against overturning. Shells attached to three or four points are also possible. The nets (Figs. 7 and 8) consist of supports buckled in one direction.

The Attachment of Nets at the Edges

The net in Fig. 9 is suspended between rigidly fixed girders subjected to bending, while in the net in Fig. 10 each cable is attached to a pylon. The net in Fig. 11 is attached to edge girders with tension-loaded lower chords and diagonals, and may consist of cables except for the compression-resistant upper chords. The net in Fig. 12 is suspended between two cables, and the net in Fig. 13 between two arches subjected to compression.

Some Examples

Figures 21 to 28 show the development of buildings with mainly simple curvature. We remind our readers of the grain silos at Albany, N.Y., although these were of sufficient weight and rigidity (see *Das hängende Dach,* Bauwelt-Verlag, 1954). In the model in Fig. 21, a net of cables and girders is suspended between abutments subjected to bending (1952).* Supports rigid in bending, as shown in Fig. 21, can be replaced by continuous shell-like stiffening mem-

14 15 18 19

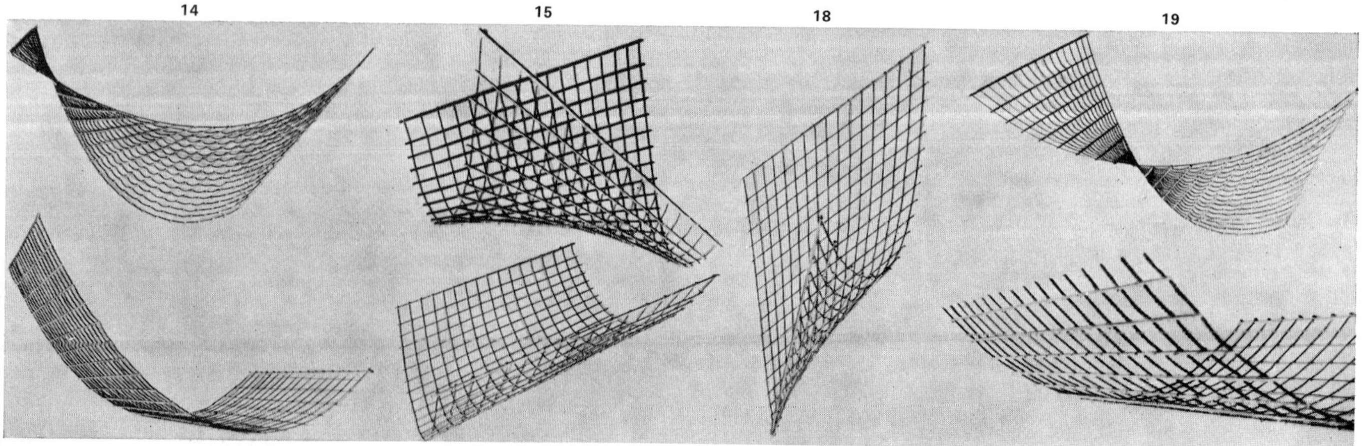

16 17 ▲ 20

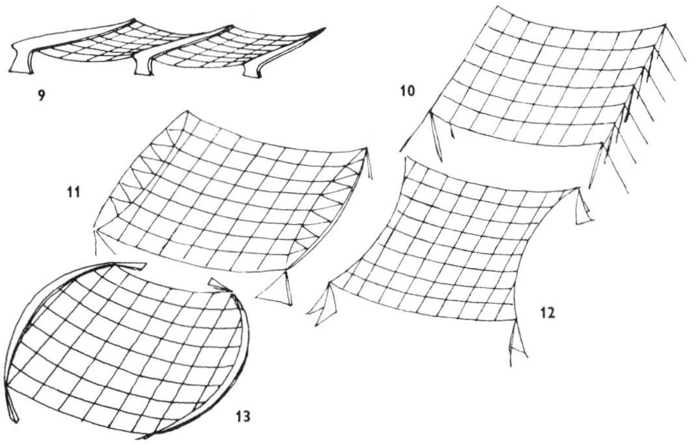

9 10 11 12 13

branes of wood, metal, light concrete, heavy concrete, or prestressed concrete (first investigated in 1950–1951).* In 1953–1954 a large aircraft hangar* (Fig. 22) was designed with a span of 100 m and a depth of 80 m. Sheet-metal girders were to be placed on cables suspended between pylons, then lined with light-concrete panels and the joints sealed. At various points and at the gates, the roof was strengthened against the effects of explosions by tension members arranged underneath (see *Dachy Wiszace* (Hanging Roofs), Arcady, Warsaw, 1959). The Schwarzwaldhalle in Karlsruhe (Fig. 23) (Schelling, Finsterwalder) was one of the first heavy suspended roofs designed in accordance with the above-mentioned principles. The aircraft hangar in Kempten (Fig. 24) was built in 1957 (Gerne, Finsterwalder).

In the same year the Wuppertal Municipal Swimming Pool (Fig. 25) was also built (Hetzelt, Leonhardt). The small Westphalian Hall in Dortmund (Höltje) (Fig. 26) has a simply curved rigid roof, like the Auditorium of Colorado State University (Hunter, Jorgensen) (Fig. 27) and Dulles Airport (Saarinen, Severud) in Washington, D.C. (Fig. 28). Photographs 23 to 28 were supplied by the architects.

The Shape of Freely Suspended Cable Nets and Membranes

Not only individual cables but also cable nets can be suspended from any frame to form either anticlastic (Fig. 1, p. 26) or synclastic surfaces (Fig. 3, p. 26). Simple curvatures (Fig. 4, p. 26) are possible only when the cables are not stressed in one direction in which they are structurally ineffective. The same applies to continuous membranes (Figs. 2, 5, and 6, p. 26). Cable nets and membranes are generally subjected to the same conditions and are often of similar or even identical shape.

Various Net Shapes

The best known nets have tetragonal meshes of regular or irregular shape. Regular shapes may be squares (Fig. 1, p. 28), parallelograms or rhombi (Fig. 2, p. 28), but also rectangles. A net with hexagonal or tetragonal meshes (Fig. 6, p. 28) can form any surface. When the cable-net surface is spatially curved, the angles at the cable intersections vary.

Freely-sagging cable-net structures with tetragonal or hexagonal meshes are not rigid in shear. Tetragonal nets with tetragonal meshes can be extended diagonally under monoaxial stress, while nets with hexagonal meshes are easily extended in any direction.

21 to 28

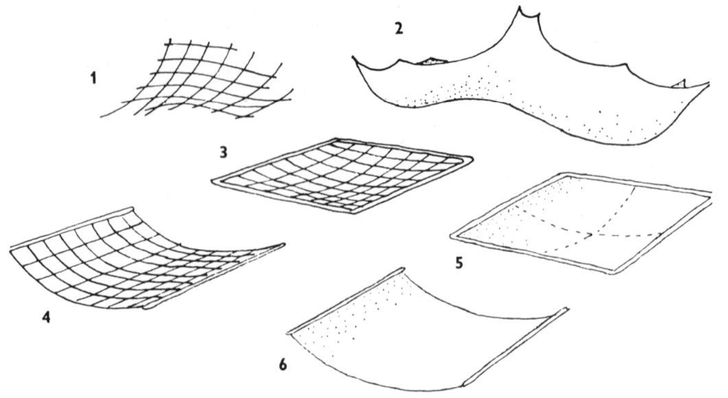

1 2 3 4 5 6

10 to 14

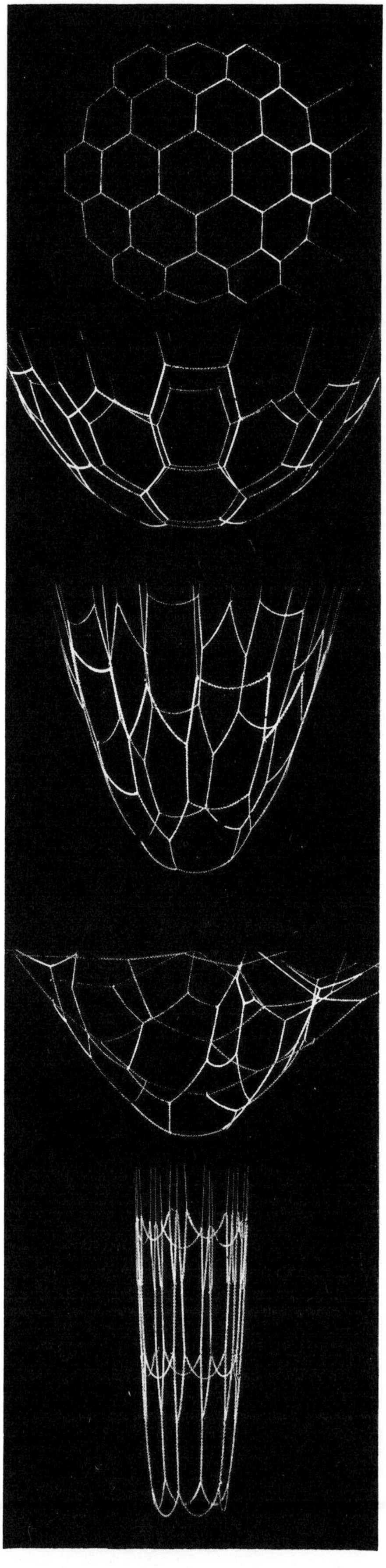

If the net is required to be rigid in shear, but the effect of the edge elements, the dead weight, or the rigidity of the net lining is not sufficient, a triangular mesh must be chosen (Fig. 5, p. 28). However, nets with uniform triangular meshes can only be simply curved. Spatially curved nets with triangular meshes must have different cable lengths in at least one direction. A freely suspended, triangular, spatially curved cable net can be obtained simply by subdividing a net with rectangular or hexagonal meshes (Fig. 5, p. 28).

A certain rigidity can be obtained in nets with tetragonal meshes by inserting stiffening cable triangles (Fig. 3, p. 28) or by means of rigid frames or panels (Fig. 4, p. 28). This also applies to nets with hexagonal meshes (Fig. 8, p. 28).

Many other regular net shapes are possible as combinations of octagonal, hexagonal, and tetragonal meshes (Fig. 7, p. 28).

Net Structures with Regular Tetragonal or Hexagonal Meshes

A net of fine cables with square meshes (Fig. 7, side view) was suspended in a square frame. Other experiments were performed using nets with hexagonal meshes. A dome (Fig. 11), whose view from below is given in Fig. 10, was obtained with a shallow symmetrical suspension. When the suspension points are moved closer together the dome becomes steeper (Figs. 12 and 14). Figure 13 shows the same net irregularly suspended, seen from the side. Figures 8 and 9 show this model as seen obliquely from below.

A suspended net with square meshes was considered* for the roof of the church in Stuttgart-Sonnenberg (Giesel, Leonhardt). This

7

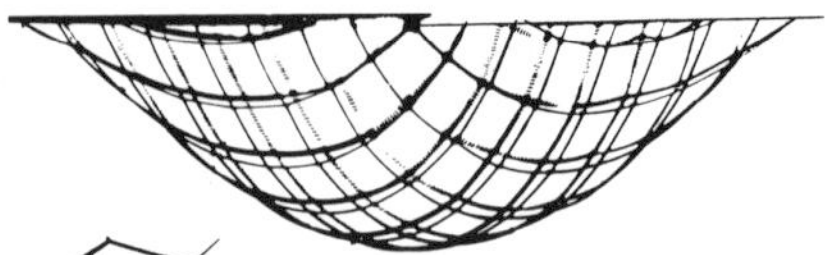

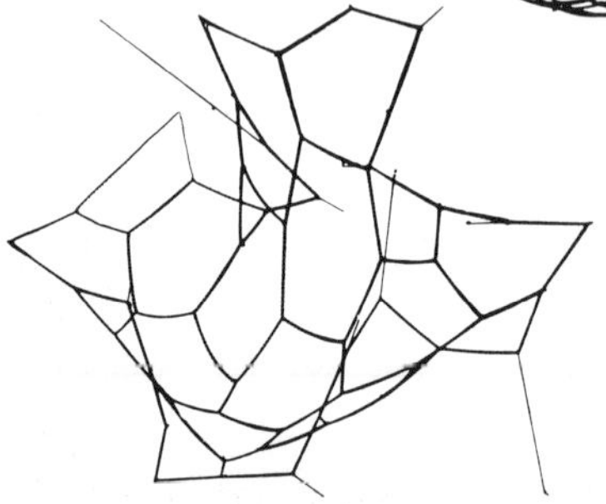

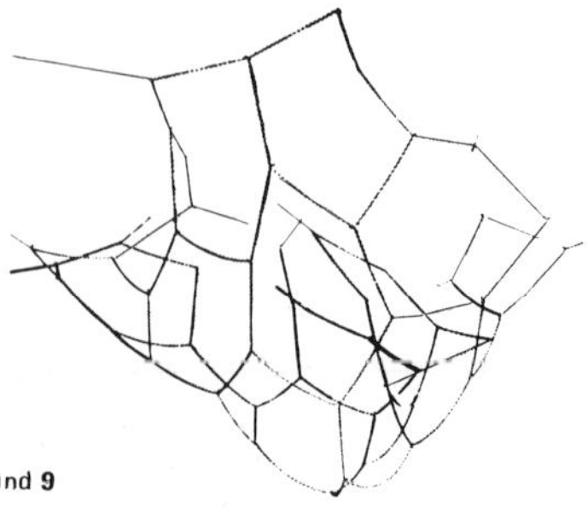

8 and 9

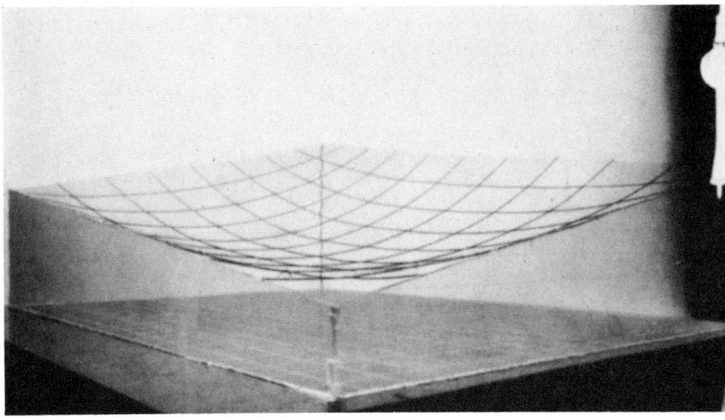

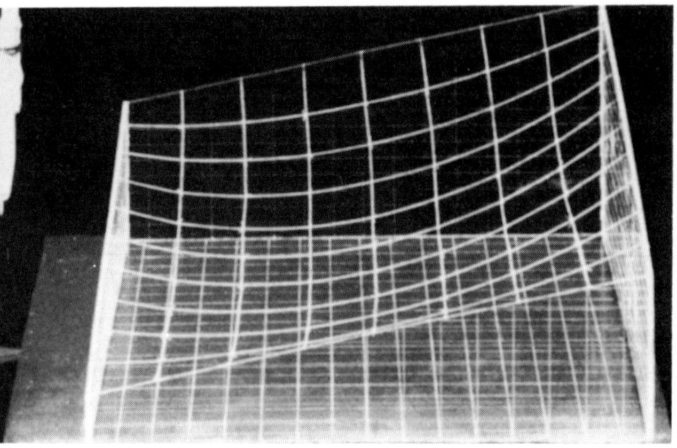

15

16 ▼ 17

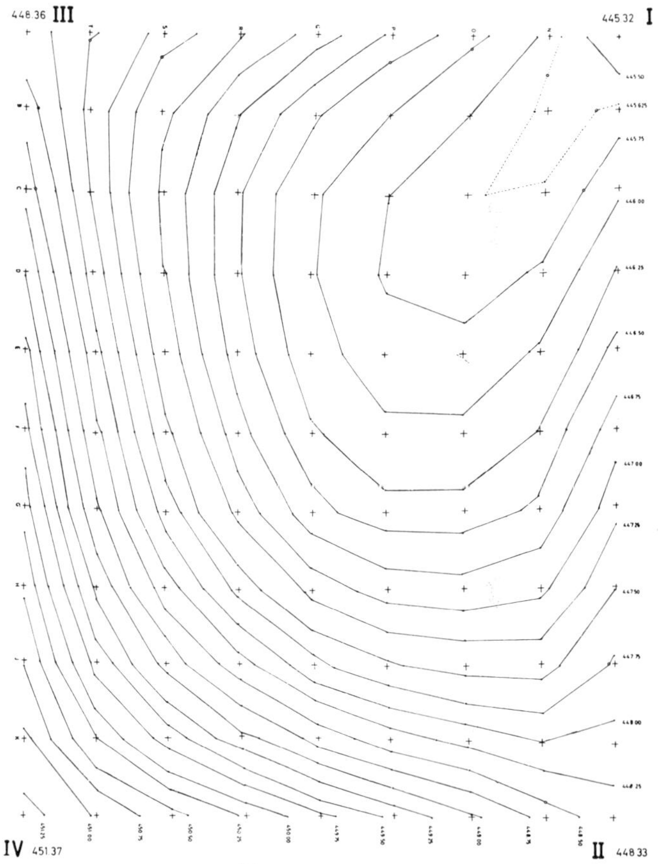

roof is suspended in an inclined plane frame of rectangular plan in such a way that outward drainage is possible via the lower corners. This can be seen from the contours (Fig. 17) and from the model photographs (Figs. 15 and 16). As in the test shown in Fig. 7, most of the surface is synclastically curved, with the shape of a suspended dome.

Experiments with tensile loads can contribute valuable information with regard to efficient design of surface structures subjected to compression. In this connection we refer to p. 160 of Vol. 1. Figure 18 is a side view of a loaded model consisting of a net with square meshes and spanning a square plan with rounded corners. Figure 19 shows a domed shell* of thin slats. A structure based on this model was erected at the Deubau in Essen in 1962 with a span of 15 m (in cooperation with Koch, Pietsch, Romberg, and the Poelzig Chair of Architecture at the Technical University of Berlin). The grid with square fields was assembled on the ground, raised by a crane and given a spatial curvature. After the ends of the wooden slats had been secured to the foundations the bolts at the net joints were tightened, thus fixing the angles, i.e., the shell was made rigid. This structure is geometrically exactly comparable to the model suspension net (see *World Conference on Shell Structures, op. cit.*).

The model in Fig. 22 was similarly designed for a dissertation at the Technical University of Berlin (Höckner, Klammer, Lindemann, and Wissel, under the guidance of the author).

18 19 ▼

20 21 ▼

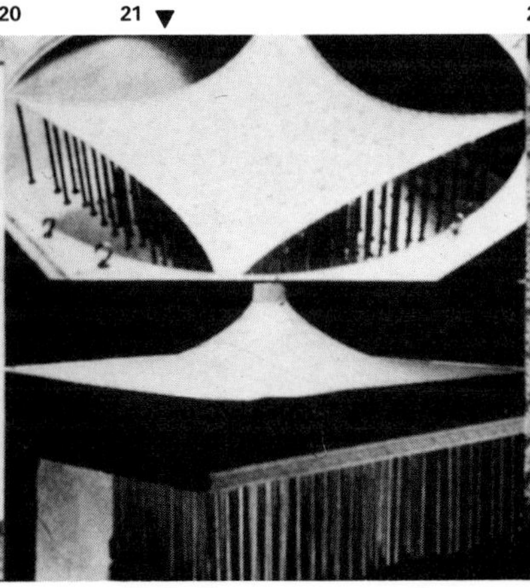

22

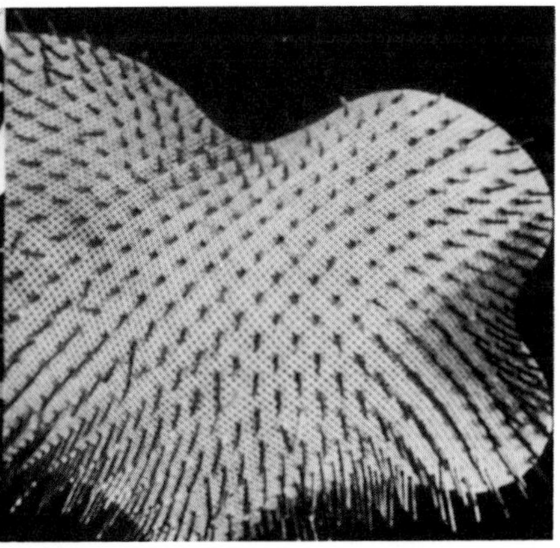

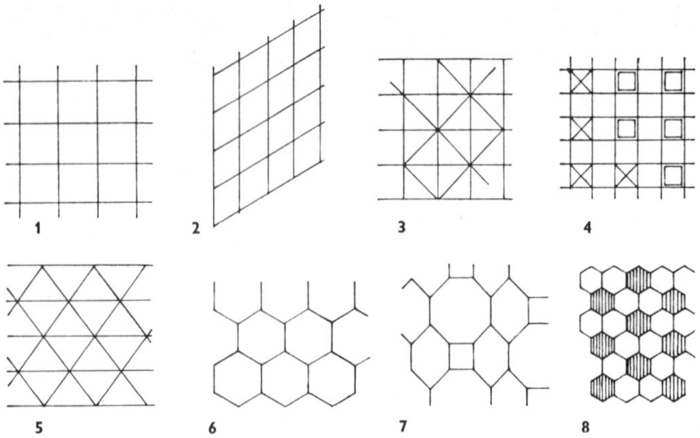

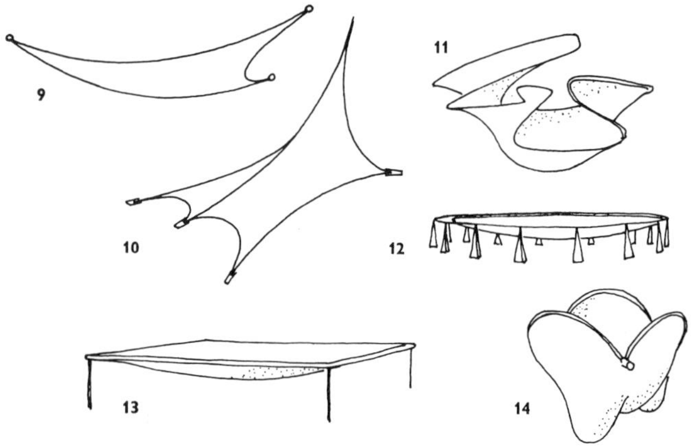

Freely Suspended Membranes

Membranes are closely related to cable nets with triangular meshes. They can take up surface stresses in every direction and assume the most varied shapes. Figure 9 shows a membrane suspended between three points. The membrane forces are transmitted to these points by edge cables. This is also evident from the test model shown in Fig. 20, p. 27 (St. Louis, 1958; see Vol. 1, p. 158). In this experiment, an initially plane rubber membrane is loaded so that a synclastic surface is obtained. When materials rigid in tension, such as sheet-metal, are used, the shape must be formed by appropriate cutting. The stress distribution is then similar.

Figure 10 shows a membrane suspended between five low points and one high point. In Fig. 11 the membrane is suspended from a frame of arbitrary shape, in Fig. 12 from a plane circular frame, and in Fig. 13 from a square frame. Arches can also be used as borders of membranes of various shapes (Fig. 14). An experiment was carried out in 1962* with students of M.I.T., (Fig. 21, p. 27): A membrane was suspended at its center and loaded by weights attached to the skin and by the weight of the outer square frame. The membrane was thus under tension while the outer frame was subjected to compression and bending. A saddle-shaped nonprestressed surface resulted. This experiment can be reversed. We then obtain a mushroom-shaped shell subjected to compressive surface forces, the frame being subjected mainly to tension, but also to bending. This experiment is very important in the study of efficiently designed mushroom shells.

Cable Nets with Nonuniform Meshes

Mesh uniformity is not an absolute requirement for cable nets, but merely facilitates their manufacture. However, cable nets can also be economically prefabricated with nonuniform meshes. Such nets can be divided into those with tetragonal (Fig. 15), hexagonal (Fig. 17), and triangular meshes (Fig. 19). Only tetragonal and hexagonal meshes can be given an arbitrary shape, proceeding, e.g., from a net which can be tensioned in a plane. Nets can also be designed in which triangular, tetragonal, pentagonal, hexagonal, etc., meshes are mixed arbitrarily.

Figure 16 shows a so-called orthogonal cable net freely suspended from a square frame. The cables of an orthogonal net form vertical planes. The families of cables are perpendicular to each other. The plan of an orthogonal cable net therefore forms a square or rectangular grid. The cable net itself is of varying mesh size, unless it is tensioned in a plane.

The cable net in Fig. 18 has square meshes only along the two central axes that are normal to each other; all other cables are curved. Experiments* carried out in 1962 with students at the University of California, Berkeley, showed that such cable nets have a highly uniform stress distribution when they are suspended at the corners. The model in Figs. 34 to 41 is a net (in accordance with Fig. 18) consisting of very fine cables. It is viewed along a diagonal at various spans (from a very flat net to a very narrow, almost folded, net

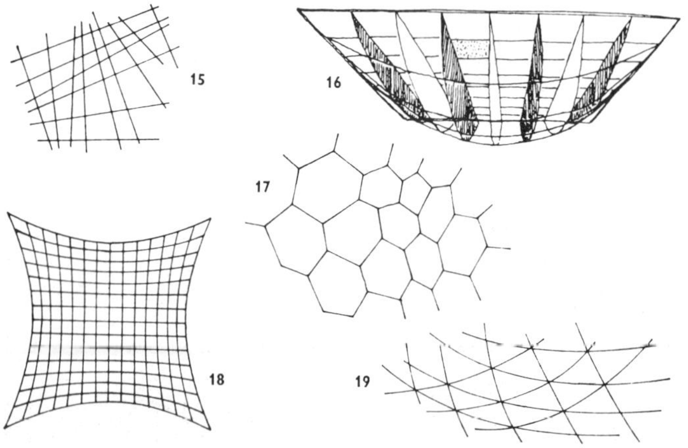

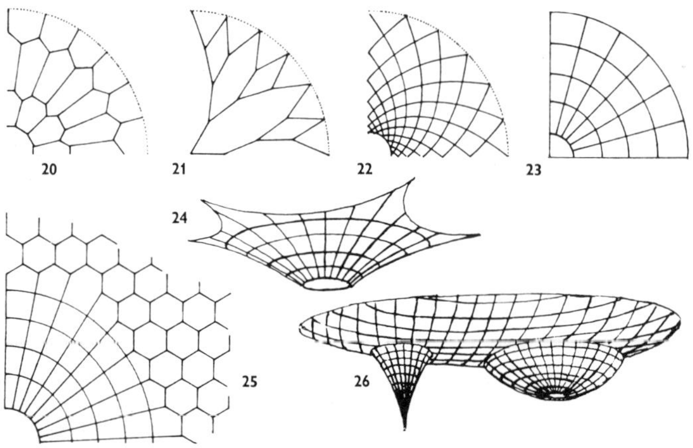

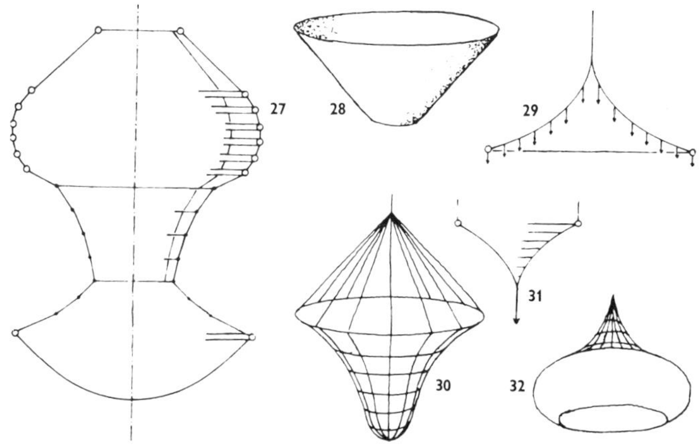

bundle). Many shapes were studied in this way, e.g., nonuniform suspension, as well as symmetrical and asymmetrical shell shapes. Figures 42 and 43 are oblique views of a symmetrical suspension. With the model in Fig. 42 as an example, an experimental geodesic shell* of the same shape (Fig. 33) was erected in the courtyard of the School of Environmental Design at the University of California at Berkeley. This was done in connection with the 1962 International Conference on Shells held in San Francisco. Of course, inversion to a shell structure under compression is not always necessary or important, since such tension-loaded suspended shapes are themselves of great practical value.

Radial-Cable Nets

The best-known form of an axisymmetrical cable net consists of radial cables, extending from the center point, and circular ring cables (Fig. 23, sector). The cable lengths of the outer ring cables are always greater than those of the inner ones, unless there are subdivisions by steps, e.g., Figs. 20 and 21. Among the many possible shapes, we mention only nets with diagonal cables (Fig. 22), forming spirals. In this way we can obtain equal angles of cable intersection and geometrically similar meshes.

Figure 24 shows a net of radial and ring cables suspended between outer edge cables. Radial-cable nets can also be inserted into nets with tetragonal or hexagonal meshes (Figs. 25 and 26).

33

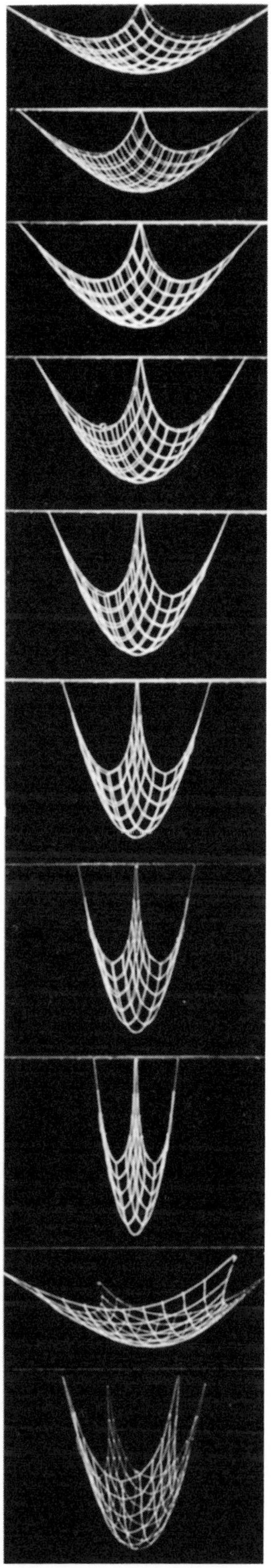

34 to 43

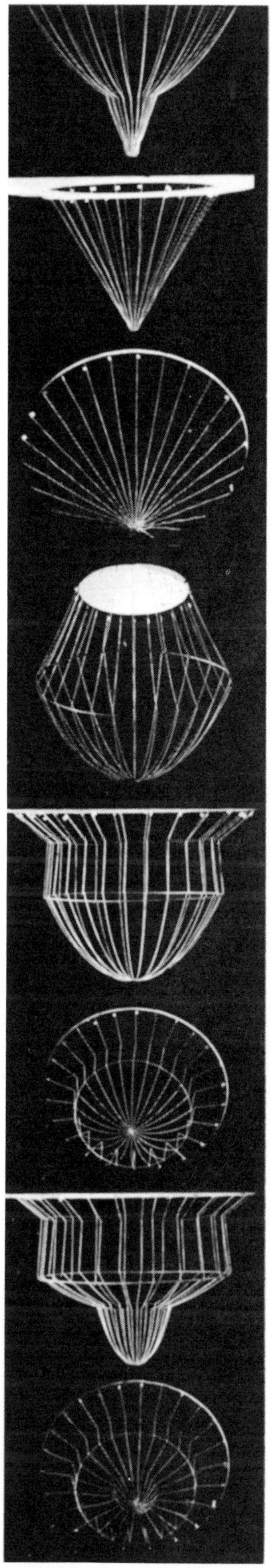

44 to 51

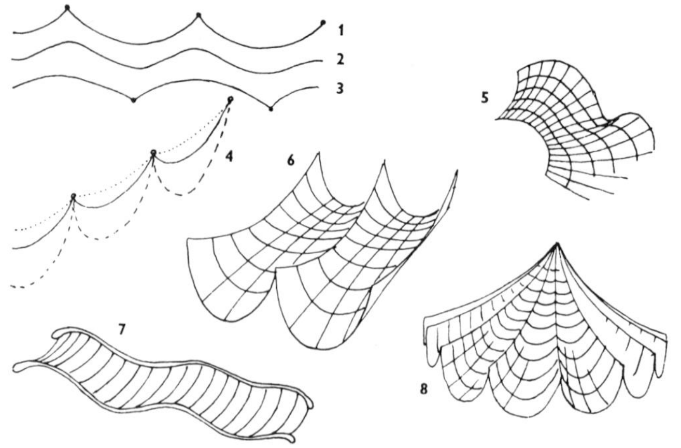

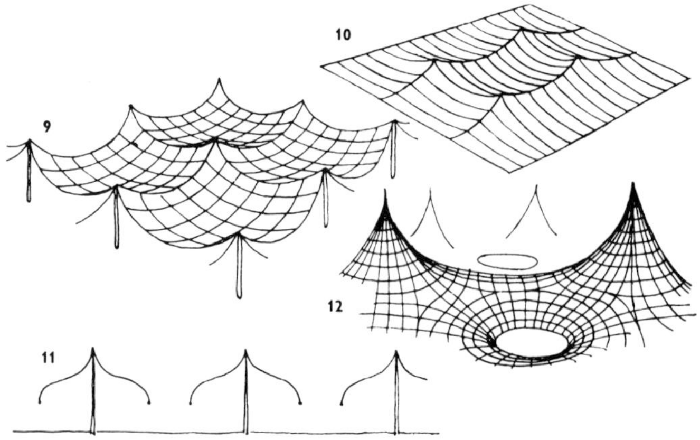

Like membranes or other cable nets, radial-cable nets may in the freely suspended state form surfaces with single curvature—conical surfaces in particular—(Fig. 28, p. 29) or with double curvature, i.e., domes or shells (Figs. 29 to 31, p. 29). The first structure with a freely suspended cone appears to have been the pavilion (Fig. 13) built by Laffaille at Zagreb in 1936 (see *Das hängende Dach, op. cit.*). Among recent buildings and designs, the Stadium in Montevideo (Fig. 14, photograph by the architect) built by Alberto rates special mention. The ceiling is lined with concrete panels that were highly stressed before the joints were sealed. When the load was removed a slight compressive prestress remained only in the roof lining. In this process, developed in 1951,* the skin of the roof acts as a continuous supporting surface retaining the advantages of the suspended dome.

Radial Nets Made of Cables and Rings Rigid in Compression

An axisymmetrical shape formed of individual cables (Figs. 23 and 24) can also be imagined as a radial-cable net when no forces act on the ring elements.

If the ring elements are shortened they become subjected to tension, and if extended, to compression. The lower part of Fig. 44, p. 29, clearly shows the ring cables to be under tension. The initially axisymmetrically arranged individual cables are pulled inward, and may form conical, (Figs. 45 and 46, p. 29) synclastic or anticlastic surfaces. If the basic shape, free of circumferential stresses (Fig. 24, p. 23) is to be extended, compression rings must be introduced (Fig. 47, p. 29). A single ring was used in this model. The model shown in Figs. 48 and 49 on p. 29 has its cables both forced apart by a ring and pulled together by a cable. An additional tension ring has been fitted in the model shown in Figs. 50 and 51 on p. 29.

Almost any axisymmetrical shape can be obtained from radial-cable nets by means of ring cables and compression rings. Figure 27, p. 29, shows an axisymmetrical shape (starting from the bottom) composed of individual cables attached to a ring (represented in the cross section by a small circle). Above the compression ring the radial cables are pulled together by seven ring cables (represented in the cross section as points). The force in the third ring cable from the bottom is greater than in the others. This causes a constriction. The cable net above and below this constriction has an anticlastic curvature and forms a hose. The cables in the uppermost quarter are again forced apart by six rigid rings. At the top the structure is suspended from a narrow ring by individual cables. All horizontal sections are circular. All vertical sections between the individual ring elements are parts of catenaries whose curvature is greater in the lower regions of the axisymmetrical body than in the upper regions.

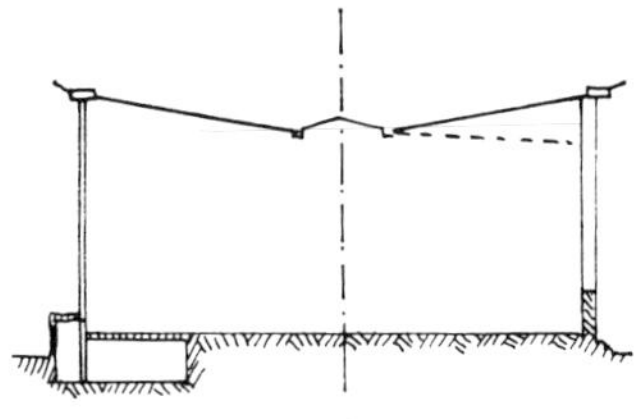
13

Spreading can also be effected by continuous shells instead of rings. The lower part of the onion-shaped body of revolution in Fig. 32, p. 29, is formed by a shell subjected to compression in the circumferential direction and to tension in the meridianal direction.

Wave-Shaped Nonprestressed Nets and Membranes

Cable nets and membranes can be arranged to form wave-shaped surfaces. The cables or cable nets can be suspended between parallel cables as shown in photographs* (Figs. 29 and 30) of models. The wave has a sharp ridge on top and is smoothly rounded at the bottom. The cross section is shown in Fig. 1. However, freely suspended cable nets forming waves rounded on top in cross section (Fig. 2) and, under certain conditions, forming ridges at the bottom (Fig. 3), are also possible. The plane of propagation of the waves may be inclined (Fig. 4, cross section with different sags).

Simply curved surfaces are exceptions in cable nets; as a rule, antielastic surfaces of double curvature are formed. Thus, Fig. 6

14

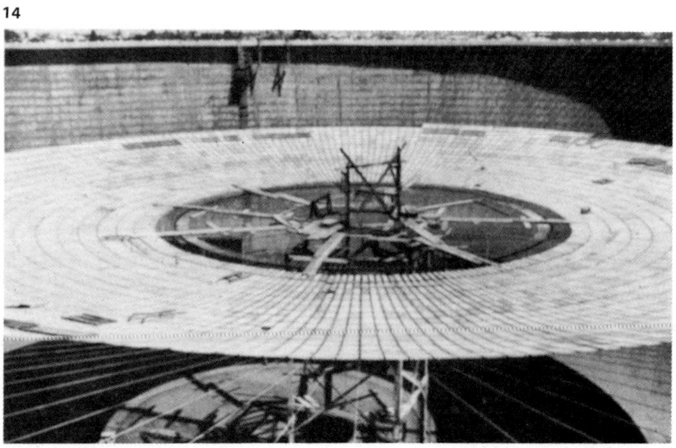

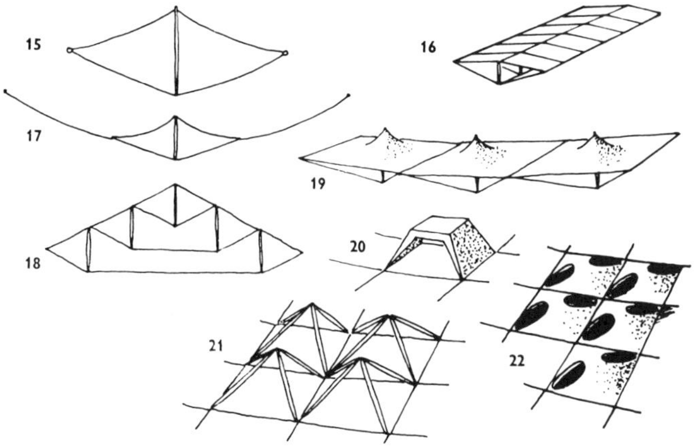

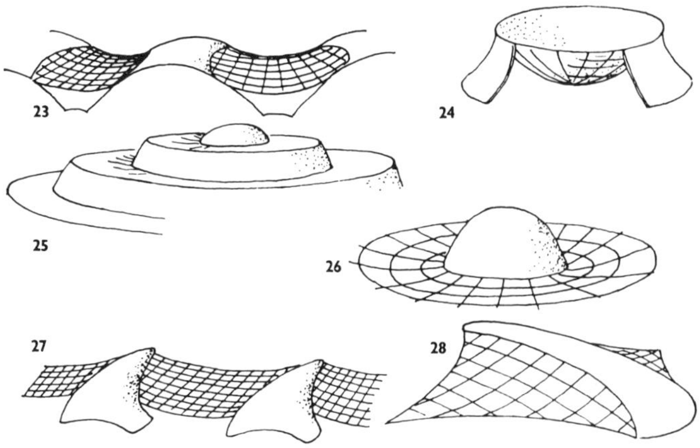

shows a cable net suspended between parallel cables. The cables form sharp ridges; the net has an anticlastic curvature. Figure 5 shows part of a circular ring segment with a smoothly curved cable net. Figure 7 shows parallel cables (or cable nets) between arbitrarily shaped edges, which are approximately parallel in this case, and Fig. 8 shows a typical radial wave shape with central support.

In the model shown in Fig. 21, p. 31, the surface formed by the cables is also wave-shaped. Other wave shapes are given in sketches 9 and 10. Prestressed wave-shaped cable nets and membrane structures, which differ greatly from nonprestressed ones, are described in detail on pp. 82 to 87.

Nonprestressed Cable Nets with Central Supports

These nets can be represented as combinations of sagging cable nets (Fig. 9), or as an addition of inserts between parallel cables forming waves (Fig. 10). However, continuous surfaces must be considered as such. Every load acting on a net causes deformations not merely within the area of application but, in attenuated form, over the entire surface, even across ridge cables under high tension.

The freely suspended form with central support and rounded openings (Figs. 11, section, and 12, view) is suited to large surface roofings with wide spans.

Struts and Shells in Cable Nets

Even nonprestressed cable systems can be extended by means of struts (Figs. 15 and 16). Such systems can be designed in practice particularly when the center of gravity of the assembled structure lies below the plane of suspension (see also pp. 80 and 81).

Figure 17 shows a cross section of an axisymmetrical roof with extended center. A circular roof can be designed with a cross section as in Fig. 18. This becomes much simpler if the system is prestressed. Linings of nonprestressed cable nets may be formed by membranes stretched underneath (Fig. 19), or by folds on top (Fig. 20). Also possible are single rods (Fig. 21) or mesh-sized shells (Fig. 22) each erected on an individual mesh.

Shells and nonprestressed cable nets can be combined in many ways. Figure 23 shows a wave-shaped roof structure in which shells form the upper parts and nonprestressed cable nets the lower parts of the wave-shaped surface. The circular structure in Fig. 24 has a radial-cable net suspended from an outer shell with reinforced rim. It resembles the Montevideo Stadium (Fig. 14) in which a nonprestressed radial-cable net is suspended from a cylindrical shell 94 m in diameter.

Figures 25 to 28 show other combinations of shells and cable nets. Either the shells are used as cable-net supports, or they are supported by the nets. Innumerable combinations are possible.

29 and **30**

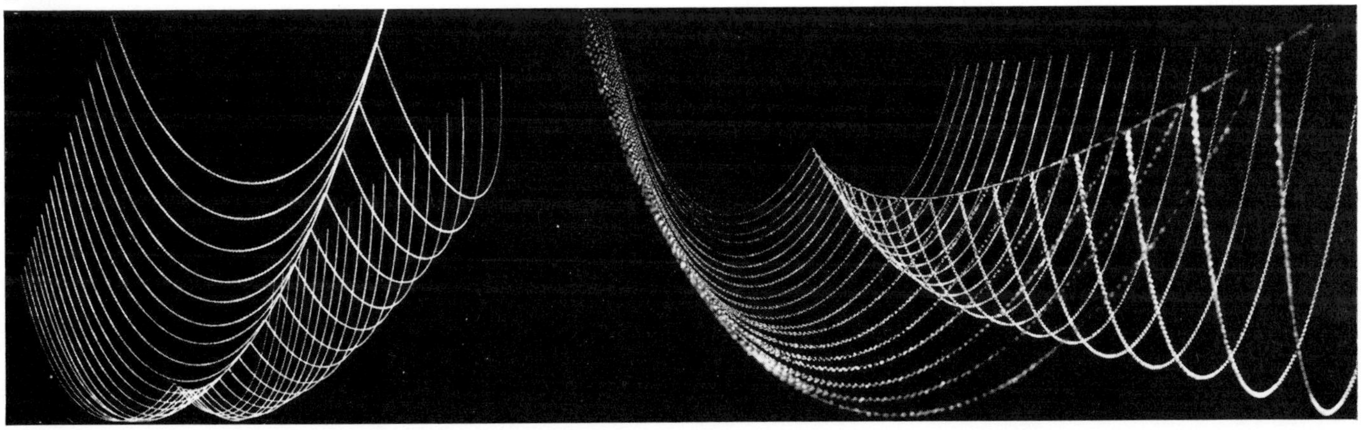

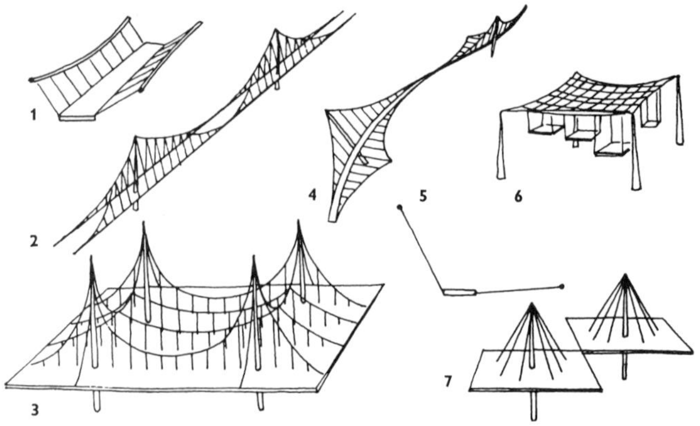

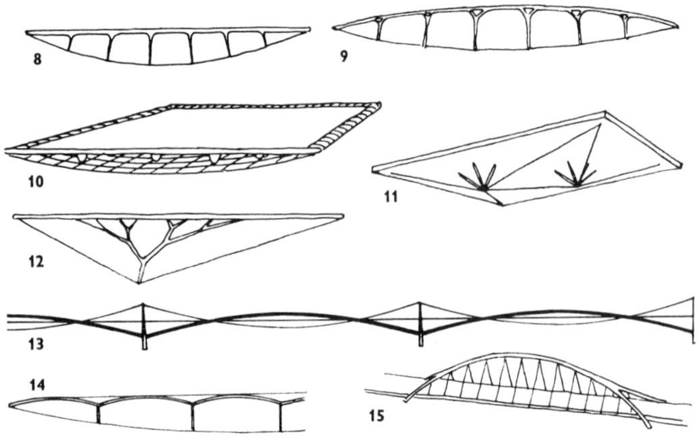

Spatial Suspended Structures

Suspension bridges with inclined bracings (Figs. 1 and 2) are considered as three-dimensional cable systems. The effects of such bracings are particularly evident in bridges with curved S-shaped roadways (Figs. 4 and 5, section through the track). Large roof surfaces, supported by several vertical or inclined braces, can also be considered as spatial systems (Fig. 3). Figure 6 shows several floors suspended from a cable net. In Fig. 7 roof panels are supported by central masts.

Beams or panels, subjected to compression and with tension members fitted underneath, usually form surface or spatial structures when interconnected. The beams in Figs. 8 and 9 act like trusses. The panel of plywood or concrete in Fig. 10 is prevented from bending by a net with short struts stretched underneath. The panel in Fig. 11 is supported similarly, though with fewer cables. The intermediate structure of the panel in Fig. 12, which transmits part of the bending forces to the cables, forms a branched-out skeleton. Arches and cables can also be combined, as in the bridge design (Figs. 13 and 15). Shells are supported from underneath in ceiling structures (Fig. 14).

Nets or membranes suspended one above another with different sags (Figs. 16 and 17) enclose a hollow space and form a spatial structure if interconnected. Figure 18 shows three superposed nets forming two hollow spaces. Struts (Fig. 19) may be inserted in the hollow space in order to take up tensile forces transmitted from the corners and edges of the cable net.

The upper net in Fig. 20 carries nearly all loads, the lower net being suspended from it. Different double- and multicable nets are possible (Fig. 21).

Cables can be used for suspended triangular trusses (Fig. 22). If arranged in series, they can be considered as spatial nets.

Freely suspended spatial cable nets with every node adequately fixed can be formed if tensile forces constantly act upon each node in at least four directions not lying in one plane. We give several basic examples of nonprestressed spatial cable nets with different suspensions. For prestressed spatial nets see pp. 94 to 96.

The cable net in Fig. 23 is suspended inside a pneumatically tensed membrane, (see Vol. 1, p. 29). However, it may also be attached to arches or shells subjected to compression (Fig. 24), to a built-in mast subjected to bending and compression (Fig. 26), or to a horizontal beam subjected to bending (Figs. 27 and 38). Suspension from a cable-net structure above (Figs. 28 and 39 to 41), is also possible. A spatial cable net can only consist of tension-loaded structures; however, it may enclose ceilings rigid in bending or have shell supports inserted (Fig. 25, top: shell; center: panel rigid in bending; bottom: suspended structure).

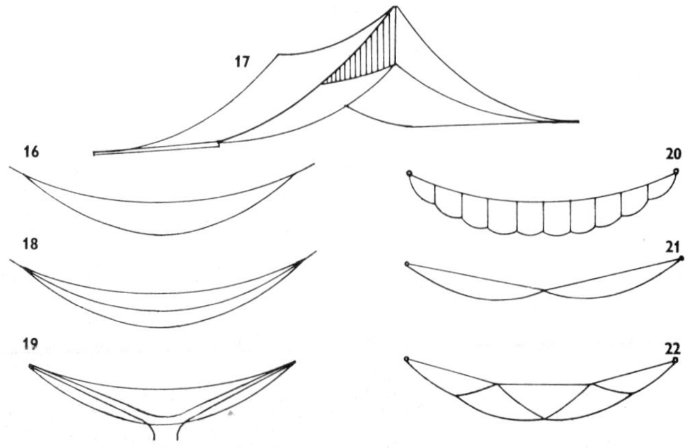

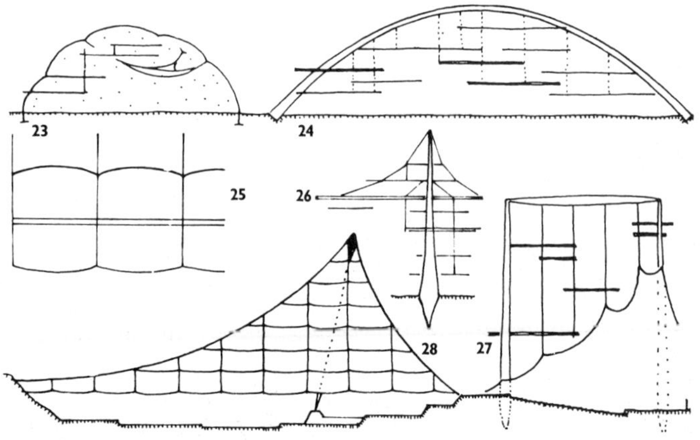

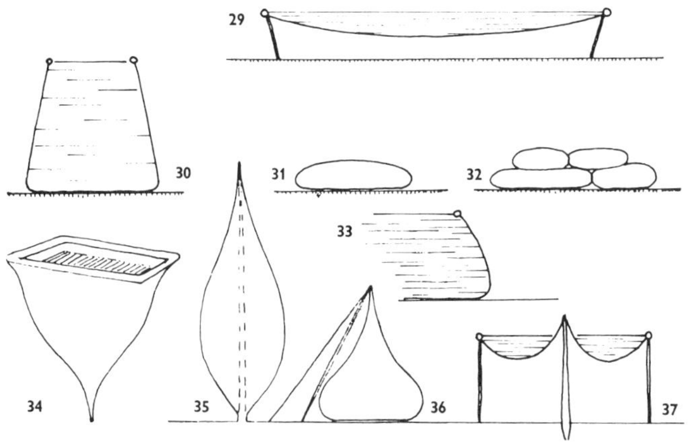

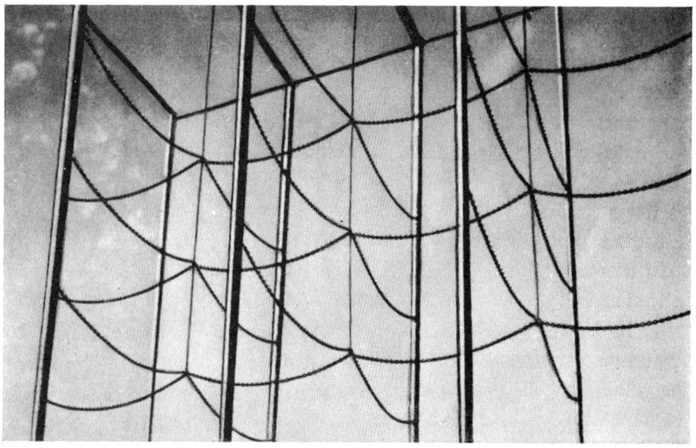
38

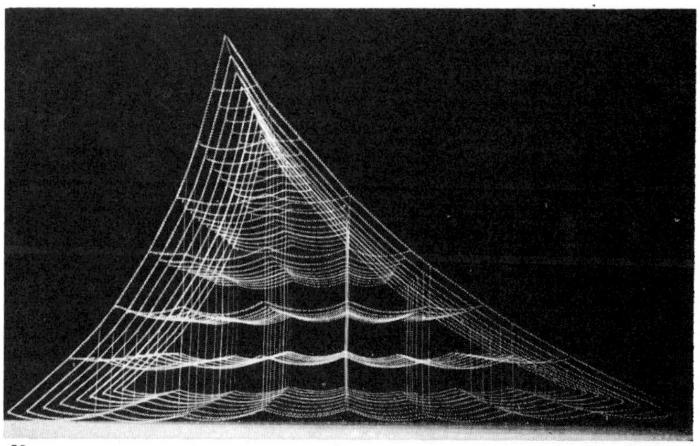
39

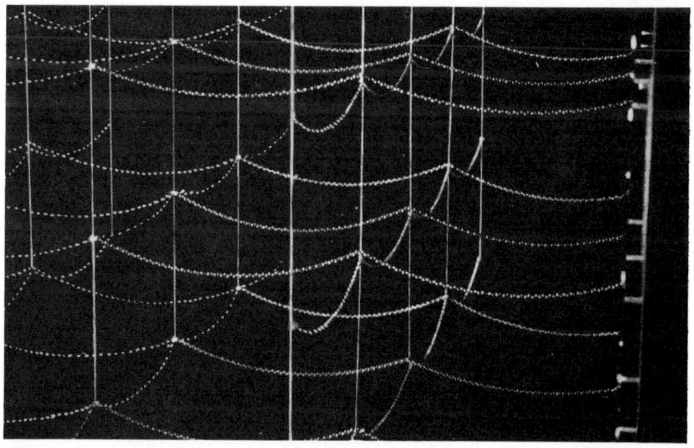
40

▼ 41

Containers for Liquids, made of Flexible Membranes

Containers for liquids, made of flexible membranes, only assume their structural shape if they are filled. The resulting three-dimensional support system was discussed in detail in Vol. 1. A few examples are given here in order to complete the subdivision of non-prestressed tension-loaded structures (see also p. 96).

A membrane filled with liquid is suspended in a horizontal frame rigid in bending (Fig. 29). The membrane is a flexible surface support, loaded by tension in two directions, and is given its shape by the liquid. This shape is determined by the cut of the membrane and by the elasticity of its material.

The same is true for the conical membrane standing upright under the pressure of a liquid (Fig. 30), and for closed containers (Fig. 31) and sandbags (Fig. 32). Buoyancy rims increase the rigidity of containers open at the top (Fig. 33). It is possible to stretch membranes of any shape in frames so as to form synclastic or anticlastic surfaces when loaded by liquids (Fig. 34). Thus an anticlastic surface is obtained when a container (Fig. 36) is held up at one point, or when it is freely suspended (Fig. 35). It is more common, however, for synclastic surfaces to result.

As an example, the membrane of the raised water tank in Fig. 37 is centrally supported.

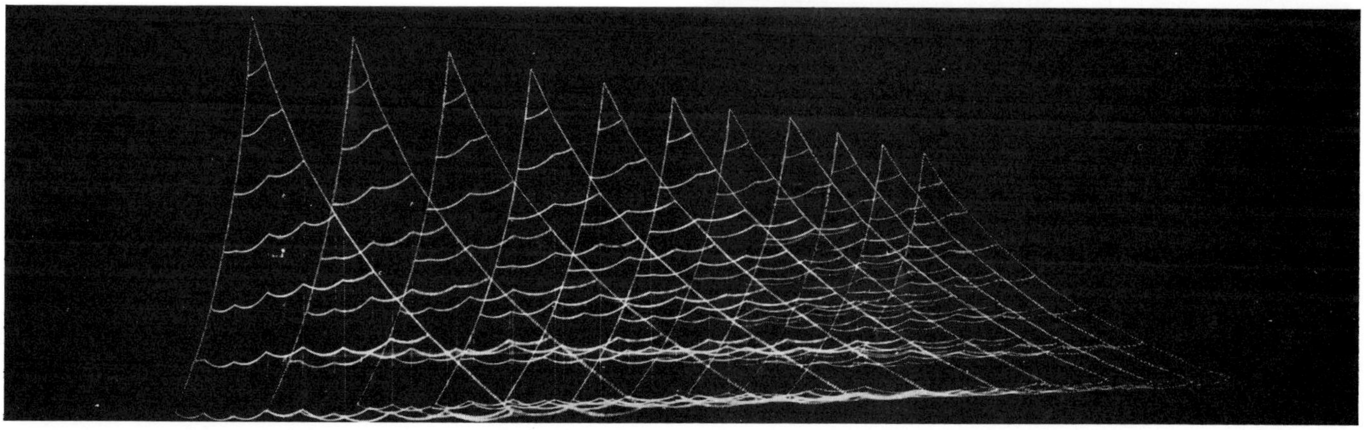

PRESTRESSED TENSION-LOADED STRUCTURES

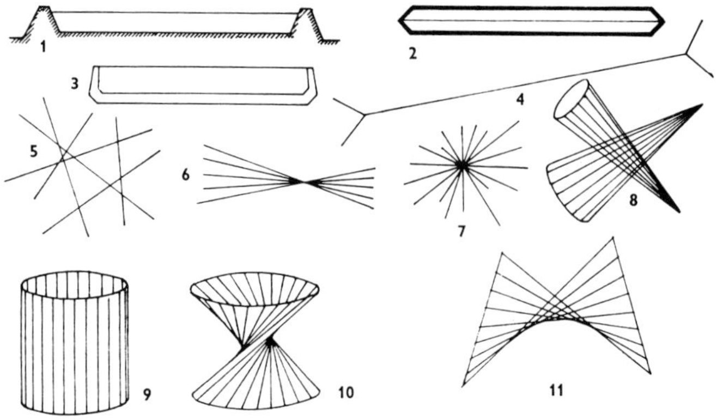

The shapes of prestressed tension-loaded structures differ, as a rule, greatly from those of nonprestressed structures. However, many transition forms complicate classification.

The individual cable is a one-dimensional support system.

Two-dimensional support systems include cable nets and membranes that may be either plane or curved. Prestressed cable nets and membranes cannot have synclastic, i.e., dome-shaped, curvature.
Prestressed spatial cable nets and membrane structures form three-dimensional support systems. They are subjected to slightly different conditions from nonprestressed tension-loaded spatial systems.

This differentiation between prestressed and nonprestressed systems is practical and obvious. However, it has the disadvantage that identical criteria, e.g., types of mesh, edge elements, internal support, etc., must be dealt with separately in both sections.

Prestressed Individual Cables

Any flexible tension-loaded line component will be called a cable. A nonprestressed and nonloaded cable does not assume any definite shape in gravity-free space. Such a cable is only given its shape by the load.

In contrast, a prestressed cable has the shape of a straight line even in the weightless state. The prestressing force is sufficient to ensure straightness even when no external load acts upon the system. When the dead weight acts, this straight line becomes a catenary, the cable being elongated in the process. The deformations of prestressed cables, due to dead weight, are small compared with those of nonprestressed cables. Prestressed cables frequently have a barely visible curvature, thus appearing to be straight. A cable is prestressed when the measured length of the nonstressed cable is less than the least distance between the points of attachment. Figure 1 shows a cable stretched between two fixed supports which do not move even during changes of temperature. When the temperature rises, the force acting in the cable decreases due to the expansion of the material; when the temperature decreases, the force increases correspondingly. The cable in Fig. 1 is arranged horizontally. It forms a straight line in the nonloaded state. When the temperature varies, the force in the cable changes in the nonloaded state, but not its position. Every point of the cable remains at the same place. Neither horizontal nor vertical displacements occur. We have the rare extreme case that temperature changes cause only variations of force or tension, but no deformations.

If a cable is additionally subjected to gravitation, the sag will change depending on the prestressing force.

Figure 2 shows a cable centrally stretched in a hollow body rigid in compression, e.g., a steel tube, the cable being a circular rod of the same material. In this case the tensile force remains constant even when the temperature fluctuates, provided the temperatures of the compression-loaded tube and of the tension-loaded cable remain equal. This is the other extreme. Temperature fluctuations cause only changes of shape, not changes of forces or stresses in the system.
In practice, synchronous temperature fluctuations in different components occur rarely. Compression-loaded components nearly always have greater mass, and thus cool more slowly than the lighter tension-loaded components. Similar conditions obtain in the system shown in Fig. 3, where a cable is stretched in a frame rigid in bending. Here too, synchronous temperature variations merely cause deformations of the entire system, without changing the prestressing force. The system expands or contracts, remaining geometrically similar, provided the materials used have identical thermal-expansion and elasticity coefficients. In the system shown in Fig. 1 every cable point remains at its place during temperature fluctuations; in the system shown in Figs. 2 and 3, however, displacements of the points are caused by the changes in length of the entire system. Yet the points remain at geometrically equivalent positions within the system.
Figures 1 to 4 show the various types of attachment of prestressed cables. In Fig. 1 a cable is stretched between two fixed abutments considered to have a mass of such magnitude that the stresses in them are small in relation to the cable force. This is true, for example, when cables are stretched between mountain slopes. The cable in Fig. 2 is attached to a system under compression, that in Fig. 3 to a system subjected to bending. The cable in Fig. 4 is stretched between other cables, and thus attached to a tension-loaded system.
Prestressed cable and membrane systems may be classified according to type of attachment or suspension. We distinguish between anchorings which are either massive, loaded by compression or by tension, or subjected to bending.
Prestressed tension-loaded and flexible components can be arbitrarily arranged in space (Fig. 5).
Two intersecting prestressed cables always form a plane.
Two nonintersecting cables need not belong to a common plane. The same holds for three or more intersecting cables. Figure 6 shows a fan that is supposed to lie in a surface; in Fig. 7 intersecting cables extend radially into space. Since a single prestressed cable is straight, only surfaces having straight lines as generators can be formed by families of cables (planes, helixes, hyperboloids, etc.). Such surfaces

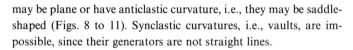

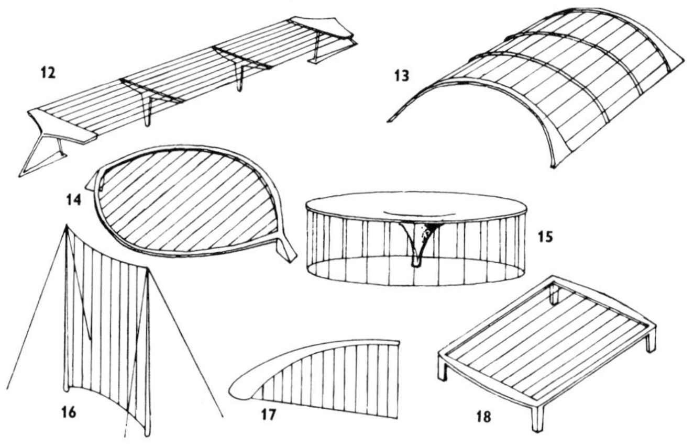

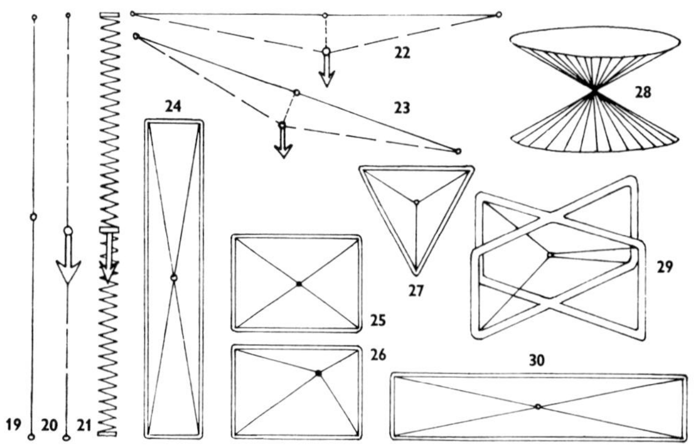

may be plane or have anticlastic curvature, i.e., they may be saddle-shaped (Figs. 8 to 11). Synclastic curvatures, i.e., vaults, are impossible, since their generators are not straight lines.

Structures with Individual Cables Forming Surfaces

Stretched surfaces formed by parallel cables are known from musical instruments, such as the piano, harp, etc. Since the strings must be highly stressed, strong frames are often required. In building construction, Maculan successfully introduced straight prestressed individual cables forming surfaces for roofs (Fig. 12). These were used particularly for railroad platform roofs with end-frames rigid in bending, firmly anchored in the foundations, and T-shaped central supports. An example would be the platform roof at Singen (Hohentwiel).

The free spans of such roof structures are limited, since the deformations under load of plane cable systems are fairly large, even when considerable tensile forces are applied. Spans of 20 m have, to the best of our knowledge, not been exceeded in roof structures.

The system shown in Fig. 13 is similar to that of Fig. 12. The cables are anchored in an arch-shaped end-frame subjected to bending. Arches in the middle permit the spans to be kept small. These arches are subjected to compression at normal loads and to tension when wind suction acts.

In Fig. 14 the individual cables are stretched in a frame shaped like two opposed parabolic arches. No moments act when the prestressing forces are uniform and all cables are equally spaced. When these and similar systems are used for structural purposes, the prestressing forces will frequently be greater in the longer cables than in the shorter ones, so as to compensate for the larger deformations under load of the longer cables.

In Fig. 15 the cables form a cylinder, and are thus stretched in a compression system. They are attached to the rim of a mushroom shell with the central column subjected to compression.

In contrast to the system in Fig. 14, Fig. 16 shows prestressed parallel cables between edge cables. The latter form parabolas when cable forces and spacings are uniform and may, e.g., form a useful support system for antennas. The parallel cables shown in Fig. 17 induce considerable bending stresses in a cantilever beam. Similarly the cables shown in Fig. 18 induce bending stresses in the two supports. The latter are braced against struts, thus forming a closed rectangular frame.

The most varied structural forms can thus be created by the use of different frame designs.

The Prestressed Cable Under Load

In principle, cable-system loads can be classified according to whether a cable transmits forces or moments. Thus, a force acting, as shown in Figs. 19 or 20, along the center line of the cable represents a force load. If the force is normal to the center line, as in Fig. 22, a moment load results. If the force acts at any other angle, a moment load is applied, which may be considered as composed of a force load and a moment load (Fig. 23). If a force parallel to the center line (Fig. 20), acts at a point on a prestressed cable (Fig. 19), the point is displaced along the center line, as are all other points of the cable, except the fixed ends. Figuratively speaking, the points slide along the center line.

Let us assume, for the sake of simplicity, that a prestressed cable consists of two tension springs (Fig. 21). It is then easy to see that when a load corresponding to the arrow acts, stresses increase in the upper windings and decreases in the lower windings. When the latter stresses vanish, the invariant prestressing force is no longer effective. The load is taken up solely by the upper springs.

In the test shown in Fig. 13, p. 36, a double rubber thread, initially 25 cm long, was loaded in stages of 5 grams. The photograph is an 18-fold exposure of the same rubber thread, moved further to the right each time the load was increased. The force-strain curve is nonlinear.

Figure 14, p. 36, shows the same double rubber thread pulled downward by another double rubber thread of the same thickness. Both threads are prestressed and extended to double length. The load was applied at the point of contact in the same stages as before. The force-strain curve of this system is initially flatter than that corresponding to Fig. 13, p. 36, and shows a break between 50 and 55 grams (after the 11th stage). At this point a slackening of the lower rubber thread is observable. In the subsequent stages only the upper thread carries the load.

In Fig. 15, p. 36 the exposures in Figs. 13 and 14 have been superposed. As long as the lower thread remains stressed, the deformations at each load stage are less than for the freely suspended thread.

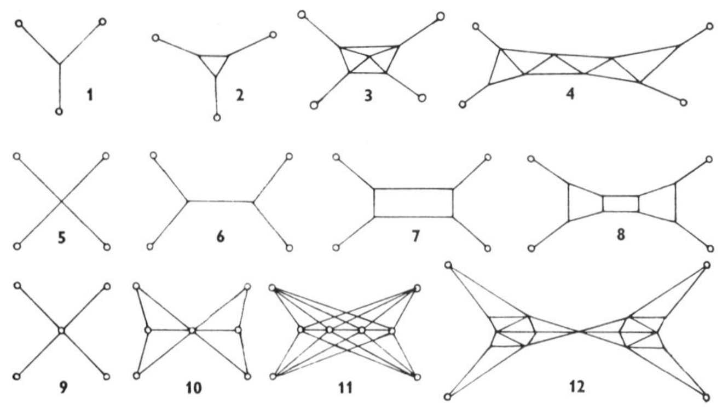

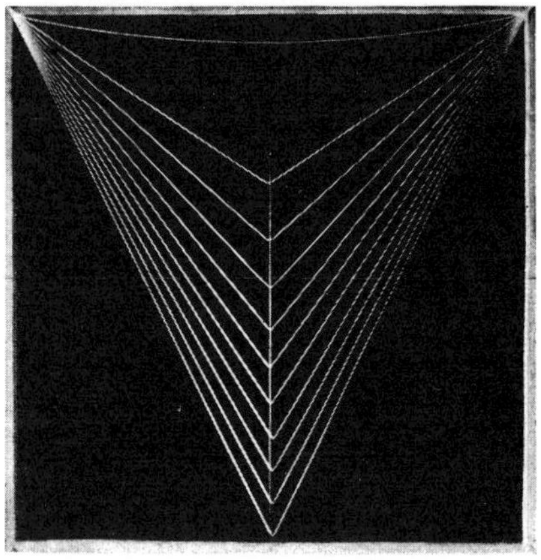

17

Figure 16 corresponds to two combined measurements as in Fig. 15, but with a material that has a linear force-strain diagram (steel-wire tension springs). The upper curve shows the deformations of the freely suspended system, and the lower curve that of the prestressed system. Both curves are linear. The slope of the lower curve is only half that of the upper curve, since double the amount of material is used to carry the load. In this case, prestressing causes the deformation per unit load to be reduced by one-half. Twice the amount of material is needed. An increase or reduction of the prestressing has no influence on the slope of the deformation curves, which remains constant. The deformation per load stage thus remains constant. Only the intersection of both curves is displaced. This means that the deformation cannot be reduced by increasing the prestressing without employing more material, i.e., increasing the cross sections.

If a prestressed cable has to transmit a moment (Fig. 22, p. 35), e.g., if a force acts normal to the cable axis, then the deformation (dashed line) depends on the cable section and on the elasticity of the material, as well as on the prestressing. The deformation varies inversely with the ratio between the prestressing and the load (Fig. 23, p. 35).

Figure 22 shows three long, thin steel springs stretched in parallel between two points lying on a straight line sloping at 45°. The springs were differently prestressed and were centrally loaded in six stages. All stages were recorded by multiple exposures. The dotted lines leading to points A, B, and C, define the path of the point of force application for the very highly prestressed spring A, the spring B, prestressed only half as much as A, and the very slightly prestressed spring C. For the latter, both vertical and horizontal displacements are greatest. When the slope is 60° (Fig. 23), the lateral deflections under the same loads are even greater. Figure 21 shows the deflections of the three springs at constant central loads, photographed simultaneously in different positions. Here too, large lateral deflections are observed at steep slopes.

If two prestressed cables, stretched in a rigid frame, are fixed at their intersection, horizontal displacements under load are prevented if the individual cable-branch lengths and angles are equal, as in Figs. 24, 25, and 30, p. 35. If the upper cable-intersection angle is very small (Fig. 24, p. 35), the system approximates that shown in Fig. 19, p. 35. If this angle is very large (Fig. 30, p. 35), the system approximates that shown in Fig. 22, p. 35.

13 14 15 16

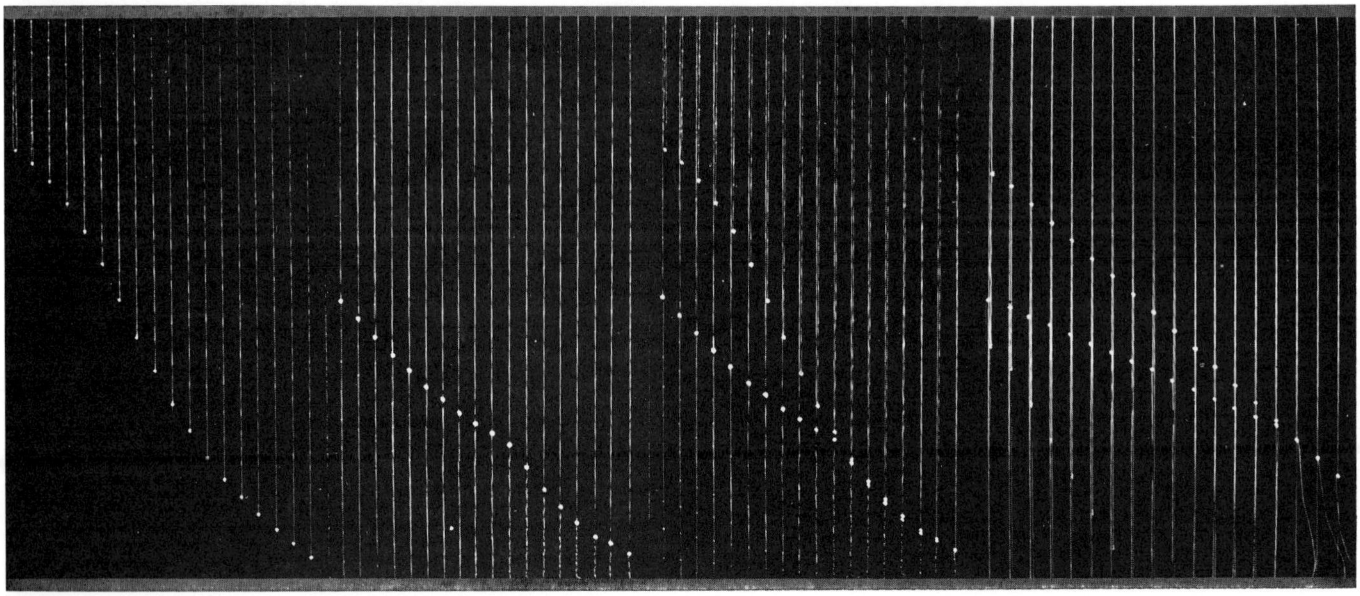

18

19

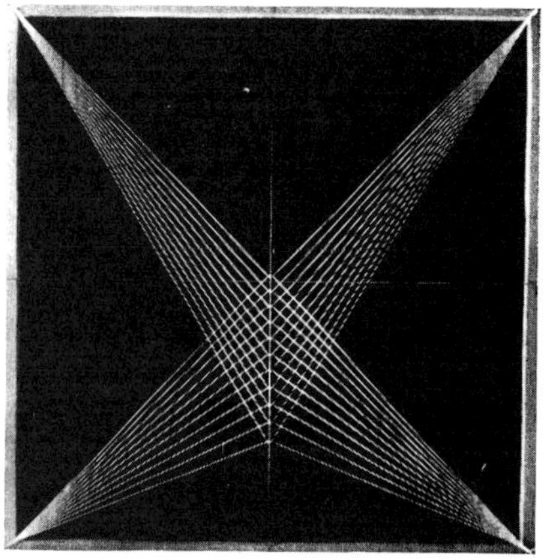

20

In contrast to the systems shown in Figs. 19 and 22, p. 35, which must be regarded as line support systems, intersecting connected cables form surface support systems composed of individual parts under line loads. The deformations are least if, as proved here, the line of action of the force lies in the surface formed by the cables. In the systems shown in Figs. 21 to 27, p. 35, the point of force application remains within the surface formed by the cable. Loads acting in any direction can be taken up. At least three cables (Fig. 27, p. 35) must lie in the surface in order to obtain such a prestressing in all directions. In the systems shown in Figs. 24, 25, 27, and 30 on p. 35, only vertical deformations can be expected under vertical loads because of their symmetrical structure; this is not so in the asymmetrical cable system shown in Fig. 26, p. 35. Here, horizontal displacements are also possible.

At least three cables (Fig. 27, p. 35) are required for a surface system; spatial systems require at least four cables (Fig. 29, p. 35). The number of cables can be increased at will as in Fig. 28, p. 35, which shows two opposed conical surfaces. This shape is formed when both the upper and the lower cables of the system in Fig. 29, p. 35, are spread conically.

The multiple exposures in Figs. 18 to 20 show the same long steel springs (with linear force-strain diagram) that were used in the tests shown in Figs. 16 and 21 to 23. The arrangement in Fig. 17 shows a nonprestressed spring suspended between the two upper corners of a square frame. Even its low weight causes deformation to a catenary. The ten other exposures show the deformations of the system under a uniformly increasing load.

Figure 18 shows the same spring connected to a second spring of equal length. We thus obtain a spring cross in a square frame, loaded as before. Both springs had to be extended to 2 times their length and are therefore prestressed. The deformations at small loads are much smaller than those seen in Fig. 17. At the two maximum loads the lower spring is already slack and ineffective; the deformations are then equal to those shown in Fig. 17. Figures 19 and 20 illustrate the effects of higher prestressing at the same loads. The deformations are much smaller.

A system according to Fig. 25, p. 35, is only effective as long as the load acts within the surface. If a load is applied normal to the surface, larger deformations must be expected. However, the two upper or the two lower cables of the system shown in Fig. 25, p. 35, can be rotated by 90°, as seen in perspective in Fig. 29, p. 35.

Plane Systems Subjected to Stresses in the Surface

The simplest surface cable system has three branches (Fig. 1). By inserting a central cable triangle (Fig. 2) the number of "fixed points" is increased to three. This number can be further increased (Figs. 3 and 4). These are triangular systems that may form extended girder-like systems (Fig. 4) particularly suited to the transmission of moments acting in the plane.

Surface support systems formed by cable branchings are based on cable nodes with four arms (Figs. 5 to 8). We thus arrive at nets with square meshes. Figures 9 to 12 show the transition to nets with triangular meshes. Under load these nets usually experience slightly smaller deformations than other nets.

21

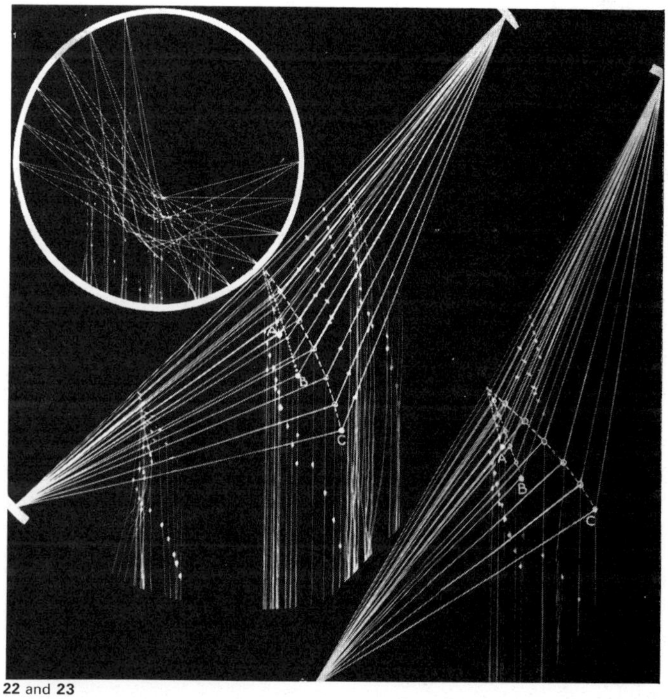

22 and 23

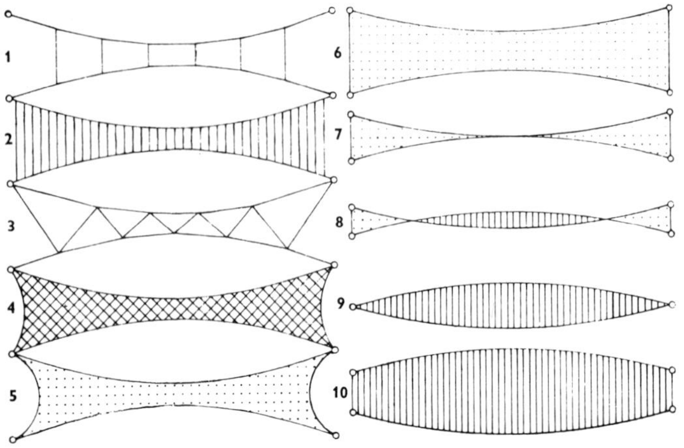

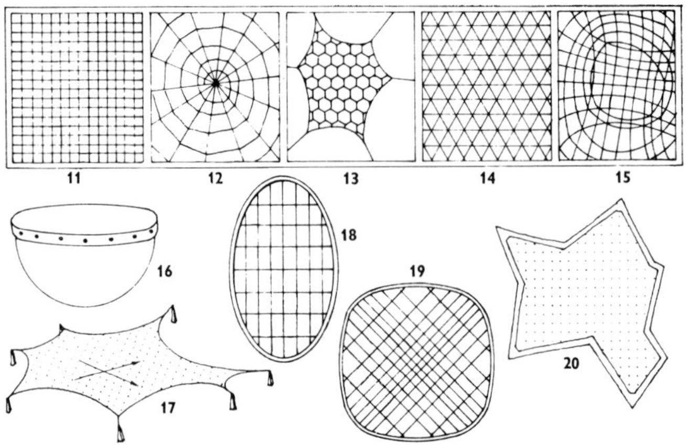

Plane Slender Cable Nets

Figures 1 to 10 show plane elongated cable nets particularly suited to transmit moments acting in the plane of the cable net ("cable frameworks" or "cable girders").

Used as roof structures, the nets are usually vertical, and can transmit vertical suction and compressive forces to the supports. The net shown in Fig. 1 consists of two curved cables interconnected by vertical short cables. Every point is fixed because of the prestressing. In Fig. 2 the spacing of the vertical connecting cables has been reduced. The upper and lower edge cables form parabola-like link polygons when the cable forces in the vertical connections are uniform. The upper and lower edge cables form an approximately polygonal structure in the triangular cable net shown in Fig. 3. A continuous curve approximating a circular arc is obtained in the net system shown in Fig. 4.

A similar system (Fig. 5) is obtained when the connection is formed by a continuous membrane instead of a cable net. Similar systems are shown in Figs. 6, 7, and 8 to illustrate different shapes obtained with identical curvatures of the upper and lower edge cables of a membrane or net. Struts can also be fitted. In Fig. 7 the upper and lower cables touch. In Fig. 8 the curves intersect in the center section so that vertical spreader bars must be fitted. In Figs. 9 and 10 the vertical net consists only of struts. Each of these cable systems is suited to specific duties. David Jawerth has successfully used the system shown in Fig. 3. One example is the Ice Rink in Stockholm-Johannishov (Fig. 37, photograph by Grafisk Stud) which has a span of 83 m.

37

Various Forms of Plane Prestressed Cable Nets

Various types of cable nets can be obtained as mentioned with reference to nonprestressed nets. This applies both to plane and to curved prestressed nets. There exist cable nets with square (Fig. 11), rectangular, or rhombic meshes, radial-cable nets (Fig. 12), cable nets with hexagonal meshes (Fig. 13, here suspended by edge cables in a frame), and nets with triangular (Fig. 14) or irregular meshes (Fig. 15). Structures intermediate between radial and square-mesh nets are possible.

Various Edges of Plane Surface Support Systems

One of the best known plane surface support systems is the drumhead. It is usually attached to a ring rigid in compression, forming the edge of a shell rigid in bending (Fig. 16). A uniformly stretched cable net acts upon its edge like a membrane. The membrane shown in Fig. 17 is bounded by cables, and that shown in Fig. 20, by a frame rigid in bending. The stresses in the cable net shown in Fig. 18 are higher in one direction than in the other. The edge, rigid in compression, forms an ellipse if no bending moments are permitted to act. The spacing of the cables in Fig. 19 varies in both directions while the cable forces are uniform, so that the stresses increase in two directions. The outer frame is not circular but forms a continuous line. Its curvature is increased at the four zones where the cable spacing is minimum.

Other Plane Cable Nets

The cable nets with square meshes shown in Figs. 21 to 24 have different edges. Figure 21 shows a large-meshed grid, rigid in bending ("skeleton"). In Fig. 22 the net is stretched between massive abutments, e.g., to close a cave. Such a net can be braced by an edge cable, or have internal openings. The bracing of plane cable nets by means of three or four cables is shown in Figs. 23 and 24. The compensating struts in Fig. 24 are arranged within the system.

The shallow elongated net in Fig. 25 is spanned between two arches. The arch thrust is taken up by a highly loaded cable. A similar

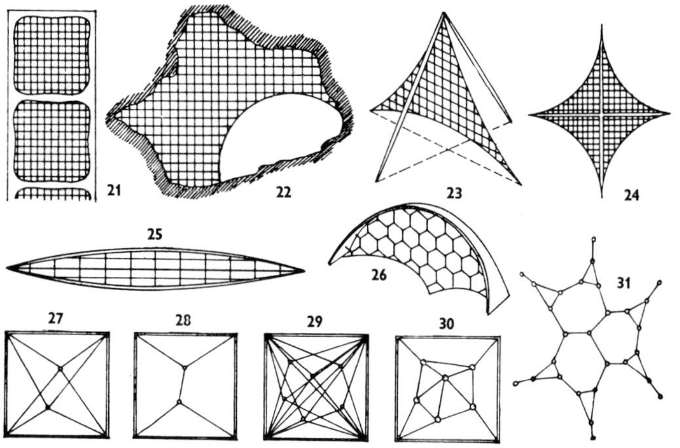

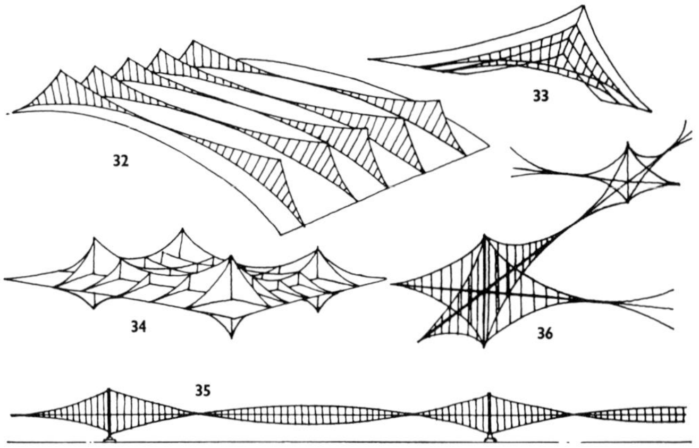

system is shown in Fig. 26. An arch is spanned by a net with octagonal meshes.

There are many ways to fix two points in a frame by means of prestressed cables (Figs. 27 and 28). The structure in Fig. 27 is a system of triangles; that shown in Fig. 28 requires less cable and is more economical in many cases. In order to fix many points (Fig. 29), each point is fixed as shown in Fig. 27, or by means of a connecting net (Fig. 30). Various net shapes of small total cable length (Fig. 31) are formed when at least three cables meet at each point. The sum of the two smallest angles between the cables must then always exceed 180°.

Composite Plane Cable-Net Systems

If we consider plane cable-net systems, especially those shown in Figs. 1 to 10, not as single structures but in conjunction with identical or similar systems (e.g., as in Figs. 32 and 33, arranged in parallel planes), we obtain three-dimensional support systems if the nets are interconnected. Prestressed three-dimensional cable nets are dealt with on p. 94 ff.

Figure 34 shows plane elongated membranes bounded by cables, which intersect at right angles. The structure shown in Figs. 35 and 36 is similar to that in Fig. 34, but contains additional struts in the central region of an otherwise purely tension-loaded net.

Prestressed Curved Cable Nets

A single pair of intersecting cables (Fig. 38) permits the fixation of a point in space (cf. Fig. 29, p. 35). If a further cable (Fig. 39) or a whole family of cables (Fig. 40) is added, we obtain a surface with a central ridge.

If two initially parallel cables intersect with two transverse cables, a spatial cable system with four fixed nodes is formed (Fig. 41), provided the attachments of the first cable pair do not lie in the same plane as those of the second pair. More cables may be added in one direction (Fig. 42) or in both directions (Fig. 43). A continuous cable net results. Prestressed cable nets always form saddle-shaped anticlastic surfaces. Synclastic curvatures are not possible. The shape of the cable net is determined by the surface stresses acting in every direction.

When the stress distribution is harmonic, the cable-net curvature is also harmonic. Every point of the net forms a node (Fig. 38). The four cables meeting at it are not coplanar. The denser the cable net, the flatter it becomes. Wire fabrics and textiles form nets with the smallest mesh. Spatially curved and prestressed, they have a wide field of application.

Spatially curved cable nets, like nonprestressed tension-loaded structures and plane prestressed cable nets, may have different shapes. The various possibilities are shown in Figs. 1 to 6, p. 40. The first shows predominantly square meshes, the second, rhombic meshes; in both cases two families of cables intersect at right or acute angles. If a third family of cables is added in such a way that the cables form the shortest connections between their ends, the resulting cable net has meshes with three to six corners (Fig. 3, p. 40). If, however, the third family of cables is stretched in such a way that it touches only the nodes of the two other families, the resulting cable net has triangular meshes. The cable nets shown in Figs. 1, 2, and 5, p. 40 are easily deformed and can be stretched in any frame. This

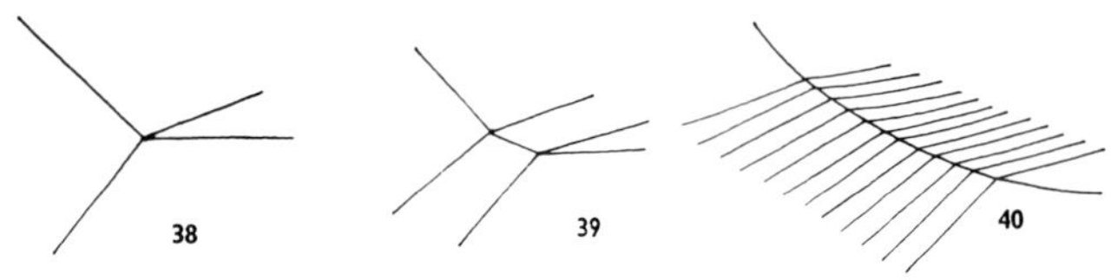

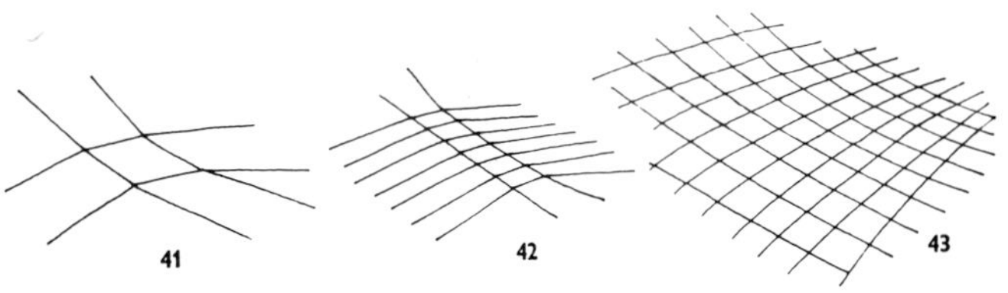

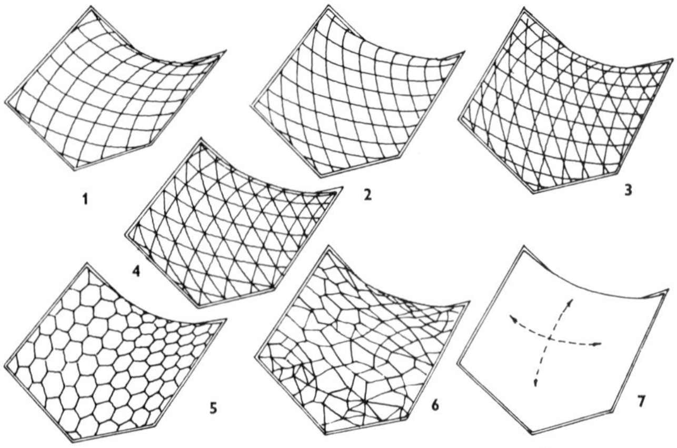

1 2 3 4 5 6 7

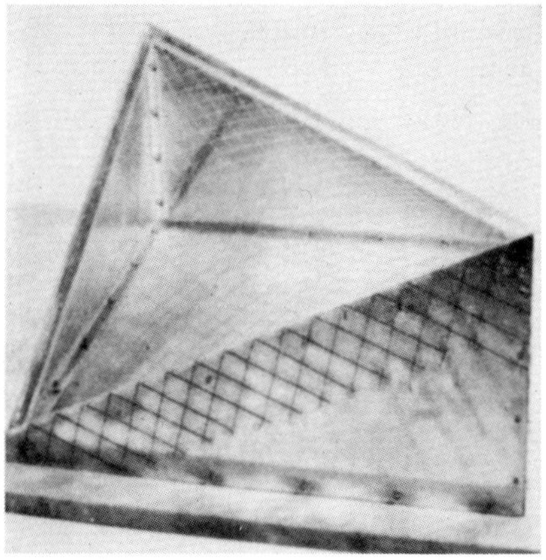

8

is not so with triangular nets. Their shape is fixed by the triangular mesh structure. Any change in shape causes elongation or unloading of cables.

In a cable net with hexagonal meshes (Fig. 5), every node is fixed in three directions, i.e., it lies in a small plane. The meshes form hexagonal cable frames that are plane only in flat nets. In other nets they form spatial cable systems. Prestressed hexagonal nets are usually less rigid than nets with triangular or tetragonal meshes. If large deformations are desired or permissible, hexagonal nets may be suitable (e.g., safety nets).

Cable nets may have any type of mesh and cable length (Fig. 6).

Nets with triangular meshes can take up shearing stresses, in contrast to nets with tetragonal meshes. Cable nets with tetragonal meshes must always be regarded as displaceable net structures, whatever the mesh size.

Nets with triangular meshes may be considered as continuous membranes when their meshes are very small (Fig. 7). Fabrics with small meshes in which the angular displacement of filaments or wires is greatly restricted through friction, adhesion, or coatings form the transition from cable nets to membranes.

Cable Nets with Tetragonal Meshes

Figures 10 to 39 show the most important forms of cable nets with tetragonal meshes.

Figure 10 shows a cable net with uniform stress distribution. As far as possible, its cables form right angles and lie along the shortest paths between the nodes. Such a net will be called a cable net of minimum cable length. We note that a nonplane cable net of minimum cable length does not assume the shape of a true minimum surface (e.g., a soap film in gravitationless space). Because of the spatial curvature, the cable spacing cannot be kept uniform at uniform cable forces, i.e., uniform surface stresses.

If the curvatures are small, a net of minimum cable length and uniform mesh structure will approximate a minimum surface.

The net of minimum cable length in Fig. 10 is suspended in a nonplane skew frame of square plan (Fig. 13). The frame has two high and two low corners. Figure 11 is a side view of the system, seen from the low corner, while Fig. 12 is an enlargement of the right-hand part of Fig. 11. Figure 13 is the plan showing the run of the cables. The development of the cable net into a plane is shown in Fig. 14. Fig. 15 shows a quarter of this developed surface, enlarged. The same presentation was used for the other net systems.

The cables in the net shown in Figs. 10 to 15 run diagonally. The longest cables thus connect the high or low corners of the frame.

9

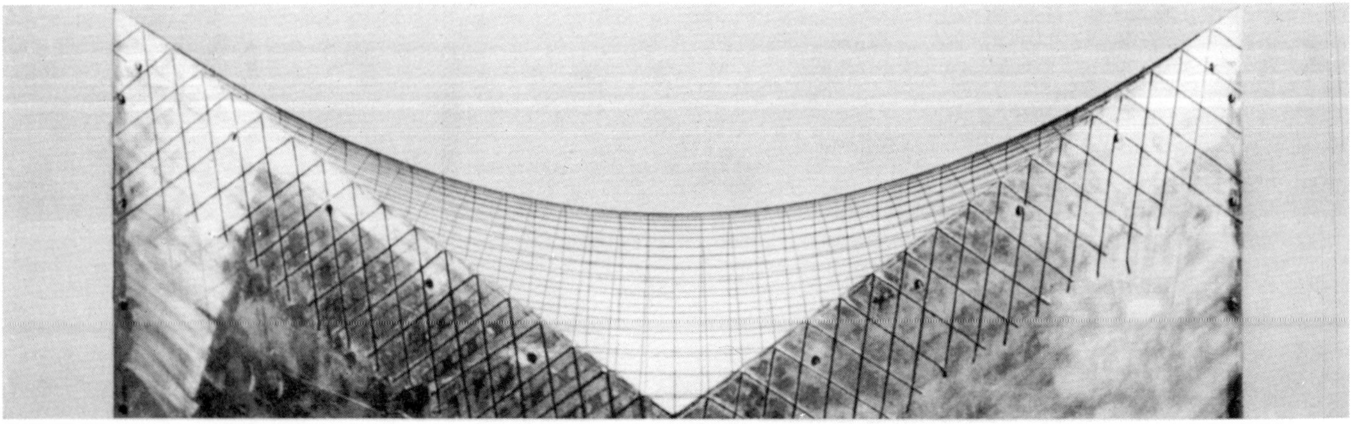

The cable spacings along the two longest cables, which form the axes of the system, are uniform (a, Fig. 12). The side view (Fig. 11) shows that the cables whose centers of curvature lie below the net (tension cables) lie in planes, since they appear as straight lines in the lateral projection. These planes are normal to the planes formed by the cables whose centers of curvature lie above the net (supporting cables).

Nets of minimum cable length need not have uniform cable spacing but may, as in the model (Figs. 8 and 9) prepared by the students at Poelzig's Seminary at the Technical University of Berlin, have uniform spacing [only] at the edge. The cable spacing along the central axes is then nonuniform, decreasing toward the center. Nets of minimum cable length form harmonically curved surfaces only if the mesh width also varies harmonically.

Figures 16 to 21 show a so-called orthogonal net, whose principal axes connect [respectively] the low and high points of the frame. All cables lie in vertical planes, as seen in side views 17 and 18, and plan 19. An orthogonal net is easier to analyze than other cable nets (see p. 108 ff.). Since the cable grid is fixed in plan, every point can be immediately defined by its height. Nevertheless, orthogonal cable nets are not regarded as practical, since, in contrast to nets of minimum cable length, their cables must be fixed at the nodes in order to oppose the forces acting when the net is stressed. Furthermore, as seen in the development (Fig. 21), the mesh width varies, increasing with the slope of the surface.

If the cables in a frame, similar to the foregoing but with acute angles, run parallel to the frame edges, the cable net is also orthogonal. This is evident from the plan in Fig. 25. The cables are straight and form a hyperbolic paraboloid. This is not a minimum surface, since the cable spacing near the edges is greater than in the middle. Hence, the surface stresses cannot be uniform. When the curvature is small the hyperbolic paraboloid approximates a true minimum surface, but often deviates greatly from that shape when the curvature is large (see Vol. 1, p. 29 ff., the analysis of membranes p. 292 et seq.).

Such a net is an exception, since it is both orthogonal and of minimum cable length. The nodes are spaced uniformly along each cable. Since the outer cables are longer than the inner ones, their node spacings are also greater (Figs. 24 and 25). While in nets of minimum cable length (Figs. 10 to 15), and in orthogonal nets (Figs. 16 to 21), the cables are disposed so as to have maximum curvature, they are straight in the cable net shown in Figs. 22 to 27.

Among the many possible and practical shapes of cable nets with tetragonal meshes, we mention those with uniform mesh size throughout the net. Thus, in the nets shown in Figs. 28 to 33 the cables run in the direction of their maximum curvature. In the nets shown in Figs. 35 to 39 the cables are only slightly curved and are

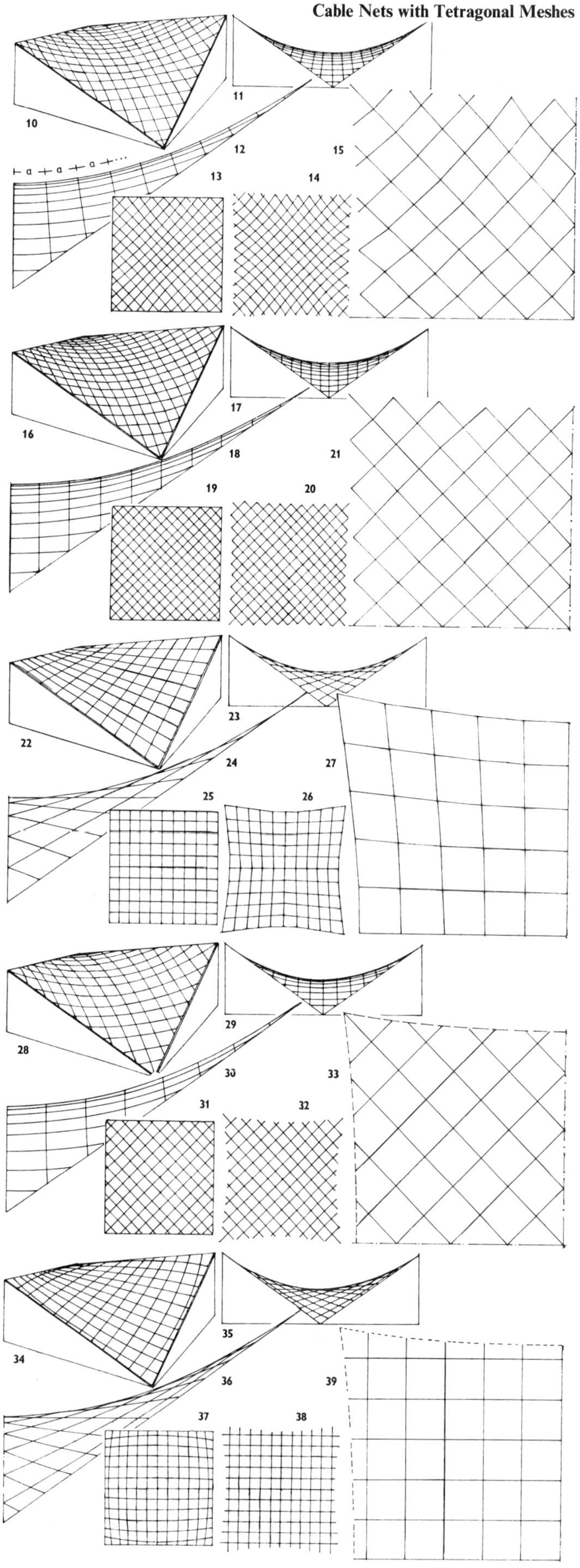

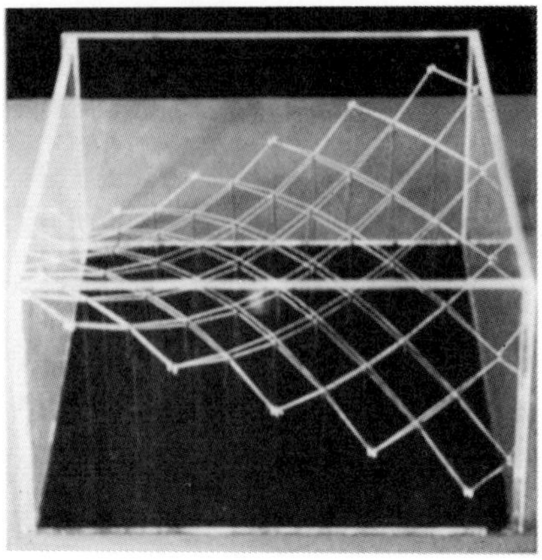
1

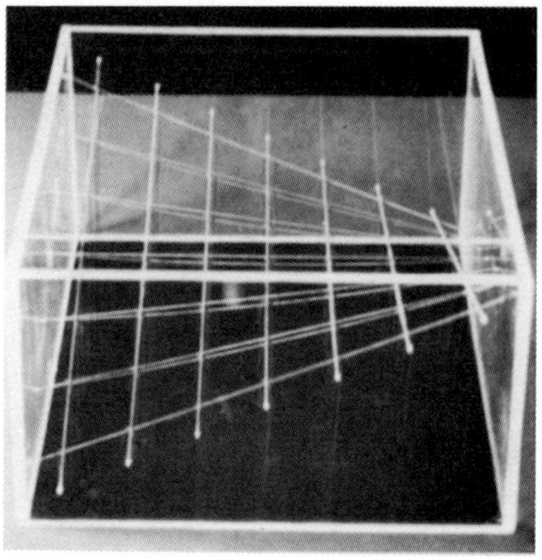
2

almost parallel. Thus, a cable net of uniform mesh size may be stretched to form a plane surface (tennis racquet, wire fence) or may be spatially curved. If the nodes are fixed, the mesh size remains constant under tension, and only the angles between the cables change. If a net is stretched so as to have mainly square meshes, exactly square meshes are obtained only in the region of two axes normal to each other.

In cable nets of uniform mesh the node spacings, measured along the cables, are equal, but not the cable spacings themselves. During angular displacements or distortions the meshes become rhombic. The cable spacings, and thus the surface areas, decrease.

Figures 34 to 39, p. 41, show a cable net of uniform mesh, in which the principal axes of the net are parallel to the frame edges. The individual cables are only slightly curved, in contrast to those shown in Figs. 28 to 33 on the same page. The frame edges are considerably longer than the central axes. Hence, more meshes fit in along the edges (see the plan in Fig. 37, p. 41, and the cuts in Figs. 38 to 39 on the same page).

The 20th Century Coliseum, designed by architect Paul Thiry and engineer Peter H. Hostmark, is an example of a structure with nets of minimum cable length. The mesh is uniform at the edge but not in the center, corresponding to Figs. 8 and 9, p. 40. The nets have a comparatively small spatial curvature (model and finished structure are shown in Figs. 3 and 4, respectively). The cable nets are bordered at the outer edges by girders rigid in bending, and in the middle by beams rigid mainly in compression. The structure measures 120 x 120 m and was the central building of the 1962 World's Fair in Seattle, Washington. See also p. 67 (photograph by Stratford).

Cable Direction in Nets with Tetragonal Meshes

A series of experiments* was performed in Berlin to determine the influence of the cable direction in saddle-shaped surfaces formed by prestressed cable nets with tetragonal meshes. These experiments were based on practical observations in order to substantiate the general theory. Comparable nets were tested under uniform point loads and their deformations determined. For ease of measuring the deformations, the "cables" used were continuous fine steel springs 1 mm in diameter and with a wire thickness of 0.1 mm (i.e., tension elements of very high elasticity). The initial shape was a hyperbolic paraboloid (Figs. 1 and 2) in a square frame. The intersections of the springs were fixed to prevent sliding under load. This was done under tension. Every cable had, therefore, the shortest possible length.

The cables were first stretched in a frame so as to run diagonally, i.e., in the direction of maximum curvature (Fig. 1). For comparison, cables were stretched at the same prestressing force and mesh width in a frame of equal size so as to have no curvature (Fig. 2).

The first test at uniform load showed that the vertical sags were almost equal in both cases.

The sags were photographically measured by double exposure and also determined with dial gages [to an accuracy of 0.001 mm]. Still closer similarity was obtained with the model shown in Figs. 5 to 7 in which the straight cables were, in plan, equal in length to those of the model shown in Figs. 8 to 10. The edges of this net were curved to obtain the same surface shapes. The models shown in Figs. 11 to 13 and 14 to 16 had the same shapes but were stretched in circular frames. The frames consisted of square or circular plexiglass tubes perforated in accordance with the pattern of the desired net boundaries.

The sum of all vertical deformations, determined from several hundred measurements, was approximately 6% less at uniform load in the models with straight cables (Figs. 6 and 12) than in the models with curved cables (Figs. 9 and 15).

The opposite occurred under a concentrated central load. The deformations of the curved cables were approximately 6 to 7% less than those of the straight cables (Figs. 7 and 11, 10 and 16).

No substantial differences were determined at the selected combination of prestressing and elasticity, within the accuracy of the measurements.

The assumption, hitherto made also by the author, that arranging the cables in nets with tetragonal meshes in the direction of maximum curvature generally increases the rigidity, may be correct for large curvatures and cable materials of small extensibility; however, at least for highly elastic and extensible cables, it can no longer be

3

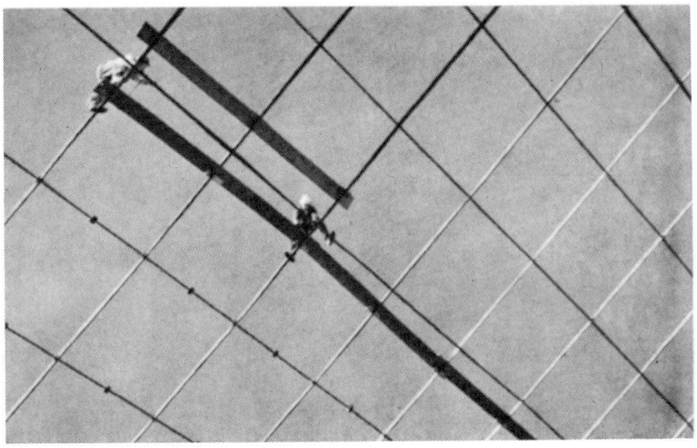

4

regarded as generally valid. The correct cable disposition depends upon cable-net curvature, frame shape, elasticity, and prestressing. The influence of the cable direction must be determined separately for each case.

Comparative investigations of nets with tetragonal and hexagonal meshes are necessary to establish better design principles for optimum net shapes. The same applies to nets with triangular meshes and to comparable membranes.

Slightly prestressed nets with tetragonal and hexagonal meshes may be deformed in the middle through angular displacements. These deformations are not caused by stretching of the material. The net frames exert a stabilizing influence near the edges.

The deformations of such nets will, therefore, be greater than those in comparable nets with triangular meshes or membranes.

When prestressing is adequate, the differences in the deformations of comparable nets under similar loads are less than expected.

Differences Between Cable-Net and Membrane Shapes

A cable net is, according to p. 12, a surface support structure consisting of one-dimensional components rigid in tension, whereas a membrane constitutes a true surface.

In the book *Das hängende Dach* a distinction was made between membrane and cable-net structures. This distinction has been largely abandoned with regard to both nonprestressed and prestressed tension-loaded surface support structures. The reason for this is that cable nets are closely related to membranes, the same design principles being applied to both. Consequently, separate discussion would lead to repetition. The shape of a prestressed cable net of uniform mesh, stretched in an arbitrary frame, is always related to the shape of a similarly stretched membrane in an identical frame. The boundary conditions, i.e., whether the edge is subjected to bending, compression, or tension, are identical, as are the internal supports or cut-outs (holes, etc.). Any basic membrane shape shown in Figs. 11 to 20 on p. 49, i.e., simple saddles, hoses, humps, or waves, can also be obtained with cable nets.

5 to 7

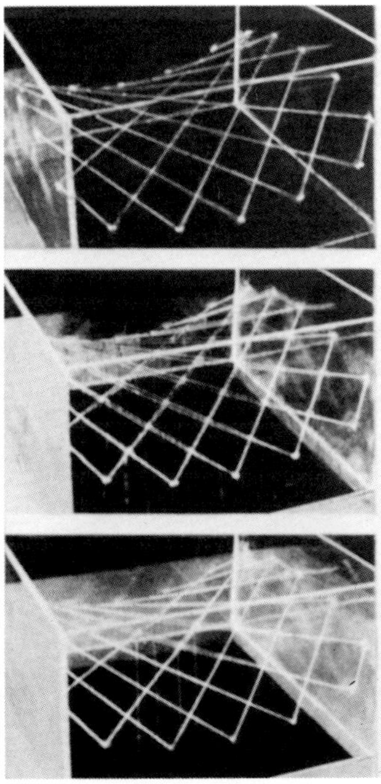

8 to 10

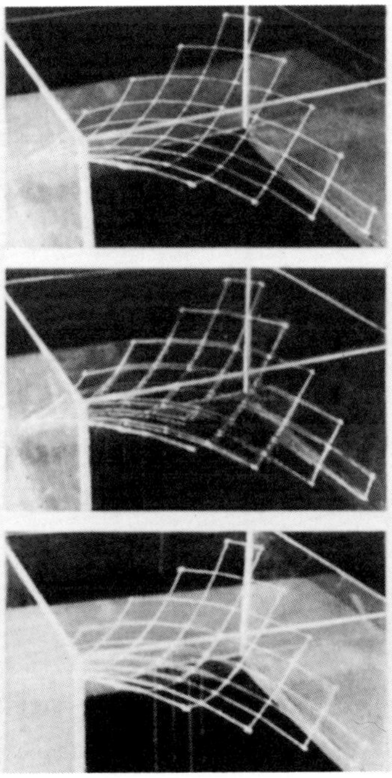

11 to 13

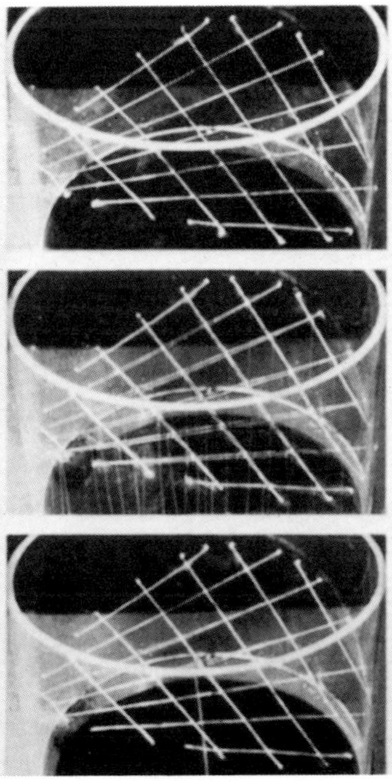

14 to 16

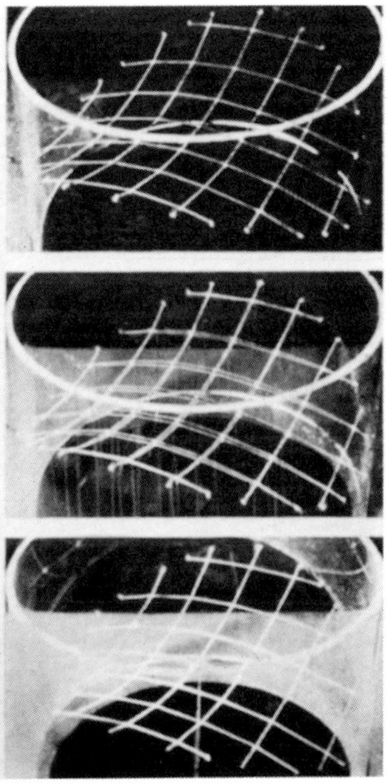

Stresses in Membranes and Flexible Surface Support Units

The state of stress in a flexible tension-loaded membrane with isotropic elastic properties can be determined fairly easily. This also applies to thin flexible shells and panels, which can take up compression and tension, if we disregard denting and buckling. However, analysis of the denting and buckling behavior of surface support structures subjected to compression may only be omitted in exceptional cases. The stress distribution in such supports is often less important than the denting and buckling behavior.

The following states of stress occur in all surface support structures of uniform thickness that are elastically isotropic, such as membranes, panels, and shells, and to a certain degree also in nets, grids, etc.

If a membrane, e.g., the skin of a drum, is uniformly stretched on all sides, the surface stresses will be uniform in all directions. Hence, there are neither principal stresses nor principal stress directions. If, for example, a circle is drawn on a plane membrane before stretching and the latter then stretched uniformly, the diameter of the circle increases, but the circle retains its shape. If, however, the membrane is stretched nonuniformly, the circle becomes an ellipse. The principal axes of the ellipse then define the directions of maximum and minimum surface stress. The extent of the deformation of the initial circle to an ellipse then depends on the difference in stresses and on the elasticity of the material. A rubber-like material will become greatly deformed, while a rigid material, such as steel-plate, will exhibit only small deviations from the initial shape.

Figure 1 is a symbolic representation of a membrane in which the tensile stress in one direction is twice as large as in the direction normal to the first. A small part of such a membrane is shown in Fig. 2, This part is cut at an angle ϕ. The normal surface tension σ (force per unit length) acts at right angles to this section.

If such a membrane is not only cut, but held together (in this case, by three clips) so that the sections do not become separated, the clips, which may be imagined to be tension cables between the membrane parts, assume a certain direction, which is that of the surface-tension resultant S. Equilibrium exists when the clips have assumed this direction. When σ and S are not in the same direction (as in this example) a force acts which tends to displace the parts in relation to each other. This force per unit length of section is the shearing surface tension τ, measured, like σ and S, in kp/cm. When σ and τ are added vectorially, we obtain the surface-tension resultant S.

The magnitudes of σ, τ, and S can be easily determined for any section. Figure 3 shows a section through a membrane corresponding to Fig. 1, whose tension σ_1 along the principal stress direction MA is twice as great as the tension σ_2 acting at right angles to it in the principal stress direction MB. The membrane is cut at an angle $\phi = 30°$, as shown in Fig. 2.

The directions and magnitudes of σ_1 and σ_2 must be known. They can be determined by calculation or measurement, using strain gages or circular marks on the membrane.

Draw a circular arc of radius σ_1, with center M to intersect the axis MB at C. By definition the normal surface tension acts at right angles to the section. Point D is obtained by making a right angle to the cut, which is represented as a dot-dash line. A perpendicular to MA through D will intersect at F, an ellipse (broken line) whose principle axes are $MA = \sigma_1$ and $MB = \sigma_2$. (This ellipse need not be drawn.)

The point on the ellipse can also be obtained as follows: A parallel to CA, drawn through D, will intersect the axis MA at E. A parallel to BA is drawn through E. This intersects the perpendicular to MA through D at F.

The length MG defines the magnitude and direction of the normal surface tension σ, the length GF the magnitude and direction of the shearing surface tension τ, and the length MF the magnitude and direction of the surface-tension resultant S. This construction is highly instructive. We can also use other methods, e.g., Mohr's stress circle.

Figure 4 shows symbolically a different stress ratio. Tension acts in one principal direction, while compression acts at right angles to it. σ_1 is positive, σ_2 is negative and half as great as σ_1.

Figure 5 shows what happens if such a surface is cut at an angle of 75°. The parts are forced together if the same clip system is used as in Fig. 2, and the membrane becomes telescoped. However, if we replace the clips by struts, we obtain the system given in Fig. 6. Equilibrium exists in both cases. The normal surface tension σ is negative, as is the surface-tension resultant S.

The tensions at the cut are determined as shown in Fig. 3. When σ_1 and σ_2 have different signs, the construction is shown in Fig. 7, where the dot-dash line represents the cut. In this case it forms an angle $\phi = 75°$ with the principal stress direction. $\sigma_1 = MA$ and $\sigma_2 = MB$ (compressive forces are considered negative). The circle, with center M and radius σ_1, intersects the σ_2 axis at C and (C).

The normal to the cut at M intersects the circle at (D). The perpendicular drawn from (D) to MA intersects at F the ellipse (broken line AB) whose principal axes are $\sigma_1 = MA$ and $\sigma_2 = MB$. Point F can also be found as in Fig. 3 by drawing a parallel to AC through D to intersect the σ_1 axis. We thus obtain point E. Through E a parallel is drawn to AB, which intersects $D(D)$ at F.

Draw a perpendicular from F to $M(D)$. This defines the magnitude and direction of the normal surface tension σ which in this case is negative and thus represents compression. We also find the magnitudes and directions of the shearing surface tension τ and of the surface-tension resultant S, which is also negative in this case. Regardless of whether a membrane or a compression-resistant elastic surface is imagined as cut so that the normal and shearing surface tensions σ and τ can be found, only the surface-tension resultant is effective and measurable in a continuous surface. The magnitude of the surface-tension resultant is always given by the tension ellipse whose principal axes represent the principal tensions.

Figure 8 is a polar diagram of (at the top) the normal surface tensions σ and (at the bottom) the shearing surface tensions τ for different angles ϕ at different ratios $\sigma_1:\sigma_2$. The outer semicircle *a* corresponds to $\sigma_1 = +1$ and $\sigma_2 = +1$. The tensions are equal and positive in all directions. There is no shear. Line *b* corresponds to $\sigma_1 = +1$ and $\sigma_2 = +0.5$. The curve is saddle-shaped. The tension σ is maximum at 0° and minimum at 90°. The shearing tension τ is very small and has its maximum at 45°.

The dot-dash line *c* represents the tensions for $\sigma_1 = +1$ and $\sigma_2 = 0$. A pronounced saddle shape results. $\sigma_2 = 0$ at 90°. The shear also vanishes at 0°, attains its maximum at 45° and again becomes zero at 90°.

Let σ_2 now be negative (compression). The tension curve for $\sigma_1 = +1$ and $\sigma_2 = -0.5$ is given by the line *d*. The normal tension σ is maximum at 0°, vanishes at about 55°, and becomes negative at still larger angles.

The last line corresponds to $\sigma_1 = +1$ and $\sigma_2 = -1$, i.e., tension in one principal direction and a numerically equal compression in the other. The resulting tension distribution is given by line *e* (dashed line). The normal tension $\sigma = 1$ at 0° vanishes at 45° and equals -1 at 90°. $\tau = 0$ at $\phi = 0°$ and $\tau = 1$ at $\phi = 45°$. This is the rare case that in the direction $\phi = 45°$ the shearing tension τ is numerically equal to the normal tensions σ_1 and σ_2. The maximum possible value of τ is obtained in this case.

Figure 9 gives σ and τ, plotted in Cartesian coordinates for the same tension ratios used in Fig. 8. The tensions corresponding to line *a* ($\sigma_1 = +1$ and $\sigma_2 = +1$) are constant. The maximum difference corresponds to line *e* ($\sigma_1 = +1$ and $\sigma_2 = -1$). It is seen that τ increases with the difference between σ_1 and σ_2.

Different tension ratios are represented in Figs. 1 and 2, pp. 46 and 47, respectively. Row *a* of Fig. 1, p. 46, represents the case of equal tensions in both principal directions, corresponding to line *a* in Figs. 8 and 9. As shown symbolically on the extreme left, $\sigma_1 = +1$ and $\sigma_2 = +1$. This means that the surface tensions are equal in all directions. This is also shown in the second diagram and in the third diagram for cuts at 30° and 75°. The fourth diagram shows the conditions that occur when such a membrane is cut at an angle of 0°. The tension resultant *r* is normal to the plane of the cut and

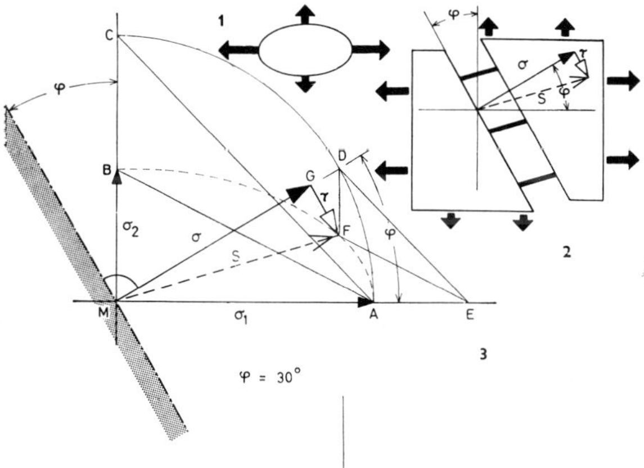

1 2 3

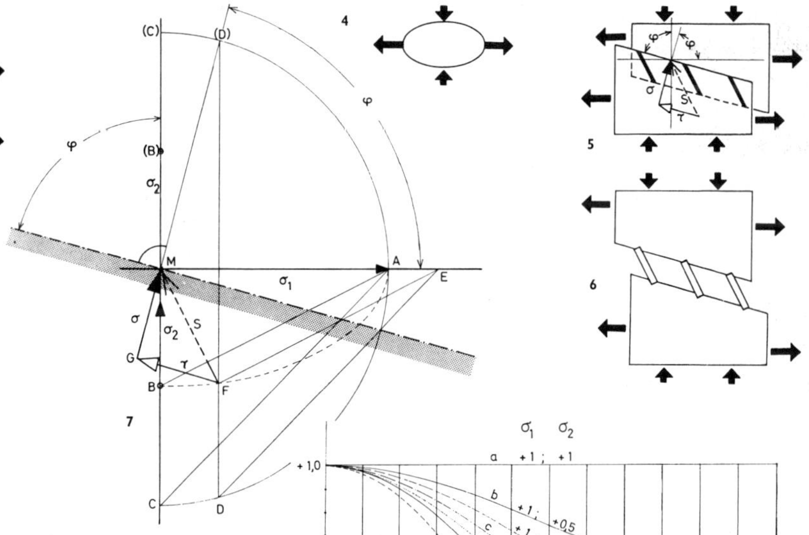

4 5 6 7

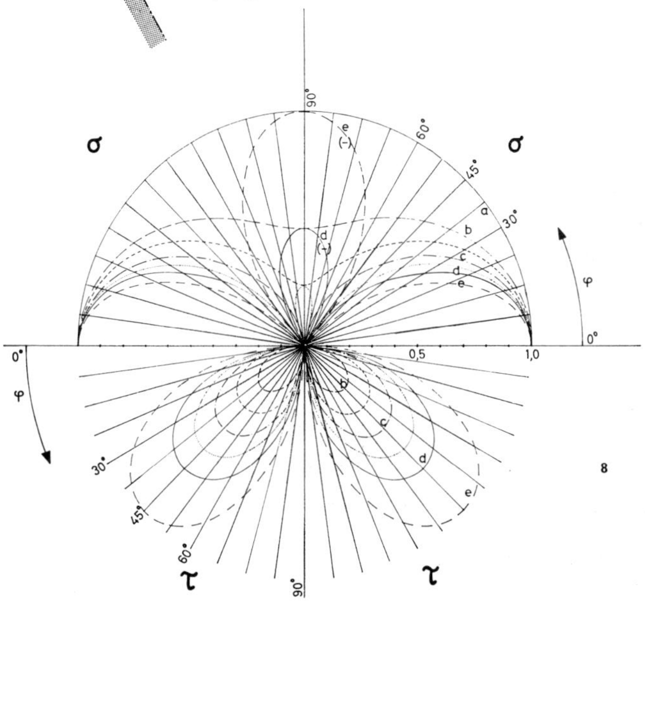

8

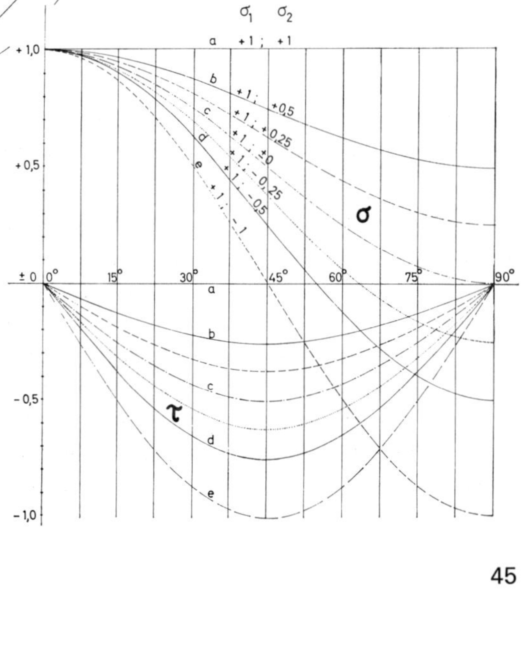

9

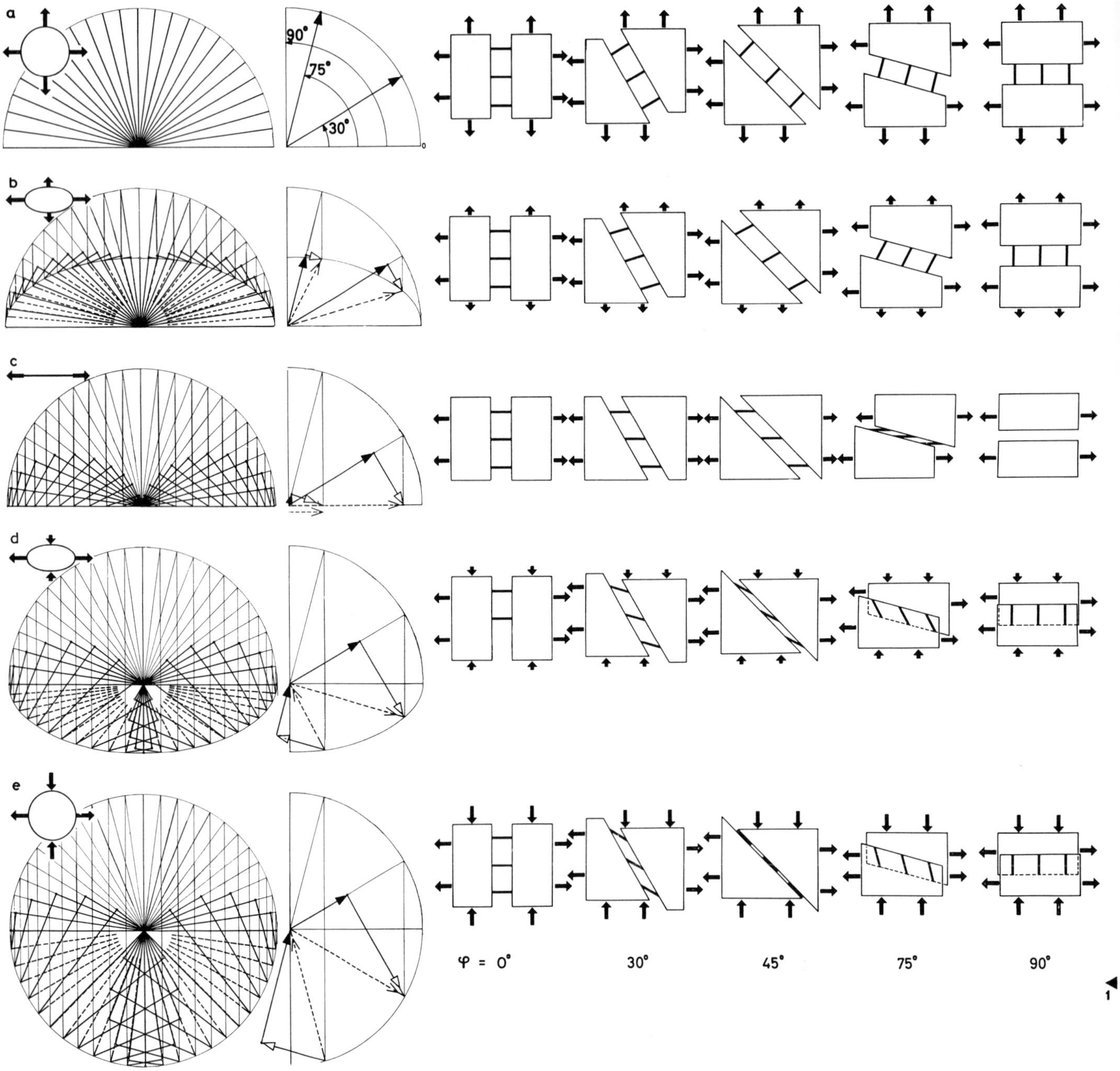

simultaneously represents the normal tension σ. This also applies to the cuts at 30°, 45°, 75°, and 90°, as shown in the other diagrams.

The tension pattern is different when the [principal] tensions are unequal. The second row (b) of Fig. 1 corresponds to $\sigma_1 = +1$ and $\sigma_2 = +0.5$; thus $\sigma_1 : \sigma_2 = 2$. The magnitudes of the normal and shearing surface tensions are given by curves b in Figs. 8 and 9, p. 45. It was shown in Fig. 3, p. 45, how normal and shearing tensions, as well as the tension resultant, are determined for $\phi = 30°$. The relationship between σ and τ is shown for $\phi = 30°$ and $\phi = 75°$ in the third diagram of row b in Fig. 1. σ is represented as a full line with a black arrowhead, τ as a full line with white arrowhead, and S as a broken line.

All σ-, τ-, and S-values are given in the second diagram of the second row. The drawings of cut membranes (fourth to eighth diagrams of the second row) show that if cuts are made at 30°, 45°, or 75° the tension resultant is not normal to the cut.

The third row (c) of Fig. 1 corresponds to $\sigma_1 = +1$ and $\sigma_2 = 0$. Tension is applied only in one principal direction. The state of stress is monoaxial. The tension resultant acts in the same direction as σ_1. This is evident from all diagrams in this row. In the last diagram of the third row ($\phi = 90°$) the tension resultant vanishes. No clips are shown, since no tensions act normal to the cut.

As shown symbolically on the extreme left of the fourth row (d) of Fig. 1, $\sigma_1 = +1$ and $\sigma_2 = -0.5$. This corresponds to line d in

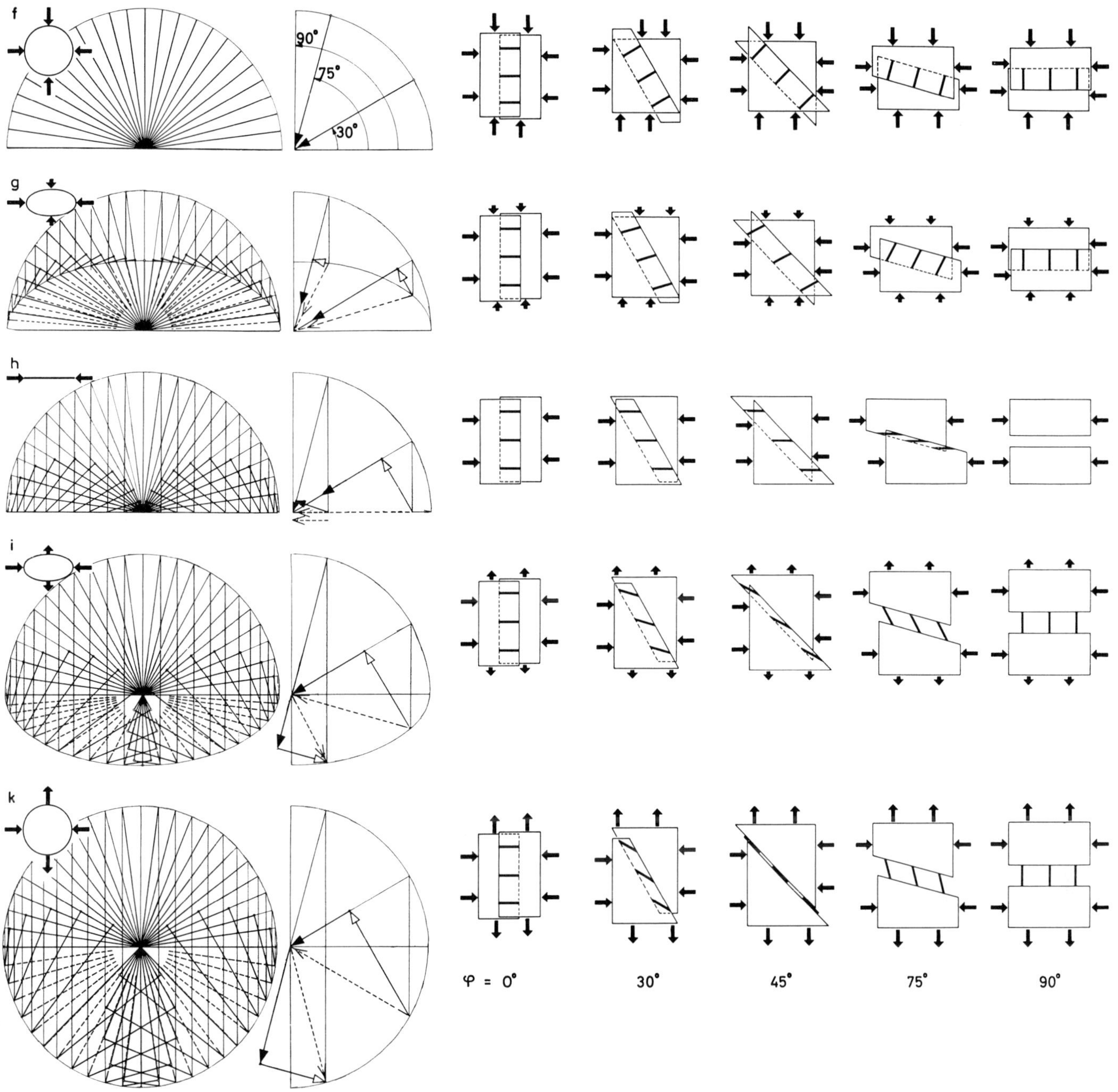

2

Figs. 8 and 9 on p. 45. For this tension ratio, σ, τ, and S were already determined for $\phi = 75°$, in Fig. 7 on p. 45. This construction is repeated in the third diagram from the left in this row. σ has a black arrowhead, τ a white arrowhead, and S is represented by a broken line. σ and S are negative, i.e., compressions. When $\phi = 30°$, σ and S are still positive, i.e., tensions. The complete diagram (second from the left in the fourth row of Fig. 1) gives the magnitudes of σ, τ, and S at intervals of 7.5°.

The fourth to eighth diagrams show that for cuts at 0°, 30°, and 45° the surface-tension resultant S is positive, but for a cut at 75° it is negative, as already shown in Fig. 5, p. 45. The two parts overlap. The tension resultant for a cut at 90° (eighth diagram of fourth row) is also negative.

The fifth and lowest row (e) of Fig. 1 corresponds to $\sigma_1 = +1$ and $\sigma_2 = -1$. The values of σ and τ were given by line e in Figs. 8 and 9 on p. 45. σ and S are positive up to angles of 45°, and negative at larger angles. This becomes evident from the diagrams in the bottom row.

Figure 2 corresponds to Fig. 1, with the signs of the tensions reversed. In the top row (f) $\sigma_1 = -1$ and $\sigma_2 = -1$. Uniform compression acts in all directions, as seen in all diagrams in this row. The second row (g) corresponds to $\sigma_1 = -1$ and $\sigma_2 = -0.5$. The [normal] surface tensions σ are negative in all directions, as are the tension resultants S. The shearing surface tensions τ reach their maximum at 45°. The diagrams resemble those of Fig. 1, p. 46, apart

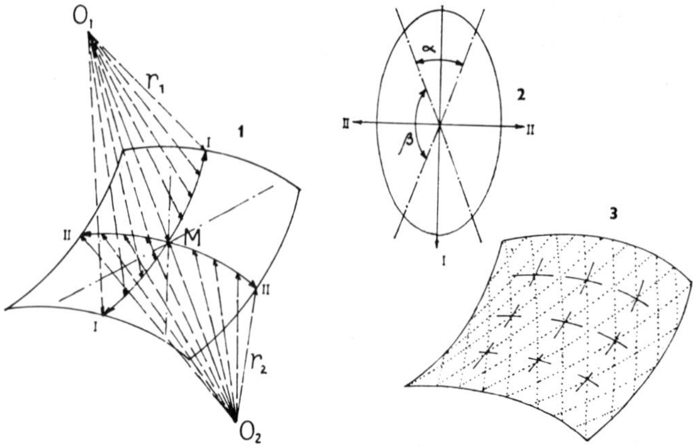

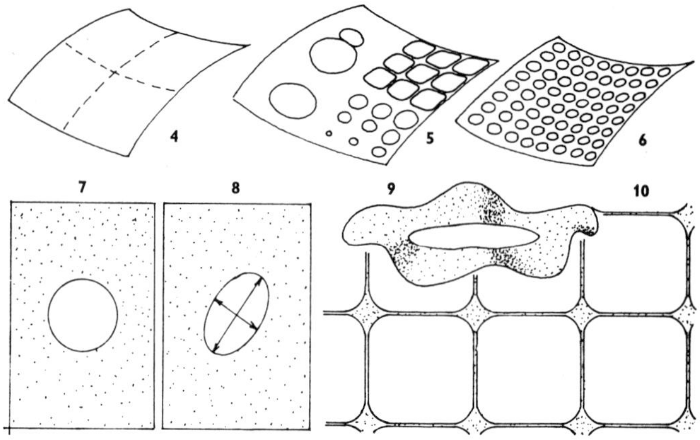

from the directions of the arrows. The same also applies to row h, for which $\sigma_1 = -1.0$ and $\sigma_2 = 0$. This is the case of monoaxial compression. The tension resultant acts in the direction of $\phi = 90°$. The fourth row (i) corresponds to $\sigma_1 = -1.0$ and $\sigma_2 = +0.5$. Although the surface-tension resultants cuts at angles of 0°, 30°, and 45° are negative (thus representing compression), they are positive for cuts at 75° and 90° (i.e., tension).

The bottom row (k) of Fig. 2 corresponds to the same tension ratio as the bottom row (e) of Fig. 1. Here $\sigma_1 = -1$ and $\sigma_2 = +1$. The surface-tension resultant is negative for cuts at 0° and 30°. At 45° $S = \tau$ and $\sigma = 0$. At angles exceeding 45° the surface-tension resultants S are positive (see also the diagrams for cuts at 75° and 90°). When flexible membranes or cable nets are used, which can only take up tension, only those diagrams are applicable in which no compression is shown. Compressive stresses can be prevented by suitable prestressing.

If an elastic membrane is stretched in a nonplanar frame it forms a nonplanar saddle-shaped surface, anticlastic at every point.

Consider a surface element as in Fig. 1. The two directions of principal curvature *I-I* and *II-II* are always mutually perpendicular. The corresponding radii of curvature are r_1 and r_2. The centers of curvature 0_1 and 0_2 lie on either side of the surface on the normal through the point of intersection of the axes at M. If the radii r_1 and r_2 are equal, the element forms a minimum surface such as can be obtained with a soap film in the no-load state. However, r_1 and r_2 may differ in magnitude. The membrane then does not form a minimum surface. Between the principal axes of curvature *I-I* and *II-II* there are two directions in which the membrane is not curved (represented by the dot-dash lines in Fig. 1).

If r_1 equals r_2 (minimum surface), the "directions of zero membrane curvature" bisect the angles between the axes *I* and *II* and intersect at right angles. When the radii of curvature are unequal (non-minimum surface) the directions of zero membrane curvature do not intersect at right angles.

The directions of principal curvature always bisect the angles between the directions of zero membrane curvature.

Consequently, it is advisable in model tests first to determine the two directions of zero curvature at a given membrane point. This can be done very accurately by placing short rulers upon the membrane and rotating them.

We thus begin by determining the directions of zero membrane curvature represented as dot-dash lines in Fig. 2, and then find the directions of principal curvature *I* and *II* by bisecting angles α and β.

A surface (Fig. 3) can always be imagined to be covered by a net of lines running in the directions of principal curvature, and by a second net of lines running in the directions of zero membrane curvature.

The latter lines are not necessarily straight. If they are curved, the radius of curvature must lie in the tangential plane.

Based on the membrane analysis in Vol. 1, Rudolf Trostel established the following important relationships: Let n_1 and n_2 denote respectively the normal surface tensions in the directions of principal curvature *I* and *II*. We then have $n_1/n_2 = r_1/r_2$ and we write: $n_1/n_2 = \mathrm{tg}^2\alpha/2$.

If the membrane is stretched in such a way that no shear occurs in the directions of principal curvature, which is the usual aim, the directions of principal curvature *I* and *II* are identical with the principal stress directions, i.e., the directions of the maximum and the minimum membrane tension. They are also the principal axes of the stress ellipse (Fig. 2), defining the magnitude of the membrane tension in every direction.

Knowledge of these relationships is very important for the design of membrane structures. This extremely simple method to determine the directions of zero curvature in the model or membrane structure enables the stress distribution in a membrane or comparable cable net to be estimated quickly, even when the absolute magnitude of the tensions is not known. The latter can usually be measured at several points without difficulty.

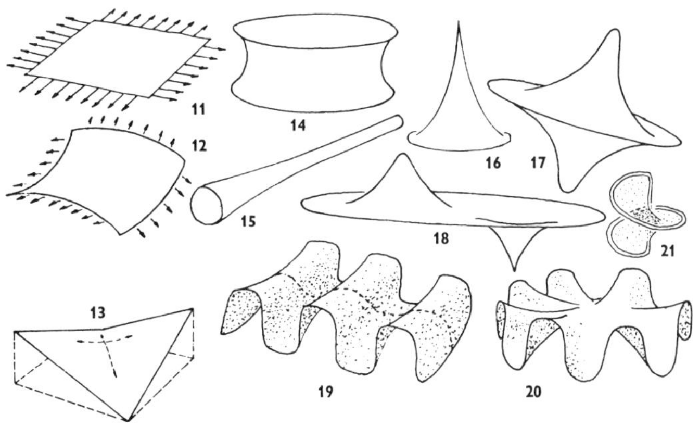

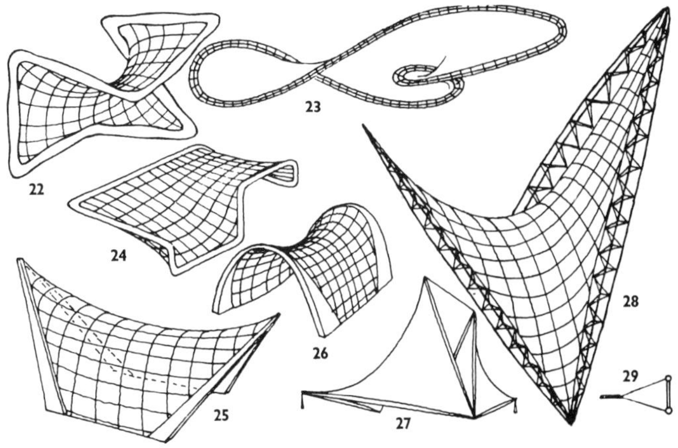

Holes in Membranes

Plane membranes can be lined at their outer and inner edges by cables that take up all membrane tensions without affecting the uniform distribution of the latter. This is also possible with spatially curved membranes. A hole cut into a membrane uniformly stressed in all directions must be circular if a tension element that cannot be subjected to bending, e.g., a cable, is to take up all stresses (Fig. 7). If the tensions differ in magnitude, the hole must form an ellipse (Fig. 8). In a spatially curved membrane the shape of the hole depends on the spatial curvature. On the other hand, the membrane itself is slightly changed in shape by being cut. For example, let a line of constant curvature be drawn on a membrane stressed uniformly in all directions. This line is a circle on a plane membrane and forms a spatially curved closed line on a spatially curved membrane. If, now, a hole is cut into the membrane and a cable attached to the edge of the hole, the spatially curved line becomes flatter, but remains a line of constant curvature. This is most pronounced with spatially strongly curved membranes, as shown in Fig. 9.

A spatially curved membrane (Fig. 4) may have holes of uniform or varying size (Figs. 5 and 6). If cables line holes so large that two adjacent holes touch, some cables will in part not border on any portion of the membrane. A membrane can be almost completely perforated by cable-lined holes, and only small parts of the former remain within a cable net (Fig. 10).

Various Shapes of Prestressed Membranes

A membrane can be analyzed as a structure on the basis of its state of stress, or, formally, in accordance with its shape.

Since force distribution and shape are closely related by the derived interdependence of curvature and stress, the formal geometrical consideration of a prestressed membrane is also one of its design.

Various surfaces may have anticlastic (saddle-shaped) curvatures, such as hoses (Figs. 14 and 15), humps (Figs. 16 to 18), wave shapes (Figs. 19 and 20), and helicoidal surfaces (Fig. 21).

When two of the conical surfaces shown in Fig. 16 are joined together they form a hollow body or "pillow structure" (Fig. 17). Conical surfaces may be adjacent, as shown in Fig. 18.

Design on the Basis of Soap Bubble Tests

A knowledge of minimum surfaces is important in the design of membrane and cable-net structures. However, minimum surfaces are not always the optimum structural shapes. A minimum surface defines only the surface of least area within a closed curve. A minimum surface is identical with a membrane everywhere uniformly stressed in all directions.

30 to 32

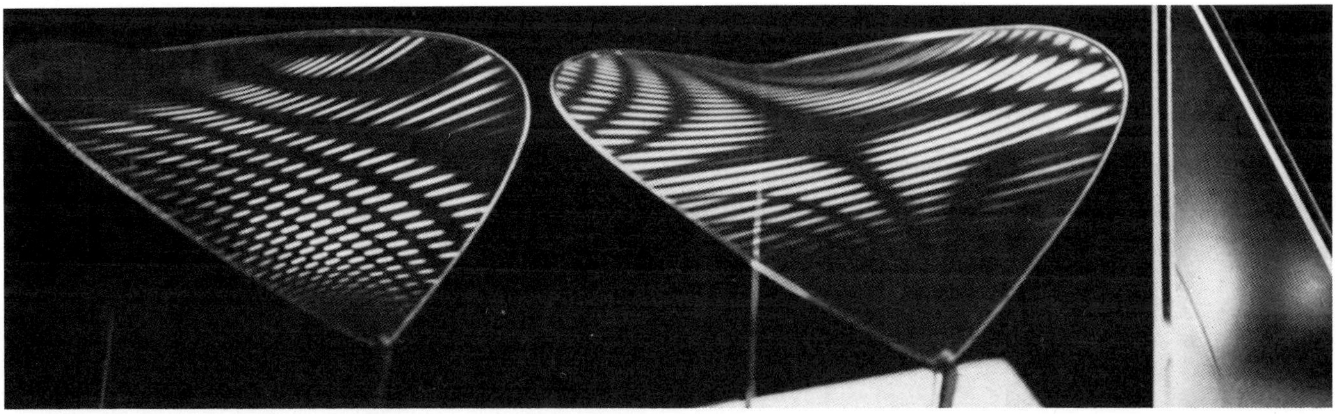

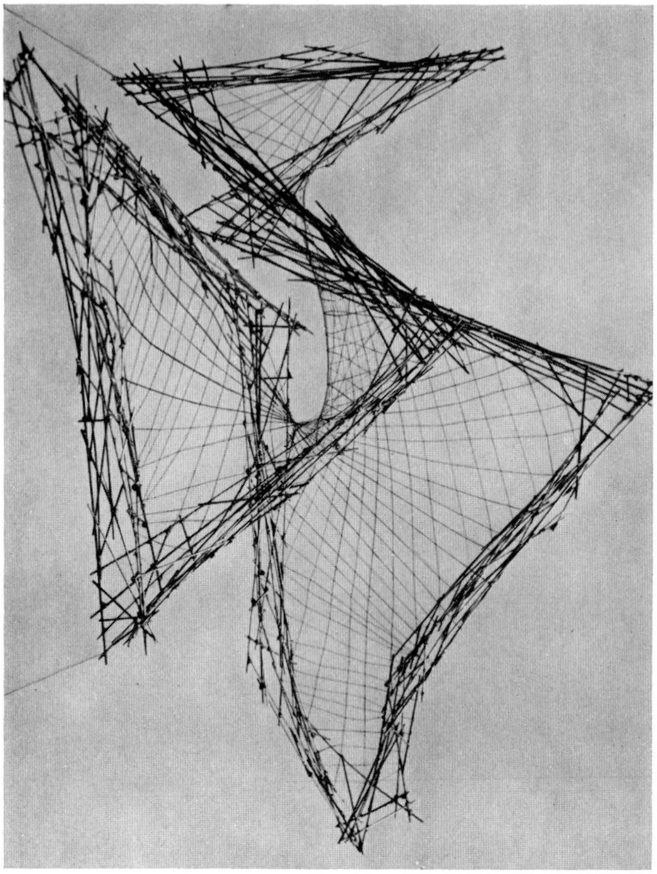

1

For the state of stress of a membrane only prestressed but not additionally loaded, the minimum surface is also the shape of the most economical surface support system if the edge members are not taken into account.

When additional loads act, the minimum surface is not always the optimum shape.

Since the amount of material required depends on the products of all forces and displacements, the carrying capacity under additional load is very important.

At uniform load the deformations are generally maximum in the central regions of a membrane or cable-net surface.

It is often necessary to change the form of the minimum surface in such a way that membrane zones requiring higher rigidity also have greater curvature.

Any deviation from the minimum surface increases the total surface area.

Determination of the minimum surface is essential despite these major reservations.

Liquid films are no longer made of soap solution, which is too viscous, but of special water-soluble foaming agents, which can form very thin, highly stressed films.

Although the preparation of soap films is usually simple, their measurement is very difficult. Methods for better visualization and illumination of soap bubbles for photogrammetric evaluation were developed between 1959 and 1962. The reflection of projections of line or point grids (Figs. 30 to 32, p. 49) permits measurement of individual surface points. Methods for visualizing contour lines or sections are being developed.

Minimum surfaces can also be approximated by rubber films if excessive curvatures are avoided. These rubber films are marked with measuring points or grids. In a project at the Cologne Federal Garden Show in 1957, a rubber membrane stretched to form a minimum surface was "set" in plaster without deformation, so that the membrane could be cut directly on the surface (Fig. 7, p. 63).

Cable Nets and Membranes with Edges Rigid in Bending

We shall now discuss prestressed membranes and cable nets with edges of various shapes.

All cable nets and membranes can be stretched in any frame that forms a closed line. Figure 1 shows a net of prestressed steel springs stretched in a steel-wire frame. The net is curved anticlastically at every point. The directions of principal curvature vary. A helicoidal surface in the middle of the cable net is particularly noteworthy.

If a membrane or cable net is stretched in a rigid frame, the latter is usually subjected to bending, regardless of whether it has corners (Fig. 22, p. 49) or is round (Fig. 23, p. 49). The frames can also be formed in such a way that only tensile or compressive stresses occur. Such frames are of particular interest, since they usually require far less material than frames subjected to bending.

We show only a few of the innumerable possibilities for stretching cable nets or membranes in frames subjected to bending. Figure 24, p. 49, shows a wave-shaped surface stretched in a frame describing a rectangle on three sides. The fourth side forms an S at right angles to the plane of the rectangle. The cable net shown in Fig. 25, p. 49, is

2

suspended between two triangular frames, rigidly fixed in the foundation. These frames are subjected to bending as are the arches shown in Fig. 26, p. 49. The bending stresses are mostly combined with normal stresses, i.e., we have bending combined with tension or compression. Membranes and cable nets stretched in frames with four straight edges (Fig. 27, p. 49) are of particular interest. The bending moments acting in the frame are considerable, compared to the compressive forces. The frame must be rigid in bending and safe against buckling.

Consequently, attempts have been made for years to reduce the material required for edge supports rigid in bending, or to eliminate them completely by the use of tension-loaded cables. When edge supports rigid in bending are necessary, lattice girders* of triangular cross section (Fig. 29, p. 49) are best for cable-net edges (Fig. 28, p. 49): Two outer braces take up the compressive stresses. The shape of the girder is selected in such a way that all diagonals and the lower brace are under tension when the cable net is sufficiently prestressed. This design enables the entire system, apart from the compression-loaded braces, to consist of tension-loaded components that are simple to make and assemble.

It is quite understandable that cable-net and membrane roofs with straight frames rigid in bending were initially given the shape of hyperbolic paraboloids. This shape is only one of many possible and offers no particular advantage in the preparation of formwork for concrete shells, for instance. However, the calculation methods developed in the 1930's for hyperbolic-paraboloid shells, primarily by Aimond and Laffaille, can be used extensively. When such shells are loaded, tensile and compressive stresses act simultaneously in different directions.

Compressive stresses can be completely prevented by the tensile prestressing of the shell. This affects the support system. A purely tension-loaded membrane can be flexible, but requires a rigid outer frame. Membranes and nets bordered by frames rigid in bending, suitable for large structures, are a comparatively recent development. The 1953 design for a Mission Church,* which appeared in *Das hängende Dach,* can be regarded as a series of shapes according to Fig. 25, p. 49. Many projects and suggestions for membranes stretched in plane or skew frames rigid in bending originated in Berlin at that time.

One of the first designs was the Exhibition Pavilion built in 1956 by Hansen and Tomascewski (Warsaw) in South America. A membrane of light tent fabric was suspended in a skew frame consisting of four fish-bellied supports rigid in bending, the web running in the direction of minimum curvature (photograph by Hansen). The membrane has the shape of a hyperbolic paraboloid.

Among the many later structures there is the French Pavilion at the Brussels World's Fair (Fig. 3), designed by Gillet and Sarger. A light net of flat parallel wire bundles was stretched in an enormous steel girder frame. We note also the small wooden pavilion (also by Sarger) on the Place de Brouquère in Brussels, and the Coliseum at the World's Fair in Seattle (Figs. 3 and 4, p. 43, and Fig. 10, p. 67), by Thiry and Hostmark.

▶ 3

Minimum Surfaces Stretched in Frames Subjected to Bending

Experiments were undertaken in the years 1960–64, in which soap films were stretched in different frames and measured photographically in order to determine their shape. Some of the results are shown on this and the following pages. Both cross sections and reflected grids were photographed (Figs. 30 to 32, p. 49).

The first photos show soap films in skew frames consisting of rods of equal length. As mentioned in Vol. 1 (see Trostel, *Analysis of Membranes*), the experimental result that

1 2 3 ▼4 8

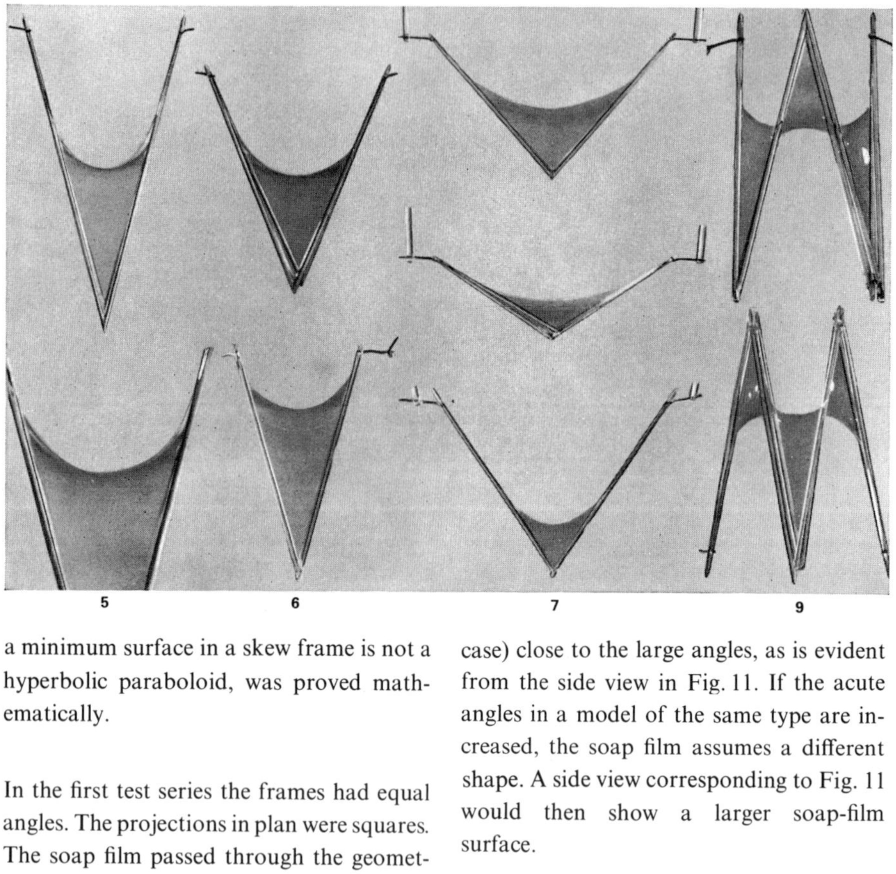

5 6 7 9

a minimum surface in a skew frame is not a hyperbolic paraboloid, was proved mathematically.

In the first test series the frames had equal angles. The projections in plan were squares. The soap film passed through the geometrical center of the system (Figs. 1 to 4), the contour being less curved near the center, i.e., flatter, than a parabola.

Figures 5 to 7 show that the deviation in shape of a soap film or minimum surface from a hyperbolic paraboloid is most pronounced if the angles of the frame are unequal, i.e., when the plan of the frame is rhombic. The center of the soap film is displaced toward the line connecting the two corners that have the larger angles. In contrast, the surface of a hyperbolic paraboloid always passes through the geometrical center of the figure, even when the frame angles are unequal.

Another minimum surface is seen in the soap-bubble test shown in Figs. 10 to 12. The frame consists of six parts of equal length. Three parts each form three sides of a square. These two open squares are joined at two points at equal acute angles. Figure 12 is a perspective while Figs. 10 and 11 are side views. The soap film near the acute angles is very flat and remains (also in this case) close to the large angles, as is evident from the side view in Fig. 11. If the acute angles in a model of the same type are increased, the soap film assumes a different shape. A side view corresponding to Fig. 11 would then show a larger soap-film surface.

The frame shown in Figs. 13 to 14 consists of eight rods of equal length. It forms a continuous line with right angles and follows the edges of a cube closed on all sides but four. Due to the symmetry of the frame, the soap film stretched in this continuous line passes through the center of the cube. This can be seen in the side view, Fig. 14. The minimum surface has a comparatively large anticlastic curvature everywhere except directly at the corners, where it is tangential to the plane formed by the two sides of the angle. At the middle of the rod it forms an angle of approximately 20° with the corresponding surface of the cube. This can also be seen in Fig. 14.

The frames shown in Figs. 8 and 9 were also constructed of 8 rods of equal length, the rods being joined at acute angles. If the angles are all equal, the minimum surface passes through the geometrical center and the center of gravity of the figure. If, as in this figure, the angles are smaller at the bottom than at the top, the minimum surface is displaced upward toward the larger angles. The curvature in the middle of the soap film is comparatively small. The radii of curvature are smallest away from the middle.

The soap film shown in Figs. 15 and 16 is stretched in a spatially curved frame of continuous curvature. This frame is related to that shown in Figs. 13 and 14. The minimum surface passes through the center of gravity of the system, since the frame is symmetrical with respect to two axes. The side view (Fig. 16) shows that at the lowest points, the membrane is not tangential to the frame, but makes an angle of about 30° with it. The uniformly stressed soap film subjects the frame primarily to bending combined with compression. Only perfectly plane frames can be subjected by soap films to pure compression without bending.

A soap film can be stretched in any frame consisting of straight or curved components, provided that it forms a closed line. The film then forms a continuous surface (Fig. 17), the frame being subjected to bending. The only exceptions are films stretched between threads instead of rigid frames (or minimum surfaces stretched as membranes between cables). In this case, the membrane and cable forces are in equilibrium (see p. 61). A symmetrical form was chosen for the frame shown in Figs. 18 and 19. It has both smooth curves and two acute angles. The soap film is only slightly curved, except near the two points of the frame.

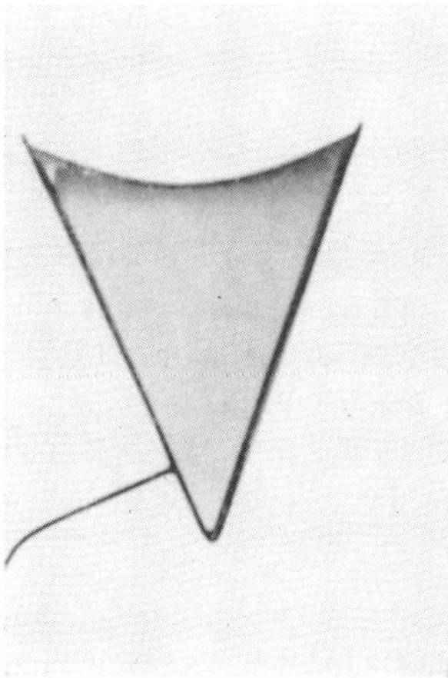

10

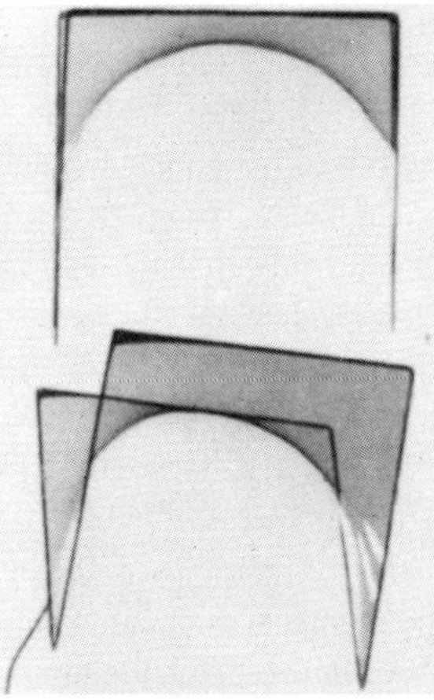

11 and 12

13 and 14

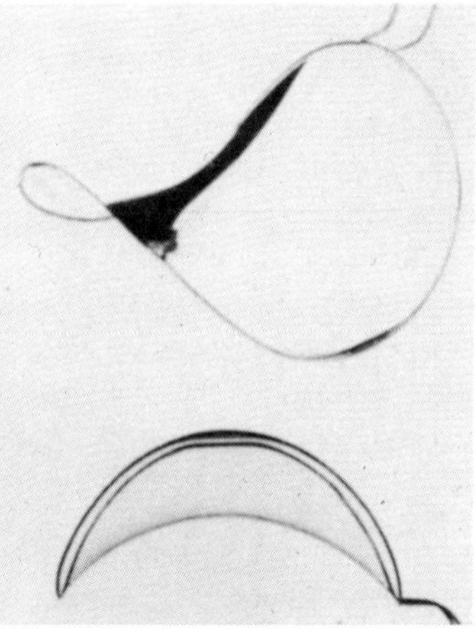

15 and 16

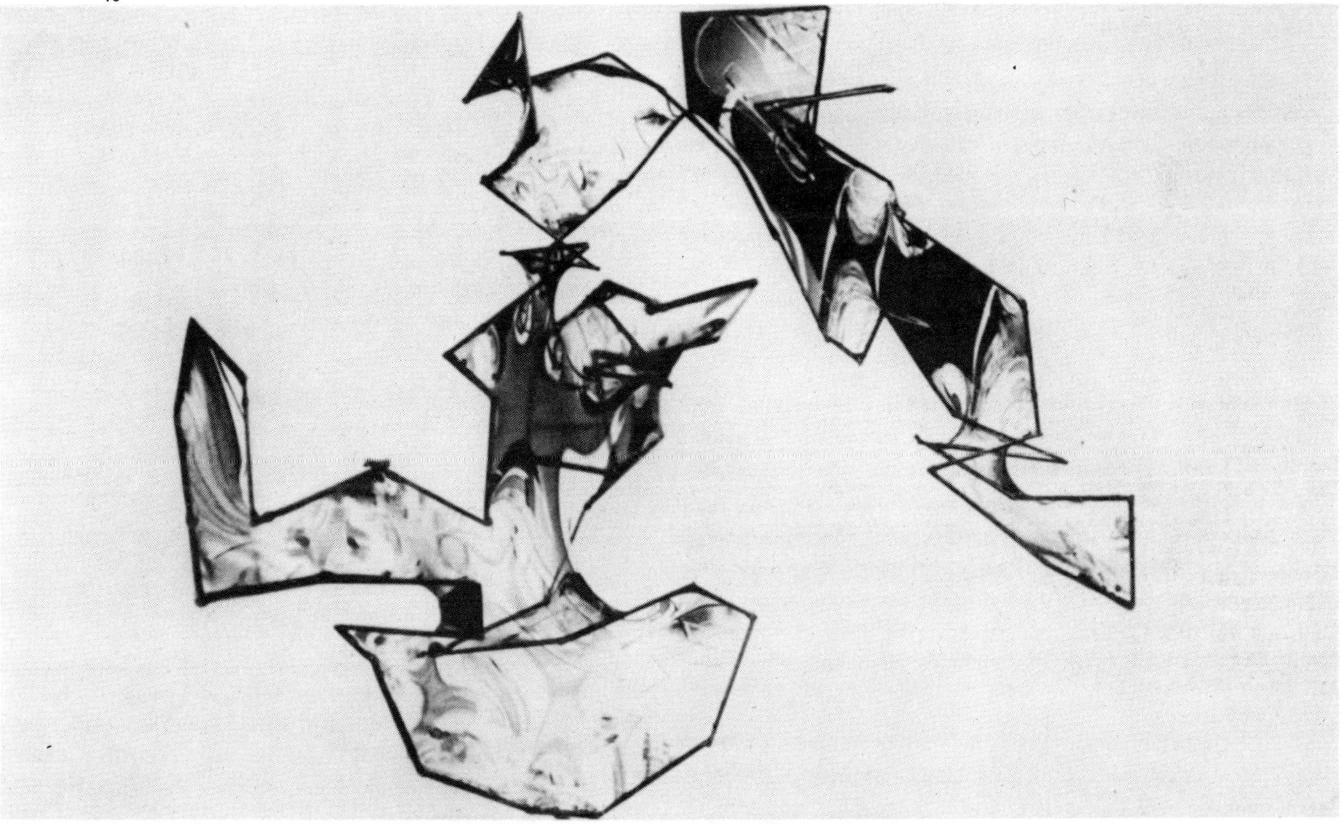

17 ▲

▼ 18 and 19

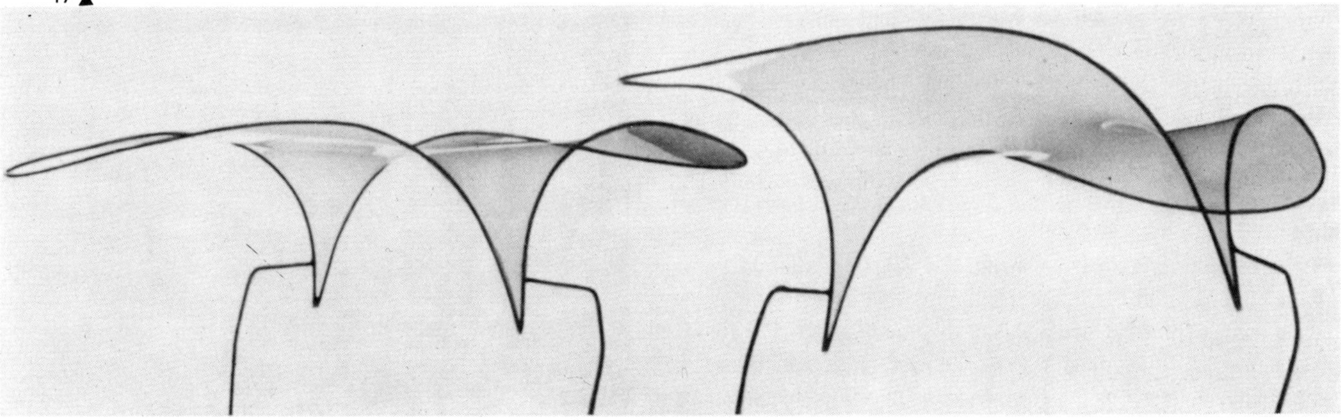

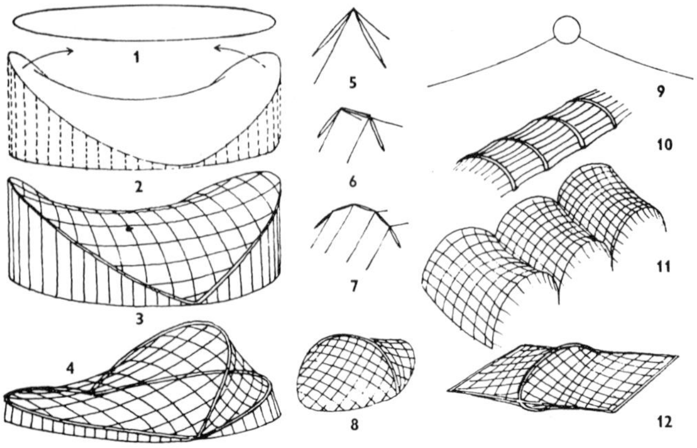

Cable Nets and Membranes with Edge Members Subjected to Compression

We have already considered edge members, rigid in compression, of cable nets and membranes. Systems with edge members subjected to compression will be discussed now. Many new designs are possible.

Only a plane circular ring can be subjected to pure compression without bending by a uniformly stressed membrane or cable net (Fig. 1). All other frames, except helixes and tension-loaded flexible edge members (p. 60 ff.) are also subjected to bending.

A ring subjected to compression is secured against buckling in its plane by the membrane itself, and can be considered as rigid in buckling. However, the membrane cannot reinforce the ring in a direction normal to that plane. The ring therefore tends to buckle in this direction, as seen in Figs. 15 and 16, p. 53. This reduces membrane surface area, and in many cases also the membrane tension. If the membrane tension remains constant, as in liquid films, initial deformation usually leads to destruction of the system through bending. This process may be described as "sudden buckling."

The edges of membranes and cable nets can be bordered by arches subjected to compression only if the tangential plane of the membrane coincides with that of the arch at the edge. This happens in the circle, and apparently also in a helix with a straight axis, in which a minimum surface is stretched. Membranes and cable nets can be stretched in such a helix so that the arch is only stressed in the direction of the radius of curvature, i.e., it is not subjected to bending. It has not yet been established whether the minimum surface in such a frame is exactly identical with a helical surface that has a straight generator. However, any differences are small (Fig. 17, p. 59).

If a circular ring enclosing a membrane (Fig. 1) is raised at two points, as shown in Fig. 2, the membrane is deformed. The membrane tends to pull the high points of the ring together. The ring is thus subjected to bending, unless otherwise supported. Buckling of the ring, as shown by the arrows, can be prevented by bracing it to the foundations, or by supporting its low-lying parts with struts.

Figure 3 shows two inclined plane arches supported by tension systems. The latter may consist of individual cables forming straight lines, or of cable nets and membranes. Two, three, four, or more arches can be joined by membranes and cable nets (Fig. 4). In this way, arches can be stiffened against buckling in any direction, and may therefore be comparatively slender. Within certain limits these arches may even be considered as a flexible chain under compression. Nevertheless, they must to a certain degree be able to resist buckling, depending on the material and cross sections of the arches and membranes or cable nets, and on the prestressing of the system. No rule exists for the slenderness ratio of arches subjected to compression that are carefully fitted into uniformly prestressed membranes or cable nets. Under favorable circumstances slenderness ratios from 1:1000 to 1:2000 are possible (ratio of smallest radius of gyration of arch section to arch length).

The stiffening of an arch is shown in Figs. 5 to 7. Figure 5 shows an arch with three hinges braced in two directions. An arch with four hinges and four braces will not collapse. The same is true for the arch with six hinges, shown in Fig. 7, and correspondingly for multihinge arches, in particular for the continuous arch between two nets or membranes, shown in Fig. 8, and in section in Fig. 9.

Arches that are almost purely subjected to compression in this way may be arranged in series (Figs. 10 and 11) or form part of other systems. Figure 12 shows a rectangular frame with two opposed arches whose thrusts are taken up by a tension member connecting the abutments. We also refer to Report No. 2 of the Development Center for Light Structures and the reprint in *Deutsche Bauzeitschrift*, No. 8, 1958, as well as to C. Roland, *Frei Otto-Spannweiten*, Ullstein-Verlag, Berlin, Frankfurt, Vienna, 1965.

An important example of a large cable net with a curved edge is the Rio Grande do Sul Pavilion in Sao Paulo that was built in 1954 for a large exhibition (Fig. 13), by the engineers Alberto Borges and Ricardo Costas Alliana. The roof has a free length of 102 m

14

13

and a maximum width of 60 m. The cables of the net run in the direction of maximum surface curvature. The design of the structure was apparently greatly influenced by that of the Raleigh Arena, as well as by the sketches in *Bauwelt* No. 14, 1952, and No. 16, 1953. The cables of the nets extend beyond the arches and are anchored directly to the foundations. The arches are thus fixed between two tension-loaded systems, and are supported by the window structures. The stiffening effect of the cables is not utilized (photograph by Tekno).

The first structure in which an arch subjected to compression was deliberately reinforced by tension-loaded prestressed membranes, was the entrance to the 1957 Federal Garden Show in Cologne,* designed in 1955–56 and built in 1957 (Engineer: Fritz Leonhardt). A slender vertical arch of 19-cm diameter steel pipes, 6 m high and with a span of 36 m, is supported on both sides by a prestressed membrane of a coated and translucent heavy fabric. A very rigid system results. Experience gained with this structure was used later (see Report No. 3 of the Development Center for Light Structures, Berlin, 1958, *Bauwelt* 30, 1957, and C. Roland, *op. cit.*).

Another important structure also built in 1957–58 was the roof over the Ice Hockey Rink of Yale University in New Haven (Figs. 14 and 15). It was designed by Eero Saarinen, and the calculations were performed by Fred N. Severud and M. Asce of Severud-Elstadt-Krueger. A vertical and extremely rigid concrete arch with a free span of 67 m carries two prestressed cable nets spanning an elongated plan 55 m in width. The stiffening effect of prestressed cable nets was apparently was not exploited. The two nets of 24 mm cables are covered with wooden boards 22 cm wide and 5 cm thick that support the insulation and the weather membrane. The arch is also supported by three pairs of cables, which connect the arch with its abutments independently of the roof membrane. This is an additional safety measure. An outstanding architect has thus tackled the problems connected with the shape of tension-loaded structures.

15

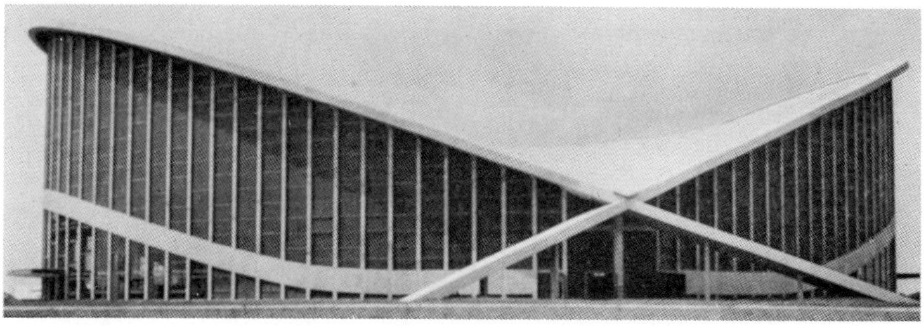

1

The Raleigh Arena (Fig. 1), built in North Carolina in 1953, was designed by Matthew Nowicki in 1950. The calculations were performed by William Henry Deitrick as chief architect and by Fred N. Severud. The multipurpose hall is used mainly for cattle shows (see *Das hängende Dach, op. cit.)*. This is an extremely important pioneering structure in the field of suspended roofs with large spans. A saddle-shaped cable net is stretched over an area of 92 m x 97 m between two inclined parabolic arches. The arches are made of reinforced concrete and rest on concrete-jacketed steel supports (photograph by the architect).

The cables of the net are between 13 and 32 mm thick at a mean mesh width of 180 cm. The calculated snow load was 122 kp/m^2 and the calculated wind suction 78 kp/m^2. The saddle shape of the corrugated sheet roof, covered with a heat-insulation layer and bitumen weather proofing, ensures drainage toward two points.

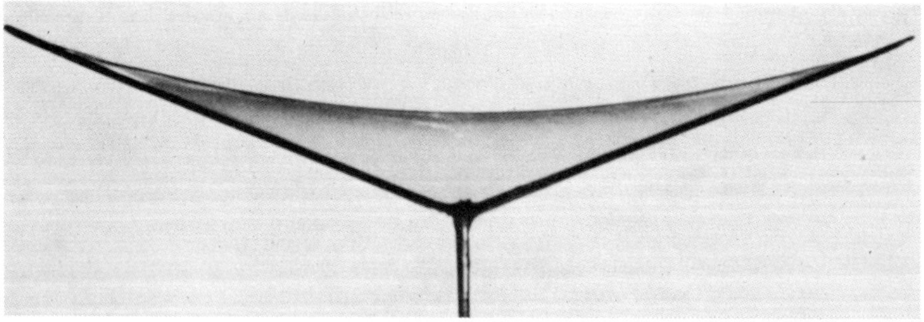

3

For a long time the Raleigh Arena was the most important structure in the field of large-span cable-net structures. It was imitated in many similar designs, none comparable with the original in quality (see p. 17).

This building provided the first significant experience with large-span cable-net roofs. Nowicki died in 1950 and did not live to see his work. Fred N. Severud carried on the development in the U.S.A., particularly with the Yale Ice Hockey Rink in New Haven, Connecticut (Fig. 15, p. 55) and the roof of the Reception Building at Dulles Airport, Washington, D.C. (Fig. 28, p. 25).

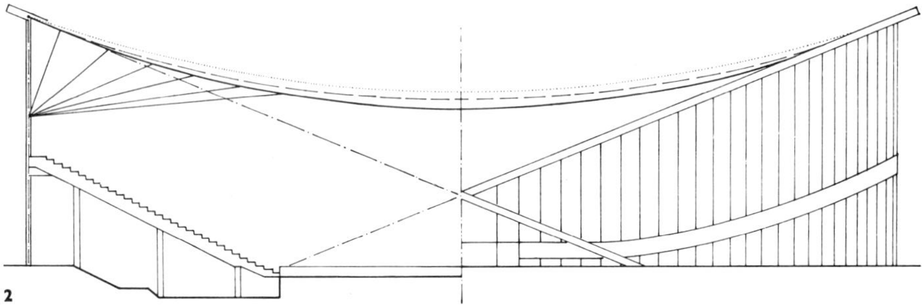

2

The author saw Nowicki's preliminary design in the Severud offices in 1950, and was thereby given the impetus to begin systematic development of tension-loaded structures.

The roof of the Raleigh Arena can be regarded as a tension-loaded surface support structure disposed between arches subjected to compression. It is not a prestressed cable net and was not designed as such. This is evident from the low position of the roof center, which necessitated cable bracings through the interior toward the vertical supports of the outer walls (Fig. 2, left). With respect to its design, the Raleigh Arena is a freely suspended cable roof (Figs. 23 and 24, p. 20, and Fig. 26, p. 21), slightly prestressed after mounting.

In the cross section of the Arena (Fig. 2) the roof is represented as a continuous line. The maximum span is 300 feet, the maximum sag of the central cable 31.3 feet. A chain, suspended between the arches so that the tangents to it at the abutments lie in the planes of the arches, which make angles of 21.8° with the horizontal, would have a sag of only 27.7 feet (dashed line) (see Fig. 26, p. 21). It was found experimentally (Fig. 3) that the minimum surface (dotted line) would have a sag of 24.9 feet.

Consequently, the roof of the Raleigh Arena differs greatly from the minimum surface. Such a roof could approximate a minimum surface if, e.g., a uniformly stressed cable net of uniform mesh were stretched between the arches.

The roof of the Raleigh Arena has a larger sag than the corresponding catenary formed by the same load in the absence of prestressing. In the central zone between the abutments the cable net has a pronounced anticlastic curvature and is slightly prestressed.

As stated on p. 21, the cable net is very flat near the apexes of the arches and has a slight simple curvature. Cables running from the roof through the interior to the supports of the sidewalls prevent movement of the roof (Fig. 2). This causes additional sag. Consequently, the curvature is slightly synclastic near the apex of the arch.

The arches rest upon the supports by dead weight.

Had the roof of the Raleigh Arena been prestressed so as to form a minimum surface, the cable net would not only have been higher in the center, but the side walls would have been under tension if the dead weight of the arches were disregarded.

Controversy over the structure and design, apparently proposed here for the first time, is not yet over. Expert judgment depends on additional knowledge. The shapes of various cable nets stretched between inclined arches have only recently been determined by model tests. Minimum surfaces were also formed and photographed, but could not be measured with sufficient accuracy. The shape has not yet been derived mathematically.

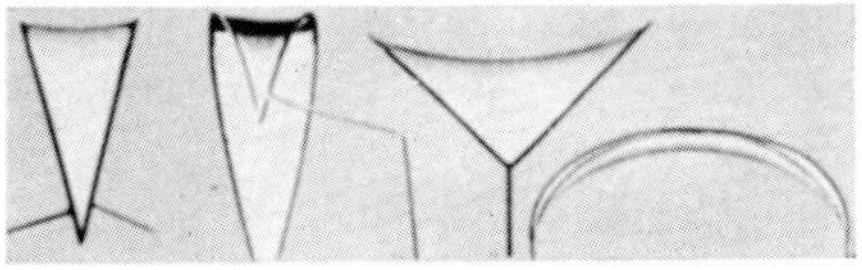

4 to 7

Figures 4 to 7 show two semicircular frames joined at their ends in such a way that their planes form an acute (Figs. 4 and 5) or right angle, (Figs. 6 and 7). Compared with the model of the Raleigh Arena, the center of the surface lies higher in relation to the span. At the corners, the minimum surface is tangential to the planes formed by the sides of the arches.

In the Church at Bremen-Grolland (Figs. 8 and 9) built by architect Carsten Schröck in 1962–63, a cable net of uniform mesh is stretched between arches so as to resemble closely the minimum surface shown in Fig. 7 (see C. Roland, *op. cit.*). The plan forms an ellipse and each arch a semi-ellipse. The roof cable net is vertical at the intersection of the arches. The walls are also prestressed cable nets with the same mesh size and prestressing as the roof. It can be seen in the model* (Fig. 8) that the highly elastic arches are completely stiffened by the prestressed nets. Model tests were carried out at a scale of 1:66 (described in detail in C. Roland, *op. cit.* pp. 60 and 61). The arches consisted of 1.0-mm diameter steel wire and had a slenderness ratio (length to radius of gyration) of 1700; the cables were made of spun glass with short measuring springs of steel wire.

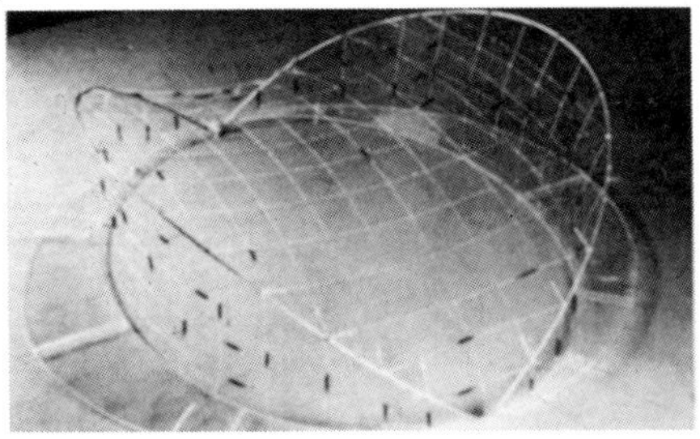

8

The model (Fig. 8) was so elastic and self-stabilizing that it could be pressed down to the base plate by a large overload, the arches being deformed to an S-shape. Sudden removal of the overload caused the model to return to its initial shape. This demonstrated clearly the stiffening effect of prestressed cable nets on arches subjected to compression.

Laminated-wood arches with extremely great rigidity were used in the finished structure; the interior is shown in Fig. 9. The engineers were Schleyer, Cassens, and Luttmann.

Despite the conspicuous disproportion between the thick arches and the cable net, this is a remarkable design, since structurally it forms one unit. There is no distinction between wall and roof. For the first time, a completely prefabricated steel cable net of uniform mesh was used, the shape of which was precisely determined in the model. The mesh length is 98 cm. The cables are arranged in pairs and are visible from the interior. They are lined with wooden panels nailed together from boards.

9

A minimum surface between three arches is shown in Figs. 10 to 12. Three semicircular arches are joined together so as to form right angles at the three points of contact. The resulting frame has three points and three arches. The minimum surface is comparatively slightly curved in the middle. This is evident from the side view (Fig. 11). A theoretically infinitesimal plane is located at the center of the system.

If we imagine a lower plane to pass through the three frame corners and an upper plane to be tangential to the arches at their apexes, the center of the surface will be much closer to the upper plane.

We should mention the work of the Scandinavian architect Bertil Zeinetz. At a quite early date he designed cable nets and membranes reinforced with cable nets stretched between three arches.

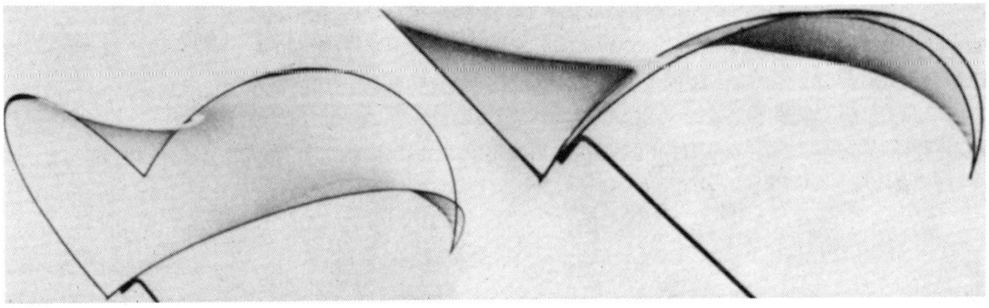

10 and 11

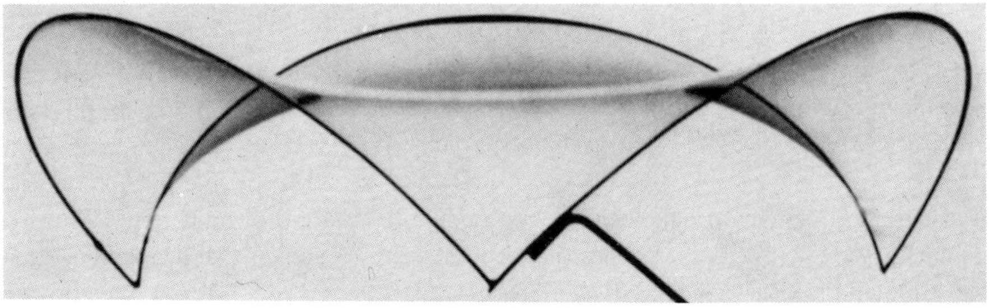

12

Single Arches with Circular Rings

Consider an arch standing centrally upright in a circular ring. If soap films (Fig. 1) are stretched on both sides of this arch, the resulting shape is related to that shown in Figs. 6 and 7, p. 57. The shape of the film does not depend upon whether one or both halves of the model are covered by the film. If only one side is covered, the arch is subjected to bending; if both sides are covered the arch is mainly subjected to compression. Figures 2 to 5 show another way of stretching soap films. The films shown in Fig. 1 tend to combine and form a third plane surface. This surface fills the upper part of the arch and forms a new line of contact with the two other films making angles of 120°. The membrane tension is uniform in this structure. Only the plane membrane acts on the upper part of the arch. If this part of the arch is not to be subjected to bending, it must be circular.

The shape of the two lower membranes and of the line of contact is not affected by changes in the shape of the arch within the plane of the upper vertical membrane. Such a frame, which may have any shape within the stated limits, can also be formed by components subjected to bending or tension.

Membranes Stretched in Two Circular Rings Intersecting at Right Angles

If a soap film is stretched in one of the four frames formed by two intersecting rings, it will assume the shape given in Figs. 4 to 7, p. 57. We can imagine this to happen simultaneously in all four frames so that a hollow space is enclosed. It is difficult to do this experimentally, since the arches are usually wetted on all sides, so that the soap films can assume a different shape of smaller total surface area.

If soap films are only stretched in two frames, as shown in Fig. 6, the resulting shape is similar to that given in Figs. 2 to 5. Only the upper plane surface is larger.

If films are stretched in all fields of this structure, the shape shown in Figs. 8 and 9 results.

Four slightly curved saddle-shaped surfaces adjoin a plane surface inclined at 45° to the planes of the frames. The resulting membrane has the least total surface area between the four frames. Let two equal rings intersect at acute angles. If soap films are then stretched in two opposite frames so that they do not touch, we obtain the known shape shown in Fig. 10. If soap films are made to cover all four fields simultaneously, the resulting structure (Figs. 11 and 12) will consist of five surfaces, related to the shape given in Figs. 8 and 9. A comparatively large plane surface occupies the middle of the frame and is bordered by four saddle-shaped surfaces.

If a soap film is stretched only between two adjoining frames, the minimum surface (Fig. 13) resembles that shown in Figs. 6 and 7. However, all three surfaces are curved in this case.

Membranes Stretched in Three Intersecting Circular Rings

Several possibilities exist if three rings intersect at equal angles at one point. Figure 14 shows a symmetrical form. It has three plane surfaces in the center, meeting at angles of 120°.

Asymmetrical forms as in Figs. 15 and 16 can also result. Measurements are required to determine which shape is the minimum surface. Whereas in a single closed frame only one minimum surface is possible, several shapes of minimum surfaces are possible when frames are added.

The Spiral Surface

If a soap film is suspended in a spiral frame with a straight axis, it will form a surface apparently identical with a spiral surface having a straight generator. If the spiral surface is a minimum surface, the outer frame is subjected only to compression. It cannot be subjected to bending, since it is a spatial curve of uniform curvature attached to a membrane of uniform tension, the radius of curvature of the frame always lying in the surface formed by the membrane. As far as is known to the author, it has not yet been proved mathematically that a spiral surface is an exact minimum surface.

In Fig. 17 the axis of the spiral surface is not formed by a straight rod rigid in bending, but by a thread which also forms a spiral. This is the rare case of a membrane suspended in a frame subjected to compression only on one side and to tension only on the other, and whose length is arbitrary.

Plane Membranes Bordered by Cable

All membranes can, as already mentioned, be stretched in frames rigid in bending or rings rigid in compression. The minimum amount of material is required for a frame that also consists of tension-loaded members, e.g., threads or cables. If the tension distribution in the membrane is uniform in all directions, the edge cables form circles. If the tension in the two principal directions differs, the cable curves are elliptic. Figures 1 to 5, p. 60, show the edges of a plane membrane under uniform tension in all directions. Figure 1, p. 60, represents a dodecagon; Fig. 2, p. 60, an octagon; Fig. 3, p. 60, a hexagon; Fig. 4, p. 60, a pentagon; and Fig. 5, p. 60 a triangle.

The force in the edge cable does not depend on the span, but only on the radius of curvature of the cable. If the tension is uniform in all directions of the membrane, $S = qr$ where S is the cable force, r the radius of curvature, and q the surface tension.

The membrane shown in Fig. 6, p. 60, is bordered by cables with equal radii of curvature, i.e., by equally stressed cables. In contrast, the membrane shown in Fig. 7, p. 60, is bordered by cables with different radii of curvature. Hence, the forces in the edge cables differ. Figure 7 shows that holes can be cut and bordered by cables in any membrane. Depending on the tension distribution, these

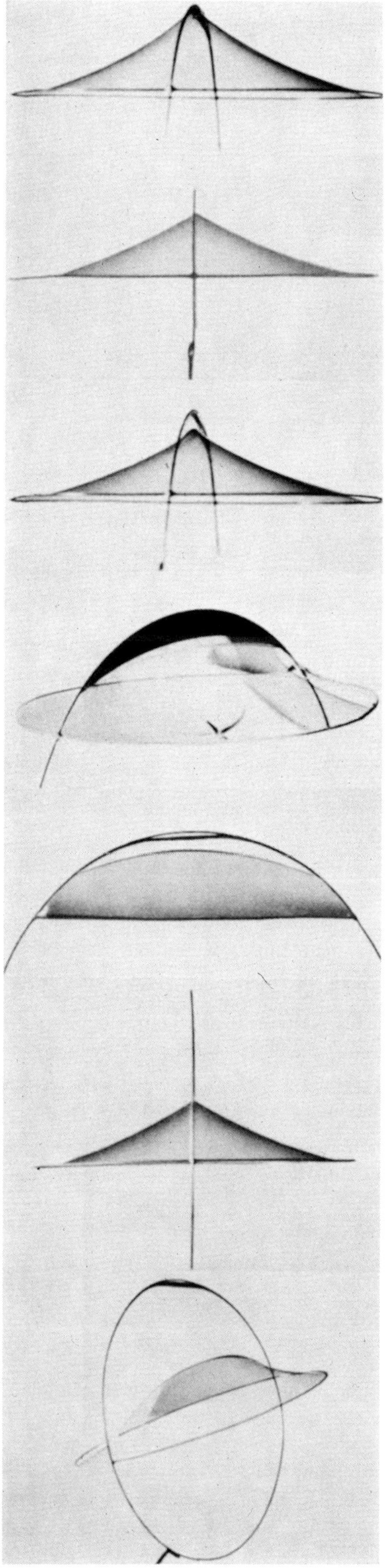

1 to **7**

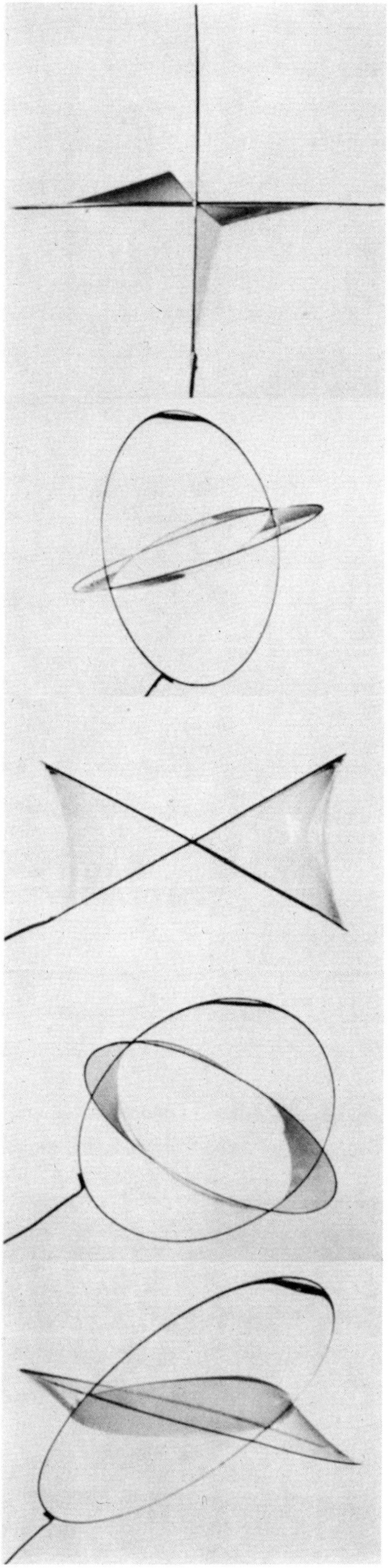

8 to **12**

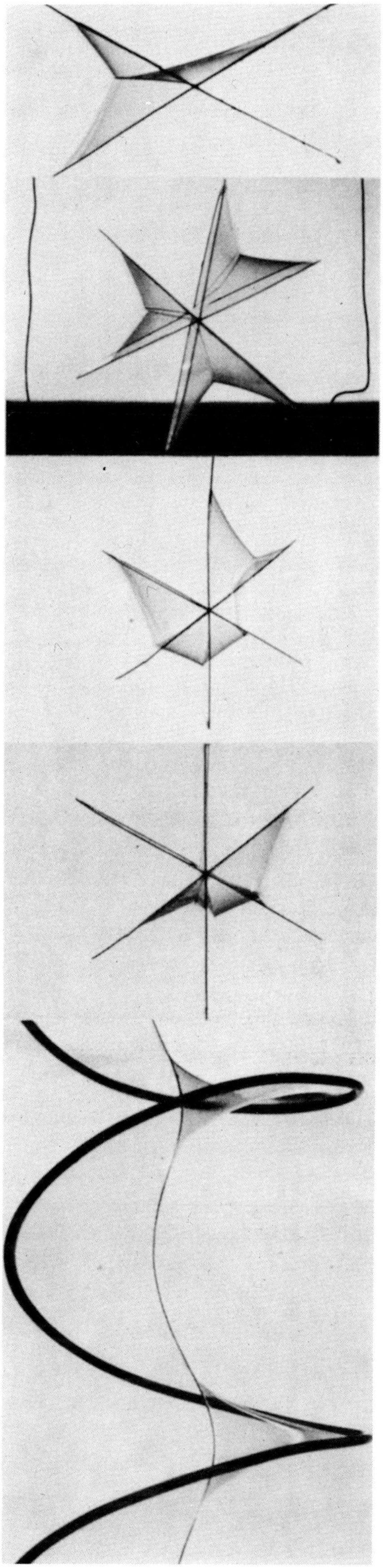

13 to **17**

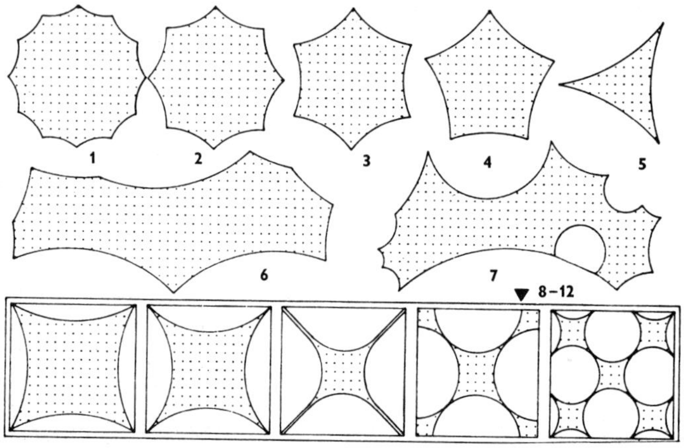

1 2 3 4 5 6 7 8–12

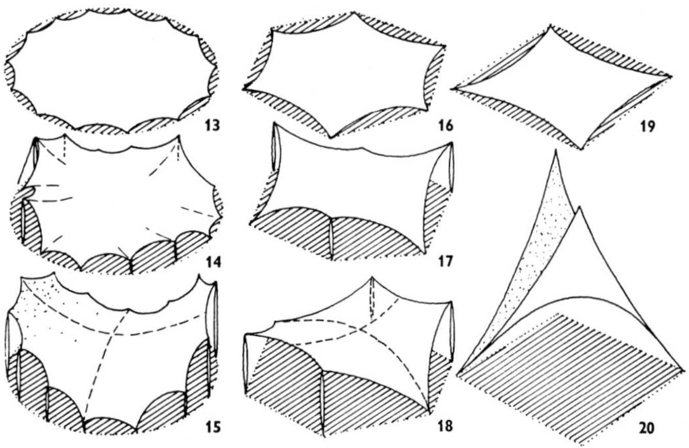

13 14 15 16 17 18 19 20

holes will be circular or elliptic. Figure 8 shows a plane membrane stretched between four points of a square frame. The radius of curvature of the cable is equal to the side of the frame. The tangents to the cables form angles of 30° at the suspension points. If the radius of curvature is only 0.7071 of the distance between the suspension points, the cables are mutually tangential at the suspension points. The membrane itself just touches the suspension points. If the cable radius is still smaller, the cables are parallel for a certain distance (Fig. 10).

Figure 11 shows the same membrane surface, but four more surfaces can be seen at the corners. The cable curvature is constant up to the edge. In the frame shown in Fig. 12, five membrane surfaces bordered by cables are suspended similarly.

The photograph in Fig. 47 is from a large test series. A soap film stretches between four flexible threads of equal length. The length of the threads was varied. In the models shown in plan in Figs. 28 to 35, the threads were lengthened by steps. This is also shown in the multiple exposure in Fig. 34. These photographs supplement the remarks concerning the sketches in Figs. 8 to 10. The soap films shown in plan in Figs. 36 to 40 are bordered by pairs of cables of different length; the resulting shapes are symmetrical to one axis. The shapes given in Figs. 41 to 46 are asymmetrical, threads of different length having been used. Figures 45 and 46 are each double exposures of two models.

Theoretical and experimental results obtained for plane cable-bordered membranes apply largely also to curved cable-bordered membranes. These will be discussed below.

Curved Prestressed Membranes and Cable Nets Stretched Between Cables

Membranes and cable nets can be stretched without difficulty between cables, i.e., between purely tension-loaded flexible nonplanar lines that form frames. In membranes under uniform tension in all directions (minimum surfaces), the edge cables form lines of constant curvature. These are not circles, as in plane surfaces, but spatial curves.

Figure 13 shows a plane membrane stretched between many points connected by cables. If several points are raised (Fig. 14), a spatially curved membrane results which is anticlastically curved everywhere. In this example, the directions of curvature vary. In Fig. 15 the points are raised in such a way that a large connected saddle results.

In Fig. 16 the number of suspension points for the edge cables of a plane surface has been reduced to six. If every other point is raised symmetrically, we obtain the spatially curved surface shown in Fig. 17; if two opposite points to the right and left of an axis of symmetry are raised, four high and two low points result (Fig. 18).

A plane membrane can be stretched from a minimum of three points, and cables can take up the membrane forces between them. However, only a membrane with cables stretched between at least four points (Fig. 19) can be spatially curved (Fig. 20).

The simplest and best known form of a curved membrane stretched between four cables* is shown in Figs. 48 to 51, of model

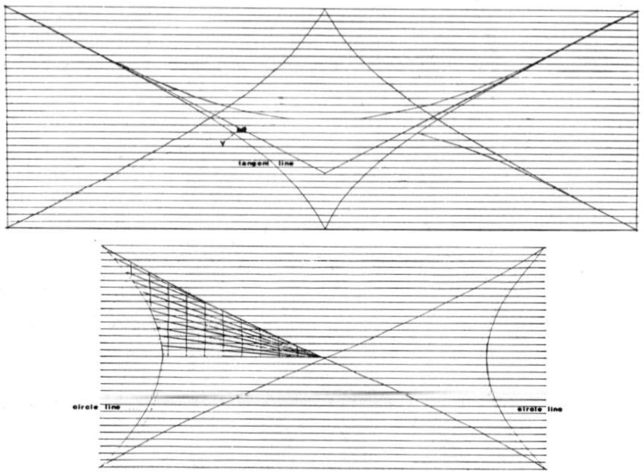

21 and 22

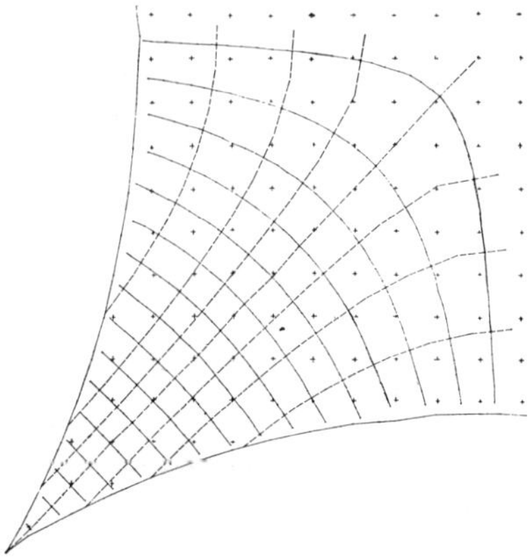

23

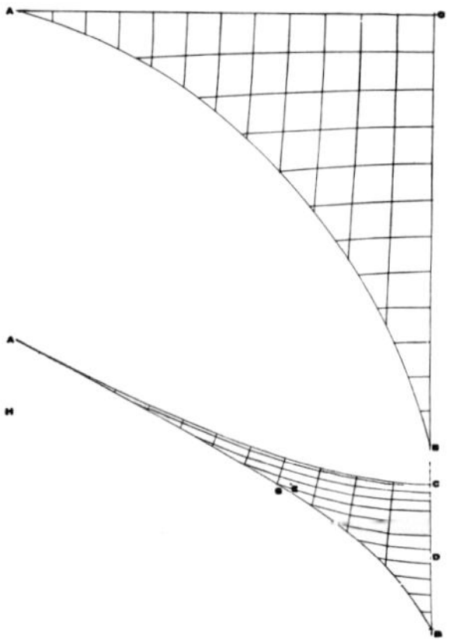

24 and 25

▼ 34

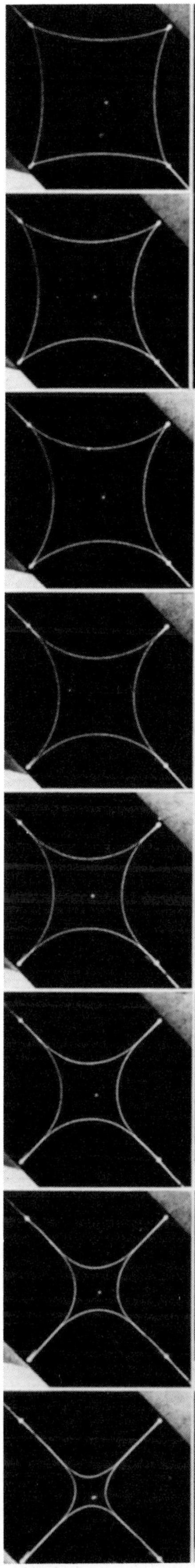

26 to 33

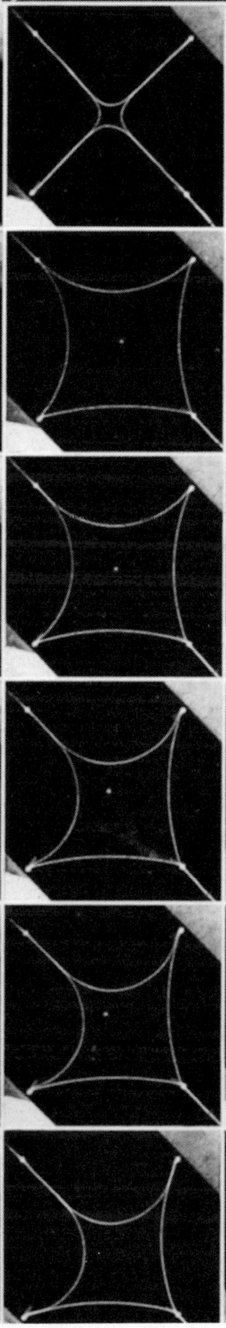

35 to 40

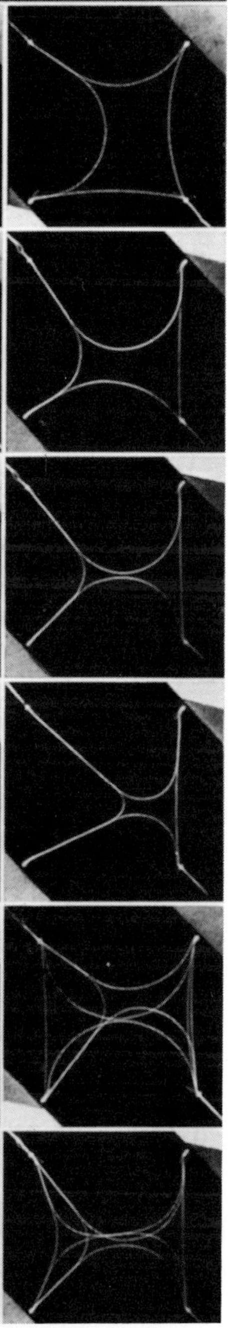

41 to 46

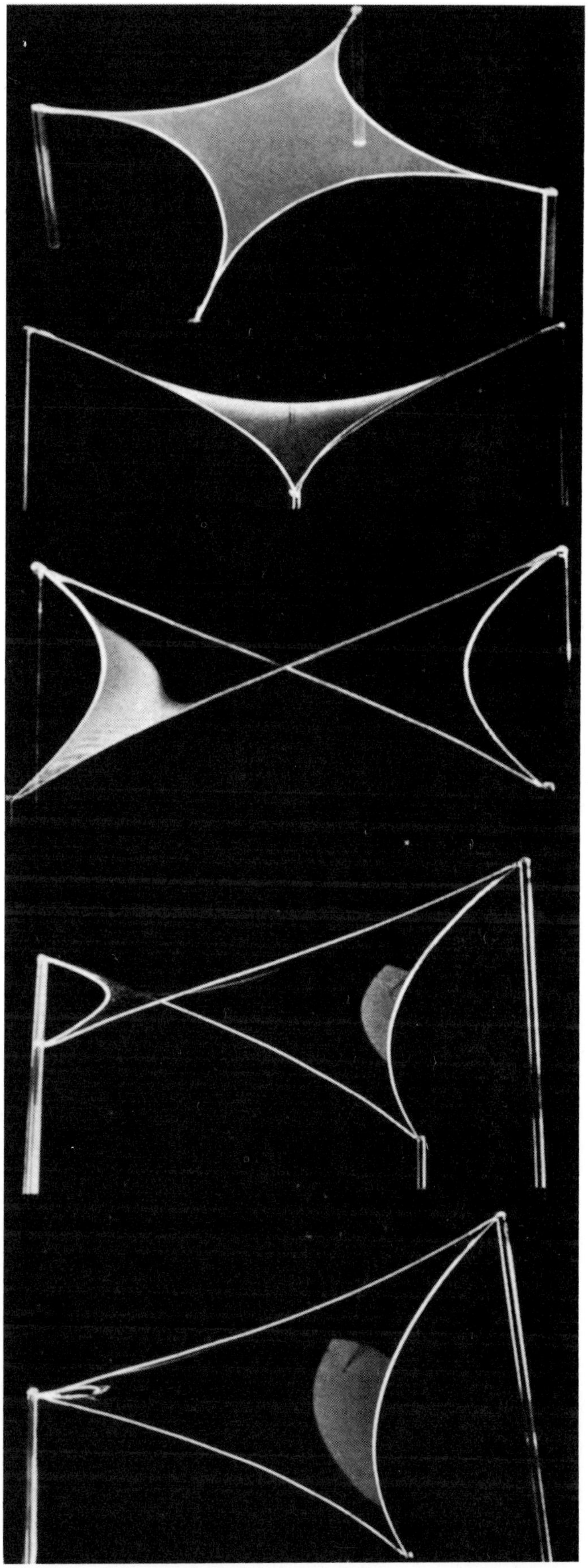

47 to 51

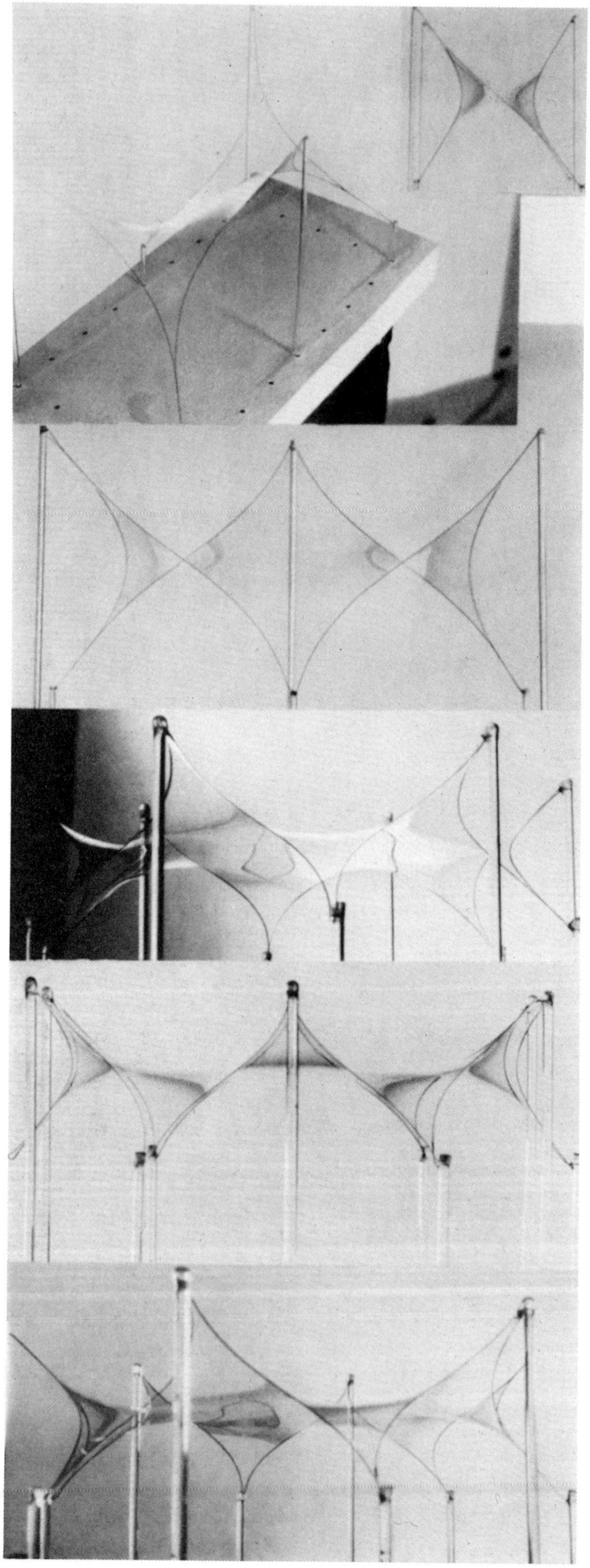

1 to 6

experiments with soap films. Figure 48 is a diagonal view and Fig. 50, a side view.

No exact mathematical derivation exists of the form of this minimum surface or of its boundaries. Since the cables influence the surface, the later is not the minimum surface in a skew frame (see Vol. 1, p. 292 ff.). Photographs in Figs. 50 and 51, p. 61, were taken so as to bring out the spatial curvature of the edge-cable curve. The cable ends in Fig. 51 lie exactly behind each other so that they coincide in the photograph. The cable appears as a loop in this projection.

Measuring tests* were performed on a large rubber membrane during a graduate seminar at the School of Architecture of Washington University, St. Louis, in 1958. The membrane was carefully stretched between cables, with highly uniform tension distribution. This permitted usable results to be obtained. Primarily, the shape was compared with that of a hyperbolic paraboloid.

A section through the high and low points, which is also a side view (Fig. 21, p. 60), clearly shows the deviations from a parabola. The sections parallel to the edges are not straight, as they would be in a hyperbolic paraboloid (Fig. 22, p. 60). The contours and the lines of maximum slope were determined in part of the plan (Fig. 23, p. 60). An experimental structure was built on the campus of Washington University according to these measurements. The membrane was formed of a fabric. A cable net based on the same measurements, also developed in St. Louis in 1958, (Figs. 24 and 25, p. 60), has similar properties. It was completely prefabricated and was erected in a few minutes. It is the first example of prefabricated tension-loaded cable-net structures intended as light, quickly assembled roofs for agricultural structures.

Only a few of the many ways of stretching membranes or cable nets between edge cables can be shown here. In the model in Fig. 1, a soap film is stretched between six threads attached at three high and three low points. This elongated surface has a saddle-shaped curvature everywhere. The section between the central high and the central low point is S-shaped, as seen in the side view in Fig. 2; at the point of inflection in the membrane center, the surface has no curvature. The edges form spatial curves of constant curvature, partly appearing as S-curves.

In Figures 4 to 6 a soap film is stretched between six low and six high points connected by threads. The points form corners of a regular dodecagon, which is practically round. The membrane does not form a large connected saddle, but rather radial waves. The membrane is only slightly curved near the centers, despite the large deformation of the frame. At the center the curvature vanishes. The curvature is maximum near the high and low points. The directions of principal curvature extend radially and concentrically to the center.

Further results appear on pp. 84 to 87. It should be noted that not every minimum surface is satisfactory for structures. Only a few of the many ways of stretching minimum surfaces between flexible edge members rigid in tension have been investigated until now.

The roof built in 1958, (Figs. 8 and 13, p. 65) over an open-air concert stage in Melbourne, Australia, is a particularly interesting prestressed cable-net roof with edge cables. It was designed by architects Yuncken, Freeman, Griffiths, and Simpson. Calculations were performed by the engineering firm of Irving and Associates. The aerodynamic consultant was Molyneux. The plan of the roof forms a triangle with sides approximately 80 m long. The strongly curved 170-m long main support cable is led over two 21-m high masts, which are in the principal support line and require, therefore, no additional guys. This had already been tried in 1957 in the small pavilion* at the Federal Garden Show at Cologne (Fig. 7). The triangular roof in Melbourne is intended to protect the orchestra and most of the audience against weather and noise from the city, and to amplify the sound of the music by reflection from the underside of the roof.

The masts are welded from steel sheets and coated with plastics. The main support cable consists of seven braids each 90 mm in diameter, and carries a net of single 35-mm diameter cables at an average spacing of 2.10 m. This prestressed cable net was covered with plywood panels 13 mm thick, coated on both sides with aluminum foil 0.4-mm thick.

7

These panels cover a surface of 3.700 m^2 and weigh 9 kg/m^2. The joints between them are sealed by 125-mm wide aluminum strips secured with selftapping screws. Good acoustics are ensured for a maximum audience of 22,000 by an echo-free loudspeaker system aided by the roof (photographs in Fig. 8, also 13, p. 65 by Sievers).

8

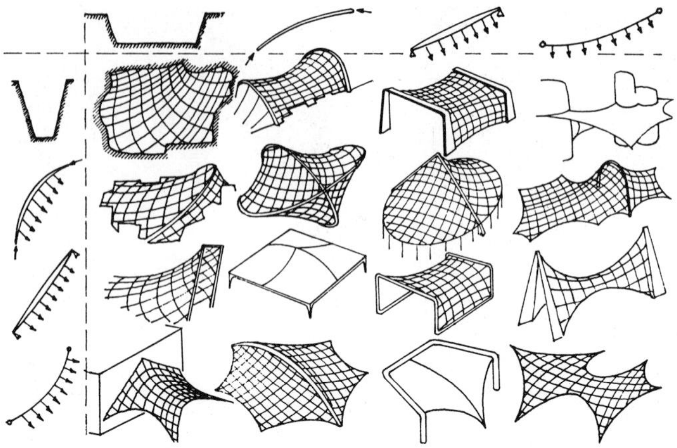

1

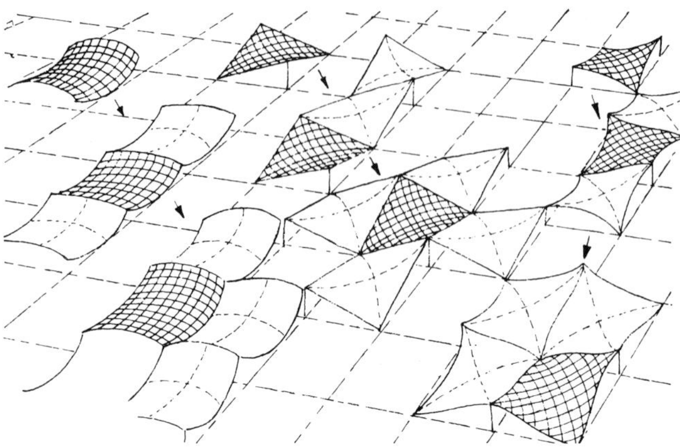

Combinations of Membranes and Cable Nets with Various Edge Attachments

Until now we have discussed cable nets and membranes that were either anchored directly to rigid abutments or whose edge elements were subjected to tension, bending, or compression. Types of anchoring and stresses of edge elements can occur in any combination. Figure 1 shows several possibilities. The first vertical column shows rigid anchorings; the second, arches subjected to compression; the third, beams subjected to bending; the fourth, tension-loaded cables forming edge elements. Each column has been similarly divided from top to bottom. The top line shows rigid anchorings, and so on.

At the intersection of the first column with the first line we see a cable net stretched across a cave, i.e., rigidly anchored on all sides.

In the second line of the first column we see a cable net anchored in the mountains and supported by an arch. The third line shows a similar net held by a frame rigid in bending, while the fourth line shows a cable net supported by a massive block on one side and bordered by tension-loaded cables on the other.

In the second column the first line shows a cable net anchored in the ground and supported by two arches. The second line shows four cable nets, also bordered by arches. The arches simultaneously form the edges. In the third line we see an outer edge, subjected to bending, combined with a central arch.

The first line of the third column shows a cable net stretched between two frames subjected to bending and directly anchored in the foundations at the sides. The second line shows two cable nets, supported by a common triangular frame rigid in bending and anchored at the edge by two arches subjected to compression. This is a combination of edges subjected to compression and to bending. The cable net shown in the third line is stretched in a continuous frame, which may be regarded as a combination of several frames subjected to bending. The sketch at the bottom of the third column shows a net bordered by cables and attached at three sides to a frame subjected to bending.

The top line of the fourth column shows a cable net stretched between massive blocks with cables at the edges. The second line of the fourth column shows a large net bordered by cables and supported by an arch. The cable net shown in the third line is suspended between two frames rigid in bending and is bordered at the lower edge by cables. The fourth line shows a combination of tension-loaded edge members.

The diagonal from top left to bottom right in this diagram shows the systems in which the kind of stress of all edge elements of a net or membrane is the same. Each combination of different kinds of stress appears in this diagram twice, once above and once below the diagonal.

3 to 6

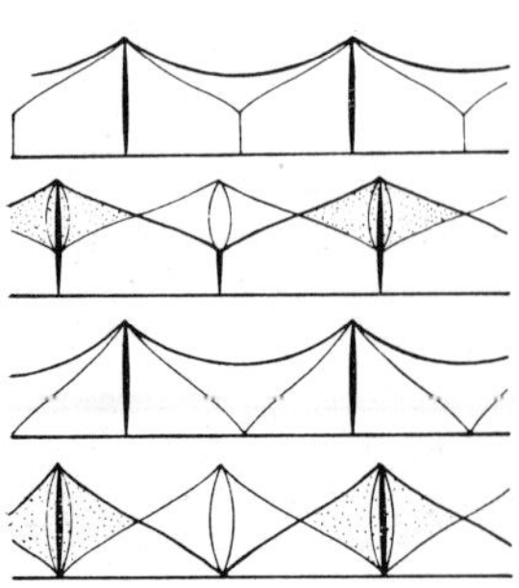

7 to 10

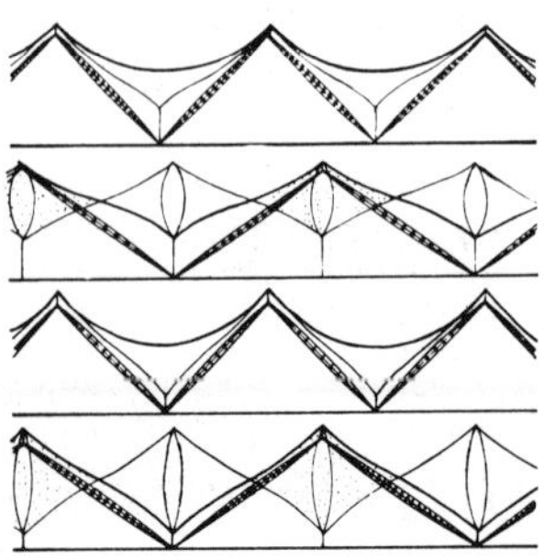

11

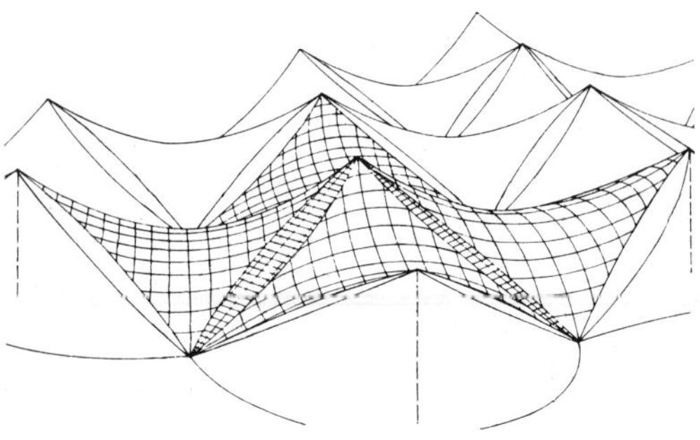

12

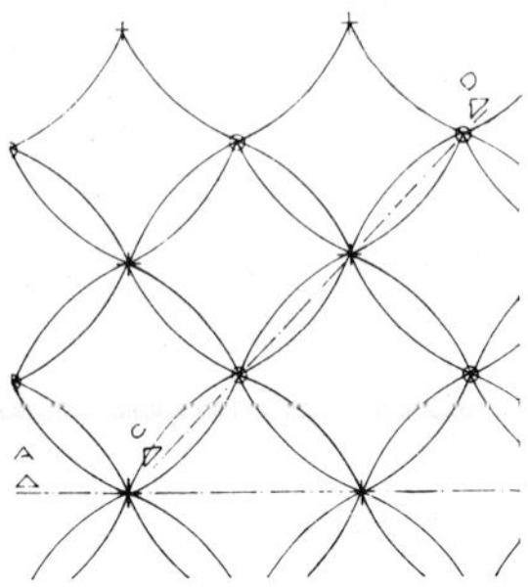

Combinations of Cable-Net and Membrane Surfaces with Various Edge Attachments

Plane or saddle-shaped cable nets or membranes can be assembled to form large structures consisting of identical components. Thus, if a structure bordered by arches (Fig. 2, top left) is connected on two sides to similar structures, we obtain a series (Fig. 2, left center). Additions on all sides are possible, so that a surface results (Fig. 2, bottom left). As already stated, arches forming edges are subjected solely to compression only when they are attached to cable nets or supporting ropes on both sides, i.e., when they form part of a large spatial system. Arches are therefore particularly suitable as cable-net supports in systems composed of identical shapes.

Figure 2, top center, shows the simple basic shape of a cable net stretched between four straight parts rigid in bending which do not lie in one plane. When similar forms are added in one direction (Fig. 2, top center), or in two directions (Fig. 2, center), the shape of the cable net remains unchanged. The bending stresses in frame components, to which two cable nets or membranes are attached, are reduced and their compressive stresses increased. Cable nets and membranes bordered by cables can also be joined. Figure 2, top right, shows a cable net stretched between four cables not lying in a plane. Such nets have been joined to form a row in Fig. 2, right center, and a surface in Fig. 2, bottom right. Four cable nets with edges are joined, with a low point in the center and four high and four low points at the edges.

The shape of every field of such a net changes when two cable nets are attached along a common connecting cable. The connecting cable appears straight in plan, if the tensions are equal, and S-shaped from the side. The initial shape remains unchanged only when the individual parts of such cable nets or membranes do not come into contact and merely have common corners. Openings then remain between the nets and the membranes, which may be closed by membranes or nets under less tension.

Such composite forms have "high" and "low" points. They are closely related and constitute a direct transition to membranes and cable nets of the same shape with central supports.

Figure 11 is a sketch of a typical composite form with closed cut-outs. Figure 12 is the plan. Composite forms are suitable for large prefabricated roofs of almost any shape when the components differ only slightly. Thus, only two elements are needed for roof surfaces as shown in Fig. 12, Figure 3 represents section A, with vertical masts subjected to compression under the high points, and tension-loaded cables under the low points of the surface. Figure 4 represents section CD. In Figs. 5 and 6 (same sections) the tension-loaded surface is anchored directly to the foundations and the cable beneath the low points omitted. Figures 7 and 8 correspond to the roof shape shown in Figs. 3 and 4, and Figs. 9 and 10 to that shown in Figs. 5 and 6. The masts are spread, and their thrust opposes the cable traction at the low points.

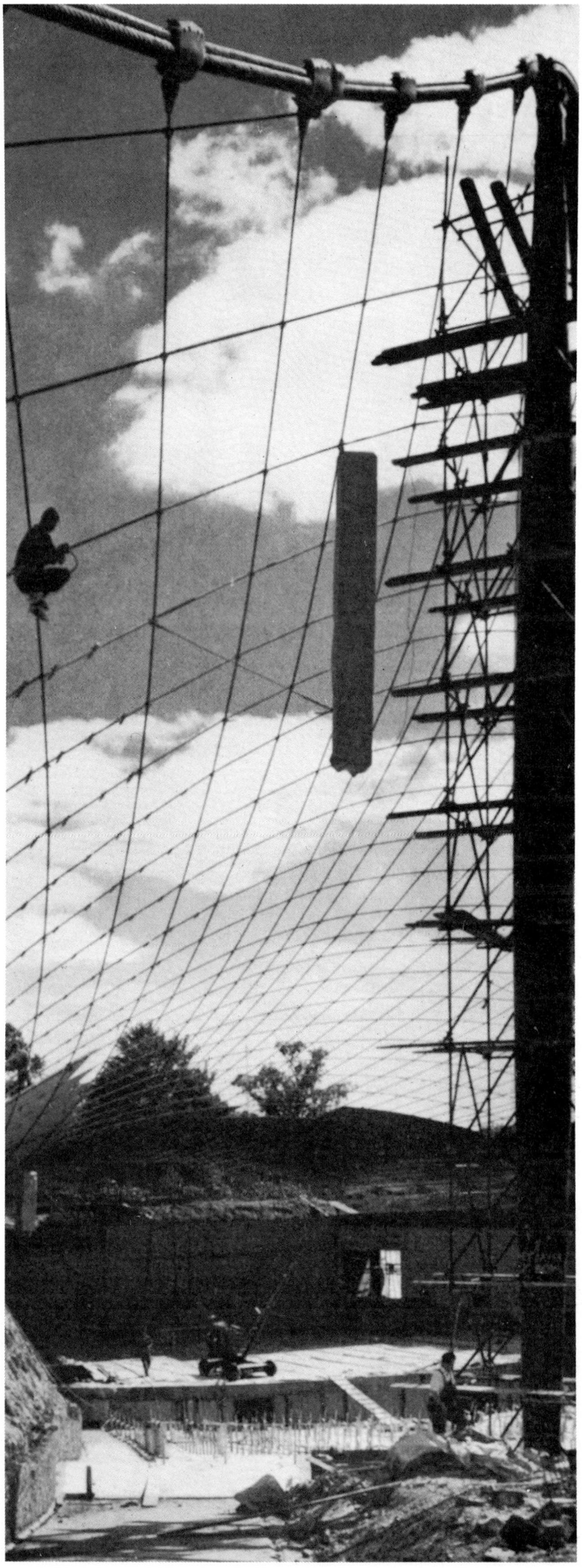

13

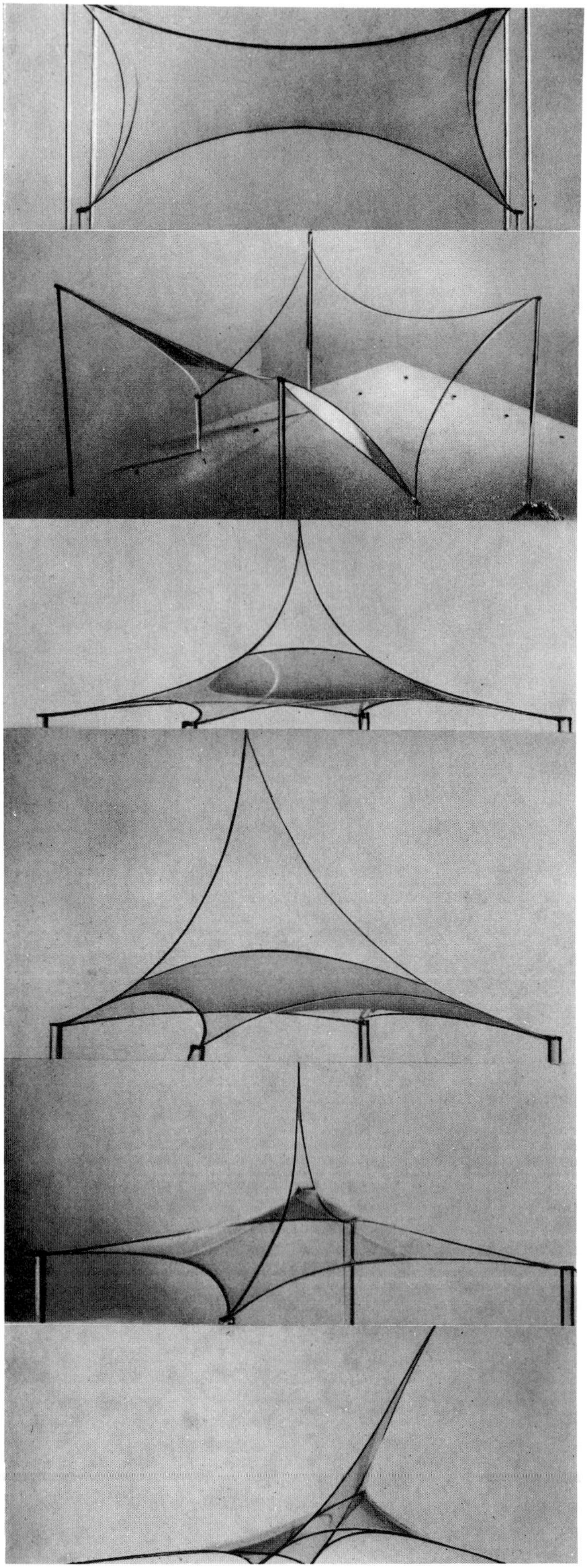

1 to 6

Soap-Film Tests with Composite Surfaces Bordered by Cables

The interaction between membrane surfaces in connected systems becomes clear in tests to determine the minimum surface. Figures 1 and 2 show threads stretched above a square plan between six points of different height. The four high points are at the corners of the square and the two low points at the midpoints of two opposite sides. The two low points are also connected by a thread. If a liquid film, such as a soap solution, is suspended in this system, two saddle-shaped surfaces are formed, which would be plane only if all six points were coplanar. The thread connecting both low points lies in one plane in a symmetrical arrangement. The curvature of this thread can be determined from the side view (Fig. 1); it is not exactly circular.

In the studies* for the Exhibition Building of Expo '64 in Lausanne, section "Neige et Rocs" (Architect: M. Saugey; see rubber-thread test shown in Fig. 7, and finished structure, Fig. 8), minimum surfaces were stretched between four low points and one high point. The high point was connected by cables to two diagonally opposed low points, so that two surfaces, each bordered by four cables, resulted. If soap films are suspended simultaneously in both surfaces, three membranes form (Figs. 3 to 7) that meet along one edge at angles of 120°. This form has the least surface area for such a cable arrangement. If the high point is raised (Fig. 4), the two bottom surfaces are only slightly affected. Only the upper surface becomes larger. It will be plane when the corners of the figure are arranged symmetrically, and spatially curved (Fig. 6) when the corners are arranged asymmetrically.

If, for example, a soap film is suspended only in the right-hand part of the model (Fig. 5), the two central ascending edge cables have a quite different curvature, and the two cables on the right also change their shape. We can also determine the minimum surfaces formed if independent but similar soap films are made to span both surfaces, each bordered by four cables.

The structures of the group "Neige et Rocs" in Lausanne approximate the above shape which has, however, a larger total surface than the minimum surfaces in the tests shown in Figs. 3 to 6.

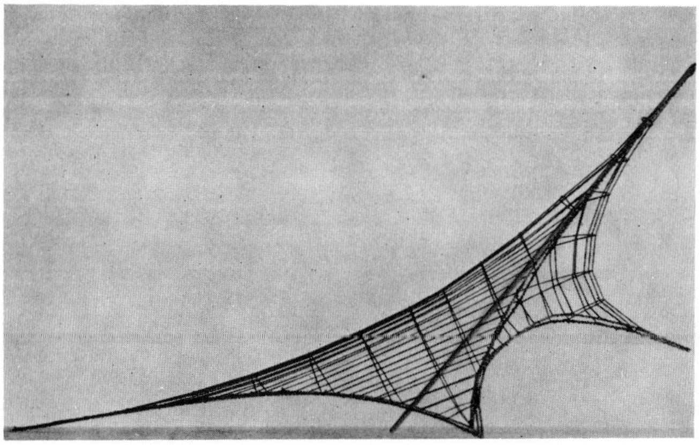

▲ 7

Examples of Joined Cable Nets or Membranes with Edges under Various Stress Conditions

The joining of cable nets with straight edges subjected to bending (Fig. 2 center, p. 64) is geometrically very simple. We obtain repetitive shapes as found by Candela and Catalano for hyperbolic-paraboloid shells. Oscar Hansen (Warsaw) stretched a series of joined membranes between supports rigid in bending for his pavilion in South America. Fig. 2, p. 50, shows the first such unit, and Fig. 9 shows the interior of the finished pavilion (photograph by Hansen). Gillet and Sarger joined two large cable-net surfaces, Fig. 3, p. 51, for the French Pavilion at the 1958 Brussels World's Fair. These surfaces were stretched between framework girders rigid in bending.

The Coliseum at the 1962 Seattle World's Fair is a further important example of joined cable nets with straight edges. It was built by architect Thiry, and engineers Hostmark and Associates (Fig. 3, p. 43).

The building has a free span of 120 m and consists of four surfaces each with sides 60 m long. The outer edge, which is rigid in bending, is a prestressed concrete beam, whereas the inner rigid connecting girders are steel structures. The cables run in the directions of principal curvature. The curvatures are comparatively small in this structure. The cable net is lined with aluminum-covered sandwich panels. This structure is now used as a sports arena for ice-hockey, basketball, and boxing, with room for 12,000 to 18,000 spectators (photograph by Seattle *Times*).

Structures with frames rigid in bending are usually much costlier than cable nets and membranes bordered by edge cables, because of the material required for the frames. However, the resulting structural separation of the individual tension-loaded support surfaces permits separate mathematical analysis of the components, and frequently facilitates design and planning.

There are many examples of joined membranes and cable nets with edges and connections subjected to tension or compression. We refer the reader to *Deutsche Bauzeitschrift* 11/1964 and C. Roland, *op.cit.*

9 ▲

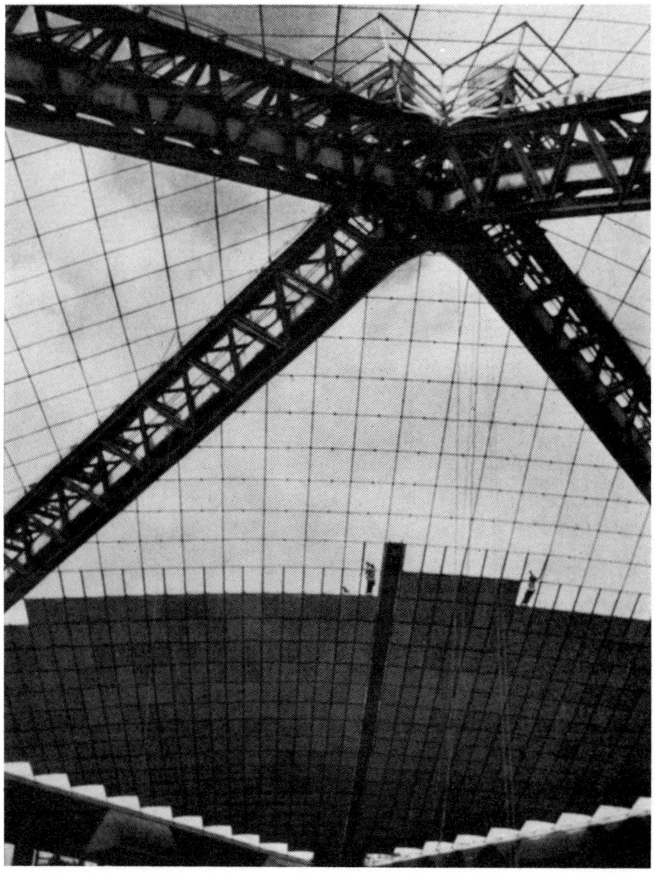

▼ 10

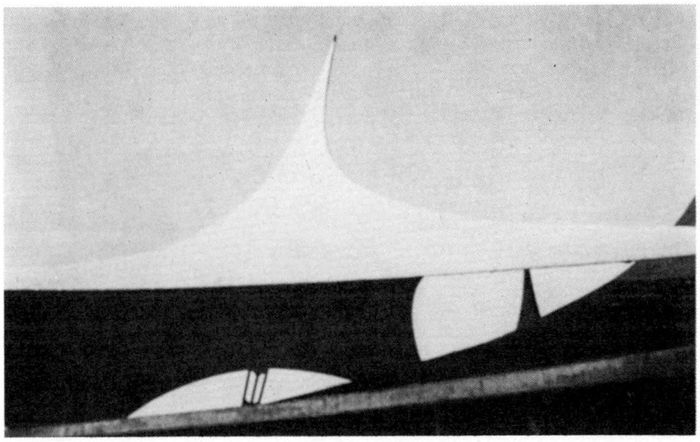

▲ 8

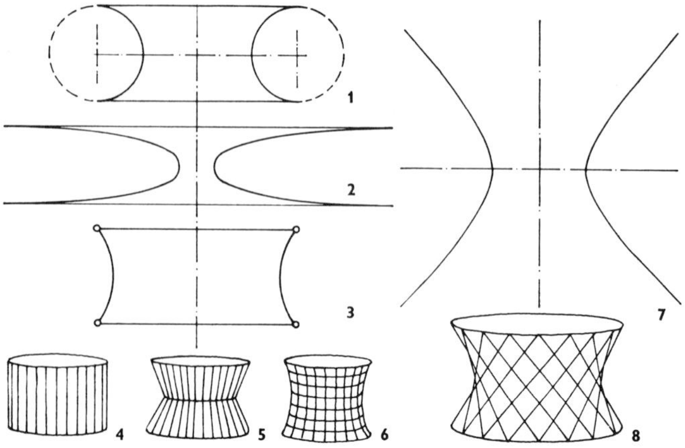

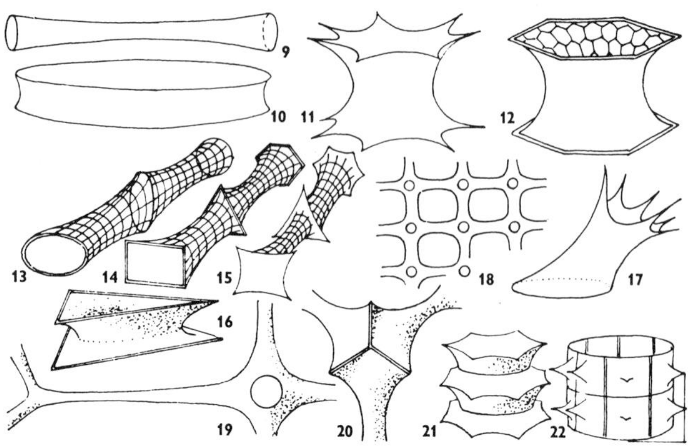

Tubular Membranes and Cable Nets

Membranes and cable nets can also be stretched to form toroidal shapes, as seen in Figs. 1 to 8. If cables are stretched in straight lines to form a cylinder (Fig. 4) and are then drawn together by an annular cable, we obtain a shape (Fig. 5) that becomes hose-shaped if more annular cables are added (Fig. 6). It is narrower at the center than at the ends. The hose surface is saddle-shaped at every point, i.e., anticlastically curved. A minimum surface, shaped like a catenoid, can be stretched between two rings (see cross section, Fig. 9). If tension is nonuniform, other forms result, e.g., the inner surface of a torus (Fig. 1), or surfaces as shown in Figs. 2 and 3, whose cross sections are ellipses or similar curves. Figure 7 shows the section of a hyperboloid which is a cable net of curved (Fig. 6) or straight (Fig. 8) cables.

We distinguish between long tubular hoses (Fig. 9) and short circular structures. Furthermore, differentiation is possible according to the edges and the inner supports. Both shapes shown in Figs. 9 and 10 are bordered by circular rings rigid in bending. A toroidal membrane or cable net may also be bordered by cables (Fig. 11), or by frames rigid in bending (Fig. 12). Circular and elliptic inner supports and edges (Fig. 13) may be subjected to compression; frames consisting of straight parts (Fig. 14) can be subjected to bending and those consisting of cables (Fig. 15), to tension.

A toroidal membrane tends to assume a round shape even between frames that are not rounded (Fig. 16).

The tubular membrane shown in Fig. 17 is an example of an asymmetrical form. It is anchored to a surface at the bottom, and bordered by cables at the top.

Tubular systems can be joined to form networks maintained in shape by external tension (Figs. 18 and 19). Such networks of flexible membranes can serve as conduit systems, since when sufficiently prestressed they retain their shape even at negative pressures, and as formwork for rigid structures. Figure 20 shows a support of three semicircular arches arranged at the intersection of three tubes. These arches are solely under compressive stress.

Figures 21 and 22 show composite forms. The form shown in Fig. 21 has been created by extending tubing at different points and connecting the outer points by a cable. Such a membrane is related to wave-shaped membranes (see pp. 82 to 87). A shape like Fig. 22 is also possible, in which membranes with high points are extended to form a hose.

A soap film stretched between two equal rings forms a catenoid (Fig. 23) whose shape depends on the distance between the rings. With increasing distance the soap film forms a constriction of increasing depth, until a maximum is attained. (In this connection, refer to p. 265 of Vol. 1.) In the test shown in Fig. 24, the film is drawn together by an inner surface. The same form can also be obtained as a hose by means of a constricting thread. In the model shown from both sides in Figs. 25 and 26, a soap film is suspended between two intersecting arches and a ring underneath, so that a tubelike continuous membrane results.

23 and 24

25 and 26

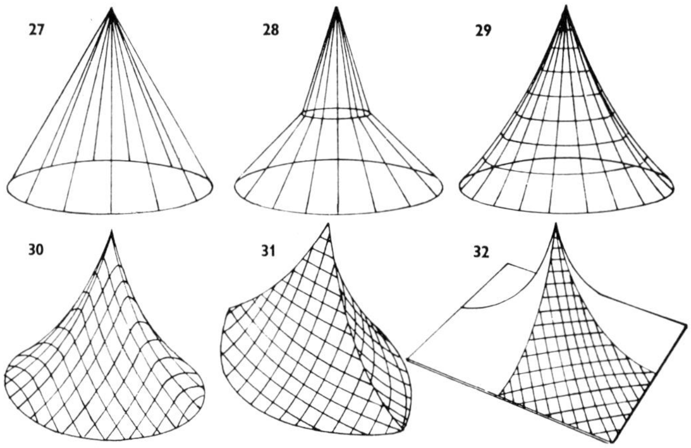

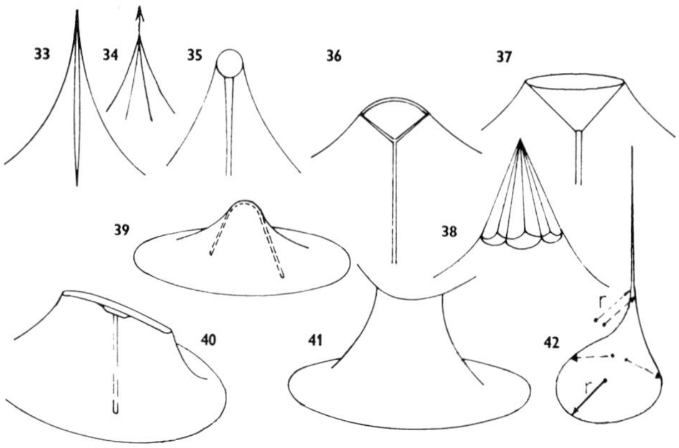

Centrally Supported Membranes and Cable Nets

Individual cables stretched from a ring toward a central raised point form a cone. If this cone is drawn together by an annular cable (Figs. 27 and 28), a constriction results, the annular cable being solely tension-loaded. Due to the action of the annular cable, the forces in the radial cables are greater in the lower than in the upper part.

A conical cable net with anticlastic curvature can be formed by means of additional annular cables (Fig. 29). Radial nets of this type have many applications.

A similar shape can be formed from a cable net with tetragonal meshes (Fig. 30). Other shapes are obtained by joining two (Fig. 31), four (Fig. 32), or more cable nets.

Every cable net can be supported at a single point, even if it is not a radial net as shown in Fig. 29. If a net with square or hexagonal meshes is secured at any point of a cable, two cables form angles with the direction of the support (mast or suspension) and can transmit forces (Fig. 33). If the net is secured at a node, three or four cables make angles with the direction of the support and can transmit forces. The cables attached directly at the point of support transmit larger cable forces than the others and should therefore be stronger.

A cable net suspended at one point does not constitute a basic problem, as, for example, is the case with membranes. The point of support of cable nets may, both in theory and in practice, be as small as desired. This is not true for membranes. Cables are line components in which forces act. Membranes form surfaces. The tensions in them are transmitted to line components. If a very thin stretched membrane is supported over a very small surface (e.g., a rubber foil supported by a needle), the tension in the membrane is extremely high at this point, since the force acting at the point of support is transmitted to the membrane along an extremely short line. With a true point load, i.e., with an infinitesimal supporting surface, and, therefore, infinitesimal edge length of the supporting surface, the membrane tensions become infinite even with a very small load when the membrane thickness is assumed to be infinitesimal. This explains why even highly resistant membranes can be easily pierced by thin needles.

Centrally supported membranes require an adequate contact line, as provided, e.g., by a sphere (Fig. 35), a supporting shell (Fig. 36), or a supporting cone (Fig. 37). The membrane is thus stressed along a line of finite length, and not at a single point.

Figure 38 shows a membrane suspended from cable loops connected to the supporting point by cables. The membrane forces are thus transmitted to the cables, i.e., to linear support elements. The central supports may be distinguished according to the stresses which they induce in the support elements (compression, bending, or tension). Support by an arch (Fig. 39) induces compression in the latter. A beam (Fig. 40) is subjected to bending and a cable (Fig. 41), to tension. A ridge is formed between two points. However, a membrane may be supported with a single cable, as seen in the soap-film test shown in Figs. 1 and 2, p. 72. The cable then forms a continuous line of constant curvature (Fig. 42). Examples of centrally supported cable nets are the early structures of Shuchov, who built four pavilions with hanging roofs (Fig. 43) at the Nizhni Novgorod Exhibition in 1896. A net consisting of straight cables spans the

▼ 43

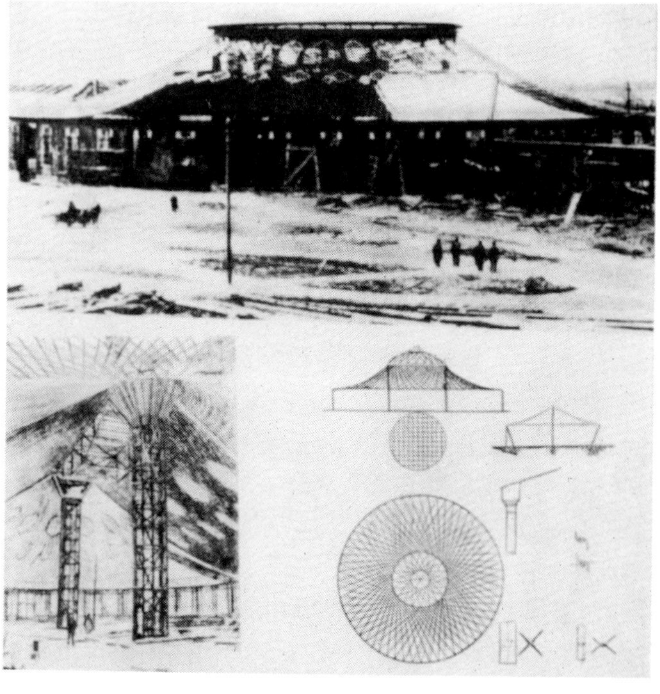

1 to **9**

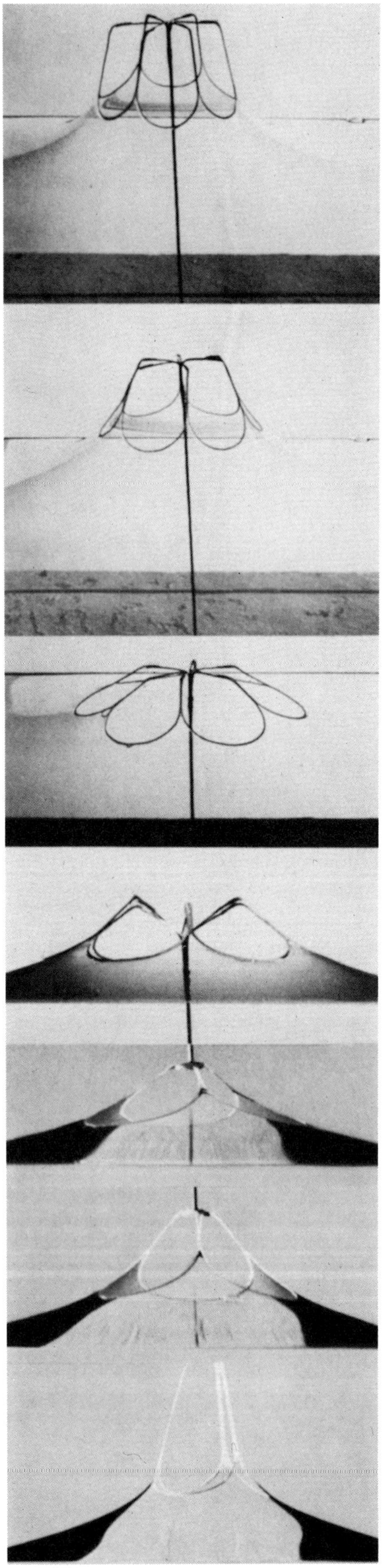

10 to **16**

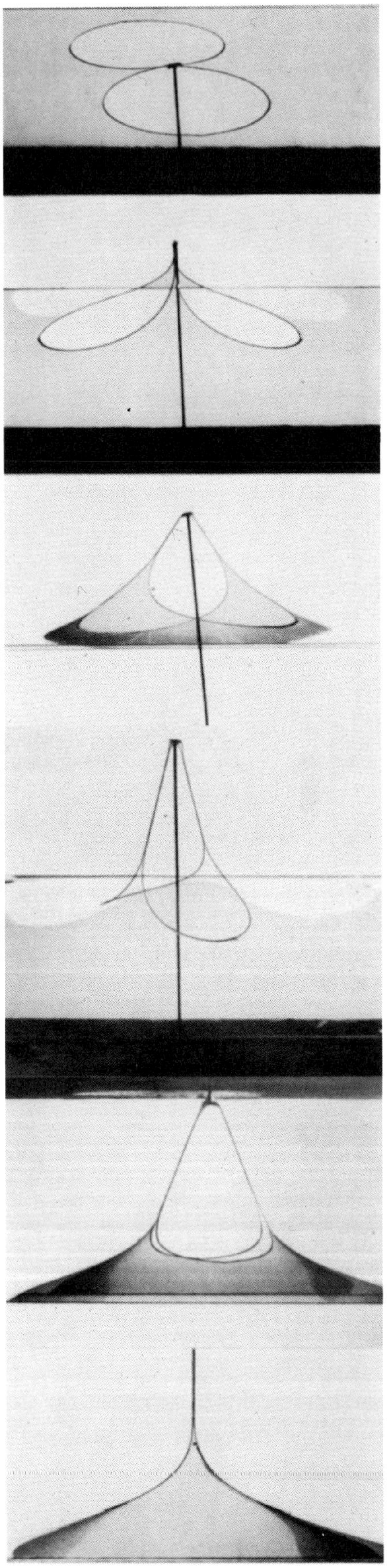

17 to **22**

outer regions of a large circular building like a hyperboloid. Other elongated pavilions have central supports and semicircular ends (see *Visyachii Pokrytie,* Russian translation of *Das hängende Dach, op. cit.;* also *Hanging Roofs, op. cit.*). The soap-film tests shown in Figs. 1 and 2 were explained by Rudolf Trostel in Vol. 1, p. 295. A film is suspended between a large and a small ring, and forms a conelike axisymmetrical surface shaped like a catenoid, with a saddle-shaped curvature at every point.

The upper ring can only be raised to a certain height above which the soap film is ruptured. This height varies directly with the diameter of the upper ring, and vanishes when the support becomes a single point.

Figures 3, 4, and 5 show a soap film stretched in a rectangular frame formed of threads. The film is deformed by forcing an off-center ring upward. The characteristic form is particularly evident from Fig. 3. Figures 4 and 5 are side views. The smallest membrane curvatures are observed near the ring.

Figures 6 to 9 show a soap film stretched between a rectangular horizontal frame at the bottom and two rings on top. This interesting shape has strong spatial curvatures, whose principal directions coincide approximately with the direction of maximum slope and with the contour lines.

It was shown by other model tests that a soap film can also be deformed with the aid of closed loops of flexible thread. The loops form flexible edges of holes in the film. Considerable deformations are possible if the loops are not too small in relation to the size of the membrane.

When six loops are used (Figs. 10 to 13) the single loops are nearly circular. Since the membrane tensions in soap films are uniform in all directions, the threads of the individual loops must form lines of constant curvature. If the membranes are curved, the loops form spatially curved lines with constant radii of curvature. Figures 12, 11, and 10 show a pole with six loops of thread being forced upward in steps.

Figure 13 is a side view of the phase shown in Fig. 12. (The shape of the pole is unimportant but the length of the thread loops can be significant.)

▲ 23

After this test a similar membrane was deformed in steps with the aid of three thread loops (Figs. 14 to 16). Here too, three lines of constant radius of curvature were formed. The torsion of these lines is greater than in the test with six loops.

In the test arrangement shown in Figs. 17 to 22, two rings were suspended in an initially plane membrane. These rings are circles (Fig. 17) in the plane state. They were then displaced by stages in relation to the initial plane. With increasing distance from the latter, the radii of curvature of the soap film and of the loops became smaller. Figures 20 to 22 show the film from various directions. Figures 21 and 22 are side views. Figure 20 is an oblique view from above.

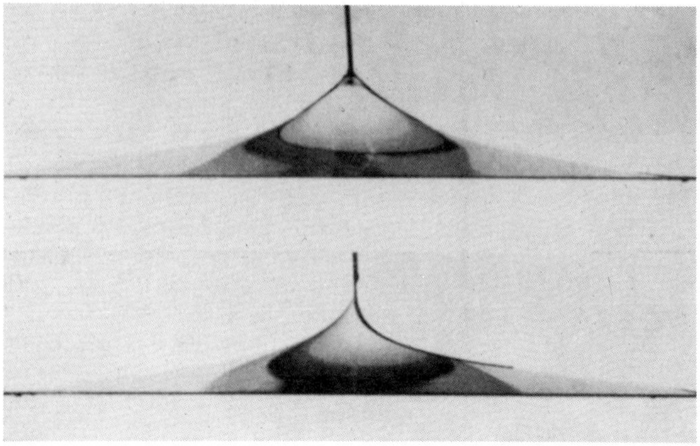

1 and 2

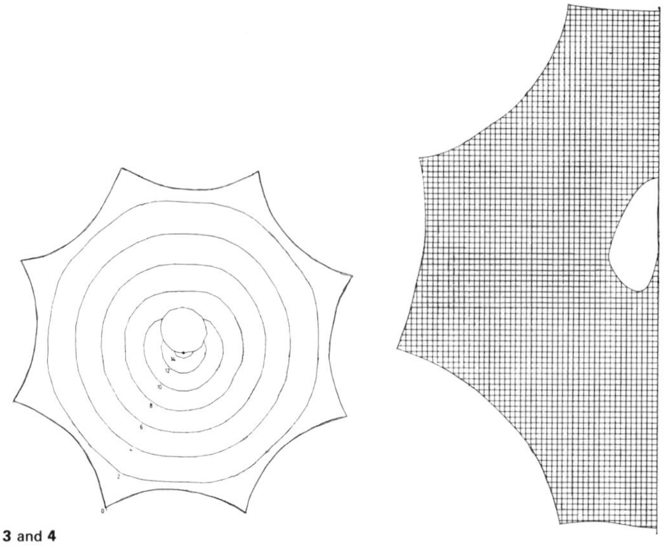

3 and 4

The most interesting test was performed with a thread loop, as shown in Figs. 1 and 2 (see Figs. 14 to 21, p. 77). The shape of the loop is independent of whether the membrane has a high or a low point. Here too, we have a spatial line of uniform curvature (Fig. 42, p. 69). Minimum surfaces with thread loops are shapes of great structural importance. By very simple means, membranes can be supported at high or at low points without increasing tension. The soap-film tests were performed in 1962 and 1963 with the aid of Bernd Friedrich Romberg. In 1964 Larry Medlin considered the problem of applying these results.

Figure 4 shows one half of a flat cable net with square uniform meshes. It has a heart-shaped opening in the center. Central opening and net edges are formed by strong cables. By raising the central point and moving the outer points together, this net can be transformed into a roof. At the same time the square meshes become rhombic. The plan with contour lines is shown in Fig. 3. The plan, obtained by measurements on a model, has the same scale as the "plane development" (Fig. 4). The high point of the model is held up by spread-legged supports. The two side views, Figs. 5 and 6, were taken with a telephoto lens and have frontal lines projected on them. Figure 5 shows the side away from the cable loop. In Fig. 6 the cable loop is on the left. The side view is not symmetrical. The cable loop, which may be described as an "eye," has the typical shape of a drop (Figs. 12 and 13). The maximum angular displacements in the cable net occur at four points near the eye. The families of cables initially intersected at right angles. Four other points with considerable angular displacements were observed in the model near the base line. The height of this cable net is greater in relation to the span than that of a comparable soap film (Figs. 1 and 2). Hence, the surface tensions in the cable net are not uniform but increase toward the top, and the cable loop no longer forms a line of constant curvature.

Figure 23, p. 71, shows a model of the first large project to be built. This is the German Pavilion for Expo 1967, Montreal (Gutbrod, Otto, Leonhardt, Kendel, Kies, Medlin). There are many other ways of centrally supporting membranes and cable nets with tension-loaded and flexible elements.

Figure 7 shows a radial net* (Fig. 29, p. 69) stretched in a net of uniform mesh. Other radial cable nets are seen in Figs. 9 to 11. These represent designs* for a Medical Academy at Ulm in 1965.

The centrally supported "cable net" with an irregular mesh structure (Fig. 8) was, by a strange coincidence, woven by a spider at the tip of the model for a crane (Fig. 2, p. 92). The radial direction is more accentuated than the annular direction.

There are very many ways of constructing cable nets with central supports. The most varied symmetrical and asymmetrical shapes are possible, provided that the prestressed cable net has an anticlastic curvature everywhere.

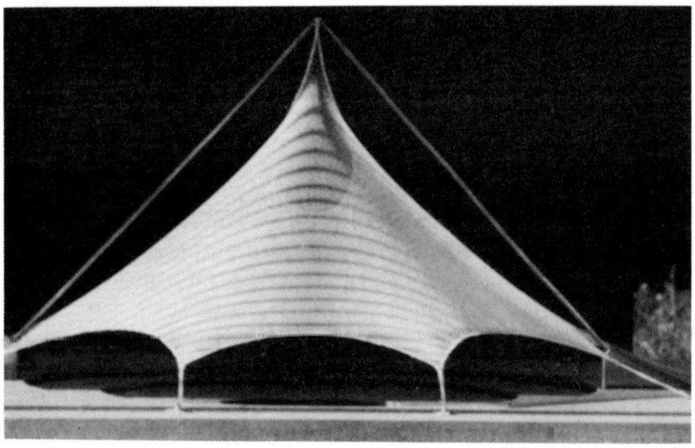

5

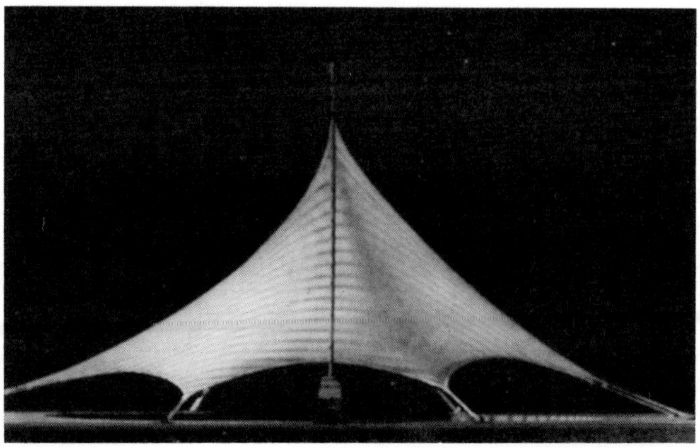

6

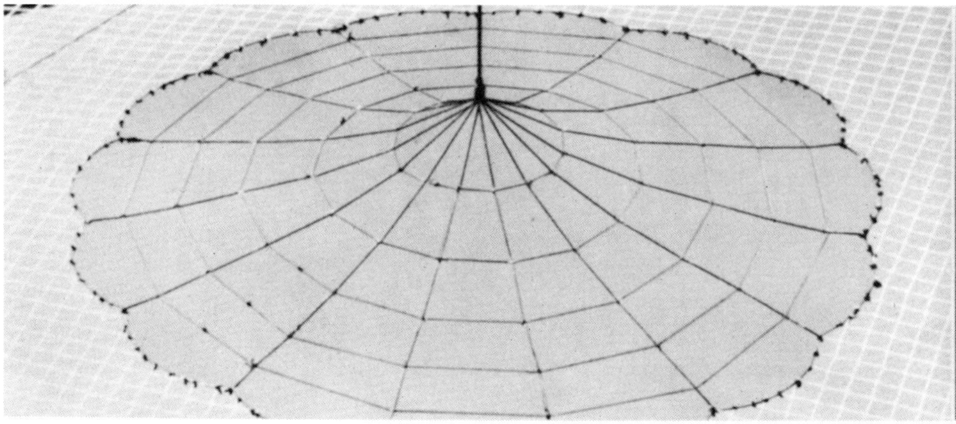

7

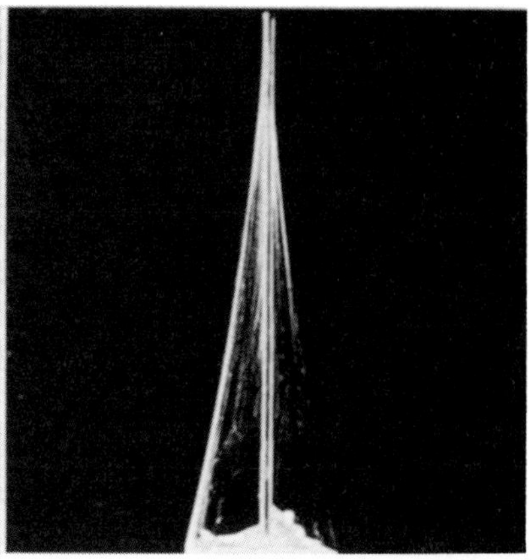

8

9

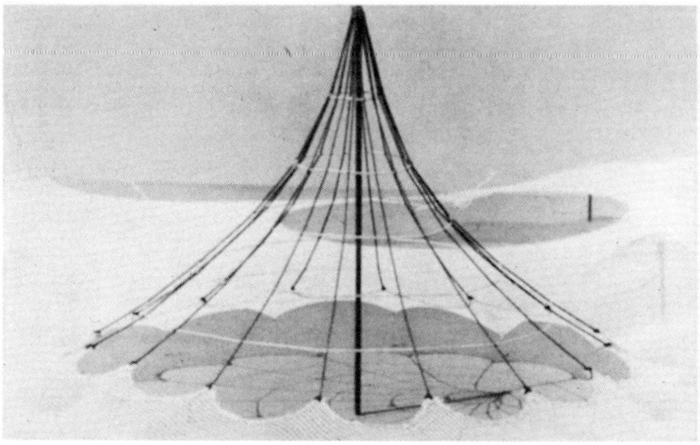

10

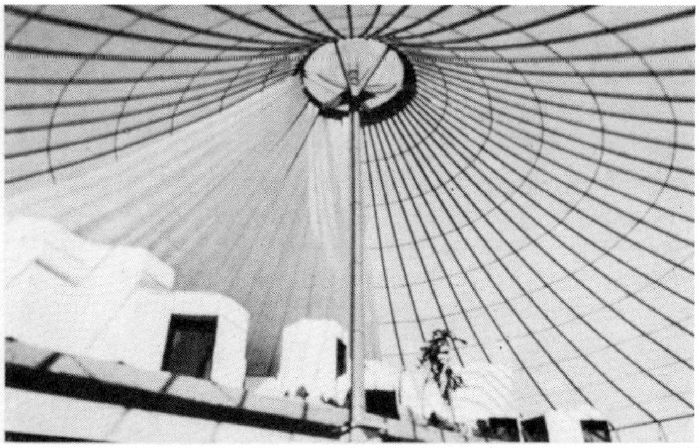

11

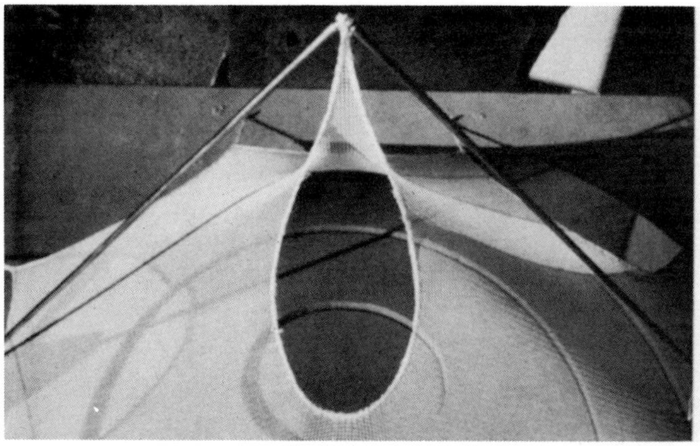

12

13

In model tests* carried out between 1960 and 1963, soap films stretched between threads were shaped like roofs with central high points (Figs. 1 to 10). In this form the membranes also have uniform surface tensions. The longitudinal cable forces are equal, since no shear is possible. Considering the tensions in the entire surface support system, in which the cables can be regarded as increasing the membrane tensions, we find that the tensions are uniform in the circumferential direction and nonuniform in the radial direction. This is because the cables are closer together in the middle than near the edge.

Almost the same shape is obtained when heavy fabric, e.g., tent canvas, is used instead of membranes. We mention the so-called Parasol Tents of L. Stromeyer and Co., developed by A. O. Maring, in which nearly straight cables form a conical tent.

If the cables are tightly stretched, as shown in Fig. 1, they will form finite angles at the apex of the cone.

If the cables are less tightly stretched than shown in Fig. 2, they will come into contact below the suspension point which they approach in parallel. Several symmetrical and asymmetrical shapes were investigated (Figs. 3 to 10). The individual fields of asymmetrical shapes have different membrane curvatures. For the sake of accuracy, we mention a minor model inaccuracy in Figs. 2 and 3: The threads used were to a certain degree rigid directly at the sus-suspension point because of the glue. In this zone the shape does not correspond to the minimum surface.

If we stretch membranes between three threads which meet at a high point, as shown in Figs. 12 and 13, we obtain minimum-surface shapes consisting of six membrane surfaces. Three plane surfaces, intersecting at angles of 120° and filling the upper region of the cable frame, are connected with three surfaces below. This figure is the minimum-surface shape for the given frame with three threads. Only when six or more threads are used are the forms shown in Figs. 1 to 10 also minimum-surface shapes. The minimum-surface shape shown in Fig. 11 results when soap films are suspended from four threads meeting at a point.

1 to 3 ▼ 6 and 7 ▼ 8 and 9 ▼

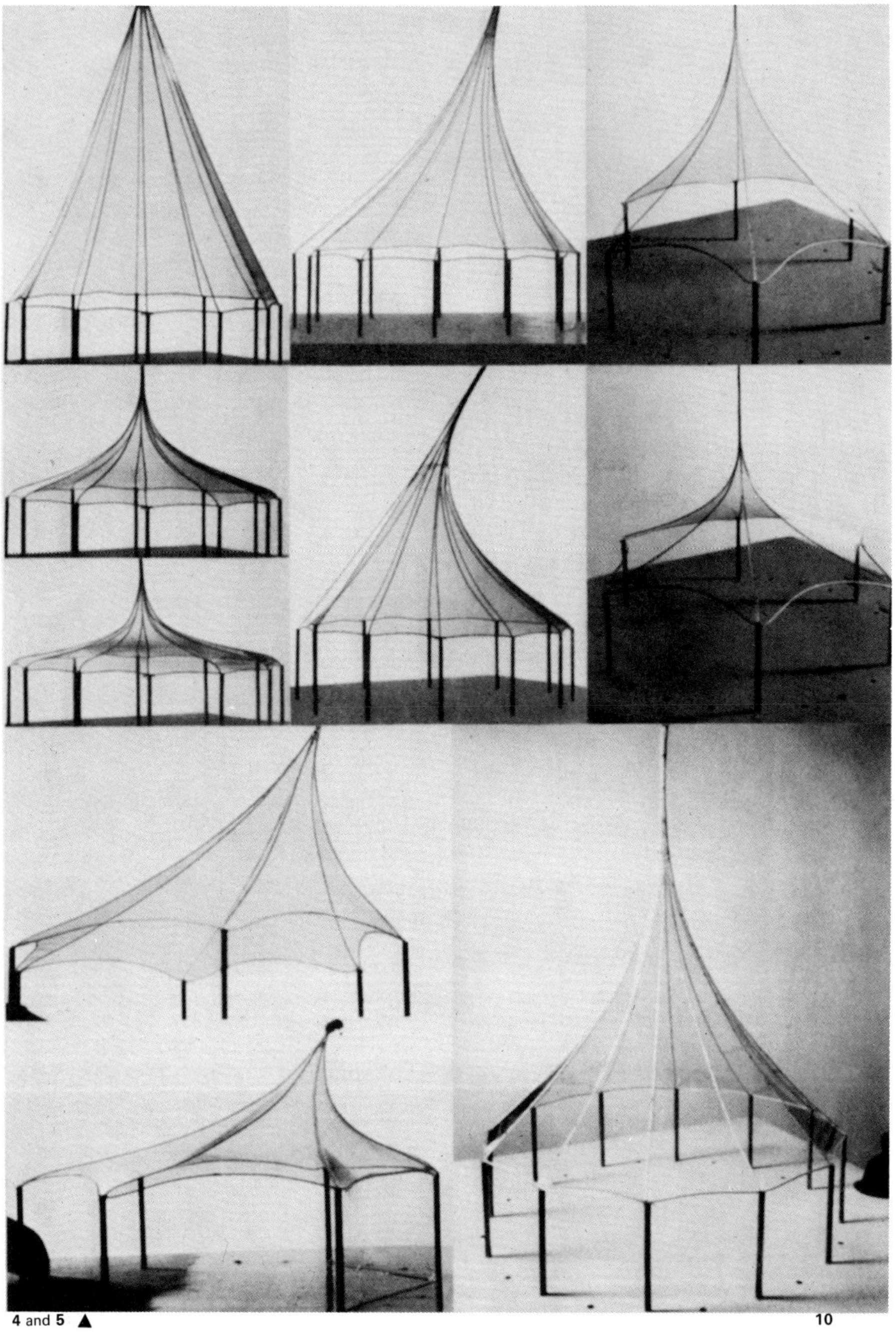

4 and 5 ▲ 10

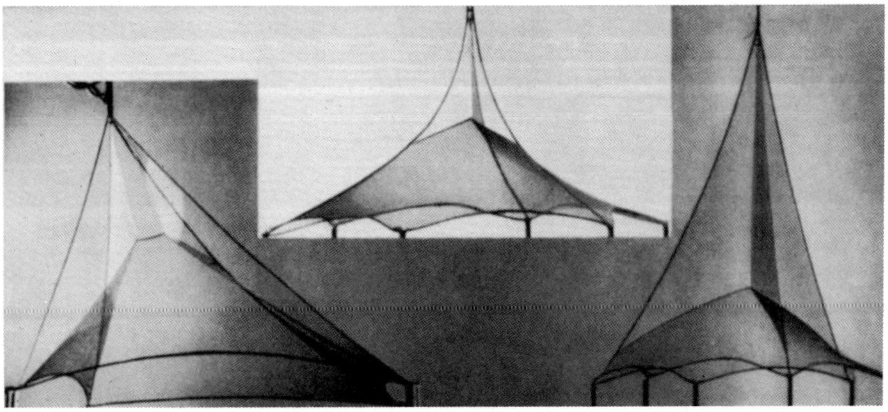

11 12 13

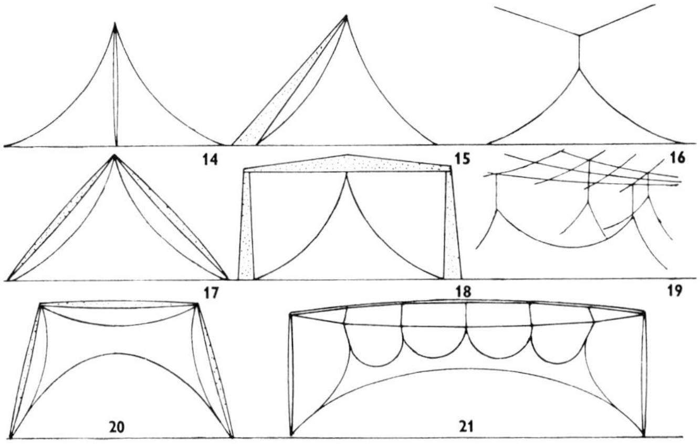

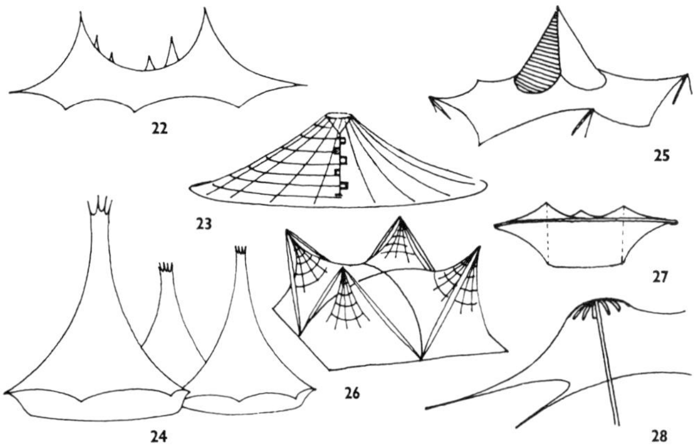

Various Supports of Cable Nets and Membranes with High Points

Structural systems, centrally supported cable nets, and membranes can be distinguished according to the manner in which forces and tensions acting at high points are transmitted. The way in which this is done does not usually affect the shape of the membrane. The simplest support is a rod subjected to compression (Fig. 14), used, e.g., for a radial cable net. The forces in the net shown in Fig. 15 are taken up by a cantilevered support subjected to bending; the interior of the structure remains unencumbered. Figure 16 shows the point of a membrane suspended from a tension-loaded cable system.

The system shown in Fig. 17 is similar to that shown in Fig. 14. The compressive forces are resolved in two or more directions. The structure shown in Fig. 18 resembles that shown in Fig. 15. The action of the high point [of the membrane] induces bending moments in a beam, and compression in two built-in supports. Figure 19 shows a membrane or cable net attached at several high points to an open cable net.

Two high points in a membrane can, for example, also be supported by three struts (Fig. 20). Studies* undertaken in 1951–1953 showed that arches with more than three hinges can be used to support cable nets at separate points. Arches with four or more hinges are prevented from collapsing by prestressing the cable nets or membranes (see Report No. 2 of the Development Center for Light Structures, *op. cit.*).

Figure 21 shows a membrane or cable-net membrane suspended at five points. The forces acting at these points were transmitted to a support system rigid in bending. This system is a framework girder consisting of components subjected to tension or compression and transmits only vertical loads to the hinged vertical struts.

Membranes with central supports have been used in tents for a long time. The four-mast circular tent of the Krone Circus (Fig. 29, photo by Stromeyer) has a diameter of 52 m. The membrane is supported at four points in the middle. The central point is suspended from a cable net, as shown in Fig. 16.

Figure 22 shows an elongated structure with two rows of high points between which a strongly curved membrane is stretched. Figure 23 is a design sketch of a large envelope with a glass-lined radial cable net supported by a central mast with a conical tip. Structures of this type can be used as large low-cost envelopes for agricultural purposes.

In the membrane structures in Fig. 24 the membranes enclose the masts like hoses. Each mast has short extended struts at its upper end. This shape was considered for a prototype of a kitchen for the main restaurant of the Interbau Berlin in 1957; the design was not carried out, however.

Figure 26 shows four high points supported by eight paired masts and forming an unencumbered interior.

Membranes that are not reinforced by cables near their points of support (Fig. 25) must be curved near these points. This can be achieved by shell-like structures, e.g., caps of sheet metal or plywood, or by elastic components, as shown in Fig. 28. Figures 23 and 26 show the membranes anchored directly to the foundations along the edge; in Figs. 22, 24, 25, and 28 the membranes are attached to edge cables. Figure 27 shows the membrane fixed to a ring rigid in bending, which also constitutes the upper boundary of a funnel-shaped wall.

29

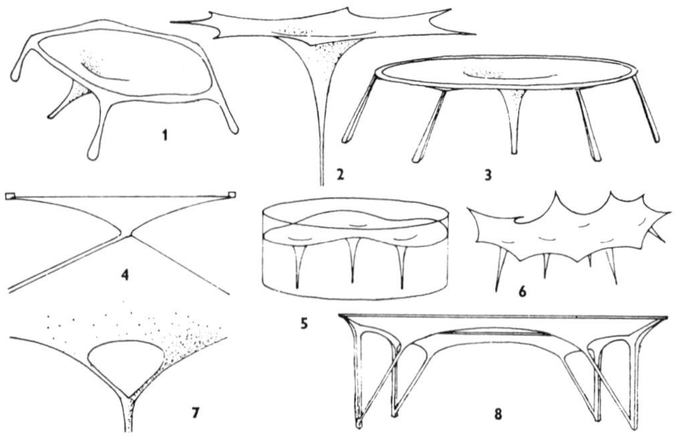

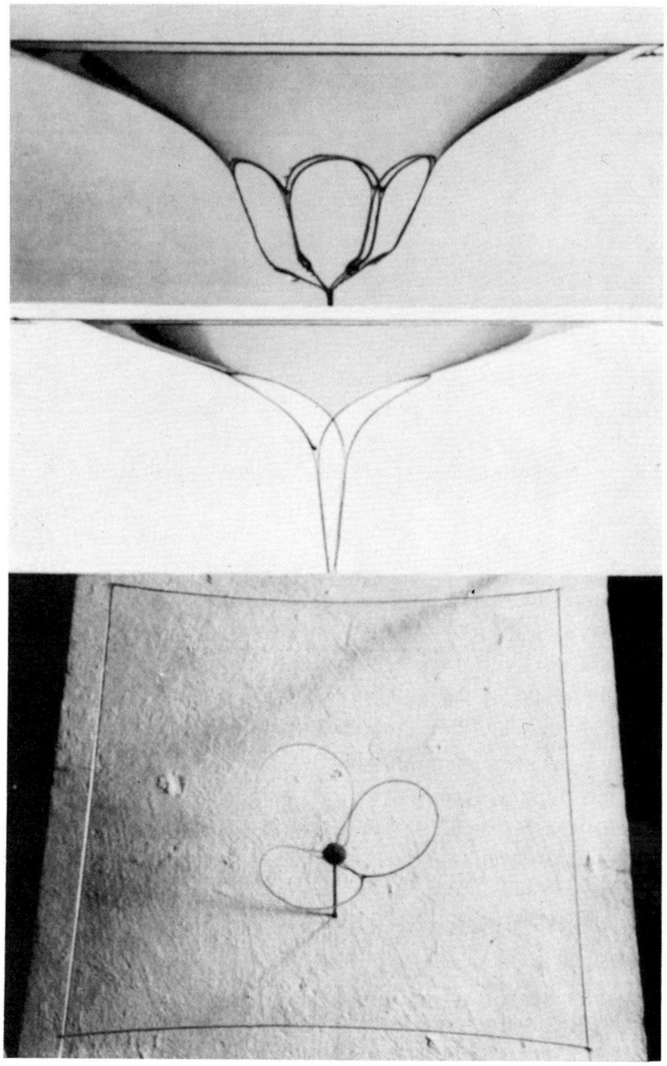

10 to 12

Membranes and Cable Nets with Low Points

Membranes with low points are, in principle, similar to structures with high points. When they are used for roofing, drainage takes place at the low points, toward which snow can slide. The resulting loads differ from those acting on membranes with high points, and call for differences in the structural details.

Membranes with low points have been thoroughly studied since 1955* and have already been used in several buildings. Various edge designs exist for membranes and nets with low points. Figure 1 shows an edge formed by a ring rigid in bending and composed of straight rods. For drainage the membrane slopes inward and downward. Figure 2 shows a shape symmetrical with respect to seven axes. The membrane is bordered at the upper edge by cables stretched between seven fixed points.

The membrane shown in Fig. 3 is suspended in a ring rigid in bending, which is mainly under compression when the membrane is flat.

9

Figure 4 shows a cross section of a membrane in which the inward drainage is not vertically downward but at a slope that forms part of the lateral bracing. The membrane is suspended in a high frame rigid in bending. A structure in which an inwardly drained tent fabric was stretched between rigid square wooden frames, was built by Stromeyer for the Swiss Agricultural Exhibition in Lausanne (Architect: Zweifel, Fig. 13). Fire hoses were used as drainage pipes and for taking up the tensile forces transmitted by four steel cables. Funnels should ordinarily have openings for cleaning. The cross section of a structure with low points is shown in detail on p. 81 of the work report of C. Roland, *op. cit.*

The outer boundary of a membrane with low points need not necessarily lie in a plane. The boundary line shown in Fig. 5 is spatially curved. In Fig. 6 the membrane is suspended between outer edge cables that do not lie in a plane.

Figure 7 shows two internal drainage points connected by hoses.

Figure 8 shows a membrane with two pairs of low points, stretched in a frame rigid in bending. The forces acting in the frame and in the membrane are transmitted via the drainage hose to a common point of the foundation.

A spider web (Fig. 9, negative) is an example of a net structure with low points. Spiders frequently construct their webs as typical cable nets and membranes with low points. As seen at the bottom right of Fig. 9, threads enclose an opening at a low point which is similar to that in the soap film shown in Figs. 14 to 21. Such webs can be compared with technical structures. They are under maximum loads when covered by dew or holding an insect.

Minimum Surfaces of Membranes with Low Points

The test series* shown in Figs. 14 to 21 was performed in 1963.

A loop of very thin and flexible thread is suspended in a square frame holding a plane soap film (Fig. 14). The loop forms a circle lying in the plane of the soap film. This proves that the liquid film is under uniform tension in all directions. In both Figs. 15 and 16 the loop is drawn downward equally far at one point and turned in different directions. When the loop is pulled down further its ends meet and become parallel (Figs. 17 to 20). The loop becomes smaller, while the height of the deformed membrane region decreases (Fig. 20). Figures 18 to 21 are accurate side views.

13

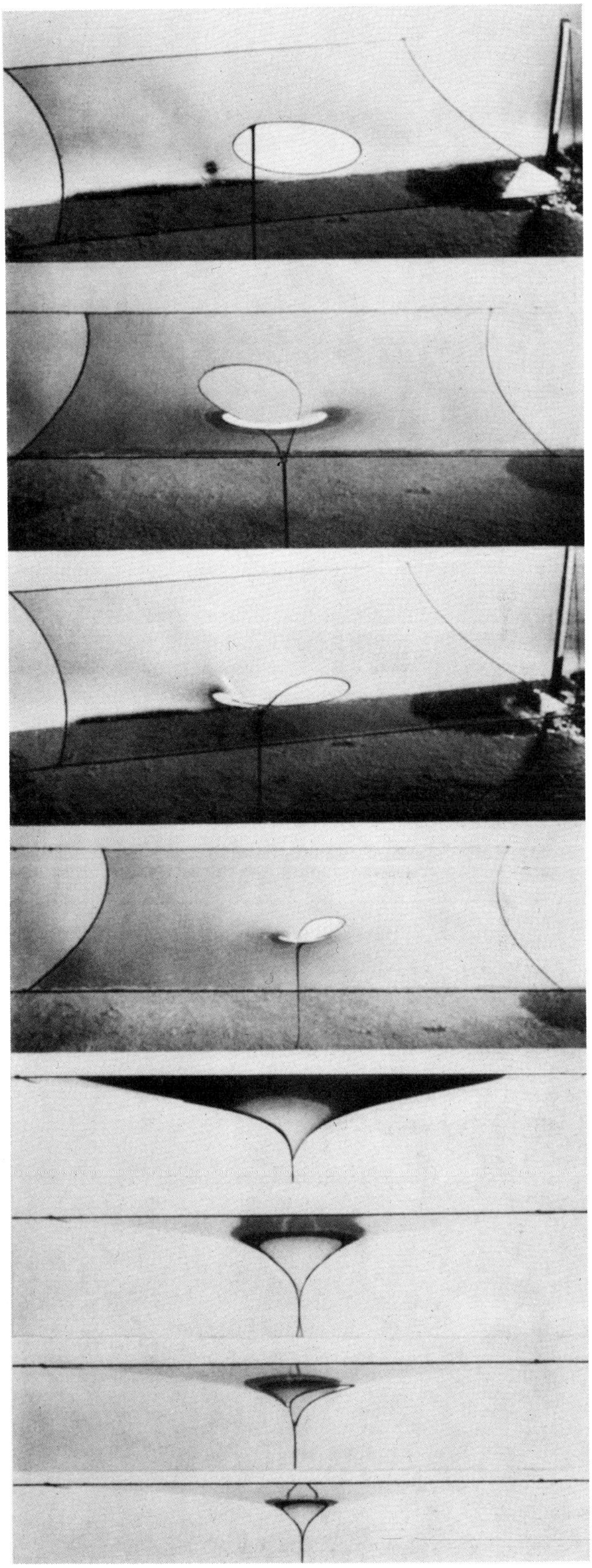

14 to 21

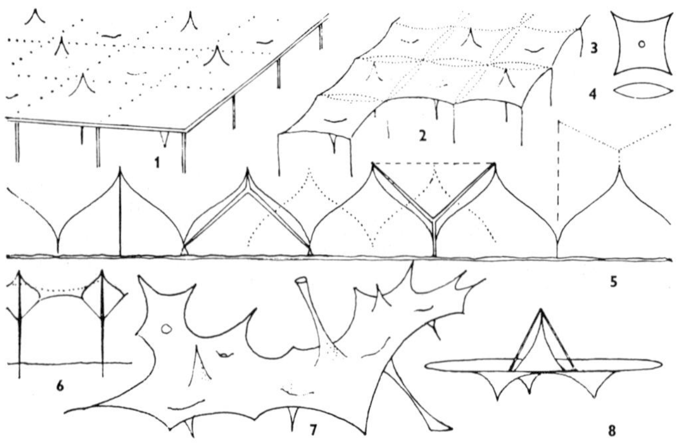

Membranes and Cable Nets with High and Low Points

Until now we have discussed membranes and cable nets with high points or with low points. The latter are, in fact, merely inversions of membranes with high points. We shall now consider membranes and cable nets in which high and low points are present in one membrane. This means that forces are transmitted to points located on both sides of a central reference surface. If, for example, a membrane is imagined as a vertical wall covering, the points of attachment protrude or are recessed. A membrane forming an essentially plane roof structure is pressed upward at several points and pulled downward at others. We note that gravity and position in space need not be considered. We have termed these structures "membranes with high and low points" only for the sake of simplicity.

These structures should, correctly, be termed "membranes and cable nets with central points of force application, pulled toward either side of an imagined central surface." Such structures are also used in branches of engineering other than building, e.g., in machinery or vehicles that change their direction constantly.

The formation of high and low points corresponds in all details to that in membranes with either high or low points. The peculiar property of surfaces with high and low points is that they can be used to form roofs of any size.

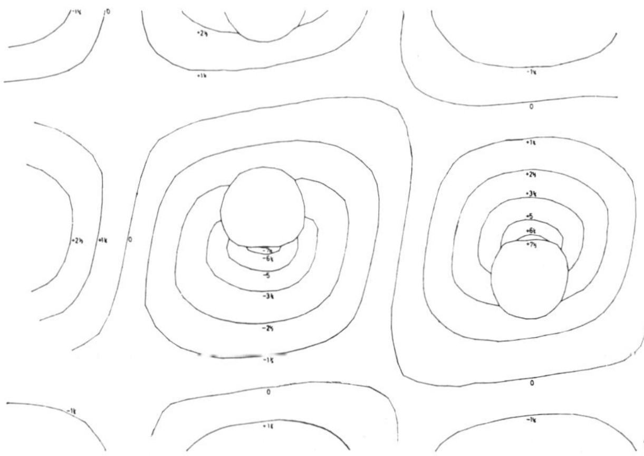

10

Membranes with high and low points can be formed from an initially plane surface of symmetry. Membranes with either high or low points are curved due to the one-sided effects of the points. Their over-all shape is cupolar or cylindrical, but not plane. Membranes with both high and low points may be curved in any way. The reference surface remains plane.

Figure 1 shows a membrane with a plane horizontal reference surface. Support points pull the membrane upward and downward at regular intervals. The shape thus recurs regularly. The edge of the membrane is suspended in a straight frame rigid in bending. The tensions and forces acting in the membrane fields with low points are equal in magnitude to those acting in the membrane fields with high points.

The boundary lines of the individual fields lie in one plane (dotted line) and form a square grid in plan.

Such membranes are anticlastic, i.e., they have a saddle-shaped curvature everywhere except at the points of inflexion midway

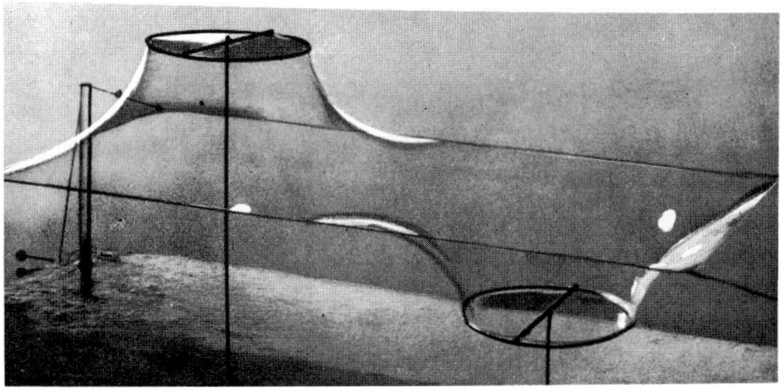

9

between the high and low points, where theoretically infinitesimal planes are formed.

All fields are similar. The membranes can therefore be built as series of components and assembled to have various plans. This is a particularly adaptable method of construction.

The surfaces with high and low points shown in Fig. 2 are bordered by cables. Such a system can also be assembled of similar parts. We need a large piece for the surface around a high or low point (Fig. 3) and a piece for the connection (Fig. 4). In this way, roof membrane systems can be connected at will without frames rigid in bending (Fig. 1), which are nearly always expensive. The grid may be square, rectangular, or rhombic. It is difficult to divide the area into triangular or hexagonal parts, since a uniformly dense distribution of high and low points is not possible. This causes the connecting lines to become curved. When the edge cables in a system according to Fig. 2 are strongly curved the membrane becomes slightly deformed at the outer edge of the system. These

11

deformations are usually so small that they can be disregarded if the material is highly elastic.

Figure 5 shows a typical cross section of a membrane with high and low points in square fields. The section passes exactly through the high and low points, i.e., in plan diagonally to the grid. The membrane has an S-shaped curvature in this cross-section. Narrow cones are formed at the high and low points, between which the curvature is slight.

The cross section in Fig. 5 illustrates various ways of supporting the high points. The first high point (from left to right) is supported by a simple straight vertical rod. The second high point is supported by two rods directly beneath the membrane. The fourth and sixth high points are supported by a Y-shaped rod system protruding above the membrane. The seventh point is suspended from a cable structure (dotted line), which is either stretched freely over the entire surface or supported as shown by the broken lines. These supports pass through the membrane at the low points and can therefore directly equilibrate the membrane forces. This is also the case for the support system of the second and third high points.

It is not necessary to combine equal numbers of high and low points. In the cross section in Fig. 6, a membrane is suspended in such a way that there are two low points for every high point. The low points are braced to the masts. This design was proposed* in the competition for a roof over the ruin of Hersfeld Abbey, for the 1958 plays.

The central reference surface of a membrane with high and low points may have any curvature (Fig. 7). Many designs are possible. Figure 8 shows a membrane with one high and three low points, connected to a circular ring rigid in compression. We refer to Caminos' studies at the School of Design, North Carolina State College (see Student Publications, School of Design, Vol. 6, No. 3, Raleigh, N.C., 1957).

In the soap-film experiment, shown in Fig. 9, a plane soap film was first suspended in a rectangular frame of tightly stretched threads. Parts of the film were then lifted or depressed by circular dies. When the design is perfectly symmetrical the minimum area around the high point is exactly equal to that around the low point. The two surfaces meet in a straight line along the axis of symmetry. The shape of the soap film remains unchanged when other similar soap films are added, every high point being adjacent to a low point, or vice versa.

As in the case of membranes with either high or low points, there are many ways to design the supports and drainage. In the shape considered here the areas near the high and low points are each braced with a cable loop.

The model shown in Fig. 12 was used to study a large cable net of uniform mesh with heart-shaped cutouts near the high and low points (cf. Fig. 4, p. 72). Such a net can be used for many purposes. All the loops in the model are open in the same direction.

The contour lines of this roof can be seen in Fig. 12. The grid of the system in this model is rhombic.

The first application of a membrane with high and low points was a roof to protect an orchestra, erected at the 1957 International Architectural Exhibition in Berlin. The membrane has one high and four low points (Fig. 11).

12

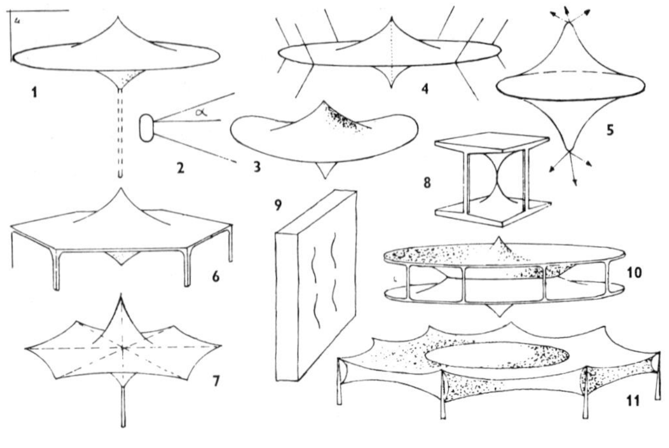

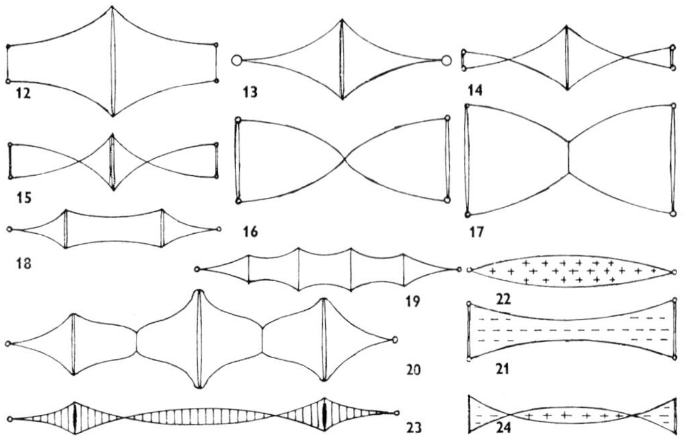

Cushion Structures

These are flat structures in which the membranes or nets enclose a shallow hollow space. We refer to the pneumatic cushion structures discussed in Vol. 1, p. 106 ff. As with other tension-loaded structures, many design possibilities exist. We therefore restrict ourselves to a few basic shapes.

One of the simplest cushion structures is obtained by stretching two plane parallel membranes in a plane ring, rigid in compression, and forcing them apart in the middle (Fig. 1). The central strut and the outer ring are then subjected to compression without bending, while the membrane is under biaxial tension. This self-contained structure requires no force equilibration by the foundations. It can be used without anchoring in a horizontal, vertical, or inclined position. Such a structure can be anchored to another structure or to the foundations in various ways. A simple method is a central support of the strut (broken lines in Fig. 1). Furthermore, suspension or support at the outer edge of the ring is possible (Figs. 4 and 6). Another way is by suspension in an external cable system connected at the center points, so that no strut is required (Fig. 5). The cushion structure shown in Fig. 4 is connected to a cable system at the edge, and that shown in Fig. 5, at the center.

Figure 2 represents the section through the edge of a structure. The smaller the angle, the less will be the stiffening effect of the membrane or cable net against lateral buckling of the ring. The outer ring, which is under compression, tends to be deformed as shown in Fig. 3. The stiffening effect of a membrane or cable net depends upon the elastic properties of the materials used and on the prestressing.

The edges of the cushions shown in Figs. 1 to 5 are under compression, while the edge of the cushion shown in Fig. 6 is subjected to bending. The cushion structure shown in Fig. 7 is suspended between tension-loaded cables. The cables may be suspended from external structures or between built-in supports rigid in bending (Fig. 11), or held apart by struts inside the cushion structure, which are under compression (shown in broken lines in Fig. 7).

Cushion structures may be either thicker or thinner at the center than at the edge. Let two membranes be stretched in a frame rigid in bending (Fig. 8). If these membranes are drawn together, tensile forces will arise at the point of contact of the membranes, and compressive forces in the two struts. Figure 9 shows a large frame on both sides of which membranes are stretched and drawn together at several points.

Combinations of cushion structures with membranes forced apart and drawn together are possible. Figure 10 shows membranes stretched in a system of two rigid rings connected by struts. Toward the periphery the membranes are drawn together, while at the center they are forced apart (see cross section, Fig. 15). The structure in Fig. 11 is similar. Two membranes are suspended in an external frame system formed by cables. The membranes are forced together near the periphery by negative pressure. In the central zone they are forced apart by positive pressure.

Figures 12 to 24 are cross sections of the principal cushion structures. Figure 13 corresponds to the structures shown in Figs. 1 to 4, 6, and 7. A frame, rigid in compression, bending, or tension, is on the outside, while in the center, a strut holds apart two membranes or cable nets. The strut in Fig. 12 is larger and the frame is broader than in Fig. 13. The frame consists of two connected rings forming a system rigid in tension. The strut in Fig. 14 is shorter than that in Fig. 13 for the same membrane shape. The two membranes intersect. The two rings of the frame are connected by struts. In Fig. 15 the penetration has been increased. In Fig. 16 the points of the membranes touch. We obtain a system as shown in Figs. 8 and 9. In Fig. 17 the frames are still further apart, and the points of the membrane are connected by a cable.

The number of struts can be increased until they are so close together (Figs. 18 and 19), that they act similarly to internal pressure (Fig. 22). We refer to the works of Le Ricolais and Zetlin. Both have contributed much to the development of cushion structures.

In Fig. 20 the membranes of a cushion are both drawn together and forced apart. Figure 23 is the cross section of a roof structure. The central lens-shaped zone is spread by struts; the peripheral zones are drawn together by cables.

The cross sections shown in Figs. 22, 24, and 21 correspond to Figs. 13, 15, and 17. The membranes are stretched by internal positive (+) or negative (−) pressure. Square, rectangular, or hexagonal cushion structures can be joined to form large surfaces.

The spoked wheels of bicycles are well-known cushion structures. Linear prestressed spokes are held in the rims that are subjected to compression.

A design* used at the 1955 Federal Horticultural Exhibition in Kassel consisted of three cushions of the type shown in Fig. 1, with wooden rings under compression and membranes of transparent plastic-coated fabric. After Le Ricolais, in particular, had studied the relevant problems intensively, a number of designs and projects were implemented in the following years. Three of these are shown here. The first is a project for an exhibition hall in Chicago with a 180 m x 180 m square plan by Bogner and Moore, carried out during a guest lectureship* at Yale in 1960. The cushion consists of two cable nets held apart by struts and suspended at the edge between cables.

Edward Stone, together with Blaton Aubert and the "Köln-Wesselinger Eisenbau", built the U.S. pavilion for the 1958 Brussels World's Fair as a cushion structure inside a ring rigid in bending and with an outside diameter of 116 m. A central cylinder holds radial cables apart like spokes of a wheel. The upper cable layer is connected with the lower layer at many points by lightly stressed cables, and carries profile rings between which transparent plastic panels are located (Fig. 26, photograph by Badjor). The pavilion was built to enclose the trees of a park. Figure 26 shows the lightness of the design.

Engineer Lev Zetlin, with the architects Gehron and Seltzer, built the Municipal Auditorium at Utica in 1959 (Fig. 27, photograph by Tranquille). This circular structure has a diameter of 80 m. It consists of a very strong outer ring of reinforced concrete and a roof with a lens-shaped cross section. Two radial cable nets are held apart at many points. The nets are differently prestressed in order to dampen vibration (see *Hanging Roofs, op. cit.;* lectures by Zetlin and Lyudkovskii).

25

26

▼ 27

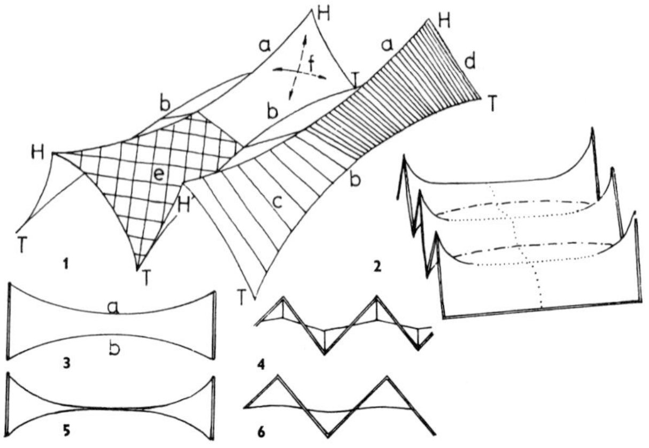

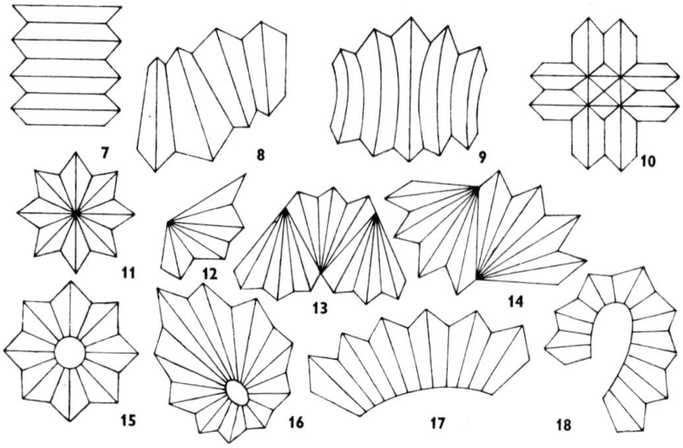

Wave-Shaped Prestressed Cable Nets and Membranes

Cable nets and membranes may also be wave-shaped. The sketch in Fig. 1 and the model* of an aircraft hangar (1955) in Fig. 33 explain the principle. Cables (a) are stretched between two parallel rows of high points (H), and cables (b), between two parallel rows of low points (T) alternating with the high points (H). Cables (a) and (b) are then connected by transverse cables (c) at short intervals. The main cables (a) and (b) are thus subjected to tension. A continuous wave-shaped cable surface is thus formed. Cables (a) form ridges and cables (b), valleys in this surface. The intervals between the transverse cables (c) can be decreased until they are close together (d). Cable nets (e) can also be stretched in the fields. They will have a saddle-shaped curvature and form the connections between cables (a) and (b). The principal directions of the cable net may be diagonal, as shown here, or parallel to the waves. Not only single cables and cable nets, but also membranes (f) can form the actual surface. The directions of principal curvature of the membrane are approximately diagonal (dashed arrows). Figure 3 is a side view of a roof according to Fig. 1, which consists of wave-shaped prestressed cable nets and membranes. The low point of cable (a) is higher than the high point of cable (b). This can be seen in the front view (Fig. 4), in which the double line is the outer edge of the roof, while the single line represents the central cross section of the roof. This section does not have as pronounced a wave shape as the edge, but its form is quite marked.

Sharp ridges in wave-shaped prestressed membranes or cable nets can be caused only by large cable forces. Thus a soap film, suspended in a frame with a pronounced wave shape on two sides (Fig. 2), has no ridges, but rather smooth wave-shaped cross sections (Figs. 5 and 6), whose curvatures are greatest near the most pronounced edge deformations and least in the middle of the film. The wave crest corresponding approximately to the ridge line H-H in Fig. 1 is shown by the dotted line in Fig. 2, while the trough bottom, corresponding to the valley in Fig. 1, is represented by dots and dashes. The central longitudinal section is indicated by points.

The side view in Fig. 5 shows the contrast to a membrane with sharp ridges, as in Fig. 3. A slightly curved surface is formed in the middle. This is also evident from the small curvature of the central longitudinal section (single line) in Fig. 6, compared with the strongly curved outer frame (double line).

The form of wave-shaped prestressed membranes and cable nets depends in the load-free state solely upon the distribution of the cable forces and membrane tensions. These membranes can be used as roofs or walls, or stretched in space at will.

Plans of Various Wave-Shaped Cable Nets and Membranes

Various plans are possible when wave-shaped cable nets or membranes are used as roofs. Figure 7 shows, symbolically, parallel waves as in Fig. 1. In this and the following sketches all ridges are shown longer, in plan, than the valleys. This creates a three-dimensional image of the structure. The ridges and valleys shown in Fig. 8 are not strictly parallel. The distances between them vary irregularly. All cables shown in Fig. 9, except the central supporting cable, are curved both in vertical and horizontal planes. [Mathematically expressed, they possess both flexure and torsion.] They thus form spatial curves. Everything stated above also applies in principle to such shapes.

Intersecting membranes are also possible. Figure 10 shows two trains of intersecting waves.

Figure 11 shows, symbolically, radial wave-shaped membranes and cable nets. The individual ridges and valleys may differ in length and be spatially curved. Figure 12 shows part of a radial wave shape used alone; parts joined to form various shapes are shown in Figs. 13 and 14.

Figure 15 shows a wave-shaped radial surface with an opening at the center. It spans an annular plan which may be asymmetrical (Fig. 16). The membrane might also be used in parts (Figs. 17 and 18). If the central cutouts are shaped and enclosed in conformity with the membrane-tension distribution (Figs. 15 and 16), no separate supports are needed. Such cutouts are usually circular or elliptic. The ends of the inner cables of circular segments (Figs. 17 and 18) must be secured.

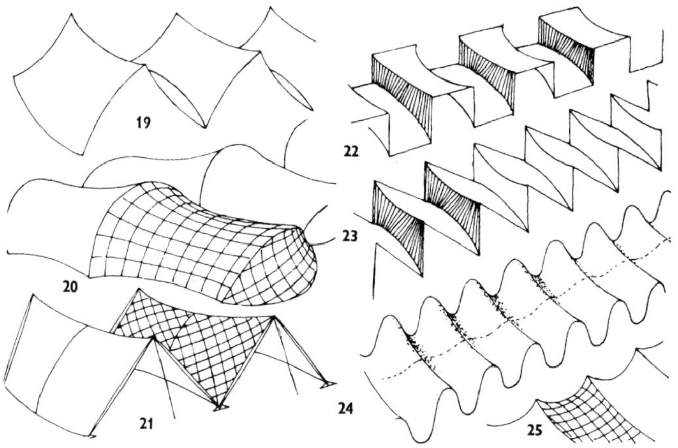

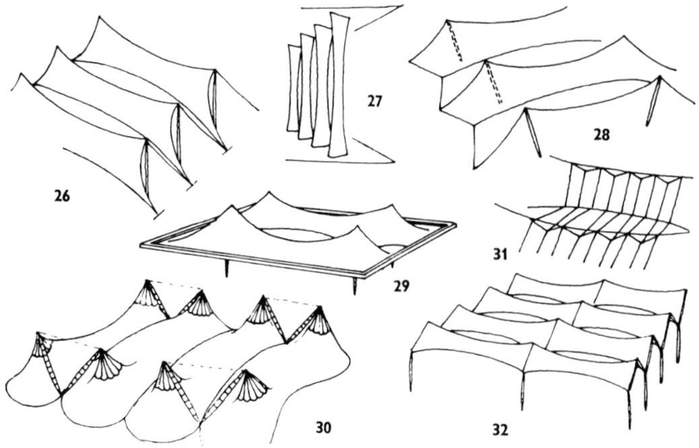

The plan given in Fig. 17 is suitable for an aircraft hangar. The upper edge of the large gate is formed by a cable.

The shape of a roof is largely determined by the form of the edge. In Fig. 19 the edge is tension-loaded and is formed by a cable; in Fig. 20 arches have been inserted into a wave-shaped cable net. We obtain a succession of arches. In Fig. 21 the edge is formed by straight beams subjected to bending. The cable net is similar in shape to that shown in Fig. 19.

Various edges are shown in Figs. 22 to 25. In Fig. 22 the edge is determined by lines forming right angles; in Fig. 23 the angles are acute. In Fig. 24 the curvature of the edge is continuous; in Fig. 25 the edge is curved downward from high points so that the resulting roof membrane has sharp ridges and gently curved valleys. Figures 22 and 23 show typical shed roofs suited for industrial structures.

Examples of Different Wave-Shaped Membranes and Cable Nets

In the roof shown in Fig. 26, membranes are stretched between ridges and bracing cables. The ridge cables connect the high points of two rows of masts, while the bracing cables are stretched directly between the foundations. The span of the bracing cables is greater than that of the ridge cables. The lateral edge cable of the membrane thus connects the head of the mast with the foundation, and guys the former. Thus no separate mast guying is needed.

Figure 27 shows a wave-shaped membrane, reinforced by cables, which connects two parallel superposed horizontal planes. This structure may, e.g., form a partition between the floors of a building, or between the floor and ceiling of a hall. Such a partition can take up stresses of different kinds, e.g., those induced by wind or internal pressure.

The structure shown in Fig. 28 has a wave-shaped roof membrane with internal supports. The ridge cable is supported by masts at two points. Ridge and bracing cables are led directly into the foundations (see Fig. 33).

A structure as shown in Fig. 30 may be described as a wave-shaped membrane, or it might be regarded as a membrane with eight high points. The masts protrude from the membrane without guying.

In the structure shown in Fig. 29, the outer edge of the roof membrane is formed by a plane frame rigid in bending. Each ridge cable is supported at two points, as in Fig. 28, but vertically, in this case. Each bracing cable is drawn downward at two points, as in membranes with internal drainage.

Wave shapes as shown in Fig. 1 may also be arranged in series side by side, so that unlimited areas can be covered in all directions (Fig. 32). The ridge cables are supported at regular intervals and drawn downward. Drainage must be provided at the low points in roof structures of this type. In the system shown in Fig. 32, the high and low points are supported by Y-shaped struts. Compound wave shapes may be suitable for very large structures, as shown in Fig. 31: The large wave-shaped roof surface is subdivided by smaller waves running normal to the direction of the large waves. Such a shape is obtained if a membrane is stretched between parallel cables (c, Fig. 1), with every other cable not directly attached to a ridge cable (a) but at a lower point. This can be done, as shown in Fig. 31, by inserting a short ridge cable exactly below the main ridge cable (a) that forms the large wave.

We can thus talk of primary and secondary waves. Secondary waves may then be subdivided into tertiary waves, and so forth.

33

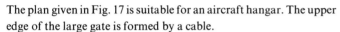

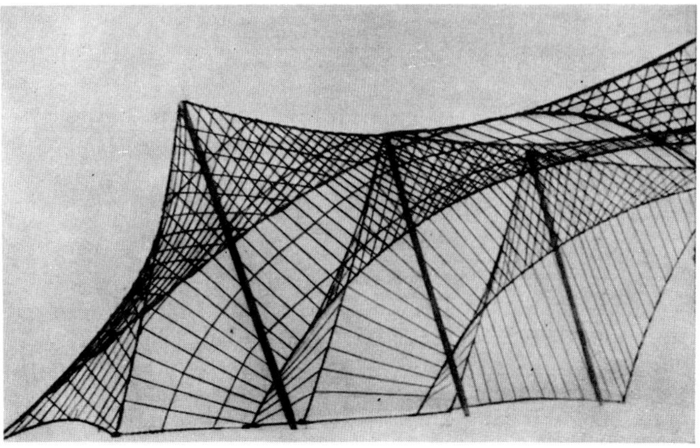

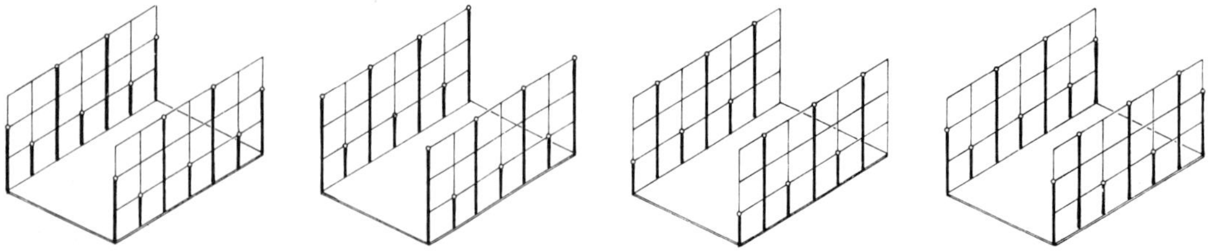

1 to 4

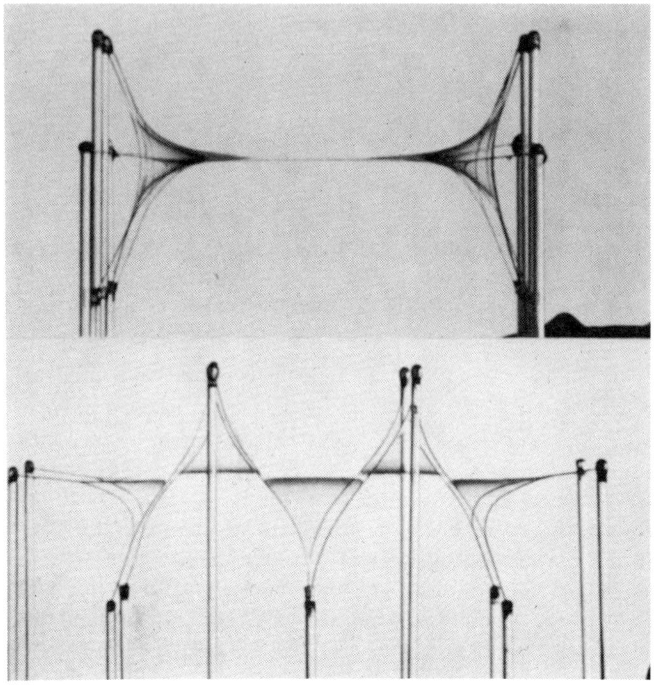

5 and 6

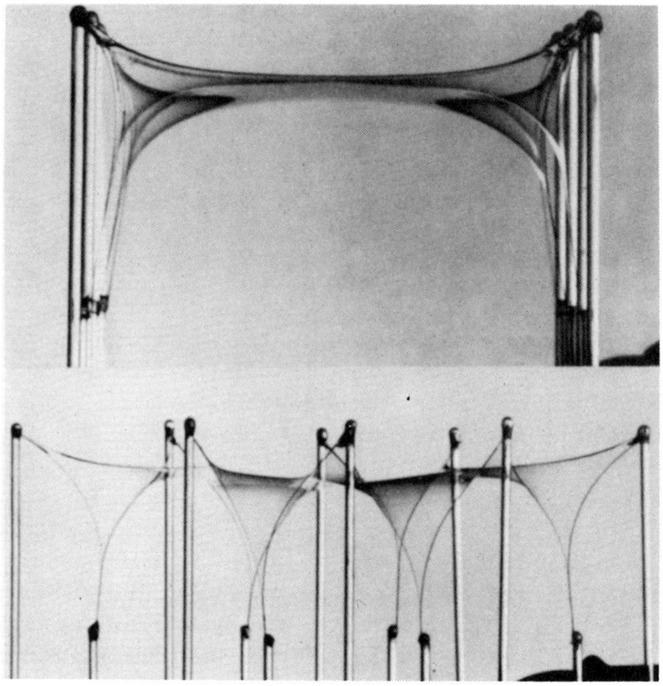

7 and 8

Wave-Shaped Minimum Surfaces Forming a Continuous Area

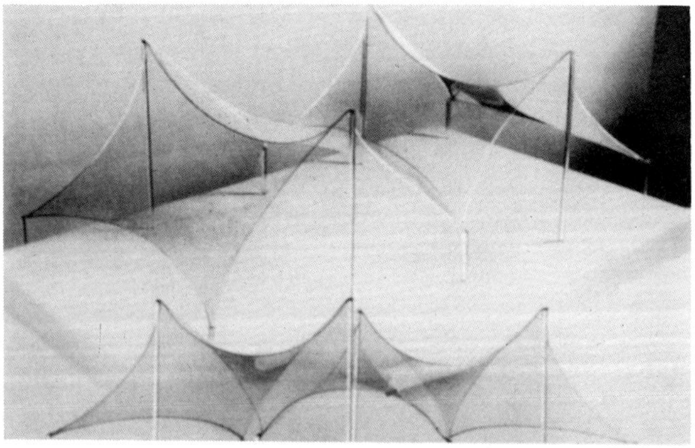

13 and 14

The influence of the boundaries upon the formation of minimum surfaces was seen most clearly in model experiments with soap films. Telescoping rods were arranged vertically on a horizontal reference plane, and their upper ends connected by threads.

Four test arrangements are shown diagrammatically in Figs. 1 to 4; the results are recorded in photographs 5 to 12.

In the first test (Fig. 1), two high, three low, and two intermediate points are arranged symmetrically on either side. The membrane thus formed is symmetrical with respect to two axes, as seen in the side views (Figs. 5 and 6). The maximum curvatures are found near the high and low points; in the middle the membrane is almost flat (Fig. 5, p. 82).

If the corner points are raised in the same test arrangement, the resulting shape will correspond to Fig. 2. Side and diagonal views are given in Figs. 7 and 8. The film is located much higher than in the first test, and is slightly more curved in the middle. A similar shape at a lower level results if [all high] points are lowered. Test arrangement and membrane are symmetrical with respect to two axes.

15

High and low points alternate on each side in the experiment shown in Fig. 3. Both lines begin with a low point and terminate in a high point. The test arrangement is symmetrical with respect to one axis only. The minimum surface between the individual points varies in height (Fig. 10). It forms an inclined surface, only slightly curved in the middle (Fig. 9, side view obliquely from below). The maximum curvatures are again found near the high and low points. The partial asymmetry, due to the varying height of the corner points, exerts considerable influence.

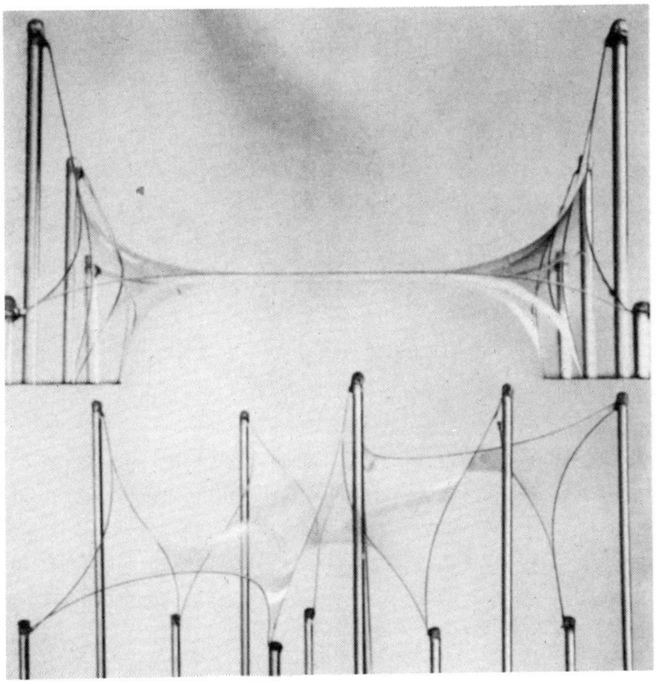

9 and 10

Three high, two intermediate, and two low points are arranged on one side in the layout shown in Fig. 4, on which the model tests shown in Figs. 11 and 12 are based. Two high, two intermediate, and three low points are arranged on the opposite side. A low point is always opposite a high point. The minimum surface (Figs. 11 and 12) is a wave-shaped surface closely related to that in the first test arrangement (Figs. 1, 5, and 6). The side views are almost identical (Figs. 5 and 11). The membrane assumes a central position; the cross sections are S-shaped. Near a high point the surface drops steeply, becomes horizontal, and again rises steeply near the opposite point. If the flexible threads are replaced by straight rods rigid in bending, and the points are similarly connected, the resulting minimum surfaces resemble those shown here.

Wave-Shaped Minimum Surfaces with Ridge and Bracing Cables

A soap film, bordered on all sides by threads, is stretched between high and low points in the test shown in Figs. 13 and 14. Three low and two high points are arranged on each side. Threads connect the points along the edge and opposite high and low points. Four surfaces are thus formed. The two outer ones have smaller curvatures than the two inner ones. The threads form ridges and valleys. The total surface area is larger than that of a soap film stretched in the same frame as a continuous surface, i.e., without ridges or valleys. The side view of this test arrangement is similar to Figs. 3 and 4, p. 82.

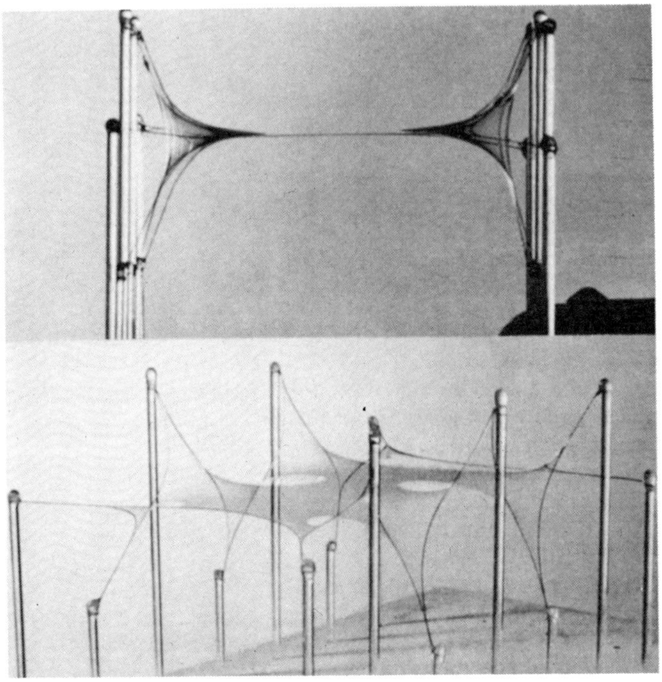

11 and 12

The aircraft hangar built by Stromeyer in 1956 is an example of a membrane with ridge and bracing cables (Fig. 15, photograph by Stromeyer). It was manufactured in large series. Other examples are the Pavilion Marie Thumas at the 1958 Brussels World's Fair (Fig. 16), designed by architects Baucher, Blondel, and Filippone, and engineers Sager, Batelier, and Gerard. Heavy fabric, similar to a membrane, was stretched between ridge and bracing cables of the hangar. Light tension-loaded fishbelly supports were used in the pavilion (photograph by Badjor).

16

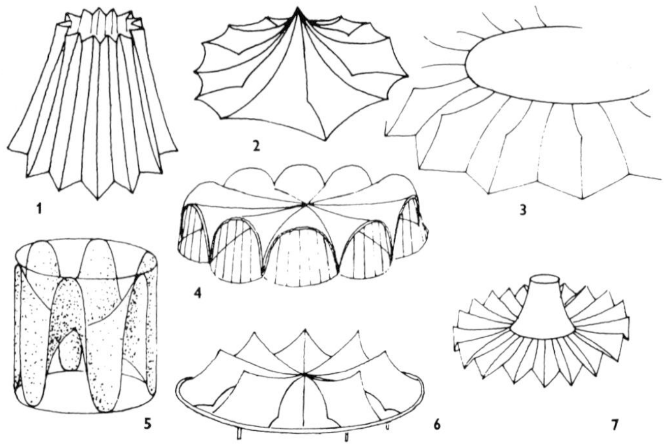

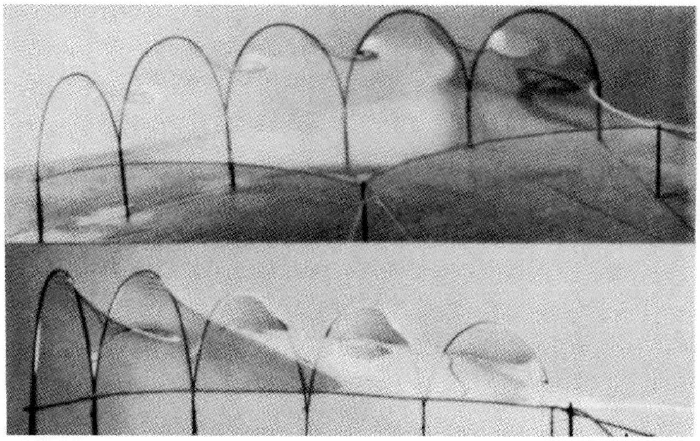

8 and 9

Radial-Wave Membranes

Some examples are given to supplement the sketches of radial-wave membranes in Figs. 11 to 18, p. 82, particularly in order to illustrate transitions and edge zones. The surface shown in Fig. 1 can be regarded either as a wave-shaped circular annulus or as a wave-shaped hose. The structure shown in Fig. 2 may be classified as a radial-wave shape or as a membrane or cable net with central support, particularly when it forms a continuous anticlastic surface around the central high point.

Figures 3, 4, and 5 show different edges. Figure 3 is a sketch of the roof over the seats of a stadium. The outer edge of the membrane is anchored directly to the foundations. The central opening is bordered by a tension-loaded flexible element, e.g., a steel cable.

The wave shape in Fig. 4 is formed by arches under compression and guyed by individual cables (see also Figs. 8 and 9). Figure 5 shows a strongly curved membrane stretched in a rigid cylinder which is thus subjected to compression and bending.

The membrane shown in Fig. 6 is suspended in a ring that is mainly subjected to compression and is subdivided by ridge and bracing cables. Masts are located below the high point of the ridge cables; tension anchorings act at the low points of the bracing cables. The structure shown in Fig. 7 is a combination of a prestressed radial-wave net with central opening carrying a hyperbolic shell rigid in bending. A tension-loaded surface support has thus been joined to one primarily subjected to compression. Innumerable similar combinations are possible.

Radial- and parallel-wave-shaped prestressed membranes and cable nets have been developed simultaneously since 1953.* The first experimental structures were built in 1954 in close cooperation with L. Stromeyer and Co. of Konstanz. A pavilion* was built in the form of a segment of a radial-wave ring at the 1955 Federal Horticultural Exhibition in Kassel. In the same year designs appeared for aircraft hangars, a roof for the Killesberg Stadium in Stuttgart, a mobile theater for 2000 people in 1955–56 for the Centre de Culture in Belgium, etc. For further examples see C. Roland, *op. cit.*

An example of a prestressed membrane with an annular wave shape is the roof over the so-called Tanzbrunnen (Dancing Fountain) in Cologne (Fig. 10), designed in 1956* and built in 1957. Later minimum-surface experiments (Figs. 11 and 12) showed the roof of this structure to be composed of almost exact minimum surfaces as formed between radial cables. Each of the twelve equal surface parts (six in mirror inversion) has an anticlastic curvature. The membrane was formed from coated heavy fabric. The directions of warp and weft coincide with those of maximum curvature. The roof has a span of 36 m and a height of 11 m.

Figures 8 and 9 show a minimum-surface experiment for a membrane structure. One side of the membrane is bordered by five arches, and the other three by cables. The wave-shaped prestressed membrane has its maximum curvature near the arches. In the middle it forms a continuous shallow saddle. The shape can be regarded as a cutout from a circular radial-wave membrane.

Combined Shapes

Saddles, tubing, humps, and waves can be combined at will. The term hump surface will be used here for all membranes and cable nets with high and low points.

The sketches in the second column of Fig. 13 are combinations with an ordinary saddle shown symbolically at the top of the column.

10 and 11

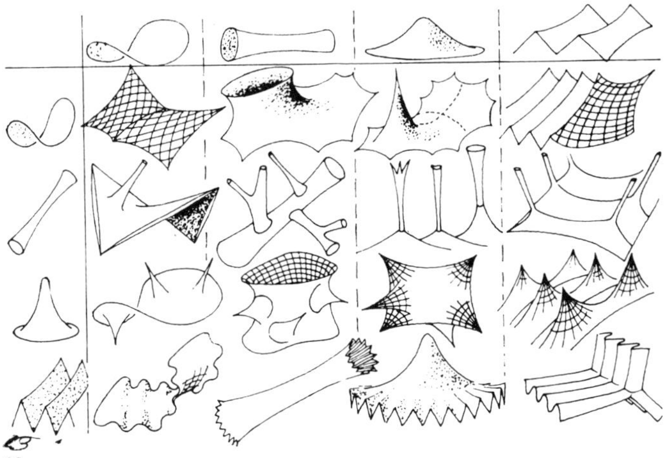

13

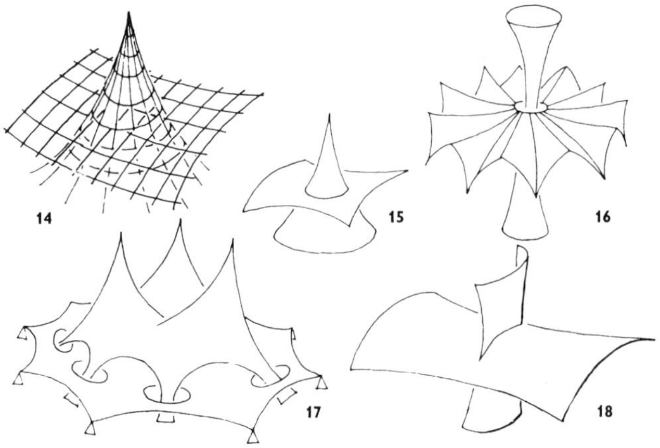

14 15 16 17 18

The first column gives the symbols of the combinations. The first combination consists of two saddles, represented as two connected cable nets influencing each other. The second combination is a saddle with a tubular membrane, and the third, a saddle and a membrane with high and low points. The last combination is a large continuous saddle with a wavy edge.

The third column shows tubes combined with saddles, tubing, humps, and waves. Tubing with a large opening becomes a saddle shape (first sketch). The second sketch shows a combination of tubes; the third shows a tubular net with humps. In the fourth sketch of this column tubing is formed by a wave shape.

The fourth column shows a hump combined with a saddle, followed by a hump whose high points end in tubes. The third sketch shows a combination of humps forming a closed hollow body. The bottom sketch in this column shows a hump with a wavy edge.

The last column shows wave shapes. A combination of a wave shape with a simple attached saddle is shown at the top followed by a wave combined with tubes and with humps. A wave combination is shown at the bottom.

Combinations of different shapes occur twice in this diagram. There are nine essentially different combinations. Sixteen different combinations are possible if we consider as principal shapes those shown symbolically in the top line. There are innumerable further variations.

Penetration Shapes

Prestressed membranes and cable nets can penetrate each other in such a way that no forces are transmitted at intersections. However, forces may also be transmitted. The supporting systems are joined along the lines of intersection, and subjected to the load together. Some examples are given. Figure 14 shows a somewhat conical cable net penetrating a saddle-shaped, slightly curved cable net. The individual cables of the nets need not touch. If both surfaces are membranes (Fig. 15), they are positively connected along the line of intersection.

Figure 16 shows a tube penetrating the center of a radial-wave roof through an opening. The two surfaces are not in contact. Figure 17 shows a flat perforated membrane stretched at the bottom around the "feet" of a central membrane with three high points. A penetration of two saddle-shaped membranes with force transmission is shown in Fig. 18. The contact line is very rigid.

12

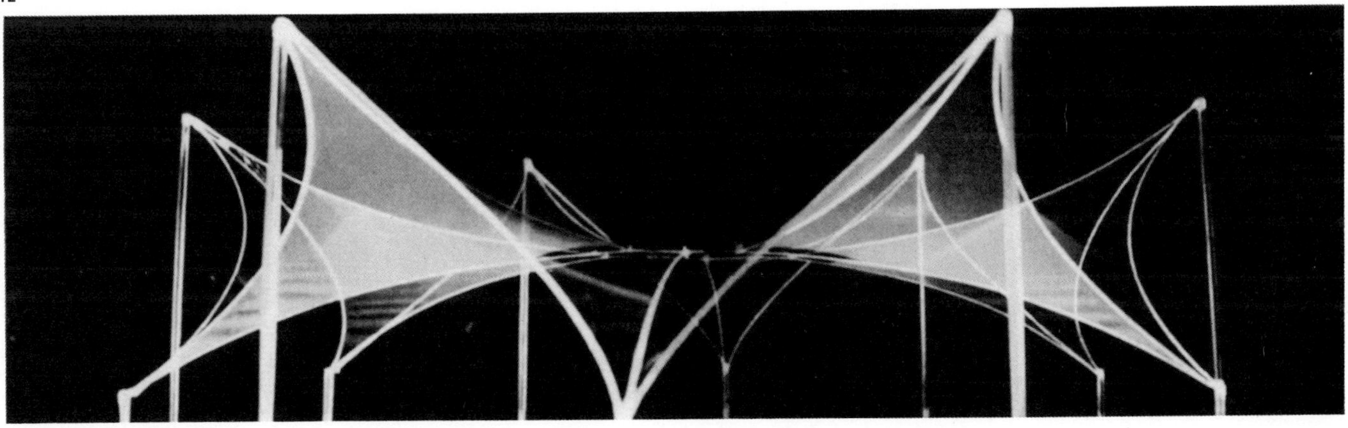

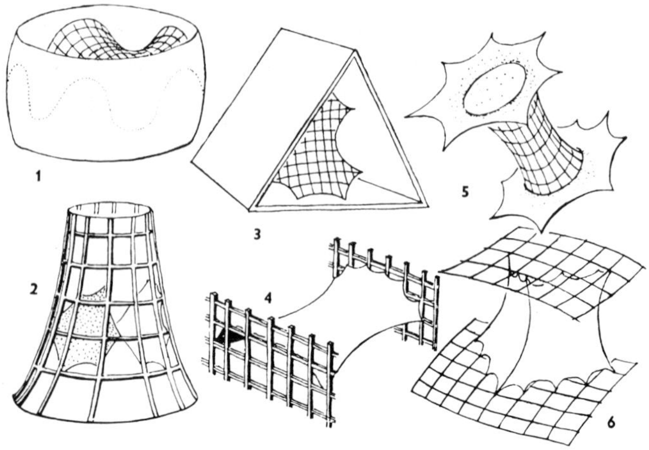

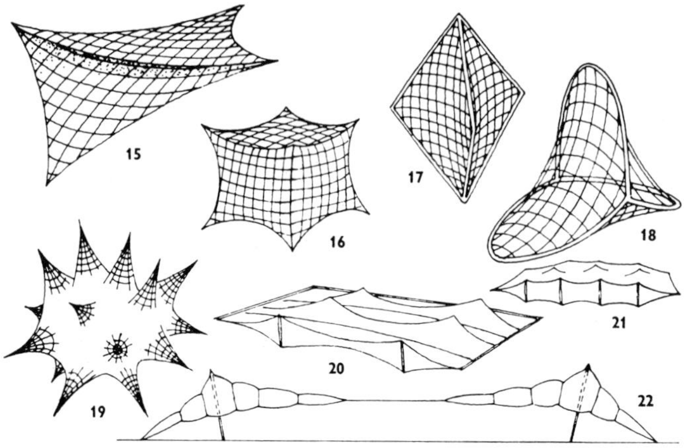

Membranes and Cable Nets Between Surface Support Structures

Membranes and cable nets may be suspended between line components such as arches under compression, beams subjected to bending, or tension-loaded cables, as well as between two-dimensional support systems (surface structures), such as shells under compression (Fig. 1), lattice shells (Fig. 2), panels subjected to bending, i.e., moments, (Fig. 3), grids of beams (Fig. 4), tension-loaded membranes (Fig. 5), or cable nets (Fig. 6).

Figure 7 shows a plane prestressed cable net anchored between eight membranes, making angles of approximately 120° with them. A similar structure is shown in Fig. 8. A tubular membrane containing a plain membrane across its diameter is stretched between two rings. The same shape can be obtained also with irregular tubing (Fig. 26). A central membrane with spatial curvature is suspended between four external membranes (Fig. 9).
Cable nets and membranes are surfaces. Even when forming part of surface support structures their edges are always (one-dimensional) lines.

The most varied shapes result (Fig. 27) when membranes are suspended in membranes in minimum-surface experiments. Figure 10 shows several intersecting plane membrane surfaces. All the membranes have the same tension and form angles of 120°, so that a regular honeycomb system results. A similar system is obtained when two plane parallel panels are connected at several points. The membrane system formed between them by means of soap films is, by virtue of the uniform membrane width, also a minimum-path system (Fig. 25). Since 1962* this test arrangement has been undergoing improvement. Important topographic and structural problems have been solved with its aid.
The wave-shaped prestressed membrane (Fig. 11) is stretched between membranes that are bordered by cables. The system shown in Fig. 12 is very similar; two wave-shaped membranes forming partitions are secured to a roof consisting of two larger prestressed membranes.
Spatial systems result when membranes are stretched in membranes or cable nets in cable nets, since the lines of contact are fixed in three directions within the planes of the membranes or cable nets. This will be discussed in detail when spatial tension-loaded systems are considered (pp. 94 to 96).
Membranes and cable nets can also be connected to pneumatically tensed membrane systems. The plane membrane shown in Fig. 13 is suspended between pneumatically tensed tubes. The spatially curved cable net shown in Fig. 14 is suspended in a pneumatically tensed membrane dome. We refer in particular to the internal partition systems described in Vol. 1, pp. 101 to 105. The enclosed tennis court (Fig. 23) was built by Stromeyer in 1963. A vertical membrane is connected from below to the bracing of a pneumatic structure. The vertical partition is braced by cables, so that a continuous interior results (photograph by Stromeyer).
Figure 28 shows a bubble under internal pressure, suspended in a spatial system consisting of twelve plane surfaces all subjected to the same tension.

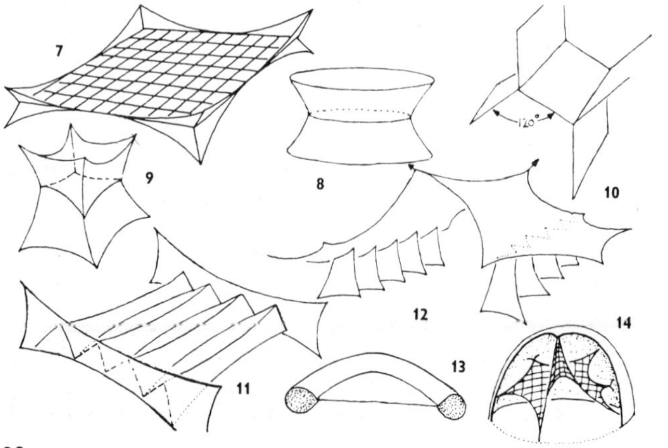

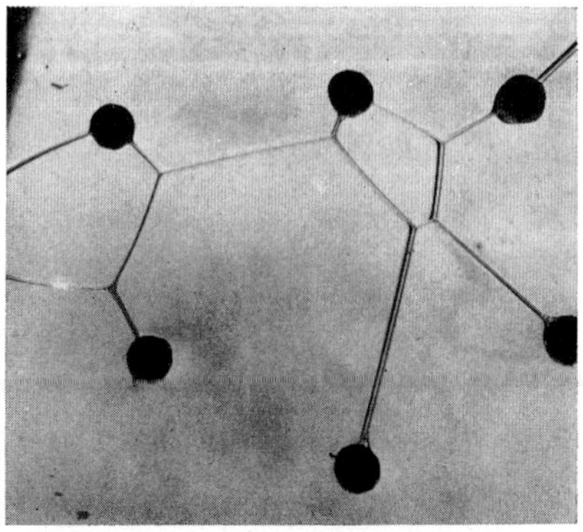
25

23

Hollow Bodies Formed by Prestressed Membranes and Cable Nets

Prestressed membranes and cable nets can form hollow bodies. Figure 15 shows a cable net stretched between four points and four edge cables. A second cable net, only half of which is shown, is suspended above it. It is connected to the same edge cables and corners as the first net but is arranged differently. The center point of the upper net is higher than that of the lower one. A shallow hollow space is formed between the two nets, which may be used for pipes or suspended rooms.

Figure 16 shows six similar nets forming a cube. Figure 17 shows three regular cable nets stretched between frames rigid in bending. A closed hollow space is thus formed.

Figure 24 shows a model by Feldkeller. Three similar cable nets are stretched in a frame as in Fig. 17.

Figure 18 shows three cable nets stretched between three arches that may be designed in such a way that they are only under compression.

The hollow spaces shown in Figs. 15 to 18 and in Fig. 24 are formed by saddle-shaped surfaces. Concentrated forces act on the continuous spherical membrane shown in Fig. 19, imparting to it a starlike shape.

Figure 20 shows how wave-shaped membranes and cable nets, which surround a shallow hollow space like a cushion, are joined together. Figures 20 to 22 refer primarily to the previously discussed cushion structures forming shallow hollow spaces (see pp. 80 and 81).

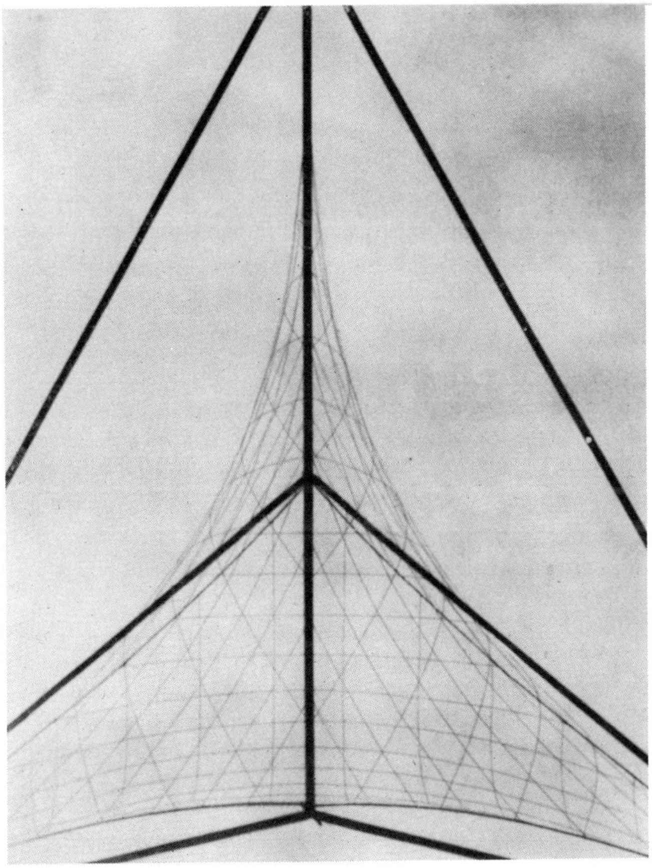

24

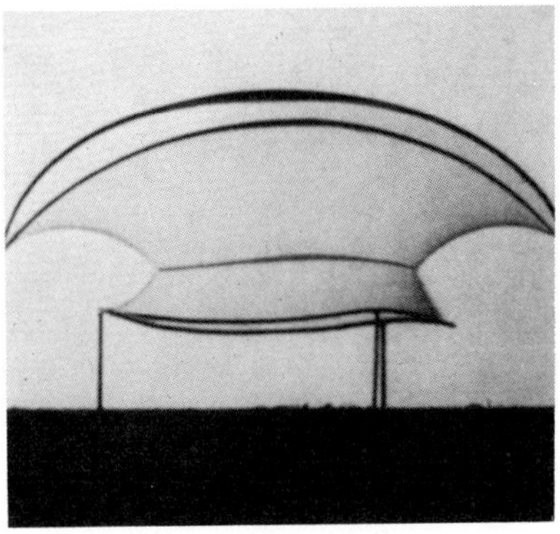

26

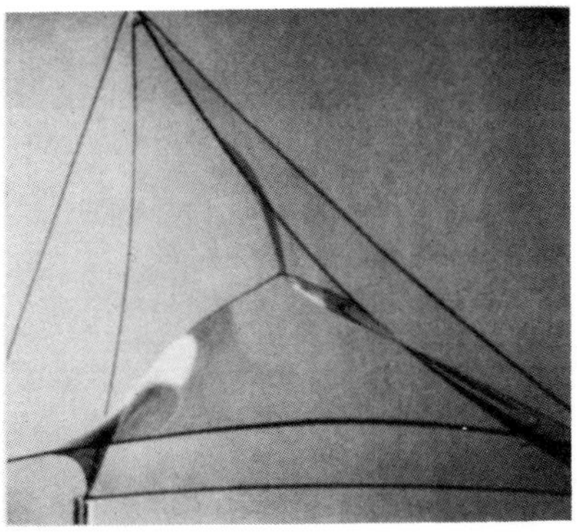

27

28

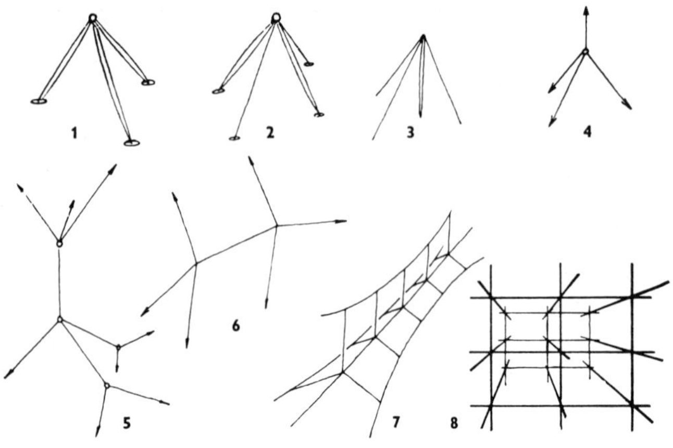

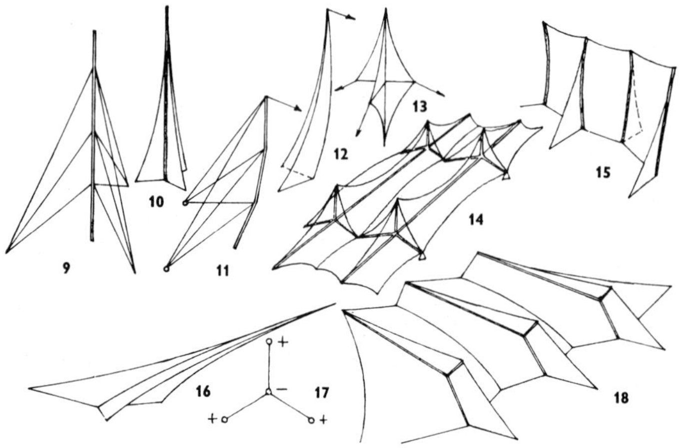

Three-Dimensional Support Systems Consisting of Prestressed Cables or Membranes

Prestressed plane membranes and cable nets are two-dimensional structures. Curved prestressed membranes and cable nets may also be regarded as two-dimensional structures, although they extend in space and are effective in three dimensions. Cable nets and membranes are by definition surface support structures. The concept "surface support structure" is justified as long as the system is large in two dimensions and small in the third.

We shall now discuss support systems that are large in all three dimensions. They consist primarily of cables, membranes, or nets, i.e., one- or two-dimensional tension-loaded elements.

A point can be fixed in space in various ways. Sketches 1 to 4 serve for explanation. A point (Fig. 1) is connected to the foundations by three rods. A force can be transmitted at the point to the rods, which are then under compression or tension.

If compression can be taken up only in two directions, a tripod as shown in Fig. 1 could tip over in the direction of the nonrigid support. Consequently, supports acting in at least four directions are necessary, as shown in Fig. 2. Two directions can take up only tension; the other two supports are rigid both in compression and tension.

Figure 3 shows a central pole that is only under compression and is guyed by three cables in three directions. The top of the pole is fixed in every direction. Forces act in four directions.

Figure 4 is similar. Cable tensions act in four directions; such a point is completely fixed in space, particularly when the cables are prestressed and no angle between the cables is larger than 180°. Cable nodes must be fixed in space in at least four directions.

Proceeding from a point as shown in Fig. 4, further branches can be added to the individual cables (Fig. 5). A spatial cable or cable-net system is formed in which cables run in four different directions from every point. Figure 6, which is similar to Fig. 5, shows a simplified cable system, with two fixed points, consisting of six cables altogether.

There are innumerable ways of designing spatial cable nets in which nodes, fixed in at least four directions, are joined together. Spatial nets may be large in one, two, or three dimensions. Figure 7 shows the system of a prestressed bridge consisting of a central straight prestressed cable secured in three directions by short equally-spaced cables. These short cables form angles of 120° and are subjected to tension by outer curved cables.

The bridge over the Gilgit between the Indus and the Karakorum (Fig. 19) consists of four cables stretched along the length of the bridge. Two cables are convex downward and two convex upward. The track runs along the two lower cables, which are only slightly prestressed. Bridges of this type can be very rigid if sufficiently prestressed. Suspension bridges with at least three prestressed main cables (prestressed three-cable bridges) need not be stabilized by dead weight or longitudinal girders rigid in bending (photograph by Ullstein).

Prestressed suspension bridges can also be built with a curved central axis (see *Dachy Wiszace, op. cit.*).

Points are frequently fixed by cables that act in six directions. Such a node is obtained when three prestressed cables cross as in the spatial net system shown in Fig. 8.

Struts Guyed in Three Directions

Compressive stresses can rarely be avoided in very high structures such as towers, or in widely overhanging roofs. Buckling, rather than actual compressive stresses, constitutes the problem.

Masts of ships have been guyed since ancient times to prevent buckling and overturning. Guyed masts can transmit large bending moments from the sails to the hull of the ship. The masts are therefore guyed not only at their tops, but also at short intervals along their height.

The design principle of the highest towers in existence is explained in Fig. 9. A light strut in the center is guyed at several points in at least three directions. The strut is rigid in bending, forming either a girder or a tube. Most towers are built of steel; some are of wood. Although thousands of such light high towers have been constructed, the possibilities of guyed towers have not been exhausted.

In theory there exists a maximum height for guyed towers. This is most probably also the greatest height attainable from the surface of the earth. However, this is no indication of the practical limit.

The maximum loads are imparted to guyed masts by one-sided wind forces acting together with dead weight. The structural workload taken up by the cables (sum of all products of length by force) often greatly exceeds that taken up by the central mast. Guyed masts are mixed systems subjected to large tensions. There are many variations of the basic principle illustrated in Figs. 3 and 9. It can be adapted to different uses without affecting its economic advantages. In the system shown in Fig. 10, the central mast is not supported by individual prestressed cables but by three membranes or cable nets bordered by cables. The cross section is shown in Fig. 17: a mast subjected to compression in the center (−), three tension-loaded cables at the edges (+), and membranes between mast and cables. In such a system all points of the mast are secured against buckling. The mast shown in Fig. 13 was designed as a support for membrane structures. The stabilization surfaces are prestressed by the tension-loaded roof surface.

Wind loads act only in the upper zone. The mast shown in Fig. 11 was designed as a support for a tension-loaded roof of wide span. The strut is angular or curved (Fig. 12). The curvature of the central mast makes it unnecessary to have guying or membrane tension in the third direction, if the mast has to carry a sufficient load in the central zone, e.g., a prestressed cable-net structure.

Figures 14, 15, 16, and 18 illustrate variations of the principle in Fig. 10. A rod under compression is secured against buckling on three sides by stressed membranes. Figure 14 shows a highly complex structure. The central frame, subjected to compression, is located inside a tension-loaded roof membrane formed of multiple surfaces. Downward buckling of the central rod is prevented by a vertical membrane, while sideward buckling is prevented by the wave-shaped roof membrane.

The struts in the vertical membrane wall shown in Fig. 15 are similarly fitted between three prestressed membranes.

The cantilever structures (Figs. 16 and 18) with slightly curved or angular struts are designed according to the same principle.

The radio transmitter at the Grosse Wannsee near Berlin (Fig. 1, p. 92) is an example of a structure with guyed masts. It is designed according to the principle illustrated in Fig. 9. The structure on the left consists of a double mast connected by a bridge and guyed on four sides. The transmitter carries a large number of short-wave antennas and is of high quality in execution and design.

▼19

1 ▼2

3 4 5 6 7

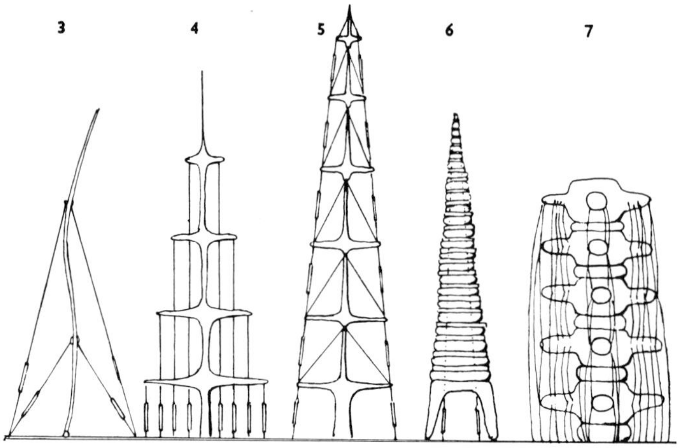

Movable Guyed Masts

Guyed masts consist of one-dimensional central elements subjected to compression and surrounded on all sides by one- or two-dimensional tension-loaded elements. They thus form three-dimensional systems most suitable for mobile structures. Many contemporary designs of high cranes for wide reaches are variations of this basic system. An elastic central rod can be bent by varying the lengths of the guys (Fig. 3). For this, all cables must be adjusted simultaneously; this is done by synchronized hydraulic presses located at the anchoring point. A similar, but much more mobile system is shown in Fig. 4. A thin elastic central strut carries cantilevers connected to the ground by means of cables. A model based on this principle was constructed in 1963*; it was intended as a design for a crane, or as a driving element for an artificial-fin drive (Fig. 2). It consists of a central strut under compression and 23 disks shaped like three-armed stars. Each disk arm carries at its end a cable slipped through holes in the disks below down to the abutment. The system is actuated by changing the cable length while maintaining a constant prestressing force. It can perform different movements at high speed and attain very small radii of curvature. Helixes, S-shapes, and wave lines are possible.

The system shown in Fig. 5 resembles that shown in Fig. 4. The controls (indicated as double lines) are located inside the system.

A rod as shown in Fig. 6 carries disks of varying elasticity, e.g., rubber disks alternating with steel disks. Each disk has at least three holes through which the cables are slipped. The structure is bent by changing the cable lengths.

In living nature the spine of a vertebrate (Fig. 7) is a guyed mobile system, approximately as shown in Figs. 2 and 4. A multiple articulated, highly flexible central rod, capable of taking up large compressive forces, is surrounded by a tension-loaded system consisting of many members, which secures the central rod against buckling and bending, while ensuring its complete mobility.

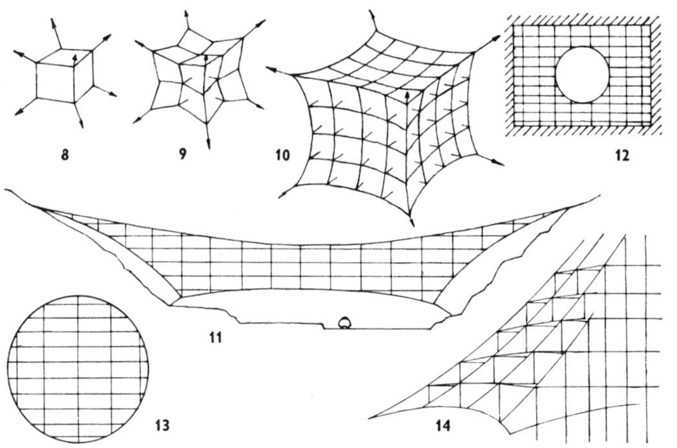

8 9 10 12 11 13 14

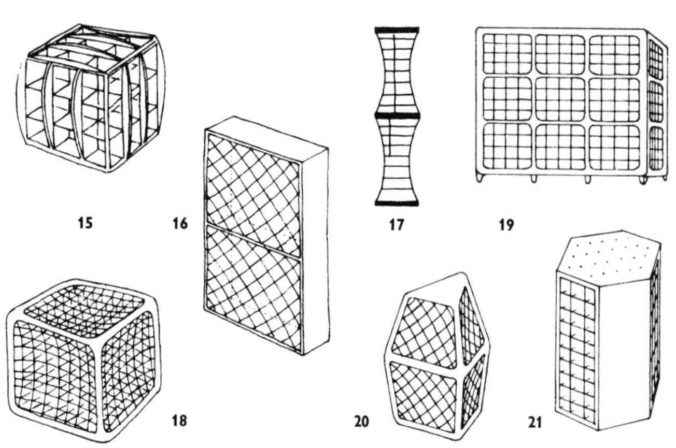

15 16 17 19 18 20 21

Prestressed Spatial Cable Nets and Their Edges

Spatial cable nets, in which every node is fixed in at least four but mostly in six directions by means of prestressed cables, have already been discussed (Figs. 1 to 8, p. 90). If eight cable forces act at the corners of a cable cube (Fig. 8), every single point is fixed in space in four directions by flexible tension-loaded elements. An additional system is inserted into this cube in Fig. 9. Further subdivision leads to a spatial net as shown in Fig. 10. This example shows that a spatial cable net can be bordered by tension-loaded elements. Fig. 11 shows a similar net stretched as a multifloor structure between mountain slopes.

Spatial cable nets can be suspended between massive anchorings, e.g., in caves or from mountains (Figs. 12 and 29, p. 95), in a spherical shell subjected to compression (Fig. 13), or between components subjected to bending. The outer skin of a spatial cable net may also act as a doubly curved surface support system (Fig. 14) which takes up all forces of the cable net and transmits them to the foundations or to fixed points.

Spatial cable nets may have large voids (Fig. 12) if the forces transmitted by the net are taken up by cable structures. Such voids are spherical or of similar shape when the force distribution in the net is uniform; they may also be cylindrical.

Spiders do not build only surface webs; some species build irregular spatial nets with many branches (Fig. 23).

The behavior of prestressed spatial cable nets has been studied since 1960 with a series of models and designs* (Figs. 22 and 29, p. 95). We refer to the work of C. Roland, to Report No. 8 of the Development Center for Light Structures, and other publications.

Prestressed spatial cable nets open up many new possibilities not previously realized. The spatial grids of these nets often have system lines similar to those of steel skeletons or spatial girder structures.

The structural and geometrical behavior of spatial cable nets can be considered quite independently of the surrounding frame structure. Thus, the net* shown in Fig. 29, p. 95, was stretched in a cavelike space (with the cooperation of Edmundo Zamboni).

The spatial cable net shown in Fig. 15 is enclosed on all sides by girders rigid in bending, which form the outline of a cube. The structure shown in Fig. 16 consists of a frame spanned by two diagonal cable nets that support an internal spatial net (see cross section in Fig. 17). A cube, whose edges are strong frames rigid in

22

23

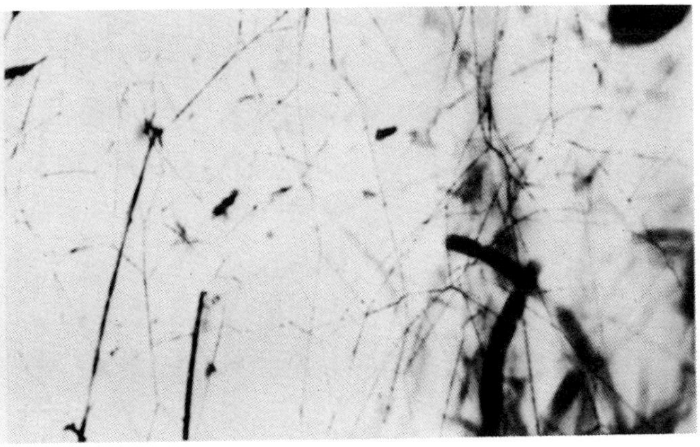

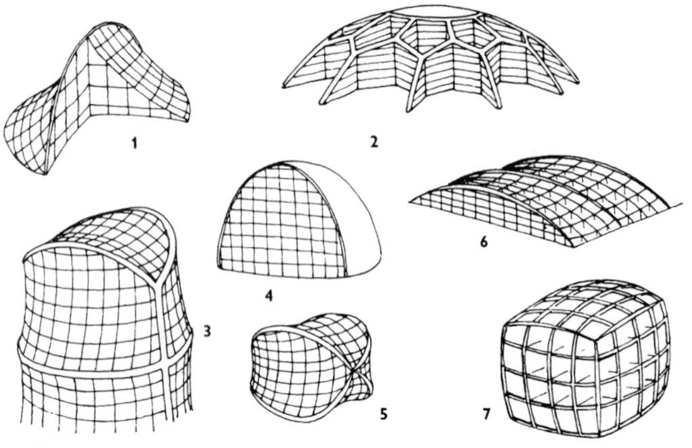

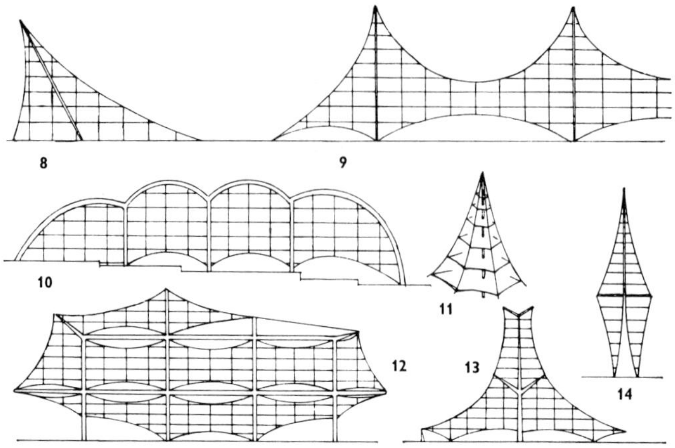

bending, has a cable net stretched on each side (Fig. 18, p. 93). The forces acting in the spatial cable net can be transmitted by the synclastically curved cable net to the edges of the cube. The structure shown in Fig. 19, p. 93, is similar; nine cubes are joined together. The outer edges are subjected to bending and compression, while the inner supports are only under compression. Figure 20, p. 93, shows a cable net of triangular plan and mesh structure, stretched in a frame rigid in bending, between diagonal cable nets with tetragonal meshes. Figure 21, p. 93, shows a spatial cable net suspended between plane panels rigid in bending. The net has triangular fields in plan.

Spatial cable nets can be inserted into almost any hollow space surrounded by cable nets. Figure 1 shows a central vertical arch with two saddle-shaped prestressed cable nets attached at the sides. An additional spatial cable net is stretched in the hollow space, subdividing the latter.

Figure 2 shows a spatial cable net supported by a wide-meshed geodesic dome. Each node of the dome is anchored to the foundations by a cable. The cables carry horizontal cable-net systems at each floor level. The spatial cable net reinforces the dome against buckling.

The external frame structure shown in Fig. 3 consists of struts and rings between which saddle-shaped prestressed cable nets are stretched. A spatial cable net is inserted between the latter.

The closed hollow body (Fig. 5) and the multifloor structure (Fig. 6) are similarly filled out with spatial cable nets. The spatial cable net shown in Fig. 4 is enclosed by a shell rigid in compression. A surface support structure under biaxial compression is thus reinforced against buckling by a prestressed spatial cable net. The inner cable net of the cube shown in Fig. 7 is supported similarly on the outside by a geodesic shell subjected to compression.

Spatial Cable Nets with Central Supports

The prestressing forces acting in a spatial cable net can be taken up at the edges either by surface support systems that are rigid in bending, compression, or tension (plane or curved, continuous or consisting of rods), or by compression-loaded structures within the cable net. The spatial cable net can then be used to reinforce the structure against buckling and bulging.

Figure 8 shows an inclined rod penetrating a spatial net suspended between the foundation and external cable nets. The net shown in Fig. 9 is supported by two vertical rods. The spatial net is not anchored to the foundations but to cables or nets at top and bottom. The boundary of the net shown in Fig. 10 is formed by a structure under compression which transmits its load to three vertical supports in the middle.

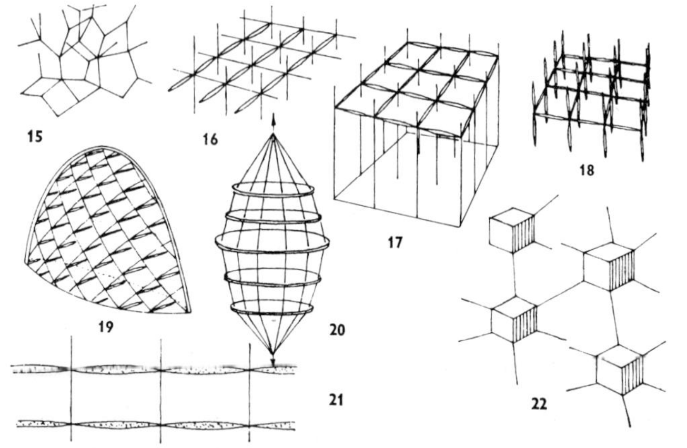

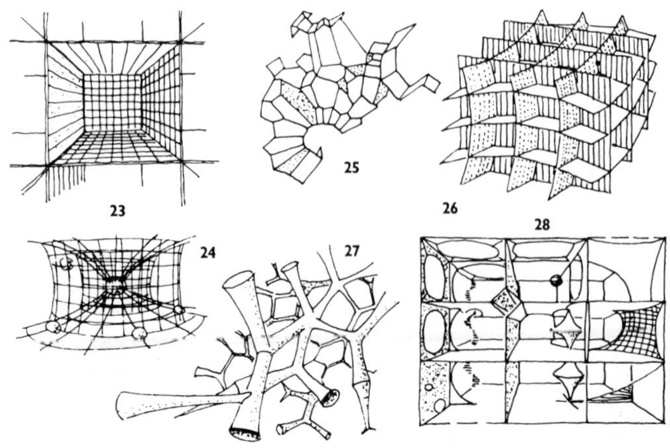

The stiffening effect of horizontal cables on a vertical central mast is illustrated in Fig. 11. The horizontal planes are formed by narrow-meshed cable nets.

Figure 12 illustrates the various design possibilities afforded by components under compression within a spatial cable net whose boundaries are formed by tension-loaded members. The central strut shown in Fig. 13 is opened out at the top and carries arms inside the net. This eliminates the need to transmit all forces acting in the spatial cable net to the masthead. The total path lengths are thus reduced. Figure 14 represents the cross section of a tall building with many ceiling panels. A horizontal compression-loaded panel in the center of the structure causes this tension-loaded structure to spread outward.

Multifloor spatial cable nets of this type are particularly suitable for structures built above rail installations or water surfaces.

Prestressed Spatial Cable Nets with Rods and Panels Rigid in Bending or Compression

Figures 15 to 18 show the transition from purely tension-loaded systems to skeletons rigid in compression or bending. The net shown in Fig. 15 is subjected to tension only. The net shown in Fig. 16 is erected on a grid of cubes. Rods that are rigid in compression or bending are fitted to it in one direction. The net shown in Fig. 17 has such rods fitted in two directions. This reduces the number of tension-loaded elements. Figure 18 shows a skeleton structure consisting only of rods.

Rods rigid in compression or bending, or surfaces, can be combined in many ways with cables to form spatial nets. Figure 19 shows two diagonally stretched surface cable nets connected to an arch and held apart by rods. A spatial system results that may be regarded as a cushion structure. Figure 20 shows a combination of cable nets in one direction and panels rigid in bending in the other. Such panels may be plane or curved.

Instead of rigid panels, a tension-loaded cushion structure can be suspended in a prestressed spatial cable net, as seen in cross section in Fig. 21 (see also p. 80). These cushions may be designed as tension-loaded prestressed structures with short struts normal to the center plane of the cushion, or as pneumatic cushions pressurized by a gas or liquid, or filled by solid particles in bulk.

29

Any solid body can be fitted into a spatial cable net and fixed in it. The body then becomes a structural component. By combining three-dimensional bodies with one-dimensional cables in a spatial arrangement, (Fig. 22), we obtain further design possibilities which have not yet been fully exploited.

Prestressed Tension-Loaded Spatial Surface Support Systems

Prestressed spatial cable nets are three-dimensional girder systems consisting of one-dimensional tension-loaded elements. In contrast, three-dimensional support systems consist of two-dimensional elements (i.e., surface supports) that are spatially assembled. The surface supports may be under compression or under tension and may form continuous surfaces such as domes, panels, and membranes, or lattice structures such as geodesic domes, lattice panels, and cable nets. We present only tension-loaded spatial support systems consisting of cable nets and membranes.

The net shown in Fig. 27, p. 94, consists of tubular hoses. It could also be called a spatial lattice structure. Various combinations are possible. Figure 28, p. 94, shows how cables, cable nets, membranes, membrane cutouts, rods, and solid bodies can be combined at will.

Foam is the most familiar example of tension-loaded membranes connected spatially. Many other forms are possible. Figure 23, p. 94, shows a spatial cable net like that of Fig. 29, p. 95, subdivided by cable nets, i.e., by surface supports forming planes. The spatial cable net shown in Fig. 24, p. 95, consists of several intersecting and interconnected curved prestressed cable nets and solid bodies forming a spatial support system of prestressed cable nets. Large structures of the most varied shapes result if touching membranes are connected spatially. The individual membrane elements are plane or curved anticlastically (Fig. 25, p. 94). The spatial support system shown in Fig. 26, p. 94, consists of nine intersecting surfaces: three are plane, three are synclastically, and three anticlastically curved. However, a single field must be either plane or anticlastically curved, unless an internal pressure acts.

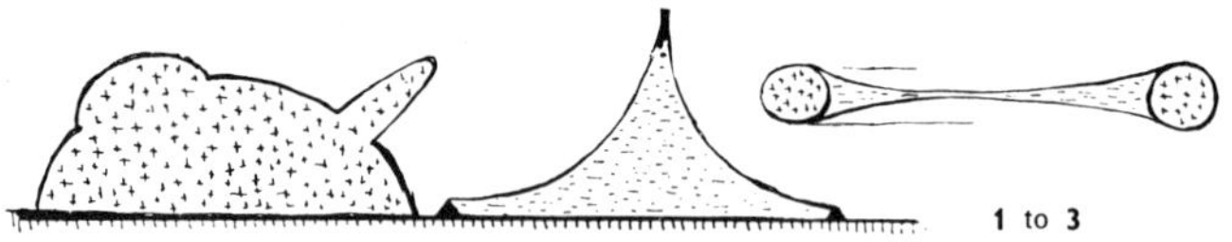

1 to 3

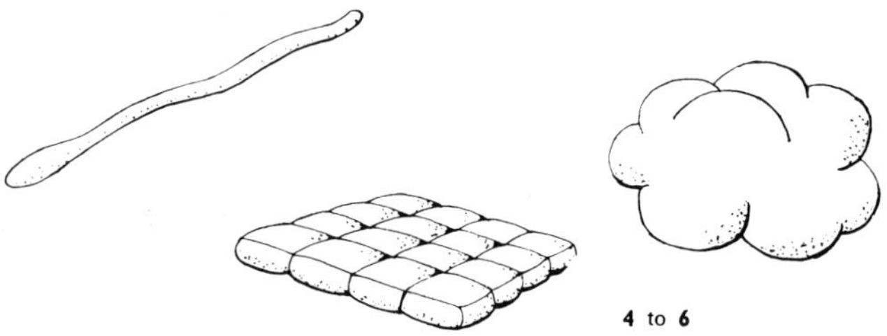

4 to 6

Prestressed Pneumatic Membrane Structures

We conclude this survey with a discussion of pneumatic structures. In these, membranes act together with gases (see p. 13). We thus obtain a three-dimensional support system with two- and three-dimensional components. We refer to the detailed discussion in Vol. 1.

There exist nonprestressed pneumatic structures, such as containers, whose state of stress depends on the weight of the liquid or other contents. They were discussed on p. 33.

Containers consisting of flexible tension-loaded membranes, closed on all sides and pressurized by gases (Fig. 1), are "prestressed pneumatic membrane structures." Stresses exist in the system even

7 to 13

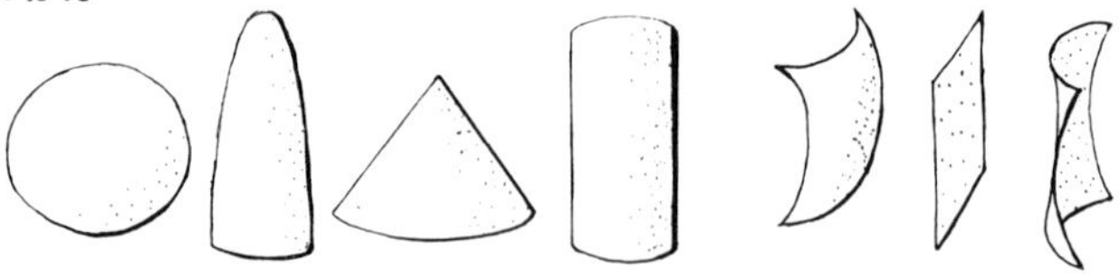

14 to 16

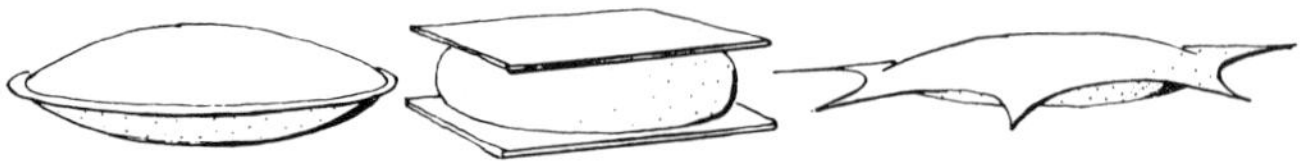

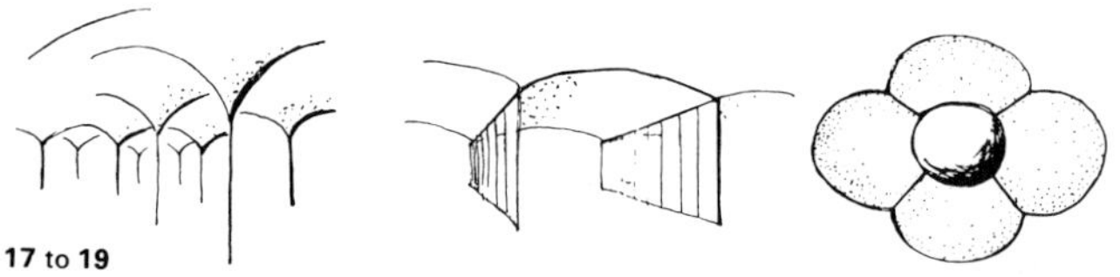

17 to 19

when no loads act. Pneumatically tensed membranes are used in mobile and stationary structures. They may be under positive (Fig. 1) or negative pressure (Fig. 2). Structures are possible in which positive and negative pressures act at the same time (Fig. 3, and Fig. 24, p. 80).

Elongated, mainly one-dimensional shapes that may be straight, curved, or angular can be formed with pneumatic structures and membranes (Fig. 4). Predominantly two-dimensional structures (Fig. 5) may be plane, simply or doubly curved, or angular. Three-dimensional structures of arbitrary shape are also possible (Fig. 6).

Structures can be subdivided according to their geometry. We distinguish between spheres, paraboloids, cones, cylinders, etc. (Figs. 7 to 9). Surfaces may be synclastic (Fig. 11), plane (Fig. 12), or anticlastic (Fig. 13). Edges may be subjected to compression (Fig. 14), bending (Fig. 15), or tension (Fig. 16). Membranes may be connected to line elements, e.g., a membrane with internal drainage anchored to cables (Fig. 17), to surfaces (Fig. 18, see also Fig. 23, p. 89), or to solid bodies (Fig. 19): a sphere is encircled and fixed by pneumatically tensed membranes.

One example is the project of a mountain observatory (Fig. 20). To the left there is a shallow pneumatically-tensed membrane dome forming a spherical segment. The membrane to the right is an ellipsoid.

20 ▼

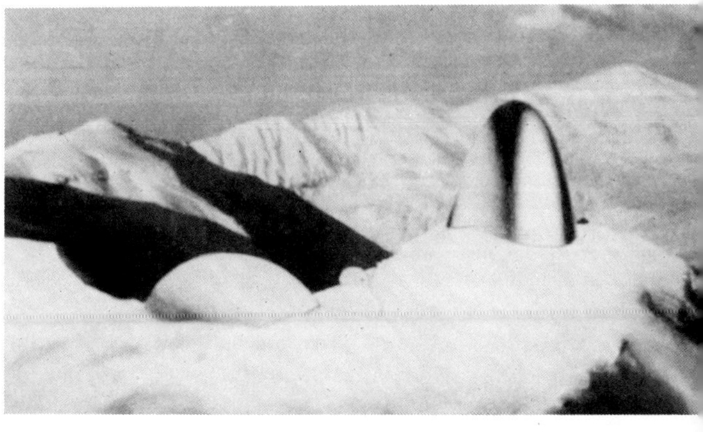

Analysis of Cables,

Cable Nets, and Cable Structures

INTRODUCTION

In order to analyze the many forms of bearing structures in which cables are used as load-carrying elements, it is convenient to subdivide the latter into several principal types. Composite structures have to be separated into their parts. According to structure and behavior under load, we can roughly distinguish between the following principal forms, where by the term "cable" is understood to be any tension member flexible in bending, such as a single wire, wire bundle, fiber, thread, thin steel section, or chain.

a. Simple (single) cables are the principal load-carrying members in hanging roofs tensioned in a single direction; pretensioned, they are also used in plane floors and roofs having small spans. They can also carry pipes, tubes, cable cranes, and ropeways, and are used as boundaries of membranes, textures, and nets. Cables also form the principal elements of many combined structures, some of which will be mentioned under e.

b. Cable nets are surface bearing structures; they consist of at least two families of intersecting cables lying within one surface. The nets are almost always spatially curved, and can be likened to membranes but have a different behavior under load.

Cable nets can be divided into several groups according to the arrangement of the cables and the surfaces formed by them. We mention nets orthogonal or nonorthogonal in plan, axisymmetrical shapes, and nets of uniform mesh. Many other forms have irregular internal structures or else do not obey simple geometrical relationships.

c. Spatial cable nets can, as extensions of surface nets, be likened to three-dimensional frameworks.

d. Cable systems forming plane bearing structures consist mainly of two cables interconnected by intermediate elements. Placed side by side or radially, they are used as connecting members; they can be likened to a plane framework.

e. Finally, we mention the various designs which are possible by combining pure tension elements with bearing members rigid in bending. These designs include suspension and inclined-cable bridges, other structures suspended from cables, cable girder nets, and beams combined with tension elements. We also note masts guyed by cables, and girders stiffened spatially by tension elements.

In accordance with the above grouping, we shall discuss four principal systems of pure cable structures that have a regular design. Figures, formulas, and tables are numbered consecutively throughout each chapter.

We shall first consider the behavior of single cables under load. Calculation methods will be given for plane cables carrying arbitrarily distributed loads; these methods can easily be extended to spatially loaded cables.

This chapter concludes with formulas for tightly pretensioned cables and with investigations of special problems.

The second chapter deals with cable nets of orthogonal ground plan. Simple calculation methods are derived from the exact theory; these methods are applicable to spatially loaded nets having arbitrary boundaries. The procedure is extended to nonorthogonal nets and may without appreciable error also be applied to other shallow cable nets that do not strictly satisfy the postulated geometrical conditions. The results of some fundamental analyses can be extended to other types of cable nets.

Application of the formulas is made clear with the aid of worked examples.

The third chapter contains formulas and calculation methods for axisymmetrical cable nets, which take into account the geometrical properties of such nets.

Various types of cable structures are discussed in the fourth chapter. In addition to general methods, formulas for frequently encountered special problems are given in closed form.

The fifth chapter will be of interest mostly to people not working in the field of statics. An attempt is made in it to describe clearly the behavior of cables and cable structures under load, with the aid of a limited number of formulas. In particular, architects may find in it some hints and bases for design.

Due to their lack of rigidity in bending, all pure cable structures are subject to comparatively large ranges of deformation under varying loads. The reason for this is that a state of equilibrium can only be attained through finite deformations. In contrast to conventional structures, primarily subjected to bending, we must here consider the equilibrium of deformed structures.

A nonpretensioned structure usually requires a comparatively large constant load for stabilization, in order to maintain the shape of the structure in the presence of negative loads (wind suction), prevent upward bulging of the roof membrane, or reduce the deformations to a minimum.

It will be shown that an appropriately designed structure can be made to take up abruptly varying loads (e.g., snow loads or wind suction) by means of pretensioned cables, the dead weight being kept very low. The distribution of the pretensioning forces and the shape of the bearing structure are interdependent.

Special emphasis has been placed upon obtaining clear calculation methods by properly selecting the coordinates and by neglecting insignificant minor effects. Thus, structures that are statically indeterminate to a high degree can be adequately analyzed by simple means (slide rules). Nevertheless, almost all formulas are valid for arbitrarily distributed loads acting in any direction; thermal expansion and displacements of the cable ends are also taken into account.

Many approximate formulas are given for design purposes; they permit the behavior under load to be determined rapidly so that preliminary design is facilitated.

The results obtained by these formulas are often so accurate that in order to effect a check, only a single typical case of loading need be analyzed in detail, and the remainder of the tedious calculation can be dispensed with.

(MS concluded in Summer 1964.)

1 SINGLE CABLES

This chapter deals primarily with the theory and analysis of novel cable structures. No complete treatment of single cables is therefore possible, nor is a new method added to those already known. The discussion extends therefore only as far as is necessary for a general understanding of the matter, which will be adequate for most problems encountered in practice.

1.1 Notations and Fundamentals

1.1.1 *Notations*

We analyze an ideal single cable, flexible in bending, with the aid of a fixed, right-handed, orthogonal coordinate system whose unit vectors are $\mathfrak{e}_x$, $\mathfrak{e}_y$, and $\mathfrak{e}_z$ (Fig. 1.1). The shape of the cable is given as an initially arbitrary curve, $\mathfrak{r}(t) = x(t) \cdot \mathfrak{e}_x + y(t) \cdot \mathfrak{e}_y + z(t) \cdot \mathfrak{e}_z$ where t is a scalar. In tensioned cables, as they occur almost exclusively in actual practice, it is advantageous to use one of the coordinates of the fixed system, e.g., x, as variable. The vector of location

$$\mathfrak{r}(x) = x \cdot \mathfrak{e}_x + y(x) \cdot \mathfrak{e}_y + z(x) \cdot \mathfrak{e}_z = \{x, y(x), z(x)\} \qquad (1.1)$$

is assumed to be single-valued and twice differentiable. In general, we shall denote differentiation with respect to x, e.g., of $\mathfrak{r}$, thus:

$$\frac{d\mathfrak{r}}{dx} = \mathfrak{r}' = \{1, y', z'\}$$

where $\mathfrak{r}'$ is assured to be finite in the entire region considered.

When an additional load is applied, the temperature changes, or the cable supports are displaced, the cable assumes a shape different from the initial shape. We introduce the displacement vector

$$\mathfrak{w} = \{u(x), v(x), w(x)\}, \qquad (1.2)$$

whose components in the x-, y-, and z- directions are positive. The new shape of the cable is thus given by

$$\bar{\mathfrak{r}} = \mathfrak{r} + \mathfrak{w} = \{\bar{x}, \bar{y}, \bar{z}\} = \{x + u, y + v, z + w\} \qquad (1.3a)$$

We then have

$$\bar{\mathfrak{r}}' = \mathfrak{r}' + \mathfrak{w}' = \{1 + u', \bar{y}', \bar{z}'\} = \{1 + u', y' + v', z' + w'\} \qquad (1.3b)$$

$$\bar{\mathfrak{r}}'' = \mathfrak{r}'' + \mathfrak{w}'' = \{u'', \bar{y}'', \bar{z}''\} = \{u'', y'' + v'', z'' + w''\}. \qquad (1.3c)$$

We have therefore to distinguish between two states: The initial state is, for practical reasons, taken as the curve assumed by the cable by virtue of its dead weight or a permanent load g. The corresponding cable forces will be denoted by the subscript g. In general, the initial state is the state of installation.

For an arbitrary load (e.g., $q = g + p$) the cable shape is given by $\mathfrak{r}(x)$; the corresponding sectional loads will be denoted by the subscript q.

The cable force will be denoted by $\mathfrak{S}(x)$ and the external load per unit length of the x-axis, by $\mathfrak{q}(x)$:

$$\mathfrak{q}(x) = q_x(x) \cdot \mathfrak{e}_x + q_y(x) \cdot \mathfrak{e}_y + q_z(x) \cdot \mathfrak{e}_z = \{q_x, q_y, q_z\}. \qquad (1.4a)$$

The total load is thus

$$\mathfrak{q} = \mathfrak{g} + \mathfrak{p} \qquad (1.4b)$$

being composed of the permanent and of the external (applied) loads.

1.1.2 *Equilibrium Conditions*

Discarding higher-order terms of the Taylor series for $\mathfrak{S}(x + dx)$ we obtain the equilibrium conditions for the cut-off cable element (Fig. 1.1):

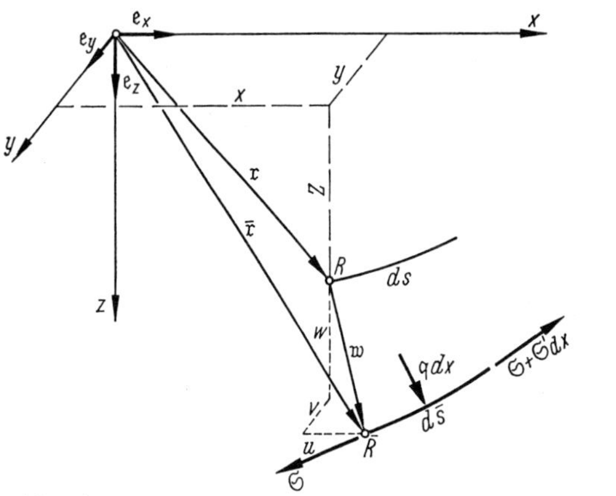

Fig. 1.1. Notations.

$$\frac{d\,\mathfrak{S}_q(x)}{dx} + \mathfrak{q}(x) = 0. \qquad (1.5a)$$

The condition that no bending moments act on the cable yields: $\bar{\mathfrak{r}}' \times \mathfrak{S}_q = 0$

This can also be written thus:

$$\mathfrak{S}_q = S_q \cdot \frac{\bar{\mathfrak{r}}'}{|\bar{\mathfrak{r}}'|}. \qquad (1.5b)$$

Here S is the magnitude of $\mathfrak{S}$, tension being assumed to be positive. It can be seen that the load vector $\mathfrak{q}$ lies in the osculating plane of the cable curve.

If we replace g by q and $\mathfrak{r}$ by $\bar{\mathfrak{r}}$, these conditions apply also to the initial state.

In order to obtain equations for the components, we introduce the x-component of $\mathfrak{S}$, which, irrespective of the actual position of the x-axis, we shall call the horizontal tension H:

$$H(x) = \mathfrak{S}(x) \cdot \mathfrak{e}_x = \frac{S(x)}{|\bar{\mathfrak{r}}'|} \cdot \bar{\mathfrak{r}}' \cdot \mathfrak{e}_x,$$

Thus, with $\bar{\mathfrak{r}}' \cdot \mathfrak{e}_x = 1 + u'$ since $u' \ll 1$,

$$H = \frac{S}{|\bar{\mathfrak{r}}'|} \quad \text{bzw.} \quad \mathfrak{S} = H \cdot \bar{\mathfrak{r}}'. \qquad (1.6)$$

Successive scalar multiplication of Eq. 1.5a by the unit vectors $\mathfrak{e}_x$, $\mathfrak{e}_y$, and $\mathfrak{e}_z$, taking into account Eqs. 1.5b and 1.6, yields

$$\left.\begin{aligned} &H_q' + q_x = 0, \\ &H_q \cdot \bar{y}'' + q_y - q_x \cdot \bar{y}' = 0, \\ &H_q \cdot \bar{z}'' + q_z - q_x \cdot \bar{z}' = 0. \end{aligned}\right\} \qquad (1.7a–c)$$

We shall henceforth assume that the permanent load applied in the initial state acts in a single direction (e.g., vertically downward). This direction is taken as the z-axis, the x, z-plane passing through both points of cable suspension. Since

$$\mathfrak{r} = \{x, 0, z\}$$

and

$\mathfrak{g} = \{0, 0, g\}$

we obtain from Eqs. 1.7

$$\left.\begin{aligned} &H_q' + p_x = 0\,, \\ &H_q \cdot v'' + p_y - p_x v' = 0\,, \\ &H_q \cdot \bar{z}'' + q_z - p_x \bar{z}' = 0\,. \end{aligned}\right\} \quad (1.8a\text{–}c)$$

For a plane cable, $v = p_y = 0$, so that Eq. 1.8b drops out. For the initial state $p = 0$ we obtain from Eqs. 1.8a and 1.8c:

$$H_g' = 0\,, \quad \text{hence } H_g = \text{const}$$

and

$$H_g\, z''(x) + g(x) = 0\,. \qquad (1.8d)$$

For $p_x = 0$ we then have also H_q= const, so that integration is easy. In this special case we obtain a clearly understandable form of the equilibrium conditions. Placing the origin at the left-hand point of suspension, and measuring the vertical deflection d from the straight line joining the suspension points, we obtain with the notations of Fig. 1.2:

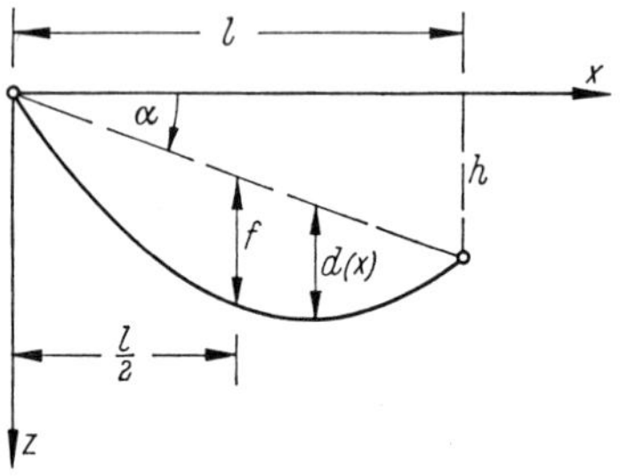

Fig. 1.2. Notation for a Plane Cable.

$$\left.\begin{aligned} &\tan\alpha = \frac{h}{l}\,, \\ &d = z - x \cdot \tan\alpha\,, \\ &\bar{d} = \bar{z} - x \cdot \tan\alpha\,. \end{aligned}\right\} \quad (1.9a\text{–}c)$$

From this, and from Eq. 1.8 follows:

$$\left.\begin{aligned} &H_q \cdot v(x) = M_y(x) \\ &\text{and} \\ &H_q \cdot \bar{d}(x) = M_z(x)\,. \end{aligned}\right\} \quad (1.10a, b)$$

Here, $M_y(x)$ and $M_z(x)$ are the bending moments due to a transverse load $q_y(x) = p_y(x)$ and $q_z(x) = g(x) + p_z(x)$ acting on a rod of length simply supported at both ends. The subscripts denote the corresponding load components and not the directions of the moment vectors. If a point of the cable curve or the horizontal tension H is known, the shape of the cable is determined.

Whereas the horizontal tensions

$$H_q = H_g + H_p \qquad (1.11)$$

are added algebraically, this superposition is not exact for the cable forces. The initial state is given, in accordance with Eq. 1.6, by

$$H_g = \frac{\mathfrak{S}_g}{|\mathfrak{r}'|}\,. \qquad (1.12a)$$

Correspondingly, when an additional load p is applied, we have

$$H_q = \frac{\mathfrak{S}_q}{|\bar{\mathfrak{r}}'|}\,. \qquad (1.12b)$$

Assuming that, like H_q, $\mathfrak{S}_q = \mathfrak{S}_g + \mathfrak{S}_p$ can also be added algebraically, we obtain by subtracting Eq. 1.12a from Eq. 1.12b:

$$H_p = \frac{\mathfrak{S}_p}{|\bar{\mathfrak{r}}'|} - \frac{\mathfrak{S}_g}{|\bar{\mathfrak{r}}'|} \cdot \frac{|\bar{\mathfrak{r}}'| - |\mathfrak{r}'|}{|\mathfrak{r}'|}\,.$$

The second term is caused by the change in direction of the force $\mathfrak{S}_g$ during displacement of the cable. The fraction denotes the strain ε (see Eq. 1.13). If the order of magnitude of $\mathfrak{S}_g$ and $\mathfrak{S}_p$ is the same, the second term can be neglected in comparison with the first term, since $\varepsilon \ll 1$ We then obtain, with sufficient accuracy,

$$H_p = \frac{\mathfrak{S}_p}{|\bar{\mathfrak{r}}'|}\,. \qquad (1.12c)$$

We note that a point R on the cable also moves in the x-direction when it is displaced to $\bar{R}$. Since the loads applied to the cable generally follow its displacements, the moments given by Eq. 1.10 are not independent of the deformations. We shall, however, exclude in this chapter displacements of the cable suspensions. When the cable is sufficiently straight, the u-displacements are small in comparison with the span, so that we can assume with sufficient accuracy that the loads at x equal those at $\bar{x}$. The moments appearing in Eq. 1.10 can then be calculated without knowing the final cable shape.

1.1.3 *Elasticity Conditions*

Due to the additional load or changes in temperature the initial length $ds = |\mathfrak{r}'|\,dx$ of the cable element becomes $d\bar{s} = |\bar{\mathfrak{r}}'|\,dx$. The strain is thus

$$\varepsilon = \frac{|\bar{\mathfrak{r}}'| - |\mathfrak{r}'|}{|\mathfrak{r}'|}\,. \qquad (1.13)$$

Using Eqs. 1.1 and 1.3b and expanding the radicals in series, retaining in the numerator only terms up to and including the second degree, we obtain

$$\varepsilon = \frac{u' + y'\,v' + z'\,w'}{1 + y'^2 + z'^2} + \frac{v'^2 + w'^2}{2\,(1 + y'^2 + z'^2)^2}\,, \qquad (1.14)$$

where the second term can generally be neglected in relation to the first.

Other authors give an expression for ε which differs slightly from the above:

$$\varepsilon = \frac{1}{1 + y'^2 + z'^2}\Big\{u' + y'\,v' + z'\,w' + \frac{1}{2}(u'^2 + v'^2 + w'^2)\Big\}\,. \qquad (1.15)$$

For its derivation, we write the length of the deformed cable element as a sum:

$$d\bar{s} = |\bar{\mathfrak{r}}'| \cdot d\,x = d\,s + \Delta\,d\,s\,.$$

We then obtain

$$d\,\bar{s}^2 = d\,s^2 + 2\,d\,s \cdot \Delta\,d\,s + (\Delta\,d\,s)^2 = [1 + y'^2 + z'^2 + 2\,(u' + y'\,v' + z'\,w') + u'^2 + v'^2 + w'^2]\,d\,x^2\,.$$

Subtracting the square of the initial length, we find

$$2\,ds \cdot \Delta\,ds + (\Delta\,ds)^2 = [2\,(u' + y'\,v' + z'\,w') + u'^2 + v'^2 + w'^2]\,dx^2. \tag{1.16}$$

Neglecting $\Delta\,ds$ in relation to $2\,ds$, we obtain $\varepsilon = \frac{\Delta\,ds}{ds}$ in the form of Eq. 1.15.

Although this equation is easier to handle than Eq. 1.14, no reason is given for neglecting $(\Delta\,ds)^2$, which for tight cables has the same order of magnitude as $(u'\,dx)^2$ on the right. Determining $\frac{\Delta\,ds}{ds}$ more accurately from the quadratic Eq. 1.16, we would obtain again Eq. 1.14.

For a monoaxial state of stress of the cable we assume for the sake of simplicity a linear stress-strain relationship (Hooke's law). For braided or spiral wire cables the effective modulus of elasticity depends on the load, but we can at first neglect the stretching of the cable if all strains are measured in relation to a state in which the cable is already loaded by g or is pretensioned (as in the structures to be discussed). For the strains caused by variations in the cable force we can then assume a modulus of elasticity E which remains constant over the stress range considered.
We thus write:

$$\varepsilon = \frac{S_p}{E\,F} + {}^t\varepsilon\,. \tag{1.17}$$

Here, E is the modulus of elasticity and F the cross-sectional area of the cable, while

$${}^t\varepsilon = \alpha_t \cdot \Delta\,t \tag{1.18}$$

is the strain due to a temperature increase $\Delta\,t$, the coefficient of linear expansion being α_t.
Combining Eqs. 1.14 and 1.17, we obtain

$$S_p = \frac{E\,F}{1 + y'^2 + z'^2}\,(u' + y'\,v' + z'\,w') + \frac{E\,F}{2\,(1 + y'^2 + z'^2)^2}\,(v'^2 + w'^2) - E\,F \cdot {}^t\varepsilon\,.$$

For practical calculations we shall discard the second term. Neglecting in Eq. 1.12c the additional inclination of the cable and setting $|\bar{\mathfrak{r}}'| = |\mathfrak{r}'|$, we obtain the horizontal tension

$$H_p = \frac{E\,F}{(1 + y'^2 + z'^2)^{3/2}} \cdot (u' + y'\,v' + z'\,w') - \frac{E\,F}{(1 + y'^2 + z'^2)^{1/2}} \cdot {}^t\varepsilon\,. \tag{1.19}$$

If the cable was initially in the x, z-plane, we have $y = y' = 0$, and the preceding expression is simplified to

$$H_p = \frac{E\,F}{(1 + z'^2)^{3/2}}\,(u' + z'\,w') - \frac{E\,F}{(1 + z'^2)^{1/2}} \cdot {}^t\varepsilon\,. \tag{1.20}$$

1.1.4 *Cable Lengths*

The length L of the cable is obtained by integration. In the initial state,

$$L_g = \int ds = \int |\mathfrak{r}'| \cdot dx = \int \sqrt{1 + y'^2 + z'^2}\,dx \tag{1.21a}$$

and when a load q is applied (neglecting u' in relation to 1), we have

$$L_q = \int d\bar{s} = \int |\bar{\mathfrak{r}}'| \cdot dx = \int \sqrt{1 + \bar{y}'^2 + \bar{z}'^2} \cdot dx\,. \tag{1.21b}$$

For a cable lying initially in the x, z-plane, we put $y' = 0$ and $\bar{y}' = v'$.
The elongation $\Delta\,L$ of the cable is given by the difference between these two expressions. On the other hand, using Eqs. 1.17 and 1.12c, we obtain

$$\Delta\,L = L_q - L_g = \int \frac{S_p}{E\,F}\,ds + \int {}^t\varepsilon \cdot ds = \int \frac{H_p}{E\,F} \cdot \mathfrak{r}'^2\,dx + \int {}^t\varepsilon\,ds. \tag{1.22}$$

If H, E, F and ${}^t\varepsilon$ are constant over the length of the cable, this is simplified to

$$\Delta\,L = \frac{H_p}{E\,F} \int \mathfrak{r}'^2\,dx + {}^t\varepsilon \cdot L_g\,. \tag{1.23}$$

Finally, for purpose of installation, the length of the completely unstrained cable is of interest. This is approximately

$$L_0 = L_g - H_g \int \frac{\mathfrak{r}'^2}{E\,F}\,dx. \tag{1.24}$$

If the stretching of the cable and the (for small stresses) comparatively large strains have to be taken into account, we must use here the effective modulus of elasticity, which may depend on the cable force, i.e., on x.

1.2 Inelastic Cable

According to the preceding section, all deformations are measured from the initial state. Our first task is therefore to determine the shape of the cable and the cable forces H or S for this state.

For cables subjected only to vertical loads, we can use graphical methods (link polygons), which will not be discussed here. The contents of the following two subsections are assumed to be known, and will only be discussed briefly.

If the vertical deflection of the cable is not very small in comparison with the span, and if the loads p are not distributed too differently from the permanent load g, then we can in some cases neglect the strains induced by p and their effects on cable shape and forces. We can then consider the load q applied to the inelastic cable.

1.2.1 *Constant Vertical Load*

For $q_z = g =$ const we obtain from Eq. 1.8 the quadratic parabola

$$z = -\frac{g}{2\,H_g}\,(x^2 + C_1\,x + C_2) \tag{1.25}$$

as the cable curve. The constants C_1 and C_2 can be determined by inserting the coordinates of the cable end points $(x_r, 0, z_r)$ and $(x_l, 0, z_l)$ with $x_r - x_l = l > 0$. The still unknown horizontal tension is found either by fixing a third point through which the cable must pass, or from the cable length.
Using the notations of Fig. 1.2, we have

$$d = \frac{g}{2\,H_g}\,(l\,x - x^2) = 4\,f\left(\frac{x}{l} - \frac{x^2}{l^2}\right). \tag{1.26}$$

The largest deflection f is in mid-span. From it we obtain the horizontal tension

$$H_g = \frac{g\,l^2}{8\,f}, \tag{1.27}$$

which can also be found from Eq. 1.10b. We give the exact expression for the cable length only for the case $\alpha = 0$. Writing

$$n = \frac{f}{l}, \tag{1.28}$$

we obtain

$$L = \frac{l}{2}\left(\sqrt{1 + 16\,n^2} + \frac{1}{4\,n}\,\text{ar sinh}\,4\,n\right). \tag{1.29}$$

The following is a simpler expression valid for sufficiently straight cables, applicable also when the end points are situated at different heights:

$$L \approx l\left(1 + \frac{8}{3}\,n^2 + \frac{1}{2}\tan^2\alpha\right). \tag{1.30}$$

1.2.2 *Loading by Dead Weight*

The load g_0 is constant along the cable curve. Per unit length of the x-axis we have $g\,(x) = g_0 \cdot \sqrt{1 + z'^2}$.

For a cable lying in the x, z-plane we obtain from Eq. 1.8d:

$$H_g \cdot z'' + g_0\sqrt{1 + z'^2} = 0.$$

The general solution (catenary) is:

$$z = -\frac{H_g}{g}\cosh\frac{g}{H_g}(x + C_1) + C_2. \tag{1.31}$$

(The subscript of g has been and will henceforth be omitted).

When $C_1 = C_2 = 0$, the origin lies at a vertical distance $\frac{H_g}{g}$ below the vertex of the cable curve. In the general case, the constants are determined by the coordinates of the cable suspension points. The horizontal tension is again found either by fixing a third point through which the cable must pass, or from the cable length

$$L_g = \int_{x_l}^{x_r}\cosh\frac{g}{H_g}(x + C_1)\,dx. \tag{1.32}$$

The calculation leads to transcendental equations. We give the results obtained for the coordinate system used in Fig. 1.2:

$$\left.\begin{aligned} C_1 &= -\frac{l}{2} - \frac{H_g}{g}\,\text{ar tanh}\,\frac{h}{L_g} \\ &\text{and} \\ C_2 &= \frac{H_g}{g}\cosh\frac{g}{H_g}\,C_1. \end{aligned}\right\} \tag{1.33a, b}$$

When both cable ends are at the same height, i.e., $h = 0$, we obtain

$$z = f - \frac{H_g}{g}\left[\cosh\frac{g}{H_g}\left(x - \frac{l}{2}\right) - 1\right], \tag{1.34}$$

where f is the maximum deflection of the cable.

When the cable length is known, we can obtain the horizontal tension (for any coordinate system) from either of the expressions

$$\cosh\frac{g\,l}{H_g} = 1 + \frac{g^2}{2\,H_g^2}(L_g^2 - h^2), \tag{1.35a}$$

$$\sinh\frac{g\,l}{2\,H_g} = \frac{g\,l}{2\,H_g}\sqrt{\frac{L_g^2 - h^2}{l^2}}. \tag{1.35b}$$

This is best done by iteration. The calculation can be found, e.g., in Heilig's paper,[1] in which the elastic horizontal displacements of the cable suspensions are also taken into account.

If in Eq. 1.34 we retain only the first two terms in the series expansion of the cosh, we obtain for small values of n the approximation:

$$H_g \approx \frac{g\,l^2}{8\,f}, \tag{1.36}$$

which is in agreement with Eq. 1.27. For $f/l = n = 0.3$, however, H_g will be about 10% too small, so that the approximation in Eq. 1.36 should only be used for straight cables.

When $n \leq 0.2$, we may assume that the cable curve, induced by the dead weight, is a parabola. The formulas of Section 1.2.1 then yield practically the same results as the expressions for a catenary.

1.2.3 *Arbitrary Load* $q_x = 0$

As before, H =const. The best approach is to proceed from Eqs. 1.10 and determine the moments M_y and M_z, acting on the equivalent beam, induced by the given load. If the deflection of the cable at a given point is known, we can easily find H. The cable length is then generally obtained from Eqs. 1.21. However, introducing the shearing forces

$$\left.\begin{aligned} Q_z &= M_z' \\ Q_y &= M_y' \end{aligned}\right\} \tag{1.37a, b}$$

acting on the equivalent beam,[2] we obtain

$$\bar{z}' = \frac{Q_z}{H} + \tan\alpha\,, \tag{1.38a}$$

when Eqs. 1.9b and 1.10b are taken into account.

Similarly, since $g_y = 0$,

$$\bar{y}' = y' = \frac{Q_y}{H}. \tag{1.38b}$$

The cable length is thus

$$L = \int\sqrt{1 + \left(\frac{Q_y}{H}\right)^2 + \left(\frac{Q_z}{H} + \tan\alpha\right)^2}\,dx. \tag{1.39}$$

If the cable length instead of the deflection is given, we estimate H and thus make a preliminary assumption about the cable shape. If the results of computation by Eqs. 1.21 or 1.39 differ from the assumed value, the calculation has to be repeated, assuming a different value of H.

We will only mention the fact that loads and cable-curve ordinates can be expressed by means of Fourier series.

1.2.4 *Arbitrary Load* $q_x \neq 0$

In this case H depends on x, so that we cannot use the integral equilibrium conditions 1.10. According to Eq. 1.4a we must assume that only the x-coordinates of the points of application of the loads are given, the other coordinates depending on the still unknown cable curve. This condition has been implicitly adopted in the

[1] R. Heilig, *Stahlbau* 23 (1954), pp. 253–258 and 283–291.

[2] For the subscripts see explanation following Eqs. 1.10.

preceding Section 1.2.3; it now becomes more explicit for horizontal loads whose lines of action are not yet determined. To solve the problem, we first determine from Eq. 1.8a the horizontal tension

$$H(x) = H_0 - \int_0^x p_x \, dx \qquad (1.40)$$

up to a constant value H_0 which must be estimated in advance, and, if necessary, corrected. The shape of the cable is determined from Eqs. 1.8b, c, in which, however, the ordinates of the cable curve still appear in their first derivatives. Usually, the loads p_x are considerably smaller than the loads p_y or in particular q_z, so that in Eq. 1.8b we can assume a mean value for v' or omit the term under consideration altogether. If in Eq. 1.8c we do not wish to estimate z' in advance, we can nearly always replace it by the magnitude $\tan \alpha$. The errors thus introduced in comparison with the exact results are small.

We then determine v and $\bar{z}$ from Eqs. 1.8b, c by integration (if necessary, numerically). The cable length is again found from Eqs. 1.21. If L is given, the entire computation is repeated for different values of H_0 until agreement is obtained.

When concentrated vertical and horizontal loads act on the cable, we first determine, according to Stüssi,[1] as before, the (here, piecewise constant) horizontal tension up to H_0. The equilibrium conditions of the link polygon then yield for each point of load application a difference equation replacing Eq. 1.8c. The resulting system of linear equations of three terms each is solved by an elegant method, due to Stüssi, in which the boundary-value problem is transformed into an initial-value problem.

1.2.5 *Permanent Load and Arbitrary Additional Load*

The equilibrium conditions in Eqs. 1.8 or 1.10 do not differ in principle in the case of a permanent load g or a total load q (which may also include temperature effects). The formulas given in the preceding subsections are therefore universally valid; we have only to use the subscripts q or g and the ordinates $\bar{\mathfrak{r}}$ or $\mathfrak{r}$. We thus consider first g (i.e., H_g) alone, and then investigate separately all possible combinations of applied loads p. The latter have to be combined with g and with any temperature effects present, the corresponding horizontal tension being H_q. Different cases of applied loads cannot be superimposed.

If H (or S at the cable end) are prescribed in magnitude by a counterweight, the cable curve can easily be determined according to Eqs. 1.10, or more generally, according to Eqs. 1.8. Usually, however, the cable end points are fixed. To determine H_q we then need to know the cable length. Since the cable is assumed to be inelastic, we have (with ${}^t\varepsilon = \text{const}$)

$$L_q = L_g (1 + {}^t\varepsilon). \qquad (1.41)$$

L_g and L_q are again obtained from Eqs. 1.21 or 1.39. This must generally be done by iteration, various values of H being assumed. From the differences in the cable-curve ordinates we obtain the change in deflections due to additional loads or temperature effects.

[1] F. Stüssi, *Statik der Seile*. Abhandl. I.V.B.H. (1940/41), p. 290.

An equation containing H explicitly is obtained when only vertical loads are present, i.e., $q_x = q_y = 0$. Proceeding from the linearized Eq. 1.14, we find for the case considered

$$\varepsilon = \frac{u' + z' w'}{1 + z'^2}. \qquad (1.42)$$

The assumption of an inelastic cable yields, according to Eq. 1.17,

$$\varepsilon = {}^t\varepsilon,$$

whence

$$u' = -z' w' + (1 + z'^2)\, {}^t\varepsilon.$$

Integrating, and postulating constancy of span $l = x_r - x_l$ when additional loads are applied, we obtain

$$\int_{x_l}^{x_r} u' \, dx = -\int_{x_l}^{x_r} z' w' \, dx + \int_{x_l}^{x_r} (1 + z'^2)\, {}^t\varepsilon \, dx = 0. \qquad (1.43)$$

Assuming ${}^t\varepsilon = \text{const}$, we can define a reference length

$$L_t = \int_{x_l}^{x_r} (1 + z'^2) \, dx. \qquad (1.44)$$

For the first integral on the right-hand side of Eq. 1.43, we have

$$\int_{x_l}^{x_r} z' w' \, dx = \Big[z' w\Big]_{x_l}^{x_r} - \int_{x_l}^{x_r} z'' w \, dx, \qquad (1.45)$$

in which the boundary terms vanish since the cable ends are fixed. On the other hand, we obtain from Eqs. 1.10b, 1.9c, and 1.3a:

$$w = \frac{M_{zq}}{H_q} - \frac{M_{zg}}{H_g}, \qquad (1.46)$$

while z'' is known from Eq. 1.8d. Eq. 1.43 thus becomes

$$H_q \left[\frac{1}{H_g^2} \int_{x_l}^{x_r} g \cdot M_{zg} \, dx + {}^t\varepsilon \cdot L_t \right] - \frac{1}{H_g} \int_{x_l}^{x_r} g \cdot M_{zq} \, dx = 0, \qquad (1.47)$$

from which H_q can be determined. This procedure, applicable for arbitrary vertical loads, permits the horizontal tension to be determined directly from the known loads without iterations. The shape of the cable is then found from Eq. 1.10b.

1.3 Elastic Cable

1.3.1 *General Observations*

In order to determine more accurately the cable forces and displacements, we must also take into account the elastic changes in length. Particularly for small deflection: span ratios, this yields results differing considerably from those obtained for inelastic cables. When cable strains are taken into account, the deflections are usually found to be larger, while the horizontal tension is less.

The statically determinate case, in which H (or S) is given by means of a counterweight, where at least one cable end can move freely beyond the fixed support, is of no practical interest.
The elasticity conditions relevant to the problem considered are: Either the cable ends do not move (or move by a prescribed amount), or the cable length is increased due to the additional load by an amount corresponding to the extent of the stretching.
Accordingly, the usual methods can be divided into two groups. For straight pretensioned cables, such as are used in "pretensioned-steel roofs," the formulas can be considerably simplified. This case will be considered in Section 1.3.4.

1.3.2 *Cable Length as Additional Condition*
The length L_q of the cable, loaded by g and p and elongated because of changes in temperature, is generally determined from Eqs. 1.21b or (for H =const) 1.39. These equations are:

$$L_q = \int_{x_l}^{x_r} \sqrt{1 + v'^2 + \bar{z}'^2}\, dx \,, \tag{1.48a}$$

$$L_q = \int_0^l \sqrt{1 + \left(\frac{Q_{yq}}{H_q}\right)^2 + \left(\frac{Q_{zq}}{H_q} + \tan\alpha\right)^2}\, dx \,. \tag{1.48b}$$

Whereas the second equation contains Q and H explicitly, in Eq. 1.48a the cable-curve ordinates have first to be found from the equilibrium conditions. In both cases the final horizontal tension must be known.
The conditions stipulated for the cable length state that the increase in L is due to thermal elongation and the elastic elongation caused by H_p. In accordance with Eq. 1.22 we must then have in general

$$L_q = L_g + \Delta L = L_g + \int \frac{H_p}{EF}(1 + z'^2)\, dx + \int {}^t\varepsilon\, dx \tag{1.49a}$$

or, in the special case when $q_x = 0$, EF =const and ${}^t\varepsilon$ =const

$$L_q = L_g\,(1 + {}^t\varepsilon) + \frac{H_p}{EF} \cdot \int (1 + z'^2)\, dx \tag{1.49b}$$

The form of these integral conditions shows that H cannot be found explicitly by this method, and that iterations are necessary.
In every case, besides the load, we know the horizontal tension $\overline{H_g}$ and the length L_g of the cable which is assumed to be initially plane.

We now estimate $H_q^{(1)} = H_g + H_p^{(1)}$ and obtain for this value the cable length $L_q^{(1)}$ from Eq. 1.48a by means of the cable-curve ordinates. When the corresponding values are inserted into Eq. 1.49a, we generally obtain a value $H_p^{(1)}$ differing from $L_q^{(1)}$. The calculation has then to be repeated for different values of H until Eq. 1.49a is identically satisfied, i.e., $L_q^{(n)} = {}^{(n)}L_q$. When H_0 is estimated according to Eq. 1.40, this procedure can also be adopted when a horizontal load q_x is present. When H =const, we can use Eq. 1.49b instead of Eq. 1.49a. The calculation then becomes shorter, since we can obtain from $L_q^{(i)}$ a new value ${}^{(i)}H_p$ with the aid of Eq. 1.49b. We then have

$$H_p^{(i+1)} = \frac{1}{2}\left(H_p^{(i)} + {}^{(i)}H_p\right)$$

which is a better approximation than $H_p^{(i)}$. The criterion for the correct determination of the horizontal tension is then $H_p^{(n)} = {}^{(n)}H_p$. Even this procedure is quite tedious, since the entire computation has to be repeated several times. We shall discuss a far more elegant procedure in Section 1.3.3, in which the required magnitudes are found directly.

1.3.3 *The Span as Additional Condition*
If only vertical forces act on the cable, we can set up (as in Section 1.2.5) an equation in which the horizontal tension is directly determined from the loads. The criterion for the correct selection of the value of H is now $\int u'\, dx = 0$.

We first rewrite Eq. 1.20 in the form

$$u' = -\, z'\, w' + \frac{H_p}{EF}(1 + z'^2)^{3/2} + (1 + z'^2)\, {}^t\varepsilon .$$

Integrating over the span l, assuming ${}^t\varepsilon$ and EF to be constant, we obtain

$$\int_{x_l}^{x_r} u'\, dx = \int_{x_l}^{x_r} z'\, w'\, dx + \frac{H_p}{EF}\int_{x_l}^{x_r}(1 + z'^2)^{3/2}\, dx + {}^t\varepsilon \int_{x_l}^{x_r}(1 + z'^2)\, dx = 0 .$$

The first integral of the right-hand side is transformed according to Eq. 1.45, while in the other two integrals we write

$$L_s = \int_{x_l}^{x_r} (1 + z'^2)^{3/2}\, dx \tag{1.50a}$$

and

$$L_t = \int_{x_l}^{x_r} (1 + z'^2)\, dx . \tag{1.50b}$$

When the cable ends are fixed, we obtain

$$\int_{x_l}^{x_r} z''\, w\, dx + \frac{H_p}{EF} L_s + {}^t\varepsilon\, L_t = 0 .$$

Inserting Eqs. 1.8d and 1.46, the equation for $H_q{}^1$ becomes[1]

$$H_q^2 \frac{L_s}{EF} + H_q\left[\frac{1}{H_g^2}\int_{x_l}^{x_r} g \cdot M_{zg}\, dx - H_g \frac{L_s}{EF} + {}^t\varepsilon \cdot L_t\right] - \frac{1}{H_g}\int_{x_l}^{x_r} g\, M_{zq}\, dx = 0 \tag{1.51}$$

For a cable rigid in tension, i.e., $EF \to \infty$, Eq. 1.51 becomes Eq. 1.47, as expected.

Stüssi proceeds from Eq. 1.15, using rough approximations for its quadratic terms. He thus obtains a cubic equation for determining H. Disregarding the influence of the quadratic terms mentioned, he finds an equation identical with Eq. 1.51.
For the frequently encountered case of constant loads we can easily calculate the integrals in Eq. 1.51. The deflection of the cable,

[1] Cf. Stüssi, *op. cit.*, p. 296.

caused by the permanent load, is

$$f_g = \frac{g\,l^2}{8\,H_g}.$$

Setting $n = f_g/l$, we obtain, using Eq. 1.26,

$$H_q^2 \frac{L_s}{EF} + H_q \left[\frac{16\,n}{3} f_g - H_g \frac{L_s}{EF} + {}^t\varepsilon\, L_t\right] - \frac{2}{3} q\, l\, f_g = 0. \quad (1.52)$$

The magnitudes defined by Eqs. 1.50 are in this case

$$L_t = l\left(1 + \frac{16}{3} n^2 + \tan^2\alpha\right) \quad (1.53a)$$

and approximately

$$L_s \approx l\,\frac{1 + 8\,n^2 + \tan^2\alpha}{\cos\alpha}. \quad (1.53b)$$

Even if the cable curve is not strictly parabolical, the expressions in Eq. 1.53 can be used as approximations.
A different procedure has been suggested by Heilig (see Section 1.2.2). Proceeding from the equilibrium position of the inelastic cable, loaded by q, two simultaneous differential equations are derived for the displacement components. Their general solution is known. The required cable forces are determined from the boundary conditions.

1.3.4 *Pretensioned Cable with Constant Vertical Load*

Cables are pretensioned in order to obviate significant deflections, particularly when they are used as load-carrying members of flat lightweight roofs. The calculations are considerably simplified in view of the very small cable inclinations. We can always set $H = S$ and determine the cable length from Eq. 1.30. We shall only consider cables whose end points are at the same height, i.e. $\alpha = 0$.
In contrast to the preceding, we assume that initially the weightless cable is straight and pretensioned to H_0. The loads g and q are then analogous; we shall therefore write p for a vertical uniformly distributed load. The total horizontal tension is thus

$$H = H_0 + H_p, \quad (1.54)$$

being composed of the pretensioning force and the horizontal tension induced by the external load. Temperature effects are included under H_p.
The equilibrium condition is[1]

$$H = H_0 + H_p = \frac{p\,l^2}{8\,f} = \frac{p\,l}{8\,n}. \quad (1.55)$$

The length of the parabolic arc, given by Eq. 1.30, yields the cable strain

$$\Delta L = \frac{8}{3} n^2 l,$$

where $n = \frac{f}{l}$. We also find from Eq. 1.22:

$$\Delta L = l\left(\frac{H_p}{EF} + {}^t\varepsilon\right).$$

[1] It should be noted that $H = H_0$ for $p = 0$.

Eliminating ΔL from these expressions, we obtain

$$H_p = E\,F\left(\frac{8}{3} n^2 - {}^t\varepsilon\right). \quad (1.56)$$

Conditions 1.55 and 1.56 form the fundamental equations of the tightly stretched cable, from which all other relationships are derived. Eliminating n, we can determine the total horizontal tension from

$$H^3 - H^2 (H_0 - E\,F\,{}^t\varepsilon) - \frac{p^2\,l^2}{24} E\,F = 0. \quad (1.57)$$

This equation can, however, only be solved after it has been reduced to the normal form; it is therefore simpler to find n first from

$$n^3 + n \cdot \frac{3}{8}\left(\frac{H_0}{EF} - {}^t\varepsilon\right) - \frac{3}{64}\frac{p\,l}{EF} = 0. \quad (1.58)$$

From this we can determine H and H_p directly with the aid of Eq. 1.55. Equation 1.58 has only one real root, which can easily be found by trial and error with the aid of the slide rule. The maximum deflection is obtained for maximum p and heating, while the maximum cable force is obtained for maximum p and cooling.
When structures are subjected to the effects of wind, we must also determine the natural frequency. When μ is the mass, per unit length of span, of the vibrating structure (cable plus roof covering), we obtain the largest natural vibration period

$$\tau = 2\,l\sqrt{\frac{\mu}{H}}, \quad (1.59)$$

which should not exceed three seconds. For this reason the design pretension must be high.

1.4 Special Problems

1.4.1 *Optimum Deflection: Span Ratio*

A symmetrical nonpretensioned cable, whose weight per unit length is $g = \gamma F$, carries a load p (e.g., roofing) per unit length. We wish to determine the optimum deflection: span ratio, without taking into account specific local conditions. We shall first determine the value of n necessary for the cable cross section or volume to become minimum.
Since we must expect large deflections, we can no longer assume the cable curve to form a parabola, but must consider a catenary. Writing

$$k = \frac{q}{H} \quad (1.60)$$

for the curvature at the apex of the cable curve, we make use of the following formulas derived from Eq. 1.31 for $C_1 = C_2 = 0$:

$$z = -\frac{1}{k}\cosh k\,x, \quad (1.61a)$$

$$z'' = -k\cosh k\,x. \quad (1.61b)$$

The origin of coordinates is in this case located at a vertical distance

$1/k$ below the apex. We then have

$$n = \frac{f}{l} = \frac{1}{k\,l}\left(\cosh\frac{k\,l}{2} - 1\right). \tag{1.62}$$

From Eq. 1.6 we obtain

$S(x) = H \cdot \sqrt{1 + z'^2} = H \cdot \cosh k\,x$,

which attains its largest value at $x = \pm \frac{l}{2}$:

$$S = H \cdot \cosh\frac{k\,l}{2} = \frac{q}{k}\cosh\frac{k\,l}{2}. \tag{1.63}$$

The cable length is found from Eq. 1.32 to be

$$L = \frac{2}{k}\sinh\frac{k\,l}{2}. \tag{1.64}$$

We note that only part p of the total load is given, the weight of the cable depending on the required cross section:

$$q = \gamma \cdot F + p. \tag{1.65}$$

The cable force depends on the permissible cable stress σ:

$$\max S = \text{perm}\ \sigma \cdot F. \tag{1.66}$$

In order to determine the deflection: span ratio for which the cable cross section becomes minimum, we note that g and q have the same effect on S. We therefore must obtain the same value of n for both. Differentiating Eq. 1.63 and equating the result to zero, we obtain

$$\frac{\partial S}{\partial k} = 0 = -\frac{q}{k^2}\cosh\frac{k\,l}{2} + \frac{q\,l}{2\,k}\sinh\frac{k\,l}{2},$$

whence

$$\frac{k\,l}{2}\tanh\frac{k\,l}{2} = 1,$$

the solution of which is

$$\frac{k_1\,l}{2} = 1.1997 \approx 1.2. \tag{1.67a}$$

The corresponding deflection: span ratio is then

$$\frac{f_1}{l} = n_1 = 0.338. \tag{1.67b}$$

Figure 1.3 shows the dimensionless magnitudes $\frac{S}{q\,l}$ and $\frac{H}{q\,l}$ as functions of n.

In this connection we shall also determine what load p, referred to its own weight, a cable can carry. We separate the total load into its two components and introduce the length

$$r = \frac{\text{perm}\,\sigma}{\gamma}, \tag{1.68}$$

which for high-quality steel amounts to about 10 km. We then obtain, using Eqs. 1.63 and 1.66,

$$\frac{p}{g} = \frac{\frac{2\,r}{l} - \frac{2}{k\,l}\cosh\frac{k\,l}{2}}{\frac{2}{k\,l}\cosh\frac{k\,l}{2}}. \tag{1.69a}$$

For $\frac{r}{l} \geqslant 25$ we can always write

$$\frac{p}{g} \approx \frac{2\,r}{l} \cdot \frac{\frac{k\,l}{2}}{\cosh\frac{k\,l}{2}} \tag{1.69b}$$

instead. The expression $\frac{k\,l}{2}\Big/\cosh\frac{k\,l}{2}$ is shown in Fig. 1.3 as a function of n.

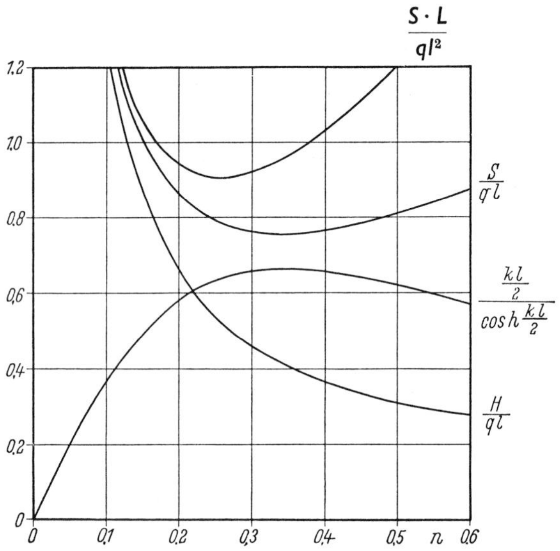

Fig. 1.3. Dimensionless Functions.

We can see that for a given cable cross section the maximum additional load is possible when $n_1 = 0.338$. When $l = 100$ m, this additional load amounts to 137 times the cable weight. This ratio is not even approximated with other types of structures, such as beams or framework, so that in view of the efficient utilization of their material, cables can be considered to be ideal load-carrying structures from the statical point of view.

When the cable volume for a given useful load is considered, we obtain the interesting result that a value of n differing from that given by Eq. 1.67b is the optimum value. Exact calculation shows that the result depends on r/l, i.e., on the properties of the material and on the span. We have, however, seen that the cable weight amounts to only a small fraction of the total load. We shall therefore consider the latter. The cable volume is, by Eqs. 1.63, 1.64 [and 1.66]

$$V = S \cdot L = \frac{q}{k^2}\sinh k\,l.$$

Differentiating with respect to k, and equating the result to zero, we obtain

$$\frac{\partial V}{\partial k} = 0 = -\frac{2\,q}{k^3}\sinh k\,l + \frac{q\,l}{k^2}\cosh k\,l$$

or

$$\frac{1}{k\,l} \cdot \tanh k\,l = 0.5.$$

This yields

$$k_2\,l = 1.915, \tag{1.70a}$$

or, inserted into Eq. 1.62,

$$\frac{f_2}{l} = n_2 = 0.258 \,. \tag{1.70b}$$

This value is less than that given by Eq. 1.67b. The dimensionless expression $\frac{S\,L}{q\,l^2}$ is shown in Fig. 1.3 as a function of n.

This theoretical analysis will not, of course, yield the most economical design of hanging roofs. Figure 1.3 shows that an excessive value of n is of less influence than a too small value. Comparison of Eqs. 1.67 and 1.70 also shows that for economy in material a smaller value of n should be selected. Although the horizontal tension is thus increased, the enclosed space (to be heated) is reduced if the cables are straighter, the cable length (and thus the roof area) is reduced, and, for equal clearances in height, the expensive structures for cable anchoring are lower.

1.4.2 *Maximum Span*

We conclude our discussion of the single cable by investigating the maximum span theoretically possible for a cable. We obtain from Eqs. 1.63, 1.65, and 1.66:

$$\sigma \cdot F = \frac{\gamma\,F + p}{k} \cosh \frac{k\,l}{2} \,.$$

Substituting $\frac{k\,l}{2}$ in accordance with Eq. 1.67a, we find

$$\max l = 1.3255 \frac{g}{q} \cdot r \,. \tag{1.71}$$

Inserting $r = 10$ km, this yields

$$\max l = 13.255 \frac{g}{q} \text{ km} \,.$$

However, the deflection is then

$$f = 4.48 \frac{g}{q} \text{ km} \,.$$

The properties of the material and the quality of the design can be judged by the maximum possible span at which the weight of the cable is just supported. If r is, without any safety factor, assumed to be the "rupture length"

$$R = \frac{\beta_z}{\delta} \,, \tag{1.72}$$

i.e., the length of a vertically suspended rod or thread which ruptures due to its dead weight, and $g = q$, we obtain

$$\max l = 1.3255\, R \,.$$

A prime-quality cable having an ultimate strength of $\beta_z = 22$ Mp/cm^2 has a rupture length of 28 km. Its theoretical maximum span is thus

$$\max \max l = 37.2 \text{ km} \,.$$

2 CABLE NETS ORTHOGONAL IN PLAN

2.1 Introduction

Nets that are orthogonal in plan (Figs. 2.2 to 2.6) fill an important place among the various forms of shallow nets. Their structure is uncomplicated, and they permit simple checks to determine the state of their installation. The cables of each family lie in the unloaded net in respectively parallel vertical planes, i.e., along the parametric curves if the cable net is represented as an ordinary Cartesian coordinate system.

Theoretical considerations and model tests show that the behavior of orthogonal nets under load differs only little from that of some other types of shallow nets. The latter can therefore also be analyzed by the formulas given here. This is true, e.g., for equal-mesh nets, in which the distances between the nodes (measured on the net surface) are equal, and for nets in which the cable curves follow the lines of principal curvature of the net surface.

At the nodes the cables can be interconnected by clamps in order to prevent relative displacements and to ensure sharing of the load by both families of cables.

Although architecturally cable-net structures are very similar to membranes and shells, they are quite distinct from the latter from the statical viewpoint. The behavior under load of cable nets is characterized by the negligibly small rigidity in shear of the space between the cables. The forces acting in a cable net cannot therefore be analyzed with the aid of the membrane theory of shells. Since textiles also have small rigidity in shear, and carry loads almost exclusively in the direction of the threads, they also in general belong statically to the (equal-mesh) cable nets. However, no sharp differentiation from membranes is possible for textiles.

The conditions are different for hanging roofs made of concrete cast in situ or of plate elements clamped together. Such structures are (at least as regards applied loads) rigid in shear and can therefore be analyzed by means of the known formulas of the membrane theory. In triangular-mesh cable nets every surface element is rigid in shear as long as no cables are slack. Unless laborious general compensation methods are used, satisfactory results are obtained by the membrane theory of shells; the sectional loads are then distributed over the cables of each of the three families in accordance with the equilibrium and deformation conditions.

This chapter is based on a previous paper[1] by the author. The analysis of orthogonal cable nets was also discussed by Roller[2] and Siev.[3] Whereas Eras and Elze[4] worked out a general numerical method for arbitrarily shaped nets, other authors restricted the problem formulated to orthogonal nets having parabolic cable curves and acted upon by uniform vertical loads. The condition of deformation continuity of both families of cables is usually satisfied only in the center of the net. It would exceed the scope of this book to give a complete bibliography on this subject: several other papers are referred to in Section 2.4.1.

The method described here is based on the geometrical conditions of the cable net, which is considered as a surface continuum. Only the net itself is assumed to have a regular structure; the boundary curves can be freely selected within the design conditions. The calculation is applicable to arbitrarily distributed loads, thermal expansion, and displacements of the cable ends. The distances between the cables may be nonuniform, the cable cross sections may vary, and the cables may be tensioned by springs. In view of the fact that the stresses in a cable can be determined more exactly than those in other load-carrying structures, such as frames and framework, in which idealization of the system to one consisting of thin rods already leads to inaccuracies, certain simplifications are permissible for cable nets. In this way, and in particular by introducing a so-called "null surface," a comparatively simple and straightforward calculation method has been developed, which can be adapted to any possible system of the type considered.

2.2 Differential Equations of the Cable Net

2.2.1 *Notation and Geometrical Fundamentals*

We base our analysis on a fixed right-handed coordinate system x, y, z with the orthonormal unit vectors $\mathfrak{e}_x$, $\mathfrak{e}_y$, and $\mathfrak{e}_z$ (Fig. 2.1).

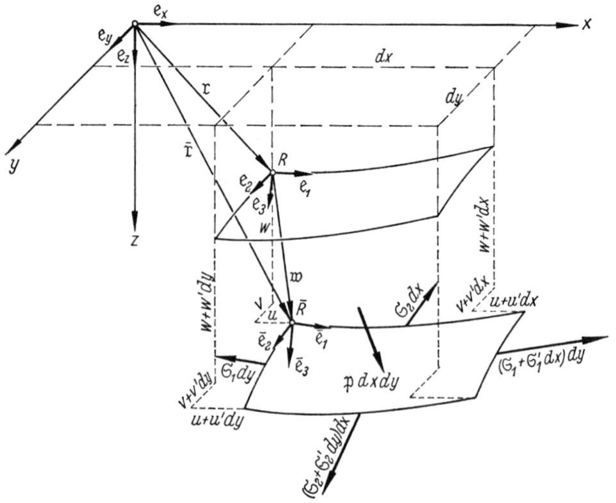

Fig. 2.1. Notation.

The net, which consists of individual tension members, is considered to be a continuum, so that a geometrical surface is analyzed.

The initial or null surface is defined as the surface that is formed by the net, in the absence of all loads (including dead weight), and

[1] F. K. Schleyer, *Über die Berechnung von Seilnetzen* (On the Calculation of Cable Nets), Dissertation, Technische Universität Berlin, 1960.

[2] Roller, *A függeszett tetöszerkezetek sztatikája* (Statistics of Hanging Roofs), Dissertation, University for Construction and Traffic Technology, Budapest, 1960; *Berechnung doppelt gekrümmter, gespannter hängender Dächer auf Grund der Theorie II. Ordnung* (Calculation of Doubly Curved Hanging Roofs Under Tension, Based on Second-Order Theory). *Bautechnik*, No. 2, 1963, pp. 48–52.

[3] A. Siev, *Stability of Prestressed Suspended Roofs*, Technion, Haifa, 1961.

[4] G. Eras and H. Elze, *Zur Berechnung und statisch vorteilhaften Formgebung von Seilnetzwerken* (Calculation and Statically Efficient Design of Cable-Net Systems). In *Hanging Roofs*, Proc. IASS, Paris, 1962.

due solely to pretensioning. Thus we need not include in the calculation those deformations and edge displacements caused by the pretensioning. The null surface of a nonpretensioned net is determined from the condition that all cables are untensioned and form straight lines between the nodes.

The null surface is defined by the vector of location

$$\mathfrak{r} = x \cdot \mathfrak{e}_x + y \cdot \mathfrak{e}_y + z\,(x, y) \cdot \mathfrak{e}_z \quad \text{or} \quad \mathfrak{r} = \{x, y, z\,(x, y)\}, \tag{2.1}$$

it being assumed that $\mathfrak{r}$ is single-valued and at least twice differentiable. In general we shall write the derivatives, e.g., of $\mathfrak{r}$, as follows:

$$\frac{\partial \mathfrak{r}}{\partial x} = \mathfrak{r}' \qquad \frac{\partial \mathfrak{r}}{\partial y} = \mathfrak{r}^{\cdot};$$

thus

$$\left.\begin{array}{ll} \mathfrak{r}' = \{1, 0, z'\} & \mathfrak{r}^{\cdot} = \{0, 1, z^{\cdot}\} \\ \mathfrak{r}'' = \{0, 0, z''\} & \mathfrak{r}^{\cdot\cdot} = \{0, 0, z^{\cdot\cdot}\} \end{array}\right\} \tag{2.2}$$

Writing

$$\left.\begin{array}{l} g_{11} = \mathfrak{r}'^2 = 1 + z'^2 \\ g_{12} = \mathfrak{r}' \cdot \mathfrak{r}^{\cdot} = z' \cdot z^{\cdot} \\ g_{22} = \mathfrak{r}^{\cdot 2} = 1 + z^{\cdot 2} \end{array}\right\} \tag{2.3}$$

we obtain the metric of the first fundamental (ground) form of the surface. The unit tangent and surface-normal vectors are then

$$\left.\begin{array}{l} \mathfrak{e}_1 = \dfrac{\mathfrak{r}'}{\sqrt{g_{11}}} = \dfrac{1}{\sqrt{g_{11}}} \cdot \{1, 0, z'\}, \\ \mathfrak{e}_2 = \dfrac{\mathfrak{r}^{\cdot}}{\sqrt{g_{22}}} = \dfrac{1}{\sqrt{g_{22}}} \cdot \{0, 1, z^{\cdot}\}, \\ \mathfrak{e}_3 = \mathfrak{e}_1 \times \mathfrak{e}_2 = \dfrac{1}{\sqrt{g}}\,(\mathfrak{r}' \times \mathfrak{r}^{\cdot}) = \dfrac{1}{\sqrt{g}} \{-z', -z^{\cdot}, 1\}, \end{array}\right\} \tag{2.4}$$

where g is the determinant of the metric tensor:

$$g = (\mathfrak{r}' \times \mathfrak{r}^{\cdot})^2 = g_{11} \cdot g_{22} - g_{12}^{\,2} = 1 + z'^2 + z^{\cdot 2} \geqslant 1\,. \tag{2.5}$$

This magnitude is also used to determine the surface element

$$d\,0 = \sqrt{g} \cdot dx \cdot dy\,. \tag{2.6}$$

The Gaussian curvature $K = (z''\,z^{\cdot\cdot} - z'^{\cdot 2}) \cdot g^{-2}$ is arbitrary, but must not change its sign in the region of the net. If $K > 0$, the surface is elliptically curved, and pretensioning of the net is impossible (cf. Section 2.3). The following expressions have been obtained for the most frequent case of a pretensioned hyperbolically curved cable net for which $K < 0$, but are in most cases also valid for nonpretensioned nets (see Section 2.5). For a cylindrical surface, $K = 0$ everywhere. Such a surface can be developed. Because of the small rigidity, pure cable nets cannot form cylindrical surfaces.

Unless the contrary is stated, all functions depend on x and y. We shall use subscripts x, y, and z for vectors or scalars referred to the fixed coordinate system, while subscripts 1, 2, and 3 will be used for magnitudes referred to the trihedron $\mathfrak{e}_1$, $\mathfrak{e}_2$, $\mathfrak{e}_3$.

When an external load is applied to the cable net, the temperature changes, or the edge points are displaced, a surface $\bar{\mathfrak{r}}$, different from $\mathfrak{r}$, is generally formed. A point

$$\bar{\mathfrak{r}} = \mathfrak{r} + \mathfrak{w} \tag{2.7}$$

then corresponds to each point of the initial surface, where, as in Eq. 1.2,

$$\mathfrak{w} = \{u\,(x, y), v\,(x, y), w\,(x, y)\} \tag{2.8}$$

is the vector of displacement of point R (Fig. 2.1).

We denote the geometrical magnitudes of the deformed surface by a stroke:

$$\left.\begin{array}{ll} \bar{z} = z + w & \\ \bar{\mathfrak{r}} = \{x + u, y + v, z + w\} & \\ \bar{\mathfrak{r}}' = \{1 + u', v', z' + w'\} & \bar{\mathfrak{r}}^{\cdot} = \{u^{\cdot}, 1 + v^{\cdot}, z^{\cdot} + w^{\cdot}\} \\ \bar{\mathfrak{r}}'' = \{u'', v'', z'' + w''\} & \bar{\mathfrak{r}}^{\cdot\cdot} = \{u^{\cdot\cdot}, v^{\cdot\cdot}, z^{\cdot\cdot} + w^{\cdot\cdot}\} \end{array}\right\} \tag{2.9}$$

$$\left.\begin{array}{l} \bar{g}_{11} = (1 + u')^2 + v'^2 + (z' + w')^2 \\ \bar{g}_{22} = u^{\cdot 2} + (1 + v^{\cdot})^2 + (z^{\cdot} + w^{\cdot})^2 \end{array}\right\} \tag{2.10}$$

$$\left.\begin{array}{l} \bar{\mathfrak{e}}_1 = \dfrac{1}{\sqrt{\bar{g}_{11}}} \cdot \bar{\mathfrak{r}}' = \dfrac{1}{\sqrt{\bar{g}_{11}}} \{1 + u', v', z' + w'\} \\ \bar{\mathfrak{e}}_2 = \dfrac{1}{\sqrt{\bar{g}_{22}}} \cdot \bar{\mathfrak{r}}^{\cdot} = \dfrac{1}{\sqrt{\bar{g}_{22}}} \{u^{\cdot}, 1 + v^{\cdot}, z^{\cdot} + w^{\cdot}\}\,. \end{array}\right\} \tag{2.11}$$

We should note that the distance of the deformed surface from the point (x_0, y_0, 0) is not $\bar{z}\,(x_0, y_0)$ but, more accurately, $\bar{z} - u \cdot \bar{z}' - v \cdot \bar{z}^{\cdot}$, all functions corresponding to the point (x_0, y_0).

2.2.2 *Equilibrium Conditions*

In contrast to other forms of cable nets, in the orthogonal cable net both families of cables lie initially in parallel vertical planes. The net forms a rectangular grid in plan (x, y-plane). The cables lie along the parametric curves $\mathfrak{r}\,(x, y_0)$ or $\mathfrak{r}\,(x_0, y)$ of the surface. We assume generally that the load-carrying cables are tensioned in the x-direction.

In practice we encounter mostly shallow nets in which the deflections of the cables are not large (approximately up to $f/l = 1/8$). This circumstance leads to considerable simplifications in the calculations. When the surface is inclined but only slightly curved, the x, y-plane of the coordinate system, instead of being horizontal, can be located so as to pass through the bisectors of the angles formed by the tangents to suitably placed sections of the surface. For the sake of simplicity we shall also call such a plane the plan.

To obtain a single-valued solution, we must consider the equilibrium of the deformed structure. It is advantageous to refer all forces, loads, and sectional magnitudes to unit plan area. Figure 2.1 shows a cable-net element of side lengths dx and dy. The initial position is shown on top, below it is shown displaced and deformed with the forces acting on it.

The cables are assumed to be perfectly flexible in bending. Hence, no moments act on them, and the cable forces are

$$\mathfrak{S}_1 \cdot dy = S_1 \cdot dy \cdot \bar{\mathfrak{e}}_1 \quad \text{and} \quad \mathfrak{S}_2 \cdot dx = S_2\, dx\, \bar{\mathfrak{e}}_2\,, \tag{2.12}$$

where $S_1 = |\mathfrak{S}_1|$ and $S_2 = |\mathfrak{S}_2|$ are the forces per unit width in plan.

The external load is

$$\mathfrak{p}(x, y) = \{p_x(x, y), p_y(x, y), p_z(x, y)\}\,, \tag{2.13}$$

referred to a unit area of the plan. Strictly speaking, $\mathfrak{p}$ (e.g., wind force) also depends on the surface deformations. However, when we consider the loads we can assume that the deformations of the structure are small. In particular, the surface elements dO and $d\bar{O}$, as well as the normal unit vectors $\mathfrak{e}_3$ and $\bar{\mathfrak{e}}_3$, before and after deformation will differ only by negligibly small magnitudes of higher order. We can thus assume that the load acting at a point $\bar{R}$ of the deformed cable net is equal to the load acting at point R of the initial surface.

However, the surface deformations can no longer be neglected when establishing the equilibrium conditions. The vector sum of all forces acting on the surface element can be found from inspection of Fig. 2.1. Only the increments of $\mathfrak{S}_1$ and $\mathfrak{S}_2$ are of interest:

$$\frac{\partial}{\partial x}(\mathfrak{S}_1\, d\,y)\, d\,x + \frac{\partial}{\partial y}(\mathfrak{S}_2\, d\,x)\, d\,y + \mathfrak{p}\, dx \cdot dy = 0\,.$$

The higher-order terms of the Taylor series for $\mathfrak{S}_1$ and $\mathfrak{S}_2$ are discarded in analogy to the theory of shells. Dividing by $dx \cdot dy$, we obtain a vector equation defining the equilibrium condition of an element cut out of the cable net:

$$\mathfrak{S}_1' + \mathfrak{S}_2^{\cdot} + \mathfrak{p} = 0\,. \tag{2.14}$$

Insertion of Eqs. 2.12 and 2.13 yields

$$\left(\frac{S_1}{\sqrt{g_{11}}} \cdot \bar{\mathfrak{r}}'\right)' + \left(\frac{S_2}{\sqrt{g_{22}}} \cdot \bar{\mathfrak{r}}^{\cdot}\right)^{\cdot} + \mathfrak{p} = 0\,. \tag{2.14a}$$

This equation differs only from the condition known from the membrane theory of shells in that no term containing the shearing force S_{12} is present. The problem cannot therefore be analyzed according to the membrane theory or any other first-order theory.

We form the component equations for three noncoplanar vectors $\mathfrak{e}$. For practical reasons the latter will be taken as $\mathfrak{e}_x, \mathfrak{e}_y$ and $\mathfrak{e}_z$. Since $\mathfrak{e}' = \mathfrak{e}^{\cdot} = 0$, we can rewrite Eq. 2.14a as follows:

$$\left(\frac{S_1}{\sqrt{g_{11}}} \cdot \bar{\mathfrak{r}}' \cdot \mathfrak{e}\right)' + \left(\frac{S_2}{\sqrt{g_{22}}}\, \bar{\mathfrak{r}}^{\cdot} \cdot \mathfrak{e}\right)^{\cdot} + \mathfrak{p} \cdot \mathfrak{e} = 0\,.$$

Taking into account Eqs. 2.9 and 2.13, we obtain

$$\left[\frac{S_1}{\sqrt{g_{11}}}(1 + u')\right]' + \left[\frac{S_2}{\sqrt{g_{22}}} \cdot u^{\cdot}\right]^{\cdot} + p_x = 0\,, \tag{2.15a}$$

$$\left[\frac{S_1}{\sqrt{g_{11}}} \cdot v'\right]' + \left[\frac{S_2}{\sqrt{g_{22}}}(1 + v^{\cdot})\right]^{\cdot} + p_y = 0\,, \tag{2.15b}$$

$$\left[\frac{S_1}{\sqrt{g_{11}}}(z' + w')\right]' + \left[\frac{S_2}{\sqrt{g_{22}}}(z^{\cdot} + w^{\cdot})\right]^{\cdot} + p_z = 0\,. \tag{2.15c}$$

If the components of $\mathfrak{p}$ are not given in the direction of the coordinate axes and per unit area of the plan, but as

$$\mathfrak{p} = p_1 \cdot \mathfrak{e}_1 + p_2 \cdot \mathfrak{e}_2 + p_3 \cdot \mathfrak{e}_3 \tag{2.13a}$$

in the direction of the surface tangents and the normal, referred to unit surface area, we make use of the following formulas:

$$p_x = \sqrt{\frac{g}{g_{11}}} \cdot p_1 - z' \cdot p_3\,, \tag{2.16a}$$

$$p_y = \sqrt{\frac{g}{g_{22}}} \cdot p_2 - z^{\cdot}\, p_3\,, \tag{2.16b}$$

$$p_z = z' \sqrt{\frac{g}{g_{11}}} \cdot p_1 + z^{\cdot} \sqrt{\frac{g}{g_{22}}} \cdot p_2 + p_3\,, \tag{2.16c}$$

or

$$p_z = z' \cdot p_x(p_1, p_3) + z^{\cdot}(p_2, p_3) + g \cdot p_3\,. \tag{2.16d}$$

We simplify Eqs. 2.15, in which the unknown cable forces are related to the equally unknown deformations ($\bar{g} \neq g$), by introducing the horizontal component H of S. Since the deformation differentials are small, we can neglect u' and $v^{\cdot}$ in comparison with unity. We thus obtain

$$H_x = \mathfrak{S}_1 \cdot \mathfrak{e}_x = \frac{S_1}{\sqrt{\bar{g}_{11}}} \cdot (1 + u') \approx \frac{S_1}{\sqrt{g_{11}}} \tag{2.17a}$$

(cf. Eq. 1.6) and

$$H_y = \mathfrak{S}_2 \cdot \mathfrak{e}_y = \frac{S_2}{\sqrt{\bar{g}_{22}}}(1 + v^{\cdot}) \approx \frac{S_2}{\sqrt{g_{22}}}\,. \tag{2.17b}$$

We already stated in Section 2.2.1 that all deformations are measured from the initial state, in which the cables are already pretensioned. The cable forces therefore consist of two components

$$S = S_0 + S_p\,, \tag{2.18a}$$

the first representing the pretensioning, the second the external loads, temperature effects, and changes in the boundary conditions (deformations of the edge members). We showed in Section 1.1.2 that the small change in direction of the cable forces S_0 during deformation can be neglected. Horizontal tensions and cable forces can then be linearly superimposed, and we have, with sufficient accuracy:

$$H = H_0 + H_p\,, \tag{2.18b}$$

$$H_{x0} = \frac{S_{10}}{\sqrt{\bar{g}_{11}}} \approx \frac{S_{10}}{\sqrt{g_{11}}}\,, \quad H_{xp} = \frac{S_{1p}}{\sqrt{\bar{g}_{11}}} \approx \frac{S_{1p}}{\sqrt{g_{11}}}\,, \tag{2.19a}$$

and accordingly for the y-direction

$$H_{y0} = \frac{S_{20}}{\sqrt{\bar{g}_{22}}} \approx \frac{S_{20}}{\sqrt{g_{22}}}\,, \quad H_{yp} = \frac{S_{2p}}{\sqrt{\bar{g}_{22}}} \approx \frac{S_{2p}}{\sqrt{g_{22}}}\,. \tag{2.19b}$$

The equilibrium conditions 2.15 become, when Eqs. 2.17 are inserted:

$$H_x' + (H_y \cdot u^{\cdot})^{\cdot} + p_x = 0\,, \tag{2.20a}$$

$$(H_x v')' + H_y^{\cdot} + p_y = 0\,, \tag{2.20b}$$

$$[H_x (z' + w')]' + [H_y (z^{\cdot} + w^{\cdot})]^{\cdot} + p_z = 0\,, \tag{2.20c}$$

in which the horizontal forces have to be resolved into H_0 and H_p. These three differential equations contain the five unknowns H_x, H_y, u, v and w, which all depend on x and y. We therefore need two more equations relating the horizontal tensions to the deformations.

2.2.3 *Elasticity Conditions*

The cable strain was obtained in Section 1.1.3 as a function of the displacements. Since $y' = 0$, we have (cf. Eq. 1.14)

$$\varepsilon_1 = \frac{u' + z' w'}{1 + z'^2} + \frac{v'^2 + w'^2}{2\,(1 + z'^2)^2} \approx \frac{u' + z' w'}{g_{11}}\,. \tag{2.21a}$$

For the y-direction we obtain similarly

$$\varepsilon_2 = \frac{v^{\cdot} + z^{\cdot} w^{\cdot}}{1 + z^{\cdot 2}} + \frac{u^{\cdot 2} + w^{\cdot 2}}{2\,(1 + z^{\cdot 2})^2} \approx \frac{v^{\cdot} + z^{\cdot} w^{\cdot}}{g_{22}}\,. \tag{2.21b}$$

Henceforth we shall neglect the second term in these expressions, which is insignificant as compared with the first.

We also give (without derivation) an expression for the changes in the angles of the surface element. The increment ϑ of the angle between the directions $\mathfrak{e}_1$ and $\mathfrak{e}_2$ is approximately

$$\vartheta \approx -\,(u^{\cdot} + v' + z' w^{\cdot} + z^{\cdot} w')\,. \tag{2.21c}$$

We shall not need this value for the statical analysis. However, it will be used, in addition to ε, when we investigate whether the roof covering selected, and in particular the sealing, can take up the expected strains and distortions.

For the formulation of Hooke's law we refer to Eqs. 1.17 and 1.18 and the relevant observations. We obtain

$$\varepsilon_1 = \frac{S_{1p}}{E_x F_x} + {}^t\varepsilon_x\,, \tag{2.22a}$$

$$\varepsilon_2 = \frac{S_{2p}}{E_y F_y} + {}^t\varepsilon_y\,, \tag{2.22b}$$

where E_x and F_x denote, respectively, the modulus of elasticity and the cross-sectional area of the member tensioned in the x-direction. The cross-sectional area is referred to the width in plan:

$$F_x = \frac{\text{Cross-sectional area of a single cable}}{\text{Distance in plan between cables}}\,. \tag{2.23}$$

Both the distances between the cables and the cross-sectional areas (even for individual cables) may be variable.

No restrictions are imposed on the temperature distribution over the cable-net surface. We can thus also assume insulation from one side. If the two families of cables are made of different materials, we may have ${}^t\varepsilon_x = {}^t\varepsilon_y$.

Combining Eqs. 2.21a and 2.22a, and taking into account Eq. 2.19a, we obtain the required relationship between horizontal tension and displacements:

$$H_{xp} = D_x\,(x, y) \cdot (u' + z' w' - g_{11} \cdot {}^t\varepsilon_x)\,. \tag{2.24a}$$

Similarly, for the y-direction,

$$H_{yp} = D_y\,(x, y)\,(v^{\cdot} + z^{\cdot} w^{\cdot} - g_{22} \cdot {}^t\varepsilon_y)\,. \tag{2.24b}$$

Here

$$D_x\,(x, y) = \frac{E_x F_x}{(g_{11})^{3/2}} = \frac{E_x F_x}{(1 + z'^2)^{3/2}} \tag{2.25a}$$

and

$$D_y\,(x, y) = \frac{E_y F_y}{g_{22}^{\ 3/2}} = \frac{E_y F_y}{(1 + z^{\cdot 2})^{3/2}} \tag{2.25b}$$

are rigidity functions which depend solely on the dimensions and mechanical properties of the cable net.

In practice the cross-sectional area of each cable remains constant over its length, so that we can assume

$$\frac{\partial}{\partial x}(E_x F_x) = 0\,, \qquad \frac{\partial}{\partial y}(E_y F_y) = 0\,.$$

Since $g_{11}' = 2\,\mathfrak{r}'\,\mathfrak{r}'' = 2\,z'\,z''$,
we obtain

$$D_x' = -\,D_x \cdot \frac{3}{g_{11}} \cdot z' \cdot z''$$

and a similar expression for the y-direction. Eqs. 2.24 can now be differentiated.

2.2.4 *Differential Equations*

We now return to the equilibrium conditions. For the initial state ($H_x = H_{x0}$, $H_y = H_{y0}$, $p_x = p_y = p_z = 0$, ${}^t\varepsilon_x = {}^t\varepsilon_y = 0$) we have assumed $u = v = w = 0$, so that from Eqs. 2.20a–c there remains

$$\left.\begin{aligned} &H_{x0}' = 0\,,\\ &H^{\cdot}_{y0} = 0\,,\\ &H_{x0} \cdot z'' + H_{y0} \cdot z^{\cdot\cdot} = 0\,. \end{aligned}\right\} \tag{2.26a–c}$$

Inserting Eqs. 2.24 and 2.18b into Eqs. 2.20, we immediately discard the terms corresponding to Eqs. 2.26. We thus obtain

$$\begin{aligned} &D_x \Big[u'' + z'' w' + z' w'' - \frac{3}{g_{11}} z' z'' (u' + z' w') +\\ &\quad + z' z'' \,{}^t\varepsilon_x - g_{11}\,{}^t\varepsilon_x' \Big] + D_y \Big[(v^{\cdot} + z^{\cdot} w^{\cdot} -\\ &\quad - g_{22}{}^t\varepsilon_y) u^{\cdot\cdot} + (v^{\cdot\cdot} + z^{\cdot\cdot} w^{\cdot} + z^{\cdot} w^{\cdot\cdot}) u^{\cdot} - \frac{3}{g_{22}} z^{\cdot} z^{\cdot\cdot} (v^{\cdot} +\\ &\quad + z^{\cdot} w^{\cdot}) u^{\cdot} + (z^{\cdot} z^{\cdot\cdot}\,{}^t\varepsilon_y - g_{22}\,{}^t\varepsilon^{\cdot}_y)\, u^{\cdot} \Big] +\\ &\quad + H_{y0} \cdot u^{\cdot\cdot} + p_x = 0\,, \end{aligned} \tag{2.27a}$$

$$\begin{aligned} &D_y \Big[v^{\cdot\cdot} + z^{\cdot\cdot} w^{\cdot} + z^{\cdot} w^{\cdot\cdot} - \frac{3}{g_{22}} z^{\cdot} z^{\cdot\cdot} (v^{\cdot} + z^{\cdot} w^{\cdot}) +\\ &\quad + z^{\cdot} z^{\cdot\cdot}\,{}^t\varepsilon_y - g_{22}\,{}^t\varepsilon^{\cdot}_y \Big] + D_x \Big[(u' + z' w' -\\ &\quad - g_{11}\,{}^t\varepsilon_x) v'' + (u'' + z'' w' + z' w'') v' -\\ &\quad - \frac{3}{g_{11}} z' z'' (u' + z' w') v' + (z' z''\,{}^t\varepsilon_x - g_{11}\,{}^t\varepsilon_x') v' \Big] +\\ &\quad + H_{x0} v'' + p_y = 0\,, \end{aligned} \tag{2.27b}$$

$$D_x\left\{(u' + z'w' - g_{11}\,{}^t\varepsilon_x)\cdot(z'' + w'') + \left[u'' + z''w' + + z'w'' - \frac{3}{g_{11}} z'z''(u' + z'w') + z'z''\,{}^t\varepsilon_x - - g_{11}\,{}^t\varepsilon_x'\right]\cdot(z' + w')\right\} + D_y\left\{(v^{\cdot} + z^{\cdot}w^{\cdot} - g_{22}\,{}^t\varepsilon_y)\times \times(z^{\cdot\cdot} + w^{\cdot\cdot}) + \left[v^{\cdot\cdot} + z^{\cdot\cdot}w^{\cdot} + z^{\cdot}w^{\cdot\cdot} - \frac{3}{g_{22}} z^{\cdot}z^{\cdot\cdot}(v^{\cdot} + + z^{\cdot}w^{\cdot}) + z^{\cdot}z^{\cdot\cdot}\,{}^t\varepsilon_y - g_{22}\,{}^t\varepsilon^{\cdot}_y\right]\cdot(z^{\cdot} + w^{\cdot})\right\} + + H_{x0}\cdot w'' + H_{y0}\cdot w^{\cdot\cdot} + p_z = 0\,. \qquad (2.27c)$$

These three simultaneous nonlinear differential equations of the second order in u, v, and w have to be integrated for the postulated boundary conditions. The cable forces are then found from Eqs. 2.24 and 2.19.

In deriving these equations we made the following simplifications:
a. In determining H according to Eqs. 2.19 and in establishing the elasticity conditions 2.24 we neglected higher powers of the deformation differentials in relation to unity. This is permissible also within the scope of the second-order theory.

b. In order to express H as $H_0 + H_p$ and to introduce H into the equilibrium conditions we had to neglect u' and $z'w'$ and correspondingly $v^{\cdot}$ and $z^{\cdot}w^{\cdot}$ in relation to unity. For instance, we obtain from Eq. 2.21a for the x-direction $\varepsilon_1 = g_{11}^{-1}(u' + z'w') < (u' + z'w')$; the relative errors are thus of the order of the cable strain ε, being determined by the material of the cable and the permissible stresses. For the most unfavorable case $\sigma = 10$ Mp/cm² and $E = 1300$ Mp/cm² (braided cable) we find $\varepsilon = 10/1300 = 0.0077 \ll 1$.

However, it is not justifiable to eliminate $u^{\cdot}$ and v' in Eqs. 2.20a, b. These magnitudes represent the changes in mesh angle, measured in plan, caused by the transverse displacement of the cables, and are, unlike the cable strains, not limited a priori. Likewise, the vertical cable inclinations w' and $w^{\cdot}$ cannot be neglected in Eq. 2.20c.
For this reason the differential Eqs. 2.27 are nonlinear despite the simplifications enumerated above. The latter introduce only insignificant errors, so that in practice Eqs. 2.27 describe accurately the problem of the orthogonal cable net.

2.3 Initial (Null) State

2.3.1 *Pretensioning*

The initial state, in which the only forces acting are caused by pretensioning, is described by Eqs. 2.26. The first two expressions state that the horizontal tensions in the initial state are constant over each cable:

$$\left.\begin{aligned} H_{x0} &= H_{x0}(y)\,, \\ H_{y0} &= H_{y0}(x)\,. \end{aligned}\right\} \qquad (2.28a, b)$$

Since both forces must be positive, we also have

$$\frac{z''}{z^{\cdot\cdot}} < 0 \qquad (2.29)$$

This is the condition necessary for pretensioning in both directions to be possible at all. The surface of the cable net must therefore have a negative Gaussian curvature everywhere (saddle-shaped surface; a plane for which $z'' = z^{\cdot\cdot} = 0$ has no practical importance). Since for any case of loading the cables must be under tension, we find that the net *has* to be pretensioned. Otherwise, the individual carrying cables would take up the negative or positive loads independently; they would thus act like single cables and would have to be analyzed as such.

If $z''/z^{\cdot\cdot} > 0$, pretensioning is not possible. A comparatively high permanent load, of about 150 kp/m², is then required to prevent upward bulging, due to wind suction, of the roof membrane. This large dead weight is generally not required to seal the enclosed space; ballast is thus added to the roof and must be transmitted through the structure to the foundations.

For pretensioned nets we can determine the surface $z(x, y)$ from Eq. 2.26c if H_{x0} and H_{y0} as well as the edge curve are given. In practice, surface and edge curve are mostly given for architectural reasons. We then have to find the pretensioning forces with which the required surface can be obtained.

2.3.2 *Analysis of Some Surfaces*

We shall now consider the pretensioning distribution in some analytically definable surfaces.

The coordinates x and y do not occur as such in Eqs. 2.26. The projection in plan of the edge curve is therefore obviously arbitrary. Since Eq. 2.26c contains only the second derivatives of z, the surfaces (which for the sake of simplicity have been drawn on a rectangular plan) may be superimposed on any inclined plane $z = a + bx + cy$, provided the cable inclinations remain moderate.

2.3.2.1 Translation Surfaces in General

The simplest representation of a curved surface, also for analysis, is the form of a translation surface

$$z(x, y) = f(x) + g(y)\,, \qquad (2.30)$$

which has to satisfy the condition

$$\frac{z''}{z^{\cdot\cdot}} = \frac{f''}{g^{\cdot\cdot}} < 0\,.$$

From Eq. 2.26c, taking into account Eqs. 2.28, we obtain

$$H_{x0}(y)\cdot f''(x) + H_{y0}(x)\cdot g^{\cdot\cdot}(y) = 0$$

or

$$\frac{H_{x0}(y)}{g^{\cdot\cdot}(y)} = -\frac{H_{y0}(x)}{f''(x)}\,.$$

The left-hand side depends only on y, the right-hand side only on x; each side is therefore separately equal to an arbitrary constant C. We give positive signs to the horizontal tensions:

$$\left.\begin{aligned} H_{x0}(y) &= C \cdot g^{\cdot\cdot}(y)\,, \\ H_{y0}(x) &= -\,C \cdot f''(x)\,. \end{aligned}\right\} \quad (2.31a, b)$$

Writing

$$\varrho\,(x,\,y) = -\,\frac{z^{\cdot\cdot}}{z''} > 0\,, \qquad (2.32)$$

we obtain

$$H_{x0}(y) = \varrho\,(x,\,y) \cdot H_{y0}(x). \qquad (2.33)$$

The magnitude of the tensions remains undetermined, and only their ratio $\varrho\,(x,\,y)$ is given.

2.3.2.2 Quadratic Parabola as Generator

If we postulate $H_{x0}(y) = H_{x0} = \text{const}$ and also $H_{y0}(x) = H_{y0} = \text{const}$, we obtain from Eqs. 2.31:

$$f\,(x) = -\,\frac{H_{y0}}{C}\,(a_0 + a_1\,x + a_2\,x^2)\,,$$

$$g\,(y) = +\,\frac{H_{x0}}{C}\,(b_0 + b_1\,y + b_2\,y^2)\,,$$

where a_n and b_n are arbitrary constants. [In fact, a_2 and b_2 are not arbitrary but equal 1/2.]

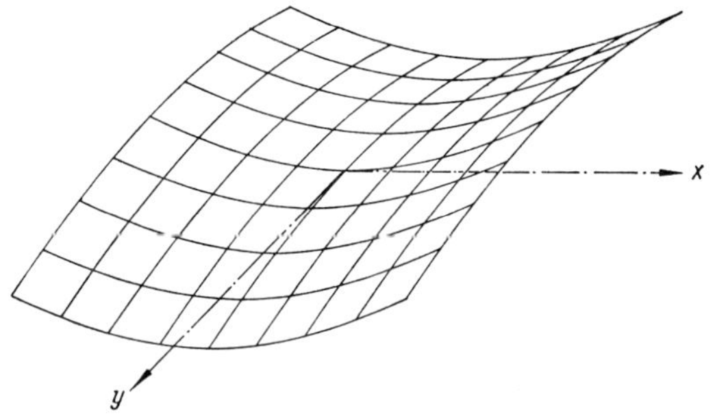

Fig. 2.2. Hyperbolic Paraboloid.

The surface obtained is a hyperbolic paraboloid (Fig. 2.2). After translation of the origin, using the same variables, we have

$$z\,(x,\,y) = -\,\frac{k_x}{2}\,x^2 + \frac{k_y}{2}\,y^2\,. \qquad (2.34)$$

The magnitudes of the curvatures at the apexes are generally denoted by k_x and k_y We then have

$$H_{x0} = C \cdot k_y\,, \qquad H_{y0} = C \cdot k_x\,,$$

$$H_{x0} = \frac{k_y}{k_x} \cdot H_{y0} = \varrho \cdot H_{y0}\,, \qquad (2.35)$$

where ϱ is independent of x and y. The cables lie along the parabolic generators.

The horizontal tensions induced by pretensioning and the curvatures z'' and $z^{\cdot\cdot}$ are constant. This surface can therefore be analyzed with particular ease. Consequently we shall therefore attempt in many cases to approximate other saddle-shaped surfaces with slight inclinations by hyperbolic paraboloids (cf. Section 2.4.5).

The particular case of an axisymmetrical paraboloid $z = a \cdot x \cdot y$ cannot be included here, since in it the cables have no curvature in the direction of the straight generator, as, e.g., the pretensioning members in the "hp shell" (Silberkuhl System).

2.3.2.3 Catenary as Generator

When the tension members have the shapes of catenaries (cf. Section 1.2.2), we obtain the surface

$$z = -\,\frac{1}{k_x}\cosh k_x \cdot x + \frac{1}{k_y}\cosh k_y \cdot y\,.$$

Equations 2.31 then yield directly

$$H_{x0}(y) = C \cdot k_y \cdot \cosh k_y \cdot y\,,$$

$$H_{y0}(x) = C \cdot k_x \cdot \cosh k_x \cdot x\,,$$

$$H_{x0}(y) = \frac{k_y}{k_x}\,\frac{\cosh k_y \cdot y}{\cosh k_x \cdot x} \cdot H_{y0}(x)\,.$$

The curvatures at the apexes of the generators are again denoted by k_x and k_y. The cables intersecting the z-axis have the smallest horizontal tensions.

2.3.2.4 Trigonometric Functions as Generators

Setting

$$z = \frac{k_x}{\alpha^2}\cos\alpha\,x - \frac{k_y}{\beta^2}\cos\beta\,y\,,$$

we obtain from Eqs. 2.31:

$$H_{x0}(y) = C \cdot k_y \cdot \cos\beta\,y\,,$$

$$H_{y0}(x) = C \cdot k_x \cdot \cos\alpha\,x\,.$$

The amount of pretensioning of the cables decreases with the distance of the latter from the origin.

The trigonometric functions cannot be continued indefinitely. Since the Gaussian curvature must be negative over the entire surface, only the region of one half-wave is possible in the x- and y-directions (Fig. 2.3).

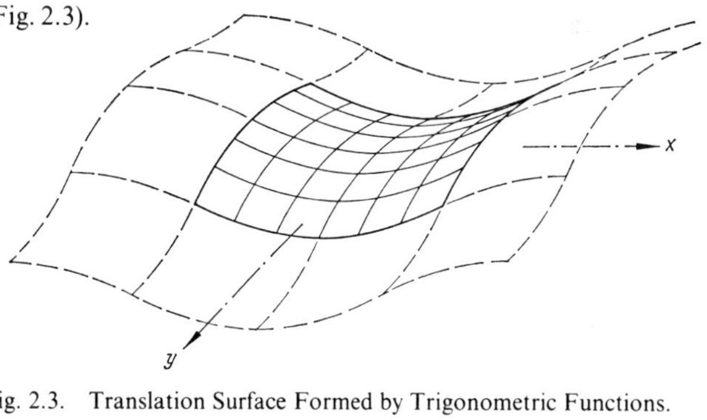

Fig. 2.3. Translation Surface Formed by Trigonometric Functions.

Thus

$$|\,x\,| \leqslant \frac{\pi}{2\,\alpha}\,, \qquad |\,y\,| \leqslant \frac{\pi}{2\,\beta}\,.$$

The edge cables are therefore not pretensioned. This theoretical limit should, however, not be approached in practice. The cables of each family should be under tension for any case of loading. For $x = \pm\frac{\pi}{2\,\alpha}$ this is not possible for the case of loading by dead weight, since $H_{y0} = 0$. We must therefore select α and β, so that we obtain approximately

$$|\,x\,| \leqslant \frac{\pi}{4\,\alpha}\,, \qquad |\,y\,| \leqslant \frac{\pi}{4\,\beta}\,.$$

2.3.2.5. Circle as Generator

Setting

$$z = -\frac{1}{k_x}\left(1 - \sqrt{1 - k_x^2 x^2}\right) + \frac{1}{k_y}\left(1 - \sqrt{1 - k_y^2 y^2}\right),$$

we obtain a translation surface whose generators are circles. We discard the negative square roots; the function is then single-valued. The origin lies at the saddle point. Eqs. 2.31 then yield

$$H_{x0}(y) = C \cdot k_y \cdot (1 - k_y^2 y^2)^{-3/2},$$

$$H_{y0}(x) = C \cdot k_x \cdot (1 - k_x^2 \cdot x^2)^{-3/2}.$$

The cables near the edges are more highly pretensioned than those passing through the origin.

2.3.2.6. Surfaces Defined as Products, in General

An interesting group of surfaces is obtained by writing

$$z(x, y) = f(x) \cdot g(y).$$

Eq. 2.26c then yields the equilibrium condition

$$H_{x0}(y) \cdot f''(x) \cdot g(y) + H_{y0}(x) \cdot f(x) \cdot g^{\cdot\cdot}(y) = 0.$$

Separating variables, we obtain

$$H_{x0}(y)\frac{g(y)}{g^{\cdot\cdot}(y)} = -H_{y0}(x)\frac{f(x)}{f''(x)}.$$

The same reasoning as in Section 2.3.2.1 leads to the independent equations

$$\left.\begin{aligned} f''(x) + \frac{H_{y0}(x)}{C} \cdot f(x) &= 0, \\ g^{\cdot\cdot}(y) - \frac{H_{x0}(y)}{C} \cdot g(y) &= 0. \end{aligned}\right\} \quad (2.36a, b)$$

We can find H_{x0} and H_{y0} when f and g are known, and vice versa.

2.3.2.7 Wave Surfaces

Assuming (as in Section 2.3.2.1)

$$H_{x0}(y) = H_{x0} = \text{const},$$

and

$$H_{y0}(x) = H_{y0} = \text{const},$$

we obtain directly from Eq. 2.36a the general solution

$$f(x) = a_1 \cos a\,x + b_1 \sin \alpha\,x,$$

where a_1 and b_1 are arbitrary constants, and $\alpha^2 = H_{y0}/C$.

Since $\sin \alpha x = \cos\left(\alpha x + \frac{\pi}{2}\right)$,

we need retain only the first term. Eq. 2.36b yields

$$g(y) = a_2 \cosh \beta\,y + b_2 \sinh \beta\,y,$$

where

$$\beta^2 - H_{x0}/C.$$

The surfaces that satisfy the condition of constant horizontal tensions are thus

$$z = a \cdot \cos \alpha\,x \cdot \cosh \beta\,y \quad (2.37a)$$

and

$$z = b \cdot \cos \alpha\,x \cdot \sinh \beta\,y. \quad (2.37b)$$

The magnitudes of the pretensioning forces are arbitrary, as before. Their ratio is $\varrho = \beta^2/\alpha^2$.

Equation 2.37a represents a saddle-shaped wave surface (Fig. 2.4), which can be continued indefinitely in the x-direction.

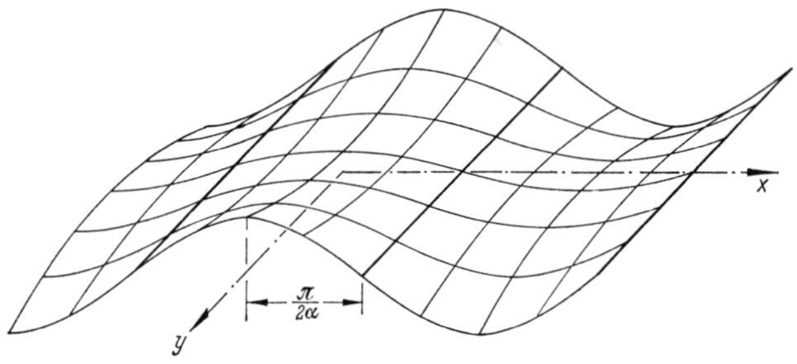

Fig. 2.4. Symmetrical Wave Surface.

If $x = \frac{\pi}{2\alpha}(1 \pm 2n)$ (where n is an integer) one cable of one family is straight; however, in contrast to the surface discussed in Section 2.3.2.4, this cable is pretensioned exactly like the others. The surface may have a straight edge along this straight line. The two families of cables interchange their duties of load carrying and tensioning from half-wave to half-wave.

The surface defined by Eq. 2.37b is periodically twisted. (Fig. 2.5). Besides the straight lines mentioned just now, it also contains a straight line $y = 0$.

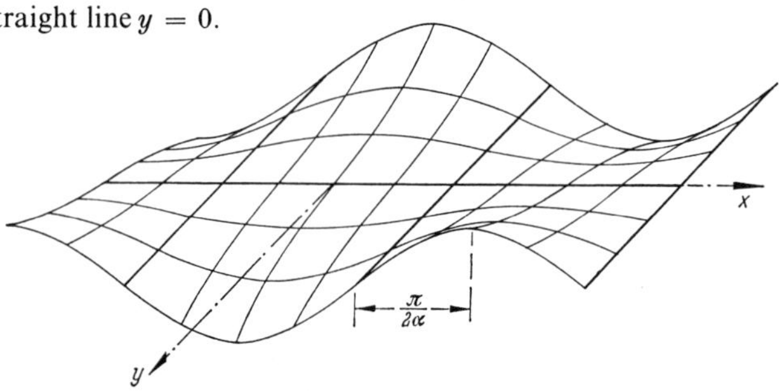

Fig. 2.5. Antimetrical Wave Surface.

With the aid of such a surface we can obtain a cable net bounded on three sides by straight lines lying in one plane. Both types of surfaces have the disadvantage that the curvature in both families of cables vanishes along the straight lines. These regions therefore tend to flap badly in the wind.

For cables extending in the x-direction over an even number of half-waves, the horizontal tensions caused by a symmetrical load (e.g., by dead weight or snow) vanish unless the points of inflection or other intermediate points are fixed in the horizontal direction. The load has then to be taken up by the cables lying in the y-direction. However, this pattern of behavior under load is obtained from the linearized theory and, in the above case, represents only a first approximation. When the horizontal displacements are taken into account it is found that a net consisting of two half-waves, as shown in Fig. 2.5, can also carry an arbitrary load. Although the cables form wave lines in both directions, a uniformly distributed vertical load can be taken up, although in this case the vertical and horizontal displacements will be fairly large. The number of calculations increases greatly in this case, since the nonlinear terms of the exact theory must be included throughout.

2.3.2.8 Biquadratic Function

The biquadratic function

$$z = c \cdot (a^2 - x^2) \cdot (b^2 + y^2)$$

represents a surface with two straight parallel edges (Fig. 2.6).

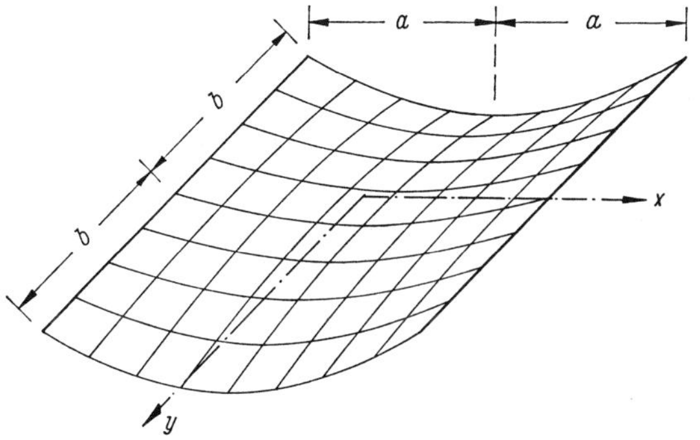

Fig. 2.6. Cable Net with Two Straight Edges.

However, it cannot form a null surface everywhere, since by Eqs. 2.36:

$$H_{x0} = C \cdot \frac{1}{b^2 + y^2},$$

$$H_{y0} = C \cdot \frac{1}{a^2 - x^2}.$$

For $x = \pm a$ this condition can be satisfied only by $H_{y0} = \infty$.

2.3.2.9 Other Surfaces

Another surface with two parallel straight edges, which is suitable for roofing rectangular rooms, is defined by the function

$$z = c \cdot \cos \alpha x \cdot (b^2 + y^2),$$

where

$$\alpha = \frac{\pi}{2a}.$$

Its appearance is similar to the surface shown in Fig. 2.6. The required pretensioning forces are

$$H_{x0}(y) = C \cdot \frac{2}{b^2 + y^2},$$

$$H_{y0} = C \cdot \alpha^2 = \text{const}.$$

The number of such examples could be increased indefinitely. A translation surface may, of course, also be of mixed form, e.g., $z = a \cos \alpha x + b y^2$.

For H_{x0} = const and H_{y0} = const we can easily transform Eq. 2.26c into the Laplacian differential equation $z'' + z^{\cdot\cdot} = 0$ so that the solutions of this equation define null surfaces with constant initial tensions. An example is the function

$$z = a \cdot x^2 \cdot y - b \cdot y^3/3,$$

for which

$$H_{x0} = b \cdot C \quad \text{and} \quad H_{y0} = a \cdot C.$$

Superposition of the principal null surfaces and the corresponding initial tensions is possible by virtue of the linearity of Eqs. 2.26.

This opens unlimited possibilities to the architect. Eqs. 2.26 can also be rewritten as difference equations and solved numerically.

No simple formulas can be given for cable nets whose boundaries depend considerably on the initial tension, as is the case when edge cables are provided. The null surface can then be determined with the aid of a model; refinements in the measured results should thereafter be introduced by means of the preceding formulas.

2.4 Principal Equations of the Orthogonal Cable Net

2.4.1 *Linearization*

The differential Eqs. 2.27, which describe the problem of a shallow arbitrarily loaded cable net, can be solved directly, if at all, only for a few special cases with certain boundary conditions. Given the same null surface and loading, the solution depends greatly on the lengths of the individual cables, i.e., on the shape of the edge.

The problem can be considerably simplified, and then analyzed by approximations, when the following restrictions are made:

We consider a simple cable-net surface, e.g., the translation surface of two parabolas;

the cables of each family have the same cross-sectional area and are equally spaced;

the edge is regular, forming, e.g., a rectangle or ellipse in plan;

no horizontal loads p_x or p_y are applied;

edge displacements are excluded;

the horizontal displacement components (which also occur with a purely vertical load) are neglected.

Equation 2.20c then yields the simple equilibrium condition

$$H_x(y) \cdot (z'' + w'') + H_y(x) \cdot (z^{\cdot\cdot} + w^{\cdot\cdot}) + p_z = 0, \qquad (2.38a)$$

which could have been obtained directly without the preceding reasoning.

We can solve this equation by trial and error, estimating the horizontal tensions as functions of y and x.[1] Where the null surface is given we can determine the deflection w from point to point. Two conditions for the cable length then determine new values of H. These will in general differ from the estimated values. The procedure is repeated until agreement is obtained; at each step we have to compute the numerous unknowns w from another linear system of equations.

[1] H. Bandel, *Das orthogonale Seilnetz hyperbolisch-parabolischer Form unter vertikalen Lastzuständen und Temperaturänderung* (The Orthogonal Cable Net of Hyperbolic-Parabolic Form Under Vertical Loads and Varying Temperatures), *Bauingenieur* 34, No. 10, 1959, pp. 394–401.

Moenaert[1] and Balgac[2] considered a shallow translation surface generated by two parabolas and subjected to a vertical uniformly distributed load. The only condition satisfied was that the center of each carrying cable had the same deflection as the center of a tension cable.

An indirect method is also possible.[1] Resolving the horizontal tensions into H_0 and H_p, and taking into account the conditions 2.26, we can rewrite Eq. 2.38a as follows:

$$H_{x0} \cdot w'' + H_{y0}\, w^{\cdot\cdot} + H_{xp}\, z'' + H_{yp}\, z^{\cdot\cdot} + H_{xp}\, w'' + + H_{yp}\, w^{\cdot\cdot} + p_z = 0 \,. \tag{2.38b}$$

In most cases we can also neglect the last two terms containing H_p. Assuming an appropriate expression for $w\,(x, y)$, which satisfies the condition $w = 0$ at the edge, we can determine H_p from the changes in cable length. Inserting these values into Eq. 2.38b, we obtain the load $p_z\,(x, y)$ corresponding to the selected function w. Conversely, we can estimate w and H_p from p_z. This procedure is restricted to a few cases for which formulas can easily be set up; the attainable accuracy depends on the number of admissible functions w. A worked example is given in Section 2.8.7.

Finally, we refer to the approximations in Section 2.6.

As already stated, we do not intend to analyze special cases; rather, a general procedure will be given by which the cable forces and deformations can be determined for any possible case of loading and boundaries. For simple special cases we then obtain considerable simplifications automatically, or become able to solve the problem by approximations.

We shall make use of Eqs. 2.20. Taking into account conditions 2.26a–c for the initial state, and resolving the horizontal tensions into H_0 and H_p, we obtain

$$H_{xp}' + H_{y0}\, u^{\cdot\cdot} + H_{yp}^{\cdot} \cdot u^{\cdot} + H_{yp} \cdot u^{\cdot\cdot} + p_x = 0 \tag{2.39a}$$

$$H_{yp}^{\cdot} + H_{x0}\, v'' + H_{xp}'\, v' + H_{xp}\, v'' + p_y = 0 \tag{2.39b}$$

$$H_{x0} \cdot w'' + H_{xp}'\,(z' + w') + H_{xp}\,(z'' + w'') + H_{y0}\, w^{\cdot\cdot} + + H_{yp}^{\cdot}\,(z^{\cdot} + w^{\cdot}) + H_{yp}\,(z^{\cdot\cdot} + w^{\cdot\cdot}) + p_z = 0 \,. \tag{2.39c}$$

If H_x and H_y are of the same order of magnitude, obviously $H_{yp} \cdot u^{\cdot} \ll H_{xp}$, hence in Eq. 2.39a, $H_{yp}^{\cdot} \cdot u^{\cdot} + H_{yp} \cdot u^{\cdot\cdot} = (H_{yp} \cdot u^{\cdot})^{\cdot} \ll H_{xp}'$, $H_{y0} \cdot u^{\cdot\cdot} \ll H_{xp}'$.

In Eq. 2.39a we first discard the terms containing H_y, and by the same reasoning, the terms containing H_x in Eq. 2.39b. In Eq. 2.39c we neglect w in relation to z. The expressions $H_{x0} \cdot w''$ and $H_{y0} \cdot w^{\cdot\cdot}$ are mostly small in comparison with the other terms; however, they cannot be neglected since otherwise no single-valued result is obtained, as will be shown.

These simplifications yield

$$\left.\begin{aligned} &H_{xp}' + p_x = 0\,,\\ &H_{yp}^{\cdot} + p_y = 0\,,\\ &H_{xp} \cdot z'' + H_{x0} \cdot w'' + H_{yp} \cdot z^{\cdot\cdot} + H_{y0} \cdot w^{\cdot\cdot} -\\ &\quad - p_x \cdot z' - p_y \cdot z^{\cdot} + p_z = 0\,. \end{aligned}\right\} \tag{2.40a–c}$$

The last equation was obtained by inserting Eqs. 2.40a, b into the simplified Eq. 2.39c.

We thus neglect in the equilibrium conditions all those terms containing the unknown H_p together with the unknown displacements, i.e., all terms in Eqs. 2.27 that contain products of the displacement derivatives. As regards Eqs. 2.40a, b, this means that the equilibrium conditions are satisfied for the undeformed structure. This statement is, however, not true for Eq. 2.40c, in which two terms containing w have been retained. Although the problem has been linearized, it has not been reduced to the ordinary first-order theory.

The results of the linearized calculations describe fairly accurately the actual behavior under load of the cable net, provided the displacements are not excessive. The terms which were discarded have the dimension of a distributed load and can thus be considered as additional loads $p^\star$:

$$\begin{aligned} p_x^\star &= (H_{y0} + H_{yp}) \cdot u^{\cdot\cdot} + H_{yp}^{\cdot}\, u^{\cdot}\,,\\ p_y^\star &= (H_{x0} + H_{xp}) \cdot v'' + H_{xp}' \cdot v'\,,\\ p_z^\star &= H_{xp} \cdot w'' + H_{xp}'\, w' + H_{yp}\, w^{\cdot\cdot} + H_{yp}^{\cdot}\, w^{\cdot}\,. \end{aligned}$$

Practical calculations show that $p_x^\star$ and $p_y^\star$ have, in general, a negligible influence on the final result. We can therefore express H_{xp}' and $H_{yp}^{\cdot}$ with the aid of Eqs. 2.40a, b:

$$\left.\begin{aligned} p_x^\star &= (H_{y0} + H_{yp}) \cdot u^{\cdot\cdot} - p_y \cdot u^{\cdot}\,,\\ p_y^\star &= (H_{x0} + H_{xp}) \cdot v'' - p_x \cdot v'\,,\\ p_z^\star &= H_{xp} \cdot w'' + H_{yp} \cdot w^{\cdot\cdot} - p_x \cdot w' - p_y \cdot w^{\cdot}\,. \end{aligned}\right\} \tag{2.41a–c}$$

When H_{xp}, H_{yp}, u, v and w have been determined according to the linear theory, the influence of the nonlinear terms can be estimated by comparing the additional loads $p^\star$ with the actual values p. This is best done by determining the load function $\mathfrak{P}^\star\,(x, y)$ from $p^\star$ (see Section 2.4.3). Edge displacements can thus also be taken into account. If $\mathfrak{P}^\star$ can no longer be neglected in relation to $\mathfrak{P}$, we can determine corrections $H_{yp}^\star, H_{xp}^\star, u^\star, v^\star$ and $w^\star$ by a repeat calculation which, except for the load, is the same as the first. The corrections have to be superimposed on the first results.

We can obtain results more quickly, and can usually neglect $\mathfrak{P}^\star$ altogether, if, with the aid of a formula, to be given later, we can first find approximate magnitudes $H_{xp}^{(1)}$ and $H_{yp}^{(1)}$ and insert these into Eq. 2.40c together with H_{x0} and H_{y0}. This yields

$$p_z^\star = (H_{xp} - H_{xp}^{(1)}) \cdot w'' + (H_{yp} - H_{yp}^{(1)}) \cdot w^{\cdot\cdot} - - p_x \cdot w' - p_y \cdot w^{\cdot}\,, \tag{2.41d}$$

where the first two terms are generally negligible.

To the corrections obtained by means of the linearized formulas there again correspond nonlinear terms $\mathfrak{w}^{\star\star}$ and $H_p^{\star\star}$ which can be found in a similar manner. In practice, however, we shall be

[1] Moenaert, *Dächer und Wände aus vorgespannten Seilen* (Roofs and Walls of Prestressed Cables), *Acier Stahl Steel* 25, 1960, pp. 299–305.

[2] E. Balgac, *Die neue Ausstellungshalle der Texilmesse in Leskovac* (The New Exhibition Hall of the Textile Fair in Leskovac), *Beton- und Stahlbetonbau* 56, No. 7, 1961, pp. 157–163.

[3] G. Eras and H. Elze, *Berechnungsverfahren für vorgespannte, doppelt gekrümmte Seilnetzwerke* (Calculation Methods for Prestressed, Doubly Curved Cable-Net Structures), *Bauplanung-Bautechnik*, No. 7, 1961.

able to omit this third (and also the ensuing) step. No general estimate of the order of the nonlinear terms can be made, although the worked example at the end of this book may give an idea on this subject.

We note that the forces acting in a cable net depend also on the displacements of the suspension points. If the cables are fixed singly or in groups, e.g., to trestles, the deformations of the latter can be calculated in advance and taken into account from the beginning when the cable net is analyzed. If the net is fixed in comparatively rigid arches the deformations of the latter can either initially be assumed to vanish, or can be obtained by preliminary calculation.

On the other hand, we can expect particularly large edge deformations if the edge members are flexible in bending or if the open cable net is totally or partially bounded by cables. These deformations depend greatly on the total cable forces acting on the edge member, and, in their turn, affect the behavior under load of the net. We shall then have to take into account values of u, v, and w obtained in a preliminary calculation. Using $\mathfrak{P}^\star$, the exact solution will be approached by iterations.

The three conditions 2.40 contain only three unknowns. The latter cannot, however, be found, since no boundary conditions are given for the horizontal tensions. We therefore have to use the elasticity Eqs. 2.24 with two further unknowns u and v. Inserting these into Eqs. 2.40, we obtain

$$[D_x (u' + z' w' - g_{11} {}^t\varepsilon_x)]' + p_x = 0\,, \tag{2.42a}$$

$$[D_y (v^{\cdot} + z^{\cdot} w^{\cdot} - g_{22} \cdot {}^t\varepsilon_y)]^{\cdot} + p_y = 0\,, \tag{2.42b}$$

$$D_x (u' + z' w' - g_{11} {}^t\varepsilon_x)\, z'' + D_y (v^{\cdot} + z^{\cdot} w^{\cdot} - g_{22} {}^t\varepsilon_y) \cdot z^{\cdot\cdot} + H_{x0} \cdot w'' + H_{y0} \cdot w^{\cdot\cdot} - p_x z' - p_y z^{\cdot} + p_z = 0\,. \tag{2.42c}$$

These expressions are, in contrast to Eqs. 2.27, linear in the load and displacement components. Several cases of loading can be superimposed.

2.4.2 *Principal Equations of the Cable Net*

The simplifications justified in Section 2.2.4, and in particular the separation of $p^\star$, gave the result that, e.g., Eq. 2.42a contains neither the displacement v nor derivatives with respect to y.

We assume that the projection in plan of the edge curve, lying on the surface $z\,(x, y)$ is an explicit function of y: In the initial state

at the left edge: $x_l = x_l\,(y)$,

at the right edge: $x_r = x_r\,(y)$.

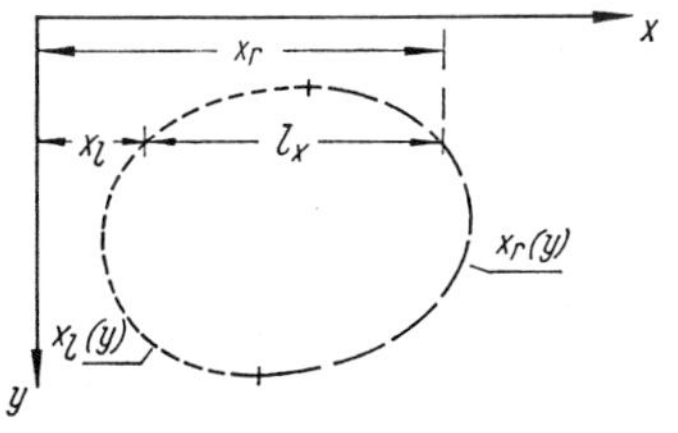

Fig. 2.7. Edge Curve as Function of y.

We assume that $x_r \geqslant x_l$ always; the span is thus positive (Fig. 2.7).

$$l_x\,(y) = x_r\,(y) - x_l\,(y) \geqslant 0\,.$$

We assume that the magnitudes of the edge-point displacements caused by a given load are known functions of y:

at the left edge: $u_{xl}\,(y)$, $w_{xl}\,(y)$,

at the right edge: $u_{xr}\,(y)$, $w_{xr}\,(y)$.

Integrating Eq. 2.40a or 2.42a, we obtain

$$H_{xp} = D_x (u' + z' w' - g_{11} {}^t\varepsilon_x) = C_1\,(y) - \int_0^x p_x\, dx\,, \tag{2.43a}$$

where C_1 depends only on y. Integrating again between the limits x_l and x_r, we obtain

$$C_1\,(y) = \Phi_x\,(y) \left\{ \int_{x_l}^{x_r} \left[\frac{1}{D_x} \int_0^x p_x\, dx \right] dx + W_x\,(y) - \int_{x_l}^{x_r} g_{11} {}^t\varepsilon_x\, dx - \int_{x_l}^{x_r} z''\, w\, dx \right\}. \tag{2.44a}$$

where

$$W_x\,(y) = [u_{xr}\,(y) - u_{xl}\,(y)] + [z_r' \cdot w_{xr}\,(y) - z_l'\, w_{xl}\,(y)]. \tag{2.45a}$$

and (cf. Eq. 2.25a)

$$\frac{1}{\Phi_x\,(y)} = \int_{x_l}^{x_r} \frac{dx}{D_x\,(x, y)} = \int_{x_l}^{x_r} \frac{(g_{11})^{3/2}}{E_x F_x}\, dx. \tag{2.46a}$$

The corresponding expressions for the y-direction are derived from Eqs. 2.40b or 2.42b. The boundary values are now functions of x (Fig. 2.8).

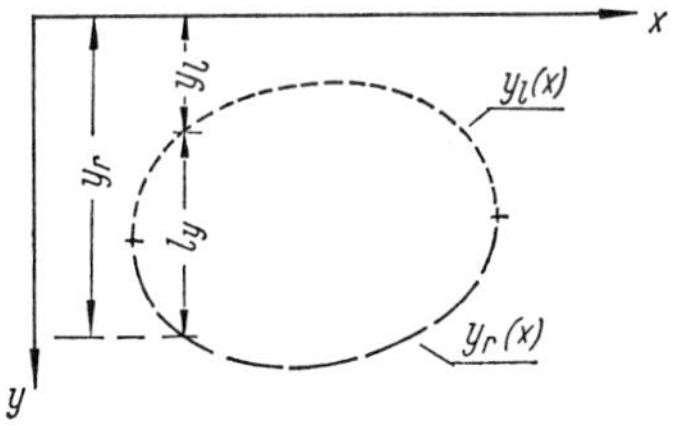

Fig. 2.8. Edge Curve as Function of x.

We find from the projection in plan $f\,(x, y) = 0$ of the edge curve:

for the left edge: $y_l = y_l\,(x)$,

for the right edge:. $y_r = y_r\,(x)$,

where $l_y = y_r - y_l \geqslant 0\,.$

The edge displacements are represented similarly:

at the left edge: $v_{yl}(x)$, $w_{yl}(x)$,

at the right edge: $v_{yr}(x)$, $w_{yr}(x)$.

Since the form of expressions 2.40a and 2.42a on the one hand, and 2.40b and 2.42b on the other, is similar, we can write immediately the results of the integrations:

$$H_{yp} = D_y (v^{\cdot} + z^{\cdot} w^{\cdot} - g_{22}{}^t\varepsilon_y) = C_2(x) - \int_0^y p_y\, dy\,, \tag{2.43b}$$

$$C_2(x) = \Phi_y(x) \left\{ \int_{y_l}^{y_r} \left[\frac{1}{D_y} \int_0^y p_y\, dy \right] dy + W_y(x) - \right.$$
$$\left. - \int_{y_l}^{y_r} g_{22}{}^t\varepsilon_y\, dy - \int_{y_l}^{y_r} z^{\cdot\cdot}\, w\, dy \right\}, \tag{2.44b}$$

$$W_y(x) = [v_{yr}(x) - v_{yl}(x)] + [z_r^{\cdot}\, w_{yr}(x) - z_l^{\cdot}\, w_{yl}(x)]\,, \tag{2.45b}$$

$$\frac{1}{\Phi_y(x)} = \int_{y_l}^{y_r} \frac{dy}{D_y(x, y)} = \int_{y_l}^{y_r} \frac{(g_{22})^{3/2}}{E_y F_y}\, dy\,. \tag{2.46b}$$

Inserting Eqs. 2.43 and 2.44 into Eq. 2.40c, we obtain after rearranging:

$$z''\, \Phi_x \int_{x_l}^{x_r} z''\, w\, dx + z^{\cdot\cdot}\, \Phi_y \int_{y_l}^{y_r} z^{\cdot\cdot}\, w\, dy - H_{x0}\, w'' -$$
$$- H_{y0}\, w^{\cdot\cdot} = \mathfrak{P}(x, y)\,. \tag{2.47a}$$

The left-hand side contains, besides w, only functions depending on the system, namely, the curvatures, initial tensions, and rigidity functions Φ. The latter depend on the cable lengths; their calculation will be discussed later.

The load function on the right-hand side includes all possible external effects (arbitrary horizontal and vertical loads, edge displacements, temperature variations):

$$\mathfrak{P}(x, y) = - z'\, p_x - z'' \int_0^x p_x\, dx + z''\, \Phi_x \int_{x_l}^{x_r} \left[\frac{1}{D_x} \int_0^x p_x\, dx \right] dx -$$
$$- z^{\cdot} p_y - z^{\cdot\cdot} \int_0^y p_y\, dy + z^{\cdot\cdot}\, \Phi_y \int_{y_l}^{y_r} \left[\frac{1}{D_y} \int_0^y p_y\, dx \right] dy +$$
$$+ p_z + z''\, \Phi_x\, W_x + z^{\cdot\cdot}\, \Phi_y\, W_y -$$
$$- z''\, \Phi_x \int_{x_l}^{x_r} g_{11}{}^t\varepsilon_x\, dx - z^{\cdot\cdot}\, \Phi_y \int_{y_l}^{y_r} g_{22}{}^t\varepsilon_y\, dy\,. \tag{2.47b}$$

We shall simplify this expression in Section 2.4.3. When the necessary simplifications are known, Eqs. 2.47 can of course also be derived differently, e.g., by the method of deformations or the method of the deformation work (Castigliano's Theorem).

When we replace H_{x0} in Eqs. 2.47 by the cable tension H_g and z by the initial deflections caused by the load g (cf. Section 1.1.1), and omit all terms corresponding to the y-direction, we can use these formulas to analyze single cables subjected to arbitrary loads. The forces, loads, and cross-sectional areas have then to be referred to the individual cables instead of to the unit width of the net.

The necessity of retaining $H_{x0} w''$ and $H_{y0} w^{\cdot\cdot}$ becomes evident from Eqs. 2.47. We prove this by rewriting Eq. 2.47a without these two terms:

$$z''\, \Phi_x \int_{x_l}^{x_r} z''\, w\, dx + z^{\cdot\cdot}\, \Phi_y \int_{y_l}^{y_r} z^{\cdot\cdot}\, w\, dy = \mathfrak{P}(x, y)\,. \tag{2.48}$$

Assume that there exists, in addition to the required solution w, at least one solution $\tilde{w}$ satisfying the homogeneous equation

$$z''\, \Phi_x \int_{x_l}^{x_r} z''\, \tilde{w}\, dx + z^{\cdot\cdot}\, \Phi_y \int_{y_l}^{y_r} z^{\cdot\cdot}\, \tilde{w}\, dy = 0\,.$$

In this case, $w_1 = w + c \cdot \tilde{w}$ would also be a solution of Eq. 2.48. The condition for $\tilde{w}$ can, however, be satisfied by an infinite number of functions, since $\tilde{w}$ appears only in the definite integrals. The solution of Eq. 2.48 is therefore not uniquely determined.

2.4.3 *Simplifications*

Up to now we have assumed the deformations to be small. Since higher powers of z' and $z^{\cdot}$ were neglected, we also restricted ourselves to moderately inclined surfaces. The magnitudes D entering in Eqs. 2.25 then vary only little, provided the cross sections of the cables are constant over their lengths. This is probably always true in practice. In addition, D_x is independent of y in translation surfaces, provided $E_x F_x$ is constant.

For a symmetrical parabolical cable curve with comparatively large relative deflection $n_x = f_x/l_x = 0.1$ we obtain at the edge:

$(1 + z_r'^2)^{3/2} = (1 + 0{,}4^2)^{3/2} = 1.25\,.$

From the apex ($z' = 0$) to the edge, D_x decreases monotonically from $E_x F_x$ to $0.8\, E_x F_x$; when $f_x/l_x = 0.05$, D_x decreases only to $0.943\, E_x F_x$.

In the repeated integral in Eq. 2.44a, D_x can be assumed to be constant throughout x without introducing a large error. We can then replace it by its mean value and write

$$\int_{x_l}^{x_r} \left[\frac{1}{D_x} \int_0^x p_x\, dx \right] dx \approx \frac{1}{D_{xm}} \int_{x_l}^{x_r} \int_0^x p_x\, dx\, dx\,.$$

This mean value is

$$\frac{1}{D_{xm}(y)} = \frac{1}{l_x(y)} \int_{x_l}^{x_r} \frac{dx}{D_x(x, y)} = \frac{1}{l_x(y) \cdot \Phi_x(y)}\,,$$

where Φ_x is the rigidity function defined in Eq. 2.46a, which will be discussed later.

The second and third terms of the load function are thus

$$- z'' \int_0^x p_x\, dx + z''\, \Phi_x \int_{x_l}^{x_r} \left[\frac{1}{D_x} \int_0^x p_x\, dx \right] dx \approx z'' \left\{ - \int_0^x p_x\, dx + \right.$$
$$\left. + \frac{1}{l_x} \int_{x_l}^{x_r} \int_0^x p_x\, dx\, dx \right\}.$$

The expression in braces on the right-hand side represents the shearing force acting on a beam of length l_x, simply supported at both ends and subjected to a vertical distributed load p_x and will be designated as $\mathfrak{Q}_x$ in Fig. 2.9:

$$\mathfrak{Q}_x = -\int_0^x p_x \, d\, x + \frac{1}{l_x} \int_{x_l}^{x_r} \int_0^x p_x \, dx \, dx \, . \qquad (2.49a)$$

Similarly, for the y-direction,

$$\mathfrak{Q}_y = -\int_0^y p_y \, d\, y + \frac{1}{l_y} \int_{y_l}^{y_r} \int_0^y p_y \, dy \, dy \, . \qquad (2.49b)$$

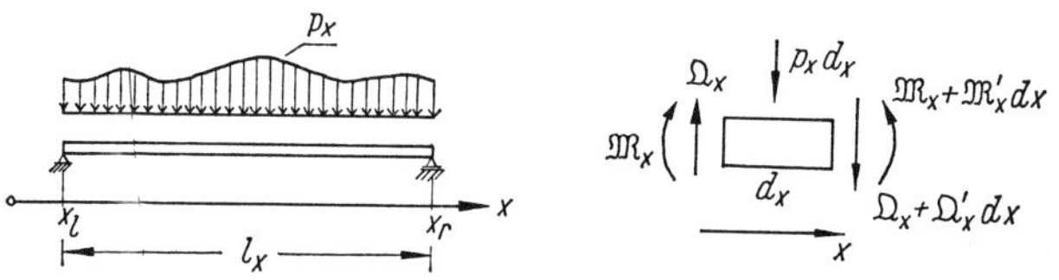

Fig. 2.9. Equivalent Beam.

The approximations introduced concern only terms containing p_x and p_y. Precisely these loads, which are generally only due to wind when the plan is horizontal, are determined from model tests or are only approximately known. In view of the inaccuracy of assuming the magnitude of these loads, the simplifications introduced are fully justified. We shall estimate the magnitude of the error in a worked example; it will be found that it amounts to only a few per cent.

Wc can also introducc approximations in the terms due to temperature changes, since g_{11} varies even less than $(g_{11})^{3/2}$ in D_x. Replacing $g_{11}(x, y)$ in Eq. 2.44a or 2.47b by its mean value

$$g_{11,m}(y) = \frac{1}{l_x(y)} \cdot \int_{x_l}^{x_r} g_{11} \cdot dx$$

and writing it in front of the integration sign, we obtain

$$\Phi_x(y) \int_{x_l}^{x_r} g_{11} \, {}^t\varepsilon_x \, dx \approx \Phi_x(y) \cdot g_{11,m}(y) \cdot \int_{x_l}^{x_r} {}^t\varepsilon_x \, dx \, ,$$

where, by Eqs. 2.46a and 2.3, in the case of constant cable cross section,

$$\Phi_x \cdot g_{11,m} = \frac{E_x F_x}{l_x} \frac{\int (1 + z'^2) \, dx}{\int (1 + z'^2)^{3/2} \, dx} \, .$$

The ratio of the integrals, both of which are taken between the same limits, can with sufficient accuracy assumed to be unity. For the parabola considered before, where $n = 0.1$, the numerator is equal to $1.0533 \, l_x$, and the denominator equal to $1.0819 \, l_x$. Even when ${}^t\varepsilon_x$ varies, the error will be negligible.

We write

$$\mathfrak{N}_x(y) = -\frac{E_x F_x(y)}{l_x(y)} \int_{x_l}^{x_r} {}^t\varepsilon_x \, dx \, , \qquad (2.50a)$$

$$\mathfrak{N}_y(x) = -\frac{E_y F_y(x)}{l_y(x)} \int_{y_l}^{y_r} \cdot {}^t\varepsilon_y \, dy \, . \qquad (2.50b)$$

Assuming tensions to be positive, we thus obtain $\mathfrak{N}_x$ as the normal force acting on a rod of length l_x whose ends are fixed, during a temperature increase of an amount corresponding to ${}^t\varepsilon_x$. $\mathfrak{N}_y$ is defined similarly.

Inserting expressions 2.49 and 2.50, Eq. 2.47b now becomes:

$$\begin{aligned} \mathfrak{P}(x, y) &= -z' p_x + z'' \mathfrak{Q}_x - z^{\cdot} p_y + z^{\cdot\cdot} \mathfrak{Q}_y + p_z + \\ &+ z'' \Phi_x W_x + z^{\cdot\cdot} \Phi_y W_y + z'' \mathfrak{N}_x + z^{\cdot\cdot} \mathfrak{N}_y \, . \end{aligned} \qquad (2.51)$$

If $w(x, y)$ is known, we obtain from Eqs. 2.43 and 2.44 the horizontal tentions caused by the load:

$$H_{xp} = \Phi_x \left(W_x - \int_{x_l}^{x_r} z'' w \, dx \right) + \mathfrak{Q}_x + \mathfrak{N}_x \qquad (2.52a)$$

and

$$H_{yp} = \Phi_y \left(W_y - \int_{y_l}^{y_r} z^{\cdot\cdot} w \, dy \right) + \mathfrak{Q}_y + \mathfrak{N}_y \, , \qquad (2.52b)$$

where, e.g., in the expression for H_{xp}, all terms except $\mathfrak{Q}_x$ are independent of x.

The horizontal displacements $u(x, y)$ are best found from Eq. 2.43a. Integrating, we obtain

$$u(x, y) = u_{xl}(y) + \int_{x_l} \frac{H_{xp}}{D_x} \, dx - \Big[z' w \Big]_{x_l} + \int_{x_l} z'' w \, dx + \int_{x_l} g_{11} \, {}^t\varepsilon_x \, dx \, .$$

When D_x is constant and Eq. 2.52a is taken into account, this leads to

$$\begin{aligned} u = {} & \frac{x_r - x}{l_x} (u_{xl} + z_l' w_{xl}) + \frac{x - x_l}{l_x} (u_{xr} + z_r' w_{xr}) - \\ & - z' w - \frac{x - x_l}{l_x} \int_{x_l}^{x_r} z'' w \, dx + \int_{x_l}^{x} z'' w \, dx + \\ & + \frac{1}{l_x \Phi_x} \mathfrak{M}_x + \frac{x - x_l}{l_x \Phi_x} \mathfrak{N}_x + \int_{x_l}^{x} g_{11} \cdot {}^t\varepsilon_x \, dx \, . \end{aligned} \qquad (2.53a)$$

Correspondingly, we obtain for the y-direction:

$$\begin{aligned} v = {} & \frac{y_r - y}{l_y} (v_{yl} + z_l^{\cdot} w_{yl}) + \frac{y - y_l}{l_y} (v_{yr} + z_r^{\cdot} w_{yr}) - \\ & - z^{\cdot} w - \frac{y - y_l}{l_y} \int_{y_l}^{y_r} z^{\cdot\cdot} w \, dy + \int_{y_l}^{y} z^{\cdot\cdot} w \, dy + \\ & + \frac{1}{l_y \Phi_y} \mathfrak{M}_y + \frac{y - y_l}{l_y \Phi_y} \mathfrak{N}_y + \int_{y_l}^{y} g_{22} \, {}^t\varepsilon_y \, dy \, . \end{aligned} \qquad (2.53b)$$

If the thermal strains ${}^t\varepsilon_x$ or ${}^t\varepsilon_y$ are approximately constant over the cable length considered, we can neglect the last two terms in Eq. 2.53a or 2.53b, respectively.

We have here introduced the bending moment of the beam shown in Fig. 2.9, when a load p_x acts on it:

$$\mathfrak{M}_x(x, y) = \int_{x_l}^{x} \mathfrak{Q}_x(x, y) \, dx \, . \qquad (2.54a)$$

Similarly

$$\mathfrak{M}_y(x, y) = \int_{y_l}^{y} \mathfrak{Q}_y(x, y)\, dy\,. \quad (2.54b)$$

In most cases a vertical, approximately uniformly distributed load acts on the cable net. We can then replace Eqs. 2.53a, b by the approximations

$$u \approx -z' w \quad \text{und} \quad v \approx -z^{\cdot} w\,. \quad (2.53c)$$

In conclusion we shall estimate the error introduced by assuming D to be constant. When a symmetrical cable net is subjected to a symmetrical load p_x, the third term in Eq. 2.47b vanishes. We therefore assume an antimetrical load

$$p_x = -p_{x0} \cdot z' = p_{x0} \cdot \xi.$$

We intersect the surface, assumed to be symmetrical, by a plane parallel to the x-axis:

$$z = -\frac{k_x}{2} x^2 = -\frac{1}{2\,k_x} \cdot \xi^2 \text{ where } \xi = k_x \cdot x\,.$$

The expression 2.25a is now expanded in series, from which, due to the rapid convergence, we retain only the first two terms. The integral entering in Eq. 2.47b is then

$$\int_{x_l}^{x_r} \left[\frac{1}{D_x} \int_0^x p_x\, dx \right] dx = \frac{p_{x0}}{30\, E_x F_x k_x^2} (10 + 9\,\xi_r^2) \cdot \xi_r^3\,,$$

whereas the approximation yields

$$\frac{1}{D_{xm}} \int_{x_l}^{x_r} \int_0^x p_x\, dx\, dx = \frac{p_{x0}}{30\, E_x F_x k_x^2} (2 + \xi_r^2) \cdot 5\,\xi_r^3.$$

The relative error is thus

$$rel F = -\frac{4\,\xi_r^2}{10 + 9\,\xi_r^2}\,.$$

It is given in the table below as a function of the slope ξ_r at the edge and the ratio $n = f/l$.

ξ_r	0	0.025	0.05	0.075	0.10	
n	0	0.1	0.2	0.3	0.4	
rel F	0	−0.4	−1.5	−3.3	−5.6	%

The error increases when the load increases towards the edge. These errors occur, however, only in the antimetrical part of the load; their influence on the total load is thus even less.

2.4.4 *Methods of Solution*

The integral-differential Eqs. 2.47 are generally solved by rewriting them as sum-and-difference equations. The plan is covered by an orthogonal lattice, the intervals $\Delta\, x$ and $\Delta\, y$ being uniform. If the intervals are taken equal to the cable distances, we obtain the exact solution, although at a great effort. At each intersection there will be a break in the cable curve.

The outermost points of the lattice will lie on the cable-net edge only in very few cases (e.g., when the nets are bounded by straight lines). We may choose these lattice points themselves as the net boundary if the intervals are sufficiently small (Fig. 2.10). When

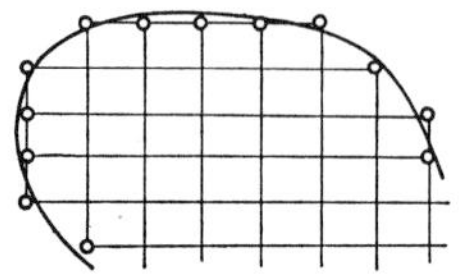

Fig. 2.10. Edge Curve and Lattice.

higher accuracy is required, the difference ratios and sums corresponding to points lying near the edge can be modified appropriately.

It can be assumed that the initial surface is always given as a function $z(x, y)$ or can be approximated by such a function; the derivatives of z can then easily be found for each lattice point. The rigidity functions Φ can also be determined in advance without difficulty. We shall therefore retain these magnitudes in the following expressions.

Each lattice point carries two subscripts: the first, 0, 1, 2, $\ldots i-1, i, i+1, \ldots n+1$ refers to the x-direction, the second, 0, 1, 2, $\ldots j, \ldots m+1$ to the y-direction.

Introducing the difference ratios

$$\left.\frac{\partial^2 f(x, y)}{\partial x^2}\right/_{ij} \approx \frac{1}{(\Delta\, x)^2} (f_{i-1,j} - 2\, f_{i,j} + f_{i+1,j})$$

and replacing the integrals by sums, we obtain for the point (i, j) the equation

$$z''_{i,j} \cdot \Phi_{x_j} \cdot \Delta\, x \sum_{i=1}^{n} z''_{i,j} \cdot w_{i,j} + z^{\cdot\cdot}_{i,j} \cdot \Phi_{y_i} \cdot \Delta\, y \cdot \sum_{j=1}^{m} z^{\cdot\cdot}_{i,j} \cdot w_{i,j} -$$
$$- \frac{H_{x0j}}{(\Delta\, x)^2} (w_{i-1,y} - 2\, w_{i,j} + w_{i+1,j}) - \quad (2.55)$$
$$- \frac{H_{y0j}}{(\Delta\, y)^2} (w_{i,j-1} - 2\, w_{i,j} + w_{i,j+1}) = \mathfrak{P}_{i,j}\,.$$

As stated in Section 2.4.1, we can increase the accuracy by introducing the approximations $H_{xp}^{(1)}$ and $H_{yp}^{(1)}$ together with H_0. These magnitudes have been omitted for the sake of simplicity.

When concentrated loads occur, they are distributed over the area $\Delta\, x \cdot \Delta\, y$

We write $w = 0$ for points at which the cable net is supported, e.g., by masts.

We can set up an Eq. 2.55 for each internal lattice point, corresponding to the number of unknowns $w_{i,j}$. The sums extend over all internal points i or j of the rows j = const or i = const. Denoting in the resulting linear system of equations the coefficient of $w_{\bar{i},\bar{j}}$ in the equation for the point (i, j) by $\delta_{i,j;\bar{i},\bar{j}}$, we obtain, by using Maxwell's theorem.

$$\delta_{i,j;\bar{i},\bar{j}} = \delta_{\bar{i},\bar{j};i,j}\,.$$

The corresponding matrix of coefficients is symmetrical. It contains zeros, since $\delta_{i,j;\bar{i},\bar{j}} = 0$, for $i \neq \bar{i}$ and $j \neq \bar{j}$ simultaneously. With a lattice of only 4·4 internal points (Fig. 2.11a) we already obtain the pattern shown in Fig. 2.11b.

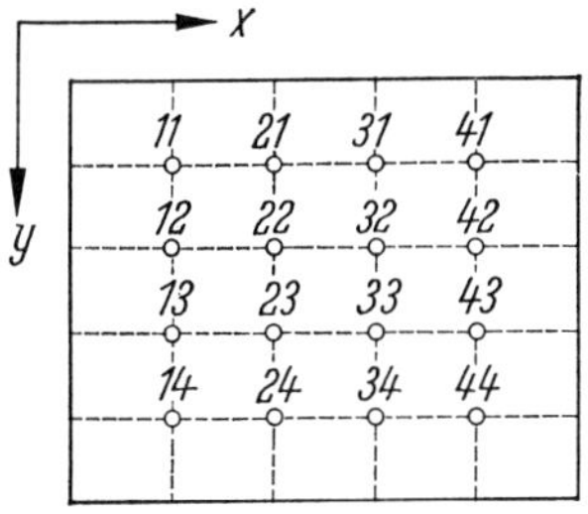

Fig. 2.11a. Lattice Points.

w_{11}	w_{12}	w_{13}	w_{14}	w_{21}	w_{22}	w_{23}	w_{24}	w_{31}	w_{32}	w_{33}	w_{34}	w_{41}	w_{42}	w_{43}	w_{44}	$\mathfrak{P}$
⊕	‡	|	|	++				—				—				$\mathfrak{P}_{11}$
‡	⊕	‡	|		++				—				—			$\mathfrak{P}_{12}$
‡	‡	⊕	‡			++				—				—		$\mathfrak{P}_{13}$
|	|	‡	⊕				++				—				—	$\mathfrak{P}_{14}$
++				⊕	‡	|	|	++				—				$\mathfrak{P}_{21}$
	++			‡	⊕	‡	|		++				—			$\mathfrak{P}_{22}$
		++		|	‡	⊕	‡			++				—		$\mathfrak{P}_{23}$
			++	|	|	‡	⊕				++				—	$\mathfrak{P}_{24}$
—				++				⊕	‡	|	|	++				$\mathfrak{P}_{31}$
	—				++			‡	⊕	‡	|		++			$\mathfrak{P}_{32}$
		—				++		|	‡	⊕	‡			++		$\mathfrak{P}_{33}$
			—				++	|	|	‡	⊕				++	$\mathfrak{P}_{34}$
—				—				++				⊕	‡	|	|	$\mathfrak{P}_{41}$
	—				—				++			‡	⊕	‡	|	$\mathfrak{P}_{42}$
		—				—				++		|	‡	⊕	‡	$\mathfrak{P}_{43}$
			—				—				++	|	|	‡	⊕	$\mathfrak{P}_{44}$

Fig. 2.11b. Matrix Scheme.

Since the determinant in the denominator does not vanish, there exists a single-valued solution.

Different methods of solution are indicated, depending on the edge, required accuracy, and availability of computers. Even when symmetry is taken into account, a large number of lattice points are needed to allow accurately for the influence of the load and, in particular, for the deformations. Direct solution of the equations is then only economical if a computer is used. The coefficients of the reciprocal matrix are the influence numbers for the deflections w. From these we can obtain the influence numbers for the horizontal tensions with the aid of Eqs. 2.52. Calculation of the coefficients δ and the load functions can also be programmed for a computer with a moderate amount of work.

The terms $\delta_{i,j;i,j}$ of the principal diagonals are larger than the others; single or block iterations can therefore be used to determine w. Convergence is quite rapid when the initial tension is high. Relaxation methods have proved of advantage when many cable nets have to be analyzed. Relaxation is obtained directly in the system by means of single steps. The same simple steps, frequently repeated, make the calculation easy to survey. The accuracy attained can be determined continually by comparing the residuals with the load functions. Since in the determination of the horizontal tensions, the deflections appear under the integration sign, an accuracy of one cm in w may be sufficient under normal conditions.

The deflections were determined with an accuracy of ± 2 mm in the example given at the end, in which the plan is fairly irregular.

Calculation of the 58 unknowns in each case of loading takes about 15 hours if a slide rule is used. Although the system was initially complicated and statically indeterminate to a high degree, use of a computer was unnecessary and would have been uneconomical.

When system 2.55 is being solved, the following has to be noted if the edge displacements w differ from zero. If the lattice point (i, j) is adjacent to the edge, the magnitudes $w_{i\pm 1,j}$ or $w_{i,j\pm 1}$ in the terms containing H_0 have to be replaced by the corresponding known boundary values. Strictly speaking, we should insert the boundary values also into the sums. If, as in Eq. 2.55, the sums extend only over the internal points, the additional term

$$z''_{i,j} \cdot \Phi_{xj} \frac{\Delta x}{2} (z_l'' \cdot w_{xl} + z_r'' \cdot w_{xr}) +$$

$$+ z^{\cdot\cdot}_{i,j} \cdot \Phi_{yi} \frac{\Delta y}{2} (z_l^{\cdot\cdot}\, w_{yl} + z_r^{\cdot\cdot} \cdot w_{yr}),$$

which does not contain $w_{i,j}$, should be added to the load function $\mathfrak{P}$. This term however can generally be neglected. The errors thus introduced are of the order of $W_x \cdot \Delta x / l_x$ or $W_y \cdot \Delta y / l_y$, i.e., they amount only to fractions of W_x or W_y.

2.4.5 *Computation of* Φ

The rigidity functions defined by Eqs. 2.46a, b have the form of definite integrals, which can be tabulated if the cable curves are given. The derivations below refer to the x-direction; for Φ_y we have to replace x by y. We assume that the modulus of elasticity and the cross section are constant over the cable length.

2.4.5.1 Quadratic Parabola

A section, parallel to the x, z-plane, through the initial surface is defined by

$$z = -\frac{k_x}{2} x^2 = -\frac{1}{2\,k_x} \cdot \xi\,,$$

where, as before, $k_x \cdot x = \xi$, k_x being the curvature at the apex of the parabola. We again denote by $x_r\,(y)$ and $x_l\,(y)$ the distances of the net edges from the apex: $l_x = x_r - x_l \geqslant 0$.

According to Eq. 2.25a

$$E_x F_x \int_{x_l}^{x_r} \frac{d\,x}{D_x} = \int_{x_l}^{x_r} (1 + z'^2)^{3/2}\, dx =$$

$$= \frac{1}{k_x}\int_{\xi_l}^{0}(1+\xi^2)^{3/2}\,d\xi + \frac{1}{k_x}\int_{0}^{\xi_r}(1+\xi^2)^{3/2}\,d\xi\,.$$

The second integral on the right-hand side is evaluated by substituting $\xi = \sinh t$. We then obtain

$$\int_0^{x_r}\frac{d\,x}{D_x} = \frac{1}{E_x F_x}\left[\frac{3}{8}\,\frac{\operatorname{ar\,sinh}\xi_r}{\xi_r} + \frac{1}{8}\,(5+2\,\xi_r^2)\sqrt{1+\xi_r^2}\right]\cdot x_r\,.$$

The function appearing in brackets depends only on the slope ξ_r at the edge. We write

$${}^{P}\lambda\,(\xi_r) = \frac{3}{8}\,\frac{\operatorname{ar\,sinh}\xi_r}{\xi_r} + \frac{1}{8}\,(5+2\,\xi_r^2)\sqrt{1+\xi_r^2}\,. \qquad (2.56a)$$

Hence

$$\frac{1}{\Phi_x} = \int_{x_l}^{x_r}\frac{d\,x}{D_x} = \frac{1}{E_x F_x}\,[x_r\cdot {}^{P}\lambda\,(\xi_r) - x_l\,{}^{P}\lambda\,(\xi_l)] = \frac{l_x\,{}^{P}\Lambda_x}{E_x F_x}\,,$$

or, finally,

$$\Phi_x = \frac{E_x F_x}{l_x\cdot {}^{P}\Lambda_x}\,, \qquad (2.56b)$$

where

$${}^{P}\Lambda_x = \frac{1}{l_x}\,[x_r\cdot {}^{P}\lambda\,(\xi_r) - x_l\cdot {}^{P}\lambda\,(\xi_l)] \geqslant 1\,. \qquad (2.56c)$$

The magnitude $l_x\cdot\Lambda_x$ is identical with the length L_s defined in Eq. 1.50a, which can also be used to analyze suspension bridges. It can be considered as the length of a straight cable in which the deformation work, due to a tension $H=1$, is equal to the work done in the curved cable.

When the net is symmetrical, we have $x_r = -x_l$ and ${}^{P}\Lambda_x = {}^{P}\lambda\,(\xi_r)$.
A satisfactory approximation for a preliminary calculation is

$${}^{P}\Lambda \approx 1 + \frac{1}{2}\,\xi_r^2 = 1 + 8\,n^2\,,$$

(cf. Eq. 1.53b).
The exact values are given in Table 2.1 and Fig. 2.12.

2.4.5.2 Catenary
From

$$z = -\frac{1}{k_x}\cosh k_x\cdot x = -\frac{1}{k_x}\cosh\xi$$

we obtain, by carrying out the same operations as for the parabola, writing ${}^{C}\lambda$ instead of ${}^{P}\lambda$:

$${}^{C}\lambda\,(\xi_r) = \frac{\sinh\xi_r}{\xi_r}\left(1+\frac{1}{3}\sinh^2\xi_r\right), \qquad (2.57a)$$

$$\Phi_x = \frac{E_x F_x}{l_x\cdot {}^{C}\Lambda_x}\,, \qquad (2.57b)$$

$${}^{C}\Lambda_x = \frac{1}{l_x}\,[x_r\cdot {}^{C}\lambda\,(\xi_r) - x_l\cdot {}^{C}\lambda\,(\xi_l)] \geqslant 1\,. \qquad (2.57c)$$

Here ξ_r and ξ_l are no longer the slopes at the edges; instead, we have $z' = -\sinh\xi$.

Values of ${}^{C}\lambda\,(\xi)$ for different values of $\xi_{r,l}$ are given in Fig. 2.12 and Table 2.1.

2.4.5.3 Circular Arc
When the cable forms a circular arc, we have, Section 2.3.2.5,

$$z = -\frac{1}{k_x}\left(1-\sqrt{1-k_x^2\,x^2}\right) = -\frac{1}{k_x}\left(1-\sqrt{1-\xi^2}\right),$$

where $1/k_x$ is the radius.

Integration yields (intermediate calculations omitted)

$${}^{K}\lambda_x = \frac{1}{\sqrt{1-\xi_r^2}}\,. \qquad (2.58a)$$

The expressions for Φ_x and ${}^{K}\Lambda_x$ correspond formally to expressions 2.56b, c; the function ${}^{K}\lambda\,(\xi_r)$ is also shown in Fig. 2.12 and given in Table 2.1.
Here again, ξ_r is not the slope at the edge; we have instead $\xi_r = k_x\cdot x_r$ or $\xi_r = x_r/\text{Radius}$.

2.4.5.4 Compilation

Table 2.1. Values of λ as a Function of ξ

$\xi_{r,l}$	Parabola ${}^{P}\lambda$	Catenary ${}^{C}\lambda$	Circle ${}^{K}\lambda$
0.00	1.00 00	1.00 00	1.00 00
0.02		1.00 02	
0.04		1.00 08	
0.06		1.00 18	
0.08		1.00 32	
0.10		1.00 50	
0.12	1.00 72	1.00 72	1.00 72
0.14	1.00 98	1.00 99	1.00 99
0.16	1.01 28	1.01 29	1.01 31
0.18	1.01 63	1.01 64	1.01 66
0.20	1.02 01	1.02 03	1.02 06
0.22	1.02 44	1.02 46	1.02 51
0.24	1.02 90	1.02 94	1.03 01
0.26	1.03 41	1.03 46	1.03 56
0.28	1.03 97	1.04 03	1.04 17
0.30	1.04 56	1.04 64	1.04 83
0.32	1.05 20	1.05 31	1.05 55
0.34	1.05 88	1.06 02	1.06 33
0.36	1.06 60	1.06 78	1.07 19
0.38	1.07 37	1.07 60	1.08 11
0.40	1.08 19	1.08 46	1.09 11
0.42	1.09 05	1.09 38	1.10 19
0.44	1.09 96	1.10 36	1.11 36
0.46	1.10 91	1.11 40	1.12 62
0.48	1.11 91	1.12 49	1.13 99
0.50	1.12 96	1.13 65	1.15 47

Fig. 2.12 appears on p. 83.

2.4.6 *Compilation of Formulas and Computation Procedure*
The formulas required for analyzing an orthogonal cable net are compiled below, where the computation procedure is also given. For ease of orientation we also indicate the numbers of the formulas.

2.4.6.1 Given Magnitudes
System: The null (initial) surface is given numerically or as a function $z = z\,(x, y)$. The edge is defined according to Figs. 2.7 and 2.8 by $x_r = x_r\,(y)$, $x_l = x_l\,(y)$ or $y_r = y_r\,(x)$ and $y_l = y_l\,(x)$. The moduli

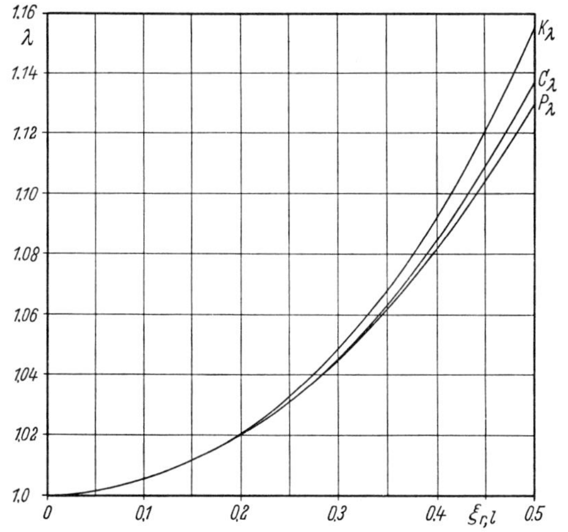

Fig. 2.12. Values of λ as a Function of ξ.

of elasticity of the cables E_x and E_y are assumed to be constant for the expected range of stresses. The cross-sectional areas F_x and F_y of the cables must already be known (Eq. 2.23). It is assumed that the cross section of each cable remains constant over its length. Should this not be the case, we can easily modify the formulas appropriately.

Loads: The external loads p_x, p_y, and p_z are referred to unit surface in plan; when the loads are given differently, transformations 2.16 apply. The edge displacements are, like the edges themselves, given both as functions of x and y (see Section 2.4.2). Temperature effects are taken into account by ${}^t\varepsilon_x$ and ${}^t\varepsilon_y$ (Eq. 1.18).

2.4.6.2 Selection of Initial Tension

We must always have

$$H_{x0}(y)\cdot z'' + H_{y0}(x)\cdot z^{\cdot\cdot} = 0. \tag{2.26}$$

Further details are given in Section 2.3.1.

2.4.6.3 Determination of the Rigidity Functions

$$\frac{1}{\Phi_x(y)} = \int_{x_l}^{x_r} \frac{(1+z'^2)^{3/2}}{E_x F_x(y)}\,dx. \tag{2.46a}$$

For certain shapes of cables we have tabulated,

$$\Phi_x(y) = \frac{E_x F_x}{l_x(y)\cdot \Lambda_x(y)} \tag{2.56b}$$

with

$$\Lambda_x(y) = \frac{1}{l_x}(x_r\cdot\lambda_r - x_l\cdot\lambda_l) \tag{2.56c}$$

in Section 2.4.5. Similar formulas apply to the y-direction.

2.4.6.4 Determination of the Load Function

$$\mathfrak{P}(x,y) = -z'\,p_x + z''\,\mathfrak{Q}_x - z^{\cdot}\,p_y + z^{\cdot\cdot}\,\mathfrak{Q}_y + p_z + \\ + z''\,\Phi_x\cdot W_x + z^{\cdot\cdot}\,\Phi_y\,W_y + z''\,\mathfrak{R}_x + z^{\cdot\cdot}\,\mathfrak{R}_y. \tag{2.51}$$

The virtual shearing forces are

$$\mathfrak{Q}_x = -\int_0^x p_x\,dx + \frac{1}{l_x}\int_{x_l}^{x_r}\int_0^x p_x\,dx\,dx, \tag{2.49a}$$

$$\mathfrak{Q}_y = -\int_0^y p_y\,dy + \frac{1}{l_y}\int_{y_l}^{y_r}\int_0^y p_y\,dy\,dy; \tag{2.49b}$$

the terms containing the edge displacements are

$$W_x = (u_{xr} - u_{xl}) + (z_r'\,w_{xr} - z_l'\,w_{xl}), \tag{2.45a}$$

$$W_y = (v_{yr} - v_{yl}) + (z_r^{\cdot}\,w_{yr} - z_l^{\cdot}\,w_{yl}); \tag{2.45b}$$

and the terms corresponding to the temperature effects,

$$\mathfrak{R}_x = -\frac{E_x F_x}{l_x}\int_{x_l}^{x_r} {}^t\varepsilon_x\,dx, \tag{2.50a}$$

$$\mathfrak{R}_y = -\frac{E_y F_y}{l_y}\int_{y_l}^{y_r} {}^t\varepsilon_y\,dy. \tag{2.50b}$$

2.4.6.5 Determination of the Deflections w

$$z''\,\Phi_x \int_{x_l}^{x_r} z''\,w\,dx + z^{\cdot\cdot}\,\Phi_y \int_{y_l}^{y_r} z^{\cdot\cdot}\,w\,dy - \\ - H_{x0}\,w'' - H_{y0}\,w^{\cdot\cdot} = \mathfrak{P}, \tag{2.47a}$$

or as sums and differences

$$z''_{i,j}\cdot\Phi_{x_j}\cdot\Delta x \sum_{i=1}^{n} z''_{i,j}\cdot w_{i,j} + z^{\cdot\cdot}_{i,j}\cdot\Phi_{y_i}\cdot\Delta y\cdot\sum_{j=1}^{m} z^{\cdot\cdot}_{i,j}\cdot w_{i,j} - \\ - \frac{H_{x0j}}{(\Delta x)^2}(w_{i-1,j} - 2\,w_{i,j} + w_{i+1,j}) - \\ - \frac{H_{y0i}}{(\Delta y)^2}(w_{i,j-1} - 2\,w_{i,j} + w_{i,j+1}) = \mathfrak{P}_{i,j}. \tag{2.55}$$

2.4.6.6 Determination of the Cable Forces

$$H_{xp} = \Phi_x\left(W_x - \int_{x_l}^{x_r} z''\,w\,dx\right) + \mathfrak{Q}_x + \mathfrak{R}_x, \tag{2.52a}$$

$$H_{yp} = \Phi_y\left(W_y - \int_{y_l}^{y_r} z^{\cdot\cdot}\,w\,dy\right) + \mathfrak{Q}_y + \mathfrak{R}_y. \tag{2.52b}$$

The above integrals should in general be replaced by the corresponding sums.

$$H_x = H_{x0} + H_{xp}, \qquad H_y = H_{y0} + H_{yp}. \tag{2.18b}$$

If nonlinear terms are neglected, we obtain immediately the cable forces:

$$S_1 = H_x\sqrt{g_{11}}, \qquad S_2 = H_y\sqrt{g_{22}}. \tag{2.17}$$

2.4.6.7 Determination of u and v

$$u = \frac{x_r - x}{l_x}(u_{xl} + z_l'\,w_{xl}) + \frac{x - x_l}{l_x}(u_{xr} + z_r'\,w_{xr}) -$$

$$- z' w - \frac{x - x_l}{l_x} \int_{x_l}^{x_r} z'' w \, dx + \int_{x_l}^{x} z'' w \, dx + \qquad (2.53a)$$

$$+ \frac{1}{l_x \Phi_x} \mathfrak{M}_y + \frac{x - x_l}{l_x \Phi_x} \mathfrak{N}_x + \int_{x_l}^{x_r} g_{11} \, {}^t\varepsilon_x \, dx .$$

The last two terms can generally be omitted.
The displacements v are found correspondingly from Eq. 2.53b.

The virtual bending moments are given by Eqs. 2.54; they are best determined at the same time as the virtual shearing forces $\mathfrak{Q}$.
When only a nearly uniform vertical load p_z acts, the horizontal displacements can be approximated by

$$u \approx - z' w , \qquad v \approx - z^{\cdot} w . \qquad (2.53c)$$

2.4.6.8 Taking into Account the Nonlinear Terms

$$\left. \begin{aligned} p_x{}^\star &= (H_{y0} + H_{yp}) u^{\cdot\cdot} - p_y u^{\cdot} , \\ p_y{}^\star &= (H_{x0} + H_{xp}) v'' - p_x v' , \\ p_z{}^\star &= H_{xp} w'' + H_{yp} w^{\cdot\cdot} - p_x w' - p_y w^{\cdot} . \end{aligned} \right\} \qquad (2.41a–c)$$

If necessary, a new load function $\mathfrak{P}^\star$ should be determined according to Eq. 2.51 for the least favorable combination of loads. Corrections for the edge displacements can be introduced simultaneously if the deformations of the edge members differ considerably from the assumed values.

The magnitude $w^\star$ can again be determined from Eq. 2.47a or 2.55. The now known magnitudes H_{xp} and H_{yp} should, for greater accuracy, be included in the left-hand side of Eq. 2.55 together with H_0. This has already been suggested in Section 2.4.1 for the first iteration step.

It will suffice in most cases to estimate the influence of $\mathfrak{P}^\star$ by means of the approximations given in Section 2.6.

2.5 Extension to Nonorthogonal and Nonpretensioned Cable Nets

2.5.1 *Nonorthogonal Cable Nets*
Until now we have assumed that the families of cables are orthogonal in plan. We shall now consider a net in which the families of cables form parallelograms with constant (acute) angles γ in plan. We introduce nonorthogonal coordinates x, y, z, the corresponding unit vectors being

$$\mathfrak{e}_x \cdot \mathfrak{e}_y = \cos \gamma \neq 0 , \qquad \mathfrak{e}_x \cdot \mathfrak{e}_z = \mathfrak{e}_y \cdot \mathfrak{e}_z = 0 .$$

The components of $\mathfrak{p}$ and $\mathfrak{w}$ are, like those of $\mathfrak{r}$. now measured in the directions of the new coordinates; the formulas of Section 2.2.1 thus remain valid. The external load is, as before, referred to unit area in plan.

The deformed surface element and the forces acting on it are represented in Fig. 2.13. The orthogonal coordinate axes are also shown for the sake of comparison with Fig. 2.1.

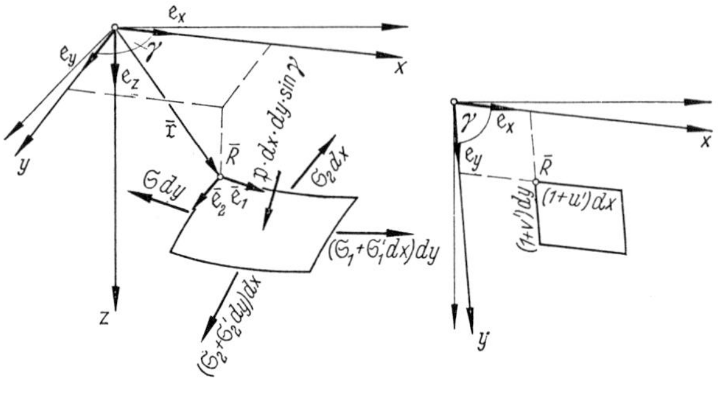

Fig. 2.13. Notations for the Nonorthogonal Cable Net.

Using Eq. 2.23, we refer the cross-sectional areas F as well as the forces S and H to unit width in plan in the direction normal to that considered. The cable forces are then

$$\mathfrak{S}_1 \, dy = S_1 \sin \gamma \cdot dy \cdot \bar{\mathfrak{e}}_1$$

and

$$\mathfrak{S}_2 \, dx = S_2 \sin \gamma \cdot dx \cdot \bar{\mathfrak{e}}_2 .$$

The load is

$$\mathfrak{p} \, dx \, dy \, (\mathfrak{e}_1 \times \mathfrak{e}_2) = \mathfrak{p} \sin \gamma \, dx \, dy .$$

The equilibrium condition for the surface element is

$$\left(\frac{S_1}{\sqrt{g_{11}}} \sin \gamma \cdot \bar{\mathfrak{r}}' \right)' + \left(\frac{S_2}{\sqrt{g_{22}}} \sin \gamma \, \bar{\mathfrak{r}}^{\cdot} \right)^{\cdot} + \mathfrak{p} \sin \gamma = 0$$

(cf. Eq. 2.14a). Since $\sin \gamma = \text{const} \neq 0$ we obtain

$$\left(\frac{S_1}{\sqrt{g_{11}}} \bar{\mathfrak{r}}' \right)' + \left(\frac{S_2}{\sqrt{g_{22}}} \bar{\mathfrak{r}}^{\cdot} \right)^{\cdot} + \mathfrak{p} = 0 ,$$

which formally coincides with Eq. 2.14a.

Obviously, all relationships previously found for the orthogonal cable net remain formally valid when F, S, and H are given by the above equations. The nonorthogonal cable net can thus be analyzed with the aid of nonorthogonal coordinates, using the same formulas as for the orthogonal net.

When the cable-net surface is given, the cables should lie in the directions corresponding to the principal curvatures, since, by Eq. 2.47a, the load-carrying capacity of the individual cables increases with increasing curvature. Since the lines of curvature are orthogonal at every point, a properly installed orthogonal cable net can take up vertical loads with the least expenditure of materials and the smallest deformations. For the (theoretical) limiting case $\gamma \to 0$ we have $y \to x$ and thus $\frac{\partial}{\partial y} \to \frac{\partial}{\partial x}$. We then obtain two parallel families of cables. Adding the equilibrium conditions 2.20a, b, we can write $p_x + p_y = \bar{p}_x$ and $H_y + H_x = H$. In this limiting case, we cannot take into account a load normal to the plane of the cable; Eqs. 18a, c for the plane cable remain valid. The homogeneous equation $H_0 z'' = 0$ then states: The cable can be pretensioned only if it is straight initially ($z'' = 0$).

2.5.2 *Nonpretensioned Cable Nets*
We have already mentioned in Section 2.3.1 that a cable net with positive Gaussian curvature cannot be pretensioned. It must be secured by permanent loads against the effects of wind suction. Both families of cables are deflected in the direction of the external load and take up the latter. The system is far more rigid than a single family of cables: all deformations are considerably smaller, in particular when the load is nonuniform.
The equilibrium conditions given in Section 2.2.2 contain no assumptions about an initial tension. The elasticity equations take into account only deformations caused by external loads and changes in temperature. Hence, all the foregoing derivations remain valid if for nonpretensioned cable nets the initial state is defined by $H_{xp} = H_{yp} = 0$ (cf. Section 2.2.1).
No single-valued solution for w can now be obtained from Eq. 2.47a. Its purely integral form gives no information about the necessarily continuous variation of $w(x, y)$. In order to "smooth out" the function w we have to insert arbitrary values for H_{x0} and H_{y0}. These are, in accordance with Eq. 2.39c, taken to be $H_{xp}^{(1)}$ and $H_{yp}^{(1)}$, chosen so as to be as close as possible to the final values H_p. They can be determined quickly by means of the approximations given in the following section.
The results are still satisfactory even when the values of $H_{xp}^{(1)}$ and $H_{yp}^{(1)}$ have been inaccurately selected (e.g., the same for all cases of loading). It was shown by means of a large number of worked examples that the curvatures w'' and $w^{\cdot\cdot}$ are very small in the center region of the surface; the terms $H_x w''$ and $H_y w^{\cdot\cdot}$ are only significant in small strips along the edge (approximately up to a distance of $l/10$ from the edge).
When the nonlinear terms are taken into account, Eq. 2.41c must in every case be replaced by Eq. 2.41d.

2.6 Approximations

2.6.1 *General Observations*
The sectional loads depend, as in every statically indeterminate structure, not only on the loads but also on the dimensions and rigidities of the system. In cable nets we encounter the additional difficulty that the magnitudes $E_x F_x$ and $E_y F_y$, as well as H_{x0} and H_{y0}, must be known before computation begins.

We therefore require a simple preliminary calculation in order to determine the order of magnitude of the sectional loads and deformations to be expected.
We assume a symmetrical cable net whose initial surface is given by

$$z = -\frac{k_x}{2} x^2 + \frac{k_y}{2} y^2, \quad \text{with} \quad \frac{k_y}{k_x} = \varrho. \tag{2.59}$$

The net is pretensioned, but the formulas below are also valid for a nonpretensioned net where $z'' < 0, z^{\cdot\cdot} < 0$ and k_y is replaced by $(-k_y)$.
In cable nets with variable curvatures we substitute appropriate mean values for k_x and k_y.
The cable rigidities are assumed to be constant; their ratio is

$$\frac{E_y F_y}{E_x F_x} = \varphi = \text{const}. \tag{2.60}$$

2.6.2 *Load p_x*
When only p_x acts, Eq. 2.52 becomes

$$H_{xp} = + k_x \Phi_x \int_{x_l}^{x_r} w\, dx + \mathfrak{Q}_x ,$$

where $z'' = -k_x$. This integral vanishes when p_x is a symmetrical function. When $p_x(x)$ is an antimetrical function, $\mathfrak{P}(x, y)$ and thus also $w(x, y)$ have a different sign in the center region of the net from that near the edges x_r and x_l. We can then neglect the integral in comparison with $\mathfrak{Q}_x$, so that

$$^{px}H_{xp} \approx \mathfrak{Q}_x , \qquad ^{px}H_{yp} \approx 0 . \tag{2.61}$$

2.6.3 *Load p_y*
Reasoning similar to that for p_x yields

$$^{py}H_{xp} \approx 0 , \qquad ^{py}H_{yp} \approx \mathfrak{Q}_y . \tag{2.62}$$

2.6.4 *Load p_z*
The vertical load is distributed nearly uniformly. We have already mentioned (in Section 2.5.2) that the terms $H_{x0} w''$ and $H_{y0} w^{\cdot\cdot}$ in Eq. 2.47a can be neglected in comparison with the others. We then obtain from Eq. 2.47b:

$$k_x^2 \Phi_x \int_{x_l}^{x_r} w\, dx + k_y^2 \Phi_y \int_{y_l}^{y_r} w\, dy = p_z .$$

We cannot determine w from this equation; however, it yields the fractions of the load $\varkappa_x \cdot p_z$ and $\varkappa_y \cdot p_z$ taken up, respectively, by the tension and by the load-carrying cables:

$$\frac{\varkappa_y}{\varkappa_x} = \frac{k_y^2 \Phi_y \cdot \int w\, dy}{k_x^2 \Phi_x \int w\, dx} = \frac{H_{yp} \cdot z^{\cdot\cdot}}{H_{xp} \cdot z''} .$$

Since the deflection curves of both families of cables are similar (cf. Fig. 2.28), we can assume

$$\frac{\int_{y_l}^{y_r} w\, dy}{\int_{x_l}^{x_r} w\, dx} \approx \frac{l_y}{l_x} .$$

Substituting Φ from Eq. 2.56b and writing $PA_x \approx PA_y$ we obtain

$$\frac{\varkappa_y}{\varkappa_x} = \frac{E_y F_y}{E_x F_x} \frac{k_y^2}{k_x^2} = \varphi \cdot \varrho^2$$

irrespective of the spans.

Since $\varkappa_x + \varkappa_y = 1$, we obtain

$$\varkappa_x = \frac{1}{1 + \varphi\,\varrho^2}\,, \qquad \varkappa_y = \frac{\varphi\,\varrho^2}{1 + \varphi\,\varrho^2} = 1 - \varkappa_x\,. \tag{2.63}$$

The horizontal tensions are thus

$$^{p_z}H_{xp} \approx \varkappa_x \cdot \frac{p_z}{k_x}\,, \tag{2.64a}$$

$$^{p_z}H_{yp} \approx -\,\varkappa_y\,\frac{p_z}{k_y} = -\,\varphi\,\varrho\,{}^{p_z}H_{xp}\,. \tag{2.64b}$$

Figure 2.14 shows $\varkappa_x$ as function of φ and ϱ.

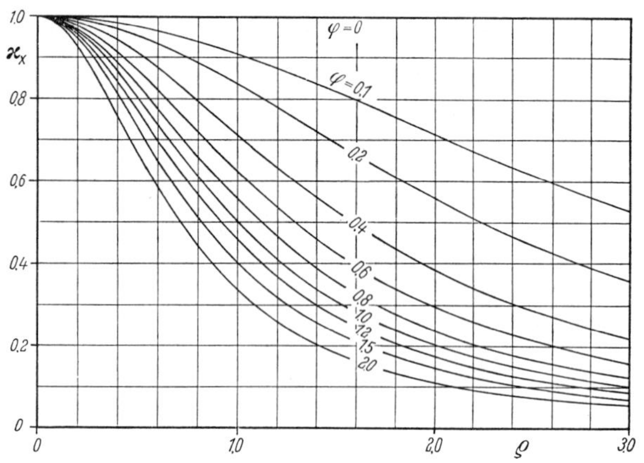

Fig. 2.14. Load Fraction $\varkappa_x$ as Function of φ and ϱ.

Substituting in Eq. 2.64a and in

$$H_{xp} = k_x\,\Phi_x \int_{x_l}^{x_r} w\,d\,x \approx \varkappa_x\,\frac{p_z}{k_x}$$

for Φ_x its expression from Eq. 2.56b and writing

$$\int_{x_l}^{x_r} w\,d\,x = w_m \cdot l_x\,,$$

we obtain an estimate of the mean deflection to be expected:

$$^{p_z}w_m = \frac{P\Lambda_x}{k_x^2\,E_x\,F_x}\,\varkappa_x\,p_z\,. \tag{2.65a}$$

The results of numerous worked examples show that for a uniform vertical load the deflection in the center of the surface is approximately

$$^{p_z}w_0 \approx (1.1 \text{ to } 1.25) \cdot w_m\,. \tag{2.65b}$$

When the net is not very shallow, w is slightly larger in the vicinity of the quarter-span points than in the center of the cable net. Equations 2.65 are obviously valid also for other loads when $\mathfrak{P}$ is constant. We must then replace p_z by $\mathfrak{P}$.

2.6.5 *Temperature Effects*

Frequently the temperature strains of a cable net, referred to the edge members, are uniform (${}^t\varepsilon_x = {}^t\varepsilon_x = {}^t\varepsilon =$const). We then have in accordance with Eqs. 2.50:

$$\mathfrak{N}_x = -\,E_x\,F_x\,{}^t\varepsilon\,, \qquad \mathfrak{N}_y = -\,E_y\,F_y\,{}^t\varepsilon\,.$$

The load term

$$^t\mathfrak{P} = +\,(k_x\,E_x\,F_x - k_y\,E_y\,F_y)\,{}^t\varepsilon$$

is then constant and can be dealt with like p_z in Section 2.6.4. We obtain in accordance with Eqs. 2.52, 2.63, and 2.64:

$$^tH_{xp} \approx -\,E_x\,F_x\,{}^t\varepsilon\,\varkappa_y\left(1 + \frac{1}{\varrho}\right) \tag{2.66a}$$

and

$$^tH_{yp} \approx -\,E_y\,F_y\,{}^t\varepsilon\,\varkappa_x\,(1 + \varrho) = \frac{1}{\varrho}\,{}^tH_{xp}\,. \tag{2.66b}$$

The deflection depends solely on $\mathfrak{P}$. Substitution for p_z in Eq. 2.65a yields

$$^tw_m = \frac{\Lambda_x}{k_x}\,\varkappa_x\,(1 - \varphi\,\varrho)\,{}^t\varepsilon\,. \tag{2.67}$$

The deformations in the cable-net center can again be estimated with the aid of Eq. 2.65b.

2.6.6 *Nonuniform Load*

The above approximation can also be used in the case of an arbitrarily distributed horizontal load. However, when p_z is nonuniform, no expression can be adduced for an estimate [of the deflections in the center].

The best method is to separate an approximately uniform "base load" that can be dealt with according to Section 2.6.4. The remaining "peak loads" can be considered by estimating magnitudes $\varkappa$, in analogy to the values $\varkappa_x$ and $\varkappa_y$ applicable to the uniform load. Using Eqs. 2.64, we then find additional (positive or negative) horizontal tensions.

A long, narrow load acting along a cable that forms part of a net is taken up mainly, but not exclusively, by the cable concerned. Cables situated directly beneath a limited region of load application will in general be subjected to larger horizontal tensions than other cables. The part of the load taken up by, e.g., cables running in the x-direction (and thus, the horizontal tension in them) increases with the fraction of the cable length directly subjected to the distributed load.

The net will often be symmetrical in at least one direction. The cable forces induced by antimetrical loads can then be determined approximately according to Section 2.7.1.

When the approximate distribution of the horizontal tensions is known, we obtain from Eqs. 2.64a and 2.65a:

$$w_m\,(y) \approx \frac{\Lambda_x}{k_x\,E_x\,F_x} \cdot H_{xp}\,(y). \tag{2.68a}$$

Similarly, using H_{yp},

$$w_m\,(x) \approx -\,\frac{\Lambda_y}{k_y\,E_y\,F_y} \cdot H_{yp}\,(x)\,. \tag{2.68b}$$

The deflections can thus be estimated even when the load is nonuniform. In any case, we have obtained satisfactory initial values for the iterative solution of system 2.55.

The procedure is demonstrated in the worked example in Section 2.9. Using the approximations, the errors in the maximum horizontal tensions amounted to only a few per cent despite the irregular plan and the sharply varying wind loads. Further details on the accuracy of the approximations are given in Section 2.8.

2.7 Behavior under Load of Cable Nets and Edge Members

2.7.1 *Symmetry Properties*

Considerable simplifications are possible by applying the linearized theory if the spatial structure is symmetrical or antimetrical with respect to a plane and if the load also has symmetrical or antimetrical properties. Henceforth we shall assume the y, z-plane ($x = 0$) to be the plane of symmetry or antimetry. The same reasoning applies if the cable net has the said properties in the y-direction. The x- and y-directions are then interchangeable.

All external effects (loads, edge displacements, temperature variations) are taken into account in Eq. 2.47a by means of the load function $\mathfrak{P}(x, y)$. Any symmetry properties of $\mathfrak{P}$ therefore affect w and H_p also. We must therefore distinguish between the cases when, on the one hand, the load function $\mathfrak{P}$, according to Eq. 2.47b or 2.51, and on the other hand, the cable net, is symmetrical or antimetrical.

The horizontal displacements are particularly large when a symmetrical load acts on an antimetrical system or vice versa. Taking into account the nonlinear terms will then yield corrections which can generally no longer be neglected in comparison with the results of the linear theory.

2.7.1.1 Symmetrical System

The geometrical conditions are:

$$z(x, y) = z(-x, y), \qquad x_r(y) = -x_l(y).$$

$\mathfrak{P}(x, y)$ is symmetrical: Obviously, $w(x, y)$ is also symmetrical. The displacement u is, considered as a *vector*, symmetrical, but the *function* $u(x, y)$ is antimetrical. For $x = 0$ we have $w = u = 0$. We can restrict ourselves to considering one half of the system ($0 \leqslant x \leqslant x_r$), for which

$$\int_{x_l}^{x_r} z'' w\, dx = 2 \int_{0}^{x_r} z'' w\, dx.$$

The integral appearing in the expression for Φ_x has in this case to be taken over the entire length $l_x = 2x_r$.

$\mathfrak{P}(x, y)$ is antimetrical: In this case $w(x, y)$ is also antimetrical. For $x = 0$ we have $\mathfrak{P}(o, y) = 0$, $w(o, y) = w''(o, y) = 0$. However, $u(o, y) \neq 0$ and

$$\int_{x_l}^{x_r} z'' w\, dx = 0.$$

If we consider only one half of the system, Eq. 2.47a reduces to

$$z^{\cdot\cdot}\, \Phi_y \int_{y_l}^{y_r} z^{\cdot\cdot} w\, dy - H_{x0} w'' - H_{y0} w^{\cdot\cdot} = \mathfrak{P}.$$

Furthermore, by Eq. 2.52a,

$$H_{xp} = \mathfrak{Q}_x,$$

since all the remaining terms vanish. All loads except p_x are thus taken up exclusively by the cables running in the y-direction.

2.7.1.2 Antimetrical System

The geometrical conditions are.

$$z(x, y) - z(0, y) = z(0, y) - z(-x, y), \qquad x_r(y) = -x_l(y).$$

For the sake of completeness we shall give the relevant formulas, although such a structure is often uneconomical since the mainly symmetrical loads (dead weight, snow) can be taken up only by one family of cables (cf. Section 2.3.2.7).

$\mathfrak{P}(x, y)$ is symmetrical: In this case $w(x, y)$ and $u(x, y)$ are also symmetrical. Since

$$\int_{x_r}^{x_l} z'' w\, dx = 0,$$

one term in Eq. 2.47a vanishes again. We can restrict ourselves to considering one half of the system, in which $w'(o, y) = 0$. Furthermore,

$$H_{xp} = \mathfrak{Q}_x.$$

The term containing $\mathfrak{N}_x$ in Eq. 2.51 is antimetrical with respect to $x = 0$. It is thus identically zero, since $\mathfrak{N}_x$ is a function only of y.

$\mathfrak{P}(x, y)$ is antimetrical: Both w and u are now antimetrical. Hence, in the center, $w(o, y) = u(o, y) = \mathfrak{P}(o, y) = 0$. Since z'' is also antimetrical, we have

$$\int_{x_l}^{x_r} z'' w\, dx = 2 \cdot \int_{0}^{x_r} z'' w\, dx.$$

We need therefore consider only one half of the system.

2.7.1.3 Compilation

The conditions that the various parts of the load function must satisfy are tabulated below.

	System symmetrical		System antimetrical	
Load:				
p_x	A	S	S	A
p_y	S	A	A	S
p_z	S	A	S	A
u_{xr}, u_{xl}	A	S	S	A
w_{xr}, w_{xl}	S	A	S	A
$t_{\varepsilon x}$	S	A	A	S
$t_{\varepsilon y}$	S	A	A	S
Load function $\mathfrak{P}$:	S	A	S	A
Results:				
w	S	A	S	A
u	A	S	S	A
H_{xp}	S	A	A	S
H_{yp}	S	A	A	S

We again remind the reader that we consider only the symmetry properties of the *functions*. A uniform load p_x acting on both halves of the structure in the direction toward the axis of symmetry is thus *antimetrical*.

The symbols denote:
S: Function symmetrical with respect to $x = 0$,
A: Function antimetrical with respect to $x = 0$.

As in other structures, any symmetry properties of the cable-net system can thus be exploited. The comparatively large number of unknowns $w_{i,j}$ can thus be reduced by one half. This makes the calculation procedure much shorter. The additional work involved in any separation of the load into parts and the superimposing of partial results is insignificant.

2.7.2 *Temperature Variations*

Let a pretensioned cable net undergo a uniform rise in temperature Δt in relation to the edge members. The load function is then according to Eqs. 2.50 and 2.51:

$$\mathfrak{P} = -\,(z''\,E_x F_x\,\alpha_{tx} + \ddot{z}\,E_y F_y\,\alpha_{ty})\,\Delta t$$

and vanishes when the expression in parentheses becomes zero, i.e., for

$$-\frac{E_y F_y}{E_x F_x}\cdot\frac{\ddot{z}}{z''}\cdot\frac{\alpha_{ty}}{\alpha_{tx}} = \varphi\cdot\varrho\cdot\frac{\alpha_{ty}}{\alpha_{tx}} = 1\,. \qquad (2.69a)$$

When the coefficients of linear expansion are equal in both families of cables, this equation can also be written as follows [using Eq. 2.26c]:

$$\frac{E_y F_y}{E_x F_x} = \frac{H_{x0}}{H_{y0}}\,. \qquad (2.69b)$$

When this condition is satisfied, no deflections and (by Eqs. 2.53) no horizontal displacements occur. The cable net thus remains at rest.

The horizontal tensions are

$${}^tH_{xp} = -\,E_x F_x\,{}^t\varepsilon\,, \qquad (2.70a)$$

$${}^tH_{yp} = -\,E_y F_y\,{}^t\varepsilon = \frac{1}{\varrho}\,{}^tH_{xp}\,. \qquad (2.70b)$$

These results also follow from Section 2.6.5, in particular Eqs. 2.66.

The deflection of a single cable always increases when the temperature rises. (This additional deflection can be of the order of the initial deflection of almost straight cables.) No deformations and strains occur in a pretensioned cable net when Eqs. 2.69 are satisfied.

This is of great benefit to the entire structure. When Eqs. 2.69 are not fulfilled, the additional deflections are always smaller than those of single cables.

Note: The complete differential Eqs. 2.27 are not exactly satisfied by writing $u = v = w = 0$ and ${}^t\varepsilon = \text{const} \neq 0$. The reason for this is that the cable force S is constant in an immovable cable subjected to a uniform change in temperature, whereas the equilibrium conditions require $H = \text{const}$. This was ignored when the last two terms were neglected in Eqs. 2.53.

2.7.3 *Safety Against Yielding*

As in other prestressed structures, the material of pretensioned cable nets is already strained even before any external load is applied. The total stresses are thus no longer proportional to the load due to dead weight and external forces.

The regulations in force in Germany concerning prestressed concrete and composite girders require proof of adequate safety when the load is increased up to the ultimate or yield stress.

Similarly, we have to show that the stresses in pretensioned cable nets remain below the yield stress for the most unfavorable combination of the following loads:

Initial tension,
Temperature variations,
Load equal to 1.6 times the sum of permanent and maximum variable loads.

The sectional loads due to the above-mentioned cases of loading must be multiplied by 1.6 when prestressed girders are considered. Analysis of cable nets is less simple.

If we assume a vertical load p_z that increases gradually, the tension cables will become slack successively beyond a certain stage. At a second stage of higher loading the carrying cables alone will take up the entire load. The intermediate stage, in which some of the tension cables are slack, can be analyzed mathematically only with great difficulty. To obtain at least a qualitative result we shall assume that all tension cables become slack simultaneously. We can represent H as a function of p_z approximately as shown in Fig. 2.15 when only the linear theory is applied.

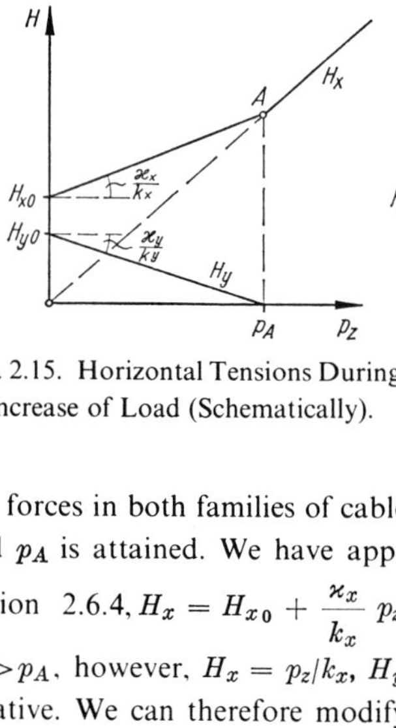

Fig. 2.15. Horizontal Tensions During Increase of Load (Schematically).

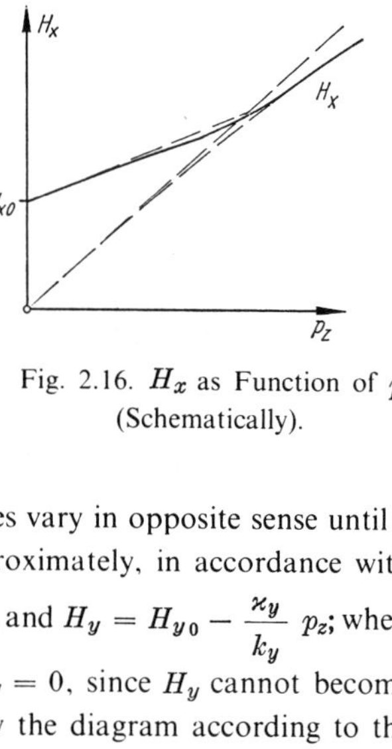

Fig. 2.16. H_x as Function of p (Schematically).

The forces in both families of cables vary in opposite sense until a load p_A is attained. We have approximately, in accordance with Section 2.6.4, $H_x = H_{x0} + \frac{\varkappa_x}{k_x}\,p_z$ and $H_y = H_{y0} - \frac{\varkappa_y}{k_y}\,p_z$; when $p_z > p_A$, however, $H_x = p_z/k_x$, $H_y = 0$, since H_y cannot become negative. We can therefore modify the diagram according to the actual behavior under load of the cables, obtaining the (also only qualitative) representation in Fig. 2.16. The function $H_x\,(p_z)$ is not exactly linear, there being a continuous transition at A instead of a slope discontinuity.

In order to assure safety against yielding we must therefore investigate first whether $H_y > 0$ or $H_y < 0$ when the load is increased. If $H_y > 0$, we determine, as before, the stresses in the cables caused by the increased load. If the calculation shows that $H_y < 0$, the entire load, without the initial tension, acts on the carrying cables, which now behave like single cables. The stresses in the latter must then be less than the yield stress of the cable material.

A similar proof must be adduced for the tension cables if the permanent load is small and wind suction large.

Safety against yielding should already be ensured in the preliminary design.

2.7.4 *Natural Frequencies*

Nonpretensioned cables and cable nets oscillate when subjected to periodic or impulsive loads. Pretensioned nets may in these cases vibrate like stretched strings. Wind gusts repeated within short intervals, or dynamic loads caused by vortex shedding have little effect on shells, since the latter are rigid in bending and have comparatively large dead weights. However, in particular with light cable nets of large span, the natural frequency may be so low, that resonance occurs. This can endanger the structure since the loads may attain values several times as great as the static loads.

We shall not consider here the problem of the wind frequencies to be expected and of the admissible limits for the natural frequencies of a roof, since too few meteorological data are available. Obviously, the vibrational behavior of a structure depends also on its dimensions. A wind gust acts considerably later on the leeward side of a building than on its windward side; hence, the roof is never subjected simultaneously to forces over its entire area. This makes it difficult to investigate the effects of wind gusts or vortices with the aid of models.

Different vibrational modes may occur, depending on the circumstances.

2.7.4.1 General Procedure

The deformations $\overline{w}\,(x, y, t)$ caused by the vibrations are referred to the state $\overline{\mathfrak{r}} = \mathfrak{r} + \mathfrak{w}$; $\overline{\mathfrak{w}}$ has, as in Eq. 2.8, the components $\overline{u}, \overline{v},$ and $\overline{w}$. Due to the action of the loads, the cable net assumes a shape differing from the initial surface when it is at rest ($\overline{\mathfrak{w}} = 0$). The horizontal tensions are then $H = H_0 + H_g$. We simplify the calculation by retaining the values of $z\,(x, y)$ and Φ which correspond to the initial state. The horizontal tensions are generally replaced by appropriate mean values.

We apply D'Alembert's principle to the fundamental equation. Equation 2.47a then yields

$$z'' \, \Phi_x \int z'' \, \overline{w} \, (x, y, t) \, dx + z^{\cdot\cdot} \, \Phi_y \int z^{\cdot\cdot} \, \overline{w} \, (x, y, t) \, dy -$$
$$- H_x \cdot \overline{w}'' \, (x, y, t) - H_y \cdot \overline{w}^{\cdot\cdot} \, (x, y, t) = \qquad (2.71a)$$
$$= - \mu \, \frac{\partial^2 \, \overline{w} \, (x, y, t)}{\partial \, t^2} \, .$$

Here μ is the mass referred (like p_z) to unit area in plan (mass = weight gravitational acceleration).

We set

$\overline{w} \, (x, y, t) = \overline{w} \, (x, y) \cdot \cos \omega \, t \, ,$

where ω is the frequency of the vibrations (circular frequency) and t is the time.

Hence

$$z'' \, \Phi_x \int z'' \, \overline{w} \, dx + z^{\cdot\cdot} \, \Phi_y \int z^{\cdot\cdot} \, \overline{w} \, dy - H_x \cdot \overline{w}'' - H_y \overline{w}^{\cdot\cdot} = \qquad (2.71b)$$
$$= \mu \cdot \omega^2 \, \overline{w} \, ,$$

where, for the sake of simplicity, we have written only $\overline{w}$ for $\overline{w} \, (x, y)$. We can consider the right-hand side to represent a virtual load:

$$\mu \cdot \omega^2 \, \overline{w} = \overline{p} \, . \qquad (2.71c)$$

This equation states that at any point of the net $\overline{p}$ is proportional to μ times the deflection. The ratio

$$\omega^2 = \frac{\overline{p}}{\mu \cdot \overline{w}} = \text{const} \qquad (2.72)$$

is the required natural frequency, from which we obtain the vibration period

$$\tau = \frac{2 \, \pi}{\omega} \, . \qquad (2.73)$$

The exact solution is obtained by rewriting Eq. 2.71b as a sum-and-difference equation like Eq. 2.55. This leads to a homogeneous system of equations in $\overline{w}_{i,j}$. When the number of unknowns is m we obtain an entire rational function of the mth degree by equating the determinant of the denominator to zero. The zeros of this function determine the required eigenvalues ω and the vibration mode.

Such a calculation must be performed on a computer if the number of unknowns is large.

This procedure is not accurate enough for the higher eigenvalues. The corresponding horizontal displacements are generally too large to be taken into account in the linearized fundamental equation.

A better procedure is to assume a virtual load $\overline{p}$ and analyze the cable net according to the method used for the other cases of load. If $\overline{p}$ was selected properly, Eq. 2.27 must be satisfied at every point of the cable net. If necessary, the calculation must be repeated with a correctly chosen value of $\overline{p}$.

The calculation yielding the smallest value of ω is the correct one. Satisfactory results are obtained if we determine the mean of all m values found in the first trial for the different points i, j:

$$\omega^2 \approx \frac{1}{m} \sum \omega^2_{i,j} = \frac{1}{m} \sum \frac{\overline{p}_{i,j}}{\mu_{i,j} \cdot \overline{w}_{i,j}} \, . \qquad (2.74)$$

The last two terms on the left-hand side of Eq. 2.71b are mostly small compared to the other terms. Since H_x is usually larger than H_{x0}, but $H_y < H_{y0}$ in every case, we can insert the approximate horizontal tensions caused by pretensioning. This leads to a system of equations similar to that corresponding to other cases of loading. We then obtain a particularly simple approximation based on the deflections $g w$ caused by the permanent load. The mass is $\mu = g/\tilde{g}$ where the gravitational acceleration is $\tilde{g} = 9.81$ m sec^{-2}. The lowest natural frequency (circular frequency) is by Eq. 2.74:

$$\omega^2 \approx \tilde{g} \cdot \frac{1}{m} \sum \frac{1}{g w_{i,j}} \, . \qquad (2.75)$$

We thus have to determine only the mean value of the reciprocal deflections caused by the permanent load, and multiply by $\tilde{g}$.

2.7.4.2 Approximations

In order to derive approximations for the natural frequencies in closed form, we assume a cable net, symmetrical in both directions, spanning a region $(l_x \cdot l_y)$ that is rectangular in plan. Following the reasoning in Section 2.6, we approximate the position at rest by the initial surface:

$$\bar{z} \approx z = -\frac{k_x}{2} x^2 + \frac{k_y}{2} y^2 .$$

The horizontal tensions $H_x(x, y)$ and $H_y(x, y)$ are replaced by constant mean values. The mass μ is also assumed to be constant. This will not introduce significant errors when the net is shallow and the roofing uniform.

Symmetrical vibrations

We shall now consider the natural frequency of a net vibrating symmetrically with respect to both the x- and y-axes. We insert in Eq. 2.71a:

$$w = w_0 \cdot \cos \alpha x \cdot \cos \beta y \cdot \cos \omega t ,$$

where

$$\alpha = \frac{\pi}{l_x}, \qquad \beta = \frac{\pi}{l_y} .$$

We then obtain

$$k_x^2 \Phi_x \frac{2}{\pi} l_x \cos \beta y + k_y^2 \Phi_y \frac{2}{\pi} l_y \cos \alpha x + \left(\frac{H_x}{l_x^2} + \frac{H_y}{l_y^2}\right) \pi^2 \cos \alpha x \cdot \cos \beta y = \mu \omega^2 \cos \alpha x \cdot \cos \beta y .$$

This equation is not satisfied for all points (x, y), in view of the integrals entering in Eq. 2.71a. We shall therefore replace the constant $2/\pi$ in the first two terms by the functions $\cos \alpha x$ and $\cos \beta y$. The total load remains unchanged.

We now substitute from Eq. 2.56b: $\Phi \cdot l = EF =$ const. (The factor $P\Lambda$ has been neglected. Its value is exactly 1.0050, i.e., nearly 1.0, when the relative deflection is $f/l = 0.1$.) The square of the lowest natural frequency is then:

$$\omega_{ss}^2 = \frac{\pi^2}{\mu}\left(\frac{H_x}{l_x^2} + \frac{H_y}{l_y^2} + \frac{k_x^2 E_x F_x}{\pi^2} + \frac{k_y^2 E_y F_y}{\pi^2}\right). \tag{2.76}$$

Siev[1] derived similar expressions by using the Rayleigh quotients. Using Eqs. 2.32, 2.60, and 2.63, we can rewrite Eq. 2.76 as follows:

$$\omega_{ss}^2 = \frac{\pi^2}{\mu}\left(\frac{H_x}{l_x^2} + \frac{H_y}{l_y^2} + \frac{k_x^2 E_x F_x}{\pi^2 \cdot \varkappa_x}\right). \tag{2.77}$$

The vibration period is obtained from Eq. 2.73.

When $k_x = k_y = H_y = 0$, we obtain the equation of a stretched string, as was to be expected.

Antimetrical vibrations

The individual cables are curved when at rest. Obviously, antimetrical vibrations with almost complete absence of stretching are possible. However, horizontal displacements can no longer be neglected in these cases.

[1] A. Siev, *Stability of Prestressed Suspended Roofs*, Dissertation, Technion—Israel Institute of Technology, Haifa, 1961.

We use Rayleigh's method to estimate the frequency of these antimetrical vibrations. The initial surface considered before is again assumed to be the resting position of the rectangular cable net.

The displacements are represented by polynomials satisfying the geometrical boundary conditions $(\bar{u} = \bar{v} = \bar{w} = 0)$

$$\left.\begin{aligned} \bar{u} &= c \frac{k_x l_x}{8} (1 + 2\xi^2 - 3\xi^4) \cdot (\eta - \eta^3) , \\ \bar{v} &= -c \frac{k_y l_y}{8} (\xi - \xi^3) \cdot (1 + 2\eta^2 - 3\eta^4) , \\ \bar{w} &= c (\xi - \xi^3) \cdot (\eta - \eta^3) , \end{aligned}\right\} \tag{2.78a–c}$$

where the dimensionless coordinates are

$$\xi = \frac{2x}{l_x} \qquad (-1 \leqq \xi \leqq +1) \tag{2.79a}$$

and

$$\eta = \frac{2y}{l_y} \qquad (-1 \leqq \eta \leqq +1) . \tag{2.79b}$$

These should not be confused with the parameters ξ_r and ξ_l in Section 2.4.5.

The functions $\bar{u}$ and $\bar{v}$ have been determined in such a way that $\bar{u}' + z' \bar{w}' = \bar{v}^{\cdot} + z^{\cdot} \bar{w}^{\cdot} = 0$ in the entire region. This can easily be proved. The first terms in Eqs. 2.21 thus vanish. We now assume that by virtue of the antimetry of the displacements, the cable forces remain constant during the vibrations. The maximum potential energy of the cable net is thus

$$U = \iint S_1 \cdot \varepsilon_1 \, dx \, dy + \iint S_2 \varepsilon_2 \, dx \, dy .$$

Inserting the (constant) horizontal tensions given by Eqs. 2.17 and neglecting z'^2 and $z^{\cdot 2}$ in comparison with unity, we obtain

$$U = \frac{H_x}{2} \iint (\bar{v}'^2 + \bar{w}'^2) \, dx \, dy + \frac{H_y}{2} \iint (\bar{u}^{\cdot 2} + \bar{w}^{\cdot 2}) \, dx \, dy .$$

For constant mass μ the referred kinetic energy is

$$\bar{E} = \frac{\mu}{2} \iint (\bar{u}^2 + \bar{v}^2 + \bar{w}^2) \, dx \, dy .$$

Integration has to be performed over the entire plan. The required frequency of the antimetrical vibrations is

$$\omega_{aa}^2 = \frac{U}{\bar{E}} . \tag{2.80}$$

Numerical evaluations of the above integrals presents no difficulties and is omitted. The result is

$$\omega_{aa}^2 = \frac{42.0}{\mu} \frac{\frac{H_x}{l_x^2}(4 + k_y^2 l_y^2) + \frac{H_y}{l_y^2}(4 + k_x^2 l_x^2)}{4 + k_x^2 l_x^2 + k_y^2 l_y^2} , \tag{2.81}$$

from which τ_{aa} follows by Eq. 2.73.

The form of Eq. 2.81 shows that ω_{aa} is not simply the second natural frequency of the symmetrical vibrations discussed before. Only in the limiting case (plane net) $k_x = k_y \to 0$ do we obtain $\omega_{aa} = 1.0315 \cdot 2 \cdot \omega_{ss} \approx 2 \cdot \omega_{ss}$.

Symmetrical-antimetrical vibrations

If the wind causes a negative pressure at one edge of the roof but a positive pressure at the other, vibrations may occur which are symmetrical in one direction and antimetrical in the other.

We assume the displacement components to be

$$\left.\begin{aligned} \bar{u} &= c\,\frac{k_x\,l_x}{8}\,(1 + 2\,\xi^2 - 3\,\xi^4)\cdot(1-\eta^2)\,, \\ \bar{v} &= -\,c\,\frac{k_y\,l_y}{3}\,(\xi - \xi^3)\cdot(\eta - \eta^3)\,, \\ \bar{w} &= c\,(\xi - \xi^3)\cdot(1-\eta^2)\,. \end{aligned}\right\} \qquad (2.82\text{a–c})$$

The vibrations are antimetrical in the x-direction. The functions were determined in such a way that, on the one hand, $\bar{u}' + z'\bar{w}' = 0$, while on the other hand, the horizontal additional tension $\bar{H}_y$ caused by the vibrations is nearly constant over the length of the cable.

We again neglect the derivatives of z in comparison with unity. We then obtain from the energy balance

$$\omega_{as}^2 = \frac{2.67}{\mu}\left(\frac{H_x}{l_x^2}\,\frac{63.0 + k_y^2\,l_y^2}{4 + k_x^2\,l_x^2} + 3.75\,\frac{H_y}{l_y^2}\right), \qquad (2.83)$$

where the intermediate steps in the calculation have been omitted.

For the sake of comparison we again set $k_x = k_y = 0$. This yields:

$$\tilde{\omega}_{as}^2 = 1.01\,\frac{\pi^2}{\mu}\left(4.2\,\frac{H_x}{l_x^2} + \frac{H_y}{l_y^2}\right).$$

Making the same assumptions as for Eq. 2.76, we would have obtained

$$\tilde{\omega}_{as}^2 = \frac{\pi^2}{\mu}\left(4.0\,\frac{H_x}{l_x^2} + \frac{H_y}{l_y^2}\right).$$

When the vibrations are antimetrical in the y-direction and symmetrical in the x-direction, we have to interchange the subscripts x and y in the above formulas.

We have here assumed the cable net to be rectangular. If this is not the case, we can obtain satisfactory results with the aid of the above formulas by considering a rectangle of equal area to that of the given surface.

Some worked examples are given in Section 2.9.

2.7.5 *Edge-Curve Shape*

The tension members of a cable net are free from moments at any point. It is therefore of interest to investigate the shape which the edge curve must assume in order that the edge members also be free from moments. The edge curve must then form the line of pressure of the three-dimensional load (dead weight, cable forces, and abutment reactions).

Two methods of design are possible:

1. Edge member completely free from moments: The cable forces vary in direction and magnitude whenever the load on the net is altered. Hence, a distinct line of action corresponds to each case of loading. This condition is satisfied by an edge cable, stretched between two fixed points, to which the ends of the net cables are fixed. Variations in the cable forces of the net cause displacements of the edge cables. These, in their turn, affect the forces acting in the net, until equilibrium is restored.

The calculation has to proceed in the following steps:

a. Analysis of the cable net without or with assumed edge deformations.

b. Determination of the deformations of the edge cable, caused by the changes in the forces acting on it.

c. Determination of the forces and deformations of the net, caused by the new displacements of the edge.

d. Renewed analysis of the edge cable.

The procedure is repeated until convergence is attained. The individual results can be superimposed if the cable net is analyzed by the linear theory; no superposition is, however, possible for the edge cable.

The edge cable can be replaced by a multijoint arch, convex in the outward direction. This labile pressure member must be stabilized not only by the cable net, but in at least one additional plane by single cables, a second cable net, or rods.

2. Edge member partially free from moments: An arch, capable of resisting bending and considered as ideally rigid in the limit, is supported at certain points in the vertical, horizontal, or both directions. The arch is analyzed separately with respect to vertical (vertical components of cable forces and dead weight) and horizontal loads (horizontal tensions in the net). In most existing structures the arch rests on numerous abutments so that the moments due to the vertical loads are small.

The horizontal tensions in the net are generally far larger. It is then most economical to give to the arch a shape corresponding to the line of pressure of a particular combined load (e.g., initial tension plus permanent load).

The arch, considered as a separate structural element, need not be safe against buckling, since the cable forces induced by its deformation oppose the latter. When the safety factor against buckling of the arch is being determined, its elastic support, i.e., the interaction of cable net and arch, must be taken into account. An approximate calculation, even when taken on the safe side, will lead to considerable savings.

We shall now determine the projection in plan of the edge curve in such a way that it forms the line of pressure of the horizontal tensions $H_x\,(y)$ and $H_y\,(x)$ acting on it.

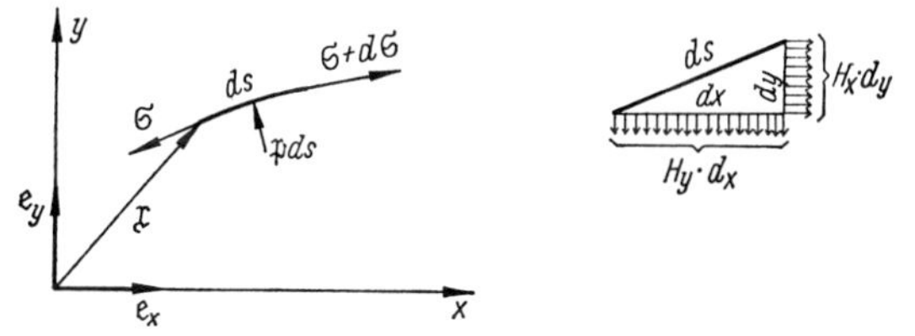

Fig. 2.17. Forces Acting on Edge Member.

Using the notations of Fig. 2.17, we proceed from the following equations:

$$d\,\mathfrak{S} + \mathfrak{p}\,ds = 0\,, \qquad d\,\mathfrak{x} \times \mathfrak{S} = 0\,.$$

These are the conditions of equilibrium and of absence of moments.

The vector quantities as defined by their components are:

$$\mathfrak{x} = \{x, y\}\,,$$

$\mathfrak{S}(x, y) = \{S_x(y), S_y(x)\}$,

$\mathfrak{p}\, ds = \{H_x(y) \cdot dy, - H_y(x) \cdot dx\}$.

The condition $ds^2 = dx^2 + dy^2$ has already been taken into account in the last equation; the minus sign denotes that both H_x and H_y are tensions acting on the same side of the curve. We obtain three differential equations which, after integration, yield the general equation of the edge curve:

$$\int\int H_y(x) \cdot dx \cdot dx + \int\int H_x(y) \cdot dy \cdot dy + a_1 x + a_2 y + a_3 = 0. \tag{2.84}$$

The three integration constants a can be determined when three points on the curve are given, or by means of other geometrical conditions.

If, for instance, H_x =const, H_y =const, we obtain

$$\frac{H_y}{2} x^2 + \frac{H_x}{2} y^2 + a_1 x + a_2 y + a_3 = 0.$$

This function represents an ellipse whose axes are parallel to the coordinate axes. It can be rewritten as follows:

$$\frac{(x - x_0)^2}{a^2} + \frac{(y - y_0)^2}{b^2} = 1, \tag{2.85}$$

where (x_0, y_0) are the coordinates of the ellipse center. The ratio of the semiaxes a and b is

$$\frac{a}{b} = \sqrt{\frac{H_x}{H_y}}. \tag{2.86}$$

One of the semiaxes is arbitrary.

The projection in plan of the edge curve of a translation surface assumes a particularly simple form if we require that the edge members be free from moments only when loaded by the initial tension. The initial surface is defined by $z = f(x) + g(y)$ (cf. Section 2.3.2). Substitution of Eqs. 2.31 in Eq. 2.84 then yields

$$f(x) - g(y) + a_1 x + a_2 y + a_3 = 0.$$

For the hyperbolic paraboloid we obtain

$$\frac{k_x}{2} x^2 + \frac{k_y}{2} y^2 + a_1 x + a_2 y + a_3 = 0,$$

which, as before, is an ellipse. The same is true for wave surfaces (Section 2.3.2.7), since for them also H_{x0} and H_{y0} are constant.

The edge curves need not have a continuous curvature at every point. When retaining points are arranged, between which the edge member has the form of one of the above curves, any shape may be obtained in plan (see Fig. 2.18).

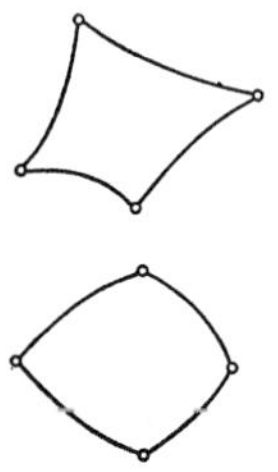

Fig. 2.18. Plans.

The above derivations are valid both for convex and for concave edges, i.e., for edge members in tension or in compression.

We can obtain a structure having no horizontal support reactions caused by vertical loads, like a continuously curved, closed rim, if the corners of the surfaces [shown in Fig. 2.18] are suitably connected by compression members.

2.7.6 *Installation of Cable Nets*

Nonpretensioned nets: The cables forming the initial surface are not in tension. When the position of any individual cable is known, its length can easily be determined from

$$L_{x0}(y) = \int ds_1 = \int_{x_l}^{x_r} \sqrt{g_{11}}\, dx \tag{2.87a}$$

or

$$L_{y0}(x) = \int_{y_l}^{y_r} \sqrt{g_{22}}\, dy, \tag{2.87b}$$

when its fixation (edge curve) is given.

When the small weight of the cables is neglected, we obtain the desired initial surface when cables of correct length are installed. A cable net of any design, including the clamped connections, can be assembled on the ground and lifted without scaffolding if the partial lengths between the intersections are determined in advance.

Pretensioned cable nets: The cable forces S_0 due to the initial tension are known in addition to the other quantities. The cable elongation caused by the initial tension is found with sufficient accuracy from Eqs. 2.19, [2.22], and 2.26:

$$\Delta L_x = H_{x0} \int_{x_l}^{x_r} \frac{g_{11}}{E_x F_x} dx. \tag{2.88}$$

If the cables are not straightened in advance, the effective modulus of elasticity must be inserted in order to take into account their straightening under tension.

The length of a carrying cable is thus

$$L_{x00} = L_{x0} - \Delta L_x, \tag{2.89a}$$

while the length of a tension cable is

$$L_{y00} = L_{y0} - \Delta L_y = L_{y0} - H_{y0} \int_{y_l}^{y_r} \frac{g_{22}}{E_y F_y} dy. \tag{2.89b}$$

The changes in cable length, occuring when tension is applied, must take into account the deformations of the edge members, which have to be determined separately. These changes in cable length can be included in an analysis of the net subjected only to dead weight.

Pretensioned cable nets can thus also be assembled on the ground before being inserted into the edge assemblies. Any necessary corrections can then be easily carried out.

2.8 Analysis of Pretensioned Cable Nets

2.8.1 *General Observations*

We shall consider a simple system, symmetrical in the x- and y-directions, in order to investigate the influence of various factors on the forces and deformations in a pretensioned cable net.

The initial surface is defined by

$$z = -\frac{x^2}{100} + \frac{y^2}{100}, \qquad -z'' = +z^{\cdot\cdot} = k_x = k_y = \frac{1}{50}\,\mathrm{m}^{-1}.$$

The spans are $l_x = l_y = 30\,\mathrm{m}$. The deflection: span ratio is thus $n = f/l = 1/13.33$. We now assume:

$$E_x F_x = E_y F_y = E\,F = 941\ \mathrm{Mp/m}\,,$$

$$H_{x0} = H_{y0} = H_0 = 2.5\ \mathrm{Mp/m}\,.$$

We shall only consider a uniformly distributed load $p_z = p$. The deflections will be determined at the 25 lattice points ($\Delta x = \Delta y = 5.0$ m) indicated in Fig. 2.19.

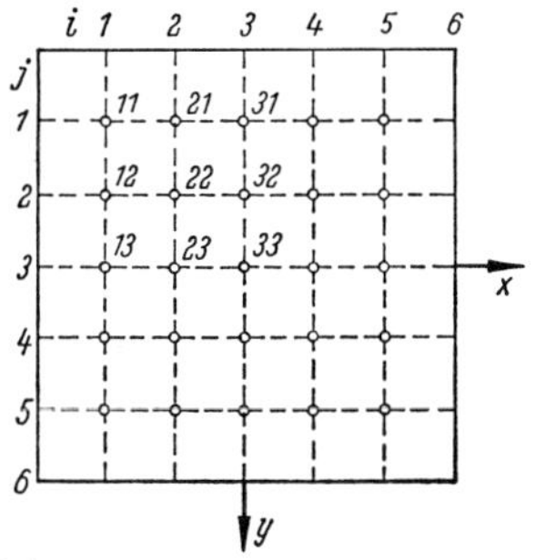

Fig. 2.19. Lattice Points.

Although the subdivision is rather coarse, we shall nevertheless obtain some fundamental results. According to the linear theory we need only determine six values of w, in view of the symmetry in both directions. We therefore solve the system of equations directly, in which one third of the matrix elements are zero. The additional load terms $\mathfrak{P}^\star$ were determined from the approximation $\mathfrak{P}^\star = p_z^\star$; they are symmetrical with respect to the coordinate axes and antimetrical with respect to the diagonals in plan. The coefficients in the equations for the determination of $w^\star$ are not symmetrical in x and y. Nine values of $w^\star$ have to be found. In the present case this was done by relaxation methods.

We shall give the results separately for variations of load, initial tension, cable cross sections, and initial surface.

The curves have the following meanings:

— · — · — Results of linearized calculations.

———— Results when $p^\star$, $w^\star$, and $H^\star$ are taken into account.

— — — — Results obtained by approximations of Section 2.6.

2.8.2 *Variation of Load*

Figure 2.20 shows horizontal tensions as functions of the load. Using the approximations 2.64 yields for $\varkappa_x = \varkappa_y = 0.5$ (with p in kp/m² and H in Mp/m)

$$H_x = H_{x0} + H_{xp} = 2.5 + 0.5 \cdot 50 \cdot 10^{-3} \cdot p = 2.5 + 0.025\,p\,,$$

$$H_y = H_{y0} + H_{yp} = 2.5 - 0.025 \cdot p.$$

The results obtained by the linearized calculation are smaller.

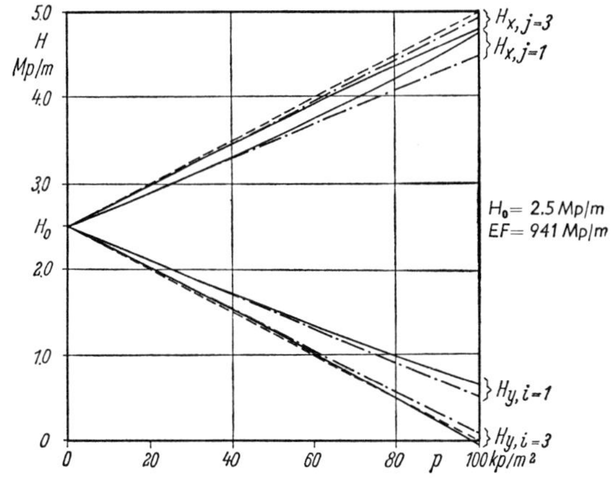

Fig. 2.20. Variation of Horizontal Tensions With Load.

Taking the nonlinear terms into account leads to a certain equalization of the horizontal tensions in the carrying cables, while the differences in H_y even increase. This phenomenon was noticed also in different forms of cable nets. All approximations err on the safe side except for H_y corresponding to $i = 3$.

We see from the ratios $H_p^\star/H_p$ shown in Fig. 2.21 that the nonlinear terms cannot in general be omitted. They must be taken into account

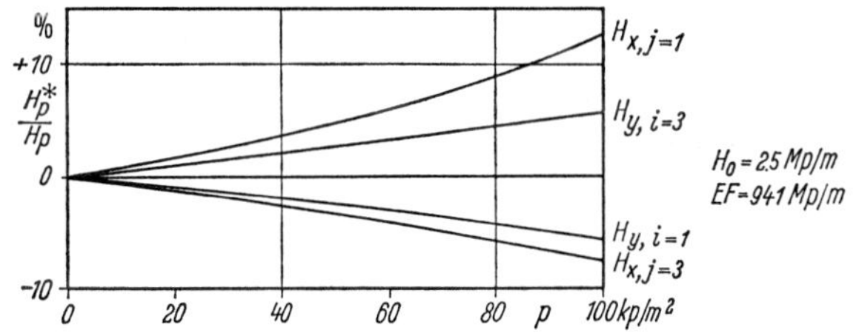

Fig. 2.21. Influence of Nonlinear Terms.

at least for the horizontal tensions of the central tension cables and of the carrying cables near the edge. This is done by an appropriate increment.

As was to be expected, the deflection w_{33} in the center of the net increases less than linearly when the load is increased (Fig. 2.22).

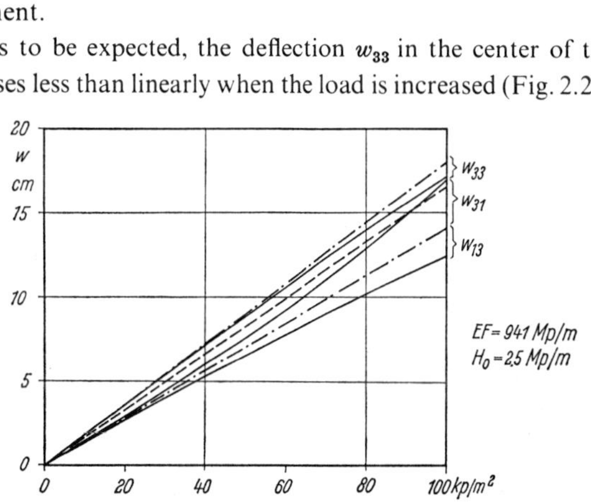

Fig. 2.22. Deformations with Increasing Load.

However, $p_z{}^\star$ causes increased deformations at some other points, e.g., at point 31.
The deflection at the net center, as determined by Eqs. 2.65, is given for comparison:

$w_0 = 1.2 \cdot 0.139\, p = 0.166\, p\,,$

Here $p = 100\ \mathrm{kp/m^2}$; thus $w_0 = 16.6$ cm. The deformations near the edge are fairly large.

2.8.3 *Variation of Initial Tension*

Figure 2.23 shows the horizontal tensions H_p and $H_p + H_p{}^\star$ calculated for $p = 33.33\ \mathrm{kp/m^2}$ and $EF = 941$ Mp/m. The positive values apply to H_x and the negative to H_y.

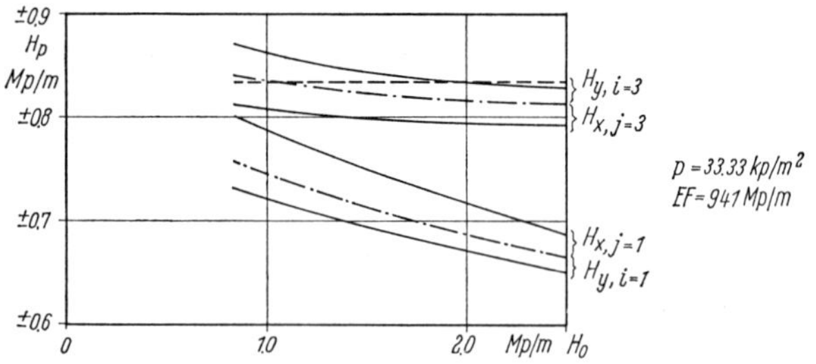

Fig. 2.23. Variation of Horizontal Tensions with Initial Tension.

The horizontal tensions decrease with increasing initial tension when the useful load remains constant. This is more pronounced for the cables near the edge.
This phenomenon can be explained easily if Eq. 2.47a is considered. Since w'' and $w^{\cdot\cdot}$ are negative for positive loads, all four terms on the left-hand side are positive. The magnitudes of the last two terms increase with the initial tensions; the deflections must therefore decrease. Equations 2.52 then yield horizontal tensions H_p, which are smaller in magnitude.

At first it appears as a paradox that the deflection in the center should increase with initial tension when the useful load is kept constant (Fig. 2.24), although evidently the net becomes more rigid. As expected, w decreases near the edges.

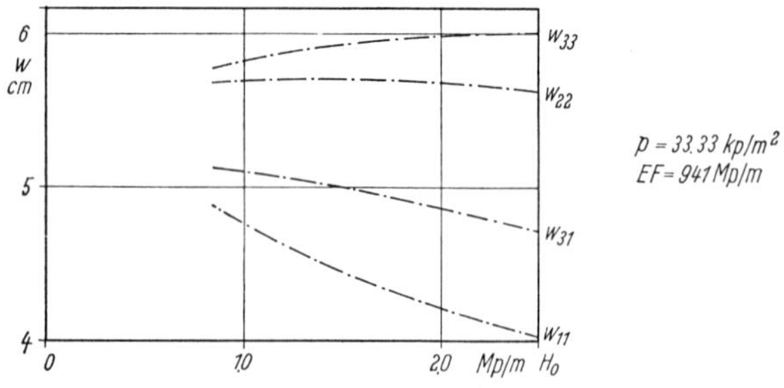

Fig. 2.24. Variation of Deformations with Initial Tension.

A property, mentioned earlier, of the deflection surfaces of cable nets becomes apparent here. With normal initial tension, the displacements w are largest near the quarter-span points (an initial tension of about 0.9 Mp/m would be required for the cable net considered to be capable of taking up a uniformly distributed load of 33.33 kp/m²). When the initial tension is high, maximum w is found approximately in the center of the surface. These qualitative changes in the deflection surface are attained by the increase of w in the center of the net.
The results of the nonlinearized analysis, which were neglected here, do not alter this pattern.

2.8.4 *Variation of Cable Cross Sections*

If we increase the cable cross sections or the modulus of elasticity (which has the same effect on the results), the deflections decrease almost hyperbolically (Fig. 2.25).

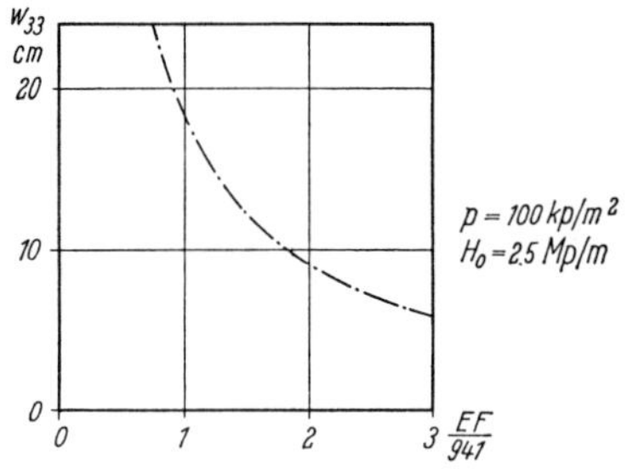

Fig. 2.25. Deformation as Function of Cable Rigidity.

However, the horizontal tensions H_p increase slightly with EF. The nonlinear terms become less important, since all deformations decrease (Fig. 2.26).

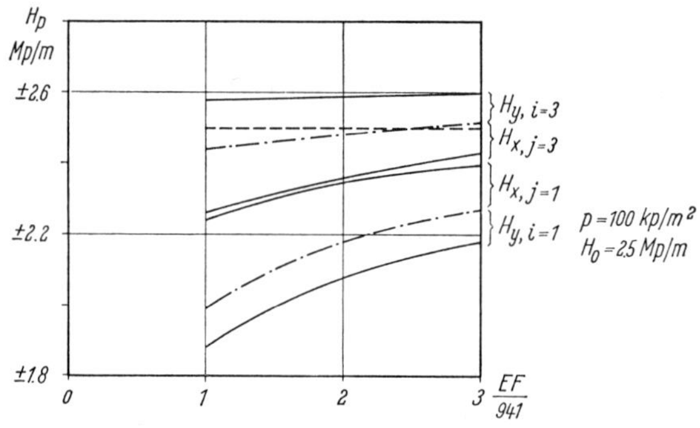

Fig. 2.26. Horizontal Tensions as Functions of Cable Rigidity.

2.8.5 *Variation of Several Magnitudes*

We shall now use the linear theory to compare two cable nets having the same initial surface and plan but different cable rigidities and initial tensions.
The magnitudes corresponding to the first net are EF, H_0 and Φ, those corresponding to the second, $\alpha \cdot EF$, $\beta \cdot H_0$ and $\alpha \cdot \Phi$.

The fundamental Eq. 2.47a is for the first net:

$$z''\, \Phi_x \int z''\, w\, dx + z^{\cdot\cdot}\, \Phi_y \int z^{\cdot\cdot}\, w\, dy - H_{x0}\, w'' - H_{y0}\, w^{\cdot\cdot} = p\,.$$

For the second net, where we write $\tilde{w}$ instead of w,

$$z''\, \alpha\, \Phi_x \int z''\, \tilde{w}\, dx + z^{\cdot\cdot}\, \alpha\, \Phi_y \int z^{\cdot\cdot}\, \tilde{w}\, dy - \beta\, H_{x0}\, \tilde{w}'' - \beta\, H_{y0}\, \tilde{w}^{\cdot\cdot} = \tilde{p} = \gamma \cdot p\,.$$

Both nets have the same deflection surface $w\,(x, y)$ if

$\alpha = \beta = \gamma =$ const.

We then have also

$$H_p = \frac{1}{\alpha}\tilde{H}_p, \qquad \text{i.e.,} \qquad \frac{\tilde{H}_p}{\tilde{p}} = \frac{H_p}{p}.$$

This result, which strictly speaking is valid only for the linearized analysis, can be generalized:

An increase of the cable rigidities alone has the same effect on the deflections as a corresponding reduction in initial tension *and* load. The ratio H_p/p remains unchanged.

When only the initial tension is increased, the deflections vary as if the cable rigidities *and* the load had been correspondingly reduced, and vice versa. The ratio H_p/p remains unchanged also in this case.

This explains why the horizontal tensions increase slightly with EF in Fig. 2.26: an increase of EF has the same effect on H_p as a reduction of the initial tension when the load is kept constant.

2.8.6 *Variation of the Initial Surface*

We shall only consider the case of an affine distortion of the cable net in the z-direction. The distortion factor is $\alpha \neq 0$, the new ordinates are therefore $\tilde{z} = \alpha \cdot z$.

All other things being equal, z'' and $z^{\cdot\cdot}$ vary linearly with α. When does not differ greatly from unity, we can neglect the (nonlinear) variation of Φ in order to obtain at least qualitative results. The first two terms in Eq. 2.47a then vary like α^2.

The affine distortion thus affects the deflection in the same way as a change in the cable rigidities to $\alpha^2 \cdot EF$. When the load is kept constant, the new deflections will be approximately w/α^2 and the new horizontal tensions approximately H_p/α. Here w and H_p are the corresponding values for the undistorted surface.

The results already available for any cable net can therefore be used for approximate deductions on the behavior under load of a second cable net similar to the first.

It is very seldom possible to perform measurements on a model made correctly to scale in all longitudinal dimensions (and cross sections) and maintain simultaneously to scale the moduli of elasticity, loads, and initial tensions. The results of this section enable us to investigate the behavior under load of a cable net with the aid of a model that is not correctly to scale in all its parts.

2.8.7 *Solution in Closed Form*

The above example of a particularly simple cable net is well suited for an attempt at finding a solution for w in closed form, (cf. Section 2.4.1) and to compare this with the more accurate results of the calculation carried out up to now. The data in Section 2.8.1 yield $\Phi_x = \Phi_y = 30$ Mp/m^2. We further assume $H_{x0} = H_{y0} = 2.5$ Mp/m and $p_z = 80$ kp/m^2 = const.

We shall first give the solution obtained by the numerical procedure employed heretofore. The deflections and horizontal tensions are shown in Table 2.2, with and without the quadratic terms of $p^\star$ being taken into account.

Table 2.2. Deflections and Horizontal Tensions Obtained by Numerical Calculation
Upper lines: Results of linearized calculation
Lower lines: Results when $p_z^\star$ is taken into account

	i	1	2	3	
j			w in cm		H_{xp}
1		9.7 11.6	11.2 12.7	11.4 13.3	+1.99 +2.15
2		11.2 10.3	13.5 13.2	14.0 13.8	+2.38 +2.30
3		11.4 10.4	14.0 13.3	14.4 13.9	+2.44 +2.32
	H_{yp}	−1.99 −1.92	−2.38 −2.43	−2.44 −2.53	Mp/m

$H_0 = 2.5$ Mp/m
$EF = 941$ Mp/m
$p_z = 80$ kp/m^2.

We write

$$w(x, y) = w_0 (1 - \xi^2)(1 - \eta^2)$$

where

$$\xi = \frac{2x}{l_x} \qquad \eta = \frac{2y}{l_y},$$

are dimensionless coordinates.

The horizontal tension is, according to Eqs. 2.52:

$$H_{xp} = -\Phi_x \cdot \int_{x_l}^{x_r} z'' w\, dx = \frac{30}{50} w_0 (1 - \eta^2) \int_{x_l}^{x_r} (1 - \xi^2)\, dx =$$
$$= 12\, w_0 (1 - \eta^2).$$

Similarly

$$H_{yp} = -12\, w_0 (1 - \xi^2).$$

Substitution in the equilibrium condition 2.39c yields

$$H_{x0} w'' + H_{xp} z'' + H_{xp} w'' + H_{y0} w^{\cdot\cdot} + H_{yp} z^{\cdot\cdot} + H_{yp} w^{\cdot\cdot} = -p_z$$

$$-\frac{5}{225} w_0 (1 - \eta^2) - \frac{12}{50} w_0 (1 - \eta^2) - \frac{24}{225} w_0^2 (1 - \eta^2)^2 -$$
$$-\frac{5}{225} w_0 (1 - \xi^2) - \frac{12}{50} w_0 (1 - \xi^2) + \frac{24}{225} w_0^2 (1 - \xi^2)^2 =$$
$$= -0.08.$$

This condition can never be satisfied at the same time for the entire region, but only for four points located symmetrically. The assumed deformation function thus corresponds to a nonuniform load.

The quadratic terms in w_0 (corresponding to $H_{xp} \cdot w''$ and $H_{yp} \cdot w^{\cdot\cdot}$) are cancelled out when the mean values of the functions are taken. We then obtain

$$w_0 = 0.229 \text{ m} = 22.9 \text{ cm}.$$

We would have obtained the same result by inserting w into Eq. 2.47a.

Hence

$$H_{xp} = 2.75 \cdot (1 - \eta^2) \text{ Mp/m},$$

$H_{yp} = -2.75 \cdot (1 - \xi^2)$ Mp/m.

The deformations are given in Table 2.3.

Table 2.3. Deflections and Horizontal Tensions Corresponding to $w = w_0 (1 - \xi^2) \cdot (1 - \eta^2)$

	i	1	2	3	
j		w in cm			H_{xp}
1		7.1	11.3	12.7	+1.53
2		11.3	18.1	20.4	+2.44
3		12.7	20.4	22.9	+2.75
	H_{yp}	−1.53	−2.44	−2.75	Mp/m

The maximum deflection exceeds by 65%, and the maximum horizontal tension by 19%, the exact values given in Table 2.2.

The load p_z corresponding to the assumed w-surface varies between 0 kp/m^2 at the edge and 120 kp/m^2 in the center. For $\xi = \pm 0.5$, $\eta = \pm 0.5$, $p_z = 90$ kp/m^2.

This solution can hardly be considered to be even a rough approximation. Even the formulas of Section 2.8.2 give more accurate results.

We obtain a slightly better approximation by writing

$$w = w_0 (1 - \xi^4)(1 - \eta^4),$$

which yields

$w_0 = 15.04$ cm,

$H_{xp} = 2.17 (1 - \eta^4)$ Mp/m, $\quad H_{yp} = -2.17 (1 - \xi^4)$ Mp/m.

The deformations and horizontal tensions are given in Table 2.4.

Table 2.4. Deflections and Horizontal Tensions Corresponding to $w = w_0 (1 - \xi^4) \cdot (1 - \eta^4)$

	i	1	2	3	
j		w in cm			H_{xp}
1		9.7	11.9	12.1	+1.74
2		11.9	14.7	14.9	+2.14
3		12.1	14.9	15.0	+2.17
	H_{yp}	−1.74	−2.14	−2.17	Mp/m

The deflection in the center of the cable net is now 8% too large and the maximum horizontal tension 6.5% too small.

The load corresponding to this w-function is 0 at the edge, 87 kp/m^2 in the center, and about 91 kp/m^2 at $\xi = \pm 0.5$, $\eta = \pm 0.5$.

When no energy considerations are taken into account, the only criterion of the suitability and accuracy of an expression for w is the difference between the given load and the load corresponding to the function w selected.

The procedure can be refined by adding some free terms to the expression for w and determining these from the conditions that, e.g., the squares of the load difference be minimal. However, the work involved in the calculations then increases considerably.

The actual errors in the determination of deflections and horizontal tensions cannot be given.

2.9 Example

2.9.1 *System and Dimensions*

We consider as an example a pretensioned cable net spanning an irregular plan (Fig. 2.27). The system is symmetrical with respect to the plane $x = 0$.

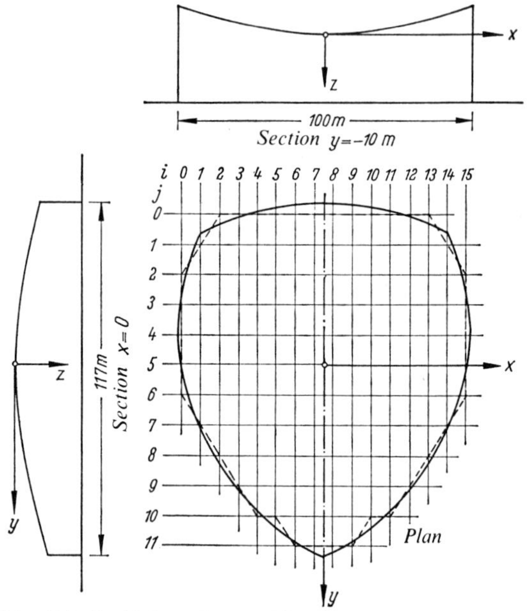

Fig. 2.27. Principal Dimensions and Lattice.

The initial surface is defined in the coordinate system shown, by

$$z = -\frac{x^2}{272} + \frac{y^2}{340}.$$

Hence

$$z' = -\frac{x}{136} \qquad z^{\cdot} = +\frac{y}{170}$$

$$z'' = -k_x = -\frac{1}{136}\,\text{m}^{-1} \qquad z^{\cdot\cdot} = k_y = +\frac{1}{170}\,\text{m}^{-1}$$

$$\varrho = \frac{k_y}{k_x} = \frac{136}{170} = 0.80.$$

The projection in plan of the edge curve was first assumed to consist of parts of ellipses having a ratio of semiaxes $a/b = 1.28$ (Cf. Section 2.7.5). The lateral arcs were later taken to coincide with the line of pressure of the load (initial tension plus permanent load); the maximum deviation from the ordinates of the ellipses is 0.4 m in the x-direction.

The deflection: length ratio of the longest carrying cable is $n_x = f_x/l_x = 1/10.9$ and of the longest tension cable, $n_y = f_y/l_y = 1/11.7$.

All cables should have the same cross sections for reasons of economy. The design provides for spiral cables of 23 mm diameter, having a cross section of 3.15 cm^2, made of St 160 according to test method DIN 69202. The effective modulus of elasticity is assumed to be uniformly $E_x = E_y = 1500$ Mp/cm^2. The distance between the carrying cables is 1.5 m and between the tension cables 1.667 m. Hence, by Eq. 2.23,

$$F_x = \frac{3.15}{1.50} = 2.10\ \text{cm}^2/\text{m} \qquad F_y = \frac{3.15}{1.67} = 1.89\ \text{cm}^2/\text{m}$$

and

$E_x F_x = 1500 \cdot 2.10 = 3150$ Mp/m ,
$E_y F_y = 1500 \cdot 1.89 = 2835$ Mp/m .

The steel requirements for the cables correspond to a (2.1 + 1.89)/10 = 0.4 mm thick sheet; they are thus very small despite the wide spans.
Numerical computation is performed with the aid of the lattice shown in Fig. 2.27, for which $\Delta x = 6.5$ m and $\Delta y = 10.0$ m. The curvilinear edge of the net was replaced by the polygon shown in broken lines.
The actual net has about 3500 cable intersections, but the displacements were calculated for only 116 points. When symmetry and antimetry are taken into account, 58 linear equations are obtained with the same number of unknown deflections $w_{i,j}$.

2.9.2 *Assumptions About Load*
Initial tensions:

$H_{x0} = 6.0$ Mp/m ,
$H_{y0} = 7.5$ Mp/m $= H_{x0}/\varrho$ (cf. Eq. (2.33)).

Permanent load:

$g = 38$ kp/m² roof surface
(of which only 3.25 kp/m² is for cables and clamps, the rest for roof covering).
Snow:
$s = 75$ kp/m² of ground area.
Temperature variation:
Temperature difference $\Delta t = \pm 15\,°$C between cable net and edge member.
$\alpha_t = 12 \cdot 10^{-6}$.
Wind loads:
Velocity head $q = 90$ kp/m², obtained by interpolation from chart No. 4, DIN 1055, for a mean elevation of 25 m above surrounding ground.
The assumed distribution of the wind coefficients is shown against the corresponding results obtained for the deflections.

The deformations of the edge members have been neglected in order to clarify the behavior of the cable net under load. One edge curve was analyzed for the case of snow load; its deformations had no significant effect on the cable forces.

2.9.3 *Preliminary Calculation*
Constants: We obtain from Eqs. 2.59, 2.60, and 2.63:

$$\varrho = \frac{136}{170} = 0,80\,,$$

$$\varphi = \frac{E_y F_y}{E_x F_x} = \frac{2835}{3150} = 0.90\,,$$

$$\varphi\,\varrho^2 = 0.9 \cdot 0.8^2 = 0.576\,,$$

$$\varkappa_x = \frac{1.0}{1.576} = 0.635\,, \qquad \varkappa_y = 1 - 0.635 = 0.365\,,$$

$$\frac{\varkappa_x}{k_x} = 0.635 \cdot 136 = 86.3\text{ m}\,, \qquad \frac{\varkappa_y}{k_y} = 0.365 \cdot 170 = 62.1\text{ m}.$$

Permanent load: The surface inclination is taken into account by assuming an average load of 39 kp/m² area in plan. We then find from Eqs. 2.64:

$H_{xp} = 86.3 \cdot 39 \cdot 10^{-3} = 3.37$ Mp/m ,
$H_{yp} = -62.1 \cdot 39 \cdot 10^{-3} = -2.42$ Mp/m .

Snow: As for permanent load:

$H_{xp} = 86.3 \cdot 75 \cdot 10^{-3} = 6.48$ Mp/m ,
$H_{yp} = -62.1 \cdot 75 \cdot 10^{-3} = -4.66$ Mp/m .

Temperature: By Eqs. 2.66:

$$H_{xp} = -3150 \cdot 12 \cdot 10^{-6} \cdot 15 \cdot 0.365\left(1 + \frac{1}{0.8}\right) = -0.47\text{ Mp/m}\,,$$

$$H_{yp} = -\frac{1}{0.9} \cdot 0.47 = -0.52\text{ Mp/m}\,.$$

Wind in y-direction: Fig. 2.29 shows that the wind coefficients have their largest magnitudes in the region of negative values of y, where we can therefore expect to find the horizontal tensions in the x-direction to have their largest absolute values. For $j = 1$ the coefficients are on the average $c = -1.0$, so that the wind suction at these points is $p_3 = c \cdot q = -90$ kp/m².
The loads are largest near the net edge. Hence, the cables running in the y-direction take up a bigger part of the wind loads than they would of a uniformly distributed load. If the horizontal components of the load are neglected and $\varkappa_x$ is assumed for this load to be equal to 0.6 for $j = 1$, we obtain from Eq. 2.64a:

$H_{xp} = -0.6 \cdot 136 \cdot 90 \cdot 10^{-3} = -7.35$ Mp/m .

Wind in x-direction: It can be expected that the largest horizontal tension, induced by the wind loads shown in Fig. 2.30, in the tension cables occurs along $i = 2$. The wind coefficients will be separated into symmetrical and antimetrical parts.
The average symmetrical part is $c_s = -0.57$; thus, $p_{3s} = -0.57 \cdot 90 = -51.3$ kp/m² and by Eq. 2.64b:
$H_{yps} = 62.1 \cdot 51.3 \cdot 10^{-3} = 3.2$ Mp/m .
The antimetrical parts act mainly along the edges $i = 0$ and $i = 15$. The average antimetrical wind load at $i = 2$ is $p_{3a} = -0.33 \cdot 90 = -30$ kp/m². The linearized analysis yields $H_{xp} = 0$ (cf. Section 2.7.1); however, the term $H_{x0} w''$ in Eq. 2.47a will still be significant. If we assume that the cables running in the y-direction take up 70% of the load, we obtain
$H_{ypa} = -0.7 \cdot p_{3a}/k_y = 0.7 \cdot 30 \cdot 170 \cdot 10^{-3} = 3.6$ Mp/m .
Neglecting the horizontal components p_x and p_y, the total load due to wind in the x-direction is for $i = 2$:
$H_{yp} = H_{yps} + H_{ypa} = 3.2 + 3.6 = 6.8$ Mp/m .
Compilation. The extremes of the horizontal tensions are given in Table 2.5.

Table 2.5. Horizontal Tensions Obtained in the Preliminary Calculation

Load	H_x	H_y	
0	+ 6.00	+ 7.50	
g	+ 3.37	− 2.42	
s	+ 6.48	− 4.66	
$\pm\Delta t$	∓ 0.47	∓ 0.52	
w	− 7.35	+ 6.8	
0 + g	+ 9.37	+ 5.08	
max	+16.32	+12.40	
min	+ 1.55 > 0	+ 0.94 > 0	Mp/m

Inclinations at the edge: When deformations are neglected, we obtain at the right-hand edge:

$$z_r' = -\frac{x_r}{136} = -\frac{50}{136} = -0.37\,,$$

at the upper edge:

$$z_l^{\cdot} = \frac{y_l}{170} = -\frac{50}{170} = -0.29\,,$$

$$\sqrt{1 + z_r'^2} = 1.07\,, \qquad \sqrt{1 + z_l^{\cdot 2}} = 1.04\,.$$

Cable stresses: According to Eqs. 2.19 and 2.3, e.g.,

$$\max S_1 = \max H_x \cdot \sqrt{1 + z_r'^2}\,,$$

The largest cable stresses are thus

$$\max \sigma_1 = \frac{\max S_1}{F_x} = \frac{16.32 \cdot 1.07}{2.10} = 8.3\ \mathrm{Mp/cm^2}\,,$$

$$\max \sigma_2 = \frac{\max S_2}{F_y} = \frac{12.40 \cdot 1.04}{1.89} = 6.8\ \mathrm{Mp/cm^2}\,.$$

The horizontal tensions are positive even in the most unfavorable case. The cables thus remain tight.

2.9.4 *Determining Deflections and Horizontal Tensions According to the Linear Theory*

2.9.4.1 System data

In the case considered, the curvatures and horizontal tensions of the net are constant in the initial state. We introduce the following notations:

$$\Delta_x^2 w_{i,j} = 2\,w_{i,j} - w_{i-1,j} - w_{i+1,j}\,,$$

$$\Delta_y^2 w_{i,j} = 2\,w_{i,j} - w_{i,j-1} - w_{i,j+1}\,.$$

The fundamental Eq. 2.47a or 2.55 then takes the form

$$A_j \cdot {}^i\sum w_{i,j} + B_i \cdot {}^j\sum w_{i,j} + C \cdot \Delta_x^2 w_{i,j} + D \cdot \Delta_y^2 w_{i,j} = \mathfrak{P}_{i,j}\,.$$

Of the four magnitudes $A \ldots D$, only A and B depend on the respective spans. Summation has to be extended over all internal lattice points of the corresponding row.

The magnitudes H_p, determined before, were not taken into account in the fundamental equation, in which only the pretensioning forces appeared (cf. Section 2.4.1). The influence of the nonlinear terms thus became clearer, and the same system of equations could be used for all cases of loading.

It was found convenient to measure w in cm and $\mathfrak{P}$ in kp/m^2. The magnitudes $A \ldots D$ are then by Eq. 2.47a:

$$A_j = 10 \cdot \Phi_{xj} \cdot k_x^2 \cdot \Delta x = \frac{10 \cdot 6.5}{136^2} \cdot \Phi_{x\,j},$$

$$B_i = 10 \cdot \Phi_{yi} \cdot k_y^2 \cdot \Delta y = \frac{10 \cdot 10.0}{170^2} \Phi_{yi}\,,$$

$$C = 10 \cdot \frac{H_{x0}}{(\Delta x)^2} = 10 \cdot \frac{6.0}{6.5^2} = 1.42\,,$$

$$D = 10 \cdot \frac{H_{y0}}{(\Delta y)^2} = 10 \frac{7.5}{10.0^2} = 0.75\,.$$

Table 2.6 shows the values of $P\Delta$, Φ, A, and B. They were obtained from Eqs. 2.56 (cf. Section 2.4.5.4).

The terms depending on i and j in the principal diagonal of the matrix are approximately 4.7, when the symmetry properties are utilized. The other terms have absolute values up to 1.208. The deflections could be found for all cases of loading with the aid of a slide rule, using relaxation methods.

The expressions for the horizontal tensions, which are of ultimate interest, contain the deflections under the summation sign. It would therefore suffice in practice to determine the deformations to within 5% of the maximum value (± 1 cm in our case). In this example the individual deflections w were determined to within ± 2 mm.

The horizontal tensions (in Mp/m) are found from Eqs. 2.52 to be

$$H_{xp} = \Phi_{x,j} \cdot k_x \cdot \Delta x \cdot {}^i\sum w_{i,j} + \mathfrak{Q}_x + \mathfrak{R}_x =$$

$$= \frac{A_j}{10^3 \cdot k_x} \cdot {}^i\sum w_{i,j} + \mathfrak{Q}_x + \mathfrak{R}_x =$$

$$H_{xp} = 0.136 \cdot A_j \cdot {}^i\sum w_{i,j} + \mathfrak{Q}_x + \mathfrak{R}_x$$

and correspondingly

$$H_{yp} = -0.170 \cdot B_j \cdot {}^j\sum w_{i,j} + \mathfrak{Q}_y + \mathfrak{R}_y\,.$$

2.9.4.2 Snow load

Table 2.7 shows the deflections and horizontal tensions obtained for $p_z = 75$ kp/m^2. The maximum values of w_i and w_j, which appear in bold type, are usually not found in mid-span. Figure 2.28 shows that the values of w remain nearly constant in the center region of the net. This deflection surface is typical for uniformly distributed loads. It is evident that the problem cannot be solved with simple expressions for $w\,(x, y)$.

Table 2.6. Constants

j	$P\Delta_x$	Φ_x	A	i	$P\Delta_y$	Φ_y	B
		Mp/m^2	kp / m^2 cm			Mp/m^2	kp / m^2 cm
1	1.049	35.54	0.125	1	1.021	46.28	0.160
2 to 6	1.065	30.32	0.106	2	1.033	34.30	0.119
7	1.049	35.54	0.125	3	1.040	30.38	0.105
8	1.035	42.57	0.149	4 and 5	1.044	27.16	0.094
9	1.023	52.61	0.185	6 and 7	1.054	24.44	0.085
10	1.007	96.23	0.338				

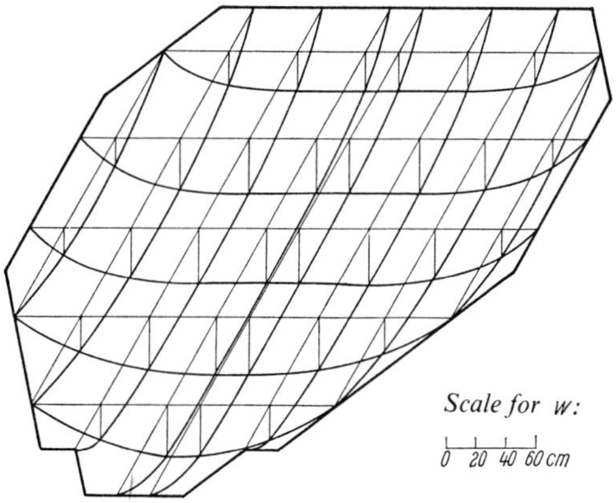

Fig. 2.28. Deflections Caused by Snow.

The approximation Eqs. 2.65 yield a mean deflection

$$w_m = \frac{1.065}{3150} \cdot 136^2 \cdot 0.635 \cdot 75 \cdot 10^{-1} = 29.8 \text{ cm}$$

and a deflection in the center of the surface

$$w_0 \approx 1.2 \cdot w_0 = 35.8 \text{ cm}.$$

2.9.4.3 Permanent load

The surface element is, according to Eq. 2.6, $d0 = \sqrt{g}\, dx\, dy$.
Using Eq. 2.5, we find the load due to the weight of roof membrane and net to be $p_z = 38 \sqrt{1 + z'^2 + z^{\cdot 2}}$.
The largest value of $\mathfrak{P} = p_z$ was 40.5 kp/m^2.
Table 2.8 gives the deflections and corresponding horizontal tensions.
Using the approximation Eqs. 2.65, we obtain for an average value $p_z = 39$ kp/m^2:

$$w_0 \approx 1.2 \cdot \frac{1.065}{3150} \cdot 136^2 \cdot 0.635 \cdot 39 \cdot 10^{-1} = 18.6 \text{ cm}.$$

If the results obtained for a snow load are multiplied by $\eta = g/s = 39/75 = 0.52$, we obtain approximately the horizontal tensions, caused by a permanent load, given in Table 2.9.
The differences between these values and the exact values in Table 2.8 are small. On the other hand, the deflections cannot be determined accurately with the conversion factor η.

Table 2.7. Deflections and Horizontal Tensions Caused by Snow

	i	1	2	3	4	5	6	7	
j					w in cm				H_{xp}
1			16.6	22.7	24.8	**25.0**	24.9	24.6	+4.71
2		18.5	25.8	30.7	32.7	**32.9**	32.8	32.4	+5.85
3		18.7	28.4	32.9	34.6	**34.8**	34.6	34.3	+6.30
4		**19.1**	**28.8**	**33.3**	**35.1**	**35.4**	35.4	35.1	+6.41
5		18.2	27.8	32.8	35.1	**35.8**	**36.2**	36.0	+6.40
6		14.8	24.4	30.5	34.1	36.0	**37.1**	**37.3**	+6.18
7			14.6	24.2	30.5	34.3	36.8	**37.7**	+6.06
8				14.4	24.3	30.6	34.9	**36.8**	+5.72
9					14.5	22.3	22.8	**33.4**	+5.03
10							17.5	**23.6**	+3.78
	H_{yp}	−2.36	−3.36	−3.95	−4.25	−4.58	−4.62	−4.78	Mp/m

Table 2.8. Deflections and Horizontal Tensions Caused by Permanent Load

	i	1	2	3	4	5	6	7	
j					w in cm				H_{xp}
1			9.1	12.3	13.2	13.1	12.9	12.7	+2.49
2		8.8	14.1	16.4	17.1	16.9	16.6	16.3	+3.06
3		10.3	15.4	17.5	18.1	17.8	17.3	17.0	+3.27
4		10.4	15.4	17.6	18.2	18.0	17.6	17.2	+3.30
5		10.0	15.0	17.3	18.1	18.2	18.0	17.6	+3.29
6		8.1	13.1	16.0	17.7	18.3	18.6	18.5	+3.18
7			7.8	12.8	15.9	17.6	18.6	19.0	+3.12
8				7.6	12.7	15.8	18.0	19.0	+2.98
9					7.7	11.8	15.7	17.9	+2.67
10							9.4	12.8	+2.04
	H_{yp}	−1.30	−1.82	−2.10	−2.21	−2.36	−2.35	−2.43	Mp/m

Table 2.9. H_p Calculated from Snow Load

j	1	2	3	4	5	6	7	8	9	10
H_{xp}	+2.45	+3.04	+3.28	+3.33	+3.33	+3.22	+3.15	+2.98	+2.62	+1.97
i	1	2	3	4	5	6	7			
H_{yp}	−1.23	−1.75	−2.05	−2.21	−2.38	−2.40	−2.49	Mp/m		

2.9.4.4 Temperature rise

We obtain from Eqs. 250 for a constant temperature rise

$$\mathfrak{R}_x = -E_x F_x \cdot \alpha_t \cdot \Delta t = -3150 \cdot 12 \cdot 10^{-6} \cdot 15 = -0.567 \text{ Mp/m},$$

$$\mathfrak{R}_y = -2835 \cdot 12 \cdot 10^{-6} \cdot 15 = -0.510 \text{ Mp/m}.$$

Eq. 2.51 thus yields

$$t\,\mathfrak{P} = \left(+\frac{0.567}{136} - \frac{0.510}{170}\right) \cdot 10^3 = +1.17 \text{ kp/m}^2 = \text{const.}$$

Multiplying the results obtained for snow load by $\eta = 1.17/75 = 0.0156$, we find the values in the second column of Table 2.10. Adding the values of $\mathfrak{R}$ obtained from Eqs. 2.52, we obtain the total horizontal tensions given in the third column.

Table 2.10. H_p Due to Temperature Rises

j		H_{xp}	i		H_{yp}
1	+0.074	−0.49	1	−0.037	−0.55
2	+0.091	−0.48	2	−0.053	−0.56
3	+0.098	−0.47	3	−0.062	−0.57
4	+0.100	−0.46	4	−0.066	−0.58
5	+0.099	−0.47	5	−0.071	−0.58
6	+0.096	−0.47	6	−0.072	−0.58
7	+0.095	−0.47	7	−0.074	−0.58
8	+0.089	−0.48			
9	+0.079	−0.49			Mp/m
10	+0.059	−0.51			

The maximum deflection found by multiplying the corresponding value for snow load by η is only

$$\max w = 0.0156 \cdot 37.7 = 0.59 \text{ cm}.$$

2.9.4.5 Wind in y-direction

The minimum horizontal tensions are determined from the wind-coefficient distribution shown in Fig. 2.29. The wind load acts everywhere normal to the roof surface in the upward direction (wind suction).

We omit resolving the wind force $p_3 = c \cdot 90$ kp/m^2 into its components p_x, p_y, and p_z, in accordance with Eqs. 2.16, as well as the determination of the virtual shearing forces $\mathfrak{Q}$ according to Eqs. 2.49. Table 2.11 gives only $p_z = p_3$ (cf. Eq. 2.16c, where $p_1 = p_2 = 0$) and the total-load function $\mathfrak{P}$. A comparison of both sets of values shows that the rather laborious computation of $\mathfrak{Q}$ and $\mathfrak{P}$ can be omitted if we assume that in the center region of the surface $\mathfrak{P} = p_3$ approximately, while at the edges we set $\mathfrak{P} \approx (1.05 \text{ to } 1.15) \cdot p_3$ depending on the slope and magnitude of the surface.

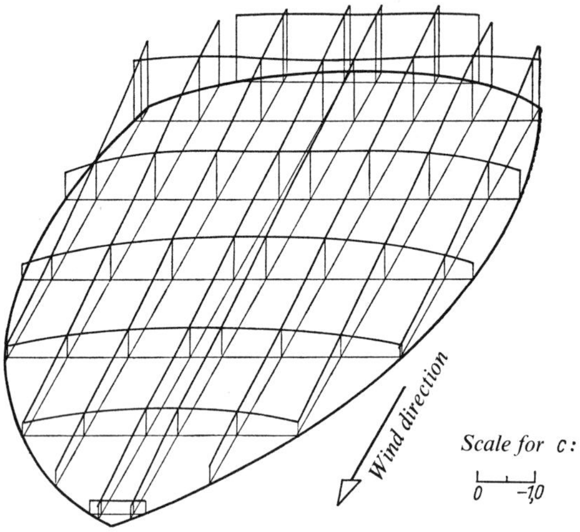

Fig. 2.29. Wind Load, Wind in y-Direction.

Table 2.11. Load Due to Wind in y-Direction
Upper rows: $p_3 = p_z$ in kp/m^2, lower rows: $\mathfrak{P}$ in kp/m^2
All values are negative

j \ i	1	2	3	4	5	6	7
1		90.0 104.3	94.5 106.2	90.0 98.7	88.2 94.9	87.2 92.5	87.2 91.8
2	70.2 82.2	80.1 89.5	82.9 89.9	81.0 85.5	79.2 82.0	78.4 79.9	78.4 79.3
3	54.0 62.2	65.7 71.7	70.2 74.4	68.4 70.5	68.4 69.1	68.4 68.1	68.4 67.4
4	41.4 47.0	52.5 56.5	58.5 61.0	58.5 59.2	63.0 62.6	63.0 61.7	63.0 61.2
5	34.2 38.5	43.2 46.2	47.6 49.3	52.2 52.5	59.4 58.7	64.0 62.5	64.0 62.0
6	22.5 24.6	35.1 37.6	38.7 40.1	45.0 45.4	52.2 51.9	54.0 52.9	56.7 55.2
8			27.0 29.3	30.6 32.4	31.5 32.7	31.5 31.2	34.2 34.8
10						27.0 29.9	27.0 29.8

The largest deflection amounts to −42.8 cm at the point $i = 4$, $j = 2$. The calculated horizontal tensions are given in Table 2.12. To these values we have to add the virtual shearing forces, which depend on i and j; their magnitude varies between −0.5 and +0.4 Mp/m.

2.9.4.6 Wind in x-direction

Figure 2.30 shows the wind-coefficient distribution on which the calculation is based. The largest absolute value is found at the point $i = 1$, $j = 4$; it amounts to −1.14 (wind suction). The load acts in the direction normal to the roof surface.

Table 2.12. H_p Due to Wind in y-Direction

j	1	2	3	4	5	6	7	8	9	10
H_{xp}	−6.90	−7.30	−6.42	−5.35	−4.51	−3.34	−2.54	−1.71	−1.10	−0.77
i	1	2	3	4	5	6	7			
H_{yp}	+1.35	+2,54	+3.12	+3.31	+3.65	+3.57	+3.69	Mp/m		

Computation is simplified by dividing the values c into parts symmetrical and antimetrical with respect to the plane $x = 0$. The two loads will be considered separately.

Some values of the load function, obtained from p_x, p_y, p_z according to Eq. 2.16 and from $\mathfrak{Q}_x$ and $\mathfrak{Q}_y$ with the aid of Eqs. 2.51, are given in Table 2.13.

Table 2.13. Load Due to Wind in x-Direction
Upper rows: symmetrical part: $\mathfrak{P}$ in kp/m², all values are negative
Lower rows: Antimetrical part: $\mathfrak{P}$ in kp/m², all values are negative, except for $i \geqslant 8$, when they are positive

j \ i	1	2	3	4	5	6	7
1		64.8 25.3	61.6 23.5	54.0 18.7	42.4 7.7	38.9 2.8	36.8 0.9
2	71.2 33.8	72.6 34.5	61.3 24.6	50.0 14.4	43.4 6.6	39.9 2.8	38.7 0.9
4	76.5 38.4	67.7 33.1	56.1 22.8	46.3 11.9	42.5 7.2	41.9 1.7	42.6 0.9
6	71.5 33.5	67.7 33.1	57.0 23.7	47.2 15.8	43.5 8.1	41.0 4.4	40.7 0.9
8			62.9 25.7	58.3 26.1	50.1 16.2	43.3 6.5	40.3 1.9
10						39.3 5.1	38.2 1.9

The differences between p_3 and $\mathfrak{P}$ were small for both parts; the ratio $\mathfrak{P}/p_3$ varied between 0.96 and 1.17.

Table 2.14 gives the horizontal tensions. We remind the reader that $H_{xp} = 0$ for the antimetrical part of the load.

The shearing forces have not been included in Table 2.14. Their extrema are

$\mathfrak{Q}_x = +\ 0.54$ Mp/m for $i = 0,\ j = 3$,
$\mathfrak{Q}_x = -\ 0.15$ Mp/m for $i = 7,\ j = 3$,
$\mathfrak{Q}_y = +\ 0.18$ Mp/m for $i = 2,\ j = 5$,
$\mathfrak{Q}_y = -\ 0.42$ Mp/m for $i = 2,\ j = 0$.

The value $H_{yp} = +\ 6.67$ Mp/m (for $i = 2$), which determines the maximum stress, is surprisingly high; this shows the large influence of high local loads.

The assumed wind coefficient has an average value of approximately $c = -1.0$. Were we, for the sake of simplicity, to replace the wind suction by a vertical load, uniformly distributed over the entire

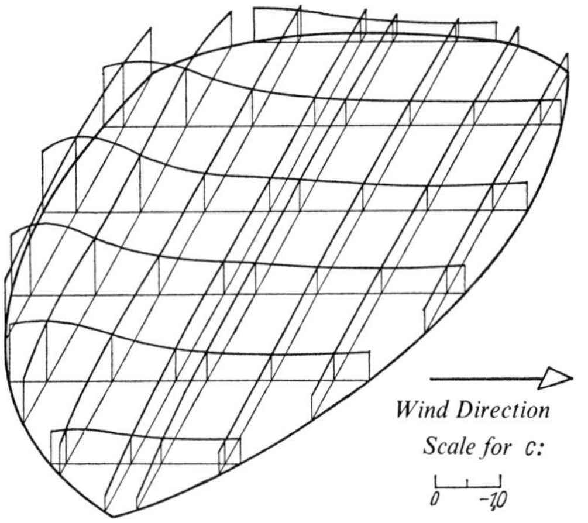

Fig. 2.30. Wind Load, Wind in x-Direction.

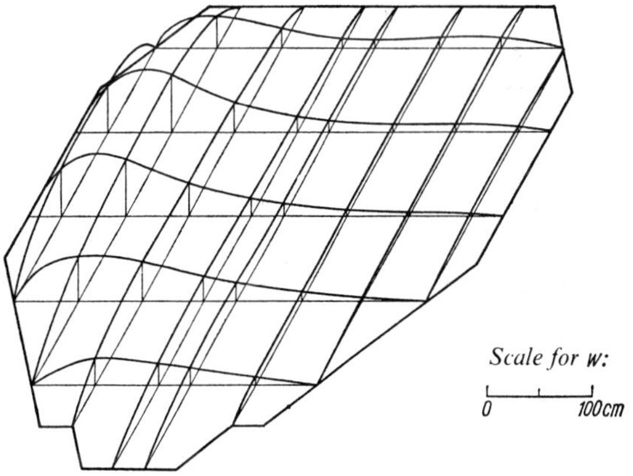

Fig. 2.31. Uplift Due to Wind in x-Direction.

Table 2.14. H_p Due to Wind in x-Direction

j	1	2	3	4	5	6	7	8	9	10
H_{xp}	−3.01	−3.99	−4.28	−4.31	−4.25	−4.13	−4.04	−3.85	−3.19	−2.12
i	1	2	3	4	5	6	7			
H_{yps}	+2.98	+3.66	+3.47	+2.94	+2.53	+2.13	+2.03	Mp/m		
H_{ypa}	+2.52	+3.01	+2.75	+2.15	+1.50	+0.77	+0.25			
H_{yp}	+5.50	+6.67	+6.22	+5.09	+4.03	+2.90	+2.28	Wind blowing from left		
H_{yp}	+0.46	+0.65	+0.72	+0.79	+1.03	+1.36	+1.78	Wind blowing from right		

surface, the above horizontal tension would be attained for $p_z = -153\ \mathrm{k/m^2}$, i.e., $c = -1.70$.
The largest uplift of the net, caused by wind suction (both parts), was found to be $w = -59.9$ cm at $i = 2$, $j = 4$. The deformation surface is shown in Fig. 2.31 so that it can be compared with the load distribution (Fig. 2.30).

2.9.5 *Influence of the Nonlinear Terms*

2.9.5.1 General observations

The influence of the nonlinear terms in Eqs. 2.39 will be shown for the two most unfavorable cases of loading, namely, permanent load plus snow and permanent load plus wind in the x-direction. Temperature variations cause only very small deformations, so that this case of loading will no longer be considered.
We shall first determine the deformations u and v by means of Eqs. 2.53. The two first and the two last terms in these equations vanish in the case considered. The second integrals will be replaced by sums according to the trapezoidal rule; the first integrals are already known sums, obtained in the computation of the horizontal tensions. The virtual moments $\mathfrak{M}$, which only act in the case of a horizontal load, are easily determined simultaneously with $\mathfrak{Q}$.

2.9.5.2 Permanent load plus snow

The horizontal displacements are shown in Fig. 2.32. With max $u = 9.8$ cm and max $v = 10.5$ cm they amount to almost 20% of the largest deflection $w = 56.7$ cm. Compared with the exact results obtained from Eqs. 2.53a, b, the approximation Eq. 2.53c yielded values that were 12 to 40% less (on the average, approximately 20%).
The smallness of the curvatures u'' and v'' of the cables caused the

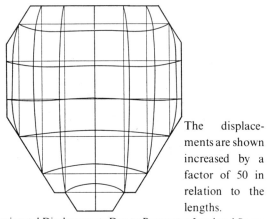

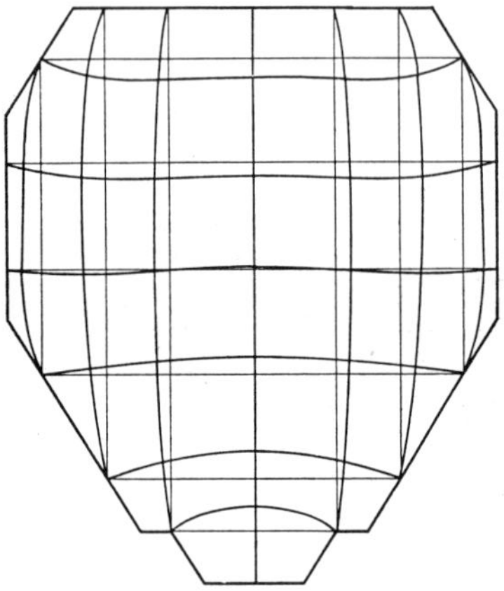

The displacements are shown increased by a factor of 50 in relation to the lengths.

Fig. 2.32. Horizontal Displacements Due to Permanent Load and Snow.

magnitudes $p_x{}^\star$ and $p_y{}^\star$, obtained from Eqs. 2.41a, b, also to be small.
The last terms in these equations are insignificant. Only at two points near the edge does $p_x{}^\star$ exceed 1.0, being equal to 1.9 and 1.5 kp/m², respectively. Almost everywhere else $p_x{}^\star$ is less than 0.2 kp/m². The values of $p_y{}^\star$ are slightly higher, also being largest near the edge: $p_y{}^\star = -8.6$ kp/m² at $i = 2$, $j = 1$. Generally, $p_y{}^\star$ is approximately equal to 2 kp/m².
We need not further consider $p_x{}^\star$ and $p_y{}^\star$, since the horizontal loads affect the load function, and thus the horizontal tensions, to a far smaller degree than the vertical loads.
Table 2.15 gives the additional loads $p_z{}^\star$ determined from Eq. 2.41c. The largest values are again found near the edge, and amount to up to 29% of p_z. The last two terms in Eq. 2.41c are insignificant. The exceptional positive value at $i = 5$, $j = 9$ shows the effect of the nearby reentrant corner at $i = 5$, $j = 10$.

Table 2.15. Additional Loads $p_z{}^\star$ Due to Permanent Load and Snow

j \ i	1	2	3	4	5	6	7
1		−22.3	+ 3.1	+12.1	+17.6	+18.0	+19.5
2	−12.2	−11.7	− 4.2	+ 0.1	+ 4.8	+ 5.7	+ 7.8
3	−30.7	−16.7	− 8.4	− 3.9	+ 0.0	+ 1.2	+ 2.5
4	−33.4	−17.5	− 9.1	− 4.8	− 0.3	− 0.8	+ 1.4
5	−29.8	−14.8	− 8.0	− 4.4	− 1.2	− 1.8	+ 0.7
6	−11.9	− 7.3	− 4.6	− 3.6	− 0.6	− 1.6	+ 0.7
7		−13.1	− 8.0	− 5.9	− 2.2	− 3.2	− 1.5
8			−10.2	− 8.0	− 1.2	− 4.0	− 3.4
9		kp/m²		−14.0	+14.2	− 2.4	− 3.1
10						−18.2	+ 2.4

Additional deflections $w^\star$ and horizontal tensions $H_p{}^\star$ were determined with the aid of the approximation $\mathfrak{P}^\star \approx p_z{}^\star$. In Eq. 2.55 H_0 was replaced by the total horizontal tensions $H = H_0 + H_p$, known from the first iteration step.
The largest deflection is $w^\star = +13.7$ cm, being 27% of w; however, in most parts of the net $w^\star$ is negative, attaining values up to -7.4 cm. A third iteration step was unnecessary.
The horizontal tensions $H_p{}^\star$, which are of prime interest, are given in Table 2.16; their magnitudes as expressed in per cents of H_p are also shown for comparison. Also in this case the differences between the horizontal tensions of the carrying cables become less (cf.

Table 2.16. $H_p{}^\star$ Due to Permanent Load and Snow

j	1	2	3	4	5	6	7	8	9	10
$H_{xp}{}^\star$	+0.58	+0.09	−0.22	−0.30	−0.28	−0.15	−0.21	−0.26	−0.06	−0.24
$H^\star/H$	+8.1	+1.0	−2.3	−3.1	−2.9	−1.6	−2.3	−3.0	−0.8	−4.1
i	1	2	3	4	5	6	7			
$H_{yp}{}^\star$	+0.67	+0.67	+0.43	+0.18	−0.11	−0.14	−0.26	Mp/m		
$H^\star/H$	−18.3	−12.9	−7.1	−2.8	+1.6	+2.0	+3.6	%		

Section 2.8.2); on the other hand, the forces acting in the central tension cables increase in absolute value.
The sectional loads are obtained by apportioning H_p^* to the permanent and the snow load and adding to the respective values of H_p.

2.9.5.3 Permanent load plus wind in x-direction
The antimetrical part of this load combination will again be considered separately.
We can expect that no significant horizontal displacements will be caused by the symmetrical part, since the weight of the cables is almost balanced by the symmetrical wind suction. The values of p^*, like the resultant deflections, have different signs within the region of the surface, varying between $+1.4$ and -3.0 kp/m^2. Apart from these peaks the additional loads are in general less than 0.5 kp/m^2, so that they can be neglected.
The antimetrical part of the wind load causes larger displacements in the x-direction, which at max $u = 9.1$ cm represent almost a third of the corresponding deflection w. These displacements are shown in Fig. 2.33. The approximation Eq. 2.53c cannot, of course, be applied to these greatly varying loads. It would exceed the scope of this book to indicate all accurately computed additional loads p^*. They amount to several kp/m^2 only at a few points near the edge. Elsewhere they are in general so small that a second iteration step is unnecessary.

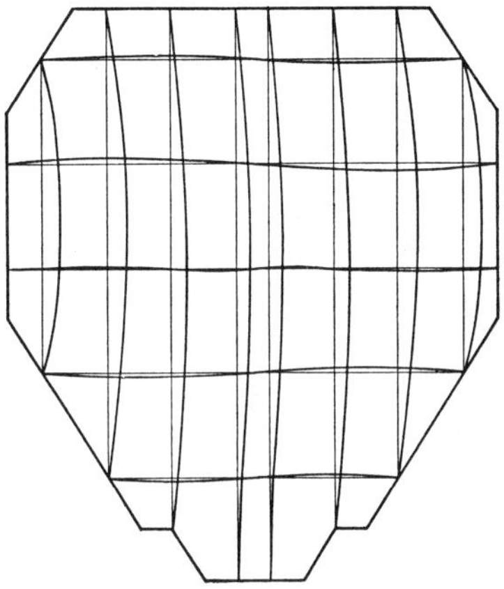

The displacements are shown increased by a factor of 50 in relation to the lengths.

Fig. 2.33. Horizontal Displacements Due to Antimetrical Part of Load Caused by Wind in x-Direction.

2.9.6 *Stress Analysis*

2.9.6.1 Horizontal tensions
Table 2.17 shows the horizontal tensions for the various cases of loading. The virtual shearing forces have not been included and will be added later. The data for permanent and snow loads contain the results of the nonlinearized calculation (Section 2.9.5.2).
The horizontal tensions in the case of wind *opposed* to the y-direction were estimated from the results of wind *in* the y-direction. In

Table 2.17. Compilation of Horizontal Tensions

H_x

j	1	2	3	4	5	6	7	8	9	10
0	+6.00	+6.00	+6.00	+6.00	+6.00	+6.00	+6.00	+6.00	+6.00	+6.00
g	+2.69	+3.09	+3.20	+3.20	+3.19	+3.13	+3.05	+2.89	+2.65	+1.96
s	+5.09	+5.91	+6.15	+6.21	+6.22	+6.08	+5.92	+5.55	+4.99	+3.62
$\mp \Delta t$	±0.49	±0.48	±0.47	±0.46	±0.47	±0.47	±0.47	±0.48	±0.49	±0.51
$W_y\downarrow$	−6.90	−7.30	−6.42	−5.35	−4.51	−3.44	−2.54	−1.71	−1.10	−0.77
$W_x\rightarrow$	−3.01	−3.99	−4.28	−4.31	−4.25	−4.13	−4.04	−3.85	−3.19	−2.12
$W_y\uparrow$						−4.5	−5.35	−6.4	−7.3	−6.9
$0+g$	8.69	9.09	9.20	9.20	9.19	9.13	9.05	8,89	8.65	7,96
max	14.27	15.48	15.82	15.87	**15.88**	15.68	15.44	14,92	14.13	12.09
min	1.30	1.31	2.31	3.39	4.21	4.16	3.23	2,01	0.86	**0.55**

H_y

i	1	2	3	4	5	6	7
0	+7.50	+7.50	+7.50	+7.50	+7.50	+7.50	+7.50
g	−1.06	−1.58	−1.95	−2.15	−2.40	−2.40	−2.52
s	−1.93	−2.93	−3.67	−4.13	−4.65	−4.71	−4.95
$\mp \Delta t$	±0.55	±0.56	±0.57	±0.58	±0.58	±0.58	±0.58
$W_y\downarrow$	+1.35	+2.54	+3.12	+3.31	+3.65	+3.57	+3.69
$W_x\rightarrow$	+5.50	+6.67	+6:22	+5.09	+4.03	+2.90	+2.28
$W_x\leftarrow$	+0.46	+0.65	+0.72	+0.79	+1.03	+1.36	+1.78
$0+g$	6.44	5.92	5.55	5.35	5.10	5.10	4.98
max	12.49	**13.15**	12.34	11.02	9.71	9.25	9.25
min	5.06	3.55	2.45	1.80	1.03	0.97	**0.61**

Mp/m

practice the actual distribution of wind forces would, of course, be determined by means of tests on models. These tests would also include investigations on whether wind blowing in any other direction would cause more unfavorable loads acting on the cable net.

The differences between the results of the preliminary calculation (Table 2.5) and the final results given in Table 2.17 are very small both for the various cases of loading and for the extreme values.

The virtual shearing forces in the cases of loading yielding the extremum horizontal tensions are:

at $i = 0, j = 5$: $\mathfrak{Q}_x = +0.01$ Mp/m (from $p_x^\star$, load $g+s$)
at $i = 7, j = 10$: $\mathfrak{Q}_x \approx -0.03$ Mp/m (from wind y)
at $i = 2, j = 0$: $\mathfrak{Q}_y = -0.42$ Mp/m (from wind $x \to$)
at $i = 2, j = 5$: $\mathfrak{Q}_y = +0.18$ Mp/m (from wind $x \to$)
at $i = 7, j = 11$: $\mathfrak{Q}_y \approx -0.02$ Mp/m (from $p_y^\star$, load $g+s$).

We then obtain finally the extremum horizontal tensions:

$$\max H_x = +15.88 + 0.01 = +15.89 \text{ Mp/m at } i = 0, j = 5$$
$$\min H_x = +0.55 - 0.03 = +0.52 \text{ Mp/m} > 0$$
$$\max H_y = +13.15 + 0.18 = +13.33 \text{ Mp/m at } i = 2, j = 5$$
$$H_y = +13.15 - 0.42 = +12.73 \text{ Mp/m at } i = 2, j = 0$$
$$\min H_y = +0.61 - 0.02 = +0.59 \text{ Mp/m} > 0\,.$$

The cables are in tension even in the most unfavorable case.

2.9.6.2 Stress analysis

max σ_1: Inclination $\bar{z}'$ at the edge at point $i = 0, j = 5$; Load $0 + g + s - \Delta t$: we write for w':

$$w_{0.5}' \approx \frac{1.5}{\Delta x}(w_{1.5} + w_{1.5}^\star) = \frac{1.5}{6.5 \cdot 100}(28.2 - 5.9)$$
$$w_{0.5}' = \quad = 0.051$$
$$z_{0.5}' = 48.75/136 \quad = 0.359$$
$$\bar{z}' = 0.410$$
$$\sqrt{1 + \bar{z}'^2} = 1.08$$
$$\max \sigma_1 = \max H_x \cdot \frac{\sqrt{1 + \bar{z}'^2}}{F_x} = 15.89 \cdot 1.08/2.10 =$$
$$\max \sigma_1 = 8.16 \text{ Mp/cm}^2 = 0.51 \cdot 16\,.$$

The maximum stress in the cable net thus attains 51% of the tensile strength of steel. Neglecting w' would have led to $\sigma_1 = 8.04$ Mp/cm².

We obtain similarly the inclination at the edge at point $i = 2, j = 0$ for the load $0 + g - \Delta t + w_x$: $\bar{z}^\cdot = -0{,}321$;

$$\max \sigma_2 = 12.73 \cdot \sqrt{1 + 0.321^2}\,/1.89 = 7.08 \text{ Mp/cm}^2 < 0.5 \cdot 16\,.$$

At $i = 2, j = 5$ we have $\bar{z}' \approx \bar{z}^\cdot \approx 0$:

$$\sigma_2 = 13.33/1.89 = 7.05 \text{ Mp/cm}^2 < 7.08\,.$$

2.9.7 *Safety Against Yielding*

An increase of the useful loads g and s, as required in Section 2.7.3, leads to (cf. Table 2.17):

$$H_y = +7.50 - 1.6\,(1.58 + 2.93) = 7.50 - 7.22 > 0$$

for $i = 2$, and

$$H_y = +7.50 - 1.6\,(1.95 + 3.67) = 7.50 - 8.99 < 0$$

for $i = 3$. Thus, H_y is positive only for $i = 1$ or 2. We therefore assume for the sake of simplicity that all tension cables become slack when the load is increased. Neglecting w and writing $\sqrt{1 + z'^2} \approx 1.1$, we obtain

$$H_x = -1.6\,(g + s)/z'' = 1.6\,(39 + 75) \cdot 10^{-3} \cdot 136 = 24.8 \text{ Mp/m},$$
$$\sigma_1 = 24.8 \cdot 1.1/2.10 = 13.0 \text{ Mp/cm}^2.$$

The maximum stresses in the tension cables occur at the load $0 + g - \Delta t + w_x$. However, the cables remain in tension when the load is multiplied by 1.6. The calculation proceeds therefore as follows:

H_y for $i = 2$ (cf. Table 2.17):

due to initial tension:			+ 7.50 Mp/m
due to temperature variation:			+ 0.56 Mp/m
due to permanent load 1.6:	−1.6	1.58 =	− 2.53 Mp/m
due to wind in x-direction 1.6:	+1.6	6.67 =	+10.67 Mp/m
		H_y =	+16.20 Mp/m

$$\sigma_2 = 16.20 \cdot 1.1/1.89 = 9.31 \text{ Mp/cm}^2.$$

2.9.8 *Natural Frequencies*

The mean spans are assumed to be

$$l_x = 90 \text{ m} \qquad l_y = 100 \text{ m}$$
$$k_x^2 \cdot l_x^2 = (90/136)^2 = 0.438 \qquad k_y^2 \cdot l_y^2 = (100/170)^2 = 0.346.$$

For $g = 39$ kp/m² and the gravitational acceleration $\tilde{g} = 9.81$ m/sec² we obtain

$$\frac{1}{\mu} = \frac{9.81}{0.039} = 251.5 \frac{\text{m}^3}{\text{Mp sec}^2}\,.$$

Load: Initial tension plus permanent load. We take the mean values of H_x and H_y from Table 2.17:

$$H_x = 9.0 \text{ Mp/m} \qquad \frac{H_x}{l_x^2} = \frac{9.0}{90^2} = 11.1 \cdot 10^{-4} \text{ Mp/m}^3$$
$$H_y = 5.4 \text{ Mp/m} \qquad \frac{H_y}{l_y^2} = \frac{5.4}{100^2} = 5.4 \cdot 10^{-4} \text{ Mp/m}^3\,.$$

We obtain from Eqs. 2.76 and 2.73:

$$\omega_{ss}^2 = \pi^2 \cdot 251.5\left(11.1 + 5.4 + \frac{3150 \cdot 10^4}{\pi^2 \cdot 136^2} + \frac{2835 \cdot 10^4}{\pi^2 \cdot 170^2}\right) \cdot 10^{-4} =$$
$$= \pi^2 \cdot 251.5\,(11.1 + 5.4 + 172.7 + 99.5) \cdot 10^{-4} =$$
$$= \pi^2 \cdot 7.26\,,$$
$$\omega_{ss} = 2.69\,\pi \text{ sec}^{-1}, \qquad \tau_{ss} = \frac{2}{2.69} = 0.74 \text{ sec}\,.$$

The first natural frequency was also determined from Eq. 2.75. The values $1/w$ were found for the 58 quantities given in Table 2.8; their sum amounts to 414/m. Hence

$$\omega^2 = 9.81 \cdot \frac{414}{58} = 70.0\,,$$
$$\omega = 8.37 \text{ sec}^{-1}, \qquad \tau = \frac{2\pi}{8.37} = 0.75 \text{ sec},$$

which is in good agreement with the above results.

For other modes of vibration we find from Eq. 2.83:

$$\omega_{as}^2 = 2.67 \cdot 251.5 \left(11.1 \cdot \frac{63.0 + 0.346}{4 + 0.438} + 3.75 \cdot 5.4\right) \cdot 10^{-4},$$

$$\omega_{as} = 1.10 \cdot \pi \sec^{-1}, \qquad \tau_{as} = 1.8 \sec,$$

$$\omega_{sa}^2 = 2.67 \cdot 251.5 \left(5.4 \frac{63.0 + 0.438}{4 + 0.346} + 3.75 \cdot 11.1\right) \cdot 10^{-4},$$

$$\omega_{sa} = 0.91\,\pi \sec^{-1}, \qquad \tau_{sa} = 2.2 \sec,$$

and similarly from Eq. 2.81:

$$\omega_{aa}^2 = 42.0 \cdot 251.5 \frac{11.1 \cdot 4.346 + 5.4 \cdot 4.438}{4 + 0.438 + 0.346} \cdot 10^{-4},$$

$$\omega_{aa} = 1.27\,\pi \sec^{-1}, \qquad \tau_{aa} = 1.6 \sec .$$

Load: Initial tension plus permanent load plus wind in x-direction. We have to assume different horizontal tensions in this case. We use the following rounded-off values, taken from Table 2.17:

$$H_x = 6.0 + 3.0 - 4.0 = 5.0 \text{ Mp/m}, \qquad \frac{H_x}{l_x^2} = 6.17 \cdot 10^{-4} \text{Mp/m}^3,$$

$$H_y = 7.5 - 2.1 + 2.0 = 7.4 \text{ Mp/m}, \qquad \frac{H_y}{l_y^2} = 7.4 \cdot 10^{-4} \text{ Mp/m}^3 .$$

The natural frequencies and vibration periods are then by Eq. 2.76:

$$\omega_{ss}^2 = \pi^2 \cdot 251.5\,(6.17 + 7.4 + 172.7 + 99.5) \cdot 10^{-4} =$$

$$\omega_{ss}^2 = \pi^2 \cdot 7.27,$$

$$\omega_{ss} = 2.70 \cdot \pi \sec^{-1}, \qquad \tau_{ss} = 0.74 \sec .$$

(The last two terms in parentheses have been taken from the results obtained for the first case of loading.)

Eq. 2.83 yields in this case:

$$\omega_{as}^2 = 2.67 \cdot 251.5 \left(6.17 \cdot \frac{63.0 + 0.346}{4 + 0.438} + 3.75 \cdot 7.4\right) \cdot 10^{-4},$$

$$\omega_{as} = 0.89 \cdot \pi = 2.79 \sec^{-1}, \qquad \underline{\tau_{as} = 2.3 \sec} .$$

The lowest frequency (longest vibration period) is thus obtained for wind in the x-direction. The net vibrations are then symmetrical in the y-direction and antimetrical in the x-direction. The vibrations cause almost no strains in the x-direction.

2.9.9 *Deformations*

The largest deflection of the cable net occurs at the load $0 + g + s$: max $w = 56.2$ cm. Hence, for $j = 6$,

$$\frac{\max w}{l_x} = \frac{0.526}{100} = \frac{1}{178} .$$

For the load $0 + g + w_x$ we find for $j = 4$:

$$\frac{\min w}{l_x} = -\frac{0.441}{100} = -\frac{1}{227},$$

for $i = 1$:

$$\frac{\min w}{l_y} = -\frac{0.36}{60} = -\frac{1}{167} .$$

As could be expected, the deflections of the cable net are considerably larger than those of beam, frame, and framework structures. They can, however, easily be reduced by increasing the curvatures of the cables or by using thicker cables.

3 AXISYMMETRICAL CABLE NETS

3.1 Introduction

Axisymmetrical cable nets differ from the orthogonal nets discussed in the previous chapter in that only cables of one family (circles) lie in parallel planes $\mathbf{z} = \text{const}$; the cables of the other family lie along the meridians of a surface of revolution; their planes intersect along the $\mathbf{z}$-axis (Figs. 3.1). These two types of cable nets are thus basically different.

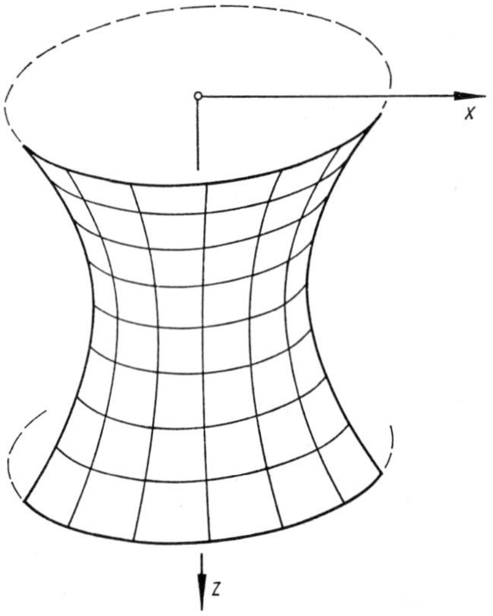

Fig. 3.1a. Erect Axisymmetrical Cable Net.

The total included angle of circular cables may attain 360°. This is impossible with shallow nets. Derivation of a simple computational procedure required that the inclinations of the cables of the other family toward the axis considered be small.

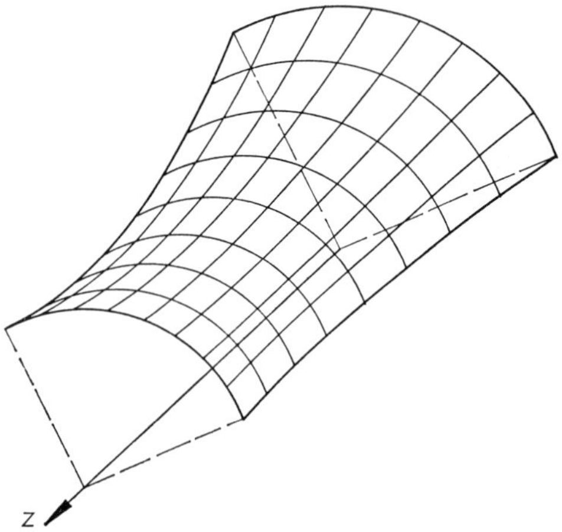

Fig. 3.1b. Recumbent Axisymmetrical Cable Net.

The formulas derived in this chapter do not therefore apply to the (more dish-shaped) radial cable nets whose meridians form angles of almost 90° with the axis.

Axisymmetrical cable nets are used in structural engineering especially for the walls of circular buildings. A closing annulus,

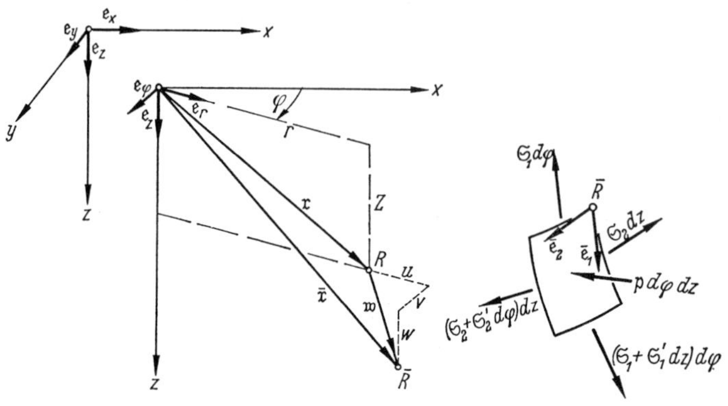

Fig. 3.2. Notation.

suitably supported by the foundations, is then required in addition to the circular foundations.

Several basic shapes can be combined if tension and compression rings are inserted [at the joints].

Although the z-axis is shown vertically in Figs. 3.1a and 3.2, this need not be so in general. Any region can be cut out from the approximately circular-cylindrical surface. Surfaces having a larger curvature in one direction (e.g., roof surfaces) can be formed and analyzed as axisymmetrical nets if the axis is arranged horizontally or at an inclination (Fig. 3.1b).

It is most convenient in this case to use cylindrical coordinates. The definitions and abbreviations of the second chapter will be largely used also in this chapter.

Many results and expressions obtained for orthogonal nets can therefore be applied in the present discussion by suitably altering the notation.

3.2 Notation and Geometrical Fundamentals

3.2.1 *Initial Surface*

We use as a fundamental system a fixed, right-handed, orthogonal coordinate system x, y, z with the unit vectors $\mathfrak{e}_x$, $\mathfrak{e}_y$, $\mathfrak{e}_z$.

The z-axis is the axis of rotation; it is positive downward in Figs. 3.1a and 3.2 but may have any direction in space (cf. Fig. 3.1b). The x, z-plane ($\varphi = 0$) is most conveniently placed at one end or, in the case of symmetry, in the center of the net.

In view of the peculiarities of the net shapes considered, we shall in addition use cylindrical coordinates with the independent variables z and φ (Fig. 3.2). We therefore introduce a second trihedron with the (orthonormal) unit vectors $\mathfrak{e}_r$, $\mathfrak{e}_\varphi$ and $\mathfrak{e}_z$, which has been rotated through the angle φ in relation to the first trihedron. Its unit vectors are related to those of the Cartesian trihedron as follows:

$$\left.\begin{aligned} \mathfrak{e}_r &= \cos\varphi\, \mathfrak{e}_x + \sin\varphi\, \mathfrak{e}_y\,, \\ \mathfrak{e}_\varphi &= -\sin\varphi\, \mathfrak{e}_x + \cos\varphi\, \mathfrak{e}_y\,, \\ \mathfrak{e}_z &= \mathfrak{e}_r \times \mathfrak{e}_\varphi = \mathfrak{e}_x \times \mathfrak{e}_y\,. \end{aligned}\right\} \qquad (3.1\text{a–c})$$

The net, consisting of individual tension members, is again considered as a continuum for the purpose of analysis. The initial (null) surface is, as before, defined as the surface $\mathfrak{r}(z, \varphi)$ (or, by virtue of axisymmetry, $r = r(z)$) which would be obtained in the absence of external loads. It will be shown later that axisymmetrical nets must generally be pretensioned. The cables are therefore subjected only to pretensioning in the initial state. If, in exceptional cases, the net is not pretensioned, all cables are slack in the initial state.
The vector of location of any point R of the net is defined in cylindrical coordinates by

$$\mathfrak{r}(z, \varphi) = r(z) \cdot \mathfrak{e}_r(\varphi) + z \cdot \mathfrak{e}_z = \{r(z), 0, z\} \quad (3.2a)$$

and in Cartesian coordinates, using Eq. 3.1a, by

$$\mathfrak{r}(z, \varphi) = r(z) \cdot \cos\varphi \cdot \mathfrak{e}_x + r(z) \sin\varphi \cdot \mathfrak{e}_y + z\, \mathfrak{e}_z. \quad (3.2b)$$

We assume that $\mathfrak{r}$ is single-valued and at least twice differentiable.
We write the partial derivatives of scalars and vectors as follows, e.g.,

$$\frac{\partial \mathfrak{r}}{\partial z} = \mathfrak{r}', \qquad \frac{\partial \mathfrak{r}}{\partial \varphi} = \mathfrak{r}^{\cdot}. \quad (3.3)$$

In the initial state the cables run along the parametric curves (coordinate lines) $z = \text{const}$ and $\varphi = \text{const}$, forming an orthogonal net.
We define, in analogy to the notation of Chapter 2, the boundaries of the cable net, i.e., the curves along which the net is fixed, by

$$\varphi_r = \varphi_r(z), \qquad \varphi_l = \varphi_l(z), \qquad \varphi_r \geqslant \varphi_l, \quad (3.4a)$$

and

$$z_r = z_r(\varphi), \qquad z_l = z_l(\varphi), \qquad z_r \geqslant z_l \quad (3.4b)$$

(cf. Figs. 2.7 and 2.8). The angle φ is measured in radians.

3.2.2 *Deformed Surface*

The displacement of a point R to its position $\bar{R}$ after deformation is described by the vector

$$\mathfrak{w}(z, \varphi) = u(z, \varphi) \cdot \mathfrak{e}_r + v(z, \varphi)\, \mathfrak{e}_\varphi + w(z, \varphi) \cdot \mathfrak{e}_z. \quad (3.5a)$$

Its components are positive in the directions of the corresponding axes of the trihedron.
The vector of location of the deformed surface is

$$\bar{\mathfrak{r}} = \mathfrak{r} + \mathfrak{w} = \{r + u, v, z + w\}. \quad (3.5b)$$

Since

$$\mathfrak{e}_r{}' = \mathfrak{e}_\varphi{}' = \mathfrak{e}_z{}' = \mathfrak{e}_z{}^{\cdot} = 0,$$
$$\mathfrak{e}_r{}^{\cdot} = \mathfrak{e}_\varphi, \qquad \mathfrak{e}_\varphi{}^{\cdot} = -\mathfrak{e}_r, \qquad r^{\cdot} = z^{\cdot} = 0,$$

the unit tangent vectors to the cable curve are (cf. Fig. 3.2)

$$\bar{\mathfrak{e}}_1 = \frac{\bar{\mathfrak{r}}'}{|\bar{\mathfrak{r}}'|} = \frac{1}{|\bar{\mathfrak{r}}'|}\{r' + u', v', 1 + w'\}, \quad (3.6a)$$

$$\bar{\mathfrak{e}}_2 = \frac{\mathfrak{r}^{\cdot}}{|\mathfrak{r}^{\cdot}|} = \frac{1}{|\bar{\mathfrak{r}}^{\cdot}|}\{u^{\cdot} - v, r + u + v^{\cdot}, w^{\cdot}\}. \quad (3.6b)$$

The unit tangent vectors $\mathfrak{e}_1$ and $\mathfrak{e}_2$ corresponding to the undeformed surface are obtained from Eqs. 3.6 by omitting all terms containing u, v, and w. Assuming the displacements to be small, we obtain with sufficient accuracy

$$\bar{\mathfrak{e}}_1{}' = \frac{1}{r''}\{r'' + u'', v'', w''\}, \quad (3.7a)$$

$$\bar{\mathfrak{e}}_2{}^{\cdot} = \frac{1}{r}\{-r - u, -v, 0\}. \quad (3.7b)$$

3.3 Derivation of the Fundamental Equation

3.3.1 *Equilibrium Conditions*

The condition that all cables be free from moments leads to the vector representation of the cable forces

$$\mathfrak{S}_1 = S_1 \cdot \bar{\mathfrak{e}}_1, \qquad \mathfrak{S}_2 = S_2 \cdot \bar{\mathfrak{e}}_2. \quad (3.8a, b)$$

A certain number of cables will always run approximately in the z-direction in a given sector $d\varphi$ or $\Delta\varphi$ of the cable net. However, the distance between these cables varies with r. It is therefore convenient to refer the cable force $S_1 = |\mathfrak{S}_1|$ to unit center angle φ (in radians) instead of to unit circumference. Thus, S_1 represents the tensile force in all cables stretched approximately in the z-direction in a sector $\Delta\varphi = 1 \hat{=} 180°/\pi = 57.296°$. On the other hand, $S_2 = |\mathfrak{S}_2|$ will be referred to unit length of the z-axis. The external load is given by

$$\mathfrak{p}(z, \varphi) = \{p_r, p_\varphi, p_z\}, \quad (3.9)$$

also referred to the units $\Delta z = 1$ and $\Delta\varphi = 1$. The components of $\mathfrak{p}$ have the directions of the corresponding unit vectors $\mathfrak{e}_r$, $\mathfrak{e}_\varphi$, and $\mathfrak{e}_z$. The load per unit area $\mathfrak{p}$ is defined thus:

$$\mathfrak{p}(z, \varphi) = \frac{1}{r(z)} \cdot \bar{\mathfrak{p}}(z, \varphi). \quad (3.10)$$

Changes in $\mathfrak{p}$, caused by deformation of the net (e.g., by wind) are neglected.
We shall now consider the equilibrium of a cable-net element $dz \cdot d\varphi$. Neglecting the higher terms in the Taylor series for $\mathfrak{S}$, we obtain

$$\frac{\partial}{\partial z}(\mathfrak{S}_1\, d\varphi)\, dz + \frac{\partial}{\partial \varphi}(\mathfrak{S}_2\, dz)\, d\varphi + \mathfrak{p}\, dz\, d\varphi = 0.$$

Substitution of Eqs. 3.8 and division by $dz \cdot d\varphi$ yields

$$(S_1\, \bar{\mathfrak{e}}_1)' + (\mathfrak{S}_2\, \bar{\mathfrak{e}}_2)^{\cdot} + \mathfrak{p} = 0. \quad (3.11)$$

The cable-force directions are in general inclined to the directions $\mathfrak{e}_z$ and $\mathfrak{e}_\varphi$. Their projections on the latter are

$$H_z = \mathfrak{S}_1 \cdot \mathfrak{e}_z, \quad (3.12a)$$

$$S_\varphi = \mathfrak{S}_2 \cdot \mathfrak{e}_\varphi. \quad (3.12b)$$

Although in Fig. 3.2 the force H_z is vertical, we shall retain the designation H for "horizontal tension." Using Eqs. 3.8a and 3.6a, Eq. 3.12a becomes

$$H_z = \frac{S_1(1 + w')}{|\bar{\mathfrak{r}}'|} \approx \frac{S_1}{|\bar{\mathfrak{r}}'|} \approx \frac{S_1}{|\mathfrak{r}'|}. \quad (3.13a)$$

Similarly, using Eqs. 3.8b and 3.6b, Eq. 3.12b defines the circumferential tension

$$S_\varphi = \frac{S_2(r + u + v^{\cdot})}{|\bar{\mathfrak{r}}^{\cdot}|} \approx S_2. \quad (3.13b)$$

The equilibrium condition 3.11 then becomes

$$\left(\frac{H_z}{1+w'}\,\bar{\mathfrak{r}}'\right)' + \left(\frac{S_\varphi}{r+u+v^\cdot}\,\bar{\mathfrak{r}}^\cdot\right)^\cdot + \mathfrak{p} = 0 . \tag{3.14}$$

Using Eqs. 3.7, we obtain immediately the component equations for the directions $\mathfrak{e}_z$, $\mathfrak{e}_\varphi$, and $\mathfrak{e}_r$, where the small higher-order terms have been omitted:

$$\left.\begin{aligned} &H_z' + \frac{1}{r}(S_\varphi w^\cdot)^\cdot + p_z = 0 ,\\ &(H_z v')' + S_\varphi^\cdot - S_\varphi \frac{v}{r} + p_\varphi = 0 ,\\ &[H_z (r' + u')]' - S_\varphi - \frac{1}{r}(S_\varphi \cdot v)^\cdot + S_\varphi \frac{u^{\cdot\cdot}}{r} + p_r = 0 . \end{aligned}\right\} \tag{3.15a–c}$$

The magnitudes H_z and S_φ consist, respectively, of parts H_{z0} and $S_{\varphi 0}$, due to initial tension, and parts H_{zp}, $S_{\varphi p}$ due to applied load, temperature variations, or edge displacements. According to Section 1.1.2 we can always write with sufficient accuracy

$$H_z = H_{z0} + H_{zp} \tag{3.16a}$$

and

$$S_\varphi = S_{\varphi 0} + S_{\varphi p} . \tag{3.16b}$$

3.3.2 *Initial State*

By definition $\mathfrak{w} = \mathfrak{p} = 0$ if only the initial tension acts on the cable net. The equilibrium conditions 3.15 for the initial surface are thus

$$\left.\begin{aligned} &H_{z0}' = 0 ,\\ &S^\cdot_{\varphi 0} = 0 ,\\ &(H_{z0} \cdot r')' - S_{\varphi 0} = 0 \end{aligned}\right\} \tag{3.17a–c}$$

or, since r does not depend on φ,

$$H_{z0} \cdot r''(z) - S_{\varphi 0}(z) = 0 . \tag{3.17d}$$

H_{z0} is thus constant over the entire cable net. Also, $r'' > 0$ for positive initial tensions; the initial surface, therefore, has a negative Gaussian curvature, like a single-sheet hyperboloid (Fig. 3.1).

In a nonpretensioned cable net r'' may have either sign. Simple reasoning leads to the conclusion that when $r'' > 0$, e.g., due to a load p_r, tensile forces will appear in one family of cables and (theoretically) compressive forces in the other; such a system cannot therefore take up loads as a cable net without pretensioning. A net, in which $r'' < 0$, bulges like a barrel; it cannot be pretensioned, is kinematically displaceable, and can only be stabilized by a permanent positive load p_r. This case is similar to the nonpretensioned orthogonal cable net, and the considerations of Section 2.5.2 are also valid here.

The initial surface that is simplest to analyze is formed by the paraboloid of revolution

$$r = a_1 + a_2 z + a_3 z^2 \quad \text{with} \quad a_3 > 0 , \tag{3.18}$$

for which [by Eq. 3.17d] H_{z0} = const in addition to $S_{\varphi 0}$ = const. No other initial surfaces will be considered.

3.3.3 *Elasticity Conditions*

The length of the element of arc is

$$|\bar{\mathfrak{r}}^\cdot| \approx \bar{\mathfrak{r}}^\cdot \cdot \mathfrak{e}_\varphi = r + u + v^\cdot .$$

According to Eq. 3.2a,

$$|\mathfrak{r}^\cdot| = r .$$

Hence, the circumferential strain is

$$\varepsilon_2 = \frac{|\bar{\mathfrak{r}}^\cdot| - |\mathfrak{r}^\cdot|}{|\mathfrak{r}^\cdot|} = \frac{u + v^\cdot}{r} .$$

On the other hand, assuming Hooke's law to be valid,

$$\varepsilon_2 = \frac{S_{2p}}{E_\varphi F_\varphi} + {}^t\varepsilon_\varphi .$$

Using Eq. 3.13b, we obtain

$$S_{\varphi p} \approx S_{2p} = D_\varphi (u + v^\cdot - r \cdot {}^t\varepsilon_\varphi) , \tag{3.19a}$$

where

$$D_\varphi = \frac{E_\varphi F_\varphi}{r} \tag{3.20a}$$

is the rigidity function, E_φ is the modulus of elasticity, and F_φ is the cross-sectional area referred to unit length of the z-axis, of the circumferential cables. The stretching of these cables, caused by temperature variations, is

$${}^t\varepsilon_\varphi = \alpha_t \cdot \Delta t . \tag{3.21}$$

The corresponding formulas for the cables running in the other direction can be obtained from Section 2.2.3 if the cross-sectional areas of the cables, as well as the forces S_1 and H_z, are referred to unit center angle. Taking into account the notation used here, we obtain from Eqs. 2.24:

$$H_{zp} = D_z (w' + r' u' - g_{11}\, {}^t\varepsilon_z) , \tag{3.19b}$$

where

$$D_z = \frac{E_z F_z}{g_{11}^{\;3/2}} \tag{3.20b}$$

and

$$g_{11} = \mathfrak{r}'^2 = 1 + r'^2 . \tag{3.20c}$$

3.3.4 *Fundamental Equation of the Axisymmetrical Cable Net*

We separate the cable forces and horizontal tensions into parts due to initial tension and applied load (cf. Eqs. 3.16). Taking into account the equilibrium conditions 3.17 for the initial state, we can rewrite Eqs. 3.15 as follows:

$$\underline{H_{zp}'} + \frac{1}{r}(S_\varphi w^\cdot)^\cdot + \underline{p_z} = 0 , \tag{3.21a}$$

$$(H_z v')' + \underline{S_{\varphi p}^\cdot} - S_\varphi \frac{v}{r} + \underline{p_\varphi} = 0 , \tag{3.21b}$$

$$\begin{aligned} &\underline{H_{zp}' r'} + H_{zp}' u' + \underline{H_{z0} u''} + \underline{H_{zp} r''} + H_{zp} u'' - \underline{S_{\varphi p}} +\\ &\quad + \underline{\frac{1}{r} S_{\varphi 0} u^{\cdot\cdot}} - \frac{1}{r}(S_\varphi v)^\cdot + \frac{1}{r} S_{\varphi p} u^{\cdot\cdot} + \underline{p_r} = 0 . \end{aligned} \tag{3.21c}$$

The underlined terms in each equation are considerably larger then the others. We linearize the system by considering the insignificant terms as additional loads that will be neglected at first. We then obtain the simple equilibrium conditions

$$H_{zp}' + p_z = 0 , \tag{3.22a}$$

$$S^\cdot_{\varphi p} + p_\varphi = 0 , \tag{3.22b}$$

$$H_{zp}\, r'' - S_{\varphi p} + H_{z0}\, u'' + \frac{1}{r} S_{\varphi 0}\, u^{\cdot\cdot} + p_r - p_z\, r' = 0\,. \tag{3.22c}$$

We retain the terms containing u'' and $u^{\cdot\cdot}$ in order to obtain a uniquely determined solution. The additional loads are

$$p_z^\star = \frac{1}{r}(S_{\varphi 0} + S_{\varphi p})\, w^{\cdot\cdot} - \frac{1}{r}\, p_\varphi\, w\,, \tag{3.23a}$$

$$p_\varphi^\star = (H_{z0} + H_{zp})\, v'' - p_z\, v' - (S_{\varphi 0} + S_{\varphi p})\frac{v}{r}\,, \tag{3.23b}$$

$$p_r^\star = H_{zp}\, u'' - p_z\, u' + \frac{1}{r}(p_\varphi\, v + S_{\varphi p}\, u^{\cdot\cdot}) - \frac{1}{r}(S_{\varphi 0} + S_{\varphi p})\cdot v^{\cdot}. \tag{3.23c}$$

We have here, as in Eq. 3.22c, substituted Eqs. 3.22a, b. We also refer the reader to Section 2.4.1. Experience shows that, if at all, only $p_r^\star$ and (with large subtended angles $\varphi_r - \varphi_l$) $p_\varphi^\star$, necessitate significant corrections.

Substituting Eqs. 3.19 in Eqs. 3.22, we obtain three linear differential equations in the three unknown displacement components u, v, and w. We can therefore superimpose different cases of loading. We first consider Eq. 3.22a, which can be integrated directly after the elasticity condition 3.19b has been inserted:

$$H_{zp} = D_z\,(w' + r'\,u' - g_{11}\,{}^t\varepsilon_z) = C_1(\varphi) - \int_0^z p_z\, d\,z\,. \tag{3.24a}$$

(We denote, as before, both the variable and the integration limit by z.) If the edge displacements u and w are given as functions of φ:

at the lower edge $z_r(\varphi)$: $u_{zr}(\varphi)$ and $w_{zr}(\varphi)$,
at the upper edge $z_l(\varphi)$: $u_{zl}(\varphi)$ and $w_{zl}(\varphi)$,

we can integrate once more. The result is

$$C_1(\varphi) = \Phi_z(\varphi)\left\{\int_{z_l}^{z_r}\left[\frac{1}{D_z}\int_0^z p_z\, dz\right] dz + W_z(\varphi) - \int_{z_l}^{z_r} g_{11}\,{}^t\varepsilon_z\, dz - \int_{z_l}^{z_r} r''\, u\, dz\right\}, \tag{3.25a}$$

where

$$W_z(\varphi) = (w_{zr} - w_{zl}) + (r_r'\, u_{zr} - r_l'\, u_{zl}) \tag{3.26a}$$

is the edge-displacement function and

$$\frac{1}{\Phi_z(\varphi)} = \int_{z_l}^{z_r}\frac{dz}{D_z} = \int_{z_l}^{z_r}\frac{(1 + r'^2)^{3/2}\, dz}{E_z F_z} \tag{3.27a}$$

the rigidity function. The last expression has been used before and is tabulated in Section 2.4.5 in the form $\Phi = E\,F/l\cdot\Lambda$.

Integration of Eq. 3.22b leads to a slightly different expression because the elasticity conditions 3.19a and 3.19b differ. We obtain first

$$S_{\varphi p} = D_\varphi\,(u + v^{\cdot} - r\,{}^t\varepsilon_\varphi) = C_2(r) - \int_0^\varphi p_\varphi\, d\,\varphi\,. \tag{3.24b}$$

A second integration yields $C_2(r)$:

$$C_2(r) = \Phi_\varphi(z)\left\{\int_{\varphi_l}^{\varphi_r}\left[\frac{1}{D_\varphi}\int_0^\varphi p_\varphi\, d\varphi\right] d\varphi + W_\varphi(r) - r\int_{\varphi_l}^{\varphi_r}{}^t\varepsilon_\varphi\, d\varphi + \int_{\varphi_l}^{\varphi_r} u\, d\varphi\right\}. \tag{3.25b}$$

Only the last integral is unknown. We have here introduced the rigidity function

$$\frac{1}{\Phi_\varphi} = \int_{\varphi_l}^{\varphi_r}\frac{d\,\varphi}{D_\varphi}\,.$$

The cables will in practice most likely have cross-sectional areas constant over their lengths; hence, by Eq. 3.20a,

$$\frac{1}{\Phi_\varphi(z)} = \frac{r}{E_\varphi\, F_\varphi}(\varphi_r - \varphi_l)\,,$$

or

$$\Phi_\varphi(z) = \frac{E_\varphi\, F_\varphi}{r(z)\cdot l_\varphi(z)}\,. \tag{3.27b}$$

Here

$l_\varphi(z) = \varphi_r - \varphi_l \geqslant 0\,,\quad l_\varphi \leqslant 2\,\pi\,,$

is not a real length, being measured in radians. This expression was chosen for the sake of conformity with

$l_z(\varphi) = z_r - z_l \geqslant 0\,.$

The actual cable length is $L_\varphi = r\cdot l_\varphi$.

In Eq. 3.25b we also used the expression

$$W_\varphi(r) = v_{\varphi r} - v_{\varphi l}\,, \tag{3.26b}$$

which takes into account the v-displacements of the edges, assumed to be known. As before, we have $v_{\varphi r}(r)$ for the right-hand edge and $v_{\varphi l}(r)$ for the left-hand edge, both being functions of r.

Substituting Eqs. 3.24 and 3.25 in the third equilibrium condition 3.22c and rearranging, we obtain the fundamental equation of the axisymmetrical cable net, which contains only one unknown displacement component (u, in the r-direction):

$$r''\,\Phi_z\int_{z_l}^{z_r} r''\, u\, dz + \Phi_\varphi\int_{\varphi_l}^{\varphi_r} u\, d\varphi - H_{z0}\, u'' - \frac{1}{r} S_{\varphi 0}\, u^{\cdot\cdot} = \mathfrak{P}(z, \varphi)\,. \tag{3.28}$$

The load function $\mathfrak{P}$, through which the effects of all applied loads edge displacements, and temperature variations are taken into account, is written out as follows:

$$\mathfrak{P}(z,\varphi) = -\,r'\, p_z - r''\int_0^z p_z\, dz + r''\,\Phi_z\int_{z_l}^{z_r}\left[\frac{1}{D_z}\int_0^z p_z\, dz\right] dz + \int_0^\varphi p_\varphi\, d\varphi - \Phi_\varphi\int_{\varphi_l}^{\varphi_r}\left[\frac{1}{D_\varphi}\int_0^\varphi p_\varphi\, d\varphi\right] d\varphi + p_r + \tag{3.29}$$

$$+ r'' \Phi_z W_z - \Phi_\varphi W_\varphi - - r'' \Phi_z \int_{z_l}^{z_r} g_{11}\, {}^t\varepsilon_z\, dz + r\, \Phi_\varphi \int_{\varphi_l}^{\varphi_r} {}^t\varepsilon_\varphi\, d\varphi .$$

We can simplify this expression by basing ourselves on [the considerations of] Section 2.4.3. The second and third terms can be written with sufficient accuracy as $r''\,\mathfrak{Q}_z$. We have here introduced the virtual shearing force acting on a straight beam of length l_z, simply supported at both ends and subjected to a distributed transverse load p_z:

$$\mathfrak{Q}_z = -\int_0^z p_z\, dz + \frac{1}{l_z} \int_{z_l}^{z_r}\int_0^z p_z\, dz\, dz \approx \approx -\int_0^z p_z\, dz + \Phi_z \int_{z_l}^{z_r} \left[\frac{1}{D_z}\int_0^z p_z\, dz\right] dz . \tag{3.30a}$$

Similarly,

$$\mathfrak{Q}_\varphi = -\int_0^\varphi p_\varphi\, d\varphi + \frac{1}{l_\varphi}\int_{\varphi_l}^{\varphi_r}\int_0^\varphi p_\varphi\, d\varphi\, d\varphi = = -\int_0^\varphi p_\varphi\, d\varphi + \Phi_\varphi \int_{\varphi_l}^{\varphi_r}\left[\frac{1}{D_\varphi}\int_0^\varphi p_\varphi\, d\varphi\right] d\varphi \tag{3.30b}$$

is the virtual shearing force acting on a beam of "length" l_φ, loaded by p_φ.

The temperature terms

$$\mathfrak{N}_z = -\Phi_z \int_{z_l}^{z_r} g_{11}\, {}^t\varepsilon_z\, dz \approx -\frac{E_z F_z}{l_z}\int_{z_l}^{z_r} {}^t\varepsilon_z\, dz \tag{3.31a}$$

and

$$\mathfrak{N}_\varphi = -r\,\Phi_\varphi \int_{\varphi_l}^{\varphi_r} {}^t\varepsilon_\varphi\, d\varphi = -\frac{E_\varphi F_\varphi}{l_\varphi}\int_{\varphi_l}^{\varphi_r} {}^t\varepsilon_\varphi\, d\varphi \tag{3.31b}$$

can be represented as normal forces acting in straight rods of lengths l_z and l_φ, respectively, caused by the temperature variations corresponding to ${}^t\varepsilon_z$ and ${}^t\varepsilon_\varphi$. Tension is considered to be positive.

Using these abbreviations, the load function defined by Eq. 3.29 now becomes

$$\mathfrak{P} = -r'\, p_z + r''\,\mathfrak{Q}_z - \mathfrak{Q}_\varphi + p_r + + r''\,\Phi_z W_z - \Phi_\varphi W_\varphi + r''\,\mathfrak{N}_z - \mathfrak{N}_\varphi . \tag{3.32}$$

The unknown function $u(z, \varphi)$ can now be determined numerically without difficulty, if the integrals on the left-hand side of Eq. 3.28 are replaced by sums and the derivatives by differences. The fundamental equation then assumes a form almost completely identical with that for the orthogonal cable net; we therefore refer the reader to Section 2.4.4.

The simplifications, discussed in detail with respect to the orthogonal cable net for the case of symmetry properties, can obviously also be applied to the net shapes considered now. The same is true for the investigation of safety against yielding.

Cable nets forming closed cylindrical surfaces ($l_\varphi = 2\pi$) have to be considered separately. No distinct structural edges φ_l and φ_r exist in these cases. We then have to select for the edge a certain meridian (if possible, in the plane of symmetry of the load) and estimate its displacements. The cable forces S and the deformations are first determined in the region of this assumed edge; thereafter, magnitude and direction of the resultant of the cable forces acting on this meridian are found. The displacement has been estimated correctly if the equilibrium and elasticity condition are satisfied for the edge cable. If this is not the case, we can either repeat the calculation, assuming suitably corrected edge displacements, or a different meridian can be chosen (e.g., one displaced by π from the former), the residual forces obtained in the first step from the equilibrium conditions being assumed to act now on the new net.

3.4 Determining the Cable Forces and Displacements

3.4.1 *Cable Forces*

When the radial displacements u have been found from Eqs. 3.28 and 3.32, we obtain from Eqs. 3.24a and 3.25a:

$$H_{zp} = \Phi_z \left(W_z - \int_{z_l}^{z_r} r''\, u\, dz\right) + \mathfrak{Q}_z + \mathfrak{N}_z , \tag{3.33a}$$

if the approximations 3.30a and 3.31a are used. The integral is known from the fundamental equation as sum.

The total cable force is thus by Eq. 3.13a:

$$S_1 = (H_{z0} + H_{zp}) \cdot \frac{|\bar{\mathfrak{r}}'|}{1 + w'} \approx \approx (H_{z0} + H_{zp}) \sqrt{1 + (r' + u')^2} . \tag{3.34a}$$

We obtain similarly from Eqs. 3.24b and 3.25b, using the abbreviations $\mathfrak{Q}_\varphi$ and $\mathfrak{N}_\varphi$,

$$S_{\varphi p} = \Phi_\varphi \left(W_\varphi + \int_{\varphi_l}^{\varphi_r} u\, d\varphi\right) + \mathfrak{Q}_\varphi + \mathfrak{N}_\varphi . \tag{3.33b}$$

The force in the circumferential cables is by virtue of $u \ll r$, $v \ll r$ and Eq. 3.13b:

$$S_2 = (S_{\varphi 0} + S_{\varphi p}) \frac{|\bar{\mathfrak{r}}^{\cdot}|}{r + u + v^{\cdot}} \approx (S_{\varphi 0}' + S_{\varphi p}) \sqrt{1 + \frac{v^2}{r^2}} . \tag{3.34b}$$

3.4.2 *Displacements v and w*

We proceed from Eq. 3.19a in order to find v (in the φ-direction) and obtain after integration

$$v(z, \varphi) = v_{\varphi l} + \int_{\varphi_l}^{\varphi_r} \left[\frac{r \cdot S_{\varphi p}}{E_\varphi F_\varphi} - u + r\, {}^t\varepsilon_\varphi\right] d\varphi . \tag{3.35}$$

Similarly, by Eq. 3.19b,

$$w(z, \varphi) = w_{zl} + \int_{z_l}^{z_r} \left[\frac{H_{zp}}{D_z} + r''\, u + g_{11}\, {}^t\varepsilon_z\right] dz - \left[r'\, u\right]_{z_l}^{z_r} . \tag{3.36a}$$

Substituting Eq. 3.33a for H_{zp} and rearranging, we obtain

$$w(z,\varphi) = \frac{z_r - z}{l_z}(w_{zl} + r_l' u_{zl}) + \frac{z - z_l}{l_z}(w_{zr} + r_r' u_{zr}) -$$
$$- r' u - \frac{z - z_l}{l_z}\int_{z_l}^{z_r} r'' u \, dz + \int_{z_l}^{z} r'' u \, dz + \qquad (3.36b)$$
$$+ \frac{1}{l_z \Phi_z}\mathfrak{M}_z + \frac{z - z_l}{l_z \Phi_z}\mathfrak{N}_z + \int_{z_l}^{z} g_{11}\, {}^t\varepsilon_z \, dz ,$$

which in some cases yields results more quickly than Eq. 3.36a which appears to be simpler. Here

$$\mathfrak{M}_z = \int_{z_l}^{z} \mathfrak{Q}_z \, dz \qquad (3.37)$$

is the virtual bending moment of the straight beam loaded by p_z (cf. Eq. 3.30a) and is best computed simultaneously with $\mathfrak{Q}_z$.

The last two terms in Eq. 3.36b can usually be neglected. The approximation

$$w \approx - r' \cdot u \qquad (3.36c)$$

will often suffice when no edge displacements occur.

3.5 Approximations

3.5.1 *General Observations*

In contrast to other statically indeterminate systems, where only the rigidity *ratios* must be given, we have to know the cross-sectional areas, the magnitudes of the initial tensions, and the shape of the cable net before the latter can be analyzed.

We shall therefore present simple approximations to be used in preliminary analyses of the most important cases of loading.

We consider a simple net with a regular edge. Its initial surface is defined by

$$r(z) = r_0 + \frac{k_z}{2} z^2 .$$

This is a paraboloid of revolution whose meridians are parabolas whose apexes lie on a circle of radius r_0. The net is bounded by the parametric curves $z_r = + l_z/2$, $z_l = - z_r$, and φ_r, $\varphi_l = - \varphi_r$, respectively.

For $r'' = k_z = \text{const}$ we obtain from Eqs. 3.17:

$H_{z0} = \text{const}, \quad S_{\varphi 0} = k_z \cdot H_{z0} = \text{const}.$

We can obtain satisfactory results for nets of different shapes and boundaries if we introduce suitable mean values.

We also assume the cable rigidities $E_z F_z$ and $E_\varphi F_\varphi$ to be constant.

3.5.2 *Load* p_z

Following the reasoning of Section 2.6.2, and changing the subscripts appropriately, we obtain with sufficient accuracy the cable forces due to p_z (generally, the weight of the wall), in the following form:

$${}^{p_z}H_{zp} \approx \mathfrak{Q}_z , \quad {}^{p_z}S_{\varphi p} \approx 0 . \qquad (3.37)$$

3.5.3 *Load* p_φ

No load in the circumferential direction $\mathfrak{e}_\varphi$ usually occurs in the case of walls; however, such a load may appear as a component of vertical loads (e.g., of dead weight or snow) in a cable net whose z-axis is not vertical. When the subtended angle l_φ is smaller than $\pi/6 = 30°$, we can write

$${}^{p_\varphi}H_{zp} \approx 0 , \quad {}^{p_\varphi}S_{\varphi p} \approx \mathfrak{Q}_\varphi . \qquad (3.38)$$

3.5.4 *Load* p_r

We set $p_r = \text{const}$ in the preliminary calculation. Neglecting the terms containing H_{z0} and $S_{\varphi 0}$ in the fundamental Eq. 3.28, we obtain for $r'' = k_z$:

$$k_z^2 \Phi_z \int_{z_l}^{z_r} u \, dz + \Phi_\varphi \int_{\varphi_l}^{\varphi_r} u \, d\varphi = p_r .$$

The left-hand side contains, as is evident from Eq. 3.22c, the two terms $- H_{zp} r''$ and $+ S_{\varphi p}$, whose ratio is

$$\frac{\varkappa_\varphi}{\varkappa_z} = \frac{S_{\varphi p}}{- H_{zp} \cdot k_z} = \frac{\Phi_\varphi \int u \, d\varphi}{k_z^2 \Phi_z \int u \, dz} .$$

Since the u-variations of both families of cables are similar, we can write

$$\frac{\varkappa_\varphi}{\varkappa_z} \approx \frac{\Phi_\varphi l_\varphi}{k_z^2 \Phi_z l_z} . \qquad (3.39)$$

When the cables form parabolas, we can make use of Eq. 2.56b (with subscripts changed appropriately):

$$\Phi_z = \frac{E_z F_z}{l_z \lambda_z} ,$$

where λ_z lies between 1.0 and 1.1 (Fig. 2.12), and Φ_φ is given by Eq. 3.27b. Hence, Eq. 3.39 becomes

$$\frac{\varkappa_\varphi}{\varkappa_z} = \frac{E_\varphi F_\varphi \lambda_z}{r k_z^2 E_z F_z} ,$$

in which only r depends on z. We now replace $r(z)$ by a suitably selected mean value r_m (this is permissible in view of the nearly straight run of the z-cables, which we assumed) and introduce the dimensionless magnitude

$$\overline{\varphi} = \frac{\lambda_z E_\varphi F_\varphi r_m}{E_z F_z} . \qquad (3.40)$$

The parts $\varkappa_z \cdot p_r$ and $\varkappa_\varphi \cdot p_r$ of the load p_r are, by virtue of, $\varkappa_z + \varkappa_\varphi = 1$ given by

$$\varkappa_z = \frac{1}{1 + \dfrac{\overline{\varphi}}{r_m^2 k_z^2}} , \qquad \varkappa_\varphi = 1 - \varkappa_z . \qquad (3.41)$$

The required cable forces are then finally

$${}^{p_r}H_{zp} \approx - \varkappa_z \frac{p_r}{k_z} , \qquad (3.42a)$$

$${}^{p_r}S_{\varphi p} \approx \varkappa_\varphi \cdot p_r = - \frac{\overline{\varphi}}{r_m^2 k_z} {}^{p_r}H_{zp} . \qquad (3.42b)$$

Denoting the ratio of the cable curvatures

$$\frac{1}{r_m k_z} = \frac{1/r_m}{k_z} = \varrho ,$$

we can find $\varkappa_z$ directly from Fig. 2.14.

We estimate the radial displacements u by combining Eqs. 3.33a and 3.42a:

$$\Phi_z k_z \int_{z_l}^{z_r} u \, dz \approx \frac{\varkappa_z}{k_z} p_r .$$

We now replace u by its mean value u_m and write out Φ_z. The result is

$$^{p_r}u_m \approx \frac{\lambda_z}{k_z^2 E_z F_z} \varkappa_z p_r , \qquad (3.43)$$

from which we can estimate the mean radial displacement due to a uniform load p_r. In the center of the surface, u will exceed this value by 10 to 20%.

3.5.5 *Temperature Variations*

For the frequent case ${}^t\varepsilon_z = {}^t\varepsilon_\varphi = {}^t\varepsilon = \text{const}$ we obtain from Eq. 3.31:

$$\mathfrak{N}_z = - E_z F_z {}^t\varepsilon \quad \text{and} \quad \mathfrak{N}_\varphi = - E_\varphi F_\varphi {}^t\varepsilon .$$

The load function is by Eq. 3.32:

$${}^t\mathfrak{P} = k_z \mathfrak{N}_z - \mathfrak{N}_\varphi = \text{const.}$$

It will be considered like p_r in Section 3.5.4. Equations 3.33 contain the terms $\mathfrak{N}$ in addition to those containing u, so that we find

$${}^tH_{zp} \approx \varkappa_\varphi \mathfrak{N}_z + \frac{\varkappa_z}{k_z} \mathfrak{N}_\varphi \qquad (3.44a)$$

and

$${}^tS_{\varphi p} \approx \varkappa_\varphi k_z \mathfrak{N}_z + \varkappa_z \mathfrak{N}_\varphi . \qquad (3.44b)$$

The radial displacements caused by temperature variations are usually insignificant and can be approximated by

$${}^tu_m \approx \frac{\varkappa_z}{k_z} \left(\frac{\overline{\varphi}}{r_m k_z} - \lambda_z \right) {}^t\varepsilon . \qquad (3.45)$$

When $k_z \mathfrak{N}_z - \mathfrak{N}_\varphi = 0$ or, in another form,

$$\frac{E_\varphi F_\varphi}{k_z E_z F_z} = 1 ,$$

no displacements occur according to the linear theory; the cable forces are then:

$${}^tH_{zp} \approx - E_z F_z {}^t\varepsilon , \qquad (3.46a)$$

$${}^tS_{\varphi p} \approx - E_\varphi F_\varphi {}^t\varepsilon = k_z {}^tH_{zp} . \qquad (3.46b)$$

We refer the reader to Section 2.7.2 for a detailed discussion of this special case.

4 CABLE STRUCTURES

4.1 Introduction

Simple slack cables are, in view of their greatly variable deformations, used in structural engineering as supporting elements only if stabilized by supporting members rigid in bending or by large permanent loads in comparison with which the useful loads are negligible.

Where sufficient height can be attained, a cable can be stabilized by a second tension member curved in the opposite sense. Due to the effect of the second cable and to the required initial tension, such structures undergo only comparatively small deformations; they are stable under the action of arbitrary loads.

We shall term these systems, which consist mainly of cables, "cable structures" in analogy with other plane structures like frameworks and suspended structures.

Some of the many possible shapes are shown schematically in Figs. 4.1–4.3. Other systems are sketched in Section 4.3.

Cable structures are arranged side by side to join rectangular halls; they carry a cylindrical roof. Installed radially, they form supporting structures for circular, elliptical, or polygonal buildings. In these cases they are usually fitted with external compression rings, often

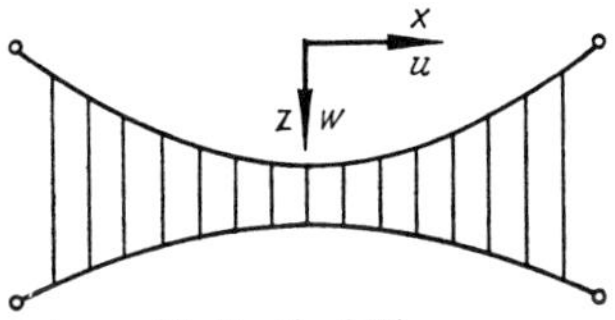

Fig. 4.1.　Cable Structure with Vertical Ties.

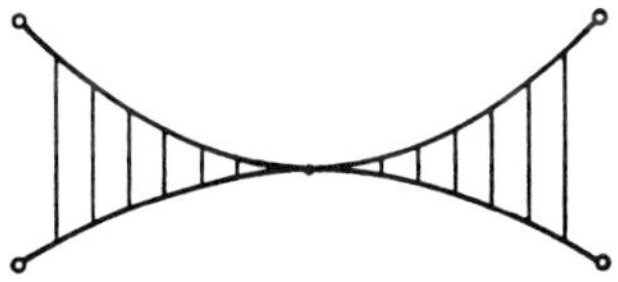

Fig. 4.2.　Cable Structure with Joined Cables.

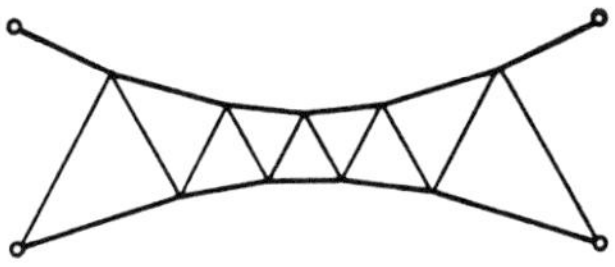

Fig. 4.3.　Cable Structure with Inclined Ties.

also with internal tension rings.

Due to differences in the computational procedure, we have to distinguish between cable structures and structures in which the two cables are not interconnected within the span. The behavior of such systems under load was investigated by, among others, Cornelius[1] and Fritz[2].

[1] W. Cornelius, *Die statische Berechnung eines seilverspannten Daches am Beispiel des US-Pavillons auf der Weltausstellung in Brüssel* 1958 (Statical Calculation of a Cable-Supported Roof, Using the U.S. Pavilion at the Brussels World's Fair, 1958, as an Example), *Stahlbau* 27, No. 4, 1958, pp. 98–103.

[2] B. Fritz, *Vom biegesteifen Fachwerksystem zum spannsteifen Seil- oder Stabhängewerke* (From the Framework System Rigid in Bending to the Cable or Rod-Suspended System Rigid in Tension), *Bauingenieur* 33, No. 6, 1958, pp. 209–212.

The advantages of cable structures were stressed by Jawerth. Some of his publications[3] contain an approximative computational procedure that is valid for three different cable shapes and the corresponding vertical loads. The resulting equations are solved by iterations.

Cable structures can be erected quite easily; their rigidity can be increased by interconnecting the two cables (Fig. 4.2) or by arranging the ties in inclined positions (Fig. 4.3).

Suitable selection of the dimensions of the system enables us to give to the loaded cable a shape corresponding to the line of action of a certain load. The deformations will be particularly small in this case and can be found in closed form.

Other arbitrary loads, including those caused by temperature variations and edge displacements, can be analyzed by means of a generally valid computational procedure, which was published in greatly abbreviated form in 1962[4]. When no horizontal load acts, the cable forces can be determined from a quadratic equation, just as for the simple cable.

A worked example demonstrates the procedure in detail.

4.2 Notations and Fundamentals

We use an orthogonal coordinate system (Fig. 4.1) to analyze plane cable structures. Experience shows that it is convenient to take, as for cable nets, the pretensioned but otherwise unloaded state of the cable structure as the initial (null) state; the deformations u (in the x-direction) and w (in the z-direction) are referred to this initial state.

We denote, as before, the cable ordinates after deformations, by

$$\bar{z} = z + w\,, \tag{4.1}$$

the horizontal tensions, consisting of initial tension and horizontal force due to applied load, by

$$H = H_0 + H_p\,, \tag{4.2}$$

and the cable forces by

$$S = H\sqrt{1 + \bar{z}'^2}\,. \tag{4.3}$$

The following subscripts will generally be used:

    1—for the upper cable (generally the carrying cable);

    2—for the lower cable (generally the tension cable);

    3—for the vertical cables (ties).

The second subscript will indicate, as before, the initial state by 0, and the sectional loads, due to the applied load, by $\bar{p}$.

The loads p_{1x}, p_{2x}, p_{1z} and p_{2z} are referred to unit length of the $\bar{x}$-axis. They act on the cable considered in the z- and $\bar{x}$-directions, respectively.

[3] E.g., D. Jawerth, *Vorgespannte Hängekonstruktion aus gegensinnig gekrümmten Seilen mit Diagonalverspannung* (Prestressed Hanging Structure of Anticlastic Cables Under Diagonal Tension), *Stahlbau* 28, No. 5, 1959, pp. 126–131.

[4] F. K. Schleyer, *Die Berechnung von Seilwerken* (The Calculation of Cable Nets). In *Hanging Roofs*, Proc. IASS Colloquium . . . Paris, 1962, North-Holland Publishing Co., Amsterdam 1963, pp. 56–61.

The ties are assumed to be infinitesimal distances apart, so that the tie forces p_3 act on the carrying and tension cables like vertical line loads, tension being positive. Inclination and strain of the ties will at first be neglected.

The equilibrium conditions for the cut-out cable element were obtained in Section 1.1.2. Introducing the appropriate subscripts, we find from Eqs. 17a, c for the upper cable:

$$H_1' + p_{1x} = 0\,, \tag{4.4a}$$

$$(H_1 \bar{z}_1')' + p_{1z} + p_3 = 0\,. \tag{4.4b}$$

Similarly, for the lower cable,

$$H_2' + p_{2x} = 0\,, \tag{4.5a}$$

$$(H_2 \bar{z}_2')' + p_{2z} - p_3 = 0\,. \tag{4.5b}$$

Last, we introduce the expressions

$$H_{1p} = -\,\Phi_1 \int z_1'' \, w_1 \, dx + \Phi_1 W_1 + \mathfrak{Q}_1 + \mathfrak{R}_1 \tag{4.6a}$$

and

$$H_{2p} = -\,\Phi_2 \int z_2'' \, w_2 \, dx + \Phi_2 W_2 + \mathfrak{Q}_2 + \mathfrak{R}_2\,, \tag{4.6b}$$

obtained from Eqs. 2.52. Unless stated otherwise, all integrals here and henceforth extend over the entire span $l = x_r - x_l$ of the cable considered. The abbreviations used in Eqs. 4.6 are already known from Chapter 2; they are constants with the exception of $\mathfrak{Q}$. We shall, however, briefly explain them once more, considering only the upper cable.

The rigidity function

$$\Phi_1 = \frac{1}{\displaystyle\int \frac{(1 + z_1'^2)^{3/2}}{E_1 F_1} dx} = \frac{E_1 F_1}{l_1 \cdot \Lambda_1} \tag{4.7}$$

depends only on the parameters of the system and is tabulated in Section 2.4.5 for certain cable shapes. Comparison with Eq. 1.50a shows that the denominator $l \cdot \Lambda$ in Eq. 4.7 is identical with the length L_s. However, the integral form of Eq. 4.7 enables us to take variable cross sections also into account.

Erect radial cable structures in circular buildings are, for reasons of design, mostly provided with internal tension rings. We assume that such a ring (of radius R) has a modulus of elasticity E_4 and a cross-sectional area F_4. The elasticity of the ring (under radially symmetrical loads) can be included in the analysis of the cable structure if n is sufficiently small as compared with the span. When n cable structures are connected to one half of the circumference, we assume virtual cable rigidity $E_i \cdot F_i = \pi / n \cdot E_4 \cdot F_4$ in the center region of the length $2R$, whence Φ is then found.

We write

$$W_1 = (u_{1r} - u_{1l}) + (z_{1r}' \, w_r - z_{1l}' \, w_l) \tag{4.8}$$

for the displacements of the right- and left-hand cable suspensions whose magnitudes must be known. The terms $\mathfrak{Q}$ are due to the horizontal loads and can, with sufficient accuracy, be considered as the shearing force of a straight beam of length l on which a vertical load p_{1x} acts (cf. Section 2.4.3):

$$\mathfrak{Q}_1(x) = -\int_0^x p_{1x}\, dx + \frac{1}{l_1} \int_{x_l}^{x_r} \int_0^x p_{1x}\, dx\, dx\,. \tag{4.9}$$

The terms $\mathfrak{R}$ take temperature variations into account, and can, with sufficient accuracy, be considered as the normal forces acting in a rod of length l both of whose ends are immovably fixed:

$$\mathfrak{R}_1 = -\frac{E_1 F_1}{l_1} \int {}^t\varepsilon_1 \, dx\,. \tag{4.10}$$

The distribution of the temperature strain ${}^t\varepsilon$ can be arbitrary, so that nonuniform insulation can be taken into account.

4.3 Initial State

By definition, we have in the initial state: $p_x = p_z = 0$, $H = H_0$, $p_3 = p_{30}$. Equations 4.4a and 4.5a then yield

$$H_{10}' = 0\,, \quad \text{thus } H_{10} = \text{const}, \tag{4.11a}$$

$$H_{20}' = 0\,, \quad \text{thus } H_{20} = \text{const}. \tag{4.11b}$$

Hence, by Eqs. 4.4b and 4.5b,

$$p_{30} = -\,H_{10}\, z_1'' = +\,H_{20}\, z_2''\,. \tag{4.12}$$

The equilibrium condition for the initial state is thus

$$H_{10}\, z_1'' + H_{20}\, z_2'' = 0\,. \tag{4.13}$$

Hence, when H_0 is positive,

$$\frac{H_{10}}{H_{20}} = -\frac{z_2''}{z_1''} = +\,\varrho = \text{const} > 0\,. \tag{4.14}$$

The two cable curves $z_1(x)$ and $z_2(x)$ are thus affine and curved in opposite sense in the region of the ties. In the region where no ties are provided, $p_{30} = 0$, and the cables are straight (Fig. 4.4). In general, the cables may have any configuration, if only Eq. 4.14 is satisfied. The magnitude of the initial tensions is arbitrary, only their ratio ϱ being given.

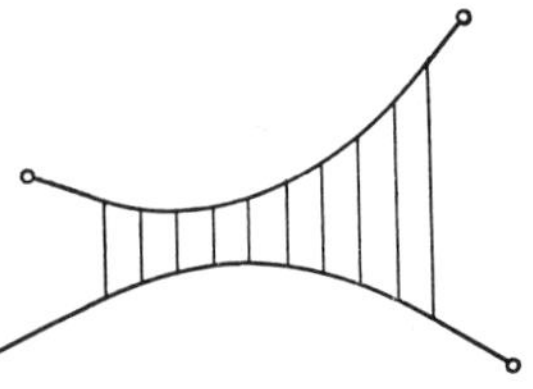

Fig. 4.4. Cable Structure with Extended Cables.

Biconvex shapes can be obtained by connecting the two cables by means of compression rods, i.e., struts (Fig. 4.5). Such designs permit proper drainage of the covering roof membrane; they offer certain advantages for the supporting structure from the statical and design viewpoints. Wave shapes can be obtained by using both tension and compression members [for the connections] (Fig. 4.6).

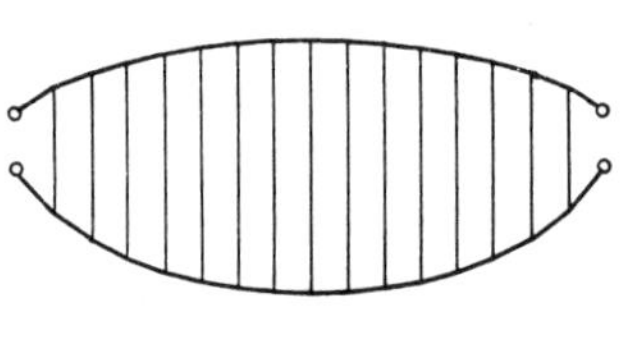

Fig. 4.5. Biconvex Cable Structure.

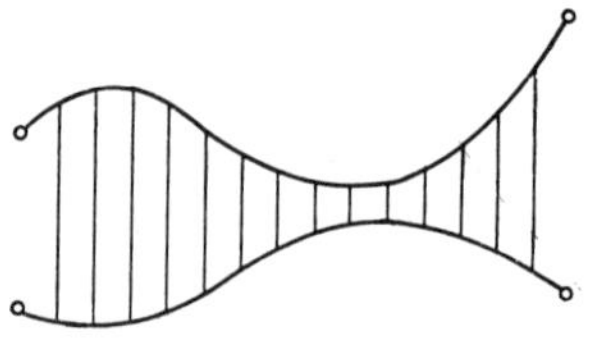

Fig. 4.6. Wave Shape.

Almost no limits are thus imposed on architectural design. However, in practice the cable inclinations to the x-axis must not exceed 25°. This restriction also leads to simple formulas.

4.4 Fundamental Equation of Cable Structures

4.4.1 *Fundamental Equation*

We shall assume that both cables have the same span $l_1 = l_2 = l$ and are interconnected by ties or struts over their entire lengths. Our considerations can, however, be extended easily to other systems also, as shown in Fig. 4.4.

The condition for deformation equality is[1]

$$w_1 = w_2 = w. \tag{4.15}$$

When the equilibrium conditions for the initial state are taken into account, Eqs. 4.4 and 4.5 can be rewritten thus:

$$H_{1p}' + p_{1x} = 0\,, \tag{4.16a}$$

$$H_{2p}' + p_{2x} = 0\,, \tag{4.16b}$$

$$(H_{1p} - \varrho H_{2p})\, z_1'' + (H_{1p} + H_{2p})\, w'' + H_{10}\left(1 + \frac{1}{\varrho}\right) w'' + + p_z - p_{1x} z_1' - p_{2x} z_2' - (p_{1x} + p_{2x})\, w' = 0\,. \tag{4.16c}$$

The last equation was obtained by adding together Eqs. 4.4b and 4.5b.

The suggested method of solution is as follows: The magnitudes H_{1p} and H_{2p} in the second term of Eq. 4.16c are replaced by (constant) values $H_{1p}^{(1)}$ and $H_{2p}^{(1)}$ which have either been obtained by approximations (cf. Section 4.6) or are estimated. Since these horizontal tensions usually differ in sign, their sum will be small. We can therefore at first assume the same value $H_p^{(1)}$ for all cases of loading or set the said sum equal to zero.

We have thus linearized the problem, and shall now discuss the different cases of loading separately

The remainders

$$\left.\begin{aligned} p_{1z}^{\star} &= (H_{1p} - H_{1p}^{(1)})\, w'' \\ p_{2z}^{\star} &= (H_{2p} - H_{2p}^{(1)})\, w'' \end{aligned}\right\} \tag{4.17a, b}$$

can (for the most unfavorable case of loading) be considered as an additional load, being taken into account like p_z in a second computational step that is, except for the load, identical with the first. We thus obtain corrections $w^\star$, $H_{p1}^\star$ and $H_{2p}^\star$ which have to be superimposed on the results of the first step. As already stated, the sum of the two H_p is mostly small; hence $p_z^\star = p_{1z}^\star + p_{2z}^\star$ also is so small that the second computational step is seldom necessary.

We obtained Eqs. 4.6 from Eqs. 4.16a, b. Substituting the former in Eq. 4.16c together with the approximate values $H_p^{(1)}$, we obtain the fundamental equation of the cable structure, from which $w\,(x)$ can be determined:

$$z_1''\,(\Phi_1 + \varrho^2\,\Phi_2) \int z_1''\, w\, d\,x - \left[H_{10}\left(1 + \frac{1}{\varrho}\right) + + H_{1p}^{(1)} + H_{2p}^{(1)}\right] w'' + (p_{1x} + p_{2x})\, w' = \mathfrak{P}\,(x)\,. \tag{4.18a}$$

The load function $\mathfrak{P}\,(x)$ on the right-hand side takes into account the effects of all applied loads, displacements of the abutments, and temperature variations. These are given separately for the upper and the lower cable:

$$\mathfrak{P}\,(x) = p_{1z} + p_{2z} - p_{1x} z_1' - p_{2x} z_2' + z_1''\,[(\Phi_1 W_1 + + \mathfrak{Q}_1 + \mathfrak{N}_1) - \varrho\,(\Phi_2 W_2 + \mathfrak{Q}_2 + \mathfrak{N}_2)]\,. \tag{4.18b}$$

When high accuracy is not required, we can omit the terms containing $H_p^{(1)}$ and w' on the left-hand side while in the load function the two terms containing z' can be neglected in comparison with the other.

We can easily determine w numerically if the integrals are replaced by sums and the derivatives by difference quotients.

The horizontal tensions are then given by Eqs. 4.6 and the cable forces by Eqs. 4.3. The parts due to initial tension have to be included in accordance with Eq. 4.2. The stresses are found from Eq. 4.3.

The dimensions of the ties are determined from the load $p_3 = p_{30} + p_{3p}$, obtained by means of Eq. 4.4b and divided over the individual ties.

We can approximate the elasticity of the ties by determining their extensions $\Delta\, l_3\,(x)$, caused by p_{3p}, and assigning these to the carrying and tension cables in accordance with the rigidities of the latter. Since $\Delta\, l_3 = w_2 - w_1$, we have $w_1 = -\Delta\, l_3 \cdot \varkappa_2$ and $w_2 = +\Delta\, l_3 \cdot \varkappa_1$ where $\varkappa$ is defined in Section 4.6.3. The integrals in Eqs. 4.6 then yield corrections for the horizontal tensions. The horizontal displacements of the individual points of the cables are determined from Eq. 2.53a, in which the subscripts 1 or 2 have to be substituted for x. Equation 2.53c may be sufficient in simple cases (cf. Section 2.4.3).

When u_1 and u_2 are known, we can find the inclination γ of the ties to the vertical. This inclination can be approximated if we assume a horizontal load $p_3 \tan\gamma$ to act on both cables. Corrections for the horizontal tensions are then obtained by means of the approximations of Section 4.6.

The inclination of very short ties can markedly affect the states of stress and deformation. With respect to its behavior under load, such a structure will take up an intermediate position between the two limiting cases of "cable structure with long ties" and "structures with joined cables" (Section 4.8).

4.4.2 *Calculation Checks*

Cable structures form plane supporting systems loaded in their planes; thus they have only three degrees of freedom. We can therefore check the results of calculations far more easily than in the case of three-dimensional cable nets. This will be done for the entire structure with the aid of the three equilibrium conditions. The errors found during this check are thus also a measure of the accuracy of the formulas and the numerical computation.

The subscripts l and r will, as before, indicate, respectively, the left and right end of the cable. Figure 4.7 shows a cable structure with the reactions at the cable abutments.

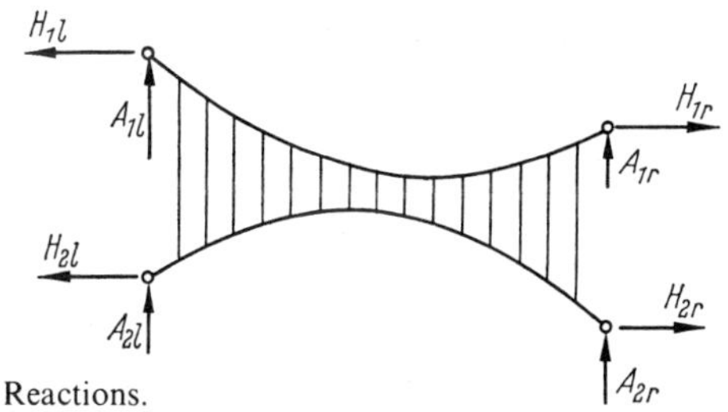

Fig. 4.7. Reactions.

[1] This condition is not satisfied for the cable abutments if, e.g., $w_{1r} \neq w_{2r}$. This incompatibility disappears when the fundamental equation is transformed into a sum-and-difference equation.

The applied loads p have been omitted. The vertical reactions on the upper cable are obtained from the condition that the cables be free from moments:

$$A_{1r} = - H_{1r}(z_{1r}' + w_{1r}')\,, \qquad (4.19a)$$

$$A_{1l} = + H_{1l}(z_{1l}' + w_{1l}')\,. \qquad (4.19b)$$

Similar formulas are found for the lower cable.

The equilibrium condition for the horizontal forces has already been satisfied by Eqs. 4.6, since $H_l - H_r = \mathfrak{Q}_l - \mathfrak{Q}_r = \int p_x \cdot dx$. Hence, a check is obtained by considering only the vertical forces. The necessary conditions are:

for the upper cable:

$$A_{1r} + A_{1l} = \int (p_{1z} + p_{30} + p_{3p})\,dx\,, \qquad (4.20a)$$

for the lower cable:

$$A_{2r} + A_{2l} = \int (p_{2z} - p_{30} - p_{3p})\,dx\,, \qquad (4.20b)$$

for the entire system:

$$A_{1r} + A_{1l} + A_{2r} + A_{2l} = \int p_z\,dx\,. \qquad (4.20c)$$

It would exceed the scope of this book to give a general formula for the equilibrium condition with respect to the moments. We suggest that a suitable reference point be chosen with respect to which the equilibrium of moments due to all external loads (p, H, A) is checked numerically.

Equations 4.19 contain the deformations w in addition to the horizontal tensions. The checks indicated are thus quite thorough.

4.5 Solutions in Closed Form

4.5.1 *General Observations*

The horizontal tensions are independent of x when no horizontal loads act on the cable structure. We can then solve the problem more quickly than by means of Eqs. 4.18.

We first integrate the equilibrium conditions, in analogy to Eq. 1.10b:

$$H_1 \cdot \bar{d}_1 = (H_{10} + H_{1p})(d_1 + w) = M_{30} + M_{3p} + M_{1z} \qquad (4.21a)$$

and

$$H_2 \cdot \bar{d}_2 = (H_{20} + H_{2p})(d_2 - w) = M_{30} + M_{3p} - M_{2z}\,. \qquad (4.21b)$$

The magnitudes d are shown in Fig. 4.8; the functions M are the bending moments due to the loads p_{30}, p_{3p}, p_{1z}, and p_{2z}, acting on

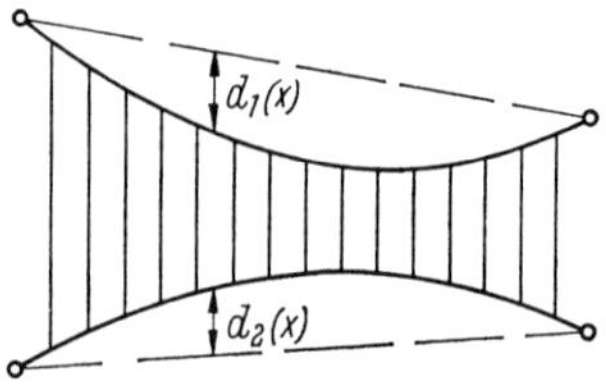

Fig. 4.8. Deflections d.

a simple beam of span l. The moments due to the loads p_{1z} and p_{2z} together form M_z.

In addition, we have to take into account the equilibrium condition for the initial state:

$$H_{10}\,d_1 = M_{30} = H_{20}\,d_2\,, \qquad (4.22)$$

which follows from Eqs. 4.21 and (after integration) from Eq. 4.12.

Equations 4.6 now take the following form if edge displacements are absent:

$$H_{1p} = - \Phi_1 \int z_1''\,w\,dx + \mathfrak{N}_1\,, \qquad (4.23a)$$

$$H_{2p} = - \Phi_2 \int z_2''\,w\,dx + \mathfrak{N}_2\,. \qquad (4.23b)$$

Hence,

$$H_{2p} = - \varphi\,\varrho\,H_{1p} + \varphi\,\varrho\,\mathfrak{N}_1 + \mathfrak{N}_2\,, \qquad (4.24)$$

where

$$\varphi = \frac{\Phi_2}{\Phi_1} \approx \frac{E_2 F_2}{E_1 F_1}\,. \qquad (4.25)$$

These conditions are sufficient to determine the four unknowns H_{1p}, H_{2p}, $w(x)$ and $p_{3p}(x)$. We omit the detailed calculation; an equation only in H_{1p} is obtained finally:

$$\begin{aligned} &H_{1p}^2(1 - \varphi\varrho) + H_{1p}\left\{\Psi_1(1 + \varphi\varrho^2) + H_{10}\left(1 + \frac{1}{\varrho}\right) + \right. \\ &\quad \left. + \mathfrak{N}_1(2\varphi\varrho - 1) + \mathfrak{N}_2\right\} + \Phi_1 \int z_1''\,M_z\,dx - \\ &\quad - \Psi_1\varrho(\varphi\varrho\,\mathfrak{N}_1 + \mathfrak{N}_2) - \left[H_{10}\left(1 + \frac{1}{\varrho}\right) + \right. \\ &\quad \left. + \varphi\varrho\,\mathfrak{N}_1 + \mathfrak{N}_2\right]\mathfrak{N}_1 = 0\,, \end{aligned} \qquad (4.26)$$

where

$$\Psi_1 = - \Phi_1 \int z_1''\,d_1\,dx \qquad (4.27)$$

depends only on the parameters of the system and has the dimensions of force.

We can obtain a simple formula by rewriting Eq. 4.26 as follows:

$$\begin{aligned} &H_{1p}^2(1 - \varphi\varrho) + H_{1p}\left\{\Psi_1(1 + \varphi\varrho^2) + H_{10}\left(1 + \frac{1}{\varrho}\right)\right\} + \\ &\quad + \Phi_1 \int z_1''\,M_z\,dx - \Psi_1\varrho(\varphi\varrho\,\mathfrak{N}_1 + \mathfrak{N}_2) \approx 0\,. \end{aligned} \qquad (4.28)$$

The terms omitted are generally small.

We shall not compare the above expression with the corresponding formulas for the single cable derived from Eq. 1.51. Only the following should be noted:

1. The coefficients of both H_{1p}^2 and H_{1p} are ordinarily positive; hence, H_p and w vary less than linearly with p_z.
2. The cable structure behaves approximately like a single cable of $(1 + \varphi\varrho^2)$-fold rigidity subjected to a $(1 + 1/\varrho)$-fold initial load.
3. Higher initial tension reduces the horizontal tensions and deflections induced by p_z[1]

The quadratic term in Eq. 4.26 is small. To obtain an accurate solution of the equation it is best to determine the unknown H_{1p} from $H_{1p} = A - B \cdot H_{1p}^2$ by iterations.

We obtain directly from Eq. 4.26 the solution for any combination of loads, since we made use of the complete equilibrium conditions

[1] Cf. Section 2.8.3.

in setting up this equation. Superposition of the individual cases of loading and subsequent corrections by the additional loads $p_z^{\star}$ are unnecessary.

After determining H_{1p} we find H_{2p} from Eq. 4.24.

The deflection w is best obtained from

$$(H_1 + H_2) \cdot w(x) = M_z(x) - (H_{1p} - \varrho H_{2p}) \cdot d_1(x), \quad (4.29)$$

derived from Eqs. 4.21 [and Eq. 4.22]. Finally, putting $H_1' = 0$ in Eq. 4.4b, we have

$$H_1(z_1'' + w'') + p_{30} + p_{3p} + p_{1z} = 0, \quad (4.30)$$

from which the forces $p_3 = p_{30} + p_{3p}$ acting in the ties can be found.

All other statements made in Section 4.41 remain valid, as do the possibilities for checking the calculation mentioned in Section 4.4.2.

We note that a moderate horizontal load has only a small influence on the displacements w. Hence, we can make use of the linearized form of the fundamental equation even when $p_x \neq 0$. In this case we separate the load p_x and consider it in accordance with the procedure in Section 4.6. The remaining effects of p_z and temperature variations are then analyzed as explained above; finally, the results are superimposed. Unless p_x is large in comparison with the (simultaneously acting) p_z, we thus obtain satisfactory, though not exact, results.

4.5.2 *Cable Curve Forms Line of Pressure of Load*

In the frequent case when the cable curves z_1 (and thus also z_2) are the lines of pressure of the load, the calculation can be shortened by first determining the deflections.

We exclude displacements of the cable ends; any (small) horizontal loads are considered separately by means of approximations.

We use the general representation

$$p_z(x) = \tilde{p}_z \cdot f(x), \quad (4.31a)$$

where $\tilde{p}_z$ is a constant.[1] Hence,

$$z_1'' = -k_1 \cdot f(x), \quad z_2'' = +\varrho \cdot k_1 \cdot f(x), \quad \varrho > 0. \quad (4.31b)$$

It is evident from the equilibrium condition that w'' also has the form

$$w''(x) = -\tilde{w} \cdot f(x), \quad (4.31c)$$

where $\tilde{w}$ is a constant having the dimension of curvature.

Integrating Eq. 4.31c twice and taking into account the boundary conditions $w_l = w_r = 0$, we obtain $w(x)$. Similar boundary conditions exist for M_z and d_1; hence, by analogy, we assume the following expressions to be valid:

$$w(x) = \frac{\tilde{w}}{\tilde{p}_z} \cdot M_z(x), \quad (4.32a)$$

$$w(x) = \frac{\tilde{w}}{k_1} \cdot d_1(x). \quad (4.32b)$$

Substituting Eqs. 4.32b and 4.27 in Eqs. 4.23, we obtain

$$H_{1p} = \frac{\tilde{w}}{k_1} \cdot \Psi_1 + \mathfrak{N}_1 \quad (4.33a)$$

and

$$H_{2p} = -\varphi\varrho \frac{\tilde{w}}{k_1} \Psi_1 + \mathfrak{N}_2. \quad (4.33b)$$

These expressions are now inserted into Eq. 4.16c. Since $f(x) \neq 0$, we find

$$\tilde{w}^2 \cdot \frac{1}{k_1} \Psi_1 (1 - \varphi\varrho) + \tilde{w} \left\{ \Psi_1 (1 + \varphi\varrho^2) + H_{10}\left(1 + \frac{1}{\varrho}\right) + \mathfrak{N}_1 + \mathfrak{N}_2 \right\} - \tilde{p}_z + k_1(\mathfrak{N}_1 - \varrho\,\mathfrak{N}_2) = 0. \quad (4.34)$$

The coefficients of this quadratic equation in $\tilde{w}$ are easier to determine than those of Eq. 4.26.

Since $\tilde{w}$ is always small, it is advisable to multiply Eq. 4.34 by powers of ten or consider l^2 as unknown.

We find H_p from Eqs. 4.33 and the deflections from Eq. 4.32b. The forces acting in the ties are finally determined from

$$p_3 = p_{30} + p_{3p} = H_1(k_1 + \tilde{w}) \cdot f(x) - p_{1z}(x). \quad (4.35)$$

We shall now apply these equations to two frequently encountered problems.

Uniformly distributed load.

The cable curves are quadratic parabolas when $f(x) = 1$. The curvatures are obtained from

$$k_1 = \frac{8 f_1}{l^2} = \frac{8 n_1}{l}, \qquad k_2 = \frac{8 f_2}{l^2} = \varrho k_1, \quad (4.36)$$

where f is the deflection in the cable center (positive, like d) and $n = f/l$.

Evaluation of the integral 4.27, leads to

$$\tilde{w}^2 \frac{k_1 l^3}{12} \Phi_1 (1 - \varphi\varrho) + \tilde{w} \left\{ \frac{k_1^2 l^3}{12} \Phi_1 (1 + \varphi\varrho^2) + H_{10}\left(1 + \frac{1}{\varrho}\right) + \mathfrak{N}_1 + \mathfrak{N}_2 \right\} - \tilde{p}_z + k_1(\mathfrak{N}_1 - \varrho\,\mathfrak{N}_2) = 0, \quad (4.37)$$

$$H_{1p} = +\frac{k_1 l^3}{12} \Phi_1 \tilde{w} + \mathfrak{N}_1,$$

$$H_{2p} = -\varphi\varrho \frac{k_1 l^3}{12} \Phi_1 \tilde{w} + \mathfrak{N}_2. \quad (4.38)$$

The forces in the ties are found from Eq. 4.35. The deflection varies parabolically, attaining its maximum

$$w_0 = \tilde{w} \frac{l^2}{8} \quad (4.39)$$

in the center of the cable.

Triangular load diagram.

A load distribution as shown in Fig. 4.9 occurs, e.g., in radially arranged cable structures of circular buildings. In this case both cables and the deflection curve are cubic parabolas.

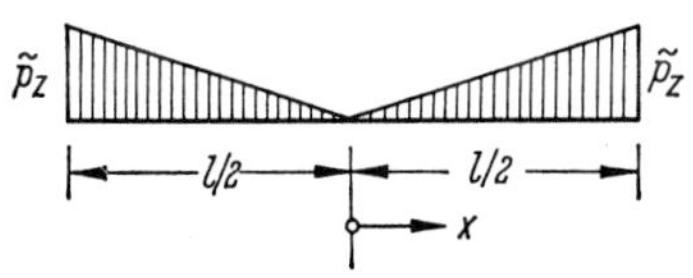

Fig. 4.9. Triangular Load Diagram.

[1] This condition is only necessary for the total load $p_{1z} + p_{2z}$, and not for each partial load.

We place the z-axis in mid-span; all formulas are valid for positive values of x; the absolute values of x have to be inserted for the left half of the structure.

Writing

$$p_z(x) = \tilde{p}_z \cdot \frac{2x}{l}, \qquad x \geqslant 0,$$

so that

$$f(x) = \frac{2x}{l},$$

we obtain

$$d_1 = f_1\left(1 - 8\frac{x^3}{l^3}\right), \qquad k_1 = +\frac{24 f_1}{l^2}. \tag{4.40}$$

The other expressions become

$$\tilde{w}^2 \cdot \frac{k_1 l^3}{80}\Phi_1(1-\varphi\varrho) + \tilde{w}\left\{\frac{k_1^2 l^3}{80}\Phi_1(1+\varphi\varrho^2) + H_{10}\left(1+\frac{1}{\varrho}\right) + \mathfrak{N}_1 + \mathfrak{N}_2\right\} - \tilde{p}_z + k_1(\mathfrak{N}_1 - \varrho\,\mathfrak{N}_2) = 0, \tag{4.41}$$

$$H_{1p} = \frac{k_1 l^3}{80}\Phi_1 \tilde{w} + \mathfrak{N}_1, \tag{4.42a}$$

$$H_{2p} = -\varphi\varrho\frac{k_1 l^3}{80}\Phi_1 \tilde{w} + \mathfrak{N}_2, \tag{4.42b}$$

$$w_0 = \tilde{w}\frac{l^2}{24}. \tag{4.43}$$

The magnitudes Φ_1 and Φ_2 depend on the shape of the cable and have to be determined from Eq. 4.7.

4.6 Approximations

4.6.1 *General Observations*

We shall now give some approximations that can be used for a preliminary analysis of cable structures. Each case of loading will be dealt with separately. The extreme values of the horizontal tensions and deformations are then found by superimposing the partial results, taking H_0 into account.

We assume both cables to have the same span and approximately parabolical shape. As before, the curvature is denoted by l in accordance with Eq. 4.36; in biconvex cable structures (Fig. 4.5) f_1 (and thus k_1) are negative. We also retain the symbol φ (Eq. 4.25).

Use of the formulas is made clear in Section 4.9 with the aid of a worked example, where the results obtained from the approximations will be compared with the exact results.

4.6.2 *Load* p_x

A horizontal load has, as with an orthogonal cable net (Section 2.6.2) little influence on the deformations. We can therefore use the following approximations for nearly straight cables:

$$\left.\begin{aligned} {}^{p_{1x}}H_{1p} &\approx \mathfrak{Q}_1, & {}^{p_{1x}}H_{2p} &\approx 0, \\ {}^{p_{2x}}H_{1p} &\approx 0, & {}^{p_{2x}}H_{2p} &\approx \mathfrak{Q}_2. \end{aligned}\right\} \tag{4.44a–d}$$

The virtual shearing forces $\mathfrak{Q}$ are found from Eq. 4.9.

4.6.3 *Load* p_z

We shall consider Eq. 4.37 when the vertical load $p_z = p_{1z} + p_{2z}$ is approximately uniform. It can be shown that the first term in braces is the most important. The quadratic term in $\tilde{w}$ is always small; when this is omitted, we obtain

$$\tilde{w}\frac{k_1^2 l^3}{12}\Phi_1(1+\varphi\varrho^2) \approx p_z,$$

where $\tilde{p}_z$ has been replaced by p_z.

We again introduce the magnitudes

$$\varkappa_1 = \frac{1}{1+\varphi\varrho^2} \quad\text{and}\quad \varkappa_2 = \frac{\varphi\varrho^2}{1+\varphi\varrho^2} = 1 - \varkappa_1 \tag{4.45}$$

which define the parts of the load taken up by the carrying and the tension cable, respectively. A diagram of $\varkappa_1(\varphi, \varrho)$ is given in Fig. 2.14.

The horizontal tensions are now found from Eq. 4.38:

$${}^{p_z}H_{1p} \approx \varkappa_1 \cdot \frac{p_z}{k_1} \tag{4.46a}$$

and

$${}^{p_z}H_{2p} \approx -\varkappa_2\frac{p_z}{k_2} = -\varphi\varrho\,{}^{p_z}H_{1p}. \tag{4.46b}$$

These formulas are, except for the subscripts, identical with the corresponding expressions for orthogonal cable nets; they can be derived also by the procedure applied in Section 2.6.4.

The maximum deflection is by Eq. 4.39:

$${}^{p_z}w_0 \approx 1.5\frac{1}{k_1^2\, l \cdot \Phi_1} \cdot \varkappa_1 p_z. \tag{4.47a}$$

Substituting for Φ_1 from Eq. 4.7, we obtain

$${}^{p_z}w_0 \approx 1.5\frac{\Lambda_1}{k_1^2 E_1 F_1}\varkappa_1 p_z. \tag{4.47b}$$

Finally,

$$p_{3p} \approx \varkappa_1 p_{2z} - \varkappa_2 p_{1z} \tag{4.48}$$

is the change in the tensile forces acting in the ties.

4.6.4 *Temperature Variations*

The constant load term corresponding to a temperature variation can be dealt with like p_z in the previous Section 4.63. We have, however, to include the terms $\mathfrak{N}$ in Eq. 4.38, which are determined from Eq. 4.10. Using the above approximations, we obtain

$${}^tH_{1p} \approx \varkappa_1\varrho\,\mathfrak{N}_2 + \varkappa_2\mathfrak{N}_1, \tag{4.49a}$$

$${}^tH_{2p} \approx \varkappa_1\mathfrak{N}_2 + \frac{\varkappa_2}{\varrho}\mathfrak{N}_1 = \frac{1}{\varrho}\,{}^tH_{1p}, \tag{4.49b}$$

$${}^tp_{3p} \approx {}^tH_{1p} \cdot k_1. \tag{4.50}$$

The deflection in the center

$$w_0 \approx -1.5\frac{\Lambda_1}{k_1 E_1 F_1}\varkappa_1(\mathfrak{N}_1 - \varrho\,\mathfrak{N}_2) \tag{4.51}$$

is thus always small in comparison with that caused by a vertical load.

When

$$\mathfrak{N}_1 - \varrho\,\mathfrak{N}_2 = 0$$

or, in the case of equal thermal strains of both cables (${}^t\varepsilon_1 = {}^t\varepsilon_2$),

$$\frac{E_2 F_2}{E_1 F_1} \cdot \varrho \approx \varphi \varrho = 1 ,$$

temperature variations have virtually no influence on the deformations of the cable structure.

Equations 4.6 and 4.18 show that, e.g., $\mathfrak{N}_1$ is of the same order of magnitude as $\Phi_1 W_1$. The above formulas can therefore also be used to estimate the horizontal tensions caused by displacements of the abutments.

4.7 Behavior of Cable Structures Under Load

4.7.1 *Symmetry Properties*

The calculation can be simplified, following the reasonings of Section 2.7.1, when the cable structure is symmetrical or antimetrical and the load function also has properties of symmetry or antimetry. The integral in the fundamental Eq. 4.18a then only extends over one half of the cable structure; this causes the number of unknowns in the corresponding sum-difference equation to be reduced to approximately one half. The observations concerning calculation of cable nets are valid also in this case.

For example, an antimetrical vertical load induces no horizontal tensions H_p in a symmetrical system; this is evident also from Eq. 4.26. Particularly large deformations can therefore be expected. If no relative displacements of the cable are possible in the center, the problem has to be analyzed in accordance with Section 4.8.

The special case $\varphi \cdot \varrho = 1$ can be achieved most simply by giving the same elasticity $E \cdot F$ and the same curvature to both cables. The sum of the two horizontal tensions is then independent of the applied load p_z. This can be of considerable advantage in the design of the supporting structure.

4.7.2 *Safety Against Yielding*

The results obtained for cable nets (Section 2.7.3) are also valid for cable structures. We need only replace the subscripts x and y by 1 and 2. Since the system considered contains only two cables, we can determine exactly the load at which one cable becomes slack.

4.7.3 *Natural Frequencies*

We have already shown the similarity that exists between the analyses of cable structures and of orthogonal cable nets. It is thus permissible to omit an exact derivation of the formulas for the natural frequencies of cable structures; the reader is referred to Section 2.7.4.

The equation of motion of the cable structure is obtained from Eq. 4.18a in a form corresponding to that of Eq. 2.71b:

$$z_1'' \, \Phi_1 \, (1 + \varphi \, \varrho^2) \int z_1'' \, \overline{w} \, dx - (H_1 + H_2) \, \overline{w}'' = \mu \, \omega^2 \, \overline{w} \, . \tag{4.52}$$

The deflection $\overline{w}\,(x)$ is measured from the state of rest $\overline{z} = z + w$ of the system under load. The magnitudes H denote, as before, the total horizontal tensions $H_0 + H_p$ and are assumed to be constant. The oscillating mass per unit length of the x-axis is $\mu = g/\tilde{g}$, where $\tilde{g} = 8.9\ \mathrm{m/sec^2}$ is the gravitational acceleration, and g is the permanent load [per unit length of the x-axis].

A simple formula for the lowest natural frequency is obtained from Eq. 2.75; the deflections found previously are substituted in it:

$$\omega^2 \approx \tilde{g} \cdot \frac{1}{m} \sum \frac{1}{{}^g w_i} \, . \tag{4.53}$$

Here ${}^g w_i$ is the deformation at point i, due to the permanent load, and m is the number of w_i determined.

Assuming the cables to be of approximately parabolical shape and g to be nearly constant, we obtain from Eq. 2.77:

$$\omega^2 = \frac{\pi^2}{\mu \, l^2} \left(H_1 + H_2 + \frac{k_1^2 \, l^2 \, E_1 F_1}{\pi^2 \, \varkappa_1} \right) . \tag{4.54}$$

The same result is obtained from Eq. 4.52.

The vibration period is

$$\tau = \frac{2 \, \pi}{\omega} \tag{4.55}$$

in every case.

4.8 Cable Structures with Joined Cables

Cable works of the form shown in Fig. 4.2 merit separate consideration. Whereas we can neglect, in general, the inclinations and strains of the ties, we must take into account a rigid connection between carrying and tension cables. This leads to an extension of the analysis.

We consider systems that are symmetrical with respect to the center of the region ($x = 0$) and neglect horizontal loads.

We separate w, H_p, and p_z into symmetrical and antimetrical parts (superscripts S and A, respectively). For constant horizontal tensions Eq. 4.16c then becomes

$$\begin{aligned} &\underline{({}^S H_{1p} - \varrho \, {}^S H_{2p}) \, z_1''} + \underline{\left[{}^S H_{1p} + {}^S H_{2p} + H_{10} \left(1 + \frac{1}{\varrho} \right) \right]} \, {}^S w'' + \\ &\quad + ({}^A H_{1p} + {}^A H_{2p}) \, {}^S w'' + \underline{{}^S p_z} + ({}^A H_{1p} - \varrho \, {}^A H_{2p}) \, z_1'' + \\ &\quad + \left[{}^S H_{1p} + {}^S H_{2p} + H_{10} \left(1 + \frac{1}{\varrho} \right) \right] {}^A w'' + \\ &\quad + ({}^A H_{1p} + {}^A H_{2p}) \, {}^A w'' + {}^A p_z = 0 \, . \end{aligned} \tag{4.56}$$

The horizontal displacements u_{1m} and u_{2m}, corresponding to the underlined terms, vanish in the centers of both cables; hence, the condition of continuity $u_{1m} = u_{2m}$ is satisfied for this part of the load, and all formulas derived in the preceding sections retain their validity.

The condition of equal horizontal displacements, corresponding to the antimetrical part ${}^A p_z$ of the load at the joint between the two cables, can be satisfied by introducing the horizontal contact force $2\,X$ (Fig. 4.10).

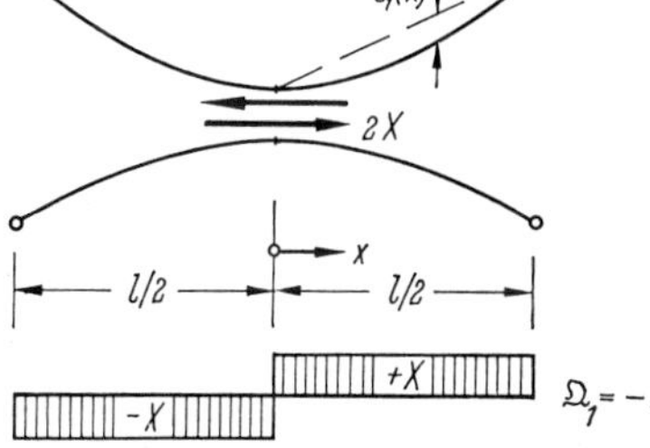

Fig. 4.10. Contact Force and Deflection e.

The integrals in Eqs. 4.6 vanish for the antimetrical part of the deformations. We then have for the right and left halves of the structure, respectively:

$$\left.\begin{array}{ll} \text{left:} & \\ {}^AH_{1p} = +\mathfrak{Q}_1 = -X, & {}^AH_{2p} = \mathfrak{Q}_2 = +X; \\ \text{right:} & \\ {}^AH_{1p} = +\mathfrak{Q}_1 = +X, & {}^AH_{2p} = \mathfrak{Q}_2 = -X. \end{array}\right\} \quad (4.57)$$

Hence, the sums $({}^AH_{1p} + {}^AH_{2p})$ in Eq. 4.56 vanish. The remainder of the antimetrical part is

$$({}^AH_{1p} - \varrho\, {}^AH_{2p})\, z_1'' + \left[H_{10}\left(1 + \frac{1}{\varrho}\right) + \right.$$

$$\left. + {}^SH_{1p} + {}^SH_{2p}\right] {}^Aw'' + {}^Ap_z = 0\,.$$

We shall now consider only the right half of the structure $0 \leqslant x \leqslant l/2$. Substituting Eq. 4.57 and integrating twice, taking account of the boundary conditions ${}^Aw\,(x = 0) = {}^Aw\,(x = l/2) = 0$, we obtain

$$\left.\begin{array}{l} {}^Aw\left[H_{10}\left(1 + \dfrac{1}{\varrho}\right) + {}^SH_{1p} + {}^SH_{2p}\right] = \\ \quad = -X\,(1 + \varrho)\, e_1 + {}^AM_z\,. \end{array}\right. \quad (4.58)$$

The magnitude e_1 introduced here denotes the deflection of one half of the upper cable, measured from the chord (Fig. 4.10), while ${}^AM_z$ is the bending moment acting on a beam of length l, simply supported at both ends and subjected to the load ${}^Ap_z$. (The beam may in this case also have the length $l/2$.)

The magnitude of X is determined from the horizontal displacements. Rearranging Eq. 2.53a and replacing the subscript x by 1 and 2, we obtain for $x = 0$:

$$u_{1m} = -\frac{X}{2\,\Phi_1} - \int_0^{l/2} z_1''\, {}^Aw\, dx\,, \quad (4.59a)$$

$$u_{2m} = +\frac{X}{2\,\varphi\,\Phi_1} + \varrho \int_0^{l/2} z_1''\, {}^Aw\, dx\,. \quad (4.59b)$$

The condition $u_{1m} = u_{2m}$ then yields, when Eq. 4.58 is taken into account, a formula for finding X:

$$\left.\begin{array}{l} X\left\{\dfrac{1}{2\,\varphi\,\Phi_1}\;\dfrac{1 + \varphi}{1 + \varrho}\left[H_{10}\left(1 + \dfrac{1}{\varrho}\right) + {}^SH_{1p} + {}^SH_{2p}\right] - \right. \\ \quad \left. - (1 + \varrho)\displaystyle\int_0^{l/2} z_1''\, e_1\, dx\right\} + \displaystyle\int_0^{l/2} z_1''\, {}^AM_z\, dx = 0\,. \end{array}\right. \quad (4.60)$$

We can now determine ${}^AH_p$, ${}^Aw$, and u_m due to the antimetrical load from Eqs. 4.57, 4.58, and 4.59.

The procedure will be explained in the following section.

4.9 Example

4.9.1 *System and Load*

The cable structure shown in Fig. 4.11 was analyzed for several cases of loading. Nonsymmetrical loads were assumed to be applied to the structure as shown in one case, and to a structure with joined cables and correspondingly shortened ties in the other case.

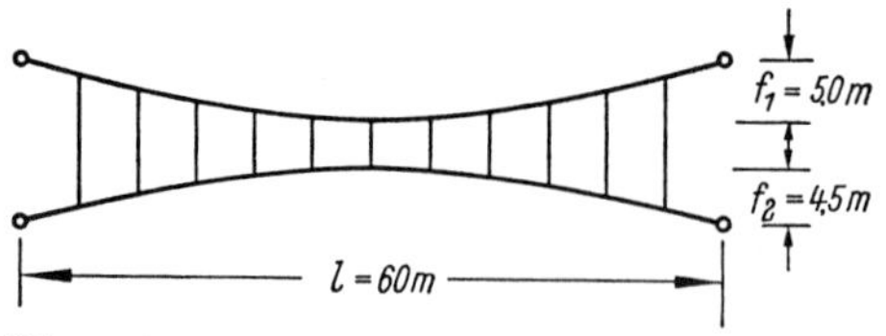

Fig. 4.11. Dimensions.

Dimensions: The cable curves are symmetrical with respect to the z-axis and form parabolas; the dimensions are:

$l = 60$ m, $\quad f_1 = 5.0$ m, $\quad f_2 = 4.5$ m.

The cross-sectional areas of the cables are:

$F_1 = 4.04$ cm², $\quad F_2 = 1.34$ cm².

The modulus of elasticity is

$E_1 = E_2 = 1600$ Mp/cm².

Load:

Initial tension $\quad H_{10} = 7.2$ Mp
$\quad H_{20} = 8.0$ Mp
Permanent load $\quad g = 0.1$ Mp/m
Variable load (snow) $\quad p = 0.2$ Mp/m (may act only on one half of the structure)
Wind suction $\quad w = -0.16$ Mp/m
Temperature variation $\Delta t = +20$°C (cooling also possible)
(No confusion between wind load and deflections appears possible.)

System parameters: We obtain from Eq. 4.36:

$$k_1 = -z_1'' = \frac{8 f_1}{l^2} = \frac{8 \cdot 5.0}{60^2} = \frac{1}{90}\ \mathrm{m}^{-1},$$

$$k_2 = \frac{8 \cdot 4.5}{60^2} = \frac{1}{100}\ \mathrm{m}^{-1}, \qquad \varrho = \frac{k_2}{k_1} = \frac{f_2}{f_1} = 0.9\,.$$

The slopes at the abutments are

$$\xi_{1r} = \frac{4 f_1}{l} = \frac{4 \cdot 5.0}{60} = \frac{1}{3}, \qquad \xi_{2r} = \frac{4 \cdot 4.5}{60} = 0.30\,.$$

Table 2.1 then yields

$$\Lambda_1 = 1{,}0565\,, \qquad \Lambda_2 = 1{,}0456\,,$$

whence by Eq. 4.7:

$$\Phi_1 = \frac{1600 \cdot 4.04}{1{,}0565 \cdot 60} = 102.0\ \mathrm{Mp/m}\,,$$

$$\Phi_2 = \frac{1600 \cdot 1.34}{1.0456 \cdot 60} = 34.2\ \mathrm{Mp/m}\,,$$

and by Eq. 4.25:

$$\varphi = \frac{34.2}{102.0} = 0.335\,.$$

Furthermore,

$$\varphi\,\varrho = 0.335 \cdot 0.9 = 0.302\,,$$

$$1 - \varphi\,\varrho = 0.698\,,$$

$$1 + \varphi\,\varrho^2 = 1.272\,.$$

By Eq. 4.45:

$$\varkappa_1 = \frac{1}{1.272} = 0.786\,,$$

$$\varkappa_2 = 0.214\,.$$

Inserting the value of the initial tension, we find

$$H_{10}\left(1+\frac{1}{\varrho}\right)=7.2\left(1+\frac{1}{0.9}\right)=15.2\ \mathrm{Mp}.$$

Equations 1.18 and 4.10 yield:

$$\mathfrak{N}_1 = -1600\cdot 4.04\cdot 12\cdot 10^{-6}\cdot 20 = -1.55\ \mathrm{Mp},$$

$$\mathfrak{N}_2 = -1600\cdot 1.34\cdot 12\cdot 10^{-6}\cdot 20 = -0.51\ \mathrm{Mp}.$$

4.9.2 *Approximative Computation*

Permanent load: We obtain from Eqs. 4.46:

$$H_{1p} = 0.786\cdot 90\cdot 0.1 = +7.07\ \mathrm{Mp},$$

$$H_{2p} = -0.302\cdot 7.07 = -2.14\ \mathrm{Mp}.$$

Hence, by Eq. 4.47a,

$$w_0 = 1.5\,\frac{90^2\cdot 0.786\cdot 0.1}{60\cdot 102.0}\cdot 100 = 15.6\ \mathrm{cm}.$$

Full variable load: We multiply the results obtained for the permanent load by

$\eta = p/g = 2.0$.

Wind suction: We multiply the results obtained for the permanent load by

$\eta = w/g = -1.6$.

Temperature rise: We obtain from Eq. 4.49:

$$H_{1p} = -0.786\cdot 0.9\cdot 0.51 - 0.214\cdot 1.55 =$$

$$H_{1p} = -0.36 - 0.33 = -0.69\ \mathrm{Mp}$$

$$H_{2p} = -0.69/0.9 = -0.77\ \mathrm{Mp}.$$

Equation 4.51 yields:

$$w_0 = +1.5\,\frac{90\cdot 1.0565}{1600\cdot 4.04}\cdot 0.786\,(1.55 - 0.9\cdot 0.51)\cdot 100 =$$

$$= w_0 = 1.9\ \mathrm{cm}.$$

Compilation:

Table 4.1. Horizontal Tensions and Deformations Obtained by the Approximate Computation

Load	H_1 Mp	H_2 Mp	w_0 cm
0	+ 7.20	+ 8.00	0.0
g	+ 7.07	− 2.14	+15.6
p	+14.14	− 4.28	+31.2
w	−11.31	+ 3.42	−25.0
$+\Delta t$	− 0.69	− 0.77	+ 1.9
$-\Delta t$	+ 0.69	+ 0.77	− 1.9
$0+g$	+14.27	+ 5.86	+15.6
max	+29.10	+10.05	+46.8
min	+ 2.27	+ 1.58	−11.3

4.9.3 *Cases of Symmetrical Loading*

Coefficients to be used in Eqs. 4.37–4.39:

$$\frac{k_1 l^3}{12}\Phi_1 = \frac{60^3\cdot 102.0}{90\cdot 12} = 2.040\cdot 10^4\ \mathrm{Mp\ m},$$

$$\varphi\varrho\frac{k_1 l^3}{12}\Phi_1 = 0.302\cdot 2.04\cdot 10^4 = 0.616\cdot 10^4\ \mathrm{Mp\ m},$$

$$\frac{k_1 l^3}{12}\Phi_1(1-\varphi\varrho) = (2.04 - 0.616)\cdot 10^4 = 1.424\cdot 10^4\ \mathrm{Mp\ m}$$

$$\frac{k_1^2 l^3}{12}\Phi_1(1+\varphi\varrho^2) + H_{10}\left(1+\frac{1}{\varrho}\right) = \frac{2.04}{90}\cdot 1.272\cdot 10^4 +$$

$$+ 15.2 = 303.4\ \mathrm{Mp}.$$

The quantity $(\mathfrak{N}_1 + \mathfrak{N}_2) = -2.06$ Mp in braces in Eq. 4.37 is small in relation to the above magnitudes and could have been neglected; however, we shall use the complete formula.

$$k_1(\mathfrak{N}_1 - \varrho\,\mathfrak{N}_2) = -\frac{1}{90}(1.55 - 0.9\cdot 0.51) = -0.012\ \mathrm{Mp}.$$

The above values are inserted into Eq. 4.37 which is then solved by trial and error with the aid of a slide rule. The horizontal tensions are thereafter obtained from Eqs. 4.38.

$g + p + \Delta t$. This combination is not considered and is not included in Table 4.1, since snow and heating do not occur simultaneously.

$g + p - \Delta t$.

$$1.424\cdot 10^4\,\tilde{w}^2 + (303.4 + 2.06)\,\tilde{w} - 0.3 + 0.012 = 0$$

$$10^4\,\tilde{w} = 9.43 - 0.00466\,(10^4\,\tilde{w})^2 = 9.05\ \mathrm{m}^{-1}$$

$$H_{1p} = 2.04\cdot 9.05 + 1.55 = +20.01\ \mathrm{Mp}$$

$$H_{2p} = -0.616\cdot 9.05 + 0.51 = -5.06\ \mathrm{Mp}$$

$g + w + \Delta t$.

$$1.424\cdot 10^4\,\tilde{w}^2 + (303.4 - 2.06)\,\tilde{w} - 0.1 + 0.16 - 0.012 = 0$$

$$10^4\,\tilde{w} = -1.59 - 0.00473\,(10^4\,\tilde{w})^2 = -1.60\ \mathrm{m}^{-1}$$

$$H_{1p} = -2.04\cdot 1.60 - 1.55 = -4.82\ \mathrm{Mp}$$

$$H_{2p} = +0.616\cdot 1.60 - 0.51 = +0.48\ \mathrm{Mp}.$$

Similarly,

$g + w - \Delta t$

$$10^4\,\tilde{w} = -2.39\ \mathrm{m}^{-1}$$

$$H_{1p} = -3.33\ \mathrm{Mp}$$

$$H_{2p} = +1.98\ \mathrm{Mp}.$$

Compilation of results obtained for horizontal tensions.

We find from the above results:

$$\max H_1 = +7.20 + 20.01 = +27.21\ \mathrm{Mp}$$

$$\min H_1 = +7.20 - 4.82 = +2.38\ \mathrm{Mp} > 0$$

$$\max H_2 = +8.00 + 1.98 = +9.98\ \mathrm{Mp}$$

$$\min H_2 = +8.00 - 5.06 = +2.94\ \mathrm{Mp} > 0.$$

Comparison with the extreme values in Table 4.1 shows that the approximations give satisfactory results. However, the exact computation leads to smaller differences between the extreme values, and thus permits a more economical design.

Largest deformations.

The extreme deflections in mid-span are, by Eq. 4.39:

$$\max w_m = 9.05\cdot 60^2\cdot 10^{-4}/8 = 0.41\ \mathrm{m} = \frac{l}{147},$$

$$\min w_m = -2.39 \cdot 60^2 \cdot 10^{-4}/8 = -0.11 \text{ m} = -\frac{l}{557}.$$

The deformation range is thus

$$\Delta w_m = 0.41 + 0.11 = 0.52 \text{ m} = \frac{l}{115}.$$

4.9.4 *Nonsymmetrical Load*

The analysis is performed only for permanent load and variable load acting on one half of the structure, which is separated into a symmetrical and an antimetrical part:

$${}^Sp_z = g + \frac{p}{2} = 0.1 + 0.1 = 0.2 \text{ Mp/m},$$

$${}^Ap_z = \pm\frac{p}{2} = \pm 0.1 \text{ Mp/m}.$$

We assume ${}^Ap_z$ to be positive for the right half of the structure.

4.9.4.1 Cables not joined

Since the horizontal tensions are independent of ${}^Ap_z$, we obtain, as above,

$$1.424 \cdot 10^4\, \tilde{w}^2 + 303.4\, \tilde{w} - 0.2 = 0$$

$$10^4\, \tilde{w} = 6.40 \text{ m}^{-1}$$

$$H_{1p} = 13.06 \text{ Mp}$$

$$H_{2p} = -3.94 \text{ Mp}$$

$$w_m = 0.29\ m$$

$$H_1 = 7.2 + 13.06 = 20.26 \text{ Mp}$$

$$H_2 = 8.0 - 3.94 = 4.06 \text{ Mp}.$$

The same results are found when Eq. 4.26 is used. We give, for comparison, the deflections at the quarter-span points. The following values have to be inserted into Eq. 4.29:

$$H_1 + H_2 = 20.26 + 4.06 = 24.32 \text{ Mp},$$

$$H_{1p} - \varrho H_{2p} = 13.06 + 0.9 \cdot 3.94 = 16.61 \text{ Mp},$$

At the left-hand quarter-span point:

$$d_1 = 0.75\, f_1 = 3.75 \text{ m}$$

$$M_z = 0.75 \cdot {}^Sp_z \cdot l^2/8 - {}^Ap_z \cdot l^2/32 =$$

$$= 0.75 \cdot 0.2 \cdot 60^2/8 - 0.1 \cdot 60^2/32 =$$

$$M_z = 67.50 - 11.25 = 56.25 \text{ Mp m},$$

whence

$$24{,}32\, w_a = 56.25 - 16.61 \cdot 3.75 = -6.04 \text{ m},$$

$$w_a = -0.25 \text{ m}.$$

Similarly, at the right-hand quarter-span point,

$$w_b = +0.68 \text{ m}.$$

Comparison with a single cable shows that for the same value of w in the center, $w_b = 0.88$ m, i.e., 13% more, with the same load.

4.9.4.2 Cables joined

The horizontal tensions in the left and right halves differ when the cables are joined in the center. The values of H_p and w_m, given above, remain valid for the symmetrical part of the load. The following expressions have to be inserted into Eq. 4.60 in order to find the contact force:

$$\frac{1}{2\varphi\Phi_1}\frac{1+\varphi}{1+\varrho} = \frac{1}{2 \cdot 0.335 \cdot 102.0}\frac{1.335}{1.90} = 0.01028 \text{ m/Mp},$$

$$H_{10}\left(1 + \frac{1}{\varrho}\right) + {}^SH_{1p} + {}^SH_{2p} = 15.2 + 13.06 - 3.94 = 24.32 \text{ Mp},$$

$$\int_0^{l/2} z_1''\, e_1\, d\,x = -\frac{1}{90}\cdot\frac{2}{3}\cdot 1.25 \cdot 30 = -0.278 \text{ m},$$

$$\int_0^{l/2} z_1''\, {}^AM_z\, d\,x = -\frac{1}{90}\cdot\frac{2}{3}\cdot 0.1 \cdot \frac{60^2}{32} \cdot 30 = -2.50 \text{ Mp m}.$$

Hence,

$$X\,\{0.01028 \cdot 24.32 + 1.9 \cdot 0.278\} - 2.50 = 0,$$

$$X = +3.21 \text{ Mp}.$$

The horizontal tensions are thus finally, in accordance with Eqs. 4.57 and 4.2,

for the left half of the structure:

$$H_{1l} = 7.20 + 13.06 - 3.21 = +17.05 \text{ Mp},$$

$$H_{2l} = 8.00 - 3.94 + 3.21 = +7.27 \text{ Mp};$$

for the right half of the structure:

$$H_{1r} = 7.20 + 13.06 + 3.21 = +23.47 \text{ Mp},$$

$$H_{2r} = 8.00 - 3.94 - 3.21 = +0.85 \text{ Mp} > 0.$$

The extreme values exceed those obtained in the preceding subsection, although they still remain below those for the full load, found in Section 4.9.3. On the other hand, the deformations are considerably less:

On the right, we have by Eq. 4.58:

$${}^Aw_b \cdot 24.32 = -3.21 \cdot 1.9 \cdot 5.0/4 + 0.1 \cdot 60^2/32,$$

$${}^Aw_b = +0.15 \text{ m} = -{}^Aw_a.$$

Using the values for w_m obtained in Section 4.9.4.1, the deflections are finally found to be,

at the left-hand quarter point:

$$w_a = 0.75\, w_m + {}^Aw_a,$$

$$w_a = 0.22 - 0.15 = +0.07 \text{ m};$$

at the right-hand quarter point:

$$w_b = 0.22 + 0.15 = 0.37 \text{ m} = \frac{l}{162}.$$

The deflection w_b has been reduced by 46% in comparison with nonjoined cables, although the maximum horizontal tension H_1 has been increased from 20.26 Mp to 23.47 Mp, i.e., by only 16%.

4.9.4.3 Calculation checks

We shall consider the equilibrium conditions (Section 4.4.2) for the last case of loading discussed (joined cables). The deformed cables form quadratic parabolas. The slopes at the abutments are thus given by

$$\frac{l}{4}\, z_{1l}' = f_1 + w_m + 2\,{}^Aw_a = 5.00 + 0.29 - 0.30 = 4.99 \text{ m},$$

$$\frac{l}{4}\, \bar{z}_{2l}' = -f_2 + w_m + 2\,{}^Aw_a = -4.50 + 0.29 - 0.30 = -4.51 \text{ m},$$

$$\frac{l}{4}\,\bar{z}_{1r}' = -f_1 - w_m - 2\,{}^A w_b = -5.00 - 0.29 - 0.30 = -5.59\ \mathrm{m},$$

$$\frac{l}{4}\,\bar{z}_{2r}' = +f_2 - w_m - 2\,{}^A w_b = +4.50 - 0.29 - 0.30 = +3.91\ \mathrm{m}.$$

The vertical reactions at the abutments are, according to Eqs. 4.19, for $l/4 = 15$ m:

$$A_{1l} = +17.05 \cdot 4.99/15 = 5.67\ \mathrm{Mp}$$
$$A_{2l} = -\ \ 7.27 \cdot 4.51/15 = -2.19\ \mathrm{Mp}$$
$$A_{1r} = +23.47 \cdot 5.59/15 = 8.75\ \mathrm{Mp}$$
$$A_{2r} = -\ \ 0.85 \cdot 3.91/15 = -0.22\ \mathrm{Mp}\,.$$

The total load is

$$\int p_z\,dx = 0.2 \cdot 60 = 12.0\ \mathrm{Mp},$$

and

$$\sum A = 12.01\ \mathrm{Mp} \approx 12.0\,.$$

The reference point for the equilibrium of moments is chosen as the point of contact between carrying and tension cables.

The moment due to the reactions is

$$M = (A_{1l} + A_{2l} - A_{1r} - A_{2r}) \cdot \frac{l}{2} + (H_{1r} - H_{1l}) \cdot f_1 -$$
$$- (H_{2r} - H_{2l}) \cdot f_2 =$$
$$= (3.48 - 8.53) \cdot 60/2 + (23.47 - 17.05) \cdot 5.0 -$$
$$- (0.85 - 7.27) \cdot 4.5 =$$
$$= -90.61\ \mathrm{Mp\,m}\,.$$

The moment due to the load is

$$M = 2 \cdot {}^A p_z \cdot l^2/8 = 2 \cdot 0.1 \cdot 60^2/8 = +90.00\ \mathrm{Mp\,m}\,.$$

The error, which is less than 1 %, is due to the expressions for the deformations which are given to only two decimal places.

4.9.5 *Natural Frequencies*

The lowest (symmetrical) natural frequency is obtained for loading by dead weight under conditions of heating. In this case

$$H_1 = 13.1\ \mathrm{Mp}, \quad H_2 = 5.2\ \mathrm{Mp}, \quad w_m = 0.165\ m.$$

We insert into Eq. 4.53 the deflections at the points dividing the span into ten equal parts; this yields:

$$\omega^2 = 9.81 \cdot \frac{1}{9} \cdot 85.9 = 93.6\ \mathrm{sec}^{-2}$$

$$\tau = 0.65\ \mathrm{sec}\,.$$

Substituting in Eq. 4.54:

$$\frac{k_1^2\, l^2\, E_1\, F_1}{\pi^2 \cdot \varkappa_1} = \frac{60^2 \cdot 1600 \cdot 4{,}04}{90^2\, \pi^2\, 0{,}786} = 370\ \mathrm{Mp}$$

we obtain

$$\omega^2 = \frac{9.81 \cdot \pi^2}{0{,}1 \cdot 60^2}(13.1 + 5.2 + 370) = 104.6\ \mathrm{sec}^{-2}$$

$$\tau = 0.61\ \mathrm{sec}$$

which is in good agreement with the value obtained from Eq. 4.53.

5 INTRODUCTION TO THE ANALYSIS OF CABLE STRUCTURES

5.1 General Observations

At the request of the publishers, we shall now attempt to explain the fundamentals of the analysis of cable structures to readers whose knowledge of mathematics and statics is insufficient to enable them to understand the complete and exact analysis.

We shall only make clear the fundamentals of the behavior of cable structures under load, compiling simple formulas that permit rapid determination of the order of magnitude of the forces, stresses, and deformations to be expected. These data will generally suffice for a preliminary design; for further details the corresponding sections of the statical part of this book should be consulted.

This "introduction" has been placed at the end of the book in order to permit reference to formulas appearing in previous sections.

As before, the term "cable" includes all tension members not rigid in bending, i.e., also wires, chains, and thin ribbons.

5.2 Single Cable

Experience shows that the shape of a cable depends on the load. Each cable curve corresponds to a certain type of loading (e.g., concentrated loads, line loads, triangular load diagrams) and vice versa.

The analysis of cables differs from that of other structures, in which the deformations are at first neglected, in that two main problems have to be solved:

1. Determination of the cable shape.
2. Computation of the forces and stresses.

Other problems, e.g., of safety and of the deformations, must also be solved.

The analysis of a cable subjected to a load $q(x)$ proceeds from the equation

$$H \cdot d(x) = M(x) . \qquad (5.1a)$$

Here M is the bending moment, due to the load, acting on a simple beam of span l (Fig. 5.1), which can be determined from handbooks.

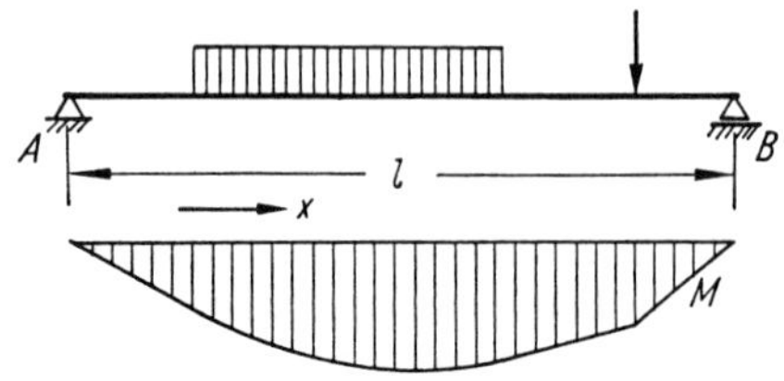

Fig. 5.1. Idealized Beam.

We denote by d (Fig. 5.2) the deflection of the cable, measured from the chord AB in the direction of the load. The quantities M, q, and d are functions of the (independent) variable x. The cable-force component normal to d is denoted by H (horizontal tension). It has the same magnitude for any value of x.

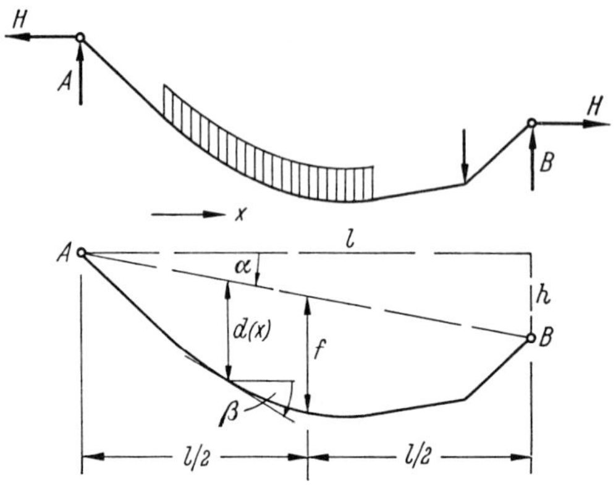

Fig. 5.2. Cable Notation.

In particular, we have at the center of the cable:

$$H \cdot f = M_m , \qquad (5.1b)$$

where f is the deflection at the center.

Equations 5.1 confirm the fact, known from experience, that the horizontal tension in nearly straight cables is, for the same load, higher than in cables with large deflections Hence, restrictions on the height of the structure lead to larger forces and heavier cables. The ratio

$$n = \frac{f}{l} \qquad (5.2)$$

varies usually between 1/8 and 1/20.

The cable force

$$S = \frac{H}{\cos\beta} \qquad (5.3a)$$

is determined from the cable curve; it is greatest at points where the cable inclination to the horizontal is maximum, i.e., at the cable ends.

The vertical abutment reactions A and B are only equal to those acting on an idealized beam when the chord AB is horizontal; the following relationships are valid in general:

$$A = H \cdot \tan\beta_A \quad \text{and} \quad B = -H \cdot \tan\beta_B . \qquad (5.3b)$$

Equations 5.1 are exact only when no inclined or horizontal loads act, since otherwise H varies with x. However, the horizontal loads (in the H-direction) acting on nearly straight cables have a much smaller influence on the cable forces and shape than the transverse loads. We shall not consider the horizontal forces now, referring the reader to Section 1.2.4.

Most problems encountered in practice can be grouped according to whether the total load is concentrated more toward the center or toward the ends of the cable (Figs. 5.3 and 5.5). Cases of uniform loading (Fig. 5.4) occupy an intermediate position; this applies also to nearly straight cables subjected to permanent loads (dead weight) where load and cable form catenaries (cosh-curves).[1]

The horizontal tensions and cable forces are obtained as functions of the total load K from the following formulas [where n is defined by Eq. 5.2]:

[1] Cf. Section 1.2.2.

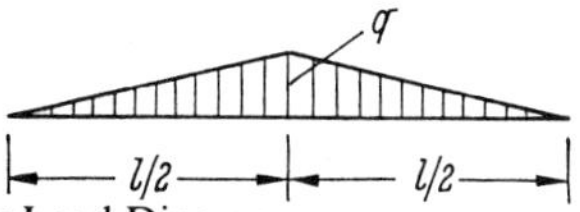

Fig. 5.3. Triangular Load Diagram.

Cable curve $z = ax^{3/2}$

$$K = \frac{q\,l}{2}\,, \tag{5.4a}$$

$$H = \frac{K}{6\,n}\,, \tag{5.4b}$$

$$\max S = \frac{H}{l}\sqrt{l^2 + (3\,f + h)^2}\,; \tag{5.4c}$$

in the special case

$$\max \overline{S} = K \cdot \frac{1}{2}\sqrt{1 + \frac{1}{9\,n^2}} = = K \cdot c_1\,(n)\,. \tag{5.4d}$$

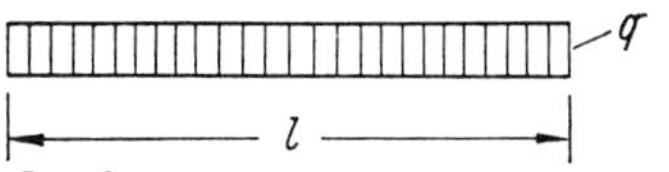

Fig. 5.4. Uniform Load.

Cable forms quadratic parabola

$$K = q \cdot l\,, \tag{5.5a}$$

$$H = \frac{K}{8\,n}\,, \tag{5.5b}$$

$$\max S = \frac{H}{l}\sqrt{l^2 + (4\,f + h)^2}\,, \tag{5.5c}$$

$$\max \overline{S} = K \cdot \frac{1}{2}\sqrt{1 + \frac{1}{16\,n^2}} = = K \cdot c_2(n)\,. \tag{5.5d}$$

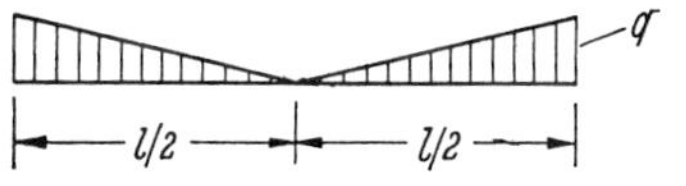

Fig. 5.5.

Cable forms cubic parabola

$$K = \frac{q\,l}{2}\,, \tag{5.6a}$$

$$H = \frac{K}{12\,n}\,, \tag{5.6b}$$

$$\max S = \frac{H}{l}\sqrt{l^2 + (6\,f + h)^2}. \tag{5.6c}$$

$$\max \overline{S} = K \cdot \frac{1}{2}\sqrt{1 + \frac{1}{36\,n^2}} = = K \cdot c_3\,(n)\,. \tag{5.6d}$$

The functions c are shown in Fig. 5.6. It is seen that the cable force is several times larger than the total load K when the cable is nearly straight.

We can separate the load into permanent and variable loads (e.g., snow): $q = g + p$. The above formulas are then valid both for g and (approximately) for q.

The cable length is approximately [cf. Eq. 1.30]

$$L \approx l\left(1 + \frac{8}{3}\,n^2 + \frac{h^2}{2\,l^2}\right). \tag{5.7}$$

An additional load p causes an increase in the horizontal tension. If the distribution of p differs from that of g, the shape of the cable will change. Superposition of forces and cable ordinates corresponding to g and the different p is then impossible, and we have to

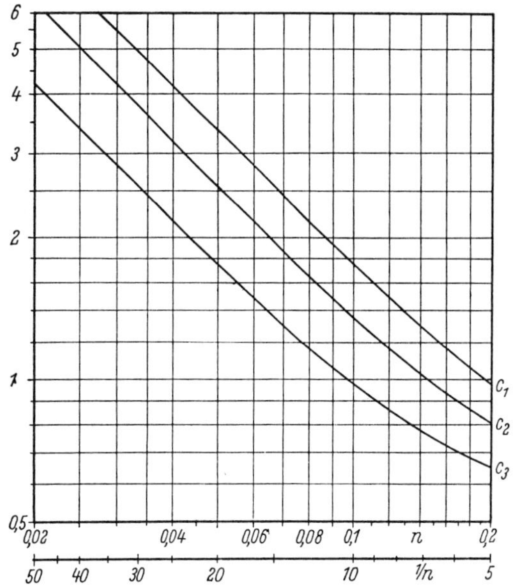

Fig. 5.6. Variation of c with n.

consider the total load q. The higher stresses cause extension of the cable. This, in turn, leads to an increased deflection, which again slightly reduces the horizontal tension. It would, however, exceed the scope of this discussion to go into details.

The deflection also changes when the cable becomes longer or shorter due to temperature variations. For the same load the cable force then increases or decreases accordingly. In most cases, however, temperature effects are insignificant.

We shall now consider only uniform loads g and p (H_g and f correspond to g). The deflection w in the center of the system is then found approximately from

$$w\left(\frac{16}{3}\,n^2 + \frac{H_g}{E\,F}\right) = \frac{p\,l^2}{8\,E\,F} + f \cdot {}^t\varepsilon\,. \tag{5.8}$$

As usual, E is the modulus of elasticity, and F the cross-sectional area of the cable, while ${}^t\varepsilon = \alpha_t \cdot \Delta\,t$ denotes the free thermal strain.

Maximum deflection occurs at the highest load with heating of the cable.

The maximum cable tension is

$$\max \sigma = \frac{\max S}{F}\,; \tag{5.9}$$

it occurs at the highest load with cooling, and must not exceed the limit permitted for the material used.

Due to the elastic deflection, S does not increase in proportion to the load applied. The safety factor of cables is thus higher than the ratio of ultimate stress to design stress.

The analysis is slightly different for pretensioned nearly straight cables or wires used as carrying elements beneath or inside light roofs. Their maximum deflection is generally determined from design considerations; their deformations caused by variable loads (e.g., snow) and temperature changes must therefore be kept within limits. The cross-sectional area and initial tension required is best determined by trial and error, using the simple formulas of Section 1.3.4.

5.3 Cable Cross

We can obtain a fairly good idea of the behavior of cable nets and structures under load by considering the cable cross (Fig. 5.7), which represents the simplest combination of two cables.

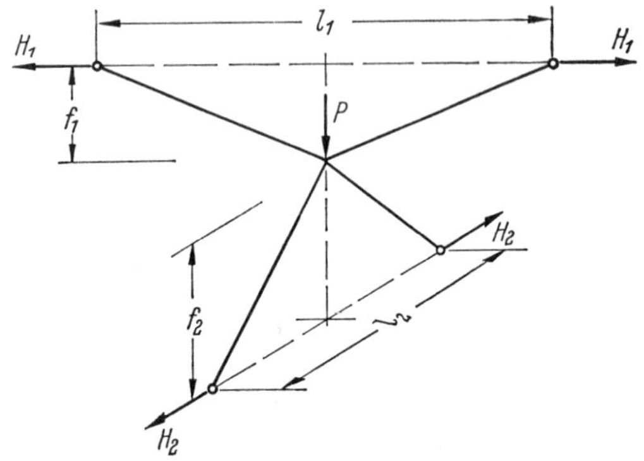

Fig. 5.7. Cable Cross.

The knot descends when a load P is applied. The upper cable becomes elongated and is subjected to tension, while the lower cable becomes shorter, i.e., it is compressed. However, such compression cannot be taken up by a flexible cable not previously under tension. An initial tension is necessary in order that both cables take up the load; this tension must thus be applied before the load.

If the load P is applied under these conditions, the tension increases in the upper cable, while the lower (tension) cable still remains in tension if it was sufficiently pretensioned; however, its tension will now be less than before.

The statement that "the initial tension in the lower cable is reduced by the load" is wrong, since the initial tension does not depend on the load applied. It would be more correct to define loading by initial tension only (without dead weight) as "initial state," superimposing on it the effects of applied loads. The deformations can be more easily determined with reference to this initial state.

The horizontal cable tensions are then (subscript 1 refers to the upper, subscript 2 to the lower cable):

$$\left. \begin{aligned} H_1 &= H_{10} + H_{1p}\,, \\ H_2 &= H_{20} + H_{2p}\,. \end{aligned} \right\} \quad (5.10a, b)$$

Here, H_0 are the horizontal tensions due solely to the initial tension, and H_p, those due to external effects (dead weight, useful loads, thermal strains, displacements of the cable ends). The cable forces are similarly composed of two parts.

The equilibrium condition for the initial state requires that the vertical force, due to H_{10} acting on the upper cable, be equal to the vertical force, due to H_{20} acting on the lower cable. We thus obtain in the case considered:

$$\frac{H_{10}}{H_{20}} = \varrho = \frac{f_2}{l_2} \cdot \frac{l_1}{f_1}\,. \quad (5.11)$$

Similar expressions can be found for other pretensioned cable structures.

The ratio ϱ of the initial tensions is thus known when the shape of the structure is given. The magnitude of the initial tension is arbitrary, but must be chosen high enough to ensure that every cable is subjected to adequate tension even in the most unfavorable case of loading. When the ratio of the initial tensions is known, the right-hand side of Eq. 5.11 is determined except for a constant factor. When one of the geometrical magnitudes, e.g., the deflection f_1, is varied, the other deflection f_2 or one of the initial tensions must be varied as well.

The infrequent case of both cables being deflected downward and carrying the load is only mentioned for the sake of completeness. Such cables cannot be pretensioned; a sufficiently large permanent load is required to prevent uplift in the case of an additional negative load (e.g., wind suction).

In order to obtain an idea of the behavior of the pretensioned cable cross under load, we shall first consider only the load P, assuming two opposite cases (we put $l_1 = l_2$ for simplicity):

a. $f_1 \gg f_2$: the upper cable forms a much larger angle and takes up most of the load. The initial tension H_{20} of the lower cable must be far higher than H_{10}.

b. $f_1 \ll f_2$: the upper cable forms only a small angle and can take up only a small part of the load most of which is carried by the pretensioned lower cable. The initial tension of the upper cable is far higher than that of the lower. The initial tensions of both cables must exceed those in case a.

The behavior under load depends also on the cable rigidities $E \cdot F$. For instance, when the upper cable is very light, only a small force acting on it is required to make the knot descend a given distance. We shall consider the limiting cases:

c. $E_1 \cdot F_1 \gg E_2 \cdot F_2$: the lower cable can take up less of the load, most of which is carried by the upper cable.

d. $E_1 \cdot F_1 \ll E_2 \cdot F_2$: the load P acts more on the lower cable, which must be under correspondingly higher initial tension.

We note that according to Eq. 5.11 the initial tensions do not depend on the cable rigidities.

Theoretical investigation of the problem shows that the ratio of the center deflections has a greater influence on the load division than the ratio of the cable rigidities $E \cdot F$. Hence, the ratios n of the two cables (or of the two cable families in cable nets) should not differ greatly.

We shall not give the exact formulas, but only mention that the cable forces vary with the applied load approximately as shown in Fig. 5.8. When S_p is positive in the upper cable, the total cable force S_1 in it increases with the load; S_p (and thus also H_p) is then negative in the lower cable.

The total load may become negative, for instance with light roofs where wind suction may exceed the dead weight.

The following load combinations determine the dimensions:

I. A maximum load max P induces a maximum cable force max S_1 and at the same time a minimum cable force min S_2: points A and B in Fig. 5.8.

II. A minimum load (negative in this case) min P induces a force S_1 in the upper cable (S_{1p} is negative) and maximum tension in the lower cable: points C and D in Fig. 5.8.

Different cases of loading occur at each of these four points when the cable structure is hotter or cooler than its supporting structure.

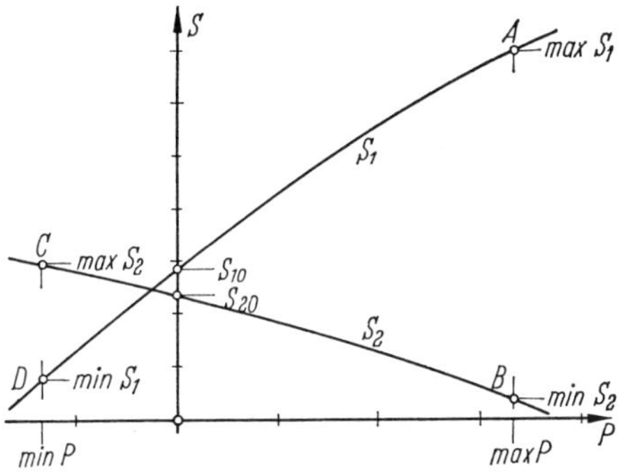

Fig. 5.8. Cable Forces as Functions of Load (Schematically)

The permissible cable forces and stresses should not be exceeded at points A and C. This condition determines the minimum cross-sectional areas of the cables. Points B and D determine the minimum initial tension. The required minimum tensions, still present in the cables in the most unfavorable case of loading, have to be determined in each case separately.
Both curves are displaced upward when the initial tension is raised; points B and D then move to the right and to the left, respectively. The cable cross can thus take up loads varying in a wider range.

5.4 Cable Nets

Cable nets are obtained by combining a large number of cable crosses, and may contain thousands of knots. The cables lie in surfaces curved in space. Since the load-carrying capacity of a cable increases with its curvature, the cables should lie in the directions corresponding to the maximum surface curvatures. We distinguish two fundamental forms in our investigations: orthogonal nets as in Fig. 2.2 (p. 113) and axisymmetrical nets as in Figs. 3.1 (p. 146). Projection in plan of the first form yields a rectangular lattice. The second form has been discussed in Chapter 3 and will not be considered here because of the less easily understood terminology.
The orthogonal net can also be used as a fundamental form for the analysis of nets that do not exactly satisfy the above geometrical conditions. Suitable mean values have to be selected in such cases; the formulas given before will then yield approximate results.
All pretensioned nets contain a family of cables deflected downward (carrying cables), which correspond to the upper cable of a cable cross. The family of tension cables behaves like the lower cable of a cable cross.

The difficulties of an exact analysis are due to the different spans and ratios n of the individual cables. In addition, cables near a rigid edge will be deformed less than those closer to the middle of the net. The forces acting in the individual cables will thus differ even when the load is uniform. Lastly, a concentrated load applied at a knot will cause displacements of all other knots, thus inducing additional tensions in all cables of the net.
It is convenient to refer the cross-sectional areas of the cables and the forces to 1 m width in plan. (The dimensions are cm^2/m and kp/m respectively.) The loads are given per m^2 area in plan. The two families of cables are distinguished by the subscripts x and y.
The exact analysis can be found in Chapter 2 and will not be repeated here. We assume for a simple preliminary calculation that the cables of each family have the same curvature k (1/m) (if necessary, a mean value is to be chosen):

$$k_x = +\frac{8\,f_x}{l_x^2}\,, \qquad k_y = +\frac{8\,f_y}{l_y^2}\,. \tag{5.12}$$

The general formula 2.26 then yields

$$H_{x0} \cdot k_x - H_{y0} \cdot k_y = 0$$

or

$$\frac{H_{x0}}{H_{y0}} = \varrho = \frac{k_y}{k_x} > 0 \tag{5.13}$$

as the condition for the initial state.

This formula is explained in the discussion of Eq. 5.11. Pretensioned cable nets must have saddle shapes; some surfaces of this type are shown in Section 2.3.2. No conditions are imposed on the edges which can be freely selected according to design and architectural criteria. The only requirement is that the edge curve lie on the surface of the cable net (cf. Section 2.7.5).

When the edges (and the initial tension) are given, the corresponding cable-net surface can generally be determined numerically. These surfaces can hardly ever be defined in closed form by functions of x and y. This causes the statical analysis to become very laborious.

The rigidity ratio of the cables of the two families is

$$\frac{E_y\,F_y}{E_x\,F_x} = \varphi \tag{5.14}$$

and should be constant over the net. The coefficients

$$\varkappa_x = \frac{1}{1 + \varphi\,\varrho^2}$$

and

$$\varkappa_y = 1 - \varkappa_x \tag{5.15a, b}$$

have been derived in Section 2.6.4. They indicate the parts $\varkappa_x \cdot p_z$ or $\varkappa_y \cdot p_z$ of the total vertical surface load p_z (permanent load, snow, wind pressure or suction) taken up by the cables of each family. The horizontal tensions are then

$$H_{xp} = \varkappa_x \frac{p_z}{k_x} \tag{5.16a}$$

and

$$H_{yp} = -\,\varkappa_y \frac{p_z}{k_y} = -\,\varphi\,\varrho\,H_{xp}\,, \tag{5.16b}$$

which must be superimposed on the corresponding values H_0 due to the initial tension. As in the cable cross, the two quantities H_p differ in sign; the total horizontal tensions are found, as in Eqs. 5.10, e.g., for the x-direction,

$$H_x = H_{x0} + H_{xp}\,. \tag{5.17}$$

The cable forces and stresses are found from expressions corresponding to Eqs. 5.3 and 5.9.

The deflection in the cable-net center is approximately

$$w \approx (1.15 \text{ to } 1.35)\frac{\varkappa_x\, p_z}{k_x^2\, E_x\, F_x}\,; \tag{5.18}$$

a deformation surface typical for a uniform load is shown in Fig. 2.28.
Nonuniformly distributed loads, e.g., local peak loads caused by wind, cause large local horizontal tensions H_p and cannot therefore be taken into account by means of these formulas.

We must nearly always also take into account horizontal loads, e.g., components of wind loads, or of the dead weight when the system is inclined. The horizontal components of the wind load acting on a shallow roof can be accounted for by multiplying the vertical wind forces by a factor of 1.1. Equations 2.61 and 2.62 apply when the horizontal loads are large. These formulas state that loads acting in the direction of any cable are almost exclusively taken up by this cable, causing additional tension at one of its ends and (theoretically) additional compression (i.e., H_p becomes negative) at the other. The horizontal tension thus varies along this cable.

Temperature changes within the range of variation usually assumed cause only small forces to act on the cable net. Deformations are practically absent when the net is stretched in a rigid frame and the cable rigidities and curvatures satisfy certain relationships.

Use of the above approximations was demonstrated in Section 2.9.3 with the aid of an example; the results were compared with those obtained by exact computation. For the latter, different methods are used which will, of course, lead to results deviating in some aspects from the above.

Certain other problems arise with pretensioned cable nets. We mention elastic and plastic deformation of the supporting structure, safety against yielding (Section 2.7.3), plastic deformation of the cables, and vibrational behavior (Section 2.7.4).

5.5 Cable Structures

We call "cable structure" a plane load-carrying structure, consisting mainly of cables and loaded in its plane, in analogy to other plane structures like frameworks and suspended structures.
The behavior under load of the cable cross (Fig.5.7) is not altered if the lower cable is placed in the plane of the upper. The fundamental forms of cable structures, as shown in Figs. 4.1–4.6, are obtained by connecting the upper and lower cables at many points by vertical ties.
Cable structures have the advantage over single cables that their shapes are fixed so that (on account of the required initial tension) they can take up positive and negative loads. The range of their deformations is small. Structures with inclined ties, and "joined" cable structures (Fig. 4.2), in which upper and lower cables are rigidly connected at one point, are particularly rigid.

A necessary condition for the initial state is that both cables (subscripts 1 and 2) have the same fundamental form (e.g., quadratic parabola) but, depending on the initial tensions, different center deflections for equal span:

$$\frac{H_{10}}{H_{20}} = \frac{f_2}{f_1} = \varrho\,. \tag{5.19}$$

The applied vertical loads p_z are again referred to unit length of the x-axis.

It follows from both theory and inspection that the behavior under load of a simple cable structure corresponds in principle to that of a single cable, cross-sectional areas and curvatures of both cables being suitably taken into account. We thus arrive at the formulas of Section 4.5, which yield accurate results fairly rapidly.
We can obtain, for preliminary calculation, the load division from

$$\varkappa_1 = \frac{1}{1+\varphi\,\varrho^2}\,, \qquad \varkappa_2 = 1 - \varkappa_1\,, \tag{5.20a, b}$$

where, as before,

$$\varphi = \frac{E_2\, F_2}{E_1\, F_1} \tag{5.21}$$

is the ratio of the cable rigidities.
The horizontal tensions due to a nearly uniform vertical load p_z are, in analogy to the formulas for the cable net,

$$H_{1p} = \varkappa_1 \frac{p_z}{k_1} = \varkappa_1 \frac{p_z\, l^2}{8\, f_1} \tag{5.22a}$$

and

$$H_{2p} = -\,\varkappa_2 \frac{p_z}{k_2} = -\,\varkappa_2 \frac{p_z\, l^2}{8\, f_2} = -\,\varphi\,\varrho\, H_{1p}\,. \tag{5.22b}$$

The curvatures k are obtained from Eqs. 5.12; putting $M_m = p_z \cdot l^2/8$ we find an expression similar to Eq. 5.1b for the single cable.
The total horizontal tensions in a pretensioned cable structure are obtained from Eqs. 5.10, while the cable forces and stresses have to be calculated from Eqs. 5.3 and 5.9, respectively.
The vertical deformations in the centers of both cables are approximately

$$w = 1{,}6\,\frac{\varkappa_1\, p_z}{k_1^2\, E_1\, F_1}\,; \tag{5.23}$$

they can be reduced by increasing either F or f_1 and f_2.
The considerations of Section 5.2 apply, *mutatis mutandis*, for the most unfavorable case of loading.

These notes may suffice for a preliminary calculation. We refer the reader to the comparatively simple formulas of Section 4.5 and to the analysis of the behavior under load of cable structures with joined cables (Section 4.8).

The formulas for cable structures contain only one independent variable. They are therefore much simpler than those for cable nets, so that the theory expounded in Chapter 4, as well as the calculation demonstrated in Section 4.9 with the aid of a worked example, can be more easily understood.

Subject and Name Index